# CIVILIZATIONS
## OF THE WORLD

## The Human Adventure

SECOND EDITION

VOLUME ONE: TO THE LATE 1600s

### Richard L. Greaves
Florida State University

### Robert Zaller
Drexel University

### Philip V. Cannistraro
Drexel University

### Rhoads Murphey
University of Michigan

HarperCollinsCollegePublishers

Executive Editor: Bruce Borland
Director of Development: Betty Slack
Project Editor: Susan Goldfarb
Assistant Art Director: Lucy Krikorian
Text Design: Delgado Design, Inc.
Cover Design: Delgado Design, Inc.
Photo Researcher: Leslie Coopersmith
Production Manager: Willie Lane
Compositor: Waldman Graphics, Inc.
Printer and Binder: R. R. Donnelly & Sons Company
Cover Printer: The Lehigh Press, Inc.

*Cover illustration: Allegory of Good Government: The Effects of Good Government in the City*, fresco by Ambrogio Lorenzetti. In the Salla della Pace, Plazzo Publico, Siena. Scala/Art Resource, New York.

*Title page photo:* Great Mosque, Jenne, Mali. Werner Forman Archive, London.

*Part-opening art:* Part One: From Egyptian papyrus of mouth-opening ceremony, New Empire (Giraudon/Art Resource); Part Two: From Koran, Maghribi script, c. 1300 (Metropolitan Museum of Art, Rogers Fund); Part Three: From Gutenberg Bible (Innervisions/Rare Books and Manuscripts Collection, New York Public Library, Astor, Lenox, and Tilden Foundations).

Color atlas in front matter copyright © Hammond Incorporated, Maplewood, N.J.

**Civilizations of the World: The Human Adventure**, Second Edition (Volume One: To the Late 1600s)

Copyright © 1993 by HarperCollins College Publishers

**Library of Congress Cataloging-in-Publication Data**

Civilizations of the world : the human adventure / Richard L. Greaves
   . . . [et al.]. — 2nd ed.
       p.  cm.
    Includes indexes.
    Contents: v. 1. To the late 1600s — v. 2. From the middle 1600s.
    ISBN 0-06-500676-3 (v. 1). — ISBN 0-06-500677-1 (v. 2)
    1. Civilization—History.  I. Greaves, Richard L.
  CB69.C576   1993b
  909—dc20                                    92-39936
                                                 CIP

93 92 91 90 9 8 7 6 5 4 3 2

# CONTENTS IN BRIEF

# CONTENTS

## CHAPTER 6   THE ROMANS   142

## CHAPTER 7    THE ANCIENT WORLD RELIGIONS    172

## CHAPTER 14  LIFE AND CULTURE IN MEDIEVAL EUROPE  360

## CHAPTER 22    THE SOCIETIES OF THE EARLY MODERN WORLD    586

# CHRONOLOGIES AND GENEALOGIES

# M A P S   A N D   G R A P H S

# P R E F A C E

The demise of the Soviet empire and the subsequent restructuring of international relations underscore the premise of this book: Our ability to relate to other cultures and peoples demands some understanding of their history and values, and without this understanding there can be no responsible citizenship, no informed judgment, and no effective commitment to seek peace and dignity for all. Americans do not live in isolation from people in Asia, Africa, Europe, Latin America, and the Middle East. Our ability to understand and respect one another necessitates an awareness of our historical roots.

*Civilizations of the World* was from its beginning a *world* history—a conscious effort to broaden the Western cultural background of most students by giving substantial coverage to all the major civilizations and by trying to place historical events, customs, and cultures in a global context. The enthusiastic reception of the first edition of *Civilizations of the World: The Human Adventure* has shown the extent to which many of our professional colleagues and their students find this approach meaningful.

## BIOGRAPHICAL PORTRAITS

World histories sometimes fail to give students a sense of personal intimacy with the subject. Migratory movements, famines and plagues, trading patterns, and imperial conquests are all important in history, but the individual also matters. Scholars used to write about the past in terms of its "great men" (rarely its women). The great figures still appear in our text, of course, as in any broad historical study. But to give a true sense of the diversity of the human achievement, we have included in most chapters biographical portraits of significant personalities from each epoch and region of the globe, not all famous in their own time but each an important reflection of it. Among them are cultural figures, such as the Greek poet Sappho, the Japanese artist Hokusai, and the German dramatist Bertolt Brecht. Others are religious leaders, such as Guatama Buddha; St. Clare, founder of the Roman Catholic order of Poor Sisters; and the Quaker pamphleteer Margaret Fell. Some were prominent in the political world: the rebel Chinese emperor Hung-wu; the South American liberator Simón Bolívar; India's Indira Gandhi; and David Ben-Gurion, a founding father of Israel. Others, such as England's Mary Wollstonecraft and the Soviet feminist Alexandra Kollontai, were especially concerned with women's rights; some, like Isabella Katz, testified to the endurance of the human spirit. All offer special insights into the times of which they were a part.

## URBAN PORTRAITS

Civilization begins with the city, and modern society is increasingly urban. We have therefore provided accounts of how cities around the world have developed. Some of the cities—Italy's Pompeii and Mexico's Teotihuacán, for example—are now in ruins, while others—Shanghai, Baghdad, Moscow—are thriving. Jerusalem, Paris, Tokyo (Edo), and Rome are revisited at different periods to give a sense of how they changed over time. Like the biographical portraits, the urban portraits are fully integrated into the narrative and provide instructors with excellent topics for discussion, essay questions, and unusual lecture themes. Students will find them intriguing subjects for term papers.

## WOMEN AND MINORITIES

This text continues to focus particularly on women and minorities. The contributions of women to both Western and non-Western societies—whether as rulers, artists and writers, revolutionaries, workers, or wives and mothers—are systematically considered. The biographical portraits are the most obvious illustrations of the attention given to women, but discussions of their contributions are also interwoven throughout the text's narrative. Special consideration is also given to the role of minorities. Four African or African-American figures are highlighted in the portraits: the dancer and social activist Josephine Baker, the African monarch Mansa Musa, Jomo Kenyatta of modern Kenya, and Dr. Martin Luther King, Jr. As one of the founders of Western civilization and a significant force throughout their history, the Jews are covered more fully in this text than in any comparable work. They are followed from their settlement in ancient Palestine to their persecution and exile under the Romans and from their medieval migrations to their return to Palestine and the founding of modern Israel. By recounting the histories of these groups, we hope to make students aware of their achievements.

## SOCIAL AND CULTURAL COVERAGE

Recent scholarship has placed considerable emphasis on social and cultural history. That scholarship is reflected throughout this text, but perhaps most clearly in two chapters that are unique among survey texts. Chapter 7, "The Ancient World Religions," offers a comparative overview of the great religions and philosophies of the ancient world, with a discussion of Islam immediately following, in Chapter 8. Chapter 22, "The Societies of the Early Modern World," provides a broad overview of such key aspects of the world's societies in the sixteenth and seventeenth centuries as marriage, the family, sexual customs, education, poverty, and crime. Moreover, at eight different points throughout the text we pause to consider four significant sociocultural themes: writing and communication, the human image, mapping, and the human experience of death. Here again are special opportunities for distinctive lectures, discussions, essay topics, and research papers.

## MAP ATLAS AND FULL-COLOR ART INSERTS

Two types of special color inserts are featured in the book. The first, included in the front matter, is an eight-page full-color atlas showing the physical characteristics of major areas of the globe. This section is intended as a reference that students can use to improve their knowledge of geography. More than 100 maps appear in the text itself.

In addition to the atlas, the combined volume includes eight full-color inserts titled "The Visual Experience," each insert featuring about eight illustrations—of painting, sculpture, architecture, and objets d'art—that are related in a meaningful way to the text's presentation of history. In the split volumes, selected color inserts are included. The text illustrations consist of a separate program of nearly 400 engravings, photographs, and other images chosen for their historical relevance.

## PRIMARY SOURCE DOCUMENTS

To enhance the usefulness of this text, we have provided not only a generous complement of maps and illustrations but also a comprehensive selection of primary sources. By studying these documents—usually four or five per chapter—students can sample the kinds of materials with which historians work. More important, they can engage the sources directly and so participate in the process of historical understanding. To emphasize the sense of history as a living discipline, we survey changing historiographic interpretations of the Renaissance, the French Revolution, imperialism, and fascism.

## READING LISTS

The discipline of history goes far beyond merely amassing raw data such as names, places, and dates. Historical study demands analysis, synthesis, and a critical sense of the worth of each source. As a guide to students who wish to hone their historical understanding and analytical skills, an up-to-date reading list is provided at the end of each chapter.

## MAJOR CHANGES IN THE SECOND EDITION

The most significant change in the second edition involves a substantial increase in the coverage of Africa and the Americas before 1500. Early Africa now has a newly written chapter (Chapter 9) of its own, as do the early Americas (Chapter 10). The latter includes innovative coverage of the Amerindians of North America as well as the Eskimos. The discussion of modern Africa in Chapter 40 has also been substantially rewritten, and recent developments in Asia, Latin America, the Middle East, Europe, and North America are discussed. To take advantage of the latest scholarship, the authors have rewritten the four chapters dealing with western Asia, Egypt, the Greeks, and the Romans (Chapters 1, 4, 5, and 6). A new biographical portrait, featuring Mansa Musa, appears in Chapter 9. The coverage of fascism has been consolidated in Chapter 37, and Chapter 38 now incorporates the origins of the Cold War. Chapter 22, on comparative social history in the early modern period, which students and professors have found highly stimulating, has been likewise revised. Other changes appear throughout the text, reflecting both new scholarship and suggestions from readers.

In revising this book the authors have benefited from the research of many others, all of whom share our belief in the importance of historical study. To the extent that we have succeeded in introducing students to the rich and varied heritage of the past, we owe that success in a very special way to our fellow historians and to the discipline to which we as colleagues have dedicated our careers.

RICHARD L. GREAVES
ROBERT ZALLER
PHILIP V. CANNISTRARO
RHOADS MURPHEY

# SUPPLEMENTS

The following supplements are available for use in conjunction with this book.

## For Instructors

- *Instructor's Resource Manual* by Richard L. Greaves and Robert Zaller. Prepared by authors of the text, this instructor's manual includes lecture themes, special lecture topics, topics for class discussion and essays, a film list, identification and map items, and term paper topics. Also included is *Mapping the Human Adventure: A Guide to Historical Geography* by Glee Wilson, Kent State University. This special addition provides over 30 reproducible maps and exercises covering the full scope of world history.

- *Discovering World History Through Maps and Views* by Gerald Danzer, University of Illinois, Chicago. Created by the recipient of the AHA's 1990 James Harvey Robinson Award for his work in the development of map transparencies, this set of 100 four-color acetates is a unique instructional tool. It contains an introduction on teaching history through maps and a detailed commentary on each transparency. The collection includes cartographic and pictorial maps, views and photos, urban plans, building diagrams, and works of art.

- *Test Bank* by Edward D. Wynot, Florida State University. Approximately 50 multiple-choice and 10 essay questions per chapter. Multiple-choice items are referenced by text page number and type (factual or interpretive).

- *TestMaster Computerized Testing System.* This flexible, easy-to-master test bank includes all of the test items in the printed *Test Bank*. The TestMaster software allows you to edit existing questions and add your own items. Tests can be printed in several different formats and can include figures such as graphs and tables. Available for IBM and Macintosh computers.

- *Grades.* A grade-keeping and classroom management software program that maintains data for up to 200 students.

## For Students

- *Study Guide* by Richard L. Greaves and Robert Zaller. Prepared by authors of the text, each chapter contains a chapter overview; map exercises; study questions; a chronology; and identification, completion, short answer, and document exercises, along with a list of term paper topics.

- *SuperShell Computerized Tutorial.* This interactive program for IBM computers helps students learn major facts and concepts through drill and practice exercises and diagnostic feedback. SuperShell provides immediate correct answers and the text page number on which the material is discussed. Missed questions appear with greater frequency; a running score of the student's performance is maintained on the screen throughout the session.

- *Mapping World History: Student Activities* by Gerald Danzer, University of Illinois, Chicago. A free map workbook featuring exercises designed to teach students to interpret and analyze cartographic materials as historical documents. The instructor is entitled to a free copy of the workbook for each copy of the text purchased from HarperCollins.

- *TimeLink Computer Atlas of World History* by William Hamblin, Brigham Young University. This HyperCard Macintosh program presents three views of the world—Europe/Africa, Asia, and the Americas—on a simulated globe. Students can spin the globe, select a time period, and see a map of the world at that time, including the names of major political units. Special topics such as the conquests of Alexander the Great are shown through animated sequences that depict the dynamic changes in geopolitical history. A comprehensive index and quizzes are also included.

# ACKNOWLEDGMENTS

The authors are grateful to Bruce Borland, history editor; Susan Goldfarb, production editor; and Bruce Emmer, copy editor. This book could not have been completed without the invaluable assistance of Judith Dieker Greaves, editorial assistant to the authors. The authors wish additionally to thank the following persons for their assistance and support: Lili Bita Zaller, Philip Rethis, Kimon Rethis, Robert B. Radin, Julia Southard, Robert S. Browning, Sherry E. Greaves, Stephany L. Greaves, and Professors Eric D. Brose, Roger Hackett, Sean Hawkins, Victor Lieberman, Winston Lo, Donald F. Stevens, Thomas Trautmann, and Edward D. Wynot, Jr.

The following scholars read the manuscript in whole or in part and offered numerous helpful suggestions:

Karl Barbir
Siena College

Robert F. Brinson
Santa Fe Community College

Christopher E. Guthrie
Tarleton State University

Craig Harline
University of Idaho

George J. Lankevich
Bronx Community College

Dennis Reinhartz
University of Texas at Arlington

Irvin D. Solomon
Edison Community College

Gerald Sorin
SUNY—New Paltz

Glee E. Wilson
Kent State University

Edward D. Wynot, Jr.
Florida State University

Donald L. Zelman
Tarleton State University

We are also indebted to the reviewers of the first edition:

Dorothy Abrahamse
California State University, Long Beach

Winthrop Lindsay Adams
University of Utah

George M. Addy
Brigham Young University

Jay Pascal Anglin
University of Southern Mississippi

Charmarie J. Blaisdell
Northeastern University

William A. Bultmann
Western Washington University

Thomas Callahan, Jr.
Rider College

Miriam Usher Chrisman
University of Massachusetts, Amherst

Jill N. Claster
New York University

Cynthia Schwenk Clemons
Georgia State University

Allen T. Cronenberg
Auburn University

John Dahmus
Stephen F. Austin State University

Elton L. Daniel
University of Hawaii at Manoa

Leslie Derfler
Florida Atlantic University

Joseph M. Dixon
Weber State College

John Patrick Donnelly
Marquette University

Mark U. Edwards, Jr.
Harvard University

Charles A. Endress
Angelo State University

Stephen Englehart
California State Polytechnic University, Pomona

William Wayne Farvis
University of Tennessee

Jonathan Goldstein
West Georgia College

Edwin N. Gorsuch
Georgia State University

Joseph M. Gowaski
Rider College

Tony Grafton
Princeton University

Coburn V. Graves
Kent State University

Janelle Greenberg
University of Pittsburgh

Udo Heyn
California State University,
   Los Angeles

Clive Holmes
Cornell University

Leonard A. Humphreys
University of the Pacific

Donald G. Jones
University of Central Arkansas

William R. Jones
University of New Hampshire

Thomas Kaiser
University of Arkansas at Little Rock

Thomas L. Kennedy
Washington State University

Frank Kidner
San Francisco State University

Winston L. Kinsey
Appalachian State University

Thomas Kuehn
Clemson University

Richard D. Lewis
Saint Cloud State University

David C. Lukowitz
Hamline University

Thomas J. McPartland
Bellevue Community College

Elizabeth Malloy
Salem State College

John A. Mears
Southern Methodist University

V. Dixon Morris
University of Hawaii at Manoa

Marian Purrier Nelson
University of Nebraska at Omaha

William D. Newell
Laramie County Community College

James Odom
East Tennessee State University

William G. Palmer
Marshall University

William D. Phillips, Jr.
San Diego State University

Paul B. Pixton
Brigham Young University

Ronald R. Rader
University of Georgia

Leland Sather
Weber State College

Kerry E. Spiers
University of Louisville

Paul Stewart
Southern Connecticut State University

Richard G. Stone
Western Kentucky University

Alexander Sydorenko
Arkansas State University

Teddy Uldricks
University of North Carolina at Asheville

Raymond Van Dam
University of Michigan, Ann Arbor

John Weakland
Ball State University

David L. White
Appalachian State University

Richard S. Williams
Washington State University

Glee E. Wilson
Kent State University

John E. Wood
James Madison University

Martin Yanuck
Spelman College

# ABOUT THE AUTHORS

*Philip V. Cannistraro.* A native of New York City, Philip V. Cannistraro, an authority on modern Italian history and culture, received the Ph.D. degree from New York University in 1971. Currently Professor of History at Drexel University, Cannistraro served as head of the Department of History and Politics from 1982 to 1986, and again from 1988 to 1990. He also taught at Florida State University and has been a visiting professor at New York University and St. Mary's College, Rome. He has lectured widely in Italy and in the United States and is American editor of the Italian historical quarterly *Storia Contemporanea.* The recipient of two Fulbright-Hays fellowships, Cannistraro is an active member of the Society for Italian Historical Studies and the American Italian Historical Association. His numerous publications include *La Fabbrica del Consenso: Fascismo e Mass Media* (1975), *Poland and the Coming of the Second World War* (with E. Wynot and T. Kovaleff, 1976), *Italian Fascist Activities in the United States* (1976), *Fascismo, Chiesa e Emigrazione* (with G. Rosoli, 1979), *Historical Dictionary of Fascist Italy* (1981), and *Italian Americans: The Search for a Usable Past* (with R. Juliani, 1989). Cannistraro has coauthored a biography of Margherita Sarfatti due to be published in 1993 and is currently writing a biography of Generoso Pope.

*Richard L. Greaves.* Born in Glendale, California, Richard L. Greaves, a specialist in Reformation and British social and religious history, earned his Ph.D. degree at the University of London in 1964. After teaching at Michigan State University, he moved in 1972 to Florida State University, where he is now Robert O. Lawton Distinguished Professor of History, Courtesy Professor of Religion, and Co-Director of the Center for British and Irish Studies. A Fellow of the Royal Historical Society, Greaves has received fellowships from the National Endowment for the Humanities, the American Council of Learned Societies, the Andrew Mellon Foundation, the Huntington Library, and the American Philosophical Society. The 22 books he has written or edited include *John Bunyan* (1969), *Theology and Revolution in the Scottish Reformation: Studies in the Thought of John Knox* (1980), *Saints and Rebels: Seven Nonconformists in Stuart England* (1985), *Deliver Us from Evil: The Radical Underground in Britain, 1660–1663* (1986), *Enemies Under His Feet: Radicals and Nonconformists in Britain, 1664–1677* (1989), *Secrets of the Kingdom: British Radicals from the Popish Plot to the Revolution of 1688–1689* (1992), and *John Bunyan and English Nonconformity* (1992). The Conference on British Studies awarded Greaves the Walter D. Love Memorial Prize for *The Puritan Revolution and Educational Thought: Background for Reform* (1969), and his *Society and Religion in Elizabethan England* (1981) was a finalist for the Robert Livingston Schuyler Prize of the American Historical Association. He was president of the American Society of Church History in 1991.

*Rhoads Murphey.* Born in Philadelphia, Rhoads Murphey, a specialist in Chinese history and in geography, received the Ph.D. degree from Harvard University in 1950. Before joining the faculty of the University of Michigan in 1964, he taught at the University of Washington; he has also been a visiting professor at Taiwan University and Tokyo University. From 1954 to 1956 he was the director of the Conference of Diplomats in Asia. The University of Michigan granted him a Distinguished Service Award in 1974. Currently president of the Association for Asian Studies, Murphey has served as editor of the *Journal of Asian Studies* and *Michigan Papers in Chinese Studies.* The Social Science Research Council, the Ford Foundation, the Guggenheim Foundation, the National Endowment for the Humanities, and the American Council of Learned Societies have awarded him fellowships. A prolific author, Murphey's books include *Shanghai: Key to Modern China* (1953), *An Introduction to Geography* (4th ed., 1978), *A New China Policy* (with others, 1965), *Approaches to Modern Chinese History* (with others, 1967), *The Scope of Geography* (3rd ed., 1982), *The Treaty Ports and China's Modernization* (1970), *China Meets the West: The Treaty Ports* (1975), *The Fading of the Maoist Vision* (1980), and *A History of Asia* (1992). *The Outsiders: Westerners in India and China* (1977) won the Best Book of the Year award from the University of Michigan Press.

*Robert Zaller.* Robert Zaller was born in New York City and received a Ph.D. degree from Washington University in 1968. An authority on British political history and constitutional thought, he has also written extensively on modern literature, film, and art. He has taught at Queens College, City University of New York; the University of California, Santa Barbara; and the University of Miami. He is currently Professor of History and former head of the Department of History and Politics at Drexel University. He has been a Guggenheim Fellow and is a member of the advisory board of the Yale Center for Parliamentary History and a Fellow of the Royal Historical Society. His book *The Parliament of 1621: A Study in Constitutional Conflict* (1971) received the Phi Alpha Theta prize for the best first book by a member of the society, and he was made a fellow of Tor House in recognition of *The Cliffs of Solitude: A Reading of Robinson Jeffers* (1983), the inaugural volume of the Cambridge Studies in American Literature and Culture series. His other books include *Lives of the Poet* (1974) and *Europe in Transition, 1660–1815* (1984). He has edited *A Casebook on Anaïs Nin* (1974) and *Centennial Essays for Robinson Jeffers* (1991) and has coedited, with Richard L. Greaves, the *Biographical Dictionary of British Radicals in the Seventeenth Century* (3 volumes, 1982–1984). With Richard L. Greaves and Jennifer Tolbert Roberts he is a coauthor of *Civilizations of the West: The Human Adventure* (1992). His recent publications include studies of Samuel Beckett, Philip Guston, Bernardo Bertolucci, and the English civil war.

## A Note on the Spelling
## of Asian Names and Words

Nearly all Asian languages are written with symbols different from our Western alphabet. Chinese, Japanese, and Korean are written with ideographic characters, plus a phonetic syllabary for Japanese and Korean. Most other Asian languages have their own scripts, symbols, diacritical marks, and alphabets, which differ from ours. There can thus be no single "correct spelling" in Western symbols for Asian words or names, including personal names and place names—only established conventions. Unfortunately, conventions in this respect differ widely and in many cases reflect preferences or forms related to different Western languages. The Western spellings used in this book, including its maps, are to some extent a compromise, in an effort to follow the main English-language conventions but also to make pronunciation for English speakers as easy as possible.

Chinese presents the biggest problem, since there are a great many different conventions in use and since well-known place names, such as Peking or Canton, are commonly spelled as they are here in most Western writings, even though this spelling is inconsistent with all of the romanization systems in current use and does not accurately represent the Chinese sounds. Most American newspapers and some journals now use the romanization system called *pinyin*, approved by the Chinese government, which renders these two city names, with greater phonetic accuracy, as Beijing and Kwangzhou but which presents other problems for most Western readers and which they commonly mispronounce.

The usage in this book follows the most commonly used convention for scholarly publication when romanizing Chinese names, the Wade-Giles system, but gives the pinyin equivalents for modern names (if they differ) in parentheses after the first use of a name. Readers will encounter both spellings, plus others, in other books, papers, and journals, and some familiarity with both conventions is thus necessary.

In general, readers should realize and remember that English spellings of names from other languages (such as Munich for München, Vienna for Wien, and Rome for Roma), especially in Asia, can be only approximations and may differ confusingly from one Western source or map to another.

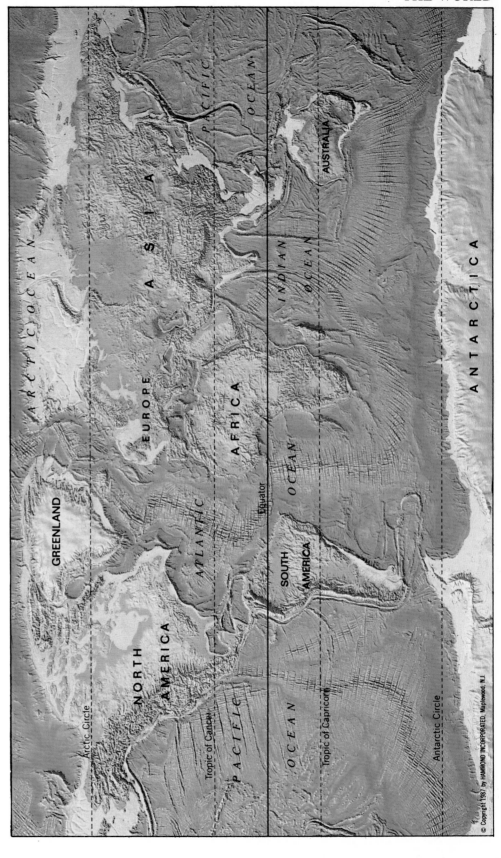

# EUROPE

© Copyright 1987 by HAMMOND INCORPORATED, Maplewood, N.J.

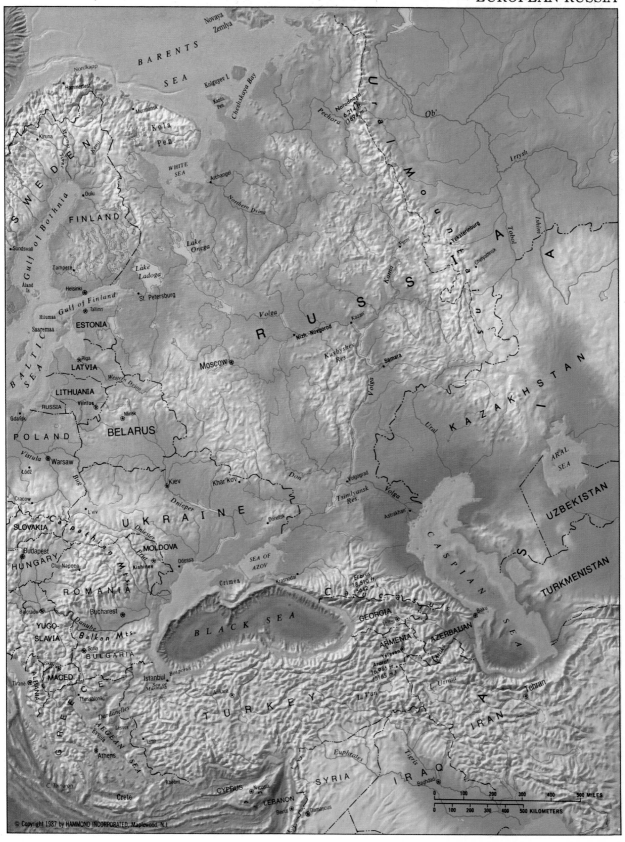

BARENTS
SEA

Novaya
Zemlya

Nordkapp
Hammerfest

Kolguyev I.
Cheshskaya Bay

Kanin
Pen.

Ural Mountains

Ob'

Irtysh

Kiruna

Murmansk

Kola
Pen.

Narodnaya
6,214 ft.
(1894 m.)
Pechora

SWEDEN

Sundsvall

Oulu

FINLAND

WHITE
SEA

Archangel

Northern Dvina

Yekaterinburg

Tobol

Ishim

Perm

S
I
B
E
R
I
A

Åland
Is.

Tampere

Lake
Onega

Chelyabinsk

Gulf of Bothnia

Lake
Ladoga

Kama

Helsinki

Gulf of Finland

St. Petersburg

Hiiumaa
Saaremaa

Tallinn

ESTONIA

Volga

R U S S I A

Nizh.-Novgorod

Kazan

BALTIC
SEA

Riga

LATVIA

Western Dvina

Moscow

Kuybyshev
Res.

Samara

Volga

Ural

K A Z A K H S T A N

LITHUANIA

Vilnius

RUSSIA

Minsk

Gdańsk

POLAND

BELARUS

ARAL
SEA

Vistula

Warsaw

Kiev

Khar'kov

Don

Volgograd

Volga

UZBEKISTAN

Łódź

Bug

Cracow

L'viv

U K R A I N E

Dnieper

Tsimlyansk
Res.

Astrakhan

SLOVAKIA

Carpathian Mts.

Dniester

Donetsk

TURKMENISTAN

Budapest

Cluj-Napoca

MOLDOVA

Kishinev

Odessa

SEA OF
AZOV

CASPIAN SEA

HUNGARY

Prut

ROMANIA

Crimea

Krasnodar

El'brus
18,510 ft.
(5642 m.)

Belgrade

Bucharest

Caucasus

Baku

YUGO-
SLAVIA

Danube

Balkan Mts.

BLACK SEA

GEORGIA

Tbilisi

AZERBAIJAN

Sofia

BULGARIA

ARMENIA

Aras

Skopje

ALBANIA

MACED.

Istanbul

Sea of
Marmara

Bosporus

Yerevan

Ararat
16,946 ft.
(5165 m.)

Tirane

Thessaloniki

GREECE

Dardanelles

Lesvos

AEGEAN
SEA

Ankara

TURKEY

L. Van

L. Urmia

IRAN

Tehran

Izmir

Evvoia

Athens

Euphrates

Tigris

C. Taínaron

Crete

Rhodes

CYPRUS

Nicosia

SYRIA

Baghdad

IRAQ

LEBANON

Beirut

Damascus

100    200    300    400    500 MILES

100   200   300     500 KILOMETERS

© Copyright 1987 by HAMMOND INCORPORATED, Maplewood, N.J.

# AFRICA

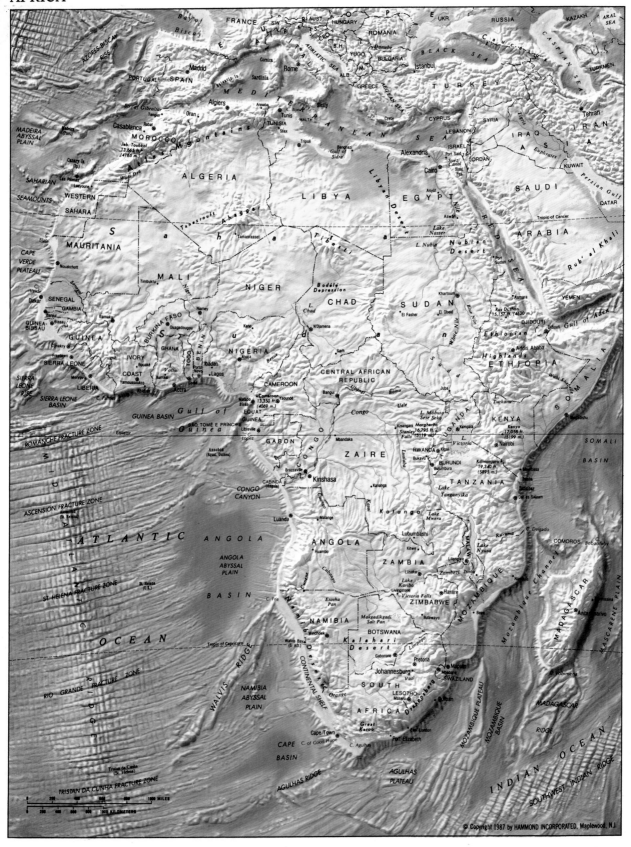

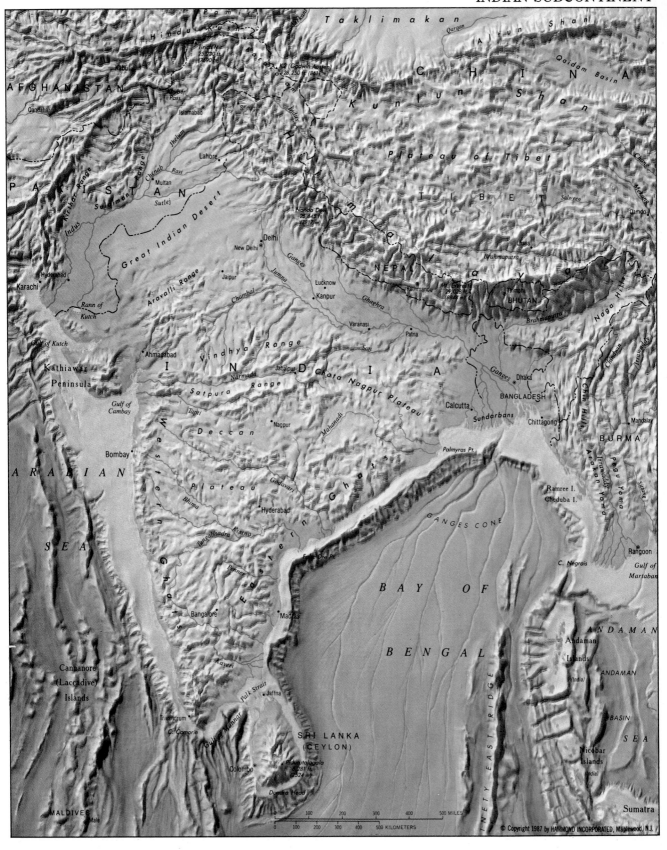

INDIAN SUBCONTINENT

AFGHANISTAN

Qandahar
Kabul
Khyber Pass
Islamabad
Srinagar
Lahore

PAKISTAN

Kirthar Range
Sulaiman Range
Indus
Hyderabad
Karachi
Rann of Kutch
Gulf of Kutch

Kathiawar Peninsula
Gulf of Cambay

Ahmadabad

Pamirs
Hindu Kush
Tirich Mir 25,230 ft (7690 m)
K2 (Godwin Austen) 28,250 ft (8611 m)
Jhelum
Chenab
Ravi
Multan
Sutlej

Taklimakan
Qargan
Altun Shan
Qaidam Basin

CHINA

Kunlun Shan

Plateau of Tibet

Salween
Gamdo
Chang
Mekong

TIBET

Lhasa
Brahmaputra

Great Indian Desert

Aravalli Range
Jaipur

New Delhi
Delhi
Ganges
Jumna
Chambal

Lucknow
Kanpur
Ghaghra

Nanda Devi 25,645 ft (7817 m)

Himalaya

NEPAL
Kathmandu
Mt. Everest 29,028 ft (8848 m)

BHUTAN
Thimphu

Brahmaputra

Naga Hills

Varanasi
Son
Patna

Ganges
Dhaka

INDIA

Vindhya Range
Narmada
Satpura Range
Tapti
Deccan
Nagpur

Chota Nagpur Plateau
Mahanadi

BANGLADESH
Calcutta
Sundarbans
Chittagong

Chin Hills
Arakan Yoma
Irrawaddy

Mandalay

BURMA

Jabalpur

Western Ghats
Plateau
Bhima
Godavari
Hyderabad
Tungabhadra
Krisna

Eastern Ghats

Palmyras Pt.

Ramree I.
Cheduba I.

Pegu Yoma
Arakan Yoma
Sittang

ARABIAN

SEA

Bombay

False Divi Pt.

GANGES CONE

C. Negrais
Rangoon
Gulf of Martaban

BAY OF

BENGAL

ANDAMAN

Andaman Islands
(India)

ANDAMAN

Pennar
Bangalore
Madras

Cannanore (Laccadive) Islands

Kaveri

Trivandrum
C. Comorin
Gulf of Mannar
Palk Strait
Jaffna

SRI LANKA (CEYLON)
Pidurutalagala 8281 ft (2524 m)

Colombo
Dondra Head

NINETY EAST RIDGE

SEA

BASIN

Nicobar Islands
(India)

MALDIVES
Male

Sumatra

100   200   300   400   500 MILES
0   100   200   300   400   500 KILOMETERS

© Copyright 1987 by HAMMOND INCORPORATED, Maplewood, N.J.

# EAST AND SOUTHEAST ASIA

© Copyright 1987 by HAMMOND INCORPORATED, Maplewood, N.J.

# SOUTH AMERICA

NICARAGUA
CARIBBEAN
Barranquilla
COSTA RICA
PANAMA
PANAMA BASIN
Malpelo I.

Pta. Gallinas
ARUBA (Neth.)
Curaçao
Bonaire
Willemstad
L. Maracaibo
Maracaibo
Caracas
Bolívar ft. (5007 m.)
VENEZUELA
Orinoco
Guri Res.
Meta
COLOMBIA
Cap.
Quito
Chimborazo 20,561 ft. (6267 m.)
ECUADOR
Guayaquil
Gulf of Guayaquil
Arauca
Vaupés
Putumayo
Negro
Japurá
Icá
Iquitos
Amazon
Javari
Jurúa
Juruá
Purus
Madeira

WEST INDIES
GRENADA
TRINIDAD & TOBAGO
Trinidad
Port of Spain
BARBADOS
Ciudad Guayana
GUYANA
Mt. Roraima 9094 ft. (2772 m.)
Georgetown
Paramaribo
SURINAME
FRENCH GUIANA
Cayenne
GUIANA PLATEAU
Guiana Highlands

DEMERARA ABYSSAL PLAIN
AMAZON CANYONS
PARA ABYSSAL PLAIN
CONTINENTAL SHELF
CEARA ABYSSAL PLAIN
Equator

Angel Fall
Negro
Manaus
Amazon
Tapajós
Xingú
Tocantins
I. de Marajó
Belém
Rep. de Tucuruí
São Luís

S e l v a s
B R A Z I L
Tapajós
Telos Pires
Araguaia
Caatingas

Planalto de Mato Grosso
BOLIVIA
Ancohuma 21,489 ft. (6550 m.)
Cochabamba
Rep. de Sobradinho
Teresina

Campo Grande
PARAGUAY
Asunción
Itaipu Res.
Vol. Llullaillaco 22,057 ft. (6723 m.)
Tropic of Capricorn
CHILE
I. San Félix (Chile)
I. San Ambrosio (Chile)
PERU BASIN
CHILE BASIN
Lima
NAZCA RIDGE
PERU-CHILE TRENCH

Goiânia
Brasília
São Francisco
Belo Horizonte
Pico da Bandeira 9,482 ft. (2890 m.)
Jequitinhonha
Brazilian Highlands
São Paulo
Rio de Janeiro
SANTOS PLATEAU
Paraná
Curitiba
I. de Santa Catarina
RIO GRANDE PLATEAU

Córdoba
Santa Fe
Rosario
Cerro Aconcagua 22,831 ft. (6959 m.)
Mendoza
Valparaíso
Santiago
Alejandro Selkirk (Chile)
I. Robinson Crusoe (Chile)
Juan Fernández Is. (Chile)
CHALLENGER FRACTURE ZONE
PACIFIC OCEAN

Paraná
Uruguay
Negro
Porto Alegre
Lagoa dos Patos
Lagoa Mirim
URUGUAY
Buenos Aires
Montevideo
La Plata
Río de la Plata
C. San Antonio

A R G E N T I N A
Colorado
Negro
Bahía Blanca
Golfo San Matías
Pen. Valdés
Chubut
Golfo San Jorge
C. Tres Puntas
Deseado
Isla de Chiloé
Archipiélago de los Chonos
G. de Penas
Bahía Grande
Reina Adelaida
Str. of Magellan
Tierra del Fuego
Cape Horn
MORNINGTON ABYSSAL PLAIN

ATLANTIC OCEAN
CONTINENTAL SHELF
ARGENTINE BASIN
FALKLAND ESCARPMENT
Falkland Islands (U.K.)
Stanley
FALKLAND PLATEAU
FALKLAND RIDGE
NORTH SCOTIA RIDGE

0   200   400   600   800 MILES
0   200   400   600   800 KILOMETERS

# History and Human Beginnings

*Anyone who closes his eyes to the past is blind to the present.*

RICHARD VON WEIZSACKER

*The study of history is the best way and, other than by bitter experience, perhaps the only way to be inoculated against the terrible simplifiers, those people who lead nations into trouble.*

GEORGE WILL

The human genus has existed for several million years, and human cultures for tens and perhaps hundreds of thousands of years. Only within the past 10,000, however, have these cultures exhibited the form that we call civilization, a word derived from *civilis*, a Latin term meaning "relating to a citizen or a state." A civilization is a culture characterized by the building of cities, the development of a complex social and political structure

**Bone harpoons from western France, about 14,000 years old. [Reproduced by Courtesy of the Trustees of the British Museum]**

1

through stratification, and the evolution of a formal economic structure through the division of labor. Civilization implies the willingness of familial groups to embrace outsiders, although clan and kinship patterns may remain important even in the most highly developed civilizations.

Civilization also came to entail the keeping of records and for this purpose the development of a system of writing. The first records were kept for the routine activities of levying taxes, taking inventories, and chronicling business transactions. But they were also maintained for compiling royal genealogies, perpetuating sacred texts, preserving the accounts of military expeditions, and recording laws, poems, and stories hitherto transmitted orally. From these latter functions evolved the idea of keeping chronologies of major events, particularly of political or religious significance, and, in time, the notion of binding these together as a narrative. Such narratives of past events came to be called *histories* by the early Greeks. History as a human activity thus grew out of the basic processes of civilization itself and, in its most developed form, is not only the record of civilization but also civilization's way of reflecting on itself. In this sense, history and civilization are inseparable. Each entails the other.

## History and the Historian

Historical study is a living process that involves the systematic discussion and interpretation of issues. It consists of far more than the simple chronicle of past events. The historian is not the mere conservator of the past but in an important sense its active shaper. To study the past is to help mold the future by providing the basis for informed judgments. The historical consciousness of modern society, even when it results in an endeavor to return to past values, is inseparable from the attempt to consider options and to make decisions. Not surprisingly, therefore, historians often differ in the philosophical approach they bring to their material. The very act of writing history entails making critical judgments and selecting events; most historians strive for objectivity and scrupulously cite the evidence on which their conclusions are based. Some historians, however, reflect a predetermined ideological position and write history with a view to proving or justifying it. All historians, of course, necessarily reflect their time and culture.

In seeking to make sense of the past, historians have focused on various key themes. Religion, for example, has often been a major factor in interpreting the past. The Christian and Islamic historians of the Middle Ages and the early modern era viewed the past through the lens of their faiths. Not all scholars have viewed religion

as a basis for historical interpretation or civilized values; the secular, rationalistic outlook of the eighteenth-century British author Edward Gibbon led him to assess Christianity's historical role in largely negative terms. Other historians, such as the classical Greek Thucydides and the sixteenth-century Florentine Niccolò Machiavelli, sought to explain earlier societies on the basis of theories of human behavior. Some, from Thucydides in classical times to the twentieth-century historian Arnold Toynbee, have searched for patterns and cycles of repetition in past events. In contrast to this has been the conviction that the study of history reveals a steady improvement in human life in accordance with a divine scheme for progress. Marxist historians have seen progress in secular terms, as a series of class conflicts that will ultimately lead to the emergence of a classless, egalitarian society. Few historians would now deny the importance of social and economic elements in the historical process, just as few would seek to explain the past primarily in terms of the actions of great men and women. Most historians, in fact, now recognize the impossibility of providing a compelling explanation of the past without giving due attention to ideological, social, economic, and political factors.

We should expect history neither to determine our future nor to impose neat patterns on the past. The aim should rather be to establish as clear an understanding as possible of past events and cultures and of the place of our own society in the historical context. This is, of course, no easy task. Rulers of all ages have manipulated the truth for their own ends, making it necessary for the historian to weigh the surviving evidence meticulously. Furthermore, the lives of vast numbers of people—the slaves of ancient Egypt or nineteenth-century America, women in the ancient and medieval eras, peasants and proletarians everywhere—are often difficult to document apart from general characteristics or broad experience.

The historical picture depends on sources that are inevitably biased, whether by deliberate attempts to distort the truth or by the chance survival of some records but not others. Better and more abundant evidence for recent times has increased the likelihood of a fuller, more accurate historical analysis of the modern world. The indescribable horrors of the forced-labor camps of Stalinist Russia and the Nazi extermination camps have been documented despite attempts to conceal or destroy the record. In assessing the history of the distant past, historians use new discoveries and sophisticated research techniques to refine the traditional picture. However, nearness or remoteness in time is not the sole criterion for historical accessibility. Much more is known about life in Athens during the fifth century B.C. than about life in Africa or North America in the fifteenth century A.D. The nature and the amount of evidence are crucial in the work of every historian.

## Fields of History

Much modern historical writing has concentrated on political institutions and practices, diplomatic relations, and warfare—subjects that have formed the traditional core of historical study. Beginning especially in the period after World War II, historians have looked increasingly to wider fields, often with the aid of new research techniques, many of them borrowed from the social sciences. Social historians are concerned with the general question of social organization and behavior in the past. Interaction between the sexes, the role of women, attitudes toward death, the rearing of children, class and kinship structure, patterns of mobility, the rules of inheritance and property, and the formation of elites are major concerns of the social historian. A special aspect of social organization is the study of urban life, one of the key distinguishing marks of civilization. Here, too, the material evidence is generally more plentiful, and shifting social patterns are easier to discern than in the more slowly changing life of the countryside. Most of the following chapters include portraits of individual cities and the lifestyles of their inhabitants. Cities have changed greatly in size and structure through the centuries, and yet over time they exhibit many common characteristics and functions.

Economic, demographic, and environmental history, too, is crucial to an understanding of the past. The movement of people, the flow of trade, the development of technology and its diffusion by contact and exchange, the fluctuations in population and in the rates of birth and death, and the changing patterns of climate all contribute to our perception of human dealings with the world, with each other, and with survival, creating and sustaining the uniquely human construct we call civilization.

The history of ideas, including religious beliefs and political ideologies, also casts light on the general principles and assumptions of society, the transmission of elite norms, the interplay and conflict between cultural values, and the common threads that unite such diverse cultural products as religion, art, science, and law. Cultural historians, in fact, concentrate on such subjects as art, architecture, music, and literature. Indeed, virtually every product of human endeavor sheds light on the period in which it was created.

## Sources and Their Interpretation

In seeking to understand the past, historians draw on a wide range of materials. These sources fall into two categories: *primary sources*, which consist of materials produced in the period under examination, and *secondary* *sources*, which comprise accounts by writers of a later age. Primary sources include a wide variety of materials, such as letters, diaries, tax rolls, treaties, statutes, birth and death registers, census returns, sermons, and court records. Historians work largely from primary sources, even as they keep abreast of findings by other scholars and incorporate those results in their own studies. Any evidence a historian uses must first be evaluated. In the words of the British historian Sir Geoffrey Elton:

> **Evaluation of all historical evidence must start from one basic question: how and with what end in mind did this come into existence? It matters whether a letter is written to a friend or an enemy; whether an account of income is prepared by a taxpayer or a tax collector; whether witnesses in a lawsuit are (as they were in the Roman-law system) called by the court or (as they were in the old [English] Common Law) supplied by the parties.[1]**

Myths constitute a special category of written evidence, though originally they were transmitted orally from generation to generation. Myths are tales that incorporate religious or supernatural notions to explain natural phenomena and social events or to express cultural values. The earliest civilizations, for instance, used myths to account for such things as floods and drought, birth and death, and gender differences. In a prescientific era, myths functioned in lieu of scientific explanations. Among the most famous myths are those that sought to explain the creation of the universe and the origin of life. Most modern scholars regard the biblical accounts of creation in the Book of Genesis as part of the corpus of ancient myth; Jewish and Christian theologians who accept this conclusion believe that the myths nevertheless point to the underlying truth of a divinely ordered creation. For the historian, myths of every sort provide valuable clues to the perpetual human effort to understand the world and our place in it.

Primary sources include much more than written records. Tools, clothing, religious artifacts, and eating and cooking utensils, for instance, tell us much about the tastes, social structure, and values of earlier societies. Fecal remains as well as foodstuffs preserved in graves and tombs can teach us much about prehistoric and ancient diets.

Such objects can often be dated with reasonable accuracy by measuring organic deposits of carbon-14, a radioactive form of carbon that disintegrates over time. This form of dating has been usable only for objects less than 50,000 years old, although current research should increase this to 100,000 years. The accuracy of radiocarbon dating has been considerably enhanced by coupling it with dendrochronology, the study of annual growth rings in trees (particularly the bristlecone pine in California's White Mountains, which date back to the seventh millennium B.C.). By subjecting ring samples to radiocarbon analysis, they can be accurately calibrated.

Items can also be dated by their position in the successive strata of objects that have accumulated over centuries at a specific location. At the Koster site, less than 50 miles from St. Louis, for example, archaeologists have identified 15 distinctive strata (called *horizons*) covering a period from approximately 6000 B.C. to A.D. 1200.

Dramatic scientific advances have resulted in other systems of dating, especially useful in working with cores of sediment from ocean bottoms and with loess (windborne soil) and microfauna deposited between glacial cycles. Measuring potassium and argon enabled scientists to determine that human fossils found at the Olduvai Gorge in Tanzania were 1,786,000 years old. Some objects can also be dated by measuring the decay of uranium, changes in the earth's magnetic field, or thermoluminescence (for such things as burned artifacts, teeth, and rocks heated by a campfire). Approximate dates for human and animal remains can also be determined by measuring the proportion of "left-handed" to "right-handed" amino acid molecules; at the time of death, the number of molecules oriented in a leftward direction begins to increase through the action of aspartic acid in a process known as amino-acid racemization.

The fine arts reveal much about the civilizations of earlier eras. Paintings, sculpture, music, and architecture reflect the values of the people who produced them as well as the audience for whom they were intended and the patrons who made their creation possible. Art is a valuable source of evidence, especially for social and religious historians. In the words of the twentieth-century American composer Carlisle Floyd, "What more accurate, more immediate access do we have to the hearts and minds of men than through what they reveal of themselves and their age in art? For art, after all is said and done, is revelation."[2]

The historian of more recent times has a wide range of additional material in the form of films, recordings, and other products of the era of mass communication. Newspapers (which originated in the seventeenth century), magazines, film, photography, popular literature, and folk songs are valuable historical evidence. In the case of recent events, oral accounts can provide significant information. A special subfield now exists called *oral history*; its practitioners interview people who participated in or witnessed historical events, thereby preserving their accounts as data for future scholars. If ancient historians must often literally dig in the soil for their information or struggle to infer the technology and commerce of a civilization from surviving coins, modern historians are frequently inundated with data. Whereas the evidence available to ancient historians is almost always less than they would like, the material available to modern historians is often more than can be evaluated. Interpreting the evidence demands appropriate ana-

lytical skills. Most historians, therefore, are trained in the methodology of at least one additional field. Social historians, for instance, must be familiar with the techniques of sociology and demography; economic historians, with statistics and economists' models; church historians, with theology and philosophy; intellectual historians, with philosophy and textual criticism; and historians of science, with scientific theory and methodology. Legal historians have often acquired formal training in the law. The controversial field of psychohistory, which attempts to apply psychological theories and models to explain the behavior of historical personalities, requires training in psychology. Historians of the ancient world work closely with archaeologists, who find and analyze such remains as pottery, utensils, inscriptions, and ruins. Anthropological studies of tribal behavior in modern times are used to formulate hypotheses about prehistoric society. In sum, historians work closely with specialists in virtually all fields to explain the past and its relationship to the present. The discipline of history is the co.. .f the modern academic community; no other discipline is so closely affiliated with so many other fields of intellectual behavior.

## Time

The ordering of time is basic to any study of the past. Events must be examined in relation to those that preceded and followed them. Yet even the simplest chronology often poses a challenge. The dating of events in ancient cultures, for example, is dependent on our knowledge of their calendar systems, which are often extremely complex, both numerically and symbolically. Such calendars are not mere units of convenience but semisacred codes that touch on the most basic questions of ordering human experience. Traces of this remain in our modern religious calendars and in such customs as observances of the equinox and Halloween.

All notions of time are relative. Our most common experience is the alternation of light and dark that we call a day, yet the periods in this alternation vary from one latitude to another, and at the poles the sun at times never sets. We mark the seasons by periods of recurrent temperature, rainfall, vegetation, and the progression of the stars, yet these too vary with geographic position.

All of these experiences have a circular character; that is, we periodically return to a point of observation from which we had moved away. At the same time, we are conscious of the linear aspect of time in the biological facts of birth, aging, and death. Our conception of time is thus a compound of circular and linear elements that combine into larger patterns of passage and recurrence. We must take account not only of things that appear to change little, if at all, such as the regular phases of the moon or the annual positions of the stars, but also of those that change rapidly and unpredictably, such as the forms of life.

A calendar is a compromise that combines both circular and linear patterns of our experience into a single system. It is based on the most immediate patterns of recurrence (days, months, seasons, years), but it imposes a linear progression on them by the device of numbering and counting. Our most general ideas about history, too, tend to be either circular or linear—or an attempt to combine the two. Circular theories of history tend to emphasize the theme of recurrently rising and falling civilizations, while linear theories stress the idea of progress, whether along an indefinite path or toward a final destination.

The Western world has used the birth of Jesus Christ and thus of Christianity as the principal dividing point in history; all historical dates are commonly expressed as B.C. (before Christ) or A.D. (Anno Domini, "in the year of our Lord"), or sometimes as B.C.E. (before the common era) and C.E. (common era). This linear system, so familiar to us (its invention dates from the sixth century), has far less cultural significance for much of the non-Western world, yet it is now universally understood and widely accepted. Nonetheless, it is by no means the only historical reference point in use today. Jewish and Muslim cultures, among others, have their own dates of origin and continue to keep their own calendars. We have adopted the Western convention in this work.

## The Origins of Humanity

Although the earth itself is approximately 4.5 to 5 billion years old, the earliest humanlike ancestors appeared several million years ago. They were hominids—primates similar to the modern human, although with considerably smaller brain capacities. Hominids walked on two feet, used tools, and ate meat. About 1.4 to 1.6 million years ago hominids evolved into *Homo erectus*, probably in temperate regions of Africa first, after which some migrated into western and southern Asia and Europe. Many anthropologists believe that *H. erectus*, with its enlarged brain (about two-thirds the size of a modern human's) evolved independently in Java, the Philippines, and China.

Because *H. erectus* used stone tools, the earliest period in the human saga is known as the Paleolithic, or Old Stone Age. During this long period, which probably began 600,000 or more years ago, tools, which were originally only primitive chips of stone, gradually became more sophisticated. *H. erectus* developed the hand ax, which could be used to chop, cut, scrape, and punch holes. Tools for scraping could also be fashioned out of flint.

Paleolithic people fed themselves with grain, fruits, vegetables, berries, roots, nuts, and game hunted with spears. Hunting large animals, such as deer, horses, and bison, required organization and communication, thus encouraging the development of speech and rudimentary social groups. These people organized themselves into bands, typically numbering several dozen persons, for the purposes of protection, the provision of food, and probably simple religious rituals. The basic social unit of this hunter-gatherer society was the family. Because of their role as gatherers and their bearing and raising of children, women were presumably the social equals of men. Nevertheless, the gradual division of labor along sexual lines contributed to a distinction of occupational roles that has lasted into the twentieth century.

In geologic terms, the Paleolithic age was roughly coterminous with the Pleistocene epoch, which extended from 2 million to approximately 10,000 years ago. During this epoch, glaciers advanced and retreated at least four and possibly as many as six or seven times, causing substantial climatic and topographic changes that required humans to adapt. They were, in other words, forced to think and thus to develop their critical capacities. Evolution therefore continued, leading to the appearance of *Homo sapiens neanderthalensis* between about 100,000 and 55,000 years ago; Neanderthal man was so named because his remains were discovered in the Neander River valley in modern Germany.

Neanderthal people lived in both caves and open-air sites, hunted mammals, and warmed themselves at large stone fireplaces. More striking was their preparation of elaborate funeral rites to deal with the needs of those who had died and presumably lived in some afterlife. Bodies were interred in graves filled with shells and ornaments made of ivory and bone, and the skin or bones of the deceased were colored with red ocher, apparently to commemorate life. The corpses themselves were buried in the fetal position, possibly to facilitate rebirth or to restrict the movements of the dead and thereby prevent them from returning to haunt the living. Thus in the process of trying to explain death, Neanderthal people seem to have developed a conception of an afterlife.

About 40,000 years ago modern humans, known anthropologically as *Homo sapiens sapiens*, first appeared. As the name implies, many anthropologists group these people with the Neanderthals, who coexisted with the new people for 5,000 or 10,000 years; both were part of one larger category, *Homo sapiens* ("wise human"). The earliest record of *H. sapiens sapiens* was found at Cro-Magnon, a cave in southwestern France. Like the Neanderthals, Cro-Magnon people were hunter-gatherers; their prey included bison, deer, rhinoceros, and mammoth. The Cro-Magnon period was marked by changes in tools, some of which were constructed of bone, ivory, and antler for the first time. Needles made of antler or bone were used to sew clothing fashioned from animal

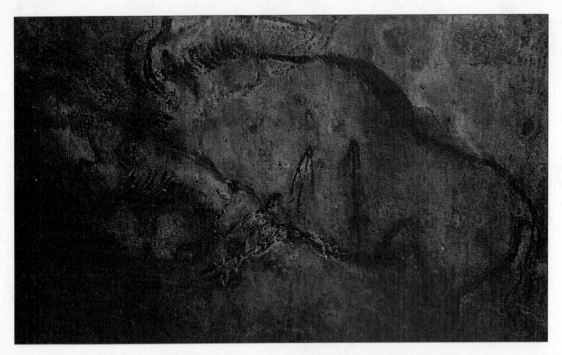

Painting of bison wounded by arrows, c. 15,000–13,000 B.C., found in the Niaux cave in southwestern France. [Ronald Sheridan/Ancient Art and Architecture Collection]

skins. Flint was used to make microliths, such as arrow tips and barbs, and spears could be fashioned from yew wood. Engraving on some antlers and bones indicates that they may have been used as ornaments.

The earliest surviving paintings come from this period and were found deep inside caves in southwestern France, particularly at Lascaux. Most of the images depict animals, such as bulls, cows, horses, bison, and deer. Because the drawings were located in the inner recesses of the caves rather than in the inhabited areas or near the mouths where natural illumination was available, they were probably associated with religious rites. Some paintings show arrows striking the animals, and others have sharp gouges in the animals' sides, as if hunters had thrown spears at them. Rarely do humans appear in these paintings, although one notable exception depicts a masked man—perhaps a priest or a hunter in disguise—wearing deer antlers, bear paws, a wolf's tail, and a lion skin.

Sculptures of humans from the same period typically depict women with enlarged breasts, thighs, and stomachs, emphasizing their reproductive role. The artists thus reflected women's crucial role as the source of life. Rarely do the statues show facial features, and some omit the head altogether; the emphasis was on fertility rather than the lifelike reproduction of physical features. Some scholars believe that these female figures reflect a primitive belief in a mother-goddess.

Drawing of a shaman or a disguised hunter wearing antlers, a bear's paws, a wolf's tail, a lion's skin, and a human beard; c. 13,000–11,000 B.C., Ariège, France. [Logan/Courtesy Department of Library Services, American Museum of Natural History]

The Laussel Venus, a stone relief carving from Les-Ezyies-de-Tarac, France. [Musée d'Aquitaine, Bordeaux]

Paleolithic people in what is now Russia and Poland lived in huts built of the bones of mammoths. [Tass/Sovfoto]

Recent archaeological research suggests that some of the people of this age, although hunter-gatherers, were the first to settle in permanent communities, with facilities for the storage of food, patterns of trade that extended over long distances, and social and political hierarchies. The existence of such hierarchies is suggested by standardized beads and pendants made by western European foragers as long as 32,000 years ago. These people also knew how to fire clay to make ceramics. In central Russia archaeologists have found the remains of elaborate settlements constructed of mammoth bones; the people who lived here some 20,000 years ago traded for materials from the Black Sea region, 500 miles away. Presumably they stored their food because their population was expanding, although this practice limited their mobility. As they settled into permanent communities, internal conflicts must have occurred, leading to the development of social and political organization to maintain order. Probably because of climatic changes, this society came to an end some 12,000 years ago, when the Europeans broke up into small bands and returned to a nomadic life.

By the end of the Paleolithic age some 10,000 years ago, the more advanced people customarily lived in shelters made of wood, hides, sod, or bones; dressed in clothing sewn from skins; used dogs to control, insofar as possible, herds of wild animals; traded with other regions; painted and sculpted; participated in primitive rituals; and buried their dead.

## Agricultural and Social Developments in the Neolithic Age

As long as there was an ample supply of animals to hunt and population remained small, incentives to raise crops and domesticate animals were few. However, as the glaciers retreated and temperatures gradually warmed, large herbivores such as mammoth and bison began to disappear in many regions of human habitation. At the same time, the human population continued to increase rapidly. Specialists estimate that population grew from 125,000 hominids 1 million years ago to 5,320,000 humans at the end of the Paleolithic age and to 133 million about 2,000 years ago. The need to expand the food supply by raising crops and grazing herds thus marked the end of the Paleolithic and the beginning of the Neolithic (New Stone Age).

Agriculture probably originated in the hill country and then was adapted to the valleys of the Tigris and Euphrates rivers in southwestern Asia and in eastern Asia Minor. Other peoples in the world, including those in Mesoamerica (Mexico and Central America), western Africa, southeastern Asia, China, and the Andes, developed agricultural techniques independently. The earliest farmers in western Asia grew wheat, barley, oats, and rye and grazed herds of sheep, goats, pigs, and cattle. People who lived near rivers or lakes could supplement their diet with fish. In time Neolithic people discovered how to brew beer from fermented grain and, in the Mediterranean region, to make wine from grapes.

Agriculture based on tropical crops, especially root crops, appeared in Southeast Asia perhaps as early as 8000 B.C. The year-round warmth and moisture of most of the region gave it strong advantages for sustained cultivation. Rice was native to this area also. Originally a swamp plant, it was adapted to upland fields or to irrigated paddies with relative ease. Pigs, chickens, and water buffalo were native to the region, and the former two soon spread among the late Neolithic cultures elsewhere in Eurasia.

Farming, in the view of some specialists, spread very slowly throughout Europe from western Asia. These experts, using carbon-14 dating, calculate that it took 1,500 years for agricultural techniques to expand from Asia Minor to central Italy and another 1,500 years to reach the central Iberian peninsula. In effect, each generation, they believe, extended the agricultural frontier an average of 11 miles, until farming populations existed throughout Europe by approximately 3800 B.C. More recently, however, some scholars have challenged this view on the basis of evidence that points to the development of European agriculture by indigenous peoples, not colonizers from western Asia. More sophisticated radiocarbon studies, for instance, have indicated that

**the spread of farming in Europe was a stop-and-start process, a series of major expansions or explosions followed by substantial pauses, and not the gradual "wave of advance" inferred in the past from a few radiocarbon dates widely spaced across Europe.[3]**

The stops and starts can, in fact, be correlated with major climatic changes and their impact on regional landscapes. Changes in climate, in other words, played a major role in the expansion of farming.

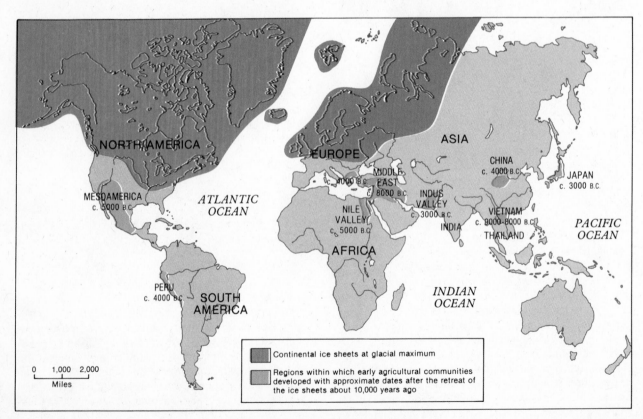

*P.1 The Development of Agriculture*

Elsewhere, the earliest settlements in India were small farming villages in Baluchistan and lower Sind that date to the fourth millennium B.C. North Africa, physically close to western Asia, soon acquired the new techniques. Fully developed Neolithic culture existed in Egypt by 5000 B.C., and from there and from western Africa farming spread gradually throughout the African continent. In the Americas agricultural communities developed more slowly than in Asia and Europe, but by about 2000 B.C. sufficient amounts of food were being grown to make permanent settlements possible.

The change from a nomadic to a settled life made possible by agriculture had both advantages and disadvantages. A greater incentive now existed to build permanent homes, with improved shelter from the elements and with room to store manufactured products. Once the crops were in the ground, many Neolithic people had sufficient free time to hone skills for making tools, cooking utensils, and clothing, thus inaugurating a technological revolution. They learned to make better tools by grinding and polishing stone rather than by chipping, and they discovered how to make pottery, fire it in kilns, and glaze it to improve its capacity to hold liquids. The domestication of sheep provided supplies of wool and thus encouraged the invention of weaving. In time Neolithic people invented the plow and the wheel, improving both agricultural yield and the ability to transport their crops. Dependence on agriculture, however, rendered these people much more susceptible to climatic fluctuations, such as drought, floods, or unseasonable freezes. Settlements also increased the likelihood of illness through greater exposure to contaminated water, excrement, spoiled food, and decaying animal entrails.

In recent decades specialists have learned much about Neolithic trading patterns through chemical and physical analyses of raw materials, such as obsidian and flint. Obsidian, a volcanic glass used for grinding and flaking, spread throughout the western Mediterranean from sources in southern Italy and Sardinia; throughout the Aegean region, mostly from the island of Melos; throughout parts of Asia Minor and as far afield as Syria and Palestine from sites in central Turkey; and throughout the Carpathians from sources in Hungary's Bukk Mountains. Generally, quantities of a given item decrease as the distance from its source increases, but in several instances large amounts of a particular material have been found a considerable distance from the source site, indicating a redistribution center. Thus Neolithic communities were probably less self-sufficient than was once assumed, just as their trading patterns were more sophisticated than was once thought. Raw materials and manufactured items were presumably exchanged for food and perhaps hides. Neolithic potters in Cornwall, at the southwestern tip of England, traded their product to people who lived in western England,

and axes made from the volcanic rock of northwestern England have been found in eastern England.

Like the Paleolithic hunter-gatherers who had established communities in central Russia, Neolithic settlers developed rudimentary forms of social and political organization. As in the Paleolithic age, the family continued to be of prime importance. Some scholars have argued that the basic unit was the extended family, embracing perhaps three generations or siblings and their spouses and children. The extended family could provide the labor necessary for wide-ranging agricultural tasks, such as clearing land or harvesting, and could ensure that the work was performed even if one or more persons became incapacitated. Against this assumption, however, is evidence that late Neolithic houses were normally too small to shelter more than the nuclear family (parents and children). Remains of larger buildings have been found, but it is unclear whether they were the homes of extended families or dwellings that housed both nuclear families and their animals, a practice still followed among some Dutch farmers. Some Neolithic villages had a single large building, generally assumed to have been a community hall.

Scholars are generally agreed that within the community little emphasis was placed on the individual. Instead the people of the village worked together, essentially as equals, to build houses, clear forests, and plant crops. Each family had access to the community's resources as need required. The emphasis, in other words, was on mutual welfare, not, as in modern Western society, productivity for the sake of social differentiation and material accumulation. Archaeological excavation in Neolithic cemeteries tends to confirm this view of a largely egalitarian society, for there is usually little differentiation in goods from one grave to the next. What we do not know, however, is whether all the deceased were interred in these cemeteries or whether Neolithic people buried only the elite.

Women played a key role in Neolithic society and may have enjoyed a higher status than men. Some scholars, in fact, believe that women were largely responsible for the agricultural revolution in the Neolithic period. Mythology suggests confirmation of this: women are associated with raising crops, men with herding animals. The Neolithic village, however, could support a larger population than the hunter-gatherer tribe, intensifying the burden on women as bearers and raisers of children in addition to their expanded agricultural duties. Women's substantial contribution to the success of the agricultural revolution may, according to some scholars, have unwittingly sown the seeds for their subsequent subjugation by men. As mythology suggests, that repression may have begun with the introduction of the animal-drawn plow, which was widely used in western Asia by 3000 B.C.; early myths associated female deities with the hoe and their male counterparts with the plow.

---

## ◉ Evidence for Prehistoric Religious Belief ◉

*The task of reconstructing religious beliefs for prehistoric people who left no written records is very difficult. Here four archaeologists outline their methodology.*

The beliefs of past societies are an integral aspect the archaeologist cannot afford to ignore, however difficult their reconstruction may seem. Burials, for example, have for some years now been interpreted as a more or less accurate mirror of life, on the assumption that a person's living status will be accurately reflected in his or her treatment at death. Ethnographic comparisons show how other factors may intrude. Belief in the impurity of death may affect the extent of ritual treatment at death as much as the deceased's social status; burial can also be an opportunity for various sorts of idealizations, inversions or distortions of social relations in life. Other insights into these important systems of belief may be offered to archaeologists by objects such as the numerous figurines of eastern Europe. Found widely on settlements and sometimes in graves, they represent animal, male and, most frequently, female beings, probably deities. Associated evidence from buildings and architectural models suggests that such cults were an important feature of daily life, with both a domestic aspect within the house and a communal aspect in shrines and temples. Models . . . suggest that temples may have been two-storeyed and impressively large. Faced with this sort of evidence, archaeologists make neat divisions between economy, society, belief and other aspects of life at their own peril.

*Source:* T. Champion, C. Gamble, S. Shennan, and A. Whittle, *Prehistoric Europe* (London: Academic Press, 1984), p. 142.

---

It is in any case worth noting that the recurring competition between the sexes, so common to much of recorded history, may not have existed, or at least was less pronounced, in the long prehistoric era.

Archaeological discoveries have made it possible to reconstruct the outlines of Neolithic religious beliefs. Numerous figurines have been unearthed in prehistoric settlements and graves throughout eastern Europe. Most of these depict females, although others portray males and animals; many probably represented deities, especially an earth mother, responsible for both human and animal fertility and agricultural yields. Neolithic Europeans worshiped both the Great Goddess, who transformed death into life and was linked with moon crescents, and the Goddess of Vegetation, her intimate companion. Religious practice was thus concerned with nature and the cycle of the seasons and occurred in both private houses and shrines or temples. Prehistoric models found in the Danube basin and in Russia indicate that some temples may have been large and even two-storied. Within these temples rituals were performed, as suggested by the large number of surviving clay statuettes depicting masked and costumed men and women.

"Myths and seasonal drama must have been enacted through the medium of the idol [the figurine], each with a different intention and with the invocation of appropriate divinities."[4] Worshipers sacrificed humans, animals, and assorted objects on altars, some of which were found in temples, others in open-air sanctuaries or caves. Archaeologists have discovered tens of thousands of miniature figurines, some of which are inscribed with assorted designs, such as spirals, chevrons, zigzags, and parallel lines; the patterns may have had religious meaning. The extensive archaeological remains pertaining to religion underscore both the extent to which Neolithic people sought to explain and deal with their environment and the growing sense of community reflected in the widespread acceptance of ritual practices.

## The Coming of Civilization

The Neolithic age, with its development of cereal cultivation and animal husbandry, permanent settlements, expanded trading patterns, and social groups, provided the roots from which civilization grew. Most Neolithic settlements were small: homesteads, with fewer than 10 people; hamlets, with populations of 10 to 50; and villages, ranging in size from 50 to several hundred inhabitants. Around 8000 B.C. the transition from village to city life began at Jericho in what was later called Palestine; 2,000 to 3,000 people lived at Jericho in multiroomed houses. They were sufficiently organized socially and politically to construct stone walls as much as 20 feet high and 6 feet thick at the base, beyond which was a ditch 25 feet wide and 6 feet deep. The extent of such fortifications suggests that warfare must have been commonplace, a thesis increasingly advanced by specialists on prehistoric Europe as well. The people of Jericho raised grain, probably with the aid of an irrigation system that used spring waters, and traded sulfur and salt for precious stones from the Sinai and obsidian from Anatolia. Their artists created portrait busts by modeling plaster over human skulls.

Comparable protocities began developing at such places as Jarmo in what is now Iraq around 7000 B.C. and at Çatal Hüyük in Anatolia. The latter, founded approximately 6700 B.C. and excavated in the 1960s, was considerably larger than Jericho. Its inhabitants raised grains, nuts, peas, apples, grapes, and oil-producing seeds; grazed sheep; and hunted deer and wild boar. Residents made pottery, baskets, and wooden vessels; crafted fine weapons from flint; wove cloth; fashioned necklaces and bracelets; and applied cosmetics as they looked into polished obsidian mirrors. Like the people of Jericho, the Çatal Hüyükans traded widely for items that included shells from the Mediterranean and stones from southern Anatolia. The walls of their religious shrines were decorated with paintings of dancers, wild animals, vultures, and funeral rituals. Their chief deity, a female, was attended by both males and females.

In addition to the gradual emergence of cities, the development of metallurgy was important for the rise of civilization. In both western Asia and the Balkans, late Neolithic people acquired the ability to smelt, hammer, and cast copper ores in the fifth millennium B.C. The earliest items fashioned of copper included personal ornaments, axes, daggers, awls, and hooks. Copper, however, is a relatively soft metal, and it was not until 3000 B.C. or shortly thereafter that metalworkers learned the technique of alloying it with tin to produce the more durable bronze. In the beginning, copper, like gold and silver, was rather scarce, and therefore objects made of it would have been prized. People fortunate enough to possess items made from gold, silver, copper, or precious stones thus distinguished themselves from other people on the basis of their wealth. Evidence for the rise of societies characterized by degrees of wealth has been found, for example, in late Neolithic graves in northern Europe, where prestigious goods such as copper daggers and beakers and fine flint battle-axes were buried in some single rather than collective graves.

Social differentiation was undoubtedly encouraged as some people mastered metallurgical technology and more sophisticated techniques of pottery making and decorating. The British archaeologist Patricia Phillips has argued that

it seems likely that the larger populations of the Late Neolithic permitted more specialization, that their density forced more complexity of social structure, and these com-

The ruins of Jericho, perhaps the world's oldest city. [British School of Archaeology, Jerusalem]

**A rock painting showing warriors, c. 8000–3000 B.C., found near Castellón, Spain.**
[Arxiu MAS, Barcelona]

plexities fuelled the demand for high-value goods to indicate their status. These goods might acquire value because of their rarity, or because of the length of time they took in manufacture.[5]

Essentially classless societies thus faded in the face of emerging distinctions based on wealth and technical skills.

A skill of a different kind involved the ability to write. Scholars may someday find that writing first appeared in southern and central Europe if it can be demonstrated that the engravings on the numerous Neolithic figurines found there are more than simple markings. At least for now, however, the earliest known writing system was devised by the people of Uruk (now Tal al-Warka), one of the principal city-states in ancient Sumer (modern Iraq). In the late Neolithic period, records were kept using small tokens in the shape of disks, spheres, half spheres, cones, and other figures, some of which were marked with incisions. Usually kept in clay containers, such tokens might be used, for instance, to represent animals in a palace herd.

Late in the fourth millennium B.C., as cities and large-scale trade developed, the use of tokens to maintain records became too cumbersome. The people of Mesopotamia substituted written images known as ideographs for the tokens. During the third millennium B.C. these ideographs evolved into a series of wedge-shaped marks that could be impressed on a clay tablet quickly and easily with a split reed. The Sumerians also wrote on stone and metal, but clay, which was plentiful in their country and was already used for building and pottery, was much easier to make marks on. Mistakes could easily be smoothed out, and the record could be made permanent by leaving the clay to dry in the sun or baking it slowly in an oven. In this form it was light and easy to carry as well. The system of wedge-shaped marks on clay is known as *cuneiform*, after the Latin word *cuneus*, which means "wedge." Cuneiform combined the use of pictographic signs (representing objects) and phonetic signs (representing sounds) with a total of some 350 characters. This method of writing was, of course, useful to keep track of financial and other transactions, including records of religious beliefs, political and military achievements, and laws.

About the time the Sumerians evolved their system

A Neolithic carving of a masked man holding a sickle and wearing rings on his arms, c. 5000 B.C. Such sickles were made of copper.
[Courtesy of Professor Marija Gimbutas]

## Notes

1. R. W. Fogel and G. R. Elton, *Which Road to the Past? Two Views of History* (New Haven, Conn.: Yale University Press, 1983), p. 92.
2. C. Floyd, "Society and the Artist," 1964 Distinguished Professor Lecture, Florida State University.
3. G. Barker, *Prehistoric Farming in Europe* (Cambridge: Cambridge University Press, 1985), p. 253.
4. M. Gimbutas, *The Goddesses and Gods of Old Europe, 6500–3500 B.C.: Myths and Cult Images*, 2nd ed. (Berkeley: University of California Press, 1982), p. 236.
5. P. Phillips, *The Prehistory of Europe* (Bloomington: Indiana University Press, 1980), p. 187.

## Suggestions for Further Reading

Barker, G. *Prehistoric Farming in Europe*. Cambridge: Cambridge University Press, 1982.

Bender, B. *Farming in Prehistory: From Hunter-Gatherer to Food Producer*. London: Baler, 1975.

Briffault, R. *The Mothers*. New York: Atheneum, 1977.

Campbell, B. *Humankind Emerging*. Boston: Little, Brown, 1979.

Champion, T., Gamble, C., Shennan, S., and Whittle, A. *Prehistoric Europe*. London: Academic Press, 1984.

Chard, C. *Man in Prehistory*. New York: McGraw-Hill, 1975.

Cohen, M. N. *The Food Crisis in Prehistory*. New Haven, Conn.: Yale University Press, 1977.

Fagan, B. *People of the Earth*. Boston: Little, Brown, 1977.

Gimbutas, M. *The Goddesses and Gods of Old Europe, 6500–3500 B.C.: Myths and Cult Images*. Berkeley: University of California Press, 1982.

Gowlett, J. *Ascent to Civilization: The Archaeology of Early Man*. New York: Knopf, 1984.

Harris, M. *Cannibals and Kings: The Origins of Cultures*. London: Collins, 1978.

Johnson, D., and Edey, M. *Lucy: The Beginnings of Humankind*. New York: Warner Books, 1981.

Keightly, D. N., ed. *The Origins of Chinese Civilization*. Berkeley: University of California Press, 1983.

Leakey, R. E., and Lewin, R. *Origins*. New York: Dutton, 1977.

Lerner, G. *The Creation of Patriarchy*. New York: Oxford University Press, 1986.

Marshack, A. *The Roots of Civilization*. New York: McGraw-Hill, 1972.

Phillips, P. *The Prehistory of Europe*. Bloomington: Indiana University Press, 1980.

Reed, C. E., ed. *Origins of Agriculture*. Paris: Mouton, 1977.

Sheratt, A., ed. *The Cambridge Encyclopaedia of Archaeology*. Cambridge: Cambridge University Press, 1980.

Sieveking, A. *The Cave Artists*. London: Thames & Hudson, 1979.

of writing, a transportation revolution was under way that provided further impetus to the emergence of civilization. The invention of the wheel enabled farmers and others to haul large quantities of goods on animal-drawn two- and four-wheeled carts. Bulky goods in particular could be moved more efficiently thanks to the invention of the sail in the fourth millennium B.C. The new means of transportation were crucial in handling the increasing amounts of agricultural produce made possible by the development of better plows (antlers replaced sticks beginning in the fourth millennium B.C.) and of the larger quantities of pottery produced after the introduction of the potter's wheel. The first peoples to combine all these developments lived in the river valleys of Mesopotamia, Egypt, and India. Civilizations developed somewhat later in China and Southeast Asia.

# The Peoples and Cultures of Antiquity

By discovering techniques for the organized cultivation of food, the world's first farmers made possible the development of civilization. By producing enough to feed a settled community and leave a surplus, they provided a basis for trade and barter. Other people, freed from the necessity of feeding themselves, could engage in different activities—administration, the organization of religion, and warfare. With the development of specialized crafts, new agricultural methods made possible large urban communities and led to the formation of states. With the need to record transactions came the invention of writing. Stratified social structures appeared together with the division of populations into rulers and ruled. As commerce developed, individuals were better able to communicate wealth and use it as a means to acquire power and influence.

In widely separated parts of the world this process produced the earliest human civilizations—in the river basins of the Tigris and Euphrates in western Asia, the Nile in Egypt, the Indus in India, and the Yellow River in China. If the causes that produced civilization were similar in each case, the characteristics of individual cultures were very different. Conditioned by factors of geography and climate, accessibility to outside influences, and, in some cases, pure chance, the forms of language, art, religion, and almost all aspects of daily life varied widely from region to region.

The application of bronze-working techniques—first in western and southeastern Asia and then in India, China, and Europe—led to further technological progress. With the notable exception of the Chinese, few other Bronze Age cultures had sizable deposits of both copper and tin, the two alloys necessary to produce bronze. This circumstance stimulated foreign trade, which was made easier by improved means of transport. Greater wealth led to aggressive economic and territorial expansion.

With the invention of iron smelting, civilization took a new turn. Discovered by the Hittites in western Asia in the mid-second millennium B.C., the technique spread to Europe and to sub-Saharan Africa, where it was possibly diffused from contacts through the upper Nile. New geographic areas began to develop in importance. In western Asia the center of civilization moved from the river basins to what is now Iran, where the Persians flourished. In India culture spread south and east. In Europe civilization gradually expanded westward to Greece and then to Italy.

By the end of classical antiquity in Europe, the world had become sufficiently small for most of the leading civilizations to be in contact with one another. At the peak of their power, the Romans controlled large tracts of Europe and Asia and traded in India and Africa and, through central Asian intermediaries, with China. Only the Americas and Australasia remained isolated from contact with outside culture.

The first 4,500 years of civilization saw a great variety of artistic and literary creations, much of which not only illuminates remote periods but also retains its power to move and delight. The chief religions of the ancient world serve as a reminder of the common ground of human experience, addressing the eternal problems of existence. ∎

# The Societies of Western Asia and Egypt

The first civilizations developed in one of the birthplaces of the agricultural revolution, western Asia and ancient Egypt, the region now known as the Middle East. Village-level agriculture had appeared earlier, in the uplands west of Mesopotamia and in mainland Southeast Asia. But the peoples of ancient Egypt and Mesopotamia were the first who systematically organized the growing of food in large permanent fields under irrigation, developed improved techniques of mining and metal processing, founded cities, and devised social, legal, and ethical systems as well as institutions of government and religion.

Such large-scale developments were greatly advanced by the discovery and use of new materials. Pottery was produced by at least 5000 B.C. in western and southeastern Asia, and soon afterward metal began to replace stone in the manufacture of tools and weapons. Copper was the earliest material employed, but the technique of alloying copper with tin to produce bronze was soon discovered, probably around 3000 B.C. It was at the fortified settlements of this new Bronze Age in Egypt and Mesopotamia that civilization in the West began. In

**Several women ruled Egypt as pharaohs in their own right. The most famous of these was Hatshepsut, shown here with a crown and a stylized beard. [Metropolitan Museum of Art, New York]**

the centuries that followed, other western Asian peoples began to form their own distinctive cultures, the most important of which were those of the Hebrews, the Hittites, and the Persians.

Egypt and Mesopotamia are dominated by great rivers—Egypt by the Nile, which regularly floods each year, and Mesopotamia by the Tigris and the Euphrates. The annual flooding of the Nile was consistent and predictable, both in its timing and in the scope of the land that it inundated. As the floodwater receded, seeds were planted in the wet soil; the new surface of fertile silt retained enough moisture to bring the crop to harvest. The Tigris and Euphrates rivers were far more irregular in their flooding and often wreaked destruction. Protection for farmland was therefore essential, as were means to irrigate the fields. Owing in part to these differences, the cultures of Egypt and Mesopotamia developed in distinctive ways, each making a special contribution to the development of civilization.

## Life Between the Rivers: The City Dwellers of Mesopotamia

The history of ancient Mesopotamia consists of a succession of peoples, each with a somewhat different but related culture. To complicate the picture, a number of other peoples played a part in Mesopotamian history, notably the Hittites to the northwest and the peoples of ancient Iran (Persia) to the east. For the most part, however, the neighboring peoples were overshadowed by the more powerful states of Mesopotamia until well into the first millennium B.C., when the Persians established their mighty empire. The lack of natural barriers opened Mesopotamia to invaders, who used surprise, superior leadership, and technology to establish dominion over the area. The political history of the region reflects these cycles of invasion both in the periodic rise and fall of the states and in the eclectic nature of Mesopotamian civilization. The foundations of this civilization rested firmly on the advanced culture of Sumer.

## Sumer

The first Sumerian settlements were farming communities that had developed around 4000 B.C. in the region between the Tigris and Euphrates rivers. The land in this area is flat, and dikes and canals had to be constructed to limit erosion during the rainy months and to collect water for the arid season. The only way for the early settlers to acquire the means for such large-scale

building projects was to pool their resources and work together for their common benefit; thus villages began to merge and new towns were born.

The need to organize and administer complex projects of this kind led to centralized control. The same necessity prompted the Mesopotamians to develop a system of writing by using images of tokens that had hitherto been employed for record keeping (see the essay "Writing and Communication (I)" on pp. 226–231). The images were marked on soft clay tablets with a split reed, and the tablets were then baked. The reeds made the distinctive wedge-shaped marks of the Mesopotamian system, known as cuneiform. With the ability to write came possibilities for trade and administration on a broader scale. The economic development this per-

Cuneiform tablet recording the foundation of the city of Aanepadda, c. 2600 B.C. [Reproduced by Courtesy of the Trustees of the British Museum]

mitted led to the growth of powerful cities. The city where modern excavation has uncovered the most spectacular treasures was Ur.

---

🪷

# URBAN LIFE IN SUMER: UR

---

Ur was the most southerly of the great Sumerian cities, lying just to the south of the Euphrates River and about 200 miles northwest of what we call the Persian Gulf. From the early third millennium B.C. its citizen-traders used the river as a means of navigating to the outer world, and the wider markets they could reach helped account for the extraordinary wealth the city accumulated. In describing Ur as a city, however, it is important to remember that in the third millennium B.C. a Sumerian city was more like a regional complex than a densely inhabited core. Ur consisted of the city itself, suburbs, and smaller, more distant villages that depended on the central administration. The whole was surrounded with agricultural lands, including barley and wheat fields, palm groves, and gardens. The exact size of Ur is not known, but Lagash, a city of comparable importance, is estimated to have had a population of 30,000 to 35,000.

For their principal building materials the Sumerians used what lay at hand. The valley of the two rivers has virtually no supplies of stone, so the builders of Ur used sun-dried bricks made from clay and straw, which long ago disintegrated into shapeless mounds. Excavations reveal that the center of the community was the temple, the dwelling place of the god who protected the town. Sumerians typically built their temples on raised mounds to prevent damage from flooding. Protected by its own walls, the temple compound housed the residences and workplaces of priests, scribes, and skilled artisans. The compound was surrounded by temples to minor deities and flat-roofed, one-story houses, the largest of which were built around inner courtyards and con-

tained shrines and family burial plots. The otherwise drab houses were decorated in places with colorful mosaics. Streets were little more than narrow, dirty lanes, and the city itself was enclosed by walls constructed of brown bricks.

The greatest monument at Ur is the ziggurat, the present form of which dates to around 2100 B.C. The word *ziggurat* means "pinnacle" or "mountaintop," and these layered artificial mountains were built from early Sumerian times throughout the Tigris and Euphrates valleys. The ziggurat at Ur consisted of a huge platform, measuring 190 by 130 feet, surmounted with terraces. Its great central staircase led to the upper terrace, which housed a temple.

It was presumably on this pinnacle that Nanna, the moon-god and patron deity of Ur, appeared to the ruler, who acted as the interpreter and conveyor of divine wishes to the citizens and as the principal servant of the gods. One of his chief duties was the building and maintenance of the temples. Several monuments show Sumerian and later Mesopotamian rulers carrying on their heads baskets filled with bricks for the construction of a new sanctuary. Nonetheless, any impression that Sumerian rulers lived austere lives is quickly dispelled by treasures retrieved from the Royal Cemetery.

In early Sumer the ruler and the chief priests shared responsibility for governing the city. But a gradual separation of palace from temple took place, and at times conflicts developed between the two sides. Nevertheless, the temple owned about a third of the land around the city of Ur, a part of which was cultivated to provide food for priests and temple employees. Some temple property was allotted to farmers, and some was leased to tenants who were required to hand back a proportion of their harvest as dues, or "tithes." Most land under secular control was probably the property of the ruler, but individuals owned their own houses, fields, and gardens. The disparity of ownership reflected social status. A high government official might possess estates of as much as 500 acres, while a simple builder owned per-

**Ziggurat at Ur, c. 2100–2000 B.C. The huge staircases led to a shrine at the top. [Hirmer Fotoarchiv, Munich]**

haps 5 acres. Apart from slaves, Sumerians of all classes could buy, sell, exchange, or rent privately owned houses, property, and livestock.

Private citizens constructed and manufactured both for the state and for one another. From Ur's earliest days its citizens had exported their manufactured products both overland and by sea. Most foreign trade was organized by the state, but on occasion wealthy private contractors received licenses to export their goods. In turn the Sumerians imported stone for the construction of their temples, and metals to decorate them and to use for tools, wood, incense, and jewels.

The population of a city such as Ur was diverse, consisting of nobles, clients of the nobility, commoners, and slaves. The king and his family, the high priests, and the chief officials in the court comprised the nobility. Below them were clients or vassals, whose service to the nobility was repaid by the right to farm small plots of land. Such services included working for the temples, on farms, and in workshops. Temples employed women, for instance, to do their spinning and weaving. At Lagash approximately one-sixth of the farmland was in the hands of the priests, who rented half of it to peasants and hired workers to farm the rest. Commoners generally owned their own land, though control of it rested in large family groups.

In ancient societies slavery typically developed as a result of military conquest. Most slaves were therefore prisoners of war or kidnapped foreigners, although some were people who had sold themselves or their children into slavery to repay debts. Owners could beat or brand their slaves, but slaves who worked hard might earn profits and in some cases purchase their freedom. They were also permitted to marry free persons; the offspring of such marriages were free. Few slaves were employed in agriculture; they tended instead to be artisans, domestic servants, and concubines. Temple slaves were often women whose responsibilities probably included spinning, weaving, and grinding flour. Ancient Mesopotamia was not economically dependent on slave labor.

Much social and economic activity involved women as well as men. Sumerian women could buy and sell property, but over the ensuing centuries the lot of women in Mesopotamia would slowly decline. At the lower end of the scale, enslaved women served as domestic servants, cooks, and concubines, while among the upper classes the ruler and his wife were surrounded by a retinue of elaborately attired court ladies. The remains of a number of these, together with their jewelry and costumes, were found in the Royal Cemetery at Ur. The ruler's wife played an important part in public life; in cities where the principal deity was a goddess, the queen often took charge of temple affairs.

Thus, in spite of obvious differences, life in a city such as Ur must have been closer to our own than might have been expected, not least in the all-pervading presence of professional administrators. Citizens today would recognize many of the attributes of a modern civil service in the bureaucrats of ancient Sumer. On the clay tablets, inscribed in cuneiform, they systematically recorded the lists of workers, payrolls, inventories, vouchers, revenues, taxes, and other details for a functioning city. Like their modern counterparts, they sought to impose their vision of order on the variety of life.

## Mesopotamian Religion

Religion permeated Sumerian civic life. Heaven and earth, the sun and the moon, and natural phenomena such as lightning and storms were all regarded as manifestations of deities. The principal holidays marked the change of the seasons. The chief annual event was the New Year, when the blistering heat of the previous summer and the winter's cold yielded to the fertile spring. The worship of the Great Mother, which evolved out of the Neolithic cult of the Great Goddess, celebrated the earth's abundance, and the sterility of the winter was attributed to the death of her partner, Dumuzi (Tammuz). His disappearance was mourned annually as the 11-day New Year festival began. At the festival's culmination, his resurrection was celebrated, together with the sacred marriage of god and goddess, renewed each spring as a symbol of hope for the coming year.

The Mesopotamians received little comfort from their religion. Life in the valley of the two rivers was harsh, and it posed a continuous struggle against the natural disasters of drought and flood. If nonetheless inhabitants preferred it to the afterlife, it was because their religion offered only darkness and dust after death, even for kings. Mesopotamian religion advanced the notion that the gods, depicted in human form, were demanding and that people were servants to them. As in many religious traditions, failure to obey the wishes of the gods was thought to bring punishment. In addition to the four creator gods—of the sky, the moving force of nature, earth, and water—were 50 "great gods" and innumerable lesser deities and demons. The appeal of Mesopotamian religion was in the possibility of obtaining the assistance of the gods, particularly Enlil, the moving force, for help in the travails of this life.

The Mesopotamians' grim vision of life is illustrated by the great Sumerian poem *The Epic of Gilgamesh*. Gilgamesh himself was an actual historical figure who ruled the city of Uruk around 2600 B.C. A series of legends grew up around his name, and these oral traditions were eventually set down in writing to become the world's first epic poem. Written in Sumerian about 2000 B.C., it was inscribed afterward on clay tablets in their own languages by the Babylonians, the Hittites, and others in western Asia.

## ◙ A Mesopotamian Account of Creation ◙

*The Sumerian poem* The Epic of Gilgamesh *circulated widely in Meso-potamia in a variety of versions and languages. This is how it begins:*

O Gilgamesh, lord of Kullab, great is thy praise. This was the man to whom all things were known; this was the king who knew the countries of the world. He was wise, he saw mysteries and knew secret things, he brought us a tale of the days before the flood. He went on a long journey, was weary, worn-out with labor, and returning engraved on a stone the whole story.

When the gods created Gilgamesh they gave him a perfect body. Shamash the glorious sun endowed him with beauty, Adad the god of the storm endowed him with courage, the great gods made his beauty perfect, surpassing all others. Two-thirds they made him god and one-third man.

In Uruk he built walls, a great rampart, and the temple of blessed Eanna for the god of the firmament Anu, and for Ishtar the goddess of love. Look at it still today: the outer wall where the cornice runs, it shines with the brilliance of copper; and the inner wall, it has no equal. Touch the threshold, it is ancient. Approach Eanna the dwelling of Ishtar, our lady of love and war, the like of which no latter-day king, no man alive can equal. Climb upon the wall of Uruk; walk along it, I say; regard the foundation terrace and examine the masonry: is it not burnt brick and good? The seven sages laid the foundations.

*Source: The Epic of Gilgamesh,* trans. N. K. Sanders (Harmondsworth, England: Penguin Books, 1960), p. 59.

Although the general vision of *The Epic of Gilgamesh* is harsh and pessimistic, the early scenes, which chronicle the exploits of Gilgamesh and his beloved friend Enkidu, are fresh and vivid. When Enkidu perishes, Gilgamesh sets out to find a way to avoid death. His quest fails. He returns home to record his adventure on a stone and by that means finds immortality. With Gilgamesh's assistance, Enkidu returns at the end of the poem with an account of the ways of the underworld, affirming the Mesopotamian belief in a shadowy, unappealing life after death. The existence of similar tales among other peoples, including the Hebrews and the inhabitants of Asia Minor and the Pacific islands, underscores the common human interest in questions of divine punishment, death, and immortality.

The story of the flood recounted in the epic has particular similarities with the later version in the biblical book of Genesis, although the tone of the scriptural account is very different. The God of the Hebrews is motivated by moral disapproval, whereas the Sumerian gods apparently send the flood to punish mortals for making too much noise and keeping the gods awake. Nevertheless, like Noah in the later Hebrew account, Utnapishtim, one of the heroes of the epic, escaped drowning by sailing the waters of death in an ark and later recounted his adventure to Gilgamesh. An earlier Mesopotamian epic titled *When the Gods Were Men*, from which the author of the *Epic of Gilgamesh* may have borrowed, recounted a similar story. The recurrence of such myths illustrates the cultural continuity that characterized Mesopotamian civilization.

## Akkadian and Babylonian Culture

Between approximately 2370 and 2130 B.C. the whole of Mesopotamia fell under the rule of King Sargon I and his descendants; his capital city of Akkad (or Agade) gives the period its name. The Akkadians had originally come from the fringes of the Arabian desert. Their new home base was to the north of the principal Sumerian cities, and their conquest and unification of Mesopotamia had a lasting effect on its political and cultural life. They also introduced a new language, of the Semitic family, which includes Hebrew, Arabic, and Aramaic. At the same time, the Akkadians preserved some aspects of Sumerian culture, including the cuneiform system of writing.

Whereas earlier Sumerian monarchs had ruled large parts of Mesopotamia, Sargon was the first to create a unified kingdom throughout the region. This he accom-

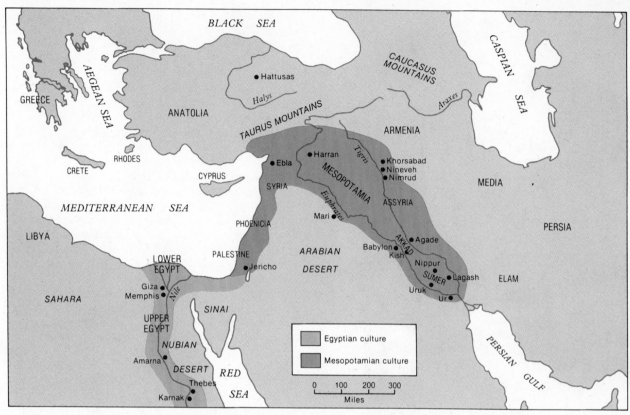

*1.1 Western Asia and Egypt*

plished by the judicious combination of military force and the establishment of a central administration. Semitic officials from Akkad served as governors throughout the kingdom, their authority reinforced by military garrisons in the subject cities. Sargon extended his rule westward into northern Syria and the Lebanon mountains (important as a source of cedar), making him the first imperialist in the Western world.

Either Sargon or his successor destroyed the Syrian city-state of Ebla, first rediscovered by archaeologists in 1964. The people of Ebla had been heavily influenced by Mesopotamian culture, as reflected in the large number of cuneiform-inscribed tablets unearthed there. From them scholars have learned much about life in northern Syria. Ebla's economy was primarily agricultural, with the emphasis on flax (for linen), barley, olive trees (for oil), vineyards, and sheepherding. Unlike southern Mesopotamia, where irrigation farming prevailed, adequate rainfall in northern Syria made it possible to dry-farm, relying on conservation of moisture in the soil without the use of irrigation. Ebla lay astride the trade routes between Anatolia and the lowland plains of Syria, enabling it to amass impressive quantities of gold, silver, and bronze. Gold and silver, in fact, were used as means of exchange, much as coinage would be later. Ebla's con-

tact with Mesopotamia was not entirely peaceful, for it engaged in a bitter economic and political rivalry with the Babylonian city-state of Mari on the banks of the Euphrates.

In the reign of Sargon's grandson, Naram-Sin (c. 2250 B.C.), rulers of individual cities were called "slaves of the king," who himself assumed the title of King of the Four Quarters of the Universe. To reinforce his authority Naram-Sin, one of the great temple builders in Mesopotamian history, demanded that he be worshiped as a god. His empire extended from Armenia south to the Persian Gulf and the Red Sea and as far westward as the Mediterranean coast.

With the sudden and violent end of Akkadian rule produced by the Guti, nomadic invaders from Iran, the cities of Mesopotamia revived earlier cultural practices. Renewed religious devotion can be seen in the many temples of this so-called Neo-Sumerian period (c. 2130–c. 2030 B.C.), especially in the statues of Gudea, the governor of the city of Lagash around 2100 B.C. Gudea, a patron of the arts, is shown in an attitude of devotion, hands tightly clasped, as he stands respectfully before the gods. The humility of the figure contrasts strongly with an earlier Akkadian portrait thought to depict Sargon.

This portrait of an Akkadian king is thought
to be of Sargon himself. [Hirmer Fotoarchiv,
Munich]

# Hammurabi,
## "King of Justice"

In the early eighteenth century B.C. Mesopotamia was
once again unified, this time under another Semitic
group, the Amorites. Their most famous king, Hammurabi (c. 1792–1750 B.C.), having defeated the Assyrians
and their allies, was determined to unify his Sumerian
and Semitic subjects, in part by codifying the legal de-

cisions rendered during his reign. Law, of course, was
important to all peoples of western Asia and Egypt, who
saw it as a means of bringing order out of chaos; as such,
it was basic to religion as well as government. Hammurabi's achievement, though not in fact a true code but
rather a collection of case laws, has nevertheless been
acclaimed as one of the earliest attempts to formulate a
legal code; the first examples date from around 2100 B.C.
Hammurabi, who formally pronounced the code, had
copies inscribed on stone slabs set up in temples to attest
to the gods' approval.

The code of Hammurabi sought to regulate the rights
and obligations of the three Amorite classes—free people, state dependents, and slaves—by establishing laws
and providing specific punishments for their transgres-
sion. The penalties, which differed according to social
status, included not only fines but also corporal punishment, mutilation, and execution; imprisonment and
forced labor were not specified.

Unlike some earlier Mesopotamian laws, Hammurabi's code did not recognize the blood feud or private
vengeance, but as in most early legal systems, its provisions were harsh. A surgeon whose patient died in the
course of a major operation was sentenced to have a
hand cut off, and architects whose faulty work caused a
building to collapse and kill a client were themselves put
to death. The operative principle was that of "an eye for
an eye," or the closest possible equivalence between a
crime and its punishment. But many penalties were exceedingly harsh. Capital punishment was meted out to
female adulterers, though a husband had the power to
pardon his wife. Incest could be punished by death or
exile. A son who struck his father could have his hand
amputated (a similar law was later incorporated in the
Old Testament). Perjurers in capital cases, rapists, many
thieves, adulterators of beer, and people who avoided
mandatory state service also faced death, as did extravagant wives.

The code spelled out the rights of husbands and
wives, of parents and children, and of masters and workers. The laws pertaining to women and children included
a number of extreme provisions: men were not only allowed to practice polygamy but also permitted to have
mistresses. They also had the power to sell their wives
and children into slavery. A husband could divorce his
wife at will, provided that he return the dowry and pay
child support if she had fulfilled her spousal responsibilities; if not, she received nothing. A wife could obtain
a divorce only by demonstrating cruelty or neglect; if she
sued and lost, she faced capital punishment. Women did,
however, retain the right to own property and enter into
contracts.

Fathers had absolute control over their children until
such time as the latter married. Marriages were arranged by the parents and sealed by a contract, sometimes while the betrothed children were very young; in

such cases, the marriage took place but the couple lived in the home of the groom's or the bride's parents until they were old enough to live on their own. Fathers could compel their daughters to become priestesses or concubines. The importance of property was underscored by a provision that prohibited a father from disinheriting his son unless the latter had twice committed major offenses.

The code also dealt with slavery. Slaves could own property, including other slaves, and sometimes ran businesses for their masters. Slaves were distinguished by branding; removal of the mark was an offense. Masters had the right to select spouses for their slaves. The spouses could be free persons, and children of half-free, half-slave marriages were born free. Slaves could purchase their freedom by accumulating or borrowing the manumission fee; the temples loaned sums for this purpose.

The legal procedures spelled out in the code reveal a concern for justice, however harsh the penalties may have been. Because the state did not initiate prosecutions, private parties had to file complaints against alleged aggressors. The judge's verdict was final, and not even he could alter it without being fined and removed from the bench. A judge who had difficulty deciding a case could resort to trial by ordeal, according to which the accused was thrown into a body of water: a guilty person was presumed to float; an innocent one would sink. In addition to the code's concern for meting out justice, it was intended above all as a deterrent to the commission of acts deemed offensive to society. By making these principles public, Hammurabi hoped to win repute as the "king of justice." Among those influenced by his code were the Hebrews, whose legal principles were eventually embodied in the Bible.

## The Beginnings of Egyptian Civilization

Egypt is a desert country, most of which can support only a pastoral economy. That it served as a breadbasket for the ancient world is due to the 4,000-mile-long Nile River, which flows north from central Africa and provides a fertile delta. Ancient Egypt was divided into two parts. Lower or northern Egypt occupied approximately 150 miles of broad, flat land in the Nile delta, from which the rest of the Mediterranean region was easily accessible. Lower Egypt had twice as much land as Upper Egypt, which, upriver, was more remote from the outside world. Upper Egypt comprised a narrow band of fertile soil that ran between high cliffs and desert on either side of the Nile for approximately 525 miles.

The sparseness of rain in both regions meant that

agriculture was possible only through extensive irrigation systems and by taking advantage of the annual flooding of the river. The Greek historian Herodotus called Egypt "the gift of the Nile," which remains an apt description. Here, as in Mesopotamia, it was possible to produce an agricultural surplus on river alluvium (silt), continually deposited by annual floods. Water from the Nile could also be manipulated to provide a controlled supply to arid areas throughout the year, and the Nile, like the Tigris and the Euphrates, also served as a vital avenue of transport to the cities, especially for the supply of food, fuel, and building materials. The Nile valley was separated from other civilizations by deserts, so Egypt was seldom menaced by outside aggressors. This allowed it to develop a homogeneous civilization of its own. Political and economic life in Egypt, as in Mesopotamia, was profoundly affected by the character of its geographic position.

Some of the rock carvings on the cliffs of the Nile valley date back to around 6000 B.C. Their depictions of hunters and animals, weapons and traps, illustrate the conditions of life before the development of civilization. As Neolithic culture began, drawings of cattle and boats appeared, but at this early period the small village communities were subject to damage caused by the floodwaters of the Nile even as they bestowed fertility. Starting around 4000 B.C. larger villages were built on higher ground out of reach of the flooding Nile. The efforts of several neighboring communities to cooperate in constructing canals and dikes to channel the waters seem to have been the original stimulus for the growth of organized districts.

As the villages joined together, the regions began to unite into two main kingdoms, Upper and Lower Egypt, "the Two Lands," and shortly before 3000 B.C. they united under a single ruler. An Egyptian priest, Manetho, the author of a history of Egypt (c. 280 B.C.), divided the vast span of Egyptian history into 31 dynasties, or periods of rule by members of a royal family. Today scholars group that history into five periods, each of roughly 500 years' duration: the Early Dynastic Period (c. 2925–c. 2575 B.C.), the Old Kingdom (c. 2575–c. 2130 B.C.), the Middle Kingdom (1938–1600 B.C.), the New Kingdom (c. 1540–1075 B.C.), and the Late Period (1075–525 B.C.), after which Egypt was absorbed into the Persian Empire. These dynastic periods were separated by times of instability and disturbance.

## Unification: The Age of the Pyramids

The Old Kingdom was an age of prosperity and innovation. New technical skills were used to construct the

WESTERN ASIA AND EGYPT

| Mesopotamia | Egypt | Other lands |
|---|---|---|
| Early Sumerians (c. 4000–c. 2370 B.C.) | Early Dynastic Period (c. 2925–2575 B.C.) | |
| ● Gilgamesh (c. 2600 B.C.) | Old Kingdom (c. 2575–2130 B.C.) | |
| Akkadians (c. 2370–c. 1950 B.C.) | ● Age of the pyramids | Hittites settle in Anatolia (c. 2000 B.C.) |
| Babylonians (Amorites, c. 1950–c. 1600 B.C.) | Middle Kingdom (1938–c. 1600 B.C.) | |
| ● Hammurabi (c. 1792–1750 B.C.) | | Semites settle in Palestine (2000–1700 B.C.) |
| | Hyksos invasion (early 1600s B.C.) | |
| | New Kingdom (c. 1540–1075 B.C.) | |
| | ● Hatshepsut (c. 1503–1482 B.C.) | |
| | ● Akhenaton (1353–c. 1332 B.C.) | |
| Assyrians (c. 1300–612 B.C.) | ● Ramses II (1279–1213 B.C.) | Exodus of Hebrews from Egypt (before 1200 B.C.) |
| | Invasion of the Sea Peoples (1100s B.C.) | Collapse of Hittite empire (c. 1190 B.C.) |
| | Late Period (1075–525 B.C.) | David rules Palestine (c. 1000–970 B.C.) |
| | | Assyrians conquer Israel (722 B.C.) |
| Chaldeans (612–539 B.C.) | | |
| ● Nebuchadnezzar (604–562 B.C.) | | Fall of Judah (586 B.C.) |
| Cyrus the Great conquers Babylon (539 B.C.) | Persians conquer Egypt 525 B.C. | Cyrus the Great (559–529 B.C.) rules Persia |

massive religious and funerary monuments for which ancient Egypt is renowned. The central authority of the divine ruler, or pharaoh, maintained the unity of the state while providing a focus for Egyptian religion and the development of a large bureaucracy of priests and officials. The Egyptians of the Old Kingdom undoubtedly had trading contacts with the Syrians and other peoples of western Asia, but these appear to have had little effect on their culture; there is scant evidence of contacts with Mesopotamia, except for an early resemblance between the Mesopotamian ziggurat and the Egyptian pyramid.

Throughout the Old Kingdom a strong pharaoh was both the symbol of and the principal reason for national unity; some of Egypt's earliest pharaohs had pyramids constructed to serve as their tombs and as sites of worship and devotion. The pharaoh Zoser commissioned the architect Imhotep to build the first pyramid during the Third Dynasty (before 2575 B.C.) as Zoser's tomb and memorial. Imhotep himself is the first architect known to history and was in later ages regarded as a god. Zoser's successors continued the tradition of building pyramids for their tombs. The great pyramid of Khufu at Giza (c. 2530 B.C.), which rises to a height of nearly 500 feet, was constructed of more than 2 million limestone blocks weighing as much as 30,000 pounds apiece. To get such stones into place the Egyptians constructed massive ramps, the height of which had to be raised as the builders progressed; the ramps themselves were constructed of quarry debris or mud brick. Blocks of stone were then pulled up the ramps on sledges that rolled over timber. When a pyramid was completed, the ramps were removed, leaving the viewers to marvel at the structure rising majestically from the desert floor.

# Gods and Priests: Traditional Egyptian Religion

The pharaoh's person was regarded as divine, his authority as equal to that of any other deity. The priests who served the pharaoh regarded themselves as the preservers of traditional religious doctrines, the most fundamental of which was the concept of divine kingship. By the time of the New Kingdom, the priests, whose office was hereditary, would become a separate caste. Each temple had a priestly hierarchy responsible for undertaking a wide variety of tasks, ranging from menial chores to religious rites. Priestesses, however, were not professionals but wives of the nobility who assisted in some of the rituals. Some priests wore special clothing that reflected their status. Religion was woven into the very fabric of Egyptian political and social life, and society reflected the Egyptian view of creation. Just as the sun god, Amon, had created the universe by

The Great Pyramids at Giza were constructed between 2650 and 2530 B.C. [Holton/Photo Researchers]

bringing order to the primeval chaos, so the pharaoh ruled the physical world.

Traditional Egyptian religious beliefs involved a bewildering variety of deities, whose rights and privileges were jealously guarded by their priests. At the time of Egypt's unification, local guardian-deities were merged into Re (or Ra), the sun god, who sailed the skies in his boat by day and combated the forces of darkness in the underworld by night. Because of the political importance of Thebes (the capital beginning about 1938 B.C.), this god absorbed the identity of the Theban deity Amon, associated with the welfare of the state, and became known as Amon-Re.

The worship of Osiris, the god of the Nile, came to offer the hope of immortality to the masses. The cult of the afterlife involved elaborate funeral rituals at which the dead would be judged and move on to the next life. Each person, it was thought, would be judged by Osiris, who would assess the good and evil that had been done in life and then determine whether the person deserved punishment or admittance to the realm of bliss. Texts were written in hieroglyphics (pictorial symbols) on writing material made from the papyrus plant and placed in the graves to assist the deceased in the examinations that marked their entrance into the afterlife; collectively these are known as *The Book of the Dead*. The following excerpt suggests the standards of ethical and social behavior to which Egyptians were supposed to aspire:

I have not done evil to mankind. I have not oppressed the members of my family, I have not wrought evil in the place of right and truth. . . . I have not brought forward my name for exaltation to honors. I have not ill-treated servants. . . . I have not defrauded the oppressed one of his prop-

erty. . . . I have made no man to suffer hunger. . . . I have done no murder. . . . I have not committed fornication. . . . I have not encroached upon the fields of others. . . . I have not caught fish with [bait made of] fish of their kind. . . . I am pure.[1]

Osiris, the god who presided over funeral rituals, was the symbol of death and rebirth. The worship of Osiris; his wife, Isis, goddess of the fertile earth; and their son Horus came in time to symbolize a sense of the afterlife beyond simple material survival; it represents the closest that Egyptian religion came to the notion of a true spiritual state. According to one common belief, Osiris was killed by his evil brother, Seth, who cut the corpse into pieces; Isis gathered them up, wrapped them in linen, and thereby brought Osiris back to life. A different Horus, the sky god, eventually defeated Seth. This Horus was typically depicted as a hawk, the form in which pharaohs were believed to ascend to heaven after they died. The Egyptians worshiped a great variety of other divinities and spirits of nature, who were responsible for all aspects of existence. The mythology and ritual they inspired affected the lives of all Egyptians on a daily basis. Several animals, such as the jackal and the cat, also had religious importance; their mummified remains have been found at a number of sanctuaries.

The differences in burial rites between the various classes reflected their social status. Even a minor royal official would spend much of his life and income preparing an elaborate tomb for himself in which he would be buried with various treasures, and the burials of the ruling family were to become legendary for their sumptuousness. Corpses were mummified because Egyptians believed that the *ka*, the spirit of life in each person,

---

## ◎ The Technique of Mummification ◎

*Since Egyptian literature provides little information about the technique of mummification, we have to rely on ancient travelers' accounts. The following one is by the Greek historian Herodotus, who visited Egypt around 450 B.C. Modern research has confirmed the accuracy of his information.*

There are a set of men in Egypt who practice the art of embalming, and make it their proper business. These persons, when a body is brought to them, show the bearers various models of corpses, made in wood, and painted so as to resemble nature. The most perfect is said to be after the manner of him whom I do not think it religious to name in connection with such a matter; the second sort is inferior to the first, and less costly; the third is the cheapest of all. All this the embalmers explain, and then ask in which way it is wished that the corpse should be prepared. The bearers tell them, and having concluded their bargain, take their departure, while the embalmers, left to themselves, proceed to their task. The mode of embalming, according to the most perfect process, is the following: they take first a crooked piece of iron, and with it draw out the brain through the nostrils, thus getting rid of a portion, while the skull is cleared of the rest by rinsing with drugs; next they make a cut along the flank with a sharp Ethiopian stone, and take out the whole contents of the abdomen, which they then cleanse, washing it thoroughly with palm wine, and again frequently with an infusion of pounded aromatics. After this they fill the cavity with the purest bruised myrrh, with cassia, and every other sort of spicery except frankincense, and sew up the opening. Then the body is placed in natron for seventy days, and covered entirely over. After the expiration of that space of time, which must not be exceeded, the body is washed, and wrapped round, from head to foot, with bandages of fine linen cloth, smeared over with gum, which is used generally by the Egyptians in the place of glue, and in this state it is given back to the relations, who enclose it in a wooden case which they have had made for the purpose, shaped into the figure of a man. Then fastening the case, they place it in a sepulchral chamber, upright against the wall. Such is the most costly way of embalming the dead.

*Source:* Herodotus, *The Histories*, vol. 2, trans. G. Rawlinson (New York: Library of Living Classics, 1928), pp. 85–86.

---

would periodically return to the body. Yet the corpse of a poor Egyptian was typically wrapped in a piece of linen and left in a cave or a pit or even in the open sand of the desert, with only a staff and a pair of sandals for the journey to the next world. Beginning in the Middle Kingdom, however, some members of the lower classes had their corpses mummified. Relatively little documentary evidence has survived about living standards among the lower classes, and they are visible to us mostly in the painted and carved scenes of the tombs, going about their work as domestic servants or farm laborers. The concept of a future life was the only shared experience that united nobles, peasants, and slaves, since the Egyptian obsession with immortality offered the hope of a good life after death to all Egyptians, regardless of status.

## Egypt in the Middle Kingdom: Consolidation, Expansion, and Decline

The ordered world of the Old Kingdom was brought to an end around 2130 B.C. as a result of several factors, notably rivalries among the provincial nobility, who now claimed offices by hereditary right, and economic strain caused by the pharaohs' exorbitant building projects and by crop failures. By challenging the unique status of the pharaohs, the courtiers provoked conflicts that led to the collapse of the monarchy. In the absence of a central authority, provincial governors attempted to seize power

The Sphinx at Giza was
commissioned by the pharaoh
Chefren to guard his tomb.
[Hirmer Fotoarchiv, Munich]

and maintain their regional independence, and not until 1938 B.C., when Mentuhotep conquered Lower Egypt and succeeded in reuniting the country, did peace return. The new royal capital was situated at Thebes, and the decorations of the tomb complex built there for the pharaoh and members of his entourage provide a vivid picture of private life at the court of a Middle Kingdom pharaoh.

The principal rulers of the Twelfth Dynasty maintained Theban domination of Egypt only by a combination of determination and brute force. Their successes at home included a massive drainage project that reclaimed 27,000 acres of arable land south of Memphis. They also developed a vigorous, aggressive foreign policy. Part of gold-rich Nubia, the land to the south of Egypt, was occupied, and the pharaoh Sesostris III himself led a military expedition into Palestine, opening up a fresh sphere of influence and new commercial frontiers. Trade links were probably established at this time with the Minoans of Crete, and evidence appears of renewed contact with Mesopotamia, perhaps through the mediation of the Syrians. Although Egyptian art and culture remained relatively untouched by foreign influence,

the Egyptians were eager to appropriate the wealth of their neighbors, by trade or conquest. By the late nineteenth century B.C. Egypt was at a peak of prosperity that made it the envy of its neighbors and lured Nubian and Semitic immigrants to its fertile valley.

The successes of the Middle Kingdom pharaohs were followed by a sharp decline in royal authority occasioned by a series of short reigns and weak rulers. Nubia threw off Egyptian rule, but a worse catastrophe occurred after 1700 B.C., when the Hyksos, a nomadic or pastoral people from western Asia with horses and war chariots, invaded the country. Fortunately for the Egyptians, the Hyksos were impressed by their civilization and adopted Egyptian religious beliefs and customs. Our knowledge of the period of the Hyksos' invasion and occupation is sketchy, partly because the invaders left little in the way of written evidence and partly because the Egyptians of the New Kingdom were understandably reluctant or perhaps unable to document life under occupation by foreigners.

For most of the seventeenth century B.C. the Hyksos apparently controlled Palestine and Syria as well as Egypt, where their power was strongest in the north. In contrast to the Egyptians, with their desire to maintain a closed society, the Hyksos seem to have encouraged the presence of foreign immigrants like themselves. It was possibly under Hyksos rule that Hebrew immigrants, preceded by Joseph, arrived in Egypt and prospered there. Not until the sixteenth century B.C. were the Hyksos driven out of Egypt and back to Palestine by King Kamose of Thebes and his brother Ahmose, founder of the Eighteenth Dynasty.

## The New Kingdom: Imperial Conquest and Religious Reform

The early pharaohs of the New Kingdom, which began with the Eighteenth Dynasty around 1540 B.C., involved Egypt internationally for the first time on a broad scale. Among the most remarkable of them was Queen Hatshepsut (c. 1503–1482 B.C.), who initially wielded power as regent to her stepson, the future Thutmose III, and then proclaimed herself pharaoh with the support of the priests of Amon. Although in general Egyptian society was male-oriented, it was by no means unusual for a pharaoh's mother to take charge of government during his minority or while he was away at war. Indeed, the custom whereby the pharaoh generally married his sister or half sister strengthened such family connections, and Egyptian religion, with its many gods and goddesses, meant that Egyptians were accustomed to respect female figures. Women were sometimes active in government at the local level too.

Hatshepsut was an unusual case. Taking the title of king, she ruled for over 20 years and left as her principal legacy one of the most massive Egyptian temples. A funerary monument for herself and her father, Thutmose I, the temple at Deir el-Bahri was designed by one of the greatest figures in Egyptian art, the architect Sen-Mut. It combined opulence of effect with extreme care for detail; its façade was decorated with colossal statues of Hatshepsut herself, which her stepson Thutmose III, who loathed her, destroyed when he became pharaoh.

Thutmose III proved to be an aggressive and forceful ruler, leading campaigns in western Asia and to the south in Nubia. By the end of his reign Palestine and Syria as far as the Euphrates were under Egyptian control, and a huge temple complex had been constructed in Nubia near Napata. The conquered territories were controlled by Egyptian garrisons, and inspectors were sent to supervise the shipping of raw materials and manufactured objects back to Egypt. Thutmose is said to have waged 17 successful campaigns; on the first one alone, 1,000 chariots and more than 400,000 bushels of wheat were captured.

The effects of the Egyptians' imperial expansion on their economy were considerable. During the Old and Middle Kingdoms, manufacturing and foreign trade had played a relatively small part in the development of Egyptian society. In part, as we have seen, this had resulted from the lack of a large commercial class whose activity might have proved a threat to the hereditary nobility. The Egyptians' agricultural self-sufficiency, too, eliminated the need to look elsewhere for basic provisions. With their new possessions throughout western Asia, however, they operated on a wider economic scale. The New Kingdom's elite, with its opulent lifestyle, provided willing customers for the foreign luxury goods that were increasingly traded for Egyptian products, including stone vessels, pottery, colored glass, and fine linens. Egyptian artisans were especially noted for their production of luxury items, including jewelry, carved ivory, enamel work, pearl inlay, perfumed oils, ointments, and even cosmetics, such as hair dyes, rouge, and eye shadow.

The general pattern of consolidation and expansion was abruptly broken by the pharaoh Amenhotep IV (1353–c. 1332 B.C.), who attempted to reform Egyptian political and religious institutions. In place of the innumerable deities of traditional religion, he encouraged the worship of a single one, the sun god Aton. In the words of the *Hymn to Aton*:

> *O sole god, like whom there is no other!*
> *Thou didst create the world according to thy*
>     *desire,*
> *Whilst thou wert alone.*

Amenhotep himself took the name of Akhenaton, "servant of Aton." To implement his revolutionary changes and to reduce the power of the priests at the royal court of Thebes, he transferred the capital to Amarna, which he called Akhetaton.

Akhenaton's attempt to encourage belief in a single deity (without necessarily denying the existence of other, lesser gods) is reflected in the culture of the Amarna period. The monumentality and idealized features of traditional art were replaced by a new lightness, in which for the first time detailed physical features were shown. The stone reliefs depicting Akhenaton, his wife Nefertiti, and their children are remarkably different from the formalized style of previous eras.

---

### ❦
### NEFERTITI, "LADY OF THE TWO LANDS"

---

Few women of antiquity were more intriguing, influential, and ultimately mysterious than Nefertiti. Egyptolo-

# ◉ Aton, the One God ◉

*This extract from the* Hymn to Aton *composed by Akhenaton illustrates the pharaoh's belief in a single divine force.*

Thou appearest beautifully on the horizon of heaven,
Thou living Aton, the beginning of life!
When thou art arisen on the eastern horizon,
Thou has filled every land with thy beauty.
Thou art gracious, great, glistening, and high over every land;
Thy rays encompass the lands to the limit of all that thou hast made;
As thou art Re, thou reachest to the end of them;
Thou subduest them for thy beloved son.
Though thou art in their faces, no one knows thy going.

When thou settest in the western horizon,
The land is in darkness, in the manner of death.
They sleep in a room, with heads wrapped up,
Nor sees one eye the other.
All their goods which are under their heads might be stolen,
But they would not perceive it.
Every lion is come forth from his den;
All creeping things, they sting.
Darkness is a shroud, and the earth is in stillness,
For he who made them rests in his horizon.

At daybreak, when thou arisest on the horizon,
When thou shinest as the Aton by day,
Thou drivest away the darkness and givest thy rays.
The Two Lands are in festivity every day,
Awake and standing upon their feet,
For thou hast raised them up.
Washing their bodies, taking their clothing.
Their arms are raised in praise at thy appearance.
All the world, they do their work. . . .

*Source:* J. B. Pritchard, ed., *Ancient New Eastern Texts Relating to the Old Testament,* trans. J. Wilson (Princeton, N.J.: Princeton University Press, 1969), p. 370.

gists have discovered almost nothing about her background other than that she was of nonroyal birth. Her parents were probably members of the court circle, and she may have been a cousin of Amenhotep IV, whose principal wife she became. During the early years of the reign, when the capital was still at Thebes, court artists depicted her twice as often as her husband, a remarkable tribute that indicated unusual political prominence. Amenhotep thought very highly of her, calling her "sweet of love" and "possessed of charm." She was a woman of striking physical beauty, as attested by her portraits and by her husband's official recognition of her as the "exquisite beauty of the sun-disk." Indeed, her name itself means "a beautiful woman has come."

Much of what we know about Nefertiti is derived from paintings, sculpture, and inscriptions. She was already very powerful before the royal court established its new capital at Amarna, and she may in fact have been the moving force behind the religious revolution for which Akhenaton is remembered. Yet despite her undoubted political influence, she is never mentioned in the diplomatic correspondence of the reign.

This bust of Nefertiti was rendered by an
artist at Amarna when she was in her mid-
twenties. [Alinari/Art Resource, New York]

The move to Amarna signaled not only a new religion
but also a higher status for Nefertiti. During the Theban
years she had often been portrayed alone, but even then
her rising fortunes were reflected in the colossal statues
of her and Amenhotep, unique in Egyptian art apart from
reigning female pharaohs such as Hatshepsut. At
Amarna the court artists habitually depicted her as the
constant companion and virtual equal of Akhenaton.
Each is shown wearing a royal crown, implying that
Nefertiti was virtually a coruler. Indeed, Akhenaton
seems to have made a special point of having artists emphasize her regal status. On one occasion she is shown

in the stance of a warrior-king, astride a fallen foe, ready
to slay him with a single blow. Most remarkably, in
one temple painting the name of Aton is written back to
front in her presence, symbolically underscoring
her eminence.

At Amarna, Nefertiti played a major role in the worship of Aton, as reflected by her adoption of the additional name of Nefernefruaton, "beautiful are the beauties of Aton." She refused to limit herself to the
traditional role of women in an Egyptian temple—ringing the sistrum, a metal rattle—but instead performed
the same rites as her husband; in most respects their
priestly roles were interchangeable. Courtiers responded by invoking her name with those of Aton and
Akhenaton in their prayers. Although she apparently
never held the office of "God's wife," she wore the costume associated with it (a clinging robe tied with a red
sash) and carried out its duties, namely the supervision
of the Mansion of the Ben-Ben, a college of choristers
and instrumentalists who provided music for religious
services. She also had a priestly duty to maintain Aton
"in a state of perpetual arousal"; since Aton was abstract,
she could do this only by alluring his son (and her husband), Akhenaton, by her erotic attire, which often consisted of open coat dresses made of transparent fabric.[2]

Apart from her religious functions, we have only tan-
talizing glimpses of Nefertiti's activities. She drove a
chariot, probably to transport herself between royal palaces, and she dispensed gold collars to worthy persons,
making them "People of Gold." Late in their reign she
and Akhenaton presided over an international pageant
at which dazzling tribute was presented to the royal couple: ivory, gold, monkeys, leopards, and shields from Nubia and the Sudan; chariots, horses, weapons, and an
antelope from Syria; ostrich eggs and feathers from Libya; incense, sandalwood, and spices from the Hittites.
This was the last occasion on which Nefertiti, Akhenaton, and their six daughters were depicted together; at
least one and possibly three of the children died in the
next two years, perhaps victims of a plague.

Nefertiti's last years are shrouded in mystery. Not
even the date of her death is known. Based on fragmentary evidence, three principal versions of Nefertiti's final
days have been suggested. One of these has her adopting the names and customs of a male pharaoh and ruling
as a coregent with her husband. An alternative theory
posits that after 1335 B.C. she took her son, Tutankhaton
(the future pharaoh Tutankhamen), and established a
virtual government in exile until she died some three
years after her husband. More credible is the view that
Nefertiti's influence waned after 1337, in part because of
Akhenaton's favoritism toward another wife, Kiya, and
in part because of the rising influence of Nefertiti's own
daughter, Meritaton, whose husband, Smenkhkare, was
appointed coregent with Akhenaton at the age of 14. If
Nefertiti outlived Akhenaton, her influence over Tut-

ankhaton probably delayed the return to the traditional religion until after her death.

## The Waning Empire

Clearly, so revolutionary a change in culture and religion as that implemented by Akhenaton and Nefertiti posed a serious threat to the priests, whose interests lay in the preservation of traditional ways. After Akhenaton's death, he was condemned as a heretic, and his name was removed from the monuments of his era. His son-in-law and successor, Tutankhamen, is perhaps the most famous of all Egyptian rulers, although for reasons that have nothing to do with his religion or politics. His unopened tomb, excavated in 1922, contained the richest hoard of Egyptian artifacts ever recovered. Tutankhamen's sweeping restoration of the old religion was carefully recorded in the temple at Karnak:

> Then his majesty made monuments for the gods, fashioning their cult-statues of genuine fine gold from the highlands, building their sanctuaries anew as monuments for the ages of eternity, established with possessions forever, setting for them divine offerings as a regular daily observance, and provisioning their food-offerings upon earth. He surpassed what had been previously. . . . He inducted priests and prophets from the children of the nobles.[3]

Akhenaton's lack of interest in foreign policy had weakened Egypt's control of conquered territories. Revolts in Egyptian possessions in Syria and Palestine were fomented by the Hittites, another imperial power in western Asia. From approximately 1300 B.C. to the end of the New Kingdom in 1075 B.C., pharaohs were involved in constant wars in which they tried, unsuccessfully, to maintain control of their overseas possessions. Ramses II (1279–1213 B.C.), perhaps best remembered for completing the magnificent temple at Karnak with its 70-foot columns, failed to conquer the Hittites, though he concluded a defensive treaty with them that left southern Syria in Egyptian hands. The splendors of Ramses' building projects notwithstanding, Egyptian might was on the wane. Shortly after 1200 B.C. Egypt itself was threatened by a new wave of migrants, known to us only as the Peoples of the Sea. Their invasions were repelled by Ramses III (1187–1156 B.C.), but only at great cost, and Egyptian imperial power continued to decline. The ever-larger building projects of the later New Kingdom seem as much attempts at restoring self-confidence as triumphal monuments.

In the last centuries of independent Egyptian history a succession of invaders attacked and occupied various parts of the country, from the Assyrians in the seventh century B.C. to Alexander the Great (331 B.C.). With its conquest by Alexander, Egypt at last became absorbed into the larger Mediterranean world.

## Egyptian Society

The ruling elite in Egypt, the apex of which was the pharaoh, included the hereditary nobility and the high priests, guardians of Egypt's religious traditions. The pharaoh's power was theoretically absolute; his commands were carried out by the advisers, scribes, and others who made up the growing bureaucracy of governing officials. At the head of the bureaucracy was the vizier, who served as the intermediary between the pharaoh and local officials, tried important cases, appointed magistrates, entertained foreign envoys, and supervised agriculture, road and building maintenance, record keeping, the army and internal security, and tax assessment and collection. The pharaoh's family formed the center of a royal court attended by the nobility. He could demand taxes ranging up to 20 percent of annual income, which were typically paid in kind, for example, in grain.

An upper middle class consisted of scribes, priests, and other court servants. The importance of scribes, who underwent a lengthy period of education to master their literary skills, was underscored by the fact that they, unlike even the priests, were not subject to forced labor or military service. The upper middle class was expanded during the New Kingdom by the addition of professional soldiers, though the officers enjoyed a status roughly equivalent to the nobility. Merchants, artisans, and farmers of substance comprised a lower middle class. In the early centuries the artisans worked primarily for the pharaoh and the nobility, but they also produced pottery, textiles, and glassware for the people. Because most of the trade was in the hands of the priesthood, the number of merchants was never great, and foreign trade in particular was a royal monopoly.

Apart from slaves, the lowest level in the social order was occupied by the agricultural laborers who farmed the Nile valley and the miners who extracted turquoise and copper in the Sinai. As throughout most of history, the life of the farmer was onerous:

> When the water is full he irrigates [the fields], servicing his equipment. He spends the day cutting tools for cultivating barley, and the night twisting ropes. His midday hour even he is in the habit of spending in farmer's work.[4]

A few laborers were independent and self-supporting, but the vast majority were essentially serfs, bound for all practical purposes to the land. They could be forced to work on state building projects, though much of this labor was recruited by persuading the people of the real or imagined benefits that would accrue from pyramids, temples, irrigation canals, and the like.

The institution of slavery in Egypt began in the Middle Kingdom, when wealthy households sometimes owned as many as 50 slaves to run their estates. Yet the use of slaves became widespread only in the New Kingdom. Most were employed on temple estates and in the mines, though some had positions in the military or in royal service. Relatively few were engaged in domestic service. Their ranks were filled by prisoners of war.

Although Egyptian society was stratified, some upward mobility was possible, especially in the Middle and New Kingdoms. This was especially so for talented people whose services were required by the state. Immigrants, including dark-skinned Nubians, had ample opportunity to enhance their social status. The best known example of social mobility is the story of Joseph, an Israelite who was sold into slavery by his own brothers; in Egypt, his managerial skills and skill in interpreting dreams eventually attracted the attention of the pharaoh, who made him overseer of the kingdom's food supplies.

The lot of Egyptian women was mixed. Although a handful ruled as pharaohs, women were generally excluded from the bureaucracy, and few became scribes. Virtually all other occupations, including business, were open to them. Women had the right to own property, even to the point that wives retained control over whatever possessions had been theirs before marriage. They could engage in financial transactions, own slaves, purchase land, and witness documents, and they had to pay taxes. Polygamy was legal, but most marriages were monogamous, and wives had the same right to a divorce as their husbands. The priesthood was open to women as well as men, and Egyptian death rituals treated both sexes equally. Egyptian women undoubtedly enjoyed a status greater than that of their western Asian contemporaries.

In general, the state supervised both the production and distribution of agricultural and manufactured products. Control of the food supply was one of the government's most important functions. It had enormous granaries and warehouses and was normally able to provide for the people when harvests were bad. From Nubia and along the Red Sea coast the Egyptians traded for ivory, incense, dwarfs, and exotic animals, and they obtained cedar from the Phoenicians. In return for such goods they exported such items as wheat, gold, and linen.

## The Legacy of Egyptian Culture

Ancient Egyptian religion and language were lost for centuries, only to be recovered by the archaeologist's spade. The earliest Egyptian writing was in the form of hieroglyphics, or pictorial symbols, which represented individual objects or actions. As early as the Old King-

dom, the Egyptians had a system of characters for the 24 consonants, although they had no way to indicate vowels. The Frenchman Jean-François Champollion finally deciphered the Egyptian hieroglyphic script by means of a trilingual inscription, the Rosetta Stone, found in the Nile delta in the early nineteenth century. Champollion compared the three languages on the stone—hieroglyphic, the demotic script of the common Egyptian people, and ancient Greek. The Rosetta Stone is, among other things, a monument to the passing of ancient Egyptian culture. The Egyptians had ceased to use the demotic script, whereas the Greek that was largely replacing it has never fallen out of use from ancient times to the present. Similarly, the beliefs that sustained the ancient Egyptians for millennia had begun to disappear along with their language.

Yet the monuments remain, and ever since their rediscovery some two centuries ago, they have fascinated the modern world. Part of the continuing appeal of Egyptian art lies in the extraordinary technical skill it often displays. In seeking to record the world around them, Egyptian artists developed techniques in painting and sculpture that permitted them to achieve a perfection of finish and a beauty of surface that remain unsurpassed. Living in or with easy access to the rocky upper valley of the Nile, they learned to use stone to produce everything from vast temple complexes to tiny figurines. Their skill at rendering the human form influenced the Greek colonizers who moved to Egypt shortly after 700 B.C. Comparison proves instructive: when the Greeks went to Egypt, they found the Egyptians producing statues not very different from those of 2,000 years earlier. The Greeks borrowed their style and in just over 100 years adapted it to their own purposes.

The Egyptians' art as a whole was primarily conditioned by the character and requirements of their religion. In addition to the images of deities, artists were commissioned to provide temples and shrines for religious ceremonies. Even the buildings or sculptures that commemorated the images, names, or deeds of real people generally served religious purposes. The largely undeviating style that resulted from the joint control of state and religion seems to have appealed to the Egyptians' cultural conservatism. In troubled times during the Middle Kingdom or the Late Period with its foreign invaders, artists tended to turn back to the certainty and security of Old Kingdom art. As late as the Roman period, architects in the Nubian city of Meroë were still building pyramids as funerary monuments.

Although the Egyptians maintained their social and political structure substantially unchanged over thousands of years, they were not completely immune to outside influences. Among them was the idea of writing, probably borrowed from the Sumerians; the adoption of the chariot, the horse, and long-range bows from the Hyksos; and the use of luxury items imported from Asia and Europe. Nevertheless, apart from the widespread use of slaves, the economic expansion of the New Kingdom had little social effect on one of the most static and rigidly stratified societies that has ever existed.

Our knowledge of Egyptian history and society was literally dictated by the ruling class in the form of the inscriptions that decorate their monuments. The awkward silence that hangs over the period of Hyksos rule serves as a reminder of how many other aspects of Egyptian life were never recorded. There is a certain irony in the fact that material objects have survived in remarkable numbers: furniture, clothes, utensils, and, of course, enough mummified ancient Egyptians to fascinate museumgoers throughout much of the world. Yet the society that made use of the couches and footstools and makeup boxes remains a mystery to us in many respects.

# The Hebrews

The history of the Hebrews is continuously intertwined with that of the other peoples of ancient Egypt and western Asia, including the Canaanites and the Phoenicians, both of whom had settled in Palestine from very early times. Much of Canaanite culture was influenced by Mesopotamia. Ugarit, the leading Canaanite city, was founded before 3500 B.C. and thrived until its destruction by the Sea Peoples around 1200 B.C. A major trading center, Ugarit enjoyed commerce with Mesopotamia, Anatolia, Egypt, and eventually Greece. The people of Ugarit pioneered the development of an alphabet made up of 30 wedge-shaped signs, each of which denoted a letter rather than a word or syllable.

By 1000 B.C. the Semitic-speaking Phoenicians, who were descended from the Canaanites, were concentrated in the area now known as Lebanon. Taking advantage of their access to the sea, the Phoenicians constructed ships capable of ranging throughout the Mediterranean. The heart of their export trade consisted of magnificent cedar and textiles dyed with a rich purple derived from a shellfish found along their coast. The Phoenicians established colonies as far away as Carthage in North Africa and Cadiz in the Iberian peninsula, where they traded for silver and tin. From the Hittites the Phoenicians learned how to smelt iron, a technology they later introduced to the Greeks and the North Africans. Another major Phoenician contribution was the development of an alphabet consisting of 22 characters, each of which represented a distinct sound; unlike the Ugaritic cuneiform alphabet, the Phoenician alphabet showed no trace of a pictographic origin. Both the Hebrews and the Greeks in turn adopted versions of this alphabet.

Like the Phoenicians, the Hebrews too had early links with Mesopotamia. The family of Abraham, the traditional founder of the state of Israel, came from Ur, and we have already met its descendants in Egypt at the time of the Hyksos. Yet the study of the early history of the Hebrews differs significantly from that of the other peoples of western Asia and Egypt. A crucial difference is the role played by written as well as archaeological evidence. Our picture of ancient Egypt and Mesopotamia is reconstituted from material remains, supplemented and at times amplified by inscriptions and surviving documents. Our principal source for the early history of the Hebrews, by contrast, is the first five books of the Old Testament, known as the Pentateuch. According to tradition, the author of the Pentateuch was Moses, a participant in the later stages of the story it tells, though the consensus of scholars is that the text we have was completed in the fifth century B.C. from oral and written traditions and laws. In places, archaeological discoveries have confirmed or filled out the biblical account; elsewhere they provide information that is missing from the Bible.

From the time of the first patriarch, Abraham, the covenant between God and the Hebrews was the dominant theme of their history. Abraham believed he had made a covenant or agreement with God that placed the Jews in a special relationship with the Creator as a "chosen people." The biblical book of Exodus records that Moses reconfirmed this covenant and on Mount Sinai received the tablets of the Law from God.*

Abraham's family settled for a while near the city of Harran in northern Mesopotamia; his descendants moved southward, living as pastoral nomads. Taking their flocks with them, they crossed the desert from one water source to the next, in general avoiding the major urban centers, always following what they perceived to be divine instructions.

At some point after 1700 B.C. these wandering nomads, driven perhaps by hunger, settled in the Nile delta. It is difficult to establish a precise date for the events that brought the Hebrews and the Egyptians into contact. Egyptian texts fail to record the presence of the Hebrews, and biblical accounts make no reference to a specific Egyptian ruler or time period. It is generally agreed, however, that the age of Hebrew prosperity in Egypt described in the story of Joseph is related to the period of Hyksos rule in the century or so following 1700 B.C. The Hyksos, themselves foreigners, were more likely to look with favor on an immigrant community. Furthermore, the Hebrews' connection with the Hyksos would help explain the Egyptian silence, both on the period itself and on the events that led to the Hebrew exodus described in the Bible, which was undertaken primarily to escape enslavement.

---

*The following account focuses on Hebrew history; Judaism as a religion is discussed in Chapter 7.

The exodus from Egypt, under the leadership of Moses, probably occurred during the reign of Ramses II (1279–1213 B.C.). Paintings of the period show "Asiatics" being used as slaves in brickmaking and other building labors, and there is archaeological evidence for a period of migration into Palestine around 1200 B.C. For the Hebrews, and for subsequent Jewish tradition, the exodus became the basis for the foundation of Israel. It demonstrated the intervention of their God, Yahweh, and was the occasion for the renewal of the covenant under the leadership of Moses.

## The Kingdom of Israel

Following Moses, the migrants traveled northeast toward their "promised land," although the final crossing of the Jordan River and the conquest of Palestine were accomplished only after Moses' death, under the leadership of Joshua. The details of the subsequent foundation and growth of the kingdom of Israel are far from clear. The biblical account is incomplete, and archaeological excavations have generally complicated rather than clarified matters. The picture is of almost two centuries of struggle between the Hebrews and other migrant peoples, particularly the Philistines, before the establishment of a Hebrew monarchy. Even then the new kingdom of Israel was far from secure. Saul, its first king, was killed in battle, and only with the accession of David, his successor (c. 1000–c. 970 B.C.), was stability established.

David was first proclaimed king by the Hebrews who lived in Judah, an arid frontier region in southern Palestine that Saul had never effectively governed. It took some seven years before David could take advantage of internal dissension in the north to unite all of Israel. Displaying considerable talent as a political and military leader, he conquered Jerusalem from a local tribe known as the Jebusites and defeated the Philistines. Jerusalem, in a nearly impregnable geographic position, became his new capital and eventually the historic center of the nation of Israel.

Unsatisfied with these achievements, David used his victorious troops to expand the frontiers of his state until it extended from the Euphrates to the Gulf of Aqaba at the head of the Red Sea; even Damascus was occupied by Hebrew troops. In a symbolic attempt to unify the disparate peoples of his empire, David married wives from the various groups; ultimately this contributed to dissension within his own family and the rebellion and death of his son Absalom. To solidify his authority, David interpreted kingship in distinctly religious terms. At his command, the ark, a fundamental symbol of the covenant between the Hebrews and their God, was enshrined in Jerusalem. There it signified the renewal of the covenant through David, "the anointed (messiah) of the Lord," and established Jerusalem as the religious as well as the political capital of Israel.

Under David's successor, his son Solomon, who reigned from around 970 to 930 B.C., Israel reached its greatest prosperity. This was in part the result of an absence of competing powers in western Asia at this time. The power of Egypt was on the wane, and the Assyrians had yet to embark on their foreign conquests. That Solomon was aware of the necessity of coming to terms with his neighbors is suggested by the fact that one of his many wives was an Egyptian, daughter of the reigning pharaoh.

Solomon sought to consolidate and extend the power of his kingdom. He expanded foreign trade by building up a large merchant fleet, manned by Phoenician sailors, that imported gold from Arabia and Ethiopia. Excavations at the port of Ezion-geber on the Gulf of Aqaba suggest the existence of a large-scale metal industry. Objects manufactured there were traded for imported foreign products and raw materials, including the famous cedars of Lebanon used in the construction of Solomon's temple, a majestic building that housed the Great Sanhedrin (the supreme rabbinic court) and served as the center of national worship. He also strengthened the power of his army by the use of iron, which was introduced throughout the Mediterranean shortly after 1000 B.C. His building projects both in Jerusalem and elsewhere in the kingdom are evidence of his ambitious intentions; the fortified city of Megiddo, with its stables for almost 500 horses, is just one of the cities he rebuilt.

## The Society of Ancient Israel

The wealthy and sophisticated city of Jerusalem provided a very different lifestyle from that experienced by the Hebrews in their long journeys and hard-won conquests. Jerusalem itself had been a small town of little importance. Now it became a major international capital, its population swollen by the crowds of workers involved in Solomon's building projects; more than 200,000 are said to have participated in the construction of the temple. Camels replaced asses as the principal means of transporting goods such as spices from Arabia, and Sardinia, with its copper refineries, and Spain, a source of mineral wealth, were accessible by sea.

The introduction of iron, perhaps borrowed from the Philistines, helped Hebrew farmers and artisans in their work. The iron-tipped plough, probably introduced during the reign of Solomon, made possible increased food production, and iron sickles speeded harvesting. Carpenters were able to replace their bronze saws and axes with sharp and efficient iron ones. The ensuing improvements in production served both the needs of an expanding Jerusalem and the increasing export trade.

Reconstruction of the temple in Jerusalem as it appeared in A.D. 41–44. [Drawing from *In the Shadow of the Temple* by Meir Ben-Dov, translation by Ina Friedman. Copyright © 1982 by Keter Publishing House Jerusalem Ltd.; English translation © 1985 by Keter Publishing Jerusalem, Ltd. Reprinted by permission of HarperCollins Publishers]

Throughout their wanderings, the Hebrews had been under strict injunction from the Law of Moses to preserve rigorous standards of hygiene. In almost every private house built at Jerusalem in the years following Solomon, there was a cistern to collect rainwater in the winter and keep it cool and clean throughout the summer. Unlike many of their contemporaries, who collected water at the nearest spring and who were accustomed to pouring refuse into open street drains, Israelite women could count on a fresh water supply, and the city was provided with underground drains. The houses themselves were constructed on two stories, a ground floor for storage and an upper level for living.

The status of Hebrew women appreciably declined as the worship of Yahweh, a male deity, replaced other gods, including Canaanite fertility deities. Before the establishment of the monarchy under Saul, women had served as prophetesses, the most famous of whom was the "judge" (or tribal leader) Deborah. The role of women decreased under the monarchy, both politically and religiously. They could not enter the inner temple at Jerusalem, and they were barred from synagogues, which developed in the sixth century B.C., in periods of ritual uncleanliness following childbirth and during menstruation. Moreover, in a society concerned about propagation, men were permitted to be polygamous. Marriages were usually arranged by the parents, with the prospective groom or his family required to compensate the bride's family; the latter did not pay a dowry. If the marriage proved unworkable, only the husband had the right to seek a divorce, and only a wife faced execution if she committed adultery. A widow who had not borne a son was required to marry her brother-in-law if her husband died. Even the creation account in Genesis 2:18–25 (unlike that in Genesis 1:27–29) placed woman in a subordinate position by proclaiming that she was created after Adam.

## The Kingdom Divided

In later ages Solomon was remembered not so much as an efficient administrator as a man of wisdom. The bib-

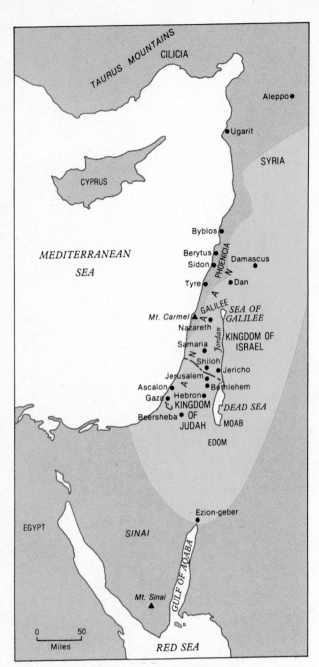

*1.2 Ancient Palestine*

Solomon's reign was the high point in Israel's political history, but it also marked the beginning of the kingdom's collapse. Fatally divided, it was a tempting prize. The Assyrians invaded and by 722 B.C. destroyed the northern kingdom of Israel and deported its leaders to Mesopotamia. The kingdom of Judah lasted until 586 B.C., when Jerusalem was destroyed by the Babylonians and the Hebrews were herded into captivity in Babylon. Some 40 years later they were permitted to return to Palestine by the intervention of the Persians, who incorporated Palestine into the Persian Empire. It was during these trying centuries that the great Hebrew prophets, including Isaiah and Jeremiah, explored the religious implications of Israel's trials in terms of divine punishment and the promise that a remnant of the Hebrew nation would be preserved. Although the pharaoh Akhenaton professed a belief in a single creator-god, it was the Hebrew prophets who first fully enunciated ethical monotheism.

# The Hittites

Unlike the Hebrews and the other Semitic-speaking peoples of western Asia, the Hittites were Indo-Europeans, members of a large group of peoples who spoke a language related to Greek, Persian, Sanskrit, and Latin. The Hittites first migrated into Anatolia, probably from central Europe or the steppes of central Asia, no later than 2700 B.C., bringing with them horses and wheeled carts. There they intermingled with earlier inhabitants. By the middle of the second millennium B.C. the Hittite kings of Asia Minor were among the most powerful of all rulers in western Asia, equals of the monarchs of Babylon and Assyria or the Egyptian pharaohs. Yet with the fall of their empire around 1190 B.C., the Hittites virtually disappear from history until they were rediscovered at the end of the nineteenth century.

The principal Hittite territory was located in what is now modern Turkey. Its capital was at Hattusas (modern Bogazkoy). From there, beginning around 1650 B.C., the Hittite kings embarked on aggressive military campaigns, pushing south across the formidable natural barrier presented by the Taurus Mountains into the more fertile territory of their southern and eastern neighbors. Sometime after 1600 B.C. they sacked Babylon with their ally, the Kassites.

These initial successes were eroded by internal feuding, and the apparent obscurity of the following century may imply that the Hittites were more concerned with defending their territory against invaders than with empire building. The powerful military leader Suppiluliumas (c. 1375–c. 1335 B.C.) put Hittite armies once again on the attack. They conquered Syria, and even the

lical account notes, however, that toward the end of his life he began to succumb to foreign influences, and the extravagance of the greatest of his monuments, the temple and the palace in Jerusalem, proved fatal to the kingdom's survival. His death was followed by a period of bitter civil war, leading to the division of the kingdom into two parts, Israel to the north, with its capital at Samaria, and Judah, with its capital at Jerusalem, to the south.

**A Hittite soldier as depicted on the King's Gate in Hattusas. [Archaeological Museum, Ankara]**

## Hittite Society and Religion

The Hittite kingdom was basically agricultural. Many of the documents from the royal archives consist of land deeds, together with laws governing farming mishaps—the escape of a pig or an accidental fire in an orchard, for example. Unlike the Mesopotamians, the Hittites could cultivate the vine, and wine, olive oil, and grain figure prominently in their records. In the fourteenth century B.C. the Hittites were also one of the first peoples to discover the technique of iron smelting, but, as we have seen, iron remained a precious metal, in short supply until about 1000 B.C. In a letter to a contemporary ruler, probably an Assyrian king, Hattusilis refused to provide supplies of iron, with the excuse that it was "a bad time for production," although he enclosed an iron dagger blade as a personal gift.

Hittite trading was widespread throughout western Asia, and much of the royal correspondence dealt with trade concessions and the protection of merchants traveling abroad. Egypt and Syria provided the principal markets, although the Hittites also traded with the Babylonians and were probably in commercial contact with the Mycenaeans, the chief Bronze Age people of the Greek mainland. Hittite objects sold or traded included bronze and iron vessels as well as gold and silver, and among the commodities Hittite merchants tried to buy was lapis lazuli, a precious blue stone mined in northeastern Afghanistan.

Like the Babylonians and other ancient peoples, the Hittites developed legal codes to organize their society. Detailed provisions were made for cases of homicide, theft, and arson as well as general conditions governing employment, property holding, and the treatment of slaves. Many of the provisions reflect the agricultural nature of Hittite society: rulings on crimes related to vineyards and orchards, offenses related to cattle, and accidents at river crossings.

Hittite society was clearly patriarchal, but unlike the Semitic-speaking peoples, the Hittites did not practice polygamy. Fathers "gave away" their daughters, and marriage was principally regarded as a financial contract. Nevertheless, young Hittite women seem to have been allowed a little more independence than their Babylonian counterparts. The initial betrothal was accompanied by a present from the future bridegroom, but if the young woman decided that she would prefer to marry someone else, she could do so, with or without her parents' consent, provided that she returned the engagement present. Various other regulations governed the treatment of widows and children; they included a provision that if a man died childless, it was the responsibility of his brother, father, or other male relative to marry and take care of his widow. Any children born of such a marriage took the name of the dead man and thus

Egyptians made peace overtures. The widow of the pharaoh (probably Tutankhamen, who had just died at the age of 18) sent a letter to Suppiluliumas begging him to send one of his sons to provide her with a new husband. Such an attractive alliance could hardly be turned down, and a Hittite prince was duly dispatched, only to be murdered en route to the Egyptian court. Suppiluliumas thus lost the opportunity to place his son on the Egyptian throne, which would have firmly linked the two empires. The career of King Hattusilis III (c. 1275–c. 1250) and his queen, the priestess Puduhepa, provides a vivid picture of power and politics in the ancient world. He was an experienced military commander in his late forties when he deposed the reigning king, his nephew, in a coup. A powerful and ruthless leader, he engaged in incessant fighting to protect the kingdom's northern frontiers and negotiated with Egypt to retain control of Syria. Royal decrees were issued jointly in the names of Hattusilis and Puduhepa, and she corresponded independently with the queen of Egypt.

## ⊕ Hittite Laws ⊕

*Hittite laws were designed for reparation rather than retribution, as these examples demonstrate.*

If anyone breaks a freeman's arm or leg, he pays him twenty shekels of silver and he [the plaintiff] lets him go home.

If anyone breaks the arm or leg of a male or female slave he pays ten shekels of silver and he [the plaintiff] lets him go home.

If anyone steals a plough-ox, formerly they used to give fifteen oxen, but now he gives ten oxen; he gives three oxen two years old, three yearling oxen, and four sucklings(?) and he [the plaintiff] lets him go home.

If a freeman kills a serpent and speaks the name of another [a form of sorcery], he shall give one pound of silver; if a slave does it, he shall die.

If a man puts filth into a pot or a tank, formerly they paid six shekels of silver; he who put the filth in paid three shekels of silver [to the owner?], and into the palace they used to take three shekels of silver. But now the king has remitted the share of the palace; the one who put the filth in pays three shekels of silver only and he [the plaintiff] lets him go home.

If a freeman sets a house on fire, he shall rebuild the house; but whatever perishes inside the house, be it a man, an ox, or a sheep, for these he shall not compensate.

*Source:* O. R. Gurney, *The Hittites* (Harmondsworth, England: Penguin Books, 1954), p. 96.

perpetuated his line. Although Babylonian law did not make this provision, a similar law existed in the ancient Jewish tradition, so that the dead man's name would not be "blotted out of Israel."[5]

As might be expected among an agricultural people, the principal Hittite deity was a weather god called Teshub. In contrast to the predictability of the Mesopotamian cycle of seasons, the weather in the Taurus Mountains in southern Asia Minor is stormy and uncertain. The son of the weather god, Telipinu, was one of the gods of agriculture, who may have become the center of a cult similar to that of Osiris in Egypt, symbolizing death and rebirth. As Hittite society developed, a complicated interweaving of deities, local and statewide, came into being, but the weather god remained the dominant figure, and Hittite kings claimed to rule as his deputy. The language of a treaty guaranteeing security throughout western Asia during the reign of Hattusilis III describes the agreement as being between "the Sun God of Egypt and the Weather God of Hatti."

mass migrations of the Peoples of the Sea, who were repelled with such difficulty by Ramses III, swept across western Asia, the Hittites were unable to keep the invaders out. With the collapse of their capital at Hattusas around 1190 B.C., the population scattered. Drought, famine, and volcanic eruptions may also have contributed to the Hittite decline. A version of Hittite culture continued in a few cities in the extreme south, in what is now Syria, but these were soon taken over by the Assyrians. The heirs of the Hittites in Asia Minor were the Phrygians, whose worship of Cybele, the Great Mother, became widespread in the Roman world, and the Lydians, who were probably the inventors of coinage. The influence of the Hittites also extended, perhaps indirectly, to the Greeks and the Romans, whose conception of the pantheon of gods was apparently shaped by Hittite mythology. In no small measure, the historical importance of the Hittites stems from their role in transmitting Mesopotamian culture to peoples of the Mediterranean.

## The End of the Hittite Empire

The treaty with Egypt may have secured the Hittites' eastern frontiers, but trouble soon developed in the west. Local governors there had revolted, and when the

## The Assyrians

The Hittites' sometime ally, the Kassites, briefly dominated Mesopotamia. Formerly nomadic, they occupied

Babylon sometime after 1700 B.C., only to fall in turn under the rule of the militaristic Assyrians, a Semitic people who evolved the last great culture of Mesopotamia. The peak of Assyrian power was between 900 and 612 B.C. The three centuries of Assyrian domination were marked by powerful and aggressive rulers whose armies were frequently on the march throughout western Asia.

The militant character of the Assyrians undoubtedly stemmed from the recurring need to defend themselves from the aggressive inhabitants of the mountains to the north. Throughout the ninth century B.C. the Assyrians carried out raids against their neighbors, including the Hittites, Phoenicians, Syrians, and Israelites. The architect of Assyrian imperialism was Tiglath-Pileser III (c. 745–727 B.C.), whose much improved army overran Babylonia, northern Syria, and Israel. Iron weapons, siege equipment (towers, rams, and mines), and troops capable of rapid deployment made his troops highly effective. So too did their discipline. But Assyrian rule provoked repeated uprisings by some of the subject peoples, who resented the payment of tribute and subjection to forced labor. By the late seventh century B.C. Assyria

had extended its control over Egypt, making the empire the largest in the world to that point in history.

Although impressive in its size, the empire lasted little more than a century. The Assyrian monarchs ruled in splendor with the aid of a vast court and bureaucracy. The very title of the sovereign reflects the sense of grandeur: "the great king, the legitimate king, the king of the world, king of Assyria, king of all the four rims of the earth, king of kings, prince without rival." Yet the monarchs were not absolute, for Assyrian cities were largely governed by councils of elders under the terms of urban charters, and powerful lords oversaw the affairs of rural districts and were responsible for raising military forces. Beyond the Assyrian homeland some of the subject peoples were ruled by Assyrian deputies, others by local leaders who were obedient to their Assyrian overlords; some, known to be loyal to Assyria, were virtually left to determine their own affairs.

The Assyrian monarchs ruled from a succession of royal capitals, each of which required extensive building programs. In the reign of Ashurnasirpal (884–859 B.C.), for instance, a huge palace was constructed at Calah (modern Nimrud) and decorated with elaborately

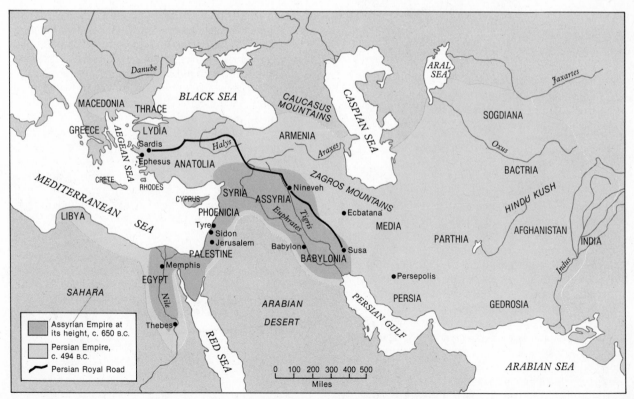

*1.3 The Empires of Assyria and Persia*

**Colossal human-headed lions such as this guarded the entrances to Assyrian palaces. [Reproduced by Courtesy of the Trustees of the British Museum]**

than-life-size statues of the king and his courtiers. Its entrance was provided with a collection of demonic figures, again of vast size. The Assyrian kings hoped by intimidation to deter their neighbors from attacking and their own subjects from rebelling. The ambassadors or petitioners who had made their way through the ceremonial halls and into the throne room faced the carved base of the king's throne, which showed Sargon standing in his war chariot over heaps of dead bodies while his soldiers piled severed heads in front of him.

The brutality inflicted by the Assyrians on their conquered enemies has obscured their accomplishments. Like the later Romans, they built roads, promoted urban development, and maintained order in a turbulent region. They forced Egypt and Babylon to open their borders to foreign trade and used units of silver virtually as coinage. Although they practiced slavery, slaves could operate their own businesses and win their freedom by faithful service. Like the Hittites, the Assyrians also played an important role in the transmission of Mesopotamian culture.

Nineveh, which had become the Assyrian capital after Sargon's death, fell in 612 B.C., and with it the Assyrian Empire. Western Asia Minor came under the control of the Medes (from Media, the ancient name for northwestern Iran) and then the Persians (from Persis, in southern Iran), while the Chaldeans of southern Babylonia dominated Palestine, Syria, and the whole of Mesopotamia. Yet even at this point the cultural fertility of Mesopotamia was not exhausted. The ancient kingdom of Babylon came under the rule of a dynasty of monarchs of whom the best known is Nebuchadnezzar and for 70 years or so underwent a remarkable cultural revival. This period, which lasted from 612 to 539 B.C., is generally called the Neo-Babylonian period, and its culture harks back across the period of Assyrian domination to that of Babylon 1,000 years earlier. The greatest building project of the age was Nebuchadnezzar's palace at Babylon, little of which has survived. The Ishtar Gate, the principal entry into Babylon, was decorated with painted and glazed bricks, giving an impression of considerable splendor, and Nebuchadnezzar's hanging gardens and 300-foot-high ziggurat made Babylon perhaps the most impressive city in the world.

carved reliefs. Under Sargon II (722–705 B.C.) a new city was built at Khorsabad, which covered almost a square mile and was surrounded by walls. The gates were provided with guard posts that could serve for defense in time of war and as customs and police posts in peacetime. Both the outer gates and the entrance doors into the palace were also protected by huge statues of the Assyrians' most powerful demons, the Lamassu, splendidly depicted as winged human-headed bulls that serve as imposing representations of Assyrian power. The palace itself was built around a large open court, with separate quarters for officers and servants, a number of temples, and the king's residential apartments. Most impressive were the state rooms, where the king received foreign ambassadors. The throne room was approached through an open courtyard lined with greater-

## The Rise of Persia

The land of the Persians had been inhabited for millennia, perhaps from as early as 15,000 B.C. Persia itself, or Iran ("land of the Aryans"), as it is now called, lies at a crossroads between the rugged lands of western Asia, the plains of central Asia, the great steppes to the northeast, and Afghanistan and the Indus valley to the east. At the heart of Persia is a high central plateau surrounded by mountains, which separate the plains of the interior from the Caspian Sea to the north and the Persian Gulf to the south. Two extensive deserts, virtually impassable in the summer, lie in the center of the immense plateau; from time immemorial they have diverted nomads from central Asia into India to the east or the Tigris-Euphrates valley to the west. The lowlands beyond the mountains receive most of the region's precipitation and thus contrast sharply with the dry interior. The land is rich in minerals, particularly iron, copper, and brilliant blue lapis lazuli. Early in its history western Iran, known then as Elam, fell under Sumerian influence. Persia as a whole, however, was only sparsely settled by prehistoric peoples throughout the centuries of Sumerian and Babylonian rule.

Around 1000 B.C., as we have seen, conditions in western Asia were generally unstable. The Egyptians had begun their decline, the Assyrians had not yet established firm rule, and the mass movements of the Peoples of the Sea had created havoc, destroying the Hittites in the process. Nor was the situation simplified by the fact that at about the same time tribes of nomadic horse-riding warriors migrated from central Asia into Iran, bringing their flocks and herds. Without horses, the prehistoric inhabitants were no match for them. Among the invading tribes were the Indo-European Medes and Persians, both of whom were related to the Aryans who settled India. The Medes and Persians were soon joined by the warlike Scythians, who had in turn been driven from the far eastern steppe, where the Huns, a people from central Asia, were at war with the Chinese.

The Medes and the Persians established a number of

The Ishtar Gate of the city of Babylon has been reconstructed in the National Museum in Berlin. [National Museum, Berlin]

small kingdoms, each of which was ruled by a king who was little more than a warlord supported by a band of warriors. Below this elite group, early Iranian society was comprised of free farmers, skilled artisans, peasants who owed labor to the king, and slaves. Trade was conducted with other peoples in the region, particularly the Assyrians to the west, who were attracted by Iranian horses and minerals. The Medes, who had settled in northern Iran, united in the late eighth century B.C., after which they imposed their rule on the Persians in the south.

An alliance of Medes and Scythians, together with the help of other nomadic tribes, sacked Nineveh in 612 B.C. and put an end to the Assyrian Empire. Throughout these tumultuous events the Persians retained their tribal identity and through a process of intermarriage and aggression established their rule over most of Iran. In 550 B.C. the Medes, weakened by their struggles to the west, were resoundingly defeated by Cyrus (559–530 B.C.), chief of the Persian tribes. The land of the Medes became Cyrus' first province, or satrapy.

About 546 B.C. Cyrus conquered prosperous Lydia and the Greek cities on the Anatolian coast, in what is now western Turkey. This gave him possession of the ports that marked the western terminus of the trade routes extending from the Aegean Sea deep into Asia. After securing his eastern frontiers by fighting that extended as far as Afghanistan and western India, he turned to the southwest and in 539 B.C. captured the venerable city of Babylon. That city, which had recently witnessed the splendid reign of Nebuchadnezzar, became an important symbol of Persian success. Cyrus included the title "king of Babylon" in his inscriptions and spent considerable time in residence there. As a conqueror he distinguished himself by his appreciation of the cultures of his new subjects; local customs and religious beliefs were not suppressed.

Cyrus' son and successor, Cambyses (530–522 B.C.), conquered Egypt in 525 B.C. and even tried to reach Carthage (modern Tunis). He failed, however, to persuade his Phoenician allies to attack their Carthaginian kinsmen. His plan to conquer Ethiopia also remained largely unfulfilled because of inadequate supplies. Cambyses was said to have been mentally unbalanced, and he was cruel enough to kill his own brother.

The accession of Darius I (522–486 B.C.) returned stability to the Persian Empire, and his reign inaugurated nearly two centuries of peaceful Persian rule. Among his accomplishments were the introduction of a uniform system of gold and silver coinage, standard weights and measures, a postal service, an imperial law code based on Mesopotamian principles, and a common calendar derived from the Egyptians'.

Darius' reign saw further attempts to extend the empire. Around 513 or 512 B.C. he sent expeditions into southeastern Europe, reaching as far as the River Danube, and into India, the northwestern portion of which became the satrapy of Hindush. Darius wanted to improve communications and trade and to that end supported an expedition, led by the Greek sailor Scylax, that sailed from the Indus River to the northern end of the Red Sea. Darius also became embroiled with the people to the far west, the Greeks, against whom he and his successor, Xerxes, launched three unsuccessful expeditions. Despite his failure to conquer the Greeks, Darius' empire enjoyed trade relations with people as far away as India to the east and Phoenicia on the Mediterranean. The Persians planned to construct a canal from the Nile to the Red Sea; had they succeeded, Alexander the Great, with better supply lines at his disposal, might have conquered India, and fifteenth-century explorers might not have sought a passage across the Atlantic Ocean to East Asia as an alternative to sailing around the African continent.

# Life and Government in the Persian Empire

The Persian Empire at its height was both wealthy and cosmopolitan. Foreign artisans worked with materials that came from Greece, Lebanon, and India to decorate the royal palaces. The Persians traded widely, using their gold coin, the daric, and maintained contacts throughout western Asia. Many of the people under their control did not speak their language, and the monuments on the Royal Road, the principal highway to cross part of the empire, were accompanied by inscriptions in Babylonian and Elamite as well as Persian. Some 1,600 miles long (the distance from New York to Dallas), the Royal Road extended from Susa in western Persia to Sardis, near the port of Ephesus, a Greek city on the Aegean. It took caravans three months to travel this road, although royal couriers, using fresh horses provided at the 111 post stations along the route, could make the trip in a week.

For all the power of their ruler, the "king of kings," the Persians' view of their monarchy differed from that of the Assyrians. The king was not an object of fear but a righteous leader, elected by all the gods. The empire was in general ruled with efficiency, justice, and tolerance. It was so large that it had to be divided into some 20 satrapies or provinces, each of which was administered by a governor (or satrap), aided by a military force under a separate commander. The governors, who were Mede or Persian nobles, were prevented from exercising inordinate power by the presence of both military officials and royal agents and spies. The king was interested primarily in receiving from the satraps appropriate tribute and recruits for the military; if those demands were fulfilled, the governors enjoyed a good deal of autonomy.

## ✿ PERSIAN CAPITALS: SUSA AND PERSEPOLIS

The principal centers of the empire were at Susa, eastern terminus of the Royal Road; Ecbatana, the former Mede capital; and ancient Babylon. Susa, which had been inhabited since Neolithic times, was situated at the foot of the Zagros Mountains, near the bank of the River Karkheh. Beginning in 521 B.C. Darius made it his principal capital for most of the year, leaving only in the summer to escape the intense heat. He ordered the construction of a citadel and a sumptuous palace as well as walls and a moat for protection. His workers were imported from many lands: stonecutters from Greece and Asia Minor, goldsmiths from Egypt, brickmakers from Babylon. So were his materials, including cedar from Lebanon, gold from Bactria, and ivory from Ethiopia. Susa became a cosmopolitan center; the biblical book of Esther is set there.

In 518 B.C. Darius began the construction of a new capital at Persepolis, a remote site in an alpine region southeast of Susa. The style of architecture and sculpture that developed at Persepolis, like that at Susa, was highly eclectic. Lacking their own architectural traditions, the Persians drew on those of others. Like the Sumerians, they employed mud brick and constructed their palaces on terraces, although they used the kind of glazed decoration found on Nebuchadnezzar's palace at Babylon. Assyrian human-headed bulls, Egyptian doorways, and even Greek columns can be found at Persepolis; some of the decorative sculpture was almost certainly produced by visiting Greek and Egyptian artists. The total effect is striking in the extensive ruins that remain.

The site of Persepolis was topped by a citadel. The lower slopes of the mountain on which it stands were leveled to allow construction on a terrace ranging 14 to 41 feet above the ground. The terrace was reached by a stairway broad enough to be used by groups of riders. Upon it were monumental public buildings, each in-

The audience hall of Darius and Xerxes at Persepolis, with the palace of Darius in the background. [Courtesy of the Oriental Institute of the University of Chicago]

tended to reinforce the general impression of splendor. The vast audience hall of the royal palace built by Darius and Xerxes between 520 and 460 B.C. was approached by an elaborate staircase lined with sculptural decoration. The reliefs showed a procession of officials, soldiers, and representatives of the assorted peoples of the empire bringing tribute to the king. The great hall was 60 feet high and contained three dozen 40-foot columns. On a retaining wall, Darius inscribed a prayer for his subjects: "God protect this country from foe, famine, and falsehood."

Darius' successors maintained the Persian Empire until it was conquered by Alexander the Great between 334 and 326 B.C. The arrival of Alexander and his troops thrust Europe and Asia into the long period of mutual influence that has lasted, despite interruptions, to our own time.

*The peoples of western Asia and Egypt achieved some of the greatest artistic and cultural innovations in history. The invention of metalworking and writing and the development of architectural techniques and drainage and irrigation systems are only the most obvious of the many technological advances of the period. These made possible the development of cities, and with them came the growth of legal systems and complex urban relationships that remain, in one form or another, the basis of our daily lives.*

*Growing economic prosperity, coupled with technological developments such as wheeled vehicles and seagoing ships that simplified long-distance travel, encouraged the expansion of trade. This in turn led, on the one hand, to stimulating contact with foreign ideas as well as goods and, on the other hand, to conflict, since what could be bought peacefully could also be taken in war. It is no accident that much of the new technology was devoted to making better weapons and stronger fortifications. Internal and external expansion required professional planners and administrators, giving rise to the new profession of bureaucrat.*

*The same drive that laid the foundations of civilized life in western Asia and Egypt was responsible for the art that helps us interpret the character and world view of each of the peoples who produced them. Some monuments are more familiar than others. The pyramids of Egypt, for example, were known to Roman soldiers and to Napoleon, whereas the Hittites and the people of Ebla have been rediscovered only within the past century. Time after time, works of art that were created in a world remote from our own succeed in communicating to us with vividness and power. The fascination they continue to exert confirms the underlying unity of human experience.*

## Notes

1. *The Book of the Dead According to the Theban Recension*, trans. E. A. Wallis Budge, in *Egyptian Literature*, ed. E. Wilson (London: Colonial Press, 1901).
2. C. Aldred, *Akhenaten: King of Egypt* (London: Thames & Hudson, 1988), p. 224.
3. J. B. Pritchard, ed., *Ancient Near Eastern Texts Relating to the Old Testament*, trans. J. Wilson (Princeton, N.J.: Princeton University Press, 1969), pp. 251–252.
4. T. G. H. James, *Pharaoh's People: Scenes from Life in Imperial Egypt* (London: Bodley Head, 1984), p. 103.
5. Deut. 25:6.

## Suggestions for Further Reading

Ackroyd, P. R. *Israel Under Babylon and Persia*. London: Oxford University Press, 1970.

Aldred, C. *Akhenaten: King of Egypt*. London: Thames & Hudson, 1988.

Bengston, H. *Introduction to Ancient History*. Berkeley: University of California Press, 1976.

Bright, J. *A History of Israel*, 3rd ed. Philadelphia: Westminster Press, 1981.

Burney, C. *The Ancient Near East*. Ithaca, N.Y.: Cornell University Press, 1977.

Cameron, A., and Kuhrt, A., eds. *Images of Women in Antiquity*. Detroit: Wayne State University Press, 1983.

Cook, J. M. *The Persian Empire*. New York: Schocken Books, 1983.

Dalley, S. *Mari and Karana: Two Old Babylonian Cities*. London: Longman, 1984.

Dandamaev, M. A. *A Political History of the Achaemenid Empire*. New York: Brill, 1989.

Davies, W. D., and Finkelstein, L., eds. *The Cambridge History of Judaism*. Vol. I: *The Persian Period*. Cambridge: Cambridge University Press, 1984. Vol. 2: *The Hellenistic Age*. Cambridge: Cambridge University Press, 1987.

De Boer, P. A. H. *Fatherhood and Motherhood in Israelite and Judean Piety*. Leiden, Netherlands: Brill, 1974.

De Gobineau, J. A. *The World of the Persians*. London: Gifford, 1971.

De Vaux, R. *The Early History of Israel*, trans. D. Smith. London: Darton, Longman & Todd, 1978.

Finley, M. I. *The Ancient Economy*. Berkeley: University of California Press, 1973.

Gurney, O. R. *The Hittites*, 2nd ed. New York: Penguin Books, 1972.

Harden, D. *The Phoenicians*, 2nd ed. New York: Praeger, 1971.

Jacobsen, T. *The Treasures of Darkness: A History of Mesopotamian Religion*. New Haven, Conn.: Yale University Press, 1976.

James, T. G. H. *Pharaoh's People: Scenes from Life in Imperial Egypt*. London: Bodley Head, 1984.

Kemp, B. J. *Ancient Egypt: Anatomy of a Civilization*. London: Routledge & Kegan Paul, 1989.

Kitchen, K. A. *The Third Intermediate Period in Egypt, 1100–650 B.C.*, 2nd ed. Warminster, England: Aris & Phillips, 1986.

Knapp, A. B. *The History and Culture of Ancient Western Asia and Egypt*. Homewood, Ill.: Dorsey Press, 1988.

Kramer, S. N. *History Begins at Sumer*, 3rd ed. Philadelphia: University of Pennsylvania Press, 1981.

Macqueen, J. G. *The Hittites and Their Contemporaries in Asia Minor*, rev. ed. London: Thames & Hudson, 1986.

Manniche, L. *City of the Dead: Thebes in Egypt*. Chicago: University of Chicago Press, 1987.

———. *Sexual Life in Ancient Egypt*. London: KPI, 1987.

Oates, J. *Babylon*, rev. ed. London: Thames & Hudson, 1986.

Oppenheim, A. L. *Ancient Mesopotamia*, rev. ed. Chicago: University of Chicago Press, 1977.

Pettinato, G. *The Archives of Ebla: An Empire Inscribed in Clay*. Garden City, N.Y.: Doubleday, 1981.

———. *Ebla: A New Look at History*. Baltimore: Johns Hopkins University Press, 1991.

Redford, D. B. *Akhenaten: The Heretic King*. Princeton, N.J.: Princeton University Press, 1984.

Rice, M. *Egypt's Making: The Origins of Ancient Egypt, 5000–2000 B.C.* London: Routledge & Kegan Paul, 1990.

Saggs, H. W. F. *Civilization Before Greece and Rome*. London: Batsford, 1989.

———. *The Greatness That Was Babylon*, rev. ed. London: Sidgwick & Jackson, 1988.

Samson, J. *Nefertiti and Cleopatra: Queen-Monarchs of Ancient Egypt*. London: Rubicon, 1985.

Sandars, N. K. *The Sea Peoples*, rev. ed. London: Thames & Hudson, 1985.

Silver, M. *Economic Structures of the Ancient Near East*. Totowa, N.J.: Barnes & Noble Books, 1987.

———. *Prophets and Markets: The Political Economy of Ancient Israel*. Boston: Kluwer-Nijhoff, 1983.

# Ancient India

India's civilization is the oldest in continuous existence. If one defines civilization as involving a writing system, metalworking, and some concentration of settlement in cities where most of the inhabitants are not farmers, the earliest such developments seem to have occurred in Mesopotamia by about 4000 B.C. and about the same time in Egypt. By about 3000 B.C. civilization in these terms had emerged in the Indus valley of India and by about 2000 B.C. in China. Mesopotamian and Egyptian civilizations came to an end by Roman times and were later superseded by the Arab conquest. The present cultures of these areas have little or no connection with ancient Sumer or the time of the pharaohs, leaving India as the oldest survivor. The Indus civilization is the clearly traceable direct ancestor of subsequent Indian civilization, and the continuities are strong.

The Indian subcontinent, as it is called, from the mountain borders of Afghanistan to the Bay of Bengal on the east and from the towering Himalayas to the

**Perhaps the best-known samples of Mauryan art are the pillars erected by the emperor Ashoka, usually bearing Buddhist edicts and surmounted by sculptured figures. This triad of royal lions in stone, still used as an official symbol of India, formed the capital of one of Ashoka's columns and effectively captures the splendor of Mauryan India. [Stella Snead/Archaeological Survey of India]**

southern tip of the peninsula, is about the size of all of Europe (excluding Russia) and is even more varied physically, linguistically, and culturally. This huge and diverse area has only briefly during its long history been united under a single ruler, and then only partly so. It is now composed of the separate states of Pakistan, India, Nepal, Bangladesh, and Sri Lanka, but within each of these political divisions remain major regional differences. For every period of Indian history it is thus difficult to generalize about this vast and varied part of the world, containing about a fifth of the world's people. Nevertheless, an underlying culture shared by inhabitants of the subcontinent, periodically enriched by new infusions, gave and still gives Indian civilization its basic identity.

Although a literate urban culture was in existence in India by around 3000 B.C. and lasted about 1,000 years, we know relatively little about it. We cannot yet decipher the marks its people inscribed on clay tablets and seals, and the evidence we have is mainly the partly excavated ruins of the very large cities they built. After the collapse of the Indus civilization, northern India was invaded, over many centuries, by a central Asian people who called themselves Aryans. They gradually became the dominant group in the north, although they intermarried with the indigenous people. By the time Alexander the Great invaded India in 326 B.C. many regional kingdoms had arisen. These were welded together into an empire by the Maurya dynasty (c. 322–c. 180 B.C.) after Alexander withdrew, which unified most of the north. A new group of invaders reunified the north under the Kushan dynasty from 100 B.C. to about A.D. 200. In the following century the indigenous Gupta dynasty restored most of the Mauryan accomplishments in the north from A.D. 320 to 550, while the south remained divided among flourishing rival kingdoms. Gupta rule collapsed around 550, as did the short-lived northern empire of Harsha by 648. Once more, India became a complex pattern of separate states. But in most of its basic elements, Indian civilization has remained continuous from the third millennium B.C. to the present.

# Origins of Civilization in India

Agriculture had evolved much earlier than civilization, probably independently in a number of places including tropical Southeast Asia, western Asia (what is now eastern Turkey, Syria, and northern Iraq), Africa, and, by about 2000 B.C., Central and South America. Agriculture in permanent fields, as opposed to a food-gathering culture, requires permanent settlement. Villages or even small towns of this sort inhabited by farmers began to emerge soon after 10,000 B.C. in southwestern Asia.

It was not far from Sumer to India, and the way was relatively easy: by ship along the sheltered coasts of the Persian Gulf and thence still following the coast to the mouth of the Indus River. The route by land across Iran and Baluchistan ran through desert with few oases, but it was used too. Neolithic developments in agriculture and the beginnings of large settled villages or towns were taking place at several locations along this land route and in the upland Baluchistan borderlands west of the Indus during the fifth millennium B.C. These developments were probably independent of Sumer but may have benefited indirectly from early Sumerian achievements. Agriculture had also appeared on the Indus floodplain by the fifth millennium and may thus have developed independently there. By 3000 B.C. or so true cities had arisen in the Indus plain and in tributary river valleys, much as early agriculture in the highlands around Mesopotamia later spread onto the riverine lowlands. As in Mesopotamia, the floodplain presented new challenges to early agriculturists: how to control river flooding, manipulate irrigation, and drain swampy land. The long experience with an evolving set of agricultural techniques ultimately made it possible to exploit the potentially rich agricultural resources of the lowlands. Consistent agricultural surpluses provided the basis for real cities, as opposed to towns; the cities were literate, metal-using, food-surplus-storing centers with a division of labor and great sophistication in the arts, in building, and in planning.

# The Indus Civilization

The chief urban centers so far discovered are Kalibangan in modern Rajasthan (probably the oldest city site yet found in India), Harappa in what is now the Pakistani part of Punjab, and Mohenjo Daro on the lower course of the Indus. All three, as well as nearly 200 smaller town or village sites from the same period scattered over an immense area from the Indus valley east to the upper Ganges and south to near modern Bombay, show similar forms of settlements, pottery, seals (for marking pieces of property), and artwork. This vast complex, extending over by far the largest area of any ancient culture, is called the Indus civilization. It clearly had a close relationship to the river and its tributaries, a situation very similar to that in Sumer and in Egypt. Like the Nile and the Tigris and Euphrates, the Indus is an "exotic" river, that is, one that originates in a well-watered area. Rising with its tributaries in the Himalayas, the source of snowmelt and heavy summer monsoonal rains, it flows across lowland Punjab and arid Rajasthan into the desert of Sind

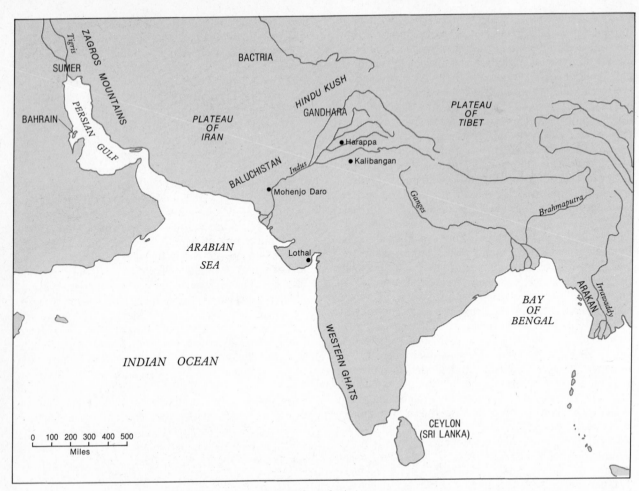

*2.1 South Asia*

to reach the sea near modern Karachi. All of this lowland area is dry, and the lower half of the Indus valley is virtually desert, as in Sumer and Egypt, so that agriculture is dependent on irrigation. Annual river floods provided both water and highly fertile and easily worked alluvium, or silt. Combined with a long growing season of high temperatures and unbroken sunshine, this was the same set of agricultural advantages that helped explain the early prominence of Egypt and Sumer after the management and use of floodwater had been mastered. The river also offered cheap, easy transport for bulky goods such as grain or building materials and together with the treeless and level plain created the access for transport that is essential for exchange and hence for the division of labor.

## Relations with Sumer

We know much less about the Indus civilization and its cities than about Sumer or ancient Egypt, in part be-

cause the Indus script has not yet been deciphered. The texts we have are incised on clay tablets and seals, as in Sumer, and contain over 300 different symbols. They may help provide some clue to who the writers were. It is plausible to assume that they were part ancestors of the present inhabitants of South India, for which there is some linguistic evidence. But the Indus script has no resemblance to cuneiform, which by at least 3200 B.C. had replaced pictographic writing in Sumer, almost certainly before the beginnings of city-based civilization in India. The clear superiority of cuneiform ensured its rapid spread. If the Indus civilization had been an outgrowth of Sumer, it would surely have used cuneiform or at least shown some connection with earlier Sumerian writing systems.

The art of the Indus people and their remarkable city planning are also completely distinctive and show no relation to Sumerian equivalents. The seals that they used are very similar to those of earlier and contemporary Mesopotamia, and we know that from at least 2500 B.C. there was trade between them. Objects from India at this period have been found in Sumer, and Sumerian objects in India. It seems likely that since seals were probably used primarily to mark property or goods, they were adopted by the Indus people in the course of their trade with Sumer. But in all other respects, their civilization was distinctively their own.

When the Indus civilization emerged is difficult to determine exactly, but it was probably around 3000 B.C. The city sites, including the three major ones at Kalibangan, Harappa, and Mohenjo Daro, were necessarily close to the Indus or its tributaries. Water levels and stream courses have changed since these cities were built some 5,000 years ago. Flooding and silt deposition have carried away, buried, or drowned most of the earliest archaeological evidence. As in the case of the Nile delta and for similar reasons, we can no longer see beginnings that may be considerably earlier than we can now prove. The earliest objects dated so far cluster around 2500 B.C., but they come necessarily from upper site levels and from a period when the urban culture was already well advanced. Especially in the emerging phase

Seal from Mohenjo Daro. The bovine figure at top right suggest the early veneration of cattle. [Borromeo/EPA: Art Resource]

Dancing girl in bronze, from Mohenjo Daro, c. 2500 B.C. The figure is stylized, even abstract, but powerfully conveys the spirit and movement of the dance. [National Museum of India, New Delhi]

of civilization, development is relatively slow. One must assume that it began many centuries before 2500, during which it evolved, built the first city levels, and acquired the form and quality evident by 2500.

We do not know what the builders of these cities called themselves or their settlements. The place names we use for them are modern—Mohenjo Daro means "place of the dead." The Greeks called the land they encountered in Alexander's time "India." This was derived from the Sanskrit *Sindhu*, the Aryan name for the river and by association the river's valley and the land beyond it. From *Sindhu* comes the Persian and modern Indian name for the country, *Hind*, and its derivatives, *Indus*, *Hindu*, and *Hindustan* (*stan* means "country").*

Trade with Sumer took place both overland and through the port of Lothal on the coast near the mouth of the Indus, where the remains of large stone docks and warehouses have been found. These were associated with a city that was clearly part of Harappan culture (a convenient shorter label for the Indus civilization). Goods from Sumer have been found there and elsewhere in Harappan India, and Harappan goods in Sumer. A site along the route between them, on Bahrain Island, has yielded both sorts of objects and seems to have supported a major trade center where many routes to and from Sumer met. Sumerian texts speak of a place called Dilmun, which was probably Bahrain, a number of days' sail southward from the mouth of their river, where were found goods from a place they called Meluha, to the east: ivory, peacocks, monkeys, precious stones, incense, and spices, the "apes, ivory, and peacocks" of the Bible. Meluha must have been India, but it is not clear whether people from Sumer went there or whether the Indus people, or some intermediary, carried their cargoes to Dilmun.

## The Cities of the Indus

Perhaps the most remarkable thing about this civilization was the planned layout of its cities, including wells, a piped water supply, bathrooms, and wastepipes or drains in nearly every house. There is no parallel for such planning anywhere in the ancient world, and indeed one must leap to the late nineteenth century in western Europe and North America to find such achievements on a similar scale. The rivers that nourished these cities were the source of their water supply, led by gravity from upstream, a technique later used by the Mughal emperors for their palaces in Delhi and Agra. The importance attached by the Indus people to personal use

of water already suggests the distinctively Indian emphasis on both bathing or washing and ritual purity. Religious remains are varied, but they include many figures that suggest an early representation of the Indian god Shiva, Creator and Destroyer, god of the harvest, of the cycle of birth, life, death, and rebirth, and also the primal yogi,[†] represented even then seated with arms folded and gaze fixed on eternity. Figures of a mother goddess, phallic images, and the worship of cattle are other elements that provide a link with classical and modern Indian civilization. Some scholars have suggested that the distinctively Indian ideas of reincarnation and the endless wheel of life were Harappan beliefs. Indeed, the roots of most of traditional and modern Indian culture can be found or guessed at in what we can piece together from the Indus culture.

The houses in these cities were remarkably uniform, suggesting an absence of great divisions in the society, arranged along regular streets in a semigrid pattern. There were a few larger buildings, including in most of the cities a large public bath, and others that were probably municipal granaries or storehouses. The art these still unknown people have left behind is strikingly varied and of high quality. Its variety may suggest that it was produced over a very long time, during which styles changed, as anywhere else in the world over 1,000 years: abstract, realistic, idealized, and so on. One of the most appealing forms is the enormous number of clay and wooden children's toys, including tiny carts pulled by tiny oxen or little monkeys that could be made to climb a string. This suggests a relatively prosperous society that could afford such nonessential production—a tribute to the productivity of its irrigated agriculture—and one whose values seem admirable. Complementing the picture, very few weapons or other indications of warfare have been found at these sites. The Indus civilization seems to have been notably peaceful and humane as well as organized and sophisticated. Cotton, indigenous to India, was woven into cloth earlier here than anywhere else. The animal sculpture and bas-relief, including the figures on many of the seals, were superbly done and include very large numbers of bovines, mainly the familiar humpbacked cattle, which suggests the importance attached to cattle and their veneration ever since in India. This and other evidence indicates that the reverence for life and the quest for nonviolent solutions that mark the consistent Indian stress on the great chain of being and the oneness of creation had emerged by Harappan times.

The chief Indus food crop was wheat, probably derived originally from areas to the west, augmented by

---

*\*India* is the label commonly used for the entire subcontinent, including the present states of Pakistan, India, and Nepal, which date in this form only from 1947, and Bangladesh, which was founded in 1971.

---

[†]One who practices yoga, the Hindu philosophy that entails a strict spiritual and physical discipline in order to attain unity with the Universal Spirit.

barley, peas, beans, oil seeds, fruits, and vegetables and by dairy products from domesticated cattle and sheep. Tools were made of bronze, stone, and wood, but in later centuries iron began to appear and was used, for example, in axle pins for wheeled carts. Rice appeared as a minor crop only toward the end of the Indus period, imported from its Southeast Asian origins as a crop plant via contact with the Ganges valley, to which it had spread earlier. Sugarcane is native to India and was first used there, especially in the well-watered Ganges valley. Riverine location was essential for irrigation but also made for recurrent problems from irregular and occasionally disastrous flooding. The remains of successive dikes speak of efforts to protect even the cities themselves against floods and major course changes, not always successfully. There was no building stone in this flat and semiarid or desert region, and the cities were built of brick, as in Sumer, some of it sun-baked and some kiln-fired, using fuel from riverside stands of trees

(which must soon have been exhausted) or brought down the rivers from forested hills and mountains upstream. The ruins of Harappa were first investigated in the 1850s by a British military engineer whose sharp eye noticed the strange dimensions of the bricks and other fragments brought to him by Indian contractors for railway ballast and the equally strange markings on some of them, samples of the Indus script, which he traced back to the site of Harappa and realized were the remains of a civilization earlier than any in India then known.

## Decline and Fall

Toward the end of the third millennium B.C. the Indus civilization began to decay. We can only guess at the reasons, but there is clear evidence of progressive shrinking of the area under cultivation or irrigation and

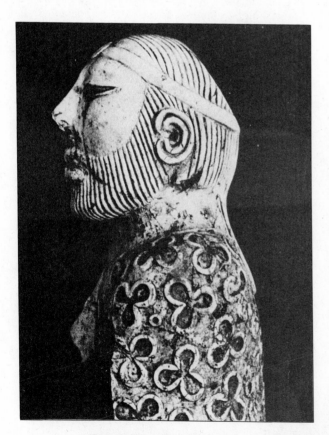 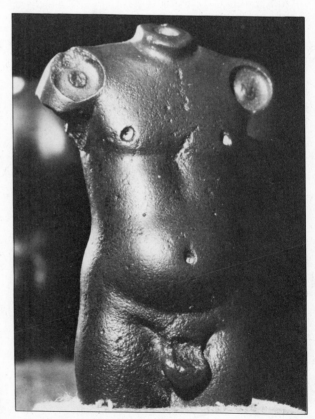

**Two strikingly different objects from the Indus civilization: a priestlike figure from Mohenjo Daro and a torso from Harappa. The highly stylized priest suggests Minoan (Cretan) art; the torso, classical Greek sculpture. That both come from the Indus civilization may suggest that they were produced at different periods and reflect stylistic changes over time. [*Left*: Stella Snead/Archaeological Survey of India; *right*: Art Resource/National Museum of India, New Delhi]**

of the urban area occupied. The port of Lothal was abandoned by about 1900 B.C., and the other major centers probably supported only a fraction of their earlier populations, huddled in a small part of the decaying city. There is also evidence of violence at some of these sites: ashes and unburied or headless corpses, victims perhaps of bandit raids against largely defenseless cities. The Indus people encountered some specific problems resulting from their desert or semiarid environment, problems that may quickly have become overwhelming. Continued irrigation of any arid area leads to the progressive buildup of salts and alkalies left behind by the evaporating water and not washed away adequately by rainfall. Irrigation also raises the water table, which may drown crop roots. When accumulated salts and alkalies reach levels toxic to plants or when the root zone is flooded, agriculture may rather suddenly come to an end. We have modern experience with both problems in many arid irrigated areas, including the drier parts of the United States.

In the Indus valley large parts of the areas cultivated in ancient times appear to have been abandoned for these reasons, as the telltale white deposits on the ancient surface indicate. In addition, recurrent flooding and course changes not only menaced the cities directly but also indirectly undermined their agricultural base by destroying or choking with silt the irrigation channels that fed the fields. Course changes could also deprive a city or an irrigated area of its water. All of this is characteristic of the behavior of exotic rivers, rising in the mountains and then flowing across a treeless desert. There is no evidence that the climate changed, as has often been asserted despite clear evidence to the contrary, but plenty to suggest that the agricultural surpluses that had built the cities and nourished their culture shrank and then disappeared, leaving only a remnant population living on a relatively primitive level in the ruins of the once great cities on what they could still wring from the remaining but far less productive fields, in addition to hunting and gathering. In this reduced state, they were less and less able to defend themselves against raiders. The Aryan invaders, arriving later, could never have seen the Indus civilization in its prime and are thus unlikely causes for its decline. The people who built it, or their descendants, probably dispersed eastward into the Ganges valley and southward into peninsular India, taking their culture and technology with them.

# The Aryans

*Aryan* is, strictly speaking, a linguistic term, but it has been used (and widely misused) to mean a people or,

even more inappropriately, a race. In the centuries after about 2000 B.C. a series of migration waves moved out from south-central Asia, including what is now Iran, to richer areas both eastward and westward. One such group was probably the seaborne invaders of Greece soon after 1100 B.C., another the Kassites who invaded and conquered Sumer, and another the Hittites who occupied northern Anatolia, while still another group moved eastward through passes in the Hindu Kush range into India sometime after about 1800 B.C. and called themselves Aryans. They spoke an early form of Sanskrit but were still preliterate, preurban, seminomadic tenders of cattle, sheep, and goats who also lived in part from hunting, plough agriculture of wheat and barley, and raiding more highly developed agricultural settlements and trade centers or routes. What little we know about them comes from their ritual hymns, the Vedas, and from the later epic poems of heroic deeds and warfare, the *Mahabharata* and the *Ramayana*, which were written down many centuries later in Sanskrit, the classical language of India. By that time the Aryans had acquired literacy, as well as the arts of agriculture, city building, and other aspects of civilization, presumably from contact and intermarriage with the more highly developed people already in India.

Vedic period culture (c. 1000–c. 500 B.C.) was, like its people, a combination of originally Aryan, Harappan, and other indigenous Indian strains. Sanskrit is the oldest written language among the ancestors of modern European languages, and it is also the direct ancestor of the languages of modern North India.* The connection was not realized until the pioneering research of a British judge in Bengal in the late eighteenth century, Sir William Jones, established the clear link among the Indo-European tongues—Greek, Latin, Celtic, Persian, and Sanskrit, as well as their modern derivatives—all of which had originally stemmed from the great migration of linguistically related peoples from south-central Asia beginning around 2000 B.C. Later research has shown that the common ancestor of the Indo-European languages was probably spoken in western Asia around 4000 B.C. and that the derived languages diverged from it as groups migrated east and, later, west.

# Aryan Domination

The Aryans had a telling advantage, despite their more primitive culture: by the time they reached India they had acquired not only metal-tipped weapons but also a light, fast war chariot with spoked wheels drawn by two

---

*Sanskrit *nava*, "ship"; *deva*, "god"; *dua*, "two"—these and many other Sanskrit words are easily recognizable as the roots of Latin and related English words (*naval, divine, dual*, for example).

or more horses, equivalent to the Greek war chariots of Homer's time, with a driver and an archer or spear thrower. Their culture glorified war, and they made a disproportionate military impact on a more peaceful Indian population. The Kassites, Hittites, Hyksos, and Mycenaeans, all possibly coming originally out of central Asia, made a similar impact with the same tactics. The horse had been known to the Indus people but was not used in fighting. The Vedas and the epics tell the story of Aryan victories over "alien" peoples, whose cities they besieged and conquered, led often by their warrior god Indra riding in his chariot with his great war bow. Like most history written by the victors, the Vedas and the epics portray the Aryans as godlike heroes and the conquered as "irreligious," inferior people. The archaeological record of the Indus civilization abundantly disproves such propaganda, but the Aryan language triumphed, presumably because, though a minority numerically, the Aryans became the ruling class of ancient India. *Arya* means "noble" or "pure" in Sanskrit; the same root word appears in the Greek *arios* ("good quality") and in the names of Iran and Eire (Ireland), illustrating the Indo-European connection.

We do not know exactly when the institution of caste, the division of Indian society into ranked status groups that could marry or eat only within the group, first appeared. One possibility is that it evolved later out of distinctions made in Vedic times between a conquering group of Aryans, insecure because of their numeric weakness, and a conquered people, although such distinctions must in time have been submerged by intermarriage and by cultural hybridization. In any case, caste distinctions and rules, including bans on intermarriage, seem not to have been widely observed until much later, perhaps as late as the fifth century A.D. The Aryan immigrants brought with them their male and warlike gods and their male-dominated culture, which slowly blended with the female goddesses and matriarchal culture of early India.

By around 1000 B.C. these Aryan-speaking groups had conquered or absorbed most of India north of the Vindhya range, which divides and protects the peninsular south and the Deccan plateau from the Ganges and Indus valleys of the north. Their language never prevailed in the south, which still speaks mainly four non-Indo-European languages collectively known as Dravidian, each with its own extensive and ancient literature. The south has also tended to resist what it still refers to as "Aryan" pressures or influences, but in fact interactions with the "Aryan" north have been a heavily traveled two-way street for thousands of years now, in religion, art, literature, philosophy, and many other aspects of culture. There is a clear north-south distinction in Indian culture, but Indian civilization is a generic whole. We can only guess at what the south was like in Vedic times. The great epics, the *Ramayana* and the *Mahabharata*,

speak of the south and Ceylon (Sri Lanka) as inhabited by savages and demons with whom the Vedic heroes were at war, in keeping with their pejorative descriptions of the people they conquered in the north. But although there were probably battles and raids, the south remained beyond Aryan control except where coastal plains at the western and eastern ends of the Vindhyas allowed easier access. Ceylon was, however, invaded by sea and settled by an Aryan-speaking group in the sixth century B.C. and about the same time by Dravidians from South India.

# Vedic Culture

The basis of traditional Indian culture and most of its details evolved in the Vedic period. We know little of that process or of worldly events. The Vedas and the epics are concerned with romantic adventure involving gods and demons or with philosophical and religious matters rather than with accounts of actual events or daily life. We know only that these centuries saw the maturation of a highly sophisticated culture, no longer simply Aryan or Aryan-dominated but Indian, which we can see in worldly terms for the first time in any detail through the eyes of Greek observers after 326 B.C., following Alexander's invasion of northwestern India. They show us a culture remarkable for its absorption in philosophy and metaphysics but also for its achievements in more mundane respects. The later classical West, like the Chinese, acknowledged India as the home of the most advanced knowledge and practice of medicine; of mathematics, including the numbering system we still use, miscalled "Arabic" (the Arabs got it from India); and of working iron and steel. Indian steel was later to be transmitted to the West, also through the Arabs, as "Damascus" or "Toledo," though the steel itself was Indian. The Indian practice of medicine, known as Ayurveda, enriched both Greek and Chinese knowledge and was widely disseminated, although it also benefited from Greek and Chinese medical practices.

These and other elements of Indian science had something to do with Vedic period assumptions about the universe and the physical world. Like some of the Greek philosophers, but even more consistently, Vedic India thought in terms of universal laws affecting all things—a supreme principle or indwelling essence, an order of nature that they called *Rta*. This order, unlike the Greek conception, was thought to exist above and before even the gods and to determine all observable and nonobservable phenomena. Modern science and technology are not conceivable without such an assumption of universal physical laws. The Greeks were on the right track in those terms, but the Indians anticipated the Greeks and probably influenced them.

## The Rise of Empire: Mauryan India

By about 500 B.C. kingdoms had emerged in the Ganges valley, already established as India's primary center of population, productivity, and commerce. This was the area traditionally known as Hindustan, which stretched from Delhi in the upper valley to Bengal near the river's mouth. Population had multiplied many times since the fall of the Indus civilization, and agriculture had spread from the Indus valley into the Ganges, a potentially more productive area watered far more plentifully by monsoonal rains and with the advantage of rich alluvial soils and a long growing season. In Harappan times the Ganges valley was still heavily forested and probably only thinly settled by hunter-gatherers. With the increasing use of iron tools after about 1000 B.C. and the rise in population, the forest was progressively cleared and most of Hindustan settled and cultivated. Growing numbers and surplus production provided the basis for the emergence of territorial states with revenue bases, officials, cities, roads, and armies.

## Alexander the Great and the Greek Impact on India

When Alexander, fresh from his conquest of the Persian Empire and eager to add what the Persians had earlier controlled in northwestern India, burst through the northwestern passes in 326 B.C. (providing thereby the first certain date in Indian history), India was composed of many rival states covering both the north and the south. Alexander encountered and defeated some of them in the Indus valley and Punjab and heard accounts of others. His campaign against Porus, king of West Punjab, with his large army and his battalions of war elephants, was the most difficult of his career. When the proud but wounded and defeated Porus was brought before him, Alexander asked how he wished to be treated. Though barely able to stand, Porus boldly replied: "As befits me—like a king!" Alexander was so impressed that he gave him back his kingdom as an ally, a pact that Porus kept to his death. Alexander's invasion was undertaken with a strong sense of mission, to unite East and West and to create a cosmopolitan fusion of cultures, a plan he had already begun to carry out by merging Greek, Persian, and Medean elements and by taking a wife and a male companion from Persia. He encouraged his 10,000 Greek and Macedonian soldiers to take Persian and Indian wives, in keeping with his larger vision, although, like most soldiers far from home, his men probably needed little urging.

The Greek impact is symbolic of the continuous link between India and the West, not only in common linguistic roots but in physical and cultural terms too. Hellenic-style art continued to be produced by the post-Alexandrian Greek kingdoms in the northwest, such as Bactria and Gandhara, and influenced the evolution of Buddhist art in India. Indian philosophical ideas circulated more widely in the West as a result of the link that Alexander's invasion strengthened. He was himself a widely curious person. Realizing the Indian penchant for philosophy, he summoned Indian scholars to instruct and debate with him and recorded much of what he learned and observed for his own teacher, Aristotle. One Indian sage whom he summoned refused at first to come, saying that Alexander's evident preoccupation with conquest and empire could leave little place for phi-

Standing Buddha from Gandhara, a Greek-ruled kingdom in northwestern India that flourished in the second and first centuries B.C. Notice the close similarity in style to Hellenistic sculpture, including the conventional representation of the folds of the garment and the generally realistic portrayal. [Lahore Museum, Pakistan]

losophy. Alexander had him brought in, and the two men apparently impressed each other enough that they became friends and companions until Alexander's untimely death in 323 B.C. Before his homesick and rebellious troops obliged him to turn back, far short of his goal of descending the Ganges to the Bay of Bengal, he made several alliances (as with Porus), set up several Hellenic kingdoms in the northwest, and received a number of Indian princes, among them the young Chandragupta Maurya, who was to found the first Indian empire and the Maurya dynasty.

## The Mauryan Conquest

By 322 B.C. Chandragupta had emerged as head of an empire that included the whole of Hindustan and most of the northwest, with its capital on the Ganges at Pataliputra, near modern Patna in what is now the state of Bihar. The age of heroic chivalry, as recorded in the Vedas and the epics, was long passed, and the time of ruthless power politics had arrived. We may also guess this from the book attributed to Chandragupta's prime minister, Kautilya, the *Arthashastra*. This is one of the earliest samples we have of what was to become a genre, a handbook for rulers with advice on how to seize, hold, and manipulate power, of which the most famous in the West is *The Prince* by Niccolò Machiavelli. The *Arthashastra* also deals with the wise and humane administration of justice, but the text we have was composed by many hands over several centuries after Kautilya's time, although he may well have been the author of a now lost original. In any case, empire building is a rough game everywhere, and the writing of such a manual fits the circumstances of the time. It is paralleled very closely by a similar text, the Book of Lord Shang, and the doctrines of Li Ssu, prime minister to China's first imperial unifier, Ch'in Shih Huang Ti, about a century later as warring states were welded into an empire by conquest.

In both India and China in the sixth century B.C. warfare and political rivalries had begun to break up the institutions and values of an earlier age. This period saw the emergence of new philosophical and religious efforts to restore the social order (Confucianism in China) or to provide an escape from worldly strife through contemplation, mysticism, and otherworldly salvation (Taoism in China, Buddhism and the Hindu revival in India). These religious and philosophical developments are dealt with in Chapter 7. We know very little about actual political forms or events in India during these centuries before the rise of the Mauryan Empire. The documents we have are, as indicated earlier, concerned almost exclusively with heroic deeds or with metaphysical and religious matters. Politics and the rise and fall of king-

## ◉ Advice to Indian Princes ◉

*The* Arthashastra, *in addition to its advice to princes on how to seize and hold power and to outwit rivals by often unscrupulous means, also stressed the responsibility of the king to take care of his people.*

> The king's pious vow is readiness in action,
> his sacrifice the discharge of his duty. . . .
> In the happiness of his subjects, his welfare.
> The king's good is not that which pleases him,
> but that which pleases his subjects.
>
> Therefore the king should be ever active,
> and should strive for prosperity,
> for prosperity depends on effort,
> and failure on the reverse. . . .
>
> A single wheel cannot turn,
> and so government is possible only with assistance.
> Therefore a king should appoint councillors
> and listen to their advice.

*Source:* A. L. Basham, *The Wonder That Was India*, 3rd ed. (New York: Grove Press, 1959), pp. 89, 98.

doms, by their nature transitory, were perhaps considered not important enough to record by comparison with the eternal quest for the mysteries of humankind and the universe, the consistent emphasis of Indian thinkers. We know the names of some of the states immediately preceding the Mauryan conquest, including the kingdom of Magadha in the central Ganges valley, which seems to have been Chandragupta's original base. But even for Mauryan India we are dependent for actual descriptions largely on Greek sources, including surviving fragments of the Book of Megasthenes, who was posted by Alexander's successor Seleucus Nicator to Chandragupta's court at Pataliputra. The book itself is lost, but later Greek and Latin writers drew on it extensively. It is the earliest description we have of India by an outsider.

## ❦
## PATALIPUTRA AND THE GLORY OF MAURYAN INDIA

In Megasthenes' time and for some two centuries or more after, Pataliputra was probably the largest and most sophisticated city and center of culture in the world, rivaled in its later days perhaps only by the Han dynasty capital at Ch'ang An and larger than anything in the West, as the Greek accounts state. It was the seat of a famous university and library, to which scholars came, reputedly, from all over the civilized world, a city of magnificent palaces, temples, gardens, and parks. Megasthenes describes a highly organized bureaucratic system that controlled the economic and social as well as political life of Mauryan India, complete with a secret service to spy on potential dissidents, suspected criminals, and corrupt or ineffective officials. But he clearly admired Chandragupta for his conscientious administration of justice and for his imperial style. The emperor presided personally over regular sessions at court, where cases were heard and petitions presented, and ruled on disputes in similar fashion on his travels around the empire. His enormous palace at Pataliputra was a splendid complex, and visitors were awed by its magnificence and by the throngs of courtiers, councillors, and guests at state receptions.

Pataliputra was surrounded by a huge wall with 570 towers and 64 gates. All mines and forests were owned and managed by the state, and there were large state farms and state granaries, shipyards, and factories for spinning and weaving cotton cloth, all supervised by appropriate government departments. To guard against corruption and favoritism, departments were supposed to be headed by more than one chief, and officials were to be transferred often. Even prostitution was controlled by the state. Megasthenes describes Mauryan India as

a place of great wealth and prosperity and remarks on the bustling trade and rich merchants. By this time, if not before, there was already an extensive seaborne trade as well, perhaps extending to Southeast Asia, and a large seaport city in Bengal, Tamralipiti, close to the mouth of the Ganges not far from modern Calcutta. Roads were essential to hold the empire together, and by Mauryan times the main trunk road of India had been built from Tamralipiti along the Ganges valley to Pataliputra, Banaras, and Delhi, through Punjab, and on to the borders of Afghanistan. Other routes branched southward, on to the mouth of the Indus, linking together all the chief cities of Hindustan. The road system was apparently well maintained, marked with milestones, provided with wells and rest houses at regular intervals, and planted with trees to provide shade. Megasthenes says that famine was unknown, although it seems more likely merely that he did not hear of it during his years there. Famine was endemic everywhere in the world, and northern India especially was prone to drought, given the fickleness of the monsoon rains.

## ❦
## THE EMPEROR ASHOKA, "BELOVED OF THE GODS"

Chandragupta died about 297 B.C.; we do not know the exact year, and one legend has it that he wearied of affairs of state and became a wandering ascetic, in the Indian tradition, for the last few years of his life. The empire was further expanded and consolidated by his son Bindusara, who maintained the Greek connection and exchanged gifts with Antiochus I, the Seleucid king of Syria. But the greatest Mauryan ruler was Chandragupta's grandson Ashoka, one of the great kings of world history. Here, however, is another reminder of the traditional Indian lack of interest in political history. Ashoka was perhaps the greatest Indian ruler ever, yet he was all but forgotten until his rediscovery by British antiquarians and archaeologists in the late nineteenth century, thanks to Ashoka's habit of inscribing his name and imperial edicts on rocks and pillars, which he set up all over his immense empire. He came to the throne about 269 B.C. and spent the first several years of his rule in military campaigns to round out the empire by incorporating the south. According to his own rock-cut inscriptions, Ashoka saw and was grieved by the carnage that his lust for power had brought about. His campaign against the Kalingas of Orissa and northern Andhra in the northern Deccan plateau was apparently a turning point. After the campaign he foreswore further territorial aggression in favor of what he called "the conquest of righteousness." Ashoka was converted to the teachings of the Buddha, who had died four centuries

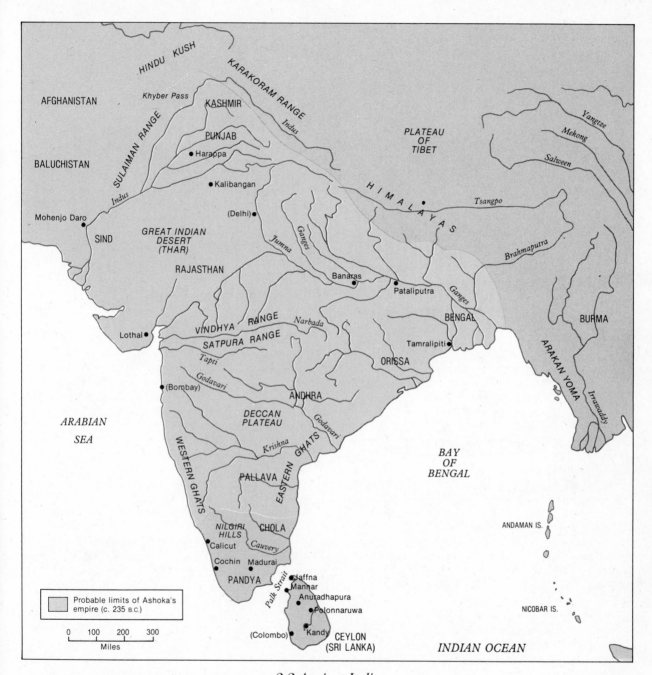

*2.2 Ancient India*

earlier, and vowed to spend the rest of his life, and his great imperial power and prestige, in spreading the Buddhist message.

The beautifully carved stones and pillars that presumably marked Ashoka's empire extend far into the south, well beyond Andhra, and may suggest that he added to his military conquests those of the spirit. We do not know to what extent the south was ruled from Pataliputra during his time, although we know that a Mauryan governor was appointed for the southern provinces. Ashoka clearly felt a sense of mission, not only to spread Buddhism but also to set an example of righteousness in government that could persuade others elsewhere to follow it. He declared that all people everywhere were his children, and he softened the harsher aspects of Chandragupta's police state methods of control. He ad-

---

### ◉ Ashoka's Goals ◉

*Ashoka had edicts inscribed on rocks and pillars at widely scattered locations all over India, stating official policy and giving instructions and advice. In one he recounts his conversion and outlines his new goals.*

When the king, of gracious mien and Beloved of the Gods, had been consecrated eight years, Kalinga was conquered. 150,000 people were taken captive, 100,000 were killed, and many more died. Just after the taking of Kalinga, the Beloved of the Gods began to follow righteousness, to love righteousness, to give instruction in righteousness. When an unconquered country is conquered, people are killed. . . . That the Beloved of the Gods finds very pitiful and grievous. . . . If anyone does him wrong it will be forgiven as far as it can be forgiven. The Beloved of the Gods even reasons with the forest tribes in his empire and seeks to reform them. . . . The Beloved of the Gods considers that the greatest of all victories is the victory of righteousness.

*Source:* A. L. Basham, *The Wonder That Was India*, 3rd ed. (New York: Grove Press, 1959), pp. 53–54.

---

vocated the ancient Indian ideal of nonviolence (adopted also by the Buddha), urged pilgrimages as a substitute for hunting, and encouraged the spread of vegetarianism. But he kept his army, law courts, and systems of punishment, including execution for major crimes, and remained an emperor in every sense, with his feet firmly in the world of politics. Nevertheless, his reign was remarkable for its humanity and its vision. The modern Republic of India appropriately adopted for its state seal the sculptured lions from the capital of one of Ashoka's pillars. Ashoka also sent explicitly Buddhist missions to Ceylon, and missionaries later went to Burma and Java. They converted the first two countries almost entirely to that faith, which they still hold, while establishing Buddhism as a new religion in much of the rest of Southeast Asia. Indian traders and adventurers, as well as priests and scholars, also carried Indian high culture in art, literature, written language, and statecraft to Southeast Asia. This cultural diffusion from India marked the beginning of literate civilization, in the Indian mode, in much of that extensive region, an origin still evident in many respects.

## Kushans and Greeks

Soon after Ashoka's death around 232 B.C., the Mauryan Empire seems to have disintegrated into civil war among provincial governors, although the Mauryan name continued through several successive rulers at Pataliputra. By 180 B.C. or so India had returned to its more traditional pattern of separate regional kingdoms. The northwest was again invaded by Greeks, descendants of groups left behind by Alexander. Northern India was subsequently invaded by new groups of outsiders, the Sakas (Scythians) from west-central Asia, and other originally nomadic peoples from east-central Asia who were driven from their pasturelands by the ancestors of the Mongols and by the rise of the first Chinese empire, the Ch'in, in the late third century B.C. One such group around 100 B.C. crossed the passes into Kashmir and down onto the Indian plain, where they defeated the Greek, Saka, and Indian kingdoms and welded most of the north into a new empire, the Kushan dynasty. The Kushans restored much of the former Mauryan grandeur, ruling also from Pataliputra, but they too declined after some three centuries, and by A.D. 200 the north was once again, like the south, a regional patchwork. The Kushans adopted and promoted Buddhism and disseminated it to their former homelands in central Asia, from which it later reached China. In other respects, like nearly all invaders or conquerors of India, they became thoroughly Indianized, including not only their adoption of the other aspects of Indian culture and language but also widespread intermarriage, adding still further to the hybrid character of the population. The most obvious and enduring legacy of the Kushans is probably the magnificent Buddhist sculpture produced under their rule and patronage. It is interesting also for the clear traces of Hellenistic artistic influence, still important in India in the time of the Kushans, deriving both from the remaining Greek-style kingdoms in the northwest and from direct contact with the Hellenic world by sea.

Throughout the centuries after Alexander, Greek

traders and travelers visited India on a regular basis. Greek ships carried Indian goods to the Mediterranean: spices, precious stones, incense, brasswork, fine cotton textiles, ivory, peacocks, monkeys, and even larger wild animals. Indian philosophers visited Mediterranean and Levantine cities, perhaps making some contribution to the Western intellectual heritage. In return, there seems little reason to doubt the claim of Indian Christians that their early church was begun by Thomas the Apostle, who probably reached India and founded there what may well be the world's oldest Christian community. The trip from Suez—or from Alexandria, where we know the apostles preached—was routine in the first century A.D. India was connected to the Greco-Roman world, and one of the apostles probably preached there in carrying out the command recorded in Mark 16:15: "Go ye into all the world and preach the gospel to every creature." To this day, a large proportion of Indian Christians, clustered in the southwest near the ports the Greeks and Romans used, carry the surname Thomas.

Our most important source for this period of Indian history is a Greek handbook for traders and travelers to India called the *Periplus of the Erythrean Sea*, dated about A.D. 80, which gives sailing directions, information on prices and sources for Indian goods, and brief descriptions of Indian culture. Large hoards of Roman coins, to pay for India's exports, and Roman pottery have been found at many ports along the west coast, from Mannar in Ceylon through Cochin and Calicut to the Bombay area and now abandoned ports south of the Indus mouth.

## Southern India

The south was protected against pressures from successive states or empires in the north by the uplifted plateau of the Deccan and its fringing mountains, the Vindhya and Satpura ranges, punctuated by the Narbada and Tapti rivers as further barriers. There was also fierce southern resistance to the repeated attempts at conquest from the north. We know very little about the lower half of India before about the time of Ashoka. By then it is clear that southern cultures and states, though divided

**The genius of Indian sculpture was well established by Harappan times but was developed further in subsequent centuries. This sandstone pillar showing Yakshis, the goddess of the life-giving waters, was carved in the second century A.D. as a love figure; the bird cage she holds signifies "I've caught him!"—as can be deduced from her sweet smile as well. [Indian Museum, Calcutta]**

into often rival groups, were fully as rich and sophisticated as those of the Aryan-influenced north. They shared what was by the third or second century B.C. a common Indian civilization, including Hinduism, philosophy, values, art forms, and material culture. The three largest political states of the south were Chola, Pandya, and Pallava, which vied with each other for regional dominance but were never able to unite the whole area under the control of any one of them. Each maintained extensive trade relations by sea, mainly with Southeast Asia, and the cultural, economic, religious, and political life of each centered in their respective capitals, which were dominated by temple complexes.

## The City of Madurai

Probably the largest and best-preserved temple complex is the former Pandya capital of Madurai. The fullest and most detailed account of any ancient Indian city is included in an early Tamil poem of the third century A.D. called *The Garland of Madurai*, which may be summarized in part as follows:

The poet enters the city by its great gate, the posts of which are carved with the images of the goddess Lakshmi. It is a festival day, and the city is gay with flags; some, presented by the king to commemorate brave deeds, fly over the houses of captains; others wave over the shops which sell toddy [a fermented drink made from the blossom of the palm tree]. The streets are broad rivers of people of every race, buying and selling in the market place or singing to the music of wandering minstrels.

The drum beats and a royal procession passes down the street, with elephants leading and the sound of conchs [shell trumpets]. An unruly elephant breaks his chain and tosses like a ship in an angry sea until he is brought under control. Chariots follow, with prancing horses and fierce footmen. Stall keepers ply their trade, selling sweet cakes, garlands of flowers, scented powder, and rolls of betel nut [to chew]. Old women go from house to house selling nosegays and trinkets. Noblemen drive through the streets in their chariots, their gold-sheathed swords flashing, wearing brightly dyed garments and wreaths of flowers. The jewels of the perfumed women watching from balconies and turrets flash in the sun.

People flock to the temples to worship to the sound of music, laying flowers before the images. Craftsmen work in their shops, bangle-makers, goldsmiths, cloth weavers, coppersmiths, flower sellers, wood carvers, and painters. Foodshops are busily selling mangoes, sugar candy, cooked rice, and chunks of cooked meat. [At this period, only the more pious Hindus were strict vegetarians.] In the evening, the city's prostitutes entertain their patrons with dancing and singing to the accompaniment of the lute. The streets are filled with music. Drunken villagers, in town for the festival, reel about in the streets. Respectable

women visit the temples in the evening with their children and friends, carrying lighted lamps as offerings. They dance in the temple courts, which resound with their singing and chatter.

At last the city sleeps . . . all but the ghosts and goblins who haunt the dark and the housebreakers, armed with rope ladders, swords, and chisels. But the watchmen are also vigilant, and the city passes the night in peace. Morning comes with the sounds of brahmins intoning their sacred verses. The wandering bands renew their singing, and the shopkeepers open their booths. The toddy-sellers ply their trade for thirsty early morning travelers. The drunkards stagger to their feet. All over the city the sound is heard of doors opening. Women sweep the faded flowers of the festival from their courtyards. The busy everyday life of the city is resumed.[1]

This gives a vivid picture of what urban life must really have been like; with few adjustments, it could serve as a description of a festival day in a small Indian city even today.

## Ceylon

The island of Ceylon (called Sri Lanka since 1975, reviving an ancient name for the country) lies within view of the tip of South India, only some 20 miles across the shallow Palk Strait via a disconnected chain of islands. Nevertheless, the two countries have always been separate politically, and Ceylon developed a distinctive culture and sense of separate identity even though it remained, understandably, a part of greater Indian culture. Sometime in the sixth century B.C. a Sanskrit- or Aryan-speaking prince named Vijaya came to Ceylon by sea from northwestern India with a large band of followers and established a kingdom. It is likely that Indian merchants had visited Ceylon earlier and perhaps settled there, but we have no record of such earlier contact. The followers of Vijaya called themselves Sinhala ("lion people") and became the dominant inhabitants of Ceylon as the Sinhalese (Singhalese). This is also the name of their Indo-European language, which is related to those of North India. The Sinhalese brought with them not only the literacy, writing forms, and religion of late Vedic North India but much of the rest of its culture and technology, including the knowledge of irrigation and the cultivation of rice. They were probably joined shortly by a second wave of settlement from Bengal, which merged with them. The Sinhalese soon displaced the earlier and far less technically developed Neolithic inhabitants of the island, the Vaddas, a few survivors of whom still live in the remoter jungles, although in the earlier centuries there was considerable intermarriage.

Beginning no later than the first century B.C. the Sinhalese constructed an extensive system of irrigated rice agriculture, centered in the northern half of the island with its capital at Anuradhapura and a secondary urban center at Polonnaruwa. This area was part of the so-called Dry Zone of Ceylon, where permanent field agriculture is impossible without irrigation but where fertile soils, level land, and an unbroken growing season of strong sun and high temperatures can produce high crop yields if water is available. Considerable rain falls there in a brief period of three months during the northeast monsoon of winter, leaving the rest of the year mainly dry. The Sinhalese kingdom constructed large reservoirs to catch the winter rain and stream runoff and then to distribute it to rice fields through an intricate system of canals. Dams also diverted water from the few year-round streams that flowed through the area. The population of the Dry Zone grew substantially, and Anuradhapura at its height about the tenth century A.D. may have contained 100,000 people or more, while Ceylon as a whole may have had as many as 3 or 4 million. Only with such a large population, controlled by the state through corvée (conscript labor), could the massive irrigation works be built and maintained and the many large palaces and temples at Anuradhapura constructed. Nowhere else in the premodern world was there such a dense concentration of irrigation facilities at such a high technical level, but it was dependent on maintaining state control over mass labor.

Ceylon was the first area beyond India to which Buddhism spread. The pious legend is that Ananda, a disciple of the Buddha, brought the message himself in the Buddha's own lifetime, but Buddhism probably did not extend beyond North India, and almost certainly not to Ceylon, until Ashoka's time in the third century B.C., when missionaries were specifically dispatched to Ceylon and Burma. The Sinhalese rapidly accepted and have retained Buddhism. They produced beautiful works of sculpture and architecture in the Buddhist-Indian tradition, including the world's largest mound temples or stupas and colossal statues of the Buddha and his disciples. The great stupa at Anuradhapura is bigger than all but one of the pyramids of ancient Egypt and is surrounded for miles by others nearly as big and by a host of beautiful and monumental stone buildings and large baths. All of this gorgeous display suggests large and consistent surpluses from the agricultural system to pay for the costs of construction and art and an economy that could spare labor for such purposes. The classical Sinhalese chronicles, compiled and preserved by Buddhist monks, deal mainly with the pious acts of successive kings, especially their building or endowing of temples, but indirectly they reflect a prosperous and generally controlled society.

Given the short and easy journey from southern India to Ceylon, continuous interaction probably began before the sixth century B.C. By or before the Christian era, the northern tip of Ceylon had been settled by people from the Dravidian Tamil-speaking area of South India, who practiced their own form of irrigated agriculture based mainly on wells. They became the dominant inhabitants of the Jaffna peninsula and the immediately adjacent parts of the north but retained their cultural ties with South India as well as their Hinduism. Immigration from South India continued for several centuries, and there was some intermarriage with the Sinhalese. These two groups of Indian immigrants, Sinhalese and Tamils, coexisted for most of Ceylon's history, until their differences exploded into a violent political issue in the 1950s (described in Chapter 40).

The Sinhala kingdom based at Anuradhapura periodically controlled the Tamil areas of the north but had to protect itself against intermittent raiding from the far larger Tamil kingdoms in South India. These raids often stimulated or increased internal dissension when rival Sinhalese claimants to the throne made common cause with the invaders, especially after about the sixth century A.D. The Chola empire, which arose in the early centuries of the Christian era in South India, launched a particularly destructive invasion of Ceylon in the eleventh century that sacked Anuradhapura in 1017. The Sinhalese capital was moved to Polonnaruwa, from which the local forces finally drove the Cholas out of the country by 1070. In the following century King Parakrama Bahu (1153–1186) unified the whole of Ceylon from his capital at Polonnaruwa, invaded South India and Burma, and constructed huge new irrigation works and public buildings that made his capital almost as impressive as Anuradhapura had been. But his death was followed by civil war and by new and especially destructive invasions from South India, which led by the thirteenth century to the virtual abandonment of the Dry Zone, whose vital irrigation works could no longer be maintained. The much reduced population clustered from then on in the protection of the hills and mountains of southeastern Ceylon, centered around the medieval capital of Kandy, and later in the lowlands around the port of Colombo.

# The Guptas and the Empire of Harsha

An imperial revival of the Mauryan model in India, the Gupta dynasty, ruled the north from about A.D. 320 to about 550. Pataliputra was again the imperial capital and seems once more to have played the role of cultural center for surrounding areas. Contact with the West appears to have diminished or ceased by this time, as the eastern Roman Empire was largely cut off from India by the rise of the Sassanid dynasty in Persia. Trade and cultural exchange, however, was still extensive with Southeast Asia, although most of it probably took place from the South Indian kingdoms of Chola, Pandya, and Pallava and from ports on the southeast coast, beyond Guptan imperial control. For much of what we know about the Gupta period, as for earlier periods, we are dependent on foreign observers. The chief source is the diary of Fa Hsien, a Chinese Buddhist monk who made the long and arduous journey to India via central Asia and the Himalayas to seek true copies of the Buddhist sutras (scriptures) and who lived and traveled there for six years in the early 400s. A typical literate Chinese, he carefully recorded what he observed, at Pataliputra and elsewhere, and gives a picture of a rich and sophisticated society and of its culturally brilliant capital in the early fifth century, when it was probably at its height.

## Life and Culture in the Guptan Period

Fa Hsien noted the peacefulness of Guptan India and the mildness of its government. His journal remarks that crime was rare and that one could travel from one end of the empire to another without harm and with no need for travel documents. He made special note of the free hospitals for treatment of the sick, supported by private donations. He also says that all "respectable" people (by which he probably means those of high caste) were vegetarians, a trend that seemed to have picked up momentum from the time of Ashoka, but that the lower orders ate meat and hence were regarded as sources of "pollution," an aspect of caste that he was the first outsider to describe. Buddhism he describes as still flourishing, but apparently in the process of being reabsorbed into the Hinduism from which it had originally sprung. In general, Fa Hsien's account shows us a prosperous, tranquil, and smoothly operating society, which probably contrasted with the turbulent China of his time.

The Gupta period was the golden age of Sanskrit literature and of classical Indian sculpture and monumental building, although unfortunately only fragments have survived. This cultural flowering was equally vigorous in the south, beyond Gupta control, and in both south and north seems to have taken the form of a renaissance of Mauryan grandeur. Kalidasa, widely acclaimed as India's greatest poet and playwright, lived and worked in the late fourth and early fifth centuries, near the peak of Gupta vigor. Many of his works have survived, as have fragments of some others. They still make fresh and en-

---

## ◉ The Port of Puhar ◉

*A graphic passage in the Tamil epic the* Silappatikaram, *of uncertain date but probably fourth or fifth century A.D., describes the port city of Puhar, not far from modern Madras, in this period a great center of foreign trade.*

The riches of Puhar shipowners made the kings of faraway lands envious. The most costly merchandise, the rarest foreign produce reached the city. . . . The sunshine lighted up the open terraces, the harbor docks, the towers with their loopholes like the eyes of deer. In various quarters of the city the homes of wealthy Greeks were seen. Near the harbor seamen from far-off lands appeared at home. In the streets hawkers were selling unguents, bath powders, cooling oils, flowers, perfume, and incense. . . . Each trade had its own street in the workers' quarter of the city. At the center of the city were the wide royal street, the street of temple cars, the bazaar, and the main street where rich merchants had their mansions . . . with warehouses of merchandise from overseas. . . . Near the sea, flags raised high toward the sky seemed to be saying: "On these stretches of white sand can be found the goods that foreign merchants, leaving their own countries to stay among us, have brought here in great ships." . . . All night lamps were burning, the lamps of foreigners who talk strange tongues, and of the guards who watch over precious cargoes near the docks.

*Source:* A. Danielou, trans., in M. Singer, "Beyond Tradition and Modernity in Madras," *Comparative Studies in Society and History* 13 (1971): 169–170.

chanting reading, as well as moving commentaries on the foibles of human existence.

## The Collapse of Gupta Rule

By A.D. 550 or so the Gupta power was destroyed by new invaders, the so-called White Huns (probably Iranians or Turks from central Asia), one more group in the long succession of ethnically and culturally different outsiders drawn to India by its wealth and sophistication and then woven into the hybrid Indian fabric. Like earlier and later invaders, they came from the west, through the only easy entrance into the subcontinent, the passes that punctuate the northwest frontier. As the linguistic tie still reminds us, India's relations were and remained overwhelmingly with the West since at least Harappan times and, except for the sea connection with Southeast Asia, hardly at all with the East and with China, the other major cultural center of Asia. Buddhism did move from India, first into central Asia and then into China by Han times, but it seems to have carried very little of Indian culture with it except for some art forms, and almost nothing of Chinese culture seems to have penetrated into India. Cotton, native to India and first woven into cloth there, spread to China only some 3,000 years later. Trade between the two societies, the other common vehicle of cultural exchange, was minimal and indirect. The reason is clear from a glance at the map: the world's highest mountains lie between India and China, and behind them the desert or alpine wastelands of Sinkiang and Tibet. It is in fact a very long and exceptionally difficult way between the centers of Indian and Chinese civilization, from the plains of Hindustan to the lower Yellow and Yangtze river valleys. The shorter route from eastern India through Burma and into mountainous southwest China (still a long way from the Chinese center) has proved even more difficult, with its combination of mountains, deep gorges, and rain forest, and has never carried more than a trickle of indirect trade.

With the collapse of the Gupta empire, India reverted once more to its regional structures. The new invaders from central Asia did not succeed in building their own empire, and for a time there was political chaos, but the first half of the seventh century saw a final indigenous effort at unification. This was the reign of Harsha (606–648), who in a series of campaigns joined the separate kingdoms of the north together and presided over a notable reflowering of Sanskrit literature and art. Harsha also encouraged Buddhism, and the Chinese Buddhist monk Hsuan Tsang visited his court, leaving a valuable account of it and of the contemporary India through which he traveled. His journal gives an admiring picture of Harsha as a charismatic, energetic, and able administrator and an impressive emperor of his domains, through which he made repeated tours to supervise its government. Like earlier and later Indian emperors, he held court wherever he went, to hear complaints and dispense justice. Like them, he lived in luxury and pomp but loved literature and philosophy and was a generous patron; he even found time to write plays himself. By this time Hsuan Tsang's account shows Buddhism declining and Hinduism again dominant, but, perhaps because of the brevity and idiosyncrasy of Harsha's rule, law and order were not as well kept as in Guptan times. Hsuan Tsang reports banditry and was himself robbed twice on his travels. Harsha's empire was so much his own creation that when he died in 648, leaving no heirs, it disintegrated into factional fighting.

| INDIA TO A.D. 648 | |
|---|---|
| c. 3000–c. 1900 B.C. | Indus civilization |
| After 2000 B.C. | Arrival of the Aryans |
| c. 1000–c. 500 B.C. | Vedic culture |
| 326 B.C. | Invasion by Alexander the Great |
| c. 322–c. 297 B.C. | Reign of Chandragupta |
| c. 269–c. 232 B.C. | Reign of Ashoka |
| c. 180 B.C. | New Greek invasions begin |
| c. 100 B.C. | Kushan invasion |
| c. A.D. 320–c. 550 | Gupta dynasty |
| A.D. 606–648 | Reign of Harsha |

## Women in Ancient India

Medieval and early modern India tended to fit the popular stereotype applied to most traditional Asian societies: heavy male dominance and female subservience or even servitude. That has been changing fast in twentieth-century Asia and was, like most stereotypes, not totally accurate even for the past. In particular, it overlooks the major part nearly all women played in the basic Asian institution of the family, a private as opposed to public role but often critically important, and it also overlooks the many women writers and performers of other public roles, including political ones. However, ancient India was substantially different from the later period of Indian history in this respect. There is much evidence to show that pre-Mauryan Indian society, especially in the south, was matriarchal; women held important economic power, property, and status, and family names often descended through the female line. This ancient pattern survives in parts of South India today. The Aryan north was from Vedic times more clearly patriarchal, and women were conventionally seen as subject to their parents, husbands, and male relatives. But they had some control over personal property, and a number of women even owned businesses. Women could not serve as priests but were free to become nuns, several of whom were notable poets and scholars. The *Upanishads*, treatises dating from about the seventh century B.C., tell the story of an exceptionally learned woman, Gargi Vacaknavi, who took an active part in discussions with the sage Yajnavalkya and outdistanced all her male counterparts. Other women attended lectures by sages and mastered the Vedas. Goddesses were as important as gods in Vedic religion, and a goddess's name was commonly recited before that of a god, a practice that still persists.

By the Mauryan era, however, the scope for women in religious and intellectual pursuits seems to have been reduced. Convention shifted to an emphasis on marriage and care of the family as the proper female role, although many upper-class women continued to be taught privately or to educate themselves, and several wrote poetry and drama that was widely read. Others learned music (both performance and composition), dancing, and painting. In early Vedic times (we know too little about society in Harappan times to speculate about it), unmarried men and women seem to have mixed freely. By the time of the *Arthashastra* (third century B.C.),

upper-class women were more circumscribed by convention, although widows were still free to marry. By late Gupta times (sixth century A.D.), restrictions on women had increased, and widows could no longer remarry. Women were to be cherished, but protected—and restricted—a trend that had apparently begun under Mauryan rule, at least in the north. In the south, women remained freer and less submissive.

The freest women in ancient India were probably the courtesans (high-class prostitutes). In many traditional societies, including India, they were usually well educated and well versed in the classics, the arts of music, dance, poetry and its composition, flower arranging, the composition of riddles and other mental puzzles, and even fencing. There were lower grades of prostitutes, but the standard was generally high. Such women were often praised for their learning and quick verbal wit, sometimes even more than for their beauty, as in China and Japan. Even the Buddha is said to have chosen to dine with a famous courtesan rather than with the city fathers, no doubt duller company. Many of the courte-

## ◉ Virtues of an Indian Wife ◉

*A passage in the* Mahabharata *extolls the virtues of a wife.*

The wife is half the man, the best of friends,
the root of the three ends of life,
and of all that will help him in the other world.
With a wife a man does mighty deeds,
with a wife a man finds courage.
A wife is the safest refuge;
a man aflame with sorrow in his soul or sick with disease
finds comfort in his wife as a man parched with heat
finds relief in water.
Even a man in the grip of rage will not be harsh to a woman, remembering that on
    her depend the joys of life, happiness, and virtue.
For a woman is the everlasting field
in which the self is born.

*Some centuries later the Laws of Manu, written about the second
century A.D., reflected the growing emphasis on the domesticity and
dependency of women.*

She should always be cheerful, and skillful in her domestic duties with her household vessels well cleaned and her hand tight on the purse-strings. In season and out of season her lord, who wed her with sacred rites, ever gives happiness to his wife, both here and in the other world. Though he be uncouth and prone to pleasure, though he have no good points at all, the virtuous wife should ever worship her lord as a god.

*Source:* A. L. Basham, *The Wonder That Was India,* 3rd ed. (New York: Grove Press, 1959), pp. 180–182.

# THE VISUAL EXPERIENCE
## Art of Ancient India and China

**Bronze mirror inlaid with gold and silver from the late Chou dynasty. Mirrors like this, highly polished to give a good reflection, were made in great quantities, especially in the Chou and Han dynasties, and were often beautifully decorated. The pierced knob in the center was to permit hanging by a cord. [Eisei-Bunko Foundation]**

The terra-cotta army of the first emperor. Ch'in Shih Huang Ti was buried in a huge underground tomb near modern Sian with an army of life-size clay figures to guard the approaches. Excavations in the 1970s brought them to light again after more than two thousand years. Each figure is a faithful representation of a real individual. [Chinese Overseas Archaeological Exhibition Corp.]

Tomb figure from northwestern China, fourth century A.D. The artistic creativity of ancient cultures was manifested in their music. From paintings and sculpture, such as this pottery figure of a woman playing bamboo pipes, musicologists can learn much about ancient music. [Chinese Overseas Archaeological Exhibition Corp.]

In this painting, attributed to Ku K'ai-chih (A.D. 344–406), an instructress is writing down directions for her pupils, ladies of the court. In China, as elsewhere, court ladies were expected to be literate and accomplished in several arts. [Trustees of the British Museum]

The art of ancient Ceylon: divine nymphs dropping flowers on the earth, from a mural of the fifth century A.D. painted on the rock face of the fortress of Sigiriya in the southern Dry Zone, preserved better than most Indian painting of this period, which it closely resembles. [Stella Sneed/Archaeological Survey of Sri Lanka]

The temple complex at Madurai in South India is one of the classic buildings saved from the Muslim onslaught that swept northern India starting in the twelfth century A.D. [Wim Swann]

This figure of a tree goddess from the second century A.D. is a fine example of the grace and voluptuousness that Indian sculptors were able to capture in stone. [C. M. Dixon]

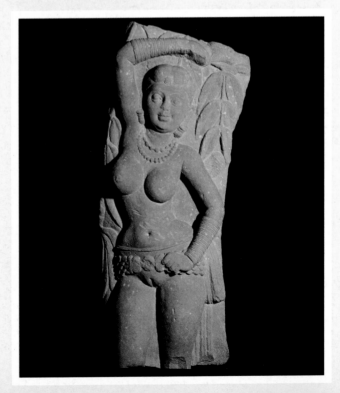

sans were celebrated poets, but most of them were considered especially sensitive and as having "great souls."

Another group of women were hereditary dancers in the service of temples; most of them also served as prostitutes, but in any case they never married, having dedicated themselves to the god, like the temple priestesses and vestal virgins of classical Greece and Rome. Dance was a particularly important religious ritual in India, as well as a beautiful art form. The god Shiva was thought to have created the world through his cosmic dance and to dance on the harvest floor as the spirit of life and of creation. From at least the Gupta period, classical Indian dance came to be associated with the temple dancers, servants of the god and a special class of women, some of whom were also prostitutes. They were honored and admired for their art but socially discriminated against. Other women were discouraged from dancing because of this association until recent years, when the classical dance forms have seen a national revival and have once again become respectable.

The custom of *sati* (suttee), wives burning themselves to death on their husbands' funeral pyres, does not seem to have extended to most widows at any period in Indian history. Although it was known in ancient India, Sumer, and China, it was uncommon. When it was practiced, it was mainly as part of the custom of burning or burying all the followers, retainers, horses, and prized possessions of a dead ruler or aristocrat with him. *Sati* was relatively rare until late Gupta times, when widow remarriage had begun to be strongly discouraged or prohibited, as it had not been before. It became more common thereafter, although it was supposed to be voluntary, as a mark of exceptional fidelity. Social and family pressure, as well as the emptiness and often the material hardship of a young widow's life, doubtless added other incentives. *Sati* horrified early Western observers, and the British tried to suppress it in the nineteenth century. Many ancient and even medieval Indian writers and poets condemned it, and in the end the Hindu renaissance and reform movement of the late nineteenth century turned educated Indian opinion against it. There is some evidence that *sati* is occasionally practiced even now.

## The Indian Heritage

The building and maintaining of empires exacts a heavy human cost everywhere. India's return to its more normal regionalism after the collapse of the Gupta empire and the death of Harsha was hardly a tragedy. But it leaves the historian, whose data are only fragmentary, to try to deal with a confused tapestry woven, like India's history and culture as a whole, of many threads. The revival of regional kingdoms did, however, encourage the continued development of the rich regional cultures that make up the Indian fabric.

Given India's size and diversity, it is not surprising that the subcontinent has only very briefly been united into a single empire, and even under Ashoka and the later rule of the British some areas remained outside imperial control. We are accustomed to thinking of Europe as properly composed of a large number of separate states and cultures, despite the heritage of common Roman rule over much of it for some four centuries and despite its common membership in the Greek, Roman, and Christian traditions. India too has long shared common traditions, including the universal spread of Hinduism, and like Europe has experienced successive efforts at unification by conquest. But the strength of separate regional cultures and states remained at least as great as in Europe, reinforced by different languages, literatures, and political rivalries. India's more recent success in building a modern state—or rather the three states of Pakistan, India, and Bangladesh—contrasts with the continued political division of Europe but still encompasses regional differences, each with its own proud tradition reaching back before Ashoka. In these terms, there is nothing improper or backward about regional separatism, for India, Europe, or any other area of the size and variety of the subcontinent. India, like Europe, would be the poorer without its array of different cultural and regional traditions. Their separate contributions in literature, philosophy, and the arts in the centuries of political disunity after the death of Harsha continued to enrich the varied tapestry of Indian civilization. But our political picture of those centuries is confusing, frequently changing, and plagued by a severe shortage of information.

Ancient and classical India as a whole had a deep respect for learning and for education, beginning with literacy and mathematics and continuing to philosophy and the study of the Vedas. But education was a privilege enjoyed only by the upper classes, and after the Vedic age for the most part only by males, as in nearly all premodern societies. As mentioned earlier, courtesans frequented by the elite classes were highly educated and widely read in addition to being accomplished dancers, singers, musicians, and poetesses; their role was to entertain their patrons in the fullest sense of the word. However, most people were peasant villagers, uninvolved with any of these upper-class matters and intent on their own active communal life. The several Greek and Chinese travelers to classical India who have left accounts describe the rural scene as productive and prosperous and compare it and the lot of villagers favorably with their own homelands. India during these centuries may have been less burdened by mass poverty or communal tensions than it is now, but we have no way to measure that. Contemporary accounts from that period could of course make judgments only in terms of what they knew of conditions elsewhere. Our modern perspectives are different. But the classical accounts we have nearly all stress the relatively high level of material well-being, the orderliness of the society, and its impressive achievements in science, technology, philosophy, and the arts. It is a tradition of which modern Indians are justly proud.

From the modern perspective, classical India seems especially noteworthy for its scientific accomplishments. Mathematics had by Gupta times been brought to a high level of sophistication, including a rudimentary algebra and a numeration system using nine digits and a zero, far more efficient than the cumbersome Roman numerals. The Arabs, who transmitted it to the West, called mathematics "the Indian art" (*Hindisat*). Later European science would have been impossible without it. Medieval Indian mathematicians after Harsha's time developed the concepts of negative and positive quantities, worked out square and cube roots, solved quadratic and other equations, understood the mathematical implications of zero and infinity, worked out the value of pi to nine decimal places, and made important steps in trigonometry, sine functions, spherical geometry, and calculus. Earlier Indian scientists anticipated the classical Greeks in developing an atomic theory of elements, basic to twentieth-century Western science, by the sixth century B.C.

Traditional Indian medicine had a very extensive pharmacopoeia and used a variety of herbal remedies and drugs discovered and used only much later in the West. Physicians appear to have understood the function of the spinal cord and the nervous system, and successful surgery included cesarean section, complicated bone setting, plastic surgery, and the repair of damaged limbs. Vaccination against smallpox was first used in Guptan India well over 1,000 years before it was tried in the West. Doctors were highly respected, and the textbook of the famous physician Caraka in the late first century A.D. includes a passage reminiscent of Hippocrates, the classical Greek physician:

> **If you want success in your practice . . . you must pray every day on rising and going to bed for the welfare of all beings . . . and strive with all your soul for the health of the sick. You must not betray your patients, even at the cost of your own life. . . . You must be pleasant of speech . . . and thoughtful, always striving to improve your knowledge.**
>
> **When you go to the home of a patient you should direct your words, mind, intellect, and senses nowhere but to your patient and his treatment. . . . Nothing that happens in the house of the sick man must be told outside, nor must the patient's condition be told to anyone who might do harm by that knowledge.[2]**

*It is more than possible that the political turmoil of invasions and internal struggles did not greatly affect the lives of most people of South Asia most of the time. For the Indians it was not particularly important to record the details of empires, kingdoms, rivalries, and political changes. We do have enough evidence to show us a sophisticated civilization, a remarkably humane set of values, and enough glimpses of the life of the common people to establish ancient and classical India as a great tradition, one of the major achievements of the human experience.*

*The Indus civilization, with major urban centers at Kalibangan, Harappa, and Mohenjo Daro, arose, flourished, and declined between 3000 B.C. and 2000 B.C. The migration of Aryan-speaking peoples from central Asia into North India after about 1800 B.C. produced Vedic culture, which became dominant in most of the north. Regional kingdoms had emerged by 500 B.C., some of which Alexander encountered when he invaded the northwest in 326 B.C. By 322 the Mauryan empire had emerged under Chan-*

*dragupta Maurya and unified most of the north from the imperial capital at Pataliputra in the central Ganges valley. Chandragupta's grandson Ashoka ruled as emperor from around 269 to 232 B.C. and extended the empire southward. Troubled by the slaughter occasioned by his conquests, he converted to the nonviolent faith of Buddhism and devoted the rest of his reign to spreading its message. The Mauryan power faded after his death, and both North and South India reverted to regional rule. New Greek and Scythian invaders in the north yielded to another dynasty of conquest, the Kushans, from around 100 B.C. to A.D. 200, while the south and Ceylon supported separate flourishing kingdoms and built impressive architectural monuments. The Gupta dynasty restored much of the Mauryan grandeur in the north from about 320 to 550, based again at Pataliputra, and Harsha from 606 to 648 reunited the Guptan empire. After his death India resumed its more typical political pattern of separate regional kingdoms, where art, learning, philosophy, and commerce continued to thrive.*

# Notes

1. A. L. Basham, *The Wonder That Was India*, 3rd ed. (New York: Grove Press, 1959), pp. 203–204.
2. Ibid., p. 500.

# Suggestions for Further Reading

Allchin, B., and Allchin, R. *The Rise of Civilization in India and Pakistan*. Cambridge: Cambridge University Press, 1982.

Auboyer, J. *Daily Life in Ancient India*. London: Weidenfeld & Nicolson, 1965.

Basham, A. L. *The Wonder That Was India*, 3rd ed. New York: Grove Press, 1959.

Begley, V., and de Puma, R. D., eds. *Rome and India*. Madison: University of Wisconsin Press, 1992.

Buck, W. *Ramayana*. Berkeley: University of California Press, 1976.

De Silva, K. M. *A History of Sri Lanka*. Delhi: Oxford University Press, 1981.

Dutt, A. K., and Selb, M. *Atlas of South Asia*. Boulder, Colo.: Westview, 1987.

Gokhale, B. G. *Asoka Maurya*. New York: Twayne, 1966.

Kalidasa. *The Cloud Messenger*, trans. F. Edgerton and E. Edgerton. Ann Arbor: University of Michigan Press, 1964.

Kautilya. *The Arthasastra*, trans. R. Shamasastry. Mysore, India: Raghuveer Printing Press, 1951.

Kosambi, D. D. *Ancient India: A History of Its Culture and Civilization*. New York: Pantheon, 1966.

Lingat, R. *The Classical Law of India*. Berkeley: University of California Press, 1973.

Liu, X. *Ancient China and Ancient India: Trade and Religious Exchange*. New York: Oxford University Press, 1988.

McCrindle, J. W., trans. *Ancient India as Described in Classical Literature*. New Delhi: Today and Tomorrow Press, 1972.

Miller, B. S., ed. and trans. *Theater of Memory: The Plays of Kalidasa*. New York: Columbia University Press, 1984.

———, trans. *The Bhagavadgita*. New York: Columbia University Press, 1986.

Murphey, R. "The Ruin of Ancient Ceylon," *Journal of Asian Studies* 16 (1957): 181–200.

Nilakanta, S. *The Cholas*, 2nd ed. Madison: University of Wisconsin Press, 1955.

———. *A History of South India*, 4th ed. Madras: Oxford University Press, 1976.

Piggott, S. *Prehistoric India to 1000 B.C.* London: Cassel, 1962.

Possehl, G. L., ed. *Ancient Cities of the Indus*. Durham, N.C.: Carolina Academic Press, 1979.

Singhal, D. P. *A History of the Indian People*. London: Methuen, 1983.

Tarn, W. W. *The Greeks in Bactria and India*. Cambridge: Cambridge University Press, 1951.

Thapar, R. *Asoka and the Decline of the Mauryas*. London: Oxford University Press, 1961.

———. *A History of India*, vol. 1. Baltimore: Penguin Books, 1966.

Van Buitenen, J. A. B., trans. *The Bhagavadgita and the Mahabharata*. Chicago: University of Chicago Press, 1981.

Wolpert, S. *A New History of India*, 3rd ed. New York: Oxford University Press, 1989.

Woodcock, G. *The Greeks in India*. London: Faber, 1966.

# The Formation of China

Chinese civilization arose largely independent of contact with or influence from other areas and early developed its own distinctive form and style. China was effectively isolated by high mountains and deserts along its northwestern, western, and southwestern borders and by the distance across the great breadth of arid central Asia. Northward lay the desert and steppe of Mongolia and the subarctic lands of Siberia and northern Manchuria. In part because of its isolation until recent centuries, the Chinese civilized tradition was more continuous, coherent, and slow to change over a longer period than any other in history.

Interaction was much easier with areas to the east, and the model of Chinese civilization later spread to Korea, Vietnam, and Japan, where it still forms a basic part of the literate cultures of those areas. East Asia as a whole is accordingly sometimes called the *Sinic* culture (from the Latin word for China).

The area also inherited most of the tradition of

An extraordinarily lifelike pottery figure from a Han dynasty tomb in Szechuan shows a groom whistling for his horse. [Innervision/ Overseas Archaeological Corporation]

Chinese agriculture as well as systems of writing, philosophy, literature, political and social institutions, and art forms. This diffusion took place, however, 2,000 years or more after Chinese civilization first began and after the establishment of the first empire in the third century B.C. This empire discarded some elements developed in earlier centuries and added others to create the model of imperial Chinese culture that subsequently spread to the rest of East Asia. But long before the beginning of the Christian era in the West, China had already produced one of the world's major civilized traditions, and the model of the Han dynasty (202 B.C.–A.D. 220) was to be reaffirmed by successive Chinese dynasties for the next 2,000 years.

## The Origins of China

We cannot fix a precise date for the emergence of a city-based, literate, metal-using civilization in China. As everywhere else, it happened over a long period of transition out of Neolithic beginnings. By about 2000 B.C., however, the late Neolithic culture we call Lung Shan, or Black Pottery, had begun to build walled settlements larger than villages, to make bronze tools, weapons, and ornaments, and to use a pictographic and ideographic script clearly recognizable as the ancestor of written Chinese. The towns and cities included large groups of nonfarmers: scribes, metallurgists, artisans, and perhaps officials, and already the Lung Shan people had learned the art of silk making, long an exclusive Chinese skill and trademark. Approximately four centuries later, around 1600 B.C., the first authenticated Chinese dynasty, the Shang, was established in the area at or near the great bend of the Yellow River where the major Lung Shan settlements had also clustered, on the North China plain. The Shang probably consolidated or arose from a combination of the previously distinct Lung Shan and Yang Shao (Painted Pottery) cultures, but they and other late Neolithic cultures may well have begun to merge considerably earlier, perhaps to form the dynasty of Hsia (Xia), which was recorded as such by traditional Chinese texts but has not yet been confirmed by archaeological finds.

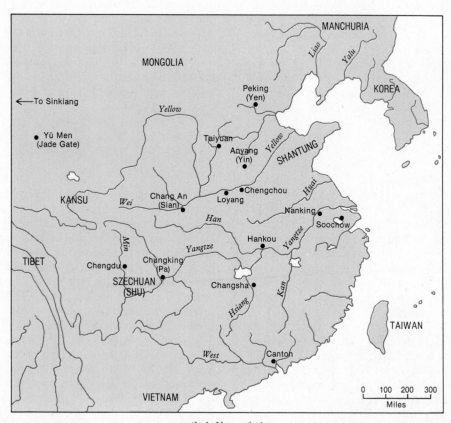

*3.1 East Asia*

Whether the Hsia was a real state and dynasty or not, the name was certainly used, and a culture of the Shang's complexity could not have appeared without a predecessor. The existence of the Shang was also discounted by modern historians despite its mention in the traditional texts giving the names of kings, until archaeological discoveries in the 1920s began to reveal its capitals and inscriptions that listed Shang kings exactly as the traditional texts had. Hsia may still be a convenient label for late Lung Shan–Yang Shao culture in the last stages of its evolution. By about 2000 B.C. Lung Shan towns were large and were surrounded by pounded-earth walls with heavy gates, clearly no longer farmers' villages and possibly organized into one or more kingdoms. What may have been a capital from this period 35 miles west of modern Chengchou (Zhengzhou), perhaps of the Hsia, had a rammed-earth wall 20 feet high and a mile square, with two bronze foundries outside the walls.

Lung Shan settlements with a similar material culture extended eastward to the sea and southward into the Yangtze valley and the south coast. The traditional Chinese texts give the names of five pre-Hsia "emperors" who are recognizable as mythological culture heroes, credited with the "invention" of fire, agriculture, animal domestication, calendrics, writing, and flood control. The last of these, the great Yü, is said to have founded the Hsia dynasty, which may tentatively be dated 2000–1600 B.C., but we know almost nothing more about it. The earliest texts we have were written many centuries later.

By Shang times, in any case, many of the elements of a distinctively Chinese culture are present. How much Shang or its Chinese predecessors owed to earlier achievements farther west has long been debated. There seems no question that wheat and later donkeys, alfalfa, grapes, and some elements of mathematics were carried to China from western Asia, but well after 2000 B.C. (The chief crop of Shang China was millet, probably an indigenous grain.) The light spoke-wheeled chariot, an important Shang weapon of war, seems also to have come in by about 1500 B.C., perhaps in some way connected with the Aryan invasions of India. Rice, water buffalo, chickens, and pigs, also not native to northern China, came considerably earlier, but from Southeast Asia via southern China. Indeed, China owed far more to diffusion from the south than from the west, especially if we consider the basic place in its economy later occupied by these originally southern imports.

In Neolithic times South China was culturally and linguistically closer to adjacent Southeast Asia than to dry, cold North China. Recent archaeological finds in the lower Yangtze (Yangzi) valley and south of the great river suggest that civilization may have emerged there as early as or even earlier than in the better-surveyed and better-preserved north. The first East Asian bronzes and the first evidence of rice cultivation so far discovered come from what is now northern Thailand and Vietnam and presumably spread from there relatively easily into neighboring South China, probably long before Shang times. By the early Shang period, there already seems to have been a good deal of cultural mixing between North and South China, although the people were ethnically and linguistically distinct.

No aspect of Shang culture suggests any connection with Mesopotamia or India, including Shang art and two further basic and conclusive elements, writing and bronze technology. Both were developed earlier in Sumer and then in India, but the earliest Chinese writing resembles neither. It is highly unlikely that the Chinese, like the Indians, would have failed to adopt or adapt cuneiform instead of developing far more cumbersome ideographic characters if they had been in contact with Mesopotamia or had imported ideas or techniques from there. And Shang China stands alone in the technical perfection, beauty, and style of its bronze work, the result of a long history of experimental progress using varying proportions of copper, tin, lead, and zinc to achieve the optimum mix. The farther one goes from the Shang centers, the cruder the bronze artifacts become; no trail leads from Sumer or Harappa.

For these and other reasons it seems clear that Chinese civilization, like Indian, was an independent innovation, already well formed before it came into effective contact with other or older centers of equal sophistication. This is also consistent with the Paleolithic and early Neolithic record, where the stone tools of China remained distinct from those produced in the area from India westward through central Asia to Europe. Chinese civilization evolved largely on its own.

## The Shang Dynasty

The Shang ruled from several successive capitals, first near modern Loyang (Luoyang), then near modern Chengchou (both close to the Yellow River), and finally, for about the last two centuries, at Anyang, which they called Yin. We do not know the extent of the Shang political domains, but cultural remains suggest that they were limited to the central Yellow River floodplain, although the Shang had or claimed vassals to the west, the east, the northeast, and possibly the south who shared much of Shang material culture. By this time wheat was beginning to share prominence with millet, and rice was also grown, though mainly in the Yangtze valley and the south. Hunting remained a subsidiary source of food in addition to domesticated cattle, pigs, and poultry. The Shang kept slaves, mainly war captives from less highly developed or subjugated groups on their borders. Slaves may have been an important part of the agricultural work force; they were also used extensively to build the cities and palaces and perhaps as troops.

Especially at Anyang, monumental building was impressive, and the city at its peak may have covered as much as 10 square miles, with nearly a dozen elaborate royal tombs complete with a variety of grave furniture. The tombs provide evidence of surplus production that could support extravagant display, including richly decorated chariots with bronze fittings and caparisoned horses to draw them; the horses had been harnessed, backed down a ramp into the underground tombs, and killed. Royal or aristocratic dead were accompanied in their burials not only by objects of use and value but also by tens or even hundreds of followers, buried as human sacrifices to serve in the afterlife and probably also as a mark of the dead person's status. Bronze vessels and weapons of great beauty and technical perfection attest to the high quality of Shang technology.

The only Shang texts we have are inscriptions used for divination, most of them incised on the flat shoulder bones of cattle or on tortoiseshells. First the bones or shells were heated until cracks appeared; then questions, or perhaps requests, were inscribed. The cracks somehow provided answers. Others of the so-called oracle bone inscriptions, like the divination texts using characters so close to classical Chinese that most can still be read, provide lists of the Shang kings and brief accounts of royal activities.

Altogether this inscriptional material gives a picture of a hereditary aristocratic society in which warfare against surrounding groups was chronic; archers used a powerful compound bow, there were ranks of spearmen, and nobles rode in light, fast war chariots similar to those of the Indo-Europeans. The royal hunt remained important and was usually a very large affair in which hundreds took part and thousands of animals perished. The inscriptions make it clear that the spirits of royal and perhaps all aristocratic ancestors demanded respectful service from the living and could intercede for them with a supreme deity—the roots of traditional Chinese "ancestor worship." Slaves were not thought to have souls or spirits and thus could safely be killed; the Shang aristocrats seem not to have thought about what might happen if they became war captives themselves. Although those at the top lived in great luxury, the houses of the common people seem to have been quite crude, often simple pit dwellings, certainly not in a class with those of the Indus civilization. Many of the divination questions ask about the weather and suggest that the North China climate then, as now, was semiarid and prone to both drought and river flooding, but there is little evidence of any large-scale irrigation, apart from what one may assume was the possible use of floodwater. North China was not as dry as the Indus valley, and the agriculture there seems to have been primarily rain-fed except perhaps in small areas adjacent to the river or on a small scale from local wells in long dry spells. Millet is highly drought-tolerant and can produce good yields when other crops might fail. The great agricultural advantage of North China was its *loess* (wind-laid alluvium), a highly fertile soil that is easily worked, and the level expanse of the largely treeless plain, which allows easy transport and exchange.

## The Chou Dynasty

Relations between the Shang and their vassals were uneasy, and chronic warfare with other groups on the margins strained Shang resources. So too did the extravagant demands of royal building and display, much of it extorted from slave laborers. The last Shang king is said to have been a physical giant and a monster of depravity who, among other cruelties, made drinking cups of the skulls of his vanquished enemies. The dynasty ended in a great slave revolt, which was joined by one of the Shang vassals, the Chou (Zhou, pronounced like *Joe*), who guarded the western frontier in the Wei valley with their capital near modern Sian (Xian). The Chou were probably an original barbarian group taken over by the Shang, tough frontiersmen who seem to have been awaiting their chance to take over the whole kingdom. About 1050 B.C. they succeeded, together with the slave rebels, defeating the last Shang king and sacking Anyang (where the king died in the flames of his own palace). By that time the Chou had absorbed most of Shang culture and technology. The victorious Chou, now fully literate, gave their own account of the excesses and oppression of the Shang as justification for their conquest and first voiced what was to become a standard Chinese justification for change: "The iniquity of Shang is full; Heaven commands me to destroy it." The Shang had lost what they called the "mandate [approval] of Heaven" by their misgovernment, and it was the duty of responsible people to overthrow them.

The Chou set up their new capital in the Wei valley, their old base. They continued and extended the Shang system of dependent vassals whereby surrounding groups and areas, soon to begin emerging as states, were linked to the Chou king by oaths of fealty that acknowledged him as sovereign. The parallel with medieval European feudalism is not exact in details, but the basic system and the reasons for it were the same: a central kingdom with ambitions to control or administer a large area beyond its own immediate territory, which it thus arranged for by contracting with local chieftains. In addition, there were needs for joint defense against surrounding enemies or raiders. The Chou appear to have subdued by means of this system a much larger

Early Chou bronzes show a trend away from abstraction and toward more lifelike representation, although the pieces remain highly ornamented. [Freer Gallery, Washington]

area than they inherited from the Shang, from the Wei valley to the sea, north into southern Manchuria, and south into the Yangtze valley. Mutual interest among evolving kingdoms, or dukedoms, as the Chou called them, may also have led them to join together in the defense of the "civilized" area against the outer barbarians and to keep order internally.

For a time this system seems to have worked reasonably well, based also on what appears to have been an institution like serfdom by which most land was cultivated under the ownership of hereditary lords, perhaps with some irrigation from shallow wells in a center plot. As in parts of medieval Europe, serfs were bound to the land and could not leave, becoming virtually the property of their lords. At both the royal Chou court and increasingly at the courts of other dependent states there was an unbroken evolution of technological and artistic development. Bronze remained the chief metal, and magnificent ritual vessels, often of great size, increasingly bore long texts recording events or decrees.

Although most writing was by now done with brush and ink on silk or on strips of bamboo, none of these perishable texts has survived, and we are dependent on much later and perhaps substantially altered copies. It is generally assumed that the central body of the Chinese classics originated in the early Chou, including the Book of Changes (*I-ching*, a cryptic handbook for diviners), the Book of Songs, the Book of Rituals, and collections of historical documents. Among the collections were the texts that give the story of the five culture-hero emperors and the Hsia dynasty, as well as a now confirmed account of the Shang and of the Chou conquest. The Chinese were already writing history and attaching characteristic importance to the keeping of records.

But fundamental changes were at work that were gradually to disrupt and then destroy the Chou structure. Iron was becoming slowly cheaper and more plentiful as technology improved, and it began to be available for agricultural implements, including iron-tipped plows, which the Chinese developed more than 1,000 years before the West. Helped by better tools, irrigation was spreading, especially in the semiarid north of China, and more and more land was being brought under cultivation. Iron axes speeded the attack on the remaining forests in the hilly margins of the north and in the Yangtze valley. Spurred by rising agricultural output, the population began to grow much more rapidly, perhaps to 20 million by the mid-Chou period. Except for recurrent years of drought, the population did not apparently outrun its food supply, and surpluses were common, providing the basis for increasing trade.

New agricultural productivity freed increasing numbers of people from farm labor to serve as artisans, transport workers, soldiers, officials, scholars, and merchants. More and more towns, now more important as centers of trade than of royal or feudal control and dominated by merchants, began to dot the plain and the richer lands to the south in the Yangtze valley, where easier transport by water further stimulated the growth of trade and of urban centers. Fixed and hereditary serfdom and the domination of a landed aristocracy came to seem less and less suited to the changing conditions, a situation that may have been in some ways similar to that in the later periods of the medieval European feudal order. At the same time many of the original Chou vassals were evolving into separate states, each with a distinctive culture. After some four centuries of Chou rule, the political, social, and economic structure began to show strains, and eventually it disintegrated.

## Warring States

In 771 B.C.* the royal capital in the Wei valley was sacked by a barbarian group from the north and the Chou king was killed. His son was installed as king the next year, but in a new and better-protected capital at Loyang, in the hope that a control point closer to the center of the royal domains would be more secure and more effective in holding the kingdom together. It was to be a vain hope. To guard the northwest borders, the old Chou base in the Wei valley was given as a fief to a

---

*From this time on, traditional Chinese dates, almost certainly inaccurate for earlier periods, are fully reliable. The earliest surviving books come from the ninth century B.C., and by the eighth century the Chou were recording eclipses of the sun, which we now know did in fact occur exactly when their records state.

loyal noble of the Ch'in (Qin) clan; five centuries later the Ch'in were to sweep away the crumbled remnants of Chou rule to found the first empire.

After 770 B.C. royal authority over the surrounding dependencies dwindled, and vassals became rival states: Ch'in to the west, Jin to the north, Yen to the northeast in the area around modern Peking (Beijing), Ch'i (Qi) to the east in Shantung (Shandong), Ch'u (Qu) to the south in the central Yangtze valley, and a number of smaller states including Shu in Szechuan (Sichuan) and Lu in Shantung, where Confucius was born and served for a time as an adviser. It is still too early to speak of any of them, even of the Chou, as "China"; each was culturally and linguistically as well as politically and perhaps even racially distinct. China as we know it emerged only under the empire of Ch'in (Qin) in the third century B.C. The Ch'in empire put its own overpowering stamp on what was to become the dominant Chinese style in statecraft and social organization for the ensuing two millennia. Our name *China* comes, appropriately enough, from the Ch'in, as the creator of the first imperial Chinese identity.

Until then no one strand dominated the assortment of people, cultures, and states that occupied what is now China. They warred repeatedly among themselves and against the various groups around their edges, still well within the borders of modern China. Technology probably passed relatively easily and quickly from group to group, and by mid-Chou most seem to have shared achievements in metallurgy, agriculture, and irrigation, as well as other arts. But in spoken and written language, in many aspects of culture, and in political identity they were as different as, say, the evolving states of late medieval Europe.

Ch'u was one of the largest such states. Its location astride the central Yangtze valley made it probably the most productive of the rival states, since its agriculture benefited from the more adequate and reliable rainfall and the longer growing season of central China as well as from the greater ease of irrigation. But it was different in character too, in particular in the size and importance of its merchant group and the role of waterborne trade and towns in its economy. Ch'u had evolved far beyond the earlier Shang pattern where power had been held by a hereditary landowning nobility and virtually the sole source of wealth was agriculture worked by slaves or serfs. Ch'u was also a naval power, with fleets on the Yangtze and its tributaries and adjacent lakes, in contrast to the land armies of the north, and even larger numbers of trading junks (riverboats). Ch'u was ultimately defeated by a coalition of northern states in a great battle in 632 B.C., and though it continued to exist, its power and further growth were greatly reduced while those of the other states rose. This may have been one of those battles that changed the course of history. A China that followed the Ch'u pattern would have been very different from what eventually emerged.

**Bronze vessels and weapons of great beauty and technical perfection attest to the high quality of Shang technology. [Freer Gallery, Washington]**

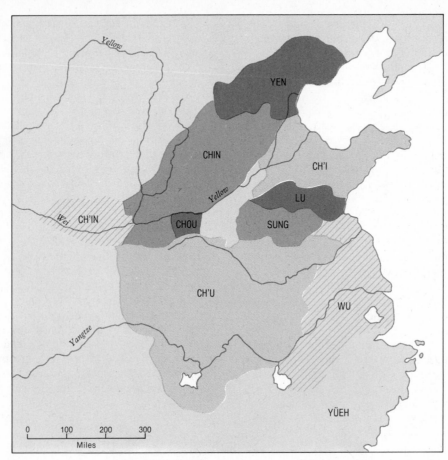

*3.2 China in the Sixth Century* B.C.

With increasing crop yields came changes in warfare. It was now possible to field large armies of men who could be spared from agriculture at least for parts of the year and could be fed on surpluses. Warfare became broader and more ruthless, and its character changed from that of earlier chivalric contests of honor between aristocrats to one of more wholesale conquest and fights for survival. The crossbow with a trigger mechanism greatly increased firepower, range, and accuracy, and by the fourth century B.C. foot soldiers were supported by armed cavalry. Such developments combined to undermine the earlier dominance of hereditary aristocrats, their chariots, and their personal retinues.

What was happening in China during this period paralleled the Indian pattern a century or so before as described in Chapter 2, where a chivalric age gave way to power struggles between states and the emergence of the Mauryan empire, based on the spread of iron, improvements in agriculture, and a population boom. As in India, bronze and copper coins minted by the state became common in this period in China, trade and cities grew rapidly, roads were built, standing armies proliferated, and the bureaucratic apparatus of the state began

to appear. All of this offered a range of new opportunities for able commoners. For many it was a positive and welcome change, but for others the passing of the old order and the great disruptions and sufferings of warfare engendered only chaos and moral confusion. Confucius, who lived at the beginning of the period of warring states, offered his prescriptions as an effort to reestablish order and what he referred to as "harmony," in an attempt to restore the values of an earlier "golden age."

❀
## CONFUCIUS THE SAGE

Confucius was born about 551 B.C. in one of the smaller states that arose out of the Chou domains in Shantung province and died about 479. He was a contemporary of the Buddha and died only a few years before the birth of Socrates. His family name was K'ung, and Chinese refer to him as K'ung Fu-tze (Kongfuzi, "Master K'ung"), which Europeans Latinized as Confucius. The

K'ung family were low-ranking aristocrats in reduced circumstances, but they were able to arrange for their son's education. Confucius made a career out of teaching, periodically serving as consultant or counselor to various feudal lords. To his pupils he taught not only literacy and the classics but also his own philosophy of life and of government. Some of his pupils won high-level jobs in state administration, but Confucius himself was never very successful in such terms, and he apparently thought of himself as a failure. In reality, he was the founder of the most successful philosophical, moral, and ethical system in human history, measured by the number of people in China, Korea, Japan, and Vietnam who followed his precepts for more than 2,500 years and who are still profoundly influenced by them.

We have nothing that the sage himself wrote and not very much direct information about him or his teachings. All we know for certain comes from a collection of discourses, or sayings, known as the *Analects*, put together rather unsystematically after his death by his disciples and hence probably not wholly accurate. Later commentaries expanded on the meaning and application of his teachings.

The picture we derive from the *Analects*, though incomplete, is of a thoughtful but very human person. He complained that he could never seem to get the right kinds of students or the kinds of appointments he yearned for. In discussing his lack of success, he commented loftily: "I don't mind not being in office; I am more concerned about being qualified for it. I don't mind not having recognition; I strive to be worthy of recognition." Yet at the same time he complained about being treated "like a gourd fit only to be hung on the wall and never put to use." He seems to have been so eager for a post as adviser that he considered working even for rebel groups, believing that, given any kind of opportunity, he could remake men and states in line with his philosophy—an attitude that Plato was to share a century later. But he also had a keen sense of the ridiculous and could even enjoy jokes on himself.

The basic message of all Confucius' teachings is that people can be molded and elevated by education and by the virtuous example of superiors. "Civilized" people so formed will *want* to do what is morally right, rather than what is merely expedient; hence they will preserve the harmony of society, which is what distinguishes humans from animals. Force and threats are ineffective controls, he asserts; only internalized values can produce correct behavior. Behavior should be modeled on that of people of superior status, beginning with the family and extending to the ruler, who thus must match power with responsibility and uprightness. For all relationships, he counsels in a variant of the Golden Rule, "Do not do unto others what you yourself would not like."

## ◉ Reflections on Social Reform ◉

*The philosopher Mo-tzu (Mozi), who was born in the fifth century B.C., while Confucius was still alive, was more interested in reforming society.*

It is the sage's business to regulate the world; he must thus know whence disorder comes in order to be capable of regulating it. . . . The origin is the lack of mutual love. . . . All the disorders of the world have this cause and this alone. . . . If mutual love prevailed universally throughout the world, no state would attack another state; no family would trouble another family; thieves and brigands would not exist; princes and subjects, fathers and sons, would all be filial and good. Thus the world would be well governed. . . . Where do ills come from? They come from hatred of others, from violence toward others. . . . The love which makes distinctions among persons causes all the ills of the world. . . . This universal love is very advantageous, and far more easy to practice than you imagine. If it is not put into practice, that is because the rulers take no pleasure in it. If the rulers took pleasure in it, I believe that men would throw themselves into it. . . . Nothing on earth could stop them. . . . To kill a man is called an unjust thing; it is a crime deserving death. To kill ten men is ten times more unjust, to kill a hundred men a hundred times more unjust. Today every prince in the world knows that this must be punished; they declare it unjust. Yet the greatest of injustices, the making of war, they do not punish. On the contrary, they glorify it and declare it just! Truly they do not know how unjust they are.

*Source:* After H. Maspero, *La Chine antique* (Paris: Presses Universitaires de France, 1927), pp. 253–254.

---

## ◉ The Path of the Sage ◉

*One of the most influential followers of Confucius was the philosopher Hsun-tzu (Xunzi, c. 300–c. 235 B.C.), who assembled his own teachings in a book that faithfully pursues the path of the sage, as the following sample indicates.*

When his horse is uneasy harnessed to a carriage, a gentleman is not comfortable in it. When the common people are uneasy under a government, a gentleman is not comfortable in his post. When a horse is uneasy, nothing is as good as calming it. When the common people are uneasy under a government, nothing is as good as being kind to them. Recruit the worthy and respectable and appoint the sincere and humble. Support filial piety and human heartedness. . . . It is traditionally said that the ruler is like a boat and the common people are the water. Water supports the boat but may also upset it.

*Source:* After C. O. Hucker, *China's Imperial Past* (Stanford, Calif.: Stanford University Press, 1975), p. 101.

---

Confucianism is a prescription for benevolence in human affairs and in government, with an essentially conservative stress on order. Nevertheless, the focus on benevolence meant that bad government should rightly be rejected, despite the threat to civil order, a point that the *Analects* repeats in several contexts. The Confucian model is the upright man who unswervingly pursues the right moral course whatever the consequences, even at the expense of his own self-interest. Master K'ung's life seems to have conformed to the model he preached. Perhaps he was, like Socrates, too outspoken to win the favor of the powerful men of his day. But his teachings and his example have far outlived the petty politics of the age in which he lived.

## The Ch'in Conquest

Ch'in, originally one of the poorest, smallest, and most remote of the Chou dependencies, seemed easily outclassed by the other contending states. Its succession of able rulers made a virtue of its relative poverty, its peasant base, and its frontier location by stressing the importance of hard work, frugality, and discipline and emphasizing agriculture and peasant soldiery rather than trade or the development of an intellectual elite. The Ch'in rulers blended these elements to create a strong military power. Its tough armies defeated those of rival states in a long series of campaigns that were kept away from the mountain-ringed Ch'in home base in the Wei valley but often devastated the more fragile economies of its trade-dependent enemies. Opponents saw the men-ace of rising Ch'in power too late to unite against it and were picked off one by one. Ch'in generals and statesmen were masters of strategy and tactics who used diplomacy, propaganda, treachery, espionage, and various forms of psychological warfare adroitly.

A series of victorious campaigns during the 230s and 220s culminated in the final defeat of all the other states in 221 B.C. North China and the Yangtze valley were united politically for the first time, and the Ch'in ruler, who now took the title of emperor (Huang Ti) as Ch'in Shih Huang Ti (Di), applied to his entire empire the systems that had built Ch'in power. Further conquests after 221 began the long Chinese absorption of the south with the acquisition of the kingdom of Yüeh (Yue) centered in the Canton (Guangzhou) delta and the route to it southward from the Yangtze, together with Yüeh territory in what is now northern Vietnam. Throughout the new domains, as in the former state of Ch'in, primogeniture (the custom whereby the eldest son inherits all of the father's property and status) was abolished, as was slavery except for minor domestic servants. The former feudal and land tenure arrangements were dissolved. Land became privately owned and was freely bought and sold. The state levied a tax on all land in the form of a share of the crop. A new uniform law code was applied to all subjects without discrimination, ending many centuries of aristocratic privilege, a reform that clearly appealed to most people. Currency, weights, measures, and forms of writing, which had varied widely among what had been separate cultures as well as states, were also unified by imperial fiat to follow the Ch'in mode, a change essential for governing a large empire. An imperial system of roads and canals was begun, and a splendid new capital was built near modern Sian (Xian) in the Wei valley. Even axle lengths for carts were standardized, so that all carts would fit the same ruts.

Probably the most spectacular and best known of the new public works projects was the Great Wall, which Ch'in Shih Huang Ti ordered consolidated from a series of much earlier walls along the northern steppe border and reconstructed as a uniform barrier with regularly spaced watchtowers. It and subsequent reconstructions (the remains currently visible date from the Ming rebuilding in the fifteenth century A.D.) constitute probably the largest single works project in human history; the Great Wall is said to be the only human construction visible from the moon. A million men reportedly died in building the Ch'in Great Wall, working as conscript labor. Ironically, the wall was never very effective in its supposed purpose of preventing nomadic incursions; end runs around it and intrigues that opened the gates made it often quite permeable. But it did serve as a symbolic affirmation of empire and as a statement of territorial and sovereign limits. The new state control over mass labor tempted the emperor to plan more and more projects of monumental scope, including the road system, the new canals (useful for transporting troops and their supplies as well as for irrigation), and his own magnificent palace and tomb, in addition to fresh conquests.

## Ch'in Authoritarianism

Agriculture was stressed as the basis of the economy and the state, with hardy peasants available in off seasons for conscript labor or for the army. Merchants were regarded as parasites and as potentially dangerous power rivals to the state. The removal of primogeniture also reduced the threat from hereditary landed power. But the chief target of the Ch'in system was the independence of intellectuals, people who ask questions, consider alternatives, or point out deficiencies. China already had a long tradition of scholars, philosophers, and moralists, of whom Confucius and his later disciple Mencius were honored examples. The Ch'in saw such people as potential troublemakers. It was an openly totalitarian state, and its sense of mission made it even more intolerant of any dissent.

Ch'in Shih Huang Ti persecuted intellectuals, buried several hundred scholars alive for questioning his policies, and ordered the burning of all books that could promote what he considered undesirable thoughts. In practice this meant most books other than trade manuals and the official Ch'in chronicles. The documents destroyed included valuable material accumulated from earlier periods. There was to be no admiration of the past, no criticism of the present, and no recommendations for the future, except the state's. These policies were profoundly contrary to the Chinese reverence for the written word and the preservation of records. They earned the emperor the condemnation of all subsequent Chinese scholars. Certainly he was a cruel tyrant, inhumane and perhaps even depraved in his lust for absolute power. But his methods, harsh though they were, built an empire out of disunity and established most of the bases of the Chinese state all the way to the present.

The emperor's policies were actually in large measure the work of his prime minister, Li Ssu, whose career closely paralleled that of Kautilya in Mauryan India and who is credited with founding a new school of philosophy called Legalism, which embodied the Ch'in policies of strict state control through the application of harsh laws. This control was augmented by a greatly expanded state bureaucracy and by rigid supervision of all education. Only values that supported the state design were taught, and practical skills were stressed over critical

The Great Wall was probably Ch'in Shih Huang Ti's most famous project. Here it is shown west of Peking, snaking along the mountain ridges separating northeastern China from Mongolia. The wall was built wide enough to allow two war chariots to pass abreast. The sections of it that remain standing date from its most recent major reconstruction under the Ming dynasty in the fifteenth century. [Werner Forman Archive]

inquiry. As in Mauryan India, there were a highly developed police system and a secret service to ferret out and punish dissidents. Travel, within the realm or abroad, was forbidden except by special permit.

China, once unified by the Ch'in, even by such ruthless means, was to cling to the idea of imperial unity ever thereafter. Each subsequent period of disunity following the fall of a dynasty was regarded as a time of failure, and each ended in the rebuilding of the empire. But one must also acknowledge the appeal of the new order that even the totalitarian methods of the Ch'in represented. By its time most people were clearly ready to break with their feudal past and to move toward a system based on achievement rather than birth. The Ch'in believed firmly that their new order was progress; they had a visionary conviction that they were creating a better society. The parallels with Communist China are striking, and indeed Ch'in Shih Huang Ti was praised as a model during the Cultural Revolution in the late 1960s. Sacrifice for an inspiring national goal has its own appeal; the end is seen to justify the means, including treachery, cruelty, and inhumanity toward the people, who are nevertheless seen as the supposed beneficiaries of the new order.

Lord Shang, an earlier Ch'in official and the true progenitor of the Legalist school, summarized state policy in classic totalitarian terms:

> Punish heavily the light offenses. . . . If light offenses do not occur, serious ones have no chance of coming. This is said to be "ruling the people in a state of law and order." . . .
>
> A state where uniformity of purpose has been established for ten years will be strong for a hundred years; for a hundred years it will be strong for a thousand years . . . and will attain supremacy. . . .
>
> The things which people desire are innumerable, but that from which they benefit is one and the same. Unless the people are made one, there is no way to make them attain their desire. Therefore they are unified, and their strength is consolidated. . . .
>
> If you establish what people delight in, they will suffer from what they dislike, but if you establish what they dislike, they will be happy in what they enjoy.[1]

In other words, in unity is strength, but the state knows best what is good for people. The major figure of the school of Legalism is the philosopher Han Fei (died 233 B.C.), who also stressed the need for severe laws and harsh punishments, the only means to establish order under the direction of the ruler. People, he taught, are naturally selfish, and they must be held mutually responsible for one another's actions.

Nevertheless, there was merit in the new equality under the law propounded by the Ch'in, new opportunities for advancement, and allure in its ambitious projects. The best illustration of the more constructive aspects of the Ch'in is the figure of Li Ping (Bing), provincial governor of the former state of Shu (Szechuan) and famed as a hydraulic engineer on many Ch'in projects, including the control works on the Yellow River. It was Li Ping who devised the best formula for minimizing the floods that had already made the Yellow River notorious: "Dig the bed deep, and keep the banks low." This helped prevent the buildup of silt in the river's bed, which over time had raised it above the level of the surrounding country and greatly worsened the destructive consequences of

## ◎ The Perils of Mindless Traditionalism ◎

*Han Fei, a Legalist philosopher, was a contemporary and sometime colleague of Li Ssu, who ultimately poisoned Han Fei as a rival. Han Fei's writings, however, survived, including the following story illustrating the folly of mindlessly following old ways instead of adapting policies to fit new circumstances.*

In a plowman's field was a tree stump. When a rabbit ran into the stump and broke its neck, the plowman left his plow and watched over the stump, hoping to pick up more rabbits. But he got no more and became the laughingstock of the whole kingdom. Wanting to apply the policies of former kings to govern people in these times belongs in the same class as watching over that stump.

*Source:* After C. O. Hucker, *China's Imperial Past* (Stanford, Calif.: Stanford University Press, 1975), p. 94.

floods. Li Ping's sound advice was finally acted on effectively only under the Communist government after 1949.

Li Ping is credited with designing and constructing the famous irrigation works at Kuan Hsien (Guanxian) in western Szechuan (Sichuan), diverting the Min River where it emerges from the mountains and enters the wide plain around the capital city of Chengdu. These works, much visited by tourists, still stand, with Li Ping's statue overlooking them. They are reputed to have saved millions of people on the Chengdu plain from drought and famine ever since. Like all big projects, they took enormous labor and hardship, mainly from conscript workers under iron discipline. According to the great Han dynasty historian Ssu Ma Ch'ien (Simaqian), Li Ping said toward the end of his life:

> People can be depended on to enjoy the results, but they must not be consulted about the beginnings. Now the elder ones and their descendants dislike people like me, but hundreds of years later let them think what I have said and done.

Li Ping's memory is still honored, while that of his emperor is reviled.

# The Han Dynasty

Ch'in Shih Huang Ti died in 210 B.C., leaving the throne to his eldest son, but Li Ssu and other counselors suppressed the news of his death for fear of uprisings and then installed the second son as their puppet. But the harshness of Ch'in rule had left the country in turmoil, exhausted the people, drained the treasury, and alienated the educated upper classes. Without their cooperation, the regime was in trouble. Rebellion had already begun in several provinces. This was soon joined by the desertion of several army commanders. In 206 B.C. rebel armies occupied the capital and burned the emperor's splendid new palace. Rival forces contended for power in the ensuing struggle, in which large groups of soldiers, workers, and former officials roamed the country. Out of this chaos there had emerged by 202 B.C. a new rebel leader, Liu Pang (Liu Bang), who founded a new dynasty, which he named the Han. Under Han rule China took the political, social, and territorial shape it was to retain until the present century. The Chinese still call themselves "People of Han," a label they carry with much pride as the heirs of a great tradition. Han imperial success, and that of later dynasties, depended, however, on retention of many of the techniques of control used by the Ch'in. The administration of an empire the size of Europe with a population of probably about 60 million could not have been managed otherwise.

Beginning with the Han, the harsher aspects of the Legalist approach of the Ch'in were softened by both common sense and the more humane morality of Confucianism. Liu Pang, who took the title Han Kao-tsu ("High Progenitor") as the first emperor, emphasized the Confucian precept that government exists to serve the people and that unjust rulers should forfeit both the mandate of Heaven and the support of the ruled. He abolished the hated controls on travel, education, and thought, lowered taxes, and encouraged learning so as to build a pool of educated men whose talents, in the Confucian mode, could be called on to serve the state. Conscription for the army and forced labor for public works such as road and canal building were retained, however, as was the administrative division of the empire into *hsien* (*xian*, counties), each under the control of an imperial magistrate. The imperial state superimposed its model in all things, including currency, weights, measures, script, and orthodox thought, on a vast and diverse area that had long been politically and culturally varied. Under beneficent rule, this system could be made to work successfully and could command general support. The early Han was a time of great prosperity and of enthusiasm for the new order.

# Expansion Under Wu Ti

The new power of the Han empire, on Ch'in foundations and with the boost of economic and population growth, tempted successive emperors to further conquests and imperial glory. Liu Pang's son and grandson continued his frugal and benevolent model as rulers, but the bitter memories of Ch'in had faded by the time of the emperor Wu Ti (141–87 B.C.). He first tightened imperial control, removed the remaining power of the lords created by Liu Pang for faithful service, and imposed regulations on trade and merchants, new taxes, and new controls over salt, iron, and the supply of grain. The last measure, which created what came to be known as the "ever-normal granary system," was intended to prevent famine by state collection of grain in good years or surplus areas, which could then be sold at low rather than inflated prices when lean years came. It was a good idea and was practiced with some success by subsequent dynasties, but, like Li Ping's projects, it was not always popular with the local producers or merchants.

Having put the imperial house in order and increased state revenues and power, Wu Ti began an ambitious program of new conquests in 111 B.C., beginning in the southeast against Yüeh in the Fukien and Canton areas, which had broken away after the fall of the Ch'in. The Yüeh kingdom had included the related people and culture of what is today northern Vietnam, and this too was now again added to the Chinese empire. Over the centuries the Vietnamese were to reassert their separate identity despite their adoption of much of Chinese culture. In Han times the people and culture of Yüeh were regarded as foreign and were very different from those of the north. More than traces of these differences remain even now, including the Cantonese language and cuisine, but the south has been an integral part of China for 2,000 years and has been largely remade in the greater Chinese image.

Turning northward after the successful southern campaign, in 109–108 B.C. Wu Ti's armies conquered Manchuria and northern Korea for the empire, while other campaigns established looser control over the still non-Chinese populations of Yunnan and Kweichou (Guizhou) in the southwest. Southern Manchuria was to remain solidly a part of the Chinese system, with large colonies, originally garrisons, planted there by Wu Ti. These became agricultural settlements in the fertile valley of the Liao River.

Similar garrisons were established in northern Korea, where there was heavy Chinese influence from Han times on. But Koreans, like the Vietnamese, remained eager to reclaim their cultural identity and independence. As in Vietnam, Korea had already developed its own civilization and was linguistically and ethnically dis-

tinct from China despite Chinese cultural influence. After the Han collapse in A.D. 220, both areas broke away from Chinese control, Korea as a nominally tributary state, Vietnam to endure later Chinese reconquest under the T'ang and then successive wars of independence until modern times, which created a heavy legacy of mutual mistrust.

China's northern and northwestern frontiers had been and were to remain troublesome for other reasons. The Great Wall had been built as a barrier, but it could not prevent infiltrations by the horse-riding nomads who occupied the steppe border zone and who periodically harried Chinese agricultural areas and trade routes. The major route for international trade was the famous Silk Road through the Kansu (Gansu) Corridor and along the northern and southern edges of the Tarim Desert in Sinkiang (Xinjiang, Chinese Turkestan), where there are widely separated oases fed by streams from the surrounding mountains. The two routes met at Kashgar at the western end of the Tarim Desert and then crossed the Pamirs into central Asia, where the trade passed into other hands on its long way to the Levant and eventually on to Rome. Silk was the main export, a Chinese mo-

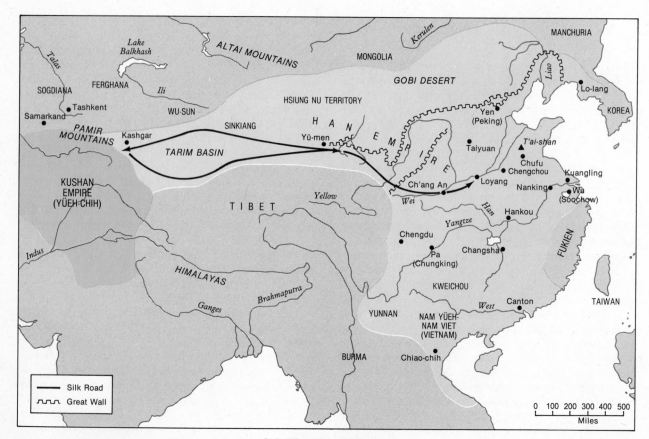

*3.3 The Han Empire*

nopoly since Lung Shan times and in great demand westward, especially in luxury-loving imperial Rome. The Romans were obliged to pay for it largely in gold, a drain that Pliny and other Roman historians felt weakened the economy and contributed to Rome's ultimate collapse in the West. It was profitable to China, and Wu Ti's pride in his new imperial power made him less willing to accept nomad interruptions of the trade and raids on Chinese territory.

The chief nomad group at this period was the Hsiung-nu (Xiong-nu), a Turkish people whose mounted mobility and cavalry tactics gave them the kind of military effectiveness later used by the Mongol leader Chinghis Khan. The Han generals complained that the Hsiung-nu "move on swift horses, and in their breasts beat the hearts of beasts. They shift from place to place like a flock of birds. Thus it is difficult to corner them and bring them under control." One can understand the frustration of the Han, but in a series of major campaigns Wu Ti defeated the Hsiung-nu, drove them for a time out of most of Inner Mongolia, Kansu, and Sinkiang, and planted colonies and garrisons in those areas and along the Silk Road, which is still marked by ruined Han watchtowers. Sinkiang and Inner Mongolia were to fall away from Chinese control in later periods whenever the central state was weak but were reclaimed by most subsequent strong dynasties as part of the empire. Non-Han groups such as the Hsiung-nu and the Mongols remained the major steppe inhabitants until the twentieth century, and another Turkish people, the Uighurs, remained the dominant oasis farmers in the desert region of Sinkiang. The Uighurs later embraced Islam and helped transmit it to China proper, where there are still a number of Chinese Muslims, concentrated in the northwest.

## China and Rome

Wu Ti sent an ambassador westward in 139 B.C., a courtier named Chang Ch'ien (Zhangqian), to try to make an alliance with other nomads against the Hsiung-nu and to scout out the country more generally. He was captured instead by the Hsiung-nu but escaped after ten years. He returned to the Han capital at Ch'ang An (Qangan) in the Wei valley, where the Ch'in had ruled, in 126 B.C. with an account of central Asia that included bits of information about India and a great empire far to the west, where the silk went. This was China's first news of Rome, but it was never to learn much more. Travelers who said they had been to Rome turned up much later at the Han court in the second century A.D., as recorded in the Han annals. The Romans knew China only as the source of silk and called it, accordingly, Seres, the Latin word for silk.

Wu Ti was tempted by Chang Ch'ien's report to add central Asia to his conquests, partly out of vainglory and partly to secure supplies of the excellent horses to be found there, which he wanted for the imperial stables and his cavalry. If he or his successors had done so, the Chinese and Roman empires or their forward troops might have met and perhaps learned from each other. In the first century A.D., with the Han still in power and still occasionally probing westward, Rome was campaigning against the Parthian kingdom in Persia. If the Romans had conquered Parthia, they might have encountered at least Han patrols or might have followed the Silk Road, which they knew about, from central Asia to the borders of China. But both armies were very far from home. Moreover, the Parthians and other central Asian groups were formidable opponents and were eager to retain their profitable role as intermediary in the silk trade rather than allow the two empires to meet. Han envoys reached the Parthians but were advised to return home, which they did.

Wu Ti's endless campaigns and his impositions on the people exhausted the country's patience and resources. One of his earlier reforms had been the establishment of imperial censors whose job it was to keep officials, even the emperor, faithful to their duty to serve the people. The censors finally convinced Wu Ti that he had neglected this basic precept and persuaded him to issue a famous penitential edict apologizing for his excesses and promising to be a better ruler, more deserving of the mandate of Heaven—and less likely to be overthrown by rebellion, which was already brewing. The institution of the censorate remained a regulatory feature of all subsequent dynasties.

Wu Ti's immediate successors, while largely abandoning further conquests, continued to press the Hsiung-nu as a defensive strategy and even sent an expeditionary force across the Pamirs into the Samarkand region in pursuit. There, in 42 B.C., on the banks of the Talas River near Tashkent in central Asia, they defeated a Hsiung-nu coalition that included mercenary troops who from the Chinese description may have been Roman auxiliaries; they had learned the Roman *testudo* formation with shields overlapping above their heads to ward off arrows and spears. The Han armies in central Asia, having marched across deserts and high mountains, were farther from their capital than regular Roman troops ever were from Rome. But this was the high point of Han power, and the empire that Wu Ti welded together was not to be significantly enlarged or altered in subsequent centuries, except for the much later incorporation of Tibet and the loss of Korea and Vietnam.

## Wider Trade Patterns

Contacts across Eurasia had probably been important during and since the prehistoric period: Sumeria may have contributed to Indian civilization (and vice versa) and to the emergence of Chinese civilization. We have no adequate archaeological data to permit more than speculation about such interchanges. Given the multiplicity and often the mutual hostility of the various cultural groups and political alliances in central Asia during the ancient and medieval periods, the passage of goods and ideas through this area, in either direction, was necessarily slow and difficult. There was certainly trade linking China and India to western Asia, Greece, and Rome. From at least 600 B.C. there was also sea trade bringing Indian and Southeast Asian spices to the Mediterranean and Europe. But except for the visits of Greek and Roman traders to the Indian west coast, the travels of a few Indian philosophers to Greece and Rome, and Alexander's invasion of India, there was no direct contact between Eastern and Western civilizations from then until the time of Marco Polo in the thirteenth century. Arab ships traded by sea, and a chain of various central Asian peoples transmitted ideas as well as goods across Eurasia, but the transmission was incomplete, and understandably some of the ideas were garbled in the process.

The Chinese and Roman empires thus remained largely in ignorance of each other except for travelers' tales, although both were of comparable size, sophistication, power, and achievements. China might have developed a different and more open attitude to the rest of the world if it had had some experience with another culture, Roman or Indian, at its own level of sophistication. Like the Chinese, the Romans were builders of roads, walls, and planned cities, synthesizers of varied cultures under an expansionist and cosmopolitan system, and contenders with "barbarians" along the fringes of their empire. The Han empire was larger, and probably richer and more populous, than either the Roman or the Indian empire, but its level of cultural and technical sophistication was probably matched by the others.

Roman traders, and before them Greeks, regularly reached the west coast of India, as mentioned in Chapter 2. Roman goods, including pottery and coins, have been found as far east as Malaya but were probably carried there by Indian or Arab merchants. Before the time of the Greeks, there was trade by both sea and land between India and Mesopotamia, but we know little or nothing about the goods shipped from west to east in that exchange; Indian exports may have been paid for largely in gold, as the Romans paid for Chinese silk. Commerce between China and the rest of Eurasia almost certainly developed later than India's trade with Mesopotamia, and there is no evidence of Chinese exports westward until the beginning of the silk route, probably during the Chou dynasty.

Chinese merchants took the silk only as far as Sinkiang, handing it over there to a long series of central Asian traders who passed it along through the thousands of miles of central and western Asia to the shores of the Mediterranean, where Syrian, Greek, and Roman merchants picked it up for transport farther west. This trade continued after the fall of the Han dynasty and was later augmented by the export of porcelain and lacquer goods, all high-value commodities that could bear the very heavy costs of such long-distance transport. The camel caravans carrying them were also exposed to frequent raids from other central Asian groups along the route, risks that further increased the prices charged for Chinese exports when they finally reached their destinations. By the eleventh century much of the Chinese export trade was also being carried by ships westward to India (and later to Africa), while Indian exports westward—fine cotton textiles, spices, gems, and other goods—continued from the earliest period through the Middle Ages to move mainly by sea, from ports on the west coast. There must have been some return flow of trade by sea from India to China, but apart from the mention of what sound like Indian merchants in ports on the South China coast, we know very little about it.

## Han Culture

The first two centuries of Han rule were a time of great cultural flowering, in poetry, painting, music, philosophy, literature, and the writing of history. Confucianism was more firmly established as the official orthodoxy and state ideology, and the famous Chinese imperial civil service system recruited men of talent, schooled in classical Confucian learning, to hold office through competitive examination regardless of their birth. Liu Pang, the founder of the Han, had been born a peasant, and thus ability and education were stressed rather than inherited status. This approach was to remain a source of strength and effectiveness for the state for the next 2,000 years. Officeholding by the scholar-gentry, who were enriched each generation by new blood rising from peasant or commoner ranks and entering the elite through the imperial examinations, became the most prestigious of all occupations. That in turn generally helped ensure that able people went into the administration and often preserved the political arena and government service from corruption, mediocrity, and ineffectiveness.

China was not free from the common problems of bureaucracy, but each new dynasty reestablished the system begun under the Han and on the whole probably managed the task of government better than many other states. Confucius, with his emphasis on duty, learning, "human-heartedness," and virtue, is to thank for this. Chinese society continued to choose that way and periodically reaffirmed the teachings of an obscure consultant to a small feudal lord in the sixth century B.C. who lived long before there was any thought of empire. Great landed-gentry families remained and periodically formed power cliques, together with court aristocrats, eunuchs, and ambitious generals—a pattern familiar from imperial Rome, Persia, and elsewhere. But the original Han ideal endured, through the rise and fall of successive dynasties, and with all its imperfections built a long and proud tradition of power combined with service that is still very much alive in China. The People's Republic is the conscious heir of an imperial past.

Han rule was briefly broken by the palace coup of the empress's nephew, Wang Mang, who made himself emperor from A.D. 9 to A.D. 23. As a model Confucian ruler, he tried to curb the resurgent power of merchants and landowning gentry. He also extended new state controls over the economy in an effort to reestablish the egalitarianism he claimed to derive from the sage's teaching. His reforms included the abolition of private estates, which had increasingly avoided paying taxes, and the nationalization of land. Such policies bitterly alienated the rich and powerful, and Wang Mang was murdered by a rebel group called the Red Eyebrows, with support from both distressed peasants suffering from a drought-induced famine and from merchant and gentry groups.

Landowning and its abuses were, of course, problems for all ancient and medieval empires. Ownership of land usually meant power and was usually (except in post-Ch'in China) passed on within the family by inheritance. Even in China the abolition of primogeniture (inheritance by the eldest son) did not always prevent powerful families from accumulating large blocks of land. Large landowners built up wealth but also threatened the supremacy of the state by their growing political power. By manipulating their influence, they often managed to reduce or avoid paying state taxes on their lands and would often also support or even constitute in themselves powerful political factions. Their tenants, the peasants who farmed the land, were often cruelly exploited, paying far more in rent and services to the landowner than the latter paid to the state. As these practices were carried to extremes, rebellion brewed, and reformers in government periodically tried to check the abuses of the large landowners, as in Wang Mang's abortive reforms. Throughout the empires of the ancient and medieval world, similar problems and similar efforts at solution can be observed, as in the case of the revolt of the Gracchi in Rome (see Chapter 6) or the reforms of Wang An-Shih in Sung China.

In A.D. 25 the Han dynasty was reestablished, under new rulers and with a new capital at Loyang, following the earlier model of the Chou and for the same reasons. It is thus known as the Eastern or Later Han, while the Ch'ang An period from 202 B.C. to A.D. 9 is called the Western or Former Han. A succession of strong and conscientious emperors restored the power, prosperity, and cultural vigor of Wu Ti's time. Learning, philosophy, and the arts flourished once more, and elite society reached new levels of affluence, elegance, and sophistication.

Bronze casting continued its development under the Han. This magnificent bronze horse from the second century A.D. shows the sophistication of Han technology and art. [Granger Collection]

Peace was reestablished along all the imperial frontiers by reconquest. In A.D. 97 a Han army marched all the way to the Caspian Sea, and its advance scouts reached either the Persian Gulf or the Black Sea. In A.D. 89 a Han army invaded Mongolia and again defeated the Hsiung-nu, probably contributing to the start of the latter's subsequent migration westward and their ultimate role as invaders of Europe as the Huns. Sinkiang, northern Vietnam, northern Korea, southern Manchuria, and Inner Mongolia were all reincorporated into the empire, trade flourished, and China gloried in its confidently reasserted power and cultural leadership.

The Later Han produced some of the most famous generals in Chinese history; those generals had repeated successes against rebellious groups on the northwest frontier. One of the best known of these is Pan Ch'ao (Ban Qao), whose brother and sister were joint authors of a famous history of the Han dynasty. Pan Ch'ao is said to have asserted that "only he who penetrates into the tiger's lair can carry off the cubs." In A.D. 73 he was sent with a detachment of troops to pacify the area south of Sinkiang. Surrounded by enemy tribal forces with whom he was attempting to negotiate, he sent part of his forces behind the enemy lines to beat drums and simulate an attack while the remainder built a huge fire in front of the barbarian fortress. The barbarians were completely surprised; many were killed as they rushed out, and many more died in the flames. The barbarian chief surrendered and renewed his oath of vassalage to China.

After the first century, landlord power and oppression grew again; Wang Mang had been right to try to curb them. Imperial relatives and powerful families jockeyed for position or influence, peasant revolts were growing, and the elite, especially those at court surrounding weak emperors, indulged themselves in luxurious living heedless of the problems around them—all echoes of the problems Rome was facing at the same time. Palace intrigues grew out of control, and eunuch groups* acquired more and more power. Generals in the provinces became rival warlords after suppressing peasant uprisings. The entire imperial structure was crumbling, and in A.D. 220 the last Han emperor abdicated. The loss of trade and revenue contributed to the fall of the dynasty, but the primary cause was self-destructive indulgence and faction fighting at court in addition to local and provincial rivalries.

Chinese control over Sinkiang was lost with the fall of the Han, by which time nearly all Chinese originally settled there as garrison troops had withdrawn, although their watchtowers and fortified bases remained, to crumble away in succeeding centuries. With the reassertion of empire under the T'ang, Sinkiang was reclaimed as imperial territory, only to fall away again with the collapse of the T'ang order, a pattern repeated under the Ch'ing (Manchu) dynasty (1644–1911). Only with the advent of modern means of communication have large numbers of Chinese again settled in Sinkiang, but the dominant inhabitants remain, as they were well before Han times, Turkish and other central Asian peoples.

## The Collapse of the Han Order

A new dynasty called Wei was proclaimed in 220, but it failed to hold the empire together, and rival dynasties soon emerged. In ensuing years the north was progressively overrun by barbarians, Hsiung-nu and other steppe nomadic groups, who sacked both Ch'ang An and Loyang by the early fourth century. The north disintegrated into a bewildering series of minor rival kingdoms under barbarian control, while the south was similarly divided into rival Chinese states.

The period from the fall of the Han in 220 to the ultimate reunification in 589 is sometimes rather misleadingly called the Six Dynasties (there were many more than six) but is better described as a long interval of disunity, invasion, disruption, intrigue, and warfare that shattered the imperial image and left most Chinese disheartened. Much of the former high culture survived,

---

*Eunuchs were men castrated as youths and hence without heirs. They were often used as courtiers (because they could not engage in intrigue on behalf of their sons) and as harem guards. However, they often formed cliques of their own and seldom used power responsibly.

### CHINA TO A.D. 589

| | |
|---|---|
| c. 2000 B.C. | Beginning of Lung Shan culture |
| c. 1600–c. 1050 B.C. | Shang dynasty |
| c. 1050–221 B.C. | Chou dynasty |
| c. 551–c. 479 B.C. | Confucius |
| c. 230–221 B.C. | Ch'in conquest |
| 202 B.C.–A.D. 220 | Han dynasty |
| A.D. 220–589 | The "Six Dynasties" |

especially in the arts, and little of it was forgotten by educated Chinese, but the period was a time of troubles. Except among the elite, many of whom fled south, most people suffered. These centuries suggest comparison with what began only a little later in the breakup of the Roman Empire and the Germanic and Hun invasions of southern Europe. In China too the period was thought of as a Dark Age, and as in Europe confidence was lost. As Europe saw the spread of a new mass religion of otherworldly salvation, Christianity, so Buddhism took root in China. The Wei dynasty, founded by an originally barbarian group, was vigorous in promoting Buddhism and left behind a rich legacy of Buddhist art, even though Wei control was limited to the north. But the imperial idea continued to appeal to Chinese pride, and in time it was to be reestablished in a new birth of unification, power, and glory, the T'ang.

## CITIES IN ANCIENT CHINA

The Shang capitals, and their immediate Lung Shan predecessors, were primarily ceremonial centers, symbols of royal authority. The late Lung Shan city on the site of modern Chengchou and the Shang capitals there, at Loyang, and at Anyang were massively walled and gated. The walls enclosed royal palaces and tombs, royal residences, quarters for priests, slaves, kept artisans, and military guards, but much of the enclosed area was not built on. Most nonroyal inhabitants and most of the workers lived in unplanned villagelike settlements outside the walls. By at least the late Shang period, the Chinese character and the spoken word for "city" were the same as those for "wall," and this has remained so to the present. Cities, in other words, were designed as statements of authority; the wall was a symbol of state or, later, imperial power and thus distinguished cities from villages or market towns. Apart from the capitals, imperial and provincial, most cities first arose as county seats, the lowest rung of national administration and, from Han times, the base of an imperial magistrate.

Chinese cities were built predominantly of wood,

## ◉ The Fall of the Han ◉

*The popular Chinese novel* Romance of the Three Kingdoms, *first written down in the fourteenth century* A.D., *tells of the fall of the Han and
the civil war that ensued. The account begins as follows:*

Empires wax and wane; states cleave asunder and coalesce. When the rule of Chou weakened, seven contending principalities sprang up, warring one with another until they settled down as Ch'in, and when its destiny had been fulfilled there arose Ch'u and Han to
contend for the mastery. And Han was the victor. . . . In a short time the whole empire
was theirs, and their magnificent heritage was handed down in successive generations till
the days of Kuang-wu, whose name stands in the middle of the long line of Han. . . . The
dynasty had already passed its zenith. . . . The descent into misrule hastened in the reigns
of the two emperors who sat on the dragon throne about the middle of the second century. They paid no heed to the good men of the court but gave their confidence to the
palace eunuchs. . . . The two trusted advisers, disgusted with the abuses resulting from the
meddling of the eunuchs in affairs of state, plotted their destruction. But the chief eunuch
was not to be disposed of so easily. The plot leaked out and the two honest men fell, leaving the eunuchs stronger than before. . . . [Some years later] the earth quaked in Loyang,
while along the coast a huge tidal wave rushed in, which, in its recoil, swept away all the
dwellers by the sea. . . . Certain hens developed male characteristics, a miracle that could
only refer to the effeminate eunuchs meddling in affairs of state. Away from the capital, a
mountain fell in, leaving a great rift in its flank. . . . But the eunuchs grew bolder. Ten of
them, rivals in wickedness, formed a powerful party. One of them became the emperor's
most trusted adviser. The emperor even called him Daddy. So the government went from
bad to worse, till the country was ripe for rebellion and buzzed with brigandage.

*Source:* After C. H. Brewitt-Taylor, trans., *Romance of the Three Kingdoms* (Tokyo: Tuttle, 1959), vol. 1,
pp. 1–2.

---

which is why little evidence remains from this early period to show what they looked like. Some written documents surviving from Chou times describe the precise
planning of all walled cities and their ritual or symbolic
importance, including their exact north-south orientation, and the arrangement and dimensions of the royal
or imperial buildings within the walls. Religious cults
such as ancestor worship and the worship of what the
Chinese called Heaven, or the Supreme Deity, were represented in every walled city by carefully placed temples.

By the time of the Han dynasty, China had nearly
2,000 years of urban experience; much of it was reflected
in the Han capital at Ch'ang An. The site was carefully
chosen by Liu Pang, the first Han emperor, but it was
not until the reign of his successor, in 192 B.C., that the
city walls were begun, of pounded earth 52 feet thick at
the base, 27 feet high, and over 3 miles long on each of
the four sides. The walls enclosed imperial palaces,
tombs, and temples to the ancestors, among other temples. The government regulated and supervised market

areas inside as well as outside the walls, and the city was
divided into 160 wards. Straight broad avenues led from
each of the major gates at the main compass points, with
an apparently less planned growth of lanes and alleys in
the wards. The ideal city form was a square, which
Ch'ang An approximated, with one major central gate
and two lesser ones on each of the four sides.

The Han now ruled an immense territory, much of it
newly conquered, especially in the south. The imperial
stamp on these new lands was achieved primarily
through the building of walled cities, county seats on the
imperial model but on a far smaller scale. Once the original inhabitants had been subdued and the land cleared,
settled, and farmed, garrison towns or fortresses gave
way to such walled county seats from which the imperial
magistrate could keep order, dispense justice, and supervise the collection of taxes and the exactions of
forced labor and military conscription.

In the hilly south such cities often had to accommodate to the terrain and sometimes altered the square

Han dynasty scientists in the second century A.D. calculated the value of pi as 3.1622 and developed a highly accurate calendar, the wheelbarrow, and a bronze seismograph for recording earthquakes. The model shown here is based on a detailed description of the original. Eight dragons at major compass points along the outer edge of the vessel respond to tremors from the appropriate direction by spitting a pearl into the mouth of the frog below. [Ronald Sheridan/Ancient Art and Architecture Collection]

built of wood, and little has survived to tell us much about them, but what accounts we have suggest that they rivaled imperial Rome in size and splendor. It is symptomatic of this vast bureaucratic empire, whose culture also put a high value on education and learning, that paper was first made there, before A.D. 100 (more than 1,000 years passed before the knowledge of papermaking spread to Europe). Another Han innovation was an early form of porcelain, one more Chinese gift to the world known everywhere simply as "china." Water-powered mills were invented in Han China, as was the basis of the modern horse breast strap and collar, which

shape somewhat. But the imperial model was apparent in all of them, including their official buildings, temples, military barracks, and regulated market areas inside and outside the walls. One can in fact chart the southward spread of Han occupation and the growth of Chinese-style agricultural settlement by noting the successive establishment of new walled county seats. They appeared first along the rivers leading south from the Yangtze and then progressively inland from the rivers. They were linked with each other and with the imperial and provincial capitals by the imperial road system begun under the Ch'in and greatly extended under the Han.

## The Han Legacy

China by Han times was highly developed technologically as well as culturally. Ch'ang An and Loyang were

Pottery figure called the "Balladeer," part of the grave furniture from a Han dynasty tomb in Szechuan. The afterlife was clearly supposed to be a happy time, replete with worldly pleasures. This figure beautifully captures the human quality of Han folk culture. [Innervisions/Sichuan Provincial Museum, China]

**Raised ceramic tile from a Han dynasty tomb, showing a festive scene with jugglers, dancers, and musicians. [Asian Archives, University of Michigan: Private Collection, Chengdu, China]**

made it possible for draft animals to pull much heavier loads more efficiently and without being choked. Lacquer had made its appearance by Wu Ti's time, and samples of fine lacquer ware have been found in Han tombs. Han dynasty alchemists invented the technique of distillation, not discovered in Europe until the fourteenth century. Artisans of the Han period built ships with watertight compartments, multiple masts, and sternpost rudders, and mariners used a magnetic compass. The circulation of the blood was also discovered in Han China; Europeans first knew of it only in the seventeenth century. Metallurgy, already well advanced, was given a further boost by the invention of a double-acting piston-bellows, something not achieved in Europe until the seventeenth century. Suspension bridges became common under the Han; it was not until the eighteenth century that they were copied in Europe.

Probably the greatest literary achievement of the Han was in the writing of history. Many Chou records destroyed by Ch'in Shih Huang Ti were reconstructed by Han scholars from memory, and the texts we have date largely from this period. New pride in empire and tradition produced the man called China's Grand Historian,

Ssu-ma Ch'ien (Simaqian, died c. 85 B.C.). His massive *Historical Records* put together materials from earlier texts in an effort to provide an accurate record of events dating back before the Shang. He added summary essays on geography, culture, the economy, and biographies of important people. A century later Pan Ku (Bangu, died A.D. 92) compiled a similarly comprehensive *History of the Han Dynasty*, which became the model for the standard histories commissioned by each subsequent dynasty, another respect in which the Han set the pattern for later centuries.

Han writers set a high standard for historical scholarship that many scholars feel was not equaled until the eighteenth century in the West. Here is another point of comparison between Han China and imperial Rome, where the writing of history also reached a high degree of cultivation and reflected a similar pride in accomplishment and the tradition that had led to it. The Roman ideal remained appealing to the European mind and still underlies much of the modern West, while in China the state system, the imperial model, and most of the other institutions and forms first established under the Han endured to shape the course of the next 2,000 years.

℩℧   ℩℧   ℩℧

*Modern civilization in China can be traced through the rise of the Shang, the first authenticated dynasty, about 1600 B.C., its conquest by the Chou about 1050 B.C., the warring-states period in the last centuries of nominal Chou rule, the Ch'in empire from 221 to 206 B.C., and the rise, flourishing, and decline of the Han from 202 B.C. to A.D. 220. The pattern of subsequent Chinese history was largely set by the achievement of the Han empire, much of it based in turn on the teachings of Confucius, who lived in the sixth century B.C. From local beginnings on the northern China plain under the Shang, the Chinese state and empire had grown by the end of the Han to incorporate most of the area within the borders of modern China. During the same centuries the traditional model of Chinese civilization was established, a model that was largely adhered to for the next 20 centuries.*

## Notes

1. J. J. L. Duyvendak, trans., *The Book of Lord Shang* (London: Arthur Probsthain, 1928), pp. 193–229 passim.

## Suggestions for Further Reading

Bodde, D. *China's First Unifier*. Hong Kong: Hong Kong University Press, 1967.

Chang, K. C. *The Archeology of Ancient China*, 4th ed. New Haven, Conn.: Yale University Press, 1987.

Creel, H. G. *The Origins of Statecraft in China*. Chicago: University of Chicago Press, 1970.

Dawson, R., ed. *The Legacy of China*. Oxford: Clarendon Press, 1964.

De Crespigny, R. *Northern Frontier Policies and Strategies of the Later Han Empire*. Canberra: Australian National University Press, 1985.

Elvin, M. *The Pattern of the Chinese Past*. Stanford, Calif.: Stanford University Press, 1973.

Fairbank, J. K. *China: Tradition and Transformation*. Boston: Houghton Mifflin, 1978.

Gernet, J. *A History of Chinese Civilization*, trans. J. R. Foster. Cambridge: Cambridge University Press, 1985.

Hsu, C. Y. *Ancient China in Transition: An Analysis of Social Mobility*. Stanford, Calif.: Stanford University Press, 1965.

———, and Linduff, K. M. *Western Chou Civilization*. New Haven, Conn.: Yale University Press, 1988.

Hucker, C. O. *China's Imperial Past*. Stanford, Calif.: Stanford University Press, 1975.

Li, C. *Anyang*. Seattle: University of Washington Press, 1976.

Liu, X. *Ancient China and Ancient India: Trade and Religious Exchange, A.D. 1–600*. New York: Oxford University Press, 1988.

Loewe, M. *Everyday Life in Early Imperial China*. New York: Putnam, 1968.

Meskill, J., ed. *An Introduction to Chinese Civilization*. Boston: Heath, 1973.

Needham, J. *Science in Traditional China*. Cambridge, Mass.: Harvard University Press, 1981.

Owen, S. *Remembrances: The Experience of the Past in Classical Chinese Literature*. Cambridge, Mass.: Harvard University Press, 1986.

Rubin, V. A. *Individual and State in Ancient China*. New York: Columbia University Press, 1976.

Schirokauer, C. *A Brief History of Chinese Civilization*. Orlando, Fla.: Harcourt Brace Jovanovich, 1991.

Schwarz, B. I. *The World of Thought in Ancient China*. Cambridge, Mass.: Harvard University Press, 1985.

Sullivan, M. *The Arts of China*. Berkeley: University of California Press, 1977.

Twitchett, D., ed. *The Cambridge History of China*. Vol. 1: *Ch'in and Han*. Cambridge: Cambridge University Press, 1986.

Wang, Z. *Han Civilization*. New Haven, Conn.: Yale University Press, 1982.

Watson, B. *Courtier and Commoner in Ancient China*. New York: Columbia University Press, 1977.

Watson, W. *Ancient China: Discoveries of Post-Liberation Archeology*. London: British Broadcasting Corporation, 1974.

Yu, Y. S. *Trade and Expansion in Han China*. Berkeley: University of California Press, 1967.

# Early and Classical Greece

Immigrants from the east arrived in the area around the Aegean Sea approximately 6000 B.C., bringing with them the newly developed agricultural techniques of the Neolithic period. For some 3,000 years life continued on a simple, pastoral basis. Around 3000 B.C. a brilliant and sophisticated Bronze Age culture began to develop, first among the Minoans of Crete and then, about 1650 B.C., among the Mycenaeans who inhabited the Greek peninsula. The Greeks of later ages knew little of those peoples because of the centuries of confusion and disorder that accompanied the decline of the Bronze Age around 1100 B.C.; they were the stuff of myths and legends rather than historical predecessors. Many Greek tales of later times are set in Bronze Age surroundings such as Thebes and Mycenae. Furthermore, the earliest Greek literary masterpieces, the works attributed to Homer, reflect a legendary interpretation of the Mycenaean past.

One of the major turning points of history in the Mediterranean region is the period around 1100 B.C., which marked the change from the Bronze Age to the Iron

This statuette of a Mycenaean woman, which dates from the fourteenth century B.C., was found on the island of Melos. [Lyvia Brown]

Age. Over the centuries that followed, a new culture began to develop in Greece that was to form the womb of Western civilization. By the fifth century B.C. Greek culture reached its zenith in the Classical Age.

## Neolithic Greece

Crossing to Europe by means of the Bosporus, people from Asia in search of new farmlands settled in northern Greece. From here some spread northwest into central Europe, while others moved south to central Greece and the rich plains of Thessaly. In time they built villages and manufactured fine pottery, often with painted decorations. These early settlers may have related the productivity of the earth to human fertility, for a number of little statues have been found, almost always of female nudes. On the Greek mainland, settlements such as Sesklo and its neighbor, Dimini, developed in relative isolation.

Meanwhile, on the island of Crete other settlers from Asia Minor founded their own communities. In many cases they chose to live in caves rather than construct drafty huts. Their pottery was elaborate and stylistically different from that of the mainland. The animals they reared included pigs, cattle, and sheep. None of these previously existed on Crete, and the transport of the original herds by sea from Asia must have presented a considerable challenge for their owners. The largest Neolithic settlement on Crete was at Knossos, the future site of the grandest of Bronze Age palaces.

The continuity of civilization at Knossos underlines the fact that the transition from stone to metal tools was gradual, producing no immediate revolution in ways of life. The Bronze Age on Crete began shortly after 2900 B.C. On the islands of the Cyclades in the eastern Aegean, bronze tools were in use by that date, and with them came other changes. The inhabitants of the Cycladic communities cut tombs in the rock or built them of stone, and with the dead they often buried weapons, a sign that the peace of the Neolithic farms was beginning to erode.

The people of the Cyclades also produced elegant sculpture, including marble statues that in many cases were buried with the dead together with weapons. These figurines, most of which represent women, vary in size from a few inches to 5 feet. The function of the statues is not clear. They may have been used as part of the funeral ceremony, and the fact that the overwhelming majority are female suggests that they too, like the earlier Neolithic figures, were forerunners of the cult of the Earth Mother.

Shortly after 2000 B.C. a new wave of invaders from the east moved into the Cyclades and eventually the Greek peninsula, to be followed by immigrants from the Balkans. The newcomers caused considerable disruption to the earlier settlers, and many of the mainland communities of this period constructed massive walls and towers to defend themselves. From the numerous warriors' graves it appears that life on the mainland was marked by frequent warfare waged between rival settlements. On Crete, however, the picture is different. Instead of retreating behind walled settlements, the population of the island, isolated from the troubles farther north, began to gather in urban centers. Here they developed the richest and most durable Bronze Age culture, that of the Minoans.

## The Minoans

In the Classical Age of the fifth and fourth centuries B.C., Crete's fame rested on its mythic past. The legendary King Minos had ruled there from his great palace at Knossos. The myths said that within the palace, at the center of a labyrinth, dwelt the Minotaur, a monster part man and part bull. To keep the monster alive Minos exacted an annual tribute from the mainlanders of seven youths and seven maidens, who were dispatched to Crete to feed the Minotaur.

In 1906, while excavating Knossos, the British archaeologist Arthur Evans discovered ancient remains. Five years later, after further excavations, he determined that the discoveries were those of a hitherto unknown Bronze Age civilization of extraordinary richness. The quantity and quality of the finds were overwhelming: ceramics, frescoes, inscriptions, and jewels. In one room Evans found a raised seat with a high back set against elaborate paintings, which he identified as the throne room of King Minos. The civilization that Evans had discovered was named Minoan after the legendary king.

The Early Minoan period (2900–2100 B.C.) was a time of slow expansion that laid the foundation for the brilliant culture of the Middle Minoan period (2100–1575 B.C.). During these later centuries the people of southern and eastern Crete constructed splendid palaces at such places as Knossos, Phaestus, and Mallia. The palaces, which included warehouses (mostly for grain, olive oil, and wine), workshops, and chapels, served as centers of government and production. The main structure of a Cretan palace was typically built around an open rectangular courtyard and contained religious shrines, public halls for banquets, and quarters for administrators. Other parts of the structure held royal living quarters and working areas for slaves and artisans. The palaces contained drainage systems and were designed to provide shade in the hot summer months and insulation against the winter cold. Surrounding the palace were the private houses of the aristocrats and chief religious leaders. Unlike royal palaces in western Asia, those on Crete were not surrounded by defensive walls. Archaeologists have unearthed no temples independent of the palace complexes.

Contacts with Egypt, Mesopotamia, and Asia Minor taught Cretan artisans to make pottery with a glasslike finish, stone vessels, and seals. Cretan pottery was soon in demand in Egypt, and Egyptian goldsmiths learned from their counterparts in Crete. The Cretans exported timber, mostly cypress, to Egypt in return for luxury items, especially ivory, precious stones, and gold. Cretan traders also maintained contacts with the Greek mainland, the islands of the Aegean, Cyprus, and probably Syria.

Around 1700 B.C. the palaces suffered severe damage, probably due to an earthquake, only to be reconstructed in an even grander manner. About a century later they were rebuilt again, probably for the same reason. These later palaces represent Minoan culture's highest achievement, and their wall paintings illustrate the elaborate court ceremonial. The Minoans left only a small amount of written material, some of it in pictographs and the rest in a syllabic script called Linear A. Although scholars cannot yet decipher more than a few words of Linear A, they believe it may have been derived from either a Semitic or an Anatolian script.

The rulers of these communities were male and apparently modeled their government on those of the kingdoms of western Asia. The principal Minoan deity, however, may have been a mother-goddess. Like the Great Mother of the Mesopotamians, she may have been a fertility figure, taking on a variety of forms associated at times with animals, at times with vegetation. The most famous religious image in Minoan art is the figure known as the Snake Goddess. The scenes of bull leaping depicted in Cretan art may reflect religious rites, which in all likelihood focused on the forces of nature; unlike the people of Çatal Hüyük, who venerated bulls, the Cretans sacrificed them. Minoan murals also suggest that men and women freely interacted in public life and that women danced publicly, perhaps in religious ceremonies or simply to entertain spectators.

At the beginning of the Late Minoan period (1575–1150 B.C.), Minoan artistic styles began to make an impact on the Greek mainland. The political and military power of the Minoans, however, was beginning to decline, and mainlanders seem to have occupied Knossos around 1460 B.C., not long after the city suffered a natural catastrophe (probably again an earthquake). In subsequent years Knossos, with a population of 50,000, subjected other palaces to its rule. Disaster—whether another natural catastrophe or an invasion is hotly debated—struck once more around 1400 B.C., after which time only small impoverished mountainous settlements survived the remaining centuries of the Bronze Age.

*Snake Goddess*, from the Temple Repository at Knossos, c. 1600 B.C. The figure probably represents a priestess rather than the goddess herself; she is wearing the characteristic Minoan open bodice and an apron, symbol of her religious function. [Hirmer Fotoarchiv, Munich]

# The Mycenaeans

The Mycenaeans, dominant in mainland Greece during the Bronze Age, are so called because the greatest and richest of their settlements was named Mycenae. Other Mycenaean communities in central Greece included Athens and Thebes, but most of their settlements were in southern Greece, an area known as the Peloponnesus. The Mycenaeans, like the Minoans, had their fame preserved in legend long before the discovery of their palaces. Their principal claim to renown was the war they launched in the later thirteenth century B.C. against the fortress of Troy on the Hellespont, whose rulers exacted tolls from passing shippers and amassed quantities of iron. The Trojan War and its consequences were celebrated in subsequent Greek poems attributed to Homer.

The German Heinrich Schliemann (A.D. 1822–1890) devoted much of his life to demonstrating that the Homeric legends were based on real events. In 1870 he began work at the site of what he believed to be Troy, in modern Turkey. During the next three years he uncovered the town's walls and gate as well as gold, silver, and bronze jewelry and weapons. On the basis of these finds, Schliemann then set out to discover the Mycenaeans who had been responsible for the Trojan War. In 1876 he excavated inside the walls of Mycenae, where he discovered the cemetery known as the Royal Grave Circle, consisting of impressive pits cut into the rock. The gold treasures found in the shafts date to 1550–1500 B.C., a time when Mycenaean power had begun to expand.

Mycenaean culture was influenced by the Minoans, particularly in its artistic style and possibly in its system of writing as well. The Minoans' Linear A script may have inspired the development of a Mycenaean script, Linear B, an early form of Greek. But unlike the Minoans, the Mycenaeans built their principal settlements, including Mycenae, Tiryns, and Pylos, on hills for defensive purposes. Their palaces were surrounded by walls, and even Mycenaean art emphasizes military motifs as well as hunting. Mycenaean kings amassed considerable wealth and governed with the aid of bureaucrats who kept records of taxes, the property and livestock of their subjects, and the stocks of assorted commodities. As the principal power in the western Mediterranean world after the decline of the Minoans, the Mycenaeans traded not only with the peoples of the Italian peninsula and Sicily but also with those of Egypt and western Asia. They even established trading colonies in the eastern Mediterranean. Commercial rivalry or a quest for iron apparently prompted the Mycenaeans to attack Troy sometime between 1250 and 1200 B.C.

Shortly after the assault on Troy, some Mycenaean palaces, including Pylos and Mycenae, were destroyed by invaders. The sea raiders who attacked the Hittite empire, Syria, Palestine, and Egypt about the same time may have been responsible. Possibly they were the Philistines, who settled in Palestine in the early twelfth century. In any event, during the twelfth century the remaining Mycenaean palaces suffered extensive damage, partly at the hands of the invaders but possibly also because of fighting among themselves. When Mycenaean power crumbled, the population began to decline sharply, the number of settlements drastically decreased, and many of the survivors migrated to safer regions, such as the mountainous area in the northern Peloponnesus, the eastern coast of Attica, the coasts of Asia Minor, the Aegean islands, and Cyprus.

*Mask of Agamemnon*, c. 1550 B.C., the death mask of one of the earliest Mycenaean rulers. It was one of five death masks found in the Royal Grave Circle. [Hirmer Fotoarchiv, Munich]

## The Homeric Epics and the Dark Age

In most important areas the Greeks of the ensuing Dark Age (c. 1100–800 B.C.) had to develop afresh almost all the techniques of the visual arts, architecture, literature, and the ability to write. All but the simplest manufacturing disappeared. Much of this decline has traditionally been blamed on the migration of Dorian-speaking Greeks into the southern part of the peninsula, but the primary cause was the series of invasions that we have noted.

Although there are no written or artistic records from the Dark Age, we can reconstruct something about life in this period from the two great epic poems that emerged from it. The *Iliad* and the *Odyssey* are traditionally attributed to Homer, but modern scholars generally agree that they were composed by a number of poets over a long period of time and possibly compiled or put into definitive form by one of them. The first version was probably produced in the ninth century B.C., and the poems were apparently in more or less their present form by 700 B.C.

Both works have the Trojan War as their background. Throughout them are fitful glimpses of the world of the Bronze Age, and some of the tales may well have been passed down from that earlier period. For the most part, though, the Homeric world reflects life in Greece during the Dark Age. The poems, especially the *Iliad*, reflect such aristocratic values as heroic combat as well as the quest for booty, but they also explore human strengths and weaknesses. The Greek historian Herodotus would later comment that Homer and the seventh-century B.C. poet Hesiod gave the Greeks their gods; certainly they shaped the vision of later generations, who saw their deities at least in part as projections of themselves, human but for their immortality.

Like *The Epic of Gilgamesh* and the Vedas, the Homeric epics were shaped orally. In their early stages the poems were recited by itinerant professional bards who traveled throughout the Greek world. Their audiences consisted of the small groups of aristocrats who ruled each community in the Dark Age. Apart from assorted clues in the epics, our impression of the lives of these communities is limited, for the most part, to the objects buried with the dead. Certainly some of the graves of the ninth and eighth centuries B.C. in the Dipylon Cemetery at Athens suggest a considerable concentration of wealth and power in the hands of a few.

## Greece and the Mediterranean

By 800 B.C. Greek civilization had entered a new phase. Literacy had been recovered, with an alphabet borrowed from the Phoenicians and adapted to the Greek tongue. Extensive trade resumed, and the pressures of a growing population produced both social conflict and colonization. Ambitious Greeks traveled overseas in search of wealth. A number of the colonies they founded, such as Syracuse in Sicily and Croton in southern Italy, grew richer and more powerful than their mother cities. Colonies were also founded in Egypt and around the Black Sea. It was perhaps inevitable that intercity rivalries accompanied the settlers, often creating tension in their

## ◉ Homer's World ◉

*In describing the scenes decorating the shield Hephaistos made for Achilles, Homer paints a picture of his own early Iron Age world.*

On it he wrought in all their beauty two cities of mortal men. And there were
   marriages in one, and festivals.
They were leading the brides along the city from their maiden chambers under the
   flaring of torches, and the loud bride song was arising.
The young men followed the circles of the dance, and among them the flutes and
   lyres kept up their clamor as in the meantime the women standing each at the
   door of her court admired them.
The people were assembled in the market place, where a quarrel had arisen, and
   two men were disputing over the blood price for a man who had been killed.
One man promised full restitution in a public statement, but the other refused and
   would accept nothing.
Both then made for an arbitrator, to have a decision; and people were speaking up
   on either side, to help both men.
But the heralds kept the people in hand, as meanwhile the elders were in session on
   benches of polished stone in the sacred circle and held in their hands the staves
   of the heralds who lift their voices.
The two men rushed before these, and took turns speaking their cases, and between
   them lay on the ground two talents of gold, to be given to that judge who in this
   case spoke the straightest opinion.

*Source:* Homer, *The Iliad*, trans. R. Lattimore (Chicago: University of Chicago Press, 1961), bk. 18, ll. 490–508, p. 388.

relations with each other and with the communities of the Greek homeland.

Simultaneously, along the coast of Asia Minor the Greek settlements founded in the Dark Age established trade links with much of western Asia; these were to have important consequences for Greek culture. After several centuries of isolation, the Greeks came into contact with the developed cultures of western Asia and Egypt, which they rapidly assimilated. So profound was the effect of western Asian art on the Greeks from the late eighth century to around 600 B.C. that the artistic style of this period is called "orientalizing."

As the Greeks continued to expand, they gradually shaped the characteristic sociopolitical institution that they called the *polis*. Each of the *poleis* was an independent political unit consisting of a town or village and the surrounding territory, the inhabitants of which were bound together in a community based on kinship relations. Geographic conditions in Greece played a crucial role in shaping these small political units, for the mountainous terrain encouraged communities to develop in relative isolation. Communication was difficult; unlike

Mesopotamia and Egypt, the Greek peninsula has no major rivers, although many communities had ready access to the sea and to the myriad islands that dot the Aegean.

The polis provided the basis for social, political, religious, and cultural life. The loyalty of its citizens toward their city was far more powerful than any sense of fellowship with other Greeks. The resulting competitive spirit eventually produced fierce rivalries. The polis was thus both the most distinctive achievement of Greek civilization and its most destructive element, nurturing both incomparable intellectual and cultural achievement and a tendency to chronic intercommunal rivalry.

Many poleis deliberately sent out colonizers as a way to release tensions and population pressures at home. The success of the colonizers often created new problems, however. The wealth made possible by colonial trade produced unsettled conditions both abroad and in the mother cities in Greece. The more prosperous the polis, the more likely a political upheaval created by the newly powerful traders, manufacturers, and farmers, who challenged the traditional elites. In these unstable

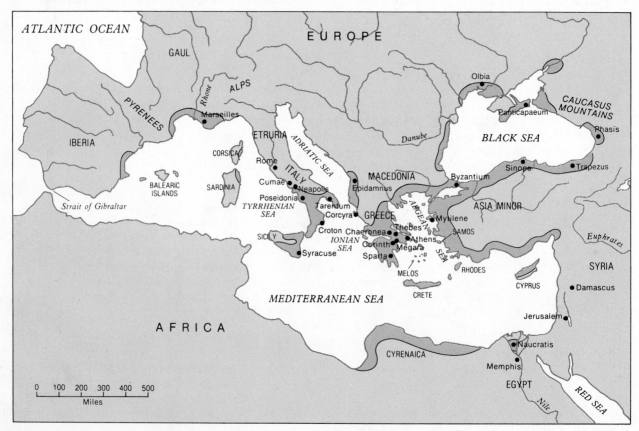

*4.1 Greek Influence in the Mediterranean, c. 550 B.C.*

conditions, power in many of the poleis was seized by local leaders with popular support. The Greeks called these revolutionary leaders "tyrants." The term was not derogatory; it meant simply those who attained office through insurrection or, sometimes, consensus. Indeed, many tyrants became famous for their public works and enlightened rule, although there was no shortage of those whose behavior explains the notoriety of the term in later times.

The experience of Corinth was typical of many poleis that willingly submitted to tyrants. Corinth was among the richest Greek cities in this period. Corinthian colonies were established in the west, and Corinthian vases, oil, and perfume were exported throughout the Mediterranean. This growth of the trading class undermined the old aristocracy, and around 655 B.C. Cypselus overthrew them and became tyrant of Corinth. Supposedly related to the ruling family he had overturned, he governed for 30 years. It was a mark of his popularity that he never had a bodyguard.

The success of Cypselus illustrates the basic conditions that made possible the phenomenon of the tyrants. On the one hand, tyranny was a form of monarchy. Not only did the tyrants wield power, but they passed it on to their descendants; Cypselus was succeeded by his son, Periander. On the other hand, the tyrants could continue to rule only if they maintained popular support. The citizen-militia that often gave them power in the first place could, and did, dislodge them if that proved necessary.

These citizen-armies were made possible by a new form of warfare that had developed in the late eighth century B.C. Previously, fighting had been undertaken by small troops of mounted horsemen and individual champions, who dueled with spears and swords. The new military style involved large numbers of armed infantrymen, called *hoplites*, who fought in a tightly organized block, or *phalanx*. As long as the phalanx remained intact, it was virtually indestructible. Because the hoplite needed only a shield, a sword, a pike, a breastplate, and leg armor, it was economically feasible to organize citizen-armies, especially since each hoplite had to provide his own equipment. The absence of a standing professional army that could be used by an oppressive ruler against his people was the ultimate guarantee of popular control. Paradoxically, therefore, the concentration of power in the hands of one person, checked by the citizen-militia, made possible a general move toward wider community participation in the affairs of government.

The social and economic discontents that gave rise to the tyrants were not always resolved as in the case of Cypselus. At Miletus in Asia Minor, the center of the earliest school of Greek philosophy, the common people rose up against the aristocrats who ruled them and slaughtered their wives and children; when the aristocrats regained power, they roasted their opponents alive.

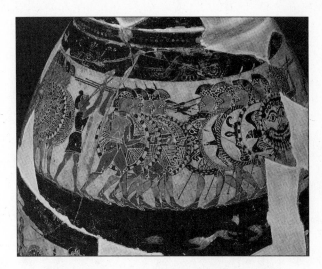

The scene painted on this Corinthian vase shows hoplites in close formation marching into battle. [SCALA/Art Resource]

A number of the tyrants were famous for their achievements. Polycrates, tyrant of Samos, commissioned a long protective harbor mole and a new water system cut through the rock, as well as an enormous temple to Hera. The aqueduct ran over 3,000 feet and carried a waterpipe in a channel 3½ feet high. At many cities, as on the island of Samos, outer defensive walls were constructed for the first time since the Mycenaean era, thereby defining the urban core, as well as reflecting the increased rivalry among the poleis.

The new merchant traders and the tyrants who ruled them were often patrons of artistic projects intended to perpetuate their memory and fame. The sculptures they commissioned were the first life-size stone figures in Western art. The earliest surviving figures, dating to the mid- and late seventh century B.C., are stiff and formalized, with flat planes and rigid stances. These figures, both male and female, showed Egyptian influence. Yet whereas Egyptian statuary emphasized the undulating surfaces of the skin, from the beginning Greek sculptors manifested their primary interest in rendering bone structure and anatomy. By the middle of the next century Greek sculptors had learned to produce works with individual character and in doing so developed a new style in art that reached its fulfillment in the Classical Age. The intermediate period beginning around 600 B.C., during which the Greeks gradually eliminated orientalizing elements from their art and developed their own style, is known as the Archaic period. It was during this period as well that pottery and vase-painting reached their highest development. Most subjects represented were mythological scenes, but many showed everyday

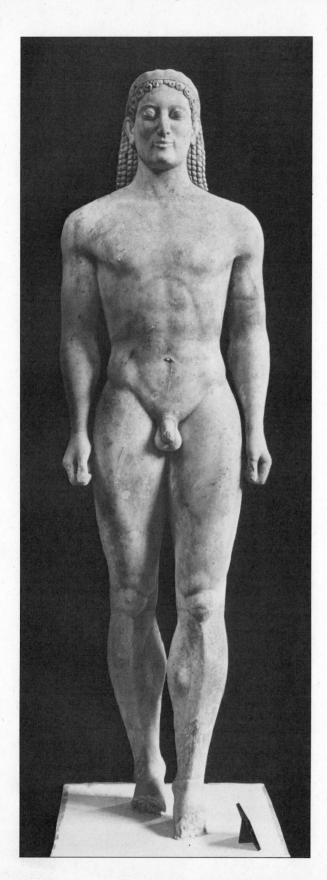

activities and events, including games and revels, and some depicted erotic acts with considerable frankness.

In literature two new forms emerged. The heroic verse of Homer had served the ruling class of an aristocratic society, with the leisure to hear about the deeds of mighty leaders such as Achilles. The poets of the age of the tyrants were more interested in individual feelings and emotions, and the medium invented to express their feelings about life, death, and love was lyric poetry.

Hesiod, who lived in Boeotia in the seventh century B.C., is chiefly remembered for his *Works and Days*, an almanac in verse that praised peasants rather than aristocrats, frugality rather than ostentatiousness, and hard work rather than heroic adventures. Himself of humble birth, he demonstrated no comparable concern for slaves or women. Wives, in his view, were either obnoxious because of their nagging or contemptible because of their unthinking obedience. Hesiod's pessimism shaped his view of history, which he saw as a relentless decline from a golden age free of toil and pain to a future overwhelmed by labor, anguish, and death in which infants would be born with gray hair, decency would perish, might would take precedence over right, and family relationships would disintegrate. Hesiod's *Theogony (Creation of the Gods)* collected many of the religious myths that reflected Hellenic belief, giving shape and coherence to the scattered stories and conflicting chronologies that profoundly influenced future generations.

Another early lyric poet was Archilochus (c. 678 B.C.), whose work exhibited antiheroic elements, as in these lines:

> Some Thracian is proudly wearing the shield I
>     left behind;
> It was a fine one, but I had to throw it into a
>     bush.
> Anyway I saved my life, so why worry about the
>     shield?
> I can always get another one just as good.[1]

---

## ❦
## SAPPHO AND THE POETRY OF LOVE

---

Although women played an important part in Greek mythology and religion, we have almost no account of their experience from their own hands. Virtually all of our

**The base of this kouros, c. 530 B.C., bears an inscription saying that the statue represents a young man, Kroisos, who died heroically in battle. The hairstyle and rigid pose reflect Egyptian influence. [Marburg/Art Resource; National Archaeological Museum, Athens]**

knowledge is derived from sources written by men, and Sappho, the first Greek woman to enshrine her personal experiences in literary form, is therefore an important exception.

Sappho was born around 612 B.C. on the island of Lesbos, where she lived most of her life. She apparently combined the domestic functions of wife and mother with her writing and teaching. She earned considerable admiration as a poet during her own lifetime and taught younger women on Lesbos. The warm bond between Sappho and her students was deep, for it recurs as a constant theme in her poetry. Her appearance itself is uncertain: one ancient authority described her as a "beautiful day," while a less complimentary commentator said that "physically she was very ugly, being small and dark, like a nightingale with misshapen wings enfolding a tiny body." A contemporary poet described her as "violet-haired, pure and honey-smiling." In the ancient world the women of Lesbos were notorious in the popular imagination for shameless, uninhibited sexual behavior. Sappho's poetry makes clear her sexual feeling for other women, but we have no evidence that her contemporaries thought this unseemly. Erotic friendship played an important role in Greek society, both between women and between men.

The principal topic of Sappho's poetry is love; the only one of her poems to survive intact is a prayer to Aphro-

**Sappho, as depicted in a Spartan mosaic dating from around the fourth century A.D. [Caroline Buckler]**

dite, the goddess of sexual love, expressing Sappho's fondness for an unnamed young woman about to be married. In other works Sappho expresses the conflicting

---

### ◉ Sappho's Poetry ◉

*This poem by Sappho exemplifies the directness and emotional intensity of her work.*

#### Seizure

*To me that man equals a god
as he sits before you and listens
closely to your sweet voice*

*and lovely laughter—which troubles
the heart in my ribs. For now
as I look at you my voice fails*

*my tongue is broken and thin fire
runs like a thief through my body.
My eyes are dead to light, my ears*

*pound, and sweat pours down over me.
I shudder, I am paler than grass,
and I am intimate with dying—but*

*I must suffer everything, being poor.*

*Source: Sappho,* trans. W. Barnstone (New York: Doubleday/Anchor Books, 1965), p. 11.

emotions of isolation and of intense erotic involvement. Her tone is distinctive, but her theme, the celebration of sexual love, is quite common in Greek culture.

Sappho's writing shows a remarkably objective self-awareness, and she makes it clear that the agony her love often causes her is worth the price. Her most outstanding gift is her skill in describing the complexity of her emotional responses. In the same way as sixth-century B.C. sculptors and painters understood the workings of the human body by portraying it, Sappho revealed the process of her personal development. In so doing, she learned to temper her feelings, and much of her work expresses the kind of resignation that is the fruit of deep self-understanding. Throughout antiquity Sappho's work evoked the highest praise. Plato described her as "the tenth muse," and the Hellenistic poet Meleager said of her poems that they were "few but roses." In Roman times poets such as Catullus and Horace imitated her forms, and from there they were passed down into the long history of European lyric poetry.

## The Growth of the Polis

The political ideal of the polis involved the devotion of the citizens to their city-state at the expense of any wider community. This had practical consequences wherever the Greeks settled. A polis that represented the collective image of its citizens needed to have impressive public buildings and, if possible, an organized town plan. In the case of the older cities of the Greek mainland, cluttered by the buildings of several centuries, planners and architects were constrained by the work of their predecessors. Where new sites were settled, however, as at Poseidonia in southern Italy (better known by its Roman name, Paestum), streets were laid in straight lines to form city blocks, intersected by other streets running at right angles. At a convenient flat space within the city was the main square, or *agora*, surrounded by the principal public buildings, where the citizens could meet both formally and informally. The inhabitants of Paestum embellished their city with impressive temples, constructed between 550 and 450 B.C.

If great buildings could give visible character to a city, so could coinage. The coins each city minted bore a figure or design that identified its origins. Corinthian coins, for example, showed Pegasus, the legendary winged horse, which, according to the myth, was born at the fountain in Corinth's main square. The citizens of Metapontum, the fertile plain of southeast Italy, chose an ear of grain as their symbol.

Coins and manufactured objects such as pottery and terra-cotta statues were used to pay for raw materials the Greeks lacked. One basic commodity, iron, was close at hand in central and northern Italy, and a thriving trade developed between the western Greek colonies and the

The scene on this fifth-century B.C. Attic vase depicts a pottery workshop; on the left a painter is decorating a vessel. [Ashmolean Museum, Oxford]

Etruscans. The individual cities often established their own trade patterns. The citizens of Aegina in central Greece transported grain from their colonies on the Black Sea back to the mother city. In some cases cities were founded precisely to serve as exchange ports, as in the case of Naucratis in Egypt.

The most complete demonstration of the sense of the Greeks' pride in their own cities was provided by the athletic festivals at which they came together to compete against one another. Olympia, Delphi, and Nemea were known as Panhellenic (all-Greek) shrines, and games were held at each of them. Victors, upon their return home, were given a civic welcome at public expense.

In all these ways individual citizens were constantly reminded of the differences between themselves and their fellow Greeks. Certain shared characteristics were never lost. The Greek language and alphabet varied slightly from one part of the Greek world to another, but not enough to prevent communication. Furthermore, although there were regional variations in Greek religious practices and beliefs, there was enough common ground to sustain the great Panhellenic sanctuaries such as Delphi. Yet apart from these common events and observances, and a shared artistic taste, even neighboring poleis failed to develop a sense of community until after the Macedonian conquest of the fourth century B.C. That conquest was a direct result of divisive civic pride and of the great fifth-century civil war that had fatally weakened them.

However flawed in practice, the Greek civic ideal represents a distinctive concept in the development of civilization. From the earliest history of Egypt and Mesopotamia, the city had represented the focus of political, economic, and technological development. For the Greeks, their poleis took on a moral significance that transcended any sense of nationhood. The polis represented a complete and self-contained way of life in which each adult male citizen had his civic and moral being. During the relatively brief period of its ascendancy as the dominant political body of the eastern Mediterranean, it nurtured a culture of astonishing fecundity, diversity, and brilliance.

## Athens and the Birth of Democracy

The greatest of the poleis was Athens, situated strategically on the Attic peninsula, with easy access to the Aegean Sea. To later ages Athens symbolized the pinnacle of Greek civilization. Its beginnings, however, were modest. While other Greek poleis were founding colonies abroad and developing politically at home, Athenian society in the eighth and seventh centuries B.C. underwent no dramatic changes. There was little or no rise in population and virtually no overseas trade. The would-be tyrant Cylon attempted to overthrow the aristocratic government in 632 or 628 B.C. but failed for lack of popular support. However, the continuing power of the wealthy aristocracy combined with the increasing poverty of the peasantry was ominous. Growing numbers of poor Athenians were reduced to the state of pledging themselves and their families as security against their debts. When they were unable to pay, they were sold into slavery, often abroad, a fate that many avoided by fleeing into exile.

The Athenian solution to this social and economic problem was characteristically daring and farseeing.

GREEK CIVILIZATION

| Period | Important events | Cultural highlights |
|---|---|---|
| Bronze Age (3000–1100 B.C.) | ● Minoan civilization<br>● Mycenaean civilization | ● Minoan frescoes and statuettes |
| Dark Age (1100–800 B.C.) | ● Calamity and recovery<br>● Development of the polis | ● Homeric epics<br>● Hesiod's poems |
| Age of Expansion (800–500 B.C.) | ● Colonization of the Mediterranean<br>● Rise of Athens, Sparta, and Corinth<br>● Age of the Tyrants | ● Lyric poets<br>● Ionian school of philosophers<br>● Archaic sculpture |
| Classical Age (500–338 B.C.) | ● Persian Wars<br>● Growth of Athenian empire<br>● Age of Pericles<br>● Peloponnesian War<br>● Spartan and Theban hegemonies<br>● Philip of Macedon conquers Greece | ● Herodotus<br>● Thucydides<br>● Aeschylus<br>● Sophocles<br>● Euripides<br>● Parthenon<br>● Myron<br>● Plato<br>● Aristotle |

Around 594 B.C. the Areopagus, a council of wealthy citizens, gave the archon (magistrate) Solon special powers to introduce sweeping reforms. The alternative was a social and political revolution. An aristocrat, a poet, and a man of wide cultural interests as well as a trader with extensive experience abroad, Solon gave shape to the development of an Athenian constitution that was to last 200 years. He abolished all agrarian debts and restored freedom to all Athenians who had been sold into slavery. To enhance the city's commercial prosperity, he reformed the coinage and encouraged skilled artisans to immigrate to Athens in return for citizenship.

In addition, Solon devised a more broadly based system of government. Athens had traditionally had a popular assembly as well as the Areopagus and an executive of nine archons, but the assembly had had little effective power. Decision making had rested in the hands of the aristocratic magistrates and the Areopagus. Under Solon's reforms, all citizens received the right to vote in the assembly, although only landowners could qualify as citizens. At the other end of the scale, high offices were no longer limited to males born within the old aristocracy but opened to all wealthy men. With the exception of poor laborers, all male citizens qualified for membership in a new Council of Four Hundred, which comprised 100 members selected from each of the four Athenian tribes. The Council discussed proposed legislation before it was submitted to the assembly for final approval or rejection.

Although hindsight suggests that these reforms were essential to the stability of Athens, Solon was not uniformly popular. The aristocrats feared for the erosion of their power, and the poorer citizens were at first disappointed and then enraged at the absence of any real redistribution of wealth or land. Ultimately disappointed by their complaints, Solon, according to tradition, castigated his fellow Athenians as "individual foxes and collective geese."

In solving old problems, Solon's reforms created new political rivalries. As competing factions jockeyed for power, Pisistratus, an aristocrat, twice attempted to seize control, failing both times. Returning with a mercenary army and new financial resources acquired from his gold-mining operations in northern Greece, he finally attained power in 546 B.C. and ruled as tyrant until 527. Large sections of the population, especially the small farmers, supported him, not least because he helped them with loans to plant their crops. His encouragement of overseas trade also aided them by providing expanded markets for their olive oil and wine. But although Pisistratus enjoyed substantial popular support and left the democratic machinery of government intact, the traditional institutions exercised no independent power.

The tyranny of Pisistratus and his sons Hipparchus and Hippias, who ruled after him until 510 B.C., marked the first sustained period of peace and economic growth in Athenian history. The peaceful conditions enjoyed at this time encouraged cultural developments, and at Athens itself the period of Pisistratus' rule was one of great artistic development. Vase painters such as Exekias and Amasis produced works of exquisite refinement and skill that were increasingly sought abroad. In sculpture, artists continued to move toward more naturalistic styles, applying their techniques not only to freestanding figures but to relief carving as well. The expanding overseas trade encouraged the arts by increasing the de-

---

### ◉ Solon on Injustice ◉

*In this fragment of verse, Solon, the reformer of Athenian political life, expresses his own perplexity at the injustices of the world.*

*In every activity there is danger, nor does anyone know,
at an enterprise's start, where he will end up.
One man, striving to do what is right, but lacking foresight,
falls headlong into great folly and great hardship,
while to another who acts wrongly, God in all things gives
pure good luck, redemption from his own thoughtlessness . . .*

*The immortals bestow rich profits upon men,
but folly often appears as the result, which when Zeus
sends it to punish, strikes now this man, now that one.*

*Source:* J. J. Pollitt, *Art and Experience in Classical Greece* (Cambridge: Cambridge University Press, 1972), p. 4.

mand for Attic pottery. To pay for an ambitious building program (including new temples), however, Pisistratus introduced a tax system based on income from land that many Athenians found oppressive.

Enamored of extravagant, pleasure-filled lives, Pisistratus' sons failed to maintain their father's legacy of civil peace. After a group of young Athenians assassinated Hipparchus in 514 B.C., Hippias employed severe repressive measures against his real and supposed enemies. In 510, however, he was driven into exile by a group of Athenian nobles led by Cleisthenes, a reformer who looked to the people for his political support. Cleisthenes' success was made possible by the assistance of

Athens' archrival, Sparta, whose army, led by King Cleomenes, helped expel Hippias. Presumably Cleomenes hoped that Hippias would be replaced by a friendly government that would be more to the Spartans' aristocratic taste. Cleisthenes, however, proved to be democratic. The Spartans, together with the more conservative Athenian aristocrats, drove him out of Athens for a brief period. In the end, however, popular will triumphed. Cleomenes and his allies reluctantly withdrew, and in 508 Cleisthenes returned to Athens.

Like Solon, Cleisthenes set out to produce a more broadly based government. The citizens were given membership in *demes*, or local districts, that were then

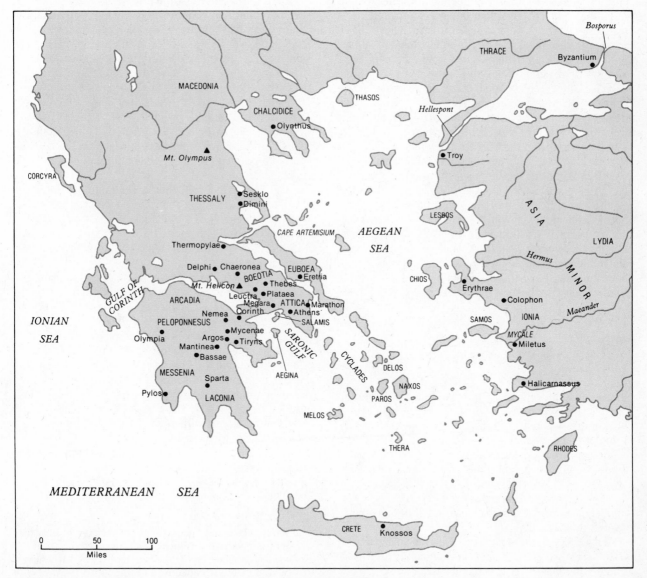

*4.2 Classical Greece*

combined in such a way as to cut across the old borders of tribes and factions. The day-to-day business of running the state was entrusted to the *Boule*, or People's Council, consisting of 500 members. Fifty men were chosen by lot from each of the city's ten new tribes and served a term of one year. Each group of 50 supervised the magistrates one-tenth of the year. The Council supervised the routine work of running the state: control of expenditures, organization of religious festivals, and superintendence of buildings and other public works. The Council also assumed the responsibility of the now defunct Council of Four Hundred to act as a steering committee for the Popular Assembly by preparing legislation for its consideration.

Under Cleisthenes' new constitution, all adult male citizens continued to serve as members of the Popular Assembly. It met three or four times a month, and major business could not be transacted unless at least 6,000 members were present. The Assembly debated all proposals put before it by the Council before passing them into law or rejecting them, thus providing for a direct exercise of sovereignty by all citizens who chose to participate. By rotating membership and offices, Cleisthenes ensured that a large number of Athenian citizens would have practical experience in civic administration. The Areopagus and the magistrates retained their aristocratic character, but with decreased authority.

When Solon had been called to power around 594 B.C., Athens was a polis of relatively minor significance. By the end of that century the Athenians had become a major political force. With the prosperity acquired during the years of Pisistratus and their newly won political freedom, they were soon to become the most energetic and influential power in the Greek world. First, however, both they and their fellow Greeks had to face a threat from a source far beyond their borders: Persia.

## The Persian Wars

In the seventh century B.C. the two principal powers to the east of Greece were Lydia and Persia. The Lydian kings were generally well disposed toward the Greeks, some of whom settled in colonies on the coast of Asia Minor, an area known as Ionia. The Greeks learned much from contacts with their eastern neighbor; coinage, probably invented in Lydia, had first been introduced into Europe around 625 B.C. Greek relations with the Persians were less friendly, although trade contacts apparently existed.

In 546 B.C. the kingdom of Lydia fell to Cyrus the Great of Persia, who added to his conquests the Greek colonies in Ionia and installed Persian governors. In 513 and 512 the Persian king, Darius (522–486 B.C.), led a great campaign to subdue southeastern Europe. The expedition was unsuccessful, however, and for the moment the Persians withdrew, preoccupied with problems in central Asia.

Discontented with their Persian governors and the taxes levied to support Persian interests, the Ionians took advantage of the temporary relaxation of imperial control. In 499 B.C. they launched a rebellion and called on their fellow Greeks to the west for help. Only the Athenians and their allies the Eretrians, inhabitants of a minor polis on the island of Euboea in the western Aegean, sent ships and men. Their support could not save the Ionians from defeat. By 494 the last city to hold out, Miletus, was sacked after a decisive naval battle off its shore.

Darius, displeased by the interference of Athens and Eretria, reportedly ordered a servant to say to him three times every day before dinner: "Sire, remember the Athenians." Revenge was not long in coming. In 490 the king's troops sailed across the Aegean and sacked Eretria. Proceeding south toward Athens, they landed at Marathon Bay north of the city to face an outnumbered Athenian army. The Athenians had desperately sought support from other Greeks in their struggle against mighty Persia, particularly from Sparta. The Spartans declined, offering the convenient excuse that the celebration of a religious festival prevented them from leaving home.

The Persians, despite their greater number, were less flexible in their tactics than the Athenians. Under the brilliant generalship of Miltiades, the Athenian soldiers outflanked the Persians and drove them back to their ships or into the marshy shore, where thousands were trampled to death.

The Persians had been stopped only temporarily. The Athenians, under the leadership of the archon Themistocles (527–460 B.C.), built new warships and fortifications and cultivated allies. When the Persians returned under Darius' son Xerxes in 480, they found a combined Greek army with some semblance of unity. The subsequent battles and the final Greek triumph represent one of the high points of Greek history. Having marched virtually unopposed through northern Greece, the Persians were blocked at the pass of Thermopylae by 300 Spartans, together with several thousand other Greek soldiers. Only treachery on the part of local Greeks enabled the Persians to encircle the defenders, who were reputedly massacred to a man. The Greek historian Herodotus, born shortly before the war began, describes the last stage of the battle:

**The Greeks under Leonidas [the Spartan general], as they now went forth determined to die, advanced. . . . They . . . carried slaughter among the barbarians, who fell in heaps. Behind them the captains of the squadrons, armed with whips, urged their men forward with continual blows.**

Many were thrust into the sea, and there perished; a still greater number were trampled to death by their own soldiers; no one heeded the dying. . . . They defended themselves to the last, such as still had swords using them, and the others resisting with their hands and teeth; till the barbarians . . . overwhelmed and buried the remnant left beneath showers of missile weapons.[2]

The Persians proceeded toward Athens, still the object of their vengeance. They found the city abandoned, occupied it, and destroyed many of its buildings. But the Athenians had brought away their fleet and treasury intact, and they engaged the Persians in the narrow straits between the Attic mainland and the island of Salamis, where Athenian experience proved decisive. A few months later, in 479 B.C., the remaining Persian land forces were defeated at Plataea.

The details of the Greeks' success were chronicled by Herodotus, whose account is the earliest surviving prose record in the West of historical events. Herodotus is often called the "father of history." His explanation of the Greek victory in his *History of the Persian Wars* shows how the Greeks explained their success: The Persian defeat was the result not only of Greek arms but also of the Persians' moral flaw—*hubris*, or excessive ambition. The Greek victory thus demonstrated the triumph of justice over brute force and proved that the gods, who had helped determine the war's outcome, were on the side of right. In Herodotus' mind, the war had been fought to preserve not only the independence of the Greek poleis but also the rule of law, which had been directly threatened by the invaders from the east. Thus the conflict was important not only for its immediate outcome but also as a source of future Greek perceptions about Asia. The war sharpened the Greeks' sense of their separate identity, and that notion of Western distinctiveness was subsequently inherited by the Romans.

Herodotus also saw the war as the beginning of three generations of trouble for the Greeks, caused at least in part by disputes among themselves. Nevertheless, the Greeks' victory had been made possible by the fact that they had managed to unite in the face of a common enemy. Their success marked the high point of Greek political cooperation, but this unity proved only temporary.

# Athens in the Age of Pericles: Democracy and Imperialism

The Athenian leader during much of the late fifth century B.C. was Pericles, whose name now symbolizes the

Cresilas carved *Pericles* around 440 B.C. (this Roman marble copy was based on the original). An idealized image rather than a realistic portrait, the sculpture shows Pericles wearing a helmet, symbolic of his office as general. [Alinari/Art Resource]

glories of Athens' Golden Age. Born to an aristocratic family around 495 B.C., Pericles entered politics and by 457 had become the unofficial leader of Athens, although he ran for public office every year like other magistrates. He devoted his efforts to glorifying Athens by constructing the majestic buildings on the Acropolis that still testify to the grandeur of his age.

Pericles did not rule Athens in the sense that a modern head of state does. The Athenians governed themselves by the participation of every adult male citizen in the Popular Assembly. Any member of this body could address it and try to convince it of his point of view. Frequently the Assembly would follow Pericles' advice, but his authority was personal, not constitutional.

## ◉ Pericles on the Government of Athens ◉

*In a speech on the occasion of the public funeral of the Athenian war
dead, delivered in the fall of 430 B.C., Pericles describes his view of the
Athenian system of government.*

Let me say that our system of government does not copy the institutions of our neighbors.
It is more the case of our being a model to others, than of our imitating anyone else. Our
constitution is called a democracy because power is in the hands not of a minority but of
the whole people. When it is a question of settling private disputes, everyone is equal before the law; when it is a question of putting one person before another in positions of
public responsibility, what counts is not membership of a particular class, but the actual
ability which the man possesses. No one, so long as he has it in him to be of service to the
state, is kept in political obscurity because of poverty. And, just as our political life is free
and open, so is our day-to-day life in our relations with each other. We do not get into a
state with our next-door neighbor if he enjoys himself in his own way, nor do we give him
the kind of black looks which, though they do no real harm, still do hurt people's feelings.
We are free and tolerant in our private lives; but in public affairs we keep to the law. This
is because it commands our deep respect.

*Source:* Thucydides, *History of the Peloponnesian War*, trans. R. Warner (Harmondsworth, England: Penguin Books, 1954), p. 117.

Few Athenians, presumably, would have disagreed
with Pericles' conviction of the superiority of their city.
He claimed, according to the historian Thucydides, that
Athens was "the school of Greece," its natural political
and cultural leader, and his plans were devoted to maintaining and increasing its greatness. His patriotism inspired him and his fellow Athenians to combine political
liberty at home for citizens with control of an empire
abroad.

## ❀
## LIFE IN PERICLEAN ATHENS

By the mid-fifth century the male citizen population of
Athens numbered about 40,000 to 45,000. Including
women and children the total population was probably
around 170,000, with perhaps the same number of
slaves. In 451, however, a law was passed limiting citizenship to those whose parents were both Athenian. The
new decree may have prevented a flood of immigration
from Athens' allies, states that remained voluntarily or
involuntarily bound to it after the Persian wars. The decree did not, however, soothe the allies' resentment of
Athens' military and political domination.

Each Athenian citizen could be called on to participate in the daily running of Athens as well as in the de-
liberations of the Assembly. Citizens had the duty to
serve as magistrates. The nine archons, who in Solon's
time had been drawn from the aristocracy, were now
chosen by lot. They had been supplemented as chief
magistrates by ten generals, who were elected by the
ten tribes. Pericles held the office of general for many
years, and during his tenure the generals played as large
a part in domestic affairs as in military operations. Except for generals and treasurers, however, virtually
every magistrate was chosen by lot. As a consequence,
even the obscurest citizen could find himself in a prominent administrative position.

Trials were held in the people's courts, or *dikasteria*.
Although the juries typically numbered 201, 401, or 501,
the Athenians did not think of them as a plurality of law
courts but as a single government body. Altogether
6,000 jurors were selected by lot, and from them the
various juries were formed. They sat in judgment on
both private and public affairs, including the evaluation
of magistrates at the conclusion of their term in office.
Treason, however, was prosecuted before the Assembly,
and homicide was tried by one of the few survivals from
predemocratic days, the Areopagus. Even in criminal
cases the prosecutors and defenders had to speak for
themselves; there were neither judges nor professional
lawyers.

Clearly, a government in which so many of its citizens

could participate required very special conditions. The average Athenian was expected to have a detailed knowledge of current affairs and the workings of the law. Financial hardship was no obstacle to holding public office, for the state paid almost all public servants an allowance to compensate for their loss of regular earnings. Thus even the poorest citizen was expected to serve as juror, member of the Council, or magistrate; only the elected officials—the generals and the treasurers—were not paid. Furthermore, all magistrates, even the generals, were fully accountable to the Council of Five Hundred for their conduct in office.

A system known as *ostracism* prevented the ambitious from acquiring too much power and reviving tyranny. Any political figure could be exiled for ten years by means of this institution. The names of suspect or unpopular persons were inscribed on fragments of pottery known as *ostraka*, and if one name appeared often enough, that person was banned. Themistocles, the hero of the resistance to Persia, was one of those proscribed; he ended his days in the Persian camp.

Athenian democracy—the word literally means "rule by the people (*demos*)"—was a remarkable and unprecedented experiment. It coincided with Athens' political and economic hegemony in Greece and its great cultural

Ostraka from the Athenian Agora, fifth century B.C. The potsherds record the names of persons whom the Popular Assembly sought to exile, among them Themistocles; his main opponent, Aristides; Pericles; and Cimon. [American School of Classical Studies at Athens: Agora Excavations]

flowering as well. It remains the wellspring of the Western democratic tradition, and although it had severe critics even in its own day, it has remained the ideal of a

# ◉ A Critical View of the Athenians ◉

*A conservative critique of Athenian life is expressed by an anonymous writer of the late fifth century B.C. known simply as the "Old Oligarch."*

Another point is the extraordinary amount of license granted to slaves and resident aliens at Athens, where a blow is illegal, and a slave will not step aside to let you pass him in the street. I will explain the reason of this peculiar custom. Supposing it were legal for a slave to be beaten by a free citizen, or for a resident alien or freedman to be beaten by a citizen; it would frequently happen that an Athenian might be mistaken for a slave or an alien and receive a beating, since the Athenian people is not better clothed than the slave or alien, nor in personal appearance is there any superiority.

Or if the fact itself that slaves in Athens are allowed to indulge in luxury, and indeed in some cases to live magnificently, be found astonishing, this too, it can be shown, is done of set purpose. Where you have a naval power dependent upon wealth we must perforce be slaves to our slaves, in order that we may get in our slave-rents, and let the real slave go free.

For my part I pardon the people its own democracy, as, indeed, it is pardonable in any one to do good to himself. But the man who, not being himself one of the people, prefers to live in a state democratically governed rather than in an oligarchical state may be said to smooth his own path towards iniquity. He knows that a bad man has a better chance of slipping through the fingers of justice in a democratic than in an oligarchical state.

*Source:* C. Starr, *The Ancient Greeks* (London: Oxford University Press, 1971), pp. 199–201.

political community of free, equal, and self-governing persons. Never, however, did it eradicate poverty. Nor did it embrace the entire community, for it excluded two large groups that together made up the majority of the adult population: women and slaves.

Roughly half of the Athenian population resided outside Athens and its nearby harbor town, Piraeus. Apart from participation in public affairs, for which approximately 50 percent of the adult citizens received state pay during at least part of the year, most Athenians worked the land. Some Athenians still owned large estates, though most were small freeholders who worked the land themselves or with the assistance of a few slaves. A third of the land was normally left fallow each year, and the Athenians had to import a staggering 75 percent of the grain needed to feed themselves. Landless Athenians depended for employment on state building projects, the craft industries, and retailing, though most of the manufacturing and commerce were controlled by resident aliens known as *metics*. The latter competed with Athenians for jobs: the stonecutters, carpenters, and unskilled laborers who built the temple known as the Erechtheum consisted of 24 Athenians, 40 metics, and 17 slaves. Wages were such that a married man with two or three children lived at the subsistence level. The state did not intervene to regulate wages or working conditions. Free time could be spent in religious festivals or at state-supported exercise grounds known as gymnasiums, but civic responsibilities were demanding for many.

## Women in Classical Athens

The first literary and dramatic representations of women we have from the ancient Western world, apart from the Hebrew Bible, are those of classical Greece. The Greeks added what the Hebrews lacked, the visual representation of women in paint and stone. The great tragic figures of the Greek stage—the avenging queen, Clytemnestra; the betrayed wife, Medea; the martyred princess, Antigone; and many others—are still the prototypes of Western drama. The magnificent representations of the female figure, including the first life-size nudes in Western art (beginning with those of Praxiteles in the fourth century B.C.), are still the acknowledged ideal of feminine beauty in Western culture. In mythology, too, women played a crucial and often commanding role, and the very name of Athens was derived from its patron goddess, Athena, whose 40-foot-high statue sat enthroned in the temple of the Parthenon.

The actual position of women in classical Greek society fell far short of these idealized images. The philosopher Aristotle reflected the prevailing view when he described women as the natural inferiors of men, born to serve and obey; he even denied them a full share in

A Roman copy of a fifth-century B.C. statue of a woman, perhaps representing a goddess. [Alinari/Art Resource, New York]

the procreation of children (their chief function), arguing that the male seed alone contained the full germ of the child, with the womb serving only as its receptacle. The role and status of women were far closer to those of slaves than those of citizens. Women had no independent legal standing and could have legal rights exercised for them only through male guardians. Marriages were generally arranged by the bride's father, who was also responsible for the wedding celebration and, of course, the dowry. A husband could divorce his wife at will, whereas women had to find magistrates to represent them. Husbands could even dispose of their wives in their wills, and the orator Demosthenes describes the case of a widow ordered to marry her husband's former slave in his will. The double standard was also applied to adultery; tolerated for men, it was regarded as automatic grounds for divorce in the case of women.

Only inside the home did women exert any authority. Within her house a woman was responsible for domestic finances, duties such as spinning and weaving, and the supervision of slaves. Even here, however, the sexes were socially segregated, with women consigned to their own part of the house while men entertained their visitors (including prostitutes and concubines) elsewhere. The woman's part of the house, the *gynaeconitis*, varied in size and complexity with the scale of the home. In small residences it consisted of one or two rooms, divided from the main section by a door that could be locked, apparently to keep the male and female slaves apart. In larger houses the woman's quarters had a separate dining room, an open courtyard, and occasionally additional suites of rooms.

The sexual life of most of the citizen-class women was as restricted as their social lives. The eroticism of Greek vase paintings is very misleading. Procreation rather than pleasure was the primary aim of marital sexuality. The Greco-Roman historian Plutarch cited a law of Solon's that required married couples to have intercourse at least three times a month, "for the same reason that cities renew their treaties from time to time." Athens and most other Greek cities supported a large population of male and female prostitutes; Corinth is said to have had 1,000 of the latter. These included the famous *hetairai*, or courtesans, who had the reputation of being cultivated companions as well as women skilled in the art of pleasure. Because hetairai were usually of metic status and did not generally come from citizen families, Athenian men desiring to beget sons who would enjoy civic rights were limited in their choice of wives to the comparatively uneducated women of the citizen class. Predictably, they also established liaisons with the more cultured hetairai as well. The division of women in Athens into a cultivated courtesan class and an uneducated citizen class suitable for providing heirs created considerable tensions. It is the hetairai who are largely represented in the vase paintings, often performing acts that were frowned on in the marriage bed. They were also sometimes represented as being beaten, raped, or otherwise abused.

Domestic occupation was viewed as good for women, but any kind of work for pay was considered socially demeaning. Women of the lower classes hired out as weavers, spinners, and wet nurses; many worked as vendors in the public market. Athenian women seldom worked at agriculture, but in periods of duress they sometimes went into the field or picked grapes in the harvest. A very few served in temples. Most upper-class women simply stayed home. It is unclear whether women were even able to attend the theaters where the tragic heroines were portrayed, but we do know that they were prohibited from acting the parts, which were played by men and boys.

## Slaves and Metics

At Athens alone the number of slaves in the late fifth century B.C. is estimated to have been between 100,000 and 200,000 people, or roughly half the population. Almost none of these were of Greek origin; many, either captured in war or bought at slave markets in Greece and western Asia, came from Asia Minor or southern Russia. They were owned by individual citizens, metics, or the state. Those who were skilled in a craft could produce work for sale, on condition that their masters received a share of the profit. Many worked in industries such as mining and quarrying or in farming. About half worked as domestic servants. Since the wealthier households had several slaves—a famous shield manufacturer, Cephalus, owned 120—many Athenian households of the poorer classes must have functioned without slave labor.

The daily life of a domestic slave differed little from that of the average Athenian housewife. It was not possible for an outsider to distinguish between slaves and free workers by their dress or their treatment. Slaves were generally considered members of the household. They were allowed to marry and produce children, who then became the property of their owners; they could save money for their old age; and when they died they were buried in the family tomb. Although no laws existed to protect them from abuse, they could seek refuge from cruel masters in legal sanctuaries. There are even cases where slaves received their freedom, went into business, and became Athenian citizens. The lot of agricultural or mine workers was far grimmer. The quarriers and miners were often worked to death, and farm laborers shared the generally uncertain and penurious conditions of their farmer-masters.

In addition to citizens and slaves there was another class in Athens, the metics. These included immigrants from other parts of the Greek world and their descendants, freed slaves and their descendants, and, after 451 B.C., the children of marriages between citizens and noncitizens. Like the slaves and female relations of citizens, they could not vote in the Assembly or serve as jurors, nor could they own houses or land, though they fought in the Athenian army and paid taxes. Metics were in general socially accepted, had freedom of worship, and were able to follow their chosen trade or profession. Many of them, in fact, played an important part in Athenian business and industry, and some acquired considerable wealth, though most were poor. They could also own slaves. The interests of metics were represented by Athenian officials known as *polemarchs*, who were appointed by lot. The opening pages of Plato's *Republic* indicate the high social esteem enjoyed by some metic families. Indeed, the metic Cephalus, who had moved from Syracuse to Athens at Pericles' urging, was included in the circle of Plato's friends.

# The Spartan Ideal

Sparta, Athens' principal rival in the Greek world, espoused different values. The champion of conservative forces in Greece, the Spartans had been warlike from the beginning of their history. Gradually they evolved a way of life based on the military ideal, to which they subordinated all other aspects of social, economic, and cultural life. Their ideals are vividly illustrated in a description of the city of Ephesus in Asia Minor when it was under Spartan control in the early fourth century B.C.:

> You could see the gymnasia full of men exercising, the hippodrome full of horsemen riding, the javelin-throwers and the archers at target practice. . . . The market-place was full of armaments and horses for sale, while the bronze-smiths and carpenters, ironworkers, leatherworkers and painters were all preparing military equipment. As a result you would truly have thought the city a workshop of war.[3]

The Spartans dominated the region around them, known as Laconia. Because all adult Spartan males were soldiers, the work of cultivation was done by the neighboring population, the *perioikoi*, and the large class of serfs, or "helots," who were owned by the Spartans, bound to the soil, and kept under strict control. Together these groups gave the Spartans an abundant supply of forced or semifree labor. This system also surrounded them with a permanently hostile population. The perioikoi enjoyed personal freedom and a measure of local self-government, but they were subject to Spartan governors and to conscription in the Spartan army. They were probably the descendants of former allies who had been reduced to subservience. The helots, descended from conquered peoples, were restive and frequently rebellious. Unlike the Athenian slaves, who were in large part integrated into the families of citizens or worked beside them in the fields, the helots had little incentive to identify themselves with the harsh and exclusive rule of their masters.

Sparta's military ideal was thus both a cause and an effect of its pattern of conquest, which left the Spartans an elite minority among a disaffected mass of serfs and subjects. But if the Spartans were hard on the people they ruled, they were demanding of themselves as well. Spartan babies were inspected at birth, and those deemed unfit were exposed to die. Children were taken from their mothers at the age of 7 to be trained in martial arts and athletics. Their clothes were scanty, their beds were hard, and their food was monotonous and strictly rationed. The training they received was calculated to increase their powers of endurance and inspire them with patriotic fervor. Students were encouraged to steal, because foraging was a military virtue, and were punished not for the act but only for failing at it. At the age of 20 each male enlisted in the army and spent the next ten years living in barracks. For the rest of his life he remained a member of a small peer group, with whom he took his meals, even though he was expected to marry by the age of 30. Girls were given a similar, though less rigorous, military education. In contrast to Athenian women, those in Sparta had legal standing, could inherit property and represent themselves in court, and played a major role in managing the large estates of the Spartan aristocracy.

At the age of 30 Spartan males were divided into two classes, "equals" and "inferiors." The equals made up the Assembly, whose principal function was to elect the 30 members of the Council. These comprised two kings, who shared power and ruled jointly, and 28 elders. The chief magistrates were the five *ephors* (overseers), who had almost unlimited powers; they could arrest and prosecute any citizen, including the kings.

In embracing this social and political system, the Spartans of classical times believed they were following a code of laws introduced by Lycurgus, a shadowy and perhaps mythical figure in early Spartan history. Even the oracle at Delphi was uncertain whether Lycurgus was a man or a god, and it is probable that the Spartan system of government developed, like that at Athens, over a period of time.

The Spartans' concern with military affairs limited their contacts with the rest of Greece and left them in relative economic and cultural isolation. Their self-sufficiency was, of course, voluntary. Indeed, the profound differences between the Athenian and Spartan interpretation of civic ideals underscore the diversity of the polis as an institution. The Athenian version of democracy produced a spirit of commercial and imperial aggressiveness and stimulated a rich culture. The Spartans left behind no art or architecture of consequence, nor did they develop a literary or dramatic tradition. Yet many Greek cities feared and mistrusted Athens' expansionism and looked to Sparta for leadership as Athenian power grew.

The Spartans' attachment to tradition, the austerity of their lives, and their rigorous adherence to the military ideal were widely admired. Many of the poleis were far more attracted to Spartan stability than to the democratic experiments of Athens. Powerful but staunchly conservative, the Spartans rarely undertook any kind of political initiative and therefore seemed less threatening to their neighbors. If they lived on the labor of serfs, they often lived less well, materially, than those who served them. Their standards of courage, loyalty, endurance, and honor were high, and the penalty for failing them was severe: disgrace and loss of citizenship. The Spartans deliberately contrasted their ascetic way of life

with what they considered the self-indulgence and reckless individualism of the Athenians; one of their kings, Agesilaus, asked what the greatest Spartan virtue was, is said to have replied, "Contempt of pleasure."

The imperial aggressiveness of Periclean Athens finally roused the Spartans and their allies to concerted action. Military sparring commenced in the 450s, but not until 431 B.C., at Corinth's urging, did Sparta declare war on Athens. The ensuing civil war lasted 27 years and ended with the defeat of the Athenian empire.

## The Peloponnesian War

By the end of the Persian Wars, Athens was the most powerful polis in the Greek world, not least because it had played a decisive part in defeating the Persians. Moreover, its essentially democratic government had proved stable and effective. Athens organized a defen-

### ◉ Spartan Bravery ◉

*In this extract from Herodotus' account of the Persian Wars, Xerxes hears high praise for the valor of the Spartans.*

Having sailed from one end to the other of the line of anchored ships, Xerxes went ashore again and sent for Demaratus, the son of Ariston, who was accompanying him in the march to Greece. "Demaratus," he said, "it would give me pleasure at this point to put to you a few questions. You are a Greek, and a native, moreover, of by no means the meanest or weakest city in that country—as I learn not only from yourself but [also] from the other Greeks I have spoken with. Tell me, then—will the Greeks dare to lift a hand against me? My own belief is that all the Greeks and all the other Western peoples gathered together would be insufficient to withstand the attack of my army—and still more so if they are not united. But it is your opinion upon this subject that I should like to hear."

"My lord," Demaratus replied, "is it a true answer you would like, or merely an agreeable one?"

"Tell me the truth," said the king; "and I promise that you will not suffer by it." Encouraged by this Demaratus continued: "My lord, you bid me speak nothing but the truth, to say nothing which might later be proved a lie. Very well then; this is my answer: poverty is my country's inheritance from of old, but valor she won for herself by wisdom and the strength of law. By her valor Greece now keeps both poverty and bondage at bay.

"I think highly of all Greeks of Dorian descent, but what I am about to say will apply not to all Dorians, but to the Spartans only. First then, they will not under any circumstances accept terms from you which would mean slavery for Greece; secondly, they will fight you even if the rest of Greece submits. Moreover, there is no use in asking if their numbers are adequate to enable them to do this; suppose a thousand of them take the field—then that thousand will fight you; and so will any number, greater than this or less."

*Source:* Herodotus, *The Histories*, trans. A. de Selincourt (Harmondsworth, England: Penguin Books, 1954), pp. 447–448.

sive alliance of Greek poleis to repulse any future Persian attack. This was the Delian League, so named because the money contributed by the member states was stored in a treasury on the island of Delos, sacred to Apollo and politically neutral.

Other poleis, including Sparta, Thebes, and Corinth, soon became suspicious that the league was intended primarily to enhance Athenian power. The Athenians, they believed, were transforming an association of free states into an empire. Their concerns were intensified in 454 B.C. when the league's funds were moved to Athens and some of the money was diverted to pay for an ambitious building program in Athens itself. The Greek world largely divided into competing camps, with Athens and the poleis that remained in the league arrayed against Sparta and its supporters.

Chief among Sparta's allies was Corinth, gateway to the Peloponnesus and the site of intersecting east-west and north-south trade routes. The importance of Acrocorinth, the awesome citadel that towers above the city, was aptly noted by the historian Plutarch:

> **It hinders and cuts off all the country south of the Isthmus [of Corinth] from intercourse, transits, and the carrying on of military expeditions by land and sea, and makes him who controls the place with a garrison sole lord of Greece.[4]**

A polis of traders and manufacturers, Corinth was also blessed with fertile soil. Like Athens, Corinth attracted immigrant artisans to its thriving economy, but unlike Athens its government was oligarchic, perhaps because of Spartan influence. Both Athens and Corinth acquired

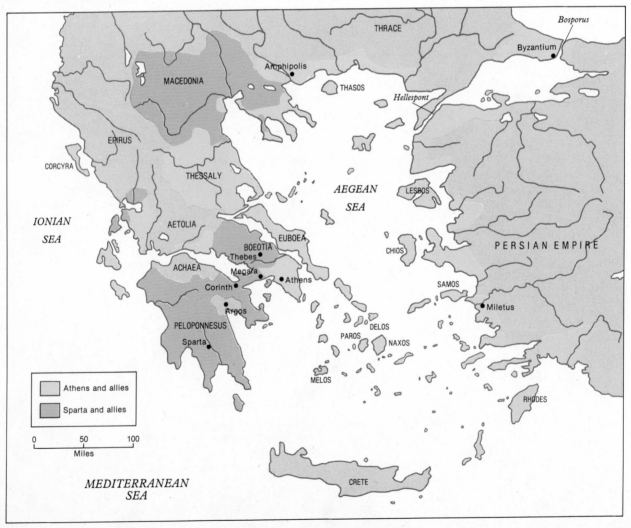

*4.3 Allies in the Peloponnesian War*

impressive empires and constructed powerful navies with which to defend them. The two poleis thus had much in common, but in the end, political considerations persuaded the Corinthians to side with Sparta. By the time the war ended, both the Corinthians and the Athenians had suffered enormously for their animosity.

Conflict between the Spartan and Athenian alliances was perhaps inevitable. The Peloponnesian War, so called after the homeland of the Spartans and their principal supporters, broke out in 431 and lasted until 404 B.C., when it ended in the defeat and occupation of Athens. Although the conflict involved virtually the whole of Greece in a generation of bitter strife, it did not result in more satisfactory or more stable conditions. It served principally to hasten the decline of the independent poleis that had proved themselves incapable of coexistence. If the war seems particularly memorable in the history of the West, it is in large part because of the detailed and authoritative account left by Thucydides, who both participated in and recorded its events.

Thucydides, born between 460 and 455 B.C., had been active in Athenian politics before the war. Elected general in 424, he was responsible for the defense of Amphipolis in northern Greece. When Sparta seized Amphipolis, Thucydides was tried in absentia and exiled. Not until 404 did he return to Athens. The purpose of his *History of the Peloponnesian War* was to narrate the events of the war to 404, but he brought it down only to 411 before his death; a later historian, Xenophon, completed the account. Thucydides was not content with a mere narrative of events. Through the use of set speeches, he analyzed the motives and reactions of the principal personalities of the struggle to give future generations an understanding of its causes. At the heart of his examination was the contrast between the restless, revolutionary Athenians and the confident, conservative Peloponnesians. Thucydides was also intrigued by the contest between Athens, a naval power, and Sparta, whose strength was on land; as a military commander he laid stress on the problems of siege warfare, troop landings, and nighttime battles. Unlike Herodotus, he deliberately avoided digressions, and he made a scrupulous effort to verify his facts, though like other ancient historians he embellished the speeches of his protagonists to clarify their motives and express what he judged to be their character. As a narrative historian, Thucydides has never been surpassed. With Herodotus, he ranks as one of the fathers of historical study.

## Strife and Stalemate

The Athenian war effort went badly at first. The Persian Wars had demonstrated the power and efficiency of the Athenian navy, but no land army in Greece was a match for the Spartans. Trusting to the strength of Athens' fortifications and the richness of its treasury, Pericles al-

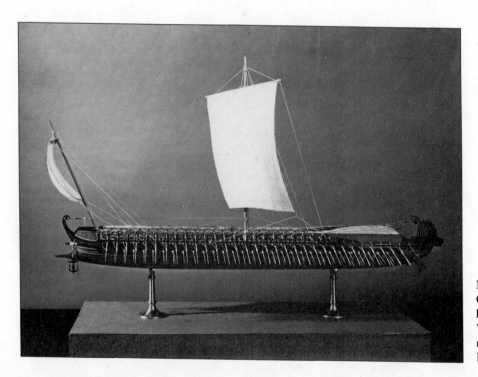

Model of a fifth-century B.C. Greek trireme (galley) of the kind used in the Peloponnesian War. It was 120 feet long and required a crew of 200. (Photo Deutsches Museum, Munich]

lowed the Spartans to ravage the countryside outside Athens and wear themselves out. Thucydides vividly depicted the strain on the Athenians:

> When they saw the army . . . barely seven miles from the city, they felt the presence of the invader to be intolerable. The devastation of their country before their eyes, which the younger men had never seen at all, nor the elder except in the Persian invasion, naturally appeared to them a horrible thing, and the whole people, the young men especially, were anxious to go forth and put a stop to it. Knots were formed in the streets, and there were loud disputes, some eager to go out, a minority resisting. . . . The people were furious with Pericles, and, forgetting all his previous warnings, they abused him for not leading them to battle, as their general should, and laid all their miseries to his charge.[5]

Meanwhile, Pericles sent the Athenian navy to do what damage it could to the Peloponnesus. For two years the Athenians withstood a Spartan siege, guaranteed food supplies by their access to the sea. The devastation of the farmlands around the city, however, drove thousands of people inside the walls. In 430 a terrible plague, still unidentifiable, ravaged the city. Perhaps as much as a quarter of the population, including Pericles himself, had perished by the time the contagion finally abated in 427.

The Athenians found themselves without an able leader to take his place. The city split into two main factions, a war party and a peace party. The latter was led by Nicias, a wealthy Athenian who used his money to provide public entertainments. His opponent was the fiery Cleon, a self-styled "watchdog of the people" and the son of a tanner. After ten years of reverses for both the Athenians and the Peloponnesians, the peace faction at Athens gained the ascendancy. In 422 Cleon was killed in action, and in 421 the combatants signed the so-called Peace of Nicias, which was supposed to last for 50 years.

By now a new generation had come to power in Athens. Chief among its leaders was the brilliant but erratic Alcibiades (c. 450–404 B.C.); handsome, wealthy, and intelligent, he was called ambitious and extravagant by his enemies. An aristocrat by birth, he seems to have despised the lower classes, although he was mistrusted by his fellow conservatives. As long as his aims seemed in the city's interest, his charm won him popular support. Even his admirers, however, learned to fear him.

## The Sicilian Expedition and the Collapse of Athens

When war erupted anew in 415 B.C., Alcibiades was one of the principal promoters of a daring scheme to invade Sicily. The Athenians' intention was twofold: by conquering the Sicilian Greek cities, they could enrich themselves with treasures and crops; at the same time, they could disrupt Sicilian trade with the Peloponnesus, especially Corinth, thereby weakening its alliance with Sparta.

A string of disasters dogged the Sicilian expedition. When Alcibiades was recalled to Athens to answer trumped-up charges lodged by his political enemies, he defected to Sparta and helped the Spartans against his own polis. By painting a menacing picture of a growing Athenian empire in the west, he induced the Spartans to send the Sicilians a volunteer force. In the spring of 414 the Athenians found themselves trapped between local units and a Spartan expeditionary force. The Athenians dispatched more troops, but when they arrived in the spring of 413, it was too late. A rout occurred, and the expedition surrendered.

The Athenians were so disheartened by this reversal that they temporarily abandoned their greatest achievement, democratic government. In 411 a revolution brought a Council of Four Hundred to power, although after a few months it too split into various factions, and by 409 B.C. democracy was restored. Alcibiades returned briefly to Athens, where, despite his earlier defection, he was welcomed as a savior. When his enemies revived the old suspicions, he again fled into exile, this time for good.

The war ended in the late summer of 405, when the Spartan navy ambushed the Athenians in the Hellespont. Of 179 Athenian ships only 9 escaped, and 4,000 Athenian prisoners were executed. Even then the city resisted a siege. But by the spring of 404 B.C. the situation was hopeless, and Athens surrendered unconditionally.

The long-term causes of the Peloponnesian War are to be found in the nature of Greek political life, which encouraged confrontation rather than unity. The temporary alliance against the Persians had proved only an exception to the tradition of intercommunal rivalry. The defeat of Athens was hailed as a victory for Greek independence, but it did nothing to foster unity among its divided states.

In the space of a few centuries the Greeks, emerging from a Dark Age characterized by a shrinking population, severe economic disruption, and cultural decline, developed one of the most brilliant civilizations in history. The core of this development was the polis, an independent sociopolitical institution that bound together the residents of a city and the surrounding territory, serving as the basis for their religious and cultural life as well as their political institutions. The ideals and the character of the respective poleis differed, ranging from the conservative, militaristic society of Sparta to the democratic, commercial, and imperialistic society of Athens. Although the latter pioneered in the development of political democracy, it limited participation to a minority of its inhabitants, excluding women, resident aliens, and slaves. Greeks of the Classical Age never solved the problem of political unity. They cooperated to repel the invading Persians, after which they organized themselves into rival alliances that ultimately took up arms against each other in the Peloponnesian War, the greatest tragedy of ancient Greek history.

By the end of the Peloponnesian War, the concept of the polis as the dominant force in the lives of its citizens, inspiring and fulfilling them, had been damaged beyond repair. The internal divisions within the Greek world ultimately produced wounds far more serious than those inflicted by the Persian invasions. In the years that followed, the Greeks moved in new political and cultural directions but failed to solve the fundamental dilemma of their disunity. That dilemma remained part of the Greek legacy, along with the magnificent achievement of its Classical Age.

## Notes

1. Archilocus, "My Goodly Shield," trans. W. R. Castle, in *Classics in Transition*, ed. P. MacKendrick and H. M. Howe (Madison: University of Wisconsin Press, 1952), vol. 1, p. 94.
2. Herodotus, *The Persian Wars*, trans. G. Rawlinson (New York: Modern Library, 1942), pp. 587–588.
3. Xenophon, in A. Powell, *Athens and Sparta: Constructing Greek Political and Social History from 478 B.C.* (Portland, Oregon: Areopagitica Press, 1988), p. 240.
4. Plutarch, in S. Hornblower, *The Greek World, 479–323 B.C.* (London: Methuen, 1983), p. 95.
5. Thucydides, *The Peloponnesian War*, trans. B. Jowett (New York: Bantam, 1960), p. 109.

## Suggestions for Further Reading

Austin, M. M., and Vidal-Naquet, P. *Economic and Social History of Ancient Greece.* Berkeley: University of California Press, 1978.

Bengston, H. *History of Greece: From the Beginnings to the Byzantine Era*, trans. and rev. by E. F. Bloedow. Ottawa: University of Ottawa Press, 1988.

Boardman, J. *The Greeks Overseas.* Baltimore: Penguin Books, 1973.

Cargill, J. *The Second Athenian League: Empire or Free Alliance?* Berkeley: University of California Press, 1981.

Charbonneaux, J., Martin, R., and Villard, F. *Archaic Greek Art, 620–480 B.C.* London: Thames & Hudson, 1971.

Demand, N. H. *Urban Relocation in Archaic and Classical Greece: Flight and Consolidation.* Norman: University of Oklahoma Press, 1990.

Dover, K. J. *Greek Homosexuality.* New York: Random House, 1980.

Drews, R. *The Coming of the Greeks: Indo-European Conquests in the Aegean and the Near East.* Princeton, N.J.: Princeton University Press, 1988.

Finley, M. I. *Early Greece: The Bronze and Archaic Ages*, 2nd ed. New York: Norton, 1982.

———. *Economy and Society in Ancient Greece*, ed. B. D. Shaw and R. P. Saller. London: Chatto & Windus, 1981.

Forde, S. *The Ambition to Rule: Alcibiades and the Politics of Imperialism in Thucydides.* Ithaca, N.Y.: Cornell University Press, 1989.

Garlan, Y. *Slavery in Ancient Greece*, rev. ed. Ithaca, N.Y.: Cornell University Press, 1988.

Garland, R. *The Greek Way of Life: From Conception to Old Age.* Ithaca, N.Y.: Cornell University Press, 1990.

Hood, S. *The Arts in Prehistoric Greece.* Baltimore: Penguin Books, 1978.

Hooker, J. T. *The Ancient Spartans.* London: Dent, 1980.

Hornblower, S. *The Greek World, 479–323 B.C.* London: Methuen, 1983.

Just, R. *Women in Athenian Law and Life.* London: Routledge & Kegan Paul, 1989.

Kagan, D. *The Fall of the Athenian Empire.* Ithaca, N.Y.: Cornell University Press, 1987.

Lacey, W. K. *The Family in Classical Greece.* Ithaca, N.Y.: Cornell University Press, 1968.

Lintott, A. *Violence, Civil Strife, and Revolution in the Classical City, 750–330 B.C.* Baltimore: Johns Hopkins University Press, 1982.

Luce, J. V. *Homer and the Heroic Age.* New York: Harper & Row, 1975.

Manville, P. B. *The Origins of Citizenship in Ancient Athens.* Princeton, N.J.: Princeton University Press, 1990.

Marinatos, S., and Hirmer, M. *Crete and Mycenae.* New York: Abrams, 1960.

Murray, O., and Price, S., eds. *The Greek City: From Homer to Alexander.* Oxford: Clarendon Press, 1990.

Ober, J. *Mass and Elite in Democratic Athens: Rhetoric, Ideology, and the Power of the People.* Princeton, N.J.: Princeton University Press, 1989.

Oliva, P. *The Birth of Greek Civilization.* Edmonton, Alberta: Pica Pica Press, 1985.

Ostwald, M. *From Popular Sovereignty to the Sovereignty of Law: Law, Society, and Politics in Fifth-Century Athens.* Berkeley: University of California Press, 1986.

Page, D. L. *Sappho and Alcaeus.* Oxford: Clarendon Press, 1955.

Pomeroy, S. B. *Goddesses, Whores, Wives, and Slaves.* New York: Schocken Books, 1975.

Schaps, D. M. *Economic Rights of Women in Ancient Greece.* Edinburgh: Edinburgh University Press, 1979.

Sealey, R. *Women and Law in Classical Greece.* Chapel Hill: University of North Carolina Press, 1990.

Snodgrass, A. M. *An Archaeology of Greece.* Berkeley: University of California Press, 1987.

———. *Archaic Greece.* Berkeley: University of California Press, 1980.

Stockton, D. *The Classical Athenian Democracy.* New York: Oxford University Press, 1990.

Strauss, B. *Athens After the Peloponnesian War.* Ithaca, N.Y.: Cornell University Press, 1986.

Willetts, R. F. *The Civilization of Ancient Crete.* Berkeley: University of California Press, 1977.

Wood, E. M. *Peasant-Citizen and Slave: The Foundation of Athenian Democracy.* London: Verso, 1988.

Zinserling, V. *Women in Greece and Rome.* New York: Schram, 1972.

# The Greek Achievement and the Hellenistic World

The Peloponnesian War marked the end of Athens' bid for political and cultural supremacy. The ensuing period of confusion was brought to an end by the appearance of a new power, the northern kingdom of Macedon. Yet the ultimate failure of the Greek political system could not diminish the cultural achievements of Greek civilization. The Greeks were pioneers in many fields of Western culture and provided the basis for a distinctively Western tradition in areas as diverse as history and sculpture, urban planning and medicine, drama and mathematics.

The world in which Greek ideas were developed was one of war and disturbance, and the Greek concern for measure in all things must be seen against that background. The Greek conviction that the pursuit of reason

**Alexander the Great. Note the strained position of the head and the emotion expressed by the eyes and the mouth. [Alinari/Art Resource: Musée du Louvre]**

could provide a basis for order in human affairs was reflected in the artistic achievements of the classical period. The essence of this classical belief was the quest for an ideal balance between mind and body and for harmony between the individual and society. The Greeks summed this up in the adage "Nothing in excess."

The Greeks believed that humans could achieve order in their lives by comprehending the causes not only of other people's actions but also of their own. This faith in reason and self-understanding was as central to Greek spiritual life as belief in divine forces. The Parthenon, the principal temple on the Athenian Acropolis, was intended to celebrate Athens as much as to honor the goddess Athena. Even in the worst of times, the belief in human potential remained central to the Greeks' vision of life. At the same time they understood the powerful forces of the irrational that were part of human nature and had to be acknowledged and pacified. If Apollo, god of the sun, represented clarity and order, he was balanced by the figure of Dionysus, god of wine, sexuality, and abandon.

The Greeks believed that human life was subject to uncontrollable forces. Such forces might be propitiated, but they could never be tamed. Chief among them was Nemesis, or destiny, from which there was no appeal. If the values of harmony and order were paramount in Greek sculpture and architecture, Greek fatalism found its outlet in the tragic drama. Even the plastic arts, however, reflected the Greek sense of the pathos and frailty as well as the nobility of human existence.

## The Visual Arts: In Search of the Human Ideal

The buildings on the Acropolis were the culmination of classical architecture. The two principal Greek architectural styles, Doric and Ionic, were both represented on the Acropolis. Both had undergone a long development. The Doric style was widespread by 600 B.C.; the Ionic, though used in the Archaic period, was not common until the fifth century B.C.

The Doric order is more austere and majestic than the Ionic and may derive from an earlier period of wood construction. A number of its features may be based on building techniques employed in the wooden structures of an earlier time. The Ionic order, by contrast, is more delicate and makes use of complex architectural details; its surface decoration is as important as its structural design. When, after the Persian Wars, the Greeks collaborated to construct the Temple of Zeus at the Panhellenic shrine of Olympia, they chose the Doric order. Built between 470 and 456 B.C., it was the largest Doric

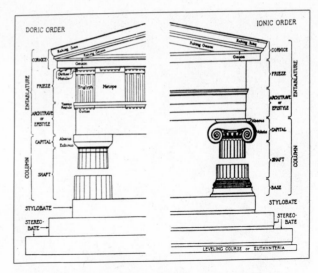

**The Doric and Ionic orders (after Grinnell). [Courtesy of Prentice Hall]**

temple in Greece. Libon of Elis, its designer, was concerned to render the classical sense of order in architectural form. The positioning of the columns and other architectural elements follows precise mathematical formulas. A similar concern for proportion can be seen in the temple of Apollo designed by Ictinos and built at Bassae in the western Peloponnesus around 450–425 B.C.

Sculptors of the Classical Age were particularly concerned with harmony. They sought to produce a fresh notion of human beauty by presenting the human form through the application of principles of symmetry and proportion. Polyclitus of Argos, one of the most important classical sculptors, invented a mathematical system of proportion in order to depict the ideal male form. His book, *The Canon* (c. 440 B.C.), argued that ideal beauty is achieved by an exact correspondence of proportion among all parts of the human anatomy. His bronze statue of a youth holding a spear, the *Doryphoros*, was intended to demonstrate this principle. Neither the book nor the original statue has survived, although later copies of the *Doryphoros* exist.

One of the great achievements of fifth-century B.C. Greek sculptors was the depiction of movement. Figures such as a woman fastening her sandal or a charioteer gripping his reins convey motion in a satisfyingly natural fashion. Such figures contrast sharply with the formal, rigid statuary of the Archaic period. The classical sculptors were largely successful in this endeavor because of their careful observation of human anatomy, particularly musculature. Subjects such as Zeus hurling a thunderbolt or an athlete poised to throw a discus were ob-

**Detail of Apollo from the center of the west pediment of the Temple of Zeus at Olympia. [Alinari/Art Resource: Olympia Museum, Greece]**

## The Athenian Acropolis

The most famous buildings of the classical period are the structures on the Athenian Acropolis. The magnificence of their design and execution is still visible. The Parthenon, the great temple to Athena, remains an unsurpassed symbol of classical achievement. Nevertheless, it was constructed in a period of conflict and division among the Greeks, its financing from the treasury of the Delian League a subject of controversy between Athens and its allies, and its sculptures completed only months before the outbreak of the Peloponnesian War. The Erechtheum, the last temple on the Acropolis to be finished, was completed in 406 B.C., scarcely a year before Athens' disastrous defeat at the Hellespont. Despite the political tensions of the classical period, the temples serve as a memorial to its highest ideals.

The natural stone outcrop known as the Acropolis made an ideal location for the temples. The site, which

viously chosen at least in part to explore the artists' anatomical interests. Naturalism was heightened by the skillful depiction of bones and muscle as though under living skin. Artists had manifestly become more sensitive to and appreciative of the natural world.

Toward the end of the fifth century B.C. both sculpture and vase painting began for the first time to exhibit an interest in portraying individuals rather than an idealized beauty. Associated with this was a more frequent depiction of aging and death as artists began to explore the psychological ramifications of mortality. Thus the subject of death and the human response to it came to be treated frequently in works of art.

The *lekythoi*, or oil flasks, used for funeral ceremonies are decorated with scenes that are among the most moving in classical art. Many show grieving figures or funerals; the background is generally white instead of the black or red favored on other painted pottery. Although the figures retain the composure of the classical style, they frequently display deep emotions. A similar individual reaction to death also characterizes the *stelai*, or grave markers, of the late fifth century, which reveal a sense of loss and resignation as well as depth of feeling.

**Painting on classical Greek vases commonly treated religious, military, and social themes, as in this fifth-century B.C. depiction of a warrior about to depart for battle facing a girl with a wine jug and an olive branch, the symbol of peace. [Ronald Sheridan/Ancient Art and Architecture Collection]**

**Grave stele from Heges. [Hirmer Fotoarchiv, Munich: National Archaeological Museum, Athens]**

rises more than 400 feet above Athens, had dominated the city's life from the Bronze Age, when it was occupied by a fortress. During the Archaic period a number of temples were built there, but the Persians destroyed them in 480 B.C. The new building program was begun in 449 under the general supervision of Phidias, the leading sculptor of the day. The most important building, the Parthenon, was begun in 447 and completed in 438. Its designers were Ictinos and Callicrates, and its name is derived from the Greek word *parthenos*, or virgin. This honored the city's patron goddess Athena, one of whose imputed qualities was virginity and whose statue, 40 feet high and encrusted with gold and ivory, adorned the interior of the Parthenon. Athena's legend was the focus of the exterior sculptural program as well. The east pediment—the triangular space supporting the roof—pictured her birth, the west pediment her contest with the sea god Poseidon for the territory of Attica. The bands of stone (friezes) above the outer colonnade portrayed Greeks battling mythical Amazons and centaurs in an allegorical representation of the triumph of civilization over barbarism, while another series showed the procession of the Panathenaic festival in which Athenians of both sexes ascended the Acropolis each year to present the goddess with a new robe. The Parthenon was severely damaged by bombardment in A.D. 1687, and the statue of Athena has long since disappeared. Tourism and pollution have replaced war as the chief threat to the citadel, and much of its surviving statuary and decoration have been removed for safety.

Sculpture was used in three sections of the building. The Ionic running band, or frieze, shows a ceremony that was held every four years at the time of the Great

**In this detail of the west-face Parthenon frieze (c. 442–432 B.C.), the speed and vigor of the horses' movement contrasts strongly with the calm, typically classical expressions of their riders. [Ronald Sheridan/Reproduced by Courtesy of the Trustees of the British Museum]**

Panathenaic festival. It depicts Athenians walking and riding in procession and others at the climax of the religious ceremonies. The balance of form, motion, and rhythm in this sculpture make it one of the most impressive masterpieces of classical art. The extant free-standing figures originally on the east and west pediments are no less striking despite their damaged condition. The group of three goddesses from the east pediment blends ideal form and natural observation, particularly in the harmony of limbs and flowing drapery. The rectangular slabs decorating the outside of the building, which are called *metopes*, show various legendary battles, including the conflict between the Lapiths, a tribe of northern Greece, and the half-human, half-animal centaurs, which for the Greeks represented the clash of civilization and barbarism.

Work on the entrance to the Acropolis, the Propylaea, began in 437 B.C. and lasted six years, although the war probably forced its architect, Mnesicles, to modify his original design. He used both Doric and Ionic columns, an uncommon practice for a classical building. The little Ionic temple of Athena Nike (goddess of victory), built between 427 and 424 B.C., is decorated with carvings that depict the earlier Athenian triumph over the Persians. The purpose of showing historical figures instead of legendary ones was no doubt intended to recall Athenian successes at a time when the city faced renewed crisis.

The Erechtheum, an Ionic temple of unusual and striking design, was built between 421 and 406 B.C. It was the site of a variety of religious ceremonies and commemorated several gods. The Erechtheum's most famous element is the south porch, whose roof is supported by the Caryatids, statues of young women, rather than traditional columns.

## Late Classical Art

Nothing comparable to the scope and ambition of the Acropolis was attempted in Greece during the century that followed Athens' defeat. The shrines at Olympia and Delphi were expanded, and new forms were devised, such as the *tholos*, or circular building. The grandest project of the age was perhaps the reconstructed Temple of Artemis at Ephesus. Many of the principal fourth-century B.C. sculptures are lost, although surviving Roman copies enable us to trace the principal stages of development in this field. The heroic, idealized facial expressions of fifth-century B.C. works gave way to a

As a result of pollution and the deterioration of the stone, the Caryatids of the Erechtheum, on Athens' Acropolis, have now been moved to the Acropolis Museum. [Wim Swann]

new and often inward sense of individualism. The sculptor Praxiteles, for example, was famous for the gentle melancholy of his figures, a mood aptly characterized by the *Hermes* at Olympia often attributed to him. His younger contemporary, Lysippus, who developed a more elongated approach to proportion and a greater naturalism, had a significant influence on later Hellenistic art.

## Tragic Drama and the Meaning of Existence

The fifth century B.C. also gave rise to the tragic drama, a form invented by the Greeks. The plays written for performance in the sanctuary of Dionysus at Athens represent classical literature at its height and the birth of theater as we know it. The three great playwrights of the era, Aeschylus, Sophocles, and Euripides, not only created a new form of human expression but also set a standard in their works that has never been surpassed.

The extant works are religious, in two senses. In the first place, the theater for which they were written was regarded as sacred to the god Dionysus, who was honored at the festival at which they were performed. In the second place, their plots, usually derived from legend, frequently deal with the interaction between mortals and gods in search of the meaning of existence. To achieve an appropriate seriousness, the style of performance was lofty and dignified. The actors, all of whom were male, thought of themselves as priests of Dionysus and wore masks, intricate costumes, and high shoes.

Greek tragedy had its origins in choral hymns honoring Dionysus and accompanying religious sacrifice, and the chorus, a group of supplemental actors who commented on the actions of the main actors, remained an important element in classical plays. In earlier works, such as Aeschylus' *Suppliant Women,* the choral group is at the center of the action. Generally, the chorus reflects on the action and its implications for the moral law, the affirmation of which is a prime function of tragedy.

The three principal dramatists illustrate the evolution of fifth-century Athenian cultural history. Aeschylus (525–456 B.C.) lived at a time when the ideals of the early classical period were still unshaken by disaster. His plays reveal an intense sensitivity to human frailty and the corrupting influence of power; he had been a soldier at Marathon in 490 B.C. Aeschylus did not abandon his belief that justice would always prevail; he recognized, however, the difficulties of gaining knowledge, for only suffering can teach the errors of human ways. Moreover, even after the lessons have been learned, they do not alter the conclusion—only a divinely inspired justice, represented by Zeus, chief of the Olympian gods, can determine the outcome.

Aeschylus' optimism persists even when he depicts scenes of violence and bloodshed. His greatest achievement is the trilogy known as the *Oresteia*, first performed at Athens in 458 B.C. The *Oresteia* is both the family saga of the royal house of Atreus and a historical romance that connects the Trojan wars with the founding of Athens. The central action of the drama is the slaying of King Agamemnon by his wife, Clytemnestra, in retaliation for his sacrifice of their daughter, Iphigenia. Their son Orestes is then ordered to avenge his father's death by killing his mother. Pursued by vengeful spirits who represent both outraged female deities and the torments of his own conscience, Orestes is finally cleared in a public trial in Athens in which the deciding vote is cast by Athena, the patron goddess of the city. The play thus traces the evolution of Greek society from a primitive monarchy ruled by blood vengeance to a citizen-state governed by law and justice.

Sophocles (c. 496–406 B.C.), a personal friend of Pericles, enjoyed great acclaim. His plays reveal a more somber view of life than those of Aeschylus, although it is more difficult to extract a consistent philosophy from his work. He is interested chiefly in character development rather than in presenting a general theme, but he tempers the tragic results of human error with a belief in human dignity and capability.

Sophocles asserts that each individual is responsible for deciding between good and evil. Yet in his plays the choice is often obscured or difficult and at times impossible to make. Sophocles was more insistent than his fellow dramatists on human helplessness in the face of divine will or destiny. The play for which he is most widely known, *Oedipus the King*, has remained the most enduring symbol of classical tragic drama. First performed in 429 B.C., it combines a unity of time, place, and action with a story that moves inexorably toward a tragic conclusion. Its poetic language is beautiful and controlled. The play is universally regarded as a work of genius, yet its meaning remains ambiguous.

The play tells the story of Oedipus, who is doomed before birth by divine decree to murder his father and marry his mother and who finally discovers that he cannot avoid his fate. The simplest conclusion to be drawn from Oedipus' story is that humans must meet their destinies, but it is unclear whether such fates are deserved. Oedipus does not consciously decide to kill his father or marry his mother, although unknowingly he does both. Why, then, should he bear the consequences of his actions? Perhaps the meaning of the play is that much of human life is subject to forces beyond our comprehension and control. In this sense, Sophocles chronicled the impotence of human will in the face of destiny and warned that humans should not expect self-reliance to provide a means of avoiding fate.

## ◉ Human Destiny: A Greek View ◉

*This chorus from Sophocles'* Antigone *expresses his complex view of human destiny.*

**Chorus.** *Happy the life that tastes not lamentation!*
*But when with the curse of God a lineage shakes,*
*From generation down to generation*
*Comes no surcease of sorrow; so, when breaks*
*The Thracian tempest and the dark surge wakes,*
*Up from the deeps it whirls the sable sand,*
*While groan, in answer to the waves, the capes of the wind-vexed land.*

*Lo, from of old the Labdacids are stricken—*
*On the sorrows of their dead new sorrows fall.*
*Each generation sees the same curse quicken,*
*Some God still ruins them, helpless. In the hall*
*Of Oedipus one hope lit, last of all,*
*One root yet living. Now, this too lies slain*
*By Hell's red dust, by a reckless tongue, by a Fury in the brain.*

*Thy power, O Zeus, who can master? What pride of man's endeavor?*
*Sleep binds Thee not (that snares all else to rest),*
*Nor the tireless months of Heaven—Time leaves Thee ageless ever,*
*Throned in the dazzling glory of high Olympus' crest.*
*But for Man, from long ago*
*Abides through the years to be*
*This law, immutably—*
*All over-greatness brings its overthrow.*

*For Hope, that wanders ever, comes oft to Man as blessing;*
*For oft she cheats, till his giddy lusts are stirred.*
*Nearer she creeps, the deceiver, till he stumbles, all unguessing,*
*In the hot fires hid beneath him. Wise is the ancient word—*
*That he whom God hath planned*
*To ruin, in his blinded mood*
*Sees evil things as good—*
*And then the coming doom is hard at hand.*

*Source:* F. L. Lucas, *Greek Tragedy and Comedy* (New York: Viking, 1968), p. 144.

The plays of Euripides (c. 485–406 B.C.), Sophocles' contemporary, reflect the profound impact of fifth-century B.C. Greek political conflict and its social repercussions. Perhaps as a consequence, his work has the most direct meaning for us. Euripides was bent on exposing the social and political injustice of his time. He acknowledges that irrational forces, symbolized by the gods, affect human life, but he refuses to respect and worship them. Indeed, his open skepticism made people suspect him of impiety. The characters in his plays often reach the limits of their endurance, and his depiction of their response reveals a keen sense of psychological portraiture.

More than any of his predecessors, Euripides displays a deep sympathy for the problems of women in a male-dominated society. Characters such as Medea and Phaedra, who seek vengeance and passion outside the norms of social life, challenge many of the fundamental assumptions of Athenian society and show the violence to which women could be driven by social constraints. Euripides' plays—together with the powerful creations of Aeschylus and Sophocles, including the vengeful

Queen Clytemnestra in the *Oresteia* and the heroine of Sophocles' *Antigone*, who defies a royal prohibition to give her brother a proper burial—offer a gallery of female characters unsurpassed in the history of Western drama.

In a world that admired Spartan militarism, Euripides hated war and its attendant misery. His play *The Suppliant Women* was apparently written in 421 B.C., when a decade of inconclusive struggle in the Peloponnesian War was temporarily halted by the Peace of Nicias. The play deals with the return of the bodies of dead warriors to their families, in particular to their wives and mothers. The scenes of mourning that he depicted were undoubtedly grimly familiar to his audience. Furthermore, the expression of grief does not terminate the violence. In the last scene, Athena announces that the heirs of the dead soldiers will launch a war of vengeance. Euripides has rejected the optimism of Aeschylus; the cycle of violence cannot be broken.

Euripides lived long enough to see his fears fully realized. Driven from Athens by a public that had little taste for reminders of their folly, he ended his days at the court of the king of Macedon. There he wrote *The Bacchae*, a work that shows the limits of the rational mind in confronting the darkness of experience. This profoundly disturbing work, which describes the killing of Pentheus, the young king of Thebes, at the hands of his mother, acknowledges that emotion can overturn the sense of balance and proportion and that religious intoxication can release powers of destruction.

Not all of Greek theater was tragic. The performances of tragedies—during festival competitions, three a day—were interspersed with bawdy farces called satyr plays and with spirited comedies. The master of Attic comedy, Aristophanes (c. 450–c. 385 B.C.), often treated satirically the same issues taken up by the tragic playwrights. His *Lysistrata*, produced in 411 B.C. after the failure of the Sicilian expedition, decries the futility of war no less than Euripides' *Suppliant Women*, but using the weapons of ridicule—in this case, a sex strike organized by the women of Athens to bring the menfolk to their senses—rather than pathos. It is an extraordinary mark of the openness of Athenian society that a work that mocked the war effort could be staged at the most critical point of the struggle.

# The Greeks and the Physical World

Science and philosophy developed together in sixth-century B.C. Greece, laying the foundations for the Western tradition in both. Since early Greek science, or *physis* (from which our word *physics* derives), was based on speculation and casual observation rather than systematic experiment, it shaded off easily into the more general attempt to describe the nature of the world of humanity that we call philosophy. The Greeks had the benefit of existing traditions of knowledge, notably Babylonian astronomy. From the beginning, however, Greek science differed from earlier traditions in attempting to provide an essentially material description of the world without assuming the intervention of divine forces. This was a radical departure from previous thought, and more than any other factor it laid the foundation for Western science.

The Greeks were not preoccupied, as we are, with the origin of the material world. They assumed that the earliest state of the universe, which they called *chaos*, was a formless flux of elements out of which an orderly, patterned condition had emerged, the cosmos in which they lived. Classical mythology had attempted to account for the transition from chaos to cosmos by the action of the gods, but the school of science that grew up in Ionia at the beginning of the sixth century B.C. sought to explain it by material processes alone.

# The Ionian School

The first major thinkers in this school, Thales, Anaximander, and Anaximenes, all residents of the city of Miletus, posed a simple yet extraordinary question: What is the world made of? The question was extraordinary because it contradicted the commonsense observation that the world is made of many quite different things. The assumption that there was a fundamental unity beneath the varied world of appearance enabled the Ionians to posit the idea of *matter*, the single, uniform stuff from which the cosmos took shape.

Thales, who lived in the early sixth century B.C. and was renowned for having correctly forecast a solar eclipse, suggested that the fundamental cosmic substance was water. Water was not only the most abundant single material in the world, but it could take solid shape by freezing and could liquefy as a gas, thus providing a basis to account for both land and atmospheric forms. What his theory apparently failed to provide was a principle of transformation that could explain these successive states. Thus from the beginning Greek science was beset with the fundamental problem of change or, in physical terms, motion.

Anaximander attempted to deal with this problem by suggesting that the world represented a warring concourse of opposed qualities—hot and cold, wet and dry, and so forth. He conceived the first state of matter as an undifferentiated mass in which antagonistic elements or their properties were latent rather than distinct. This mass he called the *apeiron*, "the boundless," a notion similar to the traditional one of chaos. Anaximander solved the problem of motion by assuming it as a primary quality of the apeiron; the universe had started not from a condition of rest but from one of turbulence and flux. This motion had gradually sorted out the apeiron into the familiar cosmos, rather like the operation of a centrifuge. The less agitated elements, being colder and wetter, had condensed into the solid earth and its oceans; the hotter and drier parts had formed the atmosphere; and those hottest of all had burst into flame, creating the sun and the starry heavens.

Anaximander boldly guessed that life had first arisen in the warm mud or slime, producing first reptiles, then land animals, and ultimately the human race. He thus hit upon the first theory of evolution, which he defended by pointing to fossilized seashells he had discovered in the mountains, and to the parallel between infant helplessness and that of certain fish species. Most remarkably, he produced a complete account of the cosmos without reference to the gods of myth; whereas earlier Greeks had used the myth of Atlas to explain how the earth could be suspended in space, Anaximander suggested that since the earth occupied the exact center of the universe, its position was maintained by an equilibrium of forces.

Anaximenes attempted to explain the existence of spirit or intelligence by positing not water but air as the primary substance. In its grosser material forms, he suggested, air constituted the basis of the physical world, whether heated into fire or condensed into earth and water; but in its most perfect and rarefied forms it was spirit, a part of which, trapped within the body, was the soul of each human and animal form. This idea of the soul as confined by the body, to be released only upon death, had a profound influence on the thought of the fourth-century B.C. philosopher Plato and through him on Christianity as well.

Pythagoras of Samos developed the idea of a spirit that survived the death of the body into a theory of the transmigration of souls similar to that taught by Buddhism (see Chapter 7), according to which souls passed into new bodies at the time of physical death. From this Pythagoras deduced the essential unity of all living things. Pythagoras also made significant contributions to mathematics and musical theory, declaring boldly that the universe exhibited the same mathematical relationships found in harmonic intervals.

## Philosophy in the Fifth Century B.C.

Greek thinkers of the fifth century B.C. were dissatisfied with the theories of their predecessors, particularly with the account of motion given by the Ionians. Heraclitus (flourished c. 500 B.C.) of Ephesus, like Pythagoras a priest as well as a philosopher, rejected the idea of any moment of creation or process of evolution; the world, he said, "is, was, and ever will be" exactly what it is at the present moment. This meant not that the cosmos was static but, on the contrary, in a continuous state of flux and creation, an idea that he expressed in his famous paradox that one "cannot step in the same river twice."

Parmenides of Elea (c. 515–c. 450 B.C.) contended, against Heraclitus, that motion was impossible since the idea of an unoccupied space through which matter could pass was logically absurd. When it was pointed out to him that things did appear to move (for example, the lips of Parmenides denying that motion existed), the philosopher replied loftily that this was merely an illusion.

Empedocles (c. 493–c. 433 B.C.), a native of Akragas in Sicily who, like Pythagoras and Heraclitus, became something of a cult figure, propounded an ambitious cosmogony based on the idea of four primary elements—earth, air, fire, and water. These elements, combined in varying proportions by the twin forces of attraction and repulsion (which Empedocles called "love" and "strife"), produced physical substances. Because chance alone determined such combinations, monstrous forms had probably been created at an earlier period, but these, failing to adapt, had perished in the struggle for existence. Empedocles thus propounded an early form not only of the Newtonian principle of gravity but also of Darwinian natural selection. His theory of the four basic elements was accepted down to the seventeenth century A.D., although two later figures, Leucippus and Democritus of Abdera (c. 460–c. 370 B.C.), put forth a rival theory that stated that all physical entities were composed of tiny, undifferentiated pellets of matter, which they called *atoms* (literally, "without parts," or indivisible).

These daring thinkers of the sixth and fifth centuries B.C., often called pre-Socratic to distinguish them from the generation of Socrates and his successors, propounded many of the basic questions that Western science would later pursue. Not surprisingly, they scandalized contemporaries by their denial of the gods; Anaxagoras of Clazomenae (c. 500–428 B.C.), who lived in Periclean Athens, was expelled from the city for asserting that the sun was not a divinity but a white-hot stone, and the sanctuaries of Pythagoras' followers in southern Italy were sacked and burned and many of their number killed. By the mid-fifth century B.C., an intellectual reaction had set in against the pre-Socratics. One theory seemed to beget another, without any certain knowledge being reached. A consequence of this was the rise of a new group, the sophists.

The sophists shunned speculation about both the physical world and the gods, concentrating instead on teaching practical skills such as the arts of persuasion and rhetoric. Their professed aim was to understand not the nature of the world but how to get along in it. Their basic presumption was summed up in the motto of one of their number, Protagoras (c. 481–c. 411 B.C.), that "man is the measure of all things." The task of humans was not to describe an objective world but to shape it to their own ends.

## Socrates

Parmenides, Protagoras, and many other figures of the middle and late fifth century B.C. would be brought to life in the dialogues of Plato, where their theories were argued back and forth. The chief protagonist of these dialogues, however, was Plato's own teacher, Socrates (469–399 B.C.), one of the most remarkable personalities of antiquity. The son of a sculptor and a midwife, he was a frank admirer of the Spartans, a familiar figure in the marketplace where he held his impromptu discussions with pupils and passersby alike, and notorious enough to be satirized in Aristophanes' play *The Clouds*. Unlike the sophists, Socrates took no payment for his teaching; unlike them as well, he claimed to be wise only in realizing the extent of his own ignorance. His teaching method, the dialectic, consisted of a series of questions and responses on a set theme. By exploring a subject from all sides and thereby refining his students' capacity to analyze and define it, Socrates hoped to guide them toward better understanding. For his own part, Socrates never offered answers but only further questions, believing that genuine knowledge could never be communicated, only discovered.

Socrates' intellectual fearlessness and his refusal to subscribe to popular opinion, as well as the association of several of his students with the hated oligarchy that ruled Athens at the end of the Peloponnesian War, made him a natural target for those seeking a scapegoat for the city's military defeat. Arraigned on charges of impiety and corrupting the young, he was sentenced to death. Few citizens expected or even desired the execution to proceed, deeming the disgrace of the conviction sufficient to discredit the aged philosopher. Socrates' friends urged him to escape, and his captors apparently gave him an opportunity to do so. But he refused, arguing that his flight would be an admission of guilt and a defiance of the law. His death, dramatically described by Plato, gave intellectual freedom its first martyr in the West.

## Plato

Plato (c. 427–c. 347 B.C.) was deeply affected by his mentor's death. In a unique tribute, he couched most of his writings in the form of dialogues in which Socrates has the chief role. By using this literary form, Plato does not expound his own philosophy but permits it to emerge dialectically, a method well suited to his striking and often paradoxical insights. How accurately he expresses his master's thought cannot be known, but it is safe to say that if the shadow is that of Socrates, the substance is surely Plato's.

The basis of Plato's philosophy is his theory of forms. All our ideas, he asserts, whether of material entities such as chairs and tables or of conceptual ones such as beauty, justice, and goodness, are intuitions of immaterial forms that are the basis of all physical and mental reality. We first perceive a physical object or intellectual category and then, through dialectical analysis, proceed to recognize the permanent form it fleetingly and imperfectly embodies.

Plato gives an example of this process in his dialogue on love, the *Symposium*. Typically, our first intuition of love is through admiration for a beautiful body, but our feeling for the person who attracts us can deepen only if we discover a corresponding beauty of soul as well. In this way we proceed from the material to the spiritual and then from the particular to the general as we gradually come to understand that what we love is the quality of goodness that manifests itself in the beloved. The beauty that attracted us at first is transitory; the basis of our permanent affection is our own aspiration to the good, and love is the desire of two persons to fulfill that aspiration in each other.

In the hierarchy of forms, goodness is the ultimate value, and later Christian philosophers, deeply influenced by Plato, would declare goodness to be the primary quality of God. If goodness is the final object of philosophy, however, the object of civil society is justice, a quest Plato pursued in his best-known dialogue, *The Republic*, composed about 374 B.C. As in other dialogues, his characters weigh various definitions of justice; some argue that it is the force of custom or the will of the strongest. Ultimately Plato settles on the idea that justice is the harmony that arises when each person is able to pursue his or her own best talent: the artisan to build, the musician to play, and the ruler to govern.

To ensure that each talent is properly developed and employed, Plato constructs a three-tiered society that resembles an idealized version of Sparta. At the top are the *guardians*, who live communally and enjoy neither family nor possessions and whose function is wisdom and rule. The guardians are assisted by *auxiliaries*, or soldiers, chosen especially for their strength and courage. The *majority*, who are permitted moderate affluence, are trained and assigned to perform the other functions of society.

Since the capacity to rule—that is, to perceive justice in its essence and apply it to the social order—is the rarest of talents, the education of the guardian elite is protracted and difficult. Only those who have demonstrated both the necessary philosophical aptitude to

## ◉ Platonic Love ◉

*In this extract from the* Symposium, *Plato describes what has often been called platonic love.*

It is necessary for the one proceeding in the right way toward his goal to begin, when he is young, with physical beauty, and first of all, if his guide directs him properly, to love one person and in his company to beget beautiful ideas and then to observe that the beauty in one person is related to the beauty in another. If he must pursue physical beauty, he would be very foolish not to realize that the beauty in all persons is one and the same. When he has come to this conclusion, he will become the lover of all beautiful bodies and will relax the intensity of his love for one and think the less of it as something of little account. Next he will realize that beauty in the soul is more precious than that in the body, so that if he meets with a person who is beautiful in his soul, even if he has little of the physical bloom of beauty, this will be enough and he will love and cherish him and beget beautiful ideas that make young men better, so that he will in turn be forced to see the beauty in morals and laws and that the beauty in them all is related.

*Source:* M. P. O. Morford and R. J. Lenarden, *Classical Mythology* (New York: Longman, 1977), p. 126.

grasp and internalize the nature of the forms and the practical ability to apply them to affairs may be entrusted with the responsibility of the state. But since the existence of these talents, as well as the lesser ones that pertain to the lower orders, can be discovered only through time, education, and testing, it is axiomatic that all citizens, both male and female, begin on a plane of equality and be educated to the limits of their ability. Plato thus combines a radical democracy of opportunity with a radical elitism of final authority to produce a society that will exemplify, as far as humanly possible, his ideal of justice.

Plato was given an opportunity to put his utopia to the test when Dionysius II, the tyrant of Syracuse in Sicily, engaged him as a personal tutor in 366 B.C. The challenge to impart his conception of justice to a man of power was irresistible, but Dionysius soon tired of the rigors of the dialectic, and Plato returned to the more receptive pupils of the Academy, the school he had founded in the groves outside Athens sacred to the hero Academus. What remained of the experiment was the warning he had given that society would not be just until kings had become philosophers and philosophers kings.

## Aristotle

Aristotle (384–322 B.C.) was Plato's chief pupil. He began as a disciple of his master but broke away to develop his own philosophy and ultimately to found his own school, the Lyceum, located in the grove of Apollo Lyceius in Athens. Unlike Socrates and Plato, Aristotle was not a native Athenian. He was born in Stagira in northern Greece, returned to tutor Alexander of Macedon, and, threatened as Socrates had been with prosecution following Alexander's death, left Athens in the last year of his life, remarking that he would not permit the city to commit a second crime against philosophy.

Aristotle's philosophy is firmly rooted in the sensible world. He rejected Plato's conception of ideal forms that lacked any direct connection with material substance. Instead he suggested that form was inherent in matter itself. Every substance, he contended, consists of a mutable stuff on which change operates—the substrate— and an unchanging form, conceived as a kind of blueprint that determines its final material form. Thus, for example, the final mature form of the child is the adult, as the oak is of the acorn. Form and matter, which had long been distinct in Greek philosophy, were thereby reunited in Aristotle's conception of substance. The world was neither static nor chaotic but a dynamic process; change was neither illusory nor random but orderly and patterned.

This conception had significant implications for the study of both the material world and human society. In rejecting the material world as illusory, Plato rejected science for philosophy, the truths of observation for the truths of contemplation. Aristotle restored science by asserting the final and indivisible reality of material substance, and by conceiving the world in terms of orderly process he gave empirical knowledge a new and far more sophisticated basis.

Aristotle's own quest for knowledge was tireless. One ancient commentator numbered his works at 400, another at 1,000. He wrote on virtually every subject: metaphysics, natural science (including separate works on physics, astronomy, meteorology, anatomy, heredity, and even the gait and movement of animals), ethics, politics, history, literature, and rhetoric. His essays on prior and posterior analytics were the founding works of Western logic, and his *Poetics* was the first systematic treatment of aesthetics. In addition, his pupils undertook a complete history of the sciences under his direction. It was no wonder that the Middle Ages called him the "master of those who know," and when the poet Dante referred to Aristotle as simply "the philosopher," readers understood at once who was meant.

Aristotle was no less interested in achieving a just society than Plato, but his approach was characteristically different. After analyzing the constitutions of some 158 Greek cities, he defined the basic types as monarchy (rule by one), aristocracy (rule by a minority), and democracy (majority rule). Each type had its own virtues and defects; the most stable form, he felt, would be one that combined the best elements of aristocracy and democracy, rewarding merit and encouraging the growth of a prosperous middle class.

Generally enlightened, Aristotle nonetheless shared some of the prejudices of his time and culture. He defended slavery, arguing that it was in the nature of some people to obey others, and unlike Plato, he held women to be naturally inferior to men. Pragmatic rather than heroic, he praised the "golden mean" in both private and political conduct and counseled against excess in any form. If his thought was less daring than Plato's, it was eminently more serviceable in the daily world. Between them, the two men set the terms for much of subsequent Western thought. The British philosopher Alfred North Whitehead remarked that Western philosophy was a mere series of footnotes to Plato, and Christianity owed much to him. As for Aristotle, it is no exaggeration to say that he created the Western intellectual curriculum, stamping and defining its various disciplines and branches of knowledge.

## The Rise of Macedon

Despite the intellectual brilliance of the fourth century B.C., the Greeks failed to find a basis for political stability. No single state could fill the vacuum left by the collapse of Athenian power, and peaceful cohabitation proved as elusive as ever. The early years of the fourth century saw divisive skirmishes among Sparta, Thebes, Corinth, and Argos that invited the intervention of the Great King of Persia. By the so-called King's Peace of 387 B.C. the Greeks bought a brief respite, but the price was high; many of the Greek cities of Asia Minor, whose freedom had supposedly been achieved by the victories in the Persian Wars 100 years earlier, were handed back to Persian rule. It was not long before Thebans and Spartans were once again fighting. In 371 B.C. Thebes defeated Sparta at Leuctra and became for a few years the dominating force in Greek politics.

Such instability was bound to attract outside intervention. The Persians were too far away and had problems in their own empire. Just to the north of the Greeks, however, lay the kingdom of Macedon, hitherto a backward land of farmers and agricultural laborers. Although the Greeks considered them barbarians, the Macedonians spoke a rough Greek dialect; and if they managed to avoid becoming entangled in Greek political feuding, it was principally because they were kept occupied defending themselves from raiders from the north.

In 359 B.C., with southern Greece still divided, Philip became king of Macedon. Over the next 20 years he gave ample evidence of his powers as an orator, general, and statesman, but perhaps his greatest asset was his ability to manipulate and outmaneuver even the most cunning Greek politicians. By negotiating with his enemies secretly and singly, Philip soon brought virtually the whole of Greece under his rule.

Before he could challenge the Greeks, however, Philip needed to secure Macedon's northern borders and restore the morale of his troops. By 356 B.C. he had already begun to look south to Athens and Thebes. After a trial expedition into Greece met with defeat, Philip retreated to Macedon to recoup. Like a battering ram, as Philip himself said, he drew back to hit harder the next time. By 349 he was ready to return to the offensive. Two half brothers of his, possible contenders for his throne, were living in the northern Greek town of Olynthus. As a pretext for action he demanded their surrender, and when they refused, he attacked and razed Olynthus in 348. In 346 Philip turned to Delphi, one of the most venerated sanctuaries in the Greek world, and seized control of the governing council. The message to the rest of Greece was clear.

Yet Philip himself always denied that he had plans to conquer Greece. There was even talk of an Athenian-Macedonian alliance that could unite the Greeks and lead them against Persia. The Athenian orator and politician Isocrates (436–338 B.C.) publicized the project in a pamphlet called *Philip*. Disunity in Athens, however, undermined the scheme. The pro-Macedonian faction at Athens found itself increasingly under pressure from a conservative majority that could not conceive of Athenian power subordinated to a barbarian king. The success of Philip's opponents at Athens unquestionably owed much to the fact that their principal spokesman was also the greatest Greek orator of the day, Demosthenes (384–322 B.C.).

Demosthenes proved a formidable opponent to Philip. A man of great energy and resolve, he had overcome a speech defect to become one of the foremost rhetoricians in Athens. Demosthenes persuaded the Athenians to levy taxes and pour money into military preparations to defend Greek liberty. In 341 the Athenians sent troops to northern Greece to attack territory held by the Macedonians, and over the following two years they continued to clash with Macedonian troops and allies; Philip could no longer delay. When the Athenians learned of the Macedonians' advance south, the city was mobilized, and Demosthenes himself went to Thebes to seek an alliance with his former enemy. At Chaeronea in 338 Philip, assisted by his son Alexander, defeated a combined Greek army. In a congress at Corinth the same year, a league of all Greek cities except Sparta proclaimed Philip its captain-general.

A year later Philip began plans to enlarge his empire even further by attacking Persia, but he was never to carry them out. In 336 he was assassinated under mysterious circumstances, perhaps through the jealousy of Olympias, Alexander's mother, for Philip's new wife. Alexander, tutored by Aristotle himself, succeeded him.

His career was to prove even more spectacular, but the loss of Philip at so delicate a stage in the reestablishment of peace was fateful for the Greeks. The new king had little interest in establishing good terms with his Greek neighbors; he was eager to invade Asia and pursue his dreams of world conquest.

## The Conquests of Alexander the Great

With the accession of Alexander in 336 B.C. the history of the Greeks was transferred to a wider stage. The spread of Greek culture throughout much of Asia was, in fact, one of Alexander's principal achievements and, unlike the empire he sought to build, one of long duration. Yet Alexander himself, however well disposed to Hellenic ideas, was not reluctant to use force to dominate the Greeks. When in 335 the Thebans took advan-

---

### ◉ A Call to Arms ◉

*Demosthenes tries to shame his Athenian audience into taking action against Philip of Macedon.*

What is the cause of these events? Not without reason and just cause were the Greeks of old so ready to defend their freedom but now so resolved on servitude. Men of Athens, there was then something in the spirit of the people which is not there now, something which overcame even Persian gold and kept Hellas [Greece] free, something which admitted defeat on neither land nor sea. Now the loss of that has ruined everything and made chaos of our affairs. What was that thing? Nothing involved or tricky. It was just that one and all hated those who accepted bribes from men who aimed to rule or ruin Hellas. To be convicted of taking bribes was a most grievous crime; yes, they punished the guilty one with the utmost severity, and there was no room for intercession or pardon. Therefore the right moment for achieving each enterprise, the opportunity Fortune often extends even to the indifferent at the expense of the vigilant, could not be bought from statesmen or from generals, any more than could our mutual good will, our distrust of tyrants and foreigners, or any such thing at all. But now these possessions have been sold off like market wares, and in exchange there have been imported things which have brought ruin and disease to Hellas.

And what are these things? Envy, if a man has received a bribe; laughter, if he admits it; indulgence for a man proved guilty; hatred for his critic; and all the other things that come from bribery. As for warships, troops, abundance of funds and equipment, and all else that may be held to form the strength of our cities, in every instance they are present in greater abundance and extent than in days gone by. But all this is being made useless, unavailing, unprofitable because of those who traffic in them.

*Source:* P. MacKendrick and H. M. Howe, eds., *Classics in Translation* (Madison: University of Wisconsin Press, 1966), vol. 1, p. 288.

tage of trouble in the north to stage a revolt, Alexander and his troops stormed the city, razed it, and sold the population into slavery. Thereafter the horrified Greeks provided no more opposition to him, and he was free to turn his attention to the campaign against Persia. By the time of his death in 323 B.C. at the age of only 33, he had extended Macedonian rule from the Adriatic to the river Indus.

The great expedition left for Asia Minor in 334 B.C. Success came quickly with a lightning victory over the forces of the Persian governors at the river Granicus, although Alexander himself was almost killed in the confusion. Pausing only to liberate the Greek cities of Asia Minor, in 333 he pushed south into Syria, where he defeated the Persians at Issus. Most of the next year was spent in a siege of Tyre. Alexander's troops finally destroyed it in time to reach Egypt by the winter. Not only did the Egyptians give way without fighting, but the oracle of Zeus Ammon prudently greeted him as the son of God and rightful pharaoh of Egypt. While in that country Alexander founded Alexandria, later to be one of the great cities of the ancient world. In 331 he moved east of the river Tigris, where he scored one of his greatest victories at Gaugamela; although vastly outnumbered, his forces penetrated the enemy lines and drove the Per-

sian king, Darius, into flight. At Persepolis, the old Persian capital, Alexander burned the royal palace, seized the treasury, and began to enlist the young men of Persia in his army.

Over the next three years Alexander battered the rugged northern and eastern sections of the Persian Empire into submission. In 326 he reached northwestern India, but after a desperate battle against the warrior king Poros and his forces (which included 200 elephants), his men would go no further. Even Alexander's drive would not persuade them to take on the kingdoms of the Ganges, and he was compelled to turn back to Persia. The main part of the expedition took the route they had followed on the outward journey, but Alexander, with a small contingent, set out to explore the desert wastes of the coast while another group went by ship. They made it back to Persia, but only with heavy losses and terrible suffering, first from thirst and then from flood. Even Alexander's iron constitution was not proof against such continued ordeals. While preparing yet another campaign, against southern Arabia, he became sick and died within ten days.

Such a life was made possible in part by the remarkable personality and restless energy that characterize his portraits and that certainly marked his career. At the

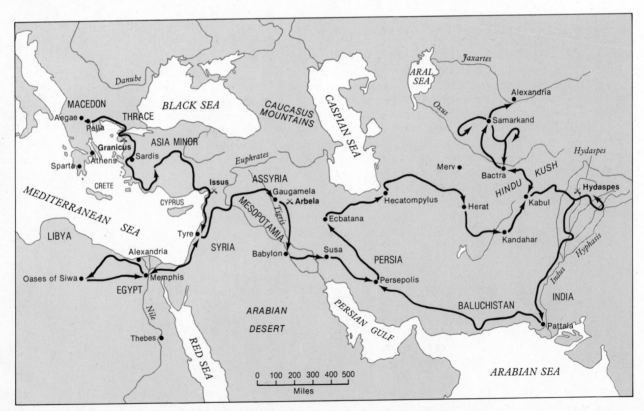

**5.1** *Alexander's Conquest of the Persian Empire, 334–323* B.C.

same time, Alexander had other virtues. Often against the wishes of his followers, he rejected the traditional Greek contempt for foreigners. From the beginning he meant his empire to be governed by principles of tolerance. The peoples whom he conquered were encouraged to retain their native laws, religions, and customs, and he himself set an example of "the marriage of east and west" by taking a Persian bride. At the same time, to unite the enormous variety of peoples involved in his conquest, he founded more than 70 cities, all of them called Alexandria or Alexandropolis (one in Egypt and another in northern Greece still survive) and all embodying the principles of Greek urban planning, architecture, and institutions. Through these strongholds many of his conquests survived the confusion that followed his death.

Alexander's critics have often observed that he never seems to have paid any regard to who would succeed him or how his empire would have been ruled on a permanent and stable basis. Apart from the cities he founded, he retained, for the most part, the administrative structure of the Persian Empire. He often employed former Persian governors, several of whom betrayed him, although in the army most of the principal officers remained Macedonian. In the detailed planning and execution of a campaign, however, he functioned efficiently. Lines of communication were kept open over very long distances with the arrival of reinforcements and medical supplies from Macedon. Such careful organization, coupled with his personal charisma, held his troops together under the most arduous conditions. Yet toward the end of his life he began to play the part of the great king with too much enthusiasm. To the discomfort of his Macedonian old guard, he wore Persian dress, required them to make obeisance before him, and even assigned Persian brides to them. It is by no means certain that, had he survived his illness, his empire would have been more permanent. His achievements still stand: the spread of Greek culture from a small corner of southeastern Europe to most of the Mediterranean and central Asian world and the memory of his life—the scope and daring of his conquests, his heroic personality, and the new world that he sought to create.

## The Hellenistic Kingdoms and the Cosmopolitan World

In the absence of a successor nominated by Alexander, disagreements among his generals after his death resulted in the breakup of the Macedonian empire. The most important of the new states were Egypt, Perga-

mum, Macedon, and the kingdom of the Seleucids, each of which fought the others until the Romans conquered them all. They continued to spread Greek culture and customs, a process called "Hellenization" after the Greek name for Greece, *Hellas*. But the resulting period, the Hellenistic Age, represented a hybrid civilization in which Greek and western Asian cultures were freely blended and exchanged.

## The Ptolemies and the Seleucids

The Egyptian city of Alexandria remained the most significant center of Greek learning. There Ptolemy, a former officer of Alexander's, proposed the creation of an institute for study and research called the Temple of the Muses—the "Museum." Ptolemy himself had bolstered his claim to power by snatching Alexander's body and burying it at Alexandria, although the tomb has never been discovered. In 305 B.C. he took the title of king and, on his death in 283, was succeeded by his son. The dynasty of the Ptolemies continued to rule Egypt until Rome's absorption of it after the reign of Cleopatra in 31 B.C.

Ptolemaic rule had little of the multiracial character of Alexander's original design. Egypt was run primarily by a Greco-Macedonian elite, and Greek remained the official business language. Cleopatra was the only Ptolemaic ruler who learned Egyptian.

The wealth accumulated by the Ptolemies became legendary—not surprisingly, given the elaborate taxing and licensing system of the state. Even beekeepers had to have a license from the king, and fishermen were required to pay a part of their catch to a representative of the royal treasury. Little or nothing of the money raised from the peasants in the form of such levies as taxes, death duties, sales taxes, and transit dues was used to improve their lot. Some was spent on maintaining the strongest navy in the Mediterranean, and the rest ended up in the royal coffers.

The former Persian territories in Asia were seized by the commander of Alexander's footguard, Seleucus, who by the time of his murder in 280 B.C. had sufficiently consolidated his power to be succeeded by his son, Antiochus. The Seleucids ruled until 83 B.C., when they were briefly replaced by Armenian kings and then annexed by Rome. Even Seleucus himself, however, had to give up Alexander's Indian conquests, and the Seleucid portion of the empire shrank rapidly. As early as 275 B.C. Antiochus held off with great difficulty an invasion of the Gauls, a tribe that had migrated from western Europe, only to become involved in futile wars with Egypt. The sheer size of the Seleucids' territory precluded the establishment of a Ptolemaic-style bureaucracy, and much of it was ruled by local governors. Anti-

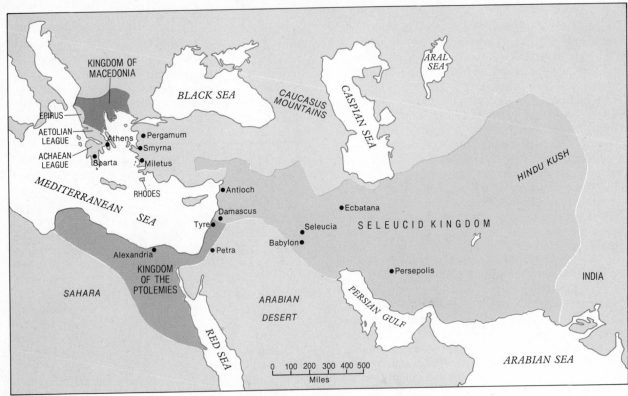

*5.2 Hellenistic Kingdoms, c. 275 B.C.*

och, the royal capital, was designed on Greek lines, and Greek continued to be spoken in Seleucid cities as far east as the river Tigris for centuries following the fall of the kingdom.

## Macedon and the Hellenistic Greeks

Macedon acquired a permanent dynasty only in 275 B.C., after several generals had fought for its possession. The eventual victor was Antigonus, a grandson of one of Alexander's commanders. His successors spent most of their time fighting with neighboring kingdoms for influence in central and southern Greece, where two competing leagues of poleis, the Aetolian and Achaean, battled each other as well as external enemies.

The vision of a single great state, Hellenic in culture but multiethnic in character, did not die with Alexander but remained alive as an ideal until the Romans unified the eastern Mediterranean and western Asia two centuries later. Alexander had prayed at a celebrated banquet for a union of all hearts and a commonwealth of Macedonians and Persians; the philosopher Zeno envisioned a universal city under one divine law; and the

word derived from this, *cosmopolitanism*, originally taken up by the Cynics to indicate their attachment to no state, was finally adopted in the Hellenized world to signify world citizenship. This remained (as it does today) an ideal rather than a reality, but it had some practical consequences for the old Greek poleis themselves, now under Macedonian domination but enjoying a certain degree of autonomy.

Honorary citizenship was increasingly conferred on foreigners, and whole cities exchanged citizenship as a mark of friendship and alliance, as in the case of Athens and Rhodes. Arbitration was extensively adopted in the third century B.C. as a means of settling boundary claims, and foreign commissioners were frequently invited to adjudicate intracity disputes, a practice that would have been almost unthinkable among the jealously divided and fiercely independent poleis of the fifth century. Leagues grew up among cities, which shared a joint army, pursued a common foreign policy, and introduced a common system of taxes, tariffs, weights, and measures.

The best known of these leagues, the Aetolian and Achaean, developed innovative federal structures that were models of cooperation. The Aetolian League, centered in the region north of the Gulf of Corinth, granted dual citizenship, its members retaining their native citizenship along with citizenship in the league. This practice was known as *sympolity*. More distant states were linked to the league by *isopolity*, according to which their citizens enjoyed Aetolian civil but not political rights. In the Achaean League, based in the northern Peloponnesus, the mutual exchange of citizenship was rare. Members of the federation shared a common coinage and uniform standards of measurement and used a system of federal courts. Both leagues had relatively democratic constitutions, with power vested in each case in an assembly, a representative council, and an elected general. The federal governments could levy taxes, raise armies, and conduct foreign policy. These and other Greek leagues of this period illustrate a trend away from the distinctive autonomy of the polis in favor of a significant degree of cooperation and unity.

Temples and sanctuaries, such as Delphi, had long been considered neutral ground, but after 270 B.C. whole cities, including Smyrna and Miletus, proclaimed their permanent neutrality, and more and more places sought the status of *asyla* (asylums), which were immune from reprisal. Obviously, these claims were not always respected, but they had a certain deterrent force. War itself became milder, at least temporarily; the old practice of slaughtering the males in a conquered city and selling the women and children into slavery was first modified into a general sale of both sexes and finally abolished altogether; when it was revived, as against Mantinea in 223 B.C., it aroused a storm of protest. In short, international public opinion had begun to develop, at least among the older Greek cities, and the idea of a world without borders, of a universal city of the spirit, persisted through Roman times until it was given its final expression in antiquity by the fifth-century A.D. Christian philosopher Augustine in his book *The City of God*.

*Athena Slaying Giant*, detail of a frieze in the altar to Zeus at Pergamum, shows the head of the giant Aleyoneus, whose hair is grasped by Athena. [National Museum, Berlin]

## Pergamum and Bactria

Pergamum, an ancient Greek polis in Asia Minor, was the most influential Hellenistic kingdom in Greek affairs. For a time it had been a Seleucid possession. Its local governor, a eunuch called Philetaerus, had used the money in the treasury to hire his own army; he was succeeded by a nephew, Eumenes I (263–241 B.C.), who governed Pergamum with the support of the Seleucids' great rivals, the Ptolemies. Under later rulers Pergamum won a reputation as a great cultural and artistic center, reaching a high point in the reign of Eumenes II (197–159 B.C.). Its chief religious shrine was the immense altar to Zeus erected by Eumenes II around 180 B.C. to commemorate the victories of his father, Attalus I, over the Gauls during the preceding century. The tangled, writhing bodies of the figures on the frieze, with their intensity of gesture and facial expression, represent one of the high points of Hellenistic art. Other Pergamene rulers reinforced their reputation as champions of Hellenism by contributing money and building projects to Athens and other Greek cities.

At the eastern end of Alexander's conquests, on the northeastern frontier of India, a new kingdom, Bactria, broke off from Seleucid rule around 250 B.C. Its control of trade routes throughout central Asia lasted until the middle of the following century and brought the descendants of Alexander's Greek mercenaries into contact with the peoples of India. Even after Bactria had been overrun by central Asian nomads, Greek-style cities such as Begram and Taxila continued to exert a cultural influence: Gandharan Buddhist sculpture, the earliest monumental Buddhist art, made use of Greek styles and techniques. Thus in the two centuries following Alexander's death the various Hellenistic kingdoms each contributed to the Hellenization of vast tracts of Asia.

In the meantime, a new political force had begun to make its presence felt in the western Mediterranean:

**A head of the Buddha, from Gandhara. The expression is classically Greek. [Scala/Art Resource: Victoria and Albert Museum, London]**

Rome. In 133 B.C. the last king of Pergamum died childless and willed his kingdom to Rome; by 31 B.C. the defeat of Cleopatra left almost the whole of Alexander's empire in Roman hands. Thus the history of the Hellenistic world became fused with that of Rome.

# Changing Economic Patterns

Although in some ways the Hellenization of western Asia produced significant social and economic changes for both natives and new arrivals, it did not cause a total revolution. The Greek poleis were, after all, famous for being able to maintain their independent character under the most trying circumstances. The citizens of the newly founded cities of the Hellenistic period continued to own the land in and immediately around the city and

used slaves or resident aliens to work for them. The rest of the land belonged to the king and was worked by peasants as it had been for centuries. The basic level of agricultural production thus remained fairly constant.

Some rulers did try to make improvements. Both the Ptolemies and the Seleucids encouraged the introduction of more sophisticated agricultural equipment, such as iron plows and more efficient oil and wine presses, and introduced new fruit and crops. One of the Ptolemies' successes was a new quick-growing wheat that gave a double harvest and a higher yield. On occasion, the extra supplies were sent to feed the urban poor, although in general the kings, or their local representatives, were unwilling to subsidize the growing urban population at their own expense. In some cases the cities tried to solve the problem of subsistence on their own. Samos, for example, set up a fund for making loans; the interest on the loans was used to purchase grain, which was then distributed free to the citizens.

Within each independent city-state, industry and manufacturing developed according to the needs and abilities of the resident artisans. Sidon was famous for its glassware, Tarsus for its linen, and Antioch for its gold and silver, as might be expected for a royal capital. The volume remained small, and there is no evidence of mass production. Most businesses were family-run, with perhaps two or three slaves. Economic power was concentrated in the hands of the royal family and a small minority of wealthy landowners who, rather than providing food to the urban centers, preferred to ornament them with new temples, porticoes, and theaters that would perpetuate the memory of their donors.

In one significant respect, however, Alexander's conquests did change economic patterns. Trade, both in manufactured goods and in raw materials, became increasingly international, and the descendants of Alexander's Greeks found themselves in commercial contact with the people of the East. The kingdom of Bactria continued to serve as a center for Greek interests in central Asia, but other trade routes were also developed. Delos and Rhodes lay on the routes connecting Greece and Italy with the east and were also a conduit for the Black Sea trade in slaves, fish, fur, wheat, and timber. To the south the great caravan routes connecting the Mediterranean with Arabia, India, and central Asia passed through Phoenician and Syrian ports.

The principal route, which ran through Seleucid territory, followed the river Tigris to the Persian Gulf and then the coast of Baluchistan to the mouth of the river Indus. Although under Seleucid control, the route was used for a while by the Ptolemies, but in time they developed their own trade route, which involved sailing around the south coast of Arabia to the Gulf of Aden. Although the route was longer, it opened up the Arabian spice market as well as that of India. The Sabaeans, the ancient inhabitants of modern Yemen, produced myrrh

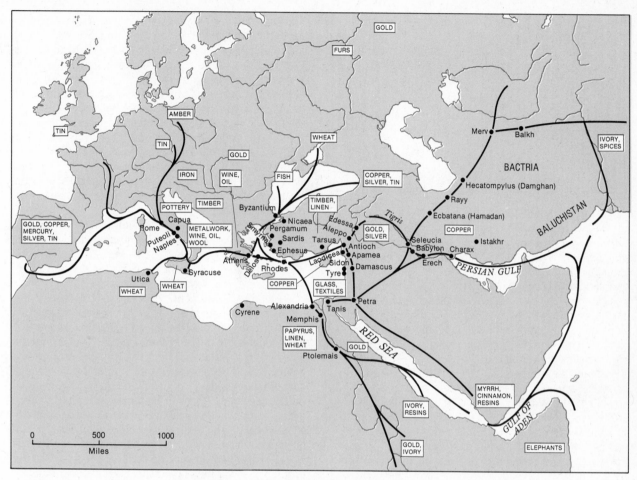

*5.3 Trade in the Hellenistic World, c. 145* B.C.

and cinnamon, both highly regarded and expensive in the west.

More complicated was the importation of elephants. After Alexander's Indian campaign, the strategic value and prestige of having elephants in a royal army appealed to his successors. The Ptolemies had a source fairly close to home, for they captured their elephants in what is now Somalia; the Seleucids, by contrast, had to import theirs from India. Nor was this ancient form of military extravagance without its problems. On a famous occasion in 217 B.C., at a battle fought between Ptolemy IV and Antiochus III, Ptolemy's forest elephants were no match for the larger Indian elephants of the Seleucid army. Terrified by the smell and the trumpeting of these beasts, according to the Greek historian Polybius, the African elephants fled.

Trade contacts such as these were sufficiently important to the Seleucids for them to station a permanent ambassador at the court of one of the Indian kingdoms, the Mauryan empire. One of the ambassadors, Megas-

thenes, wrote a detailed account of India, now lost, that circulated widely in the Greco-Roman world (see Chapter 2).

Although the cultural exchange resulting from these commercial links was limited, some mutual influence undoubtedly occurred. Many of the Greek coins minted in India have an inscription in Greek on one side and in a local script on the other. Western theories of medicine and astrology were imported into India, and some Greek settlers became assimilated into the native populations. Some were said to have become Buddhists, while others were described by a later writer as the equivalent of the warrior class in Hindu society.

All such contacts throughout Asia in the Hellenistic period were originally motivated by the desire to establish trading relations, but they also awakened curiosity in some Greek minds as to the nature of the wider world. Polybius, the Greek historian, joined a military expedition that seems to have sailed down the western coast of Africa as far as southern Morocco. Another traveler,

Pytheas, set off on a journey from the Greek city of Massilia (modern Marseilles) in 320 B.C. that took him as far north as the Arctic. From his description he seems to have reached either Iceland or the northern coast of Norway.

---

🏵

## ALEXANDRIA: CAPITAL OF THE PTOLEMIES

---

From the time of its foundation by the great conqueror in 332 B.C., Alexandria became a natural meeting place for the cultures of Europe and Asia. Its planner was Deinocrates, like Alexander a Macedonian. Laid out on a grand scale, its main street was said to be 100 feet wide and lined with shops and bazaars. The principal building complex was the royal palace, which served both as the residence of the Ptolemies and the seat of government. Surrounded by gardens and fountains, it was occupied for the most part by the Greek-speaking bureaucrats who administered Ptolemaic Egypt.

The center of Greek culture at Alexandria was the Museum, one of the major intellectual institutions of the ancient world. Within its walls were lecture halls, laboratories, observatories, a dining hall, a park, and a zoo. Its library was said to have contained over half a million scrolls, and its principal librarian was also the head of the whole organization and thus one of the most powerful figures in Alexandria. In some ways the Museum resembled a modern university, except that the scholars and scientists who worked there had no obligation to teach. They were supported by the Ptolemies to pursue their own research and to glorify the royal family.

At first the Greek community tried to keep out the native Egyptians, but as intermarriage became more common, Alexander's dream of fusing cultures became at least in part fulfilled. The Alexandrians came to think of themselves, and be thought of by others, as cosmopolitans, citizens of the world that revolved around their city. They were notorious for their rowdiness, always ready for a spectacle, fond of noisy demonstrations, rude to foreigners, arrogant, and opinionated. The Ptolemies kept them more or less contented by constructing race tracks and parks and staging lavish public festivals and sports events that were often the pretext for violent street demonstrations.

Only the Jews of Alexandria, one of the largest settlements of the Diaspora (the settlement of the Jews outside Palestine), maintained their cultural independence. Ptolemy I had encouraged the establishment of a Jewish community, and by the time of Ptolemy III (246–221 B.C.) there were three synagogues in the city. The Jewish population lived together in one district of the city and had its own governing council. The Jews were given the right to be judged by their own magistrates according to their own law, a privilege that brought some hostility from Greek Alexandrians, who felt that religion was a private matter. With time the Jews came to speak Greek, and the Old Testament was translated into that language, a version known as the Septuagint. Services at the synagogues were conducted in Greek, and many Jews took Greek names, such as Theophilus ("lover of God"). The Jews of Alexandria were allowed to own land and were often employed as tax collectors but were rarely involved in trade or moneylending. On several occasions Jewish generals led Egyptian forces, and Jewish mercenaries were not unknown.

Much of the activity at Alexandria centered around the harbor, one of the most international of its times, with traffic from the Nile and the Red Sea as well as the whole of the Mediterranean. Great quays and warehouses were constructed there, as well as Alexandria's most famous monument, the Pharos. This was a vast lighthouse, named after the small island on which it stood at the mouth of the harbor. The Pharos was 440 feet tall, and the beam of light from its lantern was intensified by a series of reflectors. A marvel of the latest technology, it became an apt symbol of the city whose port it illuminated.

There are few traces of Ptolemaic Alexandria today; owing to a change in sea level, most of the ancient city is underwater. The tomb of Alexander, a pilgrimage center for centuries, has never been found, and the Pharos was destroyed by an earthquake in the fourteenth century A.D. Yet the memory of the city's glamour and cultural activity has not altogether faded, nor has its power to fuse different cultures. One of the greatest modern Greek poets, Constantine Cavafy (1863–1933), spent his life there, and much of his work evokes the cosmopolitan world of Hellenistic Alexandria.

## Hellenistic Science and Religion

By the time of Alexander, the Greeks had discovered two basic principles of science: the use of mathematics as a means of investigating natural phenomena and the idea of establishing general truths by practical research. Both of these were applied in the development of Hellenistic science, which made greater strides than the science of any comparable period before the sixteenth and seventeenth centuries A.D.

The most important advances of the Hellenistic Age were in the life sciences—Theophrastus (c. 369–c. 285 B.C.), a successor to Aristotle at the Lyceum, founded the science of botany—and in geography and astronomy, whose study was stimulated by the conquests of Alexander and the requirements of trade. By the mid-fourth century, Heraclides of Pontus (c. 390–310 B.C.) had discovered that the earth revolved daily on its axis. The astronomer Aristarchus of Samos (c. 310–230 B.C.) wrote a treatise on the size of the sun and the moon, arguing that the sun was the center of the universe. This was regarded as impiety by most of his contemporaries, to whose view of life the earth and human existence were central. The most influential Hellenistic astronomer, Hipparchus (c. 190–126 B.C.), proposed a rival theory involving cyclical movements of the planets and measured the lunar and solar year with considerable accuracy. Hipparchus produced the first work on trigonometry, *The Table of Chords*; discovered the irregular occurrence of equinoxes; and compiled a catalog of some 850 stars. The geocentric theory eventually received its classic statement in the *Almagest* of Claudius Ptolemy, a second-century A.D. Greek scholar.

An even more remarkable figure was Eratosthenes (c. 275–194 B.C.), the head of the library at Alexandria under Ptolemy III, who measured the circumference of the earth, calculated by using a shadow to determine the angle between the Egyptian cities of Alexandria and Aswan.

Eratosthenes' calculation was made possible by the earlier work of the great geometer Euclid (flourished c. 300 B.C.). Euclid also wrote on astronomy and music, but his major achievement was *The Elements*, the most important work on geometry in antiquity. One of the most popular textbooks of all time, it was translated into Hebrew, Latin, Arabic, and western languages and has remained useful up to our time. A little later Archimedes of Syracuse worked on the geometry of cylinders and spheres and in the process established the mathematical value of pi (3.14), also discovered independently in India.

---

### ☙ ARCHIMEDES OF SYRACUSE: PRACTICAL SCIENCE IN THE ANCIENT WORLD

Perhaps the greatest figure in Hellenistic science, Archimedes (c. 287–212 B.C.) was born at Syracuse in Sicily. After completing a period of research at Alexandria, he returned to Syracuse to become chief scientific adviser to King Hieron II (265–215 B.C.). He wrote on geometry and calculus and considered that his greatest work was in theoretical mathematics. On his tomb was engraved the figure of a sphere within a cylinder, a symbol of his concern for pure, abstract form.

Yet Archimedes' chief claims to fame are based on

the practical use to which he put his knowledge. The inventor of the science of hydrostatics, the measurement and use of waterpower, he constructed a planetarium, worked by water, to represent the movements of the sun and planets around the stationary earth. He developed pulleys and a drilling system to pump out ships and to drain the fields of the Nile delta after flooding. The archetypal absentminded scientist, he was, it was said, too forgetful to eat; and when he discovered the concept of specific gravity by noticing the water he displaced in his bathtub, it is said that he leaped out and ran naked through the streets, crying "Eureka!" ("I have found it!"). When Hieron had constructed a huge ship, the *Syracusia*, Archimedes found a way of launching it and then said to the king: "Find me a place to stand and I shall move the world."

In mathematics his achievements include the invention of a system for expressing extremely large numbers and the solution of various problems relating to the cube. Although most of his work was done at Syracuse, he corresponded with the mathematicians working at Alexandria. A letter to Eratosthenes there included a complex mathematical analysis described in the form of an elegaic poem. Like many of his contemporaries, he applied his theories to the study of astronomy, and his planetarium still survived in the time of Cicero, 200 years later.

All Archimedes' skill was needed in 215 B.C., when Syracuse was besieged by the Romans. He spent his time inventing ways to defend the city, including iron gates that caught up the Roman soldiers as they advanced toward the walls and lifted them into the air, and pulleys for raising huge stones or lumps of lead to be dropped on enemy ships. Finally, in 212 an outbreak of malaria undermined the morale of both Romans and Syracusans, and the city, which the Athenians had failed to take 200 years earlier, was forced to surrender. It is said that when Archimedes realized that his beloved Syracuse was about to fall, "he wept much." The Roman soldiers, storming the city, killed him by accident. Archimedes' career became symbolic of the achievements of the Hellenistic scientists; a profoundly original thinker, he was also famous for his patriotism.

---

## Health and Medicine

The father of Greek medicine, Hippocrates, was born on the island of Cos in the mid-fifth century B.C. and traveled widely in the Greek world. His writings include case studies of various illnesses that show his concern with the practical details of curing invalids. Doctors still subscribe to the Hippocratic Oath, which prescribes a physician's ethical responsibility. Hippocrates' successors were more interested in research, which often involved dissection. According to the Roman scholar Celsus (early first century A.D.), who wrote a book about Hellenistic medicine, doctors not only dissected corpses to study their entrails but also practiced human vivisection on criminals. Whether this is true or not, Hellenistic doctors made important discoveries concerning digestion and the vascular system. The Alexandrian physician Herophilus, working in the early third century B.C., discovered that the brain was the center of the nervous system and that the arteries carried blood, and he was the first person to measure the human pulse. His dissections enabled him to discover the ovaries and perhaps also the fallopian tubes. His contemporary Erasistratus, a fellow Alexandrian, distinguished between the sensory and the motor nerves and discovered the heart's function in the circulation of the blood.

## Ruler Cults and Mystery Religions

Interest in the workings of the body did not preclude a concern for more spiritual matters, and the Hellenistic age saw a number of fundamental changes in the nature of Greek religion. From the time of Homer, traditional beliefs had centered around the Olympic pantheon, the 12 deities, including Zeus and Athena, who were thought to live on Mount Olympus in northern Greece. The Greeks thought of their gods as like themselves, distinguished only by their powers and their immortality, and they came to symbolize various human attributes: Ares, the war god, personified aggression; Aphrodite, sexual love; and so on. Over time a wide variety of local cults sprang up, and the concept of the original deities became blurred by the variations of regional practices. By the fifth century B.C. educated Greeks had begun to doubt the existence of the traditional gods. Temples were still built and rituals celebrated, but the old beliefs began to lose their power. When the Greeks came into contact with the enormous variety of Asian religions, fundamental changes occurred.

The first major development was initiated by Alexander, who claimed to be descended from Hercules and Achilles and in 324 B.C. ordered the Greek states to pay him "godlike honors." The subsequent practice of ruler worship became a feature of many Hellenistic kingdoms. In Egypt, where from time immemorial the people had been accustomed to think of their pharaoh as the incarnation of the sun god, Ptolemy I began by deifying Alexander, and his son deified both his father and himself. From then on the reigning monarch automatically became a god, and the Seleucids soon followed the example of their Egyptian rivals.

Clearly, these ruler cults served political purposes,

## ◉ Greek Medicine ◉

*In the following extract, taken from his work on epidemics, Hippocrates describes his approach to the treatment of illness.*

These are the things observed in disease from which we have learned to judge them, studying the general nature of mankind as well as the peculiarities of the individual, the disease as well as the patients, the measures taken and the physician who prescribed them. Our judgment is easier or harder in proportion to our knowledge of these matters. First of all, there is the general climate and any local peculiarities of geography and weather. Then there is the particular patient—his habits and way of life, his occupation, his age; his words, manner of speaking, talkativeness, silence; his disposition; his sleep or lack of it, the time and nature of his dreams, his gestures, his tears. Thirdly, from the onset of the disease we must consider the movements of the bowels and the urine, the spitting and vomiting; we must observe the causes of each stage in the progress of the disease, and likewise their effects, and how it finally reaches a favorable end or death. During its course we must study the patient's sweats and chills, coughs and sneezes, hiccoughs and breathing, belching and gas, and bleeding and piles. From our observation of these we must then decide what course the disease will take next.

*Source:* P. MacKendrick and H. M. Howe, eds., *Classics in Translation* (Madison: University of Wisconsin Press, 1966), vol. 1, p. 311.

reinforcing the power and prestige not only of the kings but of their dynasties as well. It is doubtful that they satisfied religious needs on any broad scale, and the conquering Macedonians and Greeks, far from exporting Greek religion to Asia, found themselves subscribing to Asian and Egyptian religions, which in many cases they carried back to Greece. The most popular cult was that of the Egyptian deities Sarapis and Isis. Sarapis was invented by Ptolemy I, who adapted the cult of Osiris, the Egyptian god of the underworld, to Greek tastes. Sarapis was a god of healing and a protector of travelers, and by the second century he was worshiped as far west as Sicily. Isis, his wife, was even more important, offering the promise of life after death to all of her initiates who had undergone certain mysterious rituals.

Other "mystery cults" also flourished, as did the practice of magic and astrology. The Greeks, with their tendency to religious eclecticism, were attracted to the mystery cults, which focused on the afterlife and offered hope in a period when the economic condition of many people had deteriorated. At the same time one of the few Greek cults that developed and spread throughout the Hellenistic period was that of Tyche, or chance, a force beyond control or understanding that dictated the fate of human existence.

Paradoxically, the sheer variety of cults and religions, from the Syrian Hadad to the Phrygian Sabazios to the Anatolian Great Mother Cybele, made the ground fertile for the development of monotheism. Hadad, after all, represented Zeus in another context, and the Greek sun god Apollo and the Egyptian sun god Helios were clearly two versions of the same idea. Thus all gods, Greek and non-Greek, might be regarded as aspects of a single universal deity.

These various strands of belief, combined with the monistic world view of Aristotle and his successors, particularly Zeno of Elea, produced the philosophical conception of a single god. This god, as developed by the school of philosophy known as Stoicism, was an object of contemplation rather than worship. Nonetheless, Stoic divinity was a significant element in the development of an idea powerfully associated with monotheism, that of universal salvation.

The one people in the Hellenistic world who already practiced a monotheistic religion were the Hebrews. Following the period of Babylonian captivity described in Chapter 1, the Hebrews had scattered throughout Asia, a process of dispersal known as the Diaspora, and had established settlements alongside those of other religions. Orthodox Jewish belief was essentially exclusive, however, and Hebrew communities were appalled at the concept of ruler worship, which inevitably brought them into conflict with the authorities. One of the consequences was the uprising of Judas Maccabaeus and his followers from 173 to 164 B.C. against their Seleucid rulers, a rebellion still commemorated in the annual Jew-

ish festival of Hanukkah. Elsewhere in Asia, Jewish settlements were more peaceful. We have already met the Jews of Alexandria, and earlier Seleucid rulers had encouraged Jewish immigration into the western part of their kingdom, Lydia and Phrygia. The Jewish community of the Greek island of Delos was able to build its own synagogue on land that had once been dedicated to Apollo. In general the Jews of the Diaspora continued to look to Jerusalem as their holy city and to pay an annual tax for the upkeep of the temple there. Nevertheless, contacts between the wide range of Hellenistic religious thought and Orthodox Judaism inevitably affected both sides; in turn, each was to play a part in the formation of Christianity.

## The Changing Status of Women

As we have seen, the social life of women in classical Greek society was essentially restricted to the household. Even in fifth-century B.C. art, there seems to have been little interest in women or their lives. The ideal form of beauty was largely represented by the male nude, and women were rarely depicted nude before the fourth century B.C. It is true that at the performances of Greek tragedies the audience, which may have included women, would see powerful female characters, such as Clytemnestra and Antigone, who often behaved more forcefully than the men whom they dominated. Yet their roles were played by males.

By the end of the fifth century B.C. the general upheaval at all levels of society brought forward new artistic and intellectual concerns. Yet it cannot be said that women's role changed to any significant degree; indeed, the turmoil of the age, together with the population movements of Alexander's time and the subsequent Hellenistic period, probably strengthened the traditional patriarchal family unit. However, late classical art and literature began to show interest in women as women.

One of the earliest examples of this can be found in Euripides' play *Medea*, probably first performed in 431 B.C. The play describes how Medea, abandoned by her husband, Jason, for a new bride, avenges herself by killing first the prospective wife and then her own two children. In the eyes of an Athenian audience, Medea labors under two crushing disadvantages: she is both a woman and a foreigner. As such she is denied her basic rights; she is married to a Greek, Jason, and has two children by him, but Athenian law did not recognize children by foreign wives as citizens. Thus Jason has no responsibility when he abandons her for a Greek wife and thereby legitimizes his children. The deserted Medea expresses all the rage, frustration, hopelessness, and loneliness that she feels as a woman. Ironically, Euripides' contemporaries, anxious to preserve the status quo, branded him a mysogynist, a hater of women.

This figurine of a woman with a fan comes from Tanagra in Boeotia, where examples of these clay statuettes were first found. [National Museum, Berlin]

By the fourth century B.C., sculptors had begun to turn to the naked female form to express concepts of ideal beauty. The most famous example was Praxiteles' much imitated Aphrodite of Cnidus. The statue combines a goddess's dignity with a clearly erotic message. We see her while she is bathing; recognizing the intrusion, she covers herself modestly with one hand—thereby drawing the viewer's attention precisely to what she seeks to conceal.

Throughout the Hellenistic period the female nude remained one of the most popular artistic subjects. In smaller statuettes, Hellenistic artists seem to have enjoyed showing various aspects of the private lives of women, from the two girls intent on their game of knuckleball to the elegant lady from Tanagra, out for a stroll. Women in public are described as well by Theocritus (c. 310–250 B.C.) in a poem set in Alexandria. Two women from Syracuse have moved to the big city and become suburban housewives; Theocritus describes their walk around town on a festival day and records their gossip and their comments on the various sights. It is inconceivable that so witty, realistic, and familiar a note could have been sounded in the fifth century B.C., whose writers showed little or no interest in women's daily life.

Change in the status of women was thus slow but perceptible. In terms of their legal and economic rights, the old barriers remained, but the Hellenistic kingdoms, with their constant evolution, made it possible for women of extraordinary character to achieve power. Arsinoë II, the wife of Ptolemy II (283–244 B.C.), instituted the custom of having the queen's portrait appear on the coinage as well as her husband's, and both she and her mother wore crowns. In the wars between Egypt and the Seleucids (276–272 B.C.) her generalship apparently succeeded in leading the Egyptian forces to victory. Not only was Arsinoë deified, but she also had a separate priestess for her own worship. Arsinoë and other Hellenistic queens and princesses began to play an increasing cultural role as well. Berenice, wife of Ptolemy III (246–221 B.C.), corresponded with the leading poet of the day, Callimachus (c. 305–c. 240 B.C.), and Stratonice, the wife of Antiochus I (280–261 B.C.), helped build the art collection at Delos.

Following such aristocratic examples, other women began to write and publish and even to appear in public. The poet Aristodama of Smyrna traveled throughout Greece in the mid-third century B.C., giving recitals and receiving honors; her brother went along as her business manager. By the end of the Hellenistic period there were even clubs for women at Alexandria and Athens, on the lines of similar organizations for men. Perhaps most important was the development of new schools of philosophy, two of which, Stoicism and Epicureanism, actively encouraged the participation of women at their meetings and made no distinction between the sexes.

## ◉ Hellenistic Women ◉

*These Hellenistic inscriptions throw light on the improving status of women in that period. The first records the gratitude of the city of Lamia to the poetess Aristodama for her public readings; in the second, King Antiochus III establishes a state cult in the name of his wife.*

Good fortune. The people of Lamia decreed: Whereas Aristodama, daughter of Amyntas of Smyrna in Ionia, an epic poetess, came to the city and gave several readings of her own poems in which she made appropriate mention of the Aetolian nation and the ancestors of the people . . . , showing zeal in her declamation, that she be a *proxenos* [protector and informal diplomatic representative] of the city and a benefactor, and that citizenship, the right to acquire land and property, grazing rights, exemption from reprisals, and safety by land and sea in peace or in war be granted to her and her children and her property for all time together with all the grants made to other *proxenoi* and benefactors. To . . . her brother and his children there shall be rights of *proxenia*, citizenship and freedom from reprisals.

King Antiochus to Anaximbrotus, greeting. As we desired to increase still further the honor of our sister-queen Laodice . . . we have now decided that, just as there are appointed throughout the kingdom high-priests of our cult, so there shall be established in the same districts high-priestesses of her also, who shall wear golden crowns bearing her image and whose names shall be mentioned in contracts after those of the high-priests of our ancestors and of us.

*Source:* F. W. Walbank, *The Hellenistic World* (Cambridge, Mass.: Harvard University Press, 1982), pp. 73, 216.

# Hellenistic Philosophy

Plato and Aristotle saw in the polis the natural unit of the human community. The Hellenistic world of empire, with its much broader political and commercial connections, called for a philosophy that could express the changed relations among individual, state, and society.

The three major schools of thought to emerge from the Hellenistic age provided different counsel for the problems of the age. Stoicism aimed at achieving inner tranquillity in a troubled world, Epicureanism advocated the cultivation of private life, and Cynicism rejected engagement with the world as such.

The most influential of the three was Stoicism. It was founded by Zeno of Elea (335–263 B.C.), who came to Athens in 313 B.C. and set up a school in the stoa or portico of the Athenian marketplace, from which the word *Stoic* derives. The Stoics believed in a ruling providence, but happiness, they emphasized, depended on avoiding desire for or dependence on things—wealth, power, fame—that were ultimately subject to the control

of others. The Stoics did not advocate withdrawal from public life but rather an ideal of disinterested service and detachment from ambition. They preached a high ethical standard, including general pacifism and the recognition of universal human equality.

Stoicism was adopted by the Romans and served as the fundamental ethical system of antiquity until the rise of Christianity, which internalized much of its teachings. Among the most important Roman Stoics was Epictetus (A.D. c. 55–c. 135), a former slave. In his *Handbook* Epictetus counsels trust in providence even in the face of dire misfortune. The philosopher, in his view, speaks for that providence, "taking the human race for his children." The Roman emperor Marcus Aurelius (A.D. 121–180), a later follower, strove for serenity and detachment despite his vast responsibilities. "Tell yourself every morning," he wrote in his *Meditations*, " 'today I shall meet the officious, the ungrateful, the bullying, the treacherous, the envious, the selfish. All of them behave like this because they do not know the difference between good and bad.' "

The philosophy expounded by Epicurus (341–270 B.C.) was geared to personal satisfaction rather than social duty. Epicurus adopted the Atomist theory of the fifth century B.C., which held that the universe was a purely material structure unaffected by the existence of the gods; he thus rejected the Stoic belief in providence. The soul, like the body, was mortal, and thus earthly happiness was the only goal of existence. This could best be achieved through the state of *ataraxia*, a condition neither agitated by excessive desire nor subject to avoidable discomfort and pain. To attain ataraxia, one should abstain from all things that made one vulnerable to disappointment and suffering, be it business, politics, or the pursuit of pleasure. Thus, whereas the serenity achieved by the Stoics was the result of an active life in the service of others, that of the Epicureans was premised on abstention from the public world. Epicureans were, of course, encouraged to associate with one another, and the school Epicurus himself founded in Athens in 306 B.C., which included women and slaves, shared a common life that included regular discussions and a monthly banquet.

The Cynics carried rejection of the world to a far greater extreme than either the Stoics or the Epicureans. Civilization, they contended, was a false creation that encumbered humans with arbitrary conventions and artificial needs. To regain a natural life, it was necessary to shun its social and material trappings entirely. Diogenes of Sinope (c. 400–c. 325 B.C.) taught by example the virtues of an ascetic life and an uncensored tongue; his defiance of convention won him the nickname "the Cynic" ("dog"), soon applied to all adherents of his philosophy. Cynicism was clearly a radical response to the social dislocation of the world in the fourth century B.C. Its following declined in the later Hellenistic period, but it revived during the Roman Empire and influenced early Christian monasticism.

Hellenistic philosophy derived ultimately from the Sophists, with their emphasis on a personal career in the world. It thus reflected a divorce between ethical and natural philosophy. For the pre-Socratics, there was no distinction between understanding the world and conducting oneself in it. By the late fourth century B.C., however, science had become a descriptive enterprise, and philosophy in large part a quest for meaning in a world ruled at best by an abstract providence and at worst by pure chance.

*The achievements of the Greeks within the relatively brief flowering of their culture were remarkable. Greek art and architecture set standards that guided subsequent artists for centuries and remain a powerful influence today. The tragic drama of fifth-century B.C. Athens is the basis of the Western theater tradition, and its archetypal heroes and heroines remain an inspiration across the entire spectrum of Western art. Greek science and philosophy, particularly in the works of Plato and Aristotle, formed much of the Western intellectual tradition. During the Hellenistic period, Greek culture spread widely across the Mediterranean and among the older societies of Egypt and western Asia,* *contact with which broadened and enriched Greek thought. The Greeks experimented with various forms of government, including democracy, and created a distinctive political unit, the polis. But their inability to resolve their disputes peacefully or to find a basis for federal union undermined the independence they so jealously protected, and after repelling Persia in the fifth century B.C., they fell prey to Macedon in the fourth. Only in the more cosmopolitan climate of the third century B.C. did the Greeks seek a wider conception of the state and the world, but the emergence of a great new power in the west, Rome, was to complete the political subjection begun by Alexander.*

## Suggestions for Further Reading

Barnes, J. *Aristotle.* Oxford: Oxford University Press, 1982.

Burkert, W. *Greek Religion.* Cambridge, Mass.: Harvard University Press, 1985.

Casson, L. *Travel in the Ancient World.* London: Allen & Unwin, 1974.

Cawkwell, G. *Philip of Macedon.* Boston: Faber & Faber, 1978.

Finley, M. I., ed. *The Legacy of Greece: A New Appraisal.* Oxford: Clarendon Press, 1981.

Green, P. *Alexander to Actium: The Historical Evolution of the Hellenistic Age.* Berkeley: University of California Press, 1990.

Hammond, N. G. L. *Alexander the Great: King, Commander and Statesman.* London: Chatto & Windus, 1981.

Haynes, D. *Greek Art and the Idea of Freedom.* London: Thames & Hudson, 1981.

Kirk, G. S., and Raven, J. E. *The Pre-Socratic Philosophers: A Critical History with a Selection of Texts,* 2nd ed. Cambridge: Cambridge University Press, 1983.

Lefkowitz, M. R., and Fant, M. B. *Women in Greece and Rome.* Toronto: University of Toronto Press, 1978.

Lesky, A. *Greek Tragic Poetry,* 3rd ed., trans. M. Dillon. New Haven, Conn.: Yale University Press, 1983.

Lloyd, G. E. R. *The Revolutions of Wisdom: Studies in the Claims and Practice of Ancient Greek Science.* Berkeley: University of California Press, 1987.

MacDowell, D. M. *The Law in Classical Athens.* London: Thames & Hudson, 1978.

Marrou, H. I. *A History of Education in Antiquity.* Madison: University of Wisconsin Press, 1982.

Morford, M. P. O., and Lenardon, P. J. *Classical Mythology,* 2nd ed. New York: Longman, 1977.

Onians, J. *Art and Thought in the Hellenistic Age: The Greek World View, 350–50 B.C.* London: Thames & Hudson, 1979.

Pollitt, J. J. *Art and Experience in Classical Greece.* Cambridge: Cambridge University Press, 1972.

Rist, J. M., ed. *The Stoics.* Berkeley: University of California Press, 1978.

Staveley, E. S. *Greek and Roman Voting and Elections.* Ithaca, N.Y.: Cornell University Press, 1972.

Walbank, F. W. *The Hellenistic World.* Cambridge, Mass.: Harvard University Press, 1982.

Wycherley, R. E. *The Stones of Athens.* Princeton, N.J.: Princeton University Press, 1978.

# The Romans

Throughout much of Asia and North Africa as well as the West, the Romans have left an indelible mark. In law, politics, religion, language, and the arts, Roman culture spread throughout an empire that stretched from the Atlantic to western Asia and from North Africa to England. The alphabet in use throughout much of our world was derived from the Roman alphabet, and the various Romance languages, such as Italian and French, are derived from Latin. The Western calendar is a modified form of one adapted from an Egyptian calendar by Julius Caesar in 46 B.C. Rome advanced fundamental political concepts, especially the republican form of government, that have influenced numerous modern states. The Romans developed sophisticated law and jurisprudence that served as the foundation of modern Continental European legal systems as well as those of the areas Europeans colonized, especially in Africa and Asia. Roman law had an impact on the English common law, much of it was employed in formulating the canon law of the Roman Catholic church, and all international and maritime law is based on it. Even the road network of

Detail of the lower bands of Trajan's Column in Rome, showing the bearded river god of the Danube and the Romans' pontoon bridge. [Leonard von Matt/ Rapho Guillumette/Photo Researchers]

modern Europe and the Middle East is based on one planned and built 2,000 years ago by the Romans.

From the beginning of their rise to power the Romans envisioned their task as one of regional and ultimately world domination. In fulfilling this vision, they carried their culture throughout much of the ancient world. Through the Romanization of diverse peoples and cultures, the Romans were able to transmit ideas they had acquired from others as well as those that they developed themselves. In particular, the two great streams of Western culture, the classical and the Judeo-Christian, spread throughout the empire. In assessing their own cultural achievements, the Romans were uncharacteristically modest. They seem to have believed that their virtues lay in efficient rule and success on the battlefield rather than aesthetic and intellectual achievements. Rome's self-appointed task was to rule the known world.

The history of Rome began with the traditional foundation of the city in the mid-eighth century B.C., but almost at once it fell under the domination of another people of ancient Italy, the Etruscans. Rome's subsequent rise to power was made possible by the impact of Etruscan rule.

## Italy Before Rome

Early in the Bronze Age the first Indo-European invaders of Italy had displaced the older inhabitants of the peninsula, who were related to the native populations of Spain and Gaul, and built their houses on platforms resting on poles. Toward the end of the Bronze Age various groups who spoke Italic dialects arrived—the Umbrians, the Samnites, and the Latins. Among the settlements of the Latins was the small village of Rome on the river Tiber, the site of which may have been inhabited as early as 1400 B.C. although its legendary founding was in 753 B.C. With the dawning of the Iron Age about 1000 B.C., a shared culture began to develop among the tribes of central Italy on the basis of manufacturing. This culture is called Villanovan, on the basis of discoveries at the village of Villanova near Bologna. It was powerfully affected in the succeeding centuries by the arrival of Greek colonists in southern Italy and the rise of an important new culture to the north, the Etruscan.

### The Etruscans

As early as Roman times scholars began to question the identity, origins, and language of the Etruscans. By 700 B.C. these people had settled in central Italy, in what was later called Tuscany. There is considerable doubt, however, as to whether they were of foreign origin or a na-

tive Italian people with a more highly developed culture. In most cases the principal Etruscan cities developed where Villanovan communities had previously existed, which would seem to support the latter theory. Yet the ancient Greeks and Romans, with few exceptions, were convinced that the Etruscans had migrated to Italy from western Asia, perhaps from the ancient kingdom of Lydia, in what is now Turkey. Much of their social life and art was strikingly Eastern in character.

As is clear from the ornate funerary objects found in tombs dating from the mid-seventh century B.C., the Etruscans were a rich and technologically sophisticated people from the beginning of their history. Their commercial connections included the Greek cities of southern Italy and the Phoenician colony of Carthage in North Africa. Indeed, throughout the seventh and sixth centuries B.C. in the western Mediterranean, the three principal trade rivals, the Etruscans, the Greeks, and the Carthaginians, formed a constantly changing series of alliances. The high point of Etruscan success came in 540 B.C. when, with Carthaginian help, they defeated the Greeks at Alalia and drove them out of the island of Corsica, off the coast of Tuscany. The price of their victory, however, was that their erstwhile collaborators, the Carthaginians, obtained control of the nearby island of Sardinia, a rich source of iron and other minerals that had formerly been in Etruscan hands. The Greeks had their revenge when, in 474 B.C., a Syracusan fleet destroyed

*6.1 Etruria*

**Lid of an Etruscan funerary urn depicting the couple whose ashes it contains. Note the characteristic Etruscan concern for vividness of facial expression and lack of interest in proportion. [Alinari/Art Resource]**

Etruscan forces off the coast at Cumae and effectively put an end to any Etruscan influence in southern Italy.

By then the Etruscans had already lost one of their strongholds in central Italy, Rome itself, which they had occupied from around 616 B.C. In 510 the Etruscan rulers of Rome were driven out by the Romans, and centuries of Etruscan decline began. The principal Etruscan cities nearest to Rome were conquered one by one: Veii in 396, Cerveteri in 353, and Tarquinia, the richest Etruscan center, in 351. The northern Etruscans submitted to the Romans without resistance, and in the wars of the third century B.C. in which the Romans fought and finally destroyed Carthage, the Etruscans provided support.

By the first century B.C. the Etruscans had been awarded the right of Roman citizenship and became absorbed into the Roman state. It is perhaps surprising that a people who had once been one of the richest and most active in the Mediterranean should have declined so rapidly. A partial explanation may be found in the nature of Etruscan society, which was divided into a small hereditary aristocracy and a large body of slaves and peasant farmers. Such a social structure, lacking flexibility, functioned successfully in the relatively stable conditions of the seventh and sixth centuries B.C. With the changing economic conditions produced by Roman expansion, however, the small number of rich Etruscan families

were unable to hold their own, let alone compete against the increasingly prosperous Romans. The pronounced gloominess of late Etruscan art may suggest a sense of imminent cultural demise.

## Early Rome

The early history of Rome is shrouded in legend. The Romans themselves celebrated the legendary foundation of their city in 753 B.C. on April 21 of each year, although there were different and irreconcilable accounts of who the actual founders had been. Modern archaeological research has done much to clarify the early stages of Roman history, but uncertainties remain, and it may never be possible to establish the precise chronology.

### From Monarchy to Republic

Recent archaeological finds of Bronze Age pottery have shown that a small community probably existed on or near Rome's Capitoline hill in the second millennium B.C., but there is no real evidence of continuity of occupation, and the Iron Age settlements of the eighth century B.C. probably represent a new beginning. The traditional founding date of 753 B.C. coincides closely with the archaeological evidence. Like other Latins, the first Romans were probably farmers and shepherds, and the simple huts discovered on the seven hills that surround Rome are similar to those of other Latin tribes to the south and east. The fertile land below was left for grazing.

As the community grew, the slopes of the hills, which were formerly used only as burial sites, became inhabited, and by the end of the seventh century B.C. the grazing land had been partially drained and settled. There are also signs of contact with the outside world, notably the importation of pottery and metalwork from neighboring Etruscan cities. Roman historians later endowed their city with a legendary founder, Romulus, who, together with his twin brother Remus, was said to have been born to Rhea Silvia, the daughter of a local king, and the war god Mars. For more than two centuries, according to tradition, the city was ruled by seven kings, first Latin and then Etruscan.

Rome as the Etruscans found it was a small country town. The new rulers built it up considerably. Etruscan engineers drained the marshy central valley and built temples, shrines, and roads. Etruscan craftsmen introduced and developed new skills and established guilds, including those of the bronze workers, goldsmiths, and carpenters. Most important of all, under Etruscan rule the Romans came into contact for the first time with the outside world. From the simple village life of a small community under the leadership of tribal chiefs they took their place in a larger cultural and political context that extended beyond Italy. It took only a century for the Romans to learn the principles of Etruscan technology, expel their former rulers, and begin their climb to power.

# The Republic: Conflict and Accommodation

With the expulsion of the Etruscans, the Romans devised a new form of government, abolishing the monarchy and founding a republic. The two principal magistrates, or consuls, were elected by all the male citizens to serve one-year terms. Throughout the first century and a half of the republic they had to be members of the Roman aristocracy. This tradition of rule by the nobility seems to have developed during the period of the monarchy, although its basis is not clear. When Rome's last king was overthrown, the closed groups of families, known as *patricians,* assumed control of the primary political and religious offices and comprised the Senate, the principal advisory body.

The remaining citizens, regardless of their wealth or education, were known as the *plebeians,* or common people. Prosperous and ambitious plebeians, who resented the patricians' political domination, joined with the poorer plebeians to force change on the ruling order, although the struggle proved bitter and protracted. By the end of the fifth century B.C. a plebeian assembly had evolved that met alongside the Senate in the Forum. The leaders elected by this body, the tribunes, represented plebeian interests and protected them from unjust treatment by state officials.

The entire citizen body, including both classes, was known as the *populus.* The patricians, who comprised about 10 percent of the population, were the landed, governing class, and the plebeians, who included soldiers, artisans, laborers, merchants, and farmers, were subject to their rule. The result of the patricians' monopoly of office, which included their assembly, the Senate, and the two chief magistrates, or consuls (elected by all citizens but chosen solely from the patriciate), was the growth of a patronage system that reinforced elite control. Patrons offered jobs, protection, and legal services, and within the closed ranks of the magistrates, advancement along the career ladder, or *cursus honorum,* depended on the sponsorship of senior officials.

Patronage provided a rough system of checks and balances, as did the principle of collegiality. Either of the consuls could reject the proposals of the other by pronouncing the word *veto* ("I forbid"); in this fashion, executive authority was limited. But as patrician factions jockeyed for popular support, the plebeians were able to wrest a series of concessions that, over a period of two centuries, successfully challenged the patrician monopoly of office and created a parallel set of plebeian institutions and magistracies.

The first of the new magistrates were the two tribunes, whose function was to represent plebeian interests in the Senate. The person of a tribune was held to be sacrosanct, and his door was to be open day and night to any citizen. In 471 B.C. the plebeians won the right to meet in their own assembly, and around 450 B.C. they compelled the promulgation of a law code, the Twelve Tables. This provided, among other things, legal recognition of the patronage system and prescribed the death penalty for patrons who violated their duties to their clients. The plebeians next won the right of intermarriage with the patricians (445 B.C.), and then of admission to some of the lesser magistracies (421 B.C.).

It was not until 367 B.C., with the passage of the Sexto-Licinian Laws, that plebeians could stand for the consulship. Any man elected to the office automatically ennobled his family, and a mixed patrician-plebeian aristocracy began to develop that encouraged the support of the poorer plebeians by distributing some of the land won in Rome's conquest of Italy. The final recognition of the plebeians' formal political equality came in 287 B.C., when the Hortensian Law made decisions of the plebeian assembly binding on the Senate and the Roman people. The patricians' slow and reluctant acceptance of the need for compromise had significant consequences for the growth of Roman power; without adjustment, Roman expansion abroad would have been impossible.

## The Unification of Italy and the Conquest of the Mediterranean

Between 509 and 266 B.C. the Romans extended their control over the Italian peninsula, aided by a number of factors. The Etruscans failed to mount any serious or organized opposition and, as we have seen, were defeated city by city. The Greeks in southern Italy, like their fellow Greeks in the homeland, were so rent by intercity feuding that they offered little unified resistance. Finally, the Romans turned to their own advantage an event that could have proved catastrophic. In 390 B.C. the Gauls, a northern Celtic people, crossed the Alps and moved into Italy. In the course of their rampaging they laid waste much of central Italy and sacked Rome. By the speed of their recovery, particularly in comparison with their Etruscan and other neighbors, the Romans proved to themselves and their fellow Latins that only they could mount a real defense of the peninsula in the face of foreign invasion.

The Latins had signed a treaty with Rome as early as 493 B.C. The formation of the Latin League in that year guaranteed the Romans some security on their immediate borders and allowed them to deal with the Etruscans and the other peoples of central Italy. The Aequi and the Volsci were defeated in 431, and with the fall of the city of Veii in 396 the collapse of the Etruscans seemed assured.

There remained, however, one of the fiercest of Italian peoples, the Samnites. This warlike tribe came originally from the rugged mountainous country to the east of Rome, but during the fifth century B.C. they had moved south into the rich land in the region below Naples abandoned by the Etruscans after the battle of Cumae in 474. For a while both Romans and Samnites were sufficiently distracted by problems elsewhere to leave each other in peace, but conflict was inevitable. The Samnite Wars, which lasted intermittently from 325 to 290, constituted the most serious challenge Rome had yet faced to its growing power. By 290 B.C., however, the Samnites had been crushed and their principal cities turned into Roman colonies.

That left the Greeks of the south the only independent group on the peninsula. Unable to agree on a plan of common defense, they turned to outside help.

The city of Tarentum (modern Taranto) invited Pyrrhus, the Greek ruler of the Adriatic Confederation of Epirus, to aid them. One of the other Greek cities in southern Italy, Thurii, appealed for Roman aid against this outside intervention, thereby giving the Romans an excuse to attack. The wars with Pyrrhus lasted from 281 to 272, and by 267 B.C. the whole of southern Italy, Greeks and native tribes alike, had submitted to Roman domination.

## The Punic Wars

The unification of the Italian peninsula brought Roman power to bear on Sicily, which had been colonized by Greeks and Carthaginians and was now after a long struggle under the control of the latter. Carthage had been founded on what is now the bay of Tunis by Phoenician emigrants in the mid-ninth century B.C. By the sixth century B.C. it had become the dominant power in the Mediterranean, with colonies extending as far as Spain. Rome and Carthage had generally enjoyed peaceful relations under a treaty of 509 B.C. that recognized their respective spheres of influence, with Sicily as a neutral zone. Carthage resembled Rome in certain respects. Ostensibly a republic, it was in fact an oligarchy based on wealth. Like the Romans, the Carthaginians had two chief magistrates, elected annually, but the government was run by the heads of prominent households who made up the Senate and the Council. They worshiped both Phoenician and Greek gods; a colossal statue of Apollo stood in the forum or chief square of Carthage, but the Carthaginians still sacrificed children to their older deity, Baal-Ammon.

With Rome bent on expansion, a confrontation over Sicily was inevitable. In 264 B.C. the Romans sent an expeditionary force to Messana (Messina) at the behest of its Greek population. Carthage responded, and the first of the three Punic Wars began, so called because the Latin for Phoenician is *Punicus*.

The First Punic War, which lasted from 264 to 241 B.C., proved to the Romans that the Carthaginians were formidable opponents. Fighting for the first time at sea, Roman forces suffered severe losses, and it was only the development of an effective Roman fleet that finally drove the Carthaginians to seek peace. The Romans were in no mood to negotiate a face-saving compromise. A war in which the Romans had for the first time to face the serious possibility of defeat seems to have reinforced both the best and worst aspects of their character. Brave, efficient, self-sacrificing, they won by virtue of their persistence and determination. Having won, though, they dictated terms of peace that humiliated Carthage, demanding both the surrender of territory and the payment of a large indemnity. In the following years, moreover, the Romans did what they could to cause trouble between the Carthaginians and their allies

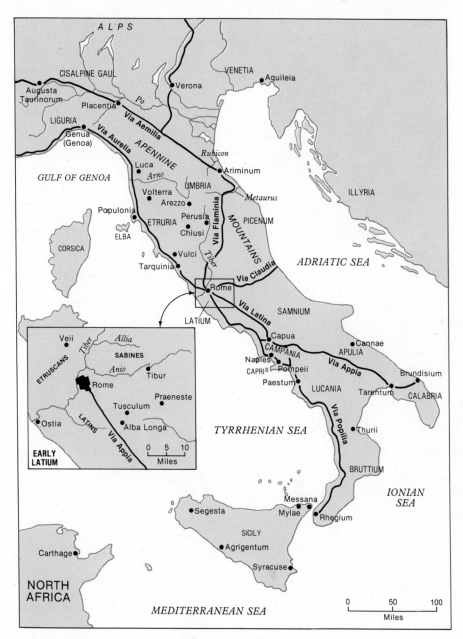

*6.2 Roman Italy*

while expanding along the eastern Adriatic shore of Illyria (modern Croatia).

In 218 B.C., hearing that a Roman expedition was marching to Spain to support a revolt against Carthaginian allies, Carthage struck back. The Second Punic War (218–201 B.C.) began with the arrival of a Carthaginian force in Italy under the leadership of perhaps the most brilliant and certainly the most famous of Carthaginian generals, Hannibal (247–c. 183 B.C.). Counting on the support of the local population, he crossed into Spain

and descended on Italy over the Alps with a huge supply train, inflicting several painful defeats on Roman forces. The last, at Cannae in 216, virtually annihilated a Roman army.

Hannibal, victory within his grasp, besieged Rome, but he was unable to sustain his momentum. His forces were a long way from home, and the Romans effectively blocked the arrival of reinforcements. The Italian population was still too fearful of Roman reprisals to aid Hannibal, and Rome remained a formidable opponent fight-

**Gold coins minted at Carthage.** [Ronald Sheridan/Ancient Art and Architecture Collection]

ing on home territory. As a result, Hannibal and his troops spent years waiting for the formation of an anti-Roman alliance that never materialized. The Romans seized the opportunity to rebuild their forces and sent a counterexpedition to North Africa to invade Carthaginian territory under the young and ambitious general Scipio.

When the victorious Romans demanded uncompromising peace terms, Hannibal returned with his troops to reinforce the Carthaginians. In 202 the entire Carthaginian army was defeated at Zama in North Africa and forced to surrender, and peace was concluded the following year. Carthage was divested of its entire empire, including Spain, and was left with only a small strip of territory around the city itself, in modern Tunisia. It was forced to pay a crippling indemnity and permanently to disband its armed forces. The once proud Carthaginians were reduced to impotence, and the expression "Carthaginian peace" entered the language, denoting a dictated settlement designed to crush an opponent permanently.

## Conquests in the East

Throughout the following century the Romans continued to fight sporadically in Spain, where they established control in a series of brutal campaigns. The helpless Carthaginians, who had attracted Roman enmity by regaining some of their former prosperity, were completely destroyed in the Third Punic War of 149–146 B.C. Their city was leveled, and its inhabitants were sold into slavery.

In theory, Roman involvement in the affairs of Greece and the Asian kingdoms was for the purpose of defending and even "liberating" the Greeks from their Hellenistic rulers. Already by the end of the third century B.C., Greek art and literature had become fashionable at Rome. Victory over the Carthaginians had fed the Romans' pride and arrogance. Triumphant in the western Mediterranean, they looked to the rich kingdoms of Asia as both potential enemies and attractive conquests. Allegedly advocating the cause of Greek freedom, first in Macedon and then in Asia, Roman forces fought a series of wars to gain control there.

The first step was to secure the Adriatic Sea, which was begun in the First Illyrian War of 229–228 B.C. In the following years the Romans became involved in a series of wars with Philip V of Macedon and Antiochus III of the Seleucid empire, and by 200 B.C. they were committed in the Hellenistic east on a massive scale. The next half century saw complex battles and negotiations in western Asia, in which territories of the Hellenistic kingdoms either gained their independence or were merged with other states. The Greek poleis threw off Macedonian domination in 197 B.C., thanks to Roman assistance.

In the case of Pergamum, King Eumenes decided that collaboration offered better prospects than opposition. Pergamum continued to serve Roman interests in Asia as a client state until 133 B.C., when Attalus III willed it to Rome in a last attempt to win favorable treatment for his people. Any illusion the Greeks may have had that Roman campaigns against Macedon or the Seleucid empire of Syria were for their benefit was shattered when a defensive league of Greek poleis was crushed at Pydna in 168 B.C. In 146 B.C. another Greek army that refused to accept Roman "liberation" was defeated at Corinth. The Romans razed the city and shipped its artworks to Rome. Other temporary beneficiaries of Roman aid also paid with their freedom. The Romans supported the Jewish revolt of the Maccabees in 167 B.C.; two centuries later, a Roman army would destroy the last vestiges of Jewish independence and burn the temple in Jerusalem.

## ◉ Hannibal: A Roman View ◉

*Livy's description of Hannibal was written some 200 years after the Second Punic War, yet it vividly conveys the Romans' wary respect for the Carthaginian general.*

Hannibal was dispatched to Spain and on his first appearance attracted the interest of the army. The old soldiers thought that a younger Hamilcar had come back to them. They saw in him the same features, the same liveliness of expression, the same fire in the eyes. But shortly his resemblance to his father was only the least among their reasons for devotion to him. Never was an individual more perfectly suited both to obedience and to command. It would be hard to say whether the commander or the army loved him more. There was no one whom Hasdrubal [Hannibal's older brother] preferred to put in charge of any assignment which demanded bravery and vigor; nor was there any leader under whom the army fought with greater confidence and daring. When danger was to be faced it was Hannibal whose spirit was the boldest, and in a crisis his strategy was the shrewdest. Under no hardship did his energy wane or his spirits flag. He could face heat or cold with equal endurance. His appetite for food and drink were controlled by hunger and not by pleasure. His waking and sleeping were not fixed by day and night. What time remained after the task in hand was done he gave to sleep, and this without any need of soft bed or quiet. Many a time he could be seen lying on the ground among the sentries and pickets off duty, covered only with a soldier's cloak. His dress was no different from that of his fellow-soldiers, but his weapons and his horses were of the finest. He was the best among cavalry and infantry alike, always the first to go into battle and the last to leave any clash of arms.

These qualities were matched by equally great flaws of character: inhuman cruelty and a worse than Punic treachery which had no regard for the truth, held nothing sacred, was stopped by no fear of the gods or scruple at breach of faith. With such an endowment of faults and virtues he served for three years in Spain under the command of Hasdrubal, omitting no experience or training suitable for a man destined to become a great military leader.

*Source:* P. MacKendrick and H. M. Howe, eds., *Classics in Translation* (Madison: University of Wisconsin Press, 1966), vol. 2, p. 296.

## The Crisis of the Republic

By the end of the second century B.C. the Romans had constructed a huge empire of subject regions, client states, and nominally free kingdoms that stretched from Spain to western Asia. They had failed, however, to develop effective systems of administration, and the consequences were often chaotic. Provincial governors were frequently inefficient and corrupt. Patricians and wealthy plebeians, enriched by their conquests, began to compete in piling up fortunes derived either from property in Italy or from the provinces.

Rome's imperial career had also affected the constitutional balance at home. The victories in the Punic Wars had enhanced the Senate's prestige. During the many years of fighting it had been necessary for some authority to make decisions quickly and efficiently, and that task had fallen to the Senate. Among the powers it assumed was the right to prolong magistrates' terms of office when conditions of war made it necessary. Furthermore, by the end of the wars the Senate had taken control of foreign policy, and the provincial governors it appointed thus had unofficial license to extort what they could from their subjects. Laws against bribery were passed in 181 and 159, but to little effect; Rome's opponent in North Africa, King Jugurtha, was advised that "at Rome everything is for sale."

The poorer plebeians had lost rather than gained from the continued warfare. Rome's new territories had been won by part-time soldiers, eager to return to their farms or businesses. In order to hold on to their conquests, the Romans now needed to maintain conscript troops outside Italy, but in many cases plebeians were unwilling to serve. On some occasions the tribune, as defender of plebeian rights, stepped in to arrest the consul conducting the conscription. In other cases the conscript had little choice. Many small plebeian farms had been swallowed up by the growth of large estates, or *latifundia*, whose wealthy owners bought public land and worked it by means of slaves made available by the wars. Thus the poorer plebeians who had survived economically by cultivating their plots had little choice other than to serve abroad or to join the growing number of unemployed in Rome. The urban mob that these social conditions produced was to prove a new and powerful force in Roman political life.

As the government of the empire grew ever more complex, divisions began to appear among the wealthy as well, both patrician and plebeian. Public contracts for tax collecting, construction work, or other projects were issued by the Senate. Because they were supposed to oversee the contracted work, senators were debarred from appointing themselves and undertaking these contracts in their own name. The rich landowners who were not members of the Senate thus became the principal group to benefit from the large sums of money spent in and received from the provinces. This new social and economic class was known as the *equestrians*, or cavalry. The provision of a horse at public expense had been a mark of honor from earlier times; now it became a property qualification to distinguish between senators, with their inherited wealth, and the new class of equestrians. Of course, the formal exclusion of senators from lucrative work in the provinces, especially tax collecting, scarcely impeded their accumulation of wealth through bribery, payoffs, and the like. With the spoils of three continents at their disposal, the patrician and equestrian classes reaped immense fortunes. Meanwhile, the gap between the propertied elite and the plebeians continued to widen.

## The Gracchi

By the last third of the second century B.C. Rome faced a number of serious and interrelated problems. The great estates required increasing numbers of slave workers, while free agricultural laborers were all but disappearing as a class. There was little chance of agrarian reform as long as the members of the Senate saw it as contrary to their own interests. In 133 B.C., facing apparent deadlock, the tribune Tiberius Gracchus attempted to introduce major changes. He recommended that the government reclaim state land that had been illegally occupied, mostly by owners of large estates. A proposed commission would distribute the repossessed farmholdings to the landless. Tiberius' plan was approved by a plebeian assembly made unusually large by the crowds of poor ex-farmers who had poured into Rome to vote for the measure. To achieve this, however, Tiberius had bypassed the Senate and illegally blocked the veto of a fellow tribune. Wealthy landowners claimed that he had acted unconstitutionally. He ran for a second term to implement the new law but was clubbed to death in street fighting on election day.

Tiberius' younger brother, Gaius, was elected tribune for 123 B.C. and again for the following year. More cautious than Tiberius, he buttressed his appeal to the plebeians by seeking the support of the equestrians. The right to collect taxes in Roman territory in Asia was for the first time put up for auction at Rome rather than meted out by the Senate, providing equestrians with the opportunity to compete for highly profitable monopolies. At the same time the membership of juries that tried provincial governors for corruption was, at Gaius' suggestion, limited exclusively to equestrians. Governors had always been drawn from the Roman Senate, and this gave the equestrians the chance to play watchdog over provincial administration and protect their own interests. Like his brother, Gaius was threatening the wealthy senatorial landowners, and despite his attempt to broaden his political base, he met with the same fate: early in 121 he and perhaps as many as 3,000 of his supporters were killed by mobs openly encouraged by the Senate.

The Gracchi demonstrated only too well that a political system that had been devised for a small city 400 years earlier was inadequate for the governance of a vast empire. Furthermore, no ambitious politician could leave out of account two new forces on the political scene: the urban mob and the standing army. The first had been used against the Gracchi. The second, a professional fighting force whose primary loyalty was not to Rome but to whichever general led and paid it, was to play a crucial role in the careers of the next generation of politicians. Indeed, the men who struggled for power right up to the end of the republic—Marius, Sulla, Pompey, and Caesar—were all highly successful field commanders in their own right and could count on the loyalty of their troops.

---

### ❧
### CORNELIA AND THE WORLD
### OF THE GRACCHI

---

In some ways even more remarkable than the Gracchi themselves was their mother, Cornelia. Born in the late 190s B.C., she was the younger daughter of Scipio Africanus, the victor of Zama, and Aemilia, whose brother Hannibal had slain. Cornelia was probably about 20 years old when she married the politically prominent plebeian Tiberius Sempronius Gracchus, who had been twice consul.

Cornelia bore Tiberius 12 children, of whom only three—the future tribunes Tiberius and Gaius and their deformed sister Sempronia—survived. Widowed around 154 B.C., Cornelia was a diligent mother, allegedly boasting that her sons, rather than her jewelry, were her true ornaments. Cicero was impressed by the care she took with their education: "We read the letters of Cornelia," he wrote, ". . . from which it appears that they were reared more on their mother's discourse than on mother's milk." Another oft-repeated story asserted that she prodded her sons toward fame by claiming to be bored with her titles and lineage; certainly she was ambitious for them.

Controversy surrounds Cornelia's role in her sons' careers. Some contemporaries claimed that it was she who had urged Tiberius to take up the agrarian problem and to go over the Senate's head to the Assembly when his reforms were stalled. Others asserted that she and Sempronia were at least partly to blame for the murder of the latter's husband, Scipio Aemilianus, who had opposed the work of the land commissioners responsible for implementing Tiberius' reforms. Later she was accused of aiding Gaius' political activities, even to the point of hiring men to impersonate harvesters and agitate for her son. That Gaius felt obliged to respond to these attacks suggests at least some substance to the allegations.

The murders of both her sons, and with them the hope for reform they represented, made Cornelia a tragic figure. Nonetheless she remained undaunted and continued to move proudly in Roman political circles as of old. At one point she rejected a marriage proposal from Ptolemy VII of Egypt, who wished the support of her eastern connections in his own dynastic quarrels. Toward the end of her life she lived at Misenum on the Bay of Naples, presiding over a celebrated literary salon.

Whether any of the writings of Cornelia have survived is unclear; Cicero, as we have seen, was familiar with some of her letters, although historians have questioned the authenticity of the fragments that remain. But her combination of ambition, fidelity, virtue, and personal modesty made her the archetypal Roman matron and one of the few figures of either sex in the later republic to win the general approbation of posterity.

## Marius, Sulla, and the Rebellion of Spartacus

Two figures, Marius the populist and Sulla the aristocrat, dominated Roman political life from Marius' first consulship in 107 to Sulla's retirement in 79. Fierce opponents, each could claim military successes, Marius in Africa and Sulla in Italy, where the latter played a large part in crushing a revolt by Rome's Italian allies in the so-called Social War of 90–88 B.C. Marius' principal contribution to Rome was his reform of recruitment procedures. During his first consulship he abolished the need for members of the army to own property; the poverty-stricken could enlist and be armed at public expense. Men who joined did so not only for the pay but also in the hope that they would receive a grant of land at the end of their service.

Both Sulla and Marius, together with their followers, were responsible for bloody purges among their opponents, which plunged Rome repeatedly into civil war; neither provided even a temporary solution to Rome's real problems. Sulla ruled as dictator until he retired in 79 B.C. This was, in fact, a constitutional position, first created after Hannibal's victory at Cannae; the holder was appointed for six months by the two consuls, with the Senate's advice, to rule the state during an emergency. Sulla imposed a new constitution that attempted a return to the conservative and elitist concepts of the early republic. He doubled the size of the Senate and strengthened its powers, limited the tribunes' right of veto, and abolished their ability to legislate and take legal action. After Sulla stepped down, faction and class conflict resumed, including an uprising by Rome's most despised class, its slaves.

Enslaving prisoners had been a Roman practice since 396, when the citizens of the captured city of Veii were taken to Rome. Throughout the second century B.C. thousands of prisoners were shipped to Italy and put to work on the great estates. Plantation workers generally toiled in chain gangs and were locked up in underground barracks at night, but it was harder to control herdsmen, who had to be left free to tend their flocks. Slave uprisings were therefore a continuous threat and made travel through remote agricultural areas unsafe. In 73 B.C. a major revolt erupted, led by the Thracian gladiator Spartacus. An initial band of 74 men quickly swelled to an army of 70,000, and only massive intervention by the Roman army crushed the rebels. Some 6,000 of them were crucified as a warning to others.

In general, however, the Romans were liberal in granting freedom to domestic slaves, if not in their treatment of them during the years of servitude. Throughout the first century B.C. thousands of slaves were freed by their owners through a process called manumission, which required them to purchase their freedom. Many of them became shopkeepers, artisans, or clerks, although some practiced their skills as teachers or doctors. The freed slaves, or *liberti*, were subject to certain legal restrictions, but their children became full citizens.

## Julius Caesar

The principal political contest of the generation following Sulla was between Pompey (106–48 B.C.), who called himself Pompey the Great and appointed himself defender of the Senate, and Julius Caesar (100–44 B.C.). Both men were military commanders as well as politicians. Pompey combined the virtues of his military calling—efficiency and good planning—with lack of principle, deviousness, and personal vanity. Caesar's talents were much more complex and versatile; some have called him Rome's greatest mind. A successful politician and orator and a lucid, elegant prose writer, he was also, as Pompey was not, a genuine political thinker. Caesar realized that the only sure way to achieve power was through military force. After making his mark in the politics of the capital between 65 and 62, he left Rome, first to serve as governor in Spain and then, in 58, in Gaul. He remained there for almost ten years and completed the conquest of the region, thereby bringing much of continental Europe north of the Alps into the orbit of Roman civilization.

Before leaving Rome, Caesar ensured his continuing influence by concluding a secret agreement in 59 B.C. to divide the power and patronage of the capital with Pompey and the wealthy businessman Crassus, who had made his political reputation by putting down Spartacus; this pact is known as the First Triumvirate. Pompey and Caesar cemented their alliance by the marriage of Caesar's daughter, Julia, to Pompey—a match that proved unexpectedly happy despite a considerable age difference. During Caesar's period in Gaul, however, both Crassus and Julia died, and Pompey, distrustful of the increasingly popular Caesar, forged close ties with the aristocrats in the Senate. When in January 49 B.C. the Senate commanded Caesar to relinquish his command, he illegally ordered his army to cross the Rubicon River, the boundary between Gaul and Italy.

Caesar's march to Rome with his victorious army made civil war inevitable. After a brief period of indecision, Pompey and his followers fled to Greece. Caesar followed him and defeated his forces at Pharsalus (48 B.C.). Pompey himself escaped to Egypt, whose ruler decapitated him and sent the embalmed head to Caesar as a means of currying favor. Caesar turned this to patriotic advantage by executing Pompey's murderers and erecting a statue to him in the Senate. Caesar spent the winter in Alexandria, where he entered into a liaison with the young queen of Egypt, Cleopatra. By the time he left, Cleopatra was pregnant. She named her son Caesarion and sent him to Rome. Although Caesar showered Cleopatra with presents and honors, he never returned.

By 46 Caesar had been appointed dictator, which gave him emergency powers to govern for up to six months. As dictator, he set about reorganizing the government both at home and in the provinces. Among his most lasting achievements was the creation of a unified code of civil law. Produced with the help of eminent legal experts, it served as a model for later times. His reformed calendar, based on the research of astronomers

**A portrait bust of Julius Caesar made in Egypt in the late first century B.C., perhaps during Caesar's stay with Cleopatra. [National Museum, Berlin]**

at Alexandria, was used in the West until the eighteenth century, and our present one, introduced by Pope Gregory XIII in 1582, is a modified form of it.

Caesar also launched an ambitious and wide-ranging series of reforms. He began an extensive public works program designed in part to take citizens off the welfare rolls and make them less susceptible to the violence that had become commonplace in Rome. To that end also he instituted a police force and relieved the overpopulation of the capital by sending 80,000 citizens into the provinces. He subsidized Italian farmers to restore the agricultural self-sufficiency of the peninsula and undertook the overhaul of provincial administration. To reduce political opposition, he packed the Senate with his own followers. But his plans had little time to take effect. On March 15, 44 B.C., he was assassinated by a band of senatorial conspirators led by a magistrate, Gaius Cassius, and the prominent aristocrat Marcus Brutus. The agony of the republic was to be prolonged for another 13 years.

## The End of the Republic

In the turmoil that followed Caesar's assassination, Mark Antony (83–30 B.C.), his former lieutenant, organized the attempt to avenge his death. He was joined by Caesar's young great-nephew, Octavius (63 B.C.–A.D. 14), whom Caesar had named in his will as his heir. On Caesar's death Octavius had arrived in Rome from the provinces to assume power. It was soon clear that Antony and Octavian (the name Octavius now took) were bound to clash. After the defeat of Caesar's assassins in 42 B.C. at Philippi in western Greece, an uneasy settlement placed Octavian in charge of the western provinces while Antony was dispatched to the east. To strengthen their ties and to protect Antony from the enticement of Cleopatra, whom he had met on an earlier tour of duty, he was persuaded to marry Octavia, Octavian's sister. A woman of firmness and tact, she seems to have curbed Antony's tendencies to sensuality and self-indulgence and maintained peaceful relations between her new husband and

Octavian. From 39 to 37 Octavia and Antony administered the eastern provinces from their base in Athens.

Three years of domestic tranquillity were enough for Antony. After a disastrous military operation in Syria, he escaped to Alexandria, where in 34 B.C. he made his union with Cleopatra official by the so-called Donations of Alexandria. This news was predictably exploited at Rome by Octavian, who depicted his rival as degenerate and corrupt. With Antony out of Rome, Octavian declared war on Egypt.

Cleopatra (69–30 B.C.) had her own ambitions. She was a Macedonian by birth and thus the successor of Alexander the Great, and her native language was Greek. Yet she also considered herself to be the successor of the pharaohs and a descendant of the sun god Re. Like Alexander, she dreamed of uniting East and West in one great empire. Her plan was to conquer Rome and with its aid create a global kingdom. But Egypt, though wealthy, had virtually no military strength. It was Cleopatra's hope to overthrow the Roman Empire by provoking civil war among the Romans, but to achieve this goal she needed a Roman ally. Her liaison with Mark Antony was a gamble that, without the equally strong resistance of Octavian, might well have produced military success.

The end for Cleopatra and Mark Antony came in 31 B.C. at the naval battle of Actium in western Greece. When Antony's forces deserted, he and Cleopatra escaped to Egypt, where Antony saw no honorable alternative to suicide. Cleopatra hesitated. A meeting was arranged between her and Octavian, perhaps so that she could make a final attempt to win him over, but this

---

THE ROMAN REPUBLIC

| Period | Important events | Major writers |
|---|---|---|
| Early Republic (509–275 B.C.) | • Founding of the republic (509 B.C.)<br>• Establishment of the Tribunate (494 B.C.)<br>• Plebeian Assembly (471 B.C.)<br>• Twelve Tables (c. 450 B.C.)<br>• Licinian-Sextian Laws (367 B.C.)<br>• Hortensian Law (287 B.C.)<br>• Unification of Italy (c. 400–275 B.C.) | • Menander (Greek) |
| Overseas Conquest (275–146 B.C.) | • First Punic War (264–241 B.C.)<br>• Second Punic War (218–201 B.C.)<br>• Wars in the eastern Mediterranean (200–146 B.C.)<br>• Third Punic War (149–146 B.C.) | • Ennius<br>• Plautus<br>• Terence<br>• Cato the Elder |
| Late Republic (146–27 B.C.) | • Reforms of the Gracchi (134–121 B.C.)<br>• First Consulate of Marius (107 B.C.)<br>• Social War (90–88 B.C.)<br>• Age of Sulla (88–79 B.C.)<br>• First Triumvirate (59–49 B.C.)<br>• Caesar's dictatorship (46–44 B.C.)<br>• Second Triumvirate (43–36 B.C.)<br>• Augustan settlement (27 B.C.) | • Lucretius<br>• Catullus<br>• Cicero<br>• Julius Caesar |

failed. Knowing that Octavian wanted only to display and humiliate her at Rome, she killed herself with a deadly serpent smuggled to her in a basket of figs. Octavian was left as sole leader of the Roman world, and his victory marked the end of the republic.

## Augustus and the Pax Romana

By the time of the battle of Actium, Rome had suffered more than a century of civil and external war. Political institutions had in large part ceased to function effectively, and much of Italy was in chaos. Yet when Octavian died in A.D. 14, Rome had attained political stability and commercial prosperity. Augustus—to use the title he assumed in 27 B.C.—formally inaugurated the empire, a period that lasted some 500 years in the West and nearly 1,500 in the East.

Augustus, remembering Caesar's fate, took great care to avoid the appearance of autocratic rule. He declined the title of *rex* (king) or dictator, preferring to be known simply as *princeps*, or first citizen, an honorific used for elder statesmen under the republic. At the same time, however, he was careful to retain the title of *imperator* (victor), which was granted to successful generals, and, like Caesar, he assumed the office of pontifex maximus when it fell vacant. In addition, when he resigned the office of consul in 23 B.C., the Senate conferred on him the powers of a tribune for life. His successors were known by the title of imperator, which has come into English as *emperor*. It is thus with Augustus that we can speak of Rome as an empire in the political sense, that is, as possessing not merely a territorial empire but an imperial form of government.

Augustus was careful to preserve republican institutions. Under his rule and that of his successors, the Senate met and Roman aristocrats continued to be elected to the consulship, but all decisions of importance originated with the emperor. Ostensibly, the form of Roman government was now a dyarchy ("rule of two") in which the Senate and the emperor cooperated to administer the empire. In fact, the emperors made as much or as little use of the Senate as they chose. As commanders in chief of the army, they could be deposed only by military revolt or assassination.

Augustus himself restored the Senate to its former standards of birth, wealth, and conduct, gave it control of Rome's civic administration, and used its members to govern the inner provinces of the empire. He was outwardly deferential to it and claimed in his autobiography

**View of the Roman Forum, with the Arch of Titus in the distance. [Graziano Paiella]**

to have "transferred the state back into the hands of the Senate and the Roman people." But he never yielded to it except in trivial matters, and he ruled directly over the outer provinces of the empire. Augustus retained Egypt, the granary of the empire, as an imperial estate; he assumed the title of pharaoh and forbade any senator to set foot there without his consent.

Augustus reorganized the army, over which he likewise retained direct control. He fixed its size at 25 legions; regularized pay, pensions, and terms of service; and deployed it at key points throughout the empire. His own security force, the 9,000-man Praetorian Guard, was sworn to personal loyalty to him. Augustus skillfully used his religious authority as well. Casting himself as the champion of traditional Roman religion, he revived a number of old priesthoods, rebuilt more than 80 temples, and encouraged the worship of Venus (as the Romans had renamed the Greek goddess Aphrodite), from whom Julius Caesar had traced his lineage. Although he was careful not to present himself as a god in Italy, he tacitly permitted himself to receive divine homage in the provinces and encouraged the erection of temples, monuments, and statues to himself and to his wife, Livia, throughout the empire.

Augustus devoted considerable attention to restoring the economic and fiscal health of the empire. The principal sources of revenue were in the provinces, and Augustus introduced new censuses to assess population, assets, and resources. He staffed the financial bureaucracy with members of the equestrian class, thus reinstating them to their traditional role and providing a buffer against senatorial corruption.

The civil wars of the late republic had taken their toll in Italy, where the principal occupation remained farming. Owners of latifundia were encouraged to diversify their crops to guard against poor years or changes in the market. Many medium-size farms specialized in the production of wine or olive oil, both of which were popular abroad and easy to export. The general rise in living standards produced by the Augustan peace led to a demand for luxury products such as peacocks and pheasants, so even a modest poultry ranch could be profitable. Augustus encouraged agriculture not only for its practical benefits but also as a symbol of the bounty guaranteed by political stability.

Italian industry flourished under Augustus, partly for obvious economic reasons and partly because the emperor seems to have favored businessmen and manufacturers rather than the ingrown, snobbish aristocracy. A style of pottery called Arretine was developed in the ceramics factories of Arezzo and other centers in central Italy; Arretine vessels were exported throughout the empire. Such demand required new, more efficient methods of production. One of the factories at Arezzo could mix 10,000 gallons of clay at a time, and similar mass production techniques were used for the extraction and working of metals. Furthermore, Augustus' building program throughout Italy stimulated demand for bricks, tiles, and other construction materials.

Augustan legislation stimulated industry and commerce throughout the provinces. Egypt, with its fine sand, became a center for glass manufacture, while Alexandria retained its importance as an international port for the buying and selling of raw materials. With a return to prosperity, the demand for luxury goods such as silk, rare fruits, and fine wines rose sharply. To some extent this could be satisfied by products from the provinces; the Greek island of Cos was famous for its silks, and dates, figs, and plums were imported from Spain. Supply stimulated yet more demand, and Roman traders found themselves exploring ever more distant markets.

In the late first century B.C., Roman sailors discovered that monsoon winds greatly aided the sea journey from Egypt to India. The trip there took some 40 days, and the speed with which commercial links grew is demonstrated by the large quantities of Arretine pottery discovered at ports on India's east coast. The Indian connection was valuable in itself, providing spices, jewels, ivory, and other exotic commodities. More important, it gave the Roman world better access to China, with its production of high-quality silk, than the dangerous overland route that passed through the territory of the warlike Parthians, the inhabitants of northeastern Persia. From the time of Augustus it was possible to transport Chinese products through Afghanistan, down the river Indus, and across the Indian Ocean to Syria and then Rome. Fashionable Romans were thus assured of luxury products, although some political leaders were concerned that the trade in luxury items seriously depleted stocks of gold and silver.

At Augustus' death the empire was peaceful, stable, and prosperous. Firm leadership and prudent reform were responsible for this. Augustus drew a clear distinction between political and administrative control. The former he kept in his own hands; the latter he dispersed as widely as the security of the empire permitted. Thus provincial autonomy and local self-government were stressed, as was respect for ethnic customs and cultures. This enabled Rome to control a very large empire with a minimum of centralized bureaucracy, and that in turn kept taxation at tolerable levels. Local self-government proved Augustus' happiest and most enduring innovation. It enabled the provinces to withstand the effects of erratic or tyrannical rulers and to prosper until the empire weakened in the third century A.D., when the Augustan system began to break down.

## Social Legislation

Much of Augustus' social reform was intended to correct the general social laxity that had developed during the

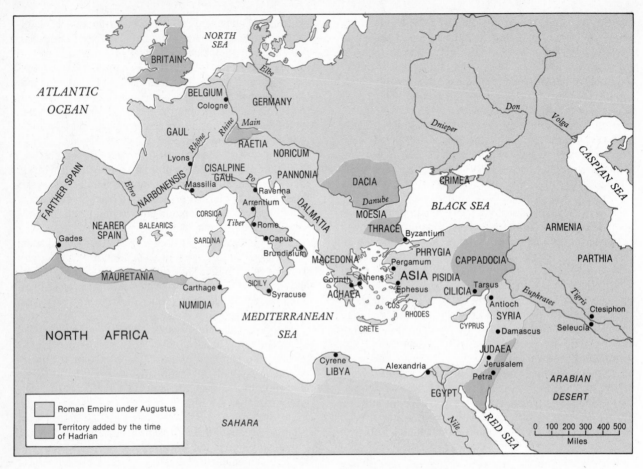

*6.3 The Roman Empire*

last century of the republic. Comprehensive laws on marriage were introduced that rewarded large families and penalized the single, the childless, and people who married beyond childbearing age. Decrees were also issued to curb promiscuity and adultery, and Augustus exercised his own paternal rights directly, sending both his daughter and his granddaughter into exile for breaches of his code. In part this legislation reflected Augustus' attempt to promote the family as a social unit and his concern with the falling population of native Roman citizens. The slaves who had been freed during the previous century represented a foreign element in Italy that the emperor saw as a potential threat. Thus in addition to his encouragement of large families, he had laws passed that specifically limited the number of slaves who could be freed by their masters.

Augustus himself lived simply and unostentatiously, at least in public, and laid great emphasis on duty to the state as well as traditional values and morality. He even exiled his daughter Julia for wanton conduct. High society must have found the new austerity difficult to adapt

to, and Augustus' successors were unable to maintain his high moral tone—nor, in most cases, were they much inclined to do so.

## Augustan Literature and Art

A masterful propagandist, Augustus made full use of the arts to reinforce the impression of peace and prosperity. Much of the art produced at Rome during his reign was official, commissioned by the state to serve government purposes. Yet if he can justly be accused of cultural manipulation, it must be admitted that the art and literature of his age are of the highest quality.

The literary period of Augustan Rome is known as the Golden Age. Perhaps the greatest poet of the age, and one of the most influential figures of the Western literary tradition, was Publius Vergilius Maro, called Virgil (70–19 B.C.). His principal work, the *Aeneid*, an epic poem in 12 books, was commissioned to give the Romans their own national epic, worthy to stand alongside the *Iliad* and the *Odyssey*. It contains passages of patriotic fervor, recounting the mythical founding of Rome by Aeneas, son of Venus, after he fled from the ruins of Troy. Inspired by Homer, Virgil consciously made his epic a Roman counterpart of Homer's works, thus firmly linking the glories of Rome to the Hellenistic cultural legacy. An earlier work of Virgil's, the *Georgics*, deals with one of the emperor's favorite themes, praising agriculture and the virtues of family life on the farm and offering practical advice on farming, forestry, and raising cattle and horses.

Among the other Roman poets of the period to praise country life was Horace (65–8 B.C.), a personal friend of both Virgil and Augustus, whose private secretary Horace became. A more worldly man than Virgil, Horace combined passion with irony to create a series of short odes that illuminated both Roman politics and his own refined sensibility. The leading prose writer of the time was Livy (59 B.C.–A.D. 17), whose *History of Rome*, also sponsored by Augustus, told the story of Rome's growth from its earliest days.

Peace and order were the goals of Augustus' administration, and the subject of one of the most complex works of art produced during his reign, the *Ara Pacis*, or Altar of Peace, which combines episodes from Rome's mythic past with representations of Augustus and his family leading the way to the ceremony at which the altar is to be dedicated to the goddess Peace. In fact, beginning with Augustus' rule, Rome was to enjoy two centuries of relative civil security, known as the Pax Romana, or Roman Peace. It was an extraordinary accomplishment, but it was not without its price. The republic, despite its corruption and strife, had represented an ideal of self-government that was now abandoned. The exile of the poet Ovid (43 B.C.–A.D. 17), the witty and irreverent author of *The Art of Love*, showed the darker side of Augustus' campaign to reform morals, and the historian Livy's refusal to take his account of Rome down to his own time for fear of giving offense was no doubt only an example of the self-censorship imposed on art, scholarship, and political expression. Throughout the first decades of the empire an underground movement of political philosophers known loosely as the "Stoic opposition" continued to discuss principles of rational government and the possibility of restoring the republic. Many of the real or imagined members of this group lost their lives during the first century of the empire. Not all Romans, in short, succumbed to Augustan propaganda or confused order with liberty.

## The Julio-Claudians

The one problem for which Augustus was unable to find a satisfactory solution was the choice of his successor.

In the end he was forced to nominate his able but unpopular stepson, Tiberius (A.D. 14–37). The first five emperors, including Augustus himself, were related to one another as members of the Julian and Claudian clans. Thus the principle of hereditary succession was implicitly established, although as early as the reign of Claudius (A.D. 41–54) the right to select the family member chosen emperor was temporarily seized by the army, a precedent that was to prove dangerous.

The Julio-Claudian emperors do not make a particularly good case for the hereditary system of government. Claudius himself was effective enough. A dedicated administrator, he also achieved what even Julius Caesar had failed to do by adding Britain to the empire. Nor did Tiberius altogether deserve the hatred with which his contemporaries regarded him. Whatever his personal idiosyncrasies, which are spelled out in lurid detail by the historians Tacitus (c. 55–c. 117) and Suetonius (c. 69–c. 160), the Augustan peace was maintained throughout his reign.

The other two Julio-Claudians, however, were a very different matter. Gaius, better known as Caligula, or "Little Boots" after a childhood nickname, came to the throne in A.D. 37 amid general relief at the passing of Tiberius. By the time of his assassination in 41, he had a reputation for criminal insanity that has endured; among his more whimsical acts was declaring a horse his prime minister. If Nero (54–68) surpassed the excesses of Caligula, and in certain respects he did, the greater length of his reign is at least in part responsible. He was protected from his worst instincts during its first five years by his mother, Agrippina, but after ordering her killed in 59, he organized a reign of terror against the aristocracy. He may not have deliberately started the great fire that destroyed Rome in 64 as legend states, but he certainly took advantage of it to build an immense palace, the so-called Golden House of Nero, and to persecute the Christians, whom he accused of starting the conflagration.

## The Flavians and the "Good" Emperors

Nero committed suicide after being proscribed by the Senate. His death was followed in 69 by a year of confusion in which no fewer than four generals made themselves emperor. The final victor, Vespasian (69–79), was the first emperor to die peacefully since Tiberius. A professional soldier, hardworking and conscientious, he did much to repair the economic confusion wrought by Nero and reasserted the Augustan policy in the provinces. He also gave Rome one of its most famous monuments by turning an artificial lake that had been made for Nero within the walls of his Golden House into the Colosseum.

Vespasian had little better luck than Augustus in finding a successor. His two sons, Titus and Domitian, were groomed to succeed him. Titus, the elder son, served his father as general in the Roman province of Judea, annexed by Rome in A.D. 6, where disturbances had broken out in the last years of Nero's reign. Vespasian himself had commanded Roman forces in 66, when the Jews of Caesarea and Jerusalem protested their lack of civil equality. The revolt at Caesarea was suppressed, but at Jerusalem the protestors remained active. In 70, Roman forces under Titus finally crushed the revolt, destroyed the temple of the Jews, and abolished the Jewish national council, the Sanhedrin.

By the time of his accession, Titus was known for his cruelty, and his well-publicized love affair with Berenice, sister of the Jewish king Julius Agrippa II, had given Rome a subject for gossip. When he came to power, he proved a modest and popular ruler, but a fever cut short his reign barely two years later. Domitian (81–96) continued his father's policies of maintaining efficient gov-ernment and improving provincial defenses and admin-istration, but, victim of his own paranoia, he constructed the apparatus of a police state, instituting a complex system of state spies and informers.

Prominent Roman political leaders could take no more. With the approval of the Senate, a group of conspirators determined that an elderly senator of unimpeachable character would be chosen to serve as immediate successor to Domitian. Aided by the Senate, he would select as his successor someone who seemed qualified for the position and adopt him as his son. The scheme worked well. Domitian was assassinated in 96 and replaced by Nerva (96–98), who was doubly qualified by his age (66) and by the fact that he was childless. Nerva in turn adopted one of the most distinguished generals and provincial administrators of his day, Trajan (98–117).

Thus merit rather than birth or brute force was responsible for a series of outstanding Roman emperors, for Trajan in his turn was to adopt as his successor the able and cultivated Hadrian (117–138). The system of adoption continued in the selection of the next two em-

**The Pantheon, Rome. The inscription, which dates the building from the third consulship of Agrippa (27 B.C.), must have been intended by Hadrian as a tribute to Agrippa's master and friend, Augustus. [Marburg/Art Resource]**

perors, Antoninus (138–161) and Marcus Aurelius (161–180). With Trajan and Hadrian, they provided an extended and much needed period of stability. Under Trajan the borders of the empire expanded to their fullest extent, and Hadrian successfully consolidated them. He traveled tirelessly throughout the provinces to see that imperial defenses and administration were strengthened. The reign of Hadrian, perhaps the most gifted and complex of all the emperors, marked a high point of Roman civilization, but it was tainted by the suppression of another Jewish revolt, led by Simon Bar-Kochba ("Son of the Star"), which ended in the extermination of most of the Jewish population of Judea (133).

---

❀✿❀

## LIFE IN THE ROMAN CAPITAL: IMPERIAL POMP AND URBAN SQUALOR

By Hadrian's reign Rome's center had become filled with temples, monuments, and public buildings, many of which have partially withstood the ravages of time, of fifth- and sixth-century invaders, and of Renaissance builders looking for bricks or marble for their own palaces and churches. Roman architecture and engineering have had a lasting effect on later styles. In particular, the Roman use of columns, arches, and domes has been widely imitated since the eighteenth century in public building in Europe and the Americas.

One of the greatest domed buildings, the Pantheon, designed by Hadrian himself, was constructed around 126. Its imposing portico (or porch), containing 16 monolithic granite columns, leads into the central rotunda, the roof of which consists of a huge concrete dome. The building is lit only by a central *oculus*, or eye, in the top of the dome. As the sun moves across the sky, its rays travel around the inside of the Pantheon, whose form thus became symbolic of the world itself.

The Forum, where the early political life of the young republic had been concentrated, remained at the heart of the city's activities. During the empire, however, effective political control passed to the emperor and his staff, who lived on the Palatine (from which our word *palace* is derived), the hill overlooking the ancient as-

---

## ◉ Life in Imperial Rome ◉

*An embittered description of life in imperial Rome was penned by the Roman satirist Juvenal.*

*So the day goes by with a lovely order of business:*
*First, this handout; then the forum, the courts of Apollo,*
*And the triumphal statues, including some lousy Egyptian's,*
*At the base of which only pissing's permitted.*
*There they go, the poor souls, old clients, weary and hopeless,*
*Though the last hope to leave is always that of a dinner,*
*They must buy cabbage now, and a little kindling to cook it.*
*Meanwhile, all by himself, on a couch unshared, their good king will*
*Gobble and guzzle the choicest products of land and ocean.*
*Down goes a whole estate; from such luxurious tables,*
*Broad and antique, down goes a whole estate at one sitting.*
*This will kill parasites off, at least; but who can endure this*
*Luxury, grudging and cheap? A whole roast boar for one gullet*
*When good custom decrees this is the fare for a party?*
*You will get yours pretty soon, when you go and undress in your bathroom,*
*Trying to ease your gut's distending burden of peacock.*
*Hence come sudden deaths, too sudden for old men to make wills.*
*What a good laugh for the town at all of the dinner tables!*
*Hear the disgruntled friends cheer at the funeral service!*

*Source:* Juvenal, *The Satires*, trans. R. Humphries (Bloomington: Indiana University Press, 1958), p. 22.

sembly place of the people. Augustus' house there (which can still be visited) is a surprisingly, if characteristically, modest structure. Domitian, with his obsessive need for protection, began the construction of a huge imperial palace, the Domus Augustana. This palace, extended by his successors, contained its own race track and incorporated a private viewing stand from which the emperor could watch the races in Rome's main public stadium, the Circus Maximus.

According to tradition, racing and blood sports had been introduced into Rome by the Etruscans. By the time of the empire, chariot races and gladiatorial combats were held on a massive scale before a vast public; in its heyday the Circus Maximus had places for more than 300,000 people. Public performers such as charioteers, musicians, and fighters were generally slaves or criminals, since no respectable citizen would perform or compete in public. Of the scandals that helped turn popular opinion against Nero, the most serious was not his murder of his mother or of his wife but his appearance in public as a musician. Prizes were very large; a successful charioteer could easily amass a fortune and become the idol of a rabid fan club. There were four teams, the Reds, Whites, Blues, and Greens, each with its ardent supporters, and rivalry was intense.

The principal stage at Rome for individual gladiatorial contests was the Colosseum, which held 50,000 spectators. There were three types of gladiators: the Samnite was heavily armed with a long oblong shield, the Thracian relied on a small round shield, and the Retiarius carried only a net and dagger in one hand and a short pronged spear in the other. In general, combats ended with the death or surrender of one of the participants. In the case of surrender it was up to the crowd (or the emperor, if he was present) to decide the loser's fate. As the empire grew and the Romans had access to more exotic creatures, animal contests (either against gladiators or between animals) became increasingly popular. In the "games" of A.D. 249, fully 1,000 pairs of gladiators fought, and among the animals killed were 32 elephants, 10 elks, 10 tigers, and 60 lions. Such entertainment reveals a darker side of Roman culture.

Emperors exploited popular tastes by organizing special games, such as the one in 249, to keep the urban masses content. This policy of "bread and circuses," by which rulers attempted to control their often unruly subjects, also entailed the construction of centers for the distribution of grain and the sale of basic commodities such as wine and oil at subsidized prices. The provision of cheap grain for the Roman masses had begun as early

Part of a large plastic scale model of Rome in A.D. 350 showing the Circus Maximus in the center and the Domus Augustana behind. Note the arches of the aqueduct. [Alinari/Art Resource]

as the tribunate of Gaius Gracchus (123–122 B.C.). By 58 B.C. free grain was being provided for any citizen who needed it, and this remained the case throughout the history of the empire. The magistracy in charge of the distribution of the grain dole, the Annona, was one of the most important public offices.

Rome was also provided with a plentiful supply of fresh water. A huge system of aqueducts connected pipes through which millions of gallons of water flowed each day; the water fed public fountains and baths as well as the private homes of the well-to-do. The street drains were covered, an improvement over the open sewers of earlier times. (After the fall of Rome, open sewers were to become the norm again until the nineteenth century.)

For all the ingenuity of its public works, however, imperial Rome was overcrowded, and life must often have been uncomfortable. Most Romans lived in apartment blocks, of which there were some 45,000. Laws regulated the height of these buildings to discourage the construction of unsound structures, but buildings sometimes collapsed, and fire was a constant hazard. The streets were crowded and noisy, and traffic jams were a frequent problem: descriptions of the squabbling and brawling between carriage drivers sound all too familiar to the modern big-city dweller. It is little wonder that at weekends and in summer, affluent Romans escaped to their rural villas. Hadrian imported all the convenience of the city to his immense villa at Tivoli, which contained libraries, theaters, baths, and quarters for hundreds of servants.

## Life in the Provinces and on the Frontier

The same dependable engineering that provided the capital with water linked the city, by means of a vast road network, to the farthest corners of the provinces. Good communications were essential for maintaining efficient government, and Roman roads are the most visible remains of the Roman achievement. The main roads connecting Rome to other parts of Italy were begun in the fourth century B.C. Rome's armies included builders who surveyed and laid roads for supplies and reinforcements in conquered territories and provinces. By the time their conquest was complete, each province was thus provided with an effective network of communications. The thousands of miles of roads were well maintained and provided with milestones, and in the time of Augustus a column was erected in the Roman Forum that displayed the distances between Rome and the principal cities of the empire.

## Provincial Life in Southern Europe, North Africa, and Asia

An empire as vast as that ruled by Trajan and Hadrian encompassed an enormous diversity of people, culture, language, and religion. The average Roman soldier or administrator probably felt most at home in Greece or the Greek cities of Asia Minor, where he was surrounded by art and architecture of the kind that had conditioned Roman taste. Athens, although no longer of political significance (its former rival, Corinth, was the capital of the Roman province of Achaea), was always a cultural and intellectual center. Augustus provided it with a fine new marketplace, and Hadrian had a public library built there. Even in the Greek world, however, there were cultural differences. The Greeks, for example, were fond of serious music, which held little interest for the Romans, and the Greeks showed no enthusiasm for gladiatorial contests. Even Greek theaters had to be adapted for the performance of Roman plays by the construction of a permanent stage set.

Elsewhere in the provinces, where local culture was less developed and new cities were built, the Romans created an environment more to their taste. Many cities in southern France and Spain still have their Roman amphitheaters, and Roman public baths were built throughout the empire. One of the most elaborate sets of baths were those at Lepcis Magna in North Africa, which rival even those of the capital for size. Like many other public works, they were paid for by a wealthy private citizen rather than by the state.

The generally mild climate of the Mediterranean region meant that life in the Roman provinces of North Africa, Spain, or western Asia was in many respects similar to that in Italy. Large public squares were adorned with temples and public buildings such as baths and theaters, and private houses often included gardens. The best-preserved of these houses can be seen at Pompeii.

### ❦ POMPEII: LIFE IN A PROVINCIAL TOWN

On August 24, A.D. 79, the volcano Vesuvius, which stands above the Bay of Naples, erupted. The lava that flowed from it and the pumice and ash that were spewed out buried a number of small towns. The most famous of these is Pompeii, located 10 miles southeast of the volcano. The finds excavated there in the past 250 years provide detailed evidence about life in a provincial town of the period—from the shrines of the religious cults and the houses and gardens to the meals Pompeiians had prepared at the time of the eruption.

Lying some 150 miles south of Rome, Pompeii was a prosperous town of 20,000 people that served both as a commercial center for its region and as a holiday resort for Romans of modest means who sought to escape the heat of summer. It provides an impressive picture of the pleasant but modest lifestyle of the provinces. Houses were spacious and comfortable, and the frescoes that decorated them were often of high quality. Many houses had private gardens, sheltered from the noise of the streets. The furniture, tableware, and other household goods were often elaborately designed.

Pompeii's layout followed the Greek system of town planning, adapted to the irregularities of its hillside. Long, narrow residential blocks were separated by narrow access roads running at right angles to the main avenues. As in all town plans of this kind, there are two principal arteries, the *cardo*, running north-south, and the *decumanus*, running east-west.

The town contained three public baths, a concert hall, a theater, and an amphitheater capable of accommodating all the citizens, as well as houses of prostitution; a famous sign in the form of an erect phallus pointed to the red-light district. The main square or forum was closed to vehicular traffic; about it were grouped public buildings, including a *basilica*, or large hall, that was the setting for Pompeii's legal and financial activities. At the opposite end of the forum was the main temple, dedicated to Jupiter. Just beyond it was another temple, consecrated to the emperor Augustus, whose memory by the first century A.D. was revered throughout the empire.

Excavation at other towns buried by Vesuvius suggests that Pompeii was far from the most prosperous site in the region. Some of the villas at nearby Herculaneum are grander than anything at Pompeii, particularly the lavish waterfront homes with large windows that opened on the view. Recent excavation at Oplontis has revealed a magnificent villa.

In addition to serving the needs of tourists, Pompeii and the neighboring towns had their own commercial life. The largest building in Pompeii's forum, for example, was neither religious nor political; it was a large hall for the clothmakers and dyers that combined storage and sales facilities with a meeting place for fabric manufacturers. Nearby was a large open market, the Marcellum, at which farmers sold their produce. At its center, where fishmongers had their stands, was a pool connected to underground sewers, in which the sellers cleaned their fish; it was found filled with scales. Other shops in the city sold utensils, wine and olive oil, and bread, including flat loaves that look like modern pizza bases. In addition to the usual artisans, Herculaneum boasted a colony of artists.

A number of toilet facilities, including a communal one across from the Marcellum, were found in Pompeii. The provision of such facilities throughout the empire was one of Vespasian's contributions to Western culture. To this day in Italy a public urinal is known as a *vespasiano*.

## Provincial Life in the North

The northern provinces present a different picture. In the rich farmland of northern France, life was concentrated not in cities but around country villas. The largest of these contained, in addition to farming establishments, small factories turning out pottery, bricks, ironwork, and other materials useful for the armies guarding the northeastern frontier against hostile Germanic tribes. The grain and wool produced by the smaller establishments served the farms themselves, which seem to have been run by slaves, and the neighboring troops.

Britain, one of the remotest provinces, was the northern frontier, for the Romans never gained control over what is now modern Scotland. Agricola, who governed Britain from A.D. 78 to 84, did what he could to Romanize the local population, and in the south Roman ideas and customs took root fairly quickly. The capital, Londinium (most of which lies beneath modern London), developed into a city of some size, and Roman villas and baths have been uncovered throughout southern England. The north, however, presented a more formidable challenge. One of the military encampments Agricola built was in modern Perthshire. The buildings, made primarily of wood, included a headquarters, barracks, granaries, a drill hall, and a hospital.

The Romans' last major extension of their frontiers is recorded in detail on the monument known as Trajan's Column. In 101 and again in 104 Trajan led expeditions to subdue the Dacians, whose territory in modern Romania lay to the east of the river Danube, previously a frontier. To celebrate Trajan's victory and the submission of the Dacians to Rome, a 125-foot column was erected in Trajan's Forum in Rome that shows the campaigns in vivid detail: the crossing of the Danube, the Roman army building camps and bridges, the harangues of Trajan, and scenes of battle and torture. Here is carved no mere celebration of Roman triumph but an almost photographic record of the endurance needed by emperor and foot soldier alike to create and maintain the empire.

## Women in Roman Society

With the growth of empire and of contact with the Hellenized East, the position of upper-class women became freer. Wealthy and aristocratic women were able to preside over literary salons and to dabble in high politics. The salons appear to have been of some cultural importance from the days of the Flavian dynasty to the empress Julia Domna (died A.D. 217). Some women won fame as orators, and political demonstrations by women were not unknown. In 195 B.C. the women of Rome gathered to demand repeal of the Oppian Law, which, having confiscated most of their gold for the war effort against Hannibal, had been prolonged into peacetime. On a similar occasion in 42 B.C., when women were taxed to pay the expenses of the civil war, a group of them burst into the Forum, and their spokeswoman, Hortensia, made an impassioned speech:

> **Why should we pay taxes when we do not share in the offices, honors, military commands, nor in short, the government, for which you fight between yourselves with such harmful results? . . . Let war with the Celts or Parthians come, we will not be inferior to our mothers when it is a question of common safety. But for civil wars, may we never contribute nor aid you against each other.[1]**

The legal position of Roman women was, as in Greece, strictly subordinate. In the intensely patriarchal culture of early Rome, the male head of the family literally had life and death powers over the members of his household. Adult males were emancipated at their father's death, but women were subject, at least in theory, to the guardianship of a male relative until marriage. Roman law assumed the incapacity of women to deal with matters of contract, property, and inheritance.

There were two kinds of marriage, with or without *manus*, the equivalent of a transfer of paternal authority to the husband. Marriages without *manus* left the bride freer but also with fewer rights. The consent of both partners was required for betrothal, but a woman could refuse a prospective husband only if she could show that he was morally unfit. With or without *manus*, the bride's father continued to exercise considerable supervision over his daughter and could, as in Greece, initiate divorce.

Divorce among the upper classes in the late republican and imperial periods was surprisingly casual. No reason was legally required for it, and no particular stigma attached to it unless scandal was involved. Despite the official exhortations to increase childbearing, infanticide and abortion were commonly practiced; in fact, infanticide did not become a moral offense until the third century A.D. Among the many advertised techniques for contraception was the suggestion that a woman hold her breath at the moment of male ejaculation.

Roman matrons were expected to master such traditional domestic skills as spinning and weaving. In practice, they left these tasks to their slaves, exercising only a general supervision of the household. With little restriction on their movements, they were able to visit, shop, and attend public functions. In this and other respects they enjoyed far greater freedom than their Greek counterparts.

At the apex of the social scale, some women enjoyed extraordinary honors. The erection of statues to the women of prominent Roman families was imitated by provincial governors, who put up likenesses of their wives. Some women were granted citizenship and even held public office in late Hellenistic Greece, a practice that continued into Roman times. A number of empresses were deified after death, becoming part of the official state religion.

For the great majority of Roman women, life was quite different. Most of these women fell into three broad categories: slaves, freedwomen, and the freeborn poor. The slaves of well-to-do families were perhaps the best off economically; they were permitted to accumulate property and even to buy other slaves. Their duties were varied, including cooking, cleaning, clothesmaking, and the care and nursing of children. More specialized slaves might serve as secretaries, ladies' maids, masseuses, entertainers, and midwives. Some acquired considerable education. Because there was always more demand for male slaves, however, slave daughters were often left to die of exposure or sold. All female slaves, whatever their function, were used sexually by their masters; Cato the censor, in addition to exercising his own prerogatives, gave his male slaves access to the women of the household in return for a fee.

Slaves might buy their freedom or be manumitted through marriage. Freedwomen comprised a large part of the Roman working class, serving as laundresses, shopkeepers, waitresses, and prostitutes or working at artisanal trades or as domestics. Some attained prosperity, but many continued to work for their former masters. Freeborn women enjoyed a higher status than any slave, even slaves who worked in the imperial household, and often wielded considerable influence. They were discouraged from marrying slaves, and in A.D. 52 a senatorial decree reduced those who did to the status of slaves of their husbands' masters. Some freeborn women purchased the freedom of male slaves in order to marry them, but this practice was subsequently outlawed. Under Constantine, finally, it was made a capital offense for a woman to cohabit with a slave, and the slave himself was to be burned to death.

Unlike notable women of the upper classes, whose lives were often commemorated, we have little biographical information about the great mass of Roman women. Their position, restricted as it was, did offer some opportunity for mobility and self-expression and in these terms compared favorably with that of the women of Han China. The epitaph of one woman, Claudia, must serve for the anonymous history of many:

Stranger, what I have to say is short. Stop and read it through. This is the unlovely tomb of a lovely woman. Her parents named her Claudia. She loved her husband with her whole heart. She bore two sons, one of whom she leaves on earth; the other she has placed beneath the ground. She was charming in conversation, yet her conduct was appropriate. She kept house; she made wool.[2]

# The Roman Achievement

The Romans' mission, as defined by Virgil, was to "rule the world, show mercy to the defeated, and strike down the proud." Their intellectual contribution to the human heritage is significant. From the beginning, Roman culture was imitative rather than original. The first Roman poet of whom anything is known is Ennius (239–169 B.C.), a writer the Romans themselves called the father of Roman poetry. Ennius adapted tragedies from Greek and used Greek metrical schemes to write his *Annals*, an epic chronicle of Rome; almost all his work is lost. The first writers whose work has survived in any quantity, the comic playwrights Plautus (c. 251–184 B.C.) and Terence (c. 195–159 B.C.), turned Greek comedies into Latin and generally adapted them to Roman tastes, with results that were lively and often earthy.

The last years of the republic produced a rich body of literature. The poetry of Catullus (c. 84–c. 54 B.C.) is renowned for its uninhibited satire and eroticism, and his account of an unhappy affair with the girl he calls Lesbia is painful and candid. *On the Nature of Things*, by Lucretius (c. 99–55 B.C.), expounds the materialist teachings of Epicurus in one of the world's greatest philosophical poems. Caesar himself left us the history of his military campaigns in Gaul, written in a simple but gripping style.

Perhaps the most representative literary and political figure of the late republic was Marcus Tullius Cicero (106–43 B.C.). A successful lawyer and politician, Cicero published many of his speeches, the rhetorical power of which serves as a reminder of the Romans' cultivation of oratory. Cicero also wrote philosophical works and took an active part in politics, but he is best remembered for the personal correspondence that he kept to be published after his death. His nearly 900 letters provide an incomparable picture of the man and his world, his political judgments, his literary tastes, and his personal relations. If they often reveal Cicero's weaknesses—his vanity, his reluctance to make decisions, and his stubbornness—they confirm his humanity and sensitivity. His weaknesses proved ultimately fatal; proscribed in 43 B.C., he was assassinated, and his severed head was nailed to the rostrum of the Senate.

The Romans also paid a good deal of attention to practical matters. Cato (234–149 B.C.) published a guide to farming, as did Varro (116–27 B.C.), Rome's first public librarian, who also wrote on language and grammar. A work from the late first century B.C., Vitruvius' *On Architecture*, influenced Renaissance architects such as

## ◉ Cicero on His Daughter's Death ◉

*Cicero's letter to his friend Atticus conveys the effect on him of his daughter's death.*

To Atticus                                                    Astura, 15 May 45 B.C.

I think I shall conquer my feelings and go from Lanuvium to my house at Tusculum. For either I must give up my property there for ever—since my grief will remain the same, though I shall become able to conceal it better—or if not it does not matter in the least whether I go there now or in ten years' time. The place will not remind me of her any more than the thoughts which consume me all the time, day and night. You will be asking me if there is no comfort to be derived from books. I am afraid that in this situation they have the contrary effect. Without them I might have been tougher; an educated man is not insensitive or impervious enough.

So do come as you wrote you would, but not if it is inconvenient. A couple of letters will be enough. I will come and meet you, if necessary. Whatever you can manage, so be it.

*Source:* Cicero, *Selected Works*, trans. M. Grant (Harmondsworth, England: Penguin Books, 1960), p. 87.

Bramante and Michelangelo. Sextus Frontinus (c. A.D. 30–104), who directed Rome's water system, wrote a fascinating treatise on aqueducts.

If the Augustan Age saw in Virgil the apex of Roman poetry, the so-called Silver Age that followed found its historian in Cornelius Tacitus (c. A.D. 55–c. 120). Many of the historical characters of the period spring to life in his works. Tiberius, Nero, and Domitian are unforgettably (if not always fairly) portrayed by a man who observed at first hand the consequences of their deeds. Tacitus' world is one of continuous action, moving from the imperial court to the battles on the frontiers. He was married to Agricola's daughter, and his biography of his father-in-law (one of the few people of whom he had anything good to say) includes an account of Roman Britain. He also provides us with the best contemporary account of the Germans in his *Germania*, based on reports related to him by travelers.

The Silver Age was characterized by satire. Petronius (died A.D. 66) poked fun at the self-importance of rhetoricians and the self-indulgence of the newly rich in his comic novel *Satyricon*. Lucan (39–65) and Juvenal (c. 60–c. 127) lampooned Roman mores in verse, as did Martial (c. 40–c. 104), whose pithy epigrams spared no vice or folly:

> *You're so alike, you're matched for life:*
> *A nitwit man, his nitwit wife.*
> *(I wonder then why it should be*
> *That such a pair cannot agree?)*[3]

Rhetoric, philosophy, natural science, and history were among the chief subjects of Roman prose. Seneca (c. 5 B.C.–A.D. 65) wrote Stoic treatises as well as tragedies in the Greek style, and Quintilian (c. 35–c. 100) composed what remained the standard work on Latin rhetoric. Pliny the Elder (23–79) left behind many volumes of a natural history, and the correspondence between his nephew Pliny the Younger (c. 62–c. 113), governor of Bithynia, and the emperor Trajan, offers a vivid picture of the daily life of a provincial administrator in Asia Minor. Tacitus' contemporary Plutarch (c. 46–c. 120) wrote a highly influential set called *Parallel Lives*, comparing Greek and Roman historical personalities. The practice of literature could be a dangerous profession in imperial Rome; Lucan and Seneca were both compelled to commit suicide by Nero, and Juvenal is said to have been exiled by Domitian.

In a sense, the greatest Roman contribution to literature was the Latin language itself. Latin was the language of the early writers of the Christian church and remained the common link between people of culture in the West virtually until our own time. It is still used for scientific nomenclature and remains the official language of the Roman Catholic church. It evolved into all the Romance languages, including French, Italian, Spanish, Portuguese, and Rumanian, and was a root of English and German as well.

The Romans were awed by the brilliance of Greek visual art, and many of their own chief monuments are marked by a dependence on classical models. Yet in at least two major fields the Romans broke new ground. Roman portraiture broke with the idealizing classical style. Taking their cue from Hellenistic examples, Roman artists learned to use physical appearance to convey character. Many of the best Roman portraits are revealing psychological documents; that of Cicero, for example, reveals his smugness as well as his humanity.

In architecture most of all, the Romans could express their need to construct and to dominate. Whereas Greek buildings were generally meant to be seen from the outside, Roman buildings consciously enclose their occupants. The Pantheon is a striking example of this, as are the imperial baths and, on an even grander scale, monumental complexes such as Trajan's Forum, which could accommodate thousands of people. The invention of concrete in the first century B.C. and the growing mastery of the principles of stress and counterstress enabled architects to experiment with forms—arches and vaults—that passed into the Western architectural tradition. The theaters, stadiums, libraries, markets, temples, and other public buildings constructed on three continents are proof of the high quality of Roman engineering.

# Roman Law and the Ideal of Justice

Beyond the Latin language itself, Rome's major contribution to civilization was its legal system, the principles of which still undergird the jurisprudence of most European countries, Quebec, Louisiana, and Latin America. As Roman law evolved, two fundamental concepts developed: that judicial decisions must be based on equity rather than on the rigid application of the law and that all persons of the same status enjoyed identical legal rights. Most cases were decided by a judge (*judex*), who applied the appropriate law (*jus*). The judge could seek the advice of a specialist learned in the law (*juris prudens*), who assisted him both in interpreting it and applying it equitably to the case at hand. Their function was carried out under the watchful eyes of citizens, since trials and suits were conducted in public.

Other magistrates, especially praetors, whose main function was to act as judges in civil cases, had the power to make and shape law by issuing edicts at the outset of their annual term. In these edicts they enunciated the principles by which they intended to interpret legislation. This practice—subject to legislative review—was more efficient than amending laws in the Senate or the Assembly to conform to changing circumstances and made for speedier justice. As the empire developed, imperial edicts began to replace praetors' edicts, signaling a further consolidation of imperial power.

Like other ancient societies, the Romans at first applied their laws—the *jus civile*, or civil law—only to themselves, leaving visiting foreigners without rights in the absence of a treaty between their state and Rome. This impeded commercial development, and magistrates built up a body of law—the *jus gentium*, or law of nations—applicable to all persons, citizen or alien. Gradually the two forms of law adopted common principles and procedures and were applied to resident aliens as well. With the extension of citizenship to most of the free population in A.D. 212, a single law covered most of the empire. Most women, as noted, were legally subordinate and subject to male guardianship, but their rights of property and consent were gradually liberalized.

## The Empire in Crisis

At its height in the mid-second century A.D., the Roman Empire extended over some 3.5 million square miles and embraced a population of about 75 million people. More than 85 percent were engaged in agriculture, but Rome itself had a population of approximately 1 million, and Alexandria in Egypt and Antioch in Syria numbered several hundred thousand inhabitants each. The 1,000 cities of the empire were connected by an extensive network of roads, some of which are still in use today; water was piped in by aqueduct. Roman law, backed by Roman legions, provided stability and security, while decentralized administration and local autonomy lightened the imperial yoke.

Yet the empire suffered from structural weaknesses. The supply of cheap labor provided by conquest and slavery was a disincentive to innovation and efficiency, but when Rome's frontiers ceased to expand, that supply began to dry up. The economy slowly contracted, underscoring the fact that its strength had lain in the acquisition of new resources rather than the development of existing ones. At the same time, unrest on the frontiers stretched the imperial army and treasury. Marcus Aurelius' unwise decision to end the system of adoptive emperors destabilized the throne; the reign of his deranged son Commodus (180–192) ended in assassination and civil war, with the Praetorian Guard at one point actually attempting to auction off the empire to the highest bidder.

## The Severi

Order was restored by Septimius Severus (193–211), an African-born general whose accession to the throne symbolized the increasingly multiracial nature of the empire and the shift in its center of gravity from Rome. Septimius spent little time in his capital; most of his reign was devoted to pacifying the frontiers, and he died campaigning in Britain in 211. With him, the dyarchy effectively came to an end. He opened the Senate to commoners while stripping it of much of its function, making the army and the civil service the main avenues to imperial preferment. But he encouraged the codification of the law under the jurist Papinian and laid the groundwork for the general extension of citizenship throughout the empire by his son and successor Antoninus, known as Caracalla (211–217). This had, among other aims, the effect of broadening the tax rolls.

As early as 161, the mounting difficulties of administering the empire had led Marcus Aurelius to divide his responsibilities with a coemperor, Lucius Verus (161–169). Septimius bequeathed the empire to both his sons, Antoninus and his brother Geta; the latter, however, was slain. Rome's dominant figure during the next several years was Septimius' widow, Julia Domna (c. 169–217), a woman of powerful character who was even spoken of as a candidate for the throne herself. The later Severi included the unpopular Macrinus (217–218), the profligate Elagabulus (218–222), and the adolescent Alexander Severus (222–235). Only Septimius died a natural death among the Severi, and with the assassination of Alexander by the army, the dynasty was extinguished. A period of near-anarchy ensued.

## The Germanic Invasions

In the 50 years from 235 to 285, more than 25 emperors were officially recognized by the Senate. Almost all were raised to power through, and sooner or later killed by, the army. These rulers had little reason to feel loyalty to Rome. They were themselves generally not of Roman origin; selected by an army that was itself increasingly non-Roman, they were unlikely to see beyond their own interests and those of their men to the state as a whole.

The empire was now under serious threat from outside. Germanic, partly Romanized tribes such as the Goths and the Alemanni penetrated its defenses. As early as 231 marauding Franks crossed the river Rhine. In 259 the city of Rome itself was almost invaded by the Alemanni. In many parts of the empire it became clear that Rome could provide no help against invaders, and some of the provinces tried to establish themselves as independent states with their own armies. Although the attempts of Gaul in 260 and Palmyra in 267 to win their

THE ROMAN EMPIRE

| Period | Major emperors | Important events | Cultural highlights |
|---|---|---|---|
| Julio-Claudians (31 B.C.–A.D. 68) | ● Augustus (27 B.C.–A.D. 14) ● Tiberius (A.D. 14–37) ● Caligula (37–41) ● Claudius (41–54) ● Nero (54–68) | ● Principate ● Founding of Christianity ● Expansion into northern and western Europe | ● Virgil ● Livy ● Ovid ● Seneca ● Philo of Judea ● Petronius ● Horace |
| Flavians (69–96) | ● Vespasian (69–79) ● Titus (79–81) ● Domitian (81–96) | ● Jewish revolt ● Growth of autocratic government ● Vesuvius eruption | ● Roman Colosseum ● Martial |
| Adoptive Emperors (96–180) | ● Nerva (96–98) ● Trajan (98–117) ● Hadrian (117–138) ● Antoninus Pius (138–161) ● Marcus Aurelius (161–180) | ● Largest geographic extent of the empire ● Bar-Kochba rebellion ● Economic expansion | ● Pantheon ● Tacitus ● Plutarch ● Lucian |
| Severi (193–235) | ● Septimius Severus (193–211) ● Caracalla (211–217) ● Alexander Severus (222–235) | ● Military autocracy | ● Baths of Caracalla ● Dio Cassius ● Clement of Alexandria |
| Barracks Emperors (235–284) | ● 26 emperors in 49 years | ● Military anarchy ● Germanic invasions ● Economic decline | ● Origen ● Neoplatonism |
| Late Empire (284–c. 450) | ● Diocletian (284–305) ● Constantine (306–337) ● Valens (364–378) ● Theodosius (379–395) | ● Tetrarchy ● Edict of Milan (313) ● Origins of Byzantine Empire ● Christianity becomes the state religion (378) | ● Jerome ● Early monasticism ● Ambrose of Milan ● Augustine |

freedom were crushed, they presaged the fragmentation of the empire. By 271 the reigning emperor, Aurelian (270–275), began the construction of a defensive wall around the city of Rome, the first since the time of Hannibal. Meanwhile, in the east, Roman armies were continually involved in repelling the Persians. In 274 Aurelian regained Roman territory in Asia, but he was assassinated before he could deal effectively with the Persian threat.

These problems had a devastating effect on the economy. Taxes increased as the value of money plunged. The constant threat of invasion or civil war made trade difficult. What funds there were went for the support of the army, and the general standard of living steadily declined. The former Hellenistic kingdoms in the east suffered less than the western provinces, since they were protected in part by their prosperity. Much of Italy's farmland ceased to be cultivated, the loss of export mar-

kets played havoc with industry, and the population of Rome diminished.

## The Reforms of Diocletian

The accession of Diocletian (284–305), the son of a Dalmatian freedman, marked the beginning of a revival that would extend the life of the empire by two centuries, but on a very different basis. The days of a unitary empire ruled by a single emperor were henceforth over, to be replaced by a system known as the *tetrarchy* ("rule of four"). Under this system, devised by Diocletian, two senior rulers, called Augusti, would share responsibility with two junior rulers, or Caesars. When an Augustus died, he was to be replaced by his Caesar, who in turn would appoint a new junior associate. Each tetrarch had his own capital and defense perimeter, but each could issue decrees binding on the empire as a whole. None of the tetrarchs based himself in Rome, a further proof of the capital's declining importance; Diocletian ruled from Nicomedia (modern Izmit) in northwestern Turkey.

Despite sharing power, Diocletian remained the dominant figure of the tetrarchy; indeed, it was only his authority that prevented immediate rivalries from breaking out. He, too, implemented the wide-ranging series of reforms that transformed the social, economic, and administrative structure of the empire. After quartering the throne, Diocletian divided the provinces, roughly doubling their number. His purpose was to tighten control, for each governor was now made responsible for the heavy new requisitions laid on the localities by the central government. The cost of the new bureaucracy alone was a heavy burden for the exhausted empire, being equivalent to the furnishing of two or three legions. The army itself was considerably expanded, chiefly with conscripts but also with levies from barbarian tribes. As a contemporary observer complained, the number of soldiers and officials in Diocletian's empire exceeded the number of taxpayers.

This remark, however exaggerated, summed up the paradox of Diocletian's reforms. On the one hand, the empire needed firm and expanded government if it was to recover from the disasters of the mid-third century; on the other hand, it lacked the resources to sustain such a government. Diocletian strove to maximize those resources and to stabilize the economy. He reformed the coinage, decreed regulation of wages and prices, and, to compensate for the lack of money in circulation, instituted taxation in kind. At the same time, he forbade all people listed on the tax rolls to leave their registered domicile and heaped such obligation on the *curiales* (local landowners conscripted into government service) that many fled.

The results of Diocletian's reforms were mixed. With secure borders, a measure of prosperity returned to the empire. Taxes were higher but more equitably and realistically levied, and with improved as well as intensified administration, public confidence was at least partially restored. But the burdens of taxation and service were heavy, and virtually the last trace of republican institutions—the only check on absolute autocracy—were swept away.

Diocletian never appeared in public but maintained an elaborate court ritual and sought to restore the prestige of the imperial office by reviving the traditional state cults, including emperor worship. This brought him into conflict with Christians, whom he vigorously persecuted. Diocletian retired from office in 305 to Split in his native Dalmatia, where he maintained one of his principal residences; he died there in 313, but not before witnessing a bloody struggle for power among his fellow tetrarchs.

## Constantine: The Last Renewal

The division of the empire begun by Diocletian was formalized by Constantine (died 337), who was acknowledged as senior Augustus in 312 after defeating his chief rival and was recognized as sole emperor from 324. Constantine extended Diocletian's reforms of the currency and the army, but he is chiefly remembered for having changed the course of Roman and subsequent Western history in two decisive ways: he transferred the imperial capital to the great new city he built on the Bosporus, Constantinople (now Istanbul), and he adopted Christianity as his personal religion. (The growth and early development of Christianity are discussed in Chapter 7.)

Constantine's conversion to the Christian faith followed a dream he had on the eve of the Battle of Milvian Bridge (312), which established his control of Italy and his preeminence as Augustus. As he related to the Christian historian Eusebius many years later, he saw in his dream a cross of light superimposed on the sun. He thereupon ordered his men to paint a monogram of Christ on their shields and attributed his subsequent victory to the favor of the Christian God as well as that of Apollo, god of the sun. Constantine continued to regard

**Head of the colossal statue of Constantine from the Basilica of Constantine in Rome.**
[Werner Forman Archive, London]

himself as under the protection of both deities, whom he sometimes appeared to regard as distinct and sometimes as aspects of a single divine power. This calculation may have been partly political, as the solar cult was still widely popular throughout the empire. It was Christianity, however, that benefited the most. Constantine granted Christians freedom of worship in 313 by the Edict of Milan, showered favor and privilege on them, and even preached on their behalf at court. In 325 he convened a church council at Nicaea that resolved doctrinal disputes (see Chapter 7). More ominously, he also denounced the Jews for the murder of Jesus, a theme that would be echoed in the patristic literature later in the fourth century. Constantine's embrace of Christianity was decisive for the fortunes of the church. Without his support it might well have remained a minority sect, as it did in neighboring Persia. With that support it became the majority religion of the Roman Empire by the middle of the century and ultimately one of the great religions of the world.

Constantinople, which the emperor named for himself, was built on the straits that separate the Black Sea from the Mediterranean, a location purportedly revealed to him in a vision, though also of clear strategic value. The city was dedicated to the Christian faith, but it was also meant as a second inauguration for the empire itself. Temples from far and wide were stripped of their ornaments to furnish the churches and public buildings of the new capital, and residents were attracted by the offer of free land and a permanent grain supply. Rome itself was to survive little more than a century after the founding of Constantinople in 330, but the city of Constantinople would serve for 1,000 years as the capital of the Byzantine Empire that succeeded it (see Chapter 8).

## The Twilight of Rome

Constantine's sons contended for control of the empire after his death. Their successor, Julian (361–363), known as the Apostate, is chiefly remembered for his attempt to revive the pagan cults and check the spread of Christianity. Julian fancied himself another Alexander and prepared an expedition against Persia. He died on the march; it was Rome's last campaign of conquest. The Sassanid dynasty of Persia pressed it in the east, while Germanic tribes ravaged the northern frontier and Moorish raiders attacked the cities of Africa. In 378 a Gothic host, itself in flight from the fierce central Asian nomads known as the Huns, destroyed a Roman army at Adrianople in Thrace.

Theodosius (379–395), the last ruler of an undivided Rome, made peace with the Goths and enrolled many of them in the Roman army. In 410, however, the Visigoths

## ◉ The Christian Empire ◉

*In this speech, delivered in 336 to celebrate the thirtieth year of Constantine's reign, the church historian Eusebius works out a theological justification for the existence of a Christian emperor and empire.*

The divine Logos [Word], which is above, throughout and within everything, visible and invisible at once, is the lord of the universe. It is from and through the Logos that the emperor, the beloved of God, receives and wears the image of supreme kingship, and so guides and steers, in imitation of his Lord, all the affairs of this world. . . . Constantine, like the light of the sun, . . . illuminates those farthest from him with his rays . . . and harnessing the four Caesars like spirited coursers beneath the single yoke of his royal quadriga, he molds them to harmony with the reins of reason and unity, guiding his team like a charioteer, controlling it from above and ranging over the whole surface of the earth illuminated by the sun, and at the same time present in the midst of all men and watching over their affairs. . . . God is the model of royal power and it is he who has determined a single authority for all mankind. . . . Just as there is only one God, and not two or three or more, since polytheism is really atheism, so there is only one emperor. . . . He has received the image of the heavenly monarchy, and his eyes lifted on high he governs the affairs of this world in accordance with the ideas of his archetype, fortified by the imitation of the sovereignty of the heavenly king.

*Source:* R. Browning, *The Emperor Julian* (Berkeley: University of California Press, 1976), p. 22.

(West Goths), under their leader, Alaric, sacked the city of Rome itself, an event that shocked the entire Roman world. For 800 years no enemy army had entered the city. Even Christians who had lived in expectation of Judgment Day were stunned. The lamp of the universe, the church, father Jerome said, had been extinguished; in this one city, he cried, the whole world had perished.

Simultaneously, the Vandals, another German tribe, invaded Gaul and Spain and established a powerful sea-faring kingdom in North Africa, from which they disrupted the supply of grain to Rome and harassed communications between the eastern and western halves of the empire. In the 420s two Germanic tribes, the Angles and the Saxons, settled in Britain, the first province abandoned by the empire, while the Alemanni and the Franks moved into Gaul. In 455 the Vandals invaded Italy by sea and sacked Rome once more. Finally, in 476 a coalition of German tribes deposed the young emperor of the west, Romulus Augustulus, and replaced him with their chieftain, Oadacer. By 500 the Angles and Saxons held Britain, northern Gaul was in the hands of the Frankish king Clovis, the Visigoths ruled Spain and southern Gaul, and the Vandals occupied Rome's former domains in northwestern Africa. The eastern portion of the empire survived and in the sixth century made unavailing attempts to recover the west. Thereafter, as Byzantium, it would pursue its own separate destiny. Rome was no more.

---

## Rome in Perspective

No historical question has been more widely debated than the decline of the western empire. The historian Ammianus Marcellinus (born c. 330) attributed Rome's ills to a loss of virtue and a decline of vital energy. Edward Gibbon (1737–1794), in his monumental *History of the Decline and Fall of the Roman Empire*, saw Rome in part as the victim of Christianity, which was alien to its spirit and diverted it from pressing civil and military problems.

More recent historians have focused on social, economic, political, and demographic factors. Some have pointed to the low productivity associated with the use of slave labor, some to the increased burden of taxation and the loss of economic mobility in the empire. Others have emphasized the contingencies of Rome's situation, including the depredations of the German tribes and the pressure of the Huns. Nonetheless, certain long-standing structural weaknesses of Roman society should be borne in mind. The Romans never resolved the economic and class divisions that had destroyed the republic. The Augustan settlement papered over these divisions, but at a cost of subsidizing an unproductive urban population whose support required continuous expansion and conquest, and with an imperial system that increased rather than diminished the army's role in politics. These underlying problems left the empire ill prepared to deal with stagnation and retrenchment.

The survival of the eastern empire must be contrasted with the collapse of Roman power in the west. If the empire's political center of gravity was the city of Rome, its economic and cultural base had always been in the eastern Mediterranean, a fact that Constantine recognized when he built his new capital on the shore of Asia. In a sense, the stronger, more viable half of the empire survived there, its history and culture continuous down to the Turkish conquest of 1453.

*The Roman Empire was the largest and most ethnically diverse political unit ever seen in the world up to its time. It stood for nearly 1,000 years and left the permanent impress of its law, its language, its culture, and its institutions on the subsequent history of the West.*

*The effects as well as the subsequent destinies of the eastern and western portions of the empire must be contrasted. From the point of view of the Hellenized east, the long centuries of Roman rule were an episode of foreign domination in a region whose civilizations stretched back thousands of years. To be sure, the passing of Rome was painfully felt, and many of its institutions were retained, but on the whole the traditions and cultures that Rome had so freely borrowed for its own only reverted to their native soil, and* *everyday life went on much as before. The major difference between the pre- and post-Roman periods was the advent of Christianity; the major change to come was the rise of Islam.*

*In the west, Rome's influence was far more formative and profound. Rome was the first civilization known to most of Europe. Its historical memory remained strong, and from medieval times down to the nineteenth century it was the chief model for Western culture, as it is still in many respects today. The classical culture of Greece remained the heritage of both East and West, but without the legacy of Rome, the Western world as we know it today would be unimaginably different.*

# Notes

1. Appian, *Civil Wars*, 4.33.
2. S. B. Pomeroy, *Goddesses, Whores, Wives, and Slaves: Women in Classical Antiquity* (New York: Schocken Books, 1975), p. 199.
3. G. Wills, ed., *Roman Culture* (New York: Braziller, 1966), p. 124.

# Suggestions for Further Reading

Balsdon, J. P. V. D. *Roman Women*. Westport, Conn.: Greenwood Press, 1975.

Birley, A. *Marcus Aurelius: A Biography*, rev. ed. New Haven, Conn.: Yale University Press, 1987.

Bradford, E. *Cleopatra*. New York: Harcourt Brace Jovanovich, 1972.

Bradley, K. R. *Slaves and Masters in the Roman Empire*. Berkeley: University of California Press, 1987.

Brendel, O. *Prolegomena to the Study of Roman Art*. New Haven, Conn.: Yale University Press, 1979.

Christ, K. *The Romans: An Introduction to Their History and Civilization*. Berkeley: University of California Press, 1984.

Cornell, T., and Matthews, J. *Atlas of the Roman World*. New York: Facts on File, 1982.

Crawford, M. *The Roman Republic*. Cambridge, Mass.: Harvard University Press, 1982.

Cunliffe, B. W. *Rome and Her Empire*. London: Bodley Head, 1978.

D'Arms, J. H. *Commerce and Social Standing in Ancient Rome*. Cambridge, Mass.: Harvard University Press, 1981.

Deiss, J. J. *Herculaneum: Italy's Buried Treasure*, rev. ed. New York: Harper & Row, 1985.

Dixon, S. *The Roman Family*. Baltimore: Johns Hopkins University Press, 1992.

Duncan-Jones, R. *The Economy of the Roman Empire: Quantitative Studies*. Cambridge: Cambridge University Press, 1982.

Dyson, S. L. *Community and Society in Roman Italy*. Baltimore: Johns Hopkins University Press, 1991.

Finley, M. I. *The Ancient Economy*. Berkeley: University of California Press, 1973.

Gardner, J. F. *Women in Roman Law and Society*. Bloomington: Indiana University Press, 1986.

Garnsey, P., and Saller, R. *The Roman Empire: Economy, Society and Culture*. Berkeley: University of California Press, 1987.

Goodenough, S. *Citizens of Rome*. New York: Crown, 1979.

Grant, M. *Cities of Vesuvius: Pompeii and Herculaneum*. Baltimore: Penguin Books, 1971.

———. *The Etruscans*. New York: Scribner, 1981.

Hanfmann, G. *Roman Art*. New York: Norton, 1976.

Heurgon, J. *The Rise of Rome to 264 B.C.*. Berkeley: University of California Press, 1973.

Hooper, F. A. *Roman Realities*. Detroit: Wayne State University Press, 1979.

Hopkins, K. *Conquerors and Slaves*. Cambridge: Cambridge University Press, 1981.

Jones, A. H. M. *The Later Roman Empire; 284–602: A Social, Economic, and Administrative Survey*. Baltimore: Johns Hopkins University Press, 1986.

Lefkowitz, M., and Fant, M. B., eds. *Women's Life in Greece and Rome*, rev. ed. Baltimore: Johns Hopkins University Press, 1982.

Luttwak, E. N. *The Grand Strategy of the Roman Empire*. Baltimore: Johns Hopkins University Press, 1976.

Macmullen, R. *Roman Social Relations, 50 B.C. to A.D. 284*. New Haven, Conn.: Yale University Press, 1981.

Millar, F. *The Emperor in the Roman World, 31 B.C.–A.D. 337*. Ithaca, N.Y.: Cornell University Press, 1977.

Pallottino, M. *The Etruscans*. Baltimore: Penguin Books, 1976.

Potter, T. *The Changing Landscape of South Etruria*. New York: St. Martin's Press, 1979.

Scullard, H. H. *Roman Politics, 220–150 B.C.* Westport, Conn.: Greenwood Press, 1982.

Syme, R. *The Roman Revolution*. New York: Oxford University Press, 1960.

# The Ancient World Religions

The earliest evidence for religious beliefs dates back to the Neanderthal people of the late Paleolithic period. Even in its most primitive forms, religion helped humans explain their natural environment, to the point of providing means, such as prayer, sacrifices, or offerings, intended to control the world around them. Appeasing the gods, for instance, was seen as a way to ward off illness or famine or perhaps to enjoy the blessings of children and fertile fields. Religion also provided a way for people to relate to each other, often hierarchically within their own society, especially since priests usually enjoyed substantial social and political status. Religious beliefs could be used as well to persuade people to obey their secular rulers and perform their vocational responsibilities. Eventually, many religions developed codes of ethical conduct to guide adherents in their dealings with each other. Thus religion was often the bond that bound a society together.

All of the religions discussed in this chapter took their particular character from the environment in which

**A classic representation of the Buddha from Japan, made of bronze and dating from the Nara period in the eighth century A.D. [Mega Press, Tokyo]**

they evolved. The Hindu concept of *dharma* and the Christian practice of monasticism paralleled the social and political realities of their respective societies. Most religions try to influence the nature of society, with varying success, and it is important to remember that none of them exists in a vacuum as pure theology. Yet by considering the principal world religions as entities and by comparing their aims and characteristics, it is possible to cast fresh light on some of the oldest human needs, hopes, and fears.

All of the world's major religions, including Judaism and Christianity, had their origins in Asia. All of them go back roughly 1,500 to 2,500 years, yet they still affect the lives of most people today. Most Communist states substituted a secular belief system, but in China, much of both Confucianism—like Taoism, more of a moral philosophy rather than a religion—and traditional folk religion survive, and in Russia and eastern Europe, traditional religion remains popular despite decades of suppression.

# Hinduism

Hinduism is the oldest world religion, and India has remained the most religiously oriented of all major cultures. Hinduism is often called a way of life, which is true but not very helpful. It is hard to define; its name means simply "Indianism," and the religious element is hard to sort out from more general cultural practice. The caste system is a good illustration. It is a Hindu practice, but it is also observed by South Asian Muslims and Buddhists. Caste has some minor religious connection but is primarily a system of social organization and is discussed as such in Chapter 22. There is no single body of writings for Hinduism like the Koran, the New Testament, or Buddha's sayings, and Hinduism had no single founder.

## Hindu Beliefs and Writings

In the broadest sense, we can define Hinduism as developing out of the complex of religious beliefs held by the people of the Indus civilization, which included the cult of Shiva, still the dominant god of Hinduism. The Aryans brought their own tribal gods, including the war god Indra and the fire god Agni,* but by the time the Vedas were first written down, many centuries later, Vedic religion was becoming a mixture of Harappan, Aryan, and Dravidian (southern Indian) elements. Composed cumulatively between about 1500 and 600 B.C., first orally and later written down, as a set of hymns, spells, and mystic poems used at sacrifices, the Vedas are the world's oldest religious texts still used in worship. The last of the Vedas, the *Upanishads* (seventh century B.C.), deal mainly with the nature of the universe and the place of humans in it. The *Upanishads* involve a sophisticated metaphysics that is characteristically Indian, a far cry from the earlier anthropomorphic (humanlike) gods of the Aryans. Asceticism and mysticism are seen in the *Upanishads* as paths to wisdom and truth.

The *Upanishads* deal also with good and evil, law, morality, and human duty and are often seen as the core of classical Hinduism. But Hinduism's main ethical text is the much later *Bhagavadgita* (second century A.D.), which tells the story of Prince Arjuna. Arjuna is faced with a rebellion led by disloyal friends, relatives, and teachers, people he has loved and respected. He knows his cause is just but cannot bring himself to fight and kill those so close to him. He stands in his chariot awaiting battle and talks to his charioteer, who turns out to be Krishna, an incarnation of the Vedic god of creation, Vishnu. Krishna tells him that bodily death does not mean the death of the soul and is thus unimportant. For any individual's life, what is important is duty, and action in accordance with duty, without attachment, personal desires, or ambition. Each person has a special role in society, and morality lies in faithfulness to that prescribed role.

This concept of *dharma*, the selfless execution of one's prescribed duty on earth, applied also to the faithful following of caste rules. Arjuna was a ruler and had to follow the ruler's dharma, which included the duty to fight to uphold his rightful power. Other roles in society entail their own, different dharmas, including that of lower castes to serve and defer to those above them and the rules associated with wives, students, parents, and others. *Karma* is the result or consequence of one's actions; faithfulness to one's dharma produces good karma or reward, while behavior contrary to dharma yields bad karma and punishment. There is much universal human wisdom in this, but it also clearly supported the social status quo of India and its maintenance by force if necessary. It has accordingly been much criticized, even by leading Hindus. In many ways it is inconsistent with other parts of Hinduism, especially the doctrine of *ahimsa,* or nonviolence and reverence for all life. Mahatma Gandhi, the leading religious figure of modern India, saw no conflict between the *Bhagavadgita* and ahimsa and took the former simply as emphasizing duty.

A broad variety of doctrine, however, is characteristic of Hinduism. Hinduism has cumulatively incorporated various ideas, texts, and practices and combines what may seem excessive emphasis on ritual with much genuine spirituality. But the concepts of dharma and karma have remained basic to Hinduism, as has the tradition

---

*Compare the Latin *ignis*, "fire," and the English *ignite*.

## ◉ Creation: Hindu Views ◉

*These selections from the* Rig Veda *illustrate early Hindu concepts of
creation. Compare them with the biblical accounts in Genesis and John.*

Let me proclaim the valiant deeds of Indra,
The first he did, the wielder of the thunder,
When he slew the dragon and let loose the waters,
And pierced the bellies of the mountains. . . .

When Indra, you slew the firstborn of dragons,
And frustrated the arts of the sorcerers,
Creating sun and heaven and dawn,
You found no enemy to withstand you. . . .

At first there was only darkness wrapped in darkness.
All this was only unillumined water.
That One which came to be, enclosed in nothing,
Arose at last, born of the power of heat. . . .

But who knows, and who can say
Whence it all came, and how creation happened?
The gods themselves are later than creation,
So who knows truly whence it has arisen?

*Source:* A. L. Basham, *The Wonder That Was India* (New York: Grove Press, 1983), pp. 248, 400.

of meditation and asceticism. Moral uprightness lies in faithfulness to dharma, and dharma is rightly different for everyone. This has helped create the tolerance for which Hinduism is noted. All faiths and all ascetic or mystic disciplines are seen as paths to truth, which is held to be universal. Gandhi said he did not object to the message of Christian missionaries but wished they could be more faithful to their dharma—that is, true Christians.

## Reincarnation

The belief in reincarnation and the immortality of the soul, probably first held by the Harappans, had reappeared by late Vedic times and became a further basic part of Hinduism. The karma produced by one's mortal life determined the next rebirth of the soul, which might be in a person of higher or lower status or even in an animal or insect. Special piety, meditation, asceticism, and understanding of eternal truth could bring escape from the endless cycle of birth and rebirth. The soul was then liberated from the cycle and achieved *moksha*, not a bodily heaven but a blissful spiritual rejoining with the godhead, whose essence was love.

Belief in reincarnation heightened reverence for all life. One's relative might have been reborn as a horse or a spider. Bovine animals were especially revered from Harappan times onward, both for their basic usefulness to people and for the obvious relation of the cow's milk with creation and motherhood. Bulls and oxen, too, were valued natural symbols of patient strength and virility, as also in Mediterranean cultures. But to Hinduism all life is sacred, and all creatures are part of the great chain of being that manifests the divine. Accordingly, pious Hindus are vegetarians, and all but the lowest castes (and the westernized) particularly avoid eating beef. Milk, curds, clarified butter, and yogurt are also used ritually in religious ceremonies.

By late Vedic times (c. 600 B.C.) the Hindu pantheon was dominated by the trinity of Vishnu, Shiva, and Brahma, all supreme deities. There developed as well, however, a bewildering variety of consorts, divine incarnations, and lesser gods, each with his or her own cult, as Hinduism continued to incorporate regional and folk religious figures and traditions. These included, among the more prominent, Ganesh, the benevolent elephant-headed son of Shiva and of his consort Parvati; Hanuman the monkey god; Lakshmi, wife of Vishnu and goddess of good fortune; Krishna, the human incarnation of Vishnu; and Kali or Durga, a consort or female equivalent to the grimmer aspect of Shiva, sometimes called the goddess of death. Kali was also a positive figure prayed to for help, especially by women.

Hinduism accepted the presence of evil and suffering in the world to a greater extent than other religions and recognized that people, themselves a mixture of good and evil, love and hate, petty and noble, selfish and altruistic, must come to terms with their own nature and with the nature of the cosmos. The major Hindu gods and goddesses thus represent both aspects, destroyers as well as creators, makers of suffering as well as bliss, true representations of the world as it is. Nevertheless, most devout Hindus, especially literate ones, have always been basically monotheistic, stressing the oneness of creation and the majesty of a single creative principle above the level of a humanlike god figure, to which access was possible without cults or intermediaries but through devotion, meditation, and mystical understanding of eternal truth. As a Hindu proverb put it, "God is one, but wise people know it by many names."

Jainism and Sikhism, reformist offshoots of Hinduism that arose respectively in the sixth century B.C. and the late fifteenth century A.D., centered on monotheism. So too did the teachings of the Buddha, in which universal truth was given no material identity, as it is not in pure Hinduism. A similar tension has existed in Christianity between concepts of the Christ as a godhead and the worship of saints and other cults.

Hinduism never developed a fixed or uniform ritual comparable with those of Christianity or Judaism. Pious Hindus recite specified prayers daily before the simple altar found in nearly all Hindu homes and may make frequent offerings of prayer, food, and flowers at one of the many temples throughout India, which are tended by people called priests. But there is no formal "service," no established ordination or clergy comparable with Christianity, and no special day for worship like the Sabbath. Brahmins—the highest and supposedly priestly caste and the exclusive keepers and reciters of the sacred rituals, mainly texts from Sanskrit Vedas and epics—are the only people who perform the rituals for death, marriage, coming of age, and intercession with the divine. These are certainly priestly functions, but such people are not seen as necessary intermediaries for laypersons. Not all Hindu Brahmins are priests, and although Hindu priests may tend temples and receive offerings, they are a far more informally constituted group than in Christianity or Judaism. There are a number of Hindu festivals, most of which are as much cultural as religious, such as the autumn Diwali, or festival of lights, and the spring festival of Holi, and there is an ancient tradition of religious pilgrimage to famous temples and sacred sites.

Hinduism is deeply rooted in the Indian tradition and in the modern sense of Indian identity, and it remains the basic guide for over 700 million people. But despite its strong elements of spirituality, Hinduism has also long recognized the importance to human life of achieving material well-being (*artha*), the responsibility of individuals to provide for their families, and the importance of interpersonal love and of sex (*kama*). Such matters are basic parts of human nature and hence accepted as good. Hinduism in effect rejects nothing that God has made but celebrates and enshrines all of life, including its creation through sex, while making much less distinction than in the West between the sacred and the profane; all are part of creation, which is divine. Hinduism's acknowledgment of the bad as well as the good things of life may perhaps have made things easier or psychologically healthier for its followers, who accept the tragedies and sufferings of life without feeling that they are somehow being "punished."

# Buddhism

The preoccupation of the *Upanishads* with eternal truth reflected a troubled world. A new hybrid India was emerging, and the rise of larger states brought an increase in the scale of warfare. Many people sought solace or escape from a harsh reality through otherworldly quests. The founders of Buddhism and Jainism, roughly contemporary figures in the sixth century B.C., pursued such a path, as they also reacted against the growing ritualization of Hinduism and its dominance by the priestly caste of Brahmins. Both urged independent access to truth through meditation and self-denial without the aid of priests or ritual, and both taught the equality of all in these terms, rejecting caste distinctions. But Buddhism and Jainism were developments within the tradition of Hinduism, and they also share the Hindu beliefs in dharma, karma, *samsara* (reincarnation), moksha (union with the godhead), devotion, and nonviolence or reverence for life. Both rejected the folk panoply of Hindu gods but reaffirmed Hinduism's basic monotheism, its nonpersonalized worship of the infinite and of the "great chain of being."

## GAUTAMA BUDDHA, THE ENLIGHTENED ONE

The founder of Buddhism was born around 563 B.C. in the Himalayan foothills region of Nepal, the son of a minor raja ("king"; compare the English word *royal*) of the Sakya clan. His family name was Gautama and his given name Siddartha, but he was also later called by some Sakyamuni ("Sage of the Sakyas"), as well as Gautama or Prince Siddartha. Until he was 29 years old, he led the conventional life of a prince, filled with earthly pleasures. At 19 he married a beautiful princess, and in due time they had a son, or so say the pious legends elaborated in great detail long after his death, as with so many religious figures. We know that he subsequently became an ascetic, wandered and taught for many years, acquired a number of disciples, founded a religious order, and died at the age of about 80 somewhere between 485 and 480 B.C. This is all we know of his life for certain. The later embroidered story of his life, replete with miraculous tales, is important as it has influenced the lives of many millions among successive generations of Asians, from India eastward.

According to this story (in its briefest form), Prince Siddartha, filled with nameless discontent, wandered one day away from his walled palace and met in quick succession an old man broken by age, a sick man covered with boils and shivering with fever, a corpse being carried to the cremation ground (Hindus have always burned their dead), and a wandering sadhu (holy man) with his begging bowl and simple yellow robe, but with peacefulness and inner joy in his face. Overwhelmed by this vision of the sufferings of mortal life, the emptiness of worldly pleasure, and the promise of ascetic devotion, Siddartha shortly thereafter left his palace, abandoning his wife and son. He became a wandering beggar, seeking after the truth and owning nothing but a rag of clothing and a crude wooden bowl to beg the bare essentials of food. For several years he wandered, wasted from fasting, until he determined to solve the riddle of suffering through intense meditation under a great tree. After 49 days, during which he was tempted by Mara, the prince of demons, with promises of riches, power, and sensual pleasures, he perceived the truth and attained enlightenment. From this moment, he was known as the Buddha, or the Enlightened One. Soon after, he preached his first sermon, near Banaras (Varanasi) in the central Ganges valley, and spent the rest of his life as an itinerant preacher with a band of disciples.

The Four Noble Truths, announced in that first sermon, formed the basis for the new faith: (1) Life is filled with pain, sorrow, frustration, impermanence, and dissatisfaction. (2) All this is caused by desire, by wanting, and by the urge for existence. (3) To end suffering and sorrow, one must be released from desire. (4) Release from desire can be gained by the eightfold path of "right conduct." The "right conduct" of the eightfold path was later defined as kindness to all living things, purity of heart, truthfulness, charity, and avoidance of faultfinding, envy, hatred, and violence. To these were added specific commandments not to kill, steal, commit adultery, lie, speak evil, gossip, flatter, or otherwise wander from the path.

Followers of the path may attain *nirvana*, or release from the sufferings of worldly existence through the endless cycle of rebirth, and achieve blissful reabsorp-

A modern sadhu, or holy man, who has renounced the world and lives by begging for food. He stands in front of a temple frieze in South India. [Stella Snead]

tion into the spiritual infinite, as the Buddha did on his death. Such perfection was, however, rare, and although the Buddha did not say so, Buddhism incorporated the Hindu concept of karma. In accordance with this, less dutiful individuals were reborn in successive existences in forms appropriate to their behavior in their most recent incarnations. Accounts of the Buddha's own teachings were recorded in a collection of texts called the Tripitaka ("three baskets"). In addition, a literature of moral tales about the life of the Buddha grew up, together with commentaries on the teachings, which are comparable in many ways to the stories of the Christian New Testament.

As with Christianity too, Buddhism remained for its first several centuries a minority religion, although the difficult discipline of the original teachings was softened somewhat so as to accommodate more followers. The conversion of Emperor Ashoka (c. 269–c. 232 B.C.) helped transform it into a mass religion, and it began to spread from India, first to Ceylon and Southeast Asia and later to China, Korea, and Japan. Within India, Buddhism survived for many centuries, although its following slowly declined from a peak reached around A.D. 100. For many, its distinction from Hinduism was gradually blurred, and except for its several monastic orders

---

## ⊕ Buddhist Teachings ⊕

*Many of the teachings attributed to the Buddha are almost certainly later additions or commentaries. Here are two rather striking passages from such Buddhist scriptures, whose closeness to the Christian Gospels is remarkable.*

A man buries a treasure in a deep pit, thinking: It will be useful in time of need, or if the king is displeased with me, or if I am robbed, or fall into debt, or if food is scarce, or bad luck befalls me. But all this treasure may not profit the owner at all, for he may forget where he hid it, or goblins may steal it, or his enemies or even his kinsmen may take it when he is not on his guard. But by charity, goodness, restraint, and self-control man and woman alike can store up a well-hidden treasure—a treasure which cannot be given to others and which robbers cannot steal. A wise man should do good; that is the treasure which will not leave him.

Brethren, you have no mother or father to care for you. If you do not care for one another, who else will do so? Brethren, he who would care for me should care for the sick.

*Source:* A. L. Basham, *The Wonder That Was India* (New York: Grove Press, 1983), p. 284.

---

and some lay devotees, Buddhism was slowly reabsorbed into Hinduism. The remaining Buddhist centers and monasteries in the central Ganges heartland were destroyed, most of the monks slaughtered, and the few survivors driven into exile by the Muslim invaders of the twelfth century. That holocaust largely extinguished Buddhism in the land of its birth.

## Hinayana and Mahayana Buddhism

Soon after Ashoka's time, Buddhism divided into two major schools known as Hinayana ("the lesser vehicle") or Theravada and Mahayana ("the greater vehicle"). Theravada Buddhism remained closer to the original faith, although it too was necessarily popularized to some extent as it spread and included more scope for the doctrine of good works. By performing good works, one could acquire "merit," which could even offset bad conduct in the building of karma; thus, for example, pious donations could make up for the bad karma of unethically acquired money. Theravada was the form of Buddhism transmitted to Southeast Asia, where especially in Burma, Thailand, Cambodia, and Laos, as well as Ceylon, it has remained the dominant religion and is paid far more than lip service even today. Nearly all young men in these countries traditionally spent two years in a Buddhist monastery, as many still do, with shaven heads, a yellow robe, and a begging bowl.

Mahayana Buddhism developed a little later, during the Kushan period in India in the second century A.D. What had begun as a spiritual discipline for a few became a mass religion for all, popularized, humanized, and provided with a variety of supports. The Buddha himself was made into a supernatural god, and there were also innumerable other Buddhas called *bodhisattvas*, saints who out of compassion delayed their entrance into nirvana in order to help those still on earth to attain deliverance. Faith in and worship of a bodhisattva also offered comfort to those who felt they needed divine help for any purpose. This in turn promoted the worship of images, including those of the original Buddha, and the development of elaborate rituals and cults. Such worship by itself, it was held, could produce salvation, as well as help in solving worldly problems.

Some forms of Mahayana Buddhism acquired a magic overlay. Bodhisattvas and their attendants were believed capable of flying through the air. Sanctity could be obtained, some held, merely by repeating ritual phrases or worshiping supposed relics of the Buddha. The Mahayana school also developed details of a bodily heaven to which the faithful would go, filled with recognizable human pleasures, while to match it, there was a gruesome hell, presided over by a host of demons, where the wicked or unworthy suffered an imaginative variety of hideous tortures. One may again compare this with analogous changes in Christianity. As with Christianity too, the popularization of Buddhism led to extensive artistic representation in painting, sculpture, and architecture, including a number of often profoundly beautiful paintings and statues of the Buddha and his

The great stupa (temple) at Sanchi in central India. Begun by Ashoka in the third century B.C., it was enlarged during the century after his death, when the outer ring and gateways were added. The stupa represents the universe as the great bowl of the sky. The small three-tiered structure on top became the basis for the pagoda form as Mahayana Buddhism spread from India to China, Korea, and Japan. [Rhoads Murphey]

attendants and a great variety of temples. The latter included the pagoda form in the Mahayana countries and the dagoba in Theravada lands.

Mahayana Buddhism was transmitted to China (via central Asia), Korea, and Japan because by that time it had become the dominant form in India. From China it spread to Tibet and Korea and from there to Japan by A.D. 500. A number of new Mahayana monastic orders and sects that developed originally in China, including the contemplative and mystical school of Ch'an Buddhism, were diffused to both countries; in Japan, the term *Ch'an* was corrupted into *Zen*, and other schools and monastic orders of Buddhism also flourished. The growth of Japanese Buddhism accelerated greatly during the period of direct Japanese contact with T'ang dynasty China (eighth century A.D.), when many Japanese Buddhist monks visited the country. In Japan and Korea too, Buddhist art flourished in a variety of forms. In the 840s the Chinese state, concerned about and covetous of the growing wealth and power of Buddhist temples and monasteries, confiscated much of it and suppressed Buddhism except as a small minority religion within a dominantly Confucian context. That was to be its fate until modern times. But in Japan Buddhism remained proportionately far more important. Buddhism is today,

at least nominally, the major religion of Japan, although most Japanese are either wholly secular or very casual followers in their adherence to any religious faith. In Korea, Buddhism survived the T'ang persecution and remained vigorous, though losing ground in the modern period to secularism, as in Japan.

# Confucianism

Many people argue that Confucianism is not a religion but merely a set of ethical rules, a moral philosophy. It is true that it specifically avoids any concern with theology, the afterlife, or otherworldly matters and true as well that most Chinese, Korean, Vietnamese, and Japanese Confucianists supplemented it with Buddhism, Taoism, or Shinto (traditional Japanese animism or nature worship), which provide a greater otherworldly structure. In the end it does not perhaps matter whether one calls Confucianism religion or philosophy; it is the creed by which millions of East Asians, close to a third of the world, have lived for over 2,000 years. Confucianism has probably made more impact on belief and behavior than any of the great religions, in the sense that most East Asians accept and follow the teachings of Confucius more thoroughly than followers of the ethical teachings of any other system of belief. Those teachings contain much common sense about human relations, but they are a good deal more than that, reflecting and shaping a highly distinctive set of values, norms, and sociopolitical patterns. Confucianism has its temples too, which serve as monuments to the doctrine even though it lacks a prescribed ritual or organized priesthood.

## Confucius and Mencius

Confucius (K'ung Fu-tze, 551–c. 479 B.C.), the son of a minor official in one of the smaller states of eastern China long before the first imperial unification, became a teacher and later an adviser to various local rulers. He never had a definite official post, and he had no discernible political influence. Like Plato, he looked for rulers who might be shaped by his advice, and like Plato, he never really found one. Several of his students became his disciples, though never as organized as in Plato's Academy; after his death, they and their students began to write down his teachings and to expand on them.

The most famous of his later followers and commentators was Meng-tzu (Mengzi), Romanized to Mencius (c. 372–c. 289 B.C.). Confucius and Mencius lived in the chaotic period of warring Chinese states and sought means for restoring order and social harmony through individual morality. Society in East Asia has always been profoundly hierarchical. The social order was seen in terms of a series of status groups and graded roles, from the ruler at the top through officials, scholars, and gentlemen to the father of the family, all of whom possessed authority over those below them but also had the responsibility to set a good example. The key element was "right relationships," carefully defined for each association: father-son, subject-ruler, husband-wife, elder brother–younger brother, and so on. Confucius and Mencius provided what became doctrinal support for such a system. It left small place for the individual but at the same time stressed the vital importance of self-cultivation and education as the only true guarantee of morality, or "virtuous behavior."

## The Confucian View

According to Confucianism, people are born naturally good and inclined to virtue but need education and the virtuous example of superiors to stay that way. Confucius emphasized "human-heartedness," benevolence, respect for superiors, filial loyalty, and learning to prevent anarchy and to achieve the "great harmony" between self and society that was his chief objective. Force and

A Ch'ing dynasty ink rubbing of Confucius, made over 2,000 years after the death of the sage. There are no contemporary portraits. [Granger Collection]

law were no guarantee of individual virtue or of social harmony, and indeed they were seen as ineffective as well as unnecessary in a properly run society. People must *want* to do right, and that can be achieved only by internalizing morality. When force or punishment have to be used, the social system has broken down.

Confucianism offered a highly pragmatic, this-worldly, and positive view of people and of society; it provided little scope for metaphysical speculation, for the supernatural, or for concepts like sin or salvation. Although Confucius and Mencius were certainly conservatives and supporters of a hierarchical social order, their doctrine also allowed for individual ability and dedication. They taught that everyone is born with the seeds of virtue and that by self-cultivation and by following virtuous examples, anyone can become a sage. This concept was incorporated later in the imperial examination system and the selection of officials from the ranks of the educated, regardless of their social origins. Confucianism also reaffirmed the right of the people to rebel against immoral or unjust rulers who had forfeited the "mandate of Heaven" by their lapse from virtue. Thus loyalty to superiors was ultimately subordinate to moral principle. This often presented individuals with a severe dilemma, especially in family situations; fathers, for example, however unjust, were rarely defied.

Natural calamities like floods, droughts, or earthquakes were commonly taken as portents of Heaven's displeasure at the unvirtuous behavior of rulers and as pretexts for rebellion, especially since they disturbed the Confucian sense of order and harmony. The natural world was seen as the model for the human world. Both ran by regular rules. Nature was a nurturing power, not a hostile one, grander and more to be admired than human works, something to which people should harmoniously adjust rather than attempt to conquer. But it was not to be looked to except as a pattern. As Confucius said, "Heaven does not speak"; it merely shows us a model of order and harmony to emulate.

Such occasional references to Heaven as an imper-sonal force superior to humanity are about as far as Confucius went beyond the human world. When disciples asked about the suprahuman world or life after death, he merely said that we had enough to do in understanding and managing human affairs without troubling about other matters. Although he did not explicitly say so, he did approve, however, of what is rather misleadingly called "ancestor worship." In folk religion, ancestors were prayed to as if they could intervene as helpers. Confucian practice merely extended respect for one's elders to those who had gone before, valuing them as models and performing regular rituals in small household shrines to keep their memory alive. It was the duty of the eldest son to perform rituals on the death of his father, keeping the ancestral chain intact through succesive generations and thus ensuring family continuity. Mencius underlined this by saying that of all sins against filiality (respect for one's parents), the greatest was to have no descendants, by which he meant male descendants, since women left their parental family at marriage and became members of their husband's family. This

## ◉ Sayings of Confucius ◉

*Sayings attributed to Confucius and printed in the* Analects *are usually brief and pithy. Here are some examples.*

- Learning without thought is useless. Thought without learning is dangerous.
- Shall I teach you the meaning of knowledge? When you know a thing to recognize that you know it, and when you do not know to recognize that you do not know, that is knowledge.
- Not yet understanding life, how can one understand death?
- The gentleman is concerned about what is right, the petty man about what is profitable.
- The gentleman's quality is like wind, the common people's like grass; when the wind blows, the grass bends.
- If one leads them with administrative measures and uses punishments to make them conform, the people will be evasive; but if one leads them with virtue, they will come up to expectations.

*The following are from the* Book of Mencius.

- Between father and son there should be affection; between sovereign and minister, righteousness; between husband and wife, attention to their separate functions; between young and old, a proper order; and between friends, fidelity.
- Nature speaks not, but the ongoing of the seasons achieves the nurturing of the ten thousand things of creation. . . . [The moral laws of society] form the same system with the laws by which the seasons succeed each other. . . . It is this same system of laws by which all created things are produced and develop themselves, each in its order and system, without injuring one another, that makes the universe so grand and impressive.

*Source:* Translated by R. Murphey.

attitude still militates against current Chinese efforts to reduce the birthrate.

In the twelfth century A.D. the Confucian philosopher Chu Hsi (Zhuxi, 1130–1200) went somewhat further in speculating about the nature of the universe, in whose operation he saw the working of abstract principles, rather like those of Plato, and a Supreme Ultimate, or impersonal cosmic force. From his time on it is appropriate to speak of Neo-Confucianism, which also sets before every person the goal of becoming a sage through self-cultivation. Like classic Confucianism before it, Neo-Confucianism spread to Korea, Vietnam, and Japan, where it became the dominant philosophy, especially among the educated.

Confucianism in general strikes a balance between individual self-development and achievement on the one hand and the subjection of the individual to the greater good of the family and society on the other. Unfettered individualism and freedom, basic values to Americans, connote in East Asia selfishness and the absence of rules or essential constraints, the result of which is social chaos, from which everyone suffers. For Confucianism, chaos is the greatest of all evils. Though officially rejected, Confucianism remains in many ways the basis of Chinese society today. It has persisted because it works, as the ethical code of probably the world's most successful society over so long a time. It is said to be a basic factor also in the phenomenal success of modern Japan, Korea, Taiwan, Hong Kong, and Singapore.

# Taoism

The second important moral or religious philosophy of traditional China was Taoism (Daoism), from the Tao (Dao), or Way. Taoism is hard to define since one of its basic axioms is silence, even inaction. It holds that the observable, rational, human world does not matter; the far greater cosmic world of nature does. Accordingly, one must seek guidance from the cosmos, which is beyond the realm of words. The chief text of Taoism, the *Tao te Ching* ("Classic of the Way"), is a cryptic collection of mystical remarks whose meaning even in Chinese is far from clear. The famous opening line is typical and may be translated as "The name that can be named is not the eternal name" or "The Way that can be spoken of is not the true Way, which is inconstant," implying, one supposes, that truth can only be expressed in language, if at all, through riddle and paradox. Much of the content is attributed to a contemporary of Confucius' known simply as Lao-tze (Laozi, "The Old One"), although the present text is not older than the third century B.C. and was probably compiled by several hands. Lao-tze is said to have debated with Confucius and to have disappeared in old age, traveling westward, where he somehow became immortal.

On one point the *Tao te Ching* is clear: "Those who understand don't talk; those who talk don't understand." This comment may well have been aimed at the Confucians, but although Taoist figures did occasionally speak or write, it was usually in riddles or in metaphors drawn from nature. All make the point that worldly strivings, especially attempts at political control, are futile and wrong. Their message is to relax, "go with the flow," stop trying to improve things, as the Confucians were always doing. The Taoists' favorite model was water, which flows around obstructions, adapts itself to what is, and seeks the lowest places. Whatever is, they said, is natural and hence good.

The other major figure of Taoism was the philosopher Chuang-tze (Zhuangzi; died c. 329 B.C.), whose still intriguing essays and parables further expound the ideas already associated with the school. One of his most delightful stories tells that he dreamed he was a butterfly and when he awoke could not be sure whether he was himself or was the butterfly now dreaming that it was Chuang-tze.

Taoism grew into a religion as it merged with folk beliefs, earlier animistic and nature worship, belief in the supernatural, and a variety of mystical practices. Taoist priests, temples, and monastic orders developed (however inconsistent with the earlier message), and the originally rather esoteric philosophy became a mass religion. Later Taoists, especially after the Han dynasty, practiced magic and alchemy and pursued the search for elixirs of immortality. Such activities put them in bad repute with proper Confucians, as did their habit of irresponsible hedonism or pleasure seeking. However, the Taoists' search for medicinal herbs and their experimentation contributed importantly to the growth of Chinese medicine and other technology. They deviated from their supposed founder's injunctions to accept nature without questioning and began instead to probe for its secrets.

As it acquired a mass following, Taoism also developed a pantheon of gods and "immortals" who offered help to people in trouble and eased the way to a Taoist version of the Buddhist heaven. Taoism became in many ways an important supplement to Confucianism, and Confucians often found parts of it attractive. It was aptly said that most Chinese were Confucian when things went well and Taoist when things went badly and in retirement or old age. Confucianism's activist and social reformist postures were well complemented by Taoism's passivity and inwardness. This dualism appealed to the old Chinese distinction between yin and yang, where yang is the strong, assertive, masculine principle of existence and yin is the passive, intuitive, feminine one. Taoists and Confucians alike agreed that both nature and humans must approximate a balance of yin and yang elements and that nature should serve as a model for humanity. But where Confucians sought to shape the world through education, Taoists urged acceptance of things as they are, confident that human meddling could not improve on cosmic truth. For them, the human world was terribly petty.

# Asian Religions: Some Reflections

Most East Asians have always been eclectic in religion, weaving into their beliefs and practices elements from different religious traditions. Confucianism and Taoism are dominant except in Japan, where Confucianism, Buddhism, and Shinto predominate. Shinto is similar to Taoism but remained closer to animism and nature worship. These complementary parts form a whole, representing the religion or philosophical outlook of nearly a third of the world. Each part of the combination has its undeniable appeal, and it is easy to understand why most people selected from all of them in their beliefs and practices. When Christian missionaries arrived in the sixteenth century, they found the religious ground already thoroughly occupied in Asia not only by Confucianism, Taoism, and Shinto but by Hinduism, Buddhism, and Islam as well. All were old and sophisticated religions or philosophies with long literate traditions.

All of these Asian religions recognized that there is evil in the world, and even evil people, but none of them ever developed the sharp dichotomy (or dualism) between good and evil that is characteristic of Zoroastrianism, Judaism, Christianity, and Islam. In the Indian and Chinese view, all of creation is the work of God ("Heaven," the creative principle), which thus necessarily includes what is perceived by humans as both good and bad. Consequently, there was no conception of "original sin" inherent in individuals, no Garden of Eden or early innocence from which people then fell into error and suffered punishment because they had broken God's rules. Evil was understood as part of God's created world, not as some human aberration. The Christian idea of sin thus had little meaning in Asia; as has often been said, "Eden was preserved in the East." Bad behavior was acknowledged and might be punished in this world and the next, but the basic presumption was that people were born and remained intrinsically good, not with built-in inclinations to "sin."

Misbehavior was seen as a failure of society, which God created imperfect, and the result of an individual's straying from the teaching and model of her or his elders or superiors, as in Confucianism, or from the established rules of her or his dharma in Hinduism and Buddhism, as made clear by priests and sages. People were seen not as morally lost when they strayed from the path but as always redeemable, through education or renewed efforts at right behavior, aided by piety, meditation, and so on. Return to virtue, or "merit," might also be won by good deeds, including charity, or simply by leading (in Christian words) "a godly, righteous, and sober life," but never by having one's "sins" magically forgiven by priestly or other ritual, since no concept of sin existed. Nor was faith or the acceptance of any creed ever seen as paramount, if important at all; people were judged by their actions.

One further distinction between all of these eastern Asian religions on the one hand and Christianity, Judaism, and Islam on the other is their acceptance of the natural world as good, as part of divine creation that is greater and more powerful than humankind but like them a part of the cosmos. People occupy a humbler place in God's creation, and it behooves them therefore to adjust, while seeking in nature the image of God, rather than in themselves. The sages and holy men who sought wisdom and the understanding of God or of the cosmos looked for it in nature, in the mountains, far from human distractions. There was no conception of the natural world as an enemy, to be fought against or overcome, as in later Christianity. Nature was instead seen as a nurturing mother or as an inspiring model. Adapting to it and understanding it were the keys both to earthly success and to spiritual and moral truth.

Such a thread runs deeply through Hinduism, Buddhism, Confucianism, Taoism, and Shinto and is far weaker, absent, or explicitly opposite in Judaism, Christianity, and Islam, as in the Book of Genesis call to the human world to "have dominion" over all the world of nature or in the nineteenth- and twentieth-century Western drive for the "conquest of nature." One might perhaps argue that Judaism, out of which Christianity and later Islam grew, was conceived in a harsher environment than the great religions of Asia farther east, where it may be easier to see nature as beneficent and nurturing and people as prospering by adjusting to, accepting, and admiring it. Whatever the reasons, Asia west of India followed a different religious path.

# Zoroastrianism and Mithraism

We know less about Zoroastrianism, the dominant religion of ancient and classical Persia (Iran), than about any of the others described in this chapter. Zoroaster, its founder, lived and preached long before the advent of preserved written records in Persia, probably between

800 and 600 B.C., and the incomplete texts we have on the belief and practice of the religion he founded come mainly from the thirteenth century A.D., although earlier texts were probably written down by the sixth century B.C. The founder's name in Persian was Zarathustra (Zoroaster was the Greek version), and his teachings are recorded and embroidered in the Avesta, but the form of the Avesta we have is only a fragmentary remnant of earlier texts and includes much later material and doctrine. To the Greeks and Romans, Zoroaster was famous as the founder of the wisdom of the Magi, mythical Iranian priest-kings. In his youth he is said to have had celestial visions and conversations with divine beings, after which he became a wandering preacher. Later he interested an eastern Iranian prince in his teachings; the prince became his protector and advocate, and the new religion became a state church.

## Zoroastrian Beliefs

Zoroastrianism was rooted in the old Iranian or Aryan folk religion, and there are some striking similarities between it and the religion of Vedic India. Both are polytheistic (professing many gods), and both worshiped Indra as well as natural forces, especially fire. Both believed in the supremacy of moral powers and of an eternal natural law and creative principle. The major difference lay in the pronounced dualism of Zoroastrianism, which divided creation into the powers of good and evil, light and darkness. Vedic India called all their gods and goddesses *deva*, and although many of them had destructive aspects, in general they were seen as good. Zoroastrianism used the closely related term *daeva* in Persian to refer to evil spirits only, which are opposed and kept in check by the forces of good and light, incorporated in the supreme deity, the sexless Ahura-Mazda. In one of several striking parallels with Judeo-Christian theology, Ahura-Mazda's original twin Ahriman was, like Lucifer, banished from heaven to hell, where he or she reigns as the principle of evil. Earlier cults, such as the cult of Mithras, the god of day, survived within Zoroastrianism and later spread to the Mediterranean.

Zoroaster is reported to have said that he received a commission from God to purify religion, in effect by transcending the earlier cults, introducing moral laws, and constructing a theory of the universe embodying the dualist principle. By his time Iranian society was based mainly on agriculture rather than hunting, gathering, or nomadism; had developed cities and towns; and was ready for a more sophisticated theology than nature worship alone or ritual cults. Ahura-Mazda is the personification not only of power and majesty but also of ethical principles for the guidance of human behavior. She or he is described in the Avesta as assisted by her or his creatures, "immortal holy ones," the forces of good sense or good principle, truth, law, order, reverence, immortality, and obedience. The history of the conflict between these good forces and the forces of evil is the history of the world. All creation is divided between these two forces, whose endless conflict has as its object the human soul. People are creations of Ahura-Mazda, but they are created free to decide and to act and can be influenced by the forces of evil. All human life and activity are part of this conflict. By a true confession of faith, by good deeds, and by keeping body and soul pure, any individual can limit the power of the evil forces and strengthen the power of goodness. Evil deeds, words, and thoughts strengthen the power of evil.

After death, each person is judged in heaven, according to the Book of Life in which all deeds, thoughts, and words are recorded. Wicked actions cannot be undone but can be balanced by good works. If the balance is favorable, the person enters paradise; if unfavorable, the eternal pains of hell. If the account is equally balanced, a kind of limbo or intermediate stage is provided, with the final lot to be decided at the last judgment. The Avesta tells us almost nothing about ceremonial worship, but it appears from early times to have centered on a sacred fire. Later development of the religion added the doctrine of repentance, atonement, and the remission of sins, administered by priests.

Zoroaster saw himself as a prophet and believed that the end of the present world and the coming of the Kingdom of Heaven were near. But for most people his doctrines were too abstract; both old and new popular deities became part of Zoroastrianism in later periods, and a priesthood developed that organized and conducted worship and laid down detailed laws for the purification of the body and soul, the conduct of good works, the giving of alms, the pursuit of agriculture, and the prohibition against either burning or burying the dead. Both soil and fire, as well as water, were considered sacred and not to be defiled by death. Bodies were to be exposed in appointed places, sometimes an elevated platform, for consumption by vultures and wild dogs. Originally there seem to have been no temples, but in later periods fire altars came into use, and these slowly evolved into more elaborate temples where sacrifices and other rituals were performed by priests. Priests were the teachers and keepers of the religion; every young believer, after being received into the religion, was supposed to choose a spiritual guide, usually a priest. Most of the changes mentioned here seem to have come about by approximately the sixth century B.C. and to have begun considerably earlier.

With the rise of the Persian Empire in the sixth century B.C., Zoroastrianism was further confirmed as the national and state religion of Iran. Under the Achemenid dynasty and its conquests, the religion spread over most of western Asia and the Turkic republics of central Asia.

After the collapse of this first empire, Zoroastrianism languished and then was restored to new vigor under the Sassanids from the third to the seventh centuries A.D., when it was again the state church; compliance with its religious laws was even enforced by the state. The Arab conquest of Iran, complete by A.D. 637, and the persecutions that followed largely extinguished Zoroastrianism in the land of its birth. In modern Iran there remain only a very few followers, now under new pressure from the rigid fundamentalism of its Muslim rulers. The chief survivors are the Parsees of the Bombay area (the name Parsee is a corruption of *Persian*), who came originally from Persia to India about the eighth century A.D., primarily to escape Muslim persecution; they still maintain most of the doctrine and practices of classical Zoroastrianism.

Zoroastrianism, as well as the cult of Mithras, which it incorporated, had a profound influence on both Eastern and Western thinking during the time of its flourishing. It has obvious similarities both with Hinduism and with Judaism and Christianity and in part even with Islam, especially its doctrines on life after death. Its basic dualistic emphasis helped shape early Christian theology, and more than traces of what was eventually labeled the "dualistic heresy" remain even in modern Christian thought, like its pre-Christian ideas about the judgment of the dead, the relationship between faith and good works, and the role of the priesthood. Arising out of more primitive cults, especially the worship of fire and of the sun, it nevertheless became through the teachings of Zoroaster and his successors a sophisticated theological, cosmological, and ethical system that was known to and admired by both Eastern and Western civilizations before or during the period when they were working out their own transition from tribal cults to mature religious thought. Although Zoroastrianism largely ceased to exist nearly 14 centuries ago, many of its ideas live on in the other great religions, a further reminder of the central role that Persian civilization played in the evolution of Eurasian culture.

# Mithraism

The worship of Mithras began as far back as the fourth century B.C. Originally Ahura-Mazda's chief aide in the battle against the powers of darkness, Mithras became the central figure in a cult that spread rapidly throughout western Asia and into Europe, arriving in Rome in the first century B.C. In the years following A.D. 100 it acquired many new adherents in Italy and other parts of the Roman Empire, attracting the lower classes, slaves, and soldiers, who took their religious customs with them when they served abroad—a temple to Mithras has been discovered in the Roman remains of London. By the late third century A.D. Mithraism was vying with Christianity

to replace the old paganism, although Constantine's support of the Christians caused Mithraism's rapid decline.

Mithraism's broad appeal was probably due to the fact that it combined the spirituality of its origins with humanizing detail. Unlike Ahura-Mazda, the remote god of light, Mithras, god of day, was born in human form on December 25 in a cave. When he grew up, he slaughtered a mythical sacred bull, whose blood fertilized the earth. After a time the god returned to heaven, where he constantly interceded with Ahura-Mazda on behalf of his followers.

Ceremonies in honor of Mithras were held in special temples known as Mithraea, which often took the form of underground caves in memory of his birth. Among the rites of initiation was baptism in the blood of a bull, which formed one of the seven stages of induction; others included the recitation of various miracles that Mithras had performed, such as ending a drought and averting a flood.

It is a measure of Mithraism's appeal that Christianity adopted a number of its external characteristics, including the symbolic date of December 25 as the birthday of Jesus—the day marks the approximate period of the winter solstice, when the sun, returning from south of the equator, is "reborn." Yet in the end Mithraism was to gain no lasting hold. One reason for this may well be that women were not accepted as initiates and played no part in the rituals or the myths. By contrast, many of the early converts to Christianity were women, and tradition has it that Constantine himself was much influenced by his mother Helena, herself a Christian.

# Judaism

Unlike Buddhists or Christians, the Jews have maintained a strong sense of ethnic as well as spiritual identity. That this identity has survived through so lengthy and so tragic a history is an indication of the strength of Jewish convictions.

From the very beginning the Jews saw themselves as special instruments of a unique providence. The vision of Abraham, whose family fled from Ur around 2000 B.C., was twofold. Abraham, the traditional founder of the Jewish people, put his faith in a God who operated in the world on principles of righteousness. At the same time he saw the Jews as appointed by his God to communicate this vision to the world. To transmit their message, the Jews found it essential to maintain their separateness from the peoples with whom they came in contact. This did not preclude the possibility of others joining the Jewish nation, but those who did so had to give tangible proof of their conversion. The symbolic representation of this was the rite of circumcision, a tradition that probably goes back to the time of Abraham. In addition, as Judaism developed, customs evolved that were intended to strengthen the sense of ethnic distinctness.

## The Covenant at Sinai

Abraham's message had stressed a universal obligation for the Hebrews to serve humanity as a "kingdom of priests." The more precise terms and conditions of this service were spelled out by Moses in the Sinai desert after the exodus from Egypt, particularly in the Ten Commandments, which laid out the basic tenets of the Jewish ethical system. The first four dealt with human obligations to God and described how Yahweh was to be worshiped. The remaining six were concerned with relationships between peoples, parents and children, husbands and wives; they also prohibited certain crimes, such as perjury, theft, and murder, which might involve strangers. Other ancient religions produced codes governing conduct, but the Ten Commandments were unique in that they were directed not only at the Jews but all peoples. They underlined the special character of the Jewish message, moreover, by forbidding the worship of nature or of images and by emphasizing that the piety and morality they outlined constituted a duty. All who abided by them would be rewarded; the disobedient would be punished.

By subscribing to the Covenant, the Jews acquired a special historical consciousness. The Ten Commandments were universal in their application, yet the Jews alone bore the responsibility of communicating the message to the rest of the world. This sense of special identity proved crucial to the survival of Judaism, and the Jews, throughout centuries of persecution.

## The Torah

The teachings that evolved from the Covenant at Sinai are known as the *Torah*, or Law. The Torah laid out the religious and moral requirements of Judaism in prescriptions and prohibitions; one of its special characteristics was the importance laid on negative commands: "thou shalt not." Jewish law aimed to cultivate a holiness that would influence not only the spiritual life of individuals but also their relationship to society. Just as the pious Buddhist was enjoined not to wander from the path by injunctions that were intended to regulate human relationships, so Jews were taught by the Torah not only about their religious duties but also about their earthly responsibilities, including an injunction to "love thy neighbor as thyself" that could apply to Jews and non-Jews alike.

As in Hinduism and Buddhism, Jewish law paid special attention to the poor and the weak. Employers were

A section from the scrolls found near the Dead Sea in 1947, probably dating from the first century B.C. They contain most of the Old Testament. [Zev Radovan]

forbidden to exploit their workers. There were complex regulations about the making and repaying of loans that were designed to protect the borrower. Unlike the Law Code of Hammurabi and the laws of the Hittites, which were intended to safeguard property, the Torah sought to protect the individual. This concern extended also to animals. Although Jews were not required to be vegetarians, as pious Hindus were, they were instructed to treat oxen and other work animals with kindness and to allow them the same rights as humans to rest on the Sabbath, the weekly day of repose. Detailed instructions concerned the preparation and consumption of food and drink and other aspects of daily life. The dietary regulations covered both foods that could and could not be eaten and the dishes and utensils with which they were prepared and consumed. This tradition, often loosely referred to as "keeping kosher," is still observed by many Jews today. In general, the aim of the Torah's social legislation was to eliminate distinctions based on rank, wealth, or birth; in the eyes of the law, all people were equal and enjoyed the same rights. This was in strong contrast to the hierarchic caste system of Hinduism or the graded society of Confucius.

In later centuries Judaic traditions often had the effect of alienating the Jews from other people among whom they lived. Even in cosmopolitan Alexandria, as we have seen, the Jewish community lived apart from the rest of the population, a tradition that, by unhappy irony, became a requirement in the ghettos of the Middle Ages in Europe. It is therefore important to remember that the Torah exhorts Jews to follow the example of their God and love all persons equally. Only by doing so, while maintaining their own Jewish character, could they truly love God. Tradition, together with the experience of prolonged exile following a brief period of nationhood, may have accentuated the Jews' sense of distinctiveness. Furthermore, their belief that they were the people divinely chosen to reveal God's love for all was often interpreted by non-Jews as a conviction of moral superiority. Yet from its beginning the message of Judaism was intended to be applicable not to the Jews alone but to all societies.

# The Prophets

The injunctions of the Torah left no doubt that people who violated the Law would be punished. Formal warning, however, was in itself insufficient to instill righteousness, and throughout the history of the foundation and subsequent collapse of the kingdom of Israel there appeared religious figures known as prophets. The word is derived from the Greek word *profetes*, meaning "one who speaks for another"; the prophets of the Old Testament thought of themselves as spokesmen for God. Inspired by their visions of God's will, they counseled and rebuked their contemporaries on every aspect of religious, moral, and political conduct.

The earliest prophets were probably unofficially attached to shrines or, during the kingdom, to the royal household. From the eighth century B.C., however, figures such as Jeremiah vigorously expressed their opposition to corruption in official religion. Calling his

people to a rigid observance of ethical monotheism, Jeremiah railed against the emptiness and hypocrisy of formal religious observance. Speaking on behalf of his God, he thundered: "Why have they provoked me to anger with their graven images and with their foreign idols?"[1] Other prophets, such as Isaiah, reminded the Jews of their unique historical mission: "Give thanks to the Lord, call upon his name; make known his deeds among the nations, proclaim that his name is exalted."[2]

Although the prophets affirmed their belief in the special destiny of the Jews, they underlined the universal nature of their message and insisted on the necessity of rigorous monotheism. The God of Israel was the only God, destined to be the God of all people. Furthermore, their messages were directed against not only religious error but also social injustice. In language that was frequently sharp, they reproved an errant people for breaking their covenant with God. In the words of Amos:

> Seek the Lord and live, lest he break out like fire in the house of Joseph, and it devour, with none to quench it for Bethel [the northern kingdom's chief sanctuary], O you who turn justice to wormwood, and cast down righteousness to the earth!"[3]

The role of the prophet as unofficial mediator between God and humanity is a special characteristic of

---

## ◎ A Prophet Calls for Social Reform ◎

*Typical of the prophetic message is the following passage from Amos, written in the eighth century B.C. The prophet is incensed by the social injustice he sees among the Hebrews.*

Listen to this, you that trample on the needy and try to destroy the poor of the country. You say to yourselves, "We can hardly wait for the holy days to be over so that we can sell our grain. When will the sabbath end, so that we can start selling again? Then we can overcharge, use false measures, and fix the scales to cheat our customers. We can sell worthless wheat at a high price. We'll find a poor man who can't pay his debts, not even the price of a pair of sandals, and we'll buy him as a slave."

The Lord, the God of Israel, has sworn, "I will never forget their evil deeds. And so the earth will quake, and everyone in the land will be in distress. The whole country will be shaken; it will rise and fall like the Nile River. The time is coming when I will make the sun go down at noon and the earth grow dark in daytime. I, the Sovereign Lord, have spoken. I will turn your festivals into funerals and change your glad songs into cries of grief. I will make you shave your heads and wear sackcloth, and you will be like parents mourning for their only son. That day will be bitter to the end.

"The time is coming when I will send famine on the land.

"People will be hungry, but not for bread; they will be thirsty, but not for water. They will hunger and thirst for a message from the Lord. I, the Sovereign Lord, have spoken."

*Source:* Amos 8:4–11a, *Good News Bible* (New York: American Bible Society, 1976).

the Jewish religion and was partly embraced by Christianity and Islam. It profoundly influenced the life and teachings of Jesus, whose fierce denunciations of the Jewish religious leaders of his day were in the tradition of Jeremiah and other prophets.

With the destruction of Solomon's temple at Jerusalem in A.D. 70 by Roman forces, the Jews lost the focal point of their worship. The temple was never forgotten; indeed, to this day pious Jews pray at the western wall of the building, known as the Wailing Wall, the only part still standing. Jewish tradition advises observant Jews to leave a tiny part of their house unfinished, perhaps a small piece of wall unplastered, in memory of Jerusalem and its temple. The very need to remember Jerusalem underlines the sense of dispersal that has permeated the past two millennia of the Jewish Diaspora ("scattering").

---

## ❁ JERUSALEM: THE HOLY CITY

The historic center of Judaism, Jerusalem is today the crossroads of three great world religions, Judaism, Christianity, and Islam, and remains sacred to each. The historic city of Jerusalem is situated dramatically on a series of hills north of the Negev desert. From its very beginnings it appears to have been a sacred city; its name derives from Shalem, a western Semitic deity of the second millennium B.C. King David captured it from a local tribe, the Jebusites, about the year 1000 B.C., and made it the capital of ancient Israel. David's successor, Solomon, greatly enlarged it and built a massive temple for the Ark of the Covenant, which David had brought with him.

The temple was a thick-walled rectangular building of squared stones and cedar beams laid out east to west, 110 feet long, 48 feet wide, and more than 50 feet high. A huge porch extended on its eastern side, and side chambers were built against the other three sides. An interior wall marked off the main hall from the sanctuary of the ark, a 30-foot cube paneled with richly carved cedar that admitted light through high lattice windows and contained a single lamp. The ark itself was surmounted by two cherubim carved from olive wood, each standing 15 feet high.

Over the centuries the city and especially the temple became the primary focus of the Jewish faith. Psalm 137 still rings with the passionate sense of loss felt by the Jewish people during their first exile from the city during the Babylonian captivity of the sixth century B.C.:

> *If I forget thee, O Jerusalem, let my right hand*
> *lose its cunning.*
> *If I forget thee, O Jerusalem, let my tongue*
> *cleave to the roof of my mouth.*[4]

After the return to Zion, a second temple, completed around 515 B.C., was built on the ruins of the first. The city too was rebuilt and flourished under successive domination by the Persians, the Ptolemaic dynasty of Egypt, and the Romans. During the Hellenistic period the Jews became widely dispersed throughout the eastern Mediterranean world, but Jerusalem remained their spiritual capital, the site of their pilgrimages, and the direction they turned to in prayer. All pious Jews, wherever they were, sent a half shekel of tribute each year for the upkeep of the temple.

Ancient Jerusalem reached the height of its splendor under the otherwise repressive rule of the Roman client-king Herod the Great (37–4 B.C.), who undertook a restoration and expansion of the temple that was completed only shortly before both the city and the temple were razed in the wake of the Jewish rebellion of A.D. 70. Despite Herod's unpopularity, even his Jewish subjects marveled at the reconstruction of their temple; one rabbi commented, "He who has not set eyes upon the structure of Herod has not seen a structure of beauty in his life." But few guessed that the fame of Herod would rest not on his public works but on the birth, late in his reign, of Jesus of Nazareth. Jerusalem was where Jesus came to preach his gospel and where on the small hillock of Golgotha outside the city walls he was crucified in A.D. 29.

Christianity made little headway in Jerusalem in the decades after Jesus' death and slow progress even after the city was once again rebuilt. It was not until its adoption by the Roman emperor Constantine early in the fourth century that the sites associated with his life were identified. The magnificent Church of the Resurrection, completed in A.D. 335, marked the beginning of Jerusalem as a Christian capital, and by the end of the fourth century it was crowded with churches, shrines, and monasteries, as well as hospices for the many thousands of pilgrims who now thronged to it. Within the church Jerusalem was elevated to the status of a patriarchate, equal in rank to the far larger cities of Alexandria, Antioch, and the new imperial capital of Constantinople. Under the Byzantine emperors, its position was unrivaled. But after a brief Persian occupation (A.D. 614–629), it surrendered to Muslim forces, ushering in the city's third phase as a religious center.

---

## The Talmud

With the temple gone and its priests scattered, Jewish worship centered on local synagogues and their teachers, or rabbis. The term *rabbi* is often applied to individuals who have undergone special study and training in religious matters. In more recent times rabbis have come to serve as the equivalent of priests or ministers of congregations, with a wide range of social and counseling responsibilities. In its original sense, however, the

Following the Jewish revolt against Roman rule in A.D. 66, Roman troops looted Jerusalem, taking such religious objects from the temple as the *menorah*, or seven-branched candlestick, and the sacred trumpets. The scene is depicted here on the Arch of Titus in Rome. [Alinari/Art Resource]

term was applied to anyone who impressed fellow Jews by the wisdom and insight with which he expounded Jewish Law.

The principal source of the Law was to be found in the biblical texts. The transformation of the written and oral accounts into a fixed canon was long and complex; the work that came to be known among Christians as the Old Testament had probably received its final form by A.D. 100. Rabbinical teachings on these biblical texts, together with legal judgments, religious duties, and other aspects of Jewish life, began to be collected and written down by the scattered Jewish communities of the Diaspora. By the middle of the fourth century B.C. the Jews of Palestine had put together a compilation of religious and ethical teachings known as the Talmud, which, together with another version of the Talmud produced slightly later in Babylon, has served ever since as the single most cohesive force in Judaism. The aim of the Talmud's creators was to use biblical interpretation and discussion as the basis for religious, moral, and legal practice that could serve all Jewish communities.

The rituals of modern Judaism still derive from the Talmud, as do marriage laws and other social customs. Until the nineteenth century, religious services made use of the Hebrew liturgy, which included psalms and other readings from the Bible, established by Talmudic scholars; Orthodox Jewish worshipers continue this practice today. The custom of the bar mitzvah (the confirmation of boys at the age of 13) and the principal holy days of the year, together with the manner in which they should be kept, all derive from the Talmud. Yom Kippur, the day of atonement for sins, the most solemn day of the year, is marked by fasting.

Firmly anchored in a tradition that goes back to the Torah and Moses' exposition of the Covenant, the Talmud is a practical guide to conduct rather than a theological treatise. Unlike the early Christian writers, who sought to provide a sound theological basis for the principles of their religion, the Talmudic rabbis concentrated almost exclusively on religious practice and questions of morality in human relationships. The Talmud teaches that faith is valuable only if it leads to ethical action. In this way Judaism has avoided many of the theological controversies that characterize the history of Christianity. In its insistence on God as pure spirit, Talmudic doctrine reaffirms a belief as old as Abraham. The Hebrew Scriptures, it is true, refer to God as one who addresses Moses and the prophets, but this manner of speaking is used only to make communication possible between God and humans: "We describe God by terms borrowed from the divine creation in order to make [God] intelligible to humans." Judaism is thus the only ancient religion that avoids the use of the visual arts and condemns the worship of "graven images." Centuries later Islam adopted similar strictures.

The goal to which obedience to God will lead is an age of righteousness on earth. Judaism believes that this period of universal peace will be ushered in by the Messiah, who will preside over the spiritual regeneration of humanity. In the words of Isaiah:

> **Of the increase of his government and of peace there will be no end, upon the throne of David, and over his kingdom, to establish it, and to uphold it with justice and with righteousness from this time forth and for evermore."[5]**

Judaism remains a minority religion outside of Israel. If its ethical influence remains strong, that is in part because such principles have proved relevant to people in a wide variety of circumstances, often adverse, from the Babylon of Nebuchadnezzar to the concentration camps of Nazi Germany. At the same time Judaism's principal religious texts, the Hebrew Scriptures, have had a profound influence on every aspect of Western culture. Many of its principles have entered the mainstream of Western culture through the religion that sprang from it, Christianity.

# Christianity

From the time of its adoption by Constantine, the history of Christianity has been inextricably linked with that of Western culture. During the centuries of its diffusion and transmission by missionaries throughout virtually the entire world, it has taken on a variety of forms. If the range of Christian belief is less varied than that of Hinduism, it is more eclectic than Judaism or, probably, Buddhism. Yet its founder, Jesus of Nazareth, was a Jew who regularly attended the synagogue on the Sabbath and on the principal Jewish religious festivals and who declared that his purpose was not to destroy but to fulfill the Jewish Law.

Virtually all that is known about the life of Jesus is contained in the Gospels of Matthew, Mark, Luke, and John. Even the date of his birth is uncertain; most modern authorities place it between 4 and 2 B.C. The Gospel writers give little information about his early life; only Matthew and Luke describe the nativity (the birth of Jesus) and his childhood.

Near the age of 30 Jesus was baptized by John, "the Baptist," a religious ascetic in the style of the earlier prophets. Fervent in denouncing the ways of his contemporaries, John predicted that one greater than he would come after him as an agent of divine judgment and identified that figure as Jesus. In taking up the life of an itinerant rabbi, Jesus continued to preach John's message that the Jews should mend their ways and return to a strict observance of the Law. He was assisted in his mission by a band of 12 male followers, who were called the apostles.

By the time of Jesus' baptism Jerusalem had become

## WORLD RELIGIONS

| | Hinduism and Buddhism | Chinese | Persian | Judeo-Christian |
|---|---|---|---|---|
| 1500–600 B.C. | Vedas | | | Exodus (c. 1250 B.C.) Reign of David (c. 1000–c. 970 B.C.) |
| 600–100 B.C. | Jainism (600–500 B.C.) Gautama Buddha (c. 563–c. 485 B.C.) | Confucius (551– c. 479 B.C.) Lao-tze (c. 500 B.C.) Mencius (c. 372– c. 289 B.C.) Chuang-tze (c. 350 B.C.) | Zoroaster (before 600 B.C.) Mithraism (before 300 B.C.) | Fall of Judah (586 B.C.) |
| 100 B.C.–A.D. 320 | *Bhagavadgita* (A.D. 100–200) Mahayana Buddhism (A.D. 100–200) | | | Jesus (c. 4 B.C.–A.D. 29) Death of Paul (A.D. 67) Destruction of the Temple at Jerusalem (A.D. 70) Edict of Milan (A.D. 313) |

the capital of the Roman province of Judea and the center for a wide variety of Jewish religious movements. The teachings of the Pharisees, who advocated strict observance of the Law, were at one extreme. The Sadducees combined Jewish traditions with those of the Greco-Roman world in a blend typical of the Hellenistic period, while the Zealots advocated violent revolution against the Romans. These groups were united in one respect: opposition to the teachings of Jesus.

The ideals that emerge in the Gospel accounts stress the importance of love and the avoidance of anger or violence. In the Sermon on the Mount, Jesus extends the traditional Jewish sympathy for the poor and the helpless: "Blessed are the meek, for they shall inherit the earth." His teaching was explicitly based on the Law;

his insistence on the importance of following its ethical content rather than merely observing its outward forms drew the anger of the Pharisees. Their attempts to trap him in a simple solution to moral dilemmas are described by the Gospel writers. When Jesus was reproached for preaching against divorce, which was permitted by Mosaic Law, he replied: "For your hardness of heart Moses allowed you to divorce your wives, but from the beginning it was not so."

Jesus' declaration that the Kingdom of God was at hand was interpreted by some of his followers as referring to contemporary political events; they believed him to be predicting the expulsion of the Romans and the refounding of David's old kingdom of Israel. The use of David's title of Messiah (*Christos*, in Greek) by Jesus'

## ◉ The Sermon on the Mount ◉

*The essence of Jesus' teaching is found in the Sermon on the Mount.*

Now when he saw the crowds, he went up on a mountainside and sat down. His disciples came to him, and he began to teach them, saying:

"Blessed are the poor in spirit,
    for theirs is the kingdom of heaven.
"Blessed are those who mourn,
    for they will be comforted.
"Blessed are the meek,
    for they will inherit the earth.
"Blessed are those who hunger and thirst for righteousness,
    for they will be filled.
"Blessed are the merciful,
    for they will be shown mercy.
"Blessed are the pure in heart,
    for they will see God.
"Blessed are the peacemakers,
    for they will be called sons of God.
"Blessed are those who are persecuted because of righteousness,
    for theirs is the kingdom of heaven.

"Blessed are you when people insult you, persecute you and falsely say all kinds of evil against you because of me. Rejoice and be glad, because great is your reward in heaven, for in the same way they persecuted the prophets who were before you. . . . Do not think that I have come to abolish the Law or the Prophets; I have not come to abolish them but to fulfill them. . . .

"You have heard that it was said, 'Love your neighbor and hate your enemy.' But I tell you: Love your enemies and pray for those who persecute you, that you may be sons of your Father in heaven."

*Source:* "The Sermon on the Mount." Scripture taken from the HOLY BIBLE: NEW INTERNATIONAL VERSION®. Copyright © 1973, 1978, 1984 by International Bible Society. Used by permission of Zondervan Publishing House.

followers thus implied that he was the successor of the great Jewish king; it was for this reason that he was condemned for blasphemy by the high priest and crucified by the Romans.

The apostles' belief in Jesus' physical resurrection was the prime factor in the foundation of a church to promote his teachings. The message of the apostle Peter's first sermon was that Jesus had died and risen to be with God and that the adherence of those who accepted his resurrection was marked by the rite of baptism. These first Christians were Jewish by birth and continued to follow the basic Jewish Law, but their belief in the divine as well as the human nature of Jesus inevitably aroused hostility and suspicion among their contemporaries. When one early convert, Stephen, was stoned to death, many of the others left Jerusalem and traveled throughout Asia, preaching and seeking converts. One of them, Thomas, is even credited by tradition with having carried Christianity to India.

## Paul and the Expansion of Christianity

The most important figure in the development and spread of Christianity was Paul (died A.D. 67), a Pharisee who had been present at the stoning of Stephen. Converted to Christianity by a vision, Paul was the first and greatest theologian of the early church. As a Jew he spoke Aramaic, the language of Jesus and his followers, but he had been brought up in the Greek city of Tarsus and was at home in the world of Greco-Roman culture. His exposition of the principal beliefs of Christianity, together with his subsequent preaching in Greece and Italy, played a major part in Christianity's rapid spread. The cohesion of the early church and its teachings, for which Paul is largely responsible, is in strong contrast to the variety of traditions that accumulated about the Buddha after his death.

According to Pauline doctrine, human failure to follow God's law was the consequence of Adam and Eve's disobedience, which corrupted all their descendants. Thus humans could achieve salvation not by living in accordance with any set of laws, Jewish or other, but only by the grace of God. The life and death of Jesus were intended, Paul taught, as a manifestation of this grace; as God's son, he suffered in order to show God's love for humanity. All who accepted Jesus' sacrifice through faith, said Paul, could thus achieve reconciliation with God.

Paul was the virtual creator of Christian theology, and his views were debated and generally accepted throughout the early church. Yet the austerity of his view of proper relations between men and women caused problems for future theologians. Women played an important part in the life of Jesus and were among his most loyal

One of the earliest surviving depictions of Jesus' crucifixion and resurrection appeared in the "Rabula Gospels" (c. 460). At the foot of the cross, Roman soldiers gamble for Jesus' robe. [Alinari/Art Resource]

and devoted supporters; a majority of those who followed him to his crucifixion were women. Nonetheless, for Paul they were required to play a subordinate social role. The devout man, he taught, should avoid them as much as possible: "It is well for a man not to touch a woman." Those who were single should remain so, Paul urged, as he himself did. Marriage was counseled in cases where sexual abstinence was impossible, but Paul warned that it tended to distract from spiritual duties by tempting the couple to think in worldly terms. Elsewhere in his writings, however, Paul compares marriage to Christ's relationship with the church. Paul's teachings have profoundly influenced social relations and sexual ethics in the West up to our time.

Paul saw Christianity as a universal religion. Unlike Judaism, it involved no traditional or ethnic barriers, and unlike Hinduism or Buddhism, its followers could become Christians only by rejecting their earlier religious beliefs. In expressing these ideas Paul used what was the universal language of his day, Greek, which had been spoken since the Hellenistic period from Italy to India. The use of Greek helped transform Christianity from an offshoot of Judaism to a universal religion by placing it on the vast stage of the Roman Empire. The other crucial factor in the transformation was Paul's insistence that converts to Christianity were not bound to follow the customs prescribed in the Jewish Law or to undergo the rite of circumcision. Paul's opinion was much debated in the first century of Christianity, but its general acceptance facilitated the conversion of Gentiles to the early church. (*Gentile* is derived from a Latin word meaning "non-Roman," thus "foreign," "pagan.")

The rich and complex character of many Hellenistic cults, with their blend of ancient Greek and Asian features, had in many ways prepared the West to accept a new religion from Asia. Throughout the Roman world, as we have seen, philosophical systems of belief such as Stoicism and Epicureanism provided satisfaction only to an elite few, while traditional Roman religion was largely an instrument of the state. Provided that they said or did nothing to question the state's authority, Paul and other Christian missionaries were free to preach their doctrines in public. Nor was there any serious chance of Jewish opposition, since the Roman forces that destroyed the temple in Jerusalem in 70 effectively ended the city's role as a religious center. Indeed, some Hellenized Jews at various places in the Roman world became enthusiastic converts, and the network of synagogues throughout the Mediterranean area and western Asia often provided a valuable platform for Paul and the other missionaries.

For its first decades the new movement functioned on a relatively informal basis, with preachers, teachers, and evangelists either self-appointed or selected by individual congregations. The community at Jerusalem remained "first among equals," while Paul continued to exercise supervision over the churches he founded. Conflict with the Roman authorities was usually avoided; Paul himself instructed Christians to obey the laws and pay taxes.

As Christian communities grew and became more active, the need for greater organization arose. Around the end of the first century the principal seat of religious authority was transferred from Jerusalem to Rome, where according to tradition Peter and Paul had founded a church. Each community had a leader, or bishop, but beginning in the fourth and fifth centuries the bishops of Rome claimed supreme authority by virtue of their reputed succession from Peter.

In addition there remained a constant need to define and explain Christian doctrine as it came into contact with adherents of other beliefs. The Gnostics, who followed a Hellenistic blend of Greek and Roman religious beliefs, posed a particular challenge. They despised the world of matter and sought salvation by escape from the flesh, like Hindu and Buddhist ascetics. Many of them eagerly adopted the belief in a divine Christ but could not accept that the divinity had become flesh in the person of Jesus. To avoid the confusion of dogma presented by Gnostic Christians and others like them, the leaders of the early church formalized their teachings.

It was in response to a Gnostic opponent of the church, Marcion (died c. 160), who refused to acknowledge the Old Testament as a source of revelation, that the Christian canon evolved. From the time that the content of the New Testament was established, this canon served as a binding force for Christians throughout the Roman Empire and has remained central to Christianity ever since. Judaism and Christianity are therefore "religions of the book" in a way that Hinduism and Buddhism are not.

The earliest Christian preachers were the apostles themselves, who chose and ordained their successors. Throughout the history of the church, its leaders have traced their mission back to the earliest Christians, and the concept of apostolic succession represents a major difference between Christianity and Judaism. The religious ceremonies conducted by the early ministers of the church were in the vernacular, and the rites included the celebration of the sacraments, visible ceremonies intended to bestow divine grace on worthy recipients. Two sacraments are retained by nearly all Christians today in one form or another: the rite of baptism and the commemoration of the Last Supper. The precise nature and number of these sacraments, however, was the subject of long debate. The Catholic church finally established the definitive number at seven, but this was repudiated by Protestant reformers in the sixteenth century.

## The Church and the Roman Empire

During the reign of Septimius Severus (193–211) figures such as Julia Domna began to take an interest in the theoretical bases of Christianity. One of the principal Christian writers of the age was Tertullian (c. 160–c. 225), who was the first to formulate the doctrine of the Trinity, whereby one God is simultaneously conceived of as Father, Son, and Holy Spirit. The detailed philosophical implications of this doctrine provided thorny problems for the church for centuries.

Two other major figures of the third century, Clement (c. 150–c. 214) and Origen (c. 185–c. 254), both of Alexandria, continued the process of synthesizing the original Jewish content of Christianity with Greek ideas and culture and making the result available to their Roman readers. Origen, however, fell victim to the first major systematic persecution of Christians, initiated by Emperor Decius (249–251). After Decius' death, Christians were able to resume their worship, but the persecution had created a new theological issue: Should the Christians who had saved themselves by making public sacrifices to local gods be forgiven and admitted back into their congregations? To deal with such cases, a system of penance evolved that was to prove one of the most striking characteristics of medieval Christianity.

Christianity's impact on the Roman Empire during its first three centuries was through the effects of personal example and moral witness rather than systematic organization and conversion. The high moral standard maintained by most Christian leaders, coupled with the willingness of many to die as martyrs, elicited reluctant admiration. The subtleties of Christian theology attracted the interest of many prominent intellectuals. Furthermore, both church and empire depended for their success on careful organization and concern for administrative detail; some church leaders, in fact, saw the empire as a force for order, making possible the performance of their own work.

By the beginning of the fourth century one out of every ten Roman citizens was at least nominally a Christian. The emperor Diocletian (284–305) attempted to control the growing faith by a series of persecutions that lasted from 303 to 311. Although the policy produced thousands of martyrs, it failed in its aim, and in 313 Diocletian's successors, Constantine and Licinius, signed the Edict of Milan, granting all citizens of the empire freedom of religious worship. Constantine subsequently introduced legislation that protected the church. Writing in the aftermath of this new partnership between church and state, the Christian writer Eusebius (c. 260–c. 339) claimed that the empire and the church were both the work of God.

Constantine's toleration for Christianity doubtless owed much to the fact that his mother, Helena, was a Christian who devoted her influence to its promotion. As an elderly woman she visited the Holy Land and helped found numerous churches there. By the late fourth century, writers began to credit her with the discovery of the "true cross" on which Jesus had been crucified.

## The Early Church and Heresy

Unlike Hinduism or Buddhism, Christianity presented a single body of doctrine, together with the requirement that adherents accept the faith in the form in which it was handed down and interpreted to them by their religious superiors. Indeed, from the time of Paul the growth of Christian influence had been aided by careful, consistent leadership. With Constantine, victory had been won, but the church paid a price for its success. Its new power and security encouraged the development of alternative views about basic Christian teachings, which had to be discussed and in most cases were prohibited in church councils. Throughout the fourth and fifth centuries various theological interpretations were proposed, only to be declared heresies. The words *heresy* and *heretic* are now often used to describe an unconventional

opinion and its holder; they were originally coined to describe someone whose beliefs were contrary to the teaching of the church and whose immortal soul was thus in danger. In this way Christian theological orthodoxy was defined in relationship to views that were deemed unacceptable. In contrast, Judaism never attempted to define heresy; Hinduism has always embraced seemingly inconsistent ideas; and Buddhism, Confucianism, and Taoism, in their different ways, were intended to be adapted to the individual's moral and spiritual needs.

The first dispute was caused by the problem that had occurred after the persecutions of Decius, namely, how people who had betrayed their faith at the time of Diocletian should be treated. The most delicate cases were those of priests who had, at the imperial command, handed over the Scriptures to be burned. A group of rigid opponents to reinstatement developed at Carthage, in North Africa; they were known as the Donatists from their leader, Donatus. In an effort to solve the controversy, Constantine summoned a council of bishops in 314 at Arles in Gaul. Although the council decided against the Donatists, it was unable to enforce its opinion. The principle of using church councils to debate and rule on theological issues, however, had been established.

Among the earliest heresies to be denounced was Arianism, first propounded by a priest from Alexandria named Arius, whose teaching concerned the divinity of Christ and the relation between God the Father and God the Son. Arius claimed that Christ was divine but did not have the same nature as the Father, who had created him. In 325, at the Council of Nicaea (an ecumenical rather than a regional gathering, as Arles had been), the Arian view was rejected; the Nicene Creed asserted that the Father and Son were fully equal, sharing one being and, together with the Holy Spirit, constituting the Trinity. This formulation met with opposition, and the debate about the Trinity and the nature of Christ still continues.

## Monasticism

Even before the establishment of Christianity as the state religion, individual Christians had turned to asceticism and solitude as a source of spiritual discipline. The tradition of withdrawal from the world to an austere life of religious devotion is also a characteristic found in Hinduism, Buddhism, and Taoism. In all three religions, monks have tended to live in communities, although solitary mystics or hermits inaugurated the Christian tradition. (*Monk* is derived from the Greek word *monos*, meaning "alone.") Anthony (c. 251–356), generally acknowledged as the father of Christian monasticism, spent some 20 years after 285 alone in the desert of Egypt. As the practice spread and communities began to develop, monastic life was organized according to a set pattern or rule. Such rules were established in Asia as early as 358 by Basil (330–379) and later in Italy by Benedict (480–547). Throughout the subsequent history of Christianity the religious orders of men and women who retired to monasteries and convents exerted a considerable influence in secular as well as sacred matters. It was through monks in the West that the Latin language and classical Latin texts were preserved, carefully copied for monastery libraries.

# The Papacy

No less important than monasticism for the history of Latin Christendom was the growth of the power and prestige of the bishop of Rome, more familiarly known as the pope (the Latin *papa* is derived from *pappas*, the Greek word for "father"). The claim to papal primacy, though based on Jesus' allusion to the apostle Peter as the rock on which the church would be built, was in fact asserted much later and only in response to the growing authority and claims of the patriarch of Constantinople. Pope Leo I (440–461), the beneficiary of an imperial Roman decree recognizing his sole jurisdiction over the Latin church, claimed to have fullness of power, presumably over the church as a whole. If the Byzantine emperors' successors had been able to continue the expansion of their rule after the sixth century, such claims might have proved worthless. But the internal problems of the Byzantine Empire and the external challenge of the Muslims destroyed whatever chance the patriarch of Constantinople had to establish himself as universal head of the Christian church and contributed to its growing split into eastern and Latin communions. The ability of the popes to maintain their independence was momentous, for they claimed to have authority superior to that of monarchs. In Eastern Orthodoxy, however, ultimate authority rested in the hands of the emperor. In practice, of course, both east and west, challenges to the authority of emperors and popes were successful from time to time.

The greatest of the early medieval popes, Gregory I (590–604), enhanced papal power by sponsoring a mission to convert the pagans of Anglo-Saxon England. The success of the mission was due in part to his instructions that pagan festival days and shrines be adapted to Christian use rather than repudiated outright. He was concerned as well with the conversion of the Lombards and with the expansion of Christianity in Spain. Contemporaries called him "God's consul" because of his administrative reforms, particularly the reorganization of papal revenues. A monk himself, Gregory wrote a biography of Benedict, thereby helping provide the impetus that made the Benedictine Rule the dominant form of monastic life by the ninth century.

# Augustine

If Paul was the first great leader in the history of the early church, Augustine (354–430) was its culminating figure and one who influenced Christian thought for centuries after his death. His writings, which draw on both Christian theology and Greco-Roman thought, deal with the most complex questions: human nature and destiny, the work of Christ as savior, and the relationship of the church to the world. His *Confessions*, an autobiographical account of his spiritual life, reasserted the teachings of Paul, in particular the unique importance ascribed to God's mercy as a means of forgiveness. In *The City of God*, written between 413 and 426 when Roman power was crumbling, Augustine claimed that God was punishing the Romans for the violence and corruption of their

**Augustine, bishop of Hippo, author of**
***The City of God*, in a detail from a painting**
**by Simone Martini. [Fitzwilliam Museum,**
**Cambridge]**

empire. The new order to emerge from this chaos should, he argued, be a Christian society, governed by principles of love and justice.

A portion of Augustine's theological writing was inspired by his opposition to Pelagius, whose writings had brought him a number of enthusiastic followers. The Pelagians believed that humans did not inherit original sin and that free will was sufficient to attain salvation. Divine grace was not limited to the preordained elect but was given to all persons; hence Pelagius' view of human nature was not pessimistic like that of Augustine. In works such as *On Original Sin* and *On Grace and Free Will*, Augustine attacked the Pelagian view. To some of Augustine's contemporaries and successors, however, his refutation presented an equally extreme picture: a world ruled by a God so omnipotent that lives were predestined, where individual acts of goodness were insignificant in the face of dependence on divine grace. Medieval theologians generally tried to steer a middle course between the two extremes, but the debate was to be renewed in the sixteenth-century Protestant Reformation, which saw the revival first of Augustinian and then of Pelagian views.

Augustine's views on sex and marriage have remained central to Catholic thought ever since his time. The only justifiable purpose of sexual relations, he believed, was the creation of children, and only within the institution of marriage. Marriage thus serves the divine will, even though people who abstain from sexual relations are of a spiritually higher order. This concept of the flawed state of the human condition is a fresh assertion of the Pauline belief in human sinfulness. Augustine remained unrivaled as an expositor of Christian theology until Thomas Aquinas in the thirteenth century. The theologians of the Protestant Reformation were inspired by the influence of Augustinian principles to seek fundamental changes in Christian practice. Martin Luther and John Calvin were both dedicated readers of Augustine.

# Women in the Ancient World Religions

The role of women in ancient and classical religious practice was roughly consistent throughout Eurasia. Most priestly functions were reserved for men, and women were often excluded from the inner sanctum of the temple, especially in Judaism. Judaism and to a degree the teachings of Paul contain an underlying bias against women, seeing them as "unclean" and hence as profaning religious ritual. In many Orthodox Jewish congregations, women were obliged to sit apart from men, concealed behind a screen. In India by classical times,

priests were exclusively male, and this was also true of Buddhism and most of Taoism. Confucianism, which largely lacked a priestly order, was explicitly male-dominated and preached the subjection of women to their husbands. Shinto, the Japanese partial equivalent of Taoism, similarly reflected the heavy male dominance of Japanese society. Nevertheless, some women played major religious roles, separate from the male priestly order, as soothsayers and priestesses in ancient and classical Greece and Rome and similarly in ancient and classical India. The Tantric version of Hinduism, in its celebration of sex as the embodiment of the life force and hence a celebration of the divine mystery, made a central role for women as the chief focus of its rituals and doctrine. In this, Tantrism may be seen as echoing very early religious veneration of women as symbols of fertility and life. Perhaps it was also, like the acceptance of temple priestesses and soothsayers in both East and West, an acknowledgment of the spiritual and intuitive qualities of women. Especially in the earlier periods, most religions (except Judaism and Islam) have imputed to women special access to the mysteries and special spiritual powers.

As Buddhism and Christianity developed, so did female devotion, and various orders of nuns were organized, counterparts to the monks of both religions and with a similar discipline. Women had in fact played a far more prominent part in the early growth of both religions than the established order recognized. The Buddha and Jesus seem to have paid as much attention to women as to men and apparently made little status distinction between them; both may indeed have been said to favor them or to regard them as more open to the message. For whatever reason, both religions quickly produced female saints in great numbers, of which the best known are the Virgin Mary and the Buddhist goddess of mercy, Kuan Yin (Kannon in Japanese), among a host of others to whom people prayed for help probably more often than to male saints. In our own time women generally (except in Judaism and Islam) play a more active role than men in religious faith and practice everywhere, as perhaps they have always done, and the Christian priesthood is in the early stages, at least within Protestant Christianity, of admitting them on equal terms.

Hinduism has always had more or less equal numbers of female and male deities, and even Shiva was provided with a female consort of equal powers, although by classical times the priesthood was closed to women and currently shows few signs of removing that bar. But Hindus still give at least equal attention to female deities and hence continue to acknowledge the special powers and insights of women. Confucianism has no deities, no saints, and no organized priesthood, although since Han times a small number of people calling themselves Confucian priests have tended the temples and conducted services centered on the veneration of Confucius the sage. These have always been men, and Confucianism barely acknowledges the existence of women. Women in Confucian countries seek religious involvement in Taoism or Buddhism, where their role is more accepted—another aspect of East Asian eclecticism in religion.

From very early times in China there was an explicit assertion of the need for balance in all things between yin (female) and yang (male); this was incorporated into Taoism and accepted by nearly all Chinese, including Confucians, although most Chinese followed both religious traditions. The persistence of this idea even in modern China indicates an acceptance of the equal importance of male and female characteristics and the essential role of both.

Religion seems to have evolved away from its earliest emphasis on women. With the rise of the first states and empires, the coming of bureaucracy, the increase in large-scale warfare, and the consequently greater importance of the warrior, males and male roles may have become more dominant, and religion may have changed accordingly. Most of the great religions subordinate or even exclude women, and most tended to justify male domination. Judaism, Confucianism, and Islam are probably the clearest examples, but only Judaism and Islam speak explicitly, and pejoratively, about women. Christianity, to some degree a blend of Judaism with other Eastern religious traditions, was clearly male-dominant. Only Buddhism and to some extent Taoism approach the ideal of gender equality.

*In spite of the obvious differences between the various religions and moral philosophies discussed in this chapter, they share some important characteristics. Each continues to influence the lives of millions of people. Whereas the worship of the gods of ancient Egypt, Assyria, or Greece has largely vanished, all the major religions and philosophies described here provide at least partial solutions to the problems of life for their followers, even though they originated in times and cultures remote from our own. The major world religions share a number of attitudes. Nonviolence and reverence for life are urged by Hindu and Christian doctrine alike. The important role played by the religious mystic and teacher is typical of virtually all present world religions. Moreover, each attempts to order human relationships in society as well as individually. In this, however,*

*they share another common characteristic, the fact that the ideal visions they propose remain, for the most part, unfulfilled.*

*In an age of rapid communications, the ancient world religions have inevitably, and often profitably, been brought into direct contact with one another. Christian priests and teachers continue to work in Asia, and in India, Mother Teresa of Calcutta, herself an Albanian, has become a symbol of practical Christian charity. At the same time, Western culture has become increasingly open to the religions of the East, with their emphasis on spiritual rather than material values. In the 2,000 years since the foundation of Christianity, only one other religion has established itself on the same global scale: Islam, whose formation and growth is discussed in the next chapter.*

## Notes

1. Jer. 8:19.
2. Isa. 12:4.
3. Amos 5:6–7.
4. Ps. 137:5–6.
5. Isa. 9:7.

## Suggestions for Further Reading

### Religions of South and East Asia

Basham, A. L. *The Origins and Development of Classical Hinduism.* Boston: Beacon Press, 1989.

Bowker, J. *Problems of Suffering in Religions of the World.* Cambridge: Cambridge University Press, 1975.

Brown, W. N. *Man in the Universe: Some Continuities in Indian Thought.* Berkeley: University of California Press, 1970.

Callicot, J. B., and Ames, R. T., eds. *Nature in Asia: Traditions of Thought.* Albany: State University of New York Press, 1991.

Campbell, J. *The Masks of God: Oriental Mythology.* New York: Viking, 1962.

Chandhuri, N. C. *Hinduism: A Religion to Live By.* New York: Oxford University Press, 1979.

Creel, H. G. *What Is Taoism? And Other Studies in Chinese Cultural History.* Chicago: University of Chicago Press, 1970.

De Bary, W. T., ed. *Sources of Chinese Tradition.* 2 vols. New York: Columbia University Press, 1964.

———. *Sources of Indian Tradition.* New York: Columbia University Press, 1958.

Embree, A. T., ed. *The Hindu Tradition.* New York: Modern Library, 1966.

Gombrich, R. F. *Theravada Buddhism: A Social History.* London: Routledge & Kegan Paul, 1988.

Harvey, B. P. *An Introduction to Buddhism.* Cambridge: Cambridge University Press, 1990.

Herman, A. L. *A Brief Introduction to Hinduism.* Boulder, Colo.: Westview Press, 1991.

Hopkins, T. *Hindu Religious Tradition.* Encino, Calif.: Dickenson, 1971.

Humphreys, C. *Buddhism.* London: Cassell, 1962.

Monro, K. W. *Reaching for the Moon: Asian Religious Paths.* Chambersburg, Penn.: Anima Publications, 1991.

Munro, D. J. *The Concept of Man in Early China.* Stanford, Calif.: Stanford University Press, 1969.

Schwartz, B. I. *The World of Thought in Ancient China.* Cambridge, Mass.: Harvard University Press, 1985.

Sharma, A., ed. *Women in World Religions.* Albany: State University of New York Press, 1987.

Taylor, R. L. *The Religious Dimensions of Confucianism.* Albany: State University of New York Press, 1991.

Thompson, L. G. *Chinese Religion.* Belmont, Calif.: Wadsworth, 1988.

## The Judeo-Christian Tradition

Bright, J. *A History of Israel,* 2nd ed. Philadelphia: Westminster Press, 1972.

Coggins, R., Phillips, A., and Knibb, M., eds. *Israel's Prophetic Tradition.* Cambridge: Cambridge University Press, 1984.

De Jonge, M. *Jesus, the Servant-Messiah.* New Haven, Conn.: Yale University Press, 1991.

Fredriksen, P. *From Jesus to Christ: The Origins of the New Testament Images of Jesus.* New Haven, Conn.: Yale University Press, 1988.

Frend, W. H. *Martyrdom and Persecution in the Early Church.* New York: New York University Press, 1967.

Grant, M. *The Jews in the Roman World.* New York: Scribner, 1973.

Grant, R. M. *Augustus to Constantine: The Rise and Triumph of the Christian Movement in the Roman World.* San Francisco: HarperSanFrancisco, 1990.

Halpern, B. *The Constitution of the Monarchy in Israel.* Chico, Calif.: Scholars Press, 1981.

Hengel, M. *Acts and the History of Earliest Christianity.* London: SCM Press, 1986.

Jacobs, L. *The Talmudic Argument.* Cambridge: Cambridge University Press, 1984.

MacMullen, R. *Christianizing the Roman Empire, A.D. 100–400.* New Haven, Conn.: Yale University Press, 1984.

Meeks, W. A. *The First Urban Christians: The Social World of the Apostle Paul.* New Haven, Conn.: Yale University Press, 1983.

Renko, S. *Pagan Rome and the Early Christians.* Bloomington: Indiana University Press, 1986.

Riches, J. *The World of Jesus: First-Century Judaism in Crisis.* Cambridge: Cambridge University Press, 1990.

Sanders, E. P. *Jesus and Judaism.* Philadelphia: Fortress Press, 1985.

Segal, A. F. *Paul the Convert: The Apostolate and Apostasy of Saul the Pharisee.* New Haven, Conn.: Yale University Press, 1990.

———. *Rebecca's Children.* Cambridge, Mass.: Harvard University Press, 1986.

Smallwood, E. M. *The Jews Under Roman Rule,* rev. ed. Leiden, Netherlands: Brill, 1981.

Smith, M. S. *The Early History of God: Yahweh and the Other Deities in Ancient Israel.* San Francisco: HarperSanFrancisco, 1990.

Watson, F. *Paul, Judaism, and the Gentiles.* Cambridge: Cambridge University Press, 1987.

Witherington, B., III. *Women in the Earliest Churches.* Cambridge: Cambridge University Press, 1988.

# PART · TWO

# The Middle Ages

The millennium that stretched from 500 to 1500 witnessed the golden age of the civilizations of China and Byzantium and the continuation of classical civilization in South India. Particularly in China and the Byzantine Empire, the great advances of the classical era flowered and spread to other societies. In Arabia, however, a new civilization, rooted in the Muslim religion, emerged in the seventh century and rapidly expanded from its Middle Eastern base into North Africa, Iberia, Iran, North India, and parts of Southeast Asia. During the mid-fifteenth century the Turks, themselves Muslims, overwhelmed the remnants of the Byzantine Empire, widening their wedge between Hindu and Buddhist Asia and Christian Europe. Thus much of the vast area from the Atlantic Ocean to Southeast Asia acquired a degree of social and cultural unity, though throughout most of India and Southeast Asia, Islam failed to supplant Hindu and Buddhist traditions.

In East Asia, China was dominant throughout this era, particularly after the T'ang dynasty began to restore Chinese unity and imperial power in the seventh century. China, however, fell under the rule of the Mongols in 1279. This Asiatic people established an enormous empire that stretched from the Pacific Ocean to the Baltic Sea, opening up vast new opportunities for trade and cultural exchange. Less than a century later, in 1368, the Chinese regained control of their land through a new dynasty, the Ming. Chinese influence extended to Korea and Japan, whose civilizations were modeled after China's. Southeast Asia, because of its uniquely important position on the trading routes, served as the principal meeting place for Buddhist and Islamic culture.

The collapse of the Roman Empire in the West left North Africa and Europe vulnerable to the Muslim invaders. Although North Africa and Iberia were lost, the reorganization of Europe, first along feudal lines and later through more centralized states, contributed to its ability to repel the Muslims despite repeated attacks that occurred as late as the seventeenth century. The politically fragmented European societies slowly recovered from the effects of Muslim and Viking invasions while relearning much of their classical heritage from their Islamic neighbors and from Jewish scholars. Such unity as there was in Europe was provided largely by the Catholic church, which played a major creative role in areas as diverse as education, agriculture, governmental organization, and the arts. Despite the stunning crises of the fourteenth century—famine, the arrival of the Black Death from Asia, and war—western Europe was sufficiently strong by the fifteenth century to launch voyages of discovery that took the European adventurers to South and East Asia, Africa, and the Americas. They came into contact with the ancient civilizations of the Sudanese and Swahili kingdoms in Africa as well as the Incas and Aztecs in America. Without realizing it, these explorers had taken the first steps that would eventually lead to the integration of the peoples of the world. ■

# Byzantium and Islam

While western Europe was being transformed by nomadic invaders after the collapse of Roman rule, the eastern half of the empire, despite initial setbacks at the hands of the Goths and the Huns, laid the foundation in the sixth century for a period of imperial brilliance. Known as the Byzantine Empire or Byzantium, its name derived from the former Greek colony of Byzantium, which Constantine had transformed into the site of his new capital, Constantinople, in 330. Strategically located on the Bosporus, part of the great water route between the Black and Aegean seas, the city, surrounded on three sides by water, was easily defended. It was also a natural site for a commercial center, since it was the crossroads for the great east-west trading routes that extended from Asia to Europe, as well as the north-south routes that reached from southern Russia into the Mediterranean. Byzantine culture, a distinctive fusion of Greco-Roman and Christian traditions, made a lasting impact on many of the peoples of eastern Europe.

After a 1,000-year history, Byzantium fell in 1453 to

**A detail from one of the eighth-century mosaics that line the walls of the Great Mosque at Damascus. [Ronald Sheridan/Ancient Art and Architecture Collection]**

the Ottoman Turks, who conquered it on behalf of Islam, the last of the world's major religions to take form. Islam began in Arabia in the early seventh century. From there it spread throughout the Middle East and beyond, into Iran, North Africa, the Iberian peninsula, and the Balkans. Virtually from the beginning, Islamic expansion brought the Arabs into conflict with their Byzantine neighbors, and as early as 674, Muslim armies made their first, albeit unsuccessful, attempt to conquer Constantinople. During the ensuing eight centuries, relations between the Muslims and the Byzantines were often characterized by hostility and periodic warfare.

# Byzantium

The Byzantine Empire was a remarkable achievement. The last of its emperors, Constantine XI, could trace the imperial succession back to the Roman emperor Augustus in the late first century B.C., although many of the institutions familiar to Augustus had long ceased to exist. Nevertheless, a remarkable continuity of culture and tradition helped make the Byzantine Empire the most durable political entity in medieval Europe. During this period it not only preserved and enhanced classical culture but also made important contributions in law, religion, commerce, and the arts. Moreover, the empire provided a crucial buffer between waves of invaders from Asia and the peoples of western Europe as they constructed new states in the aftermath of the Roman decline and the German, Viking, and Magyar invasions.

## Historical Background

In contrast to the chaos that prevailed in the Roman world in the third century, most of the ensuing 100 years was a time of peace, both externally and internally. Despite its administrative separation in the late fourth century, the empire was still regarded as a single state. The roots of the future division were, however, already present. The western part of the empire, which traditionally enjoyed political supremacy, had always been inferior to the east in terms of natural resources, population, urban centers, commerce, and industry. When, in the fifth century, it became increasingly apparent that the west could not defend itself against outside invaders, rulers in the east concentrated on protecting their own domains. Suspicion, conflict of interest, and jealousy were stronger than feelings of unity and responsibility, especially as the two halves of the empire evolved into separate states, each with its own laws and coinage. Even religion played a modest role in dividing the empire, as the Latin Christians found themselves at

odds with the Monophysites, who emphasized Christ's divinity at the expense of his humanity and who enjoyed substantial support in Egypt, Syria, Palestine, and Constantinople.

Although the eastern half of the empire survived, it did not escape the blows of nomadic invaders. As early as 378 a Visigoth army defeated the emperor Valens and the Roman army of the Danube at Adrianople. The empire, however, saved itself by allowing the Visigoths to settle in the Balkans in return for serving in the Byzantine army. Faced with the threat of an invasion by the Huns in the mid-fifth century, the government at Constantinople chose instead to pay the tribute demanded by Attila (died 453), the Huns' leader. When the Ostrogoths threatened the empire in the late fifth century, their chieftain, Theodoric (died 526), who had previously spent ten years in Constantinople as a hostage, was persuaded to invade Italy instead. Thus by the early sixth century, when the western empire had for all practical purposes ceased to exist, the Byzantine domains still embraced the Balkan peninsula, Armenia, Syria, Palestine, Egypt, and Asia Minor, the economic heartland of the empire.

## The Age of Justinian

An empire that stretched from the Nile to the Black Sea and included not only Constantinople but also Alexandria, Antioch, and Athens was not enough to satisfy Justinian (527–565), a strong-willed, pious emperor determined, as he said, "to recover the rest of our Empire, which the Romans of earlier days extended up to the limits of the two oceans, and which they lost through their indifference."[1] By the time Justinian uttered those words in 536, he had already concluded a war with the Persians on his eastern frontier, thus freeing troops to reclaim much of North Africa from the Vandals. This task was accomplished by Belisarius, the most prominent of his generals, in 533 and 534. The following year Belisarius overran Sicily, and between 536 and 540 he reconquered the Italian peninsula from the Goths. The Persians, however, violated their treaty in 540 by invading Syria and encouraging the Goths in Italy to rebel. It took another 15 years of fighting before Justinian had pacified Italy. In the meantime he dispatched an expedition against the Visigoths in Spain in 550, which soon brought the southern part of the Iberian peninsula under his rule.

The result of these campaigns was that much of the western Mediterranean had been recovered from the invaders who had occupied it. The boundaries of the ancient Roman Empire, however, were still a long way from being restored, and Justinian's campaigns had exacted a heavy toll; overtaxed, the empire was on the verge of fiscal collapse, the defenses in the east had been seri-

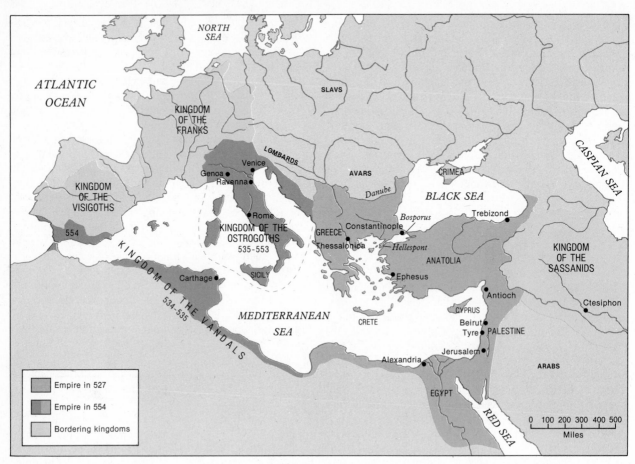

*8.1 The Byzantine Empire Under Justinian*

ously undermined, and trade with India and China had been disrupted by the fighting with Persia.

Within his empire, Justinian ruled as an agent of God, enjoying supreme authority over both church and state. Just as there was only one God, so there could be only one Christian empire governed by one emperor, himself subject to divine law alone. The imperial ideal was aptly stated by one of Justinian's contemporaries:

> Possessing a dignity, O Emperor, surpassing all others in honor, you should, above all, render honor to God, who has bestowed that rank upon you. For he has given you the scepter over terrestrial power in imitation of the celestial kingdom in order that you should teach men to cultivate justice. . . . The emperor is equal to all men in the nature of his body, but in the authority of his rank he is similar to God, who rules all. For there is no one on earth higher than he. . . . Impose on yourself the necessity of obeying the laws, since no one on earth can force you to do so.[2]

The emperor was the focal point of a partly Persian, partly Roman court ritual designed to enhance his power and image. Over the centuries the ceremonial became more and more elaborate, until it finally included ingenious mechanical contraptions, such as a throne that could be raised or lowered, a gold-plated bronze tree filled with gilded bronze birds, and gold-covered lions that roared when a visitor approached. Eventually, people who wanted an audience with the emperor not only had to prostrate themselves but were expected to kiss the monarch's foot and hand. Beginning in the seventh century the emperor styled himself *basileus*, or "ruler of all the world," a title analogous to the Persian notion of "king of kings," in addition to the title *autocrat*, or "sole ruler," to underscore his absolute power.

Keeping the church in order was a fundamental part of Justinian's imperial responsibility as well as a means of preserving unity. His concern extended even to the sexual behavior of his clergy; on one occasion he had two homosexual bishops arrested, castrated, and publicly humiliated. Generally, however, he preferred to convert dissidents to his point of view rather than impose harsh punishment. Nevertheless, a number of Manichaean heretics were burned to death in his reign when they refused to retract their belief in a strictly dualistic universe that identified goodness with the spirit and evil with matter. Thanks especially to the patronage of his wife, the empress Theodora, the Monophysites fared much better and were even guests at the royal palace, where Justinian disputed with them. The emperor went so far as to issue an imperial edict seeking a compromise between Orthodox Christians and Monophysites, who refused to distinguish between the divine and human natures in Christ. After his effort to restore unity failed, he reaffirmed his fidelity to Orthodox Christianity.

Justinian enjoyed considerable success in his reform of the law, which he deemed, like religion, a source of social and political cohesion. His goal was nothing less than

> to attempt the most complete and thorough amendment of the entire law, to collect and revise the whole body of Roman jurisprudence, and to assemble in one book the scattered treatises of so many authors, which no one else has hitherto ventured to hope for or to expect.[3]

Under the supervision of Tribonian, the highest judicial officer in the empire, a royal commission imposed order on the mass of surviving Roman imperial edicts, deleting repetitions and resolving contradictions. The new code was ready in 529, after 14 months of work. Tribonian, 16 associates, and a staff of hundreds next set about compiling a digest of Roman judicial opinion, gleaned from a corpus of 2,000 volumes. To train law students in this material, Tribonian and his colleagues prepared a handbook called the *Institutes*, which remained in use in Europe into the twentieth century. All three of these documents were in Latin, still the official language of the empire, but a volume of new laws, called *Novels*, was issued in Greek, the language of most citizens in the east. Beginning in the sixteenth century these compilations were collectively known as the *corpus juris civilis*, or "body of civil law."

Although Justinian's legal reform was intended to be a work of conservation, it offered some significant improvements, including simpler ways to convey property and inheritances and the replacement in law of the extended family with a nuclear core of parents and children. The influence of the code was profound. In the twelfth century it spread to western Europe, where the principle of mutual interest—enshrined in the phrase "that which touches all concerns all"—provided much of the basis for Western medieval law, both religious and secular. This concept contributed to the development of

representative institutions in the West during the fourteenth century and eventually to modern parliamentary government, although Byzantium itself remained autocratic. Justinian advanced other reforms to curtail administrative corruption, eliminate the sale of offices, and reform provincial government, but his lasting monument was his *Code*, *Digest*, and *Institutes*, the most significant single body of legal documents in Western history and the primary means by which the Roman legal heritage was preserved and transmitted.

---

## ❁
## THEODORA: FROM ACTRESS TO EMPRESS

**Whether or not a woman should give an example of courage to men, is neither here nor there. At a moment of desperate danger one must do what one can. . . . Flight, even if it brings us to safety, is not in our interest. . . . The purple is the noblest shroud.[4]**

With those words, the Empress Theodora persuaded Justinian not to flee from his capital in the midst of the greatest crisis of his reign. A few days earlier the Greens and the Blues, the organizations that provided charioteers and acrobats as well as avid supporters for the games in Constantinople's great stadium, the Hippodrome, had rioted. Normally fierce opponents, they made common cause against the government in January 532, setting fire to the city and besieging the imperial palace in support of two of their number, whom the government had unsuccessfully tried to hang. Shamed into action by Theodora, Belisarius and a fellow general ordered the imperial army to suppress the rioters. Before the troops were called off, some 30,000 people had been killed; at this price Justinian's throne was secured.

Justinian had married Theodora, daughter of a bearkeeper in the employ of the Greens, seven years earlier, when he was in his early forties and she in her late twenties. Before she became Justinian's mistress and eventually his wife, she had followed her older sister onto the stage, an occupation associated with promiscuity. What little we know about these years in Theodora's life comes from the poison pen of the historian Procopius, her bitter enemy. The portrait he draws is one of a courtesan and striptease artist who indulged in frequent abortions and sexual orgies. On stage, he said, "she would often undress and parade naked among the people, with only a girdle around her groin and genitals."[5] In pursuit of a better life, she became the mistress of a bureaucrat, who took her to North Africa before tiring of her. In Alexandria she met and was probably con-

Mosaic from the church of
San Vitale in Ravenna
portraying the empress
Theodora with her
attendants. [Ronald
Sheridan/Ancient Art and
Architecture Collection]

verted by prominent Monophysite clergymen. Justinian
met her after she had returned to Constantinople and
taken up a trade spinning wool. Under Roman law a man
of Justinian's rank could not marry an actress, but this
barrier was removed on Justinian's behalf in a special
edict issued by Justinian's predecessor, his uncle Justin
I. Two years after their marriage in 525, the patriarch of
Constantinople crowned Justinian and Theodora in the
church of Hagia Sophia.

As empress, Theodora generally acquitted herself effectively. She took a special interest in the prostitutes of
the capital, at one point purchasing their freedom from
their keepers and returning each to her parents with a
gold coin. She and Justinian were quick to provide aid
to the city of Antioch after it was ravaged by an earthquake in 528 and to two other towns that were similarly
victimized the following year. She also extended monetary assistance to the churches and villages of Asia Minor. She was firm and determined in her views. In addition to her work on behalf of the Monophysites in
Constantinople, she attempted, without success, to obtain the election of a pope who would look more toler-
antly on them. Her efforts to dissuade the Persians from
breaking their treaty likewise failed, but her experience
in government prepared her to run it when Justinian was
ill with the bubonic plague in 542. The empress died of
cancer six years later; her death had a major impact on
Justinian, whose last years were devoted increasingly to
religious pursuits.

# Byzantine Economy and Society

An important part of the empire's long existence and
relative stability can be attributed to its economic and
social structure. As long as its aristocracy was service-
based, its free farmers were prosperous, and its trade
was in Byzantine hands, the empire was quite strong.
But the rise of a military aristocracy, the decline of independent farmers, and the domination of trade by Italians fatally weakened the Byzantine state.

## Economic Patterns

Much of the wealth of the Byzantine Empire came from
agriculture, especially commencing in the seventh century, when manufacturing and commerce began to decline as a result of continuing warfare and a decreasing
population. During the fourth and fifth centuries the
basic agricultural unit was a large estate worked by
hundreds of sharecroppers bound to the land as *coloni*,
or serfs—peasants who were legally bound to those estates. Coloni who fled their estates were hunted down,
returned, and enslaved. During the sixth and seventh
centuries the Persian, Slavic, and Arab invasions increased the need for higher taxes and military recruits,

## ◉ Theodora: A Hostile View ◉

*In his* Secret History, *Procopius paints this extremely unflattering portrait of the empress Theodora.*

Theodora had a lovely face and was generally beautiful, but she was short and pale—not completely, but enough to seem pallid—and her expression was always serious and frowning. All time would not be enough for anyone who tried to record most of her past life on the stage. . . . Now I must speak briefly of what she and her husband did, for they never acted separately in their life together. For a long time they gave everyone the impression that they were constantly at odds in opinions and mode of life. But later it was realized that this was deliberately cultivated by them so that their subjects, far from joining together and rebelling against them, would all have different views about them. . . .

Of her body she took more care than was necessary, though less than she herself desired. She went very early to her bath and left it very late, and after her bath she went to breakfast. After breakfast she rested. At lunch and dinner she took all kinds of foods and drinks and would sleep for long periods from morning until night, and at night until sunrise. And after this self-indulgence for such long stretches of the day, she saw fit to rule the Roman Empire. If the emperor gave orders to someone for an action against her wishes, the man's affairs stood at such a state of fortune that soon afterwards he would be dismissed from his office in ignominy and destroyed in a most shameful manner.

*Source:* Procopius, *History of the Wars*, trans. A. Cameron (Boston: Twayne, 1967), pp. 311, 323.

---

thus encouraging the development of a free peasantry that could provide the necessary manpower and shoulder the increased financial burden. By the eighth century, coloni and slaves had virtually disappeared, although there were still substantial variations in the economic status of peasants. In the tenth century, however, the large lay and ecclesiastical estates began expanding again, especially when members of the landed aristocracy acquired control of the throne in the eleventh century. Many peasants were forced into a nearly servile status, particularly in the face of staggering taxes that left them heavily in debt or bankrupt.

Nevertheless, agriculture continued to develop in the eleventh and twelfth centuries, as reflected in efforts to reclaim abandoned land and in exports of grain, wine, and meat to the west. Western European visitors in this period were impressed by the abundance of grain, olive oil, wine, and cheese. Byzantine farmers were, in fact, able to produce plentiful amounts of food despite the absence of technological improvements of the kind adopted in the west, such as wheeled iron plows and scythes. During the last centuries of the empire, however, this prosperity was destroyed when peasants became valued more as sources of military manpower than as farmers. In this period the great landowners held their estates virtually tax-free in return for providing the imperial army with troops. The gross abuse of the peasantry and the consequent decline of agriculture significantly weakened the empire, whose greatest strength had been its independent farmers.

Commerce, although less important in the Byzantine economy than agriculture, nevertheless played a significant role. Constantinople was the primary center of trade between the Middle East and Asia on the one hand and Europe on the other. In the words of a twelfth-century Jewish visitor from Spain:

> **All kinds of merchants come [to Constantinople] from Babylon . . . , from Persia and Media, from all the kingdoms of Egypt, from the land of Canaan, from the kingdom of Russia, from Hungary, from the land of the Pechenegs [north of the Black Sea], from Khazaria [northwest of the Caspian Sea], from Lombardy and from Spain.**[6]

In turn, Byzantine merchants traveled as far as East Asia and Spain in the early centuries of the empire. From Asia came Chinese silk, prized by the wealthy as an alternative to abrasive, heavy wool; spices to season and sugar to sweeten food; and jewels, pearls, and ivory, imported not only to adorn the rich but also to beautify churches. Africa provided slaves as well as ivory, and the Black Sea region was a source of wheat, furs, hides, slaves, salt, and wine. From France and Italy came textiles and weapons.

## ◉ Rich Man, Poor Man ◉

*This extract from the* Life of St. John the Almsgiver *conveys something of the gap between rich and poor at Byzantium.*

Who shall say that humble John was lying under a coverlet costing 36 nomismata whilst Christ's brethren are pinched with cold? How many are there at this minute grinding their teeth because of the cold? And how many have only a rough blanket half below and half above them so that they cannot stretch out their legs but lie shivering, rolled up like a ball of thread? How many would like to dip their bit of bread into the soupwater which my cooks throw away? How many would like even to have a sniff at the wine which is poured out in my wine-cellar? How many strangers are there at this hour in the city who have no lodging-place but lie about in the market-place, perhaps with the rain falling on them?

*Source:* J. M. Hussey, *The Byzantine World* (London: Hutchinson, 1967), pp. 128–129.

In addition to these items, many of which passed through the empire en route to more distant locations, the Byzantines exported various commodities of their own, including cotton, glassware, and enamels from Syria and timber, flax, and honey from the Balkans. The greatest Byzantine export, however, was silk, whose manufacture was first learned in the mid-sixth century, thanks to two monks who smuggled silkworm eggs out of China. To feed the worms, mulberry plantations were established, mostly in Syria. In order to prevent a small number of wealthy people from monopolizing the new industry, the different stages of production were assigned to separate guilds, each of which operated under government regulation. Until the eleventh century, manufacturing and sales were limited to Constantinople, whose people therefore benefited to some degree, whether by direct employment or by lower taxes than would otherwise have been assessed. In the eleventh and twelfth centuries silk production spread to Greece, from which the Normans kidnapped silk weavers in 1147 to create their own industry in Sicily. The Byzantine emperors also enjoyed a monopoly in the production of gold embroidery and purple dye. Among the most luxurious exports from the tenth century on were cloisonné enamel plaques, intricately crafted by jewelers who soldered gold wire onto a gold backing and then filled the tiny partitions, or *cloisons*, with glass tinted by metal oxides.

By the tenth century most of the carrying trade had been taken over by foreign merchants, particularly Italians. These merchants were increasingly exempted from the 10 percent customs tax in return for providing naval assistance to the Byzantine government. The Venetians in 1082 and the Genoese in 1261 even received their own special quarters in Constantinople with extensive trading rights throughout the empire. Thus in the later centuries of the empire much of the profit of the extensive trade network that centered on Constantinople belonged to the Italians, who manipulated the economy for their own benefit. This too was a factor that contributed to the empire's decline.

## Merchants, Artisans, and the Aristocracy

Although Constantinople was the center of Byzantium's major industries and the heart of its international trade routes, the provincial towns were the home of artisans and merchants who plied their wares in rural fairs. The greatest of these fairs was held at Thessalonica, which became second in importance only to Constantinople in the last centuries of the empire. Probably larger than its famous counterpart at Champagne in France, the Thessalonica fair attracted traders from as far as Spain and France, although most merchants were native Greeks. Merchants and artisans alike were subject to a good deal of government regulation, as were bankers, lawyers, and notaries. In general, government control was designed to protect the trade guilds in the capital from nonguild artisans and peddlers and from control by powerful landowners. State inspectors monitored the quality of manufactured articles, workers' wages, the size of the shops, and the prices of goods, all for the purpose of ensuring a stable supply at regulated prices. Guilds, in other words, existed to serve the state. Government control of the guilds declined in the twelfth century, and during the later period of the empire they became more like their counterparts in western Europe, concerned primarily with their own welfare.

The notion of service to the state, which was fundamental to the guilds as they had originally been conceived, was also at the root of the Byzantine conception of nobility. Aristocrats, typically referred to as *archons*, or magistrates, enjoyed superior social status because of their service as courtiers or officials of the government. Vertical mobility was thus a characteristic of Byzantine society, unlike the feudal societies of contemporary western Europe. Not until the tenth century did a landed, hereditary nobility emerge in the empire as the result of distinctly military needs.

Defensive requirements prompted the emperors to organize their territories into military districts, called *themes*, each of which was governed by a general in charge of civil and military affairs. Troops were recruited locally and alloted grants of land in return for military service. These grants could not be sold but passed to the soldiers' sons, who assumed responsibility for military duty. The theme system had an adverse impact on the traditional service-based aristocracy but gave rise to a new military nobility, which in general was less educated and less culturally refined than the old aristocracy.

Even then, a civil aristocracy continued to exist side by side with the new military one; the former continued to function as tax collectors, judges, and heads of government offices. A number of those who served in the civil aristocracy were eunuchs—men who had been castrated, probably for criminal behavior or after being sold by destitute parents. They were popular at court because their condition precluded them from becoming emperors and because they had no independent base of power. By the eleventh century the Byzantine aristocracy even included foreigners, notably Germans, Normans, Pechenegs, and Englishmen, who served as officers in the military. Vertical mobility may have peaked in the middle of that century when deliberate efforts were made to draw large numbers of merchants and foreigners living in Constantinople into state government.

Shortly thereafter, Byzantine society underwent a major transformation when the elite families in the military aristocracy banded together through intermarriage, forming a powerful "clan" linked to the Comnenian dynasty, which governed the empire from 1081 to 1185. Those who were not part of this clan, including eunuchs and foreigners, were forced out of the military aristocracy; some found their way into the civil aristocracy, which was henceforth deemed inferior. In the late twelfth century the latter regained supremacy when Emperor Andronicus I (1183–1185) crushed the military elite who opposed his rule. Nevertheless, the last centuries of the empire were characterized less by the rule of a civil bureaucracy than by semifeudal warlords whose power was based on family networks. In general terms, Byzantium evolved from a highly centralized state to a virtually feudal society ruled by a military aristocracy. Western Europe developed in precisely the opposite direction.

# Women in the Byzantine Empire

The social role of most Byzantine women was defined within the confines of the family. From the sixth to the late eleventh century, the nuclear family, not the clan, was at the heart of the social structure. As a result, the social position of women was generally less favorable than it had been in the late Roman era. There were, of course, exceptions, such as the empresses Theodora and Irene (797–802) or the women who defied traditional standards of propriety by becoming actresses, public dancers, or courtesans. Issues of great public import, such as the controversy over the use of religious images, were debated by women as well as men. Women could also be called on to serve in an emergency, as when the governor of Attaleia in Asia Minor ordered young women to dress in men's clothing and help defend the walls when an Arab fleet attacked about 825. For the most part, however, women spent their lives in a tightly knit patriarchal family.

An examination of Byzantine laws offers substantial insight into the status of women. Except in matters pertaining exclusively to women, for instance, they could not act as witnesses in the signing of contracts. An edict of Emperor Leo VI (886–912) explains why:

> The power to act as witnesses in the numerous assemblies of men with which they mingle, as well as taking part in public affairs, gives them the habit of speaking more freely than they ought, and, depriving them of the morality and reserve of their sex, encourages them in the exercise of boldness and wickedness.[7]

Yet an eighth-century law treated husband and wife virtually as equals with respect to property and stipulated that a widow with children control all of the property in her capacity as the new head of the family. A fourth-century law pertaining to coloni who had escaped or been abducted provided for the return of males within a period of 30 years but established a lower limit of 20 years for women, presumably reflecting a lack of worth after their childbearing years were past. By law a free woman could be punished if she had sexual intercourse with a slave, but such activity on the part of a free man was not similarly prohibited.

Beginning in the late eleventh century the nuclear core broadened into an extended family as the basis of social and legal order, perhaps because of the changing outlook of the ruling Comnenian dynasty, which found its primary political support in a kinship network. Educated, politically intelligent women became more active in court and aristocratic circles. Emperor Alexius I Comnenus (1081–1118) officially shared imperial power with his mother, Anna Dalassena. In the words of Alexius' daughter, Anna Comnena, a historian, Alexius acted as if he were his mother's servant:

> He used to say and do whatever she ordered. The emperor . . . made his right hand the executor of her orders, his ears paid heed to her words, and everything which she accepted or rejected the emperor likewise accepted or rejected. . . . Alexius possessed the external formalities of imperial power, but she held the power itself.[8]

Alexius' wife, Irene, accompanied him on his military expeditions and, like other women of the age, engaged in political intrigue. A number of prominent women, including Anna Comnena, who had a special interest in Aristotle, patronized scholarship. In the late twelfth century Empress Euphrosyne governed the empire for her husband.

The greater prominence of women was accompanied by a growing disregard for traditional standards of morality in court circles, as reflected in the open practice of adultery and incest. Among the masses, however, the traditional role of the ideal spouse as submissive and generally confined to the home undoubtedly continued. Anna Comnena, herself a major public figure, observed

that the common women of her society still wore veils when they left the privacy of their homes. In Byzantium at least, the social mores of the elite were apparently slow to influence commoners.

❦

# CONSTANTINOPLE, GLORY OF THE BOSPORUS

Constantinople is located on the boundary between Europe and Asia, on a hilly peninsula between the Sea of Marmora and the Golden Horn. With a 7-mile-long inlet and a natural harbor, it had a population of perhaps 1 million in the time of Justinian. Others lived in the suburbs, which comprised outlying commercial centers, residential villages, and, along the shores of the Bosporus, resorts for the wealthy. The city was home to a rich amalgam of peoples, including Greeks, Italians, Jews, North Africans, Syrians, Armenians, Goths, and descendants of Hittites and Lydians. Among its many tongues, Greek was the normal language of daily discourse, although the imperial government and the law courts used Latin. Beginning in the early fifth century the city was protected by mammoth walls 15 feet thick and 40 feet high, stretching the length of the city.

Constantine had originally planned the capital in im-

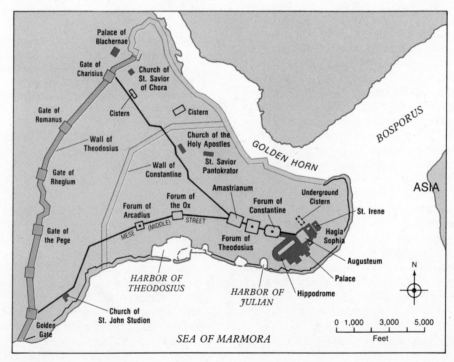

*8.2 Constantinople in Justinian's Time*

The church of Hagia Sophia was completed in A.D. 535; the minarets were added 1,000 years later by the Turks. [Wim Swaan]

itation of Rome, to the point of including seven hills within the original walls. At the heart of the city was the Augusteum, a great open square, like the Roman Forum, around which were grouped the Church of Hagia Sophia ("Holy Wisdom"), the public baths, the Senate House, and the entrances to the Hippodrome (a large oval arena) and the royal palace. The palace consisted of assorted buildings, courtyards, and gardens commissioned by various emperors and built on terraces that extended down toward the sea. A broad avenue stretched westward from the Augusteum to the Golden Gate; a second avenue branched off to the city's other principal entry, the Gate of Charisius, in the northwest. The rest of the city was a web of narrow lanes lined with houses, shops, monasteries, and hundreds of churches. The greatest of these were Hagia Sophia, where emperors were crowned, and the Church of the Holy Apostles, where they were buried.

The homes of the wealthy were multistoried structures built around circular inner courtyards, many of which had fountains. More modest homes might have simple patios, and those of the poor, constructed of wood, were constantly threatened by fire. The destitute,

often chronically unemployed, slept in the streets unless they were fortunate enough to find temporary shelter in the hostels, hospitals, and orphanages run by the churches or under arcades and other public structures kept open by the government during the winter. The impoverished could usually find food in church kitchens, although beggars were nevertheless common. All registered householders in the city could obtain bread free or at a nominal cost, and price controls were placed on other basic foods with the exception of fish, which could not be hoarded. Distribution of free bread ended, however, in 618 when the Persians conquered Egypt, a major grain supplier. The government's interest in maintaining stable food prices stemmed from the need to prevent riots, not humanitarian concerns.

The old Church of Hagia Sophia was destroyed by the rioting Greens and Blues in 532, but its replacement, commissioned by Justinian, became the city's greatest monument. The church's distinctive feature is a soaring dome resting on four arches, a feat made possible by the use of pendentives—spherical triangles that distribute the dome's weight to the arches. The dome of the Roman Pantheon, in contrast, rested on round walls.

Though the exterior of Hagia Sophia was plain, the interior was adorned with sumptuous mosaics and gold, silver, and variegated marble. Lighting was provided through numerous windows, including a ring of 40 at the base of the dome, as well as 1,000 lamps, the effect of which was spiritually uplifting. As Procopius testified, "The church is singularly full of light and sunshine; you would declare that the place is not lighted by the sun from without, but that the rays are produced within itself."[9] Hagia Sophia, he added, "overtops the whole country." It was an architectural jewel and an appropriate focal point for the Byzantine Empire. After the city was conquered by the Ottoman Turks in 1453, the church's appearance was permanently altered to meet the needs of a new faith, Islam.

## Byzantine Christianity and Culture

In contrast to the largely secular culture of the modern West, Byzantine society was framed in religious terms. Conflict between church and state in the modern sense was impossible because one Christian emperor ruled, in theory, both civilian and ecclesiastical government in a single Christian commonwealth. This form of government is usually referred to as *Caesaropapism*, a term that underscores the unity of civil and ecclesiastical power, of emperor and patriarch, in harmony with God's rule over a universal heavenly kingdom. Thus the Byzantine ideal might be summed up as one church, one creed, one sovereign.

In reality, the emperor did not possess a priestly title, nor was he able to administer the sacraments. Throughout Byzantine history emperors were periodically challenged by ecclesiastical figures, particularly patriarchs (the highest ecclesiastical officials in the Byzantine church), and religious dissidents, such as the Monophysites. No emperor was powerful enough to alter doctrine or liturgy arbitrarily, although the imperial position entitled him to mediate religious disputes. Caesaropapism did not, then, give the emperor absolute power in religious affairs. Yet despite the practical limitations on an emperor's religious authority, the ideal of a Christian emperor ruling a Christian state remained a powerful one throughout the empire's existence.

Byzantine Christianity was very conservative, with a pronounced emphasis on tradition, liturgy, and ecclesiastical pomp. All aspects of worship, from the ritual of the service to the design and decoration of churches, were intended to promote a sense of mystery and otherworldliness. Aids to worship, such as religious images and relics, were accorded special importance; purported

An ivory panel depicting the Byzantine emperor Constantine VII being crowned by Christ. [Giraudon/Art Resource]

pieces of the true cross, thorns from the crown of Jesus, and Mary's robe and shroud were especially valued. Not only was there a trade in relics, but devout Christians sometimes stole them for their churches. In light of the emphasis on otherworldly values, ascetic living was highly regarded, and monks were typically held in great esteem.

## Religious Controversy

Given the importance of religion in Byzantine society, theological disputes were virtually unavoidable. One of the most serious of these controversies erupted around 726 when Emperor Leo III (717–741), apparently concerned about divine anger when a volcano erupted in the Aegean Sea, banned the use of religious icons, such as pictures or statues of Christ and the saints, on the grounds that they were graven images. This was the view already held by Jews and Muslims, but long before the eighth century, religious images had become commonplace in both western and eastern Christendom, largely for devotional reasons but to a lesser degree as political symbols and commercial objects. For instance, when Avars and Persians besieged Constantinople in 626, the government used icons to inspire the people to defend their city.

Leo's ban incited a furious debate, known as the Iconoclastic Controversy, that lasted until 787 and then was renewed between 813 and 842. The monks in particular opposed the prohibition even in the face of persecution; some were executed, exiled, maimed, or publicly ridiculed by having to parade through the Hippodrome hand in hand with a woman. A church council upheld the iconoclastic position in 754, but 33 years later, under the influence of Empress Irene, another council accepted icons as a channel of divine grace on the condition that they be revered but not worshiped. Another empress, Theodora, widow of Theophilus, settled the issue in 843 in yet another council that reaffirmed the use of religious images.

Because the popes, the leaders of the western church, opposed the Byzantine attempt to abolish images, relations between the empire and the papacy were strained. Other factors contributed to a deteriorating relationship, including an imperial decision during the Iconoclastic Controversy to transfer ecclesiastical jurisdiction over the Balkans, southern Italy, and Sicily from the pope to the patriarch of Constantinople. There was theological conflict too when the Latin church modified the traditional creed to stipulate that the Holy Spirit "proceeds" from the Father "and from the Son" (*filioque*). In Byzantine eyes the added term *filioque* had no biblical basis and was thus unacceptable. The controversy culminated in 1054 when each side excommunicated the other, causing a schism that has never been healed. At root, however, the fundamental cause of the breach was not theology but conflicting views over the respective roles of emperor and pope in the church.

## Religion and Culture

Byzantine culture was shaped largely by religious convictions and reverence for classical antiquity. Throughout the empire's history, the educated laity were typically trained in the Greek classics, though always within a Christian framework. Among the learned, there was keen interest in the relative merits of Plato and Aristotle, with the latter attracting the greater support. Virtually all students studied the Homeric epics, and advanced studies could be pursued in philosophy, law, and medicine.

The importance of the classical tradition encouraged many writers to imitate its literary forms, such as history, satire, letters, orations, and epigrams (short poems, usually witty or barbed in tone). Byzantine writers did not produce secular, lyrical poetry of the kind written in classical Greece by Sappho, nor were they very interested in classical drama; classical tragedies were read but not performed, perhaps because of church opposition. Generally, Byzantine authors were imitative rather than creative. This conservative tone was evident in their interest in grammars, encyclopedias, and commentaries. Some literary forms, such as sermons, hymns, and the lives of saints, were intended as religious pedagogy and composed for common people; those who were illiterate could have such works read to them. Although saints' lives extolled virtue, piety, and steadfastness, they usually contained more than a little adventure and psychological drama and can still make stimulating reading. One of the finest forms of Byzantine literature was liturgical poetry, which set religious verse to music.

The most characteristic Byzantine art form was the mosaic, which, like most Byzantine literature, blended classical and Christian influences. The best mosaics typically adorned the curved surfaces of domes, semidomes, and apses and were placed to take maximum advantage of the limited light in churches. Mosaicists tilted the glass, ceramic, marble, or shell cubes that made up their pictures to create a shimmering effect. The artists illustrated both sacred and secular themes, although the advocates of iconoclasm wanted religious art restricted to abstract symbols, animals, and plants, much as in contemporary Islamic art.

Byzantine artists were also fond of painting devotional images on panels. These images were rendered

**An icon from the seventh century showing Christ as Pantocrator, or ruler of all. [Ronald Sheridan/Ancient Art and Architecture Collection]**

according to strict formal rules but often beautifully reflect the spiritual devotion of Orthodox Christians. The figures in the icons are traditionally painted frontally, to create the impression that the subjects are communicating with the viewer about the mysteries of the Christian faith.

The prevailing conservatism in the empire is reflected in art forms, which show only modest changes from the age of Justinian to the fall of the empire in the fifteenth century. Almost from the beginning, however, this empire, so rooted in the classical and Christian traditions, had been challenged by the new religion that was finally to overthrow it, Islam.

Main apse of the cathedral in Cefalu, Sicily, dominated by the figure of Christ as Pantocrator. [SEF/Art Resource]

## The Arabs

"There are," reflected the patriarch of Constantinople in the early tenth century, "two lordships, that of the Muslims and that of the Byzantines, which stand above all lordship on earth and shine out like the two mighty beacons in the firmament."[10] The new religion, Islam, had attained stature as a world religion long before the patriarch wrote. By 750, thanks in large measure to the appeal of its vision of society and the religious commitment of its adherents, Islam had spread from its homeland in Arabia into Persia and through the Middle East and North Africa as far as the Iberian peninsula.

The Arabs who carried the Islamic message from Spain to the Indus were Semites who lived along the

## ◉ In Defense of Icons ◉

*John of Damascus, an eighth-century monk, wrote this argument in favor of icons around 730.*

For the invisible things of God since the creation of the world are made visible through images. We see images in creation which remind us faintly of God, as when, for instance, we speak of the holy and adorable Trinity, imaged by the sun, or light, or burning rays, or by a running fountain. . . .

Worship is the symbol of veneration and of honor. Let us understand that there are different degrees of worship. . . .

Of old, God the incorporeal and uncircumscribed was never depicted. Now, however, when God is seen clothed in flesh, and conversing with men, I make an image of the God whom I see. I do not worship matter, I worship the God of matter, who became matter for my sake, . . . who worked out my salvation through matter. I will not cease from honoring that matter which works my salvation. I venerate it, though not as God. . . . Is not the most holy book of the Gospels matter? Is not the blessed table matter which gives us the Bread of Life? Are not the gold and silver matter out of which crosses and altar-plate and chalices are made? And before all these things, is not the body and blood of our Lord matter? Either do away with the veneration and worship due to all these things, or submit to the tradition of the Church in the worship of images, honoring God and his friends.

*Source: St. John Damascene on Holy Images,* trans. M. H. Allies (London: Burns & Oates, 1898), pp. 10–17 passim.

shores of the Arabian peninsula, in the southern high-lands, and in the oases that dotted the rest of the land. Pre-Islamic Arabia had never been politically unified. Economically, the lives of its inhabitants depended on the camel, which facilitated trade between the Mediter-ranean and India. Camel caravans had played an impor-tant role in the spice trade during the Hellenistic and Roman eras and were still important in the sixth century, when Muhammad was born.

Mecca, Muhammad's native city, was strategically lo-cated at the crossroads of the caravan routes from Pal-estine and Syria to Yemen, at the southern end of the peninsula, and from Mesopotamia to Ethiopia, in eastern Africa. There was little manufacturing or agriculture in the area, but Mecca itself was a pilgrimage center, where visitors came to worship assorted deities; the main sanc-tuary housed idols representing some 360 gods, includ-ing Allah (*al-ilah* means "the god"), a creator deity. Pil-grims, of course, contributed to the local economy, so commerce and religion were closely entwined.

## Muhammad and Islam

The precise date of Muhammad's birth is unknown, but it was probably about 570. Orphaned while a youngster, Muhammad was raised by an uncle. He worked for a while as a shepherd, lived with the nomadic Bedouins, and traveled with caravans on the Syria-Yemen route. This experience served him in good stead when the wealthy widow Khadija, who was engaged in the caravan trade, employed him to manage her business. When Mu-hammad was about 25, he married her; they subse-quently had several children and an apparently happy relationship.

A devout man, Muhammad regularly went into the hills near Mecca to pray, and there, in a cave on Mount Hira in 610, he heard a voice proclaim that he was the messenger of God and was to recite God's word. Ac-cording to Muslim tradition, the voice was that of the archangel Gabriel. For some three years, however, Mu-hammad was not fully certain of his calling, although Khadija was sympathetic and became his first convert. Others followed, including members of his own family and younger sons of prominent Mecca families. Most, however, were young people of modest background. In general they were persons sympathetic to the traditional ideals of family solidarity, honor, and generosity, as distinct from the profit-oriented values of the wealthy merchants.

The religion Muhammad founded is known as Islam ("submission"). A Muslim is one who submits to the will of Allah (God) and who fulfills the five duties known as the Pillars of Islam. The first of these is the sincere profession of the *Shahada*, a simple credal statement: "I bear witness that there is no god but God; I bear witness that Muhammad is the messenger of God." In time Mu-hammad professed strict monotheism, although at the outset of his ministry he accepted three traditional Ara-bic deities as lesser beings who could intercede with God on behalf of believers; he later renounced this view, the expression of which became known as the "satanic verses." Muhammad rejected the Christian doctrine of the Trinity, even while according respect to Jesus as a prophet:

> **The Messiah, Jesus son of Mary, was only the Messenger of God, and His Word that He committed to Mary, and a Spirit from Him. So believe in God and His Messengers, and say not, 'Three.' . . . God is only one God.**[11]

BYZANTIUM AND ISLAM: THE EARLY CENTURIES

| Byzantines | Muslims |
|---|---|
| Constantine makes Byzantium his capital (330) | |
| Age of Justinian (527–565) | |
| ● Code (529) | |
| ● Hagia Sophia (532–537) | |
| | Muhammad's vision (610) |
| | Hejira (622) |
| | Origins of Sunni-Shi'ite split (late 650s) |
| | Umayyad caliphate (661–750) |
| Iconoclastic Controversy (726–787) | Invasion of Iberia begins (710) |
| | Abbasid caliphate (750–1258) |
| | Spain breaks away (756) |
| | Moroccan independence (788) |
| | Tunisian independence (800) |
| Iconoclastic Controversy renewed (813–842) | |
| | Beginning of Fatimid rule in Egypt (969) |
| Schism between Byzantine and Roman churches (1054) | Abbasids become puppets of the Seljuk Turks (1055) |
| Comnenian dynasty (1081–1185) | Mongols overrun Baghdad (1258) |

Similar in most of these attributes to the God of Judaism and Christianity, Allah is eternal and infallible, the Light of the Heavens and the Earth, as well as the creator and ultimate judge of all people. As his servant, Muhammad was the last and greatest—the "Seal"—of the prophets, whose number included Adam, Abraham, Moses, Alexander the Great, and Jesus. Four of the prophets were transmitters of divine revelation: Moses in the Torah, David in the Psalms, Jesus in the Gospels, and Muhammad in the Koran.

The second of the Pillars is *Salat*, formal prayer at five specified times each day. Following ritual purification that involves washing, worshipers face Mecca and together move through a cycle of standing, bowing, prostration, and sitting. *Salat* often occurs in a mosque, an Arabic word meaning "place of prostration." Each mosque has a niche indicating the direction of Mecca, a raised pulpit from which sermons are preached, and, normally, a minaret from which the call to prayer is made.

Almsgiving, in the form of a mandatory tax called the *Zakat* ("purification"), is the third Pillar. It renders the rest of the believer's property religiously acceptable and is a vivid symbol of the strong sense of community among Muslims. In effect, it is viewed as a loan to God, who will repay it many times over. The fourth Pillar consists of fasting during the lunar month of Ramadan, during which time no food, drink, medicine, or sensual pleasure can be taken during daylight hours.

The final Pillar is the *Hajj*, a pilgrimage to Mecca, if circumstances allow, to visit the Kaaba, a temple that Muslims believe was built by Abraham and his son Ishmael. Some Muslims regard *Jihad* (literally, "exertion" in God's service) as a sixth Pillar. It can take two forms: the greater jihad involves an internal spiritual struggle, and the lesser jihad entails physical conflict against the enemies of Islam.

Muslims believe that the Koran (*Qur'an* in Arabic), the sacred text of Islam, contains the word of God as revealed to Muhammad. The text in its present form, which is comparable in length to the New Testament, was established about 650 by Muhammad's companions. Proper recitation of the Koran, according to Muslims, results in a special sense of divine presence. Within its pages are found social as well as religious maxims, including instructions about inheritance, dowries, and marriage. Polygamy is permitted, though the number of wives cannot exceed four. Men are generally treated as superior to women, and slavery is allowed, subject to restrictions on how slaves can be treated and when they should be freed.

> **Those your right hands own who seek emancipation, contract with them accordingly, if you know some good in them; and give them of the wealth of God that He has given you. And constrain not your slave girls to prostitution, if they desire to live in chastity.[12]**

Further guidance was expressed in the *Hadith*, traditional sayings based on recollections of Muhammad's words and acts; thousands of these have been collected. As a guide to godly living, Muslims created the *Shari'a*, or "way" of the believer, including laws governing behavior and belief.

## Sunnis, Shi'ites, and Sufis

Muhammad's teachings incited substantial opposition at Mecca, and in July 622 he moved some 200 miles north,

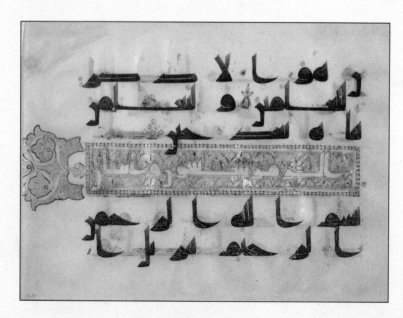

A page from the Koran, written in Kulic script. [Freer Gallery of Art, Smithsonian Institution]

to Yathrib, later called Medina. This event became known as the *Hejira*, or migration, the date of which became the first year of the Muslim era. There he remained, gathering followers and launching expeditions against Meccan caravans, until he was powerful enough to return to Mecca in 630. He died at Medina from a fever in June 632.

No provisions had been made for a successor, but upon news of Muhammad's death, his key advisers agreed that his closest friend, Abu Bakr (c. 573–634), should be the new leader, or caliph ("deputy") of the Prophet. Abu Bakr and the caliphs who succeeded him had no status as prophets but functioned as head of the Arab state, commander of the army, supreme judge, and leader of public worship. During his brief tenure as caliph, Abu Bakr imposed unity on most of the Arabian people, many of whom had reverted to their independent ways after Muhammad's death. His army successfully challenged Byzantine control of Palestine, but it was left to his successor, Umar (634–644), to conquer Jerusalem. Umar also won a series of brilliant victories against the Byzantines and Persians that carried Islam into Syria, Iraq, Iran, and Egypt before he was assassinated in 644. The new caliph, Uthman (644–656), continued the militant policy of early Islam, sending his armies across North Africa to Tunisia and northward into Armenia and Afghanistan. Muslim fleets defeated the powerful Byzantine navy, captured Cyprus, and plundered Rhodes. Uthman is primarily remembered, however, for appointing the commission that established the definitive version of the Koran. He too was slain by assassins, among them Abu Bakr's son, in 656.

The rebellious Muslims in Egypt who were responsible for Uthman's murder successfully pressed for the election of Ali (656–661), Muhammad's son-in-law and cousin, as the new caliph. His authority was challenged, however, by Muawiya (died 680), the governor of Syria and a member of the powerful Umayyad clan, whose army fought Ali's forces on the banks of the upper Euphrates River in 657. When both sides agreed to arbitration, radical idealists broke with Ali and formed their own party, the Kharijites ("seceders"). The arbitration failed, but in the aftermath of Ali's assassination by a Kharijite in 661, Muawiya had no serious rival and was proclaimed caliph at Jerusalem; he ruled, however, from Damascus in Syria.

The modern division of Islam into two main branches, the Shi'ites and the Sunni, had its origins in Ali's claim that he had been designated Muhammad's successor before the prophet died. Ali's party, or *shi'ah*, supported this claim. When Muawiya died in 680, Ali's son, Husayn, led the party in a rebellion, only to be massacred with his family by Umayyad troops the same year. In Shi'ite eyes, he was a martyr, and his death is reenacted each year in a type of passion play. Henceforth Shi'ites have accepted suffering as the characteristic lot of the true Muslim.

The core of the Shi'ite movement is the conviction that Ali was the true successor of Muhammad and thus the first *imam*, or caliph. Some Shi'ites expand the *Shahada* ("creed") by adding the phrase "and Ali is his comrade." Most Shi'ites eventually came to believe in a succession of 12 imams extending from Ali to Muhammad al-Muntazar (died 878), who reportedly disappeared into a cave, is still living, and will someday return as a savior (*Mahdi*). Until that time, Shi'ites accept only the laws and beliefs found in the Koran or set forth by a true imam, who is the beneficiary of divine revelation. In contrast, most Muslims, known as Sunni, follow the tradition (*sunnah*) established by Muhammad and the Koran; they regard the latter as complete and do not attribute special religious knowledge to their leaders. Shi'ites believe that a Muslim can perform the pilgrimage to Mecca by proxy or can substitute a visit to the tomb of a Shi'ite saint, such as Ali.

As in the case of early Christianity, some devout Muslims were attracted to an ascetic life, characterized by solitary meditation, fasting, prayer, lengthy vigils, and poverty. Some of the devout were content to wear simple woolen frocks and soon became known as Sufis, after the Arabic word *suf* ("wool"). The Sufis were mystics whose ultimate goal was union with God through love and the purification of the soul. An important means to this end is the special remembrance of God by repeating his 99 "most beautiful names," whether in a rhythmic chant, in silence accompanied by special breathing exercises, or in a dance that culminates in a swoon. In the tenth century the Sufis began organizing brotherhoods, each of which was led by a master who taught disciples and inducted them into the order. As in the case of Christian monasticism, most orders had affiliated lay members who periodically participated in the orders' religious worship. The Sufis played a major role in the spread and popularization of Islam, in part because of their willingness to incorporate local customs and beliefs into Muslim orthodoxy.

## The Umayyads at Damascus

Between 661 and 750 the Umayyad family provided the caliphs who ruled the Islamic world from their capital at Damascus. This period was marked by further Arab conquests. As caliph, Muawiya continued to battle the Byzantines, especially in eastern Asia Minor. Between 674 and 678 his troops besieged Constantinople itself, but the fortifications proved too formidable. The Arabs returned again in 717–718, only to be foiled by new defenses, a harsh winter, disease, and "Greek fire," a fearsome substance (possibly made with quicklime or distilled petroleum) that ignited on contact with water.

## ◉ Sufi Mysticism ◉

*The poet Hafiz uses the analogy of a bird to express his search for mystical reunion with the divine.*

My soul is as a sacred bird, the highest heaven its nest,
Fretting within its body-bars, it finds on earth its nest;
When rising from its dusty heap this bird of mine shall soar
'Twill find upon the lofty gate the nest it had before.
The Sidrah [Tree of Paradise] shall receive my bird, when it has winged its way,
And on the Empyrean's top, my falcon's foot shall stay,
Over the ample field of earth is fortune's shadow cast,
Where upon wings and pennons borne this bird of mine has passed.
No spot in the two worlds it owns, above the sphere its goal,
Its body from the quarry is, from ''No Place'' is its soul.
'Tis only in the glorious world my bird its splendor shows,
The rosy bowers of Paradise its daily food bestows.

*Source:* E. A. Reed, *Persian Literature: Ancient and Modern* (Chicago: Griggs, 1893), p. 329.

The assault on the city was a traumatic experience, as reflected in the reaction of the Byzantine patriarch:

> **Such dangers our city had never before experienced, and not our city only, but the whole world that is inhabited by Christians. For it may be acknowledged without any doubt that Christ's entire flock would have been in the same peril as ourselves had the godless Saracens [Muslims] attained the goal of their expedition against us [the capture of Constantinople].[13]**

By the early eighth century all of North Africa was in Muslim hands, and the first raids across the Strait of Gibraltar into the southern tip of Iberia came in 710 and 711. Because the peninsula was already in a state of political chaos, it fell completely into Muslim hands before the end of the decade. With their allies, the Berber tribesmen of North Africa, the Arabs crossed the Pyrenees into the Frankish kingdom in 718. From 720 until 759 they occupied the town of Narbonne, which served as a base for plundering expeditions. Islamic penetration north of the Pyrenees might have been more extensive had it not been for the bitter fighting that erupted between the Arabs and the Berbers in Spain and North Africa between 734 and 742 and factional struggles among the Arabs themselves. These factors were more important than the military skills of the Franks in stopping further Muslim expansion in Europe.

In the meantime, Arab armies resumed their push into Asia, reaching as far as the Indus River. In the early eighth century they established themselves in such places as Turkestan, Baluchistan, and the northwestern corner of India (now Pakistan), which to this day remains Muslim. Not until the eleventh century, however, did Turks from central Asia establish Islam as a major force in much of the Indian subcontinent.

The empire was now so extensive that the Umayyads organized it into five states, each of which was governed by a viceroy appointed by the caliph in Damascus: Iraq and the Muslim lands to the east; central and southern Arabia; eastern Asia Minor, Armenia, and the Caucasus; Egypt; and the rest of North Africa and the Iberian peninsula. The speed of the Arab conquest was such that the conquerors had to rely on existing native bureaucrats to administer the subject areas; in Spain the Jews were particularly useful in this regard. Administrative effectiveness was undermined in the later years of Umayyad rule by viceroys who tried to govern from Damascus, as well as by viceroys and subordinate provincial governors who siphoned tax revenues into their personal coffers. The tax structure itself became a major source of trouble. All free non-Muslims paid a poll (head) tax, and those with land paid a tax on it as well, whereas Arabs outside of Arabia did not. Converts to Islam were freed from the poll tax but not the land tax, a situation that caused them bitterly to resent Arab landowners in their midst.

In the end, Umayyad power was undermined by a variety of factors, including the problematic tax structure. No less important was the disaffection caused by the specter of an opulent court in Damascus, which of-

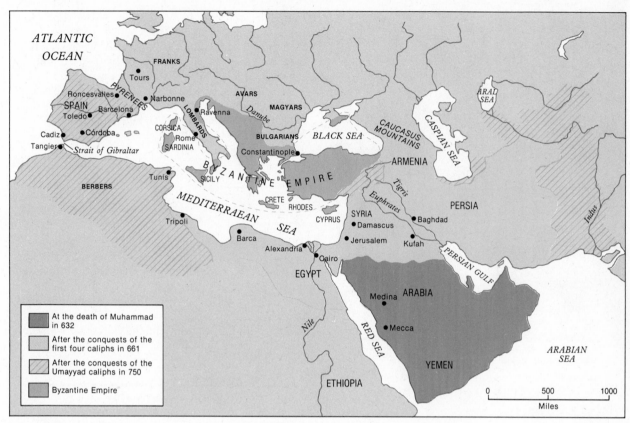

*8.3 The Expansion of Islam*

fended traditional Muslims. Shi'ites, who were strong in Iran and Iraq, and Kharijites were implacable enemies of the Umayyads. So too were the Abbasids, who claimed to be the heirs of Ali and who traced their ancestry to Muhammad's uncle. The Abbasids revolted in 747, overran Iraq in 749, and completed their conquest by taking Damascus the following year. Most members of the Umayyad family were ruthlessly slaughtered, although one fled to Spain and founded a caliphate at Córdoba. The Abbasid leader, Abu al-Abbas, who was now caliph over most Muslim areas, moved the capital to Kufah in Iraq; his brother and successor, Abu Ja'far al-Mansur (754–775), built a new capital at Baghdad.

## The Abbasids

Politically, the years of the Abbasid caliphate (750–1258) were marked by factional intrigue, violence, and the decentralization of power. Abu al-Abbas (750–754), the founder of the caliphate, referred to himself as "the Bloodletter," an apt sobriquet in view of his treatment of the deposed Umayyads. Many of his successors were no less vicious in executing Shi'ites who challenged their authority. Al-Abbas felt it necessary to surround himself with several thousand bodyguards. In the ninth century Turkish slaves, presumably more loyal to their employers, were recruited as guards, yet even they turned against the caliph, al-Mutawakkil, whom they assassinated in 861. Imperial ministers and generals openly intrigued to manipulate the succession while the caliphs themselves enjoyed court living as avidly as had the Umayyads. With tens of thousands of staff members and servants, the palace complexes in Baghdad were centers of waste, inefficiency, and decadence, their cultural splendor notwithstanding.

Under these circumstances it is no surprise that the Abbasid period was characterized by the decentralization of power and the breakup of the empire. Spain had gone its own way when the Umayyad prince, Abd al-Rahman (756–788), established an independent caliphate at Córdoba. Like its counterpart in Baghdad, it became a brilliant cultural center, only to succumb to turbulent palace guards in the mid-tenth century. The caliphate of Córdoba then fragmented into smaller Muslim states, making it easier for the Christians to begin their reconquest of the peninsula. Morocco broke away from Baghdad in 788 and was ruled by Shi'ites for two

**Central dome of the mosque at Córdoba, Spain. The dome is supported by a series of intercrossing arches. [Arxiu MAS, Barcelona]**

centuries before succumbing to the Córdoban caliphate; Tunisia became independent in 800 and in the ensuing century conquered Malta, Sicily, and Sardinia in addition to plundering the coasts of France and the Italian peninsula. Egypt pursued its own course beginning in the mid-ninth century and in 969 fell under the dominion of the Shi'ite Fatimid family of Tunisia, who ruled from the new capital of Cairo. By 1000 the Fatimid empire embraced North Africa, Syria, and much of the Arabian peninsula, but it too was undermined by inept caliphs and rebellious slave armies in the eleventh century, making possible the modest gains of Christian crusaders in the late 1090s.

The story was much the same in the east, where the aristocratic Samanid family established an independent dynasty in parts of Persia and central Asia. Iraq itself was badly shaken by revolutionary upheavals and revolts by African slaves in the late ninth century. In 945 Baghdad was occupied by the Buyids, a Shi'ite clan from Iran. For a century thereafter the Abbasid caliphs were mere puppets of the Buyids, whose rulers claimed a variety of titles, including "emir of emirs" and "king of kings." They were in turn overthrown in 1055 by the Seljuk Turks, originally from Turkestan. These new invaders also found it useful to maintain the Abbasids as figureheads, but the caliphate was extinguished in 1258 when Mongol invaders overran Baghdad and murdered the last caliph. From Baghdad the Turkish sultans ruled

Iraq, Syria, and Iran, but not until the sixteenth century would another group of Turks, the Ottomans, extend their sway throughout most of North Africa. Never, however, would any Muslim caliph exercise sovereignty on the scale of the Umayyads in the early eighth century. Despite its checkered political history, the Abbasid period is important because it marks the end of Arab dominance in the Muslim world and the emergence of Islam as an international religion.

# Islamic Civilization

The driving force in Islamic civilization was the teachings of Muhammad, but wherever Islam spread, it demonstrated a remarkable ability to assimilate native cultures. The result was the creation of a distinctive civilization, with major centers of culture in Damascus, Baghdad, Cairo, Córdoba, and, later, Delhi and Constantinople. Both the economy and the culture of the Islamic world had a substantial impact on the peoples of Europe and Asia.

## Economic Life

As a merchant himself, Muhammad gave Islam a keen appreciation of commerce and, indeed, of all forms of productive activity, provided that they were carried out in an honest, charitable spirit. Sayings attributed to him in the Hadith describe merchants as "the couriers of the horizons and God's trusted servants on earth," who, if honest, "will stand with the martyrs on the Day of Judgment." Tilling and sheepherding were occupations also created and blessed by God, but "the best of gain is from honorable trade and from a man's work with his own hands." Muhammad condemned moneychangers, prostitutes, hoarders, greedy merchants, and lenders who charged usury (interest).[14] Similar ethical maxims are found in contemporary Christian teaching and underscore the common attempt to curtail acquisitiveness and dishonesty on the one hand while instilling thrift and humaneness on the other. Yet contemporary Christianity did not place a comparable positive emphasis on commerce per se.

Muslim trade routes eventually extended from the Pyrenees to the Indus, but Muslim traders also traveled far beyond the boundaries of Islamic states, ranging as far as India, Southeast Asia, and China. Others crossed the Sahara into western and central Africa or sailed down the east coast of Africa as far as Kilwa (in modern Tanzania). They traded as well with the peoples of Byzantium and with western Europe and Russia, although much of this commerce was in the hands of Jewish and

Christian merchants. Most of the trade with Europe and Asia was undertaken by ship; however, the primary route with China, the "Great Silk Way," ran overland through northern Persia and Turkestan. Commercial growth was enhanced by the fact that non-Muslim merchants could live and work in Islamic states. Around 1285, for instance, the sultan of Egypt formally welcomed merchants "who come to his realm, as to the garden of Eden, by whatever gate they may choose to enter, from Iraq, from Persia, from Asia Minor, from the Hijaz [in Arabia], from India, and from China."[15] The fact that there were no internal tariff barriers in the Muslim world between the eighth and twelfth centuries also helped foster commercial expansion. So too did the development of bills of exchange (checks) and joint-stock companies, which enabled many people to invest in business activities, thus sharing both profits and risks.

Manufacturing in the Islamic world was extensive and varied. Linen, cotton, wool, and silk were produced, as were glass, ceramics, many varieties of metals, soaps, dyes, and perfume. Some areas were renowned for their products: Córdoba for its leather, Egypt for glass and linens, Toledo and Damascus for steel, Kufah for silk kerchiefs, Baghdad and Samarkand for porcelain, and Bukhara (in central Asia) for carpets. The Muslims learned how to make paper from the Chinese in the eighth century and subsequently founded their own mills from Samarkand to Spain. The widespread availability of paper was a stimulus to scholarship and encouraged the growth of publishing and bookstores, typically adjacent to the main mosques.

# Islamic Society

"The noblest among you in the eyes of God is the most pious," said Muhammad, "for God is omniscient and well informed." This principle could serve as a new basis for social valuation, in contrast to the traditional Arab recognition of an aristocracy based on birth and family ties. A similar position is expressed in the New Testament, but as Islam and Christianity evolved, each accommodated notions of a social hierarchy. Muhammad himself was reported to have given preeminence to the Arabs: "The best of mankind are the Arabs." "Love the Arabs," he insisted, "for three reasons: because I am an Arab, because the Koran is in Arabic, and because the inhabitants of Paradise speak Arabic."[16]

During the Umayyad period, Muslims recognized four social classes, the first of which comprised Arab Muslims, the de facto aristocracy. The government in Damascus recorded their names in a special registry and gave each Arab Muslim a regular payment from the imperial treasury. Initially, the new garrison towns, such as Cairo and Kufah, were reserved for them alone. Arab women were discouraged from marrying non-Arabs.

Non-Arab Muslims made up the second class. Because they typically affiliated themselves with an Arab clan or family, they were known as *mawali*, or clients. By the early eighth century, not only were they more numerous than the Arabs, but they resented their inferior status, especially since some of them were more educated than their Arab counterparts. Some mawali reacted by embracing Shi'ite views, while others claimed to have become Arabs through clientage. In time the Arabs of the conquered lands tended to intermarry with the mawali, giving rise to a broader definition of an Arab as one who spoke Arabic and embraced Islam.

The third class in Islamic society was comprised of free non-Muslims, primarily Jews, Christians, and Zoroastrians. Such persons, known as dhimmis, or covenanted people, received personal security and substantial local autonomy in return for accepting Muslim rule and paying additional taxes. Dhimmis were free to worship according to their own rites, engage in business activities, own property, and for the most part govern themselves through their own laws and in their own courts. They could not hold public office, bear arms, testify in court against Muslims, dress in Muslim fashion, or use saddles on their horses. One such pact, dating from about the seventh century, specifically prohibited missionary activity: "We shall not manifest our religion publicly nor convert anyone to it. We shall not prevent any of our kin from entering Islam if they wish it." The same pact also made the dhimmis' inferior status very apparent: "We shall show respect toward the Muslims, and we shall rise from our seats when they wish to sit."[17] For the most part the dhimmis were treated with more tolerance and respect than medieval European Christians accorded Jews. Repression did occur periodically, however, as when the dhimmis' commercial success threatened the Muslims, when they were suspected of collaborating with either the crusaders or the Mongols, or when they ignored the terms of their covenant.

Slaves comprised the lowest class in Islamic society. Although Muhammad had reservations about slavery, he accepted its legality. A saying in the Hadith may reveal his true feelings: "The worst of men are those who buy and sell men."[18] Muslims could not be enslaved, although conversion did not automatically bring manumission. Masters and slaves could not marry, but the former could take slaves as concubines. The children of such a union were free, and their mother enjoyed a special status, could not be sold, and was liberated when her master died. Children of slave parents, however, were born slaves.

The Islamic economy was not heavily dependent on slaves, as in the Roman Empire or the southern United States before the American civil war, but large numbers of slaves were traded and used primarily in the military or as servants. Some caliphs were the sons of slave mothers. The wealthiest Muslims possessed thousands of slaves. Captured prisoners were enslaved, but many slaves were purchased in slave markets. There were slaves of nearly all races and from a wide variety of places, including Spain, Greece, sub-Saharan Africa, India, and central Asia. Their numbers included Goths, Berbers, Iranians, Turks, and Armenians. So plentiful and varied was the supply that handbooks were prepared to guide consumers in the art of purchase. The advice included observations on the strengths and weaknesses of the various peoples: Greek women, for instance, "are good as treasurers because they are meticulous and not very generous," whereas Slavic women "live long because of their excellent digestion, but . . . are barren because they are never clean from menstrual blood."[19] Despite the popularity of slavery, Islamic teaching recommended manumission and urged that slaves be allowed to purchase their freedom.

## Muslim Women

Women in traditional Arabic society, although important in the home, were clearly subordinate to men. They could neither inherit nor claim a share of spoils won on the battlefield, and their husbands enjoyed an absolute right of divorce. In some instances baby girls were regarded with such disdain that they were buried alive at birth or killed at the age of 5 or 6. The Koran alludes to this practice—disapprovingly—in several places, as in an account of the Last Judgment, "when the buried infant shall be asked for what sin she was slain."[20]

Without question, Muhammad sought to improve the treatment of women, according them spiritual if not social equality. They were, nevertheless, to be obedient to men, into whose hands the management of affairs was entrusted.

**Men are the managers of the affairs of women for that God has preferred . . . one of them over another, and for that they have expended of their property. Righteous women are therefore obedient. . . . And those you fear may be rebellious admonish; banish them to their couches, and beat them.[21]**

The proper relationship between husbands and wives, according to Muhammad, involved love and gracious-

---

## ◉ Muhammad's View of Women ◉

*Muhammad outlined his view of female dependency in the Koran.*

And if ye are apprehensive that ye shall not deal fairly with orphans, then, of other women who seem good in your eyes, marry but two, or three, or four; and if ye still fear that ye shall not act equitably, then one only. . . .

If any of your women be guilty of whoredom, then bring four witnesses against them from among yourselves; and if they bear witness to the fact, shut them up within their houses till death release them, or God make some way for them. And if two men among you commit the same crime, then punish them both; but if they turn and amend, then let them be. . . .

Men are superior to women on account of the qualities with which God hath gifted the one above the other, and on account of the outlay they make from their substance for them. Virtuous women are obedient, careful, during the husband's absence, because God hath of them been careful. But chide those for whose refractoriness ye have cause to fear; remove them into beds apart, and scourge them: but if they are obedient to you, then seek not occasion against them. . . . And if ye fear a breach between man and wife, then send a judge chosen from his family, and a judge chosen from her family: for if they are desirous of agreement, God will effect a reconciliation between them.

When ye divorce women . . . put them not forth from their houses, nor allow them to depart, unless they have committed a proven adultery. . . . Lodge the divorced wherever ye lodge, according to your means; and distress them not by putting them to straits. And if they are pregnant, then be at charges for them till they are delivered of their burden; and if they suckle your children, then pay them their hire . . . and act generously.

*Source: The Koran, trans. J. M. Rodwell (New York: Dutton, 1909), pp. 410–430 passim.*

ness, and marriage itself was conceived contractually, with each party having both rights and responsibilities. According to the Koran, however, men were allowed to have up to four wives, but no woman was entitled to more than one husband. Behind this practice was the conviction that procreation was a fundamental purpose of marriage. "Your women," said Muhammad, "are a tillage [cultivated land] for you; so come unto your tillage as you wish."[22]

Women were exhorted in the Koran to clothe themselves circumspectly, taking special care to cover their breasts, and to "draw their veils close to them" when they left the home.[23] Such admonitions led some Muslim women to veil their faces in public and to seclude themselves within their own part of the home, known as the harem. The harem system was not new with the coming of Islam but had roots in ancient Mesopotamia. Nevertheless, it became a characteristic part of Islamic society by the late eighth century. The seclusion of women in harems or behind veils, the practice of polygamy, and a willingness to beat disobedient wives underscore the fact that Islam, though making important advances over traditional Arab society, was a long way from establishing the social equality of the sexes. This is apparent as well with respect to the inheritance of property; in pre-Islamic Arabic society, women could not inherit at all. The Koran lifted this absolute prohibition but still limited women's rights in specified circumstances.

In practice, the role of women in medieval Islam varied substantially. Some played an active part in politics, including the scheming that became a regular part of determining succession to the caliphate. The wife of the Ummayad caliph al-Walid I (705–715) interfered in political affairs to promote justice and encouraged her husband to enlarge mosques; her role was extensive enough to prompt the governor of Iraq to warn al-Walid about her influence. One of the greatest of the Abbasid caliphs, Harun al-Rashid (786–809), apparently owed his position to his fabulously wealthy mother, Khayzuran, a former slave, who bitterly opposed another son, al-Hadi (785–786), and may even have had him assassinated. Harun's wife, Zubaydah, contributed money to build an aqueduct in Mecca and took an interest in urban development, much as aristocratic Turkish women were prominent patronesses of hospitals and schools between the tenth and thirteenth centuries. Women were de facto rulers of Egypt in the 1020s, late 1040s, and 1250s.

Muslim women participated in a wide range of cultural and intellectual pursuits. During the Umayyad caliphate they provided salons in which scholars, poets, and other educated people could gather; prominent among such women was Muhammad's great-granddaughter, Sukaina. As in pre-Islamic society, some women continued to write poetry, and female professionals sang elegies at funerals. Throughout the Umayyad period, women studied both law and theology, while in the caliphate of Córdoba women as well as men taught in schools; female scholars were prominent in the towns of Muslim Spain, and some lectured at the universities of Córdoba and Valencia. Women were also active in the Sufi movement. The Abbasids employed women to spy against the Byzantines in the guise of merchants, physicians, and travelers, which suggests that they undertook such activities in their own society.

There were, of course, instances of repression. During the Abbasid caliphate the public appearances and clothing of women were increasingly regulated by government decree. Around the year 1030, they were banned from public ceremonies. In twelfth-century Seville "decent women" were prohibited from dressing like prostitutes and from "party making" among themselves, even with their husbands' permission. Some of these regulations were intended to stress female modesty. In Seville women could not run hostels because of the possibility of sexual improprieties, and they could not enter Christian churches because the priests had reputations as fornicators and sodomites. In markets they could deal only with merchants of good reputation, and they were prohibited from sitting by the riverbank in the summer in the presence of men. For the most part such regulations, though patronizing, suggest concern for the protection of women in Islamic society.

## The Muslim Synthesis in Medicine, Science, and Philosophy

The Muslims demonstrated a remarkable capacity to assimilate and advance the medical and scientific knowledge of classical antiquity. Because Muhammad himself had reportedly praised the study of medicine, the subject received considerable attention by medieval Muslim scholars, especially after the works of Galen, Hippocrates, and other classical writers were translated into Arabic. The great age of medical advances occurred in the Abbasid period, when schools of medicine were founded and hospitals were introduced; Baghdad alone had 860 physicians in the year 931.

The contributions of two men are especially noteworthy in this field: the Iranian physician al-Razi (Rhazes; died c. 925), head of the Baghdad hospital, who wrote approximately 120 medical books, including a pioneering study of smallpox and measles; and the Iranian scholar Ibn Sina (Avicenna; died 1037), whose *Canon of Medicine* synthesized classical and Islamic medical knowledge, was translated into Latin in the twelfth century, and served as the leading medical text in Europe for 500 years. Among the topics Ibn Sina explored were the contagious nature of tuberculosis, psychological dis-

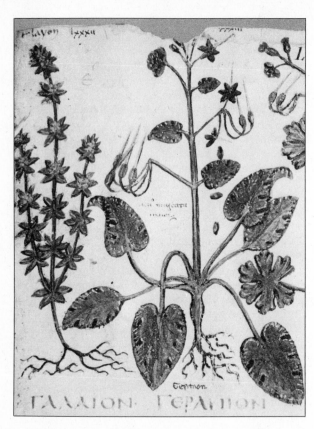

Page from a medical manuscript describing the cultivation of medicinal herbs. [Granger Collection]

tions to denote units, tens, hundreds, and so forth, and geometry and simple trigonometry from the Greeks. One of the leading scholars in this field was Muhammad ibn-Musa al-Khwarizmi, whose ninth-century treatises on arithmetic and algebra (*al-jabr*, "integration") were subsequently influential in Europe. Later mathematical work involved quadratic and cubic equations and led to the development of analytical geometry and spherical trigonometry.

Beginning primarily in the twelfth century, Muslim advances in mathematics and science spread to Europe through Sicily and Spain, where the Jews played a crucial role as cultural intermediaries. In the sixteenth century those achievements provided much of the foundation for the scientific revolution.

Islamic philosophy was heavily indebted to the works of Plato, Aristotle, and the Neoplatonists. No question was more basic to Muslim philosophers than the proper relationship of reason to revelation. The most prominent of the early Arab philosophers, Yaqub al-Kindi (died c. 870), made a conscious effort to reconcile Plato and Aristotle while insisting on the importance of knowing God and the universe as the key to immortality, a doctrine essentially derived from the Neoplatonists. When some philosophers insisted that reason was equal in importance to revelation as a means to acquire religious knowledge, al-Ghazali (died 1111) sought to restore the primacy of belief, thereby preventing Islamic doctrine from becoming the monopoly of an educated clique of theologians. God, he insisted, could reveal his mercy to the common people as well, for belief is

> a light which God bestows on the hearts of His creatures as the gift and bounty from Him, sometimes through an unexplainable conviction from within, sometimes because of a dream in sleep, sometimes by seeing the state of bliss of a pious man . . . , sometimes through one's own state of bliss.[25]

Al-Ghazali's attack on rationalist theologians prompted a defense of Aristotelian and Neoplatonic philosophy by the celebrated Ibn Rushd (Averroës, 1126–1198) of Córdoba, a judge and court physician. Like Ibn Sina, he was convinced that the truths of reason and revelation were compatible. The same truth, he argued, could be expressed either philosophically or symbolically; when, therefore, the Koran seemed to advocate an irrational belief, he resolved the apparent contradiction by interpreting the sacred texts allegorically. Through his extensive commentaries on Aristotle, which were translated into Latin in the thirteenth century, Ibn Rushd had a major impact on the development of scholastic thought in medieval universities. His views were equally influential in shaping late medieval Jewish philosophy, as reflected especially in the teaching of the Frenchman

orders, and skin diseases. One of the keys to his success was his willingness to learn from practice: "I . . . attended the sick, and the doors of medical treatments based on experience opened before me to an extent that cannot be described."[24]

The importance of experimentation was appreciated in other sciences as well. Although alchemy—the attempt to transform common metals into gold and other valuable substances—was a pseudoscience, its practitioners acquired valuable chemical knowledge and developed the world's first laboratories. Al-Razi classified all matter as animal, vegetable, or mineral and distinguished between volatile and nonvolatile substances. In the field of optics, Ibn al-Haytham (Alhazen; died 1039) of Cairo rejected the classical theory that the eye emits visual rays, arguing instead that it sees by receiving rays of light. He also devised experiments to study refraction, eclipses, and the atmosphere.

The Muslim ability to synthesize is perhaps best illustrated in the field of mathematics, where Islamic scholars adopted "Arabic" numerals from India, including zero and the placement of numbers in serial posi-

Gersonides (1288–c. 1344), a rationalist noted for his commentaries on Aristotle. The Western religious and philosophical heritage was thus greatly indebted to Islam, not least for introducing European thinkers to much of Aristotle's work.

## Islamic Literature

Medieval Muslims were extraordinarily fond of verse. Indeed, the Koran itself was written in quasi-verse form. A ninth-century Arabic scholar aptly summarized the importance of verse:

> **Poetry is the mine of knowledge of the Arabs, the book of their wisdom, the muster roll of their history, the repository of their great days, the rampart protecting their heritage, the trench defending their glories, the truthful witness on the day of dispute, the final proof at the time of argument.[26]**

Verse was the medium used by Firdawsi (c. 935–c. 1020) to compose what became the Iranian national epic, the *Shah-Nameh* ("Book of Kings"), which recounted the history of Persia's rulers from legendary times to the fall of the Sassanian dynasty in 651. Nearly 60,000 verses long, it was instrumental in establishing the definitive form of the Persian language, much as the King James Bible and the works of Shakespeare did for English.

Another Iranian poet, Shams ud-din Hafiz (c. 1325–c. 1389), composed some 500 short lyric poems, or *ghazals*, using simple language and proverbial expressions. Most have three levels of meaning: a reflection of contemporary life in the Persian town of Shiraz, with much to say about wine and love; an expression of tribute to Hafiz' courtly patrons; and an expression of his Sufi beliefs through images readily understood by Iranian readers. Hafiz' works reveal a deep sympathy for the common people, a strong dislike of hypocrisy, and a preoccupation with love:

> *When your beauty radiated on creation's morn,*
> *The world was set ablaze by love freshly born.*[27]

Hafiz influenced another major Sufi poet, Jami (1414–1492), whose mystical lyrics explored ethics and existence. His contemporary, the Indian poet Kabir (died 1518), was also a mystic. Raised as a Muslim and influenced by Hindu teachings, Kabir taught the equality of all persons and their ability to achieve unity with God through personal devotion.

Apart from the Koran, the best-known literary work in the Islamic world and in Europe was *The Thousand and One Nights*, a fabulous collection of stories from the Middle East and Asia that were originally transmitted orally, much like the ancient Homeric epics. In their extant form, most are set against the background of Baghdad during the caliphate of Harun al-Rashid or Cairo under the Fatimids. A fragment of the work existed by the ninth century, although it was another 600 years or so before a final version emerged.

Final mention must be made of history as a literary form. The greatest medieval Muslim historian was the Tunisian Ibn Khaldun (1332–1406), a pioneer of sociological methodology in explaining the past. To write history, he insisted, required a knowledge of geography, climate, economics, religion, and culture. He called attention to the necessity of evaluating documents preparatory to writing history, since all records are likely to contain inaccuracies. These errors, he explained, are caused by partisanship, overconfidence, a chronicler's failure to grasp the meaning of what he has recorded, excessive faith in one's sources, the inability to place an event in proper context, a desire to gain favor from patrons, a reliance on myth, and simple exaggeration. A sense of group consciousness was basic to Ibn Khaldun's philosophy of history; a strong communal identity enabled a people to triumph, but their civilization decayed as that spirit weakened. This theory, he felt, explained the decline of the Abbasid caliphate and the triumph of two less cultured nomadic peoples, the Seljuk Turks and the Mongols.

*The Byzantine and Islamic civilizations, thrown together by geography, lived in troubled proximity, sometimes engaging fruitfully in a commerce of goods, ideas, and values but periodically erupting into conflict and attempted conquest. Both civilizations made incalculable contributions to Western civilization by preserving and transmitting clas-* *sical culture, the Byzantines primarily in literature and the arts, the Muslims especially in science and mathematics. Religion permeated both societies, providing their foundations and shaping their outlook toward humanity and the world. Nevertheless, the Byzantine religious tradition was largely inherited from previous centuries, while the Arabs* founded a new religion, borrowing parts of the Judeo-Christian heritage. They differed as well with respect to the religious issues that most deeply divided them: Byzantines fought furiously over religious images, whereas Muslims debated the succession to the caliphate and the relationship of faith and reason. People in both societies gave great importance to the law, the Byzantines through Justinian's epic code and the Muslims through the Shari'a. Although neither society accorded women social equality, women enjoyed certain legal rights with respect to property, and they were occasionally active at the highest levels of politics and in cultural pursuits.

Economically, the Byzantine Empire was based primarily on agriculture, while the Muslim states were oriented toward trade. Although both shared certain manufacturing interests, such as silk, Muslim trade and production were generally more sophisticated than in By-

zantium. Indeed, a major source of Byzantine weakness in the later centuries of the empire was that it relinquished commerce into the hands of the Italians. Nor were Byzantine rulers successful in preserving the welfare of the free peasantry on whom the empire's strength rested; the rise of a military aristocracy seriously undermined the strength and stability of the empire. The Islamic states, in turn, were sapped by the periodic rebellion of slave armies. Both Byzantine and Muslim governments were weakened by violence, intrigue, bloated bureaucracies, and inadequate tax structures. Their conflicting imperial ambitions further undercut their strength, eventually leaving both prey to the invading Turks. The legacy of both civilizations, however, continues to shape the lives of millions of people, particularly in southeastern Europe, the Middle East, and North Africa.

## Notes

1. P. Whitting, ed., *Byzantium: An Introduction*, 2nd ed. (Oxford: Blackwell, 1981), pp. 20–21.
2. D. J. Geanakoplos, *Byzantium: Church, Society, and Civilization Seen Through Contemporary Eyes* (Chicago: University of Chicago Press, 1984), pp. 19–20. The quotation is from Agapetus, a deacon in the church of Hagia Sophia.
3. Ibid., p. 74.
4. R. Browning, *Justinian and Theodora* (London: Thames & Hudson, 1971), p. 72.
5. Geanakoplos, *Byzantium*, p. 321.
6. Ibid., p. 278.
7. Ibid., p. 304.
8. Ibid., p. 303.
9. Ibid., p. 196.
10. Ibid., p. 340 (slightly modified for clarity).
11. *The Koran Interpreted*, trans. A. J. Arberry (New York: Macmillan, 1955), vol. 1, p. 125.
12. Ibid., vol. 2, p. 50.
13. Whitting, *Byzantium*, p. 57.
14. B. Lewis, trans. and ed., *Islam from the Prophet Muhammad to the Capture of Constantinople* (New York: Walker, 1974), vol. 2, pp. 125–129.
15. Ibid., vol. 2, p. 166.
16. Ibid., vol. 2, pp. 195–196.
17. Ibid., vol. 2, p. 218.
18. Ibid., vol. 2, p. 128.
19. Ibid., vol. 2, pp. 246–247, 250.
20. *Koran Interpreted*, vol. 2, p. 326.
21. Ibid., vol. 1, pp. 105–106.
22. Ibid., vol. 1, p. 59.
23. Ibid., vol. 2, p. 128.
24. Lewis, *Islam*, vol. 2, p. 179.
25. Ibid., vol. 2, p. 21.
26. Ibid., vol. 2, p. 173.
27. *The Divan*, 87:1–2.

## Suggestions for Further Reading

Cameron, A. *Circus Factions: Blues and Greens in Rome and Byzantium*. Oxford: Clarendon Press, 1976.

Crone, P. *Meccan Trade and the Rise of Islam*. Princeton, N.J.: Princeton University Press, 1987.

Daniel, N. *The Arabs and Medieval Europe*, 2nd ed. London: Longman, 1978.

Donner, F. M. *The Early Islamic Conquests*. Princeton, N.J.: Princeton University Press, 1981.

Downey, G. *Constantinople in the Age of Justinian*. Norman: University of Oklahoma Press, 1960.

Endress, G. *Islam: A Historical Introduction*, trans. C. Hillenbrand. New York: Columbia University Press, 1988.

Every, G. *The Byzantine Patriarchate, 451–1204*, 2nd ed. New York: AMS Press, 1978.

Grabar, A. *Byzantine Painting*, trans. S. Gilbert. Geneva: Skira, 1953.

Haldon, S. F. *Byzantium in the Seventh Century: The Transformation of a Culture*. Cambridge: Cambridge University Press, 1991.

Hussey, J. M. *The Byzantine World*. Westport, Conn.: Greenwood, 1982.

———. *The Orthodox Church in the Byzantine Empire*. Oxford: Clarendon Press, 1986.

Kazhdan, A. P., and Epstein, A. W. *Change in Byzantine Culture in the Eleventh and Twelfth Centuries*. Berkeley: University of California Press, 1985.

Kitzinger, E. *Byzantine Art in the Making*. Cambridge, Mass.: Harvard University Press, 1977.

Lapidus, I. M. *A History of Islamic Societies*. Cambridge: Cambridge University Press, 1988.

Le Strange, G. *Baghdad During the Abbasid Caliphate*. New York: Barnes & Noble, 1972.

Lewis, B. *Islam: From the Prophet Muhammad to the Capture of Constantinople*. New York: Oxford University Press, 1987.

Loverance, R. *Byzantium*. Cambridge, Mass.: Harvard University Press, 1988.

# THE VISUAL EXPERIENCE
## Byzantine and Islamic Art

In this mosaic from Hagia Sophia, Justinian (left) presents the church to Mary and Jesus while Constantine (right) offers them the city of Constantinople. [Erich Lessing/Art Resource]

Detail depicting Justinian, from a sixth-century mosaic in the Church of San Vitale, Ravenna, Italy. [Scala/Art Resource]

The altar and apse of San Vitale, Ravenna, which functioned as a royal chapel for Justinian. [Scala/Art Resource]

In this mosaic from Hagia Sophia, Jesus and Mary are flanked by Emperor John II Comnenus (1118–1143) and Empress Zoe. The symbolism reflects the Byzantine view of close church-state relations. [Erich Lessing/Art Resource]

The Hejira: Muhammad flees Mecca with a companion as Jesus watches. The Muslim artist is paying homage to Islam's Christian heritage. [Edinburgh University Library]

This fourteenth-century Persian painting shows Muhammad and his disciples with Kaaba, the black rock that is sacred to Islam. [Edinburgh University Library]

A thirteenth-century Iraqi painter depicted Arab apothecaries preparing medicine. [Francis Bartlett Donation of 1912 and Picture Fund, Courtesy of Museum of Fine Arts, Boston]

Interior of the lavishly ornamented mosque at Córdoba, Spain. [MAS, Barcelona]

Maclagan, M. *The City of Constantinople.* New York: Praeger, 1968.

Magoulias, H. J. *Byzantine Christianity: Emperor, Church, and the West.* Detroit: Wayne State University Press, 1982.

Mottahedeh, R. P. *Loyalty and Leadership in Early Islamic Society.* Princeton, N.J.: Princeton University Press, 1980.

———. *The Mantle of the Prophet.* New York: Simon & Schuster, 1985.

Nicol, D. M. *Church and Society in the Last Centuries of Byzantium.* Cambridge: Cambridge University Press, 1979.

Obolensky, D. *The Byzantine Commonwealth: Eastern Europe, 500–1453.* New York: Praeger, 1971.

Rahman, F. *Islam,* 2nd ed. Chicago: University of Chicago Press, 1979.

Robinson, M. *Mohammed,* trans. A. Carter. New York: Pantheon, 1971.

Runciman, S. *The Byzantine Theocracy.* Cambridge: Cambridge University Press, 1977.

Sherrard, P. *Constantinople: Iconography of a Sacred City.* New York: Oxford University Press, 1965.

Watt, W. M. *The Majesty That Was Islam: The Islamic World, 661–1100.* New York: St. Martin's Press, 1990.

———. *Muhammad: Prophet and Statesman.* New York: Oxford University Press, 1974.

———. *Muhammad's Mecca: History in the Qur'an.* Edinburgh: Edinburgh University Press, 1989.

Wiet, G. *Baghdad: Metropolis of the Abbasid Caliphate,* trans. S. Feiler. Norman: University of Oklahoma Press, 1971.

Ziadeh, N. A. *Damascus Under the Mamluks.* Norman: University of Oklahoma Press, 1964.

# Writing and Communication (I)

One of the major elements in the development of civilization was the invention of writing. Its original purpose was probably to leave messages and to keep track of financial and other transactions, but with the ability to accumulate and preserve knowledge almost every aspect of human life was transformed. The power of the written word became vastly extended with the invention of printing, and the twentieth century has seen the discoveries of new technologies and an almost unimaginable proliferation of means of communication. These three stages—writing, printing, and mass communications—have affected the history of virtually every human civilization.

The earliest known writing system was devised by the people of Uruk (now Warka), one of the principal Sumerian city-states. In the late Neolithic period, records had been kept using small tokens in the shape of disks, spheres, half spheres, cones, and other figures, some of which were marked with incisions. Usually kept in clay containers, such tokens might be used, for instance, to represent animals in a palace herd. Late in the fourth millennium B.C., as cities and large-scale trade developed, the use of tokens to maintain records became too cumbersome. The Mesopotamians substituted written images known as ideographs for the tokens. During the third millennium B.C. these ideographs evolved into a series of wedge-shaped marks that could be impressed on a clay tablet quickly and easily with a split reed. The Sumerians also wrote on stone and metal, but clay, which was plentiful in their country and was already used for building and pottery, was much easier to make marks on. Mistakes could easily be smoothed out, and the record could be made permanent by leaving the clay to dry in the sun or baking it slowly in an oven. In this form it was light and easy to carry as well. The system of wedge-shaped marks on clay is known as cuneiform, after the Latin word *cuneus*, which means "wedge."

Cuneiform combined the use of pictographic signs (representing objects) and phonetic signs (representing sounds) with a total of some 350 characters. It was adopted by the Sumerians' Akkadian successors and was in general use in western Asia and Persia until around the middle of the first millennium B.C. Cuneiform signs formed the basis of the earliest known alphabet, which was devised around 1400 B.C. at the Canaanite city of Ugarit. An *alphabet* is a system using only phonetic symbols. The Canaanite writing system, known as North Semitic, gave rise to a large number of later alphabets, including the Arabic, Hebrew, Greek, and Latin.

Around 3000 B.C., shortly after the Sumerian inven-

Statuette of the goddess Ningal from Ur, 2080 B.C. The figure can be identified by the cuneiform inscription on the side of the throne. [University Museum, University of Pennsylvania]

tion of cuneiform, the Egyptians introduced a system of writing that is somewhat misleadingly known as hieroglyphics. The word means "sacred carved text," but Egyptian hieroglyphs were used for funerary and commemorative inscriptions as well as religious ones and were often painted or written on papyrus, a material woven from the reeds that grew along the Nile River. Whether the Egyptians were directly influenced by the Sumerians is uncertain. The sudden appearance and rapid development of hieroglyphic writing certainly

**Relief from the Old Kingdom tomb of Ptahhotep at Saqqara, showing agricultural scenes with hieroglyphic inscriptions above them. [George Holton/Photo Researchers]**

suggests contact, but the Egyptians never developed a simplified sign system like cuneiform; throughout their long history no attempt was made to change the basic hieroglyphic signs, although the cursive forms of hieratic and, later, demotic (a script devised for secular use) were introduced for speedier writing with brushpen on papyrus for business, tax, and other nonmonumental purposes.

The earliest writing in India dates back to the Indus valley civilization, which flourished between 3000 and 2000 B.C. in what is now Pakistan. Small, square sealstones were carved with picture signs, often accompanied by animals. The script has never been deciphered, however. With the disappearance of the Indus valley culture, knowledge of writing seems to have been lost for a few centuries. By 600 B.C. the Aryan in-

vaders of India had developed an alphabetic script. Under the Maurya dynasty (third century B.C.) the *Brahmi*, ancestor of all modern Indian scripts and of many others elsewhere, was firmly established and was used for numerous rock-carved edicts of the emperor Ashoka (269–232 B.C.).

Attempts have been made to link the Brahmi script with the Indus valley pictograms and thus provide it with a native origin. Most experts, however, believe that a Semitic alphabet was imported into India. Given the remarkable way the alphabet was adapted to Indian needs, this must have occurred sometime before the third century B.C., although no traces of earlier inscriptions have survived. We shall look at the early history of Brahmi when we consider the other descendants of the Semitic alphabets.

The beginning of writing in China is difficult to trace. Its first surviving appearance is in the form of divination inscriptions on shells and bones worked by the Lung Shan people around 2000 B.C. and found in far greater numbers at Anyang and other Shang sites of the late second millennium B.C. The bones were carved with divinations relating to the public and private life of the ruler: building projects, military campaigns, tribute payments, sickness, royal excursions, the weather. These oracle bones were then burned, and the position of any cracks that occurred was carefully studied, since the patterns they formed and their position in relation to the inscriptions were supposed to reveal the wishes of the sacred spirits and to predict the future. The system is known as scapulimancy. It was used in a simpler form as early as the fourth millennium B.C. both in China and elsewhere in the eastern Neolithic world. The Anyang rulers were the only people in Chinese history to add inscriptions, however; all other instances of scapulimancy were produced by drilling holes around which the cracks could form.

The writing was a highly developed series of characters that are clearly related to those still in use today. It appears already well developed on the Anyang bones, and its origins are thus obscure. The objects of everyday life were represented by simple pictures. The abstract ideas of "above" and "below" were conveyed by a short line above or below a longer line. Each character was given a phonetic sound, consisting of one syllable. In time the signs came to be used phonetically, although to avoid ambiguity picture signs remained in use. Thus a sign group conveying an action will include a hand, one conveying an emotion includes a heart, and one naming a tree includes a tree.

These composite characters, combining pictographic and phonetic signs, soon became the most common type. Most of the pictographic elements were recognizable, but many of the old phonetic signs were only approximate, and the spoken language has changed completely over such a long period, as it has everywhere. Speakers of different languages or dialects sound the characters quite differently, but the meaning is the same. By the eighth century B.C. characters had evolved beyond simple pictographic and phonetic elements and included abstract ideas in an often multiple mix of signs or in two-character combinations. The Chinese script is accordingly best labeled ideographic. The educated Chinese reader or writer, even of a newspaper, has to master several thousand characters to be literate. Furthermore, since each character represents a concept rather than a sound, there is a dissociation between the written and spoken language. But this feature had an important benefit: the fact that the standardized written language did not vary with regional dialects proved of immense value in unifying a country of such pronounced diversity. Only in the twentieth century,

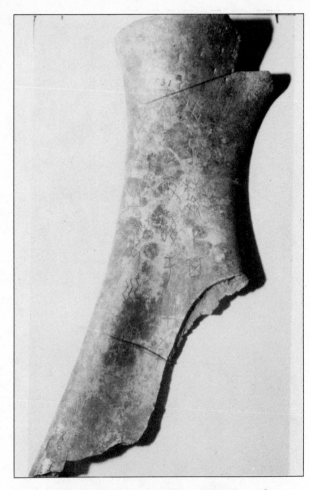

**A Chinese oracle bone with writing, from the Shang period. [Ronald Sheridan/Ancient Art and Architecture Collection]**

with the diffusion throughout China of the standard written and spoken language of Peking (Beijing) made possible by methods of mass communication, has speech become more uniform.

The Chinese system of writing remains virtually unique in retaining its nonalphabetic form. Even cultures that borrowed Chinese characters to write their own languages, such as Korean, Vietnamese, and Japanese, added a separate phonetic system for many purposes. But the Chinese characters are still used, their meaning unaffected by differences in spoken language. Most other written languages in the world developed an alphabetic system, many of them directly or indirectly based on the earliest alphabet of all, the North Semitic.

One of the earliest decipherable inscriptions in alphabetic writing is the calendar found at the Canaanite site of Gezer, dating to the eleventh century B.C.—approximately the biblical period of Saul and David. The words, roughly scratched on a schoolchild's tablet of soft limestone, consist of a poem describing the principal agricultural occupations of the seasons.

Other Semitic languages used versions of the original North Semitic alphabet, with the exception of Akkadian, which continued to employ cuneiform. Aramaic writing goes back to the beginning of the first millennium B.C. and by 500 B.C. had become the most important and widespread script of western Asia. It served as the diplomatic writing system for the western provinces of the Persian Empire and continued to be used until around the second century A.D. The square Hebrew script that is still in use today was derived from Aramaic. The Jews adopted the Aramaic language, the common tongue of the region, during the period of the Babylonian captivity. With their return, Aramaic became the vernacular of the Jews in Palestine.

After the conquest of Persia and the introduction of Greek as the official business language there, Aramaic scripts began to develop local variations; one of them, Nabatean, was to give birth to Arabic. The Hebrew version seems to have split off around 200 B.C. and began to attain uniformity in the years between 30 B.C. and A.D. 70. In the subsequent period the script was widely used in the production of biblical manuscripts and occasionally for nonliterary documents such as letters and accounts. Detailed rules developed regulating the copying of synagogue scrolls and the manner in which they should be set out. As a result, Hebrew writing has changed little since the first century A.D.

The primary diffusers of the Semitic alphabet in the Mediterranean region were the descendants of the Canaanites, the Phoenicians, who occupied the narrow coastal plain of what is now Lebanon and Syria during the first half of the first millennium B.C. The greatest traders and seafarers of their time, the Phoenicians set up commercial posts from the Atlantic to the Tigris; they are even reputed to have circumnavigated Africa. To assist their financial and trading activities they developed a form of Aramaic script for the Phoenician language that they then spread in the course of their commercial activities.

Among the peoples who came into contact with the Phoenicians were the Greeks. A form of writing had existed in the Bronze Age world of the Minoans and Mycenaeans (second millennium B.C.), but with the collapse of Mycenaen culture, knowledge of it died out. The earliest works of Greek literature, the epic poems attributed to Homer, had begun their history as oral compositions, passed from speaker to speaker without being written down, but as Greek culture developed in the eighth century B.C., an efficient writing system became necessary. The Greeks may have learned the Phoenician alphabet from contacts in the eastern Mediterranean, but it is just as likely that the transmission

occurred in the west, in Italy. Both Greeks and Phoenicians had set up trading posts there, partly to sell to Italian customers and partly to exploit the rich mineral wealth of the Italian peninsula. Throughout the seventh and sixth centuries B.C. Greek colonies were founded in southern Italy and Sicily, and the new writing system was diffused there.

Italy was to prove an important site in the transmission of the original alphabet. Italic peoples such as the Oscans and the Umbrians began to use their own versions of the Greek alphabet, as did the Etruscans of central Italy. During the Etruscan occupation of Rome (616–510 B.C.) the Greek alphabet was picked up by the Romans, who spread it throughout their empire as it grew. Every modern European language uses a form of the Roman alphabet, with the exception of Russian, Bulgarian, and Macedonian, which use a version of the Greek. Thus by the fall of the Roman Empire the Greek and Roman alphabets had become standard for all Western cultures. They have remained so ever since.

In the Arabic world there is little evidence of writing before the coming of Islam. The Nabateans, who lived

**The Gezer calendar.** [Palestine Exploration Fund]

in the Sinai region, used a version of the Aramaic script, but the oldest Arabic inscription in Nabatean characters dates only to A.D. 267. In the early period of their culture the Arabs had little need for writing, even though they were highly language-conscious and poetically gifted. Arab poets preferred to hand down their compositions orally, and each bard had at least two young companions whose task it was to memorize their master's works and continue the tradition.

With the appearance of Islam in the seventh century A.D., however, a writing system was urgently needed. Muslims felt it essential to record every syllable of the Koran with the utmost precision, and the ability to write became a skill of the highest importance. Furthermore, since strict Muslim law discouraged the painting of pictures, the Arabs began to develop the art of calligraphy (fine, ornamental writing). Within less than two centuries after the time of Muhammad, Arabic calligraphy had reached a sophistication that has been surpassed only in China, where it was highly valued as early as the Han period and was in fact considered a basic art form. Like Chinese calligraphy, several kinds of Arabic script were developed, ranging from monumental angular lettering, preferred for copying the Koran and other important works, to more cursive letters used for decorative displays. Today both types are in use, and in China calligraphic ability remains the mark of an educated person.

As Islam spread it carried the new writing with it. The enormous diversity of peoples and territories that fell under Arab rule, from North Africa and parts of Spain in the west to India and the border of China in the east, encouraged the development of local forms of Arabic script. The western style is known as Maghribi ("Western"), and a version of it was introduced into central and western Africa by Muslim traders. Other forms were adopted in Iran and Turkey.

When the Arabs carried their culture with its writing system to India, they found there, as we have seen, yet another alphabet descended from the Semitic, the Brahmi. In the strictest sense, Brahmi is not a true alphabet, since each basic consonant is accompanied by the vowel *a*. This syllabic device is due to the fact that in the early northern Indian languages, the best known of which is Sanskrit, *a* was the most common vowel sound. Other vowels were represented either by their own signs when they began a word or by signs that modified the consonants. Modern Indian scripts for the most part still use this system, although the languages of South India belong to a completely different family.

For the first centuries of its use the form of Brahmi seems to have been fairly consistent throughout India, although no manuscripts survive and the only extant examples of writing are on coins, seals, and inscriptions. Under the Gupta dynasty of the fourth century A.D., northern India developed its own version, which in due course was exported to the Buddhist centers of Chinese Turkestan. Beginning under the emperor Ashoka in the third century B.C. and in subsequent centuries, versions of the Brahmi script were also diffused, via Buddhist texts, to Ceylon (Sri Lanka), Burma, Thailand, Cambodia, and Vietnam. Each of these countries in time developed its own form of Brahmi, alphabetical systems written with added flourishes and curves that remain in use there today, although Chinese characters later displaced the Brahmi-based script in Vietnam. Thus while Muslim culture introduced one version of the Semitic alphabet into India, Buddhism was the vehicle whereby another form was transmitted even farther east.

**An eleventh-century northern Buddhist Sanskrit work written in the Nepalese version of Brahmi. [Ronald Sheridan/Ancient Art and Architecture Collection]**

In the New World the Mayans had formed a complex system of hieroglyphic writing as early as the fourth century A.D. The signs were based on pictures, and most of the surviving examples take the form of monumental inscriptions carved in stone. Not all of them have been deciphered, but for the most part they consist of archival records or religious texts, and a number attest to the Mayan interest in astronomy and the calendar. Other Mesoamerican peoples developed their own scripts, notably the Aztecs and the Mixtecs, and used them in extended manuscripts known as *codices*. These consist of long strips of animal hide or tree bark, which were folded concertina fashion, like a modern map. Most of them record mythological events, and some were preserved by the conquering Spanish of the sixteenth century. With the arrival of Europeans the Roman alphabet replaced hieroglyphic systems.

Before the invention of printing, the many systems of writing so far described provided only a limited kind of literacy. Inscriptions erected in public places were, of course, available for all to read. The Roman Emperor Augustus wrote an autobiography, *Res Gestae* ("Things I Have Done"), shortly before his death in A.D. 14, and had copies distributed throughout the empire; it was also inscribed on the bronze doors of his tomb. Muslim rulers often used the public display of passages from the Koran as a means of spreading and reinforcing the faith.

Yet such examples confirm the general limitations of literacy. Administrators, priests, and sometimes merchants—the elite in the various cultures described—needed to be able to read, both for business and governmental purposes and for preserving sacred texts such as the Bible, the sayings of the Buddha, and the Koran. Plays and poems were popular in the Greek and Roman world, and a few romantic stories were written in Greek in the second and third centuries A.D., but there is little evidence of the circulation of written literature beyond the elite in the ancient world.

## Suggestions for Further Reading

Craig, J. *Thirty Centuries of Graphic Design: An Illustrated History.* New York: Watson-Guptill, 1987.

Diringer, D. *The Alphabet.* 2 vols. London: Hutchinson, 1973.

Goody, J. *The Logic of Writing and the Organization of Society.* Cambridge: Cambridge University Press, 1986.

Gordon, C. H. *Forgotten Scripts: Their Ongoing Discovery and Decipherment,* rev. ed. New York: Basic Books, 1982.

Hosking, R. F., and Meredith-Owens, G. M. *A Handbook of Asian Scripts.* London: British Museum, 1966.

Hutchinson, J. *Letters.* New York: Van Nostrand Reinhold, 1983.

Lasswell, H. D., Lerner, D., and Speier, H., eds. *Propaganda and Communication in World History,* vol. 1. Honolulu: University Press of Hawaii, 1980.

Lockwood, W. B. *A Panorama of Indo-European Languages.* London: Hutchinson, 1972.

Logan, R. K. *The Alphabet Effect: The Impact of the Phonetic Alphabet on the Development of Western Civilization.* New York: Morrow, 1986.

Pope, M. *The Story of Archaeological Decipherment.* New York: Scribner, 1975.

Roberts, C. H. *The Birth of the Codex.* London: Oxford University Press, 1983.

Sampson, G. *Writing Systems.* London: Hutchinson, 1985.

Schmandt-Besserat, D. "The Earliest Precursor of Writing," *Scientific American,* June 1978, pp. 50–59.

Whalley, J. I. *Writing Implements and Accessories: From the Roman Stylus to the Typewriter.* Detroit: Gale Research, 1975.

# CHAPTER 9

# The Civilizations of Early Africa

The vast continent of Africa, which covers 11.7 million miles, comprises 20 percent of the earth's land surface; only Asia is larger. The birthplace of humanity, Africa became the home of numerous cultures and civilizations, including Egypt in the north, Kush and Axum in the east, Ghana and Mali in the west, and the Swahili city-states and Great Zimbabwe in the southeast. Not until the post–World War II period and the dismantling of Western imperialism, however, was there sustained scholarly interest in the preimperial history of sub-Saharan Africa. The emergence of newly independent African states and their schools and universities sparked enormous interest in the African past. We now know how rich and varied these early African cultures and civilizations were and how much contact they had with Europe, western Asia, and India, especially through extensive trading networks that transmitted not only commercial goods but culture as well.

**The tallest of the obelisks still standing at the East African city of Axum is nearly 70 feet high.** [Werner Forman Archive, London]

# Africa: From Stone to Iron

Prehistoric Africa became the center for the development of stone tools known as hand axes, which may have served for skinning and chopping up animals and other sources of food. Rich deposits of these tools have been found in eastern Africa, from whence their use spread to western Europe and India.

## The African Land

Despite this early evidence of cultural diffusion, life in much of Africa has always been affected by a degree of geographic isolation. The Sahara, of course, was not always the formidable barrier it is today. Indeed, between 5500 and 2000 B.C. open grassland areas now covered with sand were used not only by hunters but also by animal breeders and farmers. Even when changes of climate returned the last of these grasslands or savannas to their desert state, devoid of fish and game, caravans of traders used routes that crossed the central Sahara or made their way through Nubia and Egypt to and from the Mediterranean. Nonetheless, for most of recorded history the vast expanses of the Sahara, which eventually covered nearly a third of the continent, have hindered the movement of people or goods and kept contacts to a minimum.

Much of central and southern Africa is inaccessible by sea because there are few good natural harbors. Although Africa is three times the size of Europe, its coastline is actually shorter. Enormous sandbars along both the east and west coasts made navigation hazardous. Even within the continent, which stretches some 5,000 miles from north to south and an equal distance across at its widest point, transport from one region to another is difficult. Because of rapids and waterfalls, few rivers are navigable, nor are there any inland seas such as the Black or the Caspian to facilitate transportation. Deserts, rain forests, and the swamps east of the Sahara were additional barriers to travel.

To the difficulties presented by geography must be added other natural problems. Unlike Mesopotamia or India, which experienced a predictable alternation of dry and wet spells each year, the African climate is extremely irregular. Two or three years of drought may be followed by prolonged rainfall that erodes the soil (mostly clay) and washes away important nutrients. Furthermore, the regions that are hot and humid provide natural breeding grounds for insects such as mosquitoes, tsetse flies, and other parasites. Regular food production under such conditions poses formidable problems. Without it most of the early inhabitants of Africa were unable to establish the kind of widespread urbanization that, as we have seen in Asia and Europe, is normally the precondition for social and economic development and technological innovation. The only place on the African continent where the introduction of farming techniques led to an early appearance of urban civilization was Egypt, where the fertility of the Nile valley made comparatively large population concentrations possible.

In sub-Saharan Africa the most habitable areas were the three major savanna (grassland) regions, one extending across the continent south of the Sahara, known as the Sudan (Arabic for "land of the black people"; it is not to be confused with the modern state of that name); a second amid the mountains of eastern Africa; and the third ranging across southern Africa above the Kalahari desert. Between the expanses of grasslands are the tropical rain forests, parts of them virtually impenetrable and virtually all of them hazardous to humans and cattle because of such endemic diseases as sleeping sickness and malaria. Despite the often inhospitable terrain and the erratic weather, sub-Saharan Africa offered its inhabitants two distinct advantages: ample room for expansion and, until modern times, freedom from Eurasian invaders.

## Agriculture and Ironworking

The earliest peoples of Africa supported themselves by hunting and gathering. Around 5000 B.C. crop farming and animal breeding were introduced to the North African coastal regions, probably from western Asia. Farming had almost certainly begun independently in Ethiopia, the central Sudan, and the upper Niger valley. In eastern Africa, particularly Ethiopia and the Nile valley in the Sudan, local cereals such as millet and sorghum were laboriously cultivated from native wild grasses, while in the west the Bantu began to occupy the coastal rain forests, attracted there by the abundance of indigenous yams and oil palms. Animal husbandry had spread into the Sahara while that region was still lush grassland, but the emerging desert forced most of its inhabitants to migrate to the north or the south, driving their cattle with them. Many settled in West Africa and Ethiopia, and from the latter some of their descendants migrated into East Africa between 1500 and 1000 B.C. Only later did agriculture extend into southern Africa.

Throughout the whole of Africa, with the notable exception of Egypt, the transition from hunting to farming and cattle raising was a very gradual one, and in many regions both food systems probably coexisted for centuries. In addition to climate, there were two other reasons for the slow growth of agriculture. First, the native forest food plants were limited in range; only with the importation of crops from abroad such as taro (a type of yam), sugarcane, and banana and coconut trees, all native to Southeast Asia, were dependable staple crops de-

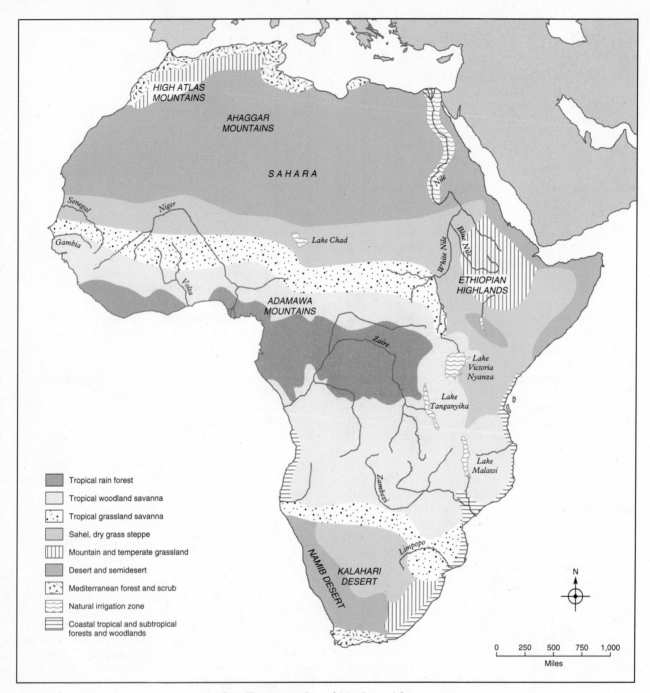

HIGH ATLAS
MOUNTAINS

AHAGGAR
MOUNTAINS

S A H A R A

Senegal

Niger

Nile

Gambia

Lake Chad

White Nile

Blue Nile

ETHIOPIAN
HIGHLANDS

Volta

ADAMAWA
MOUNTAINS

Zaïre

Lake
Victoria
Nyanza

Lake
Tanganyika

Lake
Malawi

Zambezi

Limpopo

NAMIB DESERT

KALAHARI
DESERT

N

▨ Tropical rain forest

▫ Tropical woodland savanna

⋯ Tropical grassland savanna

▨ Sahel, dry grass steppe

‖ Mountain and temperate grassland

▨ Desert and semidesert

⋯ Mediterranean forest and scrub

≈ Natural irrigation zone

≡ Coastal tropical and subtropical
  forests and woodlands

0    250    500    750    1,000

Miles

*9.1 Topography of Modern Africa*

veloped by the beginning of the first millennium A.D.
The food supply also expanded with the domestication
of chickens, ducks, and geese, all of which came from
Southeast Asia, and pigs. Second, unlike the Chinese or
the peoples of the Mediterranean and western Asia,

many of the inhabitants of sub-Saharan Africa never
worked in bronze. The peoples along the Atlantic
coast—in what became Mauritania, Senegal, and Nigeria—were exceptional in this respect, though even
their use of bronze was limited. Until the introduction of

iron shortly before 500 B.C., most African farmers were limited to stone and wood tools, the use of which rarely produced surplus crops.

Ironworking techniques were first introduced in Africa by the Phoenicians who founded Carthage and by the Assyrians who conquered Egypt. The ability to work in iron had reached Meroë in the Sudan by 500 B.C., and from there it spread slowly southward. In the meantime the West Africans learned about iron from the Carthaginians. The metal was used to manufacture such tools as picks, hoes, and axes as well as weapons (arrowpoints and spearheads). Africans who possessed these implements enjoyed obvious advantages in food production and in warfare.

# Early African Society and Culture

The chief beneficiaries of the expanding knowledge of agriculture and ironworking were dark-skinned peoples known as the Bantu. From their West African homeland in what later came to be called Nigeria and Cameroon they migrated to the south and east over a period of two millennia until they inhabited virtually all of sub-Saharan Africa apart from the southwestern savanna, the southern jungles, and the Kalahari desert. Those regions became the new home of the peoples dislodged by the Bantu—mostly the hunter-gatherers known as the San and the Khoikhoi. Two main factors accounted for the Bantu migrations: population growth, which had been sparked by the development of agriculture, and the limited ability to raise food on the central African plateau because of thin topsoil and limited water.

As the Bantu spread out through most of sub-Saharan Africa, their tribes developed a good deal of cultural variety, as attested to by the more than 400 closely related Bantu languages. Diversity was apparent too with respect to inheritance, with some groups recognizing the primacy of the female line, others the male. Despite such differences, at root the Bantu shared a common heritage in which family and kinship were especially important. Extended families grouped themselves into tribes, the chieftains of which were chosen by family elders or inherited their office and ruled with the assistance of a council of elders. The chief and elders administered laws grounded in tradition; they tried violaters, sometimes by ordeal if the testimony about their alleged offenses was inconclusive. A common form of trial by ordeal (used also in Europe) cast the accused into a body of water in the belief that the innocent would sink, whereas the guilty would float. Supreme loyalty was to the tribe, whose members were united not only to their families but also to subgroups based on age and sometimes to secret societies. As life became increasingly sedentary,

the basis of authority began to shift from kinship to residence, so that villages and then groups of allied villages assumed greater power. The more powerful tribal chiefs became kings, with the first monarchies apparently emerging in West Africa around the first century A.D. To substantiate their claims to authority the kings depicted themselves as descendants of divine ancestors, with special powers over fertility. Over time the monarchs employed a hierarchy of public officials to help them govern. Other societies continued to rely on the traditional tribal organization, with its interlocking obligations and the importance of blood ties.

Although the Bantu economy was firmly based in agriculture and cattle grazing, other occupations developed. Miners extracted iron, copper, and gold, which skilled artisans used to fashion tools, weapons, jewelry, and other items. Spinners and weavers made clothing and blankets, carpenters constructed buildings, and potters created a variety of items. Woodcarvers and basketweavers also produced their wares. In some Bantu societies the crafts were controlled by specific family groups who operated within the framework of strict regulations, but other societies operated more freely. As in Europe, the artisans themselves usually traded their goods, though as cities developed so too did merchants and trading organizations. With sedentary life also came the notion of land ownership and the emergence of patron-client relationships, typically between landlords and tenants.

The Bantu combined a strong sense of communal responsibility with religious convictions that touched virtually every aspect of life. Like the Chinese, they believed that their deceased ancestors dwelt among them in spirit, deserved respect, and influenced their lives. With all ancient peoples they also associated the forces of nature with religious spirits, whom they sought to propitiate by traditional rituals. As agriculture developed, special rituals and festivals came to be associated with specific crops, especially those, such as yams and millet, that were basic staples. Although the Bantu were not monotheistic, many were persuaded of the existence of a supreme but unknowable being.

One of the best examples of early Bantu culture has survived in terra-cotta (baked clay) figurines of humans and animals as well as depictions of fluted pumpkins produced by the Bantu who lived in central Nigeria between 500 B.C. and A.D. 200. They also had the ability to work in copper and bronze and created fine jewelry. Their representation of the human figure influenced West African artists for centuries, just as later generations copied the shapes of their houses and the layouts of their villages, thereby contributing to the pronounced sense of continuity that characterizes sub-Saharan African history. The high quality of Nok art, as this culture is known, is evidence of a considerable degree of patron-

Terra-cotta sculptures from the Nok culture, such as this head, exerted a profound influence on later African art. [Courtesy Federal Department of Antiquities, Nigeria]

age and social stability and thus of the existence of a well-organized, reasonably secure society.

# The Ancient States of the Eastern Sudan

The eastern Sudan was the home of two of the oldest kingdoms in Africa, Kush and Ethiopia, neither of whose inhabitants were ethnically, linguistically, or culturally one with the Bantu, though commercial contacts developed between them. The people of Kush were subject to Egyptian domination during much of the New Kingdom, but as Egypt declined a Kushite state emerged in the eleventh century B.C., with its capital at Napata on the upper Nile.

## The Kingdom of Kush

Beginning in the eighth century B.C. Kush extended its sway over Egypt, where its rulers established the twenty-fifth dynasty. For more than 60 years the dark-skinned Kushite monarchs governed Egypt, worshiping Egyptian deities, inscribing their names on the temples, and wearing the traditional Egyptian crown as the symbol of their authority. The Kushites now reigned over an empire that extended from the Mediterranean to the borders of modern Ethiopia and possibly beyond. But these were troubled years because of Assyrian aggres-

sion, including the temporary capture of Memphis in 670 B.C. The stone and bronze arms of the Kushites were ultimately no match for the iron weapons of the Assyrians, who drove the Kushites out of Egypt a decade later. Although Egypt was no longer theirs, Kushite sovereigns retained the style and titles of the pharaohs.

In the sixth century B.C. the people of Kush moved their capital farther south to Meroë, partly for defensive reasons but also because of its advantageous location as a trading center. Not only was the Nile navigable at this point, but Meroë was situated at the western end of a caravan route from the Red Sea and also sat astride the north-south route that extended from Egypt into the heart of Africa. At Meroë the annual rainfall was greater than at Napata, with obvious advantages for farming, and the region had abundant iron ore and the timber required for its smelting.

The economy of Meroë was varied. The kingdom became a major center of iron production for northeastern Africa. Defeat at the hands of the Assyrians had taught the Kushites the value of iron, which was useful not only for weapons but also for axes and hoes as well as spears and arrows for hunting. Judging from surviving art reliefs, many of the people farmed (mostly sorghum and millet) or grazed animals, but others were engaged in the manufacture of cloth, apparently from both flax and cotton. Hunting was also an important livelihood, as reflected in the kingdom's export trade. The Kushites exported ivory, ebony, leopard skins, ostrich feathers, and gold in exchange for products from the Mediterranean, India, and East Asia. From the Kushites the Egyptians obtained trained elephants for their army.

At first the culture of Meroë was heavily influenced by Egypt. For a time Meroë's religion and official language were Egyptian, as was its architecture, including a walled palace, great temples, and rows of pyramids in which the rulers were entombed. Gradually Meroë's culture became less Egyptianized. Local gods and shrines took their place alongside Egyptian deities, African animals (lions, giraffes, elephants, and ostriches) were featured in art, pyramids acquired distinctive flat tops, and a local language, called Meriotic but so far untranslated, replaced Egyptian. Meriotic culture became increasingly eclectic as the Kushites employed Hellenistic, Persian, and Indian motifs in such areas as architecture and sculpture.

The cultural indebtedness of the Kushites notwithstanding, their society was substantially different from that of their northern neighbors. Whereas the Egyptians were concentrated in a narrow floodplain, the Kushite population was scattered in small villages that dotted extensive fields watered by the summer rains. Political control was therefore more decentralized, with local chiefs and clan leaders exercising a good deal of authority as long as they and their people paid tribute to the king each year. The only check on the king's au-

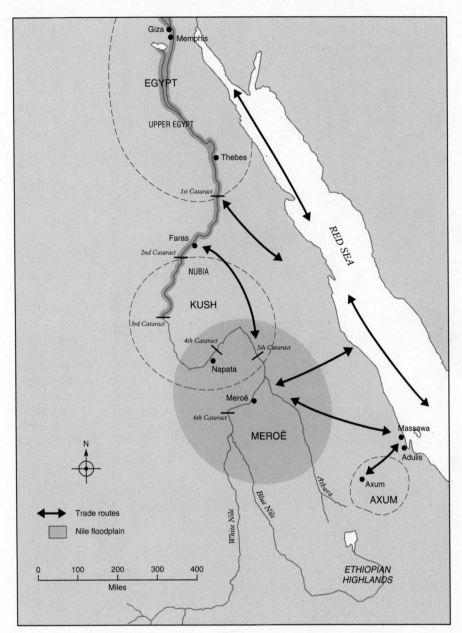

*9.2 Egypt, Kush, Meroë, and Axum, 1500 B.C.–A.D. 350*

thority was apparently the pragmatic need to retain the people's support; this was not automatic, since rulers who angered their subjects were periodically overthrown. When a new king ascended the throne, his mother, who enjoyed considerable prestige, provided both stability and continuity. Her role probably reflects a general appreciation of women among the Kushites.

The Kushite kingdom reached its peak in the first century A.D., at which time it exchanged ambassadors with the Roman Empire. The power of Kush began to

ebb in the second century as Ethiopians and desert nomads disrupted its trade routes. The iron industry declined as the forests were depleted, and the fertility of the soil was squandered by heavy farming and erosion. The economic problems of the Roman Empire, hitherto a major market for Kushite luxury goods, were also a factor in Meroë's decline. The kingdom fell in the fourth century to the Ethiopians, and the town of Meroë was abandoned. Kush's historic importance was based on its role as a country in which the cultural traditions of Egypt

This relief from a stela at Meroë depicts a Kushite queen and a ram-headed god. Note the Egyptian influence. [Werner Forman Archive, London]

mingled with those of dark-skinned Africans and where there was contact as well with the cultures of Hellenistic Greece, Rome, Persia, and India. Kush also played a crucial role in spreading the knowledge of ironworking in Africa.

## Axum, the Christian Kingdom

To the southeast of Kush lay the mountainous land of Ethiopia, where the native inhabitants were farming such grains as wheat, barley, and millet before the arrival of Semites from Yemen early in the first millennium B.C. Although the Semites had come as traders, the mountainous terrain encouraged them to take up farming. In time they intermingled with local inhabitants, creating both the ethnic and the cultural fusion that came to distinguish Ethiopia. The language of these Semites, Sabaean, gradually merged with the local tongues to form Geez, the classical Ethiopian tongue.

The Sabaeans brought with them not only the knowledge of writing but also Hebrew religious traditions, including the observance of the Sabbath and Jewish dietary regulations. The best-known example of this influence is the tradition that the Ethiopian royal line can be traced back to Menelik, son of Solomon and the queen of Sheba, and that Menelik brought the Ark of the Covenant with him to Ethiopia. The story is recounted in *The Glory of the Kings*, the most famous work in Ethiopian literature; parts of it date to the fourth century A.D. The Sabaeans had probably acquired Jewish influences when the Hebrew kingdom of Solomon expanded, sending emigrants into southern Arabia.

The state that the Sabaeans established became known as the kingdom of Axum, from the name of its capital. Taking advantage of their strategic location on the shores of the Red Sea, the Axumites profited from the trading network that extended from the eastern Mediterranean and the East African coast to Arabia and India. Like Kush, Axum had extensive contacts with Egypt and was subject to its influence. The heart of this contact was trade, since the Egyptians looked to Axum for spices, incense, and precious stones from India as well as ivory, gold, ebony, myrrh, rhinoceros horns, and elephants from sub-Saharan Africa. The traders of Axum also exported locally produced spices, frankincense (used in burials), and luxury goods made of glass, brass, and copper; most of these goods went to Egypt and the Byzantine Empire.

As Egypt declined, Axum's power increased, until by the mid-fourth century A.D. its sway extended from Kush, which was overrun by King Ezana (c. 320–c. 350), to the edge of the Horn of Africa. Axum was now the most powerful state in East Africa and the hub of the region's trade. Unlike the earlier kingdom of Kush, Axum minted its own coinage, a symbol of its political and commercial strength. In the sixth century Axum was strong enough to annex the portion of the Arabian peninsula that is now Yemen, but before the century was over, Axum's principal trade rival, Persia, had driven it from this territory.

Christianity began to make inroads in Axum as a result of trade with the Byzantine Empire, and Ezana, influenced by his tutor, a Syrian Christian named Frumentius, made it the state religion in 350. However, it took centuries for the new religion to be diffused effectively among the common people. Ethiopian Christians followed the Egyptians in embracing Monophysite theology, with its belief that the human and divine natures of Christ were fused in the Incarnation. Axum's close reli-gious ties to Egypt were also reflected in the appointment of the first bishop of Axum by the patriarch of Alexandria. The adoption of Christianity gave the kingdom of Axum a historical identity that set it apart from its African neighbors and enabled it to conduct its wars in the name of religion. The Judeo-Christian tradition made Ethiopians unique among Africans; after the Muslim conquests of the seventh and eighth centuries, only Nubia and Axum remained Christian.

Weakened by internal strife and cut off from its Mediterranean trading partners by the advance of Islam, Axum experienced economic stagnation and political chaos. The Muslims destroyed Adulis, Axum's principal port, in 710 and took over its trade routes. Moreover, much of the commerce that had once passed through the Red Sea shifted to the eastern Mediterranean and the Persian Gulf; Axum had been bypassed. Environmental factors—the depletion of forests and the erosion of soil—probably contributed to Axum's decline. The kingdom itself survived, thanks to its mountainous terrain, though it would be essentially isolated from the outside world for a millennium. Many of the Ethiopian people remained faithful to their Coptic Christianity into the twentieth century.

## ◉ Christianity in Africa ◉

*In the early sixteenth century a Portuguese visitor, Father Francisco Alvares, described the practice of Christianity in Axum.*

As they say the church of Axum is the most ancient, so it is the most revered of all Ethiopia, and the services are well conducted in it. In this church there are 150 canons, and as many monks. It has two head men; one is named *nebrete* of the canons, which means teacher, and the other *nebrete* of the monks. These two heads reside in the palaces which are within the great enclosure and circuit of the church; and the *nebrete* of the canons . . . is the principal one, and the more respected. He has jurisdiction over the canons and the laity of all this country; and the *nebrete* of the monks only hears and rules the monks. Both use kettledrums and trumpets. They have very large revenues [renderings of praise], and besides their revenues they have every day a collation [light meal] which they call *maabar* of bread and wine of the country, when mass is finished. The monks have this by themselves, and the canons also, and this *maabar* is such that the monks seldom eat other food than that. They have this every day except Friday of the Passion [Good Friday], because on that day no one eats or drinks. The canons do not take their *maabar* within the circuit of the church, and are seldom there, except at fixed hours; neither is the *nebrete* in his palace, except at some chance time when he goes to hear cases. This is because they are married, and live with their wives and children in their houses, which are very good and which are outside. Neither women nor laymen go into the enclosure of this church [but worship elsewhere].

*Source: Africa in the Days of Exploration,* ed. R. Oliver and C. Oliver (Englewood Cliffs, N.J.: Prentice Hall, 1965), pp. 77–78.

# Trading Patterns, Slavery, and Urban Development

The trading routes that extended between Egypt and its southern neighbors, Kush and Axum, were but one example of regional networks developed by Africans. West Africa was the site of others well before trans-Saharan trade began to grow dramatically in the seventh century A.D. Iron, copper, and gold as well as foodstuffs were featured objects in this commerce. Farm wives bartered goods in village markets held at regular intervals, while merchant families organized trade on a broader basis, shipping goods in canoes, on donkeys, or on the heads of porters.

As early as the first millennium B.C. daring traders, most of them desert dwellers, occasionally used horse-drawn chariots to carry goods across the Sahara. The two-month journey required knowledgeable guides, bribes to the nomads who roamed the desert, stamina to endure blinding sandstorms and limited water supplies, and patience to deal with the scorpions and the lice that lived around the oases. Much of this trade was in the hands of the Garamantes, who lived on the northern fringes of the Sahara in what is now Libya and hunted black Africans to sell into slavery, and of the Berbers, indigenous nomads who lived in the western and central regions of North Africa.

The trans-Saharan trade was revolutionized by the introduction of the camel into northern Africa from central Asia. The camel could go for several days without food or water while carrying 500-pound loads and traveling as much as 20 miles a day. But camels could carry these loads only four months a year without endangering their health.

So valuable were camels that in the Sahara people calculated their wealth in terms of the number of camels they owned. Enterprising traders developed a network of caravan routes between North Africa and the Sudan

## ◉ The Trans-Saharan Crossing ◉

*Ibn Battuta provided a vivid description of his trek across the Sahara in a caravan in 1352.*

At Sijilmasa I bought camels and a four months' supply of forage for them. Thereupon I set out . . . with a caravan including, amongst others, a number of the merchants of Sijilmasa. After twenty-five days we reached Taghaza, an unattractive village, with the curious feature that its houses and mosques are built of blocks of salt, roofed with camel skins. There are no trees there, nothing but sand. In the sand is a salt mine; they dig for the salt, and find it in thick slabs, lying one on top of the other. . . . No one lives at Taghaza except the slaves of the Massufa tribe, who dig for the salt. . . .

We passed ten days of discomfort there, because the water is brackish and the place is plagued with flies. Water supplies are laid in at Taghaza for the crossing of the desert which lies beyond it, which is a ten-nights' journey with no water on the way except on rare occasions. . . . Truffles [an edible underground fungus] are plentiful in this desert and it swarms with lice, so that people wear string necklaces containing mercury, which kills them. . . .

We came next to Tasarahla, a place of subterranean water-beds, where the caravans halt. They stay there three days to rest, mend their waterskins, fill them with water, and sew on them covers of sackcloth as a precaution against the wind. . . . The desert is haunted by demons; if the *takshif* [an advance agent] be alone, they make sport of him and disorder his mind, so that he loses his way and perishes. For there is no visible road or track in these parts—nothing but sand blown hither and thither by the wind. You see hills of sand in one place, and afterwards you will see them moved to quite another place. . . . Thus we reached the town of Iwalatan [Walata] after a journey from Sijilmasa of two months to a day.

*Source:* Ibn Battuta, *Travels in Asia and Africa, 1325–1354,* trans. H. A. R. Gibb (London: Routledge, 1929), pp. 317–319.

**The introduction of the camel around A.D. 200 revolutionized the trans-Saharan trade.**
[Victor Englebert/Photo Researchers]

between A.D. 200 and 700. Over these routes fine silk, cotton, copper (for the bronze industries), steel, glass beads from Venice, salt, figs, dates, and horses for the royal cavalries were shipped southward. Returning caravans transported gold, pepper, ivory, kola nuts, leather, cotton cloth, and slaves from West Africa. Outfitting a caravan involved great expense, including the cost of the camels and the merchandise, fees for the guide, wages for the drivers and outriders, "protection" money, and heavy tolls at both ends of the journey. The larger the caravan, the greater the security, and by the fourteenth century some caravans included as many as 12,000 camels. Substantial risks could be rewarded with enormous profits, as in the case of a fifteenth-century merchant whose fortune was estimated at 12,500 ounces of gold.

Salt, gold, and slaves were the most important items in the trans-Saharan trade. The salt, which was in great demand in West Africa, came mostly from sites in the mid-Sahara such as Taghaza, some 500 miles north of Timbuktu, where the houses themselves were built of salt blocks. At places like Taghaza slaves quarried the salt in 200-pound blocks for shipment south, where it was exchanged for gold.

Most of Africa's gold came from what is now Ghana, Nigeria, and Senegal. Men dug alluvial soil from pits or underground shafts and floated it in huge trays to the mineheads, where women extracted the gold by panning. From the mines the gold was normally transported in hollow feather quills to trading centers for conversion into ingots, coins, or jewelry and transshipment across the Sahara. By the eleventh century as much as 9 tons of gold was sent northward each year. Not surprisingly,

the mining and shipment of gold was the leading industry in black Africa.

Second only in importance to gold as an export were black slaves. From an average of 1,000 per year in the late seventh and eighth centuries, the number grew until it peaked at 8,700 per year in the tenth and eleventh centuries; by the fifteenth century it had declined to 4,300 per year. Small numbers of white slaves were transported in the opposite direction for sale to the royal courts of West Africa. Most slaves were kidnapped or seized in armed raids or warfare, often from the tribes that had not organized into states, though some rulers sold their own subjects. Monarchs desirous of increasing the size of their armies captured neighboring peoples and traded them into slavery for horses; by the fifteenth century, a horse was worth 7 to 15 slaves in Senegal. Attractive girls and eunuchs fetched the highest prices, and female slaves were generally more valuable than their male counterparts because of the high demand for harems and household servants. The human cost of the slave trade was enormous, as fatalities sustained in raids and subsequent confinement and transportation resulted in as many as five to ten deaths for every slave who reached North Africa. The Africans themselves retained many slaves for use in the fields, construction work, mining, porterage, the military, and royal harems.

The growth of the trans-Saharan trade stimulated urban development on the northern fringes of the savanna. Chief among the emerging frontier cities was Kumbi, with a population of 15,000 to 20,000 in the eleventh century. Timbuktu, Walata, Jenné, and Gao also became

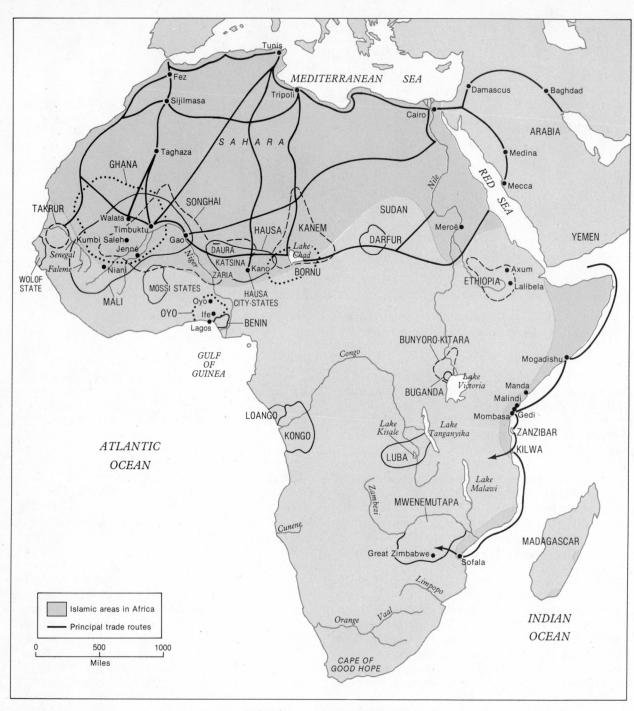

*9.3 Africa, 1000–1500*

notable cities, each of which, like Kumbi, was a commercial center with a cosmopolitan population in which Muslims and Jews mingled with black Africans. These cities were the main gateways for the expansion of Islamic culture and technology into sub-Saharan Africa, as exemplified by the construction of mosques, the introduction of writing to the western Sudan (a skill known much earlier in Kush and Axum), and, commencing in the fourteenth century, the manufacture of bricks. Muslims advised Sudanese rulers, and scholars introduced

West Africans to the rich culture of the Islamic world. Koranic schools and universities were founded, the most noted of which was Timbuktu's University of Sankoré. Graduates of these schools were especially useful to the rulers of the West African states, providing them with bureaucrats whose primary loyalty was to their sovereign rather than to their kin or their village. The importing of Islam was crucial to the development of sub-Saharan Africa.

## The States of the Western and Central Sudan

For hundreds of years before the arrival of Europeans in the fifteenth century A.D. the peoples of the western and central Sudan were governed by a series of impressive kingdoms. Monarchs proclaiming themselves divine ruled from splendid courts with the aid of councils of ministers, few of whom held their offices on an hereditary basis. The kings were therefore able to tap men of talent to administer their realms, the wealth of which derived largely from taxes and tribute. But in the end the administrations could not keep pace with territorial expansion, and the kingdoms were further weakened, like so many in early medieval Europe, by disputed successions.

## The Kingdom of Ghana

By the time the Muslims arrived in the mid-eighth century, Ghana, known as the "land of gold," was already prosperous. Located on the upper Niger River, it had emerged by the early fifth century out of a federation of farming villages. It soon developed into a powerful kingdom with the ability to dominate vassal states on its frontiers. Both economically and culturally the kingdom made a profound impression on Muslim visitors. An Arab writer of the tenth century referred to a trade contract for 20,000 gold coins, and a century later the Muslim chronicler al-Bakri, who lived at Córdoba in Spain, noted the customs duties levied by the king of Ghana on goods exported from or imported into the country. The Arabs, themselves expert and enthusiastic traders, were clearly impressed by Ghana's commercial sophistication.

The capital was located at Kumbi Saleh, in reality two adjacent towns, one for the monarch and his court and the other dominated by an enclave of foreign merchants and Muslims. The mosques and houses of the merchants in the latter were built of stone, in contrast to the mud-built structures of the native population that sur-

rounded the royal palace. In spite of continual contact with the world of Islam, Ghana maintained its cultural and religious independence until the eleventh century. Although al-Bakri underlined the fact that many of the king's advisers were Muslims (though the monarch himself was not), he described the religion of Ghana as "paganism and the worship of idols." The picture he provides is of an aristocratic society, dominated by the king and his court, that was the focus of elaborate rituals. Reflecting Ghana's key role as a supplier of gold, on formal occasions both the monarch and his retainers dressed in garments of fine cloth and bedecked themselves with gold ornaments, giving Ghana's ruler a reputation among many Africans as the "richest monarch in the world." The royal dwelling was guarded by horses whose bridles were decorated with gold and whose blankets were woven with gold thread. When the king's subjects were summoned to an audience, they approached him on their knees and with dust on their heads to express their respect. According to al-Bakri, the king maintained his power with the support of a 200,000-man army. Although this figure was surely exaggerated, Ghana's army, the core of which was an effective cavalry, was impressive.

The fundamental importance of the king, both in life and in death, is reminiscent of similar cultural patterns in ancient Egypt. According to al-Bakri, when a king died, a huge dome of wood was constructed over the site of his tomb. Buried within it were the deceased's weapons and ornaments and the plates and cups he had used in life for eating and drinking, which were filled with various foods and beverages.

The women of Kumbi Saleh and other trading cities in the western and central Sudan were respected, and some of them held positions in the government. They wore collars and bracelets, an honor accorded among males only to the king. In the cities, public nudity was common for women of all ranks, but as a matter of freedom rather than license. In the caravan town of Walata, near Kumbi Saleh, the heir apparent to the throne was the son of the king's sister rather than the king's own son, a custom known as uterine descent. Walata wives were free to take lovers. Outside the cities, the women of the western and central Sudan spent much of their time in the fields. The men typically cleared the land and prepared the fields for planting, but women did the threshing, winnowing, and milling and raised vegetables in small family plots.

The reasons for Ghana's decline in the twelfth century are murky. In the late eleventh century an invasion by the Almoravids, a strict Muslim sect of northwestern Africa, disrupted trade and damaged agriculture, but the kingdom survived until 1203, when it was destroyed by a vassal state. Shortly thereafter, its territory was annexed by Mali.

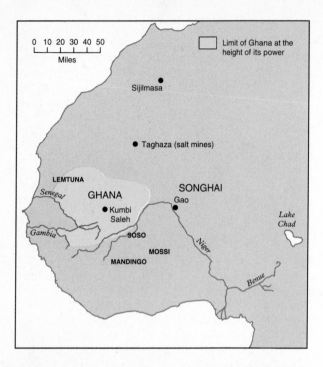

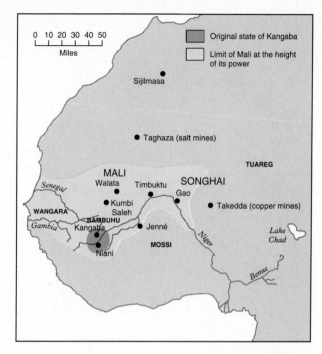

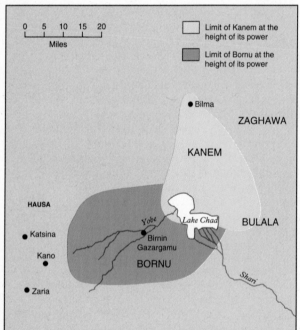

*9.4 Ancient Kingdoms of the Western Sahara*

# The Empire of Mali

The chaos that followed the collapse of Ghana enabled the people of Mali, former vassals to Ghana, to impose their domination over the western Sudan. The empire of

Mali remained the most powerful force in West Africa for two centuries (c. 1250–c. 1460). Its founder was Sundiata (c. 1235–c. 1260), who initially put together a federation in which local governors maintained their positions while acknowledging Sundiata as their monarch. With the conquest of adjacent territory by Sundiata and

Uli, his son and successor, the new kingdom combined the southern half of Ghana with Mali and parts of what is now Guinea. Uli thus controlled not only the major gold-producing areas but also the communications network provided by the upper Niger River and its tributaries. From Timbuktu, the great trading city on the southern fringes of the Sahara, to the Atlantic coast, a secure base for economic prosperity was established.

Although Sundiata owed much of his authority and success to his exploitation of traditional beliefs in his spiritual powers, he was nominally a Muslim and enjoyed the support of the predominantly Muslim merchant class. So too did Uli, a devout Muslim. The key to Mali's prosperity was the success of the merchants. Taking their cue from Muhammad, himself originally a merchant, they used their pilgrimages to Mecca and the other holy cities of the Muslim world as a means of building trade connections. Mali's products were sold through North African outlets in European markets around the Mediterranean.

Above all, the economy of Mali benefited from the fact that since the twelfth century most European communities had begun to replace copper and silver with gold as the principal unit of currency. The Christian kings of northern Spain began to use gold in imitation of the Almoravids who had settled in southern Iberia, and during the thirteenth century most of the major banking centers of western Europe adopted gold coinage. At least two-thirds of the gold that made this possible was mined in territory controlled by Mali. To facilitate commerce, Mali devised a currency system that made use of standardized weights of gold dust for large amounts and imported cowrie shells for everyday transactions.

Our picture of Mali at the height of its prosperity is considerably enlivened by the account of Ibn Battuta, an Arab traveler, of his visit in 1352–1353. Sophisticated and tireless, Ibn Battuta was no casual sightseer; by the time he made his tour of Mali, he had already visited China. Among other things, he was struck by the general safety of traveling conditions among the Malian people, asserting that there was "complete security in their country." The Malians, he said, had a greater horror of injustice than any other people and showed no mercy to those guilty of it. Part of this could presumably be ascribed to the influence of Islamic law, and Ibn Battuta comments on the zeal with which law and theology were studied. On visiting the chief judge of Niani at his home, he saw the judge's children in chains, from which they could win release only by reciting the Koran from memory.

Ibn Battuta did not approve of all aspects of life in Mali. The elaborate court ceremonials, with their hymns in praise of the king and the ritual groveling of the courtiers, met with his contempt. In general he was treated courteously, but on at least one occasion a provincial

Bearded male figure from Jenné, Mali, dating from the fourteenth century. [Founders Society, Detroit Institute of Arts]

governor kept him and his merchant companions standing and refused to speak to them except through an interpreter.

Ibn Battuta sheds light on the role of women in Ma-

## 🔘 Journey to Mali 🔘

*The following passage comes from Ibn Battuta's account of his travels in West Africa to visit the Muslim rulers there.*

I was at Malli during the two festivals of the sacrifice and the fast-breaking. On these days the sultan takes his seat on the *pempi* [ceremonial chair] after the midafternoon prayer. The armor-bearers bring in magnificent arms—quivers of gold and silver, swords ornamented with gold and with golden scabbards, gold and silver lances, and crystal maces. At his head stand four amirs [attendants] driving off the flies, having in their hands silver ornaments resembling saddle-stirrups. The commanders . . . and preacher sit in their usual places. The interpreter Dugha comes with his four wives and his slave-girls, who are about a hundred in number. They are wearing beautiful robes, and on their heads they have gold and silver fillets, with gold and silver balls attached. A chair is placed for Dugha to sit on. He plays on an instrument made of reeds, with some small calabashes [gourds] at its lower end, and chants a poem in praise of the sultan, recalling his battles and deeds of valor. The women and girls sing along with him and play with bows. Accompanying them are about thirty youths, wearing red woollen tunics and white skull-caps; each of them has his drum slung from his shoulder and beats it. Afterwards come his boy pupils who play and turn wheels in the air, like the natives of Sind. They show a marvellous nimbleness and agility in these exercises and play most cleverly with swords. Dugha also makes a fine play with the sword. Thereupon the sultan orders a gift to be presented to Dugha and he is given a purse containing . . . gold dust, and is informed of the contents of the purse before all the people. The commanders rise and twang their bows in thanks to the sultan. The next day each one of them gives Dugha a gift, every man according to his rank. Every Friday after . . . prayer, Dugha carries out a similar ceremony to this that we have described.

*Source:* Ibn Battuta, *Travels in Asia and Africa, 1325–1354,* trans. H. A. R. Gibb (London: Routledge, 1929), p. 328.

lian society. They were free, he noted, to circulate as they chose, without wearing a veil, and to select their companions. He was startled that the female slaves of the king and the provincial governors wore no clothing. Although there is no concrete historical evidence that women played an important role in Mali's political and economic life, his observations suggest a substantial difference between traditional Islamic society and that of sub-Saharan Africa.

## 🌸
## MANSA MUSA, CALIPH OF "THE WESTERN PARTS"

Mali was just past the zenith of its powers when Ibn Battuta saw it. Under Mansa ("Emperor") Musa (1312–1337), Mali's greatest ruler, it extended from Lake Chad to the shores of the Atlantic and from the Sahara to the edge of the tropical rain forest. Both north and south, local kingdoms paid regular tribute and in some cases accepted Malian governors, some of whom were members of Musa's own family. Among the lands over which Musa held sway was Songhai to the east, whose market town of Gao played a crucial role in the trans-Saharan trade. Indeed, the key to Mali's power was its domination of both trade and the gold fields in the western Sudan. Altogether, Musa ruled perhaps 8 million people.

A devout Muslim, Musa has been highly acclaimed by Islamic historians for his grand pilgrimage to Mecca in 1324–1325. During his journey he made a spectacular visit to Cairo, where he was greeted by the sultan of Egypt. Musa entered the city with a magnificent entourage that included 100 camels, each laden with 300 pounds of gold, and 500 slaves carrying golden staffs. His lavish almsgiving and purchases in the city's bazaars reportedly sparked a serious inflation that lasted years. As a result of Musa's pilgrimage, the wealth of the Sudan became legendary throughout the eastern Mediterranean.

Musa's journey had a lasting impact on West Africa. When he returned to Mali, he brought with him an architect and poet from Andalusia who subsequently introduced Arabic architectural styles to the western Sudan. A new mosque was constructed at Timbuktu, and the one at Gao was remodeled. Henceforth, major buildings were normally constructed of brick rather than pounded clay. With Musa also came a number of Islamic scholars, many of whom took up residence in Timbuktu, making it the leading cultural center in West Africa and a center of the book trade. Under Musa's patronage, Timbuktu, Jenné, and Niani became internationally acclaimed centers of theological and legal scholarship.

Under the leadership of Musa and the Islamic faith he championed, Mali made great strides. Islam helped Musa develop a literate bureaucracy, facilitated diplomatic contacts with Muslim states in North Africa, and contributed to royal authority by establishing new lines of power. Yet Musa observed the rights of local chiefs and retained many traditional African customs, including an elaborate court ritual that included magic. Musa's pride in his people is reflected in a story he told about his predecessors, who had reputedly dispatched two expeditions, one consisting of 400 ships and the other of 2,000 ships, to cross the Atlantic; only one vessel, he said, had returned from this daring feat of exploration. The reputation of Mali reached Europe, thanks in part to the work of a cartographer from Majorca, who in 1375 drew a map that depicted the ruler of Mali seated on his throne, a gold nugget and a scepter in his hands, as a Berber trader approaches.

## The Empire of Songhai

Shortly after Ibn Battuta's visit, the Malian empire began to crumble owing to palace infighting, quarrels over succession to the crown, and aggression by the neighboring Mossi, a vassal people, and the Berbers. Around 1335 the people of Songhai, who resented their Mali overlords, became autonomous, though they continued to pay tribute to Mali. By the end of the fourteenth century Songhai was a large, wealthy state. Sonni Ali (1464–1492) organized a professional army that he used to extend the borders of his kingdom, creating a sizable empire that included Timbuktu and Jenné, which fell after a seven-year siege. Sunni Ali became infamous among

The main mosque at Timbuktu is the oldest surviving one in West Africa. [Werner Forman Archive, London]

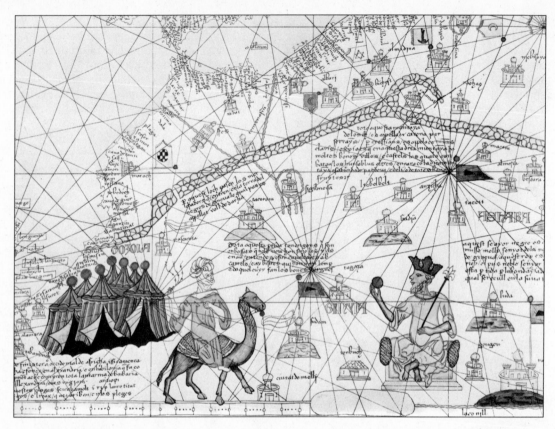

This detail of a map of Africa drawn in 1375 depicts Mansa Musa on the throne of Mali.
[Courtesy of the Trustees of the British Library]

Muslims for murdering Islamic scholars in Timbuktu who supported Mali.

The Muslims eventually got their revenge by overthrowing Sunni Ali's son and establishing a new dynasty under Muhammad Touré (1493–1528). Muhammad underscored his indebtedness to Islam by undertaking a pilgrimage to Mecca reminiscent of Musa's. Like Sunni Ali, he continued to expand the Songhai empire until it extended from the upper Niger almost to Morocco and included the salt mines of the Sahara. His greatest accomplishment was the improvement of the administrative system created by Sunni Ali, who had established a central bureaucracy and organized the empire into provinces, each directed by an appointed governor. Muhammad refined this system by establishing permanent ministries in the capital at Gao, with the head of each selected by the king and directly responsible to him. There were ministries for such major areas as the treasury, agriculture, and the army and navy.

Although Muhammad was toppled by his own sons in 1528, Songhai remained an influential power until the late sixteenth century. The Arab rulers of Morocco, fresh from victories over the Portuguese and the Turks, were eager to gain control over West Africa's gold supplies. During the period from 1590 to 1618, small bands of Arab mercenaries, armed with gunpowder and firearms, made their way across the Sahara and defeated the Songhai forces. The collapse of central government that ensued destroyed Songhai unity. The entire gold-producing area of West Africa fragmented once more into tribal kingdoms, which the Europeans found on their arrival at the end of the eighteenth century.

## Kanem-Bornu and the Hausa States

West Africa was also the home of numerous other states, among them Kanem-Bornu in the central Sudan. In its early centuries the kingdom of Kanem, located northwest of Lake Chad, derived much of its income from the slave trade. The people of Kanem exchanged captives from the south, especially young girls and eunuchs, for horses from North Africa. The horses were then used to attack Kanem's neighbors, a practice justified as jihads against the infidel. The people of Kanem kept some of the slaves to help farm the land.

EARLY AFRICA

| | Eastern Sudan | Western and Central Sudan | East Africa | South Africa |
|---|---|---|---|---|
| Before A.D. 300 | Kingdom of Kush (before 1000 B.C.–A.D. 330) | | Arrival of the Bantu (after A.D. 1) | |
| 300–1000 | Peak of Axum's power (300–710) | Kingdom of Ghana (c. 400–1203) | | Arrival of the Bantu (after A.D. 300) |
| 1000–1600 | | Empire of Mali (c. 1250–c. 1460) | Golden Age of Swahili city-states (c. 1200–c. 1600) | Great Zimbabwe (c. 1000–c. 1500) |
| | | Peak of Kanem's power (c. 1300–c. 1400) | | |
| | | Empire of Songhai (c. 1335–c. 1600) | | |

The ruler, or *mai*, of Kanem was regarded as divine, and as a god he lived in virtual seclusion. A Muslim visitor observed that the people

> **falsely imagine that he does not eat food. His people provide his food secretly, bringing it into his houses without it being known whence they bring it. If anyone of his subjects happens to meet the camels carrying it, he is immediately killed on the spot.**[1]

The *mai*'s authority was virtually unchecked, and he governed with the aid of a highly centralized bureaucracy. Descent to the throne passed through the male line, but the queen mothers and other female members of the royal family were often very powerful. In the late eleventh century the *mai* embraced Islam, after which Kanem enjoyed close relations with the Muslim states of North and East Africa.

After two centuries of expansion, Kanem reached the peak of its power in the early thirteenth century. At that time its *mai* commanded a powerful army with a cavalry that numbered 40,000. Kanem fell on hard times in the late fourteenth and fifteenth centuries because of bitter disputes among rival factions of the ruling dynasty. Bornu, a tributary state founded by Kanem southwest of Lake Chad in the previous century, became virtually autonomous. Around 1400, however, Kanem's ruling family moved to Bornu, which henceforth turned the tables on Kanem by making it a tributary state.

A resurgence of power occurred in the late sixteenth and seventeenth centuries, especially during the reign of Idris Aloma (c. 1571–1603), who reformed the government and the army. A devout Muslim, Idris Aloma replaced traditional laws with those of Islam and appointed judges empowered to enforce the Koran and the Sunna. A man of strict moral views, he condemned adultery and obscenity so stridently that contemporaries were astonished. The recipients of high office, including some slaves, were men of demonstrated loyalty to the *mai*. Idris Aloma expanded his army of cavalry and traditional infantry (hitherto armed only with bows and spears) with units of Turkish-trained musketeers and imported firearms from North Africa. These reforms enabled Idris Aloma to make Kanem-Bornu the dominant state of the central Sudan.

To the west of Kanem-Bornu were the seven principal Hausa city-states, which emerged in the eleventh and twelfth centuries. Originally villages protected by wooden stockades, they grew into impressive walled cities that ruled the surrounding territory. Their prosperity stemmed in large measure from thriving agriculture and grazing as well as from their strategic location on the trade routes linking them to the savanna and the forest states of the Guinea coast. The Hausa cities not only traded in slaves but also used them to build their walls and help farm the land. Although Islamic doctrine prohibited the enslavement of Muslims, the Hausa rulers readily traded Muslim captives for horses and firearms from North Africa.

Zaria, the southernmost city, was known for its slave raids; in the fifteenth century its most important ruler was a woman. Kano, the leading city until the sixteenth century, derived its wealth from crafts (especially leatherwork) and the manufacture of cotton textiles; much of the prized "Moroccan" leather imported by Europeans from North Africa originated in Kano. The city was eventually surpassed by Katsina, a major trading center. Each city was governed by a king, none of whom proved strong enough to unite the Hausa into a single state. Like many other West Africans, the rulers of the Hausa embraced Islam in the fourteenth century, but most commoners did not follow suit for another 400 years. Muslim scholars from Timbuktu settled at Kano and Katsina in the fifteenth and sixteenth centuries, helping the spread of Islamic culture. The prosperity of the Hausa cities continued through the eighteenth century.

## ◉ The Introduction of Islam to Kano ◉

*The coming of Islam to sub-Saharan Africa sometimes met with opposition, as in the case of Kano, a Hausa city-state. People from the Wangara district of Mali carried the message of Islam to Kano in the fourteenth century.*

When they came they commanded the *sarki* [king] to observe the times of prayer. He complied and made Gurdumus his imam [religious teacher], and Lawal his muezzin [caller to prayer]. . . . The *sarki* commanded every town in Kano country to observe times of prayer. So they all did so. A mosque was built beneath the sacred tree facing east, and prayers were made at the five appointed times in it. [One prominent man] was opposed to prayer, and when the Muslims after praying had gone home, he would come with his men and defile the whole mosque and cover it with filth. Dan Buji was told . . . to patrol round the mosque with well-armed men from evening until morning. He kept up a constant halloo. For all that, the pagans tried to win him and his men over. Some of his men followed the pagans and went away, but he and the rest refused. The defilement continued till . . . the people assented [to pray]. They gathered together on a Tuesday and prayed against the pagans until sunrise. . . . The chief of the pagans was struck blind that day, and afterward all the pagans who were present at the defilement—they and all their women. After this they were all afraid.

*Source: Africa in the Days of Exploration,* ed. R. Oliver and C. Oliver (Englewood Cliffs, N.J.: Prentice Hall, 1965), p. 24.

## The Guinea Coast: The Yoruba and Benin

To the south of the Hausa cities were the so-called forest states of the Guinea coast. Much of this region is savanna, and the peoples of this area did not inhabit the forests until they were forced to do so by population pressure. The most intriguing of these peoples were the Yoruba, who founded a state at Ife in the eleventh century. As its artistic remains indicate, it was a thriving, sophisticated state, most of whose trade was in the hands of women. The fertile soil and abundant rainfall of the region enabled the people to produce surplus cereal and root crops, leaving them with ample time and wealth to develop artistic and craft skills. The bronze and terra-cotta portraits of Ife's rulers, strikingly naturalistic, have suggested to some scholars a dependence on the art of the ancient Nok culture. The terra-cotta and metal castings were probably made for funeral ceremonies. The people of Ife presumably exported food, kola nuts (used medicinally as a stimulant), and ivory to obtain copper for their artistic endeavors from the Sahara.

In the forests southwest of Ife, most Edo-speaking peoples lived in small villages, but around the eleventh century some of them established a city-state at Benin.

By the time the Portuguese arrived in 1485, the walled city of Benin governed a prosperous state whose territory extended westward from the Niger delta to Lagos on the Atlantic coast. A Dutch visitor to the city around 1600 compared its houses and wide streets favorably with those in Amsterdam. Like Ife, Benin produced superb sculptures in bronze, terra-cotta, ivory, and wrought iron, though its figures were more conventional and stylized than those of Ife. Much of the art from both states exalts their monarchs. Benin continued to expand until the early sixteenth century, at which time it ceased to have captives to sell into slavery. Not until the eighteenth century did Benin again sell Africans—this time its own citizens—as slaves, bound now for the Americas.

## The City-States of East Africa

Unlike remoter regions to the west, the coast and offshore islands of East Africa were visited by Phoenician, Greek, Roman, Arab, and Indian traders well before the Bantu settled in the region during the first centuries A.D.

Ivory carving of a mounted Yoruba rider, probably carved at Owo in western Nigeria. [Werner Forman Archive, London]

**Typically realistic bronze sculpture of a king of Ife.** [Ife Museum, Nigeria]

The earliest traders sought ivory and tortoise shells from the indigenous Africans and in time founded their own settlements along the coast, partly to trade, partly to fish. By the early seventh century the mostly Arab merchants in these towns were shipping black slaves to Persia. The Bantu began taking up residence in the coastal communities some 300 years later, at which time some of them apparently converted to Islam. Fresh waves of immigrants—mostly Arabs, Persians, and Indonesians—arrived in the eleventh and twelfth centuries and intermarried with the Africans. The culture that

**Bronze sculpture of a king of Benin.** [Indiana University Art Museum]

evolved in these cities was a mixture of Bantu and Islamic traditions. The primary language was Kiswahili (*Swahili* means "people of the coast"), a Bantu tongue that incorporated large numbers of Arabic words and came to be written in Arabic script.

The leading Swahili city-states—Mogadishu, Kilwa, Malindi, Manda, and Mombasa—thrived on their commerce in the thirteenth, fourteenth, and fifteenth centuries. Gold (mined by the Bantu in the region of Zimbabwe), ivory, slaves, leopard skins, tortoise shells, cotton cloth, and mangrove poles (for the construction of homes around the Persian Gulf) were the main exports, in return for which the Swahili merchants imported Indian and Chinese cloth, Persian ceramics, Chinese porcelain, glassware, and beads. The slaves, captured from interior villages by raiding parties, were shipped as far afield as the Persian Gulf, India, and China. The cities also traded with the hinterland, sending such items as fish and shell beads in return for ivory and foodstuffs.

Swahili society was organized into three principal classes, the chief of which comprised the sultan and his family, high-ranking government officials, and prominent merchants. Generally wealthy, they were Muslims who were typically descended from Arab or Persian immigrants. They derived most of their wealth from overseas trade, though most of them owned sizable farms, and some of the merchants were also involved in the manufacture of cotton cloth and glass beads. Below the upper class were artisans, minor government officials, and ship captains. Like their social betters, most of them were Kiswahili-speaking Muslims; unlike the upper class, however, they were native Africans. At the bottom of the social hierarchy were the slaves, who did much of the farming and manufacturing.

The women of East Africa were generally subordinate to the men. A woman had the right to refuse to marry a particular man, but most decisions concerning marriage, including whether or not polygamy would be practiced, were made by men because they controlled the bulk of the material possessions. In a polygamous household, the wives enjoyed equal authority with their husband only if they were unanimous in their view. Men decided where and what to farm, cleared the land, and then left the women to do most of the agricultural labor while the men hunted, fought, or tended to local affairs.

The greatest of the nearly 40 Swahili city-states, Kilwa, was situated on two offshore islands to the south of Zanzibar. Around 1200 they were united under the rule of Abi bin Hasan, whose name appears on the copper coinage minted by the new state, the first of its kind in East Africa. The principal town, Kilwa Kisiwani, was constructed during his reign; its buildings, many of them of stone, include a great mosque and a royal palace. A new dynasty, the Mahdali, remained in power from the end of the thirteenth century until the arrival of Portuguese colonizers two centuries later. Under Mahdali rule, elaborate building programs were initiated. The great mosque was enlarged, and a vast palace was constructed, its great courtyard illuminated by hundreds of oil lamps. Large warehouses were built to store the cargoes shipped through Kilwa. In 1331 Ibn Battuta visited Kilwa, which impressed him as "one of the most beautiful and well-constructed towns in the world."

**The Great Mosque at Kilwa Kisiwani was built in the thirteenth century and expanded two centuries later. [Basil Davidson]**

## ◉ The City of Kilwa ◉

*A European visitor to Kilwa in the early sixteenth century provided this description of the flourishing city.*

The captain-major told the pilot to show him the port, and that he wished to go to Kilwa, which he did; and on sighting it, he entered the port with the whole fleet, which anchored round the city, which stands on an island which is surrounded and encircled by the sea water, but on the land side there is little water, which at high tide is knee-deep. The city is large and is of good buildings of stone and mortar with terraces, and the houses have much wood works. The city comes down to the shore, and is entirely surrounded by a wall and towers, within which there may be 12,000 inhabitants. The country all round is very luxuriant with many trees and gardens of all sorts of vegetables, citrons, lemons, and the best sweet oranges that were ever seen, sugar-canes, figs, pomegranates, and a great abundance of flocks, especially sheep, which have fat in the tail, which is almost the size of the body, and very savory. The streets of the city are very narrow, as the houses are very high, of three and four stories, and one can run along the tops of them upon the terraces, as the houses are very close together; and in the port there were many ships.

*Source:* G. S. P. Freeman-Grenville, ed., *The East African Coast: Select Documents from the First to the Earlier Nineteenth Century,* 2nd ed. (London: Collings, 1975), p. 66.

For much of the period before the arrival of the Europeans, the main centers of East Africa formed part of a Muslim commercial network that stretched to India and China. By the mid-thirteenth century the Muslims had consolidated their commercial monopoly in the Indian Ocean. Kilwa and other centers maintained Muslim influence in the western zone of this trading empire while also acting as a link between Islam and the indigenous peoples of Africa.

## Southern Africa

Unlike the other regions of Africa we have surveyed, southern Africa was not exposed to foreign peoples until the Portuguese came in the late fifteenth century. The earliest inhabitants of the region were people who spoke a language unrelated to Bantu called Khoikhoi. Hunter-gatherers, they depicted both themselves and their prey in rock paintings that are among the finest achievements of prehistoric African art. The Bantu reached southern Africa by the fourth century A.D., bringing with them new agricultural techniques and a knowledge of ironworking. At the artificial cave of Castle Cavern in Swaziland, pottery, smelted iron, and iron-mining tools have been found that date to the early fifth century. This and other proof of metalworking south of the Limpopo River (including iron mines) indicates that Bantu farmers and smiths had begun to make their way down the continent relatively early, coexisting with rather than conquering the hunting and gathering peoples whom they found there.

By the eleventh century hundreds of villages had been built on the high plateau of the Transvaal. Some were still in use in the nineteenth century and were seen by early missionaries to southern Africa. The buildings, made of stone, were circular, as were the fences that surrounded each house and the outer walls of the villages. Archaeologists have learned a good deal about the widespread trading patterns of this region. Copper ingots, iron implements, and salt were important items of commerce, as were such minerals as red hematite, which were used as cosmetics. The discovery of cowrie shells from the Indian Ocean indicates just how far the trading networks extended.

### ❀
### GREAT ZIMBABWE: CAPITAL OF SOUTH AFRICA'S FIRST STATE?

North of the great bend in the Limpopo River was Great Zimbabwe ("stone houses"), the capital of several successive Bantu kingdoms. The site, strategically located on the southern edge of the Zimbabwe Plateau, had been occupied since the fourth century A.D. What may have been South Africa's first state developed in the eleventh century in large measure because it was the center of gold mining and the resulting trade with the coastal communities of East Africa. Great Zimbabwe also benefited from relatively fertile land, superb building materials, adequate supplies of game, and minimal exposure to crop-devouring locusts and the tsetse flies that endangered humans and cattle.

Between the eleventh and the fifteenth centuries the rulers of Great Zimbabwe constructed enormous complexes of stone buildings. The most impressive of these was 300 feet long and 200 feet wide with a unique conical tower. Oval walls surrounded the structure, and the entire complex was encircled by an elliptical stone wall up to 32 feet in height and as much as 17 feet thick. This complex housed the elite and served as a place for the ruler and tribal representatives to intercede with ancestral spirits. After a German explorer rediscovered Great Zimbabwe in 1871, incredulous Europeans were reluctant to accept the fact that the magnificent city was the work of Africans and instead hypothesized that it was the creation of Solomon and Sheba or of the Phoenicians.

Beyond the walls the commoners lived in huts so crowded together that their eaves virtually touched. Great Zimbabwe's population may have been as large as 18,000. For all but the elite, living conditions were harsh. The absence of sanitation facilities would have meant prevalent disease, and the smoke from thousands of cooking fires would at times have enveloped the city in smog. The population's basic dietary staples were sorghum and millet, supplemented by beans and squash. The more fortunate residents also ate meat, usually beef, although some lamb, goat, and wild game were available.

By the thirteenth century the society of Great Zimbabwe had become specialized. Some people farmed; others spun cloth or mined gold (from alluvial deposits and quartz reefs), iron, copper, and tin; artisans made pottery, carved soapstone and ivory, or constructed buildings. The principal building material was granite, available locally in convenient thin slabs. Zimbabwean artisans also used a sturdy plaster known as *daga*, made of clay derived from decomposed granite; *daga* enabled the artisans to create smooth, polished surfaces as well as intricate patterns. The skill of Zimbabwean builders can still be seen in the city's walls, constructed without mortar and wherever possible without sharp corners. Other residents engaged in commerce. Through their East African trading partners the people of Great Zimbabwe imported glass from western Asia, ceramics from Persia and China, and salt and copper from neighboring

The conical tower and part of the ruins of Great Zimbabwe. [Robert Aberman/Barbara Heller Collection, London]

Africans; in turn they exported gold and gold ornaments, as well as weapons and tools made of iron.

Great Zimbabwe began to decline in the fifteenth century, apparently as the cumulative effect of declining trade, depleted soil, overgrazing, and dwindling supplies of wild game. Late in the century, a new dynasty moved the capital to a site near the Zambezi River. At that point the empire, which the newly arrived Portuguese called the Monomotapa, extended from the Zambezi to the Limpopo River and from the Indian Ocean to the Kalahari Desert in the west. Like its predecessor's, the wealth of the kingdom was based primarily on the area's gold deposits, which were now mined in open pits. Weakened by court intrigue, the empire soon splintered, leaving its people exposed to Portuguese encroachments. Great Zimbabwe, however, remained, its buildings and walls but one reminder of the rich cultural accomplishments of the African peoples in the centuries before 1500.

๚ษ        ๚ษ        ๚ษ

The early civilizations of Africa manifest striking diversity. Originally hunter-gatherers, the Africans, like many other ancient peoples, learned to raise a wide range of grains, root crops, and other vegetables. Taking advantage of such natural resources as gold, copper, ivory, ebony, and prized animal skins, they developed extensive trading networks that linked them to western Asia, India, and Europe. Urban centers emerged in the northwest, the northeast, and the southeast; some, such as Niani and Meroë, became the capitals of states, while others, such as Kilwa and Mogadishu, were loosely allied with other cities. Skilled artists, especially in Ife and Benin, carved magnificent bronze portraits, and talented sculptors throughout much of Africa worked in ivory, wood, and, especially in Great Zimbabwe, soapstone. Architects blended native motifs with designs adapted from the Egyptians, the Persians, and the Arabs. Wherever Islam spread, learning flourished; the theological and law schools of Timbuktu, Jenné, and Niani acquired international reputations. African achievements were indeed significant long before the Europeans arrived.

African civilizations also had their share of problems. Many Africans made minimal use of metal tools, probably because of discouraging geographic factors, including less fertile soils and severe climate. Moreover, they tended to abuse the environment, depleting forests, overgrazing pastureland, and exhausting the soil, all of which encouraged erosion. Many Africans depended heavily on the export of gold and slaves rather than manufactured goods. The introduction of Islam may have reduced the slave trade to some degree, but the practice remained widespread. All civilizations, of course, have mixed records. Slavery in early nineteenth-century America, for instance, was harsher than it was in Africa, and virtually all societies have failed to protect the environment. The arrival of the Europeans in sub-Saharan Africa beginning in the fifteenth century was not responsible for introducing slavery to the continent, but mounting Western demands for cheap labor greatly intensified the slave trade.

## Notes

1.  *Africa in the Days of Exploration*, ed. R. Oliver and C. Oliver (Englewood Cliffs, N.J.: Prentice Hall, 1965), p. 25.

## Suggestions for Further Reading

Ade Ajayi, J. F. *The UNESCO General History of Africa*, vols. 1–4. Berkeley: University of California Press, 1980–1988.

Asante, M. K. *Afrocentricity*, rev. ed. Trenton, N.J.: Africa World Press, 1988.

Clark, J. D. *The Cambridge History of Africa*, vol. 1: *From Earliest Times to 500 B.C.* Cambridge: Cambridge University Press, 1982.

Cockcroft, L. *Africa's Way: A Journey from the Past.* New York: St. Martin's Press, 1990.

Connah, G. *African Civilizations: Precolonial Cities and States in Tropical Africa: An Archaeological Perspective.* Cambridge: Cambridge University Press, 1987.

Crowder, M., and Ade Ajayi, J. F., eds. *A History of West Africa.* New York: Columbia University Press, 1972.

Curtin, P., et al. *African History*, rev. ed. New York: Longman, 1984.

Davidson, B. *Africa: History of a Continent.* New York: Macmillan, 1972.

———. *The African Genius.* Boston: Little, Brown, 1970.

———. *A History of West Africa, 1000–1800.* New York: Doubleday, 1966.

———. *The Lost Cities of Africa*, 2nd ed. Boston: Little, Brown, 1970.

Diop, C. A. *Civilization or Barbarism.* Brooklyn: Hill, 1991.

Dunn, R. E. *The Adventures of Ibn Battuta: A Muslim Traveler of the Fourteenth Century.* Berkeley: University of California Press, 1986.

Fage, J. D. *A History of Africa.* New York: Knopf, 1978.

July, R. W. *A History of the African People*, 3rd ed. New York: Scribner, 1980.

———. *Precolonial Africa: An Economic and Social History.* New York: Scribner, 1975.

Levitzion, N. *Ancient Ghana and Mali.* London: Methuen, 1973.

Mokhtar, G., ed. *Ancient Africa.* Berkeley: University of California Press, 1980.

Niane, D. T., ed. *Africa from the XIIth to the XVIth Century.* Berkeley: University of California Press, 1984.

Olaniyan, R., ed. *African History and Culture.* Ikeja, Nigeria: Longman, 1982.

Oliver, R. *The African Middle Ages, 1400–1800.* Cambridge: Cambridge University Press, 1981.

———, and Mathew, G., eds. *History of East Africa.* Oxford: Clarendon Press, 1963.

Pouwels, R. L. *Horn and Crescent: Cultural Change and Traditional Islam on the East African Coast, 800–1900.* Cambridge: Cambridge University Press, 1987.

Shaw, T. *Nigeria: Its Archaeology and Early History.* London: Thames & Hudson, 1978.

Shillington, K. *History of Africa.* London: Macmillan, 1989.

Trimingham, J. S. *A History of Islam in West Africa.* New York: Oxford University Press, 1962.

———. *Islam in East Africa.* Oxford: Clarendon Press, 1964.

Turnbull, C. M. *Man in Africa.* Garden City, N.Y.: Anchor/Doubleday, 1976.

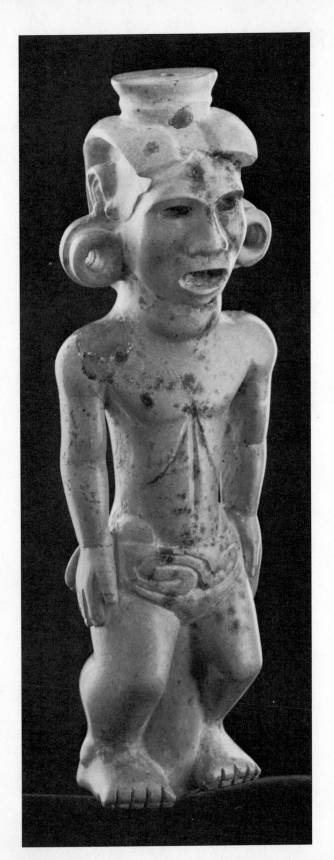

# CHAPTER 10

# The Americas to 1500

The first people in the Americas were hunter-gatherers who came from Siberia across the land bridge that is now the 56-mile-wide Bering Strait. The periodic expansion of ice sheets over much of the Northern Hemisphere had lowered sea levels worldwide as much as 300 feet, making it possible to walk from Siberia to Alaska during much of the period from about 75,000 to 10,000 years ago. Skeletal remains have enabled scholars to estimate that migrants first moved into North America more than 20,000 years ago. Southward migration brought their descendants to Mexico around 18,000 B.C., Peru by 11,000 B.C., and the tip of South America by 9000 B.C.

The pressure of expanding population and the continual search for food supplies encouraged the movement of these peoples. They supported themselves by hunting, but where natural food supplies were rich, they gradually formed settlements. The transition from a nomadic existence to agricultural communities was far more gradual than in Europe or Asia. During the period

A stone pipe from the Adena culture of the Ohio River valley. [Ohio Historical Society]

from about 8000 to 2000 B.C., which American archaeologists call the Archaic, different regions adapted themselves in various ways to their environmental resources. On both the Atlantic and the Pacific coasts of North America and on the coasts of what are now Brazil, Peru, and Chile, fishing communities began to grow. Elsewhere, as in the woodlands of eastern North America or the Andes Mountains of Peru, hunting remained the principal means of support. Although some agricultural techniques may have developed in certain regions, survival throughout the Archaic period depended on the availability of wild food.

Around 5000 B.C. or shortly thereafter the people of Mexico were growing maize (corn), beans, pumpkins, squash, chili peppers, plums, and avocados. By 2000 B.C. (and possibly much earlier) the Amerindians of Peru were raising manioc (tapioca) and potatoes. Contact between the various Amerindians enabled agricultural information to spread. Those living in Peru learned about peanuts from the lowlands of the Amazon and maize from Mesoamerica (Mexico and Central America), while the Amerindians of Mexico acquired the cultivation of manioc from the tribes of Peru. Around 1500 B.C. maize was being cultivated in what is now the southwestern United States by the ancestors of the Pueblo Indians, and sometime after 300 B.C. Indians in eastern North America had acquired this ability, long after they knew how to raise sunflowers, artichokes, and grasses.

As elsewhere in the world, the development of agriculture encouraged population growth. This was especially so in the fertile regions of Mesoamerica and Peru, as opposed, for example, to the arid lands of the American Southwest. Nevertheless, permanent villages did not appear in Mesoamerica until about 2500 B.C., several thousand years after the beginning of agriculture. This was probably because it took a long time for maize plants to become sufficiently developed to produce more per acre than wild plants. In time, reliance on maize and potatoes had the advantage of requiring less labor than the raising of grain. Surplus labor could therefore be harnessed, as in ancient Egypt and Mesopotamia, for the construction of temples and palaces as well as for the creation of sizable armies with which to expand and defend the state.

# Early Mesoamerica: The Olmecs

The first major center of civilization in the Americas developed on the hot, humid, forested lands of the Mexican Gulf Coast. The site now called San Lorenzo Tenochtitlán was first settled on a plateau around 1500 B.C.,

and on all sides the plateau was artificially extended with clay, rock, and sand. By 1200 B.C. San Lorenzo had become a major ceremonial center for a people known as the Olmecs ("rubber people," a name later bestowed on them by the Aztecs). The settlement consisted mostly of religious and governmental buildings, to be used only on formal occasions, interspersed with approximately 60 stone ornaments and carved heads. An estimated 1,000 people lived in San Lorenzo, and another 1,250 in the environs.

Following the destruction of San Lorenzo around 900 B.C., probably by invaders, the Olmecs made La Venta their ceremonial center. Founded a century earlier, the settlement at La Venta occupied an island surrounded by swamps. The principal structure was a vast stone pyramid, 110 feet high. The other buildings, spread out over a mile and a half, were decorated with elaborate stone carvings, the material for which had to be transported a considerable distance. Among the objects found in this vast temple complex were fine jade carvings, presumably left as religious offerings. When La Venta was abandoned between 600 and 500 B.C., Tres Zapotes to the northwest became the final Olmec center, a status it enjoyed until it too was abandoned at the beginning of the first century A.D.

The Olmecs' love of sculpture, which led them to seek such raw materials as jade, serpentine, and basalt, brought them into contact with other peoples and transmitted their culture. Olmec pottery and figurines have been found as far north as northern Mexico and as far south as present-day Salvador and Costa Rica. The best-known examples of Olmec art are mammoth heads, some 9 feet in height and sculpted out of basalt, that probably depicted Olmec chiefs. Olmec architecture, steles (stone-slab monuments), and altarpieces were also monumental, reflecting the fact that they were pro-

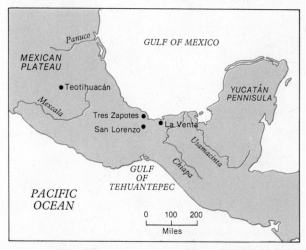

*10.1 Mesoamerica and the Olmecs*

duced by highly centralized states in which political authority was exercised by a small hereditary elite.

Olmec religion seems to have foreshadowed that of the Maya. A motif that frequently recurs and is later found among the Maya is a half-human, half-jaguar figure. Olmec deities included gods of wisdom, rain, death, fire, and spring, all of whom were worshiped by the successors of the Olmecs. A number of Olmec sculptures indicate that these people may have sacrificed humans, probably war captives but perhaps children and dwarfs as well. Judging from the remains of split, charred human bones in the refuse deposits at San Lorenzo, the Olmecs were probably cannibalistic. The religion, art, and architecture of the Olmecs left a profound impression on later Mesoamerican culture, as perhaps did their systems of writing and calculating dates, although we know little about these.

The helmet and forceful expression of this colossal Olmec head suggest that the figure may be a warrior. [Werner Forman Archive, London]

This stone figure of a woman and child is a representative example of Olmec sculpture. [Metropolitan Museum of Art, New York]

## TEOTIHUACÁN: THE FIRST GREAT CITY IN THE AMERICAS

Following the decline of the Olmecs, other major centers of civilization developed in Mexico. One of these was located in Teotihuacán, which lies on the high plateau of central Mexico, 20 miles from modern Mexico City. Another was created by the Maya, the heart of whose territory was the Yucatán peninsula and Guatemala.

Throughout most of the period from A.D. 100 to 750, Teotihuacán was the dominating force in much of Mesoamerica. Shortly before 600, when it was at its height, the city covered 8 square miles and housed a population possibly as large as 200,000, greater than any contemporary European city. Construction had begun in the first century A.D., when two great avenues were laid out at right angles to each another, dividing the area into quarters. The Aztecs later called the north-south road the Avenue of the Dead. As the city grew, it was laid out on a grid plan based on the two main arteries, with the chief ceremonial structures on the Avenue of the Dead. At the southern end stood the Pyramid of the Sun, one of the largest constructions of the ancient world (250 feet high and 650 feet square at its base), almost four times the size of the Great Pyramid of Cheops in Egypt. Its name derives from the Aztecs, who believed it to be the sun's birthplace, although it may have had an entirely different significance for the people who built it. Recent exploration indicates that there may be a huge tomb at its base, although this has never been excavated. At the opposite end stands a similar construction, the Pyramid of the Moon, approximately half the size of the Pyramid of the Sun.

Almost at the center of the city is a sunken courtyard known as the Citadel, which is surrounded by temples. In the middle of the square is another temple, dedicated to Quetzalcoatl, the sides of which are decorated with representations of the Feathered Serpent, together with the Fire Serpent, bearer of the sun across the sky. The presence of more than 20 temple complexes in the city suggests that it was governed by a priestly elite, possibly in cooperation with secular officials who employed a military force to requisition the necessary labor. Square residential compounds lined much of the Avenue of the Dead. Within the simple walls were luxurious dwellings, probably the homes of the ruling class; in them, rooms decorated with murals of ritual processions and animals such as jaguars and coyotes were ranged around a central courtyard. Workers and artisans lived on the out-

**View of Teotihuacán, with the Pyramid of the Moon in the foreground and the Pyramid of the Sun beyond, at left.**
[Gordon W. Gahan]

skirts of the city in more crowded conditions, and some of the outlying districts were reserved for foreigners.

Among the finest of Teotihuacán's manufactured goods are cylindrical vases, often covered with plaster and painted. Small figurines were mass-produced by means of clay models, and examples of both have been found throughout Mesoamerica. Much of the city's commercial preeminence came from its control of obsidian mines near the modern city of Pachuca, which supplemented the stone mined near Teotihuacán itself. In addition to production for home use, knives, blades, scrapers, and dart points were manufactured for export, and the obsidian itself was a major export item. The city had more than 400 workshops that specialized in obsidian and another 100 that manufactured ceramic, shell, and ground-stone items. Artists sculpted life-size masks out of such materials as basalt and jade. Hieroglyphics found on pottery and murals suggest that the people of Teotihuacán were literate, but if they produced written documents, none have survived.

The vast scale of the city, coupled with the presence of Teotihuacán culture over a geographic area that includes most of Mexico and Guatemala, indicates a people with expansionist aims. Future archaeological work may indicate whether they ruled an empire or whether their influence was limited to the adoption of their culture by neighboring peoples. They apparently built no forts, depots, or roads to administer an empire, but neither did the Aztecs, who were unquestionably imperialistic. Teotihuacán culture certainly influenced both the Toltecs and the Aztecs. Both the people of Teotihuacán and the Aztecs cremated their dead and worshiped some of the same deities, including Tlaloc, the rain spirit, and Quetzalcoatl, the Feathered Serpent, god of the wind. By the fourteenth century, in fact, the name Teotihuacán meant "place of the gods" in the Aztec language.

Invaders, probably from the rival city-state of Cholula to the southeast, sacked Teotihuacán about 750, burning its great houses. Yet the remnants of the city, its temples abandoned, continued to be inhabited for centuries. People lived in hovels constructed in corners of the former palaces, and the pyramids became a place of pilgrimage for the Aztecs.

## The Maya

Around the time of the early building at Teotihuacán, Maya civilization began to develop in southern Mexico and Central America. The area controlled by the Maya, which had a population of perhaps 14 million, was divided into districts, each of which was dominated by a primary center that exercised authority over a descending hierarchy of progressively smaller sites. The primary centers, of which there could be only four at any given time (one for each compass direction), varied substantially in size. Tikal, which covered 50 square miles (including residences and shallow lakes), probably housed 40,000 to 80,000 people, and El Mirador, a later center, was home to 80,000. The primary sites were religious and ceremonial centers dominated by the hereditary elite, around which were numerous house-mounds.

The so-called palaces, large structures divided into many small, cramped rooms, were uncomfortable and damp. They apparently housed the elite. The other structures were almost exclusively religious: great stone processional ways, temples, stairways decorated with painted stucco masks, and the pyramids that are the most famous characteristic of Maya architecture. The enormous ceremonial sanctuaries made use of vaults (arched roofs), an architectural feature not employed elsewhere in Mesoamerica. At Tikal the highest pyramid is 229 feet tall and decorated with sculptures of Maya warlords. The only constructions of importance at Tikal besides the temples, pyramids, and palaces are ball courts and tombs.

Ball courts became a common feature of Amerindian cities and towns in ancient Mexico and the southwestern region of what would later become the United States. Teams of players wearing pads on elbows, wrists, and knees tried to drive a hard rubber ball through one of the stone rings in the side walls of the court. Large crowds of enthusiastic spectators cheered their favorites on. The games were extremely physical and demanded considerable skill, since the balls had to be struck without being handled. Judging by surviving artwork, the games involved not only recreation but also religious ritual; some scenes depict the death god presiding over the games. For many Amerindians, this form of sport was indeed sacred.

## Maya Society, Religion, and Culture

The archaeological evidence for Maya life is enriched by the survival of written or carved texts. The Maya devised a complex system of writing based on 850 characters, some representing pictorial objects, some concepts, and others syllables. With it they recorded historical, religious, and astronomical information organized by means of an elaborate calendar more accurate than its European counterpart. The urge to record the passing of the seasons seems to have been common to many Mesoamerican peoples, but the Maya calendrical system outstrips the others in intellectual complexity. It was based on various cycles, the so-called "long count," including a 365-day solar year, a 360-day lunar year, and a 584-day year of Venus. There was also a 260-day cycle, formed

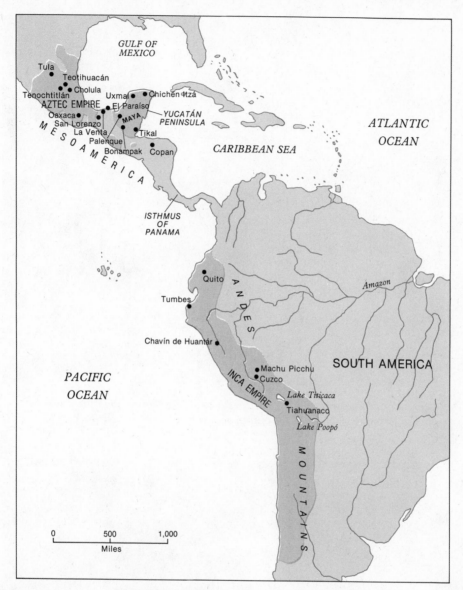

**10.2** *The Maya, the Aztec, and the Inca*

by joining 20 day names to 13 numbers—a ceremonial year, unrelated to the lunar or solar calendar and apparently antedating both. The solar year was divided into eighteen 20-day months and one 5-day month. The Maya recorded the births, marriages, and military triumphs of the rulers and their ancestors, as well as religious myths.

The importance ascribed to the Maya elite continued after their deaths. Virtually every pyramid contains a tomb in its base, presumably of a member of the aristocracy. Ancestor worship seems to have played a major role in Maya court religion, each ruler being associated with the god from whom he claimed descent. Maya warlords launched military campaigns with the help of these divine patrons, not so much to take control of enemy territory as to capture prisoners for slavery and sacrifice.

The lives of the peasants, some free, others bound to the land, were very different from those of the ruling class. Indeed, measurement of the skeletons found in royal tombs and in simple village graves shows that the nobility were much taller than their farm laborers. This may reflect a difference in ethnic origin or may simply be the result of superior nutrition; for the Maya it was proof that rulers and ruled were created separately by the gods. The villages that have been studied had no elaborate ceremonial sanctuaries, although they did have shrines. A survey of the countryside around Tikal

Temple I at Tikal, with nine levels (perhaps an allusion to the nine levels of the underworld), is a superb example of Maya architecture. [Doug Bryant/Stock]

Temple of the Inscriptions at Palenque. The pyramid design is typical of Maya architecture. There is a tomb at the base of the nine-level pyramid. [Ancient Art & Architecture Collection, London]

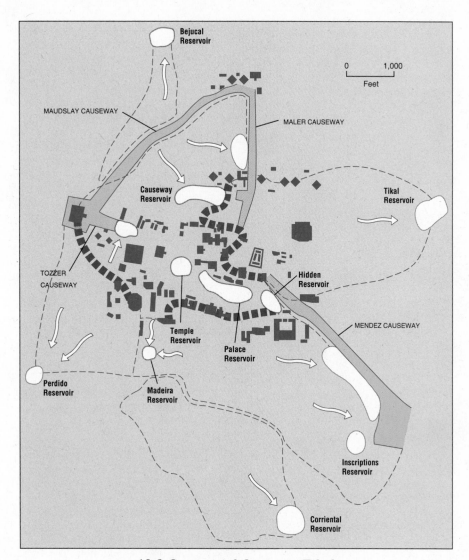

*10.3 Ceremonial Center at Tikal*

**Recent archaeological research suggests that Maya power was based in
part on effective management of water supplies. This map shows the
reservoirs (black), which were filled by catchment areas (dotted lines),
raised causeways, and drainage ditches.**

has discovered that for every 50 to 100 dwellings there
was a small religious center, dividing the residential
areas into zones. Because most of the land was swampy,
the Maya drained it with canals and in some cases piled
up soil to raise the fields above the wetlands. Some Maya
farmers used slash-and-burn agriculture: they cut and
burned trees and brush, the ashes from which fertilized
the soil for such crops as maize, beans, peppers, and
squash.

Maya women were sometimes very prominent. At
least two women—Kan Ik (583–604) and Zac Kuk (612–
615)—ruled the center at Palenque, and in other centers

women periodically governed in their own right or acted
as regents. As in medieval and early modern Europe,
leaders of centers established alliances with each other
through marriage; in the Maya world this usually took
the form of an alliance between a primary and a secondary center. In reckoning their lines of descent, Maya
aristocrats emphasized whichever line, female or male,
was more prestigious. Marriages were often arranged
by a matchmaker, sometimes while the prospective couple was very young. The Maya were monogamous, but
divorce was easily accomplished, with either spouse having the right to repudiate the other.

**A Maya woodcarving of a moustachioed dignitary or priest. [The Metropolitan Museum of Art, the Michael C. Rockefeller Memorial Collection, Bequest of Nelson A. Rockefeller, 1979]**

The Maya manufactured and exported cotton textiles to the other peoples of Mesoamerica in return for such items as jade and cacao (chocolate), the latter not only a drink for aristocrats but also a medium of exchange. Artisans made ceramics, metalware, and jewelry, while others were engaged in weaving and matmaking. Seagoing canoes were used in long-distance trading.

Maya painting, pottery, and sculpture are strikingly different from those of their neighbors. The Maya style is elaborate and complex, and the stone and wooden carvings that have survived often feature scenes of nobles accompanied by their divine protectors, together with lengthy inscriptions; the gods are highly stylized. Maya painting, unlike that at Teotihuacán, is naturalistic, showing an interest in portraiture and the lives of the aristocrats. The narrative murals discovered in 1947 at

the temple in Bonampak depict a Maya raid, the capture and sacrifice of prisoners, and a ritual dance.

The stone processional ways at Tikal and elsewhere were symbolic of the divine roads that led from the "green tree of abundance," which stood at the center of the earth; they formed a setting for ceremonies in praise of the gods. The supreme deity was Itzamna, creator of the world and lord of fire, who is frequently depicted as a snake. The most commonly portrayed of all Maya deities, recognizable by his large nose and the axe or smoking cigar in his forehead, was Bolon Tzacab, a manifestation of Itzamna. The Feathered Serpent of the Teotihuacán people and the Aztecs was worshiped by the Maya under the name of Kukulcán. Numeric subdivisions played an important role in Maya religion: there were four world directions, each with its own color and with a tree on which sat a particular bird; the heavens were divided into 13 layers and the underworld into 9. The sinister Maya underworld was ruled by gods associated with the jaguar, itself a symbol of night. To provide companions and attendants in the next world for their rulers, the Maya performed human sacrifices, using prisoners as their victims. The most common method was decapitation following torture. The Maya also practiced self-mutilation, drawing blood from wounds in ear, penis, or tongue and splashing it on pieces of bark as offerings to the gods.

## The Collapse of Maya Civilization

Around the year 800 this conservative, elitist culture went into decline. The last Maya calendar date to be inscribed was the equivalent of 909, by which time most sites had been abandoned and their populations scattered. The causes are still being debated. Overpopulation and misuse of agricultural land by overplanting or excessive burning may have been contributing factors, yet by themselves they are insufficient to account for so precipitous a collapse. The complex developments that triggered the decline probably commenced with the fall of Teotihuacán, which prompted rival Maya city-states to fight each other for control of the trade routes. Needing more people to serve in their armies and to construct monuments designed to intimidate their rivals, Maya rulers must have encouraged population growth and increased food production. The resulting situation was probably compounded by social and political unrest, leading to attacks on the elite. As the economic system broke down, large-scale agriculture collapsed, and famine ensued (as reflected in the fact that skeletons of this period, including those of some aristocrats, reveal the effects of malnutrition). Many peasants consequently died or migrated elsewhere.

A portion of the reconstructed mural from Bonampak depicting the Maya ruler in the center holding a spear. [Peabody Museum, Harvard University, photo by Hillel Burger]

## The Toltec Empire

The decline of Teotihuacán enabled a new power, the Toltecs ("reed people"), to emerge in Mesoamerica. Their capital, Tula, was a city that covered 3.5 square miles and had a population estimated between 30,000 and 60,000, with another 60,000 farmers living in the surrounding villages. Immigrants from other areas flocked to the city between 750 and 950. Tula included pyramids, a temple with sculpted stone columns, great halls, and individual statues in the form of reclining men holding sacrificial knives and round dishes on their stomachs; some scholars speculate that the hearts of sacrificial human victims were deposited in these dishes. Like the later Aztecs who admired them so much, the Toltecs displayed the skulls of their victims on wooden racks. Compared with the art of Teotihuacán, Toltec artists were much more preoccupied with human sacrifice, war, and death. Their chief deity was Quetzalcoatl, the Feathered Serpent.

The empire founded by the Toltecs was not a centralized state but rather a series of small, semi-independent kingdoms. The Toltecs used force to demand tribute from their neighbors, ruling over an empire that extended throughout most of central Mexico from coast to coast. Evidence of Toltec influence has been found as far away as Mexico's Oaxaca valley and Guatemala.

The Toltecs' best-known ruler, Topiltzin (c. 980–999), appropriated Quetzalcoatl's name as his own, apparently as part of an unsuccessful campaign to reform religion and abolish human sacrifice. Legend has it that Topiltzin's unpopular views led to his overthrow and flight from Tula. Around A.D. 1000 the Toltecs seized the Maya center at Chichén Itzá in the Yucatán and thereafter carried out a major building program patterned on that in Tula; this was done, according to the Maya, by "Kukulcán," the Maya name for Quetzalcoatl, raising the possibility that the conqueror of Chichén Itzá was Topiltzin. Legend also has it that as Topiltzin left Tula, he promised to return in 1519. When the Spanish conquistador Hernando Cortés (1485–1547) landed in Mexico that year, the stunned Aztecs were unsure whether or not he was Topiltzin.

The Toltec empire collapsed in the mid-twelfth cen-

Colossal columns from Pyramid B at Tula, showing costumed warriors ready for battle. [Werner Forman Archive, London]

## ◉ Topiltzin's Ouster and Prophecy ◉

*The story of the overthrow of Topiltzin, the ruler of Tula, was widely recounted by the Aztecs. In retelling the story, the sixteenth-century Dominican friar Diego Durán praised him for his piety and his prophetic role in preaching a New Law. Durán misidentified the Toltecs as Topiltzin's disciples.*

Topiltzin . . . was a venerable and devout person, held in deference, honored and revered as one would a holy man. . . . I saw a picture of him on an ancient paper. . . . This document showed Topiltzin with a venerable appearance: as an old man with a long red beard turning white. . . .

I have heard it affirmed that a great persecution arose against Topiltzin and his disciples and that a bitter war was waged against them, since the number of people who had accepted the New Law was great. . . . The Toltecs were not allowed to settle in any town . . . until Topiltzin made his home in Tula, where he reposed for some years, until the persecution began anew. Finally, weary of being harassed, he and his followers decided to give in to their persecutors and to depart.

Having come to this decision, Topiltzin called together the people of Tula and all his disciples. He thanked them for having allowed him to live among them and then bade them farewell. . . . He prophesied the arrival of strangers who would come to this land from the east. They wore unusual and multicolored clothing from head to foot. They used head coverings. This was the punishment which God was to send them in return for the ill-treatment which Topiltzin had received and for the shame of his banishment. In this chastisement young and old were to perish.

*Source:* Diego Durán, *Book of the Gods and Rites and the Ancient Calendar,* trans. and ed. Fernando Horcasitas and Doris Heyden (Norman: University of Oklahoma Press, 1971), pp. 57, 61–62.

Stone statue of a reclining
warrior with a bowl to hold
sacrifices, found at Chichén
Itzá in 1875. [George Holton/
Photo Researchers]

tury, and Tula itself was put to the torch. By this time
the empire had been weakened by factional strife, poor
harvests, and conflict with neighboring states, including
Cholula, and it could not cope with substantial numbers
of immigrants who sought refuge from a catastrophic
drought to the northwest. But Toltec influence lived on,
chiefly among the Aztecs, who pillaged Tula and carried
off many of its art works to Tenochtitlán, their capital.

## The Aztec Empire

The Aztecs were originally an agricultural tribe from
western Mexico who were forced by drought or population pressures to migrate into the Basin of Mexico. The
surviving Aztec histories describe their ancestors as the
chosen people of the sun god, destined to conquer and
rule in his name. In the uninhabited swampy lands
near Lake Texcoco they founded the twin towns of Tenochtitlán (the present Mexico City) and Tlatelolco in
1325 or 1345. In 1428 they began to expand their territory until their realm included much of Mexico. By 1500
the Aztec empire controlled a territory of some 125,000
square miles with a population of about 10 million
people.

The century or so of the Aztec empire is well documented, both by Spanish visitors and missionaries and
by the Aztecs' own books, or codices, some of which
escaped destruction. The latter include calendars, historical texts, works on geography and religion, and a
magnificent botanical work with drawings of medicinal
plants. Extensive records of Aztec legal disputes also
survive, and further information is provided by Spanish
administrative records.

Tenochtitlán was by far the largest city in Mesoamerica, with a resident population in 1519 estimated at
150,000 to 200,000, but the greater metropolitan area
numbered 400,000, some five times as large as contemporary London. When the Spanish arrived, King Montezuma II (1502–1520) lived in a palace of 300 rooms,
the grounds of which occupied 10 acres and included
not only the royal living quarters but also law courts,
administrative offices, an arsenal, a prison, a concert
hall, a zoo and an aviary, and quarters for 3,000 workers
and servants. The city contained hundreds of temples,
including the central complex made up of three huge
pyramids. Atop the largest pyramid, which soared to a
height of 200 feet, were twin temples to the rain and sun
gods. The sacred precinct also included smaller temples,
housing for the priests, racks for the display of the skulls
of tens of thousands of sacrificial victims, and a large
ball court. The main streets of the capital were actually

**Aztec statue of the god Quetzalcoatl in the form of a feathered serpent with a human head. [Musée de l'Homme, Paris]**

canals laid out in a grid pattern; not surprisingly, the Spaniards who witnessed this were reminded of Venice. The city also had two main markets, one of which was larger than those in Rome and Constantinople and, according to Spanish observers, accommodated 60,000 buyers and sellers on a busy day.

The high density of population in the capital and in other cities was supported by the most intensive of all Mesoamerican farming systems. Plant and animal fertilizers were employed to enrich the soil, and complex irrigation systems were developed, using terraces and canals. Especially in the area of their capital the Aztecs reclaimed swamplands and drained lakes to create productive agricultural terrain. The resulting farmland was sufficiently fertile to feed six to eight people per acre. The Aztecs' homeland was not rich in natural resources, and one of the principal motives for conquest seems to have been to gain possession of commodities such as maize and other foodstuffs, cotton cloth, incense, metal, and—the most prized of all—jade. Thus military aggression as much as trade was the primary means of economic development. The only large-scale industry that manufactured objects for export was the one that made tools of obsidian.

## Aztec Society

Like other early tribes of Africa and the Americas, the Aztecs were originally organized along kinship lines, but by the early 1500s Aztec society was stratified. At the top of the hierarchy was the king or emperor. Unlike most European monarchies, the eldest son was not the automatic heir. Instead an inner circle of nobles and high priests chose the successor from among all the ruler's legitimate sons or, if necessary, his brothers or nephews. Unlike Topiltzin of Tula, who in theory was both divine and human, the Aztec kings depicted themselves as intimate representatives of the gods but not personally divine. In this respect they were like some of the African rulers discussed earlier. The Aztec empire was a militarized state, and its kings were thought of, above all else, as warriors. By the mid-fifteenth century it was customary for a new ruler to launch his reign with a major military campaign. But the rulers were also the preeminent figures in the state religion.

Below the king were the nobles, who comprised approximately 5 percent of the population. In addition to their own hereditary estates they derived income from lands bestowed on them in return for service to the crown. From this class came the provincial governors and judges who administered the empire and the generals who preserved its security and extended its frontiers. They lived in large stone residences, wore luxurious clothes and jewelry, and ate a wide range of imported foods.

Beneath the nobility were the warriors, whose status derived from their conquests, the source of both sacrificial victims and essential commodities. The status of warrior was earned when a young soldier captured his first prisoner, and advancement to the nobility could be attained by subsequently killing or capturing four enemy soldiers. Failure to complete this assignment in several campaigns resulted in demotion to the laboring class, or *macehuales.*

The macehuales belonged by birth to one of 20 *calpullis.* Originally clans, the calpullis were eventually converted into administrative districts. Each had its own ward in the city, its own jointly owned farmland on the outskirts, its own schools (concentrating on agriculture and military training, for boys only), and its own temple. In time of war, each district provided its own military unit. Each of the calpullis also specialized in a particular craft. Unlike nobles, priests, and slaves, the macehuales had to pay taxes, but in turn they received a portion of the tribute collected from subject peoples. Although

women played no formal part in running the clan's affairs, they had a crucial role in farming. Because large numbers of men were involved in the military campaigns, the women helped plant the fields and took care of the land during the growing period, camping by the fields in brushwood huts, clearing the weeds, and driving off animal predators. Female participation in agricultural labor was undoubtedly reflected in the worship of the great earth goddess, Coatlicue, and the goddess of maize, Xilonen, who also protected the home.

Below the macehuales were the *mayeques,* mostly conquered peoples who lived as tenant farmers on the estates of the nobles; like serfs, they were bound to the land, but they were also subject to military service. At the bottom of Aztec society were the slaves, whose ranks were filled by captives, debtors, thieves, and conspirators. Aztec slaves could acquire possessions, including slaves of their own, and purchase their own freedom. Manumission was automatic if an escaped slave took sanctuary in the royal palace. The children of male slaves and free women were born free. Aztec slavery was less restrictive than that later practiced in the United States.

Aztec marriages were arranged by the families, each

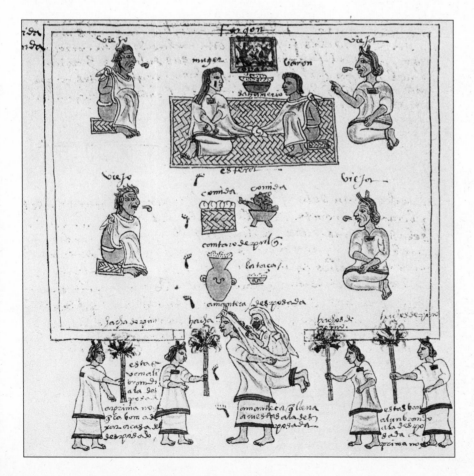

**This drawing of an Aztec marriage shows the symbolic union of the couple by the knotting of their cloaks; at the bottom, a matron carries the bride over the threshold. [Ashmolean Museum, Oxford]**

of which paid a dowry. If the girl's family expected compensation for the loss of a cook and cleaner and a potential potter or weaver, the boy's parents had to do without their son's services as a worker or a soldier who would bring home plunder. After marriage the couple were helped by their kin to build and furnish their house. Husbands and wives were expected to be faithful: women accused of immorality were physically punished by their husbands, and prostitution was permitted only in the military camps. The girls who worked there, however, were taken away and strangled as soon as they showed signs of illness or weakness, and their bodies were thrown into the swamps.

## The Gods of Human Sacrifice

The final segment of Aztec society comprised the priests. Entry to the priesthood was open to commoners, and even the two highest priests did not have to possess noble blood. Priests operated religious schools in which they educated future priests as well as the nobility, and they marched in the vanguard of the Aztec armies, possibly engaging in the fighting. Although required to be celibate, they were free to leave the priesthood and marry if they wished. In addition to their educational role, the priests spent much of their time involved in soothsaying as they tried to provide answers to the myriad questions posed to them by the people, including queries about whom to marry. There was so much demand for their services that soothsaying specialists had developed by the end of the fifteenth century. A third duty of the priests involved their responsibility to control foreign deities, a task they performed by studying the idols of conquered peoples at Tenochtitlán and subordinating them to their own gods in a conscious act of religious imperialism.

Aztec priests are best known for their role in human sacrifice, a ritual previously practiced by the Olmecs, the Maya, the people of Teotihuacán, and the Toltecs, but never on the massive scale of the Aztecs. The dedication of the great temple at Tenochtitlán in 1487 was marked by the sacrifice of between 20,000 and 80,000 prisoners, three entire tribes captured for the purpose in the mountains of central Mexico. Four columns of prisoners stood in lines stretching 2½ miles waiting for two priests to rip their hearts from their bodies; the exhausted priests finally collapsed. During the last decades of Aztec rule at least 15,000 humans a year were ritually sacrificed. The demand for victims was met by conquering more and more peoples, with a heavy premium on taking captives rather than slaying the enemy. When the Aztecs finally confronted the Spaniards, this tactic put them at a decided disadvantage.

Two factors explain the Aztecs' practice of sacrificing humans on such a scale. In part this stemmed from their conviction that the deities—especially Huitzilopochtli, the tribal warrior god and representative of the sun—responded primarily to nourishment rather than prayer, more traditional rituals, or asceticism. Without such nourishment the "fifth sun," under which the Aztecs thought they lived, would perish, ending sunlight and with it the world. The analogy was simple and direct: "Just as men go to the market to find their warm tortillas so shall our god come to market with his army, to buy sacrifices and human beings, which he can eat."[1] No less

An Aztec priest removes the heart of a sacrificial victim. [Scala/Art Resource]

⊡ **Human Sacrifice** ⊡

*This description of Aztec sacrifices was written by Bernard Díaz del Castillo, who accompanied Cortés to Tenochtitlán in 1519. The victims are captured members of Cortés' expedition.*

When we had retired almost to our quarters, across a great opening full of water, their arrows, darts, and stones could no longer reach us. . . . The dismal drum . . . sounded again, accompanied by conches, horns, and trumpet-like instruments. It was a terrifying sound, and . . . we saw our comrades who had been captured in Cortes' defeat being dragged up the steps to be sacrificed. When they had hauled them up to a small platform in front of the shrine where they kept their accursed idols we saw them put plumes on the heads of many of them; and then they made them dance with a sort of fan. . . . Then after they had danced the [Aztecs] laid them down on their backs on some narrow stones of sacrifice and, cutting open their chests, drew out their palpitating hearts which they offered to the idols before them. Then they kicked the bodies down the steps, and the Indian butchers who were waiting below cut off their arms and legs and flayed their faces, which they afterwards prepared like glove leather, with their beards on, and kept for their drunken festivals. Then they ate their flesh with a sauce of peppers and tomatoes. They sacrificed all our men in this way, eating their legs and arms, offering their hearts and blood to their idols as I have said, and throwing their trunks and entrails to the lions and tigers and serpents and snakes that they kept in the wild-beast houses.

*Source:* J. J. Norwich, ed., *A Taste for Travel* (London: Macmillan, 1986), p. 305.

important a reason was the deliberate use of human sacrifice to strike terror into the enemies of the Aztecs, whether soldiers seized in battle, ritual tribute from subject peoples, unsuccessful generals, corrupt administrators, or slaves. The Aztecs ate the arms and legs of their victims, not for normal sustenance but as part of a religious ritual, a communion with the gods, and donated the hearts and blood to their deities.

❀
## MONTEZUMA II AND THE DECLINE OF THE AZTECS

The reign of Montezuma II, who succeeded his uncle as emperor in 1502, provides an intriguing case study of imperial conquest, human sacrifice, and despotic rule. An autocratic, imposing man, his skill as a military commander and his status as a priest in the temple of Huitzilopochtli won him the crown, but 17 years later Aztec power had so weakened that the Spaniards were able to overrun much of his empire. Four principal reasons accounted for this, all of which stemmed from Montezuma's attempt to consolidate and stabilize his realm. First, although Montezuma conquered the Mixtecs in Oaxaca

and won other victories, these brought in less wealth than previous Aztec campaigns. Effort had to be expended as well on repressing rebellion within the empire, again with no significant material gain other than fresh supplies of humans for the altars of Tenochtitlán. Second, under Montezuma the long-standing rivalries with the neighboring Tlaxcaltecs and Tarascans intensified, further increasing military expenditures with nothing to show for them but more captives.

The third factor involved a profound loss of confidence in Montezuma's regime occasioned by the outbreak of a major famine in 1505 and the policies Montezuma implemented to deal with it. Since 1454 the Aztecs, trying to cope with an expanding population, had gone to great lengths to prevent famine through massive public works projects that entailed the subjugation of millions of people. In 1505 it became painfully apparent that these efforts were not enough to protect even the privileged population of Tenochtitlán. Unable to meet the needs of his people from outsiders, Montezuma demanded increased tribute from the neighboring city-states in the valley of Mexico, prompting revolt.

Finally, within Tenochtitlán itself Montezuma's consolidation measures provoked discontent. As the conquests and the accompanying patronage diminished, Montezuma removed from their posts all high officials

## ◎ The Famine of 1454 ◎

*The following account describes the 1454 famine. Food shortages sub-sequently plagued the Aztecs.*

In this year of disaster there was widespread death and thirst. And then there arrived . . . frightful packs of boars, poisonous snakes, and vultures as well. And the hunger was so great that the imperial Mexicans sold themselves, and others hid themselves away in the forest, where they lived as wood people. In that region there was nothing to eat for all of four years, so that two separate parties of the Mexicans sold themselves into slavery. It was mainly to buy slaves that the Totonacs came to Mexico with maize. . . . Before that the Mexicans had not used maize to make loaves. They crawled into holes and died any-where. The vultures then ate them, and no one buried them.

*Source:* G. Brotherston, ed., *Image of the New World: The American Continent Portrayed in Native Texts* (London: Thames & Hudson, 1979), p. 213.

who were not of noble blood and executed many, thereby making more room for the hereditary nobility. By blocking the advancement of men of talent to high office, he rigidified the class structure. Merchants who were critical of Montezuma, in part because of growing restrictions on their trade, had their property confis-cated, and they too were sometimes killed. Montezuma distributed some of their property to old soldiers in a bid for popular support. This was also the reason behind his abolition of slavery for debt, which had mushroomed because of the famine; this step won him substantial ac-claim among the poorer peasants.

Montezuma tried to disguise his increasingly des-potic rule by depicting himself as a god-king. Those ap-proaching him did so with head and eyes lowered, and his chief advisers could eat in his presence only if they stood and did not look at him. As he moved through the streets, his people had to stand motionless and stare at the ground. When Cortés observed all this, he remarked that the customs of the royal court were more splendid than those of an Asian potentate. Yet never did Monte-zuma enjoy absolute power; he could not launch military campaigns without the approval of his war council, though the council was reduced in most respects to an advisory role.

The Spanish arrived in Tenochtitlán on November 8, 1519, the ease of their entry made possible in part by Montezuma's uncertainty as to whether or not Cortés was the returning deity Quetzalcoatl; playing it safe, he sent Cortés the regalia of Quetzalcoatl and two other gods. Although Montezuma died in an Indian uprising a year later, the empire lasted until 1521. Dissension within the Aztec empire alone cannot account for the collapse. Although the Aztecs were so despised by some of their Mexican neighbors, including the Tlaxcaltecs,

that the latter refused to join them against the Spaniards, others, including the people of Tula, sustained heavy losses fighting the Europeans. The Spanish cause was also aided by superior weapons—artillery in the early battles, swords and crossbows in the later ones. In August 1521, Tenochtitlán itself was razed, ending Aztec rule.

## Early Peru: The Chavín Culture

By 2500 B.C. the inhabitants of fishing villages on the Peruvian coast had begun to raise cotton, squash, beans, and guavas. Approximately 500 years later these com-munities developed into chiefdoms, their centers domi-nated by large, presumably ceremonial buildings. Typi-cally these centers had populations of about 1,500 and were surrounded by smaller villages—a pattern later used by the Maya. At the largest of these sites, El Pa-raíso, archaeologists have found the remains of huge masonry platforms that were once part of a temple com-plex. To build these platforms, workers from surround-ing villages had to quarry and transport 100,000 tons of rock; whether forced or voluntary is unknown.

Around 1800 B.C. these communities began to ex-pand inland. The greatest of the new settlements was begun at Chavín de Huantár around 850 B.C. Some 10,600 feet above sea level in the north Peruvian Andes, Chavín was a ceremonial center, like San Lorenzo and La Venta in Mesoamerica. The buildings consisted of temple platforms containing interlinked galleries and

THE EARLY AMERICAS

| | Mesoamerica | Peru | North America |
|---|---|---|---|
| before 300 B.C. | Olmecs (c. 1500 B.C.–c. A.D. 1) | Chavín culture (c. 850–c. 300 B.C.) | Adena and Hopewell cultures (c. 800 B.C.–c. A.D. 600) |
| 300 B.C.–A.D. 100 | | | Mogollon culture (c. 300 B.C.–A.D. 1350) |
| 100–750 | Dominance of Teotihuacán (c. 100–c. 750) Maya empire (c. 100–909) | | Beginning of Anasazi culture (c. 300) Beginning of Mississippian culture (c. 500–600) |
| 750–1300 | Toltecs (c. 750–c. 1150) | | Navaho migration (after 1000) Apache migration (c. 1200) |
| 1300–1600 | Aztecs (c. 1325–1521) | Inca expansion (c. 1350–1493) Fall of Cuzco (1533) | |
| | | | Founding of the Iroquois League (c. 1570–1600) |

chambers on different levels. In the oldest part of the complex was a stele depicting one of the two main Chavín deities, the Smiling God, a figure in the form of a jaguar-man with catlike fangs and locks of hair shaped like snakes. The other Chavín deity, also with feline-human features but holding staffs in his hands, has been dubbed the Staff God. Lintels, gateways, and cornices were decorated with similar carvings, and stone human and jaguar heads were fastened on the outside wall of one of the temple platforms. The prominence of the jaguar in the Chavín cult has led some scholars to suspect that it was an offshoot of Olmec religion; a few suspect Chinese influence.

Over the succeeding centuries the Chavín cult spread throughout central and northern Peru, both in the mountains and on the coast. Chavín motifs and jaguar designs appear on the pottery and textiles of this region. Whether people embraced the new faith by choice or compulsion is not known, but the most likely explanation is that it was linked with maize crops and spread as more and more people began raising corn. Like the Olmecs' in Mesoamerica, the Chavín cult served as a unifying force as well as influencing the art and religion of subsequent Peruvian peoples. Chavín culture had vanished by 300 B.C. for unknown reasons.

# The Inca

The development and collapse of Aztec civilization in Mexico was paralleled by the history of the Inca in South America. Like their contemporaries to the north, the Inca dominated their neighbors to form a sizable empire under authoritarian rule, but it too would fall quickly to European conquerors. Shortly after Cortés' conquest of Mexico, another Spanish soldier of fortune, Francisco

Pizarro, arrived in Peru. The Inca empire he found there in 1527 stretched along the Pacific coast and through the Andes Mountains to central Chile, covering an area of more than a million square miles—twice the combined size of France, Spain, and Italy—and embracing a population estimated at between 6 and 16 million. Unlike the major civilizations of Mesoamerica, that of the Inca was not urban. Most people lived in villages or small towns that seldom had more than 1,000 inhabitants, and even Cuzco, the capital, housed only the court and a number of priests.

The most powerful of all South American peoples, the Inca passed on their history verbally from generation to generation by means of professional memorizers. The Spanish-written versions of these traditional accounts form the basis for a study of Inca history, but they need to be treated with care, since the oral tradition of the Inca produced a selective version of the facts in order to buttress the power of the ruling classes, and the Spanish accounts are inconsistent in many respects.

# The Rise of the Inca

The Andes region, where the Inca originated, is an area of varied resources. Fertile river valleys supported the cultivation of maize, beans, peppers, squash, and tomatoes; potatoes were grown on the slopes; and the high mountain plateaus provided grazing land for such animals as llamas and alpacas. The early Inca were nomads who settled throughout the Cuzco valley, moving from village to village in search of fertile land. The history of the early rulers is colored by legend, but archaeological evidence confirms that the mid-fourteenth century was marked by Inca expansion beyond the Cuzco valley. The cause may have been related to a global weather change that occurred in the mid-fourteenth century, a period known as the Little Ice Age. A diminution of rainfall in the Andes area prompted the Inca to seek land elsewhere. At the same time, they began to raid more distant peoples in search of plunder. By the mid-fifteenth century such casual raids had been converted into an aggressive policy of conquest.

Territories, once subdued, were left under the control of Inca officials and garrisons. Family rivalries within the ruling class led to further conquest, and the Emperor Topa Inca Yupanqui (1471–1493), one of the most powerful Inca rulers, led his armies into what is now the Peruvian coast, highland Bolivia, northern Chile, Ecuador, and most of northwestern Argentina. The last years of his reign were spent traveling throughout the territory he had conquered, establishing local administrations and organizing systems of tribute.

## State and Society Under the Inca

Inca society was highly stratified. The noblest aristocrats were those who could claim descent from an emperor and were called "Inca by blood." The emperor, who ruled by divine right, was allegedly descended from Inti, the sun god, and his mummified body became the object of a cult after his death. Like the Egyptian pharaohs, he married his sister but simultaneously had many wives and concubines. In an attempt to ensure a peaceful succession, one of the emperor's sons was crowned during his father's lifetime. He was expected to construct his own palace and appoint his own servants. When the reigning monarch died, his widows, concubines, and servants, all thoroughly inebriated, were killed, which had the practical effect of reducing the opportunities for opposition against the new ruler. As in Montezuma II's reign among the Aztecs, Inca sovereigns demanded extreme forms of deference, including the duty of subjects to kneel and avert their gaze as they passed, a requirement also imposed by Japanese emperors on their subjects. Even the advisers of an Inca ruler had to speak to him through a screen. At least in theory, his authority was limitless, but in practice custom undoubtedly imposed restraints.

Inca government was organized in a hierarchical chain of command. Immediately beneath the emperor, from whom all authority derived, were the four prefects of the principal territories of the empire. Often members of the imperial family, they lived in Cuzco, from where they supervised the work of the provincial governors, typically drawn from the hereditary Inca nobility. The

## ◉ Inca Royal Marriages ◉

*Marriage customs and the status of concubines at the Inca court were described by Pedro Cieza de Léon, who participated in the Spanish campaigns against the Inca and then spent three years interviewing the Inca before writing a book on their culture.*

It was ordained by them that he who became king should take his sister, being the legitimate daughter of his father and mother, as his wife, in order that the succession of the kingdom might by that means be confirmed in the royal house. It appeared to them that by this means, even if such a woman, being sister of the king, should not be chaste, and should have intercourse with another man, the son thus born would still be hers, and not the son of a strange woman. They also considered that if the Inca married a strange woman, she might do the same and conceive in adultery, in such a way that, it not being known, the child would be received as a natural born son of the lord. For these reasons, and because it seemed desirable to those who ordained the laws, it was a rule among the Incas that he amongst them all who became emperor should take his sister to wife. . . . If by chance he who became lord had no sister, it was permitted that he should marry the most illustrious lady there was, and she was held to be the principal among all his women. For none of these lords had less than 700 women for the service of their house and for their pleasure. So that they all had many children by these women, who were well treated, and respected by the people.

*Source:* Pedro Cieza de Léon, *The Second Part of the Chronicle of Peru,* trans. and ed. C. R. Markham (London: Hakluyt Society, 1883), pp. 26–27.

chieftains beneath them were generally Inca nobles or leaders of the states that the Inca had conquered. The sons of the latter were often taken to Cuzco to be trained in administration, thereby providing a constant supply of personnel while guaranteeing their fathers' loyalty. At the bottom of the bureaucracy were men selected for their ability, but all positions in the upper levels of the government were reserved for those of aristocratic birth.

The central government imposed two forms of taxation. The first consisted of service in the army or labor on public works projects; the second, called the *mit'a*, involved agricultural work, either in the fields or tending flocks, manufacturing, or mining. The Inca had no medium of exchange, unlike the Indians of Mesoamerica, who used the cacao bean. Taxes and tribute therefore had to be paid in kind. Portions of the crops and manufactured goods went into state warehouses for use by the government, the nobility, and the army, but reserves were also stored to feed the people in times of famine, as in China.

Public order was enforced by the army. Numbering 200,000, with auxiliary labor and supply units, it was efficient and disciplined. Permanent garrisons maintained order, and revolts met with fierce reprisals. The skulls of rebels were fashioned into drinking cups, and drums were made from their skins. Rebellious peoples were also moved to more distant parts of the empire and docile subjects allowed to inhabit their lands. As the empire expanded, however, rebellions became more common, and many of the peoples whom the Inca conquered later supported the Spanish.

The need for soldiers and workers was such that the state required marriage and endorsed polygamy. Young people who neglected to take mates had them selected by local officials, who annually paired off young men and women as they lined up in village plazas. The marriage ceremony involved the joining of hands (a custom also popular among European peasants) and the exchange of sandals. At the ensuing wedding feast the bride and groom each received two sets of clothing from the government, one for everyday use and the other for special occasions. The major exception to the principle of required marriage involved the "chosen women." Each year several thousand attractive girls aged 8 or 9 were selected for entry to temple schools that trained them for approximately five years in domestic activities and the performance of religious rites. Subsequently taken to Cuzco, some became imperial concubines or wives of

**The Inca city of Machu Picchu was built around the time of the arrival of the Spanish. [George Holton/Photo Researchers]**

the nobles, but most were assigned to temples and called Virgins of the Sun.

Among the achievements of the Inca empire was the creation of an effective network of paved roads that spanned nearly 19,000 miles and linked the provincial centers to the capital. As an engineering achievement, they surpassed the roads of the Roman Empire or anything constructed in Europe until the Napoleonic Age. Two main roads ran from north to south through the empire, one along the coast and the other in the highlands; several crossovers connected the two. Suspension and pontoon bridges spanned rivers, tunnels shortened distances, and stone steps or zigzags enabled travelers to navigate steep slopes. Every few miles there was a storehouse or shelter. Government runners posted along the roads carried messages or goods, but access to the roads was limited, since the Inca rulers strictly discouraged mobility. The roads, it should be noted, were constructed primarily for people on foot and animal traffic, since the Inca did not use wheeled vehicles.

The Inca had no system of writing, yet they maintained records concerning troops, work forces, and other bureaucratic matters. This was done by a special group of officials, each of whom memorized the details for which he was responsible by using a system of knotted cords. To a main rope or string were attached smaller strings of varying colors; the judicious use of sets of these strings in combination with knots enabled the officials to keep detailed records. The same group of officials was also responsible for memorizing Inca history and myths. Time was measured by a calendar that divided the year into 12 months of 30 days grouped into 10-day weeks. The remaining five days of the year were devoted to religious ceremonies at the middle and end of the year.

Much of Inca culture was centered around religious ritual, which involved an elaborate priesthood and nearly omnipresent temples, shrines, and holy places. All peoples of the empire had to worship the state deities, the highest of which, the sun god, was the ancestor of the royal family. However, the gods of the conquered tribes were incorporated into the state religion, making it possible for subject peoples to continue worshiping familiar deities. The priests periodically sacrificed humans, but normally only on such occasions as the coronation of a new ruler or the commencement of a military campaign. Boys and girls around 10 years of age were selected as victims, taken to Cuzco for a special ritual, and then returned to the provinces to be sacrificed.

## The Decline of the Inca

On the eve of the Spaniards' arrival, the Inca royal family was once again racked by feuds. Huáscar (1525–1532), the reigning emperor, was challenged by his brother, Atahualpa (1532–1533). Huáscar maintained control of the southern part of the empire, while his brother ruled Ecuador and parts of northern Peru. In the ensuing civil war Atahualpa's troops defeated the imperial army outside Cuzco in April 1532, capturing Huáscar and executing his entire family as well as his generals and officials. Within months Atahualpa, who assumed that Pizarro was the creator-god Viracocha, fell victim to the Spaniards and was strangled. After a brief interval, Pizarro and his men embarked on an undisguised conquest of the Inca empire, capturing Cuzco in November 1533. By 1535 the last rulers of the Inca were driven into the remote mountains of the interior, where their independent state lasted until 1572.

Like the Aztecs, the Inca, weakened by internal strife and perhaps territorially overextended, proved easy victims for the better-armed Spanish. Their conquest marked the beginning of the subjugation of South America and its indigenous peoples. Nonetheless, vestiges of earlier times survive within westernized forms. In particular, popular Christianity has preserved something of the color and fervor of pre-Hispanic times, and in the remoter regions tribes continue to speak a language descended from Incan.

# The Amerindians of North America

None of the hundreds of Amerindian tribes that settled throughout what is now the United States and Canada achieved civilization on the magnitude of the Maya, the Aztecs, or the Inca, but ongoing archaeological work is demonstrating that at least some of them developed impressive cultures. Most of the Amerindians north of the Rio Grande lived in relatively small temporary settlements. Virtually all of them hunted and fished, although the relative absence of large game in the southwest meant that the early tribes in that region concentrated on gathering wild foods. In time agriculture developed as the knowledge of crop raising spread northward from Mesoamerica. The men typically cleared the fields (often by burning) while the women tended the crops. Some tribes began constructing sizable permanent settlements, especially in the Ohio, Mississippi, and Rio Grande valleys.

## The Ohio Valley: The Adena and Hopewell Cultures

The Adena and Hopewell cultures were developed by a large, complex Amerindian population who lived be-

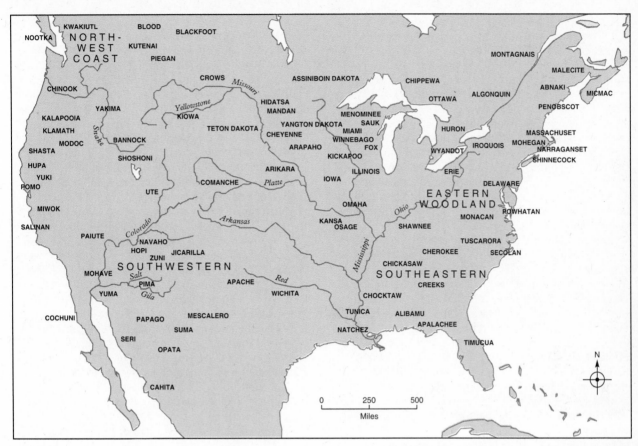

**10.4** *Amerindian Tribes, c. 1500*

tween 800 B.C. and A.D. 600 or later. Both were centered in what is now Kentucky and Ohio, although the influence of the somewhat later Hopewell culture extended from New York to the Gulf Coast and from eastern Kansas and Nebraska to the western Carolinas. The Adena people lived in round houses constructed of poles covered with woven mats, with thatched roofs, whereas the Hopewell Amerindians built round or oval houses of posts, with coverings of skins, bark, mats, or clay and thatch. Both societies expended great effort on burials, the Adena placing their dead in conical earthen mounds surrounded by earthen ramparts as much as 500 feet in diameter. Often the deceased had first been cremated, and the remains, at least of the important people, were interred with carved stone tablets, lumps of pigment, stone smoking pipes, polished stones, and similar items. Hopewellian practices were similar but sometimes grander, at least for persons of importance.

Based on these rather elaborate burial practices and evidence of public works projects, archaeologists have ascertained that the Hopewell rulers exercised considerable control over a sizable population. The ceremonial center discovered at Newark, Ohio, for instance, occu-

pied 4 square miles. The food supply must have been adequate, although there is little evidence that maize was grown. Instead there was reliance on nuts, wild grapes, and plants now considered weeds as well as fish and game. The Hopewell people either traded with or possibly extracted tribute from other Amerindians extending throughout much of what is now the United States, importing obsidian from Wyoming, copper from the northern Great Lakes, shells from the Gulf Coast, and mica (used to create silhouettes) from the southern Appalachians. In return they exported tools, figurines, pottery, and copper ornaments.

## The Mississippian Culture

Around A.D. 500 or 600 the Mississippi valley saw the development of another major culture, the precise origins of which are still under investigation. These people lived in wattle-and-daub (clay over lath) houses of varying shapes in large villages. Influenced by the cultures of Mesoamerica, they raised maize, beans, and squash and embraced a religion with planting rituals.

They sometimes buried their dead in distinctive pyramidal mounds with flat tops; the pyramids were arranged around plazas, often with palisades or earthworks surrounding the entire complex. The largest of these, at Cahokia, Illinois (near St. Louis), was gradually built up between about 900 and 1150; with a base of more than 18 acres, it reached a height of 100 feet. Altogether 85 mounds have been found at Cahokia, where the village itself was some 6 miles long. But burials could also be in cemeteries, in urns, or even beneath the floors of homes. Both burial practices and domestic architecture indicate considerable variations in Mississipian culture. Eventually this culture dominated much of the southeast and midwest, remaining influential through the seventeenth century.

Around the thirteenth century some of the Mississippian communities developed a highly ritualistic religion scholars have called the Southern Cult. They worshiped in large temples filled with such ceremonial objects as copper plates, maces, and monolithic stone axes. Among the most common symbols were the cross, the sun disk, an arrow flanked by semicircles, a human hand with an eye in the palm, and a sunburst. Artists influenced by this cult engraved mythological scenes depicting such exotic creatures as bird-people, animal deities, and plumed and winged rattlesnakes. Effigy jars often have depictions of human faces, sometimes with painted designs or tattoos, and others show the heads of sacrificial victims. Here too human sacrifice was practiced, possibly including infants. The artifacts point to a cult that apparently had a sophisticated mythology and served the needs of a well-developed society.

## The Southwest: The Mogollon, Hohokam, and Anasazi Cultures

The Amerindians of the American southwest shared one basic cultural tradition, albeit with regional variants. Each group grew maize, beans, and squash; used masonry in building its homes; and crafted superb pottery. After about 1100 A.D. even the differences faded through cultural interchange as people migrated. The fact that two of the southwestern cultures—the Hohokam and Anasazi—existed primarily on farming in a region inhospitable to it because of the water shortages indicates that they were technologically advanced.

The earliest of the three major Amerindian cultures of the southwest, the Mogollon, existed from about 300 B.C. to A.D. 1350. The heart of Mogollon territory was southwestern New Mexico. Mogollon villages, typically scattered along the summits of ridges, generally consisted of large underground ceremonial buildings and pit houses. By the eleventh century these Amerindians were constructing towns on level ground. More than other contemporary Amerindians, they based their existence fairly equally on hunting, gathering, and agriculture, probably because of the difficulties of farming in this area. Over the long course of their history they displayed little interest in innovation; Mogollon culture was highly conservative. Some scholars believe that the modern Zuni are the descendants of the Mogollon.

Hohokam culture, which developed slightly later than the neighboring Mogollon, was centered in the Salt and Gila valleys. These Amerindians too lived in pit houses, though of a different type; unlike the Mogollon, who simply put a roof over a hole, they built entire houses inside the pits. The principal Hohokam achievement was the construction of a vast network of irrigation canals, using dams to channel water from the Salt and Gila rivers. Some of the canals extended more than 30 miles and were as much as 6 to 10 feet deep and 15 to 30 feet wide. Construction and maintenance of the canals required a large work force and indicates effective social organization. The influence of Mesoamerican cultures on the Hohokam is manifest in their stepped pyramids and ball courts. The modern descendants of the Hohokam, the Pima and Papago Amerindians, live in Arizona.

The Anasazi or Pueblo culture, which emerged around A.D. 300, was possibly influenced by the Mogollon and Hohokam cultures, although the Anasazi are more remarkable for their unique development. Their earliest homes—beehive domes constructed of logs and mud mortar—were unlike anything created by contemporary Amerindians, as were their elaborate storage chambers; they grew a different variety of maize; and their pottery, unlike that of the Hohokam and Mogollon but similar to the Mississippian, was flamboyant in design. Sometime after 700 the Anasazi began growing cotton and weaving on looms. Their religious rites included ceremonies to ward off storms and crop damage and encourage fertility. By the eleventh century they too had begun to build towns, the characteristic feature of which were groups of homes constructed in the shape of squares, ells, or semicircles. In succeeding years they used mud, stone, and wood to build impressive cliff dwellings and terraced apartment houses; the largest one, containing some 500 units, was the largest residential building in North America until an apartment complex built in New York City in 1882. To grow crops they used both flood irrigation (by terracing the hills and erecting dikes) and subsurface irrigation (by constructing sand dunes at the foot of hills to hold runoff and disperse it slowly to small garden patches). At the peak of their influence Anasazi culture extended as far north as the present Idaho-Colorado border, but by 1300 the Pueblo Amerindians had been forced southward by a combination of factors that included drought, fighting between towns, and the arrival of the Navaho and

These cliff dwellings at Mesa Verde, Colorado, were constructed by the Anasazi around A.D. 1200. [Werner Forman Archive, London]

Apache. Descendants of the Anasazi still live in northern New Mexico and Arizona and parts of Utah and Colorado.

## Later Native Cultures of North America

Well before Europeans began exploring North America, other Amerindians resettled, often coming under the influence of the cultures just described. The Navaho, now the largest Amerindian tribe in the United States, migrated from the north to the southwest, possibly as early as the eleventh century, after which they borrowed heavily from the Pueblo. Somewhat later the Apache, who are close linguistic relatives of the Navaho, also began migrating to the southwest, and by the late sixteenth century they had settled in parts of what is now Arizona, Colorado, and New Mexico; they have been influenced by both the Pueblo and the Navaho. Another major tribe, the Mandan, who would later be prominent in the fur trade, had moved from the east to the Missouri valley

by the fourteenth century. In fact, all regions of what is now the United States were inhabited, however sparsely, by Amerindians in 1500.

Two groups of Amerindians can be singled out for their advanced forms of political organization, surpassing the loosely knit confederations previously established by a number of earlier tribes, including the Huron. In the southeast the Creeks organized a confederacy that united their towns according to essentially democratic principles. The towns were grouped into two divisions, the red and the white, and peace was maintained within the confederation by ball games played by towns in opposite divisions. To the north, in what is now western New York, the Iroquois developed a well-organized military confederacy, known as the Iroquois League, that impressed Europeans. According to tradition, it was founded between 1570 and 1600 with the aid of Hiawatha for the purpose of promoting peace, law, and righteousness among the five Amerindian nations that were its original members. The story of its founding was recorded in the Dekanawidah epic, which was passed down orally from generation to generation.

## ◉ The Iroquois Remedy for Anarchy ◉

*The following article, from the Iroquois Ritual of Condolence, was recited when one of the chiefs of the member nations of the confederacy died and was replaced. The key point is that death threatens unity, the cure for which is unity and compassion.*

Is not what has befallen thee then so dreadful that it must not be neglected? For, at the present time, there are wrenchings without ceasing within thy breast, and also within thy mind. Now truly, the disorder now among the organs within thy breast is such that nothing can be clearly discerned. So great has been the affliction that has befallen thee that yellow spots have developed within thy body, and truly thy life forces have become greatly weakened thereby; truly thou dost now suffer.

. . . In ancient times it thus came to pass that the Federal Chiefs, our grandsires, made a formal rule, saying, "Let us unite our affairs; let us formulate regulations; let us ordain this among others that what we shall prepare we will designate by the name Water-of-pity or compassion which shall be the essential thing to be used where Death has caused this dreadful affliction, inducing bitter grief."

*Source:* G. Brotherston, ed., *Image of the New World: The American Continent Portrayed in Native Texts* (London: Thames & Hudson, 1979), p. 252.

## The Far North: Eskimos, Aleuts, and Athabaskans

The origin of the Eskimos—or Inuit, as they call themselves—is a sharply disputed question, with some scholars suggesting that they are the descendants of a very early maritime people and others contending that they evolved in Alaska after the last ice age. Linguistically, the Eskimos are related to the Aleuts, whose origin is similarly disputed. Both groups, which diverged at least 4,000 years ago, are more closely related, both physically and linguistically, to Asians than the Amerindians

are. Whereas the Aleuts confined themselves for the most part to what we now call the Alaska peninsula and the Aleutian islands, the Eskimos spread themselves thinly across a region extending from the Bering Strait to Greenland and as far south as the Yukon.

Both peoples supported themselves by hunting and fishing. In small kayaks made of skins the Aleuts hunted seals, sea lions, and otters, and they fished for salmon in the streams. The Eskimos developed a more diverse economic base, hunting for both land and sea mammals and fishing in both fresh and salt water. Caribou, musk-oxen, walruses, whales, and fish were the staples of the Eskimo diet. In addition to kayaks, the Eskimos trans-

**This decorated object, thought to be a stabilizer for a spear shaft, was produced by an Eskimo artist before A.D. 500. [From the Smithsonian Institution exhibition *Crossroads of Continents: Cultures of Siberia and Alaska.* From the Collections of the Museum of Anthropology and Ethnography in St. Petersburg, Florida.]**

ported themselves in canoes and on dogsleds. In the early centuries A.D. the Eskimos developed a large skin boat known as an *umiak* that served as a floating platform from which they could hunt sea mammals with harpoons.

By the end of the first century B.C. the Eskimos had constructed substantial settlements near the Bering Sea. One of these, near Cape Nome, Alaska, contained approximately 400 homes; the typical house was excavated up to 20 inches deep and was covered with poles and sod for insulation against the arctic cold. Some communities included large buildings in which the Eskimos carried out their religious rites under the direction of shamans who claimed the power to heal and to predict the future. Eskimo artists carved elaborate harpoon heads, knife handles, and arrow points made from antlers and later from slate.

Below the vast expanse of tundra occupied by the Eskimos stretched the subarctic boreal forest, with its spruce, birch, and poplar. This was the homeland of Amerindians who spoke Athabaskan languages and lived primarily as nomadic hunters. Their numbers were small—perhaps only 35,000 by the sixteenth century, owing probably to difficulties in finding and developing a dependable subsistence base. In this respect they were unlike the Eskimos, with whom they normally had poor relations. For their food supplies the Athabaskans depended primarily on caribou and moose, though they also ate musk-ox, rabbit, and fish. Whereas the Eskimos could safely store their meat throughout the year because of permafrost, the Athabaskans had to smoke or dry theirs for use during the summer. They also ate berries, wild vegetables, sap, and the tender shoots of plants such as the willow.

The Athabaskans were organized into bands, each of which was a socioeconomic unit typically headed by a chief hunter. Kinship and dependency bound members together. Hunting was the province of the men, while women, children, and the elderly gathered fruits and vegetables or fished. Canoes, dogsleds, and snowshoes were the principal means of travel. The Athabaskans lived in tents made of skins and, during the winter, log huts. From antlers they fashioned arrowheads and dart points, and copper was used to manufacture knives and spearheads. The Athabaskans periodically traded with

This Eskimo mask simultaneously depicts the face of a man and a whale. The whale's tail and flipper are the man's nose and moustache, the top of its head is his chin, and its breathing hole is his mouth. The Eskimos donned such masks for the ceremonies that preceded whaling expeditions. [Field Museum of Natural History, Chicago]

the Eskimos to obtain bone and ivory knives. Athabaskan artists applied geometric designs to canoes, paddles, and moccasins and played music using drums and rattles made from caribou hooves. The Apache and Navaho who migrated into what is now the United States were part of the Athabaskan linguistic group.

*In the Americas as in Africa, prosperous and sophisticated civilizations developed well before the arrival of Europeans. Some of those in the Americas were larger than the states of Europe, just as Tenochtitlán was bigger than any European city. The more advanced societies of the Americas, like those in Africa, engaged in long-distance trade, the construction of colossal temples and pyramids, and the production of fine works of art. The social welfare program of the Inca was comparable to advanced Asian systems and generally superior to the treatment of the poor in Europe. The Amerindians demonstrated the ability to organize their societies for mammoth public works projects, including* swamp drainage for the construction of Tenochtitlán and the extensive canals of the Hohokam. Not surprisingly, the Spaniards were impressed by the Amerindian cultures, just as the Portuguese were by the coastal cities of Africa. The once popular tendency to regard the peoples of the Americas—and of Africa—as primitive natives in need of civilization was thus erroneous.

We must nevertheless avoid the temptation to lavish excessive praise on early American civilizations. Although Amerindians were enormously successful in domesticating crops, many of which were later exported to Europe, they lagged significantly in the development of farming implements, preferring to use their metal primarily for ornaments rather than tools. Nor did they develop wheeled vehicles or substantial oceangoing vessels (as distinct from rafts and dugout canoes). The practice of human sacrifice by some Amerindian cultures was appalling by modern standards.

The study of the peoples of Africa and the Americas underscores a good deal of common experience. They developed from hunter-gatherers to farmers, which encouraged sedentary life, the gradual emergence of towns, the growth of a merchant class, and the expansion of trade. These developments also affected art and religion, as the upper classes obtained sufficient leisure to engage more extensively in such pursuits. Religious beliefs focused on the relationship between humans and the natural world, and the priesthood, which claimed unique powers to deal with the gods, grew in importance. The significance of religion to Africans and Amerindians, as to most other peoples, was reflected in their art and architecture as well as in their burial practices. Intriguing comparisons can also be made between Roman, Chinese, and Inca roads; the canals of Venice, China, and Tenochtitlán; the calendars of the Europeans and the Maya; the Vestal Virgins of Rome and the Inca Virgins of the Sun; and the pyramids of Egypt, Kush, and the Amerindians.

The Americas were overrun by Europeans long before most of Africa, perhaps because the Amerindians, unlike many Africans, had been completely isolated from European culture before the arrival of Columbus. Aztec and Inca leaders were overawed by the Europeans, whereas Africans, who had long traded with outsiders, were not. The African continent, moreover, offered a considerable degree of protection to its peoples because of its deserts and rain forests and the difficulty of gaining access to the interior. Parts of Africa remained virtually untouched before the nineteenth century, whereas in the Americas the arrival of the Europeans produced massive changes that in a matter of decades substantially affected both conquered and conquerors.

## Notes

1.  F. Katz, *The Ancient American Civilizations*, trans. K. M. L. Simpson (New York: Praeger, 1972), p. 164.

## Suggestions for Further Reading

Bernal, I. *The Olmec World*, trans. D. Heyden and F. Horcasitas. Berkeley: University of California Press, 1975.

Brodo, J., Carrasco, D., and Moctezuma, E. M., eds. *The Great Temple of Tenochtitlán: Center and Periphery in the Aztec World*. Berkeley: University of California Press, 1987.

Cobo, B. *A History of the Inca Empire*. Austin: University of Texas Press, 1979.

Coe, M. D. *The Maya*, 4th ed. London: Thames & Hudson, 1987.

———. *Mexico*, rev. ed. London: Thames & Hudson, 1984.

Conrad, G. W., and Demarest, A. A. *Religion and Empire: The Dynamics of Aztec and Inca Expansionism*. Cambridge: Cambridge University Press, 1984.

Davies, N. *The Aztec Empire: The Toltec Resurgence*. Norman: University of Oklahoma Press, 1987.

———. *The Toltec Heritage*. Norman: University of Oklahoma Press, 1980.

———. *The Toltecs: Until the Fall of Tula*. Norman: University of Oklahoma Press, 1977.

Dumond, D. E. *The Eskimos and Aleuts*, rev. ed. London: Thames & Hudson, 1987.

Fagan, B. M. *The Great Journey: The Peopling of Ancient America*. London: Thames & Hudson, 1987.

Fiedel, S. J. *Prehistory of the Americas*. Cambridge: Cambridge University Press, 1987.

Gorenstein, S., ed. *Prehispanic America*. New York: St. Martin's Press, 1974.

Hammond, N. *Ancient Maya Civilization*. New Brunswick, N.J.: Rutgers University Press, 1982.

Katz, F. *The Ancient American Civilizations*, trans. K. M. L. Simpson. New York: Praeger, 1972.

Miller, M. E. *The Art of Mesoamerica: From Olmec to Aztec*. London: Thames & Hudson, 1986.

Morley, S. G., and Brainerd, G. W. *The Ancient Maya*, rev. R. J. Sharer. Stanford, Calif.: Stanford University Press, 1983.

Schele, L. *A Forest of Kings: The Untold Story of the Ancient Maya*. New York: Morrow, 1990.

———, and Miller, M. E. *The Blood of Kings: Dynasty and Ritual in Maya Art*. Fort Worth: Kimball Art Museum, 1986.

Soustelle, J. *Daily Life of the Aztecs on the Eve of the Spanish Conquest*, trans. P. O'Brian. Stanford, Calif.: Stanford University Press, 1970.

———. *The Olmecs: The Oldest Civilization in Mexico*. Garden City, N.Y.: Doubleday, 1984.

Spencer, R. F., et al. *The Native Americans*. New York: Harper & Row, 1965.

Weaver, M. P. *The Aztecs, Maya, and Their Predecessors*. New York: Academic Press, 1981.

Zantwijk, R. A. M. van. *The Aztec Arrangement: The Social History of Pre-Spanish Mexico*. Norman: University of Oklahoma Press, 1985.

# Medieval India and Southeast Asia

From the mid-tenth century, about 300 years after the collapse of the Gupta dynasty and the death of Harsha, North India endured a long period of disunion, conflict, and renewed invasions from central Asia. This era culminated in 1526 with the establishment of the Mughal Empire and a new flowering of unity and cultural brilliance. The medieval centuries of disorder and conquest, comparable in some ways to the situation in Europe after the decline of the western Roman Empire, were, however, in no way a period of universal disaster. Invasion and conquest were limited to relatively short periods of disturbance in the northern half of the subcontinent. Most people in most parts of India went on with their lives in the usual way most of the time. These centuries

**The Qutb Minar—begun in 1199 by Sultan Qutb-ud-din Aibak, completed by Sultan Iltumish (1211–1236), and repaired by Firuz Tughluq—was built to celebrate the victory of the new rulers of Delhi and also as a minaret for the adjacent mosque, since largely destroyed. The tower, 73 meters high and beautifully decorated in each segment, is one of the few monuments preserved in reasonable condition from the time of the Delhi sultanate. [Rhoads Murphey]**

also saw the vigorous continuation of the Indian artistic tradition patronized by the Guptas and by Harsha, including the construction of a great many magnificent temples and their sculpture, especially in the south. Trade flourished, particularly with Southeast Asia; wealthy merchants subsidized temple complexes and the arts in the rich urban culture of medieval India, and great literature continued to be produced. The south remained largely peaceful, but in much of the north, invasion, conquest, and warfare brought periodic misery.

# Early Islamic Influence

The new invaders from the north were part of the general expansion of Islam, and they brought with them an often harsh and intolerant version of the new religion. But they also brought Islamic and, in particular, Persian culture, including many educated Iranians, who served as scribes for the largely illiterate conquerors as well as administrators, artists, writers, and other elites. India, with its wealth, numbers, and sophistication, was an irresistible target, and both Hinduism and Buddhism

were seen as pagan creeds, to be conquered by the faith of the Prophet. The invaders' early motives and ruthless behavior were similar to those of the sixteenth-century Portuguese and Spanish invaders of Asia and Latin America in their search for riches, such as gold and spices, and for converts to Catholic Christianity. For the Muslim invaders of India, Hinduism, with its "idolatrous" worship of many gods, its tolerance, and its lack of precise scriptural doctrine, was seen as an evil to be eliminated. Their attitude to the closely related faith and practice of Buddhism was much the same. Probably the chief original motive for their invasion of India was, however, simple plunder. Many of these central Asian groups contented themselves at first with pillaging India's wealth and slaughtering "infidel" victims before withdrawing across the passes with their loot.

In time, however, Muslim kingdoms with a largely Persian courtly culture were established in much of northern India, which had far more to attract and support them than their dry, barren, and mountainous homelands. In time this new infusion of alien vigor blended with older strands of the Indian fabric.

Since the time of Ashoka and the first Buddhist missions (see Chapter 2), there has been a close connection between India and Southeast Asia. We know very little

Approaches to the Khyber Pass near the eastern border of Afghanistan. The Hindu Kush mountain range is a formidable barrier, but it is penetrable at several passes. Through them have come a long succession of invaders of India, including the Turco-Afghan carriers of Islam and various Persian cultures. [Rhoads Murphey]

about Southeast Asian systems before this time. It is possible that Indian influence there began before Ashoka, but our earliest data for Southeast Asian kingdoms come from the centuries after his reign and show a political, literate, and religious or philosophical culture already Indianized. Following the Muslim conquest of northern India, Islam was also carried to insular Southeast Asia by converts among Indian traders. These and other aspects of Indian civilization were, however, overlaid onto a well-developed preexisting base whose character was distinctly different.

Indian and Chinese influences have continued to operate on Southeast Asia up to the present. But this immense area, which embraces the present-day nations of Burma, Thailand, Laos, Cambodia, Vietnam, Malaysia, Indonesia, and the Philippines, has retained, despite regional differences, its own indigenous social and cultural forms. These evolved separately before the coming of Indian and Chinese elements. Only writing and various literary, artistic, political, and religious forms came in from India, Vietnam, and China. The social base and most other aspects of culture were less affected and indeed helped shape many aspects of the new culture. The latter part of this chapter deals with the civilization of Southeast Asia during the medieval period, after the fall of the Gupta Empire in India, when we can see for the first time in any detail the evolution of separate kingdoms and cultures in that region.

# The Muslim Advance

India at first lay beyond the wave of Islamic conquests of the seventh century, which engulfed most of the Middle East and North Africa, but Arab traders continued to bring back samples of Indian wealth. Sind, the lower half of the Indus valley, was conquered by Arab forces in the eighth century, primarily as a rival trade base. But the major advance came nearly three centuries later, from the newly converted Turks of central Asia, who had been driven westward and into Afghanistan by earlier Chinese expansion under the Han and the T'ang dynasties.

The Turkish leader Mahmud of Ghazni (971–1030), known as the "Sword of Islam," mounted 17 plundering expeditions between 1001 and 1027 from his eastern Afghan base at Ghazni into the adjacent upper Indus and western Punjab, destroying Hindu temples, sacking rich cities, killing or forcibly converting the inhabitants, and then returning to Ghazni with jewels, gold, silver, women, elephants, and slaves. His remote mountain-ringed capital became by the eleventh century a great center of Islamic culture, thanks in part to stolen Indian riches. Pillage and slaughter in the name of God did not make a good impression for Islam among most Indians,

but the austere new religion, with its promise of certainty and of equality, did appeal to some. And India attracted Mahmud's successors, as well as rival central Asian Turkish groups.

The military effectiveness of these invaders depended importantly on their mastery of cavalry tactics, true to their nomadic heritage, and their use of short, powerful compound bows of laminated wood, horn, and sinew that they could fire at a gallop on horseback. The Rajputs of Rajasthan, on the flank of the Islamic invasion route, fought relentlessly from their desert strongholds and fortified cities against these Turco-Afghan armies, which the more peaceful inhabitants of Hindustan were less able to resist. Some of the Rajputs had central Asian origins too, some centuries earlier, and hence shared an originally nomadic tradition of mounted, mobile warfare, but all Rajputs were part of a military culture of great tenacity, nurtured in the desert of Rajasthan. They were never completely overcome, but most of the rest of the north, seriously weakened by continual political division and internal conflict, was progressively conquered.

By the end of the twelfth century, Punjab and most of Hindustan (the valley of the Ganges) had been incorporated into a Turco-Afghan empire with its capital at Delhi. Delhi controlled an easy crossing place on the Jumna River where a range of hills stretched southwest and provided protection. Northward lay the barrier of the Himalayas; westward, the Thar desert of Rajasthan. Eastward the broad Ganges valley led into the heart of Hindustan, but for access to it and for routes southward, Delhi had first to be secured; all invaders from the northwest, the repeated route of entry via the Punjab, were obliged to maintain control of Delhi. Bengal was overrun in 1202, and in 1206 the Delhi sultanate was formally inaugurated. As a series of successive Islamic dynasties, it was to dominate most of North India for the next 320 years, until the rise of the Mughal Empire in 1526.

Bengal had prospered as a separate kingdom after the fall of the Gupta order. It remained the chief Indian center of Buddhism, including a great university and monastery at Nalanda, where some 10,000 monks lived and studied, and similar Hindu centers of learning and piety. Both religions and their followers were targets for the Muslim invaders. Tens of thousands of monks and other Hindus and Buddhists were slaughtered and the universities and monasteries destroyed. This catastrophe marked the effective end of Buddhism in the land of its birth. The few surviving Buddhists fled from the slaughter to Nepal and Tibet. Hindu monuments also suffered, for they violated Islamic principles forbidding the artistic representation of divine creation, including the human form.

Unfortunately for its people, northern India remained hopelessly divided among rival kingdoms, most of them small and nearly all of them in chronic conflict. In total, their armies were huge, but they seem never to have

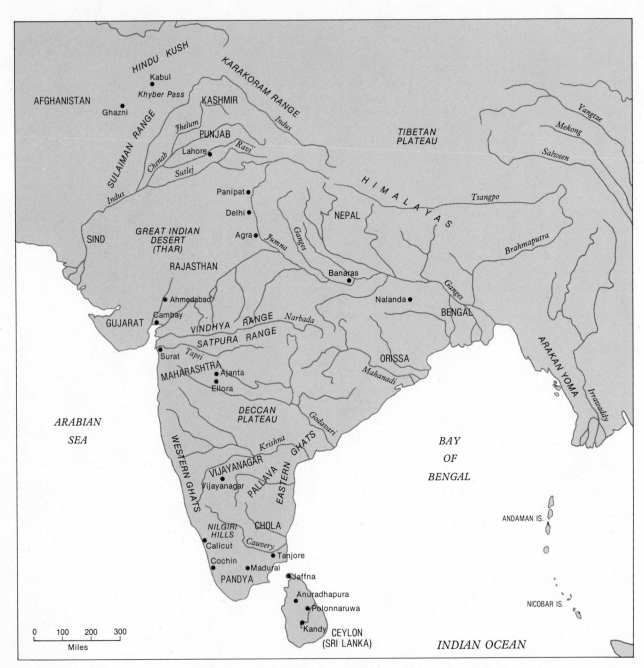

**11.1** *Medieval India*

considered a united or even partially united stand against the invaders who, like Alexander before them, defeated the few forces sent against them one by one. Even after Mahmud and his successors had established their rule over most of the north, little opposition was organized against them or against their repeated efforts to spread their conquests southward into central India and the Deccan.

# The Delhi Sultans

Successive Turco-Afghan rulers were more accepting, if not of Hinduism, then of Hindus, who remained the vast majority of the Indian population. But Hindus were treated as decidedly second-class citizens and forced to

## ◉ **Marco Polo on India** ◉

*Marco Polo visited South India on his way back from China by sea in 1293. Given his fulsome descriptions of the wealth and splendor of China, it is notable that he nevertheless called India "the noblest and richest country in the world." His account of what he saw and heard otherwise has the ring of truth and is easily recognizable as an accurate picture of many aspects of Indian society and culture.*

The people go naked all the year round, for the weather here is always temperate. That is why they go naked, except that they cover their private parts with a scrap of cloth. The king wears no more than the others, apart from certain ornaments: a handsome loin cloth with a fringe set with precious stones, so that this scrap of cloth is worth a fortune. . . . It is his task every day, morning and evening, to say 104 prayers in honor of his idols. Such is the bidding of their faith and their religion. . . . He also wears bracelets of gold studded with precious stones, and three anklets adorned with costly pearls and gems.

The people of this kingdom worship idols. Most of them worship the ox. . . . No one would eat beef for anything in the world, and no one would kill an ox. . . . They daub all their houses with cow dung. . . . Another of their customs is that they wash their whole body in cold water twice a day, morning and evening. . . . In this kingdom justice is very strictly administered to those who commit homicide or theft or any other crime. . . . It is a proof of the excellent justice kept by the king that when a nocturnal traveller wishes to sleep and has with him a sack of pearls or other valuables—for men travel by night rather than by day because it is cooler—he will put the sack under his head and sleep where he is; and no one ever loses anything by theft.

The Brahmans live longer than anyone else in the world, due to their light feeding and great abstinence. . . . Among them are certain men living under a rule who are called *yogis.* They live even longer than the others . . . and their bodies remain so active that they can still come and go as they will and perform all the services required by their monastery and their idols and serve them just as well as if they were younger. This comes of their great abstinence and of eating very little food and only what is wholesome.

*Source:* R. Latham, trans., *The Travels of Marco Polo* (Baltimore: Penguin Books, 1959), pp. 233–252.

pay a special tax as "infidels" if they refused, as most did, to convert. This was an improvement on the atrocities of the earlier raiders and followed the original Islamic practice of recognizing in other established religions a justified but inferior status.

There was no shortage of Hindu religious texts, and it was not hard in time to accept Hinduism as a sophisticated religion, not simply as "paganism." With more knowledge it was also recognized that Hinduism was basically monotheistic, like Islam, and could not be judged only on the basis of the many gods of Indian folk religion. This distinction was comparable to that between unadorned Christianity and folk practice involving many saints and local cults, as, for example, in Latin America. The head tax (*jizya*) paid by protected non-Muslims (dhimmis) was heavy—about 6 percent of an individual's total net worth annually—but it bought a degree of freedom to practice one's own religion. More-

over, the later Delhi sultans agreed to leave many of the original Hindu Indian local rulers and petty rajas in control of their domains. The sultanate thus slowly became more an Indian order and less an alien occupation. It came in time to depend increasingly on the support of India's indigenous people and, under the best of its rulers, to try to govern rather than merely to exploit.

Raids and plundering expeditions went on under the stronger rulers of the Delhi sultanate into the Deccan, south of the Ganges plain of Hindustan, but no permanent position was ever won there or elsewhere in the south. The landscape favored the Hindu defenders, beginning with the double row of mountains that mark the northern edge of the Deccan—the Vindhya Mountains and the Satpura Range—and including the Narbada and Tapti rivers, which run, respectively, in the valleys south of each range.

The Deccan itself is deeply eroded and in many areas

cut up into steep ravines and river valleys, with easily defended hills or smaller mountains in almost every part. It has seen many bloody campaigns but never a complete or permanent victory for any of the successive invaders from the north, including both the Delhi sultanate and the Mughal dynasty as well as the Guptas and Mauryas long before. The chief and most consistent Hindu defenders against the Muslim attackers were the warlike Mahrathas of Maharashtra, the arid northwestern quarter of the Deccan. They were protected by their strategically located plateau base and its mountain fringes and, like the Rajputs, had a proud martial tradition of resisting northern invasions.

The Delhi sultanate was also weakened by internal power struggles and political intrigues, which similarly plagued their Ottoman Turkish cousins later in their far larger empire. Most of the Delhi sultans were absolute rulers who tolerated no dissent and demanded total submission; most of them consequently provoked chronic revolts and plots against them, and many died by assassination, by poisoning, or in the dust of a coup or a civil war. There was no agreed method of succession, and the death of each sultan was the occasion for fighting among rivals for power.

The armies of the sultans, like those of the Ottomans and other Turkish states, owed their strength in large part to mamelukes, usually Turks bought in their youth as slaves and then trained as full-time professional fighters. They were an outstandingly disciplined force, but like many lifetime mercenaries, they were not above an interest in power and its rewards. Their commanders were often formidable contenders for political power. The ruthlessness and frequent cruelty of many of the sultans provided additional motives for revolt.

In general, the sultanate succeeded only fitfully in becoming an effective administration for the areas it controlled in the north. The records we have tell of power rivalries, intrigues at court, taxation, coups, civil wars, and abortive efforts to invade the south, but we have little evidence of the effect of these affairs on the lives of ordinary people. Political power was highly concentrated in Delhi, leaving much of the sultanate's domains under local rulers who had a good deal of autonomy. It seems likely that after the first half century or so of ruthless plunder, conquest, slaughter, and intolerance, most people in North India were left largely to themselves as long as they paid both land taxes and the *jizya*.

The main impact of the sultanate on India was probably to implant a deep mistrust of politics, government in general, and Islam in particular, where it was used as the basis of state policy. Few monuments remain from this period of northern Indian history. In broader cultural terms, however, these centuries did witness a fusion of originally Hindu elements with the Iranian influences brought in by the Turkish conquerors. Like the Mughals who followed them, they were the agents of a largely Persian culture whose richness and variety found

acceptance among many Indians. What we now think of as "traditional" Indian language, poetry, music, architecture, and painting in fact took their present forms from this fusion. Islam, and Hindu-Muslim differences, proved not to be either a bar to such cultural hybridization or a source of conflict, except where it was made an issue in political and military matters. Religious differences were ultimately far less important than other aspects of culture and proved no barrier to cultural mixing.

Islam was progressively Indianized, and over the centuries it won some converts on its own merits and through the agency of a long line of Sufi mystics (see Chapter 8) whose vision was broad enough to appeal to the Indian mystical tradition.

---

❦

# ALA-UD-DIN KHALJI, OPPRESSIVE SULTAN

The power of the Delhi sultans was severely tested by the Mongol invasion of the early fourteenth century. By this time the Turco-Afghan invaders had been partly Indianized, like so many conquerors before them, and depended more on the support of the indigenous people. It was fortunate that on the throne of Delhi was a capable ruler, Ala-ud-din Khalji (1296–1316), who, augmenting his forces with mameluke troops, drove the Mongol horsemen back into Afghanistan in a rare Mongol defeat. Ala-ud-din had usurped the throne by having his uncle murdered, after raiding the Deccan and bringing back loot, which he used to buy the loyalty of those around his uncle, Sultan Jalal-ud-din.

Ala-ud-din paid his army officers in cash and kept tight personal control over his forces. He could neither read nor write and had no tolerance for intellectuals, sophisticated courtiers, or other elites. He abolished all regular stipends and grants to the Muslim nobles, eliminating their political influence and leaving them wholly dependent on him. He outlawed wine-drinking parties, which were in any case against Muslim doctrine, fearing that revelers might plot against him. Ala-ud-din's power base was fueled by a land tax, which he raised to 50 percent of the value of each crop, and by new taxes on milk cows and houses. The crop tax tended to impoverish especially Hindus, most of whom were engaged in agriculture. Barani, the fourteenth-century Arab historian of India, quoted Ala-ud-din as saying:

> **I am an unlettered man, but I have seen a great deal. Be assured that Hindus will never become submissive and obedient until they have been reduced to poverty. I have therefore given orders that just enough shall be left them of grain, milk, and curds from year to year, but that they must not accumulate hoards or property.[1]**

# THE VISUAL EXPERIENCE
## Art of Early Africa and the Americas

The lasting impact of Christianity on Ethiopia is vividly
represented in this seventeenth-century painting of St. George
slaying a dragon, a traditional Christian theme. [British Library]

This ivory belt mask is an example of the work of the highly skilled sculptors of Benin. Their work influenced many later artists. [Reproduced by Courtesy of the Trustees of the British Museum]

A Maya ruler from the seventh or eighth century is dressed in distinctive regalia associated with warfare and spiritual struggle. ["A Ruler Dressed as Chac-Xib-Chac and the Holmul Dancer," Kimball Museum, Fort Worth, Texas]

In this mural from the Temple of the Warriors at Chichén Itzá, an advance party of Toltecs reconnoiter a Maya town from their boats. The god Quetzalcoatl watches from the upper right. [Peabody Museum, Harvard University; photograph by Hillel Burger]

This illustration from an Aztec manuscript depicts Emperor Montezuma II surrendering to Hernando Cortés. (Coloring has been added.) [Library of Congress]

This diorama depicts the Inca in the Urubamba Valley near Cuzco on the eve of their conquest by the Spaniards. Terraces enabled them to farm in the Andes, and the transportation of goods was by pack trains that traversed suspension bridges. [Field Museum of Natural History, Chicago]

The quarter-mile-long Great Serpent Mound near Cincinnati, Ohio, is a vestige of the Adena culture, the earliest of the Mound Builders. The dead were buried in log-lined tombs and earthen crematory basins at the center of effigies like that shown here. Other effigies were built in the shape of eagles, bears, and alligators. [Tony Linck]

This Anasazi mural deals with the fertility of the earth and the crucial importance of rainfall. The figures depicted, from left to right, include those of an eagle spewing forth seeds, a rainbow, and a lightning bolt; a partial figure of a corn maiden carrying a small vessel from which moisture streams into a black water jar; another corn maiden beside a water jar from which snow and rain pour forth; and the fire god. [From *Sun Father's Way* by Bertha P. Dutton (Albuquerque: University of New Mexico Press, 1963)]

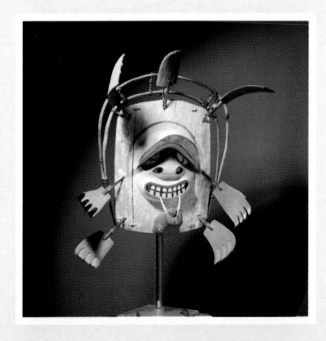

This mask of an Eskimo shaman depicts the spirit of a sea mammal. [Phoebe Hearst Museum of Anthropology, University of California, Berkeley]

---

## ◉ The Mongols: An Eyewitness Account ◉

*Even the Turco-Afghan rulers of the Delhi sultanate were appalled by the Mongols, whose invasion of India they managed to repel. Here is a description of them by a Turkish eyewitness.*

Their eyes were so narrow and piercing that they might have bored a hole in a brazen vessel. Their stink was more horrible than their color. Their faces were set on their bodies as if they had no neck. Their cheeks resembled soft leather bottles, full of wrinkles and knots. Their noses extended from cheek to cheek and their mouths from cheek bone to cheek bone. Their nostrils resembled rotten graves, and from them the hair descended as far as the lips.

*Source:* H. G. Rawlinson, *India: A Short Cultural History* (New York: Praeger, 1965), p. 224.

---

Hindus were also forbidden to possess any weapons or to ride horses. Loyalty and conformity with the sultan's decrees were further ensured by a network of spies, harsh penalties, and intricate court duplicities. He also imposed wage and price controls in Delhi and prohibited the private hoarding of gold and silver, while at the same time requiring all merchants to be licensed and their profits restricted. Peasants could sell their crops only to licensed merchants and at set prices and could retain only fixed amounts for their own use. These measures kept most prices low enough to permit soldiers and workers to live adequately on their pay, at least in the Delhi area, though merchants and peasants everywhere resented them bitterly. But the controls and taxes made it possible for Ala-ud-din to field an army that could meet and repulse the Mongol invasion.

With the Mongols defeated, Ala-ud-din resumed his looting raids in the Deccan, overcoming even some of the Rajputs and penetrating briefly as far as Pandyan territory farther south. But at his death in 1316 not only these efforts but his own family line as well came to an end; his first son was murdered by his own soldiers, and a second son abandoned all efforts at maintaining the controls established by his father and gave himself up to pleasures at court. Ala-ud-din, ruthlessly cruel and oppressive, was understandably hated and feared. His system died with him, but during his lifetime it permitted Hindustan to avoid the fate of subjugation by the Mongols. His economic controls were remarkable for their thoroughness and extensiveness, but they rested on absolute power and severe taxation, both bound to provoke resistance and ultimately to destroy them. He had bought and murdered his way to the throne with the help of the plunder brought back from his Deccan raids, but he and his successors failed to hold any part of the south or its wealth. They could maintain their authoritarian rule in the north only by bleeding the agricultural base of the economy—a prescription for ultimate disaster.

## The Tughluqs

With the collapse of Ala-ud-din's order, a new Muslim dynasty succeeded to power in the Dehli sultanate, the Tughluqs, whose founder was the son of a Turkish court slave and a Hindu woman. His son and successor, Muhammad Tughluq (1325–1351), came to the throne when a pavilion he had erected for his father collapsed, killing the father. Muhammad's regime of strict piety and his renewed efforts at carrying Islam southward may perhaps be interpreted as an attempt to expiate his sense of guilt. He ordered everyone to observe the Koranic ordinances for ritual, prayers, and Islamic doctrine and forced large numbers of troops and officials to man his drive into the Deccan, where he briefly established a secondary capital.

The endless campaigns, and taxes to support them, provoked growing rebellion as well as southern resistance. From 1335 to 1342 North India endured a seven-year drought and famine, one of the worst such periods in its history, but Muhammad was too busy with fighting, tax collecting, and the promotion of strict Islam to respond, and there was no organized effort by the state to provide tax relief or food distribution. Well over a million people died, and revolts became even more widespread, in the north as well as in the south and even in Delhi itself. Bengal broke away and declared its independence in 1338, retaining it for the next three centuries.

Muhammad was killed fighting a rebellion in Sind in 1351, and his cousin Firuz Tughluq claimed the throne, which he held until his death in 1388. Firuz proved a more constructive ruler, who largely abandoned the earlier efforts at conquest and warfare and concentrated instead on the rebuilding of Delhi, with splendid new gardens, mosques, hospitals, and colleges for the study of Islam. He also supported the construction of new irrigation schemes, including dams and reservoirs, that brought new land into production. Although a Muslim zealot like Muhammad, he cut back the sultanate's system of spies and informers, abolished torture, and tried to improve the material welfare of his subjects. But his Islamic orthodoxy and intolerance, his insistence on payment of the *jizya* tax by all "infidels," and his clear message that Hindus were second-class citizens alienated the majority. Soon after his death, the sultanate's domains broke up into warring factions.

This chaos in North India invited, as so often before, a catastrophic invasion by central Asian armies, this time led by the brutal Tamerlane (1336–1405), a Turkish leader who had already ravaged much of central Asia and the Middle East. After looting the Punjab, he entered Delhi in 1398 and systematically slaughtered whatever inhabitants he did not take away as slaves or force to carry his booty. Famine and pestilence followed in his wake. The Delhi sultanate never fully recovered from this devastating blow, and its political fragmentation accelerated. Gujarat declared its independence in 1401 and flourished under its own rulers, especially in the Gujarati capital of Ahmedabad. Gujarat had always depended on its maritime trade, westward across the Arabian Sea and the Indian Ocean and eastward to Southeast Asia, and this trade now increased still more. Many Gujaratis, including their rulers, had converted to Islam, which proved useful in trade connections both westward and eastward and made Gujarat prosperous. With their commercial profits the Gujaratis built luxurious new palaces and mosques in Ahmedabad.

## Sikandar Lodi and Ibrahim

In what remained of the Delhi sultanate, an Afghan clan, the Lodis, took the throne in 1450 and produced an effective ruler, Sikandar (1489–1517). A patron of culture and a poet, Sikandar encouraged scholarship and the compilation of books on medicine and music. Though a highly orthodox Muslim, he fell in love with a Hindu princess, and his reign saw the continued blending of the Islamic and Hindu mystical traditions. Sikandar himself was not, however, an adherent of Sufism, and perhaps to prove himself orthodox despite having a Hindu wife, he continued the Muslim policy of destroying temples and other Hindu religious art.

In North India, Sikandar's successor, Ibrahim (1517–1526), was a far less compelling figure than his father had been and was confronted by revolts in many parts of the remaining sultanate territories. The rival Rajput Confederacy grew and threatened to extinguish the sultanate altogether. Lahore, chief city of Punjab, was in rebellion, and its governor unwisely invited a new group of central Asian Turks to strengthen his hand against Sultan Ibrahim. This was the army of Babur (1483–1530), known as "the Tiger," who claimed descent from Tamerlane through his father and from Chinghis Khan through his mother. For 20 years, as his own account of his life tells us, he had "never ceased to think of the conquest of Hindustan." India's wealth and its political divisions chronically tempted Afghans, Turks, and others. Babur's outnumbered but brilliantly led forces defeated those of Ibrahim at Panipat, northwest of Delhi, in 1526, and in the next year similarly vanquished the Rajput Confederacy, now plagued by internal divisions. North India was again under alien domination, but the Mughal dynasty that Babur founded was to reach new levels of splendor and imperial achievement.

## Bhakti and Sufi: A Religious Revival

In the troubled centuries after A.D. 1000, with their shifting and periodically disastrous political changes, punctuated by invasion and bloody warfare, it is understand-

| MEDIEVAL INDIA | | |
|---|---|---|
| | North India | South India |
| A.D. 1–1000 | | Chola kingdom (c. 200–1279) |
| | | Pandyan kingdom (before 300– c. 1550) |
| | | Pallavan kingdom (c. 300–c. 880) |
| 1000–1316 | Muslim invasions begin (1001) | |
| | Delhi sultanate founded (1206) | |
| | Reign of Ala-ud-din Khalji (1296–1316) | |
| 1316–1565 | Tughlug Dynasty (1316–1388) | Empire of Vijayanagar (1336–1565) |
| | Invasion of Tamerlane (1398) | |
| | Reign of Sikandar (1489–1517) | |
| | Invasion of Babur (1526) | |

able that people turned even more fervently to religion. A new Hindu movement known as *bhakti* ("devotion") developed in the south in the tenth century, spread gradually north, and by the fourteenth century reached Bengal, where at the ancient sacred city of Banaras on the Ganges a latter-day disciple, Ramananda, preached the bhakti message of divine love. Its universal appeal as well as its solace attracted a mass following in all parts of India, including many Muslims, with its emphasis on the simple love of God and the abandonment of sectarian or rival causes. This was the Sufi message also, and Sufi Muslims helped spread the bhakti movement while they also increased the appeal of a more humane yet more mystical Islam. It was celebrated by a long series of poet-saints, probably the most beloved of whom was the blind and illiterate Muslim weaver-poet Kabir of Banaras (died 1518), a disciple of Ramananda whose moving verses on the bhakti theme have inspired many millions since his time.

The modern Indian historian D. P. Singhal sums up the history of the Delhi sultanate as follows:

The history of the sultanate of Delhi is full of dynasties which were short-lived and weak. Of the thirty-five sultans belonging to the five dynasties who sat on the throne of Delhi during a period of 300 years, nineteen were assassinated by Muslim rebels. It is almost a catalogue of kings, courts, and conquests, but it was the richest of all the Islamic states during the period. An important feature of the period was the Hindu-Muslim cultural fusion. It was not an Islamic state; it charged more than the one-fifth land tax prescribed by Muslim law, and also interest. Kingship was hereditary and not elected. The sultans were unlimited despots. Even agriculture did not flourish; no attempt was made to better the lot of the cultivators. . . . Rebellions and military expeditions were common and their political fortunes varied. The Turko-Afghan rulers lacked national support and a sound administration based on tradition, so essential for any government to survive and flourish. There was no well defined, well regulated administrative machinery under their rule. The authority of the central government, which was dominated by the ruler and military aristocracy, hardly extended beyond the capital, court, and fort. The rest of the country was in the hands of ambitious provincial governors who, having sent tribute

## ◉ Hindu Devotion ◉

*Here are some samples of the Hindu bhakti devotional literature of medieval South India.*

I am false, my heart is false, my love is false, but I, this sinner, can win Thee if I weep before Thee, O Lord, Thou who art sweet like honey, nectar, and the juice of sugar cane. Please bless me so that I might reach Thee. . . . Melting in the mind, now standing, now sitting, now lying, and now getting up, dancing in all sorts of ways, gaining the vision of the Form of the Lord shining like the rosy sky, when will I stand united with and entered into that exquisite Gem? . . . Without any other attachment, I cherished with my mind only Thine holy feet; I have been born with Thy grace and I have attained the state whereby I will have no rebirth. O benevolent Lord, worshipped and praised by the learned! Even if I forget you, let my tongue go on muttering your praise. . . . Lighting in my heart the bright lamp of knowledge, I sought and captured Him. Softly the Lord of Miracles too entered my heart and stayed there without leaving it. . . . He is not male, He is not female, He is not neuter, He is not to be seen. He neither is nor is not. When He is sought He will take the form in which He is sought, and again He will not come in such a form. How can one describe the nature of the Lord? . . . The name of the Lord will bless one with high birth and affluence; it will obliterate all the sufferings of the devotees; it will endow one with the heavenly state; it will bring success and all good things; it will perform for one more beautiful acts than one's own mother. . . . The lamb brought to the slaughterhouse eats the leaf garland with which it is decorated. The frog caught in the mouth of the snake desires to swallow the fly flying near its mouth. So is our life. . . . He who knows only the sacred books is not wise. He only is wise who trusts in God.

*Source:* W. T. de Bary, ed., *Sources of Indian Tradition,* vol. 1 (New York: Columbia University Press, 1964), pp. 349–352.

## ◉ The Bhakti Synthesis ◉

*Kabir, the blind Muslim weaver-poet of the fifteenth century, is the best-known representative of the Hindu-Muslim fusion in the bhakti movement.*

O servant, where dost thou seek me? Lo, I am beside thee.
I am neither in the temple nor in the mosque,
Not in rites and ceremonies nor in yoga and renunciation.
If thou art a true seeker thou shalt at once see Me;
Thou shalt meet Me in a moment of time.
It is needless to ask of a saint the caste to which he belongs,
For the priest, the warrior, the tradesman and all the other castes
Are all alike seeking God. The barber has sought God,
The washerwoman, and the carpenter.
Hindus and Muslims alike have achieved that end,
Where there remains no mark of distinction.
O Lord, who will serve Thee?
Every supplicant offers his worship to the God of his own creation;
None seek Him, the perfect, the Indivisible Lord.
Kabir says, "O brother, he who has seen the radiance of love, he is saved."
When I was forgetful, my true guru showed me the way.
Then I left off all rites and ceremonies, I bathed no more in the holy water.
I do not ring the temple bell, I do not set the idol on its throne
Or worship the image with flowers.
The man who is kind and who practises righteousness, who remains passive
Amidst the affairs of the world, who considers all creatures on earth
As his own self, he attains the Immortal Being;
The true God is ever with him; he attains the true Name whose words are pure,
And who is free from pride and conceit.
Look within your heart, for there you will find the true God of all.

*Source:* W. T. de Bary, ed., *Sources of Indian Tradition,* vol. 1 (New York: Columbia University Press, 1964), pp. 355–357.

or presents to Delhi, felt free to continue their autocratic rule. Their rule in turn rarely extended beyond their own courts. . . . The disintegration which began toward the close of the reign of Muhammad Tughluq was completed by [Tamerlane's] invasion and the following anarchy. The recovery of northern India under the Lodi kings was too brief to alter the picture materially.[2]

## South India

Most of India remained in fact under native control during the Delhi sultanate, including the ancient kingdoms of Pallava, Pandya, and Chola, whose rule, cultures, and literary and artistic traditions continued largely un-

broken. In much of the Deccan and the south, however, with the exception of the Chola kingdom, central state control was relatively loose, and the Hindu monarchies were organized on a semifeudal basis. Lands were held by lords as fiefs, in return for military assistance, payments in kind, and periodic attendance at court, a system similar to that in Chou dynasty China and medieval Europe. Rulers also granted tax-free estates as rewards for service. In India, as in medieval Europe, the tax burden was made heavier by grants of tax-free domains to religious orders, monasteries, and temples. These were often in fact the richest groups in the country and also received large voluntary donations, especially from merchants eager to demonstrate their piety.

The chief cities of medieval India, as of Europe, served as religious centers, grouped around a complex of temples, although supported by profits from trade, farming, and the production of artisans. The great Indian tradition of monumental architecture and sculpture flourished during these centuries, especially in the south. The major southern kingdoms alternated in their efforts to dominate all of the south, but trade continued between South India and Southeast Asia. Commercial ties served, as they had since Mauryan times, as a channel for Indian influence in the parts of Southeast Asia close to the sea. There was also some settlement by Indian colonists, who brought both Hinduism and Buddhism together with other aspects of Indian culture.

Preoccupation with the violent political scene in the medieval north, for which we have more detailed records, should not obscure the unbroken continuance and evolution of indigenous Indian civilization in the south. The south remained politically divided and periodically involved in warfare among contending states, but such problems were chronic in most societies of the time elsewhere, as in Europe. The medieval South Indian record of temple building alone, including many immense and beautiful complexes, tells a more positive tale of agricultural and commercial prosperity, a relatively orderly society and government, and a continuing emphasis on religion. Much of the urban culture was supported by merchants, and this too provides some evidence of the scope and wealth of commerce, including the maritime trade with Southeast Asia from a series of ports on the southeast coast.

## The Temple Builders

The history of South India during these centuries is in fact recorded largely in the building of temples and their records and inscriptions. Through them we know the outlines of rival and successive kingdoms; their conquests, rise, and decline; and the names of rulers and rich donors. Perhaps the greatest temple builders were the Pallavas of the western and central Deccan, who reigned from the fourth to the tenth centuries, but all of the South Indian kingdoms built temples. It was an age of faith, like the European Middle Ages, and as in Europe, Indian builders worked in stone, although many of the temples were hewn out of solid rock and consist of a series of adjoining caves, ornately decorated and with ceilings supported by carved stone pillars.

The best known and most extensive of these rock-cut temples is the complex of 27 caves at Ajanta in the central Deccan, which stretch in a crescent across an entire mountainside, and the nearby 34 cave temples at Ellora, both constructed between the fifth and the eighth centuries. The Ajanta caves were partly buried by a landslide and were rediscovered in the early nineteenth century in excellent condition by British amateur archaeologists, who marveled at the beautifully ornate friezes, sculptures, bas-reliefs, monumental figures of elephants and deities, and wall paintings.

The Pallavas and other southern dynasties who also patronized the arts built a great number of other temples. Many of them were freestanding, including the enormous complex at Madurai built by the Pandyan kingdom, the temples at Tanjore built by the Cholas, and similar clusters in other South Indian cities in a variety of styles.

Revenues from trade and productive agriculture, plus donations from the pious, helped make this extensive building possible. They also supported political power and imperial ambition. The Cholas were the most successful conquerors, fanning out from their base in southeastern peninsular India. Their economic strength depended in part on their organized success in constructing a system of excavated tanks or reservoirs to hold the monsoon rains and then distributing water to fields via canals during the long dry periods. Originally a feudatory dependency of the Pallavas, the Cholas emerged as the dominant power in South India by the tenth century and even absorbed much of the earlier Pandyan kingdom, including its capital at Madurai. They further developed the Pallavan style of temple building. The revived Pandyan kingdom continued the tradition when it supplanted Chola domination after the thirteenth century, and in the seventeenth century it completed the Madurai temple complex in the form we see today.

Throughout the classical and medieval periods, temples were the scenes of frequent festivals that included music, drama, elaborate processions, and dance. These forms of religious worship were also often combined with markets, as in the fairs of medieval Europe, and offered attractions for secular as well as religious interests. Pilgrimages to temple centers were popular, with the same mixture of devotion or piety and social entertainment, complete with storytellers and itinerant actors and jugglers as well as vendors of food, trinkets, and religious objects. Chaucer's *Canterbury Tales* could have been set in medieval South India, and pilgrimages and religious festivals of much the same sort remain an important feature of modern Indian culture.

## The Cholas

What gave the Cholas additional power for expansion during their centuries of dominance was their profitable involvement in maritime trade and their navy. Chola armies conquered most of South India, from the central Deccan to the tip of the peninsula. The Chola navy was the greatest maritime force of the surrounding oceans. It even defeated the fleet of the Southeast Asian empire of Sri Vijaya in 1025, intervening again in 1068 to defend the Malayan dependencies it had acquired.

Some of the caves at Ajanta, showing a sample of the sculptures cut out of the rock.
[Government of India Information Services]

With the help of their navy, the Cholas also invaded the northern half of Ceylon and occupied it for more than 50 years in the eleventh century. The Cholas were finally driven out of Ceylon by a great revival of Sinhalese power, which lasted until the thirteenth century. The Sinhalese capital was moved from its classical site at Anuradhapura to a new monumental capital at Polonnaruwa, and its armies in turn briefly invaded the Tamil country of the Cholas and temporarily occupied Madurai in the late twelfth century. The Sinhalese took advantage of a Pandyan revolt against the Cholas, which in itself symptomized the overall decline of Chola power and of the resurgence of rival South Indian kingdoms. By the thirteenth century Chola power had faded and the south resumed its more typical pattern of political fragmentation, although a reduced Chola kingdom remained and continued to patronize Tamil culture and to prosper eco-

nomically. The kingdom's administration was remarkable for the role played by village and district councils, which were under central supervision but retained a large measure of local autonomy.

The development of bronze casting and sculpture reached new levels of perfection in medieval South India, especially in Chola domains. The famous and exquisite figure of the dancing, many-armed Shiva was cast in eleventh-century Chola, and the form was widely copied by other Indian artists. Other pieces from this period have the same grace and beauty. These artistic accomplishments bespeak the wealth and confidence of the period. But until modern times Indians have never deemed most events of the everyday world important enough to record. Consequently, we have few accounts of day-to-day life beyond inscriptions and temple records. Indian writers concentrated on religion, philos-

Classical Indian sculpture: figures on a wall
in the temple complex at Kajuraho in central
India, c. 1000. [Rhoads Murphey]

ophy, and literature. In comparison with the eternal
questions, politics and material details seemed of little
consequence.

## Vijayanagar, Empire of Victory

Recurrent raids into the Deccan by the Delhi sultanate,
which began in the thirteenth century, helped stimulate
the rise of a new Hindu kingdom in 1336, the empire of
Vijayanagar ("city of victory"). Having organized to resist the sultanate's incursions southward and the pressures of their Muslim associates in the northern Deccan,
the founders of Vijayanagar went on to unify most of the
peninsular south under their rule. Their capital, which
bore the same name as their empire, impressed European travelers in the fifteenth and early sixteenth centuries as the most splendid in India, both larger and
more populous than contemporary Rome. The capital
depended on a huge excavated reservoir and was
adorned with numerous magnificent temples. A textbook on government written by the last great Vijayanagar king, Krishna Deva Raya (1509–1529), suggests part

of the reason for the empire's success in its advice on
how to deal with minority subjects: "If the king grows
angry with them, he cannot wholly destroy them, but if
he wins their affection by kindness and charity they
serve him by invading the enemies' territory and plundering his forts."[3] The Portuguese traveler Domingos
Paes visited Vijayanagar in Krishna Deva Raya's time
and described him as follows:

> He is the most feared and perfect king that could possibly
> be, cheerful of disposition and very merry. . . . He is a
> great ruler and a man of much justice. . . . He is by rank
> a greater lord than any, by reason of what he possesses in
> armies and territories, but he has nothing compared to
> what a man like him ought to have, so gallant and perfect
> is he in all things.[4]

Thirty-six years after the king's death, in a great battle
in 1565, a coalition of the Islamic sultanates of the northern Deccan defeated Vijayanagar with the help of the

Shiva as Lord of the Dance, cast in the
eleventh century in the Chola kingdom of
South India. With one foot crushing the
demon dwarf, the god is poised in the cosmic
dance of life, holding in one hand the drum
of awakening and in another the fire of
creation as well as destruction. With still
another hand he gives the gesture whose
meaning is "fear not." [Cleveland Museum
of Art]

new Mughal conquerors of North India, sacked and destroyed its capital city, and ended its period of greatness.

## The Eastward Spread of Islam

Buddhism and trade provided the links between India and Southeast Asia in the classical and early medieval periods, and both served as vehicles for the spread of Hinduism and other aspects of Indian civilization. But Arab traders had been active in inter-Asian trade well before the time of Muhammad and had extended their commercial networks throughout most of maritime Southeast Asia and as far east as the China coast. However, Indian converts to Islam after the founding of the Delhi sultanate were primarily responsible for carrying the new religion to insular Southeast Asia, following the long-established trade routes by sea, where they had long played a more important role than the Arabs. This included Indian merchants from Gujarat on the northwest coast and its major ports of Surat and Cambay,

which had probably been India's principal base for overseas trade since at least Mauryan times, including the trade with the Hellenic and Roman world.

These enterprises continued under the Delhi sultanate, which for some two centuries ruled Gujarat and converted some of its inhabitants to Islam. Many merchants, eager for official favor, probably chose conversion for their own financial benefit. In Southeast Asia, while there was resistance to conversion by Arabs, the long tradition of learning from Indian civilization meant that Islam was more readily accepted from Indian hands. In any case, both Indian and Arab traders spread Islam eastward along the sea routes, as earlier Indian merchants had spread Hinduism and Buddhism. Burma, Siam (Thailand), Cambodia, and Laos on the mainland remained dedicated to Buddhism, but the coastal areas of peninsular Malaya as well as insular Indonesia and the southernmost Philippines, where trading fleets had easier access, were gradually converted to Islam.

Local merchants in many of these Southeast Asian kingdoms also adopted Islam as an advantage in dealing with Muslim traders from India. In several cases local rulers were converted or chose Islam, perhaps for similar reasons, and their subjects were obliged to do likewise. Insular Southeast Asia became a patchwork of Is-

## ◉ Islamic Ideals ◉

*Key to Paradise, a guide to the good Muslim life, was compiled in the fourteenth century as an aid to newly converted Indians.*

The Prophet said that whoever says every day at daybreak in the name of God the Merciful and the Compassionate, "There is no god but Allah and Muhammad is his Prophet," him God most high will honor with seven favors. First, He will open his spirit to Islam; second, He will soften the bitterness of death; third, He will illuminate his grave; fourth, He will show the recording angels his best aspects; fifth, He will give the list of his deeds with His right hand; sixth, He will tilt the balance of his account in his favor; and seventh, He will pass him over the eternal bridge which spans the fire of hell into Paradise like a flash of lightning. . . . Keep your lips moist by repeating God's name. . . . The servant of God should make the Qur'an [Koran] his guide and his protection. On the day of judgment, the Qur'an will precede him and lead him toward Paradise. Whoever does not stay diligently close to the Qur'an but lags behind, the angel will come forth and striking him on his side will carry him off to hell. One's rank in Paradise depends upon the extent of one's recitation of the Qur'an. Everyone who knows how to read a small amount of the Qur'an will enjoy a high position in Paradise, and the more one knows how to read it, the higher one's status in Paradise. . . . The Prophet said that on the night of his ascent to heaven he was shown the sins of his people. He did not see any greater sin than that of him who did not know and did not read the Qur'an.

*Source:* W. T. de Bary, ed., *Sources of Indian Tradition*, vol. 1 (New York: Columbia University Press, 1964), pp. 386–387.

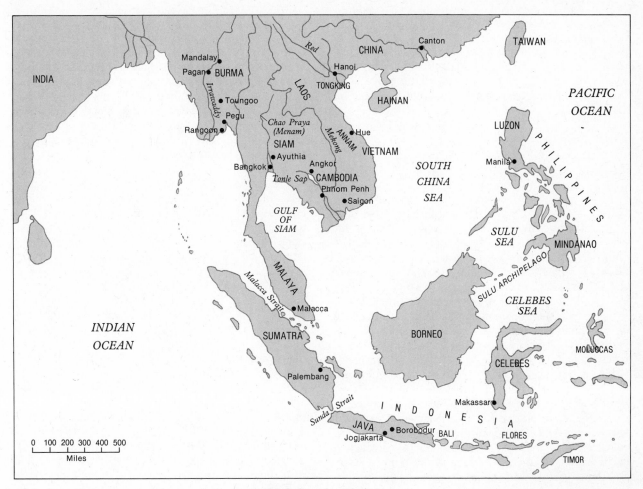

*11.2 Southeast Asia*

lamic sultanates. By the late fourteenth century, Indian and Arab Muslims largely controlled the trade of this enormous area and made converts first in Sumatra and Malaya, closest by sea to India, and in coastal ports throughout the far-flung archipelago. Malacca, on the west coast of Malaya, where it dominated the routes through the Malacca Strait, became a great center of commerce and a spearhead for the advance of Islam eastward. Nearly all trade eastward from India has always passed through the strait as the shortest and safest route, avoiding the treacherous southwest coast of Sumatra and the difficult Sunda Strait between Sumatra and Java.

In the course of the fifteenth century the new religion incorporated most of Malaya, north coastal Java, and coastal parts of the rest of the archipelago, including Mindanao, the southernmost large island of the Philippines, where it seems to have arrived early. Islam's further spread was checked in part by the almost simultaneous arrival of the Spanish in the Philippines and of the Portuguese and the Dutch in Indonesia, although away

from the coast, inland Java remained Hindu-Buddhist for another century or so, even under some nominally Muslim rulers.

By the sixteenth century only a few small and isolated areas of Indonesia outside Java retained their original animism or tribal religion, while the island of Bali, east of Java, remained Hindu, as it still is. The very different context of Southeast Asian culture, however, softened some of the more rigid aspects of Islam. This was particularly the case with regard to the treatment of women, for Southeast Asia has always been closer to gender equality than any other major culture. At the same time Islam brought, as in India, a new emphasis on the equality of all before God. In India, the Islamic practice of purdah (literally, "curtain"), whereby women must not be seen by men outside the family and must cover themselves completely when outside the house, spread also to Hindus in many parts of the north ruled by Muslim conquerors. In Southeast Asia, with its far more open society and its tradition of female equality, this custom was rejected. Many other Koranic injunctions were modified in practice, including dietary prohibitions, strict fasting during Ramadan, and rigid observance of the rule to pray five times a day facing Mecca. Indonesia has for some time been the world's largest Muslim country, but the Indonesian (and much of the Malaysian) practice of Islam is recognizably different from that in Saudi Arabia, Iraq, or Iran.

## Medieval Southeast Asia

Indian forms of dance, music, literature, art, and dramatic versions of the great Hindu epics, the *Mahabharata* and the *Ramayana*, dominated the culture of insular Southeast Asia during the medieval period, as they still do. Meanwhile, Chinese traders became more active and more numerous from the tenth century on, especially in the eastern half of the area, and founded permanent settlements of merchants in the major port cities of the Philippines and Java. Peninsular Malaya at this period was very thinly settled, and although Malay-related languages and culture were widespread throughout the archipelago, Malays remained a small group on the mainland. The traditional Buddhist monarchies of Burma, Siam, and Cambodia, centered in the productive cores of their economies in the mainland deltas and lower valleys of the great rivers, were more self-contained. They too built magnificent temple complexes in the Indian-Buddhist style, such as those in the later abandoned Cambodian capital of Angkor built by the Khmer Empire, which flourished from the ninth to twelfth centuries.

## Burma and Siam

The people of Burma and Siam include large infusions of stock originally from south China, where many of their close ethnic relatives still live. The spoken languages of both countries are distantly related to Chinese but written with an Indian-derived script. The majority inhabitants of Siam, the Thais, probably moved down over many centuries into the delta from a homeland that originally straddled the mountainous border zones of China. The origins of the people of northern Burma and to a lesser extent the lowland Burmans are similar. The civilization of both countries has been profoundly shaped, however, by the Indian models that spread to them from Ashoka's time on, including not only Buddhism but also Indian systems of writing, art, literature, philosophy, kingship, and government.

Burmans became the dominant inhabitants of Burma only after A.D. 800 and the Thais of Siam after about 1100, each displacing earlier groups who had followed

the same migratory route southward from China and Tibet. These earlier inhabitants were either assimilated or remained as minorities, a problem particularly severe in Burma and still a source of chronic tension. The Burmans and Thais occupied the productive lowlands and floodplains of the Irrawaddy in Burma and the Chao Praya (Menam) in Siam, where they founded successive capitals. Indian cultural influences were welcomed, especially since they came without political conditions or ambitions. Local rulers invited Indian advisers, priests, and administrative councillors as well as philosophers, artists, and musicians. Trade was an important source of revenue along the sea routes, but in the great river valleys of the mainland, agriculture and its revenues were the heart of the economy and the chief support of the state. The early medieval capital of Burma was at Pagan, founded about 850 in the central Irrawaddy valley, which by 1057 had incorporated the Irrawaddy basin and an upland perimeter within its boundaries.

Included in the new empire were several minority groups. Some of these were in fact culturally more advanced, especially those in the south, which had been influenced by Indian culture. The most important among them were the Mons, who gained dominion over the court and culture at Pagan until the late twelfth century and played a prominent role in Burma's overseas trade. It was via the Mons that Theravada Buddhism spread to the Burmans, together with the rest of the Mon legacy of Indian civilization. But the Pagan kingdom was utterly destroyed by the Mongol invasion of the 1280s. New waves of migrants and raiders poured into Burma, and rival kingdoms struggled against each other for control after the Mongols had withdrawn. A new Burmese dynasty emerged in the early sixteenth century at Toungoo in the southwest. By 1555, after prolonged civil wars, Toungoo had brought most of the country again under one rule.

Successive kingdoms in Burma were strongly Buddhist after the region's initial conversion, and kings competed, as in Siam, in building temples and endowing religious enterprises. Their piety did not prevent them from engaging in internal military struggles, efforts at territorial expansion, and brutal campaigns against alleged heretics, followers of Buddhist sects that were considered unorthodox. From the sixteenth century there was chronic warfare as well between Burma and Siam. But despite the denial by monarchs and armies of the Buddha's teaching of reverence for life, most people in both countries were genuinely committed to Buddhism as a culture as well as the path to personal salvation.

The Toungoo dynasty was vigorously expansionist, mainly at the expense of the Thais. The rising importance of maritime trade, in which lower Burma played a growing role, provided increased revenues to fuel conquests, and the locus of political authority shifted toward the coast. Improved guns brought in by the Portuguese gave new and often devastating firepower to Burmese expansionism. But the Toungoo order proved fragile and overextended. Its capital, now at Pegu in lower Burma, fell to rebellion and invasion in 1599, and later Toungoo rulers abandoned their claims to Thai territory, although Thai-Burmese warfare continued intermittently.

Meanwhile, the Thais had formed a state that grew in power, began eventually taking over much of the decaying Khmer Empire, and in 1431 captured the Khmer capital at Angkor. Thais had probably spilled southward across the present border of southwestern China before 1200, but the trickle became a flood after the Mongol conquest of their homeland in the late thirteenth century. By the fourteenth century they were the dominant inhabitants of the Chao Praya basin. They pushed southward and eastward against the Khmers, from whom they adopted Indian art forms, writing, and political systems while accepting Buddhism from Burma and from the earlier Mon inhabitants of the Chao Praya basin. The Thai capital was established in the mid-fourteenth century at Ayuthia on the edge of the delta, then close to the Khmer frontier and with easy access both to the Gulf of Siam and to the Mon area of lower Burma.

Ayuthia consolidated its hold on the delta and continued the Thai push southward into the thinly settled Malay peninsula and eastward into Khmer Cambodia. Thais were also a major part of the invasion that sacked the Toungoo capital at Pegu in lower Burma in 1599, but for the next two or three centuries Burmese armies generally had the upper hand in their wars with the Thais and finally sacked and destroyed Ayuthia in 1767. After a period of disorder and confusion, a new Thai dynasty, the Chakri, emerged in 1782 with a new capital at Bangkok; the same dynasty still rules present-day Thailand. Bangkok, near the seaward edge of the delta, was originally a place of marshes and tidal creeks on the Chao Praya, and the site was chosen in part because of the protection it offered against Burmese raids. With the rapid growth of maritime trade in the nineteenth century, it became a major economic center as well as the chief Thai city.

## Cambodia and Laos

The Khmer people had also probably come originally from southwestern China (or northeastern Himalayan India) and were ethnically related to the Mons. They followed the Mekong River into what is now Cambodia, probably by 100 B.C., but before they had had any lasting contact with Chinese or Indian civilizations. In Cambodia they may have founded Funan, which is described as a kingdom in Han Chinese records but was partly Indianized as well. By the third century A.D. Funan seems to have covered what is now southern Vietnam,

eastern and central Thailand, northern Malaya, and southernmost Burma. Its large fleets dominated the sea lanes and carried much of the trade moving eastward from India to China, of which it became a tributary state. Funan was probably several small loosely organized states that were overthrown by a later group of Khmers in the seventh century. They inherited its domains and in the ninth century began to build a magnificent capital and temple complex at Angkor Thom, which for several centuries thereafter was the most important city in Southeast Asia.

## ♣
## ANGKOR: CITY OF MONUMENTAL SPLENDOR

The Khmer king Yasovarman I (889–900), who began building the new capital, designed it with the help of Brahmans invited from India to legitimate his claim to divine kingship. The plan of the city reflected the structure of the world according to Hindu cosmology. It was surrounded by a wall and a moat, as the universe was thought to be encircled by rock and ocean. In the exact middle of the city, on an artificial mound, a pyramidal temple represented the sacred Mount Meru in the high Himalayas, where Shiva was said to be perpetually meditating for the eternal maintenance of the cosmic order. Numerous other temples were grouped on and around the mound, which was regarded as the center of the universe. The king declared himself Ruler of the Universe, a title, together with attendant symbols and rituals, passed on to his successors. Angkor Thom reached its final and completed form at the beginning of the thirteenth century, after the Khmers and their rulers had adopted Mahayana Buddhism. New Buddhist temples and sculptures were added, but the earlier Hindu elements remained, and the Khmers seem to have accepted both religious traditions and symbols. The financial drain of such large-scale building probably contributed to the decline and conquest of the empire only a few decades later.

The whole urban complex was a symbol of the union between king and God and of harmony between the human and divine worlds, and it was intended to ensure prosperity for the kingdom and its people as well as the authority of the ruler. Water, a further symbol of life-giving nurture, was led from the Mekong to keep the moat full and was in turn part of a much larger system of irrigation. The city formed a square about 2 miles on each side, enclosed by its walls and moat, and was entered by five huge monumental gates. Inside was the large royal palace as well as the temple complex, but little evidence remains of the other buildings, which housed the court, its officials, clerks, engineers, work-

The temple complex at Angkor in Cambodia, dating from the twelfth century. [Wim Swaan]

ers, artisans, and other inhabitants of the city. We know from surviving inscriptions that there was a large and highly organized bureaucracy.

Less than a mile to the south Suryavarman II (1113–1150) built another major temple complex a century later known as Angkor Wat (*wat* means "temple"), which replicated the arrangement and style of the temples at Angkor Thom and like them was surrounded by a moat, although Angkor Wat was smaller than the capital. Both sites were largely abandoned after the Thai invasion of 1431, and Angkor Thom itself was left in ruins. Angkor Wat was better preserved, since it was not so central a target, and remains one of the chief monuments of Southeast Asian art and architecture, reflecting the glory of the Khmer Empire at its height.

The city, and Cambodia as a whole, may have had a larger population in the thirteenth century than in the twentieth. The Mekong floodplain's fertile alluvial soil was made still more productive by an intricate hydraulic network of canals, dams, and dikes for both irrigation and flood control. Fish from the nearby Tonle Sap lake in the middle Mekong valley added to the food supply. The monsoon rains were heavily concentrated in a short summer season, when the Tonle Sap tended to overflow, leaving much of the rest of the year too dry. Flood prevention works, storage tanks, and reservoirs were carefully engineered, and canals were constructed to direct water to rice fields while protecting them from too much water. Canals were also used to transport the stone used to build Angkor Thom and Angkor Wat. The construction and maintenance of these extensive works required enormous amounts of planning and controlled labor. As the authority of the Khmer kings began to weaken and the country was invaded, dams, tanks, and canals could not be maintained. Without the productive agriculture

they made possible, the kingdom's economic base was severely reduced. The collapse of the Khmer kingdom suggests comparison with the fall of the Sinhalese kingdom in the dry zone of Ceylon two centuries earlier (see Chapter 2). In 1434, three years after the capture of Angkor, the capital was moved to Phnom Penh on the lower Mekong. The Khmer Empire never recovered its former power and glory, however, and jungle invaded the ruins of Angkor Thom and Angkor Wat. They were revealed again when French explorers stumbled on them in the late nineteenth century. The French colonial government later cleared the sites, although turmoil in Cambodia again isolated them after 1975.

The southern part of the landlocked and mountainous state of Laos had been included in the Khmer Empire during its centuries of power. Laos then came under Thai domination until the whole region was absorbed by the French colonial empire at the end of the nineteenth century. The dominant population groups of Laos are related to the Thais and the Burmese. Like these, the Laotians originally migrated from southwestern China and adopted Buddhism, but their language and culture are distinctive. The three small Lao states had to contend with Thai, Burmese, and Vietnamese incursions. Buddhism spread to Laos from Mon and Khmer sources, but Laos was chronically squeezed between expansionist states on all sides.

# Vietnam: Expansion to the South

The northern part of Vietnam, known as Tongking, in the productive basin of the Red River with its capital at

Hanoi, had been part of the pre-Han South China kingdom of Nan Yueh, or Nam Viet, which included the Canton area and was then incorporated in the Han and T'ang empires. It thus acquired a heavy overlay of Chinese civilization, becoming the only Southeast Asian state to be Sinified rather than Indianized. Below the elite level, however, Vietnamese culture remained distinctively Southeast Asian and maintained its identity.

Vietnam regained its independence after the fall of the T'ang dynasty, although it had to repel efforts at reconquest by the Mongols, the Ming, and the Manchus. During these centuries the Vietnamese were engaged in their own expansion southward, down the narrow coastal plain of Annam and eventually into the agriculturally rich delta of the Mekong in what is now southern Vietnam, a process that took nearly 1,000 years. Southward movement took place at the expense of the Indianized Champa kingdom in Annam with its capital at Hue and then of the Khmers, who originally controlled the Mekong delta and the surrounding plain.

In this long struggle, the Vietnamese drew strength from a fervent nationalism originally engendered by their efforts to resist and finally to throw off Chinese control, a 2,000-year ordeal of chronic war. But their growing empire was managed on Chinese bureaucratic lines, and their later rulers even adopted the title of emperor, although they prudently accepted the status of tributary to China. Like the Koreans and the Japanese, the Vietnamese accepted aspects of Chinese culture while resisting Chinese political control. By the early nineteenth century their empire included essentially all of the modern state, including territories conquered or detached from Cambodia and Laos, with the central and southern areas ruled from subsidiary capitals at Hue and Saigon. The delta of Tongking in the north around Hanoi and of the Mekong around Saigon, as well as the coastal plain of Annam joining them, were fertile and became highly productive under a Chinese-style system of intensive irrigated agriculture. This lent further strength to the state, helping it maintain control over a mountainous western borderland inhabited by a variety of non-Vietnamese tribal minorities in addition to Laotians and Khmers.

## Malaya, Indonesia, and the Philippines

Malay-style culture and the Malay language family are dominant not only in the Malay peninsula but also in most of insular Southeast Asia, especially the coastal areas easily accessible by sea. The peninsula itself, however, has never supported a very large population, especially compared to the larger and more productive areas of Indonesia and the Philippines, and probably did not reach half a million until the late nineteenth century. Its

mountainous and rain-forested landscape contained no extensive river valleys or productive agricultural plains, and settlement was most concentrated on the coast, where small ports were engaged in regional trade. There is no evidence of a highly developed indigenous civilization until the rise of Malacca in the fifteenth century, and Malacca itself was part of a larger system in greater Malay Southeast Asia. During the medieval period most of Malaya was first controlled by the Indonesian trading empire of Sri Vijaya, with its capital on nearby Sumatra, and later by the Thai state. Malaya was politically unified only under twentieth-century British colonial control, and most of its growth dates only from the tin and rubber booms of the same period.

In Indonesia the central island of Java, with its richly productive volcanic soils, has remained the heart of the sprawling island country. Rival kingdoms, based on agriculture, arose in Java, while larger empires based on maritime trade grew to control and profit from the sea lanes. The first and most enduring of these was the empire of Sri Vijaya, with its capital at Palembang on Sumatra, from which it could dominate the Malacca Strait, the crucial passage between east and west. It was the chief power of the archipelago from the seventh to the thirteenth centuries, despite a brief conquest by the Chola navy from southern India in the eleventh century. Mahayana Buddhism spread early to Sri Vijaya, and Palembang became a major center of Buddhist learning. Meanwhile, in central Java the Sailendra dynasty in the eighth century built a land-based state on prosperous agricultural revenues, which were also used to construct one of the world's great architectural monuments, the immense Buddhist temple at Borobodur, completed by around 825.

Borobodur, like Angkor, was a symbolic representation of the sacred Mount Meru, built up in a series of nine terraces some 3 miles in circumference and including about 400 statues of the Buddha. Indian artists and sculptors were probably involved, along with Javanese artisans. Other Javanese states built many similar temples, which combined Buddhist and Hindu iconography and symbols, as at Angkor. Interstate rivalry and the final blow of the Mongol invasion broke the empire of Sri Vijaya in the 1290s, though it survived in Sumatra. But a resurgent new Javanese state expelled the Mongols and founded the empire of Majapahit in the early fourteenth century, which succeeded to the far-flung commercial interests of Sri Vijaya and at the same time unified much of eastern and central Java. Majapahit's military success was accompanied by a cultural and literary renaissance.

Majapahit was the last of the great Hindu-Buddhist states of insular Southeast Asia. Within a century it faced aggressive competition from the new trading state of Malacca and newly Islamicized ports on the north coast of Java, which soon wrested from it control of the strait

The eighth-century Buddhist stupa at Borobodur in central Java, chief remaining monument to the Indianization of Southeast Asia before the arrival of Islam. [Brian Brake/Photo Researchers]

and nibbled away at its domination of the maritime trade eastward and of Majapahit client states in the archipelago. Islam had earlier spread to Sumatra along the trade routes from India, and the rulers of Malacca and north coastal Java adopted the new religion as a means of enhancing their commercial connections, through which they made further converts. Majapahit became merely one of many small Javanese states.

The recorded history of the Philippines begins only with Magellan's voyage in 1521, in which he claimed the islands for Spain, although a settlement was not made on Luzon, the main island, until 1565. The Philippines consist of 7,000 islands, many more than Indonesia's 3,000. Although speakers of Malay-related languages have long been dominant in the Philippines, other and probably earlier cultural groups remained in relative isolation, especially in the mountainous and heavily forested parts of the larger islands. Differences of dialect, language, and culture divided the inhabitants of most of the islands, and until recent times they lived in largely

separate worlds despite some interisland trading. No recognizable state emerged in any area before Spanish times, and there was no well-established or widely used form of writing, although Indian writing systems and some aspects of the Hindu tradition did have a minor effect over many centuries.

There was also trade contact with China, probably from Han times, but little cultural evidence remains from that early period, apart from Chinese coins and pottery shards. Islam penetrated most of Mindanao in the south, but until the Spanish occupation the religious pattern of the rest of the Philippines was dominated by a great variety of local animistic cults in the absence of any text-based religious tradition. This and the lack of anything approaching Filipino national coherence or identity made for ready conversion to Islam and to Christianity and contributed to the relative ease of the Spanish conquest. Four and a half centuries of Spanish control left the Philippines in many ways culturally, socially, and politically closer to Latin America than to Asia.

꿋   꿋   꿋

*From the late tenth century to the foundation of the Mughal dynasty in 1526, India was divided as waves of invaders from the north brought in both a new religion, Islam, and*

*a new cultural infusion. It was nevertheless a period of great artistic creativity, especially in the south, and though the records we have tell mainly of battles, kings, and con-*

*quests, they tell also of monumental building, a flourishing of the arts, and growing and profitable trade. Surpluses from this trade helped support these creations as well as the political structures and armies of numerous states. Southeast Asia was similarly divided and engaged in chronic warfare, but there too these centuries saw the building of majestic temples and the flowering of the arts, sup-*

*ported as in India by extensive maritime commerce and the taxes on yields from the fertile river valleys and deltas of the mainland and the rich volcanic soils of Java. Religion too was periodically a source of conflict, as Buddhism developed new sects and Islam spread eastward over India and most of insular Southeast Asia, profoundly changing its social and cultural character.*

## Notes

1. D. P. Singhal, *A History of the Indian People* (London: Methuen, 1983), p. 168.
2. Ibid., pp. 173–174.
3. A. L. Basham, *The Wonder That Was India* (New York: Grove Press, 1959), p. 198.
4. Ibid., p. 76.

## Suggestions for Further Reading

Andaya, B., and Andaya, L. *A History of Malaysia.* New York: St. Martin's Press, 1982.

Auboyer, J. *Daily Life in Ancient India.* New York: Macmillan, 1965.

Aung-Thwin, M. *Pagan: The Origins of Modern Burma.* Honolulu: University Press of Hawaii, 1985.

Basham, A. L. *The Wonder That Was India.* New York: Grove Press, 1959.

Briggs, L. *The Ancient Khmer Empire.* Philadelphia: American Philosophical Society, 1951.

Chand, T. *The Influence of Islam on Indian Culture.* Allahabad: Indian Press, 1954.

Chandler, D. P. *A History of Cambodia.* Boulder, Colo.: Westview Press, 1983.

Coedes, G. *The Indianized States of Southeast Asia*, ed. W. F. Vella. Honolulu: East-West Center Press, 1968.

Gesick, L., ed. *Centers, Symbols, and Hierarchies: Essays on the Classical States of Southeast Asia.* New Haven, Conn.: Yale University Press, 1983.

Groslier, B. P., and Arthaud, J. *Angkor: Art and Civilization.* New York: Praeger, 1966.

Hall, D. G. R. *A History of Southeast Asia*, 4th ed. London: Macmillan, 1981.

Hall, K. R. *Maritime Trade and State Development in Early Southeast Asia.* Honolulu: University Press of Hawaii, 1985.

Ikram, S. M. *Muslim Civilization in India.* New York: Columbia University Press, 1964.

Lieberman, V. *Burmese Administrative Cycles: Anarchy and Conquest, 1580-1760.* Princeton, N.J.: Princeton University Press, 1984.

Osborne, M. *Southeast Asia: An Illustrated Introductory History*, 3rd ed. London: Allen & Unwin, 1985.

Rawlinson, H. G. *India: A Short Cultural History.* New York: Praeger, 1965.

Reid, A. *Southeast Asia in the Age of Commerce, 1450–1680.* New Haven, Conn.: Yale University Press, 1988.

Ricklefs, M. C. *A History of Modern Indonesia.* Bloomington: Indiana University Press, 1981.

Sar Desai, D. R. *Southeast Asia, Past and Present*, 2nd ed. Boulder, Colo.: Westview Press, 1989.

Sastri, A. N. *The Cholas.* Madison: University of Wisconsin Press, 1955.

Singhal, D. P. *A History of the Indian People*, 2nd ed. London: Methuen, 1989.

Stein, B. *Peasant, State, and Society in Medieval South India.* Berkeley: University of California Press, 1980.

Taylor, K. W. *The Birth of Vietnam.* Berkeley: University of California Press, 1983.

Thapar, R. *A History of India*, vol. 1. Baltimore: Penguin Books, 1969.

Van Leur, J. C. *Indonesian Trade and Society.* The Hague: Van Hoeve, 1955.

Vlekke, B. *Nusantara: A History of Indonesia.* The Hague: Van Hoeve, 1960.

Wolters, O. L. *Early Indonesian Commerce: The Origins of Srivijaya.* Ithaca, N.Y.: Cornell University Press, 1967.

Woodside, A. *Vietnam and the Chinese Model.* Cambridge, Mass.: Harvard University Press, 1971.

Wyatt, D. *Thailand: A Short History.* New Haven, Conn.: Yale University Press, 1984.

Yazdani, G., ed. *The Early History of the Deccan.* London: Oxford University Press, 1960.

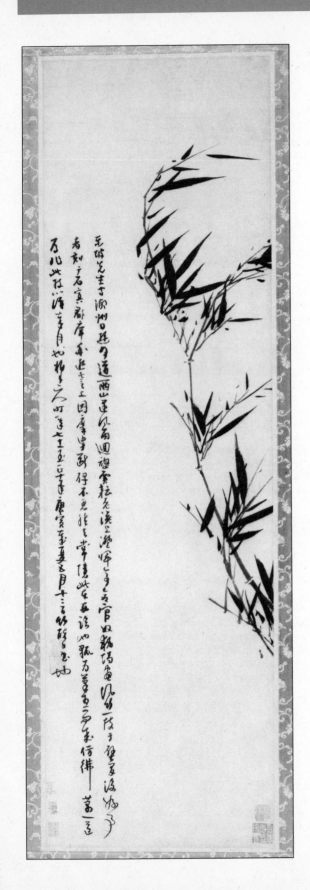

# A Golden Age in East Asia

The period from the sixth to the fourteenth centuries saw the reunification of China following a long period of division. After 600 years of renewed imperial splendor under the T'ang dynasty and its successor, the Sung (Song), China was overrun by the Mongols and ruled as part of their short-lived empire from 1279 to 1368, when a new Chinese dynasty, the Ming, restored Chinese power. During the same period, Korean civilization matured, produced a series of effective dynasties, and added innovations to the Chinese culture it had adopted from the earlier Han dynasty in China. In the eighth century Japan evolved a literate civilization on the model of T'ang China and in subsequent centuries produced a highly sophisticated court culture. Japan slowly dissolved into chronic fighting between rival clans until unity was reimposed by the founders of the Tokugawa shogunate by 1600.

*Bamboo,* by Wu Chan (Yuan dynasty). **Chinese artists loved to paint the graceful fronds of bamboo, each leaf created with a single stroke of the brush, in black ink. The techniques of bamboo painting were akin to those of calligraphy, and hence such paintings often include gracefully written text. [Freer Gallery, Smithsonian Institution]**

# Reunification in China

For nearly four centuries after the fall of the Han dynasty in A.D. 220 China was divided into many separate kingdoms, with much of the north under barbarian control. Buddhism flourished, perhaps as a response to the troubled times, and was promoted also by the Sinicized rulers of the north. The chief such kingdom, known as the Northern Wei, controlled most of North China from 386 to 534. It built a number of splendid Buddhist cave temples with statues of the Buddha and his devotees whose style, though Chinese, reveals Indian influence, as do the many pagodas, a temple form adapted from the Indian stupa.

The Chinese cultural and political tradition proper was carried on by a succession of rival dynasties vying for supremacy in the south, which was enriched by a flood of wealthy and educated refugees from the north. Nanking (Nanjing) was the chief southern capital and major urban center, but none of the southern dynasties or kingdoms was able either to unify the region or to provide strong government. Literature, philosophy, and the arts continued vigorously despite the absence of political unity, and Buddhism also became popular in the south. This was the period of both Indian Buddhist missions to China and Chinese pilgrim visits to India; it was also a time of new technological achievements, including gunpowder, advances in medicine, refinements in the use of a magnetized needle for indicating direction (the forerunner of the compass), and the use of coal as a fuel.

Most politically conscious Chinese wanted to see the Han model of greatness restored, but first the country had to be reunified and the imperial machine rebuilt. This was primarily the work of the short-lived Sui dynasty, which in 589 welded contending Chinese states together by conquest. Interestingly, the Sui base was the same Wei valley from which the Ch'in had erupted, and like the Ch'in, the Sui built roads and canals to connect their empire, radiating out from their capital at Ch'ang An.

The second Sui emperor, Yang Ti (604–618), heady with new power, is often compared to Ch'in Shih Huang Ti. He too rebuilt the Great Wall, at a cost of an additional million lives, and reconquered northern Vietnam as well as much of Sinkiang and Mongolia, although his campaign in Korea was defeated by fierce resistance. Yang Ti built a magnificent new capital at Loyang, following the model of the Chou and the Han, but at heavy expense. Perhaps his most notable project was the building of the Grand Canal, from Hangchow (Hangzhou) in the south to Kaifeng in the north, to bring rice from the productive Yangtze delta for troops and officials in semi-arid northern China. But his megalomaniacal behavior caused great suffering to his exhausted troops, forced laborers, taxpayers, and tyrannized officials. Rebellion spread, as in the last years of the Ch'in, and Yang Ti was assassinated by a courtier in 618 after only 14 years on the throne. A frontier general swept away the pretensions of the Sui heir and proclaimed a new dynasty, the T'ang. Although the new dynasty was to last nearly 300 years, it owed its success in large part to the foundations laid by the Sui, as the Han had rested on those of the Ch'in.

# The T'ang Dynasty

Under T'ang rule China achieved a new high point in prosperity, cultural sophistication and greatness, and imperial power. The cosmopolitan T'ang capital at Ch'ang An (Qangan), where the Han had ruled, was the world's largest city, with about 2 million inhabitants. The imperial civil service and the examination system were reestablished, and learning and the arts flourished.

The rebuilding of the empire exacted a price, for all its glory. Most of the Han-ruled territories were reclaimed by conquest after they had fallen away at the end of the Sui, including northern Vietnam, but Tibet, Sinkiang, Mongolia, and southern Manchuria were wisely left as tributary regions, after their inhabitants had been defeated in a brilliant series of campaigns by Emperor T'ang T'ai-tsung (Tang Taizong, 626–649). Korea again fought the Chinese armies to a standstill but accepted tributary status, and much of the mountainous southwest, home of the Thai and other groups, remained outside imperial rule. T'ai-tsung is remembered as a model ruler who fostered education and encouraged conscientious officials. In his cosmopolitan time, Buddhism was still tolerated and widely popular.

In the late seventh century a beautiful concubine of T'ai-tsung's named Wu Chao (Wuzhao) was made a consort and empress by his successor Kao-tsung (Gaozong), whom she soon came to dominate. After his death in 683 she ruled alone or through puppets and then proclaimed herself emperor of a new dynasty, the only female emperor in Chinese history. She struck at the old aristocracy, her chief opposition, and ordered many of them executed. She drew support from the Buddhist establishment, which she strongly favored and which declared her a reincarnation of the Bodhisattva Maitreya, the Buddhist messiah. Wu Chao had become a Buddhist nun after T'ai-tsung's death in 650, but she soon grew restless without greater scope for her talents. Empress Wu, as she is called, was denounced by Chinese historians, although their criticism has clear sexist overtones. She was a strong and effective, if ruthless, ruler, obviously opposed to the Confucian establishment and promoting its rival, the alien faith of Buddhism. Her being

Emperor T'ang T'ai-tsung (626–649) was a
brilliant field commander whose campaigns
reestablished Chinese control over Sinkiang
and northern Vietnam, conquered Tibet, and
even extended imperial rule into central
Asia. An astute administrator, T'ai-tsung also
restored and extended the imperial
bureaucratic system of the Han. [Granger
Collection]

a woman in addition was just too much for her opponents
to deal with, and she was deposed in a palace coup.

The gradual Sinification of the originally non-Han
south below the Yangtze valley continued under the imperial momentum. By the late T'ang most of the empire's

revenue came from the more productive south, including the Yangtze valley, and most Chinese lived in that
area. The north, where the empire had been born, suffered as always from recurrent drought, erosion, and the
silting of its vital irrigation works. But now the south,
progressively cleared of its earlier forests, more than
made up the difference. Agricultural techniques were
slowly adapted to the wetter and hillier conditions and
the far longer growing season of the south. The increasing use of human manure ("night soil") improved the
less fertile soils outside the alluvial river valleys, supporting a continued increase of population, which thus
provided still more night soil. Many northerners had fled
south after the fall of the Han dynasty; now they and
their descendants were joined by new streams seeking
greater economic opportunity than in the overcrowded
and often marginal north. Imperial tradition and the defense of the troublesome northwest frontiers kept the
capital in the north, but the south was the empire's principal economic base.

Renewing their contacts with more distant lands
westward, the Chinese found no other civilization that
could rival the Celestial Empire. The Son of Heaven, as
the emperor was called, was seen as the lord of "all under heaven," meaning the four corners of the known
world, within which China was clearly the zenith of
power and sophistication. Did not all other people the
Chinese encountered acknowledge this, by tribute,
praise, and imitation of Chinese culture, the sincerest
form of flattery?

In fact, even beyond the world the Chinese knew,
they had no equal. Rome was long gone, and the Abbasid caliphate was no match for the T'ang or its great
successor, the Sung. A coalition of Arabs and western
Turks did repulse a T'ang expeditionary force at the battle of the Talas River near Samarkand in 751, but the
battle is perhaps more significant in that some captured
Chinese transmitted the recently developed T'ang arts
of printing and papermaking to the West. The mass production of paper dated from the late first century A.D.,
although it had been invented a century earlier. Printing,
which began about A.D. 700, was first done from carved
wooden blocks a page at a time, but by 1030 the Chinese,
and only slightly later the Koreans, had developed mov-
able-type printing, with individual characters made of
wood, ceramics, or metal. Only in the fifteenth century
would this technique reach Europe.

Paper and printing were typical creations of the
Chinese, with their love of written records and of learning, literature, and painting. They were only two of China's basic gifts to the West, along with cast iron, the
crossbow, gunpowder, the compass, the use of coal as
fuel, the water wheel, paper currency, the wheelbarrow,
wallpaper, and porcelain, to mention only a few. Porcelain had appeared by T'ang times, and from it were made
objects of exquisite beauty whose refinement was never

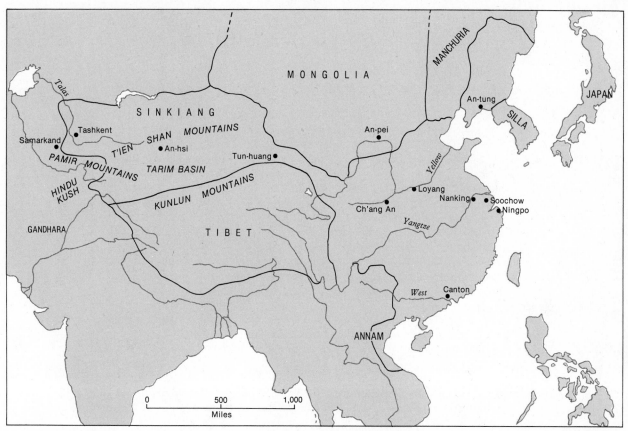

***12.1*** *China Under the T'ang*

matched elsewhere. Porcelain, silk, and later tea became China's chief exports.

The secret of making silk had been supposedly smuggled out of China by two monks at the time of the eastern Roman emperor Justinian (527–565) in the form of cocoons concealed in hollow walking sticks. But later Western silk production in Italy and France never equaled the Chinese in quality, just as European porcelain, developed in the eighteenth century, never reproduced the perfection of form and finish of the Chinese models. Silk remains a staple export to this day, although the Chinese lost ground to more uniform Japanese and later Korean silk in the nineteenth century.

Tea, largely unknown in Han times, was introduced from Southeast Asia as a medicine and an aid to meditation and began to be drunk widely in fifth-century China. It became the basic Chinese drink during the T'ang, grown in quantities in the misty hills of the south. By the eighteenth century it was a major item of export to the West. Seeds and cuttings of the tea plant were smuggled out of China by the English East India Company in 1843 to start plantation production in India and Ceylon, and tea became the world's most popular drink.

## CH'ANG AN IN AN AGE OF IMPERIAL SPLENDOR

The splendor of the T'ang and its empire was symbolized in its capital at Ch'ang An, where the Han and the Ch'in had also ruled. It was the eastern terminus of trade routes linking China with central Asia and lands beyond and also presided over the largest empire the world had yet seen, exceeding even the Han and Roman empires. People from all over Asia—Turks, Indians, Persians, Syrians, Vietnamese, Koreans, Japanese, Jews, Arabs, and even Nestorian (eastern) Christians—thronged its streets and added to its cosmopolitan quality. It was probably also the largest wholly planned city ever built, covering some 30 square miles and including within its massive walls about a million people. The imperial census also recorded nearly another million living in the urban area outside the walls.

Like all Chinese administrative centers, Ch'ang An was laid out on a checkerboard pattern, with broad ave-

# ◉ Tax Reform: A Chinese View ◉

*Yang Yen (727–781), a high official of the T'ang dynasty, wrote a memorial to the throne proposing tax reforms, which were carried out and lasted several centuries.*

When the dynastic laws were first formulated there was the land tax, the labor tax on able-bodied men, and the cloth tax on households. But enforcement of the law was lax; people migrated or died, and landed property changed hands. The poor rose and the rich fell. The Board of Revenue year after year presented out-of-date figures to the court. Those who were sent to guard the frontiers were exempted from land tax and labor tax for six years, after which they returned from service. Yet as Emperor Hsuang-tsung was engaged in many campaigns against the barbarians, most of those sent to the frontier died. The frontier generals, however, concealed the facts and did not report their deaths. Thus their names were never removed from the tax registers. When Wang Kung held the post of Commissioner of Fiscal Census during the T'ien Pao period [742–755] he strove to increase revenue. Since these names appeared on the registers and yet the adults were missing, he concluded that they had concealed themselves to avoid paying taxes. . . . The way to handle all government expenses and tax collections is first to calculate the amount needed and then to allocate the tax among the people. The income of the state would be governed according to its expenses. All households would be registered in the places of their actual residence, without regard to whether they are native households or not. All persons should be graded according to their wealth. . . . Those who have no permanent residence and do business as travelling merchants should be taxed in whatever prefecture they are located at the rate of one-thirtieth of their wealth. All practices which cause annoyance to the people should be corrected. . . . Everything should be under the control of the President of the Board of Revenue and the Commissioner of Funds.

*Source:* W. T. de Bary, ed., *Sources of Chinese Tradition* (New York: Columbia University Press, 1960), pp. 414–416.

nues running east-west and north-south to great gates at the cardinal compass points. These were closed at night, and the main avenues leading to them divided the city into major quarters. These were further subdivided by other principal streets into groups of 110 blocks, each constituting an administrative unit, with its own internal pattern of alleyways. The emperor's palace faced south down a 500-foot-wide central thoroughfare to the south gate, the one used by most visitors and all official envoys and messengers. This arrangement was designed to awe and impress all who came to Ch'ang An with the power and greatness of the empire. Kaifeng and Peking were later designed similarly, and for the same purpose.

Within the city, people lived in rectangular wards, each surrounded by walls with gates closed at night. The West Market and the East Market, supervised by the government, occupied larger blocks to serve their respective halves of the city. There and elsewhere in the city, in open spaces and appointed theaters, foreign and Chinese players, acrobats, and magicians performed dramas, operas, skits, and other amusements. Women

of fashion paraded their fancy clothing and coiffures. For men and women alike, one of the most popular pastimes was polo, which had been adopted from Persia; T'ang paintings showing polo matches make it clear that women played too. As later in India, the wealthy prided themselves on their stable of good polo ponies and their elegant turnout for matches.

Artists and sculptors also found horses popular subjects; despite their apparent mass production, T'ang paintings and clay figurines of horses are still full of life and movement. Another favorite subject for art was the endless variety of foreigners in this cosmopolitan center, depicted faithfully in both painting and figurines so that one can easily recognize, by dress and physical features, which people are being represented.

T'ang culture was worldly, elegant, and urbane, but Buddhism was still in vogue and in official favor. Buddhist temples and pagodas also gave Chinese architects an outlet for their talents, and the first half of the T'ang was a golden age of temple architecture and sculpture, the latter showing clear artistic as well as religious influences from the Indian home of Buddhism. A cosmopolitan center for all of Asia, Ch'ang An was also, like China, the cultural model for the rest of East Asia. Official emissaries and less formal visitors and merchants or adventurers came repeatedly from Korea, Japan, and lesser states to the south and west to bask in the glories of Ch'ang An and to take back with them as much as they could for building their own versions of T'ang civilization.

Persian Zoroastrians, Muslims, Jews, Indian Buddhists and Hindus, and Nestorian Christians and Byzantines from the eastern Mediterranean, representing nearly all of the great world religions, were among the city's permanent residents, all welcomed in this center of world culture and all leaving some evidence of their presence. Ch'ang An flourished for 2½ centuries, from the early seventh to the mid-ninth, when the capital, like the empire, fell into chaos. But from 618 to around 860 it shone with a cosmopolitan brilliance perhaps never equaled until modern times.

## Cultural Achievement and Political Decay

The T'ang is still seen as the greatest period of Chinese poetry, especially in the work of Li Po (Li Bo, 701–762) and Tu Fu (Du Fu, 712–770).

Some 1,800 samples of Li Po's 20,000 poems survive, including these lines:

> *Beside my bed the bright moonbeams glimmer*
> *Almost like frost on the floor.*
> *Rising up, I gaze at the mountains bathed in*
> *    moonlight:*
> *Lying back, I think of my old home.*
>
> *A girl picking lotuses beside the stream—*
> *At the sound of my oars she turns;*
> *She vanishes giggling among the flowers,*
> *And, all pretense, declines to come out.*
>
> *Amid the flowers with a jug of wine*
> *The world is like a great empty dream.*
> *Why should one toil away one's life?*
> *That is why I spend my days drinking. . . .*
> *Lustily singing, I wait for the bright moon.*
>
> *I drink alone with no one to share*
> *Raising up my cup, I welcome the moon. . . .*
> *We frolic in revels suited to the spring.*

The legend, almost certainly untrue but appealing, is that Li Po drunkenly leaned out of a boat to embrace the reflection of the moon and drowned, happy in his illusion.

Tu Fu was a more sober poet than Li Po, but equally admired. Here are some samples of his lines:

The poet Li Po (701–762) is perhaps the most appealing T'ang figure. His poetry is still learned and quoted by successive generations of Chinese. [Tokyo National Museum]

> *Frontier war drums disrupt everyone's travels.*
> *At the border in autumn a solitary goose*
> *    honks.*
> *Tonight the hoar frost will be white. . . .*
> *I am lucky to have brothers, but all are*
> *    scattered. . . .*

*The letters I write never reach them.*
*How terrible that the fighting cannot stop.*

*Distant Annam\* sends the court a red parrot,*
*Gaudy as a peach blossom and as talkative as*
*    we are.*
*But learning and eloquence are given the same*
*    treatment:*
*The cage of imprisonment. Is one ever free?*
*The capital is captured, but hills and streams*
*    remain.*
*With spring in the city the grass and trees grow*
*    fast.*
*Bewailing the times, the flowers droop as if in*
*    tears.*
*Saddened as I am with parting, the birds make*
*    my heart flutter.*
*Army beacons have flamed for three months.*
*A letter from home now would be worth a*
*    king's ransom.*
*In my anxiety I have scratched my white hairs*
*    even shorter.*
*What a jumble! Even hairpins cannot help me.*

Relatively little T'ang painting or literature has survived, apart from a few tomb walls and a few texts, but we have many accounts of the great painters of the time and of fiction writers of whose work we have only a few samples. What have survived in great abundance are the magnificent glazed pottery figures used to furnish tombs and adorn houses and palaces, probably the best-known aspect of T'ang art. Learning and the arts enjoyed a further blossoming under Emperor Hsuan-tsung (Xuanzong, 712–756) and at his elegant court. But in his old age Hsuan-tsung became infatuated with a son's concubine, the beautiful Yang Kuei-fei, who with her relatives and protégés gained control of the empire but ran it badly. Rebellion resulted, and the capital was sacked in 755. Hsuan-tsung fled south with Lady Yang, but his resentful guards strangled her as the cause of all the empire's troubles, and Hsuan-tsung abdicated in sorrow. The rebellion was finally put down, and order was restored.

Although there were to be no more outstanding T'ang emperors and the power of court factions and great families grew, the economy thrived and culture flourished. A Confucian revival occurred in the ninth century, and partly as a result, the state moved to confiscate the wealth and destroy the political power of Buddhist temples, monasteries, and monks in the 840s. Most temple and monastic properties and tax-free estates, which had grown to immense size, were taken over by the state, and most monasteries were destroyed. The move was similar to that undertaken by King Henry VIII

---

*\*Annam is central Vietnam, beyond the empire's direct rule, but, as implied here, tributary.*

of England seven centuries later, and with similar motives—the need to regain undivided power and control over lost revenues (see Chapter 17). Chinese Buddhism never recovered from this blow and remained thereafter a small minority religion in a Confucian and Taoist society (see Chapter 7). Buddhism was also resented by many Chinese because of its foreign origins, especially orthodox Confucianists and dedicated Taoists, as Christianity was to be later. Its association with Empress Wu did not help.

Like its Han predecessor, the T'ang dynasty lost effectiveness over time and was weakened by corruption. A series of rebellions broke out after 875, prompted first by a great drought in the north but spreading quickly among disaffected subjects all over the country. Rival generals or their puppets succeeded one another on the throne after 884, and in 907 the dynasty dissolved. After a period of confusion, a young general proclaimed a new dynasty in 960, the Sung, which was to last more than three centuries.

## The Sung Dynasty

In many ways, the Sung is the most exciting period in Chinese history. Later Chinese historians have criticized it because it failed to stem the tide of barbarian invasion and was ultimately overwhelmed by the hated Mongols. But it lasted from 960 to 1279, roughly the 300-year average for most dynasties, and presided over a period of unprecedented growth, innovation, and cultural flowering. For a long time the Sung policy of defending the empire's essential territories and appeasing neighboring barbarian groups with money and Chinese brides worked well. It made sense to give up the exhausting Han and T'ang effort to hold Sinkiang, Tibet, Mongolia, Manchuria, Vietnam, and even the more marginal arid fringes of northern China. These areas were all unprofitable from the Chinese point of view; they never repaid, in any form but pride, the immense costs of controlling them. Most of them were arid or mountainous wastelands thinly settled by restless nomads who took every chance to rebel and who were very effective militarily.

Vietnam and Korea had been chronic drains on China's wealth and military strength; both were determined to fight relentlessly against Chinese control but willing to accept a more or less nominal tributary status, which satisfied Chinese pride and avoided bloody struggles. The Sung wisely concentrated on the productive center of Han Chinese settlements south of the Great Wall and even accepted barbarian control of what is now the Peking area and a similar arrangement with another barbarian group in the arid northwestern province of Kansu (Gansu). Little of value was lost by these agreements,

## ◉ The "Ever-Normal Granary" System ◉

*Po Chu-i (772–846), one of China's greatest poets, was also a T'ang official. While serving as an imperial censor in 808 he wrote a memorial criticizing the "ever-normal granary" system.*

I have heard that because of the good harvest this year the authorities have asked for an imperial order to carry out Grain Harmonization so that cheap grain may be bought and the farmers benefitted. As far as I can see, such purchases mean only loss to the farmers. . . . In recent years prefectures and districts were allowed to assess each household for a certain amount of grain, and to fix the terms and the date of delivery. If there was any delay, the punitive measures of imprisonment and flogging were even worse than those usually involved in the collection of taxes. Though this was called Grain Harmonization, in reality it hurt the farmers. . . . If your majesty would consider converting the taxes payable in cash into taxes payable in kind, the farmers would neither suffer loss by selling their grain at a cheap price, nor would they have the problem of re-selling bales of cloth and silk. The profit would go to the farmers, the credit to the emperor. Are the advantages of that commutation in kind not evident? . . . I lived for some time in a small hamlet where I belonged to a household which had to contribute its share to Grain Harmonization. I myself was treated with great harshness; it was truly unbearable. Not long ago, as an official in the metropolitan district, I had responsibility for the administration of Grain Harmonization. I saw with my own eyes how delinquent people were flogged, and I could not stand the sight of it. In the past I have always wanted to write about how people suffered from this plague [but] since I was a petty and unimportant official in the countryside, I had no opportunity to approach your majesty. Now I have the honor of being promoted to serve your majesty and of being listed among the officials who offer criticism and advice. [If] my arguments are not strong enough to convince . . . order one of your trustworthy attendants to inquire incognito among the farmers. . . . Then your majesty will see that my words are anything but rash and superficial statements.

*Source:* W. T. de Bary, ed., *Sources of Chinese Tradition* (New York: Columbia University Press, 1960), pp. 423–425.

and the remarkable flowering of Sung China had much to do with its abandonment of greater imperial ambitions. What remained under Chinese control was still roughly the size of non-Russian Europe and, with a population of some 100 million, was by far the largest, most productive, and most highly developed state in the world.

The Sung capital was built at Kaifeng, near the great bend of the Yellow River. In addition to its administrative functions, it became a huge commercial entrepôt and also a center of manufacturing, served in all respects by the Grand Canal, which continued to bring rice and other goods from the prosperous south. There was a notable boom in iron and steel production and metal industries, using coal as fuel. China in the eleventh century probably produced more iron, steel, and metal goods than the whole of Europe until the mid-eighteenth century and similarly preceded Europe by seven centuries in smelting and heating with coal. Kaifeng was better located to administer and to draw supplies from the Yangtze valley and the south than Ch'ang An, whose role in frontier pacification was in any case no longer so necessary. The Sung army was large, mobile, equipped with iron and steel weapons, and well able for some time to defend the state's new borders. Kaifeng probably exceeded a million inhabitants, with merchants and artisans proportionately more important than in the past, although there were also swarms of officials, soldiers, providers, servants, and hangers-on of various sorts.

The early Sung emperors prudently eliminated the power of the court eunuchs and the great landed families and reestablished the scholar-officialdom as the core of administration. Civil servants recruited through examination had no power base of their own but did have a

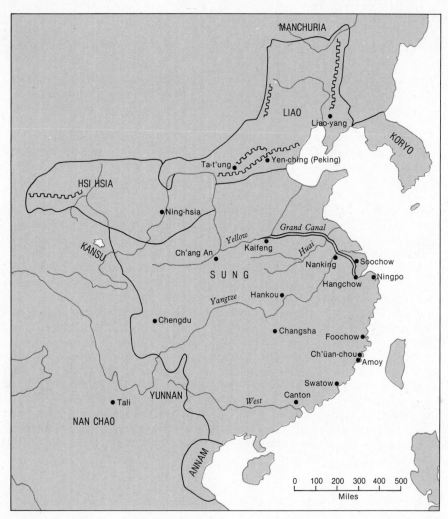

*12.2 China and Korea in 1050*

long tradition of public service and could even check the abuses of the powerful. To ensure their loyalty to the empire, their local postings were changed every three years, and they never served in their native places, lest they become too identified with the interests of any one area. In each county and at each higher level the emperor appointed both a civil administrator—a magistrate or governor—and a military official, each with his own staff, who with other officials such as tax collectors and the imperial censors or inspectors had overlapping jurisdictions and could check on each other. It was an efficient system that ensured good administration most of the time. The spread of mass printing promoted literacy and education and opened wider opportunities for commoners to enter the elite group of the scholar-gentry from whom officials were recruited or to prosper in trade.

The eleventh century was in many ways a golden age

of good government, prosperity, and creativity. Paper promissory notes and letters of credit, followed by mass government issue of paper currency, served the growth of commerce. Government officials distributed printed pamphlets and promoted improved techniques in agriculture: irrigation, fertilization, ingenious new metal tools and mechanical equipment, and improved crop strains. Population grew even beyond the T'ang levels. Painting had a glorious development, often supported by rich urban merchants as well as by the Sung court. Literature also flourished, aided by the spread of cheap printing. Fiction proliferated, some now in the vernacular. The most famous Sung literary figure is the poet-painter-official Su Shih (Su Tung-p'o, Su Dongpo, 1037–1101), perhaps the best known of China's long tradition of poetic nature lovers. It was a confident, creative time.

Su Shih was, like so many of the scholar-gentry, a

# ◉ The Confucian Revival ◉

*The Sung poet, official, and historian Ou-yang Hsiu (1007–1070) was one of several leading figures who promoted the revival of Confucianism and criticized Buddhism as alien.*

Buddha was a barbarian who was far removed from China and lived long ago. In the age of Yao, Shun, and the Three Dynasties [the golden age of China's remote past], kingly rule was practiced, [and] government and the teachings of rites and righteousness flourished. . . . But after the Three Dynasties had fallen into decay, when kingly rule ceased and rites and righteousness were neglected, Buddhism came to China, [taking] advantage of this time of decay and neglect to come and plague us. . . . If we will but remedy this decay, revive what has fallen into disuse, and restore kingly rule in its brilliance and rites and righteousness in their fullness, then although Buddhism continues to exist, it will have no hold upon our people. . . . Buddhism has plagued the world for a thousand years. . . . The people are drunk with it, and it has seeped into their bones and marrow so that it cannot be vanquished by mouth and tongue. . . . There is nothing so effective in overcoming it as practicing what is fundamental. . . . When the way of Confucius [is] made clear, the other schools [will] cease. This is the effect of practicing what is fundamental in order to overcome Buddhism. . . . These days a tall warrior clad in armor and bearing a spear may surpass in bravery a great army, yet when he sees the Buddha he bows low and when he hears the doctrines of the Buddha he is sincerely awed and persuaded. Why? Because though he is indeed strong and full of vigor, in his heart he is confused and has nothing to cling to. . . . If a single scholar who understands rites and righteousness can keep from submitting to these doctrines, then we have but to make the whole world understand rites and righteousness and these doctrines will, as a natural consequence, be wiped out.

*Source:* W. T. de Bary, ed., *Sources of Chinese Tradition* (New York: Columbia University Press, 1960), pp. 442–445.

painter as well as a poet. In several of his poems he tries to merge the two media, inviting the reader to step into the scene and be immersed in a mind-emptying union with the great world of nature. He also used dust as a symbol for both official life (dead files and lifelessness, as in our own culture) and the capital on the dusty plains of the north, where he served for many years as an official.

*Foggy water curls and winds around the brook road;*
*Layered blue hills make a ring where the brook runs east.*
*On a white moonlit shore a long-legged heron roosts.*
*And this is a place where no dust comes.*
*An old man of the stream looks, says to himself:*
*"What is your little reason for wanting so much to be a bureaucrat?*
*You have plenty of wine and land;*
*Go on home, enjoy your share of leisure!"*

*A boat, light as a leaf, two oars squeaking frighten wild geese.*
*Water reflects the clear sky, the limpid waves are calm.*
*Fish wriggle in the weedy mirror, herons dot misty foreshores.*
*Across the sandy brook swift, the frost brook cold, the moon brook bright.*
*Layer upon layer like a painting, bend after bend like a screen.*
*Remember old Yen Ling long ago—"Lord," "Minister"—a dream,*
*Now gone, vain fames.*
*Only the far hills are long, the cloudy hills tumbled, the dawn hills green.*

*Drunk, abob in a light boat, wafted into the thick of flowers,*
*Fooled by the sensory world, I hadn't meant to stop here.*
*Far misty water, thousand miles' slanted evening sunlight,*
*Numberless hills, riot of green like rain—*
*I don't remember how I came.*

## ⊛ Advice to a Chinese Emperor ⊛

*The Sung official Ssu-ma Kuang (1019–1086) was also part of the
Confucian revival and wrote a monumental general history of China.
Here is part of one of his memorials to the emperor, urging the abolition
of Wang An-shih's reforms.*

Human inclinations being what they are, who does not love wealth and high rank, and
who does not fear punishment and misfortune? Seeing how the wind blew and following
with the current, the officials and gentry vied in proposing schemes, striving to be clever
and unusual. They supported what was harmful and rejected what was beneficial. In name
they loved the people; in fact they injured the people. The crop loans, local service exemptions, marketing controls, [the] credit and loan system, and other measures were introduced. They aimed at the accumulation of wealth and pressed the people mercilessly. The
distress they caused still makes for difficulties today. Besides, there were frontier officials
who played fast and loose, hoping to exploit their luck. They spoke big and uttered bare-
faced lies, waged war unjustifiably, and needlessly disturbed the barbarians on our borders. . . . Officials who liked to create new schemes which they might take advantage of to
advance themselves . . . changed the regulations governing the tea, salt, iron, and other
monopolies and increased the taxes on families, on business, and so forth, in order to
meet military expenses. . . . They misled the late emperor, and saw to it that they themselves derived all the profit from these schemes. . . .

   Now the evils of the new laws are known to everyone in the empire, high or low, wise
or ignorant. Yet there are still some measures which are harmful to the people and hurtful
to the state. These matters are of immediate and urgent importance, and should be abolished. Your servant will report on them in separate memorials, hoping that it may please
your sage will to grant us an early decision and act upon them. . . . The best plan is to
select and keep those new laws which are of advantage to the people, while abolishing all
those which are harmful. This will let the people of the land know unmistakably that the
court loves them with a paternal affection.

*Source:* W. T. de Bary, ed., *Sources of Chinese Tradition* (New York: Columbia University Press, 1960),
pp. 487–489.

## Defeat in the North

But trouble was brewing on the northern frontiers. A
barbarian group, the Jurchen, spilled over from their
homeland in southern Manchuria in the early twelfth
century. In alliance with the Sung, in 1122 they defeated
another barbarian group that had ruled the northeastern
border area, returning it to Chinese control. The warlike
Jurchen were not overly impressed by the army of their
Sung allies, and the Sung foolishly treated them as inferiors. The Jurchen advanced southward, besieged Kaifeng, starved it into surrender, and sacked the city in
1127 after the Chinese failed to pay them an extravagant
indemnity. The war continued for a decade, with
Jurchen armies briefly penetrating south of the Yangtze.
But the Sung armies regrouped and drove them back

into northern China, finally concluding a treaty that left
the Jurchen in control of the area north of the Yangtze
valley with the Sung as a tribute-paying vassal. Now
called Southern Sung, the dynasty built a new capital at
Hangchow (Hangzhov) at the southern edge of the
Yangtze delta. The Sung had lost the north, but now they
could concentrate on China's heartland, the Yangtze valley and the south. Another century of brilliance and innovation ensued, with no loss of momentum.

## The Southern Sung Period

Cut off from normal overland trade routes through the
northwest, the Sung turned in earnest to developing sea

passages to Southeast Asia and India. Permanent colonies of Chinese merchants grew in many Southeast Asian trade centers, and ports on China's southeast coast, from Hangchow south, flourished. These included large numbers of resident foreigners, mostly Arabs, who lived in special quarters under their own headmen. Foreign accounts agree that these were the world's largest port cities at the time. Taxes on maritime trade provided a fifth of the imperial revenue, an unheard-of proportion that betokened new commercial prosperity. There was a striking advance in the size and design of oceangoing ships, some of which could carry over 600 people plus cargo, far larger than any elsewhere until modern times. The compass, an earlier Chinese invention, was a vital navigational aid, and these ships also pioneered in the use of multiple masts (important for manageability as well as speed), separate watertight compartments (not known elsewhere until much later), and the stern-post rudder, which replaced the awkward and unseaworthy steering oar. In all these respects, Sung ships presaged modern ships by many centuries. Ironically, they helped make it possible much later for Europeans to undertake the sea voyage to Asia using the compass, rudder, and masts—plus gunpowder—originally developed by China and to record their conquests and profits on Chinese-invented paper.

Domestically, too, commerce and urbanization flourished. The Yangtze delta and the southeast coast had long been China's commercial centers, thanks to their high productivity and the easy movement of goods by river, sea, and canal. An immense network of canals and navigable creeks covered the Yangtze and Canton deltas, serving a system of large and small cities inhabited increasingly by merchants managing a huge and highly varied trade. The capital at Hangchow, with its additional administrative role, grew to giant size and may have reached a million and a half in population, making it one of the world's largest cities before the age of railways. Water transport made this possible for Hangchow and other big cities, including Pataliputra, Rome, Ch'ang An, Istanbul, Edo (Tokyo), and eighteenth-century London. The proliferation of Chinese cities included for the first time several as big as or bigger than the capital and many only slightly smaller. Suchou (Soochow, Suzhou) and Fuchou (Foochow, Fuzhou) each had well over a million people, and according to Marco Polo, there were six other large cities in the 300 miles between those two. Chinese medicine became still more sophisticated, incorporating even the practice of vaccinating against smallpox, learned from Guptan India but unknown in the West until 1798.

We know a good deal about Hangchow, both from voluminous Chinese sources and from the accounts of several foreigners who visited it, including Marco Polo, who saw it only under Mongol rule after its great period had long passed. Nevertheless, he marveled at its size and wealth and called it the greatest city in the world, by comparison with which even Venice, his hometown and probably then the pinnacle of European urbanism, was, he says, a poor village. The great Arab traveler Ibn Battuta, 50 years later in the fourteenth century, says that even then Hangchow was three days' journey in length and subdivided into six towns, each larger than anything in the West. His approximate contemporary, the traveling Italian friar John of Marignolli, called Hangchow "the first, the biggest, the richest, the most populous, and altogether the most marvelous city that exists on the face of the earth."

These were all men who knew the world; even allowing for the usual hyperbole of travelers' tales, they were right about Hangchow. Its rich merchant and scholar-official community and its increasingly literate population of shopkeepers, artisans, and the upwardly mobile supported an exuberance of painting, literature, drama, music, and opera, while for the unlettered there were public storytellers in the ancient Chinese oral tradition. Southern Sung (and the Yuan or Mongol dynasty that followed it) is the great period of Chinese landscape painting, with its celebration of the beauties of the misty mountains, streams and lakes, bamboo thickets, and green hills of the south.

# Innovation and Technological Development

The Southern Sung period was also a time of technological innovation. The philosopher Chu Hsi (Zhuxi, 1130–1200), the founder of what is called Neo-Confucianism, was in many ways a Leonardo-like figure, interested in and competent at a wide range of practical subjects as well as philosophy. This was in the tradition of the Confucian scholar-gentleman, but Chu Hsi and some of his contemporaries carried what Confucius called "the investigation of things" still further into scientific inquiry. Chu Hsi's journals record, for example, his observation that uplifted rock strata far above current sea level contained marine fossils. Like Leonardo, but three centuries earlier, he made the correct deduction and wrote the first statement of the geomorphological theory of uplift. But Chu Hsi was primarily concerned with personal development. He argued that through the Confucian discipline of self-cultivation, every man could be his own philosopher and sage, a doctrine similar to Plato's.

Rapid developments in agriculture, manufacturing, and transport led to a great variety of new tools and machines for cultivation and threshing, for lifting water (pumps), for carding, spinning, and weaving textile fibers, and for making windlasses, inclined planes, canal locks, and refinements in traction for water and land car-

EAST ASIA, 600–1500

|  | China | Korea | Japan |
|---|---|---|---|
| c. A.D. 600–900 | Sui dynasty (589–618)<br>T'ang dynasty (618–907) | Paekche kingdom (c. 220–660)<br>Koguryo kingdom (c. 220–669)<br>Silla kingdom (c. 220–935) | Nara period (c. 710–794)<br>Heian era (794–1185) |
| c. 900–1200 | Sung dynasty (960–1279)<br>Jurchen invasion (1120s)<br>Chu Hsi (1130–1200) | Koryo kingdom (935–1218) |  |
| c. 1200–1500 | Chinghis Khan (1155–1227)<br>Yuan dynasty (1279–1368) | Mongol rule (1218–1364)<br>Yi dynasty (1392–1910) | Kamakura period<br>(1185–1333)<br>Ashikaga shogunate<br>(1333–1573) |

riers. Water clocks were widespread, as were water-powered mills, to grind grain and to perform some manufacturing functions. Superficially at least, thirteenth-century China resembled eighteenth-century Europe: commercialization, urbanization, a widening market (including overseas trade), rising demand, and hence both the incentive and the capital to pursue mechanical invention and other measures to increase production.

Would these developments have led to a true industrial revolution, with all its profound consequences? We will never know, because the Mongol onslaught cut them off, and later dynasties failed to replicate the conditions of late Sung society. The great English historian of early modern Europe, R. H. Tawney, warns us against "giving the appearance of inevitableness by dragging into prominence the forces which have triumphed and thrusting into the background those which they have swallowed up."[1] It is tempting to think that if the Sung had had just a little longer—or if Chinghis Khan had died young (as he nearly did many times)—China might have continued to lead the world and modern Europe might never have risen as it did.

## The Mongol Conquest and the Yuan Dynasty

The Mongols overran Southern Sung because they were formidable fighters, but they were aided by some serious Sung errors. The Mongol leader, Chinghis (Genghis) Khan (1155–1227), first attacked the Jurchen territories in the north and then the other non-Chinese groups in the northwest. In 1232 the Sung made an alliance with the Mongols to crush the remnants of the Jurchen and within two years reoccupied Kaifeng and Loyang. A year later they were desperately defending northern China against an insatiable Mongol army,

other wings of which had already conquered Korea, central Asia, the Near East, and eastern Europe.

For 40 years the fighting raged in the north, where the heavily fortified Chinese cities were both defended and attacked with the help of explosive weapons. Gunpowder had been used much earlier in China for fireworks and for warfare too as an explosive and a "fire powder." Fire arrows using naphtha as fuel and part propellant had been known in early Han times, and by the tenth century fire lances, spear-tipped bamboo tubes filled with a gunpowder propellant, were in use. In the struggle between the Chinese and the Mongols, cast-metal barrels using gunpowder to propel a tight-fitting projectile appeared, marking the first certain occurrence of cannon in warfare. This devastating new technology, especially helpful in sieges, quickly spread to Europe and was in use there by the early fourteenth century.

The Sung were fatally weakened by divided counsel and inconsistent strategies, worsened by factionalism. By 1273 the Mongols had triumphed. They soon poured into the south, where Hangchow surrendered in 1276. Resistance continued in the Canton area until 1279, when the Sung fleet was defeated in a great sea battle. During much of the long struggle it was touch and go, but the Mongols made few mistakes and the Sung many, although they put up a far longer and more effective resistance to the Mongols than any of their many other continental opponents except the Delhi sultanate of Ala-ud-din Khalji and his mameluke troops. (The Mongols' seaborne expeditions to Japan and Java left them at a serious disadvantage; their fleet was twice scattered by major storms at critical points, and their invasion attempts were abandoned.)

The Mongols could indeed never have conquered China without the help of Chinese technicians, including siege engineers, gun founders, artillery experts, and naval specialists. Chinghis died in 1227, but he had already planned the conquest of Sung China, which was completed by his grandson Kubilai (1260–1294), who fixed his capital at Peking as early as 1264 and adopted the dynastic title of Yuan. Korea, northern Vietnam, and the previously non-Chinese southwest were also conquered; southern Vietnam, Siam, Burma, and Tibet were forced to accept tributary status as vassals. The Mongol conquest of China's southwest included the defeat of the Thai kingdom of Nan Chao based at Tali (Dali) and forced a major wave of Thais out of their homeland southward into Siam, where they joined earlier migrants (see Chapter 11).

China, for all its size, constituted only a small part of the vast empire built by the Mongols (see Chapter 13). It is astounding that an area of such extent was conquered by a people who probably numbered only about a million, supplemented by a few other steppe nomads. The simple reason is that they were uniquely tough warriors, almost literally born in the saddle, used to extreme privation and exposure, and welded into an unbeatable fighting force by the magnetic leadership of Chinghis Khan, who consolidated the many warring Mongol and related tribes into a single weapon. Chinghis was born clutching a clot of blood in his tiny fist. The Mongols in his time were shamanists (animists and believers in magic), and his mother hurriedly called a soothsayer, who declared, "This child will rule the world."

The Mongols' great military advantage was mobility. Their brilliant use of cavalry tactics, controlled by the ingenious use of signal flags, plus the short but powerful compound reflex bow, which they could load and fire from a gallop, maximized their striking force. They could cover 100 miles a day in forced marches, unencumbered by a baggage train since they carried their spartan rations of parched grain and mare's milk in their saddlebags. They always traveled with spare horses, and they knew how to open a vein in the necks of the wiry steppe ponies and drink some blood, closing it again so that horse and rider could continue. Through Kubilai's time, the Mongols rarely lost an engagement, even more rarely a campaign. Men who resisted were commonly butchered, and their women and children raped, slaughtered, or enslaved.

The terror of the Mongols' record demoralized their opponents, who described them as inhuman monsters. They were expert practitioners of psychological warfare and even employed spies or agents to spread horrifying stories of their irresistible force and their ruthlessness toward resisters. Chinghis, as a true steppe nomad, especially hated cities and city dwellers and made a series of horrible examples of them, often leaving no one alive. The Mongols loved the violence and pride of conquest but had little understanding of or interest in administration, and their empire began to fall apart within a few years of its acquisition.

The period of the Mongols' rule in China, the Yuan dynasty (1279–1368), lasted a little longer only because by that time the Mongols had become considerably Sinified and had realized as well that they could not manage China without employing many thousands of Chinese. They also used many foreigners whom they felt they could trust, including the Venetian Marco Polo, who served as a minor official in China from 1275 to 1292. He and others of his contemporaries were able to reach China in this period because for the brief years of the Mongol Empire, unified control was imposed on most of Eurasia and people could travel more or less safely across it.

Marco's famous journal, like all medieval tales, includes some supernatural stories, and it was dismissed by many because it speaks in such extravagant terms about the size and splendor of Yuan China. Indeed, he soon became known as "*Il milione*," someone who told tall tales of millions of this and that. But when his confessor came to him on his deathbed and urged him to take back all his lies, Marco is said to have replied, "I have not told the half of what I saw."

## Yuan China

The Mongols ran China largely through Chinese officials, aided by a few Sinified Mongols and foreigners. The Chinese bureaucratic system was retained, leaving only the military entirely in Mongol hands. For the years of Mongol rule, Chinese culture continued its development on Sung foundations, once the country had recovered from the profound devastation of the Mongol conquest. A number of new Chinese artists restored and extended the glories of Sung landscape painting, and drama and vernacular literature flourished anew. People, especially of the scholar-gentry-official group, were understandably disheartened by the political scene and turned for solace to art and literature. Mongol rule from the new capital at Peking was exploitive and often harsh. The Mongols rebuilt the Grand Canal, neglected since the fall of the Northern Sung, and extended it to feed and supply Peking, but at a heavy cost in lives and revenue.

Kubilai proved an able ruler of his new empire but concentrated on China and became almost entirely Chinese culturally. Marco Polo gives a flattering account of his sagacity, majesty, and benevolence, a portrait that was probably no more or less accurate than his more general accounts of Yuan China. But Kubilai was followed on his death in 1294 by increasingly inept figures. Smoldering Chinese hatred of the conquerors had flared into widespread revolts by the 1330s, and by 1350 the Mongols' control of the Yangtze valley was lost, while factions of their once united front fought one another in the north. A peasant rebel leader welded together Chinese forces, chased the remaining Mongols back into the steppes north of the Great Wall, and in 1368 announced the foundation of a new dynasty, the Ming, which was to restore Chinese pride and grandeur.

## Chinese Culture and the Mongol Empire

By the late T'ang period, Chinese culture had largely acquired its present form. With the occupation and Sin-ification of most of the south, begun under the Han dynasty and completed under the aegis of the Mongols in the southwest, the state also assumed essentially its modern form. Tibet was more permanently incorporated by the Ch'ing (Qing or Manchu dynasty) in the eighteenth century, which also added Manchuria to the empire. By Sung times, the institutions of government and society had taken on outlines that persisted until the twentieth century. Civil administration was divided among six ministries, plus the censorate, and a military administration under ultimate civil control. At the top of the pyramid was the emperor, assisted by high officials. The empire was divided into provinces within the Great Wall, 18 of them by the seventeenth century, each under a governor and subdivided into prefectures and counties.

Paper flowed to and from the capital, transmitted along a network of paved roads and canals. Most decisions ultimately had to be made or approved by the emperor, which often created a bottleneck at the top. An equally important limitation was the small number of officials of all ranks. Probably no more than 30,000 governed an area the size of Europe and a population that had reached 100 million by Sung times. These administrators were indirectly augmented by unofficial but effective gentry leadership and management, even in the vast rural areas, which were beyond the power of the county magistrate to govern alone.

Still more important in the ordering of society was the family, which not only controlled people's lives but also settled most disputes and ensured harmony by virtuous example. Government controls were thus less essential. A peasant proverb summed up the self-imposed discipline of Chinese society: "Work when the sun rises, rest when the sun sets. The emperor is far away." Dynasties rose and fell, but the fundamental order of Chinese civilization persisted.

Chinese history can be readily divided into dynastic periods in what is called the dynastic cycle. The typical dynasty lasted about three centuries, sometimes preceded by a brief whirlwind period of empire building such as the Ch'in or the Sui. The first century of a new dynasty would be marked by political, economic, and cultural vigor, expansion, efficiency, and confidence; the second would build on or consolidate the achievements of the first; and in the third vigor and efficiency would wane, corruption would mount, banditry and rebellion would multiply, and the dynasty would ultimately fall. A new group would come to power from among the rebels but would rarely attempt to change the system, only its management and supervision.

Chinese culture was continuous, even during the political chaos that followed the fall of the Han. By T'ang times most of the elements of contemporary Chinese society were present. Rice was the dominant food in the diet, supplemented or replaced in the more arid parts of the north by wheat noodles, which Marco Polo is said to have brought back to Italy in the thirteenth century in a form later to become spaghetti, and steamed bread or, among poorer people, millet. Food was eaten with chopsticks, a technique adopted early by Korea and Japan, while the rest of the world ate with its fingers.

Given the size and density of population and the consequent pressure on land, poultry, eggs, meat, and fish were relatively scarce. The diet consisted largely of rice or wheat with a variety of vegetables, including beans and bean products such as curd (tofu) as a source of protein. Oxen or water buffalo were needed for ploughing and were usually eaten only when they died naturally. Pigs, chickens, ducks, and fish, however, could scavenge for their own food and thus could be more easily raised.

The Chinese cuisine is justly famous, including as it does such a wide variety of foods (the Chinese have few dietary inhibitions), flavors, and sauces. Ingredients were sliced small so as to maximize and distribute their flavor and also so that they would cook very quickly over a hot fire. As the burgeoning population cut down the forests, fuel became scarce, and people were reduced to using twigs, branches, and dried grass for cooking. The universal utensil was the thin cast-iron saucer-shaped pot (*wok* in Cantonese), which heated quickly but held the heat and distributed it evenly in a technique we now call "stir frying."

The Chinese landscape was more and more converted into an artificial one of irrigated and terraced rice paddies, fish and duck ponds, and market towns where peasants sold their surplus produce or exchanged it for salt, cloth, tools, or other necessities not produced in all villages. From T'ang times, teahouses became the common centers for socializing, relaxation, gossip, and the negotiation of business or marriage contracts. Fortune-tellers, scribes, booksellers, itinerant peddlers, actors, and storytellers enlivened the market towns and cities, and periodic markets with similar accompaniments were held on a smaller scale in most villages. All this made it less necessary for people to travel far from their native places, and most never went beyond the nearest market town. Beyond it they would have found for the most part only more villages and towns like those they knew, except perhaps for the provincial capital and of course the imperial capital.

In the south most goods and people in the lowlands moved by waterways, in the dry north by pack animals, carts, and human porters, which also operated in the

mountainous parts of the south. The wheelbarrow and the flexible bamboo carrying pole were Chinese inventions that greatly enhanced the ability to transport heavy weights, carefully balanced as they were to enable porters to wheel or trot all day with loads far exceeding their unaided capacity. All these and many other aspects of Chinese culture remain essentially unchanged today.

**Life along the river near Kaifeng at spring festival time. These two scenes come from a long scroll that begins with the rural areas and moves through suburbs into the capital, giving a vivid picture of the bustling life in and around Kaifeng, at the time the largest city in the world. The painting, by Chang Tse-tuan, was done in the early twelfth century. [Werner Forman Archive, London]**

# Korea

Korean culture, though adopting much from China, added its own innovations and retained a strong sense of separate identity, together with a fierce determination to preserve its political independence. The Korean peninsula, set off from the mainland of Asia, is separated by mountains along its northwestern frontier adjacent to Manchuria and by the gorge of the Yalu River, which marks the boundary. The Korean people probably came originally from eastern Siberia and northern Manchuria, as their spoken language, which is unrelated to Chinese, suggests. They brought with them or evolved their own culture, which was already well formed before they were exposed to heavy Chinese influence at the time of the Han occupation in the late second century B.C.

Rice, wheat, metals, written characters, paper, printing, lacquer, porcelain, and other innovations spread to Korea after they appeared in China. As in Vietnam, literate Chinese-style culture in Korea was an elite phenomenon that rested on an already developed indigenous cultural base that remained distinctive. A Chinese-style state arose in the north around P'yongyang in the century before Han Wu-ti's conquest. On the withdrawal of the Chinese military colonies after the fall of the Han in A.D. 220, Korea regained its freedom and was thenceforward self-governing (except for the brief Mongol interlude) until the Japanese takeover in 1910, although Chinese cultural influence continued and was openly welcomed.

## Three Kingdoms: Paekche, Silla, and Koguryo

Three Korean kingdoms arose after 220: Paekche in the southwest, Silla in the southeast, and Koguryo in the north, the largest and closest to China. Confucianism and Chinese forms of government, law, literature, and art spread widely throughout the peninsula, followed by Buddhism as it grew in China. But Korea's long tradition of a hereditary aristocracy in a hierarchically ordered society of privilege prevented the adoption of China's more open official system of meritocracy based on examinations. Like the Japanese, the Koreans also departed from the Chinese pattern in providing an important place for a military aristocracy.

In 669, with help from the T'ang, Silla succeeded in conquering Koguryo, after having earlier demolished Paekche. With its now united strength, Silla repelled T'ang efforts at reconquest, a remarkable feat given the power and proximity of T'ang China. As a formal Chinese vassal, Silla presided over a golden age of creativity. T'ang culture was a natural model, but in many

This masterpiece of Korean art in bronze, depicting Maitreya, the "Buddha of the future," dates from the Silla period, sixth or seventh century A.D. [National Museum of Korea, Seoul]

respects Korean adaptations were at least the equal of their Chinese models. Korean ceramics, fully as accomplished as anything produced in China, had a magnificent development, particularly in pottery and fine porcelain. This included the beautiful celadon ware with its subtle milky green jade-colored glaze, whose secret formula was admired and envied by the Chinese, though it was extinguished by the Mongol conquest of the thirteenth century and never recovered. Silla Korea also went beyond Chinese written characters and began a system of phonetic transcription, derived from the sound of characters but designed to reproduce spoken Korean. By the fifteenth century this had been further refined into the *han'gul* syllabary.

Silla control weakened by the tenth century. The kingdom was taken over by a usurper in 935, who named his new united state Koryo, an abbreviation of Koguryo and the origin of the name Korea. The Koryo capital at Kaesong, just north of Seoul, was built on the planned imperial model of the T'ang city of Ch'ang An and incorporated most of the Chinese system of government. Interest in Buddhism and its texts, as well as a refinement of Sung techniques, stimulated a virtual explosion of woodblock printing in the eleventh century, and magnificent celadon pieces were again produced. Koryo rule dissolved into civil war on the eve of the Mongol invasion, and Chinghis Khan easily overran the peninsula in 1218. The Mongols exacted heavy tribute and imposed iron rule, even forcing Koreans to aid them in their later

expeditions against Japan. But in the 1350s the Mongol empire collapsed, and in 1392 a new dynasty arose, the Yi, which was to preside over a united Korea until 1910.

# The Yi Dynasty

Under the Yi dynasty Korea continued the adaptation of Chinese civilization to a greater extent than any of its predecessors, including the incorporation of the imperial examination system, the Confucian bureaucracy, and the division of the country into eight centrally administered provinces on the Chinese model. Although Confucian ideology spread, in practice officeholding was still dominated by hereditary aristocrats. From their capital at Seoul, Yi rulers continued to accept the formal status of a Chinese tributary state, a relationship that both parties spoke of amicably as that between "younger brother and elder brother." Buddhism declined almost completely, while Confucianism and Chinese-style painting and calligraphy flourished. A group called the *yangban*, originally landowners, acquired most of the functions and status of the Chinese gentry as an educated elite but remained a hereditary class, providing both civil and military officials, unlike the Chinese model.

Korean economic development was retarded by the

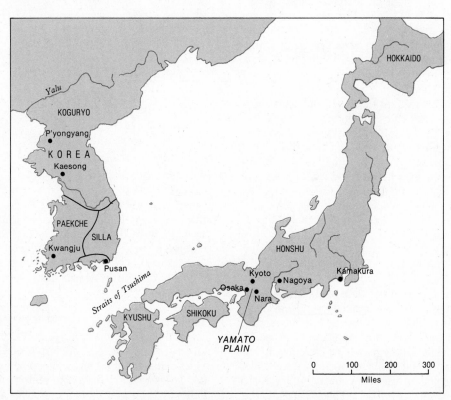

*12.3 Korea and Japan, c. 500–1000*

country's mountainous landscape, which like that of Japan and Greece is divided into separate small basins, and by its long harsh winter, especially severe in the north. Only about one-seventh of the total land area could be cultivated, and trade and concentrated urban growth were also disadvantaged. But although most Koreans remained materially poorer than most Chinese, elite culture, technology, and the arts prospered in distinctively Korean styles, including the still superb ceramics. Korean dress, house types, diet, lifestyles, marriage and inheritance customs, and the volatile, earthy, robust, spontaneous Korean temperament remained their own as well. Food was flavored by the peppery pickled cabbage called *kimchi*, as it still is. Korea's indigenous cultural fabric was basic and showed through the Chinese overlay. There was thus no risk that Korea would be absorbed into Chinese culture, and Koreans remained proud of their independence and of their own sophisticated cultural tradition.

The first century or so of Yi rule was a brilliant period in Korean and East Asian history. The fifteenth century saw a new explosion of printing, now vigorously supported by a Confucian state that put a high value on texts and learning. The Koreans further perfected the art of movable metal type, which was used among other things to reproduce the libraries burned by the Mongols and the wooden plates from which those books had been made. Eight other ambitious printing projects were carried out between 1403 and 1484. This was the first extensive use of movable type anywhere in the world. The technique originated in eleventh-century Sung China and was further developed in Korea a century or so later. In contrast, movable type printing began in Europe only in the mid-fifteenth century.

The same century in Korea also saw important new developments in mathematics and in the manufacture of astronomical instruments. More closely related to printing was the perfection of the *han'gul* alphabet and syllabary, not only to write Korean but to give the Korean pronunciation of Chinese characters as well. Traditional characters continued to be used for official documents and elite literature, but the development and popularity of *han'gul* was an affirmation of Korea's proud and confident distinctiveness.

The vigor of the Yi order was slowly weakened by bureaucratic factionalism, which the throne never really overcame. Factionalism already had a long and disruptive history in Korea, from the time of the three early kingdoms, and it progressively eroded the effectiveness and authority of the Yi state. No strong rulers emerged after the early sixteenth century, and toward its end a divided and enfeebled Korea had to face the invasion of the Japanese warlord Hideyoshi between 1592 and 1598. His army overran and ravaged the country until with aid from China the invaders were driven back almost to the coast and there stalemated. The gifted Korean admiral

*12.4 Yi Dynasty Korea*

Yi Sun-sin then repeatedly defeated Japanese naval detachments and disrupted their supply lines with his ingenious "turtle ships." These vessels, covered with overlapping plates of iron and copper and armed fore and aft with beak-shaped metal prows that could ram and sink any ship, were the first armored warships. They were powered by rowers protected by the outer "turtle shell." The invasion was abandoned when Hideyoshi died in 1598, but Korea never fully recovered from its devastation.

The Yi dynasty continued, plagued by perennial factional fighting, although it still supported learning, the arts, and major new printing projects. Considerable economic growth resulted from improved agriculture and a rising commercial sector, and population probably doubled between 1600 and 1800. Merchants began to buy their way to *yangban* (gentry) status, as did prosperous farmers. Korea thus followed the path of Sung, Ming, and Manchu China and of Tokugawa Japan. But its political and administrative health was poor, ultimately inviting Japanese intervention after 1894.

# Japan

Composed of four main islands off the southern tip of Korea, Japan had been both protected by its insularity from turmoil on the Asian mainland and to a degree also isolated from its development. The Straits of Tsushima between Korea and Japan are approximately 120 miles wide, and although Japan has been periodically involved with the mainland, the connection has never been as close as between China and other areas of East Asia or between Britain and Europe. Japan has had the advantage of a clearly separate identity and as a result of its insularity has been able to make its own choices at most periods about what it wanted to adopt from abroad. Like Korea, Japan is mainly mountainous, and settlement has remained heavily concentrated on the narrow coastal plain between Tokyo and Osaka, an area roughly equivalent to the coastal corridor between Boston and Washington, D.C. All in all, Japan is about the size of California, but the northernmost island of Hokkaido was settled by the Japanese on a major scale only in this century. Mountains also retarded Japanese economic development and political unification. As in Korea, only a little over a seventh of the country is cultivated even now, although the climate, conditioned by the surrounding sea, is far milder and better watered. Coastal sea routes have also helped link settled areas and carry trade.

## Early Culture and Development

The spoken language of the Japanese, unrelated to Chinese but in the same linguistic group as Korean, suggests that they too came originally from the Asian mainland north of China via the sea passage from Korea, although other migrants and cultural influences may have come into Japan from the tropical Pacific. The migrants slowly defeated, displaced, or absorbed the islands' original inhabitants, including a physically very different group called the Ainu, who now live as a tiny and dwindling minority on reservations on the northernmost island of Hokkaido. Early Japanese history is cloudy, in part because written records do not begin until the eighth century A.D., after Japan had adopted the Chinese art of writing from Korea. We have no firm dates before that time and can only guess when the people we now call Japanese arrived or when they emerged as a separate culture, but it was probably sometime between the

third century B.C. and the first century A.D., partly through interbreeding with earlier inhabitants. Earlier preliterate and premetallic cultures had developed in Japan, producing pottery perhaps as early as in any part of Asia. Bronze tools and weapons from China entered via Korea about the first century B.C., and implements made of iron, a technology also imported from Korea, were being produced by around A.D. 200.

It seems clear that Korea played an important role in Japan until the fifth century A.D. By the time of the first Japanese records in the eighth century, a third of the nobility claimed Korean or Chinese descent, and clearly such lineage was perceived as a mark of superiority. Close interaction with Korea continued, with large numbers of Korean artisans, metallurgists, and technologists living in Japan, as well as Korean nobles and perhaps even rulers. There were also invasions and raids in both directions, until by about 400 such violent interactions faded and the Japanese continued to move northward from the southernmost island of Kyushu, closest to Korea, onto the main island of Honshu. There they established a central core on the Yamato Plain in the Nara-Kyoto-Osaka area, where it was to remain for approximately the next 1,000 years. The imperial capital, however, was not moved northeast to Tokyo until 1868, and the frontier with the Ainu lay just north of Kyoto for centuries.

## The Nara Period

Chinese cultural infusions continued from Korea, including, sometime before 500, Chinese written characters and an increasing knowledge of Chinese culture and of Buddhism. By the end of the sixth century and increasingly in the seventh, missions were dispatched to China to observe and to bring back to Japan as much of Chinese civilization as possible. In the mid-seventh century a sweeping series of measures called the *Taika* ("Great Reform") began the process of transforming Japan and the Japanese imperial administration into a version of China's. By 710 the first permanent capital was inaugurated at Nara, a smaller-scaled copy of Ch'ang An, which presided over a modified Chinese-style government.

The ensuing century (until 794) is known as the Nara period, during which the transplantation of Chinese civilization continued, helped by successive Japanese missions to China. Currency and coins on the Chinese model were introduced. The Chinese scholars' habit of recording everything they observed was transmitted too, and important accounts of T'ang China come from Japanese sources of this period, as well as the first official histories of Japan. Buddhism spread, but Confucianism also entered from China and became important for the upper classes. As Taoism was retained in China, the original animistic and naturalistic Japanese religion of Shinto remained, in part no doubt as an assertion of Japanese distinctiveness but also because of its close connection with the imperial family. Beautiful wood-crafted Shinto shrines remain in "natural" areas even in contemporary Japan.

Artistic styles, gardens, court and official clothing, and sophisticated tastes all strove to replicate the Chinese model, and although they slowly diverged from that standard, Japanese high culture still retains the unmistakable marks of its seventh- and eighth-century Chinese origins. Even the straw mats (*tatami*) that still today cover the floor in traditional Japanese rooms, the prominence of raw fish and pickled vegetables in the diet, and the tea ceremony all came from T'ang China. Korean and Chinese artists, artisans, and technicians remained important in the Nara period as teachers and implementers of cultural reform. But Japan was a very different place, and the cultural transplant was never complete, nor did it ever penetrate very deeply into the mass of the people, most of whom remained peasants until the late nineteenth century. Unlike Chinese society, but as in Korea, descent and inherited status continued to be important, and society as a whole remained more tightly organized and more hierarchically controlled. Feudal-style lords and hereditary nobles remained the chief wielders of power. Japan tried the Chinese examination system, but, as in Korea, hereditary aristocrats undercut it by reserving most official positions for themselves. The Japanese emperor, considered divine and hence the bearer of a sacred mandate, was above politics or even administration.

# The Heian Era

In 794 a vigorous young emperor, Kammu, moved the capital to Kyoto (then called Heian), in part to break away from the growing influence of Buddhist institutions in Nara. With the support of the powerful Fujiwara family, he and his successors began to modify or discard some aspects of the Chinese model so enthusiastically adopted earlier. Art and architecture increased their characteristically Japanese concern for textures and the use of natural materials. T'ang China was in turmoil, and Japanese missions stopped going there, while new interest arose in indigenous cultural patterns. Chinese written characters were increasingly supplemented and later somewhat displaced by a phonetic system known as *kana*. Most of its symbols combined a consonant and a vowel and made it possible to transcribe spoken Japanese accurately, as Chinese characters could not do. Chinese characters remained important among the educated elite and for official use, but the *kana* system was understandably preferred for most purposes, including popular literature.

The effort to follow Chinese patterns of government was largely given up, and power came increasingly into the hands of the Fujiwara clan and its appointees or hereditary officeholders. Because the new capital was called Heian, the centuries from 794 to 1185 are called the Heian era. The period is famous for its aristocratic and court culture, where noble gentlemen and ladies devoted their lives to aesthetic refinement. The best-known Heian work is Lady Murasaki's *Tale of Genji*, considered the world's first psychological novel.

**Traditional Japanese stone garden at the Ryoanji Temple, Kyoto. Originally from T'ang China, this orderly and peaceful form of landscaping became characteristically Japanese and is still widely practiced. [Jack Deutsch]**

## LADY MURASAKI AND HEIAN COURT LITERATURE

Lady Murasaki's birth date is not known precisely, though it was probably around A.D. 978, and we are also not sure of the date of her death, probably around 1015. We do not even know her real name, since in Heian Japan it was considered improper to record the personal names of aristocratic women outside of the imperial family. It is known that she came from a junior branch of the great Fujiwara clan and that her father was a provincial governor. The name Murasaki may derive from that of a major figure in her novel, *The Tale of Genji*, or from its meaning of "purple," a pun on the *Fuji* of Fujiwara, which means "wisteria." She was far from alone as a woman author; mid-Heian period literature is dominated by women, who, particularly at court, were apparently less conventional than men. The absence of harems and extensive concubinage in Japan left women freer to express their talents in other ways.

Lady Murasaki's journal is our only source of information about her life. It records that she was a precocious child and became literate early:

My father was anxious to make a good Chinese scholar of [my brother], and often came to hear him read his lessons. . . . So quick was I at picking up the language that I was soon able to prompt my brother. . . . After this I was careful to conceal the fact that I could write a single Chinese character.[2]

But she acquired a wide knowledge of both Chinese and Japanese works and also became a talented calligrapher, painter, and musician, attainments considered suitable for an aristocratic girl. At about age 21 she was married to a much older man, a distant Fujiwara cousin, and bore a daughter. The next year her husband died, and in her grief she considered becoming a Buddhist nun but turned instead to reflection on the problem of human happiness, especially for women. Around that time, approximately the year 1001, she began work on her masterpiece, *The Tale of Genji*, which was probably nearly finished when, some six years later, she became a lady-in-waiting at the imperial court.

Her journal describes the refined and colorful life at court, as well as its less glamorous rivalries and intrigues. Both are the subject of her great novel, which combines a romantic as well as psychological approach with realistic detail and subtle insight into human behavior. *Genji* is still praised as the masterpiece of Japanese literature. Her people are real, despite the highly mannered world in which they lived, and through her journal we also have a picture of her as an extraordinarily alive, imaginative, and compelling person. A collec-

tion of her poems has also survived, which further mark her as an accomplished stylist.

*The Tale of Genji* deals with the life of a prince and his seemingly endless affairs with various court ladies. It includes careful attention to manners, dress, and court politics—perhaps not the most rewarding of subjects, but in the hands of Lady Murasaki they become not mere details but a means of revealing character. Although the hero is idealized, this is far more than a conventional romantic tale, and the portrayal of Genji as he grows older is a subtle one. Toward the end of her journal, Lady Murasaki gives us a candid glimpse of herself: People think, she wrote, that "I am very vain, reserved, unsociable . . . wrapped up in the study of ancient stories, living in a poetical world all my own. . . . But when they get to know me, they find that I am kind and gentle."[3] Perhaps she was all these things. Bold as she was in her writings, when describing herself Lady Murasaki still felt compelled to present her character in terms of the traditional "feminine" virtues.

# Political Disorder and the Rise of Feudalism

Heian court culture was delightful, no doubt, but may suggest a lack of adequate Fujiwara concern with the real world of politics. Elite life at the capital was deeply involved with elegance, refinement, and aesthetic sensitivity but gave little thought to increasingly pressing economic problems, the poverty of most Japanese, or growing political disorder. In the end Fujiwara power was undermined and finally destroyed by new families who used their private armies to become de facto rulers over lands they had originally guarded for noble families. Some of these armies, and the new group of warriors (*samurai*) with their pronounced military ethic, had developed out of frontier wars as Japanese settlement spread slowly northeastward beyond the Yamato area after the ninth century. Armed followers of Buddhist temples increasingly took part in political struggles. Armies began to interfere in factional conflicts at court or were called in by different factions, including clans within the Fujiwara family. By the twelfth century, armies had become the real powers.

## The Kamakura Period

In 1185 one of the warrior lineages, the Minamoto clan, set up a rival capital in its then frontier base at Kamakura (now a southern suburb of Tokyo). The refined culture and court-based politics of Heian were now supplemented by a less cultivated but far more politically effective system based on a combination of new bureaucratic methods, military power, and the security offered by the samurai. The samurai leaders were hereditary aristocrats who became both literate and educated and were more administrators than fighting men. Through them and other educated aristocrats Heian culture spread and in time influenced even the warrior clans. However, the rise of noble families and the samurai armies under their control led to the emergence of Japanese feudalism, a phenomenon parallel to that of medieval Europe but different from the imperial civil bureaucracy and meritocracy of China.

The emperor became increasingly a figurehead during this period, and real power rested with whoever could grasp and hold it—first the Fujiwara and then the Minamoto and other military clans. The Kamakura-based administration presided over a feudal hierarchy of warriors and nobles who were bound in fealty assured by oaths, financial and service obligations, and promises of military support. In return, the Kamakura ruler, or *shogun*, the emperor's chief military commander and agent, granted his vassal-lords hereditary rights to their lands. As in medieval Europe, this was a symptom of limited central state power, an arrangement of mutual convenience, but it was also inherently unstable as ambitious or upstart vassals sought to improve their positions or rebel against the shogun's authority. Political power was seldom unified under any single control for long. Each vassal maintained both his own group of samurai and his army, but the loyalty of these forces could not always be ensured, whether to local lords or to the shogun. The patterns that emerged in the Kamakura shogunate (1185–1333) were to dominate Japan until the nineteenth century.

In 1268 the Mongol emperor, Kubilai Khan, demanded the submission of the Japanese, and when they refused, the Mongols forced the recently conquered Koreans to build and man a fleet for the invasion of Japan, which arrived in 1274. Soon after the first landings a great storm wrecked many of the invaders' ships and forced their withdrawal. The Japanese executed subsequent Mongol envoys, and in 1281 a far larger expedition manned by both subject Koreans and Chinese arrived, only to be swept away by an even greater storm. This storm was typical of the late summer typhoons along the coasts of East Asia, though the Japanese can perhaps be forgiven for attributing their double deliverance to a "divine wind," or *kamikaze*. However, the costs of meeting the terrible Mongol threat and of the preparation that went on against an expected third expedition drained Kamakura resources and diverted large numbers of people from productive occupations. With the weakening of Kamakura power, political divisions and open revolts multiplied. In 1333 an unusually active emperor, Go-Daigo, whom the dominant faction at Kamakura had tried to depose, gathered support and attracted dissidents from the crumbling Kamakura structure. One of his commanders overran Kamakura and ended its power. But another of his supporters turned against him, put a different member of the imperial line on the throne, and had himself declared shogun.

## The Ashikaga Shogunate

The Ashikaga shoguns, who established themselves in Kyoto from 1339, were never able to build effective central control. A rival faction supporting another member of the imperial family remained in power in southwestern Honshu and could not be dislodged, while Kyushu continued under the control of one or more other groups. Civil war became endemic, and as one consequence feudal lords beyond the reach of central control supported highly profitable piracy along the coasts of China. This caused chronic trouble between the Ashikaga and the Ming dynasty. The government tried to suppress piracy, but its power to do so was inadequate. For a time the Chinese felt obliged to abandon large stretches of their own coast and pull settlements back to more easily protected sites up rivers and estuaries. From the mid-fifteenth century, political chaos in Japan was endemic, despite the country's small size and the even smaller dimensions of its settled areas. By 1467 effective Ashikaga rule was ended and much of Kyoto had been destroyed, although the emasculated shogunate continued in name. Rival Buddhist sects and their monasteries also fought bloody wars against each other with armed monks as troops. Peasant revolts and bitter conflicts among petty feudal lords continued to ravage the countryside.

Yet despite the growing political disorder, especially after 1450, the last century of the Ashikaga shogunate saw a remarkable flowering of culture. In part this was the result of a conscious fusion of aristocratic Heian traditions with those of the newer samurai culture. Millions also found solace in popular Buddhist sects, including Shin, Nichiren, and Zen, originally Chinese but adapted to Japanese tastes and styles. These popular and egalitarian or, in the case of Zen, contemplative and mystical approaches concentrated on salvation, self-cultivation, and the apprehension of eternal truths rather than on the turmoil of political life. The discipline of Zen appealed to the warrior class but also stressed unity with nature, a traditional Japanese interest. Less detached but clearly related to a turning away from worldly strife was the further blossoming of temple and palace architecture, consciously and ingeniously integrated with peaceful natural settings, of landscape gardening, and of nature painting, much of it in the Southern Sung mode. The literature of the period, meanwhile, commented on the shifting fortunes of politics and the foibles of people grasping for power or gloried in the simple beauty of nature and the joys of untroubled rural life. The shogun-ate patronized Zen as it supported art and literature, continuing the Heian tradition.

Even more specifically Japanese was the Ashikaga evolution of the tea ceremony as a graceful, soothing, contemplative, and aesthetic ritual. Although its origins too were in T'ang China, it became and remains a distinctively Japanese assertion of cultural identity and personal serenity. Delicate teahouses set in naturally landscaped gardens in unobtrusive elegance provided havens of tranquillity and aesthetic enjoyment for samurai and other members of the elite, who took additional pleasure from the exquisite beauty of the teacups. It was a striking and thoroughly Japanese counterpart to the bloody and often ruthless life of the times.

Finally, the Ashikaga era saw the evolution of traditional dances into a stylized and distinctively Japanese form, the *Noh* drama. This subtle, Zen-inspired blending of dance, gesture, speech, and costume evolved into a unique theatrical style capable of communicating rich meaning and emotion. Every step and every movement are precisely measured to achieve a state of controlled tension, a slow-moving, concentrated experience of understatement and disciplined expression.

The production of artisans, too—including, appropriately, the making of fine swords—developed still further. The arrival of the Portuguese early in the sixteenth century stimulated trade, already growing for some time, as the Europeans' more powerful vessels supplanted those of local pirates.

The Ashikaga shogunate dissolved completely into still more chaotic civil war in the 1570s, and Japan was torn by rival clans and their armies until the end of the century. In 1568 a minor but able and determined feudal lord, Oda Nobunaga (1534–1582), won control of Kyoto. He broke the military power of the major Buddhist monasteries and their fortified strongholds in the capital region, including the great fortress of the Shin sect at Osaka. As a counterweight against Buddhism, Nobunaga encouraged Portuguese and other Jesuit mission-

## ◉ Troubled Times in Japan ◉

*Political conflicts in Ashikaga Japan were echoed in literature but did not prevent continued cultural growth. This period saw the development of the haiku poetic form, evolved from an originally Chinese model but becoming in time a distinctively Japanese mode, still much used. Here are some samples, spanning roughly a century but all reflecting troubled times.*

In the hills the cries of deer,
In the fields the chirping insects.
In everything
What sadness is apparent
This autumn evening.

    Nijo Toshimoto (1320–1398)

The clouds still possess
Some semblance of order:
They bring the world rain.

    Shinkei (1407–1475)

To live in the world
Is sad enough without this rain
Pounding on my shelter.

    Sogi, a pupil of Shinkei (1421–1502)

*Source:* J. W. Hall, ed., *Japan in the Muromachi* (Berkeley: University of California Press, 1977), pp. 254, 257.

aries, but his tactics against opponents were ruthless, including the burning alive of captives and the slaughter of noncombatants.

When Nobunaga was murdered by one of his own commanders in 1582, his chief general, Toyotomi Hideyoshi (1536–1598), seized power and by the early 1590s controlled most of Honshu, Kyushu, and Shikoku, thus unifying most of Japan for the first time. A peasant by birth, Hideyoshi tried to disarm all nonsamurai to ensure that commoners were kept down and unable to challenge his authority. He nationalized and centralized the taxation system and further separated warriors from cultivators. As a self-made man, he feared the possible rivalry of others like him. His famous "sword hunt" among all commoners, in which houses were searched and all swords confiscated, reestablished rigid class lines and was accompanied by new laws prohibiting farmers or common soldiers from becoming merchants or even laborers. Hideyoshi rose to power in a period of change and instability; he saw this instability as a threat and tried to stop it. Hideyoshi seems ultimately to have

succumbed to megalomania, as evidenced by his grandiose plan for the conquest of China, for which he carried out an invasion of Korea as a first step in 1592. The story of that misadventure has already been told.

Hideyoshi at first welcomed the Christian missionaries and the profitable trade with the Portuguese, but suddenly he turned against all foreigners. He seems to have feared that Christianity was becoming a disruptive factor in Japanese society and a political menace as the foreigners, already rivals among themselves, became involved in internal conflicts and as Japanese converts developed loyalties to a foreign pope. Hideyoshi placed a ban on missionaries in 1587, but this was not strictly enforced until 1597, when he crucified 9 Catholic priests and 17 Japanese converts as an example.

In the chaos following Hideyoshi's death in 1598, Tokugawa Ieyasu (1542–1616), originally a vassal and ally of Nobunaga and then of Hideyoshi, emerged victorious in 1600 to found the far more effective and lasting order of the Tokugawa shogunate, which was to rule Japan under a centralized feudal administration until 1868.

*This chapter has summarized the renaissance of Chinese civilization after the time of troubles following the fall of the Han dynasty in A.D. 220 and the golden ages of the T'ang and the Sung until those impressive developments were cut off by the Mongol conquest late in the thirteenth century. Despite Mongol brutality, Chinese civilization continued under alien domination, and the hated invaders were eventually thrown off. Korean culture had arisen before the Han conquest and retained its distinctiveness. It borrowed heavily from Chinese civilization at the elite level while creating innovations in ceramics and printing by movable type and shaping institutions adopted from China to Korean tradition. Korea was first unified by the Silla dynasty from 669 to 995 and continued under the Koryo dynasty until it was destroyed by the Mongol invasion in 1218. Yi dynasty Korea from 1392 to 1910 saw a new burst of cultural and technological growth, although its political vigor was slowly eroded by factionalism.*

*Japanese civilization, having been largely created on the Chinese model and with Korean help, in time asserted its own separate cultural identity and produced a graceful elite culture that coexisted with rural poverty and chronic political division and conflict. Japanese feudalism and the role of the samurai evolved after the Heian period (794–1185) under the Kamakura and Ashikaga shogunates (1185–1568), but such methods were unable to unify the country or to end endemic civil war until the emergence of the Tokugawa clan in 1600. Despite political turmoil, Japan also produced great art, literature, and architecture and a refined culture for the upper classes. Chinese influence on the major East Asian societies was thus limited. Koreans and Japanese made what they took from China their own and went on to modify or develop it further in distinctive ways while retaining and building on their own indigenous culture.*

# Notes

1. R. H. Tawney, *The Agrarian Problem in the Sixteenth Century* (London: Longman, Green, 1912), p. 177.
2. All quotations from Lady Murasaki's journal are taken from Arthur Waley's introduction to his translation of *The Tale of Genji* (New York: Doubleday, 1955), pp. ix, xxi.
3. Ibid., p. xxi.

# Suggestions for Further Reading

## China

Allen, T. T. *Mongol Imperialism.* Berkeley: University of California Press, 1987.

Carter, T. F., and Goodrich, L. C. *The Invention of Printing in China and Its Spread Westward.* New York: Ronald Press, 1955.

Chaffee, J. W. *The Thorny Gates of Learning: A Social History of Examinations in Sung China.* Cambridge: Cambridge University Press, 1987.

Dawson, R. S. *Imperial China.* London: Oxford University Press, 1972.

De Crespigny, R. *Under the Brilliant Emperor: Imperial Authority in T'ang China.* Canberra: Australian National University Press, 1985.

Dien, A. E., ed. *State and Society in Medieval China.* Stanford, Calif.: Stanford University Press, 1990.

Gernet, J. *Daily Life in China on the Eve of the Mongol Invasion,* trans. H. M. Wright. London: Macmillan, 1962.

Hymes, R. *Statesmen and Gentlemen: Elites of the Southern Sung.* New York: Cambridge University Press, 1986.

Lo, W. W. *An Introduction to the Civil Service of Sung China.* Honolulu: University Press of Hawaii, 1987.

McMullen, D. L. *State and Scholars in T'ang China.* Cambridge: Cambridge University Press, 1987.

Meskill, J. *An Introduction to Chinese Civilization.* Boston: Heath, 1973.

Olschki, L. *Marco Polo's Asia.* Berkeley: University of California Press, 1960.

Rossabi, M. *Kubilai Khan: His Life and Times.* Berkeley: University of California Press, 1987.

Schafer, E. *The Golden Peaches of Samarkand: A Study of T'ang Exotics.* Berkeley: University of California Press, 1963.

Spuler, B. *History of the Mongols.* Berkeley: University of California Press, 1972.

Waley, A. *The Poetry and Career of Li Po.* London: Allen & Unwin, 1960.

Weinstein, S. *Buddhism Under the T'ang.* New York: Cambridge University Press, 1988.

## Korea

Henthorn, G. *History of Korea.* Glencoe, Ill.: Free Press, 1971.

Lee, K.-B. *A New History of Korea,* trans. E. Wagner. Cambridge: Harvard University Press, 1985.

## Japan

Berry, M. E. *Hideyoshi.* Cambridge, Mass.: Harvard University Press, 1986.

Dunn, C. J. *Everyday Life in Traditional Japan.* London: Batsford, 1969.

Duus, P. *Feudalism in Japan.* New York: Knopf, 1969.

Elison, E., and Smith, B., eds. *Warlords, Artists, and Commoners: Japan in the Sixteenth Century.* Honolulu: University Press of Hawaii, 1981.

Hall, J. W., ed. *Japan Before Tokugawa.* Princeton, N.J.: Princeton University Press, 1986.

Hane, M. *Japan.* New York: Scribner, 1972.

———. *Premodern Japan,* 2nd ed. Boulder, Colo.: Westview Press, 1990.

Keene, D. *No: The Classical Theatre of Japan.* Stanford, Calif.: Stanford University Press, 1966.

Mass, J. P. *Warrior Government in Early Medieval Japan.* New Haven, Conn.: Yale University Press, 1974.

Morris, I. *The World of the Shining Prince.* Oxford: Oxford University Press, 1964.

Reischauer, E. O. *Japan: The Story of a Nation.* London: Duckworth, 1970.

Tiedemann, A. E., ed. *An Introduction to Japanese Civilization.* New York: Columbia University Press, 1974.

Totman, C. *Japan Before Perry: A Short History.* Berkeley: University of California Press, 1981.

# The Rise of Europe

The development of a distinctively European civilization occurred during the period that extended from the Germanic invasions of the Roman Empire to the establishment of the first European empire by Charlemagne in the early ninth century. The need to defend against further Muslim attacks, as well as Magyar and Viking incursions, caused major social and political changes in Europe. After surviving the challenges of the early Middle Ages, Europeans embarked in the eleventh century on an era of vigorous growth, the basis of which was economic expansion, urban development, political unification, and religious renewal. But the High Middle Ages (c. 1050–c. 1300) were also a time of bitter conflict—between popes and sovereigns, monarchs and feudal lords, Muslims and Christians, and Christians and Jews. The clash of cultures, religions, and political ideals profoundly changed the Western world.

**The Byzantine emperor Alexius Comnenus is best known for his appeal to the West for help in fighting the Turks, thus inaugurating the crusades. [Vatican Library, Rome]**

## Migration and Transformation

Generally, the invasions that transformed Europe between the fifth and ninth centuries pitted nomads against the inhabitants of settled communities and were thus a clash of distinctive lifestyles and cultures. Much of Europe and Asia was threatened by the nomads; only remote southern China and southern India eluded their grasp. The impact of the incursions was greatest in the West, partly because the nomads tended to migrate westward, where the land was more fertile and water was more plentiful and partly because the more advanced cultures of China and India resisted transformation.

The eastern Roman Empire, with its well-defended capital at Constantinople, its thriving economy, and its strong navy, survived the invasions, but by the end of the fifth century its western counterpart was gone, its lands fallen into the hands of Germanic rulers: the Visigoths in southern Gaul and Spain; the Ostrogoths in Italy; the Franks in northern Gaul; the Angles, Saxons, and Jutes in England; the Burgundians in the Rhône valley; and the Vandals in North Africa and the western Mediterranean.

Unlike the Romans whom they conquered, the Germans were at first organized in social units, as tribes based on kinship rather than a state founded on political rights and obligations. Whereas Roman laws were written, those of the Germans were unwritten and grounded in custom. German families were responsible for the conduct of the members of their household and thus played a crucial role in upholding the laws. The Germans elected their kings or tribal leaders as well as the chiefs who led the warriors into battle. In return for serving those chiefs, the warriors received weapons, subsistence, and a share of any spoils.

The Germans were superstitious people who feared chopping down trees because they were sacred or building bridges lest they anger river spirits. As nomads, their livelihood revolved around cattle raising, but as they settled on their new lands, they turned to farming, raising grain, beans, peas, and other vegetables. Over time the Germans assimilated some aspects of classical culture, including Roman language, law, and principles of government, thus creating a distinctively European society. The fusion of Germanic and classical elements was eased by the fact that the Visigoths, Ostrogoths, and Vandals had been introduced to Christianity before they migrated into Europe. They were, however, disciples of Arian Christianity, and it was not until about 500 that the Nicene Christianity of the Latin church began to make headway among the Germans following the conversion of Clovis, king of the Franks (481–511). With the sup-

port of the Gallo-Roman population, which was loyal to Nicene Christianity, Clovis expanded the Frankish kingdom until it extended from the Pyrenees to the Rhine and beyond.

## The Franks

The dynasty Clovis founded, called the Merovingian in honor of a legendary ancestor, attempted to govern the new state by reaching agreements with powerful nobles, who received the title of count in return for serving as royal officials. Frequently, however, their primary loyalty was not to the king but to their own interests. Merovingian attempts to challenge the power of the great landed magnates by making counts of talented but landless men proved unsuccessful. The dynasty was further undermined by the physical weakness of Clovis' successors. With kings too young to rule, authority was exercised by aristocratic mayors of the palace. For much of the sixth and seventh centuries the kingdom was plagued by civil war and conflicting loyalties. Fortunately for the Franks, unity had been restored by the early eighth century, when western Europe was threatened by new invaders, the Islamic Moors from North Africa. By 711 the Iberian peninsula was theirs. Turning next to Gaul, the Moors were finally rebuffed by the Frankish mayor of the palace, Charles Martel ("the Hammer"), near Tours in 732. The battle was less significant for the Muslims, who in crossing the Pyrenees had overextended themselves, than for the Franks, whose military prowess attracted papal attention. Although Charles had recruited powerful men by offering them grants of land seized from the church, the papacy needed an alliance with the Franks, who could protect Rome from the Byzantine emperor and the Lombards. Thus the stage was set for a historically significant relationship between the Franks and the papacy.

In 751 Charles' son and successor, Pepin the Short (751–768), deposed the Merovingian monarch and claimed the Frankish throne as his own. After the fact, he obtained papal approval for his action to make his usurpation seem legitimate. He repaid the debt in 754 by defending Rome from Lombard aggression and in addition granted certain Italian lands to the papacy. By this "donation" Pepin laid the foundation for a papal state in central Italy.

## Charlemagne

The dynasty founded by Pepin became known as the Carolingian (from Carolus, Latin for Charles). Its greatest ruler was Pepin's son Charlemagne ("Charles the

Great," 768–814). An extraordinary ruler, this warrior-king established an empire larger than any in Europe between that of Rome in the third century and that of Napoleon in the nineteenth. He crushed the Lombards and claimed their crown for himself when they tried to regain the land Pepin had given to the papacy. Against the Moors his gains were modest but strategic, consisting of a *march*, or frontier district, on the southern slopes of the Pyrenees. Repeated campaigns against the Saxons gave him control of much of what is now northern Germany, and in the southeast he overran Bavaria and then pushed back the nomadic Avars, from whom he seized the tribute they had exacted from the Byzantines. The Abbasid caliph in Baghdad sent him gifts that included spices, monkeys, and an elephant.

Despite his expanding empire, Charlemagne had no capital to rival Baghdad or Constantinople, so he determined to create a "second Rome" at Aachen (Aix-la-Chapelle) in the heart of his kingdom. Its layout and principal buildings were inspired by Rome, its royal chapel by the Byzantine church of San Vitale in Ravenna. The new capital became the center of a cultural renaissance Charlemagne sponsored not only to enhance the reputation of his realm but also to improve the quality of the clergy. To direct his palace school, Charlemagne recruited one of the foremost scholars of the age, Alcuin (c. 735–804), from Anglo-Saxon England. Charlemagne chose well, for Alcuin employed a curriculum inspired by Classical Rome and refined by European writers that became the model for education throughout medieval

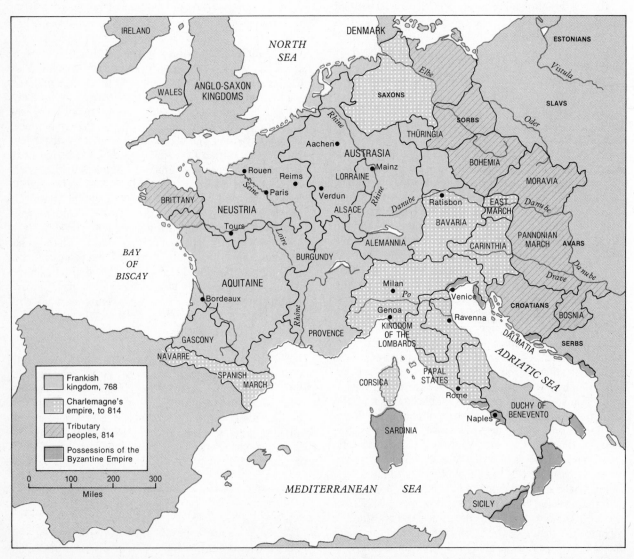

*13.1 The Empire of Charlemagne*

Europe. The seven liberal arts were divided into the trivium, comprising grammar, rhetoric, and logic, and the quadrivium, consisting of arithmetic, geometry, music, and astronomy. Other scholars were lured to Aachen, and Charlemagne, who could read but not write, acquired manuscripts of legal and religious works for his scribes to copy and distribute to the monasteries of the realm. His sister, Gisela, supervised a convent at Chelles, near Paris, that took a special interest in copying manuscripts. His scholars issued new editions of learned works and even developed a new, more readable script, called the Carolingian minuscule, from which modern scripts are derived. The manuscripts produced by these writers were studied by fifteenth-century scholars and thus influenced that later, more famous renaissance.

Charlemagne's apparent interest in being the equal of the Byzantine emperor culminated on Christmas Day in 800, against a backdrop of political intrigue. Three years earlier the emperor's mother, Irene, had blinded her son in order to rule herself. Charlemagne and Pope Leo III (795–816) seem to have regarded the Byzantine throne as vacant on the basis of Irene's sex. Some thought was apparently given to a marriage between Irene and Charlemagne, though nothing came of it. Then, in 799, the pope was kidnapped by political enemies; after he escaped, he sought Charlemagne's help to restore his control in Rome. Thus it was that the Frankish sovereign was in Rome on December 25, 800, when, following mass, Leo crowned him emperor of the Romans. The coronation strained relations with Constantinople, which claimed the imperial title solely for its own ruler. Not until 813 did both parties agree that Charles would be recognized as emperor of the Franks and the Byzantine sovereign as emperor of the Romans. For the West, the semantics were of little import, for the real significance of the Christmas coronation was the revival of the imperial tradition in the West and the question of ultimate authority raised by the way in which the crown was bestowed—from the pope to the emperor.

## Disintegration and Invasion

Had Charlemagne adhered to the Byzantine tradition, he would have bequeathed his empire to his eldest son. Instead, following the Frankish custom, he intended to divide his realm among his sons. Only one, however, survived him. Hoping to preserve most of the empire intact, Louis (814–840), Charlemagne's successor, designated his eldest son heir to the imperial title and promised his other two sons royal titles and the territories of

Aquitaine and Bavaria. Unsatisfied with this and egged on by their stepmother, the younger sons revolted against their father. By the time peace was agreed on in the Treaty of Verdun (843), Louis was dead and the empire was irrevocably fragmented. Between the western and eastern kingdoms, out of which eventually emerged France and Germany, was a middle kingdom that retained the imperial title and extended from the modern Netherlands into Italy. The middle kingdom was divided into three realms in 855.

As the Frankish states struggled to survive, new waves of invaders struck Europe. From North Africa, Arab raiders, emboldened by improved naval power, began attacking the islands of the Mediterranean and even southern France, Italy, and the great Alpine passes in what is now Switzerland. The revived militance stemmed from newly independent Muslim states in Egypt, Tunisia, and Spain following the decline of the Baghdad caliphate. Before the ninth century was over, the Mediterranean was virtually a Muslim lake.

Byzantine miscalculation was responsible for the invasion of eastern Europe by the Magyars, a nomadic people from central Asia. In 896 the Byzantines encouraged the Magyars to attack the troublesome Bulgars, but the latter outwitted the Byzantines by persuading the Pechenegs, Turkic nomads from the area around the Volga River, to attack the Magyars. Instead of fighting the Bulgars, the Magyars moved west, invading Germany, France, and Italy and plundering virtually at will. Not until 955 were they defeated by the army of the German king, Otto I, but they retained control of the great Hungarian plain. There they gradually settled down, established their own kingdom, and converted to Christianity.

A third group of invaders, the Norsemen or Vikings, came from Scandinavia, not on horseback like the Asian nomads but in swift, mobile ships. As early as 793, Viking raiders had destroyed the monastery at Lindisfarne, which had been instrumental in converting northern England to Christianity. In the century that followed, the Vikings struck freely, sacking the coastal regions of Europe and sailing up rivers to reach such cities as Paris and Hamburg. They even plundered the Muslim city of Seville in Spain and Italian towns reached by ships that sailed into the Mediterranean. Vikings struck out across the Atlantic to Iceland and Greenland, both of which they settled, and North America. The reasons for this activity varied: some Vikings were clearly in search of land for new settlements, but others apparently regarded the raids as an appropriate prelude to a settled life or as a means to establish new trade routes. Norsemen from Sweden, in fact, used the rivers of Russia to make contact with the Byzantines and the Persians.

The Vikings established settlements at Kiev in Russia, on the coast of Ireland, in northeastern England, and along the lower Seine River in northwestern France, a

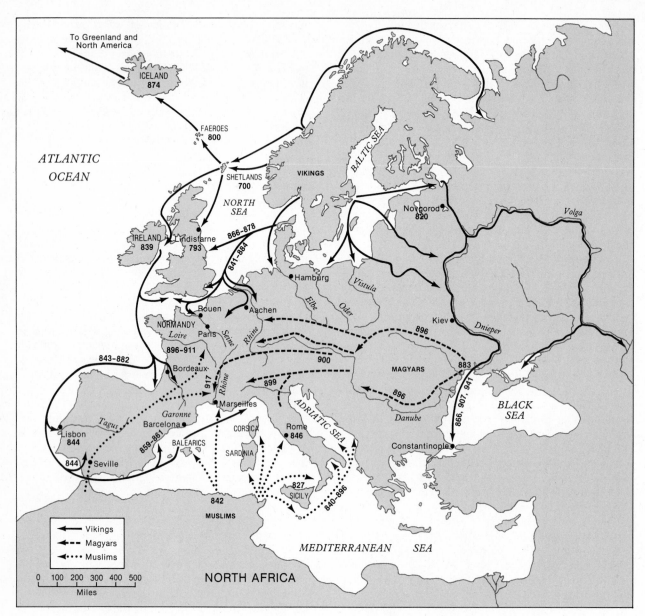

*13.2 Viking, Magyar, and Muslim Invasions*

region later called Normandy. In the eleventh century descendants from that area seized control of southern Italy and Sicily, and in 1066 William, duke of Normandy, conquered England. As the Normans settled, they embraced Christianity and European culture.

# Feudal Society

The breakup of the Carolingian empire and the impact of the various invasions caused changes in European lifestyles and governments. As royal authority ebbed, landowners were forced to turn elsewhere for protection, thereby providing the nobility with the opportunity to increase its power. The nobles ruled their districts with miniature governments of their own, dispensing justice, collecting fees, raising troops, and sometimes minting money. The heart of this way of governing was the personal bond: whereas in modern society we owe allegiance to a state, in the early medieval world allegiance was rendered to a person, and that person was in turn bound to fulfill his or her part of the contractual arrangement.

## Lords and Vassals: The Feudal Aristocracy

In the Merovingian age free landowners seeking protection offered their lands to more powerful men and agreed to serve them. The former were known as vassals. In return for their service, they were allowed to live in the lord's household or were given money or the use of land, called fiefs. Normally the most important service was military, for together the vassals comprised the lord's private army, which offered protection to its collective members. Vassals were also expected to perform other duties, such as serve on the lord's court or provide him with hospitality. As these feudal arrangements developed, various safeguards were added. In eleventh-century France, for example, the normal amount of military service required of a vassal each year was 40 days. A vassal could receive fiefs from a variety of lords, thereby raising the question of which lord had first claim on his obedience. This was resolved by designating a liege lord as the one to whom primary obedience was due. Vassals with substantial landholdings could create vassals of their own. Thus the feudal order was not a neat hierarchical arrangement but a complex web of loyalties and obligations, the total effect of which was to decentralize power.

Because fiefs were normally inherited, they could be acquired by women. Yet a woman could not perform the required military service, so she had to have a husband. Younger sons, who normally had no fief to inherit, often married such an heiress as a means of acquiring a place in the feudal order. Women exercised an important role in feudal society, managing the family estates while their husbands were away and sometimes even defending their castles or fortified manor houses if they were attacked. Legally, however, a woman could not buy or sell property or even appear in court in her own right. Yet as the wife of a noble or a knight, she enjoyed considerable status in the community and could normally expect the deference of her social inferiors, male or female.

People who held fiefs comprised the landed aristocracy, a hereditary group that ranged from the least significant vassals to powerful dukes and magnates. Wherever they ranked in this spectrum, nobles and knights were characterized by a devotion to fighting, jousting, and hunting; a lifestyle based on the labor of others; and distinctive social customs, such as the ritual dubbing of a knight. A few nobles were so powerful as to be virtually independent, but most nobles and all knights owed obligations to monarchs or princes; at the same time, all aristocrats exercised authority over others, including the peasants. The nobles could raise and command troops, and some could even coin money. All members of the landed aristocracy had the right to hold courts, even if it was only at the manorial level for the knights.

In return for these privileges the nobles and knights were supposed to protect both the church and the common people. The values espoused by the landed aristocracy included courage, loyalty, physical strength, and generosity. They measured their status in terms of the number, size, and wealth of their fiefs and the amount of authority they exercised over others, especially vassals. Their homes, ranging from castles to fortified manor houses, were another indication of their status.

The impact of the feudal order on monarchs was considerable. Although kings were normally the most substantial landowners, with vassals who owed them military and other forms of service, in some states the nobles were more powerful than their monarchical lords. In such places a king was only as dominant as his great vassals allowed him to be, for as long as they collectively refused his bidding, he had no other army to enforce his will. In Germany the substantial size of the Magyar armies meant that the nobles could not marshal adequate defenses; hence the kings actually increased their influence, as exemplified by Otto I's revival of the imperial tradition. In western Europe, by contrast, the smallness and swiftness of the Viking raiding parties enhanced the power of local lords, who could respond more quickly to the threat than the kings could. Japan experienced a similar development beginning in the twelfth century, as the emperors increasingly lost power to hereditary warrior-aristocrats; the latter's power was based, as in Europe, on the vassals who comprised their armies. In both systems, the personal bond of loyalty was crucial, and the power of the central government was clearly limited.

## The Early Medieval Peasantry

Beyond their impact on government, the invasions altered the economy of Europe. Muslim domination of the Mediterranean did not eliminate Europe's trade with the East, but it did substantially reduce shipping and profits. This in turn adversely affected European towns, particularly in coastal areas. The population of early medieval Europe became overwhelmingly rural, with peasants comprising up to 90 percent of the population.

Seeking protection and a livelihood from the large landowners, the free peasants gradually lost their lands and became dependent. Most peasants worked on large estates or manors, which became the basic social and economic unit at the local level. These manors were essentially descended from the Roman *latifundia* (see Chapter 6). In return for labor services for the owner, peasant families received the right to till tracts on the manor for their own sustenance and profit. Such arrangements allowed them considerable security—housing, land, and food—but bound them to the land; serfs (villeins) could not leave the manor without prior permission from their lord. In addition to the agricultural labor and other services that peasants owed, they were obliged to pay fines (often in produce or livestock) to the lord of the manor for the opportunity to marry someone from another manor, for a son to inherit the right to his father's lands on the manor, or for the use of the lord's mill to grind grain.

The conditions of peasant life varied greatly. Many peasants retained their freehold farms and their freedom and were quite prosperous, while others possessed few rights and were forced to endure abject poverty. The peasant diet was invariably simple, with black bread the primary staple. There was normally little meat, though poaching wild game was fairly common, and the more fortunate peasants periodically ate pork. Fish was available fresh to those who lived near water, or otherwise in salted form. The basic vegetables were cabbage, peas, carrots, turnips, and onions; fruit, apart from wild berries and nuts, was available only rarely. Peasants lucky enough to have sheep, goats, or cows could make cheese, and those with chickens could eat eggs. Southern Europeans normally drank wine, whereas their northern counterparts quenched their thirst with beer, perhaps three gallons a day or more for peasants toiling in the fields.

The typical peasant household consisted of a nuclear family—a parent or parents and children. Most peasants seem to have married in their early twenties and, with the church's encouragement, tried to raise families. Better-off peasants lived in houses with several rooms, but the poor had to make do with one-room, earthen-floored cottages. Normally constructed of mud or clay, such homes had a thatched roof, a fireplace, and no windows. The living space sometimes had to be shared with animals, and peasants lived in the knowledge that their lords had the right to raze their houses and move them elsewhere. Most peasants probably never left their village, the focal point of which was the parish church, site of most of life's major events—baptism, marriage, feast days, and funerals. The peasants had no say in the selection of their priest, a function normally exercised by the manorial lord, but most priests worked in the fields and thus had some bond with their parishioners. In time many villages organized confraternities, religious societies that combined devotion with the provision of charity and care for the sick. Standards of peasant behavior were determined by the church and the manorial lord; aside from religious obligations, manorial customs were the only law most peasants knew. But rural society was neither static nor uniform, and regional variations could be considerable. As new lands were opened up, usually by clearing forests or draining swamps, landowners lured peasant settlers by offering them improved living conditions, but for most peasants life was undoubtedly harsh.

Peasant women not only had to perform the typical child-rearing and household duties but also worked in the fields with the men and cared for the animals. On the manors the women did everything but plow. Their chief obligations in life were to bear and raise children; produce, prepare, and serve food; and manage the family's resources to enable it to exist from harvest to harvest. Women endured a life of hard toil with little amusement other than drinking, perhaps watching cockfights, and amusing themselves on the numerous holy days that dotted the church calendar. Their lives, like those of their families, must in some cases have begun to improve, however marginally, as the result of better economic conditions in the High Middle Ages.

# New Foundations: Economic Expansion

The dramatic achievements of the High Middle Ages— urban growth, the organization of guilds and universities, the construction of majestic cathedrals and guildhalls, and the revival of monarchical authority—were possible only because of the large-scale economic expansion that grew out of an agricultural revival that began in the tenth century. The development of the three-field system and crop rotation; the use of horses, properly harnessed and shoe-clad, and of fertilizer; the recovery of new land by deforestation and drainage; and the increased use of heavy wheeled plows, metal tools, and windmills permitted Europeans to produce more food with less human labor. This in turn opened up possibilities for some people to specialize in manufacturing or commerce and for some landowners to plant crops, such as flax and hemp, that were not needed for basic sustenance. Others converted their land from tillage to pasturage, specializing in sheep, cattle, or horses, sometimes even cross-breeding to improve their stock.

Agricultural and pastoral developments spurred both a rise in population and the growth of manufacturing and commerce. In the year 1000 the population of Europe, including Russia, was approximately 38 million—small in comparison to Sung China's 100 million. By the early fourteenth century, however, Europe's population had doubled. No town in western or central Europe, with the exception of several in Muslim Spain, had as many as 50,000 people in the year 1000, though in the East, Constantinople had a population of some 300,000. In the ensuing three centuries, however, agricultural and commercial advances and the economic boom fostered by the crusades made it possible for towns to develop rapidly throughout Europe. Europeans again began to participate extensively in the major trade routes that ex-

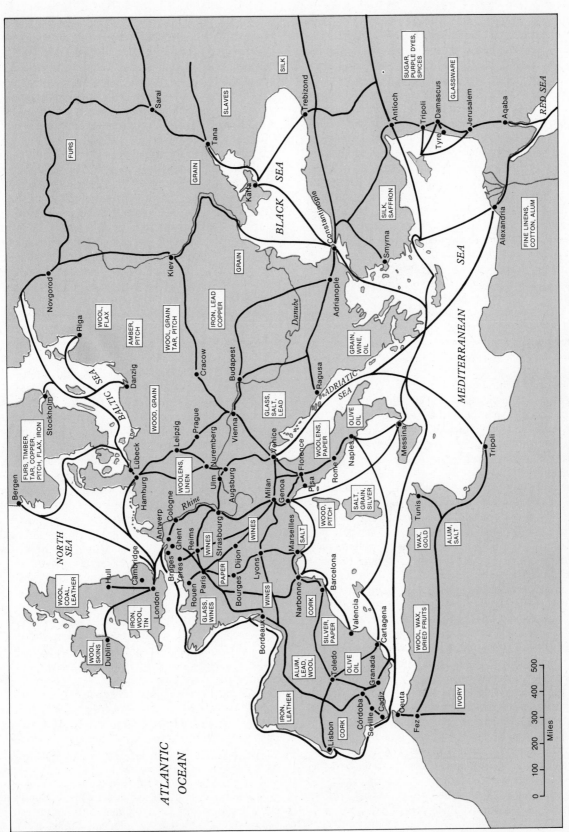

**13.3 Primary Trade Routes of Europe, c. 1300**

ATLANTIC OCEAN

NORTH SEA

BALTIC SEA

BLACK SEA

ADRIATIC SEA

MEDITERRANEAN SEA

RED SEA

*Rhine*

*Danube*

FURS

WOOL, FLAX

AMBER, PITCH

WOOL, GRAIN TAR, PITCH

IRON, LEAD COPPER

GRAIN

SILK

SLAVES

GRAIN

SILK, SAFFRON

SUGAR PURPLE DYES, SPICES

GLASSWARE

FINE LINENS, COTTON, ALUM

FURS, TIMBER, TAR, COPPER, PITCH, FLAX, IRON

WOOD, GRAIN

WOOLENS, LINEN

GLASS, SALT, LEAD

WOOLENS, PAPER

OLIVE OIL

GRAIN, WINE, OIL

WOOL, COAL, LEATHER

IRON, WOOL, TIN

WOOL, SKINS

WINES

PAPER

GLASS, WINES

WINES

WINES

SALT

WOOD, PITCH

SALT, GRAIN, SILVER

WAX, GOLD

ALUM, SALT

CORK

SILVER, PAPER

ALUM, LEAD, WOOL

OLIVE OIL

IRON, LEATHER

CORK

WOOL, WAX, DRIED FRUITS

IVORY

Bergen
Stockholm
Novgorod
Riga
Danzig
Lübeck
Hamburg
Sarai
Tana
Kaffa
Trebizond
Antioch
Tripoli
Damascus
Tyre
Jerusalem
Aqaba
Alexandria
Constantinople
Adrianople
Smyrna
Kiev
Cracow
Budapest
Prague
Leipzig
Nuremberg
Ulm
Augsburg
Vienna
Venice
Ragusa
Florence
Pisa
Naples
Rome
Messina
Tripoli
Tunis
Milan
Genoa
Cologne
Antwerp
Ghent
Bruges
Ypres
Reims
Strasbourg
Dijon
Lyons
Marseilles
Narbonne
Barcelona
Valencia
Cartagena
Hull
Cambridge
London
Dublin
Rouen
Paris
Bourges
Bordeaux
Toledo
Granada
Cádiz
Seville
Córdoba
Lisbon
Ceuta
Fez

Miles
0   100   200   300   400   500

tended from England and Scandinavia to India and China, especially the commerce that had developed in the Mediterranean in the tenth and eleventh centuries. Byzantine, Muslim, and Jewish merchants remained active throughout much of Europe, but they were soon surpassed by western Europeans, especially the Italians.

Much of the commerce of the High Middle Ages was conducted at annual fairs that lasted up to six weeks. Local markets handled weekly retail sales; the international fairs involved primarily wholesale transactions and were carefully regulated. The most influential of these were held under the aegis of the counts of Champagne six times a year. Merchants from as far away as Italy and the Balkan region were attracted to these fairs because of their strategic location at the crossroads of the European trade routes and the protection they were offered by the counts. Transactions at the fairs required the development of more sophisticated business practices, including the use of standard weights and measures, and the evolution of an international mercantile law.

Because the fairs were international in scope, money-changers were also needed. Customarily seated on benches (*bancs*), these exchange specialists became known as bankers. They accepted deposits and were instrumental in instigating the use of paper credit, which was especially helpful in facilitating the distribution of goods over long distances and in encouraging commercial transactions when bullion and coins were in short supply. Eventually governments found it advantageous to finance some of their activities by credit. These developments collectively led to the emergence of capitalism.

Commercial expansion stimulated the development of new organizations to meet the demand for products of all types and to facilitate international trade. Partnerships became commonplace, despite one serious limitation: the responsibility of each partner for the total indebtedness of the firm in the event of default. Because of this drawback, partnerships such as the Bardi and Peruzzi of Florence were usually formed only by family members, perhaps with a few close associates. An alternative was the *commenda*, a business association in which an investor provided capital to a merchant in return for a share of the profits but which limited the investor's potential loss to the funds he had invested. Merchants and artisans also organized in guilds. On a much larger scale, beginning in the twelfth century, various cities joined forces in commercial leagues designed to promote their interests. On occasion such a league, or *hansa*, became embroiled in political and military affairs. Among the most important of these confederacies were the Hanseatic League of North German cities and the Rhenish League, the leader of which was Cologne.

The increase in trade stimulated industrial production, particularly cloth manufacturing. English and Frisian cloth was sold throughout Europe by the ninth century, in Russia by the eleventh. The major textile centers of the High Middle Ages were in Flanders and eventually northern Italy. By 1300 Florence had some 200 workshops devoted to the manufacture of woolens. Less advanced than the sophisticated metal industries in China, those in Europe, which produced weapons, armor, tools, and cutlery, nevertheless expanded in this period, thanks especially to renewed interest in mining. The old Roman mines had had shafts as deep as 500 feet, but work in them had ceased in the sixth century. Until the tenth and eleventh centuries most of the digging was in shallow pits, but during the High Middle Ages mining was again pursued seriously, especially along the eastern Alps and in Bohemia, England, and northern Spain. In addition to gold and silver—crucial for the expansion of coinage—European mines produced tin, copper, mercury, iron, and coal. Productivity was gradually improved by the adoption of such technological devices as pulleys, cranks, and pumps and the harnessing of waterpower to crush the ore. Larger supplies of bullion made it possible to mint coins in higher values; pennies were increasingly coined out of copper instead of silver. Gold coins were issued by Emperor Frederick II in Sicily in 1231, followed shortly thereafter by Florence (1252), Genoa (1254), and other Italian cities.

In addition to textiles and metals, European artisans manufactured such items as leather goods, paper (primarily in Italy and Spain, although it was a Chinese invention), plate and blown glass (especially in Venice), and stained glass (France). Maritime states had shipbuilding industries, and some coastal cities, such as Venice and Marseilles, produced salt by evaporating seawater. Throughout Europe the food industry developed as people specialized in salting fish, curing meat, brewing, making wine, and milling grain. The building industry flourished, particularly beginning in the eleventh century, when it became fashionable north of the Alps to use stone instead of wood and plaster for major construction, such as cathedrals, castles, and town halls.

The manufacture of textiles and metals as well as the construction of large buildings required capital, reliable transportation, adequate supplies of raw materials, and a skilled labor force. All of this was possible only in a climate that could offer reasonable security and legal protection; hence industrial expansion and the reappearance of reasonably stable governments went hand in hand. Trade and industry provided the revenues without which effective governments could not exist, and the authorities, in turn, had to maintain conditions conducive to the further development of commerce and manufacturing. The High Middle Ages achieved dramatic progress because of the fortunate combination of agricultural expansion, technological and commercial development, and increasing political stability.

# Urban Development and Town Life

The eleventh through thirteenth centuries witnessed extraordinary urban growth in western and central Europe that provided many people with an alternative to rural living. This growth was prompted by the expansion of trade and manufacturing to meet the needs of a rising population, which was fostered in turn by the agricultural revolution and the revival of extensive commerce throughout the Mediterranean.

No single factor accounts for the development of medieval cities. Some, such as Rome, Marseilles, and Bordeaux, were rebuilt on the decayed foundations of old Roman cities and administrative centers. Ports such as Pisa and Genoa recovered in the aftermath of Lombard and Arab domination, particularly once their fleets had increased. Because the growth of cities reflected the expansion of trade, many were located at the sites of natural harbors, such as Barcelona or Naples; on major rivers, such as London (on the Thames) and Cologne (on the Rhine); or at strategic locations astride major trade routes, such as Milan, Prague, and Vienna. Some cities, such as Bruges and Cambridge, emerged where key bridges crossed rivers. Many towns developed where people congregated for protection in fortified settlements, a trend commemorated in names ending in *fort* or *furt*, *burg*, or *borough*: Frankfurt, Hamburg, Augsburg, and Edinburgh are examples. An ecclesiastical center could serve as the nucleus of an emerging town; Paris and Rouen were not only seats of bishops but also sites of important monasteries.

The largest medieval cities—Paris, Venice, Florence, Naples, Milan, and Genoa—probably never exceeded 100,000 inhabitants in the High Middle Ages, and the Flemish cities of Bruges, Ghent, and Ypres, as well as London and Cologne, were roughly half their size. Apart from Cologne, the largest German towns, such as Hamburg and Augsburg, had fewer than 30,000 people. Asian cities were much larger: in the twelfth century, China had 52 cities with more than 100,000 *households*! Ch'ang An, the imperial capital of T'ang China, the world's largest city, had some 2 million residents. In the Middle East, Cairo's population reached 500,000 by 1300, and the largest Muslim cities of late medieval Spain were nearly as big.

The traditional description of medieval European cities as overcrowded is often an exaggeration, though space within the city walls soon came to be at a premium. Beyond the walls there was open space adjacent to the city where residents could farm or build homes. Some cities erected new walls as necessary, but wall construction and maintenance consumed a considerable portion of the urban budget. It was also possible to expand vertically, and medieval builders typically made each successive story wider than the one below, with the result that many streets received little sunlight. Pollution was common, as refuse of all types, including human excrement, was routinely dumped in the streets. Horses, dogs, and oxen added their own dung. The popularity of ale was no doubt partly due to the prevalence of contaminated water (a phenomenon sometimes blamed on Jews because of the myth that their shadows polluted wells). Fires were a severe hazard wherever buildings were made of wood. In the absence of urban planning, medieval cities were like mazes, their winding streets and narrow alleys a bizarre mixture of fortified houses, shops, and the ramshackle shanties of the poor.

Whatever their drawbacks, the towns were the achievement of a new social order, the burghers or bourgeoisie—the urban merchants who took their place beside the aristocracy, the clergy, and the peasants. In some circles the newcomers were by no means welcome: a fourteenth-century English preacher thundered that "God made the clergy, knights, and laborers, but the devil made townsmen and usurers." The point, of course, was that the traditional social orders had little understanding of the merchants' role in the economy, for they neither tilled the land, provided military protection, nor ministered to spiritual needs. Although many merchants and artisans originally came from humble backgrounds, in time some of them acquired substantial wealth and eventually rivaled the aristocracy. Wedded to the land and steeped in tradition, however, most nobles treated the merchants with disdain, though in Italy the lesser aristocracy moved to the towns and allied with their inhabitants against the greater nobility and the bishops.

The lure of the towns was due in no small measure to the privileges set forth in their charters. These were usually granted by lords, nobles as well as monarchs, who were interested in potential tax revenues or income from the sale of charters. In cities such as Cologne, Mainz, and Liège, however, the townspeople had to rebel to secure their charters. The heart of the typical charter was the assurance of personal freedom for anyone who lived in the town for a year and a day. Charters typically guaranteed the people the right to hold markets and often to govern themselves, even to the point of making and enforcing their own laws to regulate commerce. Towns normally had to pay a stipulated sum to their overlords each year, but usually the citizens determined the taxes they would levy on themselves.

Although townspeople were personally free, urban governments were not democratic. Power customarily rested with the prosperous merchants and master artisans. Control was exercised not only through town councils but also through the guilds, groups of persons pursuing the same economic activity that were organized first by merchants in the eleventh century and then by

## ◉ The Rights of a French Town ◉

*The attractiveness of medieval towns was based in large part on the charters that set forth their privileges. A representative sample is found in the charter granted to the French town of Lorris, near Orléans, by Louis VII in 1155.*

1. Every one who has a house in the parish of Lorris shall pay . . . sixpence only for his house, and for each acre of land that he possesses in the parish.

2. No inhabitant of the parish of Lorris shall be required to pay a toll or any other tax on his provisions; and let him not be made to pay any measurage fee on the grain which he has raised by his own labor.

3. No burgher shall go on an expedition, on foot or on horseback, from which he cannot return the same day to his home if he desires. . . .

6. No person while on his way to the fairs and markets of Lorris, or returning, shall be arrested or disturbed, unless he shall have committed an offense on the same day. . . .

9. No one . . . shall exact from the burghers of Lorris any tallage, tax, or subsidy. . . .

16. No one shall be detained in prison if he can furnish surety that he will present himself for judgment. . . .

18. Any person who shall dwell a year and a day in the parish of Lorris, without any claim having pursued him there, and without having refused to lay his case before us or our provost, shall abide there freely and without molestation.

*Source:* F. A. Ogg, *A Source Book of Mediaeval History* (New York: Cooper Square, 1907), pp. 328–330.

artisans in the 1100s. As the craft guilds developed, they insisted on at least sharing city government with the merchant guilds. Because the guilds were so well organized, they virtually dominated government affairs, particularly since they could vote as a bloc and thereby elect their own leaders to city offices. Town government thus perpetuated the power of the guilds.

The guilds were designed to protect the interests of their members by restricting membership, limiting competition, and setting prices. In effect, a guild enjoyed a monopoly over a particular craft or trade and controlled prices; yet consumers benefited too in that the guild regulated quality. Guilds performed important social functions, such as training apprentices to become journeymen and possibly master craftsmen and guild members. Some guilds also provided basic education for members' children. The guilds aided needy members or their families, providing health care and financial assistance, particularly for victims of fire and flood as well as for widows and orphans. Some guilds, especially those involved with textiles or brewing, included women. Religion often played an important part in guild life, whether in activities honoring their favorite saints,

in charitable donations to local churches, or in the construction and maintenance of their own churches and chapels. Guilds rivaled the church in their pageantry, particularly by their great feasts and public processions. Modern-day visitors to Venice can still see some of these pageants reenacted, complete with medieval costumes.

The guilds could not absorb all who wished to enter; hence as peasants kept flocking to the towns, many could find employment only as unskilled laborers. Poorly paid, devoid of political rights, and often barely able to survive, they constituted the proletariat. Although they were nominally free, few had any chance of improving their social status.

## The Growth of Monarchy: England and France

No sovereigns made more effective use of the improved economic conditions to enhance their power than the rulers of England and France, particularly through their efforts to establish internal security and their interest in legal reform. In both countries the dominant political theme of the High Middle Ages was the struggle of the crown to establish a position of authority reasonably secure from the claims of the church on the one hand and the powerful feudal aristocracy on the other. Simultaneously, the seeds were also sown for the bitter conflict between the two countries that lasted for centuries.

## The Norman Conquest

One of the most significant dates in English history is 1066, the year William, duke of Normandy, defeated the last Anglo-Saxon monarch, Harold, at the battle of Hastings to seize the English crown. The Norman Conquest brought some fundamental changes to England, principally the imposition of a Norman-French feudal aristocracy that owed military allegiance directly to the new king and was thus more centralized than its French counterpart. The Anglo-Saxon nobility disappeared, and England was henceforth governed by Normans. Nevertheless, William shrewdly opted to retain most Anglo-Saxon laws and institutions, including some of the traditional courts and the sheriffs. The royal council, the Witan, however, was replaced by the Great Council, an advisory body and court of feudal law, and its nucleus, the Small Council, composed of the king's principal advisers and officials. One of William's most remarkable accomplishments was a detailed survey of landed property in England—the Domesday Book—probably undertaken with a view to ensuring a complete collection of taxes. William also extended royal control over the church, gradually replacing Anglo-Saxon bishops and abbots with Normans.

During the reign of William's great-grandson, Henry II (1154–1189), the territory in France under English control increased dramatically. In addition to Normandy, Henry inherited Maine, Touraine, and Anjou from his father, the count of Anjou, and added Aquitaine and Poitou by virtue of his marriage to Eleanor, duchess of Aquitaine. The Angevin empire, as all this was called, stretched from the Scottish border to the Pyrenees and included more than half of France. In feudal terms, however, Henry held his French lands as a vassal of the French king.

❁

## ELEANOR OF AQUITAINE: COURT POLITICS AND COURTLY LOVE

In her life Eleanor linked several of the major themes of the High Middle Ages—the political struggles of France and England, the crusades, and the courtly love tradition.* Born in 1122, Eleanor, the daughter and heiress of William X, duke of Aquitaine, inherited the ducal title at the age of 15. Her guardian, King Louis VI, arranged her marriage to his son, who succeeded to the French throne as Louis VII in August 1137. When Louis, a deeply pious man, set out on the Second Crusade in the summer of 1147, Eleanor too "took the cross" as her grandfather, William IX, had done in the First Crusade. At Antioch, after long conversations with her uncle Raymond, Eleanor shocked Louis by announcing that their relationship was illegitimate because of their blood ties. Whether Eleanor was now sexually unfaithful, as the king's friends charged, is impossible to prove, but Louis forced her to remain with him, and she undoubtedly was with the crusaders when they reached Jerusalem.

Papal intervention kept the royal couple together until March 1152, when their marriage was finally annulled. Happy to be rid of Louis, who was "more monk than king," Eleanor married Henry Plantagenet two months later. When Henry succeeded to the English throne in 1154, she was crowned queen of England. Having already had two daughters by Louis, she gave Henry eight more children, among them two future kings of England, Richard I and John. As a political force to be reckoned with during her first decade in England, Eleanor served as regent when Henry was out of the country. Beginning in 1163, however, she was largely reduced to ceremonial functions, and in 1168 Henry dispatched her to Aquitaine to govern her duchy. Eleven years her junior, Henry was left free to pursue an affair with his mistress. Eleanor schemed to use her children to get revenge on Henry. Unwittingly, he played into her hands in 1169 by dividing his continental lands among his sons, giving them a base from which to oppose him. An exasperated Henry finally placed Eleanor in captivity in 1174, thus keeping her from actively supporting her sons when they rebelled against him in 1183. Henry even seems to have toyed with the notion of forcing her into a convent. She appeared in court on rare occasions in the mid-1180s, but her official release came only when Henry died in July 1189.

At Poitiers in the 1160s Eleanor presided over the beginnings of the courtly love tradition, with its exaltation of women. Although experts debate the extent of her role as a patron of literature and art, the roots of courtly love were undoubtedly in her court; the tradition really flourished for the first time at the court of her eldest daughter, Marie of Champagne, patroness of Chrétien de Troyes, author of five Arthurian romances. This emphasis on love, music, and poetry was something of a family tradition that dated back to Eleanor's

---

*The crusades are discussed later in this chapter, the courtly love tradition in Chapter 14.

grandfather, William IX, reputedly the first troubadour. The troubadours who gathered at her court to sing her praises eventually spread their passionate lyrics throughout much of France, England, Spain, and Sicily.

Eleanor virtually governed England until Richard I (1189–1199), who had been estranged from his father, arrived in the country. Close to Richard, she exercised considerable power throughout his reign, especially after he was captured while returning from the Third Crusade. In addition to raising funds for his ransom, she called on the pope to help free Richard, whom she depicted as "the soldier of Christ." Four months after Richard's return, she retired to Fontevrault Abbey in western France in June 1194. She was buried there ten years later in a nun's habit.

## Law and Monarchy in Norman England

Significant reforms in law and administration were undertaken during the reigns of Henry I and Henry II. The former shifted administrative authority from feudal barons to persons of lesser rank who operated under the direction of a new official called the justiciar. The justiciar's court, known as the Exchequer, performed judicial and administrative tasks but became noted for its role as the royal treasury and the accounting arm of the government. The two kings were instrumental in the emergence of common law, a body of legal principles based on custom and judicial precedents, uniformly applicable throughout England and administered by royal judges. In contrast, the civil law that increasingly prevailed throughout much of the European continent was derived from Roman law, especially as set forth in Justinian's

*Corpus Juris Civilis.* English royal justice was not only legally superior to that dispensed in the local courts but more popular as well, and people were willing to purchase writs (legal orders) to have their cases decided by panels of jurors over which the crown's judges presided. In addition to operating a court at Westminster, the kings dispatched justices on regular circuits throughout the country. Because of the crown's role as the source of justice, the itinerant judges claimed the right to intervene in both feudal and local courts, thus furthering the notion of a common law. Henry II required residents to appear before these justices to report alleged criminals, a practice that later evolved into the modern grand jury. Henry also instituted the grand assize, which gave persons whose land titles were challenged the opportunity to have their cases judged by a jury in a royal court rather than by compurgation (the oaths of neighbors) or ordeal (trial by combat) in a feudal court.

Henry II's efforts to impose legal reforms on the church provoked a major confrontation. He was troubled in particular that the clergy had the right to be tried and sentenced in church courts, where the penalties were considerably less severe than those imposed in secular courts; a bishop's court, for instance, did not impose the death penalty. The Constitutions of Clarendon, which he issued in 1164, prohibited legal appeals to Rome without the king's permission, required that clergy convicted of a secular crime be sentenced in a royal court, and provided basic rights to laity tried in ecclesiastical courts. Thomas à Becket (1118–1170), whom Henry had appointed archbishop of Canterbury, rejected any notion of clerics' being subject to a secular court. After spending six years in exile because of his opposition, Becket was allowed to return to England, only to incur more of

**Effigy of Eleanor of Aquitaine at Fontevrault Abbey, Normandy. [Giraudon/Art Resource]**

**Knights of King Henry II murdered Archbishop Thomas à Becket in the cathedral at Canterbury in 1170. This illustration is from a fourteenth-century mansucript. [British Tourist Authority]**

Henry's wrath when he excommunicated bishops loyal to the king. When Henry, in a fit of anger, asked if no one would rid him of "this troublesome priest," four knights murdered Becket in Canterbury Cathedral. In the storm of outrage that ensued, Henry was forced to yield on two crucial points: clergy would be tried and sentenced in church courts, and appeals could still be made to the papal court.

The church and the barons each won a major victory during the reign of King John (1199–1216), who quarreled with Pope Innocent III (1198–1216) over a disputed election to the archbishopric of Canterbury. The pope, rejecting the candidates of both the king and the cathedral chapter at Canterbury, insisted on the appointment of a third candidate, Stephen Langton. When John balked, Innocent excommunicated him and placed England under an interdict, severely restricting religious services to the people. Faced with widespread unrest and the threat of a French invasion, John capitulated, even agreeing to the pope's demand that he hold England as a papal fief.

With the church controversy settled, John deter-mined to invade France to regain the territory north of the Loire River that Philip II had taken. Although John had the support of the Holy Roman Empire and Flanders, his French vassals refused to fight against Philip, their supreme lord, and Philip crushed the imperial and Flemish forces at Bouvines (1214). The financial demands of the war had forced John to use extreme measures to raise money, thereby violating the feudal rights of his barons. In June 1215 at Runnymede, on the banks of the Thames River, the barons resorted to their feudal right of armed force to compel him to accept a charter— the Magna Carta—affirming their rights. Far from being a charter of rights in the modern sense, the Magna Carta served as an affirmation of feudal principles, though some of its provisions touched the clergy, the peasants, and the townsfolk. Among other things, the charter limited feudal payments, promised the church freedom from royal interference, restricted fines on peasants, and confirmed the special privileges of London and other boroughs. The real significance of the Magna Carta was its embodiment of the principle that monarchs are subject to the law and can be constrained if they violate it. Beginning in the seventeenth century creative interpreters argued that it contained such principles as due process of law and the right of representation for those being taxed. Although John himself subsequently ignored the charter—with Innocent III's blessing—his medieval successors were repeatedly obliged to confirm revised versions of it.

Another important legal precedent was established in 1295 when Edward I (1272–1307) broadened the Great Council of nobles and prelates by summoning knights and representatives from the towns. The purpose of this Parliament, as it came to be called, was to secure support for taxes to fund a war against France. Edward justified his decision to consult this wider group on the basis of a principle used by the church in convening a general council: "What touches all should be approved by all." This principle also influenced the development of representative bodies in France and elsewhere.

## Capetian France

When Hugh Capet was elected king of France in 987, France was a patchwork of fiefs largely independent of royal authority. Hugh's own territory, the Île de France around Paris, was considerably smaller than that of the two vassals who flanked him, the duke of Normandy and the count of Champagne. Hugh, however, had two advantages over his vassals: his lordship over them in feudal theory and his consecration by the church in the coronation ceremony. The Île de France, moreover, was centrally located and the site of Paris, which in time became the greatest medieval city north of the Alps. The early Capetian monarchs improved their political for-

# ◉ The Magna Carta ◉

*The Magna Carta, to which King John of England affixed his seal, guaranteed the rights of nobles and others in a largely feudal society, but subsequent centuries interpreted the passages quoted here as guarantees of fundamental legal rights for all.*

1.  In the first place, we have granted to God, and by this our present charter confirmed for us and our heirs forever, that the English church shall be free, and shall hold its rights entire and its liberties uninjured. . . .

12.  No scutage [tax] or aid shall be imposed in our kingdom save by the common council of our kingdom, except for the ransoming of our body, for the making of our oldest son a knight, and for once marrying our oldest daughter; and for these purposes it shall be only a reasonable aid. . . .

13.  And the city of London shall have all its ancient liberties and free customs. . . . Moreover we will and grant that all other cities and boroughs and villages and ports shall have all their liberties and free customs. . . .

20.  A free man shall not be fined for a small offense, except in proportion to the gravity of the offense; and for a great offense he shall be fined in proportion to the magnitude of the offense, saving his freehold [i.e., except for the land he held without servile obligations]; and a merchant in the same way, saving [except for] his merchandise; and the villein shall be fined in the same way, saving his wainage [harvested crops set aside for seed], if he shall be at our mercy; and none of the above fines shall be imposed except by the oaths of honest men of the neighborhood. . . .

39.  No free man shall be taken, or imprisoned, or dispossessed, or outlawed, or banished, or in any way injured . . . except by the legal judgment of his peers, or by the law of the land.

40.  To no one will we sell, to no one will we deny or delay, right or justice.

*Source:* J. H. Robinson, ed., *Readings in European History*, vol. 1 (Boston: Ginn, 1904), pp. 234–237.

---

tunes by cultivating support from the church and by having their heirs crowned and given some governmental responsibility before they assumed the throne. The Capetians were fortunate in that they produced male heirs, most of whom reigned for relatively long periods. Although early Capetian authority in France was hardly extensive, it was stable. Beginning in the twelfth century the kings also wisely began to rely less on the greater nobles in the Île de France for their officials, preferring lesser nobles, clerics, and burghers whose loyalty to the throne was stronger.

By the time Philip II (1180–1223)—Philip Augustus, as he was called—became king, the gravest threat to the monarchy was posed by the English because of their extensive holdings in western France. Philip therefore devoted much of his attention to reducing English influence, an endeavor made easier by King John's domestic problems. French troops forced John to surrender

everything but Aquitaine and Gascony, more than trebling the territory under Philip's control. John's hope of winning his lands back with the help of imperial and Flemish allies was crushed on the battlefield at Bouvines in 1214.

Philip's domestic policies contributed significantly to the growth of monarchical power. Earlier kings had conferred land on local officials in return for their service, thus making many of their offices hereditary; many subsequently became venal and self-seeking. Philip restored greater royal control over local affairs by appointing new officers—known as bailiffs in the north and seneschals in the south—who worked for a salary and thus could be replaced as necessary. Moreover, they reported directly to Philip. He was careful, however, to insist that local customs be respected, a characteristic of French law until the nineteenth century. To fund his enlarged government, the king insisted on the full payment of feudal dues by his vassals, including special fees from those who did not render military service. By the end of his reign, his increase of royal revenues was no less impressive than his enlargement of the royal domain. He further enhanced his authority by issuing 78 town charters, thereby forging strong links between the townsfolk and the crown.

Philip's grandson, the saintly Louis IX (1226–1270), was distinguished by his devotion to Christian principles, symbolically represented by his washing of lepers' feet during Holy Week and his bestowal of alms to the poor. Few rulers have been as dedicated to justice, both in the workings of the royal courts and in his personal capacity as the source of French justice. One of the endearing images of medieval Europe is that of Louis sitting under an oak tree dispensing justice to all comers. More formally, Louis encouraged appeals from lower courts to the Parlement of Paris, which the king recognized as the highest tribunal in France. A concern for justice and good government also prompted Louis to appoint special commissioners to monitor the work of the bailiffs and seneschals. When conflict between wealthy merchants and artisans erupted in the towns, the king intervened to preserve order, an action that resulted in a decrease in the number of privileges the towns enjoyed. Louis made effective use of *ordonnances*, or royal decrees, to prohibit private warfare and dueling and to require the acceptance of royal money throughout France. But for all his accomplishments, Louis failed to continue Philip II's policy of reducing English influence in France.

Louis' grandson, Philip IV (1285–1314), "the Fair," was a cunning sovereign who sought to expand royal authority, in part by the vigorous use of itinerant members of the Parlement to extend royal justice throughout the realm at the expense of feudal courts. He also resumed hostilities against England, prohibiting Flemish towns from importing English wool. This endeavor failed, however, when Philip's army proved unable to defeat the rebellious Flemish cities. As military expenses mounted, Philip sought more revenue, imposing forced loans, debasing the coinage, and taxing the clergy.

This last policy sparked an explosive controversy with Pope Boniface VIII that pitted French national interests against traditional claims of papal supremacy. In his quest for funds, Philip not only expelled Jews and Italian moneylenders as a pretext to confiscate their property but also launched a vicious assault on the Knights Templars, a crusading order that had prospered from the donations of the pious and its involvement in banking activities. Accusing the Templars of assorted crimes ranging from heresy to black magic and homosexuality, Philip extracted confessions by torture and had the leading Templars burned at the stake. Although the papacy refused to allow Philip to take the Templars'

lands, he avoided having to repay the substantial debts he owed them.

The need for funds was also behind his decision to summon urban representatives to meet with his council of nobles and clergymen in 1302, thus marking the beginnings of a more representative assembly that later became known as the Estates General. In contrast to the English Parliament, the Estates General never became powerful enough to establish permanent control over the levying of taxes and thus to serve as an effective check on monarchical power. By the early fourteenth century, then, the French monarchy had substantially centralized authority at the expense of the feudal nobility, and in England, despite the success of the nobles in checking the growth of royal power in the 1200s, legal reform had done much to lay the foundation of a unified state.

## The Holy Roman Empire and the Church

Unlike their French and English counterparts, the German emperors of the High Middle Ages failed to lay the foundations of a unified German state. In part this was due to the strength of the feudal nobility and the emperors' quest to dominate Italy, but perhaps the most crucial factor was a furious struggle with the papacy that culminated in the disintegration of the Holy Roman Empire. The church's victory was made possible by reforms in the tenth and eleventh centuries that gave it new vigor and a stronger claim to moral leadership (see Chapter 14).

## Germany and the Imperial Revival

When the Carolingian empire declined in the ninth century, essentially independent duchies were established in the eastern Frankish lands. Out of this territory the Saxon duke Henry the Fowler founded the medieval German monarchy, which he governed as Henry I (919–936). His success in controlling the dukes was due partly to the freedom he allowed them in their duchies and partly to his ambitious foreign policy. He annexed Lorraine, strengthened Saxon defenses against the Magyars and Norsemen by encouraging the building of fortified towns, and urged Saxon expansion in the Slavic lands beyond the Elbe River.

The policies of Henry's son, Otto I (936–973), were basically an extension of his father's, but on a grander scale. His efforts to centralize royal power incited no less

THE MAJOR MEDIEVAL STATES, 900–1300

| England | France | Holy Roman Empire |
|---|---|---|
| Anglo-Saxons unite England politically (by 954) | Beginning of the Capetian dynasty (987) | Henry I, the Fowler (919–936)<br>• Founding of the German monarchy<br>Otto I (936–973)<br>• Founding of the empire (962) |
| Norman Conquest (1066)<br>• William I (1066–1087)<br>• Domesday Book<br>Henry II (1154–1189)<br>• Constitutions of Clarendon (1164) | | Henry IV (1056–1106)<br>• Lay investiture controversy begins<br><br>Frederick I, Barbarossa (1152–1190) |
| Richard I (1189–1199)<br>• Third Crusade<br>John (1199–1216)<br>• Magna Carta (1215) | Philip II, Augustus (1180–1223)<br>• Victory at Bouvines (1214) | Henry VI (1190–1197)<br>• Acquisition of Sicily<br>Frederick II (1212–1250) |
| Edward I (1272–1307)<br>• Expansion of the Great Council | Louis IX (1226–1270)<br>Philip IV, the Fair (1285–1314)<br>• Origins of the Estates General | Great Interregnum (1254–1273)<br>Beginning of the Habsburg dynasty (1273) |

than four rebellions, all of which he repressed. When the Magyars took advantage of the civil strife to invade Germany, Otto crushed them at Lechfeld, near Augsburg, in 955. Like his father, he appointed churchmen to offices of state, knowing they could not undermine royal authority by passing their positions to their sons. The clergy, moreover, were better educated. For its part, the church welcomed the alliance with the state, which brought not only greater influence but grants of land as well. The ecclesiastics who held those estates were responsible for providing Otto with many of his soldiers and much of his revenue.

When political turmoil in Italy offered Otto the excuse to intervene in 951, he claimed the Lombard throne as his own. Renewed conflict brought a call for his assistance from Pope John XII (955–964), who rewarded him with the imperial crown in February 962. That crown had several advantages, including the legal title to the Carolingian middle kingdom and reinforcement of Otto's supremacy over the German dukes, but it also thrust his successors into an untenable relationship with the head of a church that they had to dominate to maintain their power. The imperial policy of relying on ecclesiastical officials as the primary servants of the crown was effective so long as the papacy did not insist on appointing only those who had its approval.

Beginning in the late eleventh century the papacy attempted to assert the church's independence from secular control. The first of these popes, Leo IX (1049–1054), deposed corrupt bishops and reasserted papal supremacy over all the clergy. In 1059 a church council took a major step in freeing the papacy itself from imperial control by establishing the right of the College of Cardinals to elect future popes, a practice still in effect. In 1075 Gregory VII (1073–1085) attempted to restore the election of bishops and abbots to the church by terminating

the practice of lay investiture—the bestowal of the insignia of an ecclesiastical office by a layperson. Practically speaking, lay investiture entailed the right of the laity, such as emperors or kings, to select bishops and abbots, though this was in violation of church law and tradition. A vigorous, reformed church could hardly be established if its key officials were selected with a view to political, monetary, and family considerations rather than spiritual qualifications and if the loyalty of such persons was ultimately to the sovereign who appointed them rather than to the pope.

The immediate target of Gregory's decree was the emperor Henry IV (1056–1106), who enjoyed the support of his bishops but not of the German territorial princes. The latter stood to gain by any reduction of imperial power. Recognizing the implications of the decree, Henry had his prelates declare Gregory deposed, to which the pope responded by excommunicating Henry, absolving his subjects from their duty to obey him, and depriving the imperial bishops of their offices. Delighted with this turn of events, the renegade princes in Germany called for a council, over which Gregory would preside, at Augsburg in February 1077; its task would be to ascertain the validity of Henry's claim to the imperial crown. Unprepared to cope with a rebellion, the emperor intercepted Gregory at Canossa in Italy to seek absolution. As a priest, Gregory had to forgive the penitent Henry, thereby giving the emperor the upper hand in the civil war that ensued in Germany. Henry was in a much stronger position when Gregory again excommunicated him in 1080. Four years later Henry's troops occupied Rome, driving Gregory into exile and installing a rival or "antipope," Clement III, on the papal throne.

The investiture struggle dragged on until 1122, when Henry V (1106–1125) and Pope Calixtus II (1119–1124) agreed in the Concordat of Worms that the church

---

## ◉ Gregory VII on Papal Authority ◉

*The principles on which Pope Gregory VII and his supporters acted to reform the church and assert the supreme authority of the papacy are set forth in the* Dictatus papae *("Sayings of the Pope"), which was probably composed about 1075.*

The Roman church was founded by God alone.
The Roman bishop alone is properly called universal.
He alone may depose bishops and reinstate them.
His legate [direct ambassador], though of inferior grade, takes precedence, in a council, of all bishops and may render a decision of deposition against them. . . .
The pope is the only person whose feet are kissed by all princes.
His title is unique in the world.
He may depose emperors.
No council may be regarded as a general one without his consent.
No book or chapter may be regarded as canonical without his authority.
A decree of his may be annulled by no one; he alone may annul the decrees of all.
He may be judged by no one.
No one shall dare to condemn one who appeals to the papal see.
The Roman church has never erred, nor ever, by the witness of Scripture, shall err to all eternity.
He may not be considered Catholic who does not agree with the Roman church.
The pope may absolve the subjects of the unjust from their allegiance.

*Source:* J. H. Robinson, ed., *Readings in European History*, vol. 1 (Boston: Ginn, 1904), pp. 274–275.

---

would henceforth give prelates their offices and spiritual authority but that the emperor could be present when German bishops were elected and invest them with fiefs. In theory, at least, the clergy were now more independent of secular control, though in practice their selection and work were still very political. The real winners in the investiture struggle were the powerful territorial princes, who consolidated their hold over their own lands while imperial attention focused on Rome, and the emerging urban communes of northern Italy, which seized this opportunity to achieve a semi-independent status. In the end the biggest losers were not only the emperors but the German people, who were increasingly subjected to feudal conflict at a time when the French and English were laying the foundations of unified states.

### Papal Triumph and the Imperial Challenge

The papacy reached the zenith of its political power in the thirteenth century, but only after a renewal of its struggle with the empire. Emperor Frederick I (1152–1190), called "Barbarossa" because of his red beard, made domination of northern Italy (Lombardy) a cornerstone of his policy. Together with Burgundy, which he acquired by marriage, and his native Swabia, Lombardy would give him a solid territorial base from which to dominate Germany and Italy. Recognizing this, the pope joined with the cities of the Lombard League and the Normans in Sicily to thwart Frederick's ambitions, an end they achieved in the Peace of Constance (1183), which forced Frederick to relinquish virtually all meaningful power in the Lombard cities. The imperial cause in Italy received new life when Barbarossa's son, Henry VI (1190–1197), married Constance, heiress of Sicily and southern Italy. The papacy was now caught in the imperial vise, but rather than solidify his Italian holdings, Henry prepared to attack the Byzantine Empire. Simultaneously, he gave many of the German princes hereditary rights to their fiefs in return for their recognition that the imperial crown would likewise be hereditary rather than elective, a scheme bitterly opposed by the papacy.

Innocent III (1198–1216), arguably the most powerful of the medieval popes, took advantage of the chaos that followed Henry's untimely death to undermine the link

Innocent III, perhaps the most powerful of the medieval popes, made King John of England his vassal and helped establish Frederick II as Holy Roman emperor. This portrait is a thirteenth-century fresco in Sacro Speco Church, Subiaco, Italy. [Alinari/Art Resource]

between Germany and Sicily. Germany was thrust into civil war when the leading Hohenstaufen candidate for the imperial throne, Philip of Swabia, Henry VI's brother, was challenged by Otto of Brunswick. Although Innocent crowned Otto in 1209, the latter's attempt to control Sicily prompted the pope to excommunicate him. At the urging of the French king, Philip Augustus, Innocent recognized the hereditary claim of Henry's son, Frederick II, as king of the Romans in 1212. Philip's victory over Otto at Bouvines (1214) decided the struggle in Frederick's favor, though Frederick continued to fight with the popes over Sicily for the rest of his reign.

After Frederick's death in 1250, the papacy encouraged civil strife in Germany so successfully that between 1254 and 1273 there was no generally recognized em-

peror. Moreover, the Hohenstaufen line itself died out in 1268. The Great Interregnum, as the period without a recognized emperor was called, marked the triumph of the papacy over the empire—a victory achieved with French support. Yet half a century after the interregnum began, the French monarchy delivered a crippling blow to papal power and prestige.

## Boniface VIII and the End of Papal Hegemony

The century between the pontificates of Innocent III and Boniface VIII (1294–1303) witnessed a dramatic change in the political fortunes of the major European states, with France and England now the dominant powers. Boniface, a short-tempered, elderly man of aristocratic background, blundered seriously when, in 1296, he issued the bull (or edict) *Clericis laicos*, rejecting the right of monarchs to tax the clergy without papal authorization. Neither Philip IV nor Edward I, who were on the verge of war with each other, would tolerate such a challenge. While Edward denied legal protection to clerics who refused to pay, Philip prohibited the export of funds from France to Rome, crippling papal finances. Boniface retreated, allowing Philip the right to tax the clergy in an emergency and canonizing Louis IX for good measure.

Emboldened by the jubilee in 1300, when tens of thousands of pilgrims flocked to Rome, Boniface was ready when a new crisis erupted in 1301. When Philip had a French bishop tried in a royal court on charges of heresy and treason, the pope protested that this violated the clergy's privilege to be judged in a church court and warned Philip to submit to his authority as the vicar of Christ. Philip countered by summoning the first Estates General (1302), which protested to Rome. Boniface responded with a new papal bull, *Unam sanctam* (1302), in which he argued that God had given the church two swords: the spiritual sword, which was superior, was retained by the church, but the temporal was bestowed by the church on secular authorities to be wielded on behalf of the church and at its direction. The bull also flatly asserted that "submission on the part of every man to the bishop of Rome is altogether necessary for his salvation."

Whether *Unam sanctam* was a desperate ploy or the logical culmination of medieval papal claims is debatable, but Philip was undaunted. He dispatched his chief minister to Italy to arrest the pope, whom Philip hoped to try on fabricated charges ranging from heresy to sodomy and sorcery. Boniface was rescued by Italian loyalists, but not before he had been physically abused and the prestige of the papacy badly tarnished. In a matter of weeks Boniface was dead, and with him perished the heady days of papal supremacy. A French pope, Clement V (1305–1314), formally praised Philip's devotion, heralding the beginning of a long period in which the papacy found itself in the shadow of the French monarchy.

## The Waning of the Byzantine Empire

While western Europe was achieving remarkable political progress in the High Middle Ages, the Byzantine Empire was plagued by internal decay and external assault. In many respects the eleventh century was pivotal

---

## ◉ The Church's Claim to Supremacy ◉

*The bull* Unam sanctam, *issued by Pope Boniface VIII in 1302 during the course of his struggle with King Philip Augustus, is the classic statement of the medieval church's claim to spiritual and temporal supremacy.*

The true faith compels us to believe that there is one holy Catholic Apostolic Church, and this we firmly believe and plainly confess. And outside of her there is no salvation or remission of sins. . . .

By the words of the gospel we are taught that the two swords, namely, the spiritual authority and the temporal, are in the power of the Church. . . . The former is to be used by the Church, the latter for the Church; the one by the hand of the priest, the other by the hand of kings and knights, but at the command and permission of the priest. Moreover, it is necessary for one sword to be under the other, and the temporal authority to be subjected to the spiritual; for the apostle says, "For there is no power but of God: and the powers that be are ordained of God" [Rom. 13:1]; but they would not be ordained unless one were subjected to the other, and, as it were, the lower made the higher by the other. . . .

Submission on the part of every man to the bishop of Rome is altogether necessary for his salvation.

*Source:* F. A. Ogg, *A Source Book of Mediaeval History* (New York: Cooper Square, 1907), pp. 385–388.

in its decline. Emperor Basil II (976–1025) had secured the frontiers and brought the Balkans under Byzantine domination by defeating the Bulgars. From 1028 to 1056, however, the empire was ineffectually governed by Basil's nieces, Zoe and Theodora, who unwisely allowed imperial military strength to be sapped by supporting large landowners in their acquisition of smaller holdings. The result was the growth of a body of powerful magnates capable of fielding their own armies and posing a threat to imperial control. In effect, the empire was being feudalized.

In 1056, when the Macedonian dynasty died out, civil strife erupted until the military aristocrat Alexius I Comnenus (1081–1118) finally imposed control. In addition to weak emperors, much of the internal instability of the eleventh century was attributable to a fierce power struggle between the cultured bureaucratic elite and a wealthy aristocracy, the effects of which not only weakened the army but also undermined the government's financial stability. The lavish expenses of the imperial court and the increasing exemption of the aristocracy from taxation forced the government to devalue its coins in the mid-eleventh century.

The internal crises made it difficult for the Byzantines to cope with the pressure on their frontiers. The peoples of west-central Asia, particularly the Pechenegs who lived along the northern coasts of the Black Sea, regularly raided Byzantine territory. An even graver danger was posed by the Seljuk Turks, whose destruction of a Byzantine army at Manzikert in 1071 meant the loss of eastern Anatolia and Armenia. In the same year the Normans of Sicily drove the Byzantines out of southern Italy and attacked western Greece. Alexius Comnenus regained some of the lost territory by allying with the Venetians against the Normans and by successful military campaigns against the Pechenegs and the Turks. His military needs were so great, however, that he had to appeal to the papacy for western volunteers to fight the Turks, thus setting the stage for the crusades.

---

## The Clash of Faiths: Muslims Against Crusaders

The Turks had moved from the Asian steppes into the Islamic empire to serve in its armies. By 1055 one group of Turks, the Seljuks, had established themselves as the real rulers of the Abbasid caliphate. In the two centuries that followed their victory at Manzikert, they extended their control over most of Asia Minor, permanently changing it from a Christian to an Islamic civilization. Turkish domination extended into Armenia and Palestine as well, making it difficult for Christian pilgrims to visit the Holy Land. The Byzantine emperor, Michael VII, appealed to Pope Gregory VII for western assistance in 1073, and though the pontiff was willing to proclaim

a holy war, not least because it might reunite Christendom under his authority, the outbreak of the investiture controversy delayed the plan.

Twenty-two years later, against a background of alleged hostilities against Christian pilgrims, Byzantine envoys from Alexius Comnenus urged Pope Urban II (1088–1099) to dispatch military aid. At the Council of Clermont (1095) in southern France, the pope proclaimed a crusade to liberate the holy places, free the persecuted Christians of the East, and acquire wealth and power in a land of "milk and honey." It was better to slaughter the infidel than fellow Christians, Urban argued, and if a Christian died in the process, he would receive a plenary indulgence exempting him from the necessity of rendering satisfaction for his sins—in other words, immediate entry into heaven. To the pope's message, directed against a "pagan race," his audience responded with gusto: "God wills it! God wills it!"

The motives of the church and the crusaders varied. For the papacy the crusades offered the possibility of leadership in Europe and the opportunity to heal the breach between the eastern and western churches that had been formalized in 1054. While some crusaders were moved by spiritual considerations, including the promise of a plenary indulgence, others were motivated by stories of atrocities purportedly inflicted on pilgrims by the Muslims, the hope of material gain, the lure of adventure, the chance to escape from daily cares, or the desire to participate in an activity that quickly became fashionable. Most of the crusaders came from France, Italy, and Germany.

When Emperor Alexius appealed for assistance, he wanted western knights trained and equipped to fight, but instead the first group of crusaders, some 15,000 to 20,000 strong, were largely commoners, including women and children, devoid of military experience or suitable weapons. Inspired by faith and led by Peter the Hermit, the unruly force was hurriedly shipped from Constantinople to Asia Minor by alarmed Byzantine officials. The sultan of Nicaea's army annihilated or enslaved most of the crusaders, leaving the bones of some as a grisly warning to others who might follow. Fired by hopes of founding the New Jerusalem, the Peasants' Crusade ended in disaster, not only for the crusaders but also for the thousands of Hungarians and Jews they killed en route and the Byzantines they robbed or whose homes they burned.

Later in the same year, 1096, a much more impressive effort was made in the Crusade of the Princes, traditionally called the First Crusade. Although no monarchs participated, some of Europe's most illustrious princes were involved, including Godfrey of Bouillon, duke of Lower Lorraine; Raymond II, count of Toulouse; Robert, duke of Normandy, brother of the English king, William II; Hugh, count of Vermandois, brother of King Philip I of France; and Stephen, count of Blois, son-in-law of Wil-

## ◎ A Call to Crusaders ◎

*The crusades to bring the Holy Land under Christian control were launched by Pope Urban II's speech to the Council of Clermont in November 1095. Note the appeal to spiritual, material, and racial motives as well as the emotional tone.*

From the confines of Jerusalem and from the city of Constantinople a grievous report has gone forth and has been brought repeatedly to our ears; namely, that a race from the kingdom of the Persians, an accursed race, a race wholly alienated from God, . . . has violently invaded the lands of those Christians and has depopulated them by pillage and fire. They have led away a part of the captives into their own country, and a part they have killed by cruel tortures. They have either destroyed the churches of God or appropriated them for the rites of their own religion. They destroy the altars, after having defiled them with their uncleanness. . . .

On whom, therefore, rests the labor of avenging these wrongs and of recovering this territory, if not upon you—you, upon whom, above all other nations, God has conferred remarkable glory in arms, great courage, bodily activity, and strength to humble the heads of those who resist you? Let the deeds of your ancestors encourage you and incite your minds to manly achievements. . . .

Let none of your possessions restrain you, nor anxiety for your family affairs. For this land which you inhabit, shut in on all sides by the seas and surrounded by the mountain peaks, is too narrow for your large population; nor does it abound in wealth; and it furnishes scarcely food enough for its cultivators. Hence it is that you murder and devour one another, that you wage war, and that very many among you perish in civil strife. . . .

Enter upon the road of the Holy Sepulcher; wrest that land from the wicked race, and subject it to yourselves. . . . Undertake this journey eagerly for the remission of your sins, with the assurance of the reward of imperishable glory in the kingdom of heaven.

*Source:* F. A. Ogg, *A Source Book of Mediaeval History* (New York: Cooper Square, 1907), pp. 284–287.

---

liam the Conqueror. In all there were 5,000 to 10,000 knights, more than 25,000 soldiers, and at least that many noncombatants, both male and female, including servants, pilgrims, and prostitutes. In the hope of gaining control over whatever lands the crusaders conquered, Alexius bribed and cajoled the princes to take oaths of fealty to him, making them his vassals.

Although the Turks used scorched-earth tactics, the crusaders pushed relentlessly eastward. One branch of their army, under the command of Godfrey's brother Baldwin, captured the ancient Syrian city of Edessa, which had been ruled by Armenians, making it the first crusader state (1098). The heavily fortified city of Antioch, surrounded by 7 miles of walls, was besieged for seven months before it was finally betrayed from within and became the second crusader state. In July 1099, Jerusalem itself was conquered with the aid of equipment and supplies provided by an English-Genoese fleet. Once inside the city the crusaders massacred the inhabitants, whether Muslims or Jews, sparing neither women

nor children. It was, the victors thought, a "splendid judgment" of God.

The crusaders offered the crown of Jerusalem to Godfrey of Bouillon, who agreed only to serve as protector in deference to the kingship of Christ. Following Godfrey's death in 1100, however, his brother Baldwin became king of Jerusalem and nominal overlord of the three other crusader states, Edessa, Antioch, and Tripoli, which together formed a 500-mile strip along the coast of the eastern Mediterranean. Defending this outpost of European civilization from the hostile powers on its frontiers was therefore a matter of overriding concern, particularly since the subjects of the crusader states viewed their new rulers with hostility. Feudal knights had to be used to defend the states, but at the cost of developing a strong central government. Imposing castles were built, and the crusaders founded military orders in which the knights took the monastic vows of poverty, chastity, and obedience while dedicating their lives to the defense of the Holy Land. The Knights

Crusaders besieging Nicaea in 1097 catapult human heads at their enemies. [Bibliothèque Nationale, Paris]

Hospitalers and the Knights Templars wore distinctive dress, defended castles, and generally distinguished themselves as warriors. A third order, the Teutonic Knights, was established by German crusaders in 1198, though most of its efforts were devoted to campaigns in Hungary and the Baltic region.

The conquests of the first crusaders were possible largely because the Muslims had been disunited. In the early twelfth century, however, they began to regroup, initially under the leadership of Zenghi, governor of Mosul on the Tigris River. His capture of Edessa in 1144 sparked the call for the Second Crusade (1147–1149), which was led by King Louis VII of France and the German king Conrad III. Most of the crusaders were annihilated as they moved through Asia Minor, and the remnant, without the effective support of the suspicious defenders already in the Holy Land, failed to capture Damascus. Instead the city, which had been an ally of the crusader states, was conquered by Zenghi's successor, Nurredin, in 1154, placing Syria firmly in Muslim hands. Nurredin's forces imposed their control over Egypt in the late 1160s, setting the stage for the triumphal exploits of Saladin (1138–1193), who established himself as the master of much of the Muslim Middle East, particularly Egypt and Syria, after Nurredin's death in 1174. Thirteen years later he launched a holy war of

his own to recover Palestine, taking Jerusalem in October 1187. By 1189 the Christians held only Antioch, Tripoli, and Tyre.

The loss of Jerusalem roused Europe to launch yet another crusade, a formidable expedition led by the emperor Frederick Barbarossa, King Philip II of France, and King Richard I of England. But the emperor drowned in Asia Minor and Philip returned home after the crusaders captured the port of Acre, leaving Richard "the Lion-Hearted" to negotiate an agreement with Saladin permitting Christian pilgrims the right to visit Jerusalem. This was not enough for Pope Innocent III, who called for a fresh crusade, the Fourth (1202–1204). In return for food and transport, the crusaders acquiesced to a Venetian demand to help them reconquer the Dalmatian port of Zara, an act that resulted in the crusaders' excommunication because Zara was a Catholic city. The crusaders subsequently embroiled themselves in a disputed succession to the Byzantine throne that ended with their sack of Constantinople and the establishment of a Latin kingdom there that lasted until 1261.

As disreputable as the Fourth Crusade was, it did not quench the crusading fever. Among the later crusades, only the Sixth (1228–1229), led by Frederick II, was successful, thanks to the emperor's diplomatic skills and rapport with the Muslims. A treaty with the Egyptian

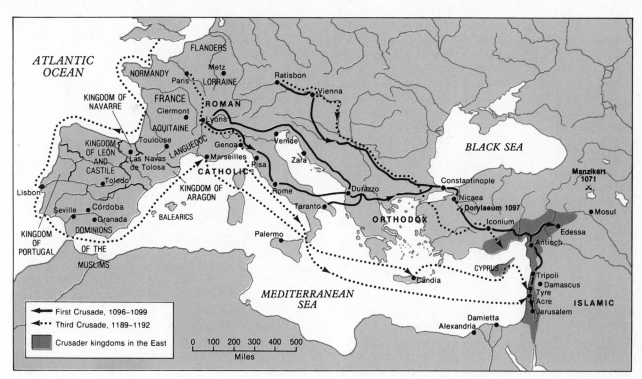

*13.4 Crusader Routes*

sultan left Jerusalem in Christian hands, but Frederick's running feud with the papacy forced him to return to Italy. Turkish forces in the employ of Egypt recaptured Jerusalem in 1244. Later crusades failed to regain the Holy Land, and in 1291 the last of the crusader possessions, Acre, was lost.

In terms of their stated objective—the conquest of the Holy Land—the crusades were a failure. The heavy expenditure in lives and resources as well as the undercutting of spiritual motives by worldly considerations cast a pall over the crusading movement. One of the most significant long-term legacies was the incitement of deep-seated religious hostility between Christians and Muslims and of Christians toward Jews. Nor did the crusades heal the breach between eastern and western Christendom, which, if anything, hardened as a result of them. In the short term the papacy probably enhanced its prestige as the spiritual leader of the West, but in the end its use of crusades to eradicate heresy in France and its deepening involvement in secular affairs began to erode its influence. The monarchs of Europe improved their position by gaining the right to levy direct taxes in order to obtain crusading funds, and perhaps Europe was subjected to a little less fighting because so many lords and knights directed their militancy against the Muslims.

There were a number of benefits from the crusades, particularly of an economic and cultural nature. The heightened contact between Europe and the Middle East stimulated commerce, especially in such commodities as fine textiles, spices, and perfumes. Expanded commerce in turn encouraged improvements in shipbuilding and banking, including greater use of letters of credit and bills of exchange. The Venetians in particular benefited from the crusades, which enabled them to become the leading shippers in the eastern Mediterranean. Although Islamic culture was already spreading to the West through the Iberian peninsula and Sicily, the crusades facilitated the exchange of ideas and the increase of geographic knowledge. The notion of "crusading" for a worthy cause lived on well past the last crusade and is still a frequently encountered concept, usually in secular guise, as well as in the Islamic notion of the *jihad*. The crusades were also significant as a chapter in the history of Western expansion and the backdrop for the great voyages of exploration that began in the fifteenth century, in part as a means of renewing the crusading movement.

## Byzantium After the Crusades

While the Europeans ruled Constantinople as a Latin kingdom, Greek refugees established a rival government at Nicaea in Asia Minor. In 1261 the Nicaean regime, aided by the Genoese, who were jealous of the privileges accorded to the Venetians by the Latin kingdom, regained Constantinople. The restored Byzantine Empire, however, was territorially smaller and economically weaker than it had been in 1200.

The empire survived for two more centuries, during which time its economy eroded and its strength was sapped by bitter social divisions. External threats were a recurring problem. A revived Latin kingdom was averted only by accident in 1282 on the eve of Charles of Anjou's planned assault. The younger brother of King Louis IX of France, Charles wanted to establish a Mediterranean empire by combining the kingdom of Sicily, which he already ruled, with the Byzantine Empire. Charles' hopes were dashed when the Sicilians massacred his French supporters during an uprising known as the Sicilian Vespers. With Byzantine financial support, an Aragonese fleet from Spain seized Sicily, ending Charles' threat to the empire. The Byzantines were not, however, able to repel the periodic incursions of the Serbs in the west and the Turks in the east. Their diminished territories in the aftermath of the Latin kingdom meant decreased resources and manpower, and the government at Constantinople was further weakened by debilitating civil wars in the 1300s. Perhaps the greatest cause of the Byzantines' decline was their inability to recover their once phenomenal prosperity, in no small measure because much of their commerce had fallen into the hands of northern Italian merchants.

# The Iberian Peninsula and the Reconquista

Although the crusaders failed to achieve a permanent hold in the Holy Land, in Europe a much longer campaign against the Muslims for the control of the Iberian peninsula was slowly being won. The *reconquista* ("reconquest") had begun in the ninth century, but by the dawn of the High Middle Ages only a thin band across the north of the peninsula was in Christian hands. Three centuries later the Muslims held only Granada at the peninsula's southern tip. Christian progress was due largely to the collapse of the caliphate of Córdoba in 1031, which had been torn by bitter internal dissension among Arabs, Jews, Berbers, and native Spaniards. As the caliphate, once the most prosperous state in Europe, disintegrated into petty principalities, the task of the knights of the cross was greatly simplified.

During the course of the High Middle Ages, three major Christian kingdoms developed in the peninsula: Castile, the largest; Aragon, in the northeast; and Portugal in the west. In addition there was a tiny Basque kingdom of Navarre in the north. During the reign of Sancho the Great of Navarre (1005–1035), Christian Spain was largely united, but Sancho viewed his state in personal terms and divided it among his four sons. Out of their inheritances eventually emerged the kingdoms of Navarre, Castile, and Aragon. The kingdom of Portugal was the result of a decision by Alfonso VI of Castile (1065–1109) to reward a Burgundian count in 1095 for his services against the Muslims. In 1143 Alfonso VII and the papacy officially recognized the count's son as a king, and Portugal henceforth pursued its own historical path. The reconquista proceeded more rapidly there than in the other Iberian kingdoms, the most crucial event being the capture of Lisbon in 1147 with the aid of an English fleet en route to the Holy Land.

The reconquista became a holy crusade in 1063, more than 30 years before Urban II proclaimed a crusade to conquer the Holy Land. In 1085 Alfonso VI conquered Toledo, the ancient Visigothic capital. Large numbers of Muslims, Jews, and Mozarabs, or Christians who had adopted Arabic culture, were incorporated into the kingdom of Castile, which promised Muslims the right to practice their religion and preserve their customs. Although Alfonso intended to be tolerant, the prospects of a Christian-Moorish civilization similar to the one that existed in thirteenth-century Sicily was doomed when the militant Almoravids invaded southern Spain from North Africa in 1096. Relations between Christians and Moors became increasingly embittered, in part because French Cluniac monks inflamed Spanish emotions and pressured Alfonso to adopt a harder line toward the Muslims. The spread of crusading zeal contributed to the Christian victories, which culminated in 1212 with the rout of the Muslims at Las Navas de Tolosa by the forces of Castile, Aragon, Navarre, and Portugal. As in the battle for the Holy Land, the crusades led to the creation of military orders in Spain. The knights of the Calatrava, Santiago, and Alcantara orders took the vows of poverty, chastity, and obedience but interpreted them in the loosest possible manner; chastity, for example, did not mean abstinence from sexual relations but marital fidelity. The orders acquired considerable power during the High Middle Ages.

The reconquista not only provided the context in which the Iberian kingdoms emerged but also helped shape their ideals and institutions. Iberian culture, especially in the Spanish states, combined Arabic influence with a fanatical religious zeal born in northern Spain of the crusading spirit. The need for fighting forces and the funds to support them during the long campaign against the Muslims resulted in the appearance of representative institutions, or Cortes, in the states of León (1188), Castile (1250), and Portugal (1254) well before the development of similar institutions in France and England, although they never acquired the power of the English Parliament. In Castile, which supplied the bulk of the men for the reconquista, the need for urban support also brought charters for the towns. Above all, the reconquista paved the way for the establishment in the fifteenth century of a unified Spain, which concluded the reconquest with the acquisition of Granada in 1492.

---

❀

## GRANADA, THE "GARDENS OF PARADISE"

Situated on the slopes of the Sierra Nevada and the banks of the Genil River, the Islamic city of Granada developed rapidly following the disintegration of the caliphate of Córdoba in 1031. As late as the ninth century Granada had been little more than a fortified village distinguished by its large Jewish population, which was so numerous that contemporaries called it "Granada of the Jews." Blessed with fertile soil and a Mediterranean climate, the population of the city grew rapidly in the High Middle Ages, rising from 20,000 in the tenth century to 26,000 in the eleventh century, about one-third the size of neighboring Seville. As the reconquista picked up speed, growing numbers of Muslim refugees fled south to Granada, enriching the city with an influx of artisans and merchants. When the monarchs of Castile and Aragon expelled thousands of Muslim agricultural workers in the 1260s, many moved to the kingdom of Granada. By the fifteenth century the population of the state had probably reached 350,000, of whom at least 50,000 resided in the capital, by then the wealthiest city in Spain.

The development of Granada began in earnest after the fall of the strife-ridden Zirids, a dynasty of North African Berbers from Tunis who had governed Granada for most of the eleventh century. They were followed by two dynasties of Berbers, the Almoravids (1090–1154) and the Almohades (1154–1228), the latter of which began the construction of major new fortifications. The city reached the peak of its glory during the rule of the Nasrid dynasty (1231–1492), which conquered Granada in 1238 and made it the capital of a new kingdom. For 2½ centuries Granada remained the only Islamic state in Iberia, but only by becoming a vassal of Castile, which exacted a tribute of 20 to 50 percent of the royal revenues and also required the Nasrid sovereigns to provide military assistance to Castile, even in the work of the reconquista. Thus the Granadans were forced to help the Castilians end Muslim rule in Seville in 1248.

As the city expanded, the role of the Jews declined. Their influence had peaked in the early eleventh century, when many Jews held fiscal and administrative offices and were prominent in the merchant community. Two Jewish financiers—Samuel ibn-Naghrilah and his son Yusuf—even served as viziers, or key administrators, for Zirid kings in the 1000s. In 1066, however, there was a violent reaction to Yusuf and other Jews in government office, which resulted in the massacre of as many as 4,000 Jews. Unlike Mozarabs, Jews were still to be tolerated in Granada, though their numbers were small by the fifteenth century.

Throughout the medieval period, Granada retained the appearance of a Middle Eastern city; one contemporary likened it to Damascus. Because of the influx of immigrants in the Nasrid period, it was extremely crowded; devoid of systematically planned open spaces, most of its maze of streets were no more than 3 to 4 feet wide. The narrow, crooked streets at least offered some protection from the intense sunlight, as did an abundance of shady gardens and courts. Aqueducts brought water to the city, including its numerous Roman-style baths. Artisans, who were grouped according to their craft in distinct quarters or streets, produced linen and silk, much of it for export. Fruits, sugarcane, and almonds were also exported to pay for the grain that had to be imported to supplement inadequate domestic crops.

The Nasrids were noted patrons of education and the arts, and their court attracted numerous learned Muslims. Mathematics, science, medicine, and literature flourished. A university was founded in the mid-1300s, and the city had no less than three important libraries. A hospital for the sick and insane was founded in 1365–1366. But perhaps the greatest monuments of Granada's golden age are the Alhambra and the Generalife. The former, constructed mostly between 1238 and 1358, was a palatial fortress replete with barracks, stables, mosques, and gardens. Built on a hilly terrace overlooking the city, the palace is richly decorated in an ornate Arabesque style with colored tiles and marble, geometric figures, and floral motifs. Its horseshoe arches, delicate columns, and graceful arcades are the culmination of Islamic architecture in Iberia. The nearby Generalife beautifully illustrates the description of paradise in the Koran as "a garden flowing with streams." Intended for summer use, the Generalife, with its pools, fountains, and rows of trees, perfectly blends building and landscape architecture. Justifiably, a fourteenth-century observer described Granada in glowing terms: "No city can be compared to it as to its exterior or interior, and no country is like it with respect to the extent of its buildings, and the excellence of its position."[1]

## Russia and the Mongol Conquest

While Christians were launching their crusades against the Muslims in the Iberian peninsula and Palestine, the

The Court of the Lions in the Alhambra is not only an exquisite walled garden but also a symbol of paradise. The four waterways that converge at the fountain represent the four rivers of paradise; the 12 lions on the fountain symbolize the signs of the zodiac. [Arxiu MAS, Barcelona]

Mongols invaded Russia, which they ruled for two centuries. Just as the initial success of the crusaders in Palestine and the advances of the Christians in Iberia were facilitated by the internal weaknesses of their Muslim enemies, so the Mongol advance was made easier by Russian disunity.

The last of the great Kievan princes, Yaroslav the Wise (1019–1054), had been a very effective ruler, extending the territory of his state, issuing the first written codification of East Slavic law, building numerous churches including the Kiev Cathedral, and supporting the translation of religious literature from Greek into Slavic. He had also strengthened ties between Russia and western Europe, in part by marrying his daughter Anna to the French king, Henry I. But Yaroslav made a fatal mistake by implementing the rota system to determine succession to the throne. According to this system, the crown passed to the senior member of the ruling family rather than to the eldest son of a deceased ruler; brothers, in other words, normally had preference over

sons. The situation was complicated by the stipulation that each prince in the royal family would be assigned to a town suitable to his place in the line of succession. When the grand prince died, each prince moved up one step to the next highest town. Instead of providing for the peaceful succession of experienced rulers, the rota system fostered dissension and occasionally violent feuding. Rather than evolving into a centralized state, Russia disintegrated into a loose confederation of essentially independent principalities.

Long before the Mongols struck, Kiev was crippled by the assaults of the militant Cumans, a nomadic people who lived in the steppes. Their attacks, which began in the 1060s, eventually severed Kiev's access by the Dnieper River to the Black Sea and trade with Byzantium. In 1203 the Cumans even sacked Kiev, already weakened by the ravages of a rival Russian prince in 1169. The attacks of the Cumans and the Pechenegs had the effect of directing Russian expansion to the forests of the north and west, away from the steppes and from contact with

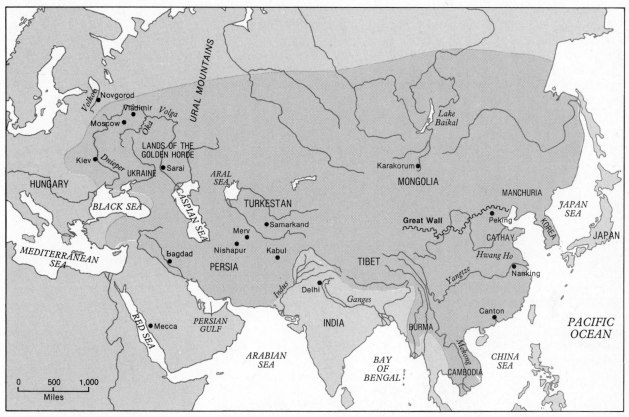

**13.5** *Mongol Empire, c. 1300*

the Byzantine Empire. Thus already by 1200 the Russians were experiencing less and less contact with the rest of Christian Europe.

The Mongols who invaded Russia in the early thirteenth century were militant nomadic tribesmen from Mongolia who had been united into a powerful confederation by Chinghis Khan (1155–1227). They had already launched assaults on China and Korea, while other military units pushed westward until they attacked the Cumans in southern Russia. In 1223 the Mongols defeated a joint Cuman-Russian army, after which they held a victory banquet on a platform beneath which they crushed the captured Russian princes. At the death of Chinghis Khan in 1227 these Mongol units withdrew to their homeland to participate in the selection of his successor, but in 1237 they returned under Chinghis' grandson, Batu, who had a huge army of 50,000 Mongols and 50,000 auxiliaries, mostly Turks. By 1240 they had overrun Russia, slaughtering all who resisted. From there they invaded Poland, Silesia, Bohemia, Moravia, and Hungary, only to pull back to Russia when another khan died in 1241. In the late thirteenth century, under the leadership of Kubilai Khan, another of Chinghis' grandsons, the Mongol Empire included not only Russia but also Iran, China, and part of Southeast Asia—the largest

empire known to this time. Within its borders new possibilities existed for peoples of different cultures to communicate with and learn from each other.

The Mongols, commonly called Tartars, Tatars, or the Golden Horde, established their western capital at Sarai on the Lower Volga River, north of the Caspian Sea. The princes of southern and eastern Russia had to pay tribute to the khans, but in return they received charters, or *yarliks*, authorizing them to act as deputies of the khans. In general, the princes were allowed considerable freedom to rule as they wished. One of them, Alexander Nevsky (died 1263), prince of Vladimir, acquired heroic status as the result of major victories over the Swedes, the Teutonic Knights, and the Lithuanians.

The Mongol incursions destroyed the last remnants of Kievan power, and henceforth medieval Russia was essentially divided into four regions. The Mongols dominated the southern steppes but exercised only moderate control over Great Russia, the region between the Volga and Oka rivers, which included the principalities of Vladimir and Moscow. Western Russia, including the Ukraine, freed itself of Mongol control in the late medieval period, only to fall under the sway of Lithuania. The Tartars had the least influence in northern Russia, where the vast principality of Novgorod extended from the Baltic Sea to beyond the Ural Mountains. Novgorod enjoyed the advantage of a strategic commercial site on the Volkov River, but most of its territory was thinly populated because of its poor soil. Immigrants who left southern Russia to escape the Mongols gravitated mostly to the northeast, where the soil was better and the rivers were more conducive to commercial development. It was this region that provided the nucleus of the modern Russian state in the late medieval period. By that time the Mongols had left their impact on the Russians in such areas as military dress and tactics, manpower levies, and the development of new trade routes. Eastern influence remained strong well into the eighteenth century, when Russian rulers made a conscious effort to westernize their country.

*In political terms, the Middle Ages witnessed the transition of England and France from decentralized feudal states to emerging national monarchies, but the course of German and Italian history was strikingly different because of the imperial ambitions of the German rulers and the determination of the papacy to rejuvenate the church by controlling episcopal appointments. Although the popes won the struggle, destroying the Hohenstaufens in the process, they in turn succumbed to growing secular concerns and the forceful resistance of the French and English monarchs.*

*The century between the pontificates of Innocent III and Boniface VIII, though one of brilliant cultural achievement, nevertheless saw the beginnings of a process that eroded papal prestige and power over secular rulers. The change in papal fortunes was mirrored in the history of the crusading movement over which they tried in vain to preside. The early successes were more than offset by subsequent failures as well as the increasingly materialistic motives of the participants. In the end, only the Iberian crusades achieved their objectives. The accomplishments of the High Middle Ages were nevertheless significant, not only with respect to the political achievements in France and England and the reforms in the church but also in terms of commerce and urban development, the founding of universities, scholastic and scientific thought, and the construction of majestic cathedrals. It is to these religious, intellectual, and cultural achievements that we turn in Chapter 14.*

## Notes

1. A. G. Chejne, *Muslim Spain: Its History and Culture* (Minneapolis: University of Minnesota Press, 1974), p. 156.

## Suggestions for Further Reading

Baldwin, J. W. *The Government of Philip Augustus: Foundations of French Royal Power in the Middle Ages.* Berkeley: University of California Press, 1986.

Barlow, F. *The Feudal Kingdom of England, 1042–1216*, 4th ed. New York: Longman, 1988.

———. *Thomas Becket.* London: Weidenfeld & Nicolson, 1986.

Barraclough, G. *The Origins of Modern Germany.* New York: Norton, 1984.

Brooke, C. *Europe in the Central Middle Ages, 962–1154.* New York: Longman, 1987.

Chapelot, J., and Fossier, R. *The Village and House in the Middle Ages*, trans. H. Cleere. London: Batsford, 1985.

Chazan, R. *European Jewry and the First Crusade.* Berkeley: University of California Press, 1987.

Chibnall, M. *Anglo-Norman England, 1066–1166.* New York: Blackwell, 1986.

Davis, R. H. C. *A History of Medieval Europe from Constantine to Saint Louis.* New York: Longman, 1988.

Day, J. *The Medieval Market Economy.* Oxford: Blackwell, 1987.

Dillard, H. *Daughters of the Reconquest: Women in Castilian Town Society, 1100–1300.* Cambridge: Cambridge University Press, 1984.

Ennen, E. *The Medieval Town*, trans. N. Fryde. New York: Elsevier North-Holland, 1979.

Fossier, R. *Peasant Life in the Medieval West.* Oxford: Blackwell, 1988.

Geary, P. J. *Before France and Germany: The Creation and Transformation of the Merovingian World.* New York: Oxford University Press, 1988.

Hanawalt, B. A. *The Ties That Bound: Peasant Families in Medieval England.* New York: Oxford University Press, 1986.

Harvey, A. *Economic Expansion in the Byzantine Empire, 900–1200.* Cambridge: Cambridge University Press, 1990.

Haverkamp, A. *Medieval Germany, 1056–1273*, trans. H. Braun and R. Mortimer. New York: Oxford University Press, 1988.

Hillgarth, J. N. *The Spanish Kingdoms, 1250–1516*, 2 vols. Oxford: Clarendon Press, 1976–1978.

Hohenberg, P. M., and Lees, L. H. *The Making of Urban Europe, 1000–1950*. Cambridge, Mass.: Harvard University Press, 1985.

Imamuddin, S. M. *Muslim Spain, 711–1492 A.D.* Leiden: Brill, 1981.

James, E. *The Franks*. Oxford: Blackwell, 1988.

Kelly, A. *Eleanor of Aquitaine and the Four Kings*. Cambridge, Mass.: Harvard University Press, 1950.

Little, L. *Religious Poverty and the Profit Economy in Medieval Europe*. Ithaca, N.Y.: Cornell University Press, 1978.

Lopez, R. S. *The Commercial Revolution of the Middle Ages, 950–1350*. Cambridge: Cambridge University Press, 1976.

Mayer, H. E. *The Crusades*, 2nd ed., trans. J. Gillingham. London: Oxford University Press, 1988.

Morgan, D. *The Mongols*. New York: Blackwell, 1986.

Morris, C. *The Papal Monarchy: The Western Church from 1050 to 1250*. New York: Oxford University Press, 1989.

Obolensky, D. *The Byzantine Commonwealth: Eastern Europe, 500–1453*. New York: Praeger, 1971.

Petit-Dutaillis, C. *The Feudal Monarchy in France and England, from the Tenth to the Thirteenth Century*, trans. E. D. Hunt. New York: Barnes & Noble Books, 1964, 1980.

Postan, M. M., and Miller, E. *The Cambridge Economic History of Europe*, vol. 2: *Trade and Industry in the Middle Ages*, 2nd ed. Cambridge: Cambridge University Press, 1987.

Reynolds, S. *An Introduction to the History of English Medieval Towns*. Oxford: Clarendon Press, 1977.

Rossabi, M. *Khubilai Khan: His Life and Times*. Berkeley: University of California Press, 1988.

Strayer, J. R. *The Reign of Philip the Fair*. Princeton, N.J.: Princeton University Press, 1980.

Warren, W. L. *King John*, 2nd ed. Berkeley: University of California Press, 1978.

# Life and Culture in Medieval Europe

The culture of Europe was forged primarily from a combination of Judeo-Christian values, classical ideals and concepts, and Germanic traditions. Yet as it developed, European culture also owed much to the Islamic world. By the High Middle Ages, European culture was vigorously creative. Commercial developments were instrumental in shaping the new outlook, as the burgeoning cities became the setting for the cathedral schools and the first universities as well as for the great symbols of the High Middle Ages, the Romanesque and Gothic cathedrals. Troubadours, university professors and students, affluent merchants, and crusaders took their place in a Europe hitherto largely confined to feudal aristocrats, peasants, and parish clergy. This was an age of spiritual renewal, as reflected in the growth of papal

**St. Clare of Assisi, disciple of St. Francis and founder of the Poor Clares, as painted by the fourteenth-century Italian artist Simone Martini. [Marburg/Art Resource]**

power, the founding of new religious orders, and the intellectual brilliance of scholastic thought. Theologians such as Thomas Aquinas attempted nothing less than a synthesis of all knowledge, both earthly and spiritual, for the greater glory of God. But although the age was one of brilliant artistic and intellectual achievement, it was no less an age whose darker side boded ill for Jews. If love, service, and civic pride inspired the building of the great cathedrals, bigotry and hate found their outlet in ruthless anti-Semitism. Nor did the status of women appreciably improve despite the overall achievements of the age and their contribution to them.

## The Medieval Church

Although Christianity was the dominant religion and played a pivotal role in the development of Europe throughout the Middle Ages and beyond, its adherents struggled to overcome a widespread belief in primitive natural forces and magic. Early medieval priests were in effect missionaries in their own parishes, though in the course of time they were successful in winning at least nominal adherence to Christianity. With its warnings of eternal damnation and its message of salvation through the sacraments, the church gradually shaped a code of conduct and a basic system of belief that was common to much of Europe. The church was, then, a key unifying force.

In their efforts to win the adherence of the people, church leaders periodically clashed with their secular counterparts when their policies conflicted. The tendency of secular authorities to rely on educated churchmen to help administer their governments raised the question of authority: To whom did such officials owe ultimate obedience? It is, however, erroneous to think of secular and ecclesiastical rulers as being in perpetual conflict, for they were commonly allies in maintaining control over their subjects. Most rulers governed with the church's blessing, while secular authorities in turn used the machinery of government and the military force at their disposal to protect the church and assist it in carrying out its policies. When conflicts did erupt, church leaders could seek support from their secular allies or have recourse to two spiritual weapons, excommunication and the interdict. Excommunication technically prohibited an offender from participating in church rites or maintaining contact with other Christians, and if the sentence was not lifted prior to one's death, the offender was eternally damned. An interdict, which could be imposed on a particular area, barred all church services with the exception of baptism and extreme unction (last rites). To be effective, these penalties had to have popular support and could not be overused.

## Monastic Communities

One of the characteristic features of medieval Christianity was the founding of religious communities in which men and women lived in relative isolation from the rest of society. Such communities were initially established in Egypt and then spread throughout the Roman Empire, including such places as Constantinople and Jerusalem. The first monastic communities in the West appeared in the late fourth and fifth centuries, the most famous of them being the two founded by John Cassian (385–440) near Marseilles in Gaul. Other monastic experiments were tried as far afield as Spain, England, and Ireland, but it was a monastery founded in Italy in 529 by Benedict of Nursia (480–547) that eventually had the greatest impact on European monasticism.

As a guide for the monks who joined him at Monte Cassino, south of Rome, Benedict wrote a rule, the intent of which was to provide for an orderly existence conducive to the complete dedication of one's life to God. Unlike some of the other early monastic leaders, Benedict did not call for extreme forms of self-denial but insisted on moderation in a life of prayer, contemplation, study, communal worship, and labor. Monks vowed to follow a life of poverty, to be chaste, to obey their superiors, and to be stable, that is, not to leave the monastery without permission. Responsibility for the direction of the monastery was placed in the hands of an abbot, elected for life by the monks and consecrated by a bishop but accountable only to the Rule and to God. The monastery was intended to be self-sufficient; hence its members had to perform a variety of tasks that ranged from farming to cooking and making clothes. Benedict's Rule did not direct monks to teach or copy manuscripts, but such tasks became necessary as novices had to be educated and as the monks required service books, Bibles, and other religious literature. By the seventh century there were communities for Benedictine nuns, who regarded Benedict's sister Scholastica as their patroness. Like the monasteries of the men, their convents spread throughout Europe in the ensuing centuries. In time the standards of some monasteries became lax as they accumulated material possessions, often the gifts of pious laity.

## Apostolic Renewal: The New Religious Orders

A new monastic order provided the foundation for religious reform beginning in the tenth century. Although the imperial revival under Otto I in the middle of that century threatened the independence of the papal office, a contemporary reform movement helped restore its vigor and spiritual leadership in the High Middle Ages.

In 910 Duke William "the Good" of Aquitaine founded a monastery at Cluny in Burgundy, with a charter guaranteeing independence from secular control. By this time control over other monasteries had fallen into the hands of feudal lords, who stripped their revenues and sold their monastic offices. To prevent this from happening at Cluny, William placed the monastery under papal protection before he died; henceforth its abbots owed their allegiance only to Rome. They insisted on major reforms in the church, including renewed emphasis on the Rule of Benedict and the monastic liturgy, an end to the sale of church offices, and the enforcement of clerical celibacy, which, though widely disregarded, had been church policy since the fourth century, in keeping with the examples of Jesus and Paul. The call to reform received a stunning response: new foundations and converted Benedictine houses swelled the total of institutions based on the Cluniac model to more than 300, all of which were administered by priors subordinate to the abbot of Cluny. The renewed sense of spiritual devotion radiated well beyond the cloister as lay believers were inspired by the Cluniac monks. The heightened devotional interest was appropriately manifested in the appearance of the first prayer books for the laity. Inspired by the prayers of Cluniac monks, the prayer books began a tradition that culminated in the production of the beautifully illustrated books of hours in the late medieval period.

The Cluniacs were the first wave of a series of reform-oriented monastic movements that swept the Latin church in the High Middle Ages. The Cistercians, founded in the twelfth century, were a Benedictine reform movement that emphasized individual devotion rather than public worship and agricultural labor rather than other forms of work. The Cistercians tended to settle in remote areas to avoid corruption by secular influences. With austerity as their ideal, the Cistercians followed a rigorous vegetarian diet that even excluded dairy products. They seldom spoke, and they worshiped in churches devoid of ornamentation. The Cistercians achieved a well-deserved reputation for their skills in making marginal lands productive. The movement reached its peak under the leadership of Bernard of Clairvaux and his successors. There were nearly 350 Cistercian abbeys by the time Bernard died in 1153, and more than 700 by 1300. Like other monastic orders, the Cistercians were less than enthusiastic about the thousands of women who wanted to become Cistercian nuns, though in the end the church resolved the issue by placing the convents under monastic supervision as a subordinate branch of the male order.

The richness of medieval Christian religious life is illustrated in the variety of orders that were founded. The Carthusians were far more rigorous than the Benedictines, insisting, for example, that each monk live in a separate cell, fast every Friday, and eat with his fellow monks only on Sundays and the major holy days. In sharp contrast to this solitary life, "canons regular" combined the monastic concept of living according to a rule with the duties of a secular priest. Thus the Augustinians ministered to the needs of the laity, both spiritually and materially. Unlike the Benedictines and Cluniacs, they refused to amass large endowments and impressive buildings, preferring instead to follow a humble lifestyle and aid the needy.

A third form of religious vocation originated in the thirteenth century with the founding of mendicant or begging orders, so called because their friars depended on alms for their living. Like the monks and canons regular, they took vows of poverty, chastity, and obedience, and they lived in communities; but unlike the monks, they devoted their lives to ministering to the laity. One of the principal mendicant orders was founded by the Spanish Augustinian Dominic (1170–1221) to fight the spread of heresy in southern France. The Dominicans, formally constituted in 1216, intended to combat heresy by preaching, education, and holy living. Their enormous contribution to Western education stems from their rule: "Day and night, whether at home or traveling, let the brethren ever be occupied with reading or meditation."

The other major mendicant order, the Franciscans,

**St. Francis of Assisi, founder of the Franciscan order of mendicants, as depicted by the thirteenth-century Italian painter Cimabue. [Alinari/Art Resource]**

was established by Francis of Assisi (1182–1226), the son of a well-to-do Italian cloth merchant. Motivated by a religious vision, Francis sold much of his father's possessions, gave the proceeds to the church, and renounced material goods. Francis and his followers, whose ideal was absolute poverty and humility, obtained papal approval for their order in 1209. The friars devoted themselves to the spiritual and material needs of the lowly, particularly in the towns. At first the Franciscans shunned learning in preference to apostolic simplicity, but their growing competition with the Dominicans gradually persuaded them to engage in scholarly endeavors. Before the century was over, both mendicant orders became prominent in the universities. Similarly, both became actively involved in missionary work among the Muslims and the Mongols.

## ST. CLARE AND THE POOR SISTERS

The life of Clare of Assisi illustrates the problems experienced by women attracted to the new religious movements. For most, including Clare, the lure was undoubtedly spiritual, though some may have been drawn to the religious life because they had little prospect of marriage, shunned the dangers of childbirth, or sought spiritual status to compensate for their declining role in medieval society. But churchmen were generally troubled by the prospect of separate female orders. How could they support themselves? Because women were excluded from the priesthood, who would provide cloistered convents with pastoral care? Women, moreover, were thought to be unusually susceptible to heresy. The problem became acute by the early thirteenth century as female groups began to organize, particularly in Italy and Flanders.

Born into a pious aristocratic family at Assisi in 1194, Clare was influenced by a mother known for her charitable deeds and pilgrimages. While her parents were arranging her marriage, Francis of Assisi secretly met with Clare to persuade her to pursue a more rigorous spiritual life. One night in March 1212, at the age of 18, she fled to a nearby chapel, where Francis received her vows to lead a life of poverty and to imitate Christ and Mary. The "Poor Clares" or "Poor Sisters" date their origins from that event. The sisters were housed in the church and convent of San Damiano, near Assisi, where Clare

## ◉ Holy Poverty: The Ideal of Francis ◉

*The ideals of Francis of Assisi are clearly reflected in his will, prepared shortly before his death in 1226. His emphasis on holy poverty contrasts with the growing wealth of the church.*

When the Lord gave me the care of some brothers, no one showed me what I ought to do, but the Most High himself revealed to me that I ought to live according to the model of the holy gospel. I caused a short and simple formula to be written, and the lord pope confirmed it for me.

Those who presented themselves to follow this kind of life distributed all they might have to the poor. They contented themselves with one tunic, patched within and without, with the cord and breeches, and we desired to have nothing more. . . .

We loved to live in poor and abandoned churches, and we were ignorant, and were submissive to all. I worked with my hands and would still do so, and I firmly desire also that all the other brothers work, for this makes for goodness. Let those who know no trade learn one, but not for the purpose of receiving the price of their toil, but for their good example and to flee idleness. And when we are not given the price of our work, let us resort to the table of the Lord, begging our bread from door to door. The Lord revealed to me the salutation which we ought to give: "God give you peace!"

Let the brothers take great care not to accept churches, habitations, or any other buildings erected for them, except as all is in accordance with the holy poverty which we have vowed in the Rule; and let them not live in them except as strangers and pilgrims.

*Source:* J. H. Robinson, ed., *Readings in European History,* vol. 1 (Boston: Ginn, 1904), pp. 393–394.

formally acquired the title of abbess in 1216, a position she retained until her death in August 1253. She attracted many followers, including two of her sisters and, after her father's death, her mother.

The problem of procuring a rule for her order, already difficult because of antifemale sentiment, was compounded by the decision of the Fourth Lateran Council in 1215 not to allow any new orders. Francis had given Clare only verbal advice and a brief "way of life," but this had not been officially recognized. In 1219, therefore, Cardinal Ugolino, the future Pope Gregory IX, provided a rule based on Benedictine and Cistercian principles: an austere life, strict seclusion from the world, and the right of the community as a whole to own property. Having already taken a vow of absolute poverty, Clare was adamantly opposed to the property provision, an issue that remained a sore point until the last days of her life. Ugolino's intent was to place all the female groups under papal protection, with a single uniform rule and with pastoral care provided by the Franciscans. Francis, however, refused to be associated with any female community apart from that of Clare at San Damiano: "God has taken away our wives, and now the devil gives us sisters," he fumed, afraid that Ugolino's scheme would ruin his order.

Despite Francis' reluctance to accept pastoral responsibility for convents, he maintained close relations with Clare, who seems to have been his confidant. On one occasion she nursed him back to health at San Damiano, during which period he wrote his famous *Canticle of the Sun*, reflecting his remarkable sense of oneness with and love of nature. Her own writings, particularly her *Testament*, reveal her strong commitment to poverty: "I was ever anxious with my sisters to preserve the holy poverty which we promised to God and the blessed Francis."[1] This commitment was especially striking since Clare and most of her followers came from aristocratic backgrounds. As she lay dying in 1253, she was visited by Pope Innocent IV, who at last approved the rule she had sought for more than three decades, which embraced a concept of poverty that allowed neither personal nor communal possessions apart from enough land on which to grow food. The continuation of the Poor Clares to the present day is largely due to the persistence and devotion of Clare, who was canonized in 1255.

## Dissidents and Heretics

The spirit of reform that swept the church substantially increased lay interest in religion, but one unintended result of this was the rapid growth of beliefs the church considered heretical (unorthodox). In the 1170s the French merchant Peter Waldo of Lyons attracted disciples by his emphasis on poverty and simplicity as well as his attack on the moral corruption of the clergy. The Waldensians, or "Poor Men of Lyons," insisted on the right of laymen to preach, rejected some of the sacraments, and accepted the Scripture alone as authoritative in religion. Moreover, they wanted translations of the Bible in the language of the people. Although they were excommunicated by the pope in 1184, the Waldensians remained popular in southern France and northern Italy.

A more serious threat to the church was posed by the Albigensians, so called because their center was the town of Albi in southern France. Their teaching viewed the universe in terms of a struggle between the forces of good and evil.* The Cathari, or "pure ones," were therefore supposed to abstain from most material things, including marriage, worldly possessions, and meat, in their quest to attain a state of perfection. Some rejected the mass, infant baptism, and even the church itself; voluntarily starving oneself to death was highly praised. Not only were the Albigensians condemned by the church, but Pope Innocent III even called for a crusade to exterminate them. Knights from northern France rallied to the call, more interested in the possibility of seizing land than uprooting heresy. The harshest fighting lasted 20 years (1209–1229) and ultimately eradicated many of the heretics.

Another weapon to combat heresy was the use of inquisitors, a practice instituted by Pope Gregory IX (1227–1241). The inquisitors' task was to convert the heretics if possible, but in any case to prevent the deadly "disease" of heresy from spreading. The Inquisition embraced the principles of Roman law, including the use of torture, such as the rack or holding the feet of the accused to hot coals. Suspects had no right to counsel, no opportunity to question witnesses, not even the right to know the charges against them. Those who refused to relinquish their heretical beliefs or were convicted a second time were subject to severe penalties, including imprisonment, loss of property, or burning at the stake. Although some inquisitors were notoriously severe, such as a Dominican who had 180 people burned on a single day in 1239, most of the accused escaped execution. Because the inquisitors were not allowed to shed blood themselves, the executions were carried out by the state, but the church nevertheless left itself open to condemnation by relying on force rather than moral suasion to maintain its spiritual supremacy.

## The World of Learning

The need to staff expanding governments with educated officials and the growth of towns, with their increasingly

---

*Such views were called Manichaean, after the third-century Mesopotamian prophet who advocated such a dualistic view of the universe.

## CHURCH AND STATE, 440–1302

| Religious orders | Major popes | Church-state relations |
|---|---|---|
| | Leo I (440–461) | Papacy claims fullness of power |
| Benedictines (529) | | |
| | Gregory I (590–604) | |
| Cluniacs (910) | | |
| | Leo IX (1049–1054) | Right of College of Cardinals to elect popes (1059) |
| Carthusians (1084) | Gregory VII (1073–1085) | Lay investiture controversy (1075–1122) |
| Cistercians (1098) | Urban II (1088–1099) | Call for crusaders (1095) |
| | Calixtus II (1119–1124) | Concordat of Worms (1122) |
| Franciscans (1209) | Innocent III (1198–1216) | |
| Dominicans (1216) | | |
| Poor Clares (1219) | | |
| | Gregory IX (1227–1241) | |
| | | Culmination of the papacy's struggle with the Hohenstaufens (1250) |
| | Boniface VIII (1294–1303) | *Clericis laicos* (1296) |
| | | *Unam sanctam* (1302) |

sophisticated businesses, their law courts, and their collection of taxes and fees, led to a greater demand for literate persons. This was a major cause of the educational revolution of the late eleventh century and the twelfth century, as was the Gregorian stress on the importance of a better-educated clergy. From the sixth century to the tenth, most schooling in Europe had been provided by the monasteries, which played a central role in the promotion of learning. There were also a few cathedral and secular schools, the latter mostly in northern Italy and southern France. These early schools were insufficient, both in number and in curriculum, to meet the needs of the towns, the expanding royal courts, and the growing ecclesiastical bureaucracy. The monastic schools, with a curriculum oriented toward biblical interpretation and commentary, were never intended to serve society as a whole.

Urban developments not only increased the demand for educated persons but also made cathedral schools accessible to more people, particularly sons of the laity. The better cathedral schools, such as those at Chartres, Rheims, and Paris, included a music school, a school for the seven liberal arts, and a more advanced school for theological studies. The seven liberal arts—grammar, rhetoric, logic, arithmetic, geometry, astronomy, and music—were regarded as the fundamental branches of knowledge. Some ecclesiastical schools even provided education in law, medicine, philosophy, and the natural sciences. At a humbler level, parish priests sometimes taught reading, writing, mathematics, and the other liberal arts. The church's growing interest in education was especially evident in the late twelfth century, when it became mandatory for every cathedral to have a school and for each to be provided with funds sufficient to educate the children of the poor without charge. In Italy,

Germany, and the Netherlands merchants took the lead in establishing municipal schools; Hamburg, Munich, and Lübeck had them by 1300. In the towns young people could also be trained as apprentices by surgeons, barbers, dentists, lawyers, notaries, architects, and artists.

In addition to the establishment of new schools, the educational revolution of the High Middle Ages also involved curricular changes. Before the eleventh century the curriculum was heavily oriented toward biblical studies, but in the 1000s the emphasis shifted to logic. As more Latin translations of Arabic and Greek works on philosophy and natural science became available, these subjects too were the object of greater attention. Writers such as the Augustinian friar Egidio Colonna, author of *On the Governance of Rulers*, called for a comprehensive curriculum that included the seven liberal arts, classical and Christian literature, philosophy, politics, economics, natural science, and etiquette. Colonna also advocated the education of women. At one level the educational revolution increased lay literacy, though only a small minority could read and even fewer could write, while at another level the revolution culminated in the founding of the first universities.

# Scholarly Guilds: The Medieval University

As growing numbers of students traveled to cities such as Paris, Bologna, and Salerno in search of the best teachers in the arts, theology, law, and medicine, formal organization became necessary to secure the rights and privileges of students and teachers. There was also a need for some form of academic recognition—a "degree"—that would enable qualified persons to teach in other cities. In a society accustomed to craft and merchant guilds, the natural solution was an academic guild, a *universitas* or corporation, that could protect the interests of faculty and students as well as issue licenses to teach. Organization was essential to assure academic standards, provide protection from townspeople inclined to overcharge students for board and room, and obtain the right of faculty and students to be tried in church rather than local courts. In southern Europe universities were initially guilds of students; in northern Europe, guilds of teachers.

The earliest universities evolved at Bologna and Paris in the mid-twelfth century, and Salerno had a medical school. In the early 1100s Bologna's reputation as the leading center of legal studies was firmly established through the work of Irnerius, who wrote commentaries on contemporary legal codes based on his familiarity with the Byzantine *Corpus Juris Civilis*, and of Gratian, whose *Decretum* became the standard text for the study of canon (church) law. At Bologna students first organized into regional groups called "nations," and these in turn eventually united to form the University of Bologna, chartered by Emperor Frederick Barbarossa in 1158. Students established regulations to govern the number, length, and content of lectures and fined or boycotted teachers who failed to cover the specified material or missed classes. The faculty, however, controlled the granting of degrees and, because of their permanence, gradually increased their authority in the university.

At Paris teachers formed a guild to control the granting of licenses to teach, at least in part because the chancellor of the archdiocese of Paris had been selling them to unqualified persons. Following a "town-gown" conflict in which several students were killed, King Philip II gave the university its charter in 1200, and the papal bull *Parens scientiarum* (1231) subsequently established institutional independence by exempting the university from the jurisdiction of the local church.

Paris was famous for its teachers of logic, philosophy, and theology. English students were among those attracted to Paris, but in 1167 worsening relations between England and France forced King Henry II to order them home. They settled at Oxford, which had its own chancellor by 1214. The growing demand for educated people in church and state, national and urban rivalries, and the search for more hospitable environments led to the founding of more universities—over 20 by 1300, more than 75 by 1500. A number of these were royal or papal foundations: that of Naples, which absorbed the medical school at Salerno, was established by Emperor Frederick II; those of Rome, by Pope Innocent IV; of Toulouse, by Pope Gregory IX; and of Seville, by King Alfonso X of Castile. Others were the result of migrating students, as in the case of Cambridge (from Oxford) and Padua (from Bologna).

Most universities were organized into four faculties: the arts, which comprised the trivium (grammar, rhetoric, and logic) and the quadrivium (arithmetic, geometry, astronomy, and music), theology, medicine, and civil and canon (church) law. The standard form of instruction was the lecture, which consisted of reading and expounding on a Latin text. A typical student listened to lectures for about seven hours a day, beginning at 5 or 6 A.M. Formal debates were also a standard pedagogical tool, but because of the expense there were few books and no libraries. Students were not examined at the conclusion of a series of lectures but at the end of a program of study, when examinations were oral and usually public. A bachelor of arts degree typically took three to six years of study and qualified one to instruct others under a master's supervision. A license to teach required several more years of study. In order to lecture as part of the arts faculty one had to become a master of arts, which required the preparation and defense of a thesis. Substantial additional study was required for a doctorate in law (up to seven years) or theology (up to 15 years).

At first universities had no permanent campuses or buildings but made do with rented rooms. To assist needy students, residence halls or "colleges" were endowed, and these eventually acquired their own instructional staff. Among the best known are the Sorbonne, founded at Paris in 1257 or 1258 by Robert de Sorbon, a royal chaplain, and Merton College, established at Oxford around 1263 by Robert Merton, who acquired the buildings from the local Jewish community. Such colleges provided the nucleus of a permanent campus. By the end of the thirteenth century the number of students—all male—at Paris exceeded 4,000, while Oxford had more than 2,000. As centers of learning, the universities attracted some of the greatest minds of the High Middle Ages.

## PARIS: MONKS, MERCHANTS, AND STUDENTS IN THE ROYAL CITY

By the time the University of Paris received its charter from Philip II in 1200, the city was in the midst of a period of dramatic growth. At the beginning of the eleventh century its outskirts had still been in ruins as the result of ninth-century Viking raids, but by 1300 the city's population had reached 100,000 and gloried in a majestic new cathedral, imposing new walls, and a flourishing commerce in addition to its university. In part the growth reflected the increasing power of the French monarchy, in part the city's strategic location at the crossroads of the trade routes between southern Europe and Flanders, or, by way of the river Seine, between east-

**14.1** *Medieval Universities*

ern France and the English Channel. Because the Capetian monarchs made Paris their capital, the city attracted both the nobility and ecclesiastical and educational institutions, thereby increasing the demand for luxury items and other goods. Parisian artisans produced a wide range of jewelry, swords, saddles, linens, and wine barrels. Merchants in turn traded these goods at the great Champagne fairs in northeastern France for Flemish and Italian woolens, Asian spices and sugar, Byzantine silks, Spanish leathers, and English tin.

The heart of Paris was the Île de la Cité, an island in the Seine whose western half was dominated by the royal palace and the exquisite Gothic chapel of Sainte-

Chapelle, built by Louis IX to house a collection of relics that allegedly included the crown of thorns, a piece of the cross, and a sample of Christ's blood. The eastern portion of the Île de la Cité became the site of the magnificent Gothic cathedral of Notre Dame ("Our Lady"), first begun in 1163. The city's commercial center, site of its guilds and principal markets, was on the right (north) bank of the Seine, extending in a rough semicircle from the Grand Pont, the great bridge, to the Île de la Cité, on which the Jewish and Lombard moneychangers had their shops. To the south, the Left Bank, or Latin Quarter, was the home of the university and of several religious orders, including the Dominicans, the Augus-

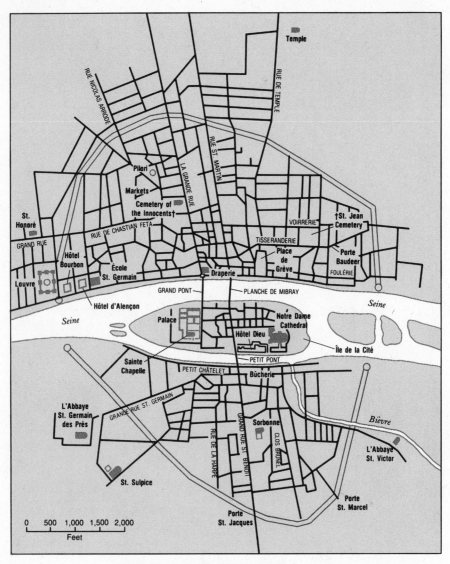

***14.2** Paris in the Thirteenth Century*

tinians, and the Carmelites. The ancient Roman walls, which were still standing in the twelfth century, enclosed only some 25 acres and were thus totally inadequate for the burgeoning city. Philip II ordered the construction of new ramparts on both banks. The resulting walls, which enclosed approximately 625 acres, were up to 20 feet high and 10 feet thick and featured 33 towers on the north bank and 34 on the south. Just beyond the wall, where the rampart met the river, stood the Louvre, a fortified palace that also functioned as a treasury, an armory, and a prison. Philip's ambitious building program also included three new hospitals to care for the needy and three aqueducts to supply the city with fresh water. He even launched a project to pave the city's main streets with 3-foot-square blocks of sandstone.

The Paris of Philip II and Louis IX was a colorful amalgam of the secular and the sacred, the royal and the common. The enforcement of the law was the responsibility of the provost of Paris, who was appointed by the crown, but in general city affairs were handled by a municipal council presided over by the master of the corporation of river merchants, the *marchands de l'eau*. Despite the presence of the crown and major religious orders, Paris was far from a puritanical city. Prostitutes were so abundant that two streets were named after them, the Rue Val-d'Amour and the Rue Pute-y-muce ("whore-in-hiding"). The churchmen of Paris themselves sometimes behaved bawdily, and in 1212 a council convened in the city tried to curtail their more outlandish behavior, including the keeping of mistresses, the Feast of the Drunken Deacons on December 26, and the Feast of Fools on January 1, when they parodied the liturgy, burned old shoes instead of incense, and marched through the streets wearing grotesque costumes.

In the thirteenth century, university students added to the local color, particularly when they demonstrated on behalf of a favorite cause, battled with the civic guards, or fought with the townsfolk or among themselves. Although lectures began at 5 A.M. and continued, with appropriate breaks, well into the afternoon, there was time in the evening for conversation and a few drinks in a tavern before retiring to modest rooms, typically in the attics of Left Bank houses. Classes met in rooms rented by the faculty, and only gradually did the university begin to acquire buildings, notably the privately endowed colleges, such as the Sorbonne, established to house, teach, and control the students. Although these were arduous years, the students lived in one of the most exciting European cities and studied under the foremost educators of their day.

## The Scholastics

Well before the evolution of the first universities, the schoolmen, or scholastics, of western Europe were engaged in a heated debate over a number of philosophical and theological issues. The scholastics, who used Aristotelian methodology and adopted the Aristotelian world view, were especially concerned with three fundamental and intimately related problems: the proper study of theological knowledge, the nature of ultimate reality, and the relationship of faith and reason.

Although the roots of Christian theology go back to the first century, only in the 1100s did the discipline of systematic theology emerge through the application of logic to the most fundamental religious questions. The leaders in this endeavor were Peter Abelard (1079–1142) of Brittany, a master in the cathedral school at Paris, and his disciple Peter Lombard (c. 1095–1160), who eventually became bishop of Paris. Their technique, known as the dialectical method, consisted of juxtaposing seemingly contradictory statements in order to encourage students to seek a logical resolution. Abelard applied this technique to theology in his book *Sic et Non* ("Yes and No"), a compilation of contradictory statements by early church fathers on a variety of religious issues. Students were encouraged to resolve the conflicts by taking into account the way words change meaning over time, the possibility of inaccurate texts, historical context, and the need to weigh the credibility of different authorities. Peter Lombard followed the same pedagogical method in his *Four Books of Sentences*, which analyzed such fundamental Christian doctrines as the Trinity, creation, the Incarnation, and the sacra-

ments. From the thirteenth century to the sixteenth, Peter Lombard's book served as the standard theological text in the universities. Traditionalists, however, condemned the logical approach to theology on the grounds that divine mysteries could not be probed by human reason and that such a method could easily lead to unorthodox thought.

The famous debate over the nature of reality reflected the indebtedness of the scholastics to classical Greek philosophy. In the eleventh century the French scholar Roscellin rejected the Platonic notion that universal concepts are real and instead insisted that reality consists only of individual things. Individual men and women are real; humanity is simply the name (*nomen*) for a mental category or concept. Roscellin and his followers thus came to be called nominalists. Because they attached primary significance to the experience of individual things through the senses, the nominalists radically altered traditional theology, which had relied heavily on philosophical concepts. Accordingly, nominalists had to assert most religious beliefs solely on the basis of faith and biblical teaching, not rational demonstration.

In contrast to the nominalists, realists such as the Italian monk Anselm (1033–1109) asserted that individual things are knowable only because they reflect universal ideas, which are accessible by reason. Realists agreed that initially an act of faith is required for things beyond the reach of the senses. "I believe," said Anselm, "so that I may know." Once beyond this, however, reason could demonstrate the existence of universal ideas and even of God. It is impossible, Anselm argued, to conceive of a being greater than God; a being who exists is greater than a being who does not exist; therefore, the idea of God must include the existence of God. The importance Anselm attached to reason did not negate Scripture but helped make logic and philosophy a fundamental part of the new systematic theology.

A middle ground in the debate over universals was advocated by a group of moderate realists that included Abelard and his student, John of Salisbury. Influenced by Aristotle, they accepted the reality of both individual things and the general ideas after which they were patterned. The idea of humanity was thus as real as the experience of individuals. The greatest of the moderate realists, Thomas Aquinas (c. 1225–1274), taught that each particular thing has the universal within it, as that which gives it its essence; by studying individual things, one can rationally discover the essence and thus formulate valid general concepts.

At the heart of the debate over universals and the dialectical method was the fundamental question of the relationship between faith (or revelation) and reason. The scholastics generally agreed that theology and philosophy are intimately related, but Franciscan and Dominican thinkers disagreed over the nature of that relationship. The great Franciscan theologians Alexander of Hales (died 1245) and his pupil Bonaventure (1221–1274), both of whom taught at the University of Paris, respected reason but put their real emphasis on revelation. To them faith was an act of the will by which one accepts revealed truth; reason is useful only to explain the truth gleaned from revelation. The leading Dominican theologians, Aquinas and his teacher Albertus Magnus (died 1280), who also taught at Paris, accorded reason a greater role than the Franciscans in the discovery of knowledge but stopped short of making revelation subordinate to reason. Because faith and reason are complementary paths, Aquinas believed that by rational processes an unbeliever can be led to the point of making a commitment of faith.

Both Alexander of Hales and Aquinas wrote lengthy *summae* (summations) in which major theological issues were rationally analyzed through a process that included the meticulous refutation of opposing viewpoints. The blending of theology and philosophy is nowhere more evident than in Aquinas' *Summa Theologica*, particularly in the sections devoted to rational proofs for the existence of God, such as the argument from an orderly universe to the existence of a Great Designer or the argument from motion to the existence of a Prime Mover, derived from Aristotle. For Aquinas, faith and reason are fully harmonious, for both are avenues to seek the one truth. The work of Aquinas thus represents the culmination of the attempt to synthesize the revealed tenets of Christianity with the rational principles of classical philosophy. Christian scholastics such as Aquinas, Jewish theologians such as Maimonides, Muslim philosophers such as Averroës, and contemporary Neo-Confucian scholars in China all stressed the importance of logical analysis to bolster traditional values. Apart from the Neo-Confucianists, they shared a heavy indebtedness to the thought of Aristotle, but in a more general sense all of them reflect the basic human quest to order existence and reaffirm basic ideals through the use of reason.

## Law and Political Thought

While the scholastics established the discipline of systematic theology, other scholars were responsible for reviving the study of Roman law in the late eleventh and

---

## ◙ Proving That God Exists ◙

*The compatibility of faith and reason in scholastic thought is reflected in Thomas Aquinas' arguments to prove the existence of God.*

God's existence can be proved in five ways. The first and clearest proof is the argument from motion. It is certain, and in accordance with sense experience, that some things in this world are moved. Now everything that is moved is moved by something else. . . . We are therefore bound to arrive at a first mover which is not moved by anything, and all men understand that this is God.

The second way is from the nature of an efficient cause. We find that there is a sequence of efficient causes in sensible things. . . . We are therefore bound to suppose that there is a first efficient cause. And all men call this God.

The third way is from the nature of possibility and necessity. There are some things which may either exist or not exist, since some things come to be and pass away, and may therefore be or not be. . . . We are therefore bound to suppose something necessary in itself, which does not owe its necessity to anything else, but which is the cause of the necessity of other things. And all men call this God.

The fourth way is from the degrees that occur in things, which are found to be more and less good, true, noble, and so on. . . . There is therefore something which is the cause of the being of all things that are, as well as of their goodness and their every perfection. This we call God.

The fifth way is from the governance of things. We see how some things, like natural bodies, work for an end even though they have no knowledge. . . . There is therefore an intelligent being by whom all natural things are directed to their end. This we call God.

*Source:* Thomas Aquinas, *Nature and Grace*, trans. and ed. A. M. Fairweather. *Library of Christian Classics*, vol. 11 (Philadelphia: Westminster Press, 1954), pp. 54–56.

**The scholastic theologian Thomas Aquinas was influenced by Aristotle (lower left) and Plato (lower right) as well as the earlier Christian thinkers shown above him. The Islamic philosopher Averroës lies vanquished at his feet. [Alinari/Art Resource]**

Germany in the 1200s. The Roman influence was not entirely positive, for it also resulted in the reintroduction of judicial torture. The impact of Roman law was greatest in the Italian states and the Iberian peninsula.

Roman principles and procedures also heavily influenced the development of the church's own law, called canon law, which was codified in the twelfth century by Gratian, an Italian monk who taught at Bologna. His influential text, the *Decretum* (c. 1140), used the dialectical method to organize and reconcile approximately 3,900 laws. Canon law in this period involved not only such religious matters as sacraments and church property but also slander, libel, morals, tithes, wills, and oaths. Gratian's codification was the prelude to a whole series of commentaries on canon law and an increasingly judicial relationship between the church and its members. In the thirteenth century, legal studies became as complex and sophisticated as scholastic theology.

The discussion of legal questions was relevant to a growing interest in political theory sparked in large measure by issues raised in the investiture controversy (see Chapter 13). As the debate over investiture intensified, theorists sympathetic to the papacy claimed ever broader papal powers until at last they asserted the pope's right to intervene in secular matters as part of his responsibility to supervise temporal sovereigns. This, of course, was unacceptable to secular rulers, whose own theorists obligingly extended the claim of royal authority until it included the duty to intervene in ecclesiastical affairs should the papacy prove incapable of reforming the church. Whereas papal writers contended that temporal sovereigns received their right to govern through the church as a divine agency, monarchical theorists insisted that such power was bestowed on the rulers directly by God. Manegold of Lautenbach (died 1085) even went so far as to argue that God's agency was not the church but the people, who were therefore entitled to withdraw their support from a tyrannical ruler. Although Manegold's theory had democratic implications, no medieval thinker espoused a philosophy of popular government. Most, in fact, would have accepted Aquinas' assertion that monarchy is preferable to other forms of government because it is the most stable.

Monarchical government was made to seem natural by the depiction of society in organic terms. The English scholar John of Salisbury (c. 1115–1180) developed the notion of the body politic, in which the sovereign is the head; the judges and governors are the ears, eyes, and tongue; the magistrates and soldiers are the hands; and the peasants are the feet. As an apologist for papal supremacy, John was then able to argue that the church is the soul of the body. Although the organic theory was often used to underscore the naturalness and stability of hierarchical society, John accepted the right of people to overthrow a tyrannical ruler on the grounds that tyranny was an abuse of the power bestowed on a ruler by

early twelfth centuries. The revival began in southern France and northern Italy as teachers and attorneys turned increasingly to the sixth-century *Corpus Juris Civilis* of Justinian for guidance. At Bologna, Irnerius and his successors lectured on the *Corpus* using the same dialectical method popularized in theology by Abelard. Their work was largely confined to glosses or comments on the *Corpus*, but commencing in the mid-twelfth century, legal scholars became more creative by exploring the general principles on which the laws were based and adapting the laws to the specific conditions of their own time and locale. There was thus a gradual blending of ideas in Roman and customary law, even in Germany and England, where customary and Roman law continued as separate entities. Roman influence was especially evident in the work of codifying and systematizing the law, such as was carried out in Saxony and southern

God. Despite the democratic implications of this theory, however, John refused to consider rulers responsible to their subjects; if tyrants were overthrown, people acted only as divine agents and not in their own right. In general, medieval thinkers preferred monarchical government but expected sovereigns to rule justly in accord with divine law. The tendency was to see society and government in positive, natural terms: the state, said Aquinas, was a natural institution, not a necessary evil as Augustine had taught in the fifth century.

## Science and Medicine

Although medieval thinkers failed to free science from its subservient position as a handmaiden to theology, they succeeded in pointing the way to a more accurate understanding of the physical universe. Scientific knowledge came to be seen not only as a reflection of divine handiwork but also as a means to improve living conditions. The expanding availability of Greek and Arabic treatises on science in Latin translation gave strong impetus to scientific study in Europe. One of the earliest interpreters of Arabic science was the twelfth-century English scholar Adelard of Bath, whose translation of Euclid's *Elements* from Arabic became the principal textbook for the study of geometry in the West. His own *Natural Questions* gave European students an insight into Arabic knowledge in such fields as astronomy, botany, zoology, and meteorology.

One of the most important contributions of medieval science was the gradual awareness of the significance of observation and experiment as the best means to acquire knowledge of the physical world. Among the early advocates of this methodology were Albertus Magnus of Paris and Robert Grosseteste (c. 1175–1253) of Oxford, both influenced by Aristotle. Grosseteste was convinced that optics, or the study of vision, was the foundation of all other scientific knowledge because light was the most basic physical substance. Accordingly, he employed an early form of the experimental method to study the rainbow. His famous pupil, the English Franciscan Roger Bacon (c. 1220–1292), proposed the dissection of pig and cow eyes in order to understand optical principles. Bacon learned that light travels faster than sound, and he was interested in the use of magnifying glasses and eyeglasses. However, he is more noted for his advocacy of experimental study than for specific contributions to scientific knowledge, and like his contemporaries he continued to attach credibility to the pseudosciences of alchemy and astrology. Bacon's oft-quoted anticipation of airplanes, submarines, and machine-powered ships were flights of fantasy, not concepts based on scientific principles like those of Leonardo da Vinci two centuries later. However, medieval scientists such as Grosseteste and Bacon did make a significant contribution by advocating the importance not only of the experimental method but also of mathematics as a key toward understanding the natural world.

Medical knowledge, too, was highly dependent on translations of Greek and Arabic works, among them the Arabic treatises of the Jewish physician Maimonides (1135–1204), much of whose career was spent in Cairo, and Avicenna, whose *Canon of Medicine* went through numerous editions. Arabic doctors had made major advances in the use of drugs, and this knowledge passed to Europeans, especially through the famous medical school at Salerno. Until it was surpassed by Montpellier in France about 1200, Salerno was the leading center of medical education in Europe, thanks largely to the presence of Greek and Arabic physicians. Among those who taught at Salerno were a number of women, including Trotula, author of the treatise *On Feminine Disorders*. Students at Salerno learned surgical techniques, though medieval operations were generally crude affairs in which modified butchers' instruments were used and amputation was common. Although anesthetics were coming into use, many patients suffered through operations deadened only by alcohol or opium. Death from shock or infection was common. The first illustrated guide to surgery was written by the Muslim Abul Kasim of Córdoba, Spain (c. 936–c. 1013), but there was no handbook of anatomy until 1316, when one was prepared by Mondino de' Luzzi, who taught at Bologna. The advance of medicine was reflected in the growth of hospitals; England had 18 in 1123 but 428 by 1300. Quarantine, however, was introduced only in 1346. Because of the interest in optics, eyeglasses became fairly common in Italy in the thirteenth century, and there were even operations for cataracts. A good deal of medieval practice, of course, was still grounded in superstition, such as the belief that sexual intercourse with a virgin would cure a man of various illnesses. Medicine remained primitive, not least because of its reliance on the ancient Greek theory of disease, according to which illnesses resulted from imbalances in the four basic "qualities" (hot, cold, wet, dry) and the four "humors" (blood, phlegm, and black and yellow bile). The best medieval treatment was often that administered by folk doctors who used herbal remedies and commonsense practices.

## The Medieval Vision

Between the eleventh and the fifteenth centuries European artists developed new styles that reflected not only their Christian faith but also the outlook first of the monastic and feudal orders and then of the expanding cities. The rampaging Vikings, Normans, and Magyars in the preceding period had destroyed many wooden churches, hence the eleventh and twelfth centuries had ample incentive to rebuild—in stone wherever possible. Perhaps even greater motivation to build stemmed from the expanding economy, the need to provide churches for pilgrims on their way to holy places, and the pious spirit engendered by the religious reforms. The cathedrals and abbey churches erected in the High Middle Ages stand as a silent but pictorially eloquent monument to the faith, resolve, and urban pride of medieval Christians.

## The Age of the Romanesque

The artistic style of the eleventh and twelfth centuries was largely shaped by the monastic revival and the militant ideals of the feudal order. The monastic reforms that commenced in the tenth century revitalized the church, giving it a new resolve to glorify God. The new style was later called Romanesque because of its similarities to classical Roman architecture. The great abbey churches that epitomize this style reflect the monastic values of order, simplicity, and otherworldliness. But the religious revival also led to a substantial increase in the number of people who undertook pilgrimages to the shrines of the saints, such as that of St. James at Compostela in northwestern Spain. The churches along the pilgrimage routes had to be larger than the traditional basilicas in order to accommodate the throngs of pilgrims. In the aftermath of the Viking and Magyar invasions, there was also a desire to make the churches stronger, with stone instead of wooden ceilings and with facades in certain cases that were reminiscent of feudal castles. Some Romanesque churches, such as that of Notre-Dame-la-Grande in Poitiers, look almost like fortresses because of their towers and thick walls.

Romanesque churches were constructed throughout Europe, although the greatest number were in France. There were regional differences as the form developed, but the Roman-style buildings shared fundamental characteristics, including a floor plan in the shape of a cross, the use of round arches and barrel (tunnel) vaults, and heavy buttresses to support the legs of the arches. The weight of the stone ceiling made it virtually impossible to cut windows into the sides of the barrel vault; hence the interior of early Romanesque churches was dark. Later Romanesque architects revived the Roman principle of the groined vault, by which intersecting arches distribute the weight of the ceiling to specific points along the wall. These points must be heavily buttressed, but windows can then be cut in the intervening spaces to illumine the interior of the church. One of the earliest Romanesque churches to use this principle was the cathedral at Durham in northern England.

To adorn the new churches, Romanesque artists revived the technique of stone sculpture, which had largely been forgotten during the eighth and ninth centuries. The figures they sculpted were intended to teach as well as to adorn, a function especially significant in an age when the overwhelming majority of the population was illiterate. Rich in symbols easily remembered by the faithful, Romanesque sculpture was a constant visual reminder of the fundamental teachings of the church. One of the most common locations for Romanesque sculpture was the semicircular space, called a tympanum, above the door of a church, which was often used to show Christ at the Last Judgment. Moreover, the columns of churches and cloisters alike were regularly topped by carved capitals depicting everything from vegetation to monsters. To some of the godly, the artists had gone too far: "I say naught of the vast height of your churches," thundered the Cistercian monk Bernard of Clairvaux, "their immoderate length, their superfluous breadth, the costly polishings, the curious carvings and paintings which attract the worshipper's gaze and hinder his attention."[2]

The monastic spirit of the Romanesque was also reflected in the paintings of the period, the most important of which were either murals in abbey churches rendered in a Byzantine style or miniatures that "illuminated" (illustrated) manuscripts. The latter were often painted by

The nave and choir of the pilgrimage church of St. Sernin in Toulouse, France (c. 1080–1120), were built using a barrel, or tunnel, vault. The interior lighting is dim and indirect. [Marburg/Art Resource]

The Romanesque sculpture in the tympanum of St. Trophime in Arles, France, is symbolic rather than naturalistic. The winged figures around Christ represent the four evangelists, Matthew, Mark, Luke, and John. [Marburg/Art Resource]

monks and nuns already devoted to copying manuscripts. Most of the identifiable manuscript illuminators in the Middle Ages were in fact nuns. Already in the sixth century the convent at Poitiers specialized in training nuns to copy and decorate manuscripts, and 200 years later two sisters, Harlinde and Relinde, founded a religious community at Maaseyck in Flanders that achieved fame for its illuminated manuscripts and gold- and jewel-bedecked tapestries.

Some medieval manuscripts depicted religious scenes; others created elaborate, intricate capital letters. Some of their work reveals a sense of humor, as in the case of the nun who depicted herself swinging on the tail of an elaborate *Q*. The miniatures in turn served as models for murals and later for the stained glass windows that decorated Gothic churches.

## The Gothic Achievement

The world of the Gothic* artist was no longer primarily that of the monastic and the pilgrim but rather that of the city and the scholastic theologian. Gothic cathedrals were triumphs of the urban spirit, a testimony to the civic pride that manifested itself in rivalries between the cities. But the Gothic achievement was equally a testimony in stone to the synthesis of theology and philosophy that the scholastics were forging. Just as reason

---

*The term *Gothic* was introduced in the fifteenth century to describe medieval architecture. Later critics liked the term because it was evocative of the spirit of the "barbaric" Goths who had sacked Rome. The accusation was unjust, but the term stuck.

became the handmaiden of faith to bridge the gap between heaven and earth, so the soaring spires and lofty vaults of the Gothic cathedral carried the vision of the worshiper logically and compellingly heavenward. The principles of scholastic theology and Gothic architecture share the conviction that reason and nature are not stumbling blocks but pathways to spiritual truth. In the Romanesque the material and the spiritual exist in an uneasy tension; in the Gothic they unite in praising God.

The principles of the Gothic style were initially worked out in the abbey church at St. Denis, near Paris, in the 1130s and 1140s. Under the direction of Abbot Suger, the goal of the architects was to construct a church that "would shine with the wonderful and uninterrupted light of most luminous windows."[3] The key was to construct a skeletal framework strong enough to support the stone roof and yet airy enough to permit the extensive use of stained glass. By using pointed instead of round arches, the architects could achieve greater height and enclose rectangular as well as square spaces. At Beauvais the groined vaulting with its supporting ribs soared to the incredible height of 157 feet, only to collapse and have to be rebuilt. The Gothic architect also introduced the flying buttress, a support that carried the horizontal thrust of the arch to heavy piers outside the church. The purpose was twofold: placing the massive piers outside the church created a more spacious interior, and the flying buttress, like the pointed arch, guided the eye of the beholder heavenward.

The abundant stained glass windows, some of which may have been done by women, give the interior of a Gothic cathedral an ethereal quality. One writer of the period likened the windows to the Bible: "Since their brilliance lets the splendor of the True Light pass into the church, they enlighten those inside."[4] Like sculpture, the windows had a pedagogical as well as an aesthetic function, and to the degree that they encouraged worship, they had a liturgical role as well. To create a window, the artist first sketched a design in chalk and then fit together cut pieces of glass. Details, such as facial features, were created by using metal oxides on the glass and firing them in a kiln. The pieces of glass were joined with lead strips, and the window was strengthened by the addition of black iron bands, which also served to separate the colors to keep them from blurring in the viewer's eye. The finished window took the place of the mosaics and murals that had decorated earlier churches. The windows were costly, but royalty, nobility, prelates, and guilds donated them as marks of their piety.

As in the Romanesque period, sculpture adorned the cathedrals, only more lavishly. The cathedral at Chartres, for instance, has more than 2,000 carved figures. In keeping with the attempt to unite the physical and the spiritual, Gothic statuary became increasingly more naturalistic both in its representation of people and in its rendering of plants and animals. Unlike their Romanesque predecessors, Gothic artists, some of whom were women, began to use human models for their statues so that their work captured elements of individual personality. Simultaneously, convention required the continued use of traditional iconographic symbols, which restricted artistic freedom but assured the ability of viewers to interpret the art's religious meaning. The range of subject matter was even more extensive than that of the Romanesque era, so much so that Gothic cathedrals, with their myriad statues and surrounding stained glass, have been likened to visual encyclopedias. In its comprehensive treatment of the natural and spiritual worlds, the Gothic cathedral was akin to the ambitious *summae* of Thomas Aquinas.

## Vernacular Culture and the Age of Chivalry

Apart from the Anglo-Saxon tradition, the literature of the early medieval period was nearly all in Latin, though a rich oral tradition created and preserved stories and poems in the vernacular, the language of the people. Easily the most important vernacular work from the early medieval period is *Beowulf*, a lengthy poem about a Swedish hero who saved the Danes from a monster and its mother. Written in England by a monk around the eighth century, *Beowulf* reflects the values of the period: loyalty, valor, and a strong sense of aristocratic worth. Surviving poems written by other authors about

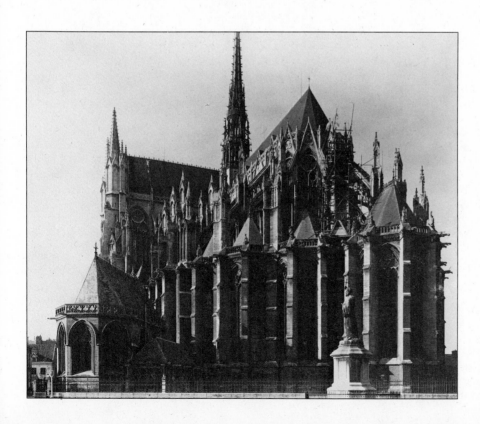

A view of the apse of the Gothic cathedral at Amiens. Tiny chapels radiate around the exterior. [Marburg/Art Resource]

The Gothic statuary on the exterior of the
Rheims Cathedral is more naturalistic than
that of the Romanesque period (compare
St. Trophime). At the left, the archangel
Gabriel informs Mary that she will give birth
to the Messiah; at the right, Mary visits
Elizabeth, mother of John the Baptist.
[Marburg/Art Resource]

the same time in northern England cover both sacred
and secular themes. The greatest of these writers, who
were influenced by monks from Ireland, was Bede (c.
673–735), a Benedictine monk commonly called "the
Venerable" because of his piety and learning. Most of
what he wrote was in Latin, including his masterpiece,
the *Ecclesiastical History of the English Nation*, the primary source of our knowledge about English history
from the time Christianity was introduced in 597 until
731. His classic was translated into Anglo-Saxon by King
Alfred the Great (871–899) and the scholars at his palace school. During Alfred's reign another major historical source was begun, a vernacular compilation of documents known as the *Anglo-Saxon Chronicle*. Thus the
early medieval writers resorted to the vernacular to explain their past as well as to entertain.

During the High Middle Ages much of the material
that had only been transmitted orally was written down,
still in the vernacular, and to this body of material were
added new works, both secular and religious. The richness of this body of vernacular literature is reflected in
the fact that it appeared in no fewer than eight major
literary forms: heroic epics, minstrel songs, courtly ro-

mances, allegorical romances, mystery and miracle
plays, pious writings, historical works, and popular stories. Although the French took the lead in developing
vernacular literature, important contributions were
made as far afield as Russia, Scandinavia, and Spain.
Latin was the language of the learned—of lawyers, ecclesiastics, and scholastics—but beginning in the eleventh century the vernacular tongues increasingly became the language of literary entertainment. Although
literacy rates remained low, these works undoubtedly
reached wide audiences as the literate read them aloud
to others.

The earliest heroic epics were the *chansons de geste*—
"songs of heroic deeds"—composed in the northern
French vernacular. In oral form they go back to the ninth
and tenth centuries, when they were used to entertain
French pilgrims traveling to the religious shrines of

The story of Roland's heroism in battling the
Muslims as recounted in the *Song of Roland*
was a favorite theme in medieval art. Roland
is shown here about to be ambushed by the
Muslims at the lower right. [Preussischer
Kulturbesitz, Handschriftenabteilung, Berlin]

southern France and northern Spain. Of the more than 80 *chansons de geste* that survive, the most popular is the *Song of Roland*, the legendary account of a Muslim attack on Charlemagne's rear guard as it retreated across the Pyrenees in 778. The forceful lines of the poem exalt the simple virtues of the feudal order: personal loyalty, militant Christian faith, and individual honor. Because Roland failed to summon help in time to save his men, he is praised for his valor and loyalty but not his wisdom. The conflict with Islam is also the setting for the famous Spanish *chanson* of the twelfth century, the *Poem of My Cid*, the fictionalized account of a chivalric lord noted for his defeat of the Moorish rulers of Andalusia and the heroic exploits that led to his conquest of Valencia. The great German epic, the *Nibelungenlied* (c. 1200), has a strikingly different flavor as it recounts the mythical quest for a hoard of Rhine gold in an atmosphere of love, treachery, and violence. Although the written version was given a Christian veneer, at root it reflects pagan Germanic mythology. In spirit it is akin to the twelfth- and thirteenth-century Scandinavian *Eddas*, which recount the stories of pagan gods and heroes, such as Thor, the god of thunder, and Frigga, the goddess of marriage, after whom Thursday and Friday are named. The counterpart of these works in Kievan Russia was

the twelfth-century *Song of Igor's Campaign*, another account of heroic exploit. Together such works represent a simple historic interest in a largely mythical past dominated by valiant heroes and heroines, a sharp contrast to the theological and metaphysical concerns of the scholastics.

French poets also took the lead in composing minstrel songs, particularly in the south, where troubadours sang their lyrical lines in the Provençal dialect. These *chansons d'amour*, or "songs of love," were immensely popular in the twelfth and thirteenth centuries throughout western Europe. Nearly 2,500 Provençal lyrics survive. Whereas the *chansons de geste* helped establish the code of knightly conduct called chivalry, the *chansons d'amour* were instrumental in popularizing the concept of courtly love. The key to this concept is the exaltation of women and love, sometimes in a platonic rather than a physical sense. The minstrels encouraged the virtual worship of the wife of someone of a higher social degree, expecting in return at least simple kindness and inner joy if not physical pleasure. A cult of courtly love was presided over at Poitiers by Eleanor of Aquitaine, wife of the English King Henry II, and in Champagne by her daughter, Countess Marie. The Germans had their counterpart to the troubadours in the *Minnesingers*

## ◙ Courtly Love ◙

*One of the most intriguing documents in the courtly love tradition is the treatise on love,* De amore, *by Andreas Capellanus, who was associated with the court of Eleanor of Aquitaine's daughter, Marie de Champagne. There is considerable debate as to whether this twelfth-century work was intended to be taken seriously or humorously.*

1. Marriage cannot be pleaded as an excuse for refusing to love.

2. A person who cannot keep a secret can never be a lover. . . .

7. If one of two lovers dies, love must be foresworn for two years by the survivor. . . .

11. It is not becoming to love those ladies who only love with a view to marriage. . . .

14. Too easy possession renders love contemptible. But possession which is attended with difficulties makes love valuable and of great price. . . .

17. A new love affair banishes the old one completely. . . .

22. When one of the lovers begins to entertain suspicion of the other, the jealousy and the love increase at once. . . .

29. Too great prodigality of favors is not advisable, for a lover who is wearied with a superabundance of pleasure is generally as a rule disinclined to love.

*Source:* J. F. Rowbotham, *The Troubadours and Courts of Love* (New York: Macmillan, 1895), pp. 245–247.

("love singers"), whose lyrics were more spiritual than those of the French *chansons*. The best known of these minstrels was Walther von der Vogelweide (Walter of the Birdmeadows, c. 1170–c. 1230), so named because birds are prominently featured in his love lyrics. A number of women similarly wrote romantic lyrics, though they did not exalt men as the male poets did women in the literature of courtly love.

The courtly love of the minstrels was united with the *chansons de geste* to create the courtly romance, the most famous of which are the late-twelfth-century works of Chrétien de Troyes about King Arthur. In these stories, the adventurous knight sought his identity in the dangerous world beyond the royal court, but if successful he could receive his just acceptance by recounting his deeds before that court. Cistercian influence in the thirteenth century led to the addition of the theme of the Holy Grail, purportedly the chalice used by Christ in the Last Supper and later taken to Britain. Thus, as the Arthurian legends spread throughout Europe, knights such as Sir Galahad and Perceval were recognizably Christian heroes. In the 1200s two French authors, William de Lorris and Jean de Meun, combined allegory and satire with the romance to create the popular *Romance of the Rose*. William's portion treats traditional troubadour themes of love in an allegorical mode—the "Rose in the Garden of Delight" is the poet's sweetheart—but Jean uses his pen to satirize everything from women to clerical celibacy.

Although most religious literature continued to be written in Latin, vernacular works began to win a wider audience. Mystery plays—religious dramas about biblical subjects, especially Christ's life—were often in Latin and in fact originated as part of the Latin liturgy. As fictitious matter was added, the plays acquired a separate identity, opening the way for vernacular versions, such as the twelfth-century French play *The Mystery of Adam*. Beginning in the fourteenth century these plays were no longer the province of the clergy but became community productions typically performed, by women as well as men, during such church festivals as Whitsun or Corpus Christi. A variation of the mystery play, the miracle play, took as its theme the life of a saint; one such was the twelfth-century English drama about St. Catherine, which must have been particularly interesting to women. The miracle and mystery plays in turn gave rise to morality plays, such as *Everyman*, which personified vices and virtues in the context of a struggle for the soul. A variety of pious literature was also composed in the vernacular during the High Middle Ages, including Francis of Assisi's *Canticle of the Sun*, a lyrical praise of God for creation, and a thirteenth-century collection of stories about Francis titled *The Little Flowers of St. Francis*.

In a more secular vein, the vernacular literature of this period included several historical works of note. Geoffrey of Monmouth's *British History* is largely given over to retelling the legendary stories of King Arthur and other fictitious tales and thus hardly qualifies as history. In contrast, Geoffrey de Villehardouin provided a historical account of the capture of Constantinople by the crusaders in 1204, which he titled *The Conquest of Constantinople*, and Jean de Joinville wrote the *History of St. Louis*, the story of the French King Louis IX. Various German chroniclers also wrote in the vernacular. French writers in particular were interested in recording popular tales—*fabliaux*—that had long been current in oral form. Alternately satirical, coarse, and amusing, the intent was usually to entertain, though some stories had a didactic purpose as well. Some were animal fables, such as the *Romance of Reynard the Fox*.

The variety of vernacular literature provides a healthy corrective to the common notion that medieval people were inordinately concerned with religious issues. Instead they demonstrated a pronounced interest in such themes as chivalry, courtly love, the mythical and mysterious past, bawdy stories, and tales of violence and romance.

# Medieval Jewry

No discussion of medieval life and culture can fail to acknowledge the significant contribution of the Jews. During the period of the Roman Empire they had migrated throughout Europe as far afield as Spain, France, Dalmatia, and the Crimea. Small Jewish communities also established themselves to the east, from Arabia and Persia to India and China. Many of the earliest Jewish settlers in the West were farmers, an occupation in which they continued for centuries in southern Europe, but most of the Jews who settled farther north engaged in commerce as town life developed. Charlemagne's government welcomed Jewish immigrants by granting them charters that guaranteed protection and privileges. The Capetian kings of France continued this policy, making France a center of medieval Jewry. The German Jewish communities were founded by immigrants from France and southern Europe beginning in the ninth century; by 1100 there were numerous Jews in the Rhineland. Few Jews emigrated to Scandinavia, and England was the last major European country where they settled, mostly after the Norman Conquest in 1066. The extensive Jewish settlements in Europe and their contributions to Jewish culture ensured that in the future the Jews would be fundamentally European in outlook.

As Europeans turned increasingly to commercial activities in the High Middle Ages, Jewish merchants found themselves slowly squeezed out of commerce and into moneylending. Because the Christian church prohibited usury—lending money at unjust rates of inter-

**Interior of the synagogue at Worms, Germany, built in 1034. [Marburg/Art Resource]**

est—many people had to obtain their loans from Jewish businessmen. When the Lombards introduced systematic banking, many Jewish moneylenders were forced to become pawnbrokers.

The crusades had a devastating impact on European Jews, thanks to the religious hatred fostered by some church leaders against non-Christian groups generally and by the anti-Semitic sermons of the friars in particular. In Europe the Jews were a tempting target, particularly to Christians inflamed by recurrent charges that Jews had murdered Christ and were sacrificing Christian children at the Passover feast. The first persecution occurred at Metz in Lorraine and then spread from the Rhineland into France and England. Christian bigotry reached as far as Palestine, where the crusaders burned an entire synagogue full of Jews in 1097. Some Jews preferred to die with swords in their hands, but many chose to commit suicide rather than be killed by Christians. In the English city of York in 1189, Jewish men killed their wives and children before turning their swords on themselves. The pattern of persecution was reinforced in the 1300s when Jews became scapegoats for the Black Death, for which they continued to be blamed well into the sixteenth century.

## ◉ The Expulsion of the Jews from France ◉

*The animosity of medieval Christians toward Jews is apparent in this account of Philip II's expulsion of the Jews from France in 1182.*

When the faithless Jews heard this edict some of them were born again of water and the Holy Spirit and converted to the Lord, remaining steadfast in the faith of our Lord Jesus Christ. To them the king, out of regard for the Christian religion, restored all their possessions in their entirety, and gave them perpetual liberty.

Others were blinded by their ancient error and persisted in their perfidy; and they sought to win with gifts and golden promises the great of the land . . . that through their influence and advice, and through the promise of infinite wealth, they might turn the king's mind from his firm intention. But the merciful and compassionate God . . . so fortified the illustrious king that he could not be moved by prayers nor promises of temporal things. . . .

The infidel Jews, perceiving that the great of the land, through whom they had been accustomed easily to bend the king's predecessors to their will, had suffered repulse, and astonished and stupefied by the strength of mind of Philip the king and his constancy in the Lord, . . . prepared to sell all their household goods. The time was now at hand when the king had ordered them to leave France altogether, and it could not be in any way prolonged. Then did the Jews sell all their movable possessions in great haste, while their landed property reverted to the crown. Thus the Jews, having sold their goods and taken the price for the expenses of their journey, departed.

*Source:* J. H. Robinson, ed., *Readings in European History*, vol. 1 (Boston: Ginn, 1904), p. 428.

The climate of hostility against the Jews was furthered by the Third and Fourth Lateran Councils. Despite the fact that the councils' decrees were not thoroughly implemented, henceforth Gentiles were not supposed to be servants of Jews, nor were they allowed to live in the same districts, a regulation that encouraged the development of separate Jewish quarters. Jews were required to wear identifying badges and attend Christian sermons designed to convert them. Christian officials censored or confiscated Jewish books and forced Jews to be present at public disputations intended to demonstrate the errors of their ways. English authorities seized synagogues on trumped-up charges that Jewish chanting disrupted Christian church services. The Holy Roman Empire asserted proprietary rights over its Jews, making them virtually the property of the crown, and other states followed suit. Many Jews fled to Poland and Lithuania, only to become the legal property of the nobility. In practice, proprietary rights had little effect on Jewish life or freedom of movement, but they provided the justification for special taxes and finally for the expulsion of the Jews from several countries. When Edward I banned the Jews from England in 1290, as many as 16,000 emigrated. Louis IX had decreed their exile from France in 1249, but the order was not implemented then. In 1306, however, Philip IV ordered their arrest, the confiscation of their property, and their ouster from France. Twice they were allowed back, only to be banned again in 1394. Because of political disunity in Germany, there was no general expulsion, but many local governments forced the Jews to flee. Spain and Sicily followed suit in 1492, Portugal in 1497, Naples in 1510 and again in 1541, and Milan in 1591. The expulsions forced the Jews eastward, particularly to Poland—where King Boleslav the Pious granted them a charter in 1264 to guarantee their liberties—and to the Ottoman Empire.

## Between Two Cultures: The Jews in Spain

One of the principal centers of Jewish culture in the medieval era was Spain, where the pre-Islamic community was strengthened by Jewish colonists and traders who followed in the wake of the Arab conquests. Jews enjoyed considerable freedom in Islamic Spain, in part because of their key role in commerce, including the slave trade, but also because of their intellectual attainments. One of the key patrons of Jewish learning was Hasdai ibn-Shaprut (c. 915–970), himself a Jew and the confidant of two caliphs. Trained in medicine and skilled in Latin as well as Arabic, Hasdai supported Jewish poets and Hebrew scholars, initiating a brilliant era of Jewish culture. The poetic revival culminated in the hymns to Zion by the physician Judah ha-Levi (1086–1141). Jewish scholars played an important part in translating Greek classics into Arabic and, beginning in the twelfth century, from Arabic into Latin. Their linguistic skills paved the way for advancements in such fields as mathematics, medicine, astronomy, and cartography. Some of the more enlightened Christian rulers, such as Emperor Frederick II and Alfonso the Wise, king of Castile, recognized the significance of these contributions and extended their patronage to Jewish scholars. Thus one of the principal avenues for the revival of classical learning in Europe came by way of the Arabs and the Jews.

The greatest of the medieval Jewish scholars was Moses ben Maimon (1135–1204), popularly known as Maimonides. Although a native of Córdoba, Spain, he spent most of his life in Cairo, where he served as court physician. As a philosopher his contributions to Judaism are comparable to those of Thomas Aquinas in Catholic theology. His major work, the *Mishneh Torah* ("Repetition of the Law"), was intended to be a *summa* of Judaism—a systematic presentation of rabbinic teachings that earned him the reputation of being a second Moses. Maimonides' approach to religion was highly rational, reflecting the influence of Aristotle and Avicenna. His *Guide to the Perplexed* includes rational arguments for the existence of God, among them the thesis that there must be an Unmoved Mover. Although his views influenced Christian scholastics, the Dominicans were finally persuaded by conservative rabbis that Maimonides' works endangered the Christian faith, and they were banned in 1234.

In Judaism, as in Christianity, there was a mystical reaction to the rationality of Maimonides and his disciples. The mystical tradition in Judaism, of course, was much older than this, dating back to the first century A.D. In the twelfth and thirteenth centuries Jewish mystics known as *Hasidim* ("Pietists") were active in the Rhineland. Probably influenced by Christian monks, they combined a penitent's life with the conviction that God can be found through humility rather than ecstatic visions. Much of the opposition to Maimonides came from mystics in Provence and Spain known as Cabalists ("Traditionalists"), who believed that every letter of the Law has some mystical meaning that can be revealed only to the initiated. Jewish and Christian mystics were one in their conviction that the deepest meaning of religion is profoundly spiritual and cannot be attained by rational processes. Thus, despite the intense animosity of many Christians toward the Jews, Christianity and Judaism were strikingly similar in the search for a rational synthesis and the subsequent reaction of those who favored a mystical approach to God. But their common quest was not strong enough to prevent the onset of bitter persecution—the dark side of the age of faith.

## Women in Medieval Society

Although medieval women were rarely subjected to the kind of persecution experienced by the Jews,* their social position began to decline around the late eleventh century, a pointed reminder that the history of civilization is not one of unbroken progress. In the early medieval period, wives of clergymen and warriors often enjoyed substantial social prominence and economic responsibility because they managed their households or estates while their husbands were away. Women were not only managers but often also owners of land, particularly in southern France and Spain, where there were no legal restrictions on a woman's right to administer family property. Within the feudal order, the development of the chivalric ideal reinforced the role of women as managers of domestic and estate affairs by stressing the male's role as a warrior and a vassal. This was truer in France and Germany, where chivalry had the greatest impact, than in Italy, where chivalric ideas were slow to win acceptance.

Throughout the medieval era women tended to enjoy greater power and prominence in periods of heavy military activity or vigorous expansion into new regions. The military campaigns of Charlemagne, the crusades to the Holy Land, and the lengthy efforts to drive the Moors out of the Iberian peninsula took men from their homes for lengthy periods and exposed them to the hazards of war and disease. Medieval records indicate that during such periods substantial amounts of property were left in the care of wives and sisters as well as the church. It was against the background of the crusades that western Europeans developed the cult of courtly love and troubadours devoted their songs to the exaltation of aristocratic ladies.

Simultaneously, however, developments in the religious and political sphere began to undermine the position of clerical wives and women of the feudal order. In religion the decline was sparked by the Gregorian reforms of the late eleventh century, which had an adverse effect on women by insisting on clerical celibacy, thereby weakening the role of women in parish activities, and by seeking to curtail the ability of the laity to nominate candidates for church offices. These reforms were not fully effective until well beyond the medieval period, but the attempts to enforce them boded ill for women. So too did the growing importance of the bishops in the High Middle Ages, a development intimately related to the revival of urban life. Bishops had no female counterparts, whereas during the period when the church had been dominated by monasteries women had achieved positions of leadership as prioresses and abbesses. Monastic life continued, of course, but power gradually shifted into the hands of the bishops. The trend toward more exclusively male leadership was encouraged by the growth of cathedral schools and universities, neither of which were open to females. Unless they had private tutors, girls could hope for education only in the convents, but from the twelfth century on these establishments were primarily interested in religious rather than academic pursuits.

The church's repressive attitude toward women became especially apparent in the thirteenth century. The religious zeal of the preceding century, which had led to the appearance of such new orders as the Cistercians, also affected women, and thousands of them organized themselves into religious communities. The male orders reluctantly agreed to provide some form of discipline, but instead of being allowed to become independent, female orders were forced to remain subservient branches of their male counterparts. In general this was because women were thought to be undisciplined, prone to heretical ideas, and less than serious in their commitment to the religious life. The Franciscans, Dominicans, and Cistercians bitterly resisted the attachment of subordinate convents, though they were overruled by the papacy. Faced with a church hierarchy determined to relegate them to subordination in all things spiritual, some women joined heretical groups such as the Waldensians, where they were permitted to preach and administer the sacraments.

Yet the influence of Christianity on medieval women was in other respects highly positive, as in the case of the attention given to the Virgin Mary, whose influence extended throughout the High and late Middle Ages. The devout exalted Mary as the Universal Mother whose love for her son was a manifestation of her love for humanity and on whose behalf she acted as an intermediary with God. The faithful credited her with performing miracles and commemorated her life with special festivals. Revered as the queen of heaven and one who was "exalted above the choirs of angels," Mary symbolized the dignity to which women could aspire. Pilgrims flocked to her shrines at such places as Chartres and Mont-Saint-Michel in France and Ipswich in England, and many churches, most notably the cathedral of Notre Dame ("Our Lady") in Paris, were dedicated to her. Numerous other churches had lady chapels in her honor. Expressions of love to the Virgin increasingly paralleled those to aristocratic women in the literature of courtly love, so that the practical effect of both movements was a tendency to idealize women.

In the secular realm, the development of stronger

---

*The main exception was the persecution of women in southern France during the Albigensian Crusade.

## ◉ Women: A Western Medieval View ◉

*The tendency of Christian thinkers to regard women as inferior is reflected in the influential* Decretum *of the jurist Gratian, written about 1140.*

Women should be subject to their men. The natural order for mankind is that women should serve men and children their parents, for it is just that the lesser serve the greater.

The image of God is in man and it is one. Women were drawn from man, who has God's jurisdiction as if he were God's vicar, because he has the image of the one God. Therefore woman is not made in God's image.

Woman's authority is nil; let her in all things be subject to the rule of man. . . . And neither can she teach, nor be a witness, nor give a guarantee, nor sit in judgment.

Adam was beguiled by Eve, not she by him. It is right that he whom woman led into wrongdoing should have her under his direction, so that he may not fail a second time through female levity.

*Source:* Gratian, *Corpus iuris Canonici,* in *Not in God's Image,* ed. J. O'Faolain and L. Martines (New York: Harper Torchbooks, 1973), p. 130.

governments did not necessarily diminish the status of women, but it effectively blocked them from many areas of political involvement. As long as state governments were ineffectual and real power resided in the great aristocratic families, women had an opportunity to assert themselves in political affairs. But as the state governments revived, particularly in the 1100s, they required the services of lawyers and clerks to staff their treasuries and courts, and women had no access to the training that prepared people for such positions.

Changing inheritance laws also adversely affected women. A woman in the feudal order was generally allowed to inherit a fief, subject to her ability to meet the feudal obligations. In practice this meant the lord's right to arrange her marriage to a suitable vassal. Because a fief typically involved military responsibilities, her husband usually assumed control of the estate. But aristocratic families were increasingly determined to preserve their power by excluding females and younger sons from any substantive inheritance in order to keep their estates intact. This was accomplished by the principles of primogeniture and the indivisibility of patrimony, by which an estate had to pass to the eldest son. Daughters received dowries and dowers, the latter being the assurance of an income during widowhood, but in turn they were excluded from inheriting a portion of the family estate. If she had no brothers, the eldest daughter could usually inherit the estate. In the thirteenth century the French awarded two-thirds of an estate to the eldest son and allowed the other children to divide the remaining third. In varying degrees, most women of the propertied order were victims of legal discrimination.

For women of humbler status, fundamental economic needs often mandated a relative equality between men and women, particularly those in rural areas who worked beside their husbands in the fields or who devoted some of their time in the home to brewing ale or making cloth to sell. In the countryside women regularly hired themselves out to bailiffs on the greater estates, where they performed virtually every form of labor except heavy plowing. Much of the sheep shearing was done by women, as were the dairy and poultry chores. Even in the towns medieval women were found in virtually all crafts—as butchers and bakers, haberdashers and shoemakers, goldsmiths and embroiderers. Masters' wives were active in many guilds, often training female apprentices. Widows regularly carried on their husbands' crafts, and those who had been married to merchants sometimes took over their business dealings. English records mention "widows of London who make great trade in wool and other things."[5]

In medieval society the range of occupations in which women were engaged was very extensive. Some women even worked in the coal and iron mines, although their pay was less than that of the men. Many women were employed in domestic service, while others managed their own shops. Urban life clearly expanded career opportunities for women, whether married or single. Whereas a landed aristocrat might leave directions in his will to place his daughter in a convent or find her a suitable spouse, an artisan was more likely to leave funds to train his daughter in a trade, usually because he could afford neither a dowry nor the funds required to place her in a convent. Many women continued to pursue their crafts after marriage, even when their husbands engaged in a different occupation. Without doubt, the female labor force was crucial to the medieval economy. The scholastic Peter Lombard may have reflected the sentiments of the commoners when he observed that God created Eve from Adam's rib rather than his head or foot because they were intended to be companions.

*The High Middle Ages was a period of notable intellectual and cultural achievement. The growth of cathedral schools and the rise of universities brought new intellectual vigor to European life and made possible the training of a better-educated clergy and officials more adept at meeting the needs of government. Scholastics made a daring attempt to synthesize all knowledge, a development that focused attention on natural science. The growth of medical schools set the stage for improved health care. Virtually all of these developments occurred in the context of an urban revival made possible by an expanding economy. The cities provided the setting for brilliant artistic achievements, particularly the age of the Gothic, which owed much to the Romanesque era. The Gothic cathedrals, resplendent with their towering spires, soaring vaults, flying buttresses, and stained glass, were the perfect visual symbol of the age of faith.*

*But for two groups—women and Jews—the High Middle Ages brought a relative deterioration in their position. Excluded from the cathedral schools and the universities, women increasingly found themselves shunted aside in politics as well. Law, medicine, and theology were forbidden areas, and women were banned from the parsonages they had once served as priests' wives. The exalted status they received in the courtly love tradition was scant compensation. The Jews, whose intellectual accomplishments influenced and were the equal of scholastic thought, were thrust into a nightmarish world of expulsion, exile, and massacre.*

## Notes

1. R. B. Brooke and C. N. L. Brooke, "St. Clare," in *Medieval Women*, ed. D. Baker (Oxford: Blackwell, 1978), p. 287.
2. E. G. Holt, ed., *Literary Sources of Art History* (Princeton, N.J.: Princeton University Press, 1947), p. 17.
3. E. Panofsky, *Abbot Suger on the Abbey Church of St. Denis and Its Art Treasures* (Princeton, N.J.: Princeton University Press, 1951), p. 101.
4. H. Gardner, *Art Through the Ages*, 7th ed., ed. H. de la Croix and R. G. Tansey (New York: Harcourt Brace Jovanovich, 1980), p. 337.
5. E. Power, *Medieval Women*, ed. M. M. Postan (Cambridge: Cambridge University Press, 1975), p. 57.

## Suggestions for Further Reading

Andreas Capellanus [André le Chapelain], *Andreas Capellanus on Love*, ed. and trans. P. G. Walsh. London: Duckworth, 1982.

Artz, F. B. *The Mind of the Middle Ages*, A.D. *200–1500*, 3rd ed. Chicago: University of Chicago Press, 1980.

Baker, D., ed. *Medieval Women*. Oxford: Blackwell, 1978.

Baldwin, J. W. *The Scholastic Culture of the Middle Ages, 1000–1300*. Lexington, Mass.: Heath, 1971.

Ben-Sasson, H. H., ed. *A History of the Jewish People*. Cambridge, Mass.: Harvard University Press, 1976.

Berman, H. *Law and Revolution: The Formation of the Western Legal Tradition*. Cambridge, Mass.: Harvard University Press, 1983.

Bogin, M. *The Women Troubadours*. New York: Paddington, 1976.

Bony, J. *French Gothic Architecture of the Twelfth and Thirteenth Centuries*. Berkeley: University of California Press, 1983.

Brooke, C. N. L. *The Medieval Idea of Marriage*. New York: Oxford University Press, 1989.

———. *The Monastic World, 1000–1300*. New York: Random House, 1974.

Bumke, J. *Courtly Culture: Literature and Society in the High Middle Ages*. Berkeley: University of California Press, 1991.

Burns, J. H., ed. *The Cambridge History of Medieval Political Thought, c. 350–c. 1450*. Cambridge: Cambridge University Press, 1988.

Bynum, C. W. *Holy Feast and Holy Fast: The Religious Significance of Food to Medieval Women*. Berkeley: University of California Press, 1987.

Cobban, A. B. *The Medieval Universities: Their Development and Organization*. London: Methuen, 1975.

Ennen, E. *The Medieval Woman*. Oxford: Blackwell, 1990.

Erickson, C. *The Medieval Vision*. New York: Oxford University Press, 1976.

Fell, C. *Women in Anglo-Saxon England*. Oxford: Blackwell, 1987.

Ferruolo, S. C. *The Origins of the University: The Schools of Paris and Their Critics, 1100–1215.* Stanford, Calif.: Stanford University Press, 1985.

Frankl, P. *Gothic Architecture*, trans. D. Pevsner. Baltimore: Penguin Books, 1963.

Gies, F., and Gies, J. *Women in the Middle Ages.* New York: Crowell, 1978.

Grodecki, L., and Brisac, C. *Gothic Stained Glass, 1200–1300.* Ithaca, N.Y.: Cornell University Press, 1985.

Gurevich, A. *Medieval Popular Culture: Problems of Belief and Perception*, trans. J. M. Bak and P. A. Hollingsworth. Cambridge: Cambridge University Press, 1988.

Haskins, C. H. *The Renaissance of the Twelfth Century.* Cambridge, Mass.: Harvard University Press, 1971.

Herlihy, D. *Medieval Households.* Cambridge, Mass.: Harvard University Press, 1985.

Keen, M. *Chivalry.* New Haven, Conn.: Yale University Press, 1984.

Kirshner, J., and Wemple, S. F., eds. *Women of the Medieval World.* Oxford: Blackwell, 1985.

Knowles, D. *The Evolution of Medieval Thought*, 2nd ed. New York: Longman, 1988.

Lawrence, C. H. *Medieval Monasticism: Forms of Religious Life in Western Europe in the Middle Ages.* New York: Longman, 1984.

Leff, G. *Paris and Oxford Universities in the Thirteenth and Fourteenth Centuries: An Institutional and Intellectual History.* New York: Wiley, 1968.

McInerny, R. *Romanesque.* New York: Harper & Row, 1978.

Moore, R. I. *The Formation of a Persecuting Society: Power and Deviance in Western Europe, 950–1250.* New York: Blackwell, 1987.

Moorman, J. R. H. *A History of the Franciscan Order.* Oxford: Clarendon Press, 1968.

Murray, D. C. *A History of Heresy.* New York: Oxford University Press, 1989.

Panofsky, E. *Gothic Architecture and Scholasticism.* New York: Meridian, 1957.

Peters, E. *Inquisition.* Berkeley: University of California Press, 1989.

Russell, J. B. *A History of Medieval Christianity: Prophesy and Order.* New York: Crowell, 1968.

Talbot, C. H. *Medicine in Medieval England.* London: Oldbourne, 1967.

# Death and the Human Experience (I)

**To every thing there is a season . . . :**
**A time to be born, and a time to die. (Eccles. 3:1, 2)**

Throughout history death has been defied or embraced, an object sometimes of fear, sometimes of hope. The earliest human ritual of which we have a record, developed by Peking man some 500,000 years ago, was associated with death, perhaps in the hope of preserving the memory of the deceased and soliciting their assistance for the living. More than 50,000 years ago Neanderthal people prepared elaborate funeral rites to deal with the needs of those who had died and presumably lived in some afterlife. Bodies were interred in graves filled with shells and ornaments made of ivory and bone, while the skin or bones of the deceased were colored with red ocher, apparently to commemorate life. The corpses themselves were buried in a fetal position, possibly to facilitate rebirth or to restrict the movements of the dead and thereby prevent them from returning to haunt the living. Thus the first human societies sought to explain death and in the process developed primitive conceptions of an afterlife.

The earliest civilizations coped with death in strikingly different ways. The Mesopotamian *Epic of Gilgamesh* (c. 2000 B.C.) suggests that the people of that region conceived of a hinterworld that existed just below the surface of the earth, a House of Darkness in which the dead were made of clay, ate dust, and endured a wretched existence. This world was neither heaven nor hell but a place bereft of light where ghostly beings, dressed like birds, fluttered their wings. To prevent the spirit of the dead from haunting the living, the Sumerians took pains to bury the corpse and provide food and drink in the grave. Offerings and prayers were made to the Mesopotamian deities, but these were intended to benefit the living rather than to obtain access to a decent afterlife. To escape his destiny in the shadowy underworld, Gilgamesh resolutely searched for immortal life but failed to find it. The sense of resignation before death was reflected in the Mesopotamians' willingness to embrace a life of physical pleasure; as Gilgamesh is advised in the poem, it is best to live the merry life, dancing and playing night and day, for old age and death are inevitable.

The Egyptians too believed in life after death, as reflected in the Pyramid Texts of the third millennium B.C., the Coffin Texts of around 2000 B.C., and later papyrus inscriptions, documents collectively known as the *Book of the Dead*. Here we find the earliest expression of belief in the idea of a divine judgment after death. The Pyramid Texts relate the story of Osiris and his resurrection, but by the time of the Coffin Texts belief in the notion of a general judgment after death was widespread. Convinced that specific fates awaited different people, the Egyptians came to fear death because of the uncertainty of their position in the afterlife. The specter of divine judgment not only spurred some to moral living but also encouraged the development of elaborate funeral rituals designed to influence the final verdict. These included lengthy prayers repudiating sin as well as artwork designed to stress the goodness of the deceased's life. One of the most common symbols of Egyptian funerary art was the scale of judgment, depicting the soul as pure enough to balance the feather of truth. A similar symbol was later used in Christian art.

The earliest Greeks viewed death as the separation of the soul (or "shade") and the *thymos*—the seat of emotions—from the body. At death the *thymos* simply disappeared, leaving the soul to enter Hades, the Land of the Dead, once the corpse had been buried or had decomposed. Existence in Hades was thought to entail anything from a senseless state to associations akin to those in life. The earliest Greeks accepted death as an inescapable evil. One could hate but not fear death, which was part of the life cycle of the community. There was no reason to dread either contact with the deceased or one's own death.

The Greek attitude began to shift in the seventh and sixth centuries B.C. in the face of changing circumstances. The tightly knit communities broke up, a sense

**A Neanderthal skeleton discovered in France in 1909 reveals that corpses were interred in the fetal position. [Musée de l'Homme, Paris]**

of individuality developed, philosophers speculated about salvation and a last judgment based on morality, and economic expansion and political upheaval increased feelings of insecurity and disorder. Consequently, the specter of death caused anxiety and stimulated a concern to perpetuate one's memory, often by inscriptions or by gravestones or other monuments. At first the depictions of the deceased on statues and gravestones followed conventional types, but gradually these evolved into actual portraits of the dead, reflecting the heightened sense of interest in the individual that was characteristic of later Greek art.

The Greeks initially believed that only a few aristocratic heroes escaped Hades, but over time the idea was broadened to include others, until finally a happy afterlife was possible for all who lived morally or were initiated into the mystery cults associated with such gods as Dionysus. Increasingly death was perceived as less a part of the community's cycle of existence than a threat to an individual.

Grappling with the meaning of death produced equally varied responses among Asian peoples. In ancient India the Vedas and the epics offered two conflicting views of death. On the one hand, death was seen as inescapable, its rule over everyone invincible. On the other, death's hold was only conditional, for each person could in theory choose from among a variety of means to attain *moksha*—release from the cycle of rebirth. Yet all but a few sages were thought to be bound to the endless wheel of such rebirth. The nature of each reincarnation was determined by the individual's behavior in the present life and could be favorably influenced by such things as an ascetic life, the acquisition of wisdom, the performance of sacrifices, and the pursuit of morality. At the very least, adherence to such means enabled the Hindu to avoid "death in life"—living in perpetual fear of death. The Hindu sages occasionally linked death with evil—a theme common in later Christianity—but in general death was accorded a natural and indispensable role in the cosmic order, for without it there would be no room for new life. Death should therefore be celebrated, the Hindus felt, not mourned, "for death is a certainty for him who has been born, and birth is a certainty for him who has died. Therefore, for what is unavoidable thou shouldst not grieve."[1]

The ability to embrace death, or at least quietly to resign oneself to it, was complicated by the Hindu belief in *samsara*, the transmigration of souls through reincarnation, which is first explicitly stated in the *Upanishads* (c. 800–c. 500 B.C.). According to this concept, death is followed by rebirth in another worldly existence, although whether this is to be viewed in positive or negative terms was largely a personal matter. Certainly for many Hindus, *samsara* was tantamount to endless "redeath." Most Hindus sought to improve

This depiction on a fifth-century B.C. tombstone of a woman holding her grandchild underscores the extent to which the Greeks, unlike the Egyptians, concentrated primarily on the beauty of life. [Deutsches Archäologisches Institut/ Kerameikos Museum, Athens]

their status in the next round of existence by embracing morality and social responsibility, whereas some sought escape from physical existence through asceticism. For them, death could be the culmination of the journey along the Way of the Gods to the world of Brahma, the absolute. This quest for release and the joyful union with the infinite in *nirvana* subsequently became a dominant theme in Buddhism.

Perhaps none have been more willing to embrace death than the Taoists in China, for whom the death of

The Hindu god Shiva and his wife, Parvati, aided by their sons, string together the skulls of the dead. One of Shiva's responsibilities was to preside over cremation grounds. [C. M. Dixon/Photoresources]

cific clans. It was the task of the living to make offerings to the memory of the dead, to undertake pilgrimages to their places of burial, and to worship or commemorate them as a family. Ancestor worship, as it is somewhat misleadingly called, was by no means unique to China but was practiced by peoples as diverse as Persians, Indians, Russians, Scandinavians, and the Bantu of southern Africa. Through ancestor worship, death was prevented from cutting the ties between the deceased and their families; hence the dead could be dealt with in traditional human ways, such as paying respect or making offerings. Unless the dead were thought to be angry or vindictive, the continuation of the familial relationship eased both the physical separation imposed by death and apprehensions about what lay beyond the grave.

The ideas discussed to this point treat death in one of three ways: as an inevitable part of the natural process, following which souls exist in a shadowy and normally unpleasant underworld; as part of an endless

an individual was insignificant in the face of the workings of the universal cosmos. Seeing themselves as a mere part of the unity of all things, they could accept death tranquilly as a manifestation of the ongoing operation of nature. "If one once recognizes his identity with this unity, then the parts of his body mean no more to him than so much dirt, and death and life, end and beginning, disturb his tranquility no more than the succession of day and night."[2]

For most Chinese, however, death was explained in the context of an extended family group that embraced the deceased, the living, and the generations yet unborn. Because the dead were seen by some to have the same needs as the living, they must be provided for, and their activities in the afterlife could in turn aid the living. Funeral ceremonies were intended to ease the passage of the spirits into the next world, yet they would symbolically dwell in graveyards, in ancestral shrines in the homes, and in temples dedicated to spe-

This fourteenth-century A.D. Japanese Buddhist scroll shows the Buddha, lying on a bier, ready to enter *nirvana* as he is mourned by gods, humans, and animals. [Museum für Ostasiatische Kunst, Preussischer Kulturbesitz, Berlin]

cycle of rebirth; or as part of an ongoing familial relationship between past, present, and future generations. A fourth way of viewing death, which originated in Judaism and was subsequently adopted by Christianity and Islam, associated it with resurrection and the notion of salvation. Like the Sumerians, the early Hebrews thought of the dead as existing in a shadowy underworld, called *sheol*, commonly linked with the tomb. Originally this was the common fate of all, good or bad, Jew or Gentile, apart from the patriarch Enoch, who "walked with God," and the prophet Elijah, who was said to have been carried to heaven in a chariot of fire. But in the late eighth century B.C., the prophet Isaiah proclaimed the resurrection of all the righteous, and nearly six centuries later the Book of Daniel asserted that even the wicked would be resurrected in order to face judgment. For the Jews, then, death became a temporary state, less important than the judgment that followed the resurrection. Thus the Hebrews, like the ancient Egyptians but unlike the Mesopotamians, stressed the importance of moral living as the necessary preparation for death and the afterlife.

Early Christianity built on this Judaic foundation, making death and resurrection only the prelude to an eternal heaven of blissful existence for the saved and endless torture in hell for the damned. Death was a foe to be conquered, but the victory came with the physical resurrection of Christ, belief in which became a cardinal tenet of the Christian faith. Because of that triumph, wrote the apostle Paul, "the dead shall be raised incorruptible. . . . O death, where is thy sting? O grave, where is thy victory?"[3] But for those who died alienated from God, death and judgment were but the fearful prelude to eternity in a lake burning with fire and brimstone.

Apart from the idea of Christ's resurrection, Islam adopted the essential features of the Christian belief in death, judgment, and reward or punishment. Death was viewed as a divinely determined act, executed by an Angel of Death or other messengers of Allah. Death itself was akin to sleep, though for unbelievers this involved agony. At the appointed time the dead would be awakened, the godly to receive the pleasures of paradise and the unbelievers to face a torment so unbearable that they would plead to be destroyed. Thus Islam, like Judaism and Christianity, regarded death as a transitory state, for which the proper preparation was righteous living.

Attitudes toward death affected decisions regarding the disposal of corpses. Cremation was common in India, Burma, and Japan, though not in China, where the people preferred to be buried in their native soil. The Etruscans, Greeks, and Romans practiced cremation (though not exclusively), but in the West it died out as the Christian belief in the physical resurrection of the body took hold. Not until the late nineteenth century did the practice again revive in Europe and America.

Christianity also introduced changes with respect to burial. The Romans, like the other peoples of antiquity, kept the dead apart to prevent them from contaminating the living. In Rome and Pompeii, for example, the deceased were buried outside the gates or beside the roads leading into the cities, but close enough to maintain the tombs and make the requisite offerings. Burial within the towns was prohibited by Roman law and the early Germanic Theodosian Code and in the teachings of the early Christian theologian St. John Chrysostom.

The prohibition of entombment within the towns began to change as Christians were martyred in North Africa. Buried in the traditional necropolises outside town walls, their tombs soon became the sites of basilicas where devout pilgrims worshiped. Other Christians wanted to be buried nearby, thus leading to the association of churches and burial plots. By the mid-sixth century it was possible to inter a corpse within a church, thus reversing the ancient attempt to separate the living from the dead. In fact, in medieval Europe cemeteries were not only places of burial but also, because the adjacent churches themselves were social centers, sites for dancing, gambling, concerts, and business transactions. Sometimes homes were even built in cemeteries. The proximity of the living and the dead in medieval Europe was also manifest in charnel houses, normally galleries that bordered churchyards and housed skulls and bones stacked neatly or arranged artistically for the living to contemplate.

Such customs point to a society in which life and death were viewed harmoniously—a society willing to accept the inevitability of death rather than depict it as a frightening event. The calmness of the deathbed ritual reflected a fundamental faith in the church's ability to care for the souls of the deceased and in the ultimate triumph of resurrection over death. A leading historian has called this view "tamed death," an attitude prevalent among the common people of the West into the nineteenth century.

Beginning in the eleventh and twelfth centuries a new attitude began to take hold among the intellectual and social elite. In part this stemmed from a desire to have funerals reflect material wealth and status. More important, the new outlook in Europe manifested a growing attention toward individuals, as reflected in the revival of funeral inscriptions, which had fallen into disuse around the fifth century; the popularity of requiem masses for individuals; and the reappearance of effigies and death masks. Individual responsibility was also emphasized, as special stress was placed on the Last Judgment, with the deeds of each person weighed on the great scales. This outlook was also accompanied by a change in funerary art, as decomposing cadavers—worm-ridden corpses—began to appear, mostly in the fifteenth century. Against the background of the Black Death, there was thus a new horror of dying and a longing for earthly life that had previously been man-

In *Death and the Miser*, Hieronymus Bosch (c. 1450–1516) depicts the futile efforts of an angel to persuade a dying knight to forsake his riches for Christ. The painting reflects the medieval preoccupation with death and judgment. [National Gallery of Art, Washington, Samuel H. Kress Collection]

ifest only rarely in the medieval West. This preoccupation with the fate of the individual has been called the "death of the self," an attitude that persisted in elite circles until the eighteenth century.

## Notes

1. *Bhagavadgita* 2:27, in *Religious Encounters with Death: Insights from the History and Anthropology of Religions,* ed. F. E. Reynolds and E. H. Waugh (University Park: Pennsylvania State University Press, 1977), p. 92.
2. Chuang-tze, 2:48, in H. G. Creel, *What Is Taoism? and Other Studies in Chinese Cultural History* (Chicago: University of Chicago Press, 1970), p. 42.
3. 1 Cor. 15:52, 55.

## Suggestions for Further Reading

Ariès, P. *The Hour of Our Death,* trans. H. Weaver. New York: Knopf, 1981.

———. *Images of Man and Death,* trans. J. Lloyd. Cambridge, Mass.: Harvard University Press, 1985.

———. *Western Attitudes Toward Death: From the Middle Ages to the Present,* trans. P. M. Ranum. Baltimore: Johns Hopkins University Press, 1974.

Boase, T. S. R. *Death in the Middle Ages.* New York: McGraw-Hill, 1972.

Bowra, C. M. *The Greek Experience.* New York: World, 1957.

Brandon, S. G. F. *The Judgment of the Dead: A Historical and Comparative Study of the Idea of a Post-Mortem Judgment in the Major Religions.* New York: Scribner, 1967.

Creel, H. G. *What Is Taoism? and Other Studies in Chinese Cultural History.* Chicago: University of Chicago Press, 1970.

Harrah, B. K., and Harrah, D. F. *Funeral Service: A Bibliography of Literature on Its Past, Present and Future, the Various Means of Disposition and Memorialization.* Metuchen, N.J.: Scarecrow Press, 1976.

Miller, A. J., and Aeri, M. J. *Death: A Bibliographical Guide.* Metuchen, N.J.: Scarecrow Press, 1977.

O'Shaughnessy, T. *Muhammad's Thoughts on Death.* Leiden: Brill, 1969.

Paxton, F. S. *Christianizing Death: The Creation of a Ritual Process in Early Medieval Europe.* Ithaca, N.Y.: Cornell University Press, 1990.

Reynolds, F. E., and Waugh, E. H. *Religious Encounters with Death: Insights from the History and Anthropology of Religions.* University Park: Pennsylvania State University Press, 1977.

Vermeule, E. *Aspects of Death in Early Greek Art and Poetry.* Berkeley: University of California Press, 1979.

Whaley, J., ed. *Mirrors of Mortality: Studies in the Social History of Death.* London: Europa, 1981.

# CHAPTER 15

# Crisis and Recovery in Europe

Famine, pestilence, war, and death—the four horsemen of the Apocalypse—ravaged Europe with unprecedented fury in the fourteenth century. The devastation inflicted by the bubonic and pneumonic plague, recurring famine, and the Hundred Years' War contributed to serious economic decline and a change in people's outlook. The prestige of the papacy suffered too when its headquarters shifted to Avignon, which proved to be the prelude to the most scandalous schism in the history of the western church. Nevertheless, around 1450 Europe began to experience a dramatic revival as population growth resumed, commerce and manufacturing ex-

The fourth horseman of the Apocalypse: "And I saw, and behold, a pale horse, and its rider's name was Death, and Hades followed him: and they were given power over a fourth of the earth, to kill with sword and with famine and with pestilence and by wild beasts of the earth" (Rev. 6:8). To the people of the fourteenth and fifteenth centuries, this prophecy seemed to be coming true in their own age. [Giraudon/Art Resource]

panded, and the states of western Europe and Russia attained greater unity and built strong central governments. In Italy, Germany, Hungary, and Poland, however, territorial princes and cities prevented the growth of centralized states. Europe in the fourteenth and fifteenth centuries moved from an age of adversity to one of recovery and in doing so laid the foundations for the early modern era.

## Famine and the Black Death

From the late tenth through the thirteenth centuries the population of Europe grew as farmers expanded the amount of land under cultivation and increased the supply of food. But neither the population growth nor the food supply increased uniformly, and marginal settlements, where the possibility of extreme hunger was always high, arose throughout Europe. Even in the more prosperous agricultural regions, poor distribution facilities often resulted in pockets of famine. By 1300 the population had expanded so rapidly that most Europeans faced grave peril should the fragile agricultural economy be disrupted by unfavorable changes in the weather patterns. The warming trend that characterized the period from the mid-eighth to the mid-twelfth centuries was reversed as Europe entered what climatologists call the Little Ice Age, which lasted approximately two centuries. In the late thirteenth century heavy rains and unexpected freezes began to wreak havoc with the food supply. The threat of famine, which became more pronounced in the 1290s, culminated between 1315 and 1317 in the greatest crop failures of the Middle Ages. Soaring grain prices placed food beyond the reach of many, especially in urban areas, where sometimes as many as one in ten died from starvation or malnutrition. Marginal lands had to be abandoned as the poor sought relief in towns or in more productive regions, thereby increasing the strain on the food supply. As famines continued to recur throughout the fourteenth century, the most serious consequence was the debilitating effect of chronic and severe malnutrition on much of the population. Physically weakened, most Europeans were highly vulnerable to disease, especially tuberculosis.

The bubonic plague is caused by bacteria that live in an animal's blood or a flea's stomach and is thus easily transmitted, particularly by fleas on rats. The first symptom in a human is a small, blackish pustule at the point of the flea bite, followed by the swelling of the lymph nodes in the neck, armpit, or groin. Then come dark spots on the skin caused by internal bleeding. In the final stage the victim, convulsed by severe coughing spells, spits blood, exudes a foul body odor, and experiences severe neurological and psychological disorders. Bubonic plague, however, was not always fatal, especially if the pus was thoroughly drained from the boil; up to half its victims survived. A more virulent form of the plague—the pneumonic variety—was transmitted by coughing and was nearly always fatal. Both forms devastated Europe.

Plague had ravaged the Byzantine Empire in the 540s and eventually extended from central and southern Asia to Arabia, North Africa, and the Iberian peninsula and north as far as Denmark and Ireland. Some 200,000 people may have died in Constantinople alone between the fall of 541 and the spring of 542. When this outbreak finally ended in 544, more than 20 percent of the people of southern Europe had died. Further outbreaks followed for another 200 years, after which Europe was free of most epidemic diseases until the mid-fourteenth century. But the bacterial strains responsible for the plague continued to survive in the Gobi Desert of Mongolia. From there the plague was transmitted both east and west by nomadic tribesmen, perhaps forced to move their flocks to new regions when hot winds began drying up the pastures of central Asia.

The plague reached epidemic proportions in the Gobi Desert in the late 1320s and from there may have spread first to China. The Chinese had already been weakened by famine brought on by drought, earthquakes, and then flooding in the early 1330s. The Black Death followed, reducing the population nearly 30 percent (from 125 million to 90 million) before the end of the century. By 1339 the plague had begun its westward march, carried slowly but widely by migrating central Asian rodents and more rapidly by traders along the caravan routes and shipping lanes.

The impact on Asia and the Middle East was devastating. According to one chronicler, "India was depopulated; Tartary, Mesopotamia, Syria, [and] Armenia were covered with dead bodies; the Kurds fled in vain to the mountains."[1] Constantinople and Alexandria were struck in 1347; both cities suffered heavy losses, the latter witnessing perhaps 1,000 deaths a day in early 1348. It was worse in Cairo, one of the largest cities in the world with its population of 500,000; there some 7,000 probably died each day at the peak of the plague. By 1349 it had spread throughout the Muslim world, killing a third of the people and possibly as many as half of those who lived in towns.

The Black Death was brought to western Europe when a Genoese ship carrying infected rats from the Crimea docked at Messina, Sicily, in October 1347. Within months the plague struck the great ports of Venice and Genoa, then spread throughout the rest of Italy, devastating Florence especially. By the end of 1348 most of France and the southern tip of England had been hit, and a year later the infected areas stretched from Ireland

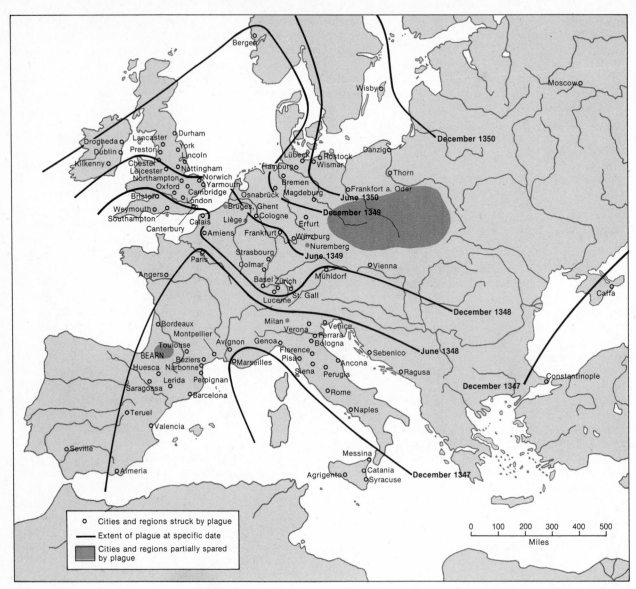

*15.1 Spread of the Plague in Europe*

and Norway to Würzburg and Vienna. The plague moved relentlessly through northern Germany and Scandinavia, finally reaching western Russia in 1351 and 1352. Severe outbreaks again struck Europe in 1362 and 1375. Until the end of the fifteenth century no decade passed without at least one outbreak, and the plague continued to pose a serious threat to Europeans for two centuries after that. Surviving records are inadequate to determine accurate mortality figures, but the Black Death of the late 1340s probably claimed 25 million lives, perhaps a third of Europe's population. No war in history has destroyed so large a percentage of the people.

Europeans had no knowledge of the cause of the plague, though many attributed it to something mysterious in the atmosphere; many Christians were convinced it was divine punishment for their sins. Some fled from the towns to the countryside, where the pestilence was less frequent. Officials of port cities tried in vain to turn away ships carrying signs of the infection, and some towns barred visitors in the hope of keeping the plague at bay. Reaction among the people varied considerably. Convinced of imminent death, some opted for the unbridled pursuit of sensual pleasures, while others turned to ascetic extremes, such as the itinerant flagellants, who ritualistically whipped themselves, wore penitential dress, and bore crucifixes. Others turned to black magic

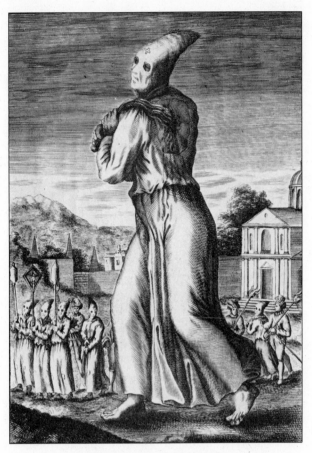

**A procession of flagellants during the Black Death. Note the bare backs and the whips. [Lauros-Giraudon/Art Resource]**

and witchcraft, while some shunned anything Asian or blamed the Jews, many of whom were massacred. At Basel the bodies of slain Jews were floated down the Rhine in wine casks; 2,000 were slaughtered in Strasbourg, 600 in Brussels. People who tried to cure the sick relied on bleeding, cauterizing the boils, applying assorted substances to draw off the poison, and administering soothing potions. Many physicians fled, so the clergy often ministered to the sick and thus suffered extensively themselves. Entire Dominican friaries in Tuscany and Languedoc were decimated, and perhaps a third of the German clergy perished.

The social and economic effects of the plague were profound. In several respects the Muslim response to the Black Death differed from that of Christians. Whereas the latter were preoccupied with guilt and fear, Muslims tended to regard the plague, like the *jihad*, or holy war, as an opportunity to achieve martyrdom and thus as a vehicle of divine mercy. "Their wounds had been similar" to those of holy warriors, said one Islamic tradition, "so they joined the martyrs."[2] Unlike the Christians, the Muslims therefore thought it was wrong to flee from a plague-stricken area, though in part this may also have involved some realization that flight could spread the disease. Theologically, however, Muslims denied that the plague was contagious, inasmuch as it was supposed to be divinely bestowed on a community deserving of special favor. Europeans, in contrast, were firmly convinced that the plague was infectious. The practical result was that Christians feared the Black Death, whereas the Muslims tended to accept it as they accepted such disasters as droughts and floods.

In the Middle East the immediate effect of the plague was a sharp rise in wages for laborers and a decrease in rents and income for the propertied classes. Yet there was no long-term improvement in the living standards of rural workers, particularly in Egypt and Syria, because a large increase in military needs to defend the region meant heavier taxes. Only in the case of urban workers did income rise sufficiently to bring an increase in real wages. In Europe hundreds of villages were severely depopulated or disappeared altogether, reducing the value of land and driving up wages as the labor supply plummeted. As in the Middle East initially, peasants who survived found their services in greater demand and could obtain better terms from their landlords or find more accommodating ones elsewhere, while others moved into the towns as artisans. Falling rents and rising wages prompted landowners to seek legislation fixing wages at low levels and restricting access to urban occupations. A French ordinance of 1351 limited wage increases to no more than a third of the preplague level, while the more ambitious English Statute of Laborers of the same year fixed wages at the pre-1349 rates and prohibited the employment of cheap female workers in place of men. Spanish, Portuguese, and German governments made similar attempts to control wages, but none was very effective. The French and the English also enacted measures to curtail the rising cost of food.

## Catastrophe and Rebellion

In Europe the dislocation caused by the plague, coupled with the restrictive measures against the peasants and the artisans, contributed to explosive unrest in the late fourteenth century. In 1358 many peasants in northern France joined in uprisings known as the Jacquerie (*Jacques* was a name nobles used to address a peasant). Already embittered by efforts to limit their wages, the peasants were angered by heavy financial exactions to support French forces in the Hundred Years' War and by marauding bands of mercenaries from whom the nobles offered them no protection. The peasants began their rampage in May, killing, raping, burning, and destroying a number of castles. They had, however, neither strong leaders nor a program of reform. Priests, craftsmen, and lesser merchants joined them before the nobles ruthlessly suppressed the rebellion throughout the summer by means of widespread massacres. In the end, some 20,000 died.

Social revolt erupted in England in 1381, fueled by the peasants' resentment at efforts to restrict their economic advances, long-standing bitterness over aristocratic cruelty toward them, and governmental efforts to impose a poll or head tax to pay for the war against France. Peasants in the south, where the rebellion broke out, were also upset by French raids on their lands. Led by the priest John Ball and the journeyman Wat Tyler, the revolt soon spread throughout much of the country as urban workers joined the peasants. The killing and destruction was stemmed only when the young king, Richard II (1377–1399), met with the rebels and promised reform. Instead the nobles regrouped and carried out a campaign of retribution. Radical rebel demands—the equality of all men before the law, the granting of most church property to the people, and the end of mandatory peasant labor on the lords' demesnes (personal lands)—were not met, though the government ceased collecting the head tax.

The Jacquerie and the Wat Tyler rebellion are but the most famous examples of the revolts that swept parts of Europe in the century after the Black Death first appeared. The peasants of Languedoc rose up in 1382 and 1383, Catalonian peasants were frequently in arms, and peasants and miners rebelled in Sweden in 1434. Much of the unrest erupted in the cities, where artisans de-manded more political power and where the working poor were chained in poverty by repressive guilds. The greatest urban revolt was that of the *ciompi* (cloth workers) in Florence in 1378, but there were uprisings as well in Paris and Rouen in France, at Ghent in Flanders, at Brunswick and Lübeck in the Holy Roman Empire, and at Barcelona and Seville in Spain. No other period in the Middle Ages experienced as much social unrest as the century 1350–1450.

## The Hundred Years' War

Between 1337 and 1453 the English and the French engaged in a series of armed conflicts collectively known as the Hundred Years' War, though in fact the two countries spent less than half this period in actual fighting. Each side went to war because it felt the other threatened its security and blocked its rightful ambitions. The war began when King Edward III of England (1327–1377) claimed the French throne as his own. The last three Capetian monarchs, the sons and heirs of Philip IV, had died without leaving a male heir. Although Edward III, Philip's maternal grandson, was the closest male heir, the French nobles supported the claim of Philip of Valois, a cousin of Philip IV's sons. At first Edward accepted the decision and even swore the vassal's oath of fealty to Philip at Amiens for his holdings in Aquitaine. English involvement in France, however, stood

On the left the English rebel Wat Tyler is slain as Richard II watches, while on the right the king calms a mob of angry peasants. [British Museum]

## ◎ Peasant Rebellion: ◎
## A Call for Communalism

*The English peasants who rebelled in 1381 were motivated in part by resentment against the landed aristocracy. One of those who encouraged such hostility was the priest John Ball, whose views reflect a basic communalism.*

Ah, ye good people, the matters goeth not well to pass in England, nor shall not do till everything be common, and that there be no villains [serfs] nor gentlemen, but that we may be all [made one] together, and that the lords be no greater masters than we be. . . . We be all come from one father and one mother, Adam and Eve: whereby can they say or show that they be greater lords than we be, saying by that they cause us to win and labor for that they dispend? . . . They dwell in fair houses, and we have the pain and travail, rain and wind in the fields; and by that that cometh of our labors they keep and maintain their estates: we be called their bondmen, and . . . [unless] we do readily them service, we be beaten; and we have no sovereign to whom we may complain, nor that will hear us nor do us right. Let us go to the king.

*Source:* G. C. Macaulay, ed., *The Chronicles of Froissart,* trans. J. Bourchier, Lord Berners (London: Macmillan, 1924), p. 251.

squarely in the way of the ambition of the French sovereigns to extend their authority throughout the country. No less important as a cause of the war was Anglo-French rivalry over Flanders. Its count was Philip's vassal, but Flemish towns depended on English wool for their textile industry. English support for the Flemings when they rebelled against their count threatened French domination in the region, whereas French control jeopardized English trade. Another grievance was France's support for the Scots, which prevented the English from exercising lordship over their northern neighbors.

As the two sides embarked on war, France was seemingly the stronger, with greater wealth and a population three times the size of England's. The French had the advantage of fighting on terrain they knew, but this in turn subjected their peasants to the ravages of war. The French kings, moreover, had to cope with the fact that some of their own subjects—the Burgundians, the Flemish, and the Gascons of Aquitaine—allied with the English at various times during the war. For most of its duration the French monarchs were unable to provide either strong military leadership or sound fiscal policies to finance the fighting. The English, despite the popular support marshaled by Edward III and a string of impressive military victories, were unable to inflict a total defeat on France because they had neither the manpower nor the funds to dominate such a vast land. In the end the English were largely reduced to a policy of intimidation, which failed in the face of renewed French resolve.

England's early victories were the result of the military superiority of its longbowmen, who could lay down a barrage of arrows powerful enough to pierce French armor at a distance of up to 200 yards. The effectiveness of the English archers was demonstrated at Crécy in 1346, at Poitiers a decade later, and at Agincourt in 1415. Although the French also had longbows, they failed to use them effectively. The turning point of the war came in 1429 as the English besieged Orléans. Charles, the sickly dauphin (crown prince), his plight desperate, gambled on an illiterate peasant girl from the village of Domrémy who claimed to have been sent by heavenly messengers. Accompanied by fresh troops dispatched by the dauphin, Joan of Arc, though only 17, inspired the French with a vision of victory. The English in any event were on the verge of withdrawing from Orléans, but Joan's sense of divine mission and the dauphin's decision to accept the royal crown as Charles VII in May 1429 gave the French new life. When the Burgundians captured Joan a year later, the English hoped to discredit her by having her tried and executed as a heretic, but instead they created a martyr. A posthumous trial found her innocent in 1456, and in 1920 she was canonized as a saint. In the years that followed her death in 1431, the French, with the Burgundians at their side after 1435, relentlessly drove the English out of France, leaving them in 1453 with only Calais.

Joan of Arc as she may have looked, shown here holding a banner with the fleur-de-lis, the royal emblem of France. [Giraudon/Art Resource]

The French victory was facilitated by the growth of national feeling and the effective use of gunpowder and heavy artillery. Not only were the new cannons useful in besieging fortifications, but they also demoralized enemy forces and frightened their horses. In the end the war was beneficial to the French monarchy, for during its course the kings acquired both a monopoly on the sale of salt, the *gabelle* or tax on which became a major source of royal income, and the right to impose other taxes, including a direct tax called the *taille*, without the approval of the Estates General. These funds were necessary to support the standing army introduced in the war. In contrast, the English monarchs were able to maintain the war only by repeatedly seeking parliamentary approval for taxation, thereby making Parliament an indispensable part of the government. By the war's end the principle was established that neither taxes nor other forms of legislation could be implemented without parliamentary approval, and Parliament had taken the first steps to hold royal officials accountable to them or risk impeachment. England and France thus began to follow strikingly different paths of monarchical government, the former eventually culminating in constitutional monarchy, the latter in absolute rule.

The social consequences of the war were profound. In both countries the rural economy was hit hard by the loss of men to the recurring campaigns, especially as the population fell sharply because of the Black Death. In addition to the soldiers killed in battle, the English callously murdered thousands of French civilians. The war brought higher taxes, disrupted trade, and contributed to the shortage of manpower on the farms of both countries. The change in the manner of fighting had significant long-term effects. Both the longbow and the use of guns enhanced the value of commoners on the battlefield and thus encouraged the development of larger armies. Those armies in turn required greater and greater financial support from the state in contrast to the smaller feudal forces. The cannons meant major changes in the construction of city walls, which had to be much thicker. At the same time, however, siege trains capable of attacking towns were generally beyond the reach of all but sovereigns and the greater princes; the military changes thus contributed to the evolution of more unified states. Economically, the demand for cannons, guns, and ammunition sparked the growth of the armaments industry and the mining companies that provided it with the necessary raw materials. Thus in the long run the socioeconomic effects of the war were more important than its territorial consequences.

## The Spiritual Crisis of the Late Medieval Church

Against a backdrop of widespread misery caused by famine, pestilence, and war, the medieval church was rocked by scandal and division in the late fourteenth and early fifteenth centuries, precisely at a time when strong spiritual leadership was desperately needed. The French king, Philip IV, emboldened by his earlier victory over Pope Boniface VIII, successfully pressured Pope Clement V (1305–1314), himself French, to move the seat of the papacy from Rome to Avignon in 1309. Although an imperial city under papal control, Avignon was not only on the French border but was French in language and culture. The papacy remained at Avignon until 1377, a period usually referred to as the Babylonian Captivity, an allusion to the period in which the ancient Hebrews were held captive in Babylon. Avignon had the advantage of freeing the popes from the turmoil then disrupting Rome and the Papal States, but it also placed the papacy under a greater degree of French influence. Of the 134 cardinals appointed during the Avignon period, 111 were French. The English, the Germans, and many Italians were displeased at the specter of a papacy in the shadow of French power, and Rome was particularly hard hit because its economy had rested so heavily on papal revenues. But perhaps most of the resentment against the Avignon popes stemmed from their efforts to create new sources of income to offset decreased revenue from the Papal States. The collection of annates, usually the first year's income from an ecclesiastical position, or expectatives, a fee for the right to be appointed to a particular ecclesiastical position when it became vacant, created the impression that the popes were more concerned with material than spiritual matters.

Disillusion with the papacy became even more pronounced as a result of the great schism that scandalized the church from 1378 to 1417. In 1377 Pope Gregory XI (1370–1378), persuaded by Catherine of Siena and Bridget of Sweden, moved the papal court back to Rome. When he died a year later, Roman mobs intimidated the cardinals to elect an Italian pope who would keep the papacy in Rome. The cardinals obliged with the reform-minded Urban VI (1378–1389), but five months later a group of mostly French cardinals declared Urban's election void and elected a rival pope, Clement VII, a cousin of the French king, Charles V. Europeans had witnessed schisms before, but nothing like the spectacle that now divided Christendom, largely along political lines. Clement, ruling from Avignon, had the support of France and its allies, Castile, Aragon, Naples, and Scotland, whereas Urban was backed by England, Portugal, Flanders, and the Holy Roman Empire. The Bohemians, Hungarians, Poles, and Scandinavians also supported the Roman pope. As each pope claimed to be the true vicar of Christ and condemned the other, the schism raised serious questions about the validity of priests' authority and the sacraments they administered. In addition to casting disrepute on the leaders of the church, the schism encouraged the spread of heresy and mysticism, with its stress on the inner life of the spirit rather than church matters and liturgy.

When it became apparent that neither the Roman nor the Avignonese pope would yield to his rivals in the interest of unity, reformers called for a church council to end the scandal. Advocates of reform contended that a council of the church exercised authority superior to that of a pope and was ultimately responsible for faith and unity. In its attempt to limit papal power, this Conciliar theory drew on a medieval intellectual tradition that in the past had been very controversial. In 1324, for instance, Marsiglio of Padua, the rector of the University of Paris, had argued in his *Defender of the Peace* that because the people are the ultimate source of authority in church and state, a church council is superior to the pope. Marsiglio went even further, insisting that the church's power was entirely restricted to spiritual matters; hence the pope had no claim to temporal authority. By reducing the church to a community within the state, he challenged its traditional claim to superiority. Although the church condemned Marsiglio's theories in 1327, his ideas provided a useful arsenal for those intent on disputing papal primacy. Among the most important

of these were theologians at the University of Paris, especially Jean Gerson and Pierre d'Ailly, who espoused Conciliar arguments as the means to end the papal schism.

With the support of most monarchs, a group of cardinals representing Rome and Avignon summoned a council to meet at Pisa in 1409. There both popes were deposed and a new one chosen, but because neither pope accepted the council's action, there were now three claimants to Peter's chair. The embarrassing schism was resolved only when a new council met in the German city of Constance beginning in 1414. It took three years and the energetic support of Sigismund, the Holy Roman Emperor, to restore unity through the election of an Italian cardinal as Martin V (1417–1431). One of the three feuding popes resigned, but the others had to be deposed. The church subsequently regarded the Roman popes as the legitimate line. In addition to ending the schism, the Council of Constance issued two decrees supporting Conciliar views, the first of which asserted that a general council of the church derived its authority directly from Christ and thus could compel the obedience of popes "in matters pertaining to the faith, the extinction of the schism, and the form of the church." The second decree called for the next two councils to meet after intervals of five and seven years and subsequent ones every decade. The council also addressed the question of heresy, particularly the problem of John Hus.

## The Challenge of Heresy: Wyclif and Hus

Symptomatic of the church's problems in the fourteenth and early fifteenth centuries was the enthusiastic reception in England and Bohemia of ideas that challenged the very core of orthodox teaching. The Oxford professor John Wyclif (c. 1330–1384) not only denied papal claims to temporal power, as Marsiglio of Padua had done, but also demanded that prelates (cardinals, archbishops, and bishops) relinquish their political offices and that the church divest itself of its property. In the tradition of Francis of Assisi, he insisted that the clergy should devote themselves to poverty and piety. On the crucial question of authority, Wyclif insisted that it rested in the Bible alone, which, he argued, should be in the language of the people. In this spirit he began preparing an English version of the Bible. Wyclif also called for the abolition of many traditions, including pilgrimages, the sale of indulgences, the veneration of saints, and the doctrine of transubstantiation—the belief that the substance of the bread and wine miraculously becomes the body and blood of Christ in the Eucharist. Convinced that the true church was composed only of people divinely predestined to believe in God, Wyclif

## ⊗ Marsiglio on the Power of the People ⊗

*In his* Defender of the Peace, *Marsiglio of Padua makes a strong case
for the people as the fundamental source of authority and the maintenance of peace as the primary task of a government.*

The authority to make laws belongs only to the whole body of the citizens . . . or else it
belongs to one or a few men. But it cannot belong to one man alone . . . for through ignorance or malice or both, this one man could make a bad law, looking more to his own
private benefit than to that of the community, so that the law would be tyrannical. For the
same reason, the authority to make laws cannot belong to a few; for they too could sin . . .
in making the law for the benefit of a certain few and not for the common benefit, as can
be seen in oligarchies. . . . Since all the citizens must be measured by the law according to
due proportion, and no one knowingly harms or wishes injustice to himself, it follows that
all or most wish a law conducing to the common benefit of the citizens. . . .

   It is hence appropriate . . . that the whole body of citizens entrust to those who are prudent and experienced the investigation, discovery, and examination of the standards, the
future laws or statutes. . . . After such standards, the future laws, have been discovered and
diligently examined, they must be laid before the assembled whole body of citizens for
their approval or disapproval. . . . The laws thus made by the hearing and consent of the
entire multitude will be better observed, nor will anyone have any protest to make against
them.

*Source:* Marsilius of Padua, *Defensor pacis*, trans. A. Gewirth (Toronto: University of Toronto Press, 1980),
pp. 48, 54–55.

---

daringly argued that salvation was independent of the
institutional sacraments, and he denied both papal and
clerical power to excommunicate the righteous from the
true church. Wyclif's clear distinction between the spiritual church of true believers and the corrupt temporal
institution presided over by the popes appealed to Christians disgusted by the events of the 1300s. Wyclif enjoyed powerful support among aristocrats in England,
who saw in his teachings the possibility of acquiring the
church's wealth. Many of his ideas were condemned,
and he was expelled from Oxford. Wyclif's followers,
known as Lollards, kept his ideas alive in England well
into the sixteenth century despite heavy persecution. Ultimately they helped prepare the ground for the Protestant Reformation.

   Wyclif's ideas were carried to Bohemia by Czech students studying at Oxford and by members of the household of Anne of Bohemia, who married King Richard II
of England in 1381. The leader of the Bohemian reformers, John Hus (1369–1415), rector of the University of
Prague, embraced some of Wyclif's teachings, especially
his concept of the true church as a body of saints and
the need for sweeping reforms. Hus, whose views struck
a responsive chord among Czech nationalists resentful
of the domination of foreign ecclesiastics, enjoyed the

backing of King Wenceslas, brother of the Emperor Sigismund. When Sigismund offered Hus a guarantee of
safe conduct in order to discuss his views at the Council
of Constance, Hus accepted, though he had already
been excommunicated. The council, which had previously condemned Wyclif's tenets, accused Hus of heresy. He was tried and convicted, turned over to Sigismund's officials, and burned at the stake in 1415;
promises made to heretics, Sigismund was assured,
were not binding. A year later Hus' disciple, Jerome of
Prague, met the same fate. Their militant followers, fired
in part by Czech patriotism, mounted a fierce rebellion
that lasted from 1421 to 1436. In the end the Bohemians
were left with considerable authority over their own
church, an example that was not lost on Martin Luther
a century later as he pondered the need for reform in
the German church.

## The Late Medieval Outlook

The crises of the fourteenth and early fifteenth centuries
had a striking effect on people's outlook: famine, plague,

## ◎ A Corrupt Clergy: Wyclif's Indictment ◎

*John Wyclif's attack on the moral evils of the clergy struck a responsive chord among many Englishmen.*

We should put on the armor of Christ, for Antichrist has turned his clerks [clergymen] to covetous and worldly love, and so blinded the people and darkened the law of Christ, that his servants be thick, and few be on Christ's side. And always they despise that men should know Christ's life, . . . and priests should be ashamed of their lives, and especially these high priests, for they reverse Christ both in word and deed. . . .

O men that be on Christ's half, help ye now against Antichrist! for the perilous time is come that Christ and Paul told [of] before. . . . For three sects fight here, against Christian[s]. . . . The first is the pope and cardinals, by false law that they have made; the second is emperors [and] bishops, who despise Christ's law; the third is these Pharisees [i.e., friars]. . . . All these three, God's enemies, travel in hypocrisy, and in worldly covetousness, and idleness in God's law. Christ help his church from these fiends, for they fight perilously.

*Source:* J. H. Robinson, ed., *Readings in European History*, vol. 1 (Boston: Ginn, 1904), pp. 497–498.

---

and war influenced the cult of death and decay; the Hundred Years' War affected the cult of chivalry and the growth of national literature; and the Babylonian Captivity and the papal schism prompted social criticism and the views of nominalists and mystics.

## The Cult of Death

The preoccupation with death induced by the massive fatalities resulting from famine and plague manifested itself in various ways. In the minds of the pious, greater attention was given to the Last Judgment, a popular motif in both art and literature. A few church walls still feature murals of the Last Judgment dating from this period. Others found solace in the Pietà, a depiction of Mary holding the dead Christ in her arms—a poignant symbol for grieving parents who shared her sense of personal loss and the hope of resurrection. Painters commonly depicted figures of death, and sculptors placed skeletal figures instead of traditional effigies on tombs. Nothing, however, more graphically reveals the fascination with death than the *danse macabre*, the dance of death that was not only portrayed in art but also acted out as an eerie drama and celebrated in poetry. The *danse macabre* may, in fact, be related to the psychological and neurological disorders that accompanied the plague. A recurring theme in these representations is the equality of all persons in death, a sharp counterpoint to a society preoccupied with social hierarchy. There was no more vivid reminder of this than the Churchyard

of the Innocents in Paris, where skulls and bones were heaped by the thousands along the cloister walls.

## The Chivalric Ideal

Juxtaposed with this cult of death and decay, with its democratic implications, was another cult, more positive in outlook and restricted in its social appeal—the cult of chivalry. Here was a code for knights and nobles, the last gasp of a way of life and warfare gradually being pushed into the shadows by new methods of fighting, the rising mercantile order, and a gradual shift in importance from ancestry to talent as the key to a successful political career. The late medieval cult of chivalry, with its idealized knights and exalted ladies, was the swan song of the old order. The chivalric code exalted war, but there was nothing particularly glorious when England's peasant archers cut down the cream of the French knighthood at Crécy, Poitiers, and Agincourt. Efficiency, technology, and discipline replaced bravado, loyalty, and dignity on the battlefield, a change that ultimately revolutionized and depersonalized warfare by shifting the burden from the landed elite to the masses. As if to protest the passing of the old order, the aristocracy put greater emphasis on the trappings of chivalry: pageants, tournaments, and glitter. When Francis I of France and Henry VIII of England met in 1520, chivalric trappings were so extravagant that contemporaries described the scene as a "field of cloth of gold." Extravagance and overstatement were indicative of the fact that

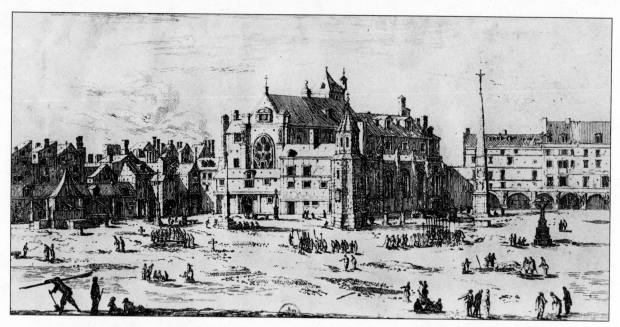

This sixteenth-century Flemish illustration depicts the churchyard of the Church of the Innocents in Paris. On its walls was a painting of the Dance of Death, below which skulls and bones were neatly stacked for public viewing. [Giraudon/Art Resource]

chivalry, once primarily a military code of conduct, had been transformed into an elegant charade, a form of escapism.

## National Literatures

The Hundred Years' War encouraged the further development of national vernacular literature. There are, of course, earlier examples of medieval literature in native tongues, such as the *Song of Roland*, the *Nibelungenlied*, and the poetry of the troubadours, but the contributions of Dante, Chaucer, and Villon were critical in shaping national languages out of regional dialects. All three writers sharply criticized late medieval society and the church.

Dante Alighieri (1265–1321), who held various civic offices in his native Florence before being forced into exile in 1301 by a rival political faction, spent the last two decades of his life traveling throughout Italy in search of patrons. Embittered by the divisiveness of the Italian states, Dante used these years to write in defense of the vernacular and to compose his epic poem, *The Divine Comedy* (1310–1321), so named because it progresses from a fearsome vision of hell in the first part, the *Inferno*, to a happy ending as the reader is guided through purgatory to paradise. The scenes from hell, peopled with everyone from actual popes and priests to politicians and queens, are used by Dante to condemn such

evils as ecclesiastical corruption, political treachery, and immorality. On other levels the journey is an allegory of the Christian life and a pictorial *summa* of medieval ethical and religious teachings akin in spirit to the scholastic *summae* of Thomas Aquinas.

Disenchantment with contemporary society, especially the church, is also reflected in Geoffrey Chaucer's *Canterbury Tales* (1387–1400). The son of a wine merchant, Chaucer (c. 1340–1400) fought in the Hundred Years' War before serving in various capacities as a royal official. It was probably on a mission to Florence that he learned of Dante's work, which influenced his own writings. Many of his poems, such as *The Legend of Good Women*, deal with the theme of love, while others, such as *The Parliament of Fowls*, may reflect contemporary political events. In the characters, anecdotes, and moral fables of *The Canterbury Tales* he probed English society, making particularly incisive and satirical comments about the foibles and hypocrisy of ecclesiastics. The thrust is similar in a nearly contemporary work titled *The Vision of Piers Plowman*, usually attributed to William Langland (c. 1330–c. 1400). The work's 11 poetic visions reflect the crises of the 1300s, especially as they affected the peasants, and are highly critical of the failings of the church even while reaffirming faith in Christian principles.

The poetry of the Frenchman François Villon (1431–c. 1463) is the voice of the downtrodden and criminal element in a society thrown into turmoil by the

## ◉ Death and Decay ◉

*François Villon's poetry reflects not only his own experiences among the lowly and the criminal in France but also the fifteenth century's fascination with death and decay.*

Death makes one shudder and turn pale,
Pinches the nose, distends the veins,
Swells out the throat, the members fail,
Tendons and nerves grow hard with strains.
O female flesh, like silken skeins,
Smooth, tender, precious, in such wise
Must you endure so awful pains?
Aye, or go living to the skies.

*The following lines were written while Villon was under sentence of death; he describes the fate that awaits his body.*

The rain has washed us through as through a sieve,
And the sun dried us black to caricature;
Magpies and crows have had our eyes to rive
And made of brows and beards their nouriture.
Never we pause, no moment's rest secure,
Now here, now there, as the winds fail or swell,
Always we swing like clapper of a bell.
Pitted as thimble is our bird-pecked skin.
Be not of our ill brotherhood and fell,
But pray to God we be absolved of sin!

*Source: The Complete Works of François Villon,* trans. J. U. Nicolson (New York: Covici Friede, 1931), pp. 32, 108.

---

Hundred Years' War. A convicted murderer, thief, and brawler as well as a graduate of the University of Paris, Villon was in and out of jail and was for a time under sentence of death. The themes of his ballads range from the ways of the Parisian underworld and his drinking companions to meditations on the beauty of life as he contemplated the skeletons in the Churchyard of the Innocents. The specter of death stalks much of his work, reflecting the popularity of this theme in the fifteenth century.

## Nominalists and Mystics

While the great vernacular writers criticized their social and religious world, William of Ockham (c. 1290–1349), an English Franciscan theologian, mounted a sweeping challenge to the scholastic teaching that prevailed in the universities. Ockham asserted that only individual things, not essences or universals, were real and knowable, a philosophical theory known as nominalism. Knowledge could therefore be attained by direct experience rather than by philosophical speculation. Contrary to the scholastics, he argued that the principal doctrines of Christianity, such as the existence of God and the immortality of the soul, were incapable of rational proof and had to be affirmed on the basis of faith alone. By removing the rational basis for Christian belief, Ockham opened the way to skepticism, a path followed by some of his disciples. Ockham's principles convinced him that the popes could not possess absolute authority, even in matters of faith; hence he contributed to Conciliar theory by insisting on the supremacy of general councils.

The rational and institutional approach to Christianity was also challenged by mystics, who urged the importance of seeking God within oneself. One of the most influential mystics was the Dominican friar Meister Eckhart (c. 1260–1328), a German, who taught that the mystical union of the human and the divine could be achieved in the soul through the purifying work of divine grace. Because the views of both Eckhart and Ockham were sufficiently different from traditional teaching, they had to defend themselves against charges of heresy before the papal court at Avignon, and Eckhart had to recant.

The real strength of late medieval mysticism was among the laity, particularly in Germany and the Netherlands. There the Dutchman Gerhard Groote (1340–1384) founded a movement known as the *devotio moderna* ("modern devotion"), which combined a strong sense of morality with an emphasis on the inner life of the soul rather than liturgy and penitent acts such as fasting and pilgrimages. After his death his followers established the Brethren and the Sisters of the Common Life—lay believers who lived in strictly regulated religious houses and devoted themselves primarily to the education of young boys. Some of the most influential religious leaders of the late fifteenth and sixteenth centuries, including Erasmus of Rotterdam, studied in these schools. The literary classic of this movement, Thomas à Kempis' *Imitation of Christ*, was a devotional handbook that emphasized personal piety and ethical conduct. Its message that "a humble husbandman who serves God is better than a proud philosopher" reflected a widespread desire among the laity to find relief from the material problems of their age through simple piety.

## Economic Recovery

Europe recovered from the calamities of the fourteenth and early fifteenth centuries in large measure because of renewed population growth, economic diversification, and technological inventions spurred by the labor shortages resulting from the Black Death. As the population began to return to its former levels in the late fifteenth and sixteenth centuries, there was once again an abundant labor supply as well as improved productivity and greater economic diversification. Merchants increasingly branched out into fields as varied as banking, textile and weapon manufacturing, and the mining of iron ore and silver. The Germans modernized the mines by harnessing horsepower and waterpower to crush ore, operate their rolling mills, pump water from mine shafts, and run the lifts. Blast furnaces were constructed to make cast iron. Dutch fishermen learned to salt, dry, and store their fish while at sea, thus enabling them to stay out longer and increase their catch. The Hundred Years' War, as we have seen, stimulated the armaments industry, and the invention of movable metal type not only led to a new industry in printing but also greatly encouraged the manufacture of paper.

The textile industry experienced some growth in this period. The production of woolens in Flanders and the cities of northern Italy, however, declined in the fifteenth century, primarily because the English monarchs made a concerted effort to build up their native wool industry by imposing low export duties on cloth and high ones on raw wool. Woolen manufacturing also expanded in France, Germany, and Holland, and new textile industries such as silk and cotton began to develop. In Venice some 3,000 persons were involved in the production of silk, 16,000 in the manufacture of cotton. Several thousand were employed in the Venetian arsenal, the greatest shipyard and probably the largest industrial establishment in Europe.

The growth in manufacturing went hand in hand with a dramatic increase in commerce and the rise of great merchants and their organizations. The latter included the seven major guilds in Florence, the six merchant corporations known as the *Corps de Marchands* in Paris, and the 12 Livery Companies in London. Firms in Europe's leading commercial centers established branch offices in other cities, and exchanges or bourses were opened to facilitate financial transactions. Banking houses developed rapidly; Florence had 33 in 1472. There were state banks in such places as Genoa, Venice, Augsburg, Hamburg, and Barcelona. As rulers as well as merchants found themselves in need of loans, the demand for credit grew, thus undermining the hostility of the medieval church to most interest charges. The Genoese pioneered the development of insurance, especially for merchants engaged in seaborne trade. The dominant role of northern Italians in banking was aided by the fact that the most stable coins of this period were Florentine florins and Venetian ducats.

Ships in the Mediterranean trade called at the Italian ports of Pisa and Genoa as well as at Marseilles and Narbonne in France and Barcelona in Aragon, but the heart of this commerce was really Venice. Its 3,300 ships, some of them capable of carrying as much as 250 tons of cargo, plied the waters from the North Sea and Spain to North Africa, Syria, and the Black Sea. In contrast, Genoa, itself a major maritime power, had 2,000 ships. Cloth from Europe was traded in the East for spices, dyes, sugar, silks, and cotton. Shipping in northern Europe was mostly the province of the Hanseatic League, whose members included Lübeck, Danzig, and Hamburg. Their ships ranged from Scandinavia and Russia to England, Flanders, and northern Italy. From the states of the Baltic and the North Sea they obtained fish, timber, naval stores, grain, and furs in exchange for wine, spices, and cloth. Much of the commerce moved through the ports of the Low Countries; in 1435 an average of 100 ships a day docked at Bruges. In the late fifteenth and sixteenth centuries the power of the Hanseatic League began to wane, partly owing to internal problems but mostly because of the growing power of states such as England and Denmark, whose merchants demanded an end to Hansa privileges and a greater role in the carrying trade.

## Political Renewal: The Quest for Unity and Authority

Economic revival was accompanied in western Europe and Russia by the development of relatively strong centralized states. The political crises of the era of adversity had increased the need for state governments to raise substantial tax revenue. Such revenue made it feasible to think in terms of a professional army rather than a feudal levy, but this in turn increased the costs of government. So too did the growth of royal bureaucracies, which were essential not only to raise the revenue but also to administer the more unified realms. Greater unity was in general beneficial to the business community; hence the monarchs typically found important allies in the towns. Urban support was translated into tax revenues (though many French towns enjoyed exemptions), an enlarged pool from which government officials could be selected, and political backing in the drive for sovereignty.

The decline of particularism—the dominance of local and regional authorities rather than a central government—was in most respects a blow to the landed aristocracy, but they were appeased by exemptions from most taxes and frequent appointments to political office. The landed elite were also prominently represented in the national assemblies, where they enjoyed power and prestige greater than that bestowed on urban delegates. The achievement of national sovereignty was possible in large measure because the power of the landed aristocracy was not so much crushed as altered: in the new system, many of them became staunch supporters of the crown, not its traditional enemy. In the case of Russia and Spain, the development of a centralized state was carried out as part of a drive to expel hitherto dominant invaders—the Mongols in Russia and the Muslims in Spain.

## The Rise of Muscovy

During the period of Mongol domination, Russia was a conglomeration of feudal principalities, but in the fourteenth century the princes of Moscow began to "gather the Russian land" by expanding their borders through marital alliances, inheritance, purchases, and conquests. In this process they were aided by three factors: the strategic location of Moscow near tributaries of the Volga and Oka rivers, Mongol reliance on the Muscov-

ites to collect tribute from other Russians, and the support of the Russian Orthodox church, whose metropolitan archbishop made Moscow the religious capital of the Russians in the fourteenth century. As Mongol power declined late in that century, the Muscovite princes ceased to be agents for the Mongols and took up the mantle of patriotic resistance. Their new role was made abundantly clear when Grand Prince Dimitri defeated the Tatars, as the Russians called the Mongols, in 1380 at Kolikovo, southeast of Moscow. The war of liberation continued well into the fifteenth century, during which time Moscow was besieged numerous times. Even after the Mongols were driven out, their influence pervaded many areas of Russian life, including military organization, criminal law, the system of tax collection, and above all the principle of unqualified obedience to the state. In a very real sense, Russian sovereigns ruled much as the Mongol khans had.

The foundation of a strong Russian state was laid by Ivan III, known as Ivan the Great (1462–1505), who was determined to prevent the recurrence of the factional struggles that had plagued his father's reign. To counterbalance the power of the hereditary boyars, or nobles, Ivan created a class of serving aristocracy by offering them lifetime grants of land in return for their service, a practice somewhat akin to that used earlier in the feudal states of western and central Europe. Ivan also enhanced his status as the result of his marriage to the Italian-educated Zoë, niece of the last Byzantine emperor, Constantine XI (died 1453). Henceforth Ivan began to refer to himself as the successor of the Byzantine emperors, adopting the Byzantine double eagle as the symbol of Russia, introducing Byzantine ceremonies at court, and calling himself Autocrat and Tsar ("Caesar"). At Zoë's urging, Italian architects were commissioned to design the Kremlin, a fortresslike palace befitting the tsar's pretensions to grandeur. Russian scholars contributed to the new image by asserting that Moscow was the third Rome (after Rome and Byzantium, each of which had fallen) and thus the center of Christianity. In the words of one Russian apologist, "The tsar is in nature like to all men, but in authority he is like to the highest God."

Ivan expanded the boundaries of his state, first by conquering the republic of Novgorod, a trading center with access to the Baltic Sea. Seizing approximately 80 percent of the former republic's land, he retained possession of more than half of it and used the rest to expand his serving aristocracy. In the process he exiled thousands of boyars, merchants, and smaller landowners. In 1500 he invaded Lithuania, hoping to conquer Smolensk; although he failed in this objective, by 1503 he had successfully expanded his borders to the west.

Above all, Ivan consciously advanced his claim to be ruler "of all the Russias," a title that even the prince of Lithuania had recognized in 1492. Unlike his predecessors, who limited their claim of ownership to royal estates and their inhabitants, Ivan asserted an unprece-

Russia in 1325
Expansion to 1389
Expansion to 1462
Expansion to 1533

*15.2 The Expansion of Russia*

dented right to all Russian lands. It was in this context that Ivan issued a new code of laws—the Sudebnik—for the Russian people in 1497. Ivan can justly be regarded as the founder of the modern Russian state and the architect of an absolute tsardom.

## The Spain of Isabella and Ferdinand

The unification of Spain was made possible by the marriage in 1469 of Isabella, the future queen of Castile (1474–1504), and Ferdinand, the future king of Aragon (1479–1516). Of the two kingdoms, Castile was by far more populous and wealthier. It was, moreover, an expanding state as it continued the campaign to reconquer Granada from the Muslims, a goal finally achieved in 1492. That done, Spain could turn its attention to overseas exploration, a pursuit in which the Portuguese had already taken the lead.

The marriage of Isabella and Ferdinand did not effectively unite the two countries, each of which spoke a different language and retained its own laws, taxes, monetary system, military, and customs. The two sov-

**The marriage of Ferdinand of Aragon and Isabella of Castile made the unification of Spain possible.** [Arxiu MAS, Barcelona]

ereigns left Aragon largely alone, free to keep its provincial assemblies, the Cortes, although royal supervision was exercised through viceroys appointed by the crown. Understandably, the monarchs concentrated on Castile, whose Cortes supported their quest for order and whose new council was the principal agency for the implementation of royal policy. In the work of centralization the sovereigns had the support of the towns, which were liberally represented in the Cortes, and of the hidalgos—knights who did not enjoy the tax-exempt status of the nobles and therefore sought employment from the crown. A number of the hidalgos served as *corregidors*, administering local districts, performing judicial functions, and supervising urban affairs. Although the role of the nobles in the government was somewhat reduced, they still exercised considerable influence through the powerful military brotherhoods established in the twelfth century, the Santiago, Calatrava, and Alcántara. To bring them under greater royal authority, Ferdinand became the head of each of the three great brotherhoods. The Mesta, the organization of large sheep farmers, also had to be controlled, for its pay-

ments were a primary source of royal revenue in the period before Spain began importing large quantities of American bullion.

The deeply devout Isabella and the pragmatic Ferdinand made the Catholic church a key instrument in their centralizing work. Isabella's most important minister, Cardinal Francisco Ximenes (c. 1436–1517), carried out a program of reform centering around the restoration of ecclesiastical discipline, thus reinforcing central authority. In 1482 Pope Sixtus IV granted the sovereigns the *real patronato* ("Royal Patronage"), giving them the right to make the major ecclesiastical appointments in Granada; this was later extended to Spanish America and then to Spain as a whole. Even more striking as a demonstration of royal authority in religion was the campaign of Isabella and Ferdinand to enforce religious orthodoxy. Although the Inquisition had been introduced into Spain by a papal bull in 1478, it soon became an instrument controlled by the crown and run by the queen's confessor, Tomás de Torquemada (died 1498). In 1492, the year Isabella and Ferdinand entered Granada in triumph, the Jews were given the option of being baptized as Christians or losing their property and going into exile; approximately 150,000 left. Ten years later Ximenes persuaded Isabella to expel professing Muslims. Jews and Muslims who converted—*Conversos* and *Moriscos*, respectively—were subject to the terrors of the Inquisition if their sincerity was doubted. Spain achieved religious unity, but at the cost of expelling or alienating productive minorities, curtailing intellectual freedom, and destroying toleration.

## England: The Struggle for the Throne

By the time England concluded the Hundred Years' War in 1453, royal authority, already checked by the growth of parliamentary power in the areas of legislation and taxation, had been undermined by bastard feudalism. By this practice a small group of powerful nobles who controlled much of the country's landed property used their wealth to employ private armies through a practice known as livery and maintenance. The retainers in their hire wore distinctive clothing (livery), served primarily for pay rather than for the use of land as in the traditional feudal arrangement, and could expect legal assistance—often involving intimidation or bribery—if they got in trouble while serving their lord. Many of these retainers were recruited from the ranks of soldiers who had fought in the Hundred Years' War. The powerful magnates who hired these private armies exerted enormous influence on the monarchs through the royal Council and commanded strong support from their followers in Parliament. These circumstances made it possible for Henry of Bolingbroke, a grandson of Edward III, to force the abdication of Richard II, another grandson, in 1399. Parliament dutifully confirmed Bolingbroke's assumption of the crown as Henry IV (1399–1413), the first ruler of the house of Lancaster.

The reign of Henry IV's grandson, Henry VI (1422–1461), who became king at the age of 9 months, was conducive to the further growth of the magnates' power during his regency and then during the bouts of insanity that afflicted him as an adult. The result was the outbreak of civil war between the feuding factions, the houses of Lancaster and York. In the sixteenth century this came to be known as the Wars of the Roses when William Shakespeare, in *Henry VI*, assigned the symbol of the Tudor dynasty, a red rose, to the Lancastrians; the Yorkist symbol was a white rose. Henry's queen, Margaret of Anjou, was unwilling to see power pass to Richard, duke of York, great-grandson of Edward III and heir apparent before the birth of Henry's son. Richard's son, Edward IV (1461–1483), finally succeeded in capturing the throne in 1461 and forcing Henry VI to abdicate. The house of Lancaster staged a brief comeback in 1470–1471, though Edward soon regained control, after which Henry VI mysteriously died in the Tower of London.

The Wars of the Roses were over, giving Edward the opportunity to improve his position by carefully shepherding his finances, establishing firm control over the Council, and expanding royal authority in Wales and northern England. At his death in 1483 his brother Richard, regent for the young Edward V, had the new king and his brother imprisoned. They too died mysteriously, possibly at the instigation of their uncle, who assumed the throne as Richard III (1483–1485). Although Richard suppressed one rebellion provoked by the renewal of factional strife, in 1485 Henry Tudor, who was remotely related to the house of Lancaster, invaded England with French backing and defeated Richard in the battle of Bosworth Field. Once again Parliament willingly recognized the victor's claim to the throne, and Henry's marriage to Edward IV's daughter, Elizabeth of York, helped heal the reopened wounds dividing the English ruling order.

Henry VII (1485–1509) resumed the task of strengthening royal authority that Edward IV had begun, notably by making the crown financially secure and building up a modest surplus in the treasury. Instead of increasing taxes, he made effective use of income from crown lands, judicial fees and fines, and feudal dues such as wardship rights. He also avoided costly foreign adventures, with the exception of a brief and futile invasion of France in 1492 in an attempt to keep Brittany independent. Apart from token forces, Henry had no standing army, but he made good use of unpaid justices of the peace drawn from the ranks of the gentry to maintain order in the counties, thereby reducing the crown's dependence on the nobility. Henry also used his Council, which could sit as a court (called the Star Chamber), to maintain order and impose swift justice; people cited before it had no right to legal counsel and could be compelled to testify against themselves. Like Edward IV, he selected men for the Council because of their loyalty to him rather than their status as magnates. He negotiated two strategic alliances, one of which involved the marriage of his daughter Margaret to James IV of Scotland. From that line came the Stuart dynasty, which governed both countries in the seventeenth century and unified them in the kingdom of Great Britain in 1707. The second alliance involved the marriage of Henry's elder son, Arthur, to Catherine of Aragon, daughter of Ferdinand and Isabella. After Arthur died of tuberculosis, Henry arranged for Catherine's marriage to his younger son, Prince Henry. When in the late 1520s the latter tired of Catherine, who had failed to provide him with a male heir, he set in motion the events that led to England's break with the Catholic church. By the time of his death in 1509, Henry VII had imposed substantial order and unity on England and, in the Statutes of Drogheda (1495), had made the Parliament and laws of Ireland subject to English control as well.

## Valois France

Charles VII (1422–1461) laid the foundation for the recovery of the French monarchy in the late fifteenth century, not least by his victory over the English in the Hundred Years' War. Despite the large size of the kingdom, the continued presence of feudal traditions and local privileges, and the existence of a representative assembly, the Estates General, the French kings were at last in a position to unify the country, aided by a new spirit of national feeling. Because of the war Charles had been able to form the first French standing army, supported by the *taille*, a direct tax for which he did not have to seek the approval of the Estates General after 1439. In fact, meetings of the Estates were very rare between 1441 and 1614, after which there were no sessions until 1789. In 1438 Charles had also brought the French church firmly under royal control in a pronouncement called the Pragmatic Sanction of Bourges. It set forth "Gallican liberties" (similar to the *real patronato* later introduced in Spain) such as the right of the French church to choose its own prelates and an end to the payment of annates to Rome.

Once England was defeated, the greatest threat to the French monarchy was the duchy of Burgundy, whose dukes, Philip the Good (1419–1467) and Charles the Bold (1467–1477), entertained thoughts of making their state a powerful middle kingdom between France and the Holy Roman Empire. Their lands included not only the duchy of Burgundy in eastern France but also the Franche-Comté, Flanders, and other areas of the Netherlands. To establish a viable middle kingdom, Charles the Bold attempted to conquer Alsace and Lorraine, thereby linking Burgundy with the Low Countries, the major source of his extensive wealth. The French king, Louis XI (1461–1483), responded to this threat by subsidizing the armies of the Swiss Confederation, who defeated and killed Charles in 1477. In the absence of a male heir, his Burgundian lands were seized by France, though Charles' daughter Mary and her new husband, Maximilian of Habsburg, retained possession of the Low Countries. The royal domains were increased again in 1480 and 1481 when Louis inherited the Angevin lands of Anjou, Maine, and Provence. Only Brittany remained beyond the pale of his authority, but that was remedied in 1491 when his son and heir, Charles VIII (1483–1498), employed military force to compel Anne, duchess of Brittany, to marry him.

Although the crafty Louis XI had shunned war wherever possible in favor of diplomacy and intrigue, Charles VIII recklessly involved France in a disastrous attempt to dominate Italy. The stage had been set when Louis succeeded not only to the Angevin lands in France but also to the Angevin claim to the throne of Naples, now occupied by the Aragonese. Louis had wisely done nothing about the claim, though he had involved himself in

The French king Louis XI was a homely man who enjoyed a game of chess. He significantly expanded the royal domain by acquiring the duchy of Burgundy. [Ronald Sheridan/ Ancient Art and Architecture Collection]

the political affairs of northern Italy. Charles, however, was determined to assert his Neopolitan claim, and in 1494 he invaded Italy, thus precipitating a great power struggle for control of the Italian peninsula that lasted 65 years. By February 1495 he had reached Naples, where he was crowned in May. Although the duke of Milan, Ludovico il Moro (1451–1508), had encouraged the French invasion as a means of weakening his own enemies—Naples, Florence, and the papacy—he soon recognized that a French presence in Italy threatened everyone. He threw his support to the newly formed League of Venice, consisting of the empire, the papacy, and the Venetians, which forced Charles out of Italy.

Charles' successor, Louis XII (1498–1515), was likewise determined to pursue his Italian ambitions. This time the French had papal support, for Pope Alexander VI (1492–1503) was primarily interested in weakening the Venetians, who were competing with him for domination of central Italy. Louis obtained the support of Ferdinand of Aragon by offering to partition Naples with him. Louis' primary goal was the conquest of Milan, which he claimed as his own because his mother had been a member of the Visconti family, which ruled the duchy until 1447. Ludovico was accordingly accused of usurping the ducal title and imprisoned for the rest of his life by the French—perhaps a fitting end for the man who had first encouraged French intervention in Italy.

Once Pope Julius II (1503–1513) had secured the Papal States, he enlisted Spain, Venice, the Swiss Confederation, and the Holy Roman Empire in a Holy League to drive France out of Italy, an end they accomplished in 1513. Under Francis I (1515–1547) the French returned again in 1515, this time sparking a series of wars with the Habsburgs that drained France financially and damaged the prestige of the monarchy. Nevertheless, as in the case of the Hundred Years' War, military needs and financial demands led to the continued expansion and centralization of the royal administration, thus strengthening the king's hold on the realm and laying the foundation for the subsequent development of absolutism in France.

## Italy: Papal States and City-States

While Russia and the western European states were developing stronger, more centralized governments in the fifteenth century, in Italy, Germany, Hungary, and Poland regional states and princes consolidated their power, effectively blocking the emergence of nations. The struggle in the High Middle Ages between the papacy and the Hohenstaufen emperors left the Italians without a strong government capable of extending its sway throughout the peninsula. Nor did any state possess a theoretical claim to serve as the nucleus for a unified nation. From Rome the popes governed the Papal States, a band extending across central Italy, but their claims to authority were international in scope. The popes themselves did not acquire their position by hereditary succession but by an elective process that was not limited to Italians. The papacy's temporal authority in Italy was severely reduced during the Avignon period and further damaged during the great schism. Beginning with Martin V, the fifteenth- and early-sixteenth-century popes were therefore preoccupied with reestablishing their temporal power. Popes such as Alexander VI of the Spanish Borgia family and Julius II were less spiritual leaders than temporal princes willing to use any means to extend their power. Alexander relied heavily on his son Cesare, who had few moral principles, while Julius personally led his forces into battle.

In the fourteenth and fifteenth centuries the communal governments of northern Italy experienced substantial internal tensions resulting from economic and social changes. Rapid urban growth, the development of textile industries, and the rise of a sizable proletariat excluded from the hope of prosperity by privilege-conscious guilds created such strife that Milan and Florence turned to men who were virtual despots to preserve order. So too did some of the smaller cities, such as Mantua. Often these despots were *condottieri*, mercenary generals whose hired armies provided them with the force necessary to keep order. In the south the kingdom of Naples and Sicily had problems of a different nature because of foreign domination. In 1282 the Sicilians revolted against their French Angevin rulers and turned for assistance to Aragon. Throughout the fourteenth century the Angevins and the Aragonese contested southern Italy until, in 1435, Alfonso the Magnanimous of Aragon drove the Angevins out of Naples. As we have seen, it was the decision of Charles VIII of France to reassert the Angevin claim that led to the French invasion of Italy in 1494.

## The Duchy of Milan

From its strategic position in the heart of the Po valley and at the base of the trade routes leading across the Alps into northern Europe, Milan developed rapidly as an industrial center specializing in textiles and arms. The medieval commune suffered, however, not only from social tensions but also from a struggle for power between Guelph (propapal) and Ghibelline (proimperial) factions. Under the leadership of the Visconti family the Ghibellines triumphed in 1277, effectively ending communal government and establishing despotic rule. The Visconti—dukes of Milan beginning in 1395—employed *condottieri* to extend their control in the Po valley. The last of the Visconti dukes, Filippo Maria, introduced the mulberry plant, laying the foundation for Milan's silk industry.

When Filippo died without a male heir in 1447, the Milanese revived communal government, but their so-called Ambrosian Republic proved unable to govern effectively. Thus in 1450 the *condottiere* Francesco Sforza, Filippo Maria's son-in-law, reestablished ducal rule. Apart from extending Milan's control over Genoa, Francesco attempted to maintain a balance of power in Italy among the five principal states: Milan, Venice, Florence, Naples, and the Papal States. To this end he was an architect of the Italian League (1455), which also included some of the lesser states and was in part designed to prevent French aggression. Thus when Francesco's son Ludovico connived with Charles VIII of France to intervene in Italian affairs, he foolishly undermined his father's policy, thereby contributing not only to the devastating wars that ensued but to the demise of

*15.3 Italy, c. 1494*

the Sforza dynasty as well. After the French were ousted, the family's rule was briefly restored between 1512 and 1535, at which time the Holy Roman Emperor Charles V acquired Milan.

---

### ⚜ CATERINA SFORZA, THE DESPOT OF FORLÌ

The complex world of fifteenth-century Italian politics is reflected in the career of the sensuous and beautiful Caterina Sforza (c. 1463–1509), daughter of Francesco

Sforza's son, the second duke of Milan. Although she received a humanist education (see Chapter 16), she displayed no interest in classical authors or philosophical issues, but she was intrigued by history as well as riding and dancing. For political reasons Caterina's father arranged her marriage to Pope Sixtus IV's nephew, Girolamo Riario. The pope subsequently gave them control of the towns of Forlì and Imola, northeast of Florence, but Caterina's husband was assassinated by political rivals in 1488. She retained power by ruling in her son's name, thanks to assistance from the armies of Milan and Bologna, and avenged her husband's murder by staging a spectacle of brutality in which the bodies of some of the conspirators were dismembered and scattered in the

Caterina Sforza, countess of Forlì. [Marburg/
Art Resource]

his son, Cesare Borgia, plotted to increase their control over the Papal States, particularly the region that included Caterina's lands. Her main ally, Milan, was preoccupied in 1499 with the threat of a new French invasion, thanks to a pact between France and Venice signed in February. A month later the pope, calling Caterina a "daughter of iniquity," claimed her lands. Negotiations with Niccolò Machiavelli, the Florentine envoy, failed to achieve an effective alliance, nor were the assassins she dispatched to kill Alexander VI successful. Cesare Borgia's army struck in the autumn, forcing Caterina to send her children and treasures to Florence for safety. She retreated to a fortress with her troops, destroying all buildings in the area that might shelter the enemy, cutting down the trees, and flooding the marshes. Italy watched as the papal army relentlessly attacked until she was finally captured—and raped by Cesare—in January 1500. For a year she was imprisoned in a Roman dungeon. Without support from any major Italian state, her efforts to regain her territories failed, forcing her to seek refuge in Florence. Her last years were spent attending to her household, her garden, her horses, and her soul. Contemporaries called her the "Amazon of Forlì," a tribute to her ability to hold her own in a political world governed by the ethics of power.

## Florence and the Medici

Bitter social conflict disrupted Florence throughout the fourteenth and early fifteenth centuries. Thanks to its banking houses and its textile industry the city was typically prosperous in this period, though it suffered severely when England's Edward III repudiated his debts and caused major banking houses to fail and again when 50,000 of its 80,000 inhabitants died in the plague. The periodic crises intensified social tensions that were already present. In part the turmoil was caused by an unusual degree of social mobility in Florentine society. The older nobles, the *grandi*, had been effectively excluded from power in 1293 through a constitution called the Ordinances of Justice, the work of the newly rich capitalists who dominated the seven greater guilds. In 1343 they in turn were successfully challenged by the craftsmen of the lesser guilds and their allies, the shopkeepers and small businessmen. The *ciompi* had their turn in 1378, when they revolted and won the right to organize their own guilds and have a say in political affairs. Feuding between the lesser guilds and the *ciompi* enabled the wealthy merchants to regain control in the early 1380s under the leadership of the Albizzi family. When the Albizzi blocked the rise of new capitalists to power but could not win a war against neighboring Lucca, they were exiled in 1434 by partisans of the Medici family.

Cosimo de' Medici (1389–1464) and his successors, who dominated Florentine politics except for brief inter-

piazza of Forlì. That done, she sought to restore unity to her possessions by launching an extensive program of public building in Forlì, including a lavish park.

Although a campaign to extend her territory to the northeast failed because of opposition from Venice, her importance was such that she was courted by all the major Italian states. When the French invaded Italy in 1494, Caterina, fearful of Venice, refused to join the Holy League against France, opting instead for a neutrality that favored the French and their Florentine allies. The assassination of her lover in 1495 prompted her to instigate another bloody vendetta, but it also opened the way for her secret marriage a year or two later to Giovanni de' Medici, second cousin of the Florentine ruler Lorenzo the Magnificent. About this time she underwent a period of spiritual searching in which she wrote to the reformer Girolamo Savonarola, who urged her to seek redemption through pious works and just rule.

Caterina's final period of political crisis began in 1498 when the Venetians raided her lands, but she was saved by military aid from Milan and the outbreak of fighting between the Venetians and the Florentines. While Caterina was occupied with Venice, Pope Alexander VI and

vals until 1737, governed as despots by manipulating republican institutions, often from behind the scenes. In addition to working with Francesco Sforza to create a balance of power in Italy and prevent French aggression, Cosimo introduced a graduated income tax and curried favor among the lesser guilds and workers. His grandson, Lorenzo the Magnificent (1449–1492), was the object of an assassination plot by the Pazzi family that killed his brother Giuliano while the two were worshiping in the cathedral at Florence in 1478. The plot had the support of Girolamo Riario, Caterina Sforza's husband, as well as Pope Sixtus IV. The pope resented the Medici's alliance with Venice and Milan, which was intended to block the extension of his authority in the northern Papal States. Although the assassination attempt failed, Lorenzo had to defend Florence against an attack by papal and Neapolitan forces. His son Piero was less able, and as a result of territorial concessions made to the French in 1494, he was ousted by the Florentines. Republican government was restored and for four years a spirit of religious frenzy prevailed under the sway of the fiery Dominican Girolamo Savonarola (see Chapter 16). The republic's alliance with France isolated Florence from other Italian states, but in 1512 Pope Julius II persuaded the Florentines to join the Holy League against Louis XII and allow the Medici to return.

Bust of Lorenzo de' Medici by Verrocchio. [National Gallery of Art, Washington, Samuel H. Kress Collection]

## ❧ VENICE: THE REPUBLIC OF ST. MARK

In sharp contrast to the Florentines and the Milanese, the Venetians enjoyed a remarkable degree of social and political stability, in large measure because the merchant oligarchy that governed the republic was a closed group limited to families listed in the Golden Book. This register of more than 200 names included only families represented in the Great Council prior to 1297. Venice had neither a landed nobility nor a large industrial proletariat to challenge the dominance of its wealthy merchants, and the republic, because of its relative isolation, had not become embroiled in the Guelph-Ghibelline feud that left cities such as Florence with a tradition of bitter factionalism. There was never a successful revolution in Venice.

The Venetian government was a tight-knit affair. The 240 or so merchant oligarchs who sat in the Great Council elected the Senate, the principal legislative body, as well as the ceremonial head of state, called a *doge*, and other government officials. The most powerful body in the state was the annually elected Council of Ten, which met in secret, focused on security, and in an emergency could assume the powers of all other government officials. To the Venetians' credit, the merchant oligarchy disdained despotic rule, thereby maintaining the support of those excluded from the political process.

In the fourteenth and fifteenth centuries the Venetians engaged in a program of expansion that made them a commercial empire. This involved a bitter contest with Genoa for control of trade in the eastern Mediterranean, a struggle that ended with Genoa's defeat in 1380. In the meantime, the Venetians embarked in 1329 on a campaign to acquire territory in northern Italy to assure both an adequate food supply and access to the Alpine trade routes. Conquering such neighboring states as Padua and Verona brought the Venetians face to face with Milan and the Papal States, both of which were also expanding, as well as with the Habsburgs and the Hungarians, who were unsettled by Venetian expansion around the head of the Adriatic. The struggle on the mainland diverted crucial resources from the eastern Mediterranean, where Turkish expansion in the late fifteenth century gravely threatened Venetian interests. More dangerous than the lengthy war with the Turks (1463–1479) was the threat posed to Venice by the League of Cambrai, formed in 1508 and 1509 by Pope Julius II to strip Venice of its territorial acquisitions. Members of the league included Emperor Maximilian, Louis XII, and Ferdinand of Aragon. Although the league

## ◎ The Glories of Venice ◎

*The civic pride of the Venetians is manifest in the 1423 deathbed oration of the doge Tommaso Mocenigo, which was delivered to a group of senators.*

This our city now sends out in the way of business to different parts of the world ten millions of ducats' worth yearly by ships and galleys, and the profit is not less than two million ducats a year. . . . Every year there go to sea forty-five galleys with eleven thousand sailors, and there are three thousand ship's carpenters and three thousand caulkers. . . . There are one thousand noblemen whose income is from seven hundred to four thousand ducats. If you go on in this manner you will increase from good to better, and you will be the masters of wealth and Christendom; everyone will fear you. But beware . . . of waging unjust war. . . . Everyone knows that the war with the Turks has made you brave and experienced of the sea; you have six generals to fight any great army, and for each of these you have . . . enough [men] to man one hundred galleys; and in these years you have shown distinctly that the world considers you the leaders of Christianity. You have many men experienced in embassies and in the government of cities, who are accomplished orators. You have many doctors of divers sciences, and especially many lawyers, wherefore numerous foreigners come here for judgment of their differences, and abide by your verdicts. You mint coins, every year a million ducats of gold and two hundred thousand of silver. . . . Therefore, be wise in governing such a State.

*Source:* P. Lauritzen, *Venice: A Thousand Years of Culture and Civilization* (London: Weidenfeld & Nicolson, 1978), p. 87.

seized some of Venice's Italian lands, a reprieve came when the pope, increasingly fearful of French ambitions, negotiated peace preparatory to forming the Holy League against France. Venice was still an important state, but Turkish expansion coupled with the discovery of new trade routes to Asia eroded its role as a Mediterranean power.

At the peak of its influence in the fifteenth and early sixteenth centuries, Venice was a city of striking contrasts. The fabulous wealth of the merchant oligarchy was reflected in the palatial houses that lined the Grand Canal, none more glittering than the Ca' d'Oro (1421–1440), with its polychrome marble and gilded paint. Living space in the city was at a premium, hence not even the wealthiest patricians could acquire spacious lots. Away from the Grand Canal there was no special residential district for the merchant oligarchy, whose homes were scattered throughout the city. Venice had its poor, but generally there was employment for them, particularly in the shipbuilding, textile, and fishing industries. Food prices were regulated, and grain was periodically distributed without charge to the needy, but there was considerable reluctance to provide regular relief until 1528, when the city was inundated with refugees because of famine and war. The Venetians traded

in slaves, and some blacks were kept in Venice as household servants, though the slave trade declined as the Turks pushed the Venetians out of the Mediterranean. The Venetians were mostly tolerant of the foreign minorities who settled in the city, but that attitude did not fully extend to the Jews. In the late fourteenth century the Jews of Venice were required to wear yellow badges, and beginning in 1423 they could not own real estate. Finally, in 1516 the Jews were forced to live in a special district known as the ghetto. It was, however, unthinkable to exclude them from the republic, as they had been from Spain, for the community required their medical expertise and their ability to provide funds, particularly in time of war. Venice was more tolerant of the Jews than were other Italian states.

## The Holy Roman Empire

The destruction of imperial power in the thirteenth century during the struggle between the Holy Roman Empire and the papacy left Germany badly divided. When the princes ended the Great Interregnum (1254–1273) by placing Rudolf of Habsburg (1273–1291) on the imperial throne, they were not interested in creating a strong centralized government that would diminish their own influence. Although the Habsburgs dreamed of creating a strong dynastic state, their own dominions were limited to Austria, giving them little control over the princes and towns in other regions. The virtual independence of the more powerful princes was confirmed in 1356 when Emperor Charles IV issued the Golden Bull, affirming that the empire was an elective monarchy. Henceforth new emperors were chosen by four hereditary princes, each of whom was virtually sovereign—the count palatine of the Rhine, the duke of Saxony, the margrave of Brandenburg, and the king of Bohemia—and three ecclesiastical princes—the archbishops of Cologne, Mainz, and Trier. In the century and a half that followed, lesser princes emulated the seven electors by establishing a strong degree of authority within their own states, a process that involved them in a struggle with the knights and administrative officials who wanted virtual independence for their fiefs. In Germany the territorial princes triumphed over both the emperor and the knights. Their power was reflected in the Imperial Diet, a representative assembly whose three estates comprised the electoral princes, the lesser princes, and the imperial free cities. Similar assemblies existed in the principalities. The Swiss took advantage of weak imperial authority to organize a confederation of cantons, or districts—13 by the early 1500s—that were essentially independent.

Although Habsburg power within the empire was weak, Maximilian negotiated a series of strategic marriage alliances that vastly increased the family's power. His own marriage to Charles the Bold's daughter, Mary of Burgundy, had led to the acquisition of the Low Countries, and the marriage of his son Philip to Ferdinand and Isabella's daughter Joanna made it possible for Maximilian's grandson Charles to inherit Spain and its possessions. Emperor Charles V (1519–1556) thus ruled the Habsburg lands in Germany, the Low Countries, Spain, Spanish territories in the New World, and the Aragonese kingdom of Naples and Sicily; no larger dominion had existed in Europe since the time of Charlemagne.

Spanish possessions in Italy brought Charles V into a bitter confrontation with the French king, Francis I, who was no less determined to press his own Italian claims. Although Charles was also concerned with the threat of advancing Turkish armies on the Danube, in 1525 he crushed the French at Pavia, near Milan, capturing Francis and forcing him to relinquish both his Italian claims and the duchy of Burgundy. Francis quickly reneged and allied with the Turks, who defeated the Hungarian army at Mohács in 1526. When the major Italian states (except Naples) allied with France in the League of Cognac, the imperial armies again invaded,

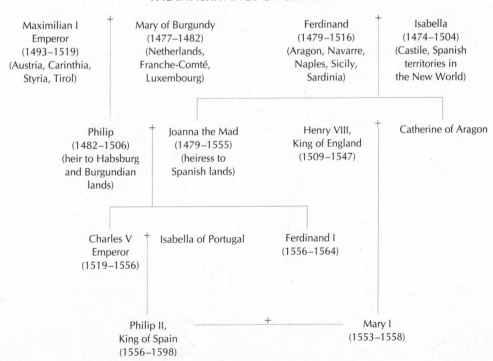

THE INHERITANCE OF CHARLES V

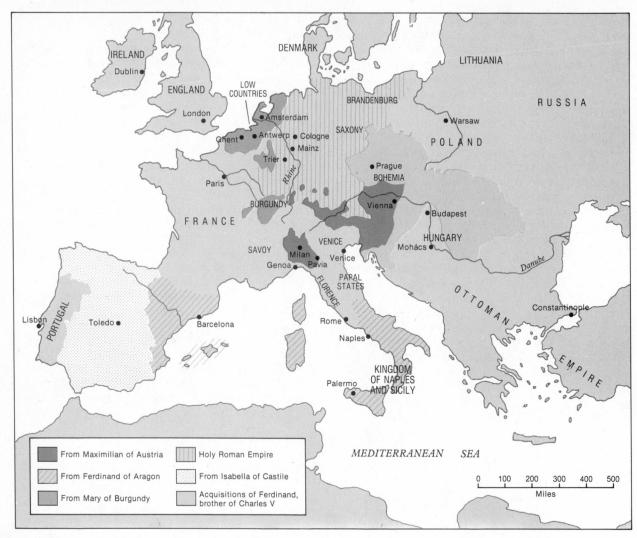

**15.4** *The Empire of Charles V*

this time sacking Rome in 1527 when their pay was late, an event that was widely regarded as the major atrocity of the sixteenth century. Louise of Savoy and Margaret of Austria negotiated a peace, the terms of which restored Burgundy to France. A year later, however, Pope Clement VII recognized Habsburg domination in Italy by crowning Charles both emperor and king of Italy, the last time the two crowns were bestowed on the same person. Although Francis renewed the war against Charles twice more (1536–1538, 1542–1544), not even an alliance with the Turks and German Protestant princes was sufficient to achieve a decisive military victory. When the Habsburg-Valois wars finally ended in 1559, Milan and Naples remained under Habsburg control. The Habsburgs, however, had failed to establish a unified state in Germany.

## Eastern Europe

Although the Hungarians had developed a reasonably strong state in the 1200s, during the following century they were weakened by a dynastic struggle involving Bavarian, Bohemian, and Angevin claimants; the Angevins triumphed with the support of the papacy. There were further problems due to the frequent absences of King Sigismund (1387–1437) from the country, partly because of his campaigns against the Turks and partly because of his responsibilities as Holy Roman Emperor (1433–1437). In 1458 the nobles gave the crown to Matthias Corvinus (1458–1490), son of the great military leader János Hunyadi, who had successfully repulsed the Turks. Matthias increased royal authority through administrative and judicial reforms, higher taxes, and the creation of a standing army. Abroad he used Hungary's new power to conquer Bohemia, Moravia, and Austria. Following his death, however, a disputed succession enabled Maximilian to regain Austria and to bring Hungary into the imperial orbit by two dynastic marriages involving his grandchildren, Mary and Ferdinand. The nobles subsequently took advantage of weak rulers to disband the standing army. As in Germany, the real struggle in Hungary then took place between the magnates and the lesser nobility. Although the latter won their claim to equality in the eyes of the law, in practice the magnates were dominant.

Poland was an immense state—the largest in Europe after its union with Lithuania in the late 1300s—but it too failed to establish a strong central government. The position of the nobles was enhanced when King John Albert (1492–1501), in need of funds, allowed a national diet composed only of nobles to impose taxes on the towns and peasants. His successor accepted a statute requiring the diet's approval of all new legislation, further eroding royal authority. Although Sigismund II (1548–1572) allied with the lesser nobles in order to curtail the power of the magnates, his death without an heir enabled the nobles to assert their right to elect a successor. Henceforth Poland was in fact as well as in theory an elective monarchy in which real power rested in the hands of the nobility.

*Politically, the fifteenth and early sixteenth centuries were a major watershed in European history. The failure of the Italians, Germans, Hungarians, and Poles to establish strong centralized states left them vulnerable to their neighbors and a perpetual source of temptation to expansionist-minded states. In contrast, the newly unified states of western Europe found themselves in an excellent position to take advantage of the economic possibilities opened up by the great voyages of discovery. It took the combined economic and military resources of these states to prosper in the expanding global trade. Nevertheless, although the Italian states failed to unify, their impressive economic growth, historical tradition, and sense of civic independence enabled them to provide intellectual and cultural leadership for Europe in the Renaissance.*

## Notes

1. R. S. Gottfried, *The Black Death: Natural and Human Disaster in Medieval Europe* (New York: Free Press, 1983), p. 36.
2. M. W. Dols, *The Black Death in the Middle East* (Princeton, N.J.: Princeton University Press, 1977), p. 113.

## Suggestions for Further Reading

Allmand, C. *The Hundred Years' War: England and France at War, c. 1300–c. 1450.* Cambridge: Cambridge University Press, 1988.

Barraclough, G. *The Origins of Modern Germany.* New York: Norton, 1984.

Becker, M. B. *Florence in Transition*, 2 vols. Baltimore: Johns Hopkins University Press, 1967–1968.

Contamine, P. *War in the Middle Ages*, trans. M. Jones. New York: Blackwell, 1984.

Crummey, R. O. *The Formation of Muscovy, 1304–1613.* New York: Longman, 1987.

Dollinger, P. *The German Hansa*, trans. D. S. Ault and S. H. Steinberg. Stanford, Calif.: Stanford University Press, 1970.

Dols, M. W. *The Black Death in the Middle East.* Princeton, N.J.: Princeton University Press, 1977.

Gillingham, J. *The Wars of the Roses: Peace and Conflict in Fifteenth-Century England.* London: Weidenfeld & Nicolson, 1981.

Goodman, A. *A History of England from Edward II to James I.* New York: Longman, 1977.

Gottfried, R. S. *The Black Death: Natural and Human Disaster in Medieval Europe.* New York: Free Press, 1983.

Guenee, B. *States and Rulers in Later Medieval Europe*, trans. J. Vale. Oxford: Blackwell, 1985.

Hale, J. R. *Florence and the Medici: The Pattern of Control.* London: Thames & Hudson, 1977.

Hay, D. *Europe in the Fourteenth and Fifteenth Centuries*, 2nd ed. New York: Longman, 1989.

Holmes, G. *Europe: Hierarchy and Revolt, 1320–1450.* New York: Harper & Row, 1975.

Hook, J. *Lorenzo de' Medici.* London: Hamilton, 1984.

Huizinga, J. *The Waning of the Middle Ages*. Garden City, N.Y.: Doubleday, 1954.

Kenny, A. J. P. *Wyclif*. New York: Oxford University Press, 1985.

Lane, F. C. *Venice: A Maritime Republic*. Baltimore: Johns Hopkins University Press, 1973.

Larner, J. *Italy in the Age of Dante and Petrarch, 1216–1380*. New York: Longman, 1980.

Leff, G. *The Dissolution of the Medieval Outlook: An Essay on Intellectual and Spiritual Change in the Fifteenth Century*. New York: New York University Press, 1976.

McNeill, W. H. *Plagues and Peoples*. Garden City, N.Y.: Anchor/Doubleday, 1976.

Mollat, M., and Wolff, P. *The Popular Revolutions of the Late Middle Ages*, trans. A. L. Lytton-Sells. London: Allen & Unwin, 1973.

Post, R. R. *The Modern Devotion*. Leiden: Brill, 1968.

Renouard, Y. *The Avignon Papacy, 1305–1403*, trans. D. Bethell. London: Faber & Faber, 1970.

Swanson, R. N. *Church and Society in Late Medieval Europe*. Oxford: Blackwell, 1989.

Tierney, B. *Foundations of the Conciliar Theory*. Cambridge: Cambridge University Press, 1955.

Vale, M. *The Angevin Legacy and the Hundred Years' War, 1250–1340*. Oxford: Blackwell, 1990.

Waley, D. *The Italian City-Republics*, 3rd ed. New York: Longman, 1988.

———. *Later Medieval Europe from Saint Louis to Luther*, 2nd ed. New York: Longman, 1985.

Wood, C. T. *Joan of Arc and Richard III: Sex, Saints, and Government in the Middle Ages*. New York: Oxford University Press, 1988.

# New Horizons: The European Renaissance

The social, political, and economic developments of the Renaissance era described in Chapter 15 were most apparent in the changes they wrought on the culture of the Middle Ages: a fresh approach to the heritage of "pagan" antiquity and a new attempt to blend its values with those of Christianity; the rise of court- and city-sponsored scholars known as humanists, whose espousal of ancient values was linked to the secularization of political power; and a new style in the arts that reflected these changes. At the heart of the cultural renaissance was a shift in the way some people viewed themselves, based on a fresh evaluation of the legacy of classical antiquity. Yet the new intellectual and artistic expression of the Renaissance remained deeply rooted in the past and coexisted with a centuries-old medieval vision. Construction of the largest Gothic cathedral in Italy was still under way in Milan in the mid-1490s when

**Petrarch is usually recognized as the first of the Renaissance humanists. [Marburg/Art Resource]**

417

Leonardo da Vinci, working nearby, painted the Last Supper. By then the new developments in thought, education, and the arts we call the Renaissance had been developing for a century and a half. Interpreting the Renaissance has always posed a special but intriguing challenge to students of history, particularly in light of the fact that no comparable phenomenon occurred in the advanced Asian societies, which enjoyed cultural continuity.

## The Urban Setting of the Renaissance

The Renaissance originated in fourteenth- and fifteenth-century Italy, which, unlike the rest of Europe, had an essentially urban culture. In Italian towns, where wealth was crucial in establishing one's social status, the emergent capitalists increasingly sought to patronize persons of intellectual and aesthetic talent, partly as a demonstration of piety, partly as an indication of cultural refinement, and partly as a manifestation of civic pride. When these conditions combined in Florence with a special sense of civic and historical awareness, particularly of the value of humanistic ideals as a unifying element in the face of external dangers from rival city-states, the stage was set for the Renaissance.

It is easy to understand why the Renaissance, inspired by the classical world, should have begun in Italy, with its abundance of classical monuments; but at first glance it is somewhat more difficult to explain why it developed first in Florence. Unlike Rome, Florence had few classical remains, nor did it possess the advantages of a port and a maritime economy like Genoa and Venice, which might bring it into contact with new currents of thought. The Venetians enjoyed not only a lucrative trade with the eastern Mediterranean but also close cultural ties with the Greeks. Even Milan was better situated because of its strategic position for trans-Alpine trade.

Florence's principal advantage was its location astride the trade route between Rome and the north, a route familiar to the many pilgrims who flocked to the Holy City. Because of its location, Florence was coveted by the expansionist Visconti rulers in Milan, and Florentine efforts to preserve the independence of their city fostered civic pride and a stronger awareness of their historical heritage. In turn, their interest in Greek and Roman politics reinforced their fascination with classical ethics, literature, and education. Writers and artists tested themselves against Roman models, hoping to find in a glorious past the inspiration to meet the challenges of the present. The humanists, moreover, saw them-

selves as living in a postmedieval world, reuniting themselves with the ancient world. In so doing, they created the notion of the thousand-year Middle Ages.

## 🌸 FLORENCE: A PANORAMA

The thirteenth century had been one of economic growth for Florence, especially in the fields of finance and textiles. Florentines established themselves as the preeminent bankers of Europe as well as tax collectors for the papacy. Using wool imported from England and Spain, they manufactured high-quality cloth for the markets of western Europe and the eastern Mediterranean. Two major catastrophes in the fourteenth century—the bankruptcies caused when King Edward III of England repudiated his debts and the devastation of the plague—failed to destroy the city's determination to prosper. Its economy was organized around 21 guilds, of which the most important were the wool manufacturers, the wool finishers, the silk manufacturers, and the bankers.

The political, social, and economic life of the city was dominated by the patricians, whose wealth enabled them to purchase land and contract marriages with the landed aristocracy, thus expanding the city's sway over the countryside. As we saw in Chapter 15, the traditional aristocracy had been ousted from its domination of the city by the great guilds in 1293, but in the late fourteenth century the guilds were in turn challenged by an alliance of artisans, shopkeepers, and owners of small businesses. Throughout this period of turmoil the patricians and guilds patronized humanists and artists, in part to encourage civic unity. When the conservative patricians feuded among themselves in the 1430s, a faction led by Cosimo de' Medici triumphed, leaving the Medici family in control of Florence for the rest of the Renaissance era, except for the brief republican periods in 1494–1512 and 1527–1530. Even during these periods the Medici continued to support scholars and artists.

Florence underwent striking changes during the Renaissance period. Located on the banks of the Arno River—torrential in the winter, a trickle in the summer—the city was surrounded by fertile fields and picturesque hills. Beyond them to the north lay the Apennines, while Pisa and the sea lay down the Arno to the west. The city had the appearance of a walled forest, particularly after the last of its three walls was erected between 1284 and 1328. Nearly 40 feet high and 6 feet thick, the outer wall had 73 towers and was surrounded by a moat. By the mid-1200s there were over 275 other towers and tall buildings within the city, partly because of the need for space but mostly because towers were symbols of aristocratic power as well as refuges during the vendettas that plagued Italian society. Some towers were as high

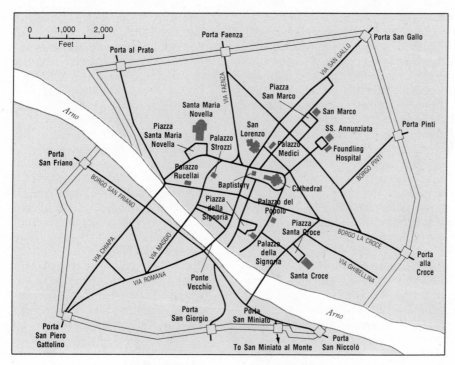

**16.1** *The Florence of the Medici*

as 230 feet, roughly the equivalent of a modern 20-story building. On the eve of the Renaissance the towers were reduced in size when the patricians, who dominated the urban economy, triumphed over their landed aristocratic rivals. From the late thirteenth century the more substantial homes were built for merchants with different needs and tastes. The great fire of 1304, the result of feuding between rival Guelph factions, destroyed some 1,700 houses and resulted in a major rebuilding effort. After the bubonic plague killed 50,000 of the city's 80,000 inhabitants in the mid-1300s, recovery was slow, and by 1500 Florence had only grown to between 50,000 and 70,000 inhabitants, or roughly half the size of Venice and Milan.[1]

Well into the Renaissance period Florence's main buildings made it visually a Gothic city. The great cathedral, begun in 1296, was Tuscan Gothic, apart from the innovative dome added in the fifteenth century, which heralded the beginning of Renaissance architecture. The cathedral manifested civic pride and reflected Florence's rivalry with Pisa and Siena, each of which was also building a cathedral. The Florentines were determined to exceed the greatest classical monuments:

**The Florentine Republic, soaring ever above the conception of the most competent judges, desires that an edifice should be constructed so magnificent in its height and in its beauty that it shall surpass anything of the kind produced in the time of their greatest power by the Greeks and Romans.[2]**

Two of Florence's most beautiful churches, Santa Croce and Santa Maria Novella, were rebuilt in the Gothic style by the Franciscans and Dominicans, respectively, in the 1200s. The two major palaces, the Palazzo del Pòpolo and the Palazzo della Signoria, are also Gothic and fortresslike in appearance. Erected in 1255, the former (now called the Bargello) was the residence of the captain of the people, who commanded armed societies representing the people's interests during periods when they exercised political dominance over the nobility. The Palazzo del Pòpolo was also a meeting place for the city's councils. The Palazzo della Signoria (commonly known as the Palazzo Vecchio, or "old palace") was begun in 1299 to house the guild representatives who governed the city. The palaces and chapels constructed during the Renaissance contrast sharply with the Gothic structures, symbolizing a new outlook and a changing set of values.

## The Patronage of Arts and Letters

Support for humanists and artists in the Renaissance came principally from guilds and religious brotherhoods, the state, and wealthy families and oligarchs.

Clergymen and merchants of more modest means also provided some backing, but their support appears to have had no significant impact on the development of the new scholarship and artistic styles. Persons with newly acquired wealth patronized artists and scholars as a means of demonstrating their status and enhancing their reputation. This meant commissions for painters to depict religious themes that incorporated portraits of the donors, for architects to design funeral chapels, and for sculptors to create impressive tombs.

As guild and civic patronage declined in the early fifteenth century due to an economic recession, families and individuals increasingly supported artists, writers, and scholars, thus increasing the scope for innovative themes and styles, particularly ones that reflected the values and interests of the patrons. All of this helped improve the artists' own social and economic status. In the medieval period they were commonly regarded as mere artisans, but by the early sixteenth century some artists had become well-to-do. The best known were much in demand, and a highly sophisticated appreciation had developed of their individual styles and talents. Some became famous and acquired a wide following, thus inaugurating the modern Western cult of the artist. Giorgio Vasari recorded anecdotes about them and facts about their careers in his book of biographical sketches, *The Lives of the Painters*. Florence, with its status-conscious patricians, its deep-rooted civic pride, its historical interest in classical Rome, and its willingness to embrace new concepts and styles, became the first setting for the Renaissance.

Before long, Rome and Milan also became important centers of patronage. Because the economy of Rome relied for the most part on the papacy, it had suffered a period of decline when the popes and their vast bureaucracy resided at Avignon. Without major manufacturing and removed from the principal trade routes, Rome stagnated economically, its population declined, and its government proved unable to control the lawless. The early-fifteenth-century popes thus had their hands full trying to restore order, though prosperity returned with the papal administration. Pope Nicholas V (1447–1455), himself a humanist, used church funds to beautify the city. Papal patronage brought Renaissance painters such as Fra Angelico (1387–1455) to Rome from Tuscany, sponsored the philologist Lorenzo Valla (1405–1457), and established a major library of classical authors. With Pope Sixtus IV (1471–1484) and his nephew, Pope Julius II (1503–1513), providing patronage to the greatest artists of their age, Rome supplanted Florence as the heart of the Renaissance during Julius' pontificate.

The Renaissance spread to Venice under strikingly different circumstances. The Venetian merchant oligarchy, primarily concerned with affairs of the republic and lucrative foreign trade, was still heavily influenced by Byzantine taste in the fourteenth and early fifteenth centuries. Because merchants returning from the Middle East brought art objects for St. Mark's Cathedral, the styles of the eastern Mediterranean were familiar. Byzantine mosaics adorned the interior of St. Mark's as well as the churches of neighboring Ravenna. Nevertheless, Renaissance ideals began to make headway as Florentine artists worked in nearby Padua, which the Venetians dominated politically, and as humanists won the support of the Venetian Senate for their printing press. Two technical developments—the introduction of oil-based paints from the Flemings about 1475 and the use of canvas—were important to the development of Renaissance painting. The new canvases were far more adaptable to the humid Venetian climate than the traditional wood or plaster and thus could readily be used to decorate religious and civic buildings. The Senate, churches, and charitable societies patronized painters such as Giovanni Bellini (c. 1430–1516) and his family. In Venice the Renaissance adapted to the merchant oligarchy's luxurious tastes and fondness for pageantry, thereby setting a rather different course from the Renaissance in Florence and Rome.

## The Humanists

The bond that knit humanists together was a commitment to study classical literary texts for their own sake rather than as handmaidens to Christian theology. The goal of such study, basic to the Renaissance, was nothing less than the revitalization of political, social, and religious institutions through the infusion of classical values. Humanists were engaged not in sponsoring a rebirth of the classics but in reorienting their approach toward them. An awareness of the thought and art of classical antiquity had never been completely lost in the medieval period and in fact had grown substantially since the late eleventh century. The reorientation that began in the 1300s entailed a shift in emphasis from the study of theology and metaphysics to the study of grammar, rhetoric, poetry, ethics, and history.

The humanists generally espoused two basic ideals: reverence for the full scope of "pagan" as well as Christian antiquity and belief in the distinctiveness of the individual, though the civic humanists of the early fifteenth century tended to subordinate the individual to the city-state. In contrast to the medieval tendency to seek virtue through solitude, the humanists sought virtue in the public sphere. Although Italian humanists focused almost exclusively on secular things, and some even assumed a personal attitude of religious skepticism, most remained traditional Catholics. Their interest in pagan literature gave way to a concern for early biblical and patristic literature, especially north of the Alps, where they were determined to blend humanistic and Christian concerns. Many Italian humanists deemphasized ritual and sacrament. Instead they stressed such temporal concerns as the performance of civic duties, the fulfillment of which brought a civic renown that pushed the medieval quest for spiritual immortality into the shadows.

## The Age of Petrarch

The earliest humanists addressed the needs of the social groups that emerged triumphant in the political struggles within the Italian city-states in the fourteenth century. As these groups consolidated their hold on power, they were ready to embrace a new psychological consciousness oriented largely toward worldly ends rather than the otherworldly ideals that had dominated the medieval outlook. The humanists provided the flattering self-image the patricians sought by praising the worth of the individual, the dignity of political affairs, secular accomplishments, and even the pursuit of personal glory. The success of the humanists was directly related to the existence of a responsive audience of the social and po-

litical elite, an audience warmly receptive to the humanist use of eloquence to validate the lifestyle and public role of the patriciate.

The most prominent of the early Renaissance humanists, Petrarch (Francesco Petrarca, 1304–1374), son of a political exile from Florence, gave up the study of law to devote himself to a public literary career, a vocation that he virtually invented. Fascinated by classical antiquity, he wrote biographies of famous Romans and composed *Africa*, a Latin epic in the style of the *Aeneid* to honor the Roman general Scipio Africanus. He even penned letters to his classical heroes—Horace, Livy, Virgil, and especially Cicero—and published them as *Letters to the Ancient Dead*. His best-known work is a charming collection of love sonnets in Italian to Laura, a married woman in Avignon. For more than 20 years he idealized her, always from a distance, until she died in the plague in 1348. Although much of Petrarch's work was secular, he made some efforts to harmonize classical and Christian teachings. Cicero's Stoic concepts, he thought, were compatible with the Gospel, and he used a series of dialogues with St. Augustine to explore his own feelings of sin and guilt. Contemptuous of both scholastics and the uneducated, committed to the criti-

---

### ◉ Petrarch on Petrarch ◉

*As an elderly man, Petrarch pondered his life and the values of a humanist. Like many humanists, he developed a strong interest in religion in his later years.*

I have always possessed an extreme contempt for wealth; not that riches are not desirable in themselves, but because I hate the anxiety and care which are invariably associated with them. . . . Nothing displeases me more than display, for not only is it bad in itself and opposed to humility, but it is troublesome and distracting. . . .

The greatest kings of this age have loved and courted me. They may know why; I certainly do not. With some of them I was on such terms that they seemed in a certain sense my guests rather than I theirs. . . . I fled, however, from many of those to whom I was greatly attached; and such was my innate longing for liberty that I studiously avoided those whose very name seemed incompatible with the freedom that I loved.

I possessed a well-balanced rather than a keen intellect—one prone to all kinds of good and wholesome study, but especially inclined to moral philosophy and the art of poetry. The latter, indeed, I neglected as time went on, and took delight in sacred literature. Finding in that a hidden sweetness which I had once esteemed but lightly, I came to regard the works of the poets as only amenities.

Among the many subjects that interested me, I dwelt especially upon antiquity, for our own age has always repelled me, so that, had it not been for the love of those dear to me, I should have preferred to have been born in any other period than our own.

*Source:* F. A. Ogg, ed., *A Source Book of Mediaeval History* (New York: American Book Company, 1907), pp. 471–472.

cal study of manuscripts, and concerned about his reputation with posterity, Petrarch was an exemplar for later humanists.

Petrarch's divergence from an essentially medieval outlook is evident when he is compared with the greatest figure of the previous generation, Dante Alighieri (1265–1321). Exiled from Florence with Petrarch's father, Dante foreshadowed one aspect of the Renaissance by using vernacular Italian for his masterpiece, *The Divine Comedy.* Petrarch subsequently expressed the ideal of a unified Italian motherland in the poem *Italia mia* ("My Italy"). But Dante's *Divine Comedy* more closely reflects the spirit of Thomas Aquinas' *Summa Theologica* than the ideals of the humanists. Its three-line stanzas symbolizing the Trinity, its treatment of the present life as a preparation for eternity, and its traditional interpretation of sins and virtues are evocations of the medieval world. The subordinate role of classical knowledge in Dante's scheme is apparent when Virgil, after guiding Dante through hell and purgatory, is replaced for the journey through paradise by Beatrice, a symbol of revelation. Beatrice also figures prominently in Dante's *Vita nuova* ("New Life"), his spiritual autobiography. Unlike Petrarch's love for Laura, which is intensely personal and secular, Dante's lifelong passion for Beatrice is symbolic of Christ's love for his church. The two types of love reflect the difference between the medieval and Renaissance outlooks.

Petrarch's friend and student, Giovanni Boccaccio (1313–1375), is remembered for his *Decameron,* a collection of 100 short stories related by ten young people who fled the plague that ravaged Florence in 1348. The racy tales were mostly borrowed from classical, medieval, and Eastern sources. Unlike Geoffrey Chaucer, who used some of the same material in *The Canterbury Tales,* Boccaccio gave his work a more secular flavor by omitting the usual moral commentary. Boccaccio's most substantive work, an encyclopedia of classical mythology titled *Genealogy of the Gods,* maintains the medieval fascination with allegory but is humanistic in its praise of poetry and its assertion that learning remakes the natural person into the civil person. Like other humanists, Boccaccio was convinced that he was part of a new age, for Petrarch, he said, had "cleansed the fount of Helicon," the abode of the mythical classical muses, "swampy with mud and rushes, restoring its waters to their former purity."[3]

## Civic Humanists

The second stage of humanism, which lasted from approximately 1375 to 1460, was staunchly committed to the proposition that humanistic scholarship must be brought to bear on public affairs. Cicero, one of the humanists' heroes, had after all been an active statesman in the Roman republic. Civic humanists held community service in high regard as a justification for the positions and privileges of the patriciate. Learning thus became a tool to benefit society as well as a means to assert political influence. Taking note of their predecessors' interest in rhetoric, the civic humanists extolled it as the basis for a new standard of nobility to which patricians were urged to aspire. Rhetoric, which entailed not only eloquence but also the application of knowledge to specific problems, could reputedly preserve society and mold good citizens by making law and morality effective. Eloquence became a way of life, as relevant to princes and ruling elites as to poets and teachers, not least because it made possible a strong degree of self-confidence.

The civic humanists espoused a belief in political liberty for a broadly defined elite and in civic patriotism, which in Florence involved a concerted attempt to preserve the city's freedom from Milanese aggression. In the late fourteenth and early fifteenth centuries Florence had three chancellors who were civic humanists: Coluccio Salutati, Leonardo Bruni, and Poggio Bracciolini. During his 31-year chancellorship, Salutati, a disciple of Petrarch, boasted that Florence was the "mother of freedom," a theme echoed by Bruni and Poggio. Bruni's *History of Florence* was written in the conviction that history involves the use of examples to teach philosophy and

HIGHLIGHTS OF THE ITALIAN RENAISSANCE

| Philosophical influences | Letters | Arts |
|---|---|---|
| Early Humanists (1325–1375) | ● Petrarch<br>● Boccaccio | ● Giotto |
| Civic Humanists (1375–1460) | ● Bruni<br>● Vergerio<br>● Christine de Pisan | ● Masaccio<br>● Ghiberti<br>● Donatello |
| Neoplatonists, Machiavelli,<br>   Guicciardini (1460–1576) | ● Ficino<br>● Pico<br>● Castiglione<br>● Vittoria Colonna | ● Botticelli<br>● Leonardo da Vinci<br>● Raphael<br>● Michelangelo<br>● Titian |

that "the careful study of the past enlarges our foresight in contemporary affairs." The political liberty extolled by the civic humanists was never fully realized in Renaissance Florence, however, and such liberty as did exist was sharply reduced after Cosimo de' Medici began to dominate city politics in 1434. Faced with the realities of the Medici oligarchy, which effectively undermined constitutional government, the humanists accepted Medici patronage and generally retreated from the political arena to their scholarship and contemplation.

## The Florentine Academy and the Neoplatonists

The decline of the civic humanists and the flowering of Neoplatonism in late-fifteenth-century Florence marked the beginning of humanism's third stage. Instead of a primary concern with the problems and duties of civil life and a preoccupation with such works as Aristotle's *Ethics* and Plutarch's *Lives*, interest shifted to Plato and the ideal of the contemplative life. The seeds of this transformation had been planted in the 1390s when the Greek scholar Manuel Chrysoloras taught Greek in the city; among his pupils was the civic humanist Bruni. Bruni subsequently translated Plato and other classical and Christian authors. Greek studies received a further impetus in 1439 when hundreds of Greeks came to Ferrara and Florence to attend an ecumenical council. At the urging of one of them, Cosimo de' Medici eventually endowed an academy near Florence in 1462. The academy provided the setting for philosophical discussions presided over by Marsilio Ficino (1433–1499). The atmosphere was semireligious: the disciples sang hymns praising Plato, burned a lamp before his bust, and adopted as their motto "Salvation in Plato." Ficino himself prepared editions of the works of Plato and Plotinus.

Renaissance Neoplatonism was a fascinating, eclectic mixture of ideas from classical thought, Christian dogma, and astrology. Ficino and his followers stressed the uniqueness of humankind, including personal worth and dignity as well as the power to transform oneself spiritually by choosing the good. Above all, each person was free, though one's sphere of action was circumscribed by the stars. Those who chose to pursue the higher things of life aspired to the release of their souls from the perishable world of matter. The Neoplatonic ideal was otherworldly; the Neoplatonic experience, emotional. Neoplatonism's moving force was love, and its direction was the rational life. To know God was the ultimate goal, attainable only by separating from the material world. The Neoplatonists were deeply sensitive to beauty, which they intimately associated with truth and goodness, all of which were earthly manifestations of Platonic forms. The Neoplatonic love of symbolic allegory, Christian mysticism, and beauty made the philosophy attractive to such Renaissance artists as Botticelli, Raphael, and Michelangelo.

Through their eclectic, mystical philosophy, the Florentine Neoplatonists effectively moved beyond the range of traditional humanists. The latter's shift of emphasis from metaphysics to ethics was reversed by the Neoplatonists, but without returning to the traditional and orthodox philosophical views of the medieval scholastics. The Neoplatonists also broke with the civic humanists by turning their backs on public affairs and the campaign for political freedom—perhaps a prudent choice in the treacherous political atmosphere of Medici Florence. Nevertheless, something of the original humanist ideal remained in their respect for human dignity and the freedom to choose one's destiny. This ideal was expressed most eloquently in the *Oration on the Dignity of Man* by Ficino's disciple, Pico della Mirandola (1463–1494). Drawing on his vast reading in Jewish, Christian, and Arabic works, the erudite Pico accorded humans a special rank in the universal chain of being where they could ponder the plan of the universe and marvel at its beauty. Although Renaissance Neoplatonism was quietist in its avoidance of political activism, it was nevertheless radical in its rejection of church hierarchy in favor of an emphasis on individual enlightenment.

## Education and Scholarship

The central goal of a humanist education was to develop the virtuous individual, one who would live a moral, disciplined life not only for personal enrichment but also for the benefit of society. This education, however, was intended for the socially elite, not commoners. A number of humanists urged major changes in the educational curriculum, particularly at the secondary level, in order to accomplish this end. An education focusing on the humanities was deemed to have the greatest practical relevance for daily living because it addressed the whole person. The humanist ideal in education was neatly summarized by Pietro Paolo Vergerio (1370–1444), a student of Chrysoloras and a friend of Bruni:

> We call those studies *liberal* which are worthy of a free man; those studies by which we attain and practice virtue and wisdom; that education which calls forth, trains, and develops those highest gifts of body and of mind which ennoble men, and which are rightly judged to rank next in dignity to virtue only. . . . Amongst these [studies] I accord the first place to history, on grounds both of its attractiveness and of its utility.[4]

For the humanists virtue entailed not only the fundamental principles of morality but also an ethical ideal that encompassed both self-determination and an awareness of personal worth. Vergerio and his colleagues drew extensively on classical authors such as Quintilian in developing this concept of a humanist education.

One of the leading Renaissance educators, Vergerio's friend Vittorino da Feltre (died 1446), established a model secondary school at Mantua called the Happy House. Scholarships enabled the children of the poor to attend, and unlike many other schools girls were welcome. The curriculum included the humanities, religion, mathematics, drawing, and physical education—riding, fencing, swimming, and martial skills. Appropriate attention was given to proper diet and dress, so that education was concerned with the whole of life.

The ideas of the humanist educators are reflected in the Renaissance's most influential handbook of manners, *The Book of the Courtier* (1527) by Baldassare Castiglione (1478–1529). Deliberately limited in scope as a guide for aristocrats in the service of their prince, the book depicts the ideal courtier as someone knowledgeable in Greek, Latin, and the vernacular. His accomplishments would also range from music and poetry to dancing and sports. In sharp contrast to the image of a courtier as a hard-drinking, arrogant swordsman, Castiglione's courtier is a well-mannered, cultivated, and versatile gentleman, as much at home in the salon and the concert chamber as in the halls of power. The cour-

tier, moreover, must be an educator—not of young people but of the prince, who must be taught the ways of virtue, especially temperance. Many of the same qualities are to be found in the aristocratic lady who, said Castiglione, should be adorned with "admirable accomplishments." Nevertheless, she was to shun "manly" sports such as riding and tennis as well as musical instruments that required ungainly physical effort, such as trumpets, fifes, and drums. While Castiglione idealized women as objects of courtly love, in practice he expected them to maintain an appropriate degree of subservience to men. *The Book of the Courtier* was immensely influential throughout Europe and was still widely consulted as a guide to aristocratic bearing in the eighteenth century. It marked a turning point in the refinement of manners that left a permanent mark on the European upper classes.

Another fundamental concern of the humanists was the search for accurate texts from classical Greece and Rome. This quest encouraged the humanists to ransack archives to find as many early manuscripts as possible. To produce good texts they had to develop critical tools, especially philology (the study of the origins of language), paleography (the study of ancient manuscripts), and textual criticism. Lorenzo Valla used the principles of textual criticism to demonstrate that the eighth-

## ◉ Aristocratic Women ◉

*Baldassare Castiglione's* Book of the Courtier *reflects the humanist interest in shaping the aristocratic woman to please the men. Note here how the courtier is expected to teach her as well as to revel in her beauty.*

Many faculties of the mind are as necessary to woman as to man; likewise gentle birth, to avoid affectation, to be naturally graceful in all her doings, to be mannerly, clever, prudent, not arrogant, not envious, not slanderous, not vain, not quarrelsome, not silly, to know how to win and keep the favor of her mistress and of all others, to practice well and gracefully the exercises that befit women. . . . Beauty is more necessary to her than to the courtier, for in truth that woman lacks much who lacks beauty. Then, too, she ought to be more circumspect and take greater care not to give occasion for evil being said of her. . . .

Let him obey, please and honor his lady with all reverence, and hold her dearer than himself, and prefer her convenience and pleasures to his own, and love in her not less the beauty of mind than of body. Therefore let him take care not to leave her to fall into any kind of error, but by admonition and good advice let him always seek to lead her on to modesty, to temperance, to true chastity. . . .

In such fashion will our courtier be most acceptable to his lady, and she will always show herself obedient, sweet and affable to him, and as desirous of pleasing him as of being loved by him.

*Source:* B. Castiglione, *The Book of the Courtier,* trans. L. E. Opdycke (New York: Scribner, 1901), passim.

century Donation of Constantine was a forgery. Some experts already suspected that this document, by which Emperor Constantine (died 337) allegedly endowed the papacy with vast lands, was fraudulent, but Valla laid any doubt to rest by demonstrating that it contained language and references unknown in Constantine's day. His exposure of the Donation was a triumphant exhibition of the powers of humanist scholarship in challenging tradition and the political authority that rested on it.

Valla also used his command of classical languages to prove that there were errors in the official version of the Bible, the Latin Vulgate. Because of his belief in the supremacy of faith over reason, however, his loyalty to the church was not shaken. Thanks to the patronage of Pope Nicholas V (1447–1455), himself a humanist, he was even appointed apostolic secretary. Valla's application of philological and historical techniques to the Donation and the Vulgate provided the foundation for major advances in textual criticism in the sixteenth century, particularly in the field of biblical scholarship, as reflected in the work of Desiderius Erasmus.

## Humanists Outside Italy

The ideals of the Italian humanists were carried beyond the Alps in the late fifteenth century by students, scholars, and merchants. The rapid development of the printing industry, particularly in the Rhineland cities, also facilitated the spread of humanist scholarship. The great pioneers were the German Peter Luder (c. 1415–1474), a hard-drinking poet whose insistence on the importance of classics in the curriculum helped make the University of Heidelberg a leading center of humanist thought, and the Dutchman Rudolf Agricola (c. 1443–1485). After spending ten years in Italy, where he was deeply influenced by Petrarch's writings, Agricola gathered a group of humanist disciples at Heidelberg. His goal was to surpass the Italians in classical learning, wresting from "haughty Italy the reputation for classical expression which it has nearly monopolized . . . and aim to it ourselves." His wide-ranging interests extended from philosophy and Greek to mining, a subject on which he wrote a treatise.

In England, too, the humanists carried their message to the universities. Both William Grocyn (c. 1466–1519), who lectured at Oxford, and Thomas Linacre (c. 1460–1524), who taught at Cambridge and was interested in classical medicine, had studied in Florence. Among Grocyn's friends were three of the greatest humanists of the sixteenth century, his pupil Thomas More, John Colet, and Erasmus (all discussed in Chapter 17). The English were also acquainted with humanist ideals through the presence of Italian scholars at the royal court. Other Italian humanists took their views to the courts of Spain, Hungary, and Poland, where the University of Cracow achieved eminence as a center of humanist studies.

Humanist ideas had already begun to penetrate France before its armies invaded Italy in 1494, but the military adventure heightened interest in Italian scholarship and the arts. Early French humanists such as Guillaume Budé (1468–1540) and Lefèvre d'Étaples (1455–1536) knew Greek and had varied interests. In addition to writing about Byzantine law and ancient coinage, Budé persuaded King Francis I to found a library at Fontainebleau, the origin of the famous Bibliothèque Nationale in Paris. Lefèvre, who had studied at Florence and Padua, was noted for philological and biblical studies, particularly his *Commentary on the Epistles of St. Paul*. His emphasis on grace, faith, and predestination may have influenced the Protestant reformer John Calvin, though Lefèvre never left the Catholic church.

The literary accomplishments of the French humanists are exemplified by Marguerite d'Angoulême (1492–1549), sister of Francis I, and François Rabelais (c. 1495–1553), successively a Franciscan friar, a Benedictine monk, and a secular priest and medical doctor. Marguerite's prolific writing ranged from poetry to religious treatises, but her most famous work was the *Heptaméron*, a collection of 70 short, racy stories akin to Boccaccio's *Decameron*. Rabelais' *Gargantua* and *Pantagruel*, tales about giants enamored of life and drinking, offer a satirical portrait of sixteenth-century society peppered with humanist insights about the human condition. Gargantua's advice to his son Pantagruel is a fitting summary of the humanists' exhortation to their disciples: "I urge you to spend your youth making the most of your studies and developing your moral sense."

## Women and Renaissance Culture

More than 30 women humanists of the Renaissance have been identified, though few wrote major works. This was probably due more to social barriers than to a lack of creative talent. Women almost never attended a university. They thus had no opportunity to enter the learned professions, although there was a female doctor of medicine at Salerno, Italy, in 1422. Women humanists typically acquired their education from their fathers or from private tutors, which effectively eliminated all but those of princely, aristocratic, or patrician status. During the early Renaissance their intellectual careers were confined to their late teens and early twenties if they opted to marry, for marital obligations and spousal pressure made intellectual commitments extremely difficult. The advent of printing, however, provided literate women with the opportunity to pursue a variety of studies, including medicine, religion, and the classics—a devel-

After Christine de Pisan's husband died when
she was only 25, she supported herself and
her three children as a writer. Among her
patrons were Philip the Bold, duke of
Burgundy, and Queen Isabella of Bavaria.
[Bavarian State Library, Munich]

orative presences who added gracefulness to their
households.

The contributions of learned Renaissance women
were varied. Many wrote Latin letters, orations, treatises, and poems. Alessandra Scala of Florence had a
command of Greek equaled by few Western scholars.
The ranks of humanist poets embraced such women as
Christine de Pisan (c. 1364–c. 1431), a French writer of
Italian descent whose works included a biography of
King Charles V of France, and Lucrezia Tornabuoni,
mother of Lorenzo the Magnificent and author of religious hymns. As the Renaissance extended north of the
Alps, more young women received a humanist education
and took up their pens to write literary, religious, and
historical works. The range of topics available to women
was, however, restricted by social custom since most
secular subjects were thought to be the province of men.
Even in the religious realm women were expected to
confine themselves to hymns and poems, devotional
works, and translations. "Great things by reason of my
sex I may not do," admitted the English translator Anne
Locke. Thus humanist education tantalized bright young
women even as society thwarted their ambitions by
tightly hedging in their possibilities for intellectual
expression. No wonder Christine de Pisan lamented that
she had not been "born into this world as a member of
the masculine sex." She found consolation in her prolific
writings, for these enabled her to reflect that "now I am
truly a man."

opment often reflected in paintings of the Annunciation
showing Mary reading a book. The usual alternative to
marriage—entry into the religious life—was tantamount
to rejecting the world in favor of a book-lined cell. For
intellectually gifted young women the choice was difficult, more so because men typically regarded learned
women as intellectual oddities, male minds in female
bodies. An educated woman was often thought to have
exchanged female concerns, such as needles and wool,
for male ones, such as pens and books.

Although male humanists praised women in general,
they usually preferred that learned women remain safely
unwed and likened them to Amazon queens and armed
warriors or viragos. In the courtly love tradition of the
Middle Ages men were supposed to please the ladies,
whereas in the Renaissance women were molded to satisfy the gentlemen. As the Renaissance ideal of learning
spread, girls and young women of the upper estates received better educations than their medieval counterparts, but the classical material they studied reinforced
notions of male superiority. Their education was to enable them not to enter the learned professions but to act
as ladies of the court, patronesses of the arts, and dec-

## VITTORIA COLONNA, POET AND PHILOSOPHER

One of the most gifted Renaissance women, Vittoria Colonna belonged to a powerful Roman family with vast
holdings in the Papal States and southern Italy. Among
her relatives were a pope and 30 cardinals. Born in 1492
at Marino, near Rome, she was the daughter of Fabrizio
Colonna, grand constable of the kingdom of Naples. Although her marriage at the age of 19 to the marchese
of Pescara, a Spaniard, had been arranged for political
reasons 15 years earlier, she nevertheless fell in love
with him. Often absent on military service, the marchese
died in 1525, leaving her childless. In his memory Vittoria wrote sonnets idealizing him as a saint despite the
fact that he had been faithless to her, contemptuous of
Italians, and treasonous in his political dealings. Imbued
with Neoplatonic concepts, Vittoria envisioned a reunion
with him in a better, spiritual life. Her love sonnets, written in the tradition of Petrarch, won her acclaim in humanist circles, particularly from the great literary stylist
Pietro Bembo and from Castiglione, who gave her a
manuscript of his *Courtier* to critique.

## ◉ The Case for Educating Young Ladies ◉

*One of the most gifted women writers of the Renaissance, Christine de Pisan argued on behalf of offering girls the same educational opportunities as boys.*

If it were customary to send little girls to school and to teach them the same subjects as are taught to boys, they would learn just as fully and would understand the subtleties of all arts and sciences. Indeed it may be they would understand them better . . . for just as women's bodies are more soft than men's, so too their understanding is more sharp. . . . If they understand less it is because they do not go out and see so many different places and things but stay home and mind their own work. For there is nothing which teaches a reasonable creature so much as the experience of many different things.

[Rectitude personified next speaks to Christine.] Your father, who was a natural philosopher, was not of the opinion that women grow worse by becoming educated. On the contrary, as you know he took great pleasure from seeing your interest in learning. Your mother, however, who held the usual feminine ideas on the matter, wanted you to spend your time spinning, like other women, and prevented you from making more progress and going deeper into science and learning in your childhood. But as the proverb says, what nature gives may not be taken away. So you gathered what little drops of learning you could and consider them a great treasure and are right to do so.

*Source:* J. O'Faolain and L. Martines, eds., *Not in God's Image* (New York: Harper Torchbooks, 1973), pp. 181–182.

---

Vittoria's religious sonnets reflect both her ascetic piety and her Neoplatonism, which together sought to liberate the spirit by subduing the flesh. In Neoplatonic imagery she expressed her hope to "mount with wings" in order to reach true light and love. Hers was an intensely personal experience: "I write," she said, "only to free myself from my inner pain." Her sonnets manifest a keen interest in church reform, a concern she shared with a number of her friends, including Cardinal Contarini, a chief architect of the Catholic Reformation. Although one of her closest friends, Bernardino Ochino, ultimately defected to the Protestants, she remained loyal to the Catholic church.

Vittoria found a kindred spirit in Michelangelo, whom she met shortly after he had begun painting the Sistine Chapel ceiling in 1508. He was Vittoria's "most singular friend" and she his "love," capable of causing "a withered tree to burgeon and to bloom." Their intimacy, in which Michelangelo found spiritual solace and artistic inspiration, was not sexual. They corresponded extensively and exchanged sonnets, the tone of which is reminiscent of Petrarch's sonnets to Laura, but in an unmistakably Christian context. Michelangelo wrote madrigals and painted at least three works for her and probably a portrait as well. He must have been sympathetic to her ascetic convictions, which were so pronounced after her husband's death. She fasted and wore hair shirts until Cardinal Reginald Pole, a key figure in the Catholic Reformation, persuaded her to adopt a more moderate course. She spent much of the period between 1541 and her death in 1547 in monasteries, a reminder that many Renaissance humanists saw their religious and humanist principles as fully compatible.

## Machiavelli and the Culture of Power

The evolution of the humanist movement is nowhere more apparent than in its attitude toward history. Initially the humanists were preoccupied with the recovery of classical Roman texts that they could use as a standard against which to measure their own society. They then broadened their horizon to the study of classical history with a view to using its lessons as a guide to human affairs and the improvement of political and social institutions. Lorenzo Valla's use of textual criticism exemplifies the humanists' refinement of scholarly techniques. Finally, in the sixteenth century, disillusioned by their inability to reshape the present by the application of historical ideals, humanist historians relinquished their belief in the ability of simple virtue to triumph over external forces. Those who thought in theological terms explained such forces as the will of God directing human history. Instead of examining the past with a view to improving the present, most historians and their readers increasingly used the historical record to justify their religious beliefs or the political ambitions of their respective states.

The disillusionment characteristic of the sixteenth-century humanist historians was a product of earlier conditions, particularly in northern and central Italy. The failure of republican government in Florence and the French invasion of 1494 virtually demolished the hopes of the earlier humanists. Power replaced virtue as the cardinal principle in the conduct of human affairs, particularly in the thought of Niccolò Machiavelli (1469–1527). He was in his twenties when the French invaded Italy, prompting the ruler of Florence, Piero de' Medici, to try to save the city by territorial concessions. For this the Florentines overthrew Piero, revived their republican government, and rallied to the reforming message of the impassioned Dominican friar Girolamo Savonarola (1452–1498). For four years the Florentines were caught up in a frenzy of revivalism directed against materialism, immorality, corruption, and godlessness. Bonfires claimed everything from sumptuous clothing and stylish wigs to books and works of art. By 1498 the zeal had ebbed, and Savonarola, having infuriated the immoral Alexander VI by his candid criticism, was burned as a heretic on trumped-up charges. The Council of Ten, which assumed the direction of Florentine affairs, made Machiavelli its secretary and one of its diplomats. Fascinated by the practice of statecraft, the young official traversed Italy conducting the business of his republic. His career was abruptly terminated in 1512 when the Medici returned to Florence and ousted the republican government. Machiavelli himself was tortured and sent into exile.

In his enforced idleness he reflected on the political problems of Italy and its history in his principal works, *The Prince* and the *Discourses on Livy*. Machiavelli brought to his writing not only a knowledge of Roman history and the works of such humanist historians as Bruni and Poggio but also considerable firsthand experience of the realities of contemporary politics and diplomacy. *The Prince* (1513), dedicated to Lorenzo de' Medici, grandson of Lorenzo the Magnificent, has sometimes been interpreted as if it were a satire on the politics of despotism. On the contrary, it reflects the sober realism of a middle-aged diplomat and a theoretical brilliance that has earned Machiavelli a reputation as the founder of modern political science. *The Prince* has rightly been called "the greatest of all theoretical explorations of the politics of innovation",[5] its primary theme deals with the "new prince"—the political innovator who

has just seized power—and his dealings with his subjects, some of whom have been ousted from power, while others expect rewards he cannot bestow.

The Medici now dominated not only Machiavelli's beloved Florence but even Rome, where Leo X (1513–1521), Lorenzo the Magnificent's son, had just become pope. Machiavelli intended to prod the Medici into embracing an ethic of power shorn of religious or ethical limitations as the only effective means to achieve a stable, secure Italy free of "barbarian" intervention. His was a creed of action, not reflection, of pragmatism rather than idealism. He praised Roman republicanism because it had been a successful tool of power and praised republican government in general if it embodied *virtù*, or inner strength. As he pondered the meaning of history, he concluded that it was shaped by a recurring cycle of events; instead of evolution and progress, there was mere repetition.

Although Machiavelli did not regard historical study as a quest for virtue, he reflected humanist influence in a variety of other ways; for him, as for Bruni, history is a storehouse of examples and should be studied to ascertain both the causes and the cures of current problems. Because history repeated itself, present ills could be treated by imitating solutions that were successful in the past. Everything in the present and the future had a counterpart in antiquity, the happiest time in history. Machiavelli's concept of the imitation of antiquity is an extreme application of the humanist tendency to venerate the classical world. One can find similar parallels in Confucian thought. In formulating his principles of statecraft, Machiavelli ransacked classical history to find material for his argument and also drew on his own practical experience in politics. Between them he found justification for the political principles that make *The Prince* famous: Be deceitful and cunning in dealing with rivals; do as people actually do rather than as they ought to do; regard the state—the prince—as supreme, recognizing that the end justifies the means; always place military security first; avoid neutrality, especially in dealing with other states; instill fear in one's subjects as the best means to compel obedience; undertake great enterprises to divert attention from internal problems. Such was the culture of power, and in espousing it Machiavelli broke with the traditional model of the good ruler, whether Confucian, Aristotelian or Judeo-Christian.

Machiavelli's Florentine contemporary, Francesco Guicciardini (1483–1540), surpassed him as a historian, particularly in his determination to discover the reasons for human behavior and explore the way institutions work. His first *History of Florence*, written during the republican era, characterized Lorenzo the Magnificent as a tyrant, but two decades later he found Lorenzo's Florence preferable to the now discredited republic. His attitude changed even more in his last work, a *History of Italy*, in which Lorenzo was glorified, reflecting Guic-

## ⊡ Machiavelli's Advice ⊡ to a Renaissance Prince

*The advice Machiavelli tendered in* The Prince *reveals a degree of cynicism based on his experience in Renaissance politics.*

How praiseworthy a prince is who keeps his promises and lives with sincerity and not with trickery, everybody realizes. Nevertheless, experience in our time shows that those princes have done great things who have valued their promises little, and who have understood how to addle the brains of men with trickery; and in the end they have vanquished those who have stood upon their honesty. . . .

For a prince, then, it is necessary . . . to appear merciful, trustworthy, humane, blameless, religious—and to be so—yet to be in such measure prepared in mind that if you need to be not so, you can and do change to the contrary. . . . A prince, and above all a prince who is new, cannot practice all those things for which men are considered good, being often forced, in order to keep his position, to act contrary to truth, contrary to charity, contrary to humanity, contrary to religion. Therefore he must have a mind ready to turn in any direction as Fortune's winds and the variability of affairs require. . . .

Hate is incurred as much by means of good deeds as of bad. Therefore . . . if a prince wishes to keep his position, he is often forced to be not good, because when that group—whether the masses, the soldiers, or the rich—which you decide you need to sustain yourself, is corrupt, you have to adapt yourself to its nature in order to please it. Then good works are your enemies.

*Source:* N. Machiavelli, *The Chief Works and Others,* trans. A. Gilbert, vol. 1 (Durham, N.C.: Duke University Press, 1965), pp. 64, 66, 72.

---

ciardini's disillusionment with the inability of the Italian states to unify against foreign aggression. The optimism of the early humanists—their faith in the ability to shape states and their leaders—was abandoned in the face of hostile external forces and the assumption of power by men with the trappings of Renaissance culture but without the ideals of humanistic virtue. Although Guicciardini was the better historian, Machiavelli had a much greater historical impact because of the popularity—and notoriety—of *The Prince*, with its calculated disregard of traditional morality and its pithy, provocative appeal to political "realism."

## The Printing Revolution

Machiavelli's *Prince* was too scandalous to be published during his lifetime, but other works of Renaissance scholarship were printed despite some humanist opposition to putting learned works in the hands of commoners. Movable metal type, developed in Germany in the fifteenth century, was vastly superior to the technique of block printing. The Chinese and Koreans, of course, had already invented movable type, but it had less appeal to them because their scripts consisted of thousands of different characters. Metal type was more durable as well as more flexible than wooden blocks because individual letters could be reused in new combinations. By 1300 linen paper, which had been introduced from East Asia through the Islamic world, was in common use, thus setting the stage for the new presses. Johann Gutenberg of Mainz, one of the pioneers of the new technology, published his first known work, an indulgence proclamation by Pope Nicholas V, in 1454. The first of his magnificent Bibles appeared two years later. The new press spread rapidly throughout western and central Europe; by 1500 there were 73 in Italy, 50 in Germany, 39 in France, 24 in Spain, and smaller numbers in other countries.

The fact that Italy had more presses than any other country was largely due to the impact of the Renaissance, despite humanist misgivings about putting learned works in the hands of the masses. The finest press was that of the humanist Aldus Manutius in Venice. His Aldine Press published at least 30 first editions of Greek classics, a tremendous benefit to Renaissance

In this sixteenth-century print shop, the men at the left are setting type, their colleague at the center rear is inking a plate of type, the man at the right is printing a sheet on the press, and the youth in the foreground is setting the wet sheets out to dry. [Bettmann Archive]

scholarship. Aldus also founded an academy of his own in Venice that was especially devoted to encouraging humanist authors and editors. The nucleus of the academy consisted of Greek exiles whose knowledge of classical Greek civilization thus found its way into print and henceforth became available to scholars throughout the West. The influential northern humanist Erasmus of Rotterdam (c. 1466–1536) perfected his Greek during a stay with Aldus.

The changes brought about by the printing press reached virtually every aspect of life. As the price of books fell and their number increased, there was a greater incentive to acquire and improve reading skills. The expansion of the literate population in turn offered new opportunities to writers and eventually freed some from the need to find and please wealthy patrons. Religious topics, works on astrology, and popular tales were prominent on the early book lists, as were editions of the Bible, especially once vernacular versions became common in the sixteenth century. The press proved a boon to scholarship by making more accurate editions possible, by standardizing maps and images as well as texts, and by encouraging cross-cultural interchange. Ideas spread with greater rapidity, and there was more inducement to develop new theories. Codifying and cataloging became commonplace, and the use of running titles at the top of each page, regular page numbering, and indexing helped order the thoughts of readers. Printing also increased the likelihood of a document's preservation. Through printing, collections of laws and ordinances became available to a wider public, with beneficial effects for the practice of law as well as for public discourse about political affairs. By the sixteenth cen-

tury, however, both church and state found it necessary to step up their censorship. The advent of printing made propaganda possible, and in the seventeenth century newspapers began replacing the pulpit as the primary source of news in urban areas. Printing also increased the reputation—or infamy—of authors and eventually made it possible for some writers, such as the English dramatist Aphra Behn (c. 1640–1689), to earn a living by their pens alone. Gutenberg and his colleagues thus set in motion one of the most sweeping revolutions in history.

# The Fine Arts

The Renaissance ushered in significant changes in artistic style and taste, reflecting the absorption of humanist ideals. The most prominent hallmarks of Renaissance painting and sculpture—fascination with classical themes, expressions of individualism, a more self-confident embracing of secular themes—reflected humanist concerns. Technical advances in painting were also possible after oil-based paints were brought to Italy from Flanders in the late fifteenth century. Painters had previously worked in fresco, which involved the application of pigment to wet plaster, and tempera, which entailed mixing pigments with a sizing, such as eggs. Oils enabled the painter to achieve a detail, clarity, and permanence of color not possible with fresco or tempera. Renaissance artists also achieved the ability to give the illusion of dimensionality by using gradations between light and dark to model their figures and by applying mathematical principles to create the visual illusion of objects receding into space.

The Renaissance in the fine arts was greatly facilitated by an expansion of patronage, especially by lay people. Not only did this lead to an increased demand for paintings and statues, but the expanded circle of patrons—towns, guilds, religious brotherhoods, patricians, aristocrats, and church leaders—broadened traditional tastes and themes, thus leading to a new richness and diversity in art. The dictates of patrons also popularized the intermingling of sacred and secular, instances of which are apparent earlier in the stained glass and statuary of the Gothic cathedrals. Some patrons wanted their portraits included alongside those of the Virgin and saints, as testimony to their piety as well as their wealth, though again there are instances of this in the Middle Ages. The blending of secular and sacred is also seen in the rather free interchanging of style and organization between classical and religious themes: Venus is represented as a secularized Mary, Mary as a spiritualized Venus. The inquisitive mind of the humanists combined with the sundry tastes of patrons to encourage a greater range of artistic expression.

## Early Renaissance Painting

In the Middle Ages, painting was the least developed of the principal fine arts. Giotto (c. 1266–1337), a Florentine, revitalized it and provided the bridge between the medieval era and the early Renaissance. Boccaccio overstated the case when he praised Giotto for reviving painting after it had "been in the grave" for centuries, but Giotto's contributions were rightly recognized when he was made head of the cathedral workshop in Florence, an honor previously accorded only to architects and sculptors. In a series of frescoes on the walls of a chapel in Padua depicting the life of Christ, Giotto's narrative power, evocation of human emotion, and use of spatial depth turned the chapel walls into a stage on which the central events of the Christian faith were acted out. His work was seen as the harbinger of a new era; in the words of Giorgio Vasari, he ushered in the "good modern manner." Although none of Giotto's immediate disciples equaled their master, his frescoes on the walls of Florentine chapels became textbooks for later generations of Renaissance painters, including Masaccio and Michelangelo.

The frescoes of the Florentine artist Masaccio (1401–1428) revolutionized painting. His treatment of the nude figures of Adam and Eve being expelled from the Garden of Eden displays a naturalism and psychological penetration very different in spirit from Giotto's paintings. Both here and in a masterly fresco of the Trinity, the Virgin, and St. John, Masaccio links the Christian

In Masaccio's *Holy Trinity* (1428), God the Father holds the cross while the Holy Spirit descends in the form of a dove. Mary is to the left of the cross, St. John is to the right, and below them are the kneeling donors. Masaccio's use of linear perspective gives the fresco a striking sense of depth. [Alinari/Art Resource]

and the classical by setting his scenes against a Roman arch. These two paintings demonstrate a dramatic advance in the ability to render a sense of depth, and the expulsion scene in particular is notable for its use of shading, a technique known as *chiaroscuro*, which enhanced the pictorial effect by conveying the reflection of light from three-dimensional surfaces. Masaccio's discoveries encouraged his contemporaries and successors to continue experimenting, and Michelangelo himself was among those who sketched Masaccio's work in order to learn his techniques.

The impact of Neoplatonism on Renaissance painting is manifest in the works of the Florentine Sandro Botticelli (1444–1510), a tanner's son. Through his Medici patrons he came into contact with Marsilio Ficino and the Florentine Academy. His famous paintings of Venus—emerging from the sea on a giant shell, celebrating the arrival of spring in the company of Mercury and Cupid, or reclining with Mars as mythological lovers—reflect the Neoplatonic notion of Venus as the source of divine love. But Botticelli, the poet of lyrical beauty, sometimes had to paint more mundane subjects at the behest of his Medici patrons. After they crushed the revolt of the Pazzi in 1478 they commissioned him to depict the execution of the rebels as a warning to others; the painting was destroyed after the Medici were forced into exile.

## Later Renaissance Painting: A New Phase

The early Renaissance achievements in rendering the human figure, three-dimensionality, chiaroscuro, and individualized portraiture became the foundation of the mature period of Renaissance painting that began in the late 1400s and lasted approximately a century. The late Renaissance is distinguished as an era in which the great artists combined creative talents with intense individuality, thereby producing a highly personal style. At the end of the fifteenth century there was a noticeable rise in the status of leading artists, the result of which was greater freedom from the dictates of patrons. Information about the artists was disseminated more widely, and the great ones were increasingly thought of in terms of genius and referred to as "divine." Leonardo da Vinci, said Vasari, manifested *grazia divina*—divine grace. Interest in and respect for the artist's personality grew, and two artists—the sculptor Benvenuto Cellini and the painter Albrecht Dürer—even wrote autobiographies, expressing the Renaissance fascination with the individual. It became increasingly common too for artists to paint their own portraits, and Dürer even depicted himself nude. The elite who could afford art valued the artist's development of a distinctively personal style, especially in the case of artists who acquired international reputations. When Titian left Venice in 1547 to paint Holy Roman Emperor Charles V at Augsburg, he was besieged with requests from people who wanted to own one of his works. In the late Renaissance more people collected art, thus encouraging the notion that a cultured person should own a few paintings or bronze statues.

## Leonardo da Vinci

Although no single painting or date marked a sharp cleavage between the early and late Renaissance, Leonardo da Vinci's *Virgin of the Rocks*, done in the early 1480s, can claim to be the first late Renaissance painting. By this point in his career Leonardo (1452–1519) had already developed a keen interest in nature. In the *Virgin of the Rocks* (see "The Visual Experience: Art of the Renaissance"), for instance, he chose a semidark grotto with an abundance of plant life and a pool for his setting. Although the natural details are faithfully rendered, the total effect is one of mystery and poetic vision—of a psychological world. Coming as it did against a tradition of artistic development dedicated to rendering nature faithfully, the *Virgin of the Rocks* is an intensely personal statement by the artist, as is his famous portrait of the Mona Lisa (*La Gioconda*), with its dreamlike background expressive of the personality of the subject.

About the time he was working on the *Virgin of the Rocks*, Leonardo left Florence and his native Tuscany for Milan, where he acquired the duke's patronage. There he painted his masterpiece, *The Last Supper*, on the wall of a church refectory, unfortunately using an experimental paint that has decayed over the years. The key to this masterful study in human psychology lies in Leonardo's philosophy of art: "A good painter has two chief objects to paint—man and the intention of his soul. The former is easy, the latter hard, for it must be expressed by gestures and the movement of the limbs."[6] For Leonardo, gestures reveal the inner drama as the disciples react to Christ's stunning statement that one of them will betray him. Space is mathematically ordered through the use of recurring rectangles, especially on the walls and ceiling, and the placement of the disciples in groups of three, united by their gestures. The serene Christ, his arms outstretched and his head framed against a window of symbolic light, is in the shape of a pyramid, Leonardo's favorite organizing device, while Judas, his profile rendered in symbolic darkness, has not been separated from the rest of the disciples as had been usual in earlier paintings of the same theme, such as Giotto's famous fresco. The innovation is deliberate; the psychological insight, unsurpassed.

Leonardo's genius as a painter was only one of his many interests. He is the supreme example of the Renaissance ideal—a virtuoso whose intellectual curiosity led him into a host of fields. His notebooks contain ideas and sketches for military inventions, many of which were not realized for centuries, including submarines, turbines, and prototypes of a tank and a helicopter. His studies of human anatomy were based on the dissection of more than 30 corpses. After examining fossils discovered in the mountains, he concluded that the biblical account of creation was inaccurate. An accomplished ri-

## ◉ Leonardo on Art and Nature ◉

*The Renaissance determination to return to the sources, whether in nature or in classical antiquity, is evident in Leonardo da Vinci's insistence that a painter must study the natural world rather than merely imitate the works of his predecessors.*

The painter will produce pictures of small merit if he takes for his standard the pictures of others, but if he will study from natural objects he will bear good fruit. As was seen in the painters after the Romans who always imitated each other and so their art constantly declined from age to age. After these came Giotto, the Florentine, who—not content with imitating the works of Cimabue, his master—being born in the mountains and in a solitude inhabited only by goats and such beasts, and being guided by nature to his art, began by drawing on the rocks the movements of the goats of which he was keeper. And thus he began to draw all the animals which were to be found in the country, and in such wise that after much study he excelled not only all the masters of his time but all those of many bygone ages. Afterwards this art declined again, because every one imitated the pictures that were already done; thus it went on . . . [until] Masaccio showed by his perfect works how those who take for their standard any one but nature—the mistress of all masters—weary themselves in vain.

*Source:* E. G. Holt, ed., *Literary Sources of Art History* (Princeton, N.J.: Princeton University Press, 1947), pp. 178–179.

der and a lover of horses, he sketched dozens of them preparatory to designing a gargantuan (but unfinished) equestrian statue for the Sforza family. Town planning, architecture, botany, music, and optics were among his wide-ranging interests. Above all he was supremely self-confident; after he listed his talents in military engineering for the duke of Milan, he added: "I can do in painting whatever may be done, as well as any other, be he who he may."[7]

## Raphael, Michelangelo, and the Roman Renaissance

After Julius II became pope in 1503, the center of the Renaissance shifted from Florence to Rome. Julius used his patronage to make the city the artistic and intellectual capital of the West. Raphael Sanzio (1483–1520), a native of Umbria in central Italy, studied various works of Leonardo and Michelangelo in Florence before going to Rome. Commissioned by Julius to paint frescoes in several rooms of the Vatican Palace, Raphael reflected the synthesis of the classical and the Christian in the Renaissance by juxtaposing two magnificent scenes, one linking the earthly and heavenly churches by the sacrifice of the mass, the other an assembly of classical philosophers and scientists grouped around Plato and Aristotle. The faces in the latter work include those of Leonardo and Michelangelo as well as his own, a characteristic late Renaissance touch. Raphael is also renowned for a series of gentle Madonnas that carefully blend naturalism with idealized beauty.

Michelangelo Buonarroti (1475–1564), another native son of Tuscany, was already in Rome to paint the ceiling of the Sistine Chapel when Raphael arrived in 1508. Deeply influenced by Neoplatonism, the temperamental Michelangelo created a massive work (128 by 44 feet) fusing Hebrew and classical themes. Christianity is only implicitly present in the sense that the pagan sibyls and the Hebrew prophets were thought to point to the advent of the Messiah. The work abounds in symbolism: the Neoplatonic contrast between light and darkness, spirit and matter; the recurring triads, basic to the numeric symbolism of Neoplatonism; the relationship of earthly knowledge (pagan sibyls) and divine revelation (Hebrew prophets); and the tree imagery in the central panels, which is both biblical, as in the tree of good and evil, and an allusion to Julius II's family name, Della Rovere ("of the oak tree"). Michelangelo's painting *The Last Judgment* on the east wall of the chapel was added much later, between 1532 and 1541, and reveals the somber, deeply religious mood that characterized the final period of the artist's life, as well as his fascination with Dante.

In the central panel of this portion of Michelangelo's Sistine Chapel ceiling (1508–1512),
God gives the spark of life (a Neoplatonic concept) to Adam. [Marburg/Art Resource]

## Titian and the Venetian Renaissance

In their basic conviction that art must transcend nature, Michelangelo and Titian (c. 1487–1576) were in full accord, yet their paintings are strikingly different. In contrast to Michelangelo's preoccupation with statuesque figures and Neoplatonic symbolism, Titian epitomizes Venice's fascination with light and color, reflecting the play of light on its waterways and palatial buildings. An immensely prolific and successful artist, Titian was appointed painter to the republic of Venice, and he enjoyed the patronage of numerous sovereigns and aristocrats, among them Emperor Charles V. Titian's themes range from devout Christian subjects to sensuous reclining nudes, from classical mythology to contemporary portraits. His is an elegant art, befitting the clients for whom

he painted. Only in his late paintings, such as his depiction of Christ being crowned with thorns, does he forsake vibrant colors and rich textures in favor of subdued tones and gloomy light. Like Michelangelo, Titian spent his last years engaged in deep religious introspection. At the personal level, both men manifested the Renaissance origins of the religious reform movements that swept Europe in the sixteenth century.

## Sculpture: From Virtuosity to Introspection

In sculpture as in painting, Renaissance artists strove to achieve greater naturalism, individualization, and, in sculptural reliefs, a keen sense of depth. Sculptors such as Lorenzo Ghiberti (1378–1455) and Donatello

(1386–1466) influenced contemporary painters as they pioneered these developments. Ghiberti's crowning achievement, the bronze doors of the baptistery in Florence, were intended to imitate nature in the classical Greek style. As Michelangelo later did on the Sistine Chapel ceiling, Ghiberti used only scenes from the Old Testament in his ten panels, flanked with portrait busts of pagan sibyls and Hebrew prophets as the heralds of Christ's coming. He succeeded brilliantly in fulfilling his commission from city officials and the guild of merchants to produce a work with "the greatest perfection, the most ornamentation, and the greatest richness."[8]

Ghiberti's pupil, the Florentine Donatello, exhibited a bold, revolutionary style that is evident in his bronze statue of David, the first freestanding nude sculpture since antiquity. Wearing only a shepherd's hat and military leggings, David, with his idealized face and physique, is the antithesis of Donatello's melancholy, emaciated figure of Mary Magdalene. In his portrayal of her as a time-ravaged penitent, there is no hint of the usual Renaissance preoccupation with beauty, for Donatello's outlook has become more introspective, his concern with matters of the spirit more predominant. In the works of Donatello, Leonardo, and Michelangelo a steady progression can be seen from an early concern with innovation and virtuosity to a later preoccupation with inward states and spiritual experience.

Michelangelo's first love was sculpting, an art he approached through his Neoplatonic convictions in the belief that his task was to liberate the living figure encased in a block of marble. Like Donatello, Michelangelo in his early years produced statues of sublime beauty, as if he were perfecting rather than duplicating nature. Instead of pursuing mathematically ordered perfection in the manner of Leonardo, he relied on inspiration to determine ideal proportions. His success is apparent in two majestic works completed in his twenties: the Pietà, in which Mary's youthful face is as supremely beautiful as Raphael's Madonnas, and a towering statue of David, resolutely awaiting Goliath, the heroic physique in every sense an idealized rendition of male anatomy. To Vasari—as to the Florentine government which commissioned the work—Michelangelo's David was a political symbol indicating that Florence "should be boldly defended and righteously governed, following David's example." Michelangelo's last works stand in vivid contrast to these idealized, confident statues. The Pietàs of his final years are unfinished, two of them partially smashed by his own hand. One Pietà includes the figure of Nicodemus, the Pharisee who had asked Jesus how a person could "be born when he is old"; Nicodemus was in fact a self-portrait of Michelangelo, whose own searching in these years was for the assurance of spiritual rebirth. The late Pietàs were a plea for his own redemption, the culmination of the Renaissance quest for individual fulfillment at the deepest, most personal level.

The vivid realism of Donatello's wood statue of the aged penitent Mary Magdalene (1454–1455) is roughly comparable to the realism of Japanese sculptors in the Kamakura period (thirteenth and fourteenth centuries). [Alinari/Art Resource]

## Women Artists

Although relatively little is known about women artists in this period, some achieved both acceptance and a degree of fame. Michelangelo, for instance, took a special interest in the painter Sofonisba Anguissola (c. 1535–1625) of Cremona, whose five sisters also painted. Vasari visited their household and described the works of each woman. For nearly two decades Anguissola, who specialized in individual and group portraits, painted at the court of King Philip II of Spain. The English monarch Henry VIII patronized a number of women painters, paying one of them—Levina Teerling (c. 1515–1576), a manuscript illuminator—even more for her work than he paid the famous portraitist Hans Holbein. Royal patronage was also bestowed on Catharina van Hemessen (1528–c. 1587) of the Netherlands, who enjoyed the support of Queen Mary of Hungary and painted some intriguingly introspective portraits. In the area of sculpture the leading woman artist was probably Properzia Rossi (c. 1490–1530) of Bologna, whose work is reminiscent of the sculptural reliefs of Ghiberti. That women artists

were active and relatively prosperous during the Renaissance is unmistakable, although it is difficult to reconstruct their contributions because so many of their works were subsequently lost or destroyed.

# Architecture and Classical Inspiration

Inspired by the architectural principles and motifs of classical antiquity, Renaissance architects rejected the Gothic style in favor of one that recalled the arches, columns, capitals, and ordered simplicity of Greco-Roman buildings. The artist who pioneered Renaissance architecture, the Florentine Filippo Brunelleschi (1377–1446), solved the greatest architectural puzzle of the fif-

The Cathedral of Santa Maria del Fiore dominates the skyline of Florence. Begun in the Tuscan Gothic style, the church, with its gleaming marble exterior, is crowned by Brunelleschi's dome, a triumph of Renaissance architecture. The companile (bell tower) was designed by Giotto. [Wim Swann]

teenth century—the design and construction of a suitable dome for the cathedral in Florence—by meticulously studying ancient Roman buildings, particularly the Pantheon. His solution was to build an inner dome to support the massive outer dome, thus avoiding the supports that had become unsightly to the tastes of his time, to use a drum below the dome to contain its outward thrust, and to place a lantern atop the dome to stabilize the entire structure. The result was not only technologically innovative but also aesthetically pleasing, as anyone who views Florence from the surrounding hills can attest. Brunelleschi's other designs, including a chapel for the Pazzi family and the Foundling Hospital in Florence, are even more distinctly Renaissance in spirit, with their graceful arches and their concern with classical order.

When Michelangelo set about to design the dome for St. Peter's Basilica in Rome, he studied Brunelleschi's dome. Other architects had already worked on St. Peter's, including Donato Bramante and Raphael, and Michelangelo's main contribution was the soaring dome. It was intended to crown a church in the shape of a Greek cross, with four equal arms, but in the early seventeenth century the western arm was extended into a long, traditional nave, upsetting the careful balance that Bramante and Michelangelo had envisioned. Michelangelo regarded his work on St. Peter's as both a divine commission and an offering of his talents to God: "It was God who laid this charge upon me. . . . I undertook it for the love of God, in whom is all my hope."[9]

Like Brunelleschi, Andrea Palladio (c. 1518–1580), the leading architect of the Venetian Renaissance, made a special trip to Rome to study classical buildings. Convinced that the numeric ratios basic to musical harmony were found throughout the universe and were thus derived from God, Palladio designed his buildings to embody mathematical symmetry. His specialty was the rural villa, of which his best-known example is the Villa Rotunda near his native Vicenza, not far from Venice. The building, mathematically perfect, is cubic, with an interior cylinder, a saucer-shaped dome, and four matching Ionic porches reminiscent of Greek temple façades. Numerous eighteenth-century architects were influenced by Palladio, particularly in Italy, England, and North America. Renaissance architecture provided the inspiration for some of the most famous buildings in the new American republic, including the Capitol, which reflects the influence of Michelangelo's dome, and Thomas Jefferson's house at Monticello in Virginia, which is indebted to Palladio.

## Northern Art

North of the Alps the transition from Gothic to Renaissance came in the fifteenth century. Pioneering Flemish

Jan van Eyck's heavily symbolic painting *The Arnolfini Wedding* (1434) is typical of late medieval–early Renaissance Flemish art. [National Gallery, London]

artists took advantage of the discovery of oil paints to develop an artistic style that was primarily concerned with capturing realism by depicting intricate details; surface appearances mattered more than form, anatomy, or motion. The fascination with detail is evident in the work of Jan van Eyck (c. 1390–1441). In his portrait of the Medici banker Giovanni Arnolfini and his bride, his ties to the medieval world are still apparent in the painting's traditional symbolism: the dog represents fidelity, the single burning candle the all-seeing Christ; the statue on the bedpost is St. Margaret, patron saint of childbirth, and the shoes have been removed to symbolize the holy ground of the sacrament of matrimony. Although the work is suffused with religious meaning, in the last resort the painting is about the union of two individuals and the status they enjoy—concerns common to Italian Renaissance painters of this period.

While these artists concentrated on external appearances, the Dutch painter Hieronymus Bosch (c. 1450–1516) created symbolic scenes so imaginative that spe-

Compare Pieter Brueghel's *Wedding Dance* (1566), a rustic scene full of robust peasants, with the bourgeois couple painted by van Eyck. Brueghel's paintings do not exhibit the usual Flemish concern with sharp detail. [Detroit Institute of Arts]

cialists are still attempting to decipher his meaning. The world of his *Garden of Earthly Delights* is peopled with emaciated nudes, unnatural beasts, flying creatures, biting toads, burning ruins, couples making love, and exotic instruments of torture. At first sight the work appears medieval in its inspiration, but in fact Bosch was daringly individualistic in allowing his imagination to engage in flights of fantasy with unmistakable sensual and sexual overtones. The intent, however, was clearly to warn viewers of the consequences of erotic pleasure as their eyes moved from the Garden of Eden on the left, through the depiction of sensual joys in the center panel, to the fires of hell on the right. Artistic creativity triumphed over the bonds of tradition, but without sacrificing the customary moral message.

Renaissance art culminated in the work of the Flemish painter Pieter Brueghel the Elder (c. 1525–1569), whose circle of friends apparently included some humanists. Although he visited Italy, he was never very impressed by classical art but instead was influenced by Bosch and other painters of the Netherlands. He was intrigued by peasant life and by landscapes, particularly the Alpine scenery he saw on his Italian trip. His delightful peasant scenes celebrate folk customs such as dances and wedding feasts, often with a touch of humor. There was a serious side to Brueghel, who used his works to condemn religious bigotry and Spanish barbarity in the Netherlands. The inscriptions on his copper engravings were so outspoken, in fact, that he had his wife destroy them as he neared death. Brueghel's almost total lack of interest in classical models and his contin-

ued use of traditional symbolism and moralizing underscore the fact that northern Renaissance artists retained far more of the medieval heritage than their counterparts in Italy.

## Perspectives on the Renaissance

"Out of the thick Gothic night our eyes are opened to the glorious torch of the sun," wrote the French writer François Rabelais, reflecting the Renaissance belief in the birth of a new age of cultural brilliance following a millennium of darkness and ignorance. Petrarch contrasted the "ancient" world, the period before the Roman emperors adopted Christianity, with the "modern" era, which he described as a time of barbarism and darkness. Thus was born the unfortunate notion of the Dark Ages. To one fifteenth-century Florentine businessman the compendious writings of the medieval scholastics darkened learning by their "subtleties and confusion." It was thus a natural step to describe the new epoch as a *rinàscita*—a rebirth or renaissance, a term adopted by Vasari to describe the renaissance of the arts. Vasari was on solid ground when he cited the dramatic changes that had occurred in the fourteenth and fifteenth centuries in painting, sculpture, and architecture. The notion of the Renaissance was expanded by later historians to include not only developments in philosophy and literature but virtually every aspect of civilization from statecraft to the economy.

A tendency to exalt the Renaissance developed in the eighteenth century, as reflected in the French philosopher Voltaire's willingness to depict Italy as the successor to the glories of classical Greece. The corollary of this was the denigration of the Middle Ages, which appeared to Voltaire as a dark age of irrationality and superstition. The romantics who followed, however, evaluated the Middle Ages more positively, taking their inspiration from its religious culture and finding their historical roots in medieval states rather than the classical heritage. But the Renaissance was once again thrust to the fore in a remarkably influential book by the Swiss historian Jacob Burckhardt (1818–1897), *The Civilization of the Renaissance in Italy*. First published in 1860, Burckhardt's book develops the Renaissance as an age dominated by the revival of classical antiquity, the development of a pronounced individualism (the awareness and expression of personality), and a fresh discovery of the world of nature and humankind. This was possible, he argued, only because of the genius of the Italians, "the first modern people of Europe who gave themselves boldly to speculations on freedom and necessity." Thus, according to Burckhardt, the Renaissance as a distinctive epoch in the history of civilization was born in the political turbulence that engulfed Italy in the fourteenth and fifteenth centuries. By the time that Burckhardt had finished his wide-ranging exploration of this age, he had provided a synthesis in which the Renaissance amounted to nothing less than a major turning point in European history.

Burckhardt's emphasis on the glories of the Renaissance was taken a step further by the English literary critic John Addington Symonds, whose seven-volume study, *The Renaissance in Italy* (1875–1886), sharply distinguished between the Middle Ages, which he likened to the shores of the Dead Sea, and the Renaissance. The history of the latter he exalted as "the history of the attainment of self-conscious freedom." The Renaissance, he contended, was the seedbed of the essential qualities that distinguish the modern from the ancient and medieval worlds, especially the emancipation of reason from its medieval bondage.

The sharp break drawn by Burckhardt and Symonds between the Middle Ages and the Renaissance was challenged by medieval specialists, whose research demolished the stereotype of the Middle Ages as a time of ignorance and "semibarbarism." Claiming to find the roots of the Renaissance in the twelfth century, some medievalists asserted that the Renaissance should be considered the last phase of the Middle Ages, not the beginning of the modern world. In 1927 the American historian Charles Homer Haskins published *The Renaissance of the Twelfth Century*. Pointing to such phenomena as the revival of the Latin classics and Roman law, the recovery of Greek science and philosophy, and the beginnings of the European universities—a revival of learning in the fullest sense—Haskins argued that the more famous Italian Renaissance was in reality the culmination of a movement that had begun in the late eleventh century and continued without a major break into the early modern period. We err, he argued, if we attempt to draw too sharp a distinction between successive periods of history. Haskins' attack on the Burckhardt-Symonds school did not deprecate the achievements of the Renaissance. Some medievalists did, however, pointing out that in many respects, such as its emphasis on magic and the occult, the Renaissance was actually less "rational" than the Middle Ages, and its science less advanced than in the thirteenth and fourteenth centuries. Even the term *Renaissance*, one medievalist contended, is detrimental to historical understanding because it has discouraged the study of the Middle Ages and obscured the truth that modern life owes far more to the medieval era than to classical Greece and Rome.

After World War II, Wallace Ferguson asserted a compromise interpretation according to which the Renaissance was an age of transition between the medieval and modern eras. Basic to this argument is the conviction that the changes that occurred in the Renaissance were profound, encompassing a transformation of institutions, outlook, culture, and economies. Although some critics objected that all periods involve transition, advocates of this view insisted that, taken together, the changes produced a distinctive cultural period that is neither medieval nor modern, though elements of both can be found in it.

The debate continues today. Much of the discussion has concentrated on the nature of Renaissance humanism, which has been variously defined as an educational system focusing on Greek and Roman classics, a cult of rhetoric and oratory, a philosophical method of rational inquiry, a philosophy of human dignity and individualism, or scholarly endeavor devoted to establishing new criteria of political liberty and civic responsibility.

In the face of so many interpretations, historians have come to realize that humanists were in reality a diverse group of individuals whose concerns were far from identical. The simplest definition of humanism treats it as the *studia humanitatis*, the study of grammar, rhetoric, poetry, history, and ethics in classical texts as distinct from the scholastic emphasis on logic and metaphysics. By this interpretation, humanism is an academic movement rather than a philosophy or a pattern of life based on the quest to imitate classical antiquity. Scholars generally recognize the medieval interest in the classics but distinguish the scholastics' selective approach—picking and choosing things that supported the Christian world view—from the humanist attempt to use all of antiquity as a means of challenging medieval assumptions and reconciling the full legacy of Western culture with its religion.

Another group of historians traces the origins of humanism to the political conditions in Italy and the need to develop a predominantly secular interpretation of government in order to throw off the bondage of the church. One exponent of this view contends that the evolutionary process of Renaissance humanism "began with the secularization of government itself and inevitably went on to engulf society at large."[10] Political conditions, particularly in Florence, provide the basis for a different interpretation: that the leaders of the city-states encouraged the emphasis on the glories of classical antiquity to assert their own political identity and to unite the people behind their rule. Humanistic ideals in this view were welcomed because they healed rifts between competing social groups and unified the community in the face of threats from other city-states. Whereas Burckhardt and Symonds highlighted the individual, a number of recent studies stress the civic nature of humanism and the importance of social groups such as the patriciate.

*Although initially the intellectual and artistic developments in the Renaissance were the province of the socially elite, in the long run many commoners enjoyed them as well. Statues and paintings were displayed in churches, civic buildings, and town squares, and such architectural gems as the Florence Cathedral and St. Peter's Basilica were of course open to the public. Michelangelo's statue of David was placed in front of the Palazzo della Signoria, and statues by Donatello were publicly displayed in Florence and Padua. As printing spread, books became less expensive, making it possible for the literary achievements of the Renaissance to reach a wider audience than anyone could have anticipated in 1400. Because husbands or wives could read to families, and masters to apprentices,*

*the high levels of illiteracy were less a barrier to the dissemination of literature than might be imagined. As humanist ideas were accepted into the curriculum and new schools were founded, Renaissance teachings reached a wider and wider audience. Despite the unwillingness of many humanists to support a liberal education for the masses, the Renaissance was the first step in an educational revolution that swept Europe beginning in the sixteenth century. The Renaissance concern with accurate texts, the keen interest in the classical world (the birthplace of Christianity), and the spread of the printed word also contributed to the Protestant Reformation in the same century. So did the humanist interest in reviving Christianity and integrating it with the culture of antiquity.*

## Notes

1. L. Martines, *Power and Imagination: City-States in Renaissance Italy* (New York: Knopf, 1979), p. 168.
2. P. G. Ruggiers, *Florence in the Age of Dante* (Norman: University of Oklahoma Press, 1964), p. 43.
3. J. B. Ross and M. M. McLaughlin, eds., *The Portable Renaissance Reader* (New York: Viking, 1968), pp. 124–125.
4. W. H. Woodward, *Vittorino da Feltre and Other Humanist Educators: Essays and Versions* (Cambridge: Cambridge University Press, 1912), pp. 102, 106.
5. J. G. A. Pocock, *The Machiavellian Moment* (Princeton, N.J.: Princeton University Press, 1975), p. 154.
6. A. Blunt, *Artistic Theory in Italy, 1450–1600* (London: Oxford University Press, 1964), p. 34.
7. E. G. Holt, ed., *Literary Sources of Art History* (Princeton, N.J.: Princeton University Press, 1947), p. 170.
8. Ibid., p. 90.
9. Ibid., p. 197.
10. W. Ullmann, *Medieval Foundations of Renaissance Humanism* (London: Elek, 1977), p. 9.

## Suggestions for Further Reading

Antal, F. *Florentine Painting and Its Social Background.* New York: Harper & Row, 1975.

Baron, H. *The Crisis of the Early Italian Renaissance: Civic Humanism and Republican Liberty in the Age of Classicism and Tyranny,* rev. ed. Princeton, N.J.: Princeton University Press, 1966.

Baxandall, M. *Painting and Experience in Fifteenth-Century Italy.* New York: Oxford University Press, 1988.

Brucker, G. A. *Renaissance Florence,* rev. ed. Berkeley: University of California Press, 1983.

Chabod, F. *Machiavelli and the Renaissance*, trans. D. Moore. London: Bowes & Bowes, 1958.

Clark, K. *Leonardo da Vinci: An Account of His Development as an Artist*. Baltimore: Penguin Books, 1967.

De Grazia, S. *Machiavelli in Hell*. Princeton, N.J.: Princeton University Press, 1990.

Eisenstein, E. L. *The Printing Press as an Agent of Change: Communications and Cultural Transformations in Early Modern Europe*, 2 vols. Cambridge: Cambridge University Press, 1979.

Ferguson, W. K. *The Renaissance in Historical Thought: Five Centuries of Interpretation*. Boston: Houghton Mifflin, 1948.

Gilbert, F. *Machiavelli and Guicciardini: Politics and History in Sixteenth-Century Florence*. Princeton, N.J.: Princeton University Press, 1965.

Goldthwaite, R. A. *The Building of Renaissance Florence*. Baltimore: Johns Hopkins University Press, 1980.

Hale, J. R. *Renaissance Europe: Individual and Society, 1480–1520*. Berkeley: University of California Press, 1978.

Herlihy, D. *Medieval and Renaissance Pistoia*. New Haven, Conn.: Yale University Press, 1967.

Holmes, G. *Florence, Rome and the Origins of the Renaissance*. Oxford: Clarendon Press, 1986.

———. *The Florentine Enlightenment, 1400–1450*. New York: Pegasus, 1969.

Hook, J. *Lorenzo de' Medici: A Historical Biography*. London: Hamilton, 1984.

King, M. L. *Venetian Humanism in an Age of Patrician Dominance*. Princeton, N.J.: Princeton University Press, 1986.

Klapisch-Zuber, C. *Women, Family, and Ritual in Renaissance Italy*. Chicago: University of Chicago Press, 1985.

Kristeller, P. O. *Renaissance Thought: The Classic, Scholastic, and Humanistic Strains*. New York: Harper & Row, 1961.

———. *Renaissance Thought and Its Sources*. New York: Columbia University Press, 1979.

Labalme, P. H., ed. *Beyond Their Sex: Learned Women of the European Past*. New York: New York University Press, 1980.

Levey, M. *Early Renaissance*. Baltimore: Penguin Books, 1967.

———. *High Renaissance*. Baltimore: Penguin Books, 1975.

Maclean, I. *The Renaissance Notion of Woman*. Cambridge: Cambridge University Press, 1980.

Martines, L. *Power and Imagination: City-States in Renaissance Italy*. New York: Knopf, 1979.

———. *The Social World of the Florentine Humanists, 1390–1460*. Princeton, N.J.: Princeton University Press, 1963.

Muir, E. *Civic Ritual in Renaissance Venice*. Princeton, N.J.: Princeton University Press, 1980.

Murray, P., and Murray, L. *The Art of the Renaissance*. London: Thames & Hudson, 1978.

Niccoli, O. *Prophecy and People in Renaissance Italy*, trans. L. G. Cochrane. Princeton, N.J.: Princeton University Press, 1990.

Partner, P. *Renaissance Rome, 1500–1559: A Portrait of a Society*. Berkeley: University of California Press, 1977.

Ralph, P. L. *The Renaissance in Perspective*. New York: St. Martin's Press, 1973.

Ross, J. B., and McLaughlin, M. M., eds. *The Portable Renaissance Reader*. New York: Viking, 1953.

Ruggiers, P. G. *Florence in the Age of Dante*. Norman: University of Oklahoma Press, 1964.

Stephens, J. *The Italian Renaissance: The Origins of Intellectual and Artistic Change Before the Reformation*. New York: Longman, 1990.

Stinger, C. S. *The Renaissance in Rome*. Bloomington: Indiana University Press, 1985.

Ullmann, W. *Medieval Foundations of Renaissance Humanism*. London: Elek, 1977.

Weinstein, D. *Savonarola and Florence: Prophecy and Patriotism in the Renaissance*. Princeton, N.J.: Princeton University Press, 1970.

# The Human Image (I)

Across the ages and around the globe, from the prehistoric cave dwellers of Europe and the rock painters of Africa to our own century of abstract painting and sculpture, every culture has represented the human figure in its art. Successive generations of artists in each civilization have used a rich variety of styles and techniques, but their efforts reveal the common concerns that underlie the human experience.

The meaning of a statue or a painting can be understood fully only in its historical context, for works of art have different functions, depending on the religions, the philosophies, and the values of the culture that produces them. Yet the focus of most artistic traditions has been on the human figure. How one culture has portrayed human beings in its art tells much about the society in which the artist worked. Thus while experts often debate the exact meaning or purpose of a particular work of art, broad cultural patterns can easily be discerned by comparing the artistic treatment accorded the human figure. In a very real sense, art serves as a language by which civilizations communicate their concerns and aspirations as they explore the meaning of existence.

The earliest known representations of the human figure were carved perhaps 30,000 years ago in central Europe. The exaggerated breasts and roundness of the body in these female figures suggest that they served as fertility images; they typically have no facial features. The remains of an ivory statue of the so-called Brno Man in present-day Czechoslovakia dates from approximately the same period but reveals much more attention to the head, which has deep-set eyes and short hair. The Brno Man seems to have been part of a burial ritual.

The unknown sculptors who executed these early Paleolithic (Old Stone Age) works rendered the human figure with a naturalism that was not true of the cave art painted 15,000 years later. The powerful realism that makes the cave paintings of France and Spain famous was devoted almost exclusively to the depiction of animals, and human figures were rarely painted or carved on the walls. When humans were represented, they often appear as abstract forms such as boxes with sticks for arms and legs.

The Addaura finds of Sicily are a rare exception. These caves contain human figures dating from 10,000 to 8000 B.C. incised in outline into the rock face. The nature of the scene is unknown, but the images are exceptionally supple and expressive. Indeed, no earlier wall art renders the human figure with such grace, and, judging from surviving evidence, several thousand

**Man from Brno, Czechoslovakia. [Moravian Museum, Brno]**

years passed before such skill in representing humans occurred again.

The shift from hunting and gathering to a farming culture that ushered in the Neolithic (New Stone) Age around 8000 B.C. saw the first permanent village com-

*Ritual Dance*, rock engraving, c. 10,000 B.C., cave of Addaura, Monte Pellegrino, Palermo, Italy. [H. W. Janson]

munities created in western Asia. Humans began to view themselves and their world differently, and a much more sophisticated skill in depicting the human figure emerged. At Jericho, just north of the Dead Sea, archaeologists have uncovered sculptured heads dated to 7000 B.C., made by refashioning human skulls with colored plaster and seashell eyes. These heads, which appear to have been placed above graves, were modeled with great skill, and some had painted features. They may represent the first attempts at individual portraiture.

When compared across many cultures and long stretches of time, all these representations of the human figure suggest the varieties of ritual and belief common to early civilizations. Indeed, clay statues of fertility goddesses made in Anatolia around 6000 B.C. bear a remarkable resemblance to figures from Romania produced 1,000 years later, and both appear quite similar to the Venus of Willendorf, carved 20,000 years earlier.

One of the most extraordinary representations of the human form in Neolithic art is a male figure, also from Romania (c. 4000 B.C.). Modeled from dark clay, the

**Man from Cernavoda, Romania.** [EastFoto/ Sovfoto]

features and limbs of the small statue are reduced to a stark, bold design that conveys a forceful sense of monumentality in miniature form. The man is seated on a stool and holds his head between his hands, a Neolithic "thinker" captured by the artist in the universal pose of contemplation 6,000 years before the French sculptor Auguste Rodin created his famous version of the same subject.

Ancient Egypt, which enjoyed political unity for more than 2,000 years, produced a remarkably consistent artistic culture obsessed with continuity and permanence. Statues of the pharaohs show the basic Egyptian approach to rendering the human figure: the anatomy and drapery are realistic, but the features are highly idealized, conveying not an individual portrait but the notion of divine power. Less formal portraits of ordinary people, however, are exceptionally lifelike, showing the facial features of a real person.

Egyptian artists adhered to strict rules for representing the human body. They generally rendered the body according to exact proportional ratios between its parts. The poses of the figures are often almost anatomically impossible, with shoulders facing the front while heads and legs face to the right. Despite this stylization, Egyptian artists were capable of achieving great naturalism, as in the relief of Akhenaton, Nefertiti, and three of their children.

The civilization of the Indus valley in the same period (c. 3000–1500 B.C.) stands in sharp contrast to Egyptian culture. Its cities developed no large-scale public art such as the pyramids or the monumental statues of the pharaohs, and the works that survive are small and delicate. A male torso found at Harappa, carved in limestone sometime between 3000 and 2000 B.C., suggests a civilization with markedly different values. The highly skilled sculptor has captured the texture of youthful flesh, softly and sensuously depicted in the swelling body. Contrasted to the rigidity of Egyptian statues, this torso appears to be a living, moving body. Nowhere else was the human figure represented at such an early date with such sensitivity.

In the ancient Aegean the human figure ultimately achieved what is probably its most famous representation. The painting and sculpture of Crete from around 1500 B.C. show influence from Egypt, yet very few human figures were depicted in explicitly religious or political postures in Minoan art. The major exceptions are the strange snake-goddess statues, which must have been worshiped by an unknown cult.

In depicting the human figure, Greeks soon became engrossed in the search for order and ideal beauty, which they saw as complementary aspects of life. Nowhere is this better illustrated than in the freestanding statues of nude young men known as *kouroi* ("youths") produced in Archaic Greece. The pose is stiff, with head held high, eyes focused straight ahead, broad shoulders, narrow waists, arms held down at the side with clenched fists, and one leg striding. The purity, simplicity, and balance of the anatomical form, almost abstract in its conception, must surely have been a deliberate effort to equate natural beauty with divine order through the representation of the human form—for the Greeks made no distinction between the physical features of humans and those of gods.

The principal subject and the greatest achievement of classical Greek art was its treatment of the nude body, which it presented with increasingly greater freedom and suppleness. Indeed, Greek artistic triumphs, such as Praxiteles' *Hermes with Dionysus* or the later *Venus de Milo* and the winged *Victory of Samothrace*, have so conditioned us to equate beauty with the human form that Western art has been concerned with the depiction of human beings ever since.

Because their art sought to achieve a sense of the ideal, the early Greeks left little in the way of actual portraiture, which was introduced into Western art during the later Hellenistic period. The Romans excelled at portraying not only the physical likenesses of real people but their character and psychology as well. Roman art generally lacked the universal sensuousness and idealized beauty of the Greeks and was more concerned with a straightforward rendering of civic and political values. Much Roman sculpture and statuary in the imperial period was devoted to representing the emperor, a practice begun by Augustus, who was keenly aware of its propaganda value. Roman imperial art was never as monumental as Egyptian art had been, but it contrasted strongly with that of the Greeks, who regarded statues of their rulers as vulgar and stamped their likenesses only on coins. But not all Roman art was official, and there was a particularly keen interest in portraiture. In relief sculpture and in portrait busts, Roman depictions of the human form are marked by a direct rendering of individual features and characteristics.

The image of the Buddha, which was to dominate much of Asian art, was first depicted in human form at the time when the Romans were producing portraits of their civic leaders. Because doctrine held that the Buddha—the "enlightened one"—eventually achieved transcendence of the senses and of self, he had been depicted for centuries only by means of abstract symbols. But a new school of Buddhist thought that emerged in the first century A.D. conceived of the Buddha as an eternal god and provided him with a host of divinities, known as bodhisattvas, to assist him. The need for icons as visual aids to this new creed became apparent. Competition with Hinduism, which practiced the worship of personalized deities, also led to the adoption of a human image for the Buddha.

**Head of the Buddha from Gandhara, third century** A.D. **[Victoria and Albert Museum, London]**

Among the earliest images of the Buddha were third-century statues produced in the border region comprising much of modern day Afghanistan and Pakistan, where Greek and Roman cultural influences were strong. The features of these Buddhas suggest a sensual spirituality that would be a trademark of Indian art. A more purely Indian classical style emerged in the fifth century under the Guptas, where statues that have no equivalent in the West portray the Buddha as more a divine essence than a real person. As Buddhist influences spread eastward into China, Southeast Asia, and Japan, images of the Buddha were fashioned according to local artistic conventions and styles.

Aside from Buddhist influences, early Chinese art generally avoided depictions of the human figure. Taoist philosophy stressed that humans were not dominant in nature but merely a part of it, so secular

Chinese art preferred landscapes and animals to portraits. The excavation of imperial tombs from the Chin dynasty (221–207 B.C.) unearthed a stunning collection of more than 500 life-size clay warriors. From the Han dynasty on, emperors were painted in lifelike portraits, as were famous sages, such as Confucius and Lao-tze. Portraits of courtiers and court ladies were also important, although often as part of large scenes of court life and the palace world.

In the millennium from the fifth to the fifteenth centuries, the human figure predominated almost everywhere in art, largely to serve religious or political purposes. The major exception was Islamic art, where Arab tradition and Muslim doctrine generally proscribed the representation of living things. The Koran, however, specifically prohibited only statuary, and some Islamic painting did portray human figures. After about 800, Muslim theologians launched a campaign against representation, arguing that an artist who made images of living things usurped the divine creative act. The human figure disappeared thereafter in large-scale art for public display, although it survived in miniatures, manuscript illuminations, and private art, in large part as a result of the influence of non-Muslim artists.

In the medieval West and in Byzantium two religious images—Christ and the Virgin Mary—dominated painting and sculpture. Although these images varied greatly in artistic style and emphasis from century to

century and from one region to another, they served to convey basic precepts of Christian belief. In the early-sixth-century mosaics of the Byzantine city of Ravenna, Christ still appears as the beardless and youthful miracle worker of early Christian art, but he was later transformed into the bearded, lean-faced image that became familiar throughout the Christian world.

A similar transformation occurred in representations of the Virgin Mary as the Madonna, the mother of Christ. Byzantine icons conformed to strict formal rules of design that were repeated over and over. They reveal a stiffness of treatment and an almost abstract quality that is related to mosaic art. The northern Gothic imagination transformed the serenity of the icon into a highly expressionistic *Pietà* whose agonized faces and grotesque wounds evoke the horror of Christ's grief-stricken mother. During the Renaissance, Italian painters produced serene and often sensual Madonnas that depict a mother and child with only muted reference to Christian symbolism.

Indian artists of the same period, intent on rendering an inner spirituality, ignored the Western obsession with the lifelike, giving their work instead a peculiar tension between spirituality and sensual beauty. A seventh century wall painting of a bodhisattva presents an exquisite vision of harmony, the personification of compassion and tenderness, that is in marked contrast to Western paintings of the Virgin Mary or of Christ

*Miracle of the Loaves and Fishes,* mosaic, c. 504.
[Alinari/Art Resource]

*Pietà*, **German, early fourteenth century.**
**[Marburg/Art Resource]**

and torsos. Large-scale figure sculpture came to Japan with the introduction of Buddhism, as can be seen in the enormous Buddha and bodhisattva statues from the eighth century.

Unique artistic cultures also developed in Africa and Central America. Near the village of Nok, in northern Nigeria, the discovery of terra-cotta sculpture testifies to a thriving civilization as early as 400 B.C. Besides representations of animals, startling human figures and large heads were produced. The heads are highly stylized, generally cylindrical or conical, but each one has expressive features that clearly suggest individual personalities. These clay works were no doubt modeled after wood carvings, for many suggest the carved masks so familiar in African art.

Although Nok culture disappeared after the third century A.D., it seems to have exercised an important and lasting influence on the later cultures of West Africa. Terra-cotta and brass heads were found at Ife, in southwestern Nigeria, dating probably from the twelfth century. Human features are brilliantly rendered in these masterpieces. These and similar heads are no

from the same period. Similarly, Chinese statues of bodhisattvas from the T'ang dynasty reveal the beauty of the figure in the traditional Indian pose. Even in Hindu religious sculpture, so filled with symbolic images, Indian artists remained faithful to the sensuous quality of their artistic traditions. A bronze statue from around 1000 A.D. shows the graceful four-armed figure of Siva Nataraja dancing within a flaming halo, creating a magnificent three-dimensional effect.

In Sung China, the major representation of a human figure, after the Buddha, was Kuan-yin, the bodhisattva of mercy, who is generally shown as a sexless deity in either male or female form. But a glazed pottery statue from the same period demonstrates that the Chinese were equally capable of the most straightforward representation.

No native deities were depicted in Japanese art before the Buddha, and the only earlier human likenesses were terra-cotta figures from the fourth to the sixth centuries consisting of human heads atop tubelike limbs

*Bodhisattva of Mercy*, **Chinese, eleventh or twelfth century. [Nelson-Atkins Museum of Art, Kansas City, Missouri]**

**Head of a Nigerian queen, twelfth or thirteenth century. [Museum of Antiquities, Ife, Nigeria]**

**Wrestler, c. 400 B.C. [Doug Bryant/DDB Stock Photo]**

**The Toltec god Chacmool, c. 1200, found at Chichén Itzá. [Andrew Rakoczy/Art Resource]**

doubt idealized forms rather than portraits. Such sculptural traditions apparently evolved in West Africa without outside influences; indeed, European artists produced no works of equal subtlety during this period.

In marked contrast to the refinement of African sculpture stand the early carvings of Central America. Although the Olmecs of Mexico were capable of sophisticated works, such as a stone wrestler that dates from around 400 B.C., or small jade figures of infants, nonetheless their culture seems to be more aptly characterized by the colossal monolithic heads made during the same period.

Later cultures in the region, such as the Toltecs, also created striking stone sculptures and carved reliefs that often appear intimidating. Thus the god Chacmool is

# THE VISUAL EXPERIENCE
## Art of the Renaissance

Giotto's *Lamentation*, a fresco painted for the Scrovegni Chapel in Padua, is one of the most eloquent depictions of grief in early Renaissance art. [Scala/Art Resource]

The Neoplatonic concern with beauty is apparent in this celebration of spring, *Primavera* by Sandro Botticelli. The Venus figure in the center represents spring; Mercury and the three Graces are to the left; at the right, a nymph being chased by the wind god Zephyr is transposed into the goddess Flora (in the flowered dress) while Cupid hovers above. [Scala/Art Resource]

Leonardo da Vinci's *Virgin of the Rocks* masterfully combines the artist's intense interest in natural phenomena and human anatomy with traditional religious devotion. [Giraudon/Art Resource]

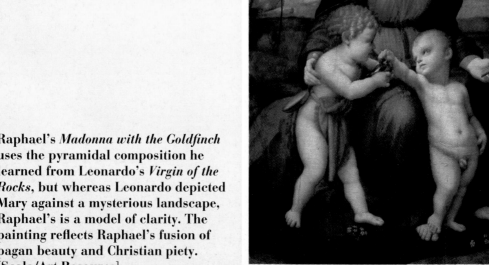

Raphael's *Madonna with the Goldfinch* uses the pyramidal composition he learned from Leonardo's *Virgin of the Rocks*, but whereas Leonardo depicted Mary against a mysterious landscape, Raphael's is a model of clarity. The painting reflects Raphael's fusion of pagan beauty and Christian piety. [Scala/Art Resource]

Michelangelo's depiction on the Sistine Chapel ceiling of the first sin and Adam and Eve's expulsion from Eden underscores the Neoplatonic contrast between the physical (evil) and the spiritual (good). [Scala/Art Resource]

This dramatic painting of the Annunciation by Titian shows the archangel Gabriel announcing to Mary that she will give birth to the Messiah. [Scala/Art Resource]

Sofonisba Anguissola painted her three sisters playing chess in 1555. She provided a role model for other Italian women who sought careers in art. Approximately fifty of her works, most of them portraits, have survived. [Jerzy Nowakowski; National Museum, Poznan, Poland]

Hieronymus Bosch's depiction of hell is the right panel of his *Garden of Earthly Delights*. Bosch was a narrative painter whose visions provoked the imagination. These scenes suggest the dangers of sensualism, such as an undue fondness for music or sexual pleasure. [Scala/Art Resource]

frequently rendered as a reclining human figure in severely foreshortened geometric shape, whose expression suggests a hostile and forbidding countenance.

Since the first Paleolithic carvers had worked their primitive sculptures tens of thousands of years earlier, the human figure had been depicted in a great variety of styles, but for broadly similar purposes. It served as a religious icon or political symbol, as a way of representing ideal beauty or activity, or as a means of commenting on the human condition. Although every generation has addressed these themes anew, the art of the modern world has remained constant to their expression.

## Suggestions for Further Reading

Breckenridge, J. D. *Likeness: A Conceptual History of Ancient Portraiture.* Evanston, Ill.: Northwestern University Press, 1968.

Clark, K. *The Nude: A Study in Ideal Form.* Princeton, N.J.: Princeton University Press, 1956.

De Dilva, A., and Von Simson, O. *Man Through His Art,* Vol. 6: *The Human Face.* New York: Graphic Society, 1968.

Garland, M. *The Changing Face of Beauty.* New York: Barrows, 1957.

Kubler, G. *The Art and Architecture of Ancient America.* Harmondsworth, England: Penguin Books, 1962.

Lee, S. *A History of Far Eastern Art.* New York: Abrams, 1974.

Leroi-Gourhan, A. *Treasures of Prehistoric Art.* New York: Abrams, 1967.

*Man: Glory, Jest, and Riddle: A Survey of the Human Form Through the Ages.* San Francisco: M. H. de Young Memorial Museum, California Palace of the Legion of Honor, and San Francisco Museum of Art, 1965.

Mayor, A. H. *Artists and Anatomy.* New York: Artist's Limited Edition, 1984.

Mode, H. *The Woman in Indian Art.* New York: McGraw-Hill, 1970.

Relouge, I. E., ed. *Masterpieces of Figure Painting.* New York: Viking, 1959.

Richter, G. *The Portraits of the Greeks,* rev. R. R. R. Smith. Oxford: Phaidon, 1984.

Rowland, B. *The Art and Architecture of India.* Baltimore: Penguin Books, 1967.

Schultz, B. *Art and Anatomy in Renaissance Italy.* Ann Arbor, Mich.: UMI Research Press, 1985.

Segal, M. *Painted Ladies: Models of the Great Artists.* New York: Stein & Day, 1972.

Smart, A. *The Renaissance and Mannerism in Italy.* New York: Harcourt Brace Jovanovich, 1971.

Walker, J. *Portraits: 5,000 Years.* New York: Abrams, 1983.

Wentinck, C. *The Human Figure in Art from Prehistoric Times to the Present Day,* trans. E. Cooper. Wynnewood, Pa.: Livingston Publishing, 1970.

Willett, F. *African Art: An Introduction.* New York: Praeger, 1971.

# PART · THREE

# The Early
# Modern World

The early modern world began with crisis and renewal in three of its major civilizations—those of western Europe, the Islamic regions, and China—and catastrophe for a fourth, the Aztec and Inca cultures of the Western Hemisphere.

In Europe, recovery from the demographic disaster of the Black Death had just been achieved when the Catholic church, the dominant social institution of Europe for 1,000 years, was challenged and riven by a movement of protest and reform—hence the name it took, the Protestant Reformation—which touched off a century and a quarter of internecine warfare, both within and between states, and left a permanently divided Christianity in western Europe.

Despite the scars left by the Reformation, Europe began a remarkable career of expansion and conquest in the early modern period that was to make it the dominant world civilization by the nineteenth century. Following their discovery of the Western Hemisphere—named by Europeans "the Americas"—Spanish and Portuguese adventurers rapidly conquered the Aztec and Inca empires, whose populations were soon decimated by exploitation and epidemic. Within Europe itself, a population increasingly urban and (after the development of movable type) literate had begun to come under the sway of centralized state bureaucracies and a new economic regime, capitalism, based on mobile labor, expanded commerce, and production for profit. The sixteenth and seventeenth centuries also saw a reconceptualization of the physical world, the scientific revolution, that was to transform human understanding of and relation to the natural environment.

Europe itself faced challenge from the east, where a new Islamic empire, that of the Ottoman Turks, extinguished the 1,000-year Christian empire of Byzantium, occupied much of southeastern Europe as well as the Middle East, and twice stood before the gates of Vienna. More loosely governed than the states of Europe, but also less politically divided, the Ottomans presided over a brilliant cultural and religious revival and showed again the remarkable capacity of Islam to achieve rapid unification and expansion. The Mughal dynasty in India and the Safavids in Iran produced a new age of prosperity and cultural splendor in south-central Asia.

While Europe and the Islamic world were both expanding, a new Chinese dynasty, the Ming, threw off the Mongol yoke of the early fourteenth century and inaugurated a golden age in the world's most populous and prosperous state. After probing westward by sea as far as Africa, the Ming turned inward. Commercialization and urbanization grew, and the arts flourished. A brisk and lucrative foreign trade nonetheless continued, mainly with Southeast Asia but also with the West through Muslim and Venetian intermediaries. By the sixteenth century, Jesuit missionaries had reached China, as had the first Western trading ships, which began to clash in the waters of Japan and Southeast Asia. ∎

# The Reformation

The forces unleashed in the Reformation struck deeply at the roots of Western values and shattered the fragile unity of medieval Christendom. Sparked by reformers who raised profound questions concerning conscience and authority, the new movements were successful because of favorable political and social conditions in the sixteenth century that supported alternative Christian views. The crisis of conscience that marked the dismantling of medieval Christendom was a poignant one for reformers on all sides of the struggle. In a society where belief and conduct had always been regulated by authority from above, the rival claims of Christian leaders initiated a period of militant zeal and frightening upheaval. Since neither camp proved able to impose its views on its opponents, the West was henceforth divided by competing ecclesiastical institutions, antagonistic creeds, and conflicting claims to religious authority.

**Archbishop Thomas Cranmer was burned at the stake in Oxford on March 21, 1556, after reaffirming his Protestant faith. [Ronald Sheridan/Ancient Art and Architecture Collection]**

Fear, doubt, and outright hostility led to persecutions and witch-hunting, but the Reformation was also an age in which the goals of religious renewal were embodied in high ideals and noble visions.

## The Late Medieval Church

The medieval church derived considerable strength from its ability to renew itself from within. The Gregorian reform of the eleventh century, subsequent monastic reforms, and the founding of the mendicant orders in the thirteenth century all gave vitality to the church. In the early fifteenth century, reformers successfully ended the Papal Schism at the Council of Constance, but further reform attempts generally failed. The major reason was lack of effective papal leadership. Fifteenth-century popes were occupied not only with their roles as Italian princes and as patrons of the arts but also with the challenge to their power posed by the reformers. Renaissance popes proved unwilling to address the deep-rooted problems that reform movements, particularly that of John Hus in Bohemia, sought to redress. Although the better popes were capable administrators and notable patrons of the arts, none instituted major ecclesiastical reforms, and Pius II (1458–1464) even prohibited appeals to church councils.

### Lay Piety

Demands for reform were made by persons intent on preserving the unity or spiritual supremacy of the church, not on destroying it; theology was not an issue for them, save in the cases of heretical groups such as the Hussites in Bohemia or the Lollards in England. Particularly in German-speaking lands, popular piety remained strong and was probably increasing. Visitors from Italy were impressed by the people's devotion, much of which was rooted in traditional family piety. The development of the printing press dramatically increased the circulation of religious material, though Bibles were still fairly expensive on the eve of the Reformation. Some 10,000 different sermons, mostly in Latin, were in print by 1500, and popular manuals for religious devotion encouraged spiritual training in the home.

The growth of piety was also reflected by the fact that more churches were constructed in German lands in the fifteenth century than in any preceding period. Religious clubs or organizations for laypersons were founded at a striking pace in the fourteenth and fifteenth centuries. Typical of these were the Brethren of the Common Life, established in the Netherlands in the fourteenth century, and the Brotherhood of the Eleven Thousand Vir-

Hans Holbein the Younger's rendering of the Dance of Death reflects the fifteenth- and early-sixteenth-century preoccupation with dying, which was in part responsible for the piety and religious concern of this period. In this panel a child is snatched by death. [Giraudon/Art Resource]

gins, founded at Cracow and Cologne a century later. While some brotherhoods, such as the Common Life, were involved in education, most were associations to foster piety through communal praying and singing. In large measure, then, the Reformation was possible because the heightened sense of religious awareness among the people, often expressed outside the institutional church, was not matched by reform of the chronic problems.

### Institutional Decay

Two of the most critical problems of the church involved the quality and training of the clergy and ecclesiastical finances. Although the moral standards and educational preparation of the ministry did not substantially decline in the fifteenth century, many people, particularly north of the Alps, were growing impatient with priests who were sometimes flagrantly immoral or semiliterate, particularly as the educational level of many laypersons began to rise. The problem was compounded by the moral laxity of many of the church's leaders, including Pope Alexander VI (1492–1503) and numerous cardinals and prelates. In an age acutely conscious of mortality, there was a demand for spiritual shepherds capable of relieving fears and providing religious guidance. Sensitivity to such needs was often lacking among the higher clergy—notably the archbishops and bishops—who were normally younger sons from aristocratic families pursuing ecclesiastical careers for wealth and political power and had little contact with commoners.

At the level of the parish priesthood, minimal incomes made it difficult to recruit educated men, although some able individuals fostered the growth of popular piety. As a result, most parish priests were drawn from the lowest ranks of society. In the absence of seminaries, the parish priests received on-the-job training from neighboring colleagues and were ill-prepared to instruct parishioners in the complex teaching of the church. The church's future welfare required the recruitment of dedicated priests, an educational program to train them, their effective supervision by bishops, adequate salaries, and the expulsion of unfit men from the priesthood.

The problem of attracting able men at the parish level was directly related to defects in the church's economic structure and officialdom. Although the church was an immensely wealthy institution with vast landholdings, its riches were unequally distributed. In contrast to the opulent lifestyles enjoyed by the archbishops and bishops, most parish priests barely eked out a living; some administrators in the church improved their positions by holding multiple benefices (church livings), a practice that normally detracted from religious duties. Others never visited their parishes but hired poorly paid vicars to perform their duties. Beneficed priests were also in the awkward position of obtaining income from their parishioners by collecting tithes (usually paid in goods, such as wheat) and fees (for baptisms, marriages, and burials). Because tithes were mandatory, they often caused disputes and resentment, particularly among the poor or those dissatisfied with the absenteeism and the low moral and educational levels of the priests. In Germany and Switzerland, peasants and artisans in the fifteenth and sixteenth centuries often condemned these abuses. In addition to the abolition of serfdom and a decrease in rents, they demanded religious reforms, including a reduction of church lands and clerical wealth. In the resulting uprisings, flags depicting a peasant's shoe beside Christ on a white cross symbolically united religious and social protest.

## Christian Humanists and the Quest for Reform

The need for institutional reform in the church was a dominant theme of the Christian humanists of northern Europe. To the principles of the Italian humanists they fused the teachings of primitive Christianity in the hope that they might achieve a return to the purity of the early church and its simple but deep-rooted faith. Many northern humanists placed special emphasis on the study of biblical languages and the publication of accurate scriptural texts. Likewise, the humanist attack on corruption and meaningless ceremony in the church prepared the way for Protestant demands for reform and a justification for the break with Rome. Yet the older generations of northern humanists generally remained loyal to Catholicism. In England, Sir Thomas More chose death over renunciation of the church when the latter was demanded of him by King Henry VIII. However, many in the younger generation, such as John Calvin and William Tyndale, found their humanist principles compatible with Protestantism. Indeed, humanists and Protestants each looked to the past as the basis for their proposed reforms—humanists to the classical world, Protestants to the early church—and both shared a deep interest in history.

## The Challenge of Hebrew Scholarship: Reuchlin and Hutten

One of the leading biblical scholars among the Christian humanists was Johann Reuchlin (1455–1522), a German authority on Hebrew language and thought. He ran afoul of a converted Jew named Johann Pfefferkorn, who had Emperor Maximilian's authorization to examine Jewish materials in order to identify ones that attacked Christianity. With the support of Dominican scholastics in Cologne, Pfefferkorn attempted to suppress all Jewish literature on the basis of its hostility to Christianity, but Reuchlin objected because Jewish texts had religious and cultural value. When Maximilian condemned his attacks on Pfefferkorn in 1512, Reuchlin retaliated by branding his enemies "pigs" and "children of the devil." Pfefferkorn had the backing of several leading theological faculties, but Reuchlin was defended by a number of German humanists, particularly Ulrich von Hutten and Crotus Rubeanus. These two men wrote the satirical *Letters of Obscure Men* (1515), which purportedly came from the pens of Pfefferkorn's friends and made them appear ridiculous. Hutten, who had once condemned Pope Julius II as the "pest of the world," regarded the papacy as the source of Christendom's troubles. A German patriot, he applauded when Martin Luther attacked the pope's authority to issue indulgences in 1517.

## Erasmus, Prince of the Humanists

The greatest Greek scholar among the northern humanists was Desiderius Erasmus of Rotterdam (c. 1466–1536), a pupil of the Brethren of the Common Life and later a student at the University of Paris. Much of his scholarly career was spent in Basel, though he was widely traveled and visited England several times. One of the great triumphs of Renaissance scholarship was his edition of the New Testament in Greek, first published in 1516. In its preface, he made an eloquent plea for Bibles in the vernacular: "I would that even the lowliest women read the Gospels and Pauline Epistles. . . . Would that . . . the farmer sing some portion of them at the plough."[1] Erasmus thus anticipated one of the major accomplishments of the Protestant Reformation, the bringing of the Bible to the common people.

Erasmus' religious beliefs are summarized in his idea of a "philosophy of Christ," by which he meant a disciplined life of love and service for God and other people. In contrast to the complexities of the scholastics, Erasmus stressed the simple teachings of Jesus; the heart of religion was faith and love in action, not ritualistic observance. In his great classic, the *Praise of Folly*, he mercilessly satirized such Catholic practices as pilgrimages, the veneration of relics, the sale of indulgences, and the mechanical use of the rosary. Erasmus condemned war as a denial of Christian love and insisted that peace was essential for the spread of education and scholarship. He even condemned war against the Turks on the ground that any victories they might win against Europeans were divinely ordained as a means to chastise Christians. Nowhere is his repudiation of the philosophy of might more evident than in his *Education of a Christian Prince* (1516), written for Charles of Habsburg, the future Emperor Charles V. Erasmus' ideal ruler—devoted to peace, guided by honesty and right religion, concerned for the welfare of his people—was diametrically opposed to Machiavelli's prince. Erasmus was the epitome of a Christian idealist: "We may shortly behold," he wrote in 1517, "the rise of a new kind of golden age. So great is the heaven-sent change we see in the minds of princes, who bend all their powers to the pursuit of peace."[2]

## The Humanists in England

John Colet and Sir Thomas More, both friends of Erasmus, were the leading Christian humanists in England. Colet (c. 1466-1519) founded St. Paul's School for boys

Hans Holbein painted Erasmus of Rotterdam, the influential Christian humanist whose stinging criticism of abuses in the Catholic church helped set the stage for the Protestant Reformation. Erasmus himself, however, remained a Catholic. [Metropolitan Museum of Art, New York]

in London, with a curriculum devoted to the critical study of Latin and Greek as well as religion. Colet's scriptural expositions were noted for their attention to historical context and literal meaning, and some of his sermons fearlessly denounced corruption in the church.

More (1478–1535), an able diplomat and later Lord Chancellor for Henry VIII, depicted the model society of a Renaissance humanist in *Utopia* (1516), a shrewd work of social criticism coupled with autobiographical reflections. His book envisioned a communal society in which "life and work [are] common to all," education is universal and compulsory, and crime is largely nonexistent because there would be no extremes of wealth and poverty. Utopia ("nowhere" in Greek) was a tolerant society in which one enjoyed the freedom to believe as one wished, so long as one did not coerce others or use religion to promote sedition. There is tragic irony in the fact that More, who was beheaded for refusing to accept

# ◉ A Bible for the People ◉

*In* The Paraclesis, *Erasmus argued for the importance of having the Bible translated into the language of the people. This was directly related to his belief in the essential simplicity of the Christian message.*

I greatly dissent from those men who would not have the Scripture of Christ translated into all tongues that it might be read diligently by private and secular men and women, as though Christ had taught such dark and insensible things that they could only be understood by a few divines, or else as though the pith and substance of the Christian religion consisted chiefly in this, that it be not known. Peradventure it is most expedient that the counsels of kings should be kept secret, but Christ would have his counsels and mysteries spread abroad as much as possible. I desire that all women should read the Gospel and Paul's epistles, and I would to God they were translated into the tongues of all men, so that they might not only be read and known by the Scots and Irishmen, but also by the Turks and Saracens. Truly it is one degree to good living, yea the first . . . to have a little sight into the Scripture, though it be but a gross knowledge . . . and that some should err and be deceived. I would to God the plowman would sing a text of the Scripture at his plow, and the weaver at his loom. . . . I would that all the communication of the Christian should be of the Scripture, for in a manner we ourselves are such as our daily speech is.

*Source:* Erasmus, *An Exhortation to the Diligent Study of Scripture* (London, 1529), pp. 8–9 (edited to conform with modern usage).

Henry VIII's headship over the English church, dreamed of a day when a ruler would recognize that it was "arrogant folly for anyone to enforce conformity with his own beliefs by means of threats or violence."[3] Yet More himself had supported the persecution of heretics in his capacity as Henry's chancellor. In the end, More, like Erasmus, found Protestant theology unacceptable, but his call for reform helped pave the way for the Reformation.

## Luther and the German Reformation

The event that triggered the Protestant Reformation—or Revolt, as Roman Catholics often call it—was associated with the church's financial policy as well as popular piety. Late in 1514, Pope Leo X revived a campaign originally launched by Julius II to rebuild St. Peter's Basilica in Rome, the money for which was to be raised partly through the sale of indulgences. An indulgence cancelled or reduced the temporal punishment for sin. Retribution and forgiveness for one's sins were the central focus of the sacrament of penance, which included confession and the performance of prescribed penalties. Catholic theology advanced the belief that few people lived such exemplary lives that the remission was complete. Most Christians therefore had to be purified in purgatory after they died before they could enter heaven. Beginning in 1476, the papacy claimed the power to reduce the time that souls spent in purgatory by transferring to them the surplus good deeds of Christ and his saints (stored in the "treasury of merit"). This it would do for anyone who purchased indulgences, usually in return for monetary gifts to the church. As early as the thirteenth century, the papacy had sold indulgences as a source of income, though reformers at the Council of Constance in 1415 protested this practice. It continued, partly because so many shared in the profits and partly because many common folk sincerely believed that their money could speed their loved ones or themselves through purgatory.

In the spring of 1517, the papacy completed preparations for the sale of indulgences in northern Germany. However, a university professor in the Saxon town of Wittenberg, Martin Luther (1483–1546), raised serious questions about indulgences and soon challenged the authority of the papacy itself. No issue was more central to the Reformation than this question of authority.

# Luther: The Early Years and the Attack on Indulgences

Luther's father, an ambitious miner who became part owner of a mine, provided a good education for his son, including a year's study with the Brethren of the Common Life. As Luther prepared to study law after graduating from the University of Erfurt, he was deeply troubled by religious doubts. Terrified by a lightning storm, he promised St. Anne, the patron of miners, that he would become a monk in return for his safety, and shortly thereafter he became an Augustinian friar. Although the rigors of the monastic routine brought no relief from his deep-seated fears of divine wrath, he remained in the order.

A trip to Rome on Augustinian business in 1510 confirmed Luther's feeling that the church was too worldly and needed reform. As he prepared lectures on the Bible at the University of Wittenberg, to whose faculty he had been assigned, he became convinced that no amount of human effort could save a person from the awesome judgment of God; salvation (or justification) could come only through the divine gifts of grace and faith. Luther vividly likened the human condition to that of a worm trapped in the ordure of the bowels, unable to escape unless God plucked the soul from the filth. From this conviction of salvation by faith alone, Luther gained the spiritual strength to become a religious leader, although personal fears continued to plague him. More than 15 years later he confessed that he was still terrified when he heard God called "just." It was this unusual sensitivity to human unworthiness and the need for divinely bestowed faith that made him rebel at the commercialism of the indulgence hawkers, particularly Johann Tetzel, who dramatically evoked the appeal of relatives suffering in purgatory: "Pity us, pity us. We are in dire torment from which you can redeem us for a pittance."[4]

Although Luther had criticized indulgences in 1516, it was not until the people of Wittenberg purchased them from Tetzel the following autumn that his views attracted serious attention. Intended at first only for academic debate, the 95 theses that Luther issued on October 31, 1517, challenged belief in papal authority to release souls from purgatory. Finding no scriptural authority for indulgences, Luther insisted that believers received full forgiveness for their sins through faith and repentance, not letters of indulgence. Within weeks, the theses were translated from Latin into German, printed, and distributed throughout Germany, creating a sensation. Summoned to Rome for examination on charges of heresy, Luther instead received a hearing in Augsburg, thanks to the intervention of his prince, Frederick of Saxony. As one of the seven electors of the Holy Roman Empire empowered to select a successor when the aged Maximilian died, Frederick was a man Pope Leo X dared not

alienate. For political reasons, then, no effective action was taken to suppress Luther, who gained vital time to work out the implications of his views on authority and salvation by faith.

# Toward a New Theology

In a debate at Leipzig with the papal spokesman Johann Eck in 1519, Luther moved closer to an open break with the church by rejecting the authority of the pope and the infallibility of church councils and by referring with approval to John Hus, the Bohemian heretic. Further reflection led Luther to write three reform manifestos in 1520. Their publication broadcast his views widely and was enormously effective in winning support for them. The first of the treatises was the *Address to the Christian Nobility of the German Nation*, an appeal to the emperor, the German princes and knights, and the imperial cities to cast off papal bondage. In a work with pronounced nationalistic overtones, Luther repudiated three fundamental papal claims: superior jurisdiction over temporal powers, the sole authority to interpret Scripture, and the exclusive right to summon a general council of the church.

In his second treatise, *On the Babylonian Captivity of the Church*, Luther rejected four of the sacraments for which he found no biblical basis, retaining only baptism, the Lord's supper, and penance (which he later dropped). Here too he set forth his concept of the priesthood of all believers, repudiating the traditional Catholic distinction between the clergy and the laity: "We are all equally priests . . . we have the same power in respect to the Word and the sacraments."[5] He conceded that to preach required the church's approval, thereby preserving a sense of order. Finally, in *The Liberty of the Christian Man*, Luther explained his doctrine of salvation by faith alone, insisting that good deeds were necessary fruits of this faith. On these principles Protestantism was founded.

Before the last two of these treatises appeared, Pope Leo issued a bull, *Exsurge domine*, commanding Luther to retract his assertions or be excommunicated. Luther and his supporters responded to this challenge by publicly burning copies of the bull and the canon law. Luther finally received a formal hearing in April 1521, three months after his excommunication, when he appeared before the imperial Diet at Worms. The decision to leave the safety of Saxony was an act of courage, despite a guarantee of safe conduct from the new emperor, Charles V. As Luther knew, a similar promise had not saved Hus from the flames a century earlier. Expecting to debate his views before the Diet, Luther was stunned when ordered to retract his statements without an opportunity to defend himself. To the emperor and the nobles Luther responded the following day: "I am neither

## ◉ Luther on Justification by Faith ◉

*One of Luther's strongest statements of the doctrine of justification by faith alone appears in his commentary on Paul's epistle to the Galatians. First published in 1535, the commentary was based on lectures delivered at the University of Wittenberg four years earlier.*

We imagine as it were two worlds, the one heavenly and the other earthly. In these we place these two kinds of righteousness, being separate the one far from the other. The righteousness of the law is earthly and hath to do with earthly things, and by it we do good works. But as the earth bringeth not forth fruit except first it be watered and made fruitful from above . . . even so by the righteousness of the law, in doing many things we do nothing, and in fulfilling of the law we fulfil it not, except first, without any merit or work of ours, we be made righteous by the Christian righteousness, which nothing appertaineth to the righteousness of the law, or to the earthly and active righteousness. But this righteousness is heavenly and passive: which we have not of ourselves, but receive it from heaven: which we work not, but apprehend it by faith; whereby we mount up above all laws and works. Wherefore like as we have borne (as St. Paul saith) the image of the earthly Adam, so let us bear the image of the heavenly (1 Cor. 15:49), which is the new man in a new world, where is no law, no sin, no sting of conscience, no death, but perfect joy, righteousness, grace, peace, life, salvation, and glory.

Why, do we then nothing? Do we work nothing for the obtaining of this righteousness? I answer: Nothing at all.

*Source:* Martin Luther, *A Commentary on St. Paul's Epistle to the Galatians,* ed. P. S. Watson (Westwood, N.J.: Revell, 1953), p. 25.

able nor willing to revoke anything, since to act against one's conscience is neither safe nor honest."[6] The break with Rome was now complete, for Luther had rejected the fundamental Catholic doctrine of the combined authority of Scripture and tradition. Neither pope nor church councils could be the final court of appeal, as authority resided in the Bible and the conscience of the believer, duly enlightened by the Holy Spirit through Scripture. The emphasis on individual conscience became one of the most important elements in the Protestant tradition.

Although the emperor was unmoved by Luther's stand, he honored the safe conduct. Taking no chances, Frederick hid Luther in his castle at Wartburg, where Luther, disguised as "Sir George," translated Erasmus' Greek New Testament into German. Excommunicated by the church and outlawed by the empire, he could not return to Wittenberg for nearly a year. He remained there until his death in 1546, secure only because of political and religious rivalries within the empire and Charles' preoccupation with military campaigns against the French and the Turks.

## Religion and Social Reform

Luther's program of reform had major religious and social consequences. Refusing to recognize the Roman church as the true church of Christ, he set out to establish an institution that conformed to his view of the New Testament. He and his supporters rejected prayers to the saints, the veneration of relics, indulgences, and pilgrimages because they regarded them as superstitious and unscriptural. The monasteries in Lutheran territories were dissolved, resulting in a major redistribution of wealth that ultimately improved the social position of the wealthier urban citizens as well as the princes and the aristocracy. Mandatory celibacy for the clergy was also ended. Regarded by Catholics as a superior state, celibacy now was given no more importance than marriage, which gained a new dignity. Luther himself married a former nun, Katherine von Bora, who bore him six children. The effects of these changes on women were mixed, for although wives were no longer regarded as inferior to celibate women, the closing of nunneries

The propaganda war between Protestants
and Catholics made effective use of the
printing press, as in the case of Hans
Holbein's woodcut depicting Luther as the
"German Hercules." Having vanquished such
Catholic teachers as Thomas Aquinas and
William of Ockham, Luther uses his cudgel
to thrash the Cologne inquisitor who attacked
Reuchlin, the Hebrew scholar.
[Zentralbibliothek, Zurich]

deprived women of a vocational option. Fathers, however, could no longer place their daughters in convents to avoid providing dowries for them.

In most respects Luther's view of women was traditional, predicated on their subordination to men and a belief in the inferiority of their abilities. They should, he said, "remain at home, sit still, keep house, and bear and bring up children." But even though he regarded wives as subject to their husbands, he viewed them as partners in marriage. Because Luther made the family the focal point of society and church, wives had a new dignity. Thus Luther accepted women's spiritual equality with men, but he refused to allow them a formal role in the preaching or teaching ministry of the church or in politics. Nevertheless, some women became active in the spread of Lutheranism. Argula von Grumbach, who came from an aristocratic Bavarian family and had a humanist education, distributed Lutheran books, conducted religious services in her home, and corresponded with Luther. Elizabeth of Braunschweig converted people in Hanover and Göttingen to Lutheranism and furthered the Protestant cause in letters to political leaders. But Argula's and Elizabeth's roles in the Lutheran movement owed more to their aristocratic status than to Luther's encouragement of female activity.

In Lutheran churches the sermon was accorded a prominent place, services were conducted in the vernacular, and congregational participation was increased, especially through the singing of hymns. The more active role of the laity and the significance attached to the sermon led to greater attention to education. Luther wanted a primary school in every parish and a secondary school in every sizable town, with provision for the education of girls as well as boys. With his colleague Philip Melanchthon, he urged civil authorities to establish and support schools, drawing especially on the wealth obtained by the closing of monasteries and other Catholic institutions. Because of the importance of the Bible, which Luther insisted must be in the vernacular, Protestantism became a major incentive to the growth of literacy.

At first, the religious confusion of the opening years of the Reformation brought a reduction in the number of students, especially at the universities; enrollment at the University of Vienna fell from 661 students in 1519 to 12 in 1532. An alarmed Erasmus complained that "wherever Lutheranism prevails, there learning disappears." But Luther and his colleagues successfully pressed civic officials and territorial princes to establish new schools. The Lutherans had several outstanding educational reformers, including Johannes Bugenhagen, who organized school systems in Germany and Denmark that included separate institutions for girls. The most influential Lutheran educator was Johannes Sturm, whose secondary school (called a "gymnasium") at Strasbourg became the pattern for similar schools throughout Europe. Divided into ten grades, the curriculum included Latin, Greek, religion, and logic. Lutherans also founded new universities in Germany, including those at Marburg and Jena. Luther's own university at Wittenberg attracted 16,000 students between 1520 and 1560, of whom a third were foreigners.

## The Growth of the Lutheran Movement

Luther's views spread rapidly, aided by the printing press, the reformer's own eloquence, the zeal of numer-

## ◉ A Lutheran Woman Speaks Out ◉

*Argula von Grumbach, one of Luther's most prominent female disciples, was undaunted by the traditional domination of males in theological matters. In 1523 she wrote a stinging letter rebuking the faculty of the University of Ingolstadt for condemning a young Lutheran teacher.*

Where do you read in the Bible that Christ, the apostles, and the prophets imprisoned, banished, burned, or murdered anyone? You tell us that we must obey the magistrates. Correct. But neither the pope, nor the Kaiser, nor the princes have any authority over the Word of God. You need not think you can pull God, the prophets and the apostles out of heaven with papal decretals drawn from Aristotle, who was not a Christian at all. I am not unacquainted with the word of Paul that women should be silent in church (1 Tim. 1:2) but, when no man will or can speak, I am driven by the word of the Lord when he said, "He who confesses me on earth, him will I confess and he who denies me, him will I deny" (Matt. 10; Luke 9). . . . I would be willing to come and dispute with you in German and you won't need to use Luther's translation of the Bible. . . . I send you not a woman's ranting, but the Word of God.

*Source:* R. H. Bainton, *Women of the Reformation in Germany and Italy* (Minneapolis: Augsburg, 1971), pp. 97–98, 100.

ous German merchants, especially in the Hanseatic towns, and the prospects for material gain by people who coveted Catholic lands and wealth. Various German princes as well as cities such as Hamburg and Magde-

**Medallion depicting Argula von Grumbach, one of Luther's leading female supporters. [Government Coin Collection, Munich]**

burg requested that Luther's friends and pupils fill their pulpits and lecterns. The work of reform went forward by winning the support of established leaders, not by revolution. For this reason, Luther himself strenuously opposed any attempt to alter the political order.

In the German cities the reform typically followed a threefold course, beginning with the preaching of Protestant tenets, followed by the growth of popular support and finally by the backing of the magistrates. While the reformers recognized that the last step was critical, the magistrates were cautious, not wanting to introduce religious change until they were assured that it would not destroy traditional social ties. The magistrates were also pressured by Charles V to remain Catholic. When some finally decided to support Protestantism, they did so with deliberation, stretching out the work of reform over a period of years: 11 in Constance, 13 in Nuremberg, 21 in Osnabrück. Wary of creating new popes, the magistrates were frequently unwilling to grant the preachers all the changes they sought. In Strasbourg, for instance, Martin Bucer's attempt to transfer control of the city's religious and moral life to the church was rejected. Some magistrates inaugurated the religious change with debates rigged so that the Protestants prevailed, as happened at Nuremberg and Constance. Because of their concentration, urban populations were especially open to the influence of popular preaching and the Protestant works that flowed from the press, the results of which were evident in the demonstrations of voting support often accorded the Protestants in the early 1530s.

Luther himself corresponded with Hussite leaders in Bohemia, and his doctrines were preached as far afield as Hungary, Prussia, and the Netherlands. Beyond the German states, however, only the Scandinavian lands adopted Lutheranism, which suited the political needs of the kings of Denmark and Sweden as they worked to unify their countries. Adopting Lutheranism made it possible for them to confiscate ecclesiastical lands and assert greater authority over the clergy. As a province of Denmark, Norway too became Lutheran, and Protestant teachings spread as well into Finland. Within Germany, Luther's views provoked bitter divisions that ultimately led to social upheaval and civil war.

Initially the German peasants regarded Luther as a leader who would help them attain not only their religious goals but social reform as well. The success of Luther's movement was tied, however, to the support of princes, nobles, and wealthy burghers, without whose backing he would have been subjected to the power of the empire and the church. Thus despite his sympathy for many peasant demands—which included reduced rents, the abolition of serfdom, and an end to unlawful punishment—he preached patience when peasants rebelled in southern and central Germany in the summer of 1524. He refused to support their call for the termination of serfdom on the grounds that such action not only violated biblical respect for property but "would make all men equal, and turn the spiritual kingdom of Christ into a worldly external kingdom." As the Peasants' Revolt became increasingly violent the following year, Luther reacted against the killing, arson, desecration of churches, and destruction of property. In May 1525 he published his pamphlet *Against the Rapacious and Murdering Peasants*, urging the nobility in God's name to "cut, stab, and strangle" the rebels. The peasants were crushed with dreadful severity: some 300 were beheaded in front of the town hall at Frankenhausen, and altogether the Peasants' Revolt claimed between 70,000 and 100,000 lives.

Although Luther's support for the nobles tied his movement to the conservative social order, Catholics seized on the revolt to accuse Lutheranism of fomenting social rebellion. In 1525 and 1526 both sides organized defensive leagues, but Charles V, who remained steadfastly Catholic, was prevented from crushing the Protestants by hostilities with the French, with whom he fought four major wars over northern Italy and Naples between 1521 and 1559. He was preoccupied too by the advancing Turkish forces of Suleiman the Magnificent (1520–1566), which soundly defeated the Hungarians at Mohács in 1526 and advanced to the very gates of Vienna before retreating.

Political and military pressures forced Charles to allow the German princes a degree of religious toleration at the Diet of Speyer the same year. When he revoked this freedom in 1529, the Lutheran princes and urban delegates protested, giving birth to the term *Protestant*. In response to Charles' demand at the 1530 Diet of Augsburg that Lutherans return to the Catholic fold, the Protestant princes organized the Schmalkaldic League to defend themselves. Although the emperor defeated the league in 1547, his armies were in turn vanquished five years later, forcing him to return to a policy of limited religious toleration. Finally, in 1555 both sides agreed in the Peace of Augsburg that each prince had the right to determine whether the people of his territory would be Catholic or Lutheran. Only in some of the German cities where toleration was already practiced did the people themselves retain the right to choose their own faith. Northern Germany became mostly Lutheran, as did Württemberg and most of the cities of the south, though much of southern Germany remained loyal to Catholicism.

## The Reformed Tradition

While Lutheranism developed in the German states, a different variety of Protestantism emerged in Switzerland. There, under the leadership of Ulrich Zwingli in Zurich and later John Calvin in Geneva, the Reformed tradition distinguished itself from Lutheranism by simpler forms of worship, emphasis on the weekly sermon rather than the celebration of the Lord's supper (undertaken only four times a year rather than weekly), greater stress on moral discipline, and a denial of Christ's physical presence in the Lord's supper. In Switzerland, a loose confederation of 13 independent states (cantons) and allied areas, there was widespread disenchantment with conditions in the church, stemming mostly from the impact of the Christian humanists and the reforming spirit kindled by the Councils of Constance (1414–1418) and Basel (1431–1449). Although the cantons were overwhelmingly Catholic, feelings against abuses in the church ran so strongly that in 1520 the Swiss diet ordered the execution of anyone selling church offices. Along with the desire for reform, there were mounting protests in the cantons against the recruitment of Swiss men for foreign military service.

### Ulrich Zwingli and the Swiss Reformation

The son of a peasant and village magistrate, Ulrich Zwingli (1484–1531), the founder of the Reformed tradition, was educated by humanists at Bern, Vienna, and Basel. Intellectually he was a disciple of Erasmus. After serving as a chaplain to Swiss mercenaries, he was moved by their heavy losses to condemn such employment. As a priest in the Great Minster at Zurich, Zwingli became an outspoken critic of indulgences. While comforting the sick during an outbreak of the plague in 1519, his own illness deepened his religious convictions and ultimately spurred his interest in reform. In 1522 he condemned fasting during Lent as unscriptural and reformed the liturgy. Finding no biblical evidence for clerical celibacy, he denounced it and married a poor widow. "I know of no greater scandal," he wrote caustically, "than that priests are not allowed to take lawful wives but may keep mistresses if they pay a fine."[7] In a series of public debates, he called for a return of the church to its original simplicity and for the peaceful removal of all images, relics, and altars. Because he allowed only psalm singing in church, the minster organ was chopped into pieces. For Zwingli, nothing was acceptable in religion unless it was revealed in Scripture.

From Zurich the reform movement spread by 1529 to Bern and Basel, as well as beyond the confederation to the German cities of Strasbourg and Constance. Civil war between Catholics and Protestants briefly erupted in 1529, after which Zwingli met with Luther to forge a Protestant union. At Marburg, however, the two leaders strongly disagreed on the nature of the Lord's supper. Zwingli, believing that Christ was present only spiritually in the sacrament, rejected Luther's insistence on a "real" (physical and spiritual) presence. The failure at Marburg was followed by renewed civil war in Switzerland when, despite Zwingli's protests, the Protestant cantons blockaded the Catholic districts in 1531, forcing them to fight or starve. Zwingli died in the battle of Kappel that year, and his body was quartered and burned because he was considered to have been a heretic. Leadership of the reform movement in Zurich was taken up by his son-in-law, Heinrich Bullinger. Following the war, the right of each canton to decide its own religion was recognized.

# John Calvin

The Reformed tradition founded by Zwingli became a major international force under the guidance of John Calvin (1509–1564), the son of a French attorney and secretary to the bishop of Noyon. After a broad education in theology, law, classical languages, and humanistic studies at the Universities of Paris, Orléans, and Bourges, Calvin joined Catholic humanists in Orléans and Paris interested in religious reform in the late 1520s. Shortly after his conversion to Protestantism, he was briefly imprisoned in 1534 and then forced into hiding.

When the French government stepped up the persecution of Protestants that autumn, Calvin fled to Basel, where he met Bullinger and other reformers. There he wrote the classic of Reformation Protestantism, the *Institutes of the Christian Religion* (1536). In it he provided a thorough introduction to a Protestant view of the

Christian faith, concentrating on the nature and work of God, the redemption of sinners, and the role of the church and sacraments in the Christian life. On a trip to Strasbourg later that year, he stopped in Geneva, which had just ended Catholic worship under the leadership of Guillaume Farel. Needing assistance, Farel pressured Calvin to stay, threatening him with God's wrath until he became "terrified and shook." Together they imposed a public confession of faith on citizens to distinguish the devout from the unfaithful, called for educational reform, and punished immorality. These measures, coupled with changes in worship and the abolition of holy days, provoked such strong resentment that the two men were exiled in 1538.

Settling in Strasbourg, Calvin became the pastor of a congregation of French exiles, lectured at Johannes Sturm's gymnasium, and revised his *Institutes*. Influenced by the teachings of Paul and Augustine, Calvin proclaimed that because human nature was totally corrupt, belief in God was impossible without the irresistible gift of faith. Only those chosen by God before creation—the elect—received this gift; all others—the reprobate—were left to their sins and condemned to eternal damnation. In his mind, the doctrine of predestination revealed not only God's justice and majesty but also his mercy in providing salvation for the elect despite their unworthiness. Too much inquiry into this doctrine was discouraged:

> Let them remember that when they inquire into predestination they are penetrating the sacred precinct of divine wisdom. If anyone with carefree assurance breaks into this place, he will not succeed in satisfying his curiosity and he will enter a labyrinth from which he can find no exit.[8]

Like Luther and Zwingli, Calvin accepted the authority of Scripture alone, which he regarded as "a declaration of the word of God," and refused to consider the teachings of the early church fathers and church councils as equally binding. He insisted, however, that only those enlightened by the Holy Spirit could properly understand the Bible. With other Protestants, Calvin recognized only two sacraments, baptism and the Lord's supper; his concept of the latter was closer to Zwingli's idea of a spiritual presence than to Luther's view. Influenced by the Strasbourg reformer Martin Bucer, Calvin developed a "democratic" plan for church government that called for the election of ministers by the congregation and the joint participation of ministers and popularly elected lay elders in running the church. Calvin's stress on the disciplined moral life and a godly society made his movement a potent force.

One of the most important themes in Calvin's thought was his treatment of vocation as a Christian duty, a concept he shared with other Protestants. He gave all legitimate professions a sense of Christian purpose, so that

## ◉ **Eternally Chosen, Eternally Damned** ◉

*Calvin's* Institutes of the Christian Religion, *perhaps the finest theological work of the Protestant Reformation, put great emphasis on the sovereignty of God. The most famous manifestation of this was Calvin's insistence that God determined the eternal destiny of each person before the creation of the world.*

We shall never be clearly convinced as we ought to be, that our salvation flows from the fountain of God's free mercy, till we are acquainted with his eternal election, which illustrates the grace of God by this comparison, that he adopts not all promiscuously to the hope of salvation, but gives to some what he refuses to others. Ignorance of this principle evidently detracts from the Divine glory, and diminishes real humility. . . .

Predestination we call the eternal decree of God, by which he has determined in himself, what he would have to become of every individual of mankind. For they are not all created with a similar destiny; but eternal life is foreordained for some, and eternal damnation for others. . . .

We affirm that this counsel, as far as concerns the elect, is founded on his gratuitous mercy, totally irrespective of human merit; but that to those whom he devotes to condemnation, the gate of life is closed by a just and irreprehensible, but incomprehensible, judgment. . . .

The will of God is the highest rule of justice; so that what he wills must be considered just, for this very reason, because he wills it. When it is inquired, therefore, why the Lord did so, the answer must be, Because he would. But if you go further, and ask why he so determined, you are in search of something greater and higher than the will of God, which can never be found.

*Source:* John Calvin, *Institutes of the Christian Religion*, trans. J. Allen (Philadelphia: Presbyterian Board of Christian Education, 1928), vol. 2, pp. 140–165 passim.

one's job became a principal means of serving God. To work was to worship. This outlook brought new dignity to occupations as diverse as business, the crafts, and agriculture. The artisan no less than the minister, Calvin insisted, was divinely called to his vocation.

Calvin's view of wealth was equally significant for economic development. In his judgment, God intended that money be used to better the human condition, and thus, within limits, usury (or interest) had a positive function. Like Luther, Calvin was conscious of the plight of debtors, but if charging interest was consistent with the good of the community, usury was acceptable. Interest rates, however, could never be excessive. Luther, by contrast, prohibited all usury as unscriptural with the exception of loans by which the borrower prospered. For Calvin the governing economic principle was always the mutual responsibility of citizens for the common welfare. Although he never sanctioned the unlimited acquisition of wealth or equated riches with godliness, his emphasis on work and discipline in the context of Christian vocation as well as his limited acceptance of usury were compatible with the growth of a capitalistic economy.

## ❀
## GENEVA IN THE AGE OF CALVIN

After the election of men favorable to his cause, Calvin returned to Geneva in 1541. The city was the largest in its region, with a population of approximately 10,000. Under Calvin, Geneva became the international center of Reformed Protestantism and attracted more than 5,000 religious refugees from France, Italy, England, and Scotland, many of whom were artisans and merchants who contributed to the city's prosperity. Among the newcomers were many booksellers and printers, who helped make Geneva one of Europe's foremost publication centers. Throughout most of the 1500s, books were the city's primary export and were only supplanted late in the century by the export of silk, an industry introduced by Italians. Because Geneva had little industry of its own apart from printing, the economy was based on commerce. Its artisans produced mostly for the local market rather than the export trade.

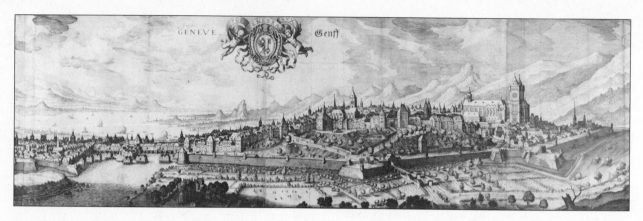

**Geneva in the late sixteenth century, its skyline dominated by St. Peter's Cathedral.
[British Library]**

Genevans prized their independence, which they achieved on the eve of Calvin's arrival by rebelling from Savoy. The heart of Genevan government was its three councils: the 25-member Little Council served as an executive body, the Council of Two Hundred determined municipal policy, and the Council of Sixty conducted foreign relations. Under Calvin's leadership, these institutions protected the Protestant church, safeguarded property, and imposed moral standards on private behavior. Although Calvin himself never held political office, his advice was sought on such matters as foreign policy, taxes, and military defense.

The councils approved his ecclesiastical ordinances, establishing four offices in the church: pastors, teachers, elders, and deacons (who were responsible for poor relief and assisting the sick). Each of the 12 elders was assigned a district in Geneva and required to oversee its families. Through the Consistory, composed of the ministers and elders, Calvin imposed strict discipline on the people for such offenses as absence from church, sexual immorality, swearing, drunkenness, bawdy songs, card playing, and even criticizing Calvin himself. More serious offenses were turned over to the city government. Between 1542 and 1546 fully 76 persons were banished and 58 executed for heresy, adultery, blasphemy, and witchcraft. In the quest to make Geneva an example of godliness, the Consistory even questioned children about the conduct of their parents. Discipline and obedience were crucial.

As the years passed, Calvin, like Luther, grew even more intolerant of opposition and demanded that his critics be punished. The intolerance of the two leaders, like that of most of their fellow reformers, grew out of their belief in the need for a unified Christendom and was the practical result of the need to define the churches they had created. In 1552 Calvin persuaded the city councils to declare that his *Institutes* contained the "pure doctrine" and should not be questioned. The extent to which

Calvin's supporters would go in defending his theology became apparent the next year when the Spanish physician and lay theologian Michael Servetus (1511–1553) visited Geneva, thoroughly scandalizing the citizens by his views. The author of works attacking the doctrine of the Trinity, the baptism of infants, and original sin, he was already a man whom the Catholics regarded as a heretic. After a trial in which he clashed with Calvin personally, Servetus was burned at the stake. Calvin's treatment of him was praised by Catholic and Protestant leaders alike. From 1555 until his death in 1564, Calvin ruled Geneva with little opposition.

Geneva made a determined effort in this period to deal with the needy. Before Calvin's arrival, the small medieval hospitals were reorganized into the Hospital of the Holy Spirit, which cared for the elderly, the sick, the indigent, and widows and orphans. Outside the city walls was a smaller hospital for victims of the plague. Responsibility for the main hospital was vested in the deacons, who obtained funding from the city government as well as from private charity. Support for the hospital was sometimes the largest item in the city budget. In addition to providing free care for the needy in the hospital, every medical doctor was required, beginning in 1569, to treat the poor without charge.

Calvin supervised a sweeping reform of the school system that replaced the old secondary schools with a gymnasium patterned after Johannes Sturm's in Strasbourg. A new academy, established to train superior students for leadership in church and state, developed into the modern University of Geneva. Beginning in 1536, all children had to attend primary school, but girls were barred from the secondary level. No reformer was more aware than Calvin of the value of education to instruct young people in religious beliefs.

Like Luther, Calvin accepted the traditional notion of female inferiority and the subject position of women in marriage. He too recognized their spiritual equality but refused to allow women a ministerial role in the church. In the secular sphere, when a woman inherited a crown, Calvin interpreted the event as a divine reproach to men. Apart from their responsibilities in the home, women were assigned the task of educating the young. In practice, however, Calvinist women of aristocratic background were prominent in the movement. Jeanne d'Albret, mother of King Henry IV of France, was a leader of the Huguenots (as the French Calvinists were called), while Madeleine Mailly, Comtesse de Roye, worked on behalf of the Huguenot cause with both the French government and German Protestant princes. Yet in Geneva, Calvin neither allowed women to serve as deaconesses nor favored their participation in city government, although his own wife was virtually his partner in the work of religious reform.

Under Calvin, Geneva was the focal point of an expanding network of reformers who carried his message as far afield as France, the Netherlands, England, Scotland, and even Hungary. With its strict morality and religious fervor, Geneva was the nerve center of a militant, determined Protestantism.

# The Radical Reformation

Although both the Lutheran and Reformed traditions appealed to Scripture as their authority and worked to restore the church to its original simplicity, as early as the mid-1520s radical critics expressed dissatisfaction with the extent and pace of reform. In their judgment, Luther and Zwingli had compromised their principles in order to win the support of the powerful. Most of the radical critics became known as Anabaptists ("Rebaptizers"), a group that quickly became an abomination to the propertied classes and the major religious groups.

## The Anabaptists

In 1523 Conrad Grebel (1498–1526), a follower of Zwingli and a member of a prominent patrician family in Zurich, became impatient with the slowness of reform. The following year he attacked Zwingli's view of baptism, insisting that the rite must be confined to believing adults as a mark of their spiritual rebirth. After a public debate in January 1525, the Zurich town council ruled in favor of Zwingli, but Grebel and his followers—the Swiss Brethren—refused to conform. For their defiance, they faced banishment or execution by drowning, a cruel parody of their baptismal practices and a poignant reminder of how intolerant some Protestants could be toward others. The Brethren rejected the traditional concept of a state church in favor of congregations composed of be-

lievers alone. Accepting the Lord's supper as a simple meal to commemorate Christ's death, they celebrated it in private homes. Of more concern to the landed classes, the Brethren insisted that pastors must be chosen by individual congregations and supported by voluntary gifts, not tithes. Because so many tithes were now paid directly to laymen rather than to the clergy, the Anabaptist call for voluntary tithing was viewed by both clergy and laity as an attack on property rights. Equally radical was the Brethren's insistence on separating from the evil world, which entailed a refusal to participate in civil government or military service, both of which involved the taking of life. They also declined to pay taxes for military purposes and rejected oaths, which traditionalists regarded as basic to the maintenance of law and order. In the eyes of the authorities, the Anabaptists were dangerous social revolutionaries, while religious leaders not only detested their theological views but also feared that the separation of church and state that the Anabaptists advocated would lead to the secularization of society.

# The Kingdom of Münster and Its Consequences

Initially the Anabaptists were not identified with any social group, but in the aftermath of the Peasants' Revolt in Germany they attracted large numbers of peasants and artisans. In 1534 the Anabaptists seized control of the German city of Münster, where they expelled or persecuted all who disagreed with them. Under the leadership of a charismatic Dutch tailor, John of Leiden, they founded a theocratic kingdom, based on the laws of the Old Testament. Polygamy was practiced, and John himself took 16 wives. Initially, an unmarried woman had to accept any marriage proposal, though female opposition finally became so intense that women were given the right to decline offers. A woman, however, could have only one husband and faced capital punishment for adultery. In Münster all property was held in common. Within the city walls there was wild anticipation that King John would soon rule the world in preparation for the second coming of Christ, but the rest of Europe was appalled. The armies of the Catholic bishop of Münster and the Protestant Philip of Hesse, acting together, recaptured the city in 1535, executed the Anabaptist leaders, and publicly displayed their bodies as a warning to others. The Münster fiasco intensified the persecution of Anabaptists throughout the Holy Roman Empire, which in 1529 had revived an old Byzantine law making rebaptism a capital offense. By the early 1600s, several thousand Anabaptists had been executed.

Persecution encouraged the migration of Anabaptists to other areas, particularly the Netherlands, Poland, Bohemia, and Moravia. Shunning the excesses of Münster, these groups distinguished themselves by their quiet piety and strict morality. The most prominent of these sects was the Mennonites, founded by Menno Simons (1496–1561), whose followers eventually spread as far as Russia and North America.

## Spiritualists and Rationalists

During the heady days of the early Reformation, a handful of radicals claimed to be prophets bearing special revelations from God. One of the most prominent was the revolutionary Thomas Müntzer (died 1525), who accepted only the authority of the Holy Spirit and endorsed the use of violence to advance the Gospel. Offering to raise 30 squads to slaughter the ungodly, Müntzer urged the elector Frederick to establish a new kingdom for the faithful. Exiled from Saxony, he preached social revolution in southern Germany and helped incite the Peasants' Revolt, during which he was executed. Spiritualists from Zwickau near the Bohemian border favored the slaughter of all the ungodly in Europe, whether at their own hands or by the Turks. In contrast to such men, Sebastian Franck (c. 1499–c. 1542) was an intellectual who rejected Lutherans and Anabaptists alike for their dogmatism. Repudiating the authority of the Bible, he argued for a religion based entirely on the inner life of the Spirit and free from all dogma and sacraments.

Whereas the Spiritualists were essentially mystics, another group of Protestant radicals advocated a religion that was predominantly rational and ethical. Distinguishing themselves by their rejection of the Trinity, they criticized predestination and original sin and favored religious toleration. In addition to Servetus, the leading rationalists included Lelio Sozzini (1525–1562) and his nephew Faustus (1539–1604), whose followers, the Socinians, were found primarily in Poland and England. There they helped prepare the foundation for seventeenth-century Deism, the ancestor of modern Unitarianism. One of the greatest literary works of the radical Reformation was Sebastian Castellio's *Concerning Heretics and Whether They Should Be Punished by the Sword of the Magistrate*. Castellio (1515–1563) condemned Calvin for supporting Servetus' execution and offered a ringing defense of religious toleration. To burn a heretic, he asserted, "is not to defend a doctrine, but to kill a man."[9] The legacy of the religious radicals was the concept of religious freedom, an idea slow to win acceptance because of the conviction that religious diversity led to the breakdown of the social and political order.

## The English Reformation

In contrast to the reform movements instigated by Luther, Zwingli, and Calvin, the Reformation in England was fundamentally an act of state rather than the work of a religious leader. The relative ease with which the break with Rome was accomplished owed much to widespread dissatisfaction with the Catholic church and to the work of early reform movements. Popular hostility toward the clergy had grown because of their tithes and fees, and many people were disillusioned by priestly ignorance and immorality. Animosity was particularly strong among the Lollards, the underground group whose radical views, inherited from John Wyclif in the fourteenth century, were spread by itinerant cloth workers. Many Lollards embraced Lutheran ideas in the 1520s, and their literature was published by Protestants to demonstrate that their own pleas for reform were firmly rooted in the English past. Lutheran cells were formed at Oxford and Cambridge, and from them Protestant theology began to infiltrate the clergy. In London a covert group of merchants known as the Christian Brethren spread the Protestant message, which they had learned as traders on the Continent. With their support, William Tyndale (c. 1492–1536) translated the New Testament and the Pentateuch into English, with marginal notes that stridently attacked the papacy and the Catholic priesthood. Many early Protestant leaders in England had been educated as humanists and were deeply influenced by Erasmus. Well before the Reformation, English humanists such as John Colet had made strong pleas for reform, unwittingly helping prepare the way for the break with Rome.

## The King's "Great Matter"

The state's decision to reject papal authority was not made primarily for religious reasons. The strong-willed King Henry VIII (1509–1547), the second of the Tudor rulers, had been married since 1509 to Catherine of Aragon, by whom he had one surviving child, Princess Mary. The prospect of leaving the new dynasty in a woman's hands raised fears of another dynastic struggle like the fifteenth-century Wars of the Roses. The fact that Henry had become infatuated with Anne Boleyn, a lady of the court, contributed to his decision to seek a new wife and produce a male heir. But to marry Anne required a church-approved annulment of his marriage to Catherine. The latter's position was strengthened by the fact that the army of her nephew, Emperor Charles V, controlled Rome in 1527 and temporarily held the pope prisoner. Unable to act freely, Clement VII delayed the annulment hearings. Exasperated, Henry summoned Parliament in 1529 to bring pressure on the pope, correctly anticipating that it would demand reforms. But the pope remained unresponsive.

Henry cowed the English clergy by threatening to punish them for enforcing papal authority in the church courts. Giving in, they recognized the king as head of

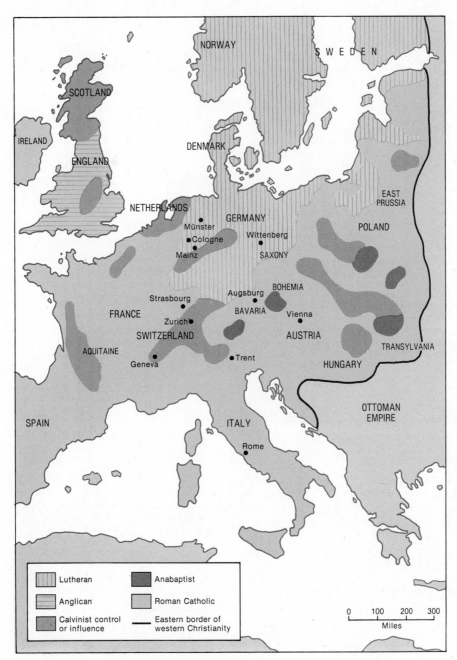

**17.1** *The Division of Christendom, c. 1550*

the English church "as far as the law of Christ allowed." Under the leadership of Henry's new adviser, Thomas Cromwell (1485–1540), a friend of the English Lutherans, Parliament renewed its complaints against religious abuses. When Henry learned in January 1533 that Anne was pregnant, he secretly married her without waiting to resolve the status of his marriage to Catherine. In March, Parliament passed the Act in Restraint of Appeals, drafted largely by Cromwell, which prohibited legal appeals to Rome without royal permission. Asserting that "this realm of England is an empire," the act affirmed the country's legal independence of all foreign authority. Two months later the new archbishop of Canterbury, the Protestant Thomas Cranmer (1489–1556), moved the Convocation of the Clergy to declare Henry's marriage to Catherine null and void, and on June 1 Anne

**Henry VIII of England. [National Portrait Gallery, London]**

low, with a banquet and a joust. Four months later Anne was executed on trumped-up charges of adultery and incest with her brother. In reality, Henry could forgive neither her arrogance nor her failure to bear him a son.

Although Henry generally remained loyal to Catholic dogma, Protestants welcomed certain changes in the Church of England. An officially approved translation of the Bible in English by Miles Coverdale was published in 1535, and the following year Cromwell ordered that every church have a copy of the Bible in English and Latin. Between 1536 and 1540 the monasteries were dissolved and their properties confiscated by the crown. Some of the land was sold, enabling the lesser aristocracy (or gentry) in particular to expand their holdings. Because the monasteries had been centers of education and hospitality, the social effects of their dissolution were profound. Although some theological concessions were temporarily made to Protestants for political reasons, the king's conservative religious ideals were reflected in the Six Articles of 1539. Except for papal supremacy, they supported Catholic teachings on the sacraments, the celibacy of priests, and vows of chastity. The religious position of the Church of England in this period is best described as Henrician Catholicism, or Catholicism without monastic institutions or obedience to Rome.

Boleyn was crowned queen of England. Three months later she gave birth to Princess Elizabeth.

## Royal Supremacy

Most of the changes during Henry's reign involved the seizure of papal authority by the crown rather than theological issues as on the Continent. Church funds previously paid to Rome now went to the English government. The king received the right to make appointments to all major church offices, as well as the final authority for all ecclesiastical legislation. In the 1534 Act of Supremacy, Parliament recognized the king as "the only supreme head in earth of the Church of England." To deny him this title was treason. An act of succession recognized the children of Henry and Anne as heirs to the throne. For refusing to accept the succession and the royal supremacy in the church, Sir Thomas More and Bishop John Fisher, Catherine's outspoken supporter, were executed in 1535. Catherine remained loyal to the Catholic faith until her death in 1536—an event celebrated by Henry and Anne, both brightly clad in yel-

## The Edwardian Reformation

After Henry's death in 1547, the Church of England became increasingly Protestant. Henry was succeeded by his 9-year-old son, Edward VI (1547–1553), whose mother, Jane Seymour, Henry's third queen, had died after childbirth. Real power rested at first in the hands of the king's uncle, Edward Seymour, duke of Somerset. Under his direction Parliament repealed the Six Articles and dissolved the chantries, which were endowments to support priests who said masses for the dead. In 1549 Parliament passed an act of uniformity requiring all ministers to use the *Book of Common Prayer*, an English liturgy prepared by Archbishop Cranmer. When Somerset failed to suppress rioting peasants in 1549, he was overthrown by John Dudley, soon to be duke of Northumberland. Under his leadership the English church became even more firmly Protestant. A second act of uniformity required clergy and laity alike to use the revised *Book of Common Prayer*, which simplified the worship service and required ministers to wear only a plain black robe and a white vestment. Communion tables replaced stone altars, and confession was made by the congregation as a whole rather than individually to priests. Royal approval was also given to the Forty-two Articles, a Protestant confession of faith.

The Edwardian Reformation, however, was secure only as long as the king lived, for the heir apparent, Prin-

THE REFORMATION

| Protestants | Catholics | Cultural highlights |
|---|---|---|
| | Oratory of Divine Love (1494) | |
| | | More's *Utopia* (1516) |
| | | Erasmus' Greek New Testament (1516) |
| Luther's Ninety-five Theses (1517) | | |
| Founding of the Anabaptists (1523–1524) | | Grünewald (c. 1460–1528) |
| | Capuchins (1528) | Dürer (1471–1528) |
| | Barnabites (1530) | |
| | Somaschi (1532) | Michelangelo's *Last Judgment* (1532–1541) |
| Act of Supremacy, England (1534) | | |
| Kingdom of Münster (1534–1535) | Ursulines (1535) | |
| Calvin returns to Geneva (1541) | Society of Jesus (1540) | Holbein (1497–1543) |
| First *Book of Common Prayer* (1549) | Council of Trent (1545–1563) | |
| Peace of Augsburg (1555) | Marian reaction in England (1553–1558) | |
| Scottish Reformation (1560) | | |
| Elizabethan settlement (1559–1563) | | Palestrina (c. 1525–1594) |

cess Mary, was a determined Catholic. As Edward lay dying of tuberculosis in 1553, Northumberland tried desperately to save himself by preventing Mary from becoming queen. He persuaded Edward to name as his heir Lady Jane Grey, Northumberland's daughter-in-law and a great-granddaughter of Henry VII. But when Edward died in July, the English people overwhelmingly supported Mary as the rightful ruler. As Northumberland was brought into London following his capture, "all the streets [were] full of people, which cursed him, and called him traitor without measure."[10] A month later he died on the scaffold as the new queen prepared to introduce the Counter-Reformation, already under way on the Continent.

## The Catholic Revival: A Church Militant

The spirit of reform prevailed within the Catholic church as well as outside it, partly stimulated by the shock of the Protestant secession. The demands for change were matched by a determination to maintain the ideals of the medieval church. Conciliarism, the major source for reform in the late medieval period, had lost much of its force by the early 1500s. The Fifth Lateran Council (1512–1517), meeting in Rome, adopted no significant reforms. Efforts to improve the church, however, were under way in various states, including France, where Cardinal Georges d'Amboise (died 1510) imposed more effective discipline on the monasteries. In Spain, Queen Isabella's confessor, Cardinal Francisco Ximenes (c. 1436–1517), the archbishop of Toledo, improved ed-

ucation for the clergy, placed tighter controls on errant priests and monks, and encouraged humanist learning at the new University of Alcala.

A characteristic feature of Catholic revival was the founding of new organizations, beginning with the Oratory of Divine Love, established in Italy in 1494. Composed of clergy and laity, its members emphasized piety and charitable work for the poor and the sick. The Capuchins (1528), inspired by Francis of Assisi's ideal of poverty, devoted themselves to helping the common people. Other new orders, such as the Barnabites (1530) and the Somaschi (1532), focused on the problems of poverty and disease. The Somaschi, who founded hospitals and orphanages, also took an interest in the plight of prostitutes. The role of women in the Catholic revival is reflected in the Congregation of the Holy Angels (an auxiliary of the Barnabites), the Capucines (the female counterpart of the Capuchins), and the Ursulines, who specialized in educating young women.

## ❦ ANGELA MERICI AND THE URSULINES

The new sense of spiritual dedication that was reviving the Catholic church is exemplified in the life of Angela Merici, the daughter of a minor country gentleman. Born in 1474 in the republic of Venice, she was orphaned at age 10. As a young woman she was deeply influenced by the piety of local nuns and recluses as well as by the devotional activities of the Oratory of Divine Love. She took part as a layperson in the work of the Franciscans but did not take formal vows. Merici devoted herself to charitable work, helping the sick and the poor as well as teaching girls. While praying in the fields in 1506, she had a vision in which she was promised that "before your death, you will found a society of virgins." Ten years later she established a school for girls, primarily to teach the catechism.

At Brescia in 1531, Merici, now partially blind, recruited a dozen young women as teachers, and in 1535, when the group had grown to 28, she founded the Company of St. Ursula (Ursulines). Like the Franciscans, she rejected the concept of a cloistered order in favor of social activism, insisting that her religious sisters live and work among the people. Because of the novelty of this idea, the pope did not approve her order until 1565, after her death. Although no formal vows were required, Merici's rule demanded poverty, chastity, and obedience. Each sister was allowed to live in her own home and work with her family and neighbors. Until her death in 1540, she served as superior general of the Ursulines. Her *Testament and Souvenirs* expresses her ideals, especially gentleness and concern for others. Her movement had more than doubled in size by 1536 and became the greatest teaching order for women.

## Ignatius of Loyola and the Jesuit Order

The most influential of the new orders, the Society of Jesus, was founded by Ignatius of Loyola (1491–1556), the son of a Basque nobleman. A French cannonball shattered his right leg as he fought in Charles V's army at Pamplona in 1521. Profoundly influenced during his recovery by biographies of Francis and Dominic, he dedicated his life to serving the Virgin Mary. After a period of meditation in monasteries and study at the Universities of Alcala and Paris, Ignatius and a small band of disciples vowed to go to the Holy Land to convert Muslims. Finding the way to Palestine blocked by fighting between the Venetians and the Turks, they preached instead to the Italians. Ignatius' constitution for a new order, which reflected the trend toward centralized government in this period, was approved by Pope Paul III in 1540. Governed by a general directly responsible to the pope, the order was highly structured in order to supervise its active, mobile apostles. Although the traditional monastic vows were required, Jesuits were exempt from the typical duties of monks, such as reciting the church offices. The society's purpose was to advance and defend the Catholic faith.

The Jesuits concentrated on four activities. To persuade secular rulers to suppress Protestantism, they served as confessors and propagandists in Catholic courts. To keep the masses loyal to the Catholic faith, the Jesuits stressed confession, achieving some popularity because of their principle that there is "no sin without specific intent" to commit it. The society was partic-

Ignatius of Loyola, founder of the Society of Jesus. This is an engraved copy of a portrait originally painted in 1584 by Alonzo Sanchez Coello under the direction of a former associate of Ignatius'. [SEF/Art Resource]

ularly successful in its efforts to improve education, especially at the secondary level, where strict discipline and obedience to the church were emphasized. After surveying the educational facilities of the church and finding the secondary schools wanting, the Jesuits launched a program to build new schools (or "colleges"). By 1640 there were approximately 520 of these secondary schools in Europe, teaching some 150,000 boys. Up to half of the students were the children of peasants and artisans, who paid no tuition. The curriculum was based on the *Ratio studiorum* ("plan of studies"), which sought to combine the best of humanist teaching with traditional Catholic beliefs, and to instill in students a strong sense of obedience to the church. Instruction was in Latin and occasionally Greek but not the vernacular. Classical texts were edited to remove "pagan" elements, and explanatory notes interpreted everything from the Catholic perspective. To motivate learning, competition was encouraged: student against student, class against class, school against school. Jesuit schools were highly successful in providing church and state with educated officials and in helping check the expansion of Protestantism.

Finally, the Jesuits, determined to carry their message throughout the world, dispatched missions to Asia,

Africa, and North and South America as well as to such European states as England and Poland. Their leading missionary, Francis Xavier (1506–1552), who preached in India, Ceylon, the Moluccas, and Japan, died half frozen and starved as he prepared to enter China. By 1557 the Jesuits had missions in the Congo, Morocco, and Ethiopia, and they also worked in Florida (1566) and Virginia (1570) as well as Brazil, Peru, and Mexico. Late in the century the Jesuit Matteo Ricci established the nucleus of a Christian church in China at Peking (see Chapter 18), and another Jesuit, Benedict de Goes, disguised as an Armenian merchant, crossed the Khyber Pass and traveled through Afghanistan and Turkistan to China. Between 1581 and 1712 no fewer than 376 Jesuits sailed for China, although a third of them died en route. The most influential Jesuit missionary to India, Roberto de Nobili (1577–1656), who was knowledgeable in Sanskrit and the Vedas, permitted his converts to retain some of their cultural traditions, such as the celebration of Hindu feasts, as long as they embraced the fundamental principles of Christianity. At times he even wore the clothing of a Brahman ascetic. This willingness to tolerate non-Western cultures coupled with their knowledge of Western science and technology helped make the Jesuits very effective missionaries.

The religious experience of Ignatius provided the basis for his *Spiritual Exercises*, a handbook to develop self-mastery and spiritual discipline. The *Exercises* call for a period of intense self-examination and meditation, at the culmination of which the disciple experiences a sense of unity with God through the surrender of mind and will. In contrast to Protestantism, which stressed the importance of the individual conscience, Ignatius emphasized the church's authority: "To be right in everything, we ought always to hold that the white which I see, is black, if the Hierarchical Church so decides it."[11] This unqualified devotion and obedience to the church was at the heart of the Catholic revival.

## The Council of Trent and the Inquisition

Catholic reformers were anxious for the papacy to convene a general council to deal with the Protestant challenge and make needed changes, but the popes, fearing a loss of their power and preoccupied with political concerns, were slow to act. Pope Paul III, a humanist who appointed a number of reformers to the College of Cardinals and even offered a cardinal's hat to Erasmus, finally yielded to pressure from Charles V and summoned a council. Convened in 1545 at Trent in northern Italy,

## ◉ Obedience: The View of Ignatius ◉

*One of the dominant features of Ignatius of Loyola's thought was his emphasis on discipline and order. In this 1553 letter to Jesuits in Portugal, he returns to the theme of obedience that was fundamental to his Spiritual Exercises.*

We may the more readily allow other religious orders to surpass us in the matter of fasting, watching, and other austerities in their manner of living, which all of them devoutly practice. . . . But in the purity and perfection of obedience and the surrender of our will and judgment, it is my warmest wish, beloved brethren, to see those who serve God in this Society signalize themselves. . . .

Make it a practice to recognize Christ our Lord in any superior you may have, and with all devotion, reverence and obey the Divine Majesty in him. This will seem the less surprising if you take note that St. Paul bids us obey our civil and pagan superiors as we would Christ, from whom flows all legitimate authority. . . .

He who wishes to make an absolutely complete offering of himself must in addition to his will include his understanding, which is the . . . highest degree of obedience. The result will be that he not only identifies his will with that of the superior, but even his thought, and submits his own judgment to the superior's judgment, to the extent that a devout will can bend the understanding.

*Source:* Ignatius of Loyola, *St. Ignatius' Own Story: As Told to Luis González de Cámara, with a Sampling of His Letters,* trans. W. J. Young (Chicago: Regnery, 1956), pp. 111–115 passim.

**The Council of Trent in session, 1562–1563. The cardinals and papal legates sit prominently on the left, flanked by archbishops on their right. [British Museum]**

it met intermittently until 1563 and was dominated by conservative Italians loyal to the papacy, although in the early stages there was also some sympathy for the Protestants. Neither the laity nor the lower clergy were allowed to vote at its sessions.

In matters of theology, the council firmly reasserted all the doctrines challenged by the Protestants. On the crucial issue of authority, it reaffirmed the importance of both Scripture and tradition, "with an equal pious devotion and reverence" to each. It recognized the Latin Vulgate as the official version of the Bible, with the church having the sole right to determine its "true sense and interpretation." The doctrine of salvation by faith and good works was asserted. All seven sacraments

were acknowledged, and the wine in the Eucharist was reserved for the clergy alone. The council reaffirmed the central Catholic doctrine of transubstantiation—the belief that the substance of the bread and wine miraculously become the body and blood of Christ in the Eucharist—thereby rejecting the Lutheran doctrine that the bread and wine coexist with Christ's body and blood and the Reformed emphasis on the spiritual presence alone of Christ in the Lord's supper. It insisted on celibacy for the clergy, reaffirmed the invocation of saints and the veneration of relics, and refused to abolish indulgences and the doctrine of purgatory, despite their role in igniting the Protestant revolt. The theological interpretation of the Thomists, the disciples of Thomas

Aquinas, prevailed, and the council therefore marked the triumph of the tradition-minded scholastics over the reforming Catholic humanists in the church.

In addition to settling the church's theology, the council reformed church discipline. Henceforth, every bishop, unless he had a papal dispensation, was required to live in his diocese and supervise his clergy. To improve the education of priests, a seminary was to be established in every diocese. Selling ecclesiastical offices and appointing relatives to church positions were condemned. Such reforms brought a new spirit of determination to the church in its struggle with Protestantism.

As Catholicism regained the offensive, the church launched the Roman Inquisition in 1542 at the urging of Loyola and Giampietro Cardinal Caraffa (1476–1559). As head of the Inquisition, Caraffa directed a commission of six cardinals empowered under Roman law to use torture, accept hearsay evidence, and keep the accused ignorant of the charges against them. The Inquisition was especially effective in stamping out Protestantism in Italy, but it also stifled intellectual life and even closed down the University of Modena in 1546. One of the Inquisition's most notable victims was the Dominican monk Giordano Bruno, who was burned at the stake in Rome in 1600 for unorthodox views about God and for teaching that the universe is infinite and contains innumerable suns and planets like our own (see Chapter 24). The Sacred Congregation of the Holy Office, which oversaw the Inquisition, also imposed its *Index of Prohibited Books*. Among the works it banned were Erasmus' writings, vernacular translations of the Bible, Boccaccio's *Decameron*, and *The Prince* by Niccolò Machiavelli. To Protestants, the *Index* and the Inquisition were further proof that Catholicism was the church of the Antichrist, as Luther had argued.

# The Counter-Reformation in England

Mary Tudor's accession to the English throne in 1553 provided the Catholics with a golden opportunity to recover an entire state that had been lost to Protestantism. Following the advice of her cousin Charles V to proceed slowly, she began by having Parliament repeal the religious legislation of Edward VI's reign. This action, coupled with the announcement of her impending marriage to Charles V's son, Philip of Spain, provoked a Protestant rebellion led by Sir Thomas Wyatt. After the revolt was crushed, Parliament repealed the antipapal legislation of Henry VIII, and in November 1554 England was officially reconciled to the Catholic church. Most of the lands previously confiscated from the church were not, however, returned. Prodded by the zealous queen, Parliament also revived a fifteenth-century law allowing the

church to condemn and the state to burn heretics. Nearly 300 Protestants died in the flames, most of them laborers and more than 50 of them women. The most famous victim, former Archbishop Cranmer, had been coerced into retracting his Protestant beliefs, but as the fire was lit his courage returned: holding the hand that had signed the retraction in the flames, he reaffirmed his Protestantism. Accounts of the martyrs hardened Protestant commitments. The words of the martyred Hugh Latimer were prophetic: "We shall this day light such a candle, by God's grace, in England, as I trust shall never be put out."[12]

Faced with persecution, some 800 Protestants fled to the Continent, where most settled in such Reformed cities as Geneva, Zurich, Strasbourg, and Frankfurt. In exile, John Foxe collected material for his *Acts and Monuments*, an immensely popular history of Christian martyrs from the early church to his own day. Other exiles prepared a new edition of the Bible in English—the Geneva version (1560)—complete with marginal notes attacking Catholicism and advocating Calvinism. Until it was finally supplanted by the Authorized (King James) version in the next century, the Geneva Bible was probably the most influential book in England. Three other exiles—John Ponet, John Knox, and Christopher Goodman—made lasting contributions to political theory by advocating the revolutionary idea that common people have the right to overthrow tyrannical and idolatrous rulers, a theory also espoused by the Jesuits against Protestant sovereigns. Knox, however, reflected traditional thinking in *The First Blast of the Trumpet Against the Monstrous Regiment of Women*, which argued that women normally have no right to govern.

The Counter-Reformation failed in England largely because of the intense revulsion the burnings caused and also because Mary had no Catholic heir. The unpopularity of Mary's marriage to Philip, symbol of Catholic orthodoxy and Spanish imperialism, also contributed to the failure. If Mary had been able to give birth to the heir she desperately wanted, Catholicism might have regained its dominance in England, but the accession in 1558 of Elizabeth I, Mary's half sister and the daughter of Anne Boleyn, destroyed the English Counter-Reformation. The foundation of the Elizabethan religious settlement was an act of supremacy that made Elizabeth supreme governor of the church and an act of uniformity that required the use of the *Book of Common Prayer*. In 1563 the queen issued the Thirty-nine Articles, a revised version of Edward VI's doctrinal statement. England thus moved firmly into the Protestant orbit, followed by Scotland under the leadership of John Knox in 1560. Throughout Catholic Europe, however, Catholicism was successfully reinvigorated by its new orders—especially the Society of Jesus—and by the reforms of the Council of Trent.

## The Reformation and the Jews

The repressive side of the Catholic Reformation had an immediate and negative impact on European Jews. They were less affected by the Protestant Reformation, in part because they had been evicted from Geneva in 1490, well before Calvin's era, as many had been from German cities. In the earliest stages of the Reformation, Luther expected the Jews to convert to his movement, but when they failed to do so, he became increasingly hostile toward them. Finally he insisted that the German princes deport them to Palestine or at least force them to return to agricultural occupations and prohibit them from practicing usury. Luther even demanded that Jewish books be confiscated and synagogues burned. In the course of the Catholic Reformation the plight of the Jews similarly worsened as the hitherto tolerant papal position was reversed. Beginning in 1553, the Talmud was publicly burned in Italy, and two years later Caraffa, now Pope Paul IV, issued a bull ordering that the Jews be segregated in their own quarter (the "ghetto"), which was to be enclosed with high walls and, at night, locked gates. Jews were banned from the professions, prohibited from employing Christian servants, refused the right to own real estate, and forced to wear yellow hats as a badge. Although the Jews were not expelled from the Papal States, they could live only in cities such as Rome and Avignon under close supervision. The ghetto concept gradually spread until it became a hallmark of European Jewish life.

As the persecution of the Jews intensified in Reformation Europe, substantial numbers migrated to Poland, where rulers such as Sigismund I (1506–1548) tolerated minorities. The number of Jews in Poland rose from 50,000 in 1500 to 500,000 in 1650. In some of the bigger towns, such as Cracow and Lublin, large ghettos developed. Polish Jews generally enjoyed far greater choice of occupation than Jews in western Europe, and they were permitted substantial self-government in matters involving Jewish law.

## The Witch-Hunt

In striking contrast to the idealism that characterized much of the Protestant movement and the Catholic revival, the Reformation helped spread a terrifying new wave of cruelty and popular hysteria. The age of spiritual renewal paradoxically contributed to the most extensive period of witchcraft persecutions in Western history, sparked in large measure by the breakdown of religious

An attack on the Jews of Frankfurt in 1614 illustrates the virulence of recurrent anti-Semitism in Europe. [Marburg/Art Resource]

unity. Belief in witches originated in ancient times, and the medieval church had organized those ideas into a systematic demonology. Witchcraft persecutions began in the context of the thirteenth-century crusades against the Albigensians and were revived by the papacy in 1484. Within two years a handbook, the *Malleus Maleficarum* ("The Hammer of the Wicked"), appeared with instructions for the discovery and interrogation of witches. Twenty-nine editions were published by 1669, testifying to the continuing interest in witchcraft.

## Reformers and Witches

At the heart of the witch-hunt was an unquestioned acceptance of the reality of the Devil and the pervasive effects of his influence in the world. Luther, for instance, claimed to have had repeated confrontations with Satan, many of which he described in anal terms. On one occasion he threatened to defecate in his pants and hang them around the Devil's neck to drive him away. In Protestant propaganda the pope became the personification of the Devil. Determined to win and hold the people's allegiance, the reformers intensified the belief in the widespread presence of satanic influence by repeatedly linking Catholicism with Satan. To Luther, monasticism was the Devil's "sweet latrine," and monks were attacked on the grounds that they had made a pact with Satan to obtain supernatural powers. For this reason, Luther believed that witches must be burned. In Geneva, Calvin appealed to the Bible (Exod. 22:18) as a divine sanction for the execution of witches. As Protestant preachers took their gospel of justification by faith into new areas of Europe, they carried with them demands for the persecution of witches. Lutherans introduced the witch-hunt to Denmark, northern Germany, and Bavaria, and Calvinists carried it to Scotland and Transylvania.

Catholic persecution of witches had begun, as we have seen, even before the Reformation. Protestant attempts to associate the papacy with Satan were countered by Catholic charges that Luther and his colleagues were tools of the Devil. Catholics also drew on late medieval demonology to justify their accusations of witchcraft. The persecution of witches increased as the intensity of religious hostility provoked by Catholics and Protestants grew. Persecution was especially vicious in areas, such as the Rhineland and Bavaria, that were re-

conquered from the Protestants. Chief among the Jesuits in this work was Peter Canisius (1521–1597), whose activities ranged from popular evangelism and the founding of Jesuit colleges to demands for the trial of witches. Witch burnings also followed in the wake of the Catholic recapture of Poland and Flanders, but in areas where Catholic uniformity was not effectively challenged, such as Italy and Spain, reported incidents of witchcraft were apparently fewer. Burning witches—like burning heretics—became a means of purging society of evil, of purifying the community while the reformers cleansed the church.

## Choosing the Victims

Although men as well as women could be accused as witches, most victims were female, probably because of the medieval notion that as the "weaker sex" they were more susceptible to the Devil's enticements. In England women were apparently accused more often than men because they were more likely to resist economic and social change. Of the 291 persons accused of witchcraft

---

### ◉ Women and Witchcraft ◉

*The popular handbook on witchcraft* Malleus Maleficarum *attempted to explain why so many women were accused of being witches. These deprecatory views of female inferiority and frailty were widespread in this period.*

As for the first question, why a greater number of witches is found in the fragile feminine sex than among men; it is indeed a fact that it were idle to contradict, since it is accredited by actual experience. . . .

For some learned men propound this reason; that there are three things in nature, the Tongue, an Ecclesiastic, and a Woman, which know no moderation in goodness or vice; and when they exceed the bounds of their condition they reach the greatest heights and the lowest depths of goodness and vice. . . .

Others again have propounded other reasons why there are more superstitious women found than men. And the first is, that they are more credulous; and since the chief aim of the devil is to corrupt faith, therefore he rather attacks them. . . .

The second reason is, that women are naturally more impressionable, and more ready to receive the influence of a disembodied spirit; and that when they use this quality well they are very good, but when they use it ill they are very evil.

The third reason is that they have slippery tongues, and are unable to conceal from their fellow-women those things which by evil arts they know; and, since they are weak, they find an easy and secret manner of vindicating themselves by witchcraft. . . .

To conclude. All witchcraft comes from carnal lust, which is in women insatiable.

*Source:* M. Summers, trans., *Malleus Maleficarum* (London: Rodker, 1928), pp. 41–44, 47.

in the English county of Essex in the period 1560 to 1680, fully 268 were women. Although many of the victims were stereotypical older widows or spinsters, younger women were often persecuted on the Continent, and there are cases of men and children suffering as well. To extract confessions, torture was often used (except in England), which led to more accusations and executions. Convicted witches were normally burned on the Continent and hanged in England. During the course of the witch-hunt, from the mid-sixteenth to the mid-seventeenth century, the number of victims probably reached 30,000. Only as religious passions waned, social upheaval receded, and a new spirit of rationalism took hold in the mid-1600s did the hunt die down.

Although the witchcraft trials were in large measure due to the breakdown of religious unity, religion alone cannot account for the full force of the persecutions. The social and economic changes that occurred in the West beginning in the fifteenth century created enormous tension, adding to the uncertainties and hostility resulting from the religious upheavals. A growing population, increasing poverty, devastating crop failures, and a rising crime rate made many people fearful and insecure. They continued to find scapegoats for their problems in social nonconformists—witches, Jews, and homosexuals, all of whom were persecuted. The link between them was sometimes explicit: Jews, for instance, were often accused of witchcraft. The witch-hunt was a result of credulity and uncertainty produced by widespread socioeconomic changes and group jealousies as well as passionate religious rivalries.

## The Cultural Impact of the Reformation

Protestantism had a significant impact on the arts in the areas it dominated, whereas the effects of the Catholic revival on culture were not generally visible until the late sixteenth century. Because Protestantism, especially the Reformed tradition, adopted a negative attitude toward the use of images and the veneration of saints, artists in Protestant regions found virtually no demand for religious statues and little interest in paintings for churches. They adapted by catering to the growing secular market for paintings and providing artwork for the burgeoning publishing industry. Similarly, although architects initially were not needed by Protestant leaders, who took over their churches from the Catholics, they found an outlet for their talents by designing palatial residences for princes and nobles. Henry VIII's palace at Hampton Court and Francis I's château at Chambord, both of

which reflected the growth of the centralized state, provided further impetus for such building. The Protestant rejection of the mass and the general simplification of the church service created a demand for suitable music, particularly hymns and psalm settings. The artistic impact of the Reformation on the Catholic church was more delayed, but its influence was strongly felt in the revival of the church after the Council of Trent and in the seventeenth-century movement known as the baroque (see Chapter 24).

## Grünewald, Dürer, and Holbein

The dilemma that the Reformation posed for the artist is illustrated by the career of Matthias Grünewald (c. 1460–1528), a German who became court painter for the archbishop of Mainz. A man of many talents in the Renaissance tradition, he supervised the rebuilding of the archbishop's castle. His major work, an altarpiece for the monastic church at Isenheim in Alsace, was finished on the eve of the Reformation. The massive altarpiece, with its flanking panels closed, depicts the anguish of Christ on the cross, his body discolored, his feet blackened, and his flesh lacerated. With the panels opened, however, the inner pane reveals the triumphant resurrected Christ bathed in the glow of an eerie red light. Other altar paintings followed for Catholic patrons. Yet Grünewald himself became a Lutheran, and in 1525 he participated in the Peasants' Revolt. The archbishop of Mainz dismissed him for his beliefs in 1526, and he spent his last years in Protestant Saxony. Only his skills as an artist and his willingness to paint traditional altarpieces had enabled him to obtain Catholic patronage despite his Lutheran sympathies.

Born in the German city of Nuremberg, Albrecht Dürer (1471–1528) became the greatest artist of the German Renaissance. Twice he went to Italy, bringing back to Germany an understanding of Renaissance ideals and techniques. He was one of the first non-Italian artists to acquire an international reputation and the first northern artist to provide a rich account of his life through self-portraits, personal correspondence, and a diary. In addition to his paintings, he produced superb woodcuts and engravings; his illustrations for books and his sale of prints to ordinary folk helped make him a wealthy man. His woodcut *The Four Horsemen of the Apocalypse*, done near the turn of the century, reflects the popular apocalyptic spirit of northern Europe.

A Christian humanist in the early 1500s, Dürer captured the spirit of his friend Erasmus' *Handbook of a Christian Knight* in his engraving *Knight, Death, and the Devil*. His own spiritual doubts were resolved when he embraced Lutheranism: "If God helps me to meet Mar-

**Albrecht Dürer's engraving *Knight, Death, and the Devil* (1513) reflects the confidence of humanists in the ability of the Christian faith to triumph over the enemies of humankind. [Museum of Fine Arts, Boston]**

tin Luther," he wrote in 1520, "I shall carefully draw his portrait and engrave it on copper as a lasting remembrance of this Christian who helped me out of great distress."[13] After his conversion, his style became more austere. His engraving of the Last Supper and his painting of four apostles (John, Peter, Paul, and Mark) reveal the simple style of his Protestant years. Quotations from Luther's German New Testament appear on the twin frames of *The Four Apostles*. Like Grünewald, Dürer continued to accept commissions from Catholic patrons after his conversion, although he hoped to establish a distinctively Protestant tradition of monumental art.

The son of an Augsburg painter, Hans Holbein the Younger (1497–1543) achieved prominence as the greatest portrait painter of the sixteenth century. Like Dürer, he was a friend of Erasmus (whose portrait is one of Holbein's masterpieces) as well as a book illustrator. Holbein settled in Basel, but when the Protestant reform created a hostile atmosphere for artists there, Erasmus recommended him to Sir Thomas More in

England. Henry VIII commissioned some of his most famous portraits, including those of the king himself and of three of his six wives, Anne Boleyn, Jane Seymour, and Anne of Cleves. Among Holbein's most fascinating works are 41 woodcuts depicting the late medieval "dance of death" and a series of drawings satirizing abuses in the Catholic church. Holbein died of the plague in 1543, but his influence on English portraiture continued for decades.

## Music and the Reformation

Although Protestant reformers repudiated the ornate polyphonic masses of the late medieval period, they retained music in the worship service. To Luther, music was "an endowment and a gift of God" that made people cheerful and chased away the Devil. Luther himself composed at least eight hymns, including the still popular "A Mighty Fortress Is Our God," and wrote sacred texts for German folk tunes. A Lutheran hymnal appeared in 1524. Although Zwingli's radical liturgical reform led to the destruction of church organs in Zurich, the year after his death a new organ was built in the minster and congregational singing was introduced. In Geneva, Calvin approved of psalm singing, and the practice quickly spread throughout the Reformed churches. One of the main objections to traditional religious music was the difficulty of understanding the words, which prompted English reformers in the 1560s to condemn most choral music. To most people, however, the simplification of religious music was a matter of regret:

> What shall we now do at church, since all the saints are taken away, since all the goodly sights we were wont to have, are gone, since we cannot hear the . . . chanting, and playing upon the organs, that we could before?[14]

The Catholics too were concerned that elaborate musical compositions were obscuring the sacred texts. The Council of Trent enacted regulations designed to encourage simplicity as well as to ban the use of secular themes in religious works. Polyphony, however, was not prohibited, so long as the words of the mass could be clearly understood. After the council, the Roman Curia urged an end to the use of lay singers as well as all instruments except the organ in religious services, but compliance was never complete. The challenge to blend simplicity with musical beauty was brilliantly met in the masses and motets, or sacred compositions, of the Italian composer Giovanni Palestrina (c. 1525–1594), whose works, often sung by unaccompanied choirs, manifest a sense of monumental grandeur. His work reflected the achievements of the Renaissance composers and remained the model for Catholic devotional writers down to the nineteenth century.

The changes in art and music that occurred in the first half of the sixteenth century reflect the effects of the religious convulsions that shook Europe. Henceforth the West was permanently divided in its religious beliefs and institutions. Yet out of that diversity eventually came the demands for freedom of religion and thought that are now fundamental to the concept of liberty. In other ways, too, the Reformation made significant contributions to the quality of Western life. Better education and improved care for the needy and the helpless were direct fruits of Protestant and Catholic idealism. But there was a dark side to the Reformation era, manifested in the religious wars to which the bellicose attitudes of Protestant and Catholic alike led. For more than a century the hostilities rooted in rival religious convictions parodied the love that was at the core of Christian teaching. This aspect of the Reformation was also reflected in brutal religious persecutions and in witchcraft trials and burnings. The Reformation era dramatically pitted the authority of religious institutions against the claims of individual conscience. Unresolved in the sixteenth century, this clash remained a source of tension well into modern times. The fervency of the religious debate had global implications as well, particularly as Catholic missionaries carried their message to Asia, Africa, and the Americas.

## Notes

1. Desiderius Erasmus, "The Paraclesis," in *Christian Humanism and the Reformation: Selected Writings*, ed. J. C. Olin (New York: Harper & Row, 1965), p. 97.
2. *The Correspondence of Erasmus*, trans. R. A. B. Mynors and D. F. S. Thompson, vol. 4 (Toronto: University of Toronto Press, 1977), p. 261.
3. Sir Thomas More, *Utopia*, trans. and ed. R. M. Adams (New York: Norton, 1975), p. 80.
4. R. H. Bainton, *Here I Stand: A Life of Martin Luther* (New York: Abingdon-Cokesbury, 1950), p. 78.
5. Martin Luther, "The Babylonian Captivity of the Church," in *Three Treatises* (Philadelphia: Muhlenberg Press, 1960), p. 248.
6. V. H. H. Green, *Luther and the Reformation* (New York: Capricorn Books, 1964), p. 98.
7. G. R. Potter, *Huldrych Zwingli* (London: Arnold, 1978), p. 24.
8. John Calvin, *Institutes of the Christian Religion*, ed. J. T. McNeill, trans. F. L. Battles, vol. 2. (Philadelphia: Westminster Press, 1960), pp. 922–923.
9. Sebastian Castellio, "Contra libellum Calvini," in *Concerning Heretics*, ed. R. H. Bainton (New York: Columbia University Press, 1935), p. 271.
10. C. Wriothesley, *A Chronicle of England During the Reigns of the Tudors, from A.D. 1485 to 1559*, vol. 2, ed. W. D. Hamilton (London: Camden Society, 1877), p. 91.
11. *The Spiritual Exercises of St. Ignatius*, trans. E. Mullan, ed. D. L. Fleming (St. Louis: Institute of Jesuit Sources, 1978), p. 234.
12. D. M. Loades, *The Oxford Martyrs* (London: Batsford, 1970), p. 220.
13. W. Strauss, ed., *The Complete Drawings of Albrecht Dürer*, vol. 4 (New York: Abaris Books, 1974), p. 1905.
14. R. L. Greaves, *Society and Religion in Elizabethan England* (Minneapolis: University of Minnesota Press, 1981), p. 458.

## Suggestions for Further Reading

Bainton, R. H. *Erasmus of Christendom*. New York: Scribner, 1969.
———. *Women of the Reformation in Germany and Italy*. Minneapolis: Augsburg, 1971.
Benesch, O. *The Art of the Renaissance in Northern Europe: Its Relation to the Contemporary Spiritual and Intellectual Movements*, rev. ed. London: Phaidon, 1965.
Bossy, J. *Christianity in the West, 1400–1700*. New York: Oxford University Press, 1985.
Bouwsma, W. J. *John Calvin: A Sixteenth-Century Portrait*. New York: Oxford University Press, 1987.
Caraman, P. *Ignatius Loyola: A Biography of the Founder of the Jesuits*. San Francisco: Harper, 1990.
Cohn, N. *The Pursuit of the Millennium*, rev. ed. New York: Oxford University Press, 1970.
Dickens, A. G. *The English Reformation*. London: Batsford, 1964.
Edwards, M. *Luther's Last Battles*. Ithaca, N.Y.: Cornell University Press, 1983.
Erikson, E. H. *Young Man Luther: A Study in Psychoanalysis and History*. New York: Norton, 1962.
Evennett, H. O. *The Spirit of the Counter-Reformation*. Notre Dame, Ind.: Notre Dame University Press, 1970.
Gäler, U. *Huldrych Zwingli: His Life and Work*, trans. R. Gritsch. Philadelphia: Fortress Press, 1986.
Ginzburg, C. *The Night Battles: Witchcraft and Agrarian Cults in the Sixteenth and Seventeenth Centuries*, trans. J. Tedeschi and A. Tedeschi. London: Routledge & Kegan Paul, 1983.
Grimm, H. *The Reformation Era, 1500–1650*, 2nd ed. New York: Macmillan, 1965.
Hsia, R. P. *Social Discipline in the Reformation*. London: Routledge & Kegan Paul, 1990.
Jensen, D. *Reformation Europe: Age of Reform and Revolution*. Lexington, Mass.: Heath, 1981.
Kingdon, R. M., ed. *Transition and Revolution: Problems and Issues of European Renaissance and Reformation History*. Minneapolis: Burgess, 1974.

Levack, B. P. *The Witch-Hunt in Early Modern Europe*. New York: Longman, 1987.

Loades, D. *Mary Tudor*. Oxford: Blackwell, 1989.

Martz, L. L. *Thomas More: The Search for the Inner Man*. New Haven, Conn.: Yale University Press, 1990.

McGrath, A. E. *The Intellectual Origins of the European Reformation*. Oxford: Blackwell, 1987.

Monter, E. W. *Calvin's Geneva*. New York: Wiley, 1967.

——. "Women in the Age of Reformation." *Becoming Visible: Women in European History*, ed. R. Bridenthal and C. Koonz. Boston: Houghton Mifflin, 1987.

Oberman, H. *Luther: Between God and the Devil*, trans. E. Walliser-Schwarzbart. New Haven, Conn.: Yale University Press, 1989.

——. *The Roots of Anti-Semitism in the Age of Renaissance and Reformation*, trans. J. I. Porter. Philadelphia: Fortress Press, 1984.

O'Connell, M. R. *The Counter-Reformation, 1559–1610*. New York: Harper & Row, 1974.

Ozment, S. E. *The Age of Reform (1250–1550): An Intellectual and Religious History of Late Medieval and Reformation Europe*. New Haven, Conn.: Yale University Press, 1980.

——. *The Reformation in the Cities: The Appeal of Protestantism to Sixteenth-Century Germany and Switzerland*. New Haven, Conn.: Yale University Press, 1975.

Potter, G. R. *Huldrych Zwingli*. London: Arnold, 1978.

Russell, P. A. *Lay Theology in the Reformation: Popular Pamphleteers in Southwest Germany, 1521–1525*. Cambridge: Cambridge University Press, 1986.

Scarisbrick, J. J. *The Reformation and the English People*. Oxford: Blackwell, 1984.

Skinner, Q. *The Foundations of Modern Political Thought*, Vol. 2: *The Age of Reformation*. Cambridge: Cambridge University Press, 1978.

Spitz, L. *The Religious Renaissance of the German Humanists*. Cambridge, Mass.: Harvard University Press, 1963.

Sprunger, K. "God's Powerful Army of the Weak: Anabaptist Women of the Radical Reformation." *Triumph over Silence: Women in Protestant History*, ed. R. L. Greaves. Westport, Conn.: Greenwood Press, 1985.

Strauss, G. *Luther's House of Learning: The Indoctrination of the Young in the German Reformation*. Baltimore: Johns Hopkins University Press, 1978.

Warnicke, R. M. *The Rise and Fall of Anne Boleyn: Family Politics at the Court of Henry VIII*. Cambridge: Cambridge University Press, 1989.

Williams, G. H. *The Radical Reformation*. Philadelphia: Westminster Press, 1962.

The illustration shows text in Gothic script reading:

-28-

oximo Kfebruio: jg 16. Als
ro her Jacob fugger kam: doch
C. Zenex jg19. verschriben wo

Mayland
Jnspruck
Nurmberg
Antorff
Lisbona

HER·IACOB·FV
reich·con

19.iax·8·mo:·8·tag

# The Age of European Discovery

The century and a half from 1450 to 1600 was one of the most extraordinary periods in Western history. The religious convulsions that shattered Christian unity and helped spur a global missionary effort occurred in the context of daring voyages of exploration and the beginnings of extensive trade that laid the foundation for a world economy. By 1450 the West, which had long lagged behind the more culturally and technologically sophisticated Indians and East Asians, developed the technological innovations, forms of commercial organization, and spiritual and materialistic ideals that enabled it to dominate much of the world by the nineteenth century. Mastery of the high seas was the key to global expansion, and the financial support and incentives for

The greatest of the merchant-capitalists was Jakob Fugger of Augsburg, shown here with his chief accountant in 1519. The signs on the walls identify Fugger branches in such cities as Lisbon, Cracow, Rome, and Innsbruck. [Herzog Anton Ulrich Museum, Brunswick, Germany]

this endeavor were made possible by the development of merchant capitalism and the increasing centralization of European states. The shift in trade routes from the Mediterranean to the Atlantic paved the way for Spain and Portugal, and later England, France, and the Netherlands, to become major powers.

## Europe on the Eve of Exploration

By the mid-fifteenth century Europe was on the road to recovery after the demographic catastrophe caused by the Black Death. One of the most crucial elements in the revival was a new and rapid growth in population. Demographers are still analyzing evidence, but the broad outlines of this growth are now well established. Between 1460 and 1620 the population of Europe nearly doubled, to approximately 100 million people. In some places, particularly the cities of western Europe, the rise was even sharper. Antwerp grew from 20,000 in 1440 to 100,000 in 1560, and Rome doubled its population, also to 100,000, between 1526 and 1600. This demographic growth increased the pressure on land and food as demand outstripped supply, thus spurring inflation while preventing many Europeans from rising above the subsistence level. Demographic recovery also meant the end of the period of improved conditions for the peasantry brought on by the Black Death in the mid-1300s. Simultaneously, however, the rising population provided not only an abundant labor supply but also economic incentives for agricultural improvements, commercial expansion, and overseas exploration and settlement. Population growth thus provided much of the impetus for economic expansion.

## Land Tenures and Agricultural Development

The devastation of the population by the Black Death and, in France, the Hundred Years' War (1337–1453) resulted in a shortage of peasant labor and a decrease in the amount of land under cultivation. For many peasants in western Europe the resulting demand for their services made it possible to escape the bonds of serfdom, trading the security of the old system for freedom and its attendant risks. Those who rented lands might profit by their industry, but they were also subject to potentially ruinous increases in rent. Whether the landlord or the tenant prospered was normally determined by the terms on which the land was held, as well as by tax obligations. Long-term leases, which some English

peasants enjoyed, were usually beneficial to the holders. Tenants in parts of France and western Germany whose tenure could be inherited might likewise prosper, for they were free to farm the land and sell the produce as they saw fit in return for a fixed payment to their landlords. In parts of Italy and France, short-term leases, which required the peasants to pay a fixed share of their crops to landlords, were common and helped the latter keep pace with rising food costs. Peasants without secure tenure, however, faced a troubled future in which the value of their services was as uncertain as their ability to continue working the land. Such tenants were at the mercy of landlords, who had to choose between opportunities for economic advancement and traditional obligations for their tenants' welfare.

Landed aristocrats whose tenants could inherit tenure or had long-term leases suffered a loss in real income as prices rose faster than rents. The lesser aristocracy often reacted by supporting wars and overseas conquest because of the prospect of new lands and financial gain. When the reconquest of the Iberian peninsula from the Moors was completed in 1492, the interest of the Spanish hidalgos, or lesser nobles, shifted to the New World. Other aristocrats, especially in France and England, shored up their finances by forming strategic alliances—typically by marriage—with rising merchant families, who shared their wealth in return for social prestige. Although some of the old nobility bitterly resented this infusion of new blood into their ranks, those who formed such alliances brought the landed elite into a closer relationship with the emerging world of overseas exploration and capitalistic investment.

Landlords whose tenants did not enjoy secure tenure had a wider range of options. This was especially the case in Spain, Portugal, southern Italy, parts of England, eastern Germany, and Poland. Some lords were content simply to raise rents at will—"rack-renters," they were called by bitter peasants and social critics. The more enterprising, however, took advantage of their power to embark on new economic ventures. In some instances this meant enclosing their lands, evicting their tenants, and converting from tillage to the pasturing of sheep. More often it meant an end to the old open-field system of farming, in which land was divided into strips and production was largely for the local market, in favor of larger, more productive farms that produced commercially for the wider marketplace. These new farms required the employment of agricultural hands, usually for subsistence wages, in place of peasants with a degree of personal attachment to the land. In many places agriculture thus became a commercial endeavor. This pattern was not equally distributed. It occurred often in England but rarely in Spain, where most hidalgos thought anything pertaining to business was beneath their dignity as warriors. In eastern Germany, Poland, and Russia landlords took advantage of western Europe's inability to feed itself by enclosing their lands in order to produce large quantities of grain for export. Unlike the English, they did not evict their peasants but forced them into gradual serfdom. The extent of western Europe's inability to feed itself in the face of rising population is amply demonstrated by the fact that approximately 6 million tons of grain had to be imported from the Baltic region between the mid-1500s and the mid-1600s.

The changes in the period from 1450 to 1600 caused substantial agrarian unrest in the English Midlands and eastern Europe, where large-scale commercial agriculture became commonplace, and throughout western Europe, where most peasants worked small plots and often worried about the security of their holdings. The Peasants' Revolt in 1524–1525, which Martin Luther denounced, was but one manifestation of this discontent. Commercial farming, however, was essential if the expanding population, particularly in the towns, was to be fed from the mid-sixteenth century on.

# Commercial Innovation and Expansion

The economic depression that gripped Europe in the fourteenth and early fifteenth centuries had been beneficial to the towns in certain respects. Despite urban riots, declining production caused by the drop in population, and war, the price of manufactured goods and wages for skilled workers generally rose while the cost of grain declined, thus increasing overall urban prosperity.

Merchants adapted to the new conditions by developing stronger organizations, diversifying their activities, and improving business procedures. Temporary partnerships, neither efficient nor conducive to expansion, were replaced by permanent companies, often formed around prominent families such as the Medici in Florence or the Fuggers in Augsburg. These firms were vulnerable during recessions when borrowers defaulted on their loans. Businessmen who survived learned to break up their firms into several independent partnerships. The importance of diversification was also recognized, as merchants engaged in a combination of commerce, banking, manufacturing, and sometimes overseas trade. Diversification encouraged the development of new industries: linens in Cambrai, iron in Liège, and weapons in Milan, among others. Economic growth was enhanced by more widespread use of double-entry bookkeeping, which uses parallel columns to balance credits and debits, and bills of exchange, which facilitate the transfer of large sums of money without risking the shipment of currency or bullion. These developments helped provide the capital accumulation that made exploration and the growth of overseas trade possible.

No family better illustrates the success of the new merchants than the Fuggers of Augsburg. By the time Jakob Fugger became a merchant in 1478, the family had been conducting business in the city for a century, mostly trading in the spices and silks that came through Venice. Jakob Fugger branched out into banking and mining, acquiring virtual control of the silver mines in the Tirol through his loans to the Habsburg emperors Maximilian I and Charles V. His company also dominated the copper supply in Europe by its acquisition of Hungarian mines and the construction of processing plants. To help repay his loans, Charles V gave the Fuggers a lease for the revenues of the Spanish orders of knighthood, which included the mercury monopoly in Spain. As bankers for the papacy, the firm handled the sale of the indulgences that Luther attacked in 1517. At his death in 1525, Jakob Fugger was the richest merchant-banker in Europe. By 1545 the Fugger firm had become the largest in Europe, a distinction that had belonged to the Medici in Florence a century earlier. The Fugger fortune, however, was more than five times as large as that of the Medici in 1440. Fugger trading posts extended in 1525 from the Mediterranean to the Baltic and from Cracow to Lisbon.

In the fifteenth century the western end of the trade in eastern spices and silks was still dominated by the Venetians. Goods from eastern Asia and the Moluccas (the Spice Islands) were taken to Malacca on the Malay peninsula, where they were transferred to Arab or Indian ships for transport to the Malabar coast of western India. From there the cargoes were taken either by way of the Persian Gulf and the Euphrates River to Beirut and Aleppo, Syria, or through the Red Sea and overland to Alexandria, Egypt. From Aleppo, Beirut, and Alexandria the Venetians dominated the trade as it passed into Europe.

The heart of this commerce was spices, a crucial item for the preparation of meat in an age that lacked refrigeration and for the general enhancement of foods that were otherwise monotonously dull or tainted. Fresh meat was commonly available only in the fall; during the rest of the year, most people who had beef ate the salted variety, which spices made more palatable. Spices were also used for medicines, perfumes, and incense in religious ceremonies. As population increased, the demand for spices intensified. Most of them came from southern and eastern Asia: pepper from India, the East Indies, and West Africa; cloves from the Moluccas; nutmeg and mace from the East Indies; cinnamon from Ceylon; and ginger from China and the Malabar coast. In addition to spices, there was also commerce in cotton cloth from India; silk, porcelain, and rhubarb (used medicinally) from China; and precious stones from India, Tibet, and Ceylon. Despite the enormous expense of conducting

---

## ◉ Fugger Money: The Price of Power ◉

*Merchants who loaned money to princes often ran a considerable risk,
but in addition to interest on loans they might acquire valuable favors
or monopolies. When, in April 1523, Jakob Fugger had to press Emperor
Charles V to repay his debts, the Habsburg ruler was reminded that he
owed his crown at least in part to Fugger money.*

Your Imperial Majesty doubtless knows how I and my kinsmen have ever hitherto been
disposed to serve the House of Austria in all loyalty to the furtherance of its well-being and
prosperity; wherefore, in order to be pleasing to your Majesty's grandsire, the late Emperor
Maximilian, and to gain for your Majesty the Roman crown, we have held ourselves
bounden to engage ourselves towards divers princes who placed their trust and reliance
upon myself and perchance on no man besides. We have, moreover, advanced to your
Majesty's agents for the same end a great sum of money, of which we ourselves have had
to raise a large part from our friends. It is well known that your Imperial Majesty could not
have gained the Roman crown save with mine aid, and I can prove the same by the writings of your Majesty's agents given by their own hands. In this matter I have not studied
mine own profit. For had I left the House of Austria and had been minded to further
France, I had obtained much money and property, such as was then offered to me. How
grave a disadvantage had in this case accrued to your Majesty and the House of Austria,
your Majesty's royal mind well knoweth.

*Source:* R. Ehrenberg, *Capital and Finance in the Age of the Renaissance: A Study of the Fuggers and Their
Connections,* trans. H. M. Lucas (New York: Harcourt, Brace, n.d.), p. 80.

---

this trade, including heavy tolls and the risk of lost cargoes, the profits were substantial. There was, then, ample incentive to discover new routes to the East, particularly since so much of the spice trade had fallen into the hands of the Muslims and was monopolized in the Mediterranean by the Venetians.

## The Search for New Trade Routes

The voyages of exploration that began in the late fifteenth century were impelled by crusading zeal against the Muslims and the quest for profit. However, they would not have been possible without various technological developments that were no less significant than the later inventions that led to the Industrial Revolution. Europeans already possessed some knowledge of Asia, thanks largely to the thirteenth-century travels of Franciscan missionaries and merchant-explorers such as Marco Polo. But only the sea afforded an opportunity to establish direct commercial links with the sources of spices, cotton, linen, and other goods. Direct sea contact

required improvements in ships, weapons, and navigational tools.

## Technology and Seafaring

Oars powered the galleys that plied the Mediterranean, giving them independence from the wind but requiring too much human labor to make arduous overseas voyages feasible. The galleys of Venice and Genoa could range the coast of the eastern Atlantic from Morocco to Flanders by the thirteenth century, but they were unsuited for exploration on the high seas and lacked the cargo space to make long voyages practicable. By 1400 the maritime states of Europe had developed large, broad-beamed ships powered primarily by square-rigged sails. Because such ponderous vessels generally had to sail with the wind, their maneuverability was severely restricted. By studying Arab ships that were capable of sailing the Indian Ocean and by borrowing multiple masts and sternpost rudders from the Chinese, the Portuguese developed a new vessel, a two- or three-masted caravel that combined square-rigged and lateen sails. Although the caravels were relatively small, the use of square-rigged sails, multiple masts, and stern-post

**This model of a four-masted caravel illustrates the triangular lateen sails. Caravels were not large vessels. [National Maritime Museum, Greenwich, England]**

rudders instead of awkward steering oars eventually made it possible to build ships large enough to make long voyages profitable and gave them greater speed when running with the wind, while the lateen sail (a smaller triangular sail somewhat like those on modern sailboats) permitted greater maneuverability and the capacity to sail at an angle to the wind instead of only with it. The masts were subsequently combined on larger vessels, including warships, and this became the norm in Europe. Most of the ships the Portuguese used to explore the West African coast were caravels, but beginning in the 1490s larger ships were also used.

The ability of the new vessels to sail the high seas rather than merely hug the shoreline created immediate navigational problems, but these were surmountable with instruments already at hand. The compass, originally Chinese but in use in the West by the thirteenth century, enabled a navigator to steer a course; the astrolabe facilitated the determination of latitude by measuring the approximate height of the sun and stars. However, the accuracy of the astrolabe and its successor, the quadrant, was adversely affected by the rolling of the ship. Portuguese navigators commonly hugged the coasts of Africa, landing every few days to use their instruments on shore.

Navigation was also aided by the increased sophistication of maritime charts known as *portolani*, prepared primarily from firsthand observations of sailors rather than by academic geographers. In the 1400s the work of geographers was dominated by Ptolemy's *Geography*, a book that dated from the second century A.D. Among its major errors were the invention of a southern continent that linked Africa and China, miscalculations concerning the size of the earth, and the notion that the Southern Hemisphere could not be navigated because of its excessive heat. The *portolani* mapped coastlines, including those of rivers and harbors. When the Portuguese explored the West African coast, they prepared similar charts, thereby adding to the fund of useful geographic knowledge.

In addition to developing better ships and navigational devices, Europeans acquired naval mastery by adapting artillery to their vessels and by gradually improving naval gunnery and the equally critical ability to maneuver their still small ships for maximum military advantage. This gave them a considerable advantage over Arab galleys and the often larger Chinese junks. Galleys relied on the traditional tactics of ramming or sailing alongside and boarding, while the cannon—developed first in twelfth-century China—though often heavier on Indian and Chinese ships than those on European vessels, were fixed and could not be effectively aimed. The Venetians pioneered the Western use of naval artillery in the fourteenth century, but the Portuguese were the first westerners to recognize the value of directing fire against an enemy's ships rather than the soldiers they carried. The capabilities of the new armaments were demonstrated when Vasco da Gama bombarded the Indian port of Calicut in 1502 and when the Portuguese destroyed an Indian fleet near Diu in western India in 1509, thereby asserting their right to sail the Indian Ocean.

# The Motives for Portuguese Expansion

Portuguese expansion was originally viewed in terms of a new crusade against the Muslims. In this regard the Portuguese hoped to establish an alliance with the legendary and mythical Prester (Elder) John, reputedly an enormously wealthy ruler whom some Europeans identified with the emperor of Ethiopia, others with the emperor of China. With his help they hoped to establish a new front in the centuries-old war against the "infidel." Their second goal, however, was to bypass Islamic middlemen by going directly to Guinea in West Africa for gold and pepper. Given the scarcity of bullion in Europe, the Portuguese hoped to increase their power by monopolizing the gold trade with the Ashanti and Fanti peoples of the Gold Coast. Initially, then, the voyages did not stem from a desire to discover new lands or a search for a direct route to the spices and wealth of eastern and southern Asia. On the contrary, Portugal's first move— the successful capture in 1415 of the Muslim city of Ceuta in northern Morocco—launched a program of African expansion. The Portuguese thus initiated the European attempt to expand Western military, commercial, and religious sway to regions far away from the Holy Land.

After 1415 Prince Henry the Navigator (1394–1460), younger son of King John I of Portugal, began dispatching frequent expeditions to explore the western coast of Africa. The knowledge his mariners gained was examined by the scientists and cartographers he patronized at Sagres on Cape St. Vincent in southwestern Portugal. As a result of these voyages, in the 1460s and 1470s Portugal established relations with the rulers of West Africa and constructed forts and trading stations. By 1500 the Portuguese had replaced the Muslims as the dominant commercial power in this region, and gold was now imported directly to Lisbon and Antwerp. In the fifteenth century the Portuguese also developed plantations on their islands in the eastern Atlantic, including São Tomé on the Gulf of Guinea, where they forced black slaves to grow sugarcane for export to Europe. Portuguese traders sent more than 1,000 slaves a year to Lisbon in the late 1400s, and by 1530 the traffic in slaves was more valuable than the shipments of gold. From the Africans the Portuguese also obtained ivory, ebony, and pepper in return for copper dishes and cheap fabrics and jewelry.

## Voyages of Exploration

Inspired by the work of Prince Henry, the Portuguese extended their vision to the East, particularly with the support of the prince's grandnephew, King John II (1481–1495), himself a geographer. In 1487 the voyages of exploration along the West African coast culminated when Bartholomeu Dias successfully sailed around the African cape, which was soon named "Good Hope." It was another decade, however, before Vasco da Gama had a fleet of four ships ready to strike out for India. Indian (and earlier Chinese) ships had long been trading across the Indian Ocean; hence da Gama was able to hire an Indian pilot in East Africa to guide him to India. Da Gama arrived at Calicut on the Malabar coast in May 1498 after a voyage of 10½ months from Lisbon. Neither the Hindu rulers nor the Arab merchants were particularly pleased to see the Portuguese, who represented a threat to their domination of the spice trade. For their part the Portuguese were unimpressed by the Indians: although "well disposed and apparently of mild temper," at first sight they seemed "covetous and ignorant." The women, however, were described, from a clearly racist perspective, as generally "ugly and of small stature."[1] Portuguese fleets, spurred on by the 3,000 percent profit realized by da Gama's voyage, sailed again in 1500 and 1502. The 1500 voyage was notable because Pedro Cabral, blown off course in a storm, sailed far enough westward to reach Brazil. Da Gama's bombardment of

Calicut on the 1502 voyage was a clear signal that European presence in the East could not be established without the threat of military power.

Although Prince Henry had been interested in exploring the Atlantic, the Portuguese missed the opportunity to sponsor the voyages that led to the European discovery of the Americas. As early as 1484 the Genoese sailor Christopher Columbus (1451–1506) tried unsuccessfully to persuade John II to support a westward expedition, the ultimate goal of which was to find a sea route to the Indies. Not until 1492 did Columbus find backing when the Spanish rulers Ferdinand and Isabella, concerned about recent Portuguese discoveries of the eastern sea route to Asia, gave him their support after the conquest of Granada. With a fleet of three ships, Columbus reached what were probably the Bahamas in October 1492 but mistakenly identified them as "the islands which are set down in the maps at the end of the Orient." Searching for Japan, which he estimated to be

**This recently discovered portrait of Christopher Columbus, attributed to the Spanish artist Pedro Berruguete, a contemporary, is believed to be the most accurate depiction of the explorer.**
[Grazia Neri Agency]

## ◉ The Amerindians: Columbus' View ◉

*In February 1493 Columbus wrote a fascinating letter recording what he and his crew saw when they arrived in the New World. To Columbus, of course, these were Asian islands that he thought would yield substantial quantities of gold, spices, cotton, and mastic (a resin). Most of the letter is devoted to a description of the "well-formed" Indians and their reaction to Columbus' men.*

In thirty-three days, I passed from the Canary Islands to the Indies. . . . There I found very many islands filled with people innumerable, and of them all I have taken possession for their highnesses, by proclamation made and with the royal standard unfurled, and no opposition was offered to me. . . .

Many times it has happened that I have sent ashore two or three men to some town to have speech, and countless people have come out to them, and as soon as they have seen my men approaching they have fled, even a father not waiting for his son. And this, not because ill has been done to anyone; on the contrary, at every point where I have been and have been able to have speech, I have given to them of all that I had, such as cloth and many other things, without receiving anything for it; but so they are, incurably timid. It is true that, after they have been reassured and have lost their fear, they are so guileless and so generous with all they possess, that no one would believe it who has not seen it. . . .

I took by force some of them, in order that they might learn and give me information of that which there is in those parts, and so it was that they soon understood us, and we them, either by speech or signs, and they have been very serviceable. I still take them with me, and they are always assured that I come from Heaven. . . . The others went running from house to house and to the neighboring towns, with loud cries of, "Come! Come to see the people from Heaven!"

*Source:* C. Jane, trans. and ed., *Select Documents Illustrating the Four Voyages of Columbus,* vol. 1 (London: Hakluyt Society, 1930), pp. 2, 8, 10.

only 2,400 miles west of Europe, he discovered Cuba and Hispaniola. From the latter he acquired a small quantity of gold and some jewelry by bartering with the natives, whom he called "Indians" (people of the Indies). Although he made three subsequent voyages, Columbus was convinced until his death in 1506 that he had discovered a sea route to eastern Asia. He carried some 1,500 settlers on his second voyage, but not until his third trip (1498) did the first Spanish women migrate to the New World.

For his exploits Columbus wanted to be honored as "the Admiral of the Ocean Sea," yet increasingly in his later years he also thought of himself as one who was divinely ordained to help Spain liberate the Holy Land. Reflecting the late medieval belief that the end of the world was imminent, he was convinced that God had made him "the messenger of the new heaven and the new earth of which he spoke in the Apocalypse of St. John . . . and he showed me the spot where to find it."[2]

When the Portuguese learned of Columbus' initial voyage, John II, unwilling to believe that the explorer had landed in eastern Asia, laid claim to the new territory on the grounds of their proximity to the Azores. Ferdinand and Isabella thereupon appealed to the pope, the Spaniard Alexander VI, who awarded the new discoveries to Spain. The pope also drew a line of demarcation approximately 300 miles west of the Azores and the Cape Verde Islands, giving Spain the rights of exploration to territory west of the line. In the Treaty of Tordesillas (1494), John II persuaded the Spanish to move the line some 800 miles farther west. Although no one apparently realized it at the time, Brazil fell into the Portuguese sphere of influence because of the change.

The significance of what Columbus had found became apparent only as other explorers made new findings. Sailing for England in 1497 and 1498, the Venetian John Cabot discovered the region of Cape Breton and Labrador, where he found an abundance of fish but no

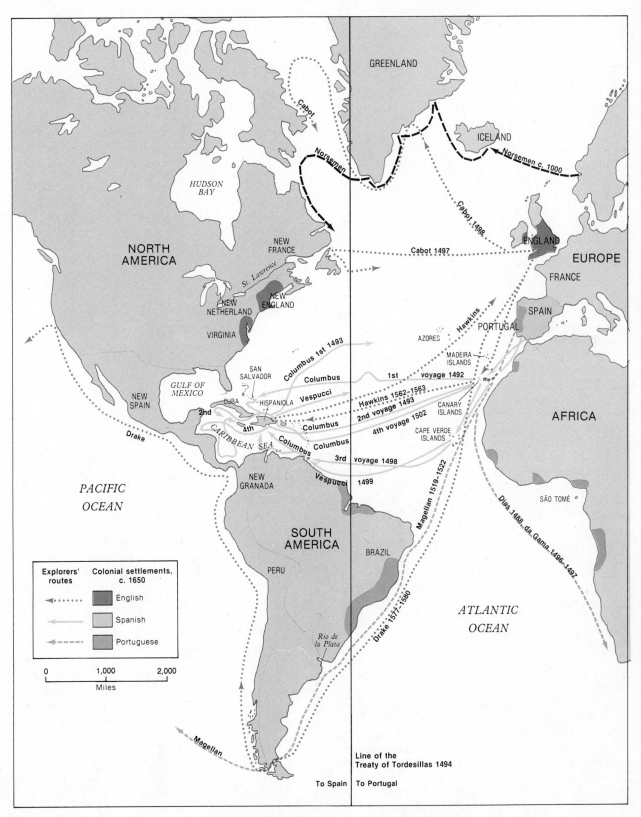

**18.1** *Voyages of Exploration to the Americas*

spices. Undeterred, Cabot was convinced that he had almost reached Japan, where he mistakenly thought "all the spices of the world have their origin, as well as the jewels."[3] It was not Cabot or Columbus who persuaded Europeans to accept the discovery of a new continent but the Florentine Amerigo Vespucci (1454–1512), a geographer who participated in Spanish and Portuguese voyages that extended from Cape Hatteras in modern North Carolina to the Rio de la Plata, the modern border between Argentina and Uruguay. His published letters popularized the idea of the New World, which came to be called America in his honor.

Accepting the presence of new continents did not dissuade European rulers from their belief in the viability of a western sea route to Asia by which the Portuguese monopoly of the spice trade could be broken. The key, they reasoned, was the discovery of a western passage. The Spaniard Vasco Núñez de Balboa's accidental sighting of the Pacific Ocean in 1513 as he was searching for gold on the isthmus of Panama stimulated interest. Ultimately, the Portuguese mariner Ferdinand Magellan (1480–1521) found a westward route in 1519 by taking a small Spanish fleet through the foggy and dangerous straits near the southern tip of South America that now bear his name. From there he sailed across the Pacific to the Philippines, where he and 40 of his men were killed. Magellan's navigator, Juan Sebastián del Cano, made his way with the two remaining caravels to the Moluccas, where he took on a load of cloves. Rather than risk the Straits of Magellan a second time, del Cano and a skeleton crew of 18 returned to Spain by way of the Indian Ocean and the Cape of Good Hope. The other ship was captured by the Portuguese as it attempted to sail back across the Pacific to Mexico. In this fashion Magellan's crew accomplished the first circumnavigation of the globe. It took three years to complete and imposed terrible hardships on the crews, who suffered from scurvy and were forced to eat rats, sawdust, and hides on the long passage across the Pacific.

For a time Spanish hopes to dominate the Moluccas quickened, but it soon became apparent that the Spaniards were no match for the Portuguese in the East. In 1529 Emperor Charles V, preoccupied by his wars with the French, sold Spain's rights in the Moluccas to Portugal. By that time Spain already had more than it could manage in America, although it retained the Philippines and began a 300-year link between Manila and its New World empire centered in Mexico. The Manila galleon, as it was called, carried yearly shipments of Mexican and Peruvian silver from Acapulco to Manila and Chinese silk, lacquer, and porcelain back to both New and Old Spain. Manila grew as an entrepôt, or intermediary center, for trade with China, and New World silver flowed into the Chinese market with major consequences for the Ming and Ch'ing dynasty economy and its growing commercialization. New World crops, especially potatoes and maize, also entered China via Manila and helped make possible subsequent major increases in population.

## Westerners in Asia and Africa

Portuguese and later Dutch settlements in Africa were incidental to the drive into Asia but served as way stations and provisioning bases along the sea route. Although the Portuguese extended the slave trade from West Africa to Brazil and sought a few other African goods, including gold, they did not penetrate inland and their coastal bases were few and scattered. Access to the interior was made more difficult by mangrove swamps, rain forests, or steep cliffs as well as by hostile African states, and the few Portuguese settlements were confined to tiny footholds on the coast or offshore islands. Their primary objective was indicated by the names they gave to their two main African bases. Algoa Bay ("to Goa," now Port Elizabeth in South Africa) and Delagoa Bay ("from Goa," now Maputo in Mozambique). Both names were derived from Goa, the administrative center of Portugal's Asian enterprise established in 1510 on the west coast of India and for which the African bases were to serve as provisioning stops.

## The Portuguese and Africa

The gold, and later the slaves, that the Portuguese obtained from scattered parts of the coasts of West and East Africa were important sources of profit, but the Portuguese established permanent African bases only in Angola on the southwest coast and at Algoa and Delagoa. In addition, they seized and occupied Madeira, the Azores, the Cape Verde Islands, and a few other offshore bases. Their presence greatly increased the slave trade, already thriving in Africa, by opening additional markets, especially in the New World. The Portuguese impact on several African societies went far beyond their relatively small power and numbers. They tried repeatedly to extend their power inland and on some occasions sacked and burned African towns or cities and pillaged overland trade routes. Although they could occasionally raid the interior, the Portuguese lacked the means for establishing control there, and their chief objective remained the Indies.

Cape Verde, where the city of Dakar now stands, was reached only after traversing the long, waterless desert coast of the northwest. Farther south, the kingdoms of Ghana and Benin offered trade at coastal ports, although the main commodities, gold and slaves, came from far-

**Situated on the Tagus River, Lisbon became one of Europe's busiest ports in the sixteenth century because of Portugal's trade with Africa and Asia. By the end of the century, however, much of this trade had shifted to Antwerp. [Granger Collection]**

ther inland. Much of the interior of West Africa was controlled by the empire of Mali, centered at Timbuktu on the upper Niger River. Gold and slaves moved from Timbuktu north across the great desert by camel caravans to the Mediterranean. The arrival of the Portuguese at the coast marked a shift of trade routes toward West African ports, from which European and New World markets could be reached more easily and cheaply. Timbuktu and the Mali empire slowly declined as the coastal centers of trade grew more rapidly in the centuries following the start of European expansion.

Persisting southward in their long search for a sea route to the Indies, the Portuguese found the dense rain forests of the Congo region impossible to penetrate. Inland navigation on the great river was blocked by falls and rapids, where the Congo tumbles off the steep escarpment that rises only a few miles from the coast around nearly the whole of Africa. The same problem hampered access from the east coast. Along the Congo coast, ivory and slaves were available to traders, but the coastal cultures were less highly developed than many of those inland, of which the Portuguese learned little except that they were the source of most of the trade goods. The coasts of Angola and Southwest Africa were part of the great southern desert and thus somewhat easier to penetrate, but also less rewarding. Having come this far south along the coast, however, the Portuguese badly needed a base for supply and refitting; they finally established one at Luanda in Angola by 1530. Once Bartholomeu Dias had made it around the Cape of Good Hope in 1488 and was followed a decade later by Vasco da Gama, the road to the Indies lay open and the bases in Mozambique on the east coast were more useful. The Portuguese traded and raided northward along the East African coast and for a time even tried to control Mombasa in what is now Kenya. Somali resis-

tance, as well as competition and opposition from the long-established Arab traders in coastal East Africa, soon ejected the Portuguese except as traders. The Europeans were resented for their arrogance and aggressiveness. Their efforts to move inland from Mozambique and to open the area to Jesuit missionaries were ultimately repelled by the African kingdom of Vakaranga, although the Europeans continued to buy slaves and other goods on the coast.

## Traders in Asia

For over two centuries after Europeans made contact with Asia by sea they remained insignificant on the Asian scene, a handful of people the natives dismissed as barbarians. At sea and along the Asian coasts they had the upper hand, but their power on land extended little beyond the range of their naval guns. The Portuguese and later the Dutch built a strong position in the spice trade, but in Asian commerce as a whole, even its seaborne component, their role was minor. They bought spices and a few other goods in preexisting markets at established ports, such as Calicut, where they had already been collected by Asian traders, and then hauled them to Europe. The Portuguese never and the Dutch only much later had an involvement in production, and both continued to compete as traders with numerous Chinese, Indian, Southeast Asian, and Arab entrepreneurs, who did the bulk of the assembly. Only in the transporting of Asian goods to Europe did they have a monopoly, and there the Portuguese in time faced intense competition from the Dutch and the English (see Chapter 19). As if to emphasize their role as ocean carriers with their improved ships for long voyages, the Portuguese developed a highly profitable trade between

China and Japan, carrying Chinese silks and porcelains (and some Southeast Asian spices) from the Canton area to Nagasaki in southwestern Japan and bringing back Japanese silver and copper for China. They, and later the English, also found profit in hauling Southeast Asian and Chinese goods to India and exchanging them for Indian cottons, which had an even larger and more eager market in Europe.

Recognizing their weakness on land or in trade competition with Asian and Arab merchants, Europeans built on their strength at sea by occupying and fortifying coastal footholds at key points along the sea routes. Ideally these were in areas on the fringes of the great Asian empires or where the local power was weak or could be persuaded to grant privileges in return for favors. The latter often included Western naval help against pirates, rebels, or small rival states. The Portuguese seized Goa on the Indian west coast in 1510 and soon made it into their major Asian base. The small area around the city was not then part of any powerful Indian state. The Portuguese saw they had little hope of controlling the larger ports farther south, such as Calicut, although they did establish some smaller bases elsewhere on the Malabar coast in the west. From Goa, however, their ships could patrol the entire coast and essentially control Indian Ocean trade. Goa was a logical choice as the administrative center of the extensive Portuguese trade network farther east, and it prospered so much on the profits of that trade that it became known as "Golden Goa."

A commercial empire stretching another 6,000 miles east by sea, through all of Southeast Asia (except the Philippines) and on to China and Japan, required other bases too. The most obvious control points over the sea lanes eastward from India were Colombo in Ceylon (now Sri Lanka) and Malacca in Malaya. The Palk Strait between India and Ceylon was too shallow for shipping, and the route around Sumatra and through the Sunda Strait between Sumatra and Java was longer and plagued by reefs and currents, with no safe harbors along the Sumatran west coast. Traffic to and from East Asia was therefore funneled through the Straits of Malacca. The Portuguese seized the town of Malacca, commanding the straits, in 1511, but Malaya at that period was thinly settled and relatively unproductive. Malacca's role was primarily strategic, although it did some entrepôt business to and from Southeast Asia. Colombo, which the Portuguese also fortified after establishing themselves there about 1515, was able to draw on the nearby production of cinnamon, which the Ceylonese made from the bark of a rain forest tree, and thus played a commercial role as well.

For trade with China and Japan, the Portuguese somewhat later established their chief base at Macao, at the seaward edge of the Canton delta. There they could be a little freer of the restrictions imposed on foreign merchants at Canton by the Ming government and be tolerated by the Chinese authorities, enough to permit modest fortifications and a small permanent settlement. From the Chinese point of view, these unruly and barbaric foreigners were in any case better shunted off to such a remote neck of land and closed off by a wall (which still stands) where they could not make trouble and where they could govern themselves according to their own customs. In the sixteenth century the Ming were still close to the height of their power and effectively excluded all foreigners except for tribute missions and a handful of traders at the fringes. There was no comparable Portuguese territorial base in Indonesia, where in any case no large state existed at this time. The Portuguese dominated the spice trade and excluded rival Europeans by intimidation of local sultans, alliances or treaties with others, and a scattered string of forts as far east as Ternate and Amboina in the Moluccas.

The shape and nature of the Portuguese commercial empire is clearly defined by its emphasis on strategically located ports, most of them already long in existence, and on domination of the sea lanes. The Portuguese controlled no territory beyond the immediate area of the few ports named, and traded in the hundreds of other ports in competition with Asian and Arab traders. Even so, their effort was overextended, and by the latter part of the sixteenth century they could no longer maintain what control they had earlier established. Their home base was tiny as well as poor; it could not provide either manpower or funds to sustain the effort required to maintain their overseas stations against competition. As the century ended, they were rapidly being ousted by the Dutch in Southeast Asia and were soon to be eliminated as serious competitors in the rest of the Asian trade by the other rising European power, the English. Many Portuguese stayed on, picking up crumbs of trade and also operating as pirates. As in Africa, they had from early days married local women, and from the seventeenth century virtually all of them in Asia were Eurasians, though commonly carrying Portuguese names and retaining the Catholic faith to which they had been converted. To this day names such as Fernando or de Souza are common in coastal South India, Sri Lanka, Malacca, and Macao. As the power of the Portuguese faded, their bases were no longer a threat, which is why Portugal retained formal sovereignty over Goa until it was forcibly reclaimed by India in 1961. The fiction of Portuguese control is maintained even today for Macao, an arrangement that suits the Chinese government for the present.

## Religious Concerns

From the beginning, the crusade against Islam and the winning of souls for the Catholic church had been Por-

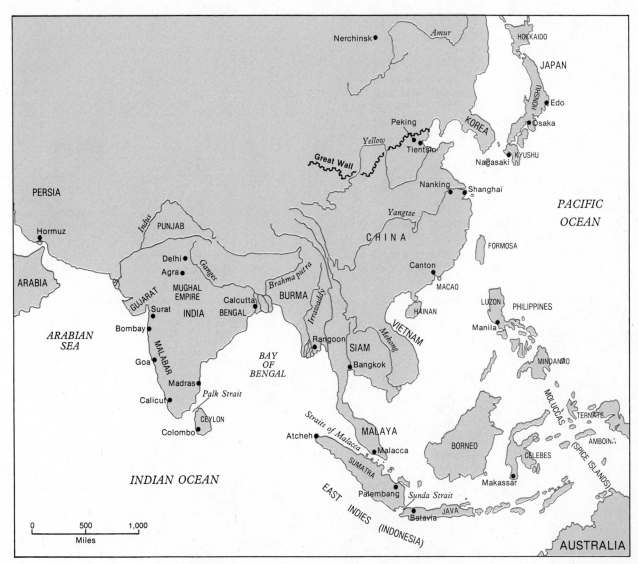

**18.2** *Asia in the Age of Early European Expansion*

tuguese goals equal to trade in importance. When Vasco da Gama arrived in Calicut in 1498 and was asked what he sought, he is said to have replied, "Christians and spices." His ships carried missionary priests, and their effort played a major role in the 1500s. In 1511, after Affonso de Albuquerque (1453–1515), chief architect of the Portuguese commercial empire in Asia, had been named viceroy of the Indies in 1508, he wrote of his plan to capture Malacca:

> The first aim is the great service which we shall perform to our Lord in casting the Moors out of this country and quenching the fire of the sect of Mohammed. . . . And the other is the service we shall render to the king . . . in taking this city, because it is the source of all the spiceries

and drugs which the Moors carry every year. . . . For I hold it certain that if we take this trade of Malacca away from them, Cairo and Mecca will be entirely ruined, and Venice will receive no spiceries unless her merchants go and buy them in Portugal.[4]

When Albuquerque took Malacca, he massacred all the Muslims but tried to make allies or friends of the few other inhabitants. In insular Southeast Asia, by now predominantly Muslim, these were not attitudes or policies calculated to ingratiate the Portuguese. Their cruel practice of conversion by torture, their pitiless extortion, and their slaughter of "heathen" Hindus and Buddhists as well as their ancient Muslim foes earned them hatred. The Portuguese record during their century of power in

Asia is at least as horrendous as that of the Spanish in the New World, and their decline was regretted by no one.

The Chinese remained aloof from these Western maritime and commercial rivalries and kept their distance at Canton, where European traders were not even permitted to enter the city but did their business outside the walls during the six-month trading season and then were obliged to depart until the next year. Successive Portuguese, Dutch, and English efforts to break these restrictions by trading elsewhere on the China coast were repelled, as Europeans did not have the means to challenge the Dragon Throne. (Dutch and English involvement in Asia are discussed in Chapter 19). The sixteenth-century missionary effort to penetrate China was more successful, at least for a time. For the Jesuits, as for all later missionary groups, China was the chief goal, if only because of its immense population, its so-

phisticated culture, and the knowledge that it lacked an indigenous religion of salvation. Successive Jesuit efforts to enter the country failed after Francis Xavier died off the south China coast in 1552, still cherishing the dream of converting China's millions.

---

### ❦ MATTEO RICCI: MISSIONARY TO THE MING COURT

The pioneer of the Jesuit effort in China was Matteo Ricci. He was born at Ancona in 1552, where he soon demonstrated his scholastic ability and magnetic personality. At the age of 16 he went to Rome to study law and at 19 entered the Society of Jesus, where he distinguished himself in mathematics and geography. In 1577

---

## ◉ A European View of China ◉

*Asians did not think much of Europeans, especially in this period, when they could easily be seen as crude ruffians. An Italian traveler to early-seventeenth-century India, Niccolò Manucci, recorded Indian views that agreed closely with those of the Chinese, Japanese, and other Asians. They believed that Europeans "have no polite manners, that they are ignorant, wanting in ordered life, and very dirty." The Europeans, however, were far more positive about Asia, which they had come so far to seek, in terms of both its wealth and its civilization. Here is a sampling of a Jesuit's account of China in 1590.*

There are such a number of artificers ingeniously framing sundry devices out of gold, silver, and other metals . . . and other matters convenient for man's use, that the streets of cities being replenished with their shops and fine workmanship are very wonderful to behold. . . . Their industry does no less appear in founding of guns. . . . To these may be added the art of printing . . . and with marvelous facility they daily publish huge multitudes of books. . . . You may add two more, that is to say navigation and discipline of war, both of which have been in ancient times most diligently practiced. . . . The people of China do above all things profess the art of literature, and learning it most diligently, they employ themselves a long time and the better part of their age therein. . . . Graduates of the second degree are elected in each province, and a certain number . . . ascend to the highest pitch of dignity. . . . Out of this order the chief magistrates are chosen. . . . Magistrates bear office for the space of three years, yet for the governing of each province men of another province are selected . . . [so that] judges may give sentence with a far more entire and incorrupt mind than if they were among their own kinsfolk and allies. . . . Over and besides all these there is an annual magistrate [the imperial censor] . . . whose duty it is to make inquisition of all crimes, and especially the crimes of magistrates. . . . Hence it is that all magistrates . . . are kept within the limits of their callings.

*Source:* N. Manucci, "An Excellent Treatise of the Kingdome of China," in *The Principal Navigations,* vol. 2, ed. R. Hakluyt (London, 1600), pp. 88–97 passim. The manuscript was written in Macao and captured by the English on its way to Lisbon.

he determined to pursue his career in the East and arrived in Goa the following year. After finishing his religious training, he taught in the college there until 1582, when he was called to Macao to prepare himself for the challenge of China. There he began diligent study of written and spoken Chinese and in 1583 became the first Jesuit to enter China, although at first only as a "guest" in Kwangtung province near Canton. There he continued his study of the Confucian classics and in 1589 built a church in the Chinese architectural style. By this time he had discovered that priests of any kind were associated with the now despised Buddhists, and he therefore adopted the dress as well as the manner and education of a Confucian scholar.

Ricci was a compelling person, tall and vigorous with flashing blue eyes, a curly beard (which assured the Chinese of his sagacity), and a resonant voice. What impressed them most, however, was his remarkable learning, combining as it did most of contemporary Western achievements, including cartography, and a thorough mastery of the classical Chinese corpus. He also had a phenomenal memory and made use of a variety of mnemonic devices to assist it. This was a tremendous help to a scholar, especially for learning Chinese characters. Ricci was accordingly much sought after by Chinese who wanted to succeed in the imperial examinations or wanted their sons to do so. This enhanced his acceptability, as did his success in dissociating himself from the Portuguese traders at Macao. In 1595 he and his missionary colleagues were permitted to move north to the Yangtze valley and in 1601 to establish their permanent base at Peking.

The reigning emperor, Ming Wan-li, had become incompetent and concerned only with pleasures; the court was corrupt and full of scheming factions. Ricci finally caught the emperor's fancy by presenting him with two clocks and a clavichord, a precursor of the piano. When asked to demonstrate it, Ricci composed some "edifying" madrigals for his majesty to sing. Later he was given a special imperial stipend and was accepted at court as an outstanding and useful scholar. As the first missionary to China and one who fully understood how Chinese society worked, Ricci concentrated on the well-placed. To avoid alienating them and to make Christianity more understandable and appealing, he represented it as a system of ethics similar to and compatible with Confucianism, leaving out such potentially upsetting parts as the crucifixion, the virgin birth, and the equality of all persons. He also avoided discussion of Christian theology. This abbreviated version of the faith got the Jesuits in trouble with Rome later on, but it made excellent sense if the aim was to interest the Chinese. Ricci avoided preaching or overt efforts at conversion, and when he died in 1610, he was buried at Peking in a special plot granted by the emperor. He and his colleagues won few converts, but they saw their role as preparing

Matteo Ricci with a Chinese convert to Christianity, Li Paulus, who translated European works on astronomy from Latin into Chinese. [New York Public Library]

the ground for a later assault by easing the Chinese into accepting the less controversial parts of Christianity and by masquerading as Confucian scholars. With his sharp mind, vast erudition, and winning personality, Ricci was an ideal person for such a role, but interest in him as a scholar never led to an equivalent interest in the religion he came to China to plant.

Such success as Ricci and his successors achieved was largely the result of their use of some of the new fruits of the European Renaissance as a lure, especially early clocks, improvements in the calendar, maps of the world, astronomy, and glass prisms. Such things intrigued the Chinese and ingratiated the Jesuits at court as learned men. By now they had necessarily learned not only the Chinese language but also the full deportment of the Confucian scholar as the vital credential for acceptance. They also understood that in this hierarchical society, the key to missionary success was to convert the people at the top, especially the emperor, and that preaching to the masses would only earn them a reputation as troublemakers. Aided by their Confucian guise as men of learning, they made some converts among gentry and court officials, but though they interested successive emperors, they never converted many Chinese. Western technology was more appealing than Western religion; this has remained true into our own times. In the end, the Jesuit effort was undermined by the pope, who refused to permit their softening of Catholic doctrine or the acceptance of some Confucian rites in order to avoid offending potential converts. The controversy simmered for years, but the ground had been cut out from under the Jesuits, and they were ultimately expelled in the early eighteenth century. Meanwhile, their accounts of China became an important source of Western knowledge.

## The Russian Advance in Asia

Russian expansion across Siberia was slow but involved permanent Russian occupation and domination of this vast territory and its technologically less developed peoples, whose numbers were also small. By 1637 the Russians had reached the Pacific coast north of what is now Vladivostok, but they were behind the western Europeans in making direct contact with China. Early Russian explorers followed the major Siberian rivers, but these flow northward into the Arctic. Gradually a network of fortified garrisons and trading posts spread eastward. When the Amur River was reached, it was eagerly used as an easier route leading to more productive areas and to the sea. Russian presence in the Amur valley came to Chinese attention when northern Manchurian tribes, tributary vassals of the Ch'ing dynasty, appealed for help. Mongol groups were also trading with the Russians, which further alarmed the Chinese. Two successive Russian embassies to Peking, in 1654 and 1676, requesting trade privileges, refused to perform the required prostrations before the emperor and were sent away. By the 1680s the Ch'ing, now having consolidated their power within China, began to establish new routes and military colonies in the Amur region and put naval ships on the river itself. The Russians were quickly chased out, and a large Ch'ing army besieged the one remaining Russian fortress. The Russians now agreed to negotiate and sent an ambassador to their major post at Nerchinsk, on an upper Amur tributary but still within Siberia.

The treaty concluded there in 1689 confirmed the Amur region as Chinese and obliged the Russians to destroy their remaining fortress but accepted limited Russian trade rights by camel caravan to Peking, in part because the Chinese court wanted to maintain the supply of fine Russian furs from Siberia. A later treaty in 1727 excluded Russia from Mongolia and further delimited the boundary between Russia and China, leaving the Russians only Siberia. The Ch'ing emperor K'ang Hsi would not deal directly with "barbarians," still less go to

them, so he sent as his representatives two Jesuits from the court, whom he deemed appropriate agents for the management of such affairs. Nevertheless, the Treaty of Nerchinsk treated both sides as essentially equal sovereign states. It was the only such treaty China agreed to with a Western state until the nineteenth century, when China was forced to abandon the pretense of political superiority and accept inferior status. Until 1842 the various "sea barbarians" could be treated as savages, though Russia as a rival and adjacent land power had to be dealt with differently. Fear of Russia and its ambitions remained a fixture in the Chinese mind and was later intensified by Russian expansion into Manchuria.

The Catholic missionary drive in Asia met with the greatest success under the Spanish in the Philippines, where there was no sophisticated indigenous religious tradition to oppose it. The Japanese too, as a small, remote, and, in their own view, less developed people, were far more open than the Chinese or the Indians to new ideas, even of foreign origin. Where Chinese, and often Indians, with their cultural pride and self-confidence, tended to dismiss anything foreign as undesirable, the Japanese remained curious and sought opportunities to learn, as they had done from T'ang China. The sixteenth century, sometimes called "Japan's Christian century," saw significant numbers of Christian converts as well as a flourishing trade with Europeans, centered in Nagasaki but also at Osaka, Edo (Tokyo), and other ports. After missionary work in Goa and the East Indies, Francis Xavier spent two years (1549–1551) in Japan preaching, teaching, and disputing with Buddhist monks. But Christians were soon branded troublemakers. Rival Catholic religious orders contended with one another, often violently, as did the Portuguese, Spanish, Dutch, and English. Their ships and arms were often used in domestic Japanese factional fighting and intrigue, and Christianity was also seen as corrupting the Confucian loyalty of the Japanese and making converts potential subversives. Christianity was suppressed by 1640; thousands of converts were crucified, and all foreigners were expelled. The Japanese were forbidden to go abroad, and contact with the world beyond China was limited to one Dutch ship a year, allowed to trade only on an island in Nagasaki harbor.

The first burst of Western activity in Asia thus ended with only minor success. It was the Europeans who sought out the East, because Europe, poor and backward by comparison with the riches of Asia, was eager for contact. Columbus carried with him on his first voyage a copy of Marco Polo's journal, with its account of the immense wealth of Cathay; the riches of India and Southeast Asia were even better known via Arab traders. The discovery of the New World was thus an accidental incident on the road to Asia. In terms of power, the Europeans were no match for the great Asian empires or even for lesser states, and they had nothing desirable to offer in trade with the more sophisticated economies of the East. This was to inhibit European contacts for several more centuries. The Europeans had to be content with a few tiny and insecure footholds on the coast, where they competed with Asian and Arab merchants. Sometimes, at the whim of the Asian states, they were thrown out and had their goods confiscated.

Only at sea were the Europeans powerful—hence in part the Dutch success in controlling most of the trade of insular Southeast Asia—and there they tended to cancel one another out as rivals. Their chief commercial advantage was in the carrying trade, where their ships made them competitive but where they served mainly Asian markets. Soon after the Portuguese arrival, Asian shipbuilders on the Indian west coast began to adopt a Western-looking rig in the hope of scaring off pirates, sometimes adding dummy gun ports for the same purpose. Although Portuguese power subsequently faded in the face of Dutch and English competition, often forcing the Portuguese into piracy, the Asians continued to acknowledge Western superiority at sea. As the first British consul at Shanghai was to remark over three centuries later in 1843: "By our ships our power can be seen, and if necessary, felt."[5] This was to remain the principal basis of Western success in Asia throughout the centuries from 1498 to the end of colonialism in the ashes of the Second World War. In the early period, however, Asians saw Westerners as clever with ships but ignorant, dirty, contentious, drunken, uncivilized, and treacherous. To Asia's later cost, they were largely ignored. That seemed reasonable enough in the splendid and confident context of Mughal India, Ming and Ch'ing China, and Tokugawa Japan, and it remained so for another two or three centuries, until these Asian orders declined while Europe began to ride the wave of new industrial and technological power.

# The European Conquest of the Americas

While the Portuguese fashioned a commercial empire in the East, the Spanish imposed a colonial empire on much of Mexico and South and Central America. Faced with uncertain economic prospects at home, the hidalgos who led the assault on the Aztecs and the Inca came in search of gold, but they were also deeply influenced by the crusading ideal and saw this adventure as a means of serving God. The combination of materialistic and spiritual motives was potent enough to provide them with the confidence to take on civilized peoples who vastly outnumbered them. In the end, however, the keys to their success were their technological superiority and the fact that both the Aztecs and the Inca were the over-

lords of a vast Amerindian population, some of whom actually fought on the side of the Spaniards. The Aztecs and Inca were also at a disadvantage because their empires, unlike those in Africa, were highly centralized and thus ill-suited to keep up resistance once their rulers had fallen.

# Conquistadors, Aztecs, and Inca

The first of the great triumphs of the Spanish conquistadors began in 1519, the same year that Magellan set out on his historic voyage. Under the command of Hernando Cortés (1485–1547), a former law student who had participated in the conquest of Cuba, a force of some 600 men, 16 horses, and a few cannon landed in Mexico near Veracruz (which Cortés founded). Although the Amerindians resisted him at first, Cortés gradually won them over, aided by his Amerindian mistress and translator, Doña Marina. With the aid of 1,000 Tlaxcala Amerindians, the long-standing enemies of the Aztecs, he advanced on the capital at Tenochtitlán, an impressive city whose population of approximately 90,000 was nearly the equal of Europe's largest cities. Dominated by an enormous temple, pyramids, and the royal palace, the city was built on mud dredged from Lake Texcoco. Impressive for its orderly streets and canals, its open squares bustling with commerce, and its whitewashed public buildings, Tenochtitlán was ruled by the war-chief Montezuma from 1502 to 1520. In a society dominated by war, all able-bodied Aztec men received military training. So many warriors died in battle that the Aztecs had to practice polygamy. Bearing children was therefore highly regarded, and a woman who died in childbirth received the same ceremonial rites as a warrior who perished on the battlefield. The main motive for the warfare was the need to acquire victims with which to appease the sun god, who fed on blood obtained by ripping out the hearts of living people. Women were rarely among the sacrificial victims. In practical terms, human sacrifice functioned as a means to terrorize subject Amerindians, which helps explain their unwillingness to defend the Aztecs against Cortés.

Despite initial threats from the Aztecs, Cortés was allowed to enter the capital peacefully, but in a matter of days he used the pretext of an attack on his garrison at Veracruz to imprison Montezuma. An Indian uprising in which Montezuma was killed forced Cortés to flee in July 1520, but 13 months later he regained Tenochtitlán with the help of the Tlaxcala. The fighting destroyed most of the city, but amid its ruins the Spaniards built Mexico City, complete with a Catholic cathedral and, in 1551, the University of Mexico.

The attack on the Inca was commanded by Francisco Pizarro (c. 1474–1541), a former associate of Balboa.

## ◉ The Splendors of Tenochtitlán ◉

*When Cortés' party entered the Aztec capital of Tenochtitlán, it was
cordially received and given a tour of the city. An eyewitness account by
a member of the party records the city's splendor and teeming life.*

When we arrived at the great market place . . . we were astounded at the number of people and the quantity of merchandise that it contained, and at the good order and control that was maintained, for we had never seen such a thing before. Each kind of merchandise was kept by itself and had its fixed place marked out. Let us begin with the dealers in gold, silver, and precious stones, feathers, mantles, and embroidered goods. Then there were other wares consisting of Indian slaves both men and women; and I say that they bring as many of them to that great market for sale as the Portuguese bring negroes from Guinea. . . .

So we stood looking about us, for that huge and cursed temple stood so high that from it one could see over everything very well, and we saw the three causeways which led into Mexico. . . . We saw the bridges on the three causeways which were built at certain distances apart through which the water of the lake flowed in and out from one side to the other, and we beheld on that great lake a great multitude of canoes, some coming with supplies of food and others returning loaded with cargoes of merchandise; and we saw that from every house of that great city and of all the other cities that were built in the water it was impossible to pass from house to house, except by drawbridges which were made of wood or in canoes; and we saw in those cities Cues (temples) and oratories like towers and fortresses and all gleaming white, and it was a wonderful thing to behold.

*Source:* B. Díaz del Castillo, *The True History of the Conquest of New Spain,* ed. G. Garcia, trans. A. P. Maudslay, 5 vols. (London: Hakluyt Society, 1908–1933), 2: 70–71, 74–75.

With a force of only 180 men and 27 horses he set out in 1531 to conquer an empire ruled by Atahualpa with his army of 30,000. The overconfident Atahualpa agreed to meet with Pizarro, whom he seriously underestimated. Pizarro took him prisoner, extracted an enormous ransom, and then executed him for allegedly murdering his half brother. In 1533 Pizarro captured the Inca capital at Cuzco in the Peruvian Andes, after which the remaining Inca maintained a tiny but independent state high in the mountains at Machu Picchu. To maintain better communications with other Spanish authorities, Pizarro founded Lima on the coast of Peru in 1535. The University of San Marcos was established there 16 years later under a grant from Emperor Charles V. Conquest of the Inca was facilitated by the dissatisfaction of subordinate Amerindians with Inca domination, as well as by internal dissension among the Inca themselves.

## Spanish Rule in the Americas

Virtually from the beginning, the Spanish confronted difficult legal questions concerning the status of the Amerindians. The problem was compounded by religious considerations, for the papal decision in 1493 that recognized Spain's claim to most of the Western Hemisphere also made the Spaniards responsible for the conversion of its inhabitants. As Spanish subjects and, in time, Christians, what legal rights did they possess? The conquerors, vastly outnumbered by their subject population, sought an essentially feudal form of government, with considerable local autonomy for their own colonists, and the right to treat the Amerindians as forced laborers. In sharp contrast, the influential Dominican friar Bartolomé de las Casas contended that as fellow Christians and subjects of the Spanish crown, the Amerindians were entitled to full legal rights and protection. Although the Spanish government was unwilling to provide the colonists much autonomy, it gave selected conquistadors and other Spaniards the right to collect tribute from specified villages and to impose forced labor. Those who exercised this power—the *encomenderos,* or protectors—were required to render military service and pay the salaries of the clergy. Because of abuses, this system was modified in the mid-sixteenth century. The authority to compel labor was transferred to colonial officials, and forced workers were paid according to a

*18.3 Colonial Empires in America, c. 1600*

fixed rate. Legally, the Amerindians could not be enslaved, but in practice their situation was little different
from slavery.

Administration of the Spanish empire in America was
directed by two viceroys who received their instructions
from the Council of the Indies in Spain. The viceroyalty
of New Spain, with headquarters in Mexico City, embraced Spanish territories in North America, the West
Indies, Venezuela, and the Philippines, and the viceroyalty of Peru, governed from Lima, included the rest of
Spanish South America. Under the viceroys were lesser
provincial governors. Both the viceroys and the lesser
governors shared authority with conciliar courts known
as *audiencias*, which gave them advice and had the

power to overturn their decisions. This system of checks and balances safeguarded royal prerogatives, but it also deprived colonial government of administrative efficiency.

# The Economy of Spanish America

Nothing was more important in determining the pattern of Spanish settlement than the sites of gold and silver deposits and the availability of native labor to mine them. On his first voyage, Columbus had found gold in Hispaniola, and more was soon discovered in Cuba and Puerto Rico. At first the gold was obtained from shallow diggings or extracted from streambeds. Such mining, however, was labor-intensive, and as the Amerindian population declined, it became more profitable to graze cattle or raise sugarcane. Many Amerindians soon died because of forced labor or diseases introduced by the Spanish. The conquest of the Aztecs and Inca, whose gold artifacts were seized and melted down, was of enormous economic importance because it led to the discovery of rich silver deposits in the 1540s. The greatest of these was an extraordinary mountain of silver at Potosí, in the Andes, discovered in 1545. By 1570 Potosí had a population of 120,000, nearly the same as Paris. The introduction of the latest technology by German miners—a water-powered stamp mill and a mercury amalgamation process that purified the silver—made the mines so productive that silver became the most im-

portant export to the mother country. By 1570 no less than 97 percent of the bullion shipped to Spain was silver. As the output of European mines declined in the late sixteenth century, the flow of silver from the New World continued to increase, rising in the 1590s to more than 10 million ounces a year. Altogether, according to official accounts, the Spanish treasure fleets transported 180 tons of gold and 16,000 tons of silver to Seville between 1500 and 1650. Much of the wealth, 20 percent of which went to the crown as the "royal fifth," was used to pay for imports, service the royal debt, and finance war.

No less significant, particularly for the future history of the Americas, was the introduction of large estates. Some, the haciendas, were used to rear animals or raise cereal crops, but in tropical regions sugar and tobacco plantations were established, patterned after the sugar plantations of Atlantic islands such as the Azores and the Canaries, which had in turn been influenced by Genoese plantations in Cyprus and Crete. Unlike the haciendas, which used Amerindian workers, the primary laborers on the plantations were African slaves. Although both the plantation system and the trade in African slaves predated the Spanish conquests in the Americas, the success of the conquistadors opened up vast new markets for the sale of blacks. Africans were accustomed to working in tropical climates, possessed some immunity from the diseases that ravaged the Amerindians, and had lower mortality rates in the New World than even the Europeans. By the eighteenth century the British were the main suppliers for this slave

**Cerro Rico, the fabulous mountain of silver at Potosí in Bolivia. Potosí itself, at an altitude of 13,700 feet, is one of the world's highest cities. Its population reached 160,000 in 1650 and then declined sharply. [Harvard College Library]**

market, followed by the French, but the Portuguese, Spanish, Dutch, Danes, and Americans also participated.

In Spain, the economic effects of its new colonial empire were a mixed blessing. Seville, which enjoyed a monopoly of trade with the colonies, prospered for several centuries. Ultimately, however, its prosperity and economic potential were undermined by the heavy hand of the Spanish government, which overregulated everything, and by the reluctance of the Spaniards to seize the commercial opportunities their empire made possible. The French historian Fernand Braudel has observed:

> The latent defect in the Spanish imperial economy was that it was based on Seville—a controlled town rotten with dishonest officials and long dominated by foreign capitalists—and not on a powerful free town capable of producing and carrying through a really individual economic policy.[6]

There was some new manufacturing in Spain, but in general Spaniards continued to rely on France and the Netherlands for their goods. Nor did large numbers of Spaniards emigrate to America, the total number amounting to some 100,000 in the entire sixteenth century. The influx of bullion into Spain, while seemingly a great economic advantage, was so badly mismanaged that for many Spaniards the most direct result was a spiraling cost of living. The quadrupling of prices in the 1500s, in part because of the increase in bullion, adversely affected the living conditions of many Spaniards.

## The Impact of Spanish Imperialism

In retrospect, the most dramatic effect of Spanish domination in the New World was the catastrophic decline in the Amerindian population, one of the greatest demographic disasters in history. By 1510 nearly 90 percent of the Amerindians of Hispaniola were dead, while in Mexico the Amerindian population, which had numbered 11 million, fell by more than 75 percent. Famine and ruthless exploitation accounted for some of the deaths, but the biggest killer was disease, especially smallpox. The fact that Europeans introduced universities and printing to the New World and that Spanish law and Christianity ended the Aztec practices of human sacrifice and polygamy was small comfort in the face of such suffering. Although Aztecs and Inca suppressed other Amerindians, the Spanish exploitation of the native inhabitants and the introduction of slave plantations were hardly an improvement, though the Amerindians were treated better than the blacks. Because of the shortage of Spanish women, intermarriage with Amerindians was so frequent that the descendants of mixed marriages—the mestizos—eventually outnumbered both the Spaniards and the Amerindians.

## The Portuguese in Brazil

Portugal concentrated on its commercial empire in Asia and paid relatively little attention to Brazil in the early 1500s, particularly since no gold or silver was found there. The region, however, did produce brazilwood, used in making red dye. The threat of Spanish incursion and the intrusion of the French into the brazilwood trade forced the government in Lisbon to act in 1533. It organized Brazil into 15 hereditary fiefs, the holders of which—the *donatários*—enjoyed sweeping powers, including the right to levy internal taxes and bestow grants of land. When most of the *donatários* proved ineffectual, the Portuguese king imposed a centralized administration under the direction of a governor general, who took up duties in 1549. After Spain's conquest of Portugal in 1580, Spanish-style colonial administration, headed by a viceroy, was introduced in Brazil.

As in the Spanish colonies, there was controversy over the treatment of the Amerindians. Jesuit missionaries worked tirelessly to convert and settle them in Christian villages. Their efforts ran counter to the needs of settlers who established sugar plantations in northern Brazil in the late 1500s. Brazil, in fact, became the world's leading producer of sugar in the early seventeenth century. In 1574 the Portuguese government resolved the dispute between the Jesuits and the plantation owners by allowing the former to protect residents of their Christian villages, while giving settlers the right to enslave Amerindians captured in war. Unable to procure sufficient labor in this manner, the colonists increasingly relied on African slaves.

The French, too, were interested in Brazil, and in 1555 they occupied the harbor of Rio de Janeiro. When the colony refused to honor its initial promise of religious toleration, potential Protestant settlers in France and Switzerland lost interest. After the Portuguese captured the French garrison, they founded the town of Rio de Janeiro in 1567. Large numbers of Portuguese Jewish immigrants subsequently settled in Brazil, where they found some freedom for the exercise of their religion.

## The North Atlantic States and the Americas

The Portuguese were the first to profit from John Cabot's discovery of the cod fisheries off Newfoundland. For the masses, salted fish was a vital item in the diet, particularly during the winter and on the frequent fast days throughout the year when the Catholic church prohibited the eating of meat. Because the herring fisheries in the Baltic, monopolized by the Hanseatic League of North German merchants, were declining as the fish shifted their spawning grounds to the North Sea, there was a ready market for cod to feed the growing population. Although Portugal claimed Newfoundland, French and English fishermen were soon hauling in catches from its waters. In addition to providing needed food, the development of new fisheries led to the beginning of the fur trade with the Indians and to an increase in the number of ships and mariners capable of sailing the Atlantic.

As their naval expertise improved, the English were determined to participate in the spice trade, the immense profits of which were enjoyed by the Portuguese and the merchants of Antwerp. Unwilling to challenge Portugal's control of the route around the Cape of Good Hope, the English opted to search for a northeast or northwest passage to Asia, encouraged by Magellan's discovery of a southwest route. Accordingly, Sir Hugh Willoughby and Richard Chancellor set out in 1553 to find a northeast passage. Two of the ships became icebound and their crews froze to death, but Chancellor took the third ship through the White Sea to Archangel. From there he traveled overland to the court of Tsar Ivan the Terrible in Moscow. His trip resulted in the establishment of the Muscovy Company (1555), which pursued a small direct trade between England and Russia. Subsequent attempts by the English and the Dutch to find a northeastern passage were unsuccessful, as were English efforts beginning in 1576 to find a northwestern route. The latter, however, led to the discovery of Hudson Strait and Hudson Bay and to additional sources of fur in the adjacent territory.

As the search for a northern passage progressed, the English turned their attention to the possibility of trade with Spain's American colonies, notwithstanding the fact that the Spaniards considered unauthorized trade illegal. In 1562 John Hawkins, son of a Plymouth merchant, launched the English slave trade with the backing of a private syndicate. In Hispaniola he traded the 300 or 400 slaves he had acquired in Sierra Leone for hides and sugar. Impressed by the potential of this trade, Queen Elizabeth I and several of her privy councillors quietly helped finance his successful second voyage in 1564–1565. In the face of mounting Spanish hostility, Elizabeth permitted Hawkins to sail again in 1567, but this time the Spanish fleet captured or destroyed three of his five ships in the Mexican harbor of San Juan de Ulúa. As relations with Spain worsened, the English restricted their activity in the New World primarily to privateering—government-approved piracy—for the rest of the century. During his circumnavigation of the globe in 1577–1580, Francis Drake challenged the Spanish sphere of dominion by claiming California, which he called New Albion, for England. In the 1580s Sir Walter Raleigh's pioneering attempt to found an English colony near Roanoke Island (now part of North Carolina) resulted in dismal failure, but the experience proved valuable for later colonial endeavors. The French, whose activities in the New World in the sixteenth century consisted largely of plundering Spanish shipping, were equally unsuccessful in attempting to establish a colony in Florida in the early 1560s.

The ability of the English, French, and Dutch to make inroads into Spanish America was largely determined by the economic and political events of the late sixteenth century. England's successful war with Spain (1585–1604) severely crippled the latter and provided substantial freedom of action to the Dutch. France, disrupted by a long and bitter civil war, began to build the strong monarchy and economy necessary for colonial expansion only in the 1590s. In all three states, a key to future success in colonial expansion and the emerging global economy was the development of aggressive capitalism.

## The Economy in the Age of Exploration

In the fifteenth and sixteenth centuries the European economy underwent dramatic changes that helped chart the course of modern economic development. The most important characteristics of this change involved not only the founding of commercial and colonial empires but also the rapid growth of capitalism and a price revolution triggered by an expanding population.

## Merchant Capitalism

Capitalism involves three elements: (1) the acquisition and investment of capital to obtain profit, (2) private ownership of the principal means of production and distribution, and (3) a division in the productive and distributive process between the owners of the capital (the employers) and the laborers. Capitalism cannot exist without the capacity and the willingness to invest and to take risks, which in turn presupposes the possibility of significant profits. The medieval concepts of the just price and the wrongfulness of usury (interest on loans purely for profit) were thus impediments to capitalistic development. Medieval theologians had generally recognized the right of a lender to additional compensation beyond the principal if he incurred a loss by forgoing the use of his money. The acceptability of reasonable interest was gradually extended until, in the sixteenth century, bankers regularly paid interest of 5 to 12 percent on deposits and merchants routinely operated on credit. The expansion of capitalistic activities was also furthered by the increased use of bills of exchange, improved facilities for interregional trade, stable coinage, and an adequate and affordable labor supply. Finally, the rise in prices was a stimulus to capitalistic investment as merchants and others with surplus wealth opted to seek profits through investment rather than to spend their money on consumables.

As the European states centralized in this period, they exercised a threefold influence on capitalism. First of all, their own demands—for weapons, supplies, and luxury items—created an expanding market for merchant capitalists, who were quick to realize the potential for profits. Second, the encouragement of overseas commercial and colonial activity by the governments of the maritime states was a major incentive to invest in such ventures. Finally, these governments introduced economic policies intended to strengthen their respective states. Collectively, these policies constitute what is sometimes referred to as "mercantilism," or the "mercantile system," as Adam Smith called it in 1776.

At the heart of mercantile policy was the principle of state regulation, which was designed primarily for the benefit of the state itself. Free enterprise—the right of merchants and manufacturers to respond to market conditions as they deem best—was not part of mercantile capitalism. Both rulers and merchants who profited from business dealings with the state accepted economic controls as necessary. However, some of these controls, particularly those creating monopolies, became increasingly unpopular in the late sixteenth and seventeenth centuries among the people, who blamed them for high prices. Governments used controls to ensure the availability of strategic items, to provide order in the economy, and to regulate commerce with other states. Economic regulation was thus an important facet of the campaign to impose greater order on the early modern state. The most common controls were tariffs on imported goods, subsidies (grants) to strategic industries, and monopolies, which conveyed the exclusive right to manufacture, sell, or trade in a specific commodity. Some also attempted to regulate the export of raw materials, such as wool and leather. In 1572 French royal edicts banned the export of various raw materials, and England tried a variety of expedients in the sixteenth and early seventeenth centuries to reduce the export of raw wool in order to encourage domestic manufacturing.

Some proponents of mercantile capitalism were convinced that the strength of the state depended on the acquisition of considerable supplies of bullion. To accomplish this, they favored strict controls on foreign commerce in order to produce a favorable balance of trade, whereby the value of exports exceeded the value of imports. The Dutch, who dominated the carrying trade, recognized the sterility of this concept and instead pursued a policy geared to maximize the volume and value of trade. Profit, they recognized, was obtained by increasing trade, not hoarding bullion. The English converted to this view for a time in the 1600s but then reverted to a protectionist policy. The Spanish, who wanted to amass bullion, had to use it instead to finance their wars and the conspicuous consumption of their elite and to import goods that they were unwilling to manufacture. Supporters of the bullionist theory tried to reduce the export of bullion by encouraging the immigration of skilled artisans, thereby reducing the need of the host country for imports and perhaps even creating new export commodities from the goods the immigrants manufactured.

Government intervention in the economy was not always beneficial, as in the case of most monopolies. An English scheme designed by the merchant Sir William Cokayne to dye and finish cloth before exporting it to the Continent, though supported by the crown, was so disastrous that it helped provoke a depression. Nevertheless, mercantile policies helped France build a stronger economy in the 1600s by expanding trade and assisting farmers, and both the English and the Dutch benefited by allowing religious refugees, especially Huguenots, to immigrate in the sixteenth and seventeenth centuries. Government intervention also had positive results as companies received charters to trade with Asia, Africa, and America; as internal barriers to trade gradually ended (though France was a major exception); and as new industries were subsidized. The implementation of policies was complicated not only by the lack of experience in dealing with a capitalistic economy but also by spiraling prices and corruption.

## The Price Revolution

Inflation is a fact of modern life; Europeans in the sixteenth century were unprepared for the rises in prices that occurred, at varying rates, throughout Europe. By today's standards the inflation rate was low, often hovering around 2 percent per year, though in some years the rate was much higher. Moreover, prices varied greatly from region to region, especially over the short run. In Spain prices quadrupled in the sixteenth century, and the figure was nearly as great in England. Inflation began later in Italy, where prices doubled by 1600. The greatest increases came between the 1540s and 1570s when bad weather and crop failures added additional pressures to the inflationary spiral and when the impact of American bullion began to be felt. For a long time many historians attributed the rise in prices to the influx of bullion from the New World, but recent research has confirmed the fact that the main cause was a rise in population and thus in demand without a corresponding increase in output, thereby creating shortages of goods and services. The shortages in turn put pressure on prices, as did the expansion of the money supply because of the large quantities of imported bullion. War destruction, crop failures, and the requirements of expanding governments also contributed to a demand that outstripped production.

Food prices rose approximately twice as much as those of other goods, with wheat costing roughly five times more in the early 1600s than it had in the late 1400s. Rising food prices caused severe hardship for the poor and acted as a brake on population growth by the mid-seventeenth century, but they also spurred the development of the Atlantic fisheries and commercial agriculture. Prices, however, rose faster than agricultural yield. In England in the late 1500s rising grain prices curtailed the earlier trend of converting arable land to pasture. Economic conditions encouraged the Dutch not only to continue reclaiming land from the sea but also to develop the techniques of crop rotation. Traditionally, a third of the land had been left fallow each year on a rotating basis in order to restore fertility, but the Dutch discovered that the same end could be achieved by periodically planting beans or peas (to return nitrogen to the soil) and grazing animals, whose manure acted as fertilizer. The adoption of crop rotation by the English and the French in the late seventeenth and eighteenth centuries was crucial to the growth in agricultural productivity that made the Industrial Revolution possible.

# Industrial and Commercial Development

The growth of merchant capitalism led to a major reorganization of the means of producing textiles, the demand for which increased as the population grew. In the cities of the Netherlands and northern and central Italy, merchant capitalists distributed raw wool from England or raw silk from Asia and western Europe to master artisans. These craftsmen, who still belonged to their own guilds, typically owned their shops, though not the materials on which they worked. Then, beginning in the late sixteenth century, English capitalists altered the system by distributing raw wool directly to village workers for spinning, dyeing, and weaving. From the merchants' standpoint, this system of "putting out" the work to villagers had the advantage of bypassing the traditional guilds with their controls over working conditions, wages, and prices. Because the labor was undertaken in the workers' cottages rather than in shops, the merchants' overhead was lower. In contrast to the guild system, however, the workers had no hope of improving their condition by completing an apprenticeship, and the division between employer and worker gradually became permanent. The price revolution provided additional incentive for the expansion of this system as the cost of goods outpaced the rise in wages. Thus the introduction of the domestic system of textile production could bring substantial profits to the merchant capitalists but increasingly sharpened the division between the

The Flemish painter Jan Gossaert, commonly known as Mabuse (c. 1478–1532), depicts a merchant recording his business transactions; other records hang on the cabinet behind him. [National Gallery of Art, Washington, Ailsa Mellon Bruce Fund]

haves and have-nots as workers were exploited. The domestic system, which regularly involved entire families working together in the home, gradually spread throughout western Europe until it was phased out by the introduction of factories in the Industrial Revolution. By that time rural workers were manufacturing not only textiles but cutlery, buttons, gloves, and household goods as well.

Merchant capitalists were also responsible for innovative new forms of business organization intended primarily to take advantage of the trade opportunities with Asia, Africa, and America. The partnerships and family firms of the medieval period were simply not in a position to raise sufficient capital to fund these voyages. With government approval, merchants began banding together as "regulated" companies with a monopoly on a particular item or trade with a given area. Even so, the amount of capital was limited to what the merchants themselves could raise. The solution was the formation of the joint-stock company, an organization of investors rather than an association of traders. Funds came not only from the business community but also from the aristocracy and government officials, and management was in the hands of directors experienced in commercial affairs. The firms were normally awarded monopolies and tended to concern themselves at first with overseas trade and colonization. The English (1600), Dutch (1602), French (1664), and others had East India companies organized on a joint-stock basis by private businessmen with government encouragement. Other companies were formed for such endeavors as colonizing Virginia and Massachusetts and trading furs in North America.

✿

## ANTWERP'S GOLDEN AGE

No city more clearly reflected the opportunities and the glory of the age of exploration than Antwerp. In the late fifteenth and sixteenth centuries it stood at the crossroads of Europe, the hub of trade between England and the Continent, the Baltic and the Mediterranean. In terms of international commerce, Antwerp enjoyed the position formerly held by Venice. An awed Venetian envoy observed: "I was astounded and wondered much when I beheld Antwerp, for I saw Venice outdone."[7] Antwerp's dominant position among a host of secondary towns moved the Belgian historian Henri Pirenne to refer to the Netherlands—which in the sixteenth century included what is now Belgium as well as Holland—as its "suburb." Antwerp was a major cultural center as well. The German artist Albrecht Dürer was impressed by the city as well as by the "wonderful works of art" from Mexico that he viewed there on his last visit in 1521. The great Flemish painters Pieter Brueghel the Elder (c. 1525–1569) and Peter Paul Rubens (1577–1640) lived in Antwerp. Rubens, famed for his historical scenes, classical allegories, and sensuous nude figures, was the most eagerly sought-after painter of his time and the first to accumulate a substantial fortune through his art. He served as well as an ambassador from the archducal court of the Spanish Netherlands (later called Belgium), particularly to England.

Antwerp's rise to commercial greatness was facilitated by its geographic advantages. In the late 1400s the preeminence of Bruges as a trading center was undercut when the Zwyn River silted up. Antwerp, situated on the Scheldt River, thereupon became the leading port and commercial center in the Netherlands. Antwerp's rise

## ◉ Antwerp's Prosperity ◉

*When the Florentine traveler Ludovico Guicciardini visited Antwerp in the mid-1500s, he was thoroughly impressed by its commercial activity. Here he tries to explain why the city was so prosperous.*

The causes of the great wealth that Antwerp is grown to, are three. The first [is] the two markets that are in Antwerp, the one whereof begins fifteen days before Whitsuntide. . . . The other . . . begins the second Sunday after Our Lady Day in August. . . . Each of these markets endures six weeks, all the which time no man is subject to any arrest for debt. . . . There are also at Antwerp besides these markets two great horse fairs . . . and likewise two of leather and skins of all sorts, which follow immediately after the horse fairs.

The second cause of the wealth of Antwerp is this . . . : The king of Portugal, having partly by love, partly by force, drawn all the traffic of spices in Calicut and the isles adjacent thereunto into his own hands, and having brought them to Lisbon, sent his factor [agent] with spices to Antwerp, by which means it drew all nations thither to buy spices. . . . Afterwards in the year 1516 divers [foreign] merchants . . . departed from Bruges to go and dwell at Antwerp, and after them others. . . .

The third cause of the wealth of Antwerp . . . [is that the citizens have] marvelously fortified their town, for the safety both of it and of all merchants trafficking to it, so that it is now free from all danger and thought impregnable, by means whereof, a great multitude of noblemen and gentlemen come to dwell in the town.

*Source:* L. Guicciardini, *The Description of the Low Countreys* (London: Peter Short for Thomas Chard, 1593), pp. 26–27 (edited to conform to modern usage).

**Merchants gathered at the Antwerp Bourse, built in 1531, to transact their business. The portico surrounding the courtyard rested on 38 sculptured columns, each unique, and the upper level housed shops. The building was destroyed by fire in 1581. [New York Public Library]**

was also aided by Bruges' insistence on maintaining outmoded commercial regulations; by its hostility to the Burgundian dukes, who turned their attention to Antwerp; and by Habsburg favoritism toward Antwerp in the collection of customs duties. Many of the city's major buildings were constructed in the period of prosperity that ensued, including the great Gothic cathedral of the Holy Virgin (begun in the 1300s), the castle, the Renaissance town hall, and the Bourse, the center of foreign exchange. So great was the expansion that in 1542 a third set of costly city walls had to be constructed. With a population of 100,000 in the mid-sixteenth century, Antwerp was one of the largest cities in Europe.

Commencing in the late 1400s, the shift in the center of European commerce from Venice and the cities of the Hanseatic League brought more than 1,000 foreign businesses to Antwerp. It became the hub of the Portuguese spice trade, the northern headquarters of the Fugger family, and the center for the import of English cloth. Its bustling harbor handled as many as 500 ships a day, and more than 1,000 freight wagons arrived in the city each week carrying the overland trade. Recognizing the amount of capital necessary to participate in the spice trade, as early as 1505 the king of Portugal allowed the merchants of Antwerp to purchase a sizable cargo in the Indies and transport it directly to Antwerp in Portuguese ships. The Fuggers were among those who participated

in this venture and the ensuing expansion of the spice trade. Antwerp also imported large quantities of raw materials for use in its own industries, especially cloth manufacturing and finishing. Antwerp artisans pioneered in the production of "new draperies," a lighter and less expensive material than traditional woolen broadcloth, and they also manufactured silk, velvet, and similar luxury goods. Antwerp designers determined European fashions. Like Geneva, Antwerp was a center of the printing industry, boasting approximately 50 print shops in the mid-1500s. The English Bible translators William Tyndale and Miles Coverdale worked for a time in Antwerp, and by the late sixteenth century its printers were among the leading publishers of Counter-Reformation literature.

Antwerp, facing growing commercial competition from the English, became a casualty of the religious wars that plagued much of Europe in the late sixteenth century (see Chapter 19). In 1576, as the Netherlands struggled against Spanish domination, Antwerp was plundered by Spanish troops, and 6,000 of its citizens were slaughtered. The people rallied, expelled the Spaniards, and were governed by Calvinists until 1585, when the Spanish regained control and exiled the Protestants. Antwerp's troubles enabled Amsterdam to replace it as the leading commercial center of Europe in the seventeenth century.

Antwerp was the first city to serve as the hub of a worldwide commercial network. By the time the city began to decline, the underpinnings of a global economy had been established, and political and economic power was beginning to shift northward from Spain and Portugal to England, the Netherlands, and France. Compared to the tempo of economic change in earlier centuries, the speed with which the global economy developed in this period was remarkable. Europeans experienced a social and economic revolution in the late fifteenth and sixteenth centuries. The emergence of merchant capitalism provided striking opportunities for the acquisition of wealth and power. In England progressive aristocrats recognized this and profited by their association with the business community, whereas in Spain the hidalgos' resistance to commercial activity contributed to that nation's declining economy. Simply put, Spain squandered the opportunities that had been presented by its early dominance in the Americas.

As most western European rulers centralized their states, they adapted to the economic changes by formulating policies designed to control or expand trade. The governments of France, England, and the Netherlands were especially successful, and the resulting wealth was the basis of their growing power in the late 1500s and 1600s. Indeed, one of the effects of the commercial revolution was the increased ability of states to field large, better-equipped armies.

The lives of countless ordinary people changed, slowly but dramatically. The domestic system of manufacturing eventually created significant numbers of workers who had no reasonable prospect of improving their position. Many continued to live at the subsistence level despite shifting from agriculture to manufacturing. To feed the expanding population, commercial agriculture blossomed, aided by the introduction of crop rotation and the further enclosing of land. For many, however, the general living standard declined in the face of bad harvests, higher taxes, the adverse effects of war on the economy, and capitalistic developments, especially on the farms. Colonial expansion, however, brought Europeans new foods—tomatoes (called "love apples" and initially thought to be poisonous), lima beans, maize, squash, potatoes, and chocolate—and in turn the people of the New World were introduced to horses, cattle, and the Eurasian diseases that largely wiped them out. The development of global trade patterns also gave Europeans readier access to such items as tea, coffee, chocolate, and sugar. As sugarcane cultivation spread from the eastern Mediterranean to the eastern Atlantic and then to the New World, so did the slave trade through the agency of the Portuguese and the Spanish. The slave trade was not a European invention, for it was already thriving among the Africans. Nevertheless, for the enslaved Africans and the ravaged natives of America, European expansion often had cruel results. In Europe the discovery of new continents and the increased contact with Africa and Asia forced a rethinking of traditional views. As travelers and explorers documented their observations, a more accurate understanding of the physical world began to replace myth and superstition. The developments of this period also marked the first steps toward a Western hegemony in the world that has lasted into the twentieth century.

## Notes

1. C. D. Ley, ed., *Portuguese Voyages, 1498–1663* (New York: Dutton, 1947), p. 28.
2. P. M. Watts, "Prophecy and Discovery: On the Spiritual Origins of Christopher Columbus's 'Enterprise of the Indies,'" *American Historical Review* 90 (February 1985): 102.
3. D. B. Quinn, ed., *New American World: A Documentary History of North America to 1612*, Vol. 1: *America from Concept to Discovery: Early Exploration of North America* (New York: Arno Press and Hector Bye, 1979), p. 97.
4. G. F. Hudson, *Europe and China* (London: Arnold, 1931), p. 201.
5. R. Murphey, *The Outsiders: The Western Experience in India and China* (Ann Arbor: University of Michigan Press, 1977), p. 21.
6. F. Braudel, *Civilization and Capitalism, 15th–18th Century*, Vol. 1: *The Structures of Everyday Life: The Limits of the Possible*, trans. S. Reynolds (New York: Harper & Row, 1979), p. 514.
7. C. Wilson, *The Transformation of Europe, 1558–1648* (Berkeley: University of California Press, 1976), p. 62.

## Suggestions for Further Reading

Andrews, K. R. *Trade, Plunder and Settlement: Maritime Enterprise and the Genesis of the British Empire, 1480–1630.* Cambridge: Cambridge University Press, 1984.
Ball, J. N. *Merchants and Merchandise: The Expansion of Trade in Europe, 1500–1630.* London: Croom Helm, 1977.

Boxer, C. R. *The Dutch Seaborne Empire, 1600–1800*. London: Knopf, 1965.

———. *The Portuguese Seaborne Empire, 1415–1825*. New York: Knopf, 1969.

Braudel, F. *Civilization and Capitalism*, trans. S. Reynolds, 3 vols. New York: Harper & Row, 1979–1984.

Cipolla, C. M. *Before the Industrial Revolution: European Society and Economy, 1000–1700*, 2nd ed. New York: Norton, 1980.

———. *Guns and Sails in the Early Phase of European Expansion, 1400–1700*. London: Collins, 1965.

Cole, J. A. *The Potosí Mita, 1573–1700: Compulsory Indian Labor in the Andes*. Stanford, Calif.: Stanford University Press, 1985.

Curtin, P. D. *Cross-cultural Trade in World History*. Cambridge: Cambridge University Press, 1984.

Davis, R. *The Rise of the Atlantic Economies*. London: Weidenfeld & Nicolson, 1973.

Diffie, B. W., and Winius, G. D. *Foundations of the Portuguese Empire, 1415–1580*. Minneapolis: University of Minnesota Press, 1977.

Elliott, J. H. *The Old World and the New, 1492–1650*. Cambridge: Cambridge University Press, 1970.

Gibson, C. *The Aztecs Under Spanish Rule: A History of the Indians of the Valley of Mexico, 1519–1810*. Stanford, Calif.: Stanford University Press, 1964.

Hemming, J. *The Conquest of the Incas*. New York: Harcourt Brace Jovanovich, 1970.

Israel, J. I. *Dutch Primacy in World Trade, 1585–1740*. New York: Oxford University Press, 1989.

Kling, B. B., and Pearson, M. N., eds. *Europeans in Asia Before Dominion*. Honolulu: University Press of Hawaii, 1979.

Kriedte, P. *Peasants, Landlords and Merchant Capitalists: Europe and the World Economy, 1500–1800*. Leamington, England: Berg Press, 1983.

Lockhart, J. M. *The Men of Cajamarca: A Social and Biographical Study of the First Conquerors of Peru*. Austin: University of Texas Press, 1972.

MacLeod, M. J. *Spanish Central America: A Socioeconomic History, 1520–1720*. Berkeley: University of California Press, 1973.

Mannix, D. P., and Cowley, M. *Black Cargoes: A History of the Atlantic Slave Trade, 1518–1865*. New York: Viking, 1962.

McAlister, L. N. *Spain and Portugal in the New World, 1492–1700*. Minneapolis: University of Minnesota Press, 1984.

Meilink-Roelofsz, M. A. P. *Asian Trade and European Influence in the Indonesian Archipelago, Between 1500 and About 1630*. The Hague: Nijhoff, 1962.

Mintz, S. W. *Sweetness and Power: The Place of Sugar in Modern History*. New York: Viking, 1985.

Morison, S. E. *The European Discovery of America: The Northern Voyages, A.D. 500–1600*. New York: Oxford University Press, 1971.

———. *The European Discovery of America: The Southern Voyages, A.D. 1492–1616*. New York: Oxford University Press, 1974.

Murray, J. J. *Antwerp in the Age of Plantin and Brueghel*. Norman: University of Oklahoma Press, 1970.

Nef, J. *The Conquest of the Material World*. Chicago: University of Chicago Press, 1964.

Parry, J. H. *The Age of Reconnaissance*, 2nd ed. New York: New American Library, 1966.

———. *The Discovery of the Sea*, 2nd ed. Berkeley: University of California Press, 1981.

———. *The Establishment of European Hegemony, 1415–1715*. New York: Harper & Row, 1961.

———, ed. *The European Reconnaissance: Selected Documents*. New York: Walker, 1968.

Pearson, M. N. *Merchants and Rulers in Gujarat: The Response to the Portuguese in the Sixteenth Century*. Berkeley: University of California Press, 1976.

Ricci, M. *China in the Sixteenth Century: The Journals of Matthew Ricci, 1583–1610*, trans. L. J. Gallagher. New York: Random House, 1953.

Rice, E. F., Jr. *The Foundations of Early Modern Europe, 1460–1559*. New York: Norton, 1970.

Schurz, W. L. *The Manila Galleon*. New York: Dutton, 1939.

Souza, G. B. *The Survival of Empire: Portuguese Trade and Society in China and the South China Sea, 1630–1754*. Cambridge: Cambridge University Press, 1986.

Spence, J. D. *The Memory Palace of Matteo Ricci*. New York: Viking, 1984.

Tracy, J. E., ed. *The Rise of Merchant Empires*. Cambridge: Cambridge University Press, 1990.

Wallerstein, I. M. *The Modern World System: Capitalist Agriculture and the Origins of the European World Economy in the Sixteenth Century*. New York: Academic Press, 1974.

# Maps and Their Makers (I)

One of the most basic tasks of all human communities, from nomad bands to settled civilizations, is to orient the group to the locations of things. To situate resources, to mark off shelter and defense, to establish territorial limits—all are essential to group survival. The idea of accomplishing these tasks by drawing a map evolved long ago among many different peoples. Human beings were making maps long before they developed the ability to symbolize their speech in writing.

From early times, too, maps appear to have been used not only to mark off known places but also to theorize, and sometimes fantasize, about unknown ones. Modern armchair travelers who open maps to stimulate their imaginations about faraway places are exercising the same faculty as ancient mapmakers who populated the scrolls and edges of their charts with dragons and monsters. Maps thus invite us not only to define but also to extend the world. They are the instruments of our curiosity as well as our knowledge, our dreams as well as our science.

The growth of our knowledge has made mapmaking—cartography—an ever more important part of modern civilization. Somewhere in the world at this moment, a topographic or geodesic survey is making our understanding of the earth more precise; somewhere, a telescope is scanning the heavens, and a satellite or a space vehicle is beaming back information about interstellar space that will go into a map. Scientists and physicians speak of mapping the brain and the living cell, and psychologists, the human mind. As a tool as well as a metaphor, mapping is one of the principal functions of our culture, in some ways as basic as speech.

The universality of mapmaking is one of its most striking characteristics. The Eskimos of North America carved coastal maps of extraordinary accuracy on animal skins and wood. The Marshall Islanders of the South Pacific lashed sticks and cane fibers together to indicate wind and wave patterns at sea, inserting stones or pieces of coral to designate islands. The Spanish conqueror Cortés made his advance through Central America with the aid only of native maps, and the British explorer James Cook navigated the South Seas with a chart made for him by a Tahitian that covered nearly 3,000 miles. Australian aborigines made rudimentary maps, and European cave dwellers incised maps on cave walls.

Perhaps the oldest surviving map is a clay tablet found at Nuzi in northern Iraq, dating from c. 2300 B.C. It is a cadastral survey, a map of property lots made for purposes of taxation. Many of the surviving maps from the second millennium B.C. are city plans,

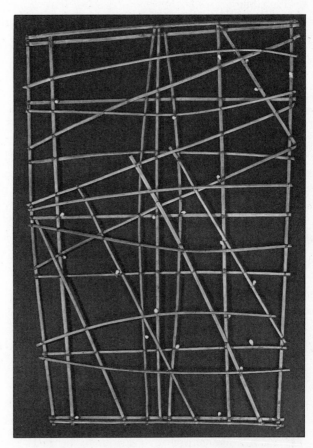

This ingenious map of the Marshall Islands in the South Pacific records wind and tidal patterns. The islands themselves are marked by inserts of coral. [British Museum]

such as the highly detailed one for the city of Nippur on the Euphrates, which shows the major temples, the river itself, the central park and canal, moats, walls, and the city gates. There is no reference to a Chinese map before the seventh century B.C. and none extant before the second century B.C., but the splendid examples excavated in Hunan province in 1974 suggest that Chinese cartography may be as ancient as any, and as sophisticated. Drawn on silk for the king of Changsha, they depict much of modern Hunan and regions as far south as the South China Sea. The first map gives the names of all cities and provinces and indicates major topographic features including more than 30 rivers. The second map, a military one, shows walled fortresses, military encampments, supply depots, and observation towers. Both the detail of the maps and the intricate use of symbols and legends suggest a highly developed tradition of cartography.

The earliest maps, then, were local and functional. The first people to attempt to map the world as a whole appear to have been the Babylonians. Their interest in the earth may have derived from their fascination with the heavens, which had for them, as for most peoples, a deep religious significance. The Babylonians depicted the sky as a vast circle, charting some 5,000 stars. In doing so, they introduced the first systematic measurement into mapping. The Babylonians had long before devised a calendar of 360 days, which they had divided into 60-minute hours and 60-second minutes. They hit on the idea of applying the same number system for measuring the circle, dividing it into 360 degrees, the degrees into minutes, and the minutes into seconds. Applying this to the heavens, they were able to plot the locations of the stars.

The Babylonians likewise conceived of the earth as round. In what appears to be the earliest surviving world map, it is depicted as a flat circular disk with Babylonia in the center and its neighbors, the Assyrians and the Chaldeans, to the east and the southwest, respectively. Beyond that single landmass lay a great, globe-encircling ocean, from which rose seven islands. These in turn formed a bridge to an outer circle or Heavenly Ocean, the abode of the ancient gods. Fanciful and symbolic, this first world map was an exercise in cosmography as much as cartography.

Not long after, the Ionian philosopher Anaximander produced the first world map in the Greek-speaking world. The slightly later map of Hecataeus (c. 501 B.C.), who is credited with having compiled the first manual of geography, was used by Aristagoras of Miletus in soliciting the help of Sparta against the Persian Empire at the time of the Ionian revolt. The Spartan king, Cleomenes, was attracted by the prospect of spoil from Persia's neighbors, but when he learned that they lay three months' journey away, he ordered Aristagoras out of Sparta by nightfall.

Herodotus, the source of this story, himself proposed locating geographic sites by means of parallels and meridians. By the end of the fifth century B.C., the idea of maps had become familiar enough so that a character in Aristophanes' comedy *The Clouds* (produced in 423 B.C.), carried one on stage and pointed out Athens on it. In the next two centuries the geographic horizons of the Greeks expanded considerably, notably through the conquests of Alexander and the travels of Pytheas to Britain and the Low Countries. The actual size of the world remained a matter of conjecture, however, until Eratosthenes (275–194 B.C.), the librarian of Alexandria, conceived the brilliant scheme of measuring the angle of shadow cast by the sun at noon in Alexandria and computing it against the known distance to an-

**On the oldest surviving world map, earth, ocean, and heaven are linked. This Babylonian vision of the cosmos dates from the sixth century B.C. [British Museum]**

other site on the same meridian in Egypt, where the sun's rays were reportedly vertical at noon on the day of the summer solstice. Assuming (as the ancient mathematician Pythagoras had) that the world was a perfect sphere, Eratosthenes was able to calculate its circumference as 250,000 stadia, or about 28,000 miles. None of Eratosthenes' factual assumptions was quite right—the two sites were not precisely on the same meridian, the distance between them was not measured exactly, and the earth is not a perfect sphere—but his method was basically sound, and his result was only about 3,000 miles off. For the first time, human beings had a tolerably accurate notion of the size of their planet, based not on fancy or guesswork but on scientific measurement. The news was not especially pleasing to Hellenistic geographers, however. It meant that three-quarters of the globe was unknown to them.

This vast expanse, *terra incognita* ("unknown earth"), as the Romans called it, did not remain unpopulated for long. Solinus, a grammarian of the third century A.D., imagined a race of horse-footed men to the east in Asia with ears so long that the flaps covered their entire bodies, making clothes unnecessary. Other men were said to have only one leg with a giant foot. In Germany, Solinus asserted, there were birds whose feathers glowed in the dark, while Libya was the home of the cockatrice, which crept along the ground like a crocodile on its forequarters but was hoisted in the rear by lateral fins. Mythical kingdoms abounded as well, such as that of Prester (Elder) John, a Christian monarch reputedly descended from the Magi who ruled a land in which one of the rivers flowed directly from Paradise. When several expeditions failed to discover this kingdom in the East (Marco Polo reported it conquered by Chinghis Khan), cartographers obligingly shifted it to Africa, where it figured on maps for several centuries. A less benign vision was that of the land of Gog and Magog, whose terrifying hordes, first prophesied by Ezekiel, were feared by Christian and Muslim alike. Some mapmakers placed the savage tribes in southern Russia, while a Syrian tale held that Alexander the Great had sealed them off, presumably in India, behind a wall of iron and brass. Ibn-Khaldun, a fourteenth-century Arab geographer and historian, apparently confused the wall of Gog and Magog with the Great Wall of China.

As the Babylonians had placed themselves at the center of the earth and as medieval Christians placed Jerusalem there, so too did the Chinese regard their "Middle Kingdom" as the center of things. Legend had it that two men had walked from the court of the fabled Emperor Yu, first from north to south and then from east to west, and found the earth equidistant at all points from the imperial palace. We do not know how the Chinese may have embellished their own *terra incognita*, but their high standard of mapmaking was maintained and advanced. P'ei Hsiu (Bei Xiu, A.D. 224–271), author of the *Six Principles of Cartography*, constructed a map of China for the emperor Wu Ti on a scale of about a third of a mile to an inch; it covered 18 sheets. An even more finely detailed map was produced in the eighth century: measuring 33 by 30 feet, it took 16 years to complete. In the eleventh century, Shen Kuo (Shen Guo) produced the first relief map, modeled in wax.

The most important ancient cartographer in the West was Claudius Ptolemy (c. 90–c. 168), who, like Eratosthenes, was the librarian of Alexandria. In his two principal works—the *Almagest*, a compendium of astronomy and mathematics, and the *Geographia*, which, with its large world map and 26 regional ones showing some 8,000 places, was the world's first atlas—he attempted to survey the whole of the cosmos. Like Eratosthenes, Ptolemy had better ideas than information. He devised the notion of dividing maps into areas

of latitude and longitude, and he was the first to orient maps to the north. But he lacked precise instruments for celestial angle measurement and timekeeping that were essential to accurate siting, and he was dependent for much of his information on travelers' reports that, as he well knew, were often both boastful and sketchy. The Ptolemaic world consisted of three continents—Europe, Asia, and Africa. Of these, only Europe was shown in full outline, and even here, guesswork or inaccurate reporting was evident; the shape of Britain (Albion), for example, was grossly distorted, and Scandinavia (Scandia) was shown as an island. Nonetheless, Ptolemy's map was by far the best representation of the known world available to Western or Islamic cartographers for more than 1,300 years, and it became the standard reference, particularly in Arab lands.

Two of Ptolemy's errors were to have fateful consequences. Like most educated people of his time, he rejected the hypothesis of the third-century B.C. astronomer Aristarchus that the sun was the center of the universe and placed the earth there instead. He also underestimated the circumference of the globe, accepting Poseidonius' calculation of 18,000 miles instead of Eratosthenes' older but more accurate one. The result of this, amplified by the expanded idea of Asia brought home by Marco Polo, was to persuade Christopher Columbus that the Indies were relatively close to western Europe. That mistake uncovered the New World, whose inhabitants had their own highly complex systems of mapping and measurement.

The first large map depicting the New World in its relation to Europe was made in 1500 by Juan de la Cosa, who accompanied Columbus on his second voyage. De la Cosa, like Columbus, was still unsure that the New World was not connected to Asia. But in 1507 a German cartographer, Martin Waldseemüller, produced the first map suggesting that "America," as he baptized the southern half of the New World in honor of the explorer Amerigo Vespucci, was actually a continent, separated from Asia by an unknown ocean. Waldseemüller's truncated depiction of the Western Hemisphere was hopelessly inadequate, and his "Ocean Orientalis" was only a fraction of the actual Pacific Ocean. But his daring guess was right. For the first time, even if only in the roughest configuration, the true shape of the world was known. Six years later, Vasco Núñez de Balboa made the first sighting of the western Pacific, and six years after that Ferdinand Magellan undertook the first circumnavigation of the globe. Magellan's heroic voyage cost him his life (he was killed in a skirmish with natives in the Philippines); only one of his five ships survived, and 35 of his 280 sailors. With what they brought back, however, the Portuguese cartographer Diego Ribero was able to produce a map that conveyed not only the true shape but also an approximation of the true proportions of the world.

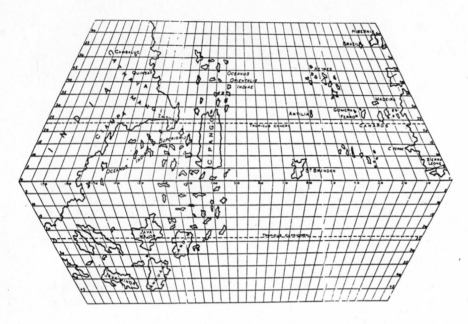

A sketch of the map used by Columbus on his first voyage to the New World in 1492. The cartographer estimated the distance to the "Indies" as little more than that from Portugal to the Azores. "India" and "Cathay" (China) were represented as part of a single undifferentiated landmass. The large island of "Cipango" represents Japan. [Library of Congress]

From this point on, discovery proceeded apace, as explorers and cartographers worked together. The dimensions of Africa had finally been realized in the fifteenth century, when Prince Henry of Portugal—the famous Henry the Navigator—had explored the west coast of Africa, partly in hopes of finding a sea route around it to India, partly in quest of the kingdom of Prester John. The daunting length of Africa had led Columbus to try a crossing of the Atlantic instead, but in 1498 Vasco da Gama sailed around the Cape of Good Hope and reached India. By the mid-sixteenth century the real dimensions of North and South America had begun to appear on maps, and the influence of Ptolemy at last faded. It was no longer permissible, as it had still been only a generation or two earlier, to mix fact and fancy, discovery and tradition. Rulers in quest of gold and merchants of silk and spices demanded accuracy and completeness of their maps. What the historian J. H. Parry has called the age of reconnaissance had begun.

The dependence of mariners on the accuracy of their maps for voyages of increasing distance and duration highlighted a problem that Ptolemy had grappled with: how to represent the reality of a three-dimensional globe on a flat, two-dimensional surface. Ptolemy had divided his world into lines of longitude and latitude, thus forming a grid whose intersections would enable one to plot any point on the globe; but on that globe itself, of course, the lines were curved, not straight, converging in the case of longitude at the two poles and varying widely in length in the case of latitude. Ptolemaic maps had attempted to compensate for this by drawing curvilinear lines, but while this was of some help with lines of latitude, it still left parallel rather than converging lines of longitude. Model globes themselves were helpful, but any large enough to show sufficient detail for navigational purposes were far too large to carry.

A practical solution was devised by a Flemish car-

This huge, splendidly carved Aztec stone calendar, which stood atop the Aztec temple at Tenochtitlán, was used to make complex astronomical measurements, including the calculation of eclipses. [Paolo Koch/Photo Researchers]

tographer, Gerhard Kremer (1512–1594), better known as Gerardus Mercator. Mercator abandoned the Ptolemaic compromise of curving lines to draw a grid of perfectly straight ones. At the same time, he extended the distance between the lines of latitude at an increasing rate from the equator to the poles. This widened the distortion both of distance and of representation, particularly in the polar regions: thus, on a Mercator map, the island of Greenland appears considerably larger than the continent of South America, although in reality it is only one-eighth as big. But the map was of vital advantage to mariners in one respect. It enabled them to plot direction and to chart their voyages from home port to final destination on a straight line. Mercator's new map was first published in 1569, and his system is still in use.

By the late sixteenth century, the shape, dimension, and much of the outline of the world had been revealed. Shortly thereafter, the shape of the heavens would begin to disclose itself as well.

## Suggestions for Further Reading

Bagrow, L. *A History of Cartography.* London: Watts, 1964.

Bricker, C., and Tooley, R. V. *A History of Cartography: 2500 Years of Maps and Mapmakers.* London: Thames & Hudson, 1969.

Brown, L. A. *The Story of Maps.* Boston: Little, Brown, 1980.

Harley, J. B., and Woodward, D., eds. *The History of Cartography.* Chicago: University of Chicago Press, 1987.

Kopal, Z. *Widening Horizons: Man's Quest to Understand the Structure of the Universe.* New York: Taplinger, 1970.

Parry, J. H. *The Age of Reconnaissance.* 2nd ed. New York: New American Library, 1966.

Schlee, S. *The Edge of an Unfamiliar World: A History of Oceanography.* New York: Dutton, 1973.

Thrower, N. J. W. *Maps and Man.* Englewood Cliffs, N.J.: Prentice Hall, 1972.

Wilford, J. N. *The Mapmakers.* New York: Knopf, 1981.

# CHAPTER 19

# State-Building and Revolution

Emboldened by the wealth of its new empire, Spain made a major bid in the late sixteenth century to establish domination in western Europe. This was largely the outgrowth of the determination of both Charles V and Philip II to rule their inherited territories and of the equally strong resolve of the English and the French to prevent the expansion of Habsburg power. The Netherlands, Portugal, England, Italy, and France were all threatened by a militant Spanish imperialism imbued with the spirit of the Counter-Reformation. By the end of the century Philip II had largely failed in his quest, although fighting continued in the Netherlands, and Portugal remained firmly under Spanish rule. Two decades after Philip's death in 1598, the Thirty Years' War erupted. Most of Europe was involved in what proved to be one of the bloodiest wars in the continent's history. The wars, internal tensions and rebellions stemming from the increasing burdens of government centraliza-

**A pious, brooding, bookish man, Philip II was described by an English admirer as "the most potent monarch of Christendom." [National Portrait Gallery, London]**

tion and taxation, and competing religious ideologies both within and across borders contributed to a series of crises in the mid-1600s that threw almost every major European state into turmoil.

# Philip II and the Quest for Spanish Hegemony

Spain's bid for supremacy in the late 1500s was a natural outgrowth of earlier Habsburg policy, the development of political absolutism, the religious zeal of the Counter-Reformation, and the wealth and power created by its new colonial empire. It was also made possible by the division of the vast and unwieldly Habsburg domain between two crowns. When Emperor Charles V abdicated and retired to a monastery in 1556, the imperial crown was bestowed on his brother, Ferdinand I (1556–1564), who also inherited the Austrian Habsburg territories. The Spanish throne went to Philip II (1556–1598), together with the territories of the Netherlands, Milan, Naples, Spanish America, and lesser places. His wife ruled England in her own right as Mary I (1553–1558). Vast though they remained, Spain's dominions still had a clear center of authority in the court of Madrid.

Spanish power in the reign of Philip II became possible in part at the expense of France. Charles V's troubles with the Lutherans and the Turks had prevented him from attaining a permanent victory over his archenemy, King Francis I of France (1515–1547). For most of their reigns the two monarchs quarreled, particularly over northern Italy. After the Habsburg forces captured Francis at the battle of Pavia in 1525, Charles held him prisoner in Spain until he signed a treaty surrendering both the duchy of Burgundy and his Italian claims. When Francis repudiated the treaty, the struggle was renewed. Both rulers had died by the time this phase of the Habsburg quest for dominance ended in 1559 with the Treaty of Cateau-Cambrésis. The treaty, which confirmed Spanish possession of Milan and Naples, ended 65 years of fighting in northern Italy.

In 1559 Philip II's prospects for the extension of Spanish Habsburg hegemony were good. The Treaty of Cateau-Cambrésis, which recognized Spanish mastery in Italy, required Spain to yield nothing of consequence in return. Although Philip's attempt after Mary's death to win the hand of the English queen, Elizabeth I, had been politely rebuffed, the new treaty included a proviso for his marriage to Elizabeth of Valois, the 13-year-old daughter of the French king, Henry II (1547–1559). Henry's accidental death in a tilting match during the treaty ceremonies brought his feeble son, Francis II (1559–1560), briefly to the French throne. Two of his equally weak brothers followed. Not until the late 1590s

would a strong monarch again govern France. Spain was without peer in Europe.

Although the work of centralizing had been under way in the major western European states since the late 1400s, the Spain that Philip inherited was still far from unified. Unlike England, where a single parliament served as a unifying bond, Spain had a separate assembly called the Cortes for Castile, each of the three regions of Aragon, and Navarre. France and the Netherlands similarly had regional states, but in both cases there was an Estates General, albeit weak, to represent the country as a whole. Philip made no attempt to create such a body in Spain but instead governed each of the three states—Aragon, Castile, and Navarre—independently. In Castile, the largest state with 7 million inhabitants, the aristocracy was tax-exempt and thus had little reason to strengthen the Cortes. Because the nobility of Aragon had a tradition of greater independence and political power, Philip seldom summoned its Cortes. The states of Aragon and Navarre, with a population exceeding a million, were in any event less important than populous Castile, whose townspeople and peasants bore the brunt of Philip's taxation. In the end, these taxes virtually destroyed Spanish manufacturing.

Although Philip had no Cortes for Spain as a whole, central authority was administered by local agents appointed by the crown. The English monarchs accomplished this function in the early Tudor period by expanding the authority of the justices of the peace. Similarly, in Castile, Isabella increased the responsibilities of the corregidors, who supervised the town councils.

The distinctive feature of Spanish government was the system of higher councils Philip used to supervise the affairs of his far-flung empire. Although the English sovereigns also used councils, the English conciliar structure was less elaborate and powerful than the Spanish. In England the Privy Council advised the monarch, helped administer the realm, and performed certain judicial functions, and there were councils for the north and for Wales. Philip, whose domain was much more extensive and scattered, had a major council for each region of his empire: Castile, Aragon, the Netherlands, Italy (Milan and Naples), and Spanish America. Viceroys carried out the instructions of these councils. There were also specialized councils to handle such matters as state affairs, finance, war, and the Inquisition. Although the councils convened in Madrid, there were so many of them that Philip rarely attended. Nevertheless, his bookish, bureaucratic temperament moved him to spend long hours poring over the mountain of paperwork his officials produced. Philip became heavily embroiled in the details of government, devoting enormous time to writing marginal comments on the papers he studied. Distrustful of his officials and jealous of his power, he played his officers against each other and set

*19.1 Europe, c. 1560*

up a system of checks and balances that made Spanish administration ponderous and inefficient.

Although Philip apparently hoped to wield absolute power based on the idea that his subjects owed him unquestioning obedience as a right and a Christian duty, in practice a top-heavy administrative system, a privileged aristocracy, regional traditions, and limited revenues circumscribed his authority. The nobles paid only sales taxes, and though Philip taxed merchants and professionals, there were fewer of them proportionately in Spain than in other western European countries. The bulk of the taxes therefore fell on those least able to pay, the peasants. The result was insufficient revenue, forcing Philip to declare bankruptcy three times during his reign. Because the government protected the ships that transported New World bullion to Spain, it was entitled to a royalty of 20 percent, but smuggling decreased the potential value of this revenue, and the king mortgaged much of what he did receive to finance military campaigns. Like the English monarchs in the early 1600s, he raised some money by selling offices and titles, and he also received income from crown lands and the sale of papal dispensations. None of this, however, compensated for the loss of funds that would have been obtained by properly taxing the nobility. In Castile alone, 300 tax-exempt nobles owned more than half the land. The king's habitual indebtedness was thus a passive restraint on his power exercised by the nobility.

## THE SPANISH CITADEL: MADRID AND THE ESCORIAL

The development of absolute government and the bureaucracy to administer it made a permanent capital necessary. "It was right," said one observer, "that so great a monarchy should have a city which could function as its heart—a vital center in the midst of the body, which ministered equally to every state in time of peace and war."[1] Unlike Charles V, who frequently moved around his empire, Philip favored a sedentary life, though when he settled the capital at Madrid in 1561, he had no apparent intention of making it permanent. Located on a plateau at an altitude of more than 2,000 feet, its major advantages were its healthy climate and its centrality. The city had a population of only 25,000 in 1561, but by the early 1600s it had quadrupled in size. Madrid's rise adversely affected Valladolid and Toledo, the latter a beautiful medieval city whose population of more than 50,000 decreased by two-thirds during Philip's reign. By the mid-seventeenth century Madrid was the only Spanish city whose population was substantially larger than it had been in the 1500s.

Madrid's growth was not the result of new industry but of bureaucratic expansion and the capital's attraction to younger sons of the nobility, declining hidalgos, and impoverished workers in search of a living. In a futile attempt to curb the growth of the city, the crown ordered the nobles to return to their estates in 1611, hoping the hangers-on would follow. Gypsies were also attracted to the city despite repeated attempts to expel them. Urban growth in Madrid was relatively easy because of ample space. The city was enclosed only with a mud wall to denote its boundaries, and as late as the nineteenth century there was still open space inside the walls. The city's importance as a financial center grew in the 1600s, particularly after the collapse of the large fairs at Medina del Campo. Although Madrid had neither a university nor a bishop, it became a leading cultural center in the early seventeenth century.

The site selected for Philip's massive new palace, the Escorial, was in the rocky hills some 30 miles northwest of Madrid. The building had been planned because of a provision in Charles V's will that his son construct a "dynastic pantheon" to house the bodies of Spanish sovereigns. In the octagonal Pantheon of the Kings, the gray marble coffins now rest four high along the walls. Philip, a deeply religious man, took a direct interest in the design, at one point admonishing one of the architects, Juan de Herrera, to remember the basic ideals of "simplicity of form, severity in the whole, nobility without arrogance, majesty without ostentation." The Escorial took two decades to build (1563–1584). Laid out in the shape of a gridiron, which probably reflected the influence of Italian Renaissance palace architecture, the gray stone building housed a Hieronymite monastery, a royal mausoleum where Charles V was interred, a large domed church inspired by Michelangelo's plan for St. Peter's in Rome, a library, and the royal palace and apartments. From a window in the apartments Philip could look out on the high altar in the chapel.

## The Culture of the Spanish Counter-Reformation

The spirit of religious austerity revealed in the Escorial reflected the severer side of the Catholic Reformation. The Spanish Inquisition, founded in 1478, rigorously persecuted Protestants and other suspected heretics, even twice imprisoning Ignatius of Loyola, the founder of the Jesuit order. The extent of its power was demonstrated when it jailed Bartolomé de Carranza, the archbishop of Toledo and primate of Spain, for 17 years on falsified

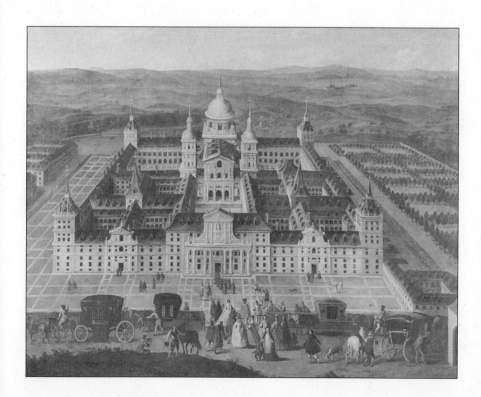

**Philip II's palace, the Escorial, as it appeared in the seventeenth century. According to a popular legend, the ground plan symbolized the gridiron on which St. Lawrence, whom Philip admired, was martyred. Philip tried to find the martyr's head to keep at the palace as a relic. [Réunion des Musées Nationaux/Louvre]**

charges of heresy. Obsessed with the need to keep the Spanish church pure, Philip supported the Inquisition and on five occasions even attended *autos-de-fé,* or "pageants of faith," religious rites at which sinners and heretics performed acts of penance or were executed. The Spanish Inquisition averaged 1,000 cases a year during his reign. The Inquisition also supervised the converted Jews known as Conversos who remained in Spain. The king himself was anti-Semitic, as reflected in his belief that "all the heresies which have existed in Germany and France . . . have been sown by the descendants of Jews."[2]

When Philip struck at the Moriscos—the Christianized Moors of Granada—by banning their language, customs, and distinctive dress, he incited a rebellion in 1568 that lasted until 1570. Subsequent efforts to assimilate the Moriscos were largely unsuccessful, and in the early 1600s they were deported by the tens of thousands. Altogether the number of Jews and Moors expelled from Spain between 1492, when they were given the option of becoming Christians or going into exile, and 1609 probably exceeded half a million. Philip also exiled the Jews from northern Italy much as his father had expelled them from Naples in 1544. Some 300,000 Conversos survived the threat of the Spanish Inquisition and remained active in professional and commercial activities, though most lived in their own districts.

Despite the brutal repression that characterized Spanish religious policy and comprised an important facet of absolutism, there was a positive side to Spanish piety in this period. This is beautifully manifested in the work of the mystics Teresa of Avila (1515–1582) and John of the Cross (1542–1591), both of whom were of Converso ancestry. Teresa, whose father was a hidalgo and whose seven brothers were colonial officials in America, was a Carmelite nun. Much of her work was devoted to the Carmelite Reform, an order dedicated to recapturing the original spirit of Carmelite austerity. She shared her religious experience in an autobiography, and in writings such as *The Way of Perfection* and *Exclamations of the Soul to God* she described the progress of the Christian soul toward its goal of unity with the divine. John of the Cross, a Carmelite monk who assisted Teresa in her reforming work, expressed his mystical experiences in poetry and in a meticulous analysis of mysticism. Together they inspired humble Spaniards to maintain their devotion to the Catholic church; their emphasis on the spiritual life probably helped the masses cope with their poverty.

Philip's favorite painter was Titian, the late Renaissance Venetian master famous for his sumptuous colors. For more than a quarter of a century Titian supplied Charles V and Philip with paintings. A number of these depicted mythological themes, often including sensuous female nudes. Like most of his contemporaries, Titian and presumably the pious Philip as well saw no contradiction between their veneration of the Virgin Mary and their appreciation of physical beauty in the Venus figures.

Directly as well as through his brilliant successor at Venice, Tintoretto (1518–1594), Titian influenced the painter whose work best captures the spirit of the Spanish Counter-Reformation, Domenico Theotokopoulos (1541–1614), known as El Greco ("the Greek"). Born in Crete, El Greco studied in Venice before moving to Spain in the 1570s. His first work for Philip allegorized the Holy League against the Turks by depicting Philip, the pope, and the doge of Venice kneeling before the "Holy Name" of Jesus. The king commissioned him to paint an altarpiece, the subject of which was the decision of St. Maurice, a commander in the imperial Roman army, to die rather than worship the traditional Roman deities. Displeased with the extent to which El Greco departed from the more straightforward Venetian style, Philip rejected the work. Most of El Greco's paintings convey the tension between the spiritual and material realms through spiral composition—swirling motion that drives the eye upward—and elongated figures. By accentuating color rather than form, he heightened the spiritual sense and created an art more emotional than intellectual or naturalistic. Thus the canvases of El Greco reflect the spiritual ecstasy expressed in the writings of Teresa and John of the Cross.

Although religion dominated much of the culture of Counter-Reformation Spain, other themes were popular as well, especially in literature and drama. The great masterpiece of Spanish literature, *Don Quixote,* was the work of Miguel de Cervantes (1547–1616), a surgeon's son who spent most of his creative life in Madrid. Captured while fighting against the Turks, he was enslaved in Algiers. Following his ransom, he finally turned to writing plays for the Madrid theater, but success eluded him until he published *Don Quixote* in 1605. A satire of the popular chivalric romances, the book entertained readers by humorously juxtaposing the idealist Don Quixote with the realist Sancho Panza. Despite Sancho's warnings, Don Quixote pursued his "righteous warfare" to rid the world of "accursed" giants, which in fact were windmills and sheep—the visions, said Sancho, of one who had "mills of the same sort in his head."

The success that eluded Cervantes on the stage was achieved by the prolific Lope de Vega (1562–1635), author of 1,500 plays by his own count. His works fall into two categories: heroic plays dealing with Spanish history and legend and comedies of manners and intrigue. Several of his plays break down the stereotyped image of the secluded Spanish lady. Some of Lope's women reject love and marriage, pursue careers, and even become outlaws. One of his most important themes deals with the king as the fount of justice and protector of the poor. Reflecting the spirit of his age, his plays demonstrate respect for the crown and the church.

## Spain and the Mediterranean

The wars in which Cervantes and Lope de Vega fought—the former against the Turks, the latter against the English—represent the two spheres of military activity that occupied Philip. Attention was focused on the Muslims in the Mediterranean during the first part of his reign and later on the Protestants in the North Atlantic. With the Ottoman Turks already in control of three-quarters of the Mediterranean coastline, their seizure of Cyprus from Venice in 1571 alarmed Europe. Spain, Venice, and the papacy responded by forming the Holy League to attack the Turks. The league's fleet of 300 ships and 80,000 men, most of them Spanish, engaged the Turks near Lepanto in Greece. The league won a decisive victory—the first major one in centuries over a Muslim fleet—in this last great battle between oar-propelled ships. The significance of Lepanto lay primarily in its impact on European morale and its check on Islamic expansion. The Turks, however, quickly rebuilt their fleet and refused to be driven from the western Mediterranean, though henceforth they concentrated on North Africa and never regained the superiority they had once enjoyed.

Philip's second major foreign policy triumph came in 1580 when he annexed Portugal and its empire. The death of the Portuguese king without a direct heir gave Philip, whose mother had been a Portuguese princess, his opportunity. After bribes and promises had won the support of the nobility and higher clergy for his own succession, the Spanish army completed the conquest. Philip ensured peace by leaving Portuguese officials to administer the realm and by generally leaving the people alone. The Spanish, however, failed to exploit their victory by coordinating the economic policy of the two countries and their empires. Spain's failure to unify the Iberian peninsula by anything more than a common crown made it possible for Portugal to recover its independence in the next century. During the period that the two crowns were united, large numbers of Portuguese Jews emigrated to Spain, where persecution had become less intense. The annexation also gave Philip additional ships and Atlantic ports, which were sorely needed for his campaigns in the Netherlands and France and for his armadas against the English.

## Rebellion in the Netherlands

The revolt of the Netherlands was the first significant setback to Philip II's dream of Habsburg hegemony in western Europe and the New World. The Low Countries were the wealthiest region in Europe and the center of the developing global economy, and its people were accustomed to considerable local autonomy and religious

**The Battle of Lepanto marked the first major European naval victory over the Turks. Some 600 ships were involved. [National Maritime Museum, London]**

diversity. Unlike Charles V, who had been raised in the Netherlands, Philip spoke no Dutch, disliked the Netherlands, and did not set foot there after 1559. The roots of the rebellion against Spanish authority were bound up in his attempt to impose a more centralized and absolute government. The first crucial step occurred when the Catholic church in the Netherlands was reorganized. By expanding the number of bishops from 4 to 18 and nominating them himself, Philip strengthened his hold over the church. Determined to impose religious uniformity in the Netherlands, Philip ordered that the decrees of the Council of Trent be enforced. The Protestants responded with the Compromise, a covenant pledging to resist the decrees of Trent and the Inquisition. Leading members of the council of state, which helped Philip's regent, Margaret of Parma, govern the Netherlands, protested in vain. When several hundred nobles presented their grievances to Margaret in 1566, one of her courtiers derided them as beggars. Making the epithet a badge of honor, the rebel battle cry became "Long live the beggars!"

Although the nobles had set the stage for rebellion by their protests, initially they failed to lead it. Instead the first outbreak of violence came in the summer of

1566 when Calvinists attacked the symbols of Catholicism. In a frenzy of iconoclasm—the "Calvinist Fury"—they ransacked Catholic churches, shocking almost everyone by their destructiveness. Unable to keep order, Margaret was replaced by the ruthless duke of Alva, who professed a willingness to destroy the country rather than see it fall into the hands of heretics. Backed by an army of 10,000, he attempted to enforce absolute rule through a special tribunal called the Council of Troubles. Because it executed thousands of heretics, confiscated their property, and imposed heavy new taxes, Netherlanders called it the Council of Blood. Thousands fled.

The heavy-handed Spanish tactics were enormously expensive. With Alva and his successors finally mobilizing 65,000 men and more for their campaigns, the tax revenue from the Netherlands was diverted to the war. Even this was insufficient, but Philip could not provide additional funds from Spain. The result was chronically unpaid troops prone to rebel against their own officers; more than 45 mutinies occurred between 1572 and 1607.

Instead of cowing the Netherlanders, Alva's cruelty prompted them to rally around William the Silent, prince of Orange (1533–1584). William was a *politique*, someone who allowed political circumstances rather than re-

## ◎ The "Calvinist Fury" ◎

*The revolt in the Netherlands commenced with an outburst of violent iconoclasm in 1566. An English observer describes the "Calvinist Fury."*

When . . . [the priests] should have begun their service, there was a company [that] began to sing psalms, at the beginning being but a company of boys, whereupon the margrave and other . . . lords came to the church and rebuked them. But all in vain, for . . . as soon as they turned their backs, they [went] to it again, and the company increased. . . . They broke up the choir. . . .

After that, they began with the image of Our Lady . . . and utterly defaced her and her chapel, and after [that], the whole church, which was the costliest church in Europe, and [they] have so spoiled it that they have not left a place to sit. . . . And from thence, part went to the parish churches and part to the houses of religion, and made such dispatch as I think the like was never done in one night. . . .

Coming into Our Lady church, it looked like a hell, where were above 1,000 torches burning, and such a noise, as if heaven and earth had gone together, with falling . . . images and beating down of costly works. . . . From thence I went . . . to all the houses of religion, where was the like stir, breaking and spoiling all that there was. Yet, they that did this never looked towards any spoil, but broke all in pieces and let it lay underfoot. So that, to be short, they have spoiled and destroyed all the churches, as well nunneries as others, but as I do understand they neither said nor did anything to the nuns. . . . In divers places in Flanders they have [done] and do the like.

*Source:* J. W. Burgon, *The Life and Times of Sir Thomas Gresham, Knt.*, vol. 2 (London: Jennings, 1839), pp. 138–140 (edited to conform to modern usage).

ligion to dictate his allegiance. Originally a Lutheran, he had converted to Catholicism as a child in order to receive his inheritance, but he returned to the Lutheran fold in 1567 and became a Calvinist in 1572. As stadholder, or governor, of the northern provinces of Holland, Utrecht, and Zeeland, where Calvinism was strong, he had a natural base of support. He also had the allegiance of a group of pirates and patriots who called themselves "sea beggars" and preyed on Spanish shipping. In the spring of 1572 they captured Brill and other ports in Holland and Zeeland, providing a haven to which Calvinists in other provinces fled. When the Spaniards besieged Leiden the following year, the rebels opened the dikes, forcing the Spanish army to flee before the advancing floodwaters.

The high point of rebel fortunes came in 1576 after unpaid Spanish troops sacked Antwerp. The "Spanish Fury" left more than 7,000 dead and persuaded the largely Catholic provinces in the south to ally with the primarily Protestant areas of the north. All but 4 of the 17 provinces united in the Pacification of Ghent (November 1576), and the others joined in the Union of Brussels (January 1577). The religious question was settled by leaving each region free to make its own policy. The Spanish, however, refused to quit, and by 1579 Philip's new commander, the duke of Parma (Margaret's son), had regained a large degree of control by combining military victories in the south with an appeal to Catholic Netherlanders to stand firm with Spain. The ten southern provinces, organized as the Union of Arras, made their peace with Philip, but under William's leadership the seven northern and largely Protestant provinces, the Union of Utrecht, declared their independence in 1581.

Even as Parma's forces advanced northward, the Dutch cause was jeopardized when a Catholic partisan assassinated William in 1584 with the pope's blessing. Unwilling to see the Protestant cause in the Netherlands crushed, the English stepped into the breach, sending a small army in 1585. The French too provided assistance. Whatever chance Philip had to destroy the Dutch rebels was lost when he became directly embroiled in war against England. By 1593 the Spaniards had been driven out of the northern provinces, though fighting continued until 1609. War resumed in 1621, and not until 1648 did the Spanish formally recognize the independence of the Dutch Republic.

## The English Challenge

Well before Elizabeth I's decision to send an army to the Netherlands, relations with Spain had been deteriorating. On the queen's part the reasons for the hostility were less religious than political and economic. The English wanted to trade with Spain's American colonies, and the attack on John Hawkins' third expedition had

set off a series of hostile economic moves on the part of both states between 1568 and 1573. The Netherlands were also a source of friction. Although Elizabeth was reluctant to support rebels and was not committed to Dutch independence, she was unwilling to accept either a massive Spanish military presence in the Netherlands or Dutch reliance on the French, which could result in French domination of the entire Channel coast.

Relations between Elizabeth and Philip were further complicated by the problem of Mary Stuart, queen of Scotland (1542–1567), widow of the French king Francis II, and a member of the powerful French Catholic family of Guise. As the great-granddaughter of the first Tudor king, Henry VII, Mary claimed the English throne, insisting that Elizabeth, as Anne Boleyn's daughter, was illegitimate. Mary, however, had fallen on hard times in Scotland because of a scandalous marriage to the earl of Bothwell, the probable murderer of her husband, Henry Lord Darnley. Irate Scottish Protestants, including the reformer John Knox, forced Mary to abdicate in 1567. After her escape to England a year later, she remained under arrest for 19 years in remote castles. Although Elizabeth tried to negotiate her return to the Scottish throne, Mary supported plots for her overthrow. In 1584 a conspiracy involving the Spanish ambassador helped set the stage for English intervention against Spain in the Netherlands. When royal officials intercepted a letter from Mary in 1586 encouraging yet another assassination attempt, Elizabeth agreed to have Mary stand trial. She was unanimously found guilty, and Elizabeth reluctantly authorized her execution in February 1587. Philip had determined to invade England well before Mary's death, but her execution and the Protestantism of her son, King James VI of Scotland, gave him an excuse to claim the English throne as his own. He based that claim on his descent from a granddaughter of the fourteenth-century English King Edward III.

Because Philip had insufficient funds to mount a direct seaborne assault, his plan called for a fleet to control the English Channel while Parma's veterans invaded England from the Netherlands. Preparation of the armada was delayed when Sir Francis Drake's daring attack on Cadiz in April 1587 destroyed some 20 ships and crucial supplies. During the interval, Spain's experienced admiral, the marquess of Santa Cruz, died. His successor, the duke of Medina Sidonia, had neither confidence in himself nor adequate experience. "I am always seasick," he protested, "[and have] no experience of seafaring or war."[3] When the two fleets met in July 1588, they were roughly equal in size, though the English vessels had greater maneuverability and superior long-range guns. Because the Spaniards used a crescent-shaped formation, the English were unable to get into position to use their guns effectively until they finally broke up the enemy formation by launching six burning ships against it. The Spaniards fled north through the Channel, suffering major losses when they rounded northern Scotland and were struck by Atlantic gales. Philip lost nearly half his ships, but an English force sent by Elizabeth to destroy the rest disobeyed her orders, giving Philip a reprieve. In the ensuing years two more armadas were readied to attack England, but storms prevented either from reaching its target. Until peace was officially concluded in 1604, both sides concentrated on helping their allies in the French civil war.

## The French Civil War

The struggle in France had begun in 1562 when soldiers of the duke of Guise slaughtered a congregation of Huguenots, or Reformed Protestants, at Vassy in Champagne. The Guise family—patrons of a militant, zealous Catholicism—were political rivals of the Bourbon and Montmorency-Chatillon families, both of whom supported the Huguenots. Because the crown of France was in the hands of a minor, Charles IX (1560–1574), his mother, Catherine de' Medici, exercised authority. To preserve her power, she played a shrewd game of shifting alliances, working first with one and then the other of the factions. Although this helped prevent either side from dominating the other, it also kept France in a state of political and religious instability.

The "wars of religion" in France were at root a struggle for political dominance in which religion, itself a potent and divisive factor, was used to justify the fighting and to attract adherents. The controversy split the aristocracy, more than 40 percent of which was Huguenot. The Protestants also enjoyed a good deal of support in urban areas, though only in Dauphiné and Languedoc

did they comprise a majority of the population. In France as a whole, more than 90 percent of the people were Catholic, but the Huguenots benefited from aristocratic support and a strong religious organization. The religious struggle was marked by intermittent periods of peace, assassinations, and the involvement of foreign troops, including English and German forces who aided the Huguenots in the early years.

The worst atrocity of the war—the St. Bartholomew's Day massacre in August 1572—grew out of Catherine's fear that the Huguenots were becoming too powerful. One of their leaders, Admiral Gaspard de Coligny, had persuaded Charles IX, who had come of age, to intervene in the Netherlands on behalf of the Protestants. Fearful of a Franco-Spanish war, Catherine was determined to reverse this decision. Huguenot power was also on the increase because of the marriage in August of the king's sister, Marguerite of Valois, to a prominent Huguenot, Henry of Navarre. Four days later an assassination plot that had Catherine's blessing wounded Coligny. Fearful of Huguenot reprisals, Catherine persuaded the king to sanction the execution of Protestant leaders on trumped-up charges that they were plotting his overthrow. Shortly before dawn on August 24, Coligny and other leading Huguenots were assassinated, and by daybreak militant Catholics were slaughtering Protestants. At least 3,000 were butchered in Paris, where bloody corpses bobbed in the Seine, and perhaps 20,000 in all of France. News of the massacre pleased Pope Gregory XIII and King Philip II, who celebrated with special religious services.

The massacre temporarily ended French intervention in the Netherlands but failed to destroy the Huguenot cause. As the Huguenots plotted revenge, Henry of

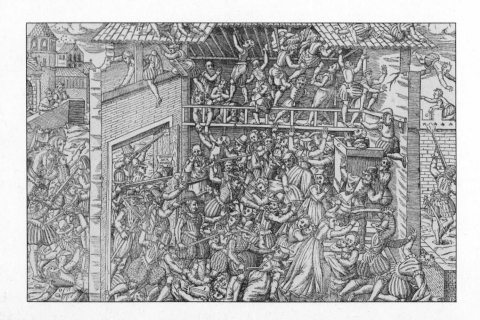

The massacre of a congregation of Huguenots at Vassy by followers of the duke of Guise in March 1562 ignited a civil war in France that lasted until 1596. [Bibliothèque Nationale, Paris]

## ◎ The St. Bartholomew's Day Massacre: ◎ Papal Reaction

*News of the St. Bartholomew's Day massacre in August 1572 prompted rejoicing in Catholic circles, including the papacy itself. An observer describes Pope Gregory XIII's reaction.*

Although it was still night, I immediately sent to his Holiness to free him from the tension, and so that he might rise to the wonderful grace, which God had granted to Christendom under his pontificate. On that morning there was a consistory court . . . and as his Holiness had such a good piece of news to announce to the Holy College, he had the dispatches publicly read out to them. His Holiness then spoke about their contents and concluded that in these times, so troubled by revolutions, nothing better or more magnificent could have been wished for; and that, as it appeared, God was beginning to turn the eye of his mercy on us. His Holiness and the college were extremely contented and joyful at the reading of this news. . . .

On the same morning . . . his Holiness with the whole College of Cardinals went to the church of Saint Mark, to have the *Te Deum* sung and to thank God for granting so great a favor to the Christian people. His Holiness does not cease to pray God, and make others pray, to inspire the Most Christian King [Charles IX] to follow further the path which he has opened and to cleanse and purge completely the Kingdom of France from the plague of the Huguenots.

*Source:* W. F. Reddaway, ed., *Select Documents of European History*, Vol. 2: *1492–1715* (New York: Holt, n.d.), pp. 94–95.

Guise in 1576 organized the Catholic League, which soon received financial support from Philip II. By the mid-1580s the league controlled Paris, forcing King Henry III (1574–1589) to adopt desperate means to save his crumbling authority: the assassination of Henry of Guise and his brother, a cardinal in the Catholic church. Although the king allied with Henry of Navarre in an effort to crush the Catholic League, he was assassinated in July 1589.

With Henry of Navarre now claiming the throne as Henry IV (1589–1610), the civil war entered its final stage. Unprepared to see France governed by Protestants, Philip II not only continued to back the Catholic League but also ordered his army to invade France. Elizabeth I, determined to prevent France from falling under Spanish hegemony, sent her troops to Henry's aid. A *politique* rather than a convinced Huguenot, Henry finally decided in 1593 that peace was possible only if he converted to Catholicism. The pope absolved him of his heresy, and Paris finally opened its gates to him, though Philip continued the struggle until 1598. In the latter year Henry provided some solace to his Huguenot allies by issuing the Edict of Nantes, giving Protestants liberty of conscience, full civil and political rights, and control of 100 fortified towns. Catholicism, however, was rec-ognized as the official religion of France, and Protestant worship was prohibited in the Paris area.

Although France was saved for Catholicism, from Philip's standpoint the 1590s was a decade of military disaster. Spain had no power in France, the Dutch Netherlands were virtually irretrievable, and the English, exultant in their victory over the armada in 1588, had checked Spain on the seas. By the time of Philip's death in 1598, the Spanish quest for hegemony had been blunted, though the Spaniards retained the southern Netherlands and continued to battle the Dutch until 1609.

## The Age of the Queens

The second half of the sixteenth century is notable as an age of unusual political prominence for women in western Europe. Mary I (1553–1558) and Elizabeth I (1558–1603) in England and Mary Stuart in Scotland (whose effective rule was from 1561 to 1567) governed as queens, while other women exercised power as regents: Mary of Guise in Scotland (1554–1560), Margaret of Parma in the Netherlands (1559–1567), and Catherine de' Medici in France beginning in 1560. Women, of course, had governed before, sometimes very successfully, as in the case of Queen Isabella of Castile (1474–1504), cofounder of a unified Spain. Although some Renaissance writers had recognized women's ability to govern, men were still quite reluctant to accept their authority. The classic statement of this view was a treatise by John Knox, architect of the Protestant Reformation in Scotland, titled *The First Blast of the Trumpet Against the Monstrous Regiment of Women* (1558), which argued that female rule was contrary to divine and natural law, though God occasionally made an exception. The queens had their defenders, but even supporters of women's right to rule were unwilling to admit women to governing bodies or deliberative assemblies. No woman sat in the English or Scottish royal councils or Parliaments during the reign of these queens; government remained an essentially male preserve throughout Europe.

Elizabeth I in particular exerted an enormous impact on England, not only by thwarting Spanish ambitions and supporting Protestantism but also by creating an atmosphere conducive to brilliant cultural achievements. The glorious image of her rule, which she assiduously cultivated, is reflected in the literary masterpieces of Edmund Spenser (c. 1552–1599), whose allegorical poem *The Faerie Queene* exalted "the most excellent and glorious person of our sovereign the queen, and her kingdom in Fairy Land," and William Shakespeare (1564–1616). The self-confidence and exuberance that radiated from England after the Spanish were repelled is eloquently expressed in Shakespeare's *Richard II*:

> *This royal throne of kings, this scepter'd isle,*
> *This earth of majesty, this seat of Mars,*
> *This other Eden, demi-paradise,*
> *This fortress built by Nature for herself . . .*
> *This blessed plot, this earth, this realm, this*
>     *England.*

In no small measure England's achievements were attributable to its queen. During the early 1600s the image of Elizabeth—more exalted in death than in life—proved to be more than her successors, James I and Charles I, could emulate.

## Europe in Crisis

As Spanish ascendancy waned, Europe became preoccupied with the Thirty Years' War and the general crisis of authority that followed it in the mid-1600s. The two problems were directly related, for the unparalleled destruction inflicted in the Thirty Years' War, much of it by undisciplined troops, underscored the need to bring

Elizabeth I, painted by George Gower around 1588. The upper left shows the English fleet; the upper right, the Spanish armada being destroyed by gales. Elizabeth often wore a stylish wig and coated her face with a white cosmetic that blanched the skin. [Marquess of Tavistock, Trustee of the Bedford Estate]

armies and warfare under strict control. Ultimately, monarchs and nobles found it to their advantage to work together to determine policy and implement discipline. By 1660 there was also a consensus that even religious convictions had to be subordinated to the maintenance of order. The period 1600–1660 was thus a major watershed in European history.

## The Thirty Years' War

Germany, a patchwork land of some 360 independent political entities, became the killing field of Europe in a great war triggered by a dispute involving the role of the Austrian Habsburgs as Holy Roman emperors. The compromise Peace of Augsburg (1555) that had ended the first round of religious warfare in Germany had given no rights to Calvinists, whose growing strength, particularly in the Palatinate (see Map 19.1), alarmed the Lutherans. There was considerable tension too between Protestants and Catholics because of changes in religious allegiance. When the Catholic rulers of ecclesiastical principalities became Protestant, Catholics demanded that they surrender both their religious office and their lands, but Lutherans refused. After the Protestants organized the Evangelical Union in 1609 and their opponents responded with the Catholic League, Germany was divided into two armed camps.

The event that sparked the fighting occurred when the Habsburg Ferdinand of Styria, king of Bohemia, curtailed religious toleration for Protestants and Hussites. In May 1618, Bohemian nobles registered their protest by throwing two of Ferdinand's advisers out of a castle window in Prague; their lives were saved when they landed in a pile of manure. A year later the rebels deposed Ferdinand as their king and gave the crown to a Calvinist prince, Frederick V of the Palatinate, son-in-law of King James I of England. Had the rebels succeeded in establishing a Protestant on the Bohemian throne, Protestants would have had a majority of the seven votes needed to elect future emperors. Ferdinand, who had become emperor in August 1619, had little choice but to reassert his control over Bohemia.

At first the war went well for Ferdinand. In addition to receiving the help of Catholic armies from Spain and Bavaria, he got the assistance of Lutheran Saxony, whose elector was more interested in acquiring land in the Palatinate than in religious solidarity with his fellow Protestants. After Frederick was defeated at the Battle of White Mountain in 1620, he fled Bohemia, leaving his Protestant supporters to face Ferdinand's wrath. The Dutch, who were alarmed by Spain's presence in the area, provided Frederick with funds to keep fighting, but his small principality was overwhelmed. After the Danes entered the war in 1625, Ferdinand's new general, Albrecht von Wallenstein, invaded Denmark, leaving starvation and destruction in his wake. Danish lands were returned on the condition that Denmark refrain from intervening in Germany.

With Ferdinand on the verge of establishing total con-trol over his empire, the Swedish king, Gustavus Adolphus, invaded Germany. He was supported militarily by Brandenburg and Saxony and financially by the Dutch and the French, both of whom were threatened by Habsburg expansion. Using innovative tactics that increased the mobility of his army, Gustavus Adolphus crushed the imperial forces in 1631. The fighting was carried into Catholic regions, especially Bavaria, whose residents were subjected to calculated brutality—rape, pillage, torture, and murder. In November 1632 the armies of Gustavus Adolphus and Wallenstein confronted each other at Lützen in Saxony in one of the bloodiest battles of the war. The Swedish king was killed, but neither side was strong enough to defeat its enemies in the ensuing months. Wallenstein was assassinated in 1634.

The final and most destructive period of the war (1635–1648) reverted to a dynastic struggle that pitted the Habsburg powers, Austria and Spain, against the French and the Swedes. The real victims were the German people. "Every soldier had his favorite method of making life miserable for peasants," noted one observer, "and every peasant had his own misery."[4] The city of Marburg was occupied no fewer than 11 times. As peasants fled before the marauding armies, the destruction of crops triggered famine. The loss of population was catastrophic: 40 percent in rural areas, 33 percent in the cities. The overall population of the empire decreased by as much as 8 million during the war.

An end to the fighting was finally achieved by the Peace of Westphalia in 1648. The sovereignty of each

The French artist Jacques Callot (1592–1635) created a series of 24 etchings titled *The Miseries of War*, one of the most moving statements of the horror that gripped Germany in the Thirty Years' War. The etchings reflect a dramatic change of mind on Callot's part, for his earlier works glorify warfare. This etching depicts the hanging of thieves, a vivid reminder of the fate that awaited German peasants unlucky enough to get caught stealing what they needed to stay alive. [New York Public Library]

German state was recognized; altogether there were now some 300 entities with sovereign rights and nearly 1,500 minor lordships. Each prince, whether Catholic, Lutheran, or Calvinist, could determine the religious beliefs of his subjects, who had no choice but to accept or emigrate. The treaty also recognized the independence of the Swiss Confederacy and the Dutch Republic, but it did not end hostilities between France and Spain, which lasted until the Treaty of the Pyrenees in 1659. Just as Spain's quest for hegemony was doomed by Philip II's defeats in the 1590s and confirmed by the Treaty of the Pyrenees, so the bid of the Austrian Habsburgs to dominate central Europe was wrecked in the Thirty Years' War. Not until 1871 would the Germans achieve political unity. The war also had disruptive effects on the domestic politics of the major European states, thereby contributing to the midcentury crises.

# Rebuilding France: Foundations of Bourbon Rule

France's ability to act decisively in the Thirty Years' War and ultimately to impose peace terms on Spain in 1659 was made possible by the rebuilding of its institutions in the aftermath of the Huguenot wars. Beginning with Henry IV, the first Bourbon monarchs pursued a course of absolutism in politics and mercantilism in economics. In the Bourbon view, stability mandated a thoroughly centralized state capable of maintaining order at home and fielding large armies. But absolutism also entailed the recognition that monarchical power was bound up with the preservation of a privileged class of royal officials and landed aristocrats. Continental absolutism was built on the notion of an ascending order of social privilege, at the apex of which was the monarch. Anything that undermined this pyramid of power thus undercut royal absolutism.

Centralization could be accomplished only at the expense of local and special interests, which were sometimes strained severely by the burden of financing a war. The attempt to impose royal absolutism coincided with the costly struggle to prevent the establishment of Spanish or Austrian hegemony. By the 1640s grinding taxation, aristocratic discontent, and resistance to centralized control had built to the crisis point and erupted in a new civil war, the Fronde.

Although no monarch came close to achieving total power in this period, there was growing interest in the concept of absolute rule, particularly in its national, monarchical form. The French political theorist Jean Bodin had stressed the importance of a sovereign power whose authority was beyond challenge, though he also insisted that monarchs were responsible to God for their actions. Building on this traditional notion, various seventeenth-century thinkers asserted that kings and queens derived their right to govern directly from God and were therefore above human law. Seemingly, the apostle Paul had provided the foundation for this theory when he taught that earthly powers were ordained by God. The concept that sovereignty was divinely bestowed suited the needs of rulers intent on centralizing their control, for they were in a position to claim the unquestioning obedience of their subjects as both a right and a Christian duty. Political theorists such as Bodin and the Englishman Robert Filmer drove home the argument for divine right absolutism by likening the monarch to a father. Though widely embraced, divine right theories were applied with more success in France than anywhere else in the 1600s, and even there not without a struggle.

When Henry IV temporarily ended the Huguenot wars in 1598, he revived the goals of the Renaissance sovereigns Francis I and Henry II, who had aimed at centralizing royal authority and expanding French territory. Although he opted not to summon the Estates General after 1593, he took care to secure the support of the more powerful aristocrats—the nobility of the sword—especially by strategic bribes. Offices were traditionally sold in France, but Henry took the practice one step further by allowing his principal bureaucrats, the nobility of the robe, to pay a voluntary annual fee called the *paulette* that made the offices hereditary. These men, most of them members of the bourgeoisie, were thus closely linked to the expansion of the government.

Henry faced daunting economic problems. He was nearly 300 million livres in debt, with annual revenues amounting to only half that amount. His finance minister, the clever duke of Sully, repudiated part of the debt, renegotiated a lower rate of interest on the balance, and rigorously sought new sources of revenue, such as the *paulette*. As a proponent of mercantile policies, Sully established monopolies on salt, gunpowder, and mining. France was already a food-exporting nation, and Sully strengthened agriculture by building more bridges, roads, and canals. To reduce the export of bullion for luxury items, new laws restricted the use of gold and silver, and royal factories were constructed to produce such luxury goods as silk, satin, tapestries, and crystal. By 1601 the budget was balanced.

When Henry was assassinated by a Catholic ideologue in 1610, the throne passed to his 9-year-old son, Louis XIII (1610–1643). The regency was in the hands of Louis' mother, Marie de' Medici. Because she relied on her Italian favorites for advice, disgruntled nobles and troubled Huguenots threatened a resumption of civil strife. Marie tried to defuse the crisis by summoning the Estates General in 1614, but internal feuding rendered it impotent, and it was not called again until 1789. For ten years France lacked an energetic government, but Marie maintained a semblance of peace by lavishing pensions and bribes on the nobles and allowing them a greater role in provincial affairs.

The appointment of Cardinal Richelieu (1585–1642) as the king's chief adviser in 1624 once more meant a strong hand at the controls of government. Nobles who defied royal edicts were imprisoned and some even executed, and their castles were destroyed. Responsibility for local administration was transferred from the nobles to *intendants*, commissioners appointed by the crown who held their posts at the king's pleasure. Their responsibilities included tax collection, the administration of justice, military recruitment, and local defense. To deal with the rebellious Huguenots, Richelieu besieged one of their key strongholds, La Rochelle, for 14 months until it surrendered. Other Huguenot towns were overrun by royal forces. In 1629 Richelieu ended the political and military rights given to the Huguenots in the Edict of Nantes, although they retained religious freedom. Richelieu also enhanced French power by building effective Atlantic and Mediterranean fleets. His policies, however, were expensive and required deficit financing. Occupied with his centralizing schemes and the Thirty Years' War, Richelieu failed to undertake desperately needed tax reform. As the cost of French military involvement in Germany increased, rising taxes underscored the unfairness of the burden on the peasants. Richelieu faced tax riots throughout France, to which he reacted with increased repression.

The death of Richelieu in 1642 and Louis XIII a year later left the 5-year-old Louis XIV on the throne and real power in the hands of Richelieu's protégé, Giulio Mazarin (1602–1661), a Sicilian cardinal and the illicit lover—or secret husband—of the regent, Anne of Austria. A foreigner and a powerful churchman, he was thoroughly disliked. Discontent was especially pronounced because of the effects of centralization on local authority and Mazarin's inability to pay interest on the loans that financed French participation in the Thirty Years' War. So depleted were royal finances that some officials had not been paid for four years. The situation was made worse by famine, especially in the late 1640s, when many peasants lost their holdings to bourgeois creditors.

Against this backdrop of economic dislocation and political unrest, the Parlement of Paris, France's main law court and a stronghold of the nobility of the robe, called for reform, including the abolition of the office of *intendant*, a habeas corpus law, the right to approve taxes, and an end to the creation of new offices. Mazarin arrested the leaders of the Paris Parlement, inciting an uprising that forced the king and the cardinal to flee. Unwilling to sanction popular rebellion, the Parlement of Paris came to terms with Mazarin in the spring of 1649, but the uprising spread nevertheless. The end of the Thirty Years' War enabled prominent nobles of the

## ◈ Richelieu's Plan for Reform ◈

*After Cardinal Richelieu became Louis XIII's principal minister in 1624, he outlined conditions in France and his program of reform.*

At the time when your majesty resolved to admit me both to your council and to an important place in your confidence for the direction of your affairs, I may say that the Huguenots shared the state with you; that the nobles conducted themselves as if they were not your subjects, and the most powerful governors of the provinces as if they were sovereign in their offices.

I may say that the bad example of all of these was so injurious to this realm that even the best regulated *parlements* were affected by it, and endeavoured, in certain cases, to diminish your royal authority as far as they were able in order to stretch their own powers beyond the limits of reason.

I may say that everyone measured his own merit by his audacity; that in place of estimating the benefits which they received from your majesty at their proper worth, all valued them only in so far as they satisfied the extravagant demands of their imagination; that the most arrogant were held to be the wisest, and found themselves the most prosperous. . . .

I promised your majesty to employ all my industry and all the authority which it should please you to give me to ruin the Huguenot party, to abase the pride of the nobles, to bring back all your subjects to their duty, and to elevate your name among foreign nations to the point where it belongs.

*Source:* J. H. Robinson, ed., *Readings in European History,* vol. 2 (Boston: Ginn, 1906), pp. 268–270.

sword to march their forces against Mazarin. Among them was a leading member of the Bourbon family, the prince of Condé. In Bordeaux artisans and lawyers seized control of the city government, and urban and agrarian uprisings broke out elsewhere. Mazarin had to flee again in February 1651; two years passed before he could safely return to Paris. Ultimately, the Fronde collapsed because the *frondeurs* were too fragmented in their goals. The prospect of a France divided into feudal principalities was unpalatable to the nobility of the robe, while neither they nor the nobility of the sword were interested in the plight of the peasants and the urban workers. The crisis in France passed because the leaders of the Fronde, occupied with their narrow self-interests, failed to forge a cohesive movement for reform. The cause of constitutional monarchy in France was then dormant for more than a century.

## Spain: Disillusionment, War, and Revolt

As in France, Spain during the reigns of Philip III (1598–1621) and Philip IV (1621–1665) experienced mounting reaction against centralization, economic hardship, and the impact of foreign war, all of which finally triggered open rebellion. The economic problems stemmed from several factors. Seventeenth-century Spain experienced a severe decline in population: Castile and Aragon dropped from 10 million to 6 million, a percentage decrease greater than that in any other European country, including the war-torn German states. The reasons for the decline are not altogether clear, but they include plague, crop failures, mismanaged financial resources, and a decline in the wealth coming from Spain's overseas empire. Between the 1600s and the 1650s, bullion shipments to Spain decreased more than 80 percent, due mostly to the decimation of the Amerindian population and the loss of its forced labor. The Spaniards failed to compensate for this loss of income by developing new industries. When Spain renewed the war against the Dutch in 1621 and subsequently became embroiled in the Thirty Years' War, the government had to squeeze funds from an already overburdened people. The price of elusive glory abroad was grinding poverty at home.

Philip IV's chief minister, the count of Olivares (1587–1645), embarked on a plan of reform designed to increase revenues and rationalize the administration, thereby enhancing Spain's military capabilities. "Kings," he proclaimed, "cannot achieve heroic actions without money."[5] He increased the church's tax burden and reduced the number of officeholders, but in Castile the Cortes blocked his attempt to introduce new direct taxes. Administratively, he wanted to impose uniform laws on the semiautonomous Spanish kingdoms and make each provide its fair share of taxes and troops. Olivares' Union of Arms called for the creation of a reserve army of 140,000 men drawn from every royal dominion. His reduction of regional autonomy and redistribution of some of Castile's burden to other provinces touched off revolts. The first rebellion erupted in the northern province of Catalonia in June 1640, triggered by the billeting of Castilian and mercenary soldiers sent north to repel a French invasion. Rebellious peasants, overtaxed clergy hostile to Castilian domination, and rioting urban mobs joined forces. When Barcelona revolted, the royal viceroy was murdered, but the Catalans had no effective rebel leaders. They tried to establish an independent republic, but dependence on French funds forced them to acknowledge Louis XIII as king. Disillusioned with foreign rule, the insurgents lost heart, and the revolt collapsed when Barcelona's citizen army was defeated in 1652. The Catalan nobles, who had deserted the rebel cause rather than risk their wealth and rank, had their privileges confirmed by Philip IV.

Revolts against Spanish rule also occurred in Portugal, Naples, and Sicily. Resentment against Castilian rule and financial support for Spanish wars triggered a national war of liberation in Portugal in December 1640. The nobles restored the Portuguese monarchy, the Lisbon masses rose in support, and a French fleet provided naval protection. Funded by the profits of the Brazilian sugar fleet, the Portuguese continued defiantly until Spain finally recognized their independence in 1668. In contrast, the government suppressed the 1647 revolts in Sicily and Naples in a matter of months. The Sicilians wanted their local privileges restored and the new taxes abolished, but they were leaderless. The rebellion in Naples began with attacks on anything Spanish and quickly developed into a class war of peasants against landlords. When not even the French were willing to lend support, a Spanish fleet restored order.

The crises of the 1640s made it apparent that Spain could no longer afford the foreign policy of a great power. The Treaty of the Pyrenees in 1659, though it involved only modest territorial losses to France on the frontiers and in the Spanish Netherlands, was nevertheless humiliating. The nobles came to dominate the monarchy, particularly after the inept Charles II became king in 1665. Spanish institutions, however, were sufficiently strong to enable the country to survive Charles' reign and the subsequent accession of a Bourbon dynasty, and in the eighteenth century Spain once again became a major power.

## The Dutch Republic and the House of Orange

Although the Dutch had to renew their fight for independence between 1621 and 1648, they were unusual in their ability to keep the state solvent. Severe political tensions existed, but with rare exceptions they were resolved without recourse to violence.

The principal source of friction was the role of the House of Orange in Dutch politics. Because each of the seven Dutch provinces normally chose the prince of Orange as its stadholder, or governor, he was not only the symbol of national unity but often the most powerful man in the country as well. The Dutch had an Estates General to which each of the provinces elected representatives. Delegates to this body traditionally split, some supporting the House of Orange and a militant foreign policy, others favoring a greater degree of provincial autonomy and peaceful relations with foreign countries in order to improve trade. In the early 1600s Jan van Oldenbarneveldt, founder of the Dutch East India Company and the most important representative in the Estates of the province of Holland, challenged Maurice of Nassau, from 1618 the prince of Orange, on the issue of resuming the war with Spain when the truce expired in 1621. The conflict had religious overtones, for Oldenbarneveldt and his supporters opposed the efforts of Calvinists to drive Arminians—Protestants who rejected Calvin's doctrine of predestination in favor of free will—out of the state church and the universities. With the support of the Calvinists, Maurice used the army to purge Oldenbarneveldt's supporters from the town governments in the province of Holland, and in 1619 Oldenbarneveldt himself was executed for high treason.

His main supporters, including the great philosopher and jurist Hugo Grotius (1583–1645), architect of the concept of international law, were condemned to life imprisonment.

The conflict between Holland and the House of Orange erupted again in 1648 when William II became stadholder. Unlike the Hollanders, William opposed peace negotiations with Spain and supported King Charles I of England in his conflict with Parliament. A compromise was reached when William's cousin threatened Amsterdam with an army. After William died unexpectedly in 1650, the Hollanders and their allies took over the government, maintaining their supremacy until a French invasion in 1672 necessitated the return of a strong military leader from the House of Orange.

Although the restoration of the republic in 1650 was a quasi-revolutionary event, the Dutch avoided a civil war and enjoyed continued prosperity. When Antwerp declined in the late 1570s, Amsterdam moved quickly to establish itself as the center of European commerce. By the mid-seventeenth century the Dutch operated more than half of the world's commercial vessels. Using raw materials from Scandinavia, the shipyards of Amsterdam built Europe's most efficient ships, including large vessels for the transoceanic trade and inexpensive flat-bottomed freighters known as *fluiten* ("flyboats"). In addition to trading and shipbuilding, the economy of Amsterdam was based on banking, insurance (including the first life insurance policies), printing, and manufactur-

A meeting of the Estates General at The Hague in the Netherlands in 1651, painted by Dirck van Delen. [Rijksmuseum, Amsterdam]

ing. Artisans finished cloth, made jewelry, brewed beer, dressed leather, processed tobacco, and cut diamonds. Other towns became famous for particular products, such as Delft for ceramics, Haarlem for linens, and Schiedam for gin. The Haarlem area also achieved fame by cultivating tulips, which were first imported from the Ottoman Empire. Jews, who benefited greatly by the normally tolerant religious atmosphere in the Netherlands, played a prominent role in the Dutch business community, especially banking. The Dutch, in short, were economically the most progressive Europeans in the seventeenth century, and the people of Amsterdam enjoyed the highest per capita income in Europe. Although there were a substantial number of poor, whose ranks were swollen by immigrants and refugees, the Dutch provided enough relief to stave off the misery that attended political crises in other European states in the mid-1600s.

# Early Stuart England: From Consensus to Conflict

Alone among the European states, England experienced not only a severe crisis but a revolution in the 1640s and 1650s as well. Under Elizabeth I (1558–1603) and James I (1603–1625), who also governed Scotland as James VI (1567–1625), England attained religious stability and a reasonably effective working relationship between crown and Parliament. Elizabeth's Protestant settlement withstood the challenge of Catholics, nearly 200 of whom she executed for treason, and of a handful of radical Protestants who repudiated the state church. James, raised as a Calvinist, disappointed English Puritans who wanted further reforms in the established church, including a better-educated clergy with higher moral standards, stricter sabbath observance, and an end to such "unscriptural" customs as the sign of the cross in baptism and the wedding ring. They also demanded the reform of church courts, especially the High Commission, which could compel accused persons to testify against themselves and tried them without a jury. James agreed only to a Puritan request for a new translation of the Bible into English, the so-called King James version of 1611.

The work of centralization was carried forward, particularly through the appointment of lords lieutenant and their deputies in the counties. Because England had no standing army, local defense was in the hands of these men, but as long as the crown appointed local magnates, the system worked well. Central authority was also enhanced by the use of conciliar courts, especially the Star Chamber, which evolved out of the judicial activities of the king's Council, and the Court of High Commission, which originated in Elizabeth's reign and enforced the laws and doctrine of the Church of England.

Although the war against Spain (1585–1604) was pop-ular, its cost forced Elizabeth to adopt measures that reduced future income, such as the sale of various crown lands. In most respects she handled her Parliaments superbly, though at the end of her reign a controversy over royal grants of monopolies embittered relations as anger over their abuse mounted. Finances were increasingly a problem for James, especially with respect to foreign policy. Dreaming of the glory of the 1580s, his Parliaments were willing to support a naval war against Spain but had little desire to become embroiled directly on the Continent in the Thirty Years' War on behalf of James' son-in-law, Frederick V. Nor did they understand the king's desire to establish an alliance with their traditional enemy, Spain, by means of a marriage involving Prince Charles and a Spanish princess. The proposed match was crucial to James' dream of a partnership between Catholic Spain and Protestant England that could serve as the vehicle to maintain peace in Europe.

James, who thought that kings were "God's lieutenants upon earth" and sat on "God's throne," heightened concern by actions that seemed to challenge traditional constitutional procedures. Chronically short of funds, he sought additional revenue by levying a special import duty, an "imposition," without parliamentary approval. Although the courts decided in his favor on the grounds that import duties were part of his prerogative to determine foreign policy, some members of Parliament were irate. James also provoked controversy by dismissing one of his chief justices, Sir Edward Coke, for attempting to assert judicial independence. The king subsequently imprisoned Coke and a fellow member of the House of Commons for drafting a "protestation" asserting Parliament's right to speak freely on such subjects as "the arduous and urgent affairs concerning the king, state, and defense of the realm, and of the Church of England," including areas that had traditionally been reserved to the crown.[6] Yet when James died in 1625, he left a country whose tensions were still largely contained beneath the surface.

The consensus that Elizabeth had achieved was rapidly undermined by the policies of James' son, Charles I (1625–1649). Unable to conclude an agreement to marry a Spanish princess, he was determined to go to war against Spain, though a distrustful Parliament refused to give him sufficient funds. An expedition that tried to repeat Sir Francis Drake's brilliant 1587 raid on Cadiz not only failed but provoked outrage when the unpaid, sick, and wounded troops returned to the streets of Plymouth. Charles blundered further by going to war against France while still fighting Spain. With his finances depleted, he tried to raise money by forced "loans," billeting his troops in private homes to compel payment. Led by Coke, critics in the House of Commons responded in 1628 with the Petition of Right, which demanded that no taxes be levied without parliamentary consent, no person be imprisoned without knowing the charge, no troops be billeted in private homes without the owners' consent, and martial law not be imposed in peacetime. The king accepted the document in principle in return for further taxes. In 1629, however, a bitter attack on newly appointed Arminian bishops who supported Charles led to Parliament's dismissal, although only after critics held the speaker of the House of Commons in his chair while they passed resolutions condemning Catholicism, Arminianism, and taxes that lacked parliamentary approval. The Arminian position that Puritans and others found so offensive rejected the Calvinist doctrine of predestination, insisted that Christ died for all persons rather than the elect alone, and affirmed the freedom of each person to accept or reject divine grace.

For 11 years Charles ruled without a Parliament, raising revenue by a variety of unpopular expedients that stretched his legal powers. One of these was "ship money," a tax traditionally levied on coastal areas for naval expenses but now extended to the entire kingdom. Charles also sold monopolies, titles, offices, and crown lands. During this period religious grievances continued to mount, with much of the hostility directed at Charles' French Catholic queen, Henrietta Maria, and his Arminian archbishop of Canterbury, William Laud. Committed to the principle that a unified state required unity in religion, Laud vigorously persecuted his Puritan critics. They in turn attacked his Arminian theology and his emphasis on liturgy rather than preaching. When Charles and Laud attempted to force the English liturgy on the Presbyterian Scots, the latter rebelled. The militia units Charles dispatched to restore order were woefully inadequate, and the king was forced to summon Parliament.

In the cultural atmosphere of the English royal court, the leading painter was Rubens' disciple Anthony Van Dyck (1599–1641), who painted King Charles I and his queen, Henrietta Maria. Charles, by his ineptitude, and his wife, by her Catholicism, contributed to the outbreak of civil war in England. [Bridgman/AA Resource]

## The English Revolution

Historians hotly debate the nature and causes of the English revolution. Some contend that it was only a civil war, while others perceive a full-scale revolution that altered the structure of government, religion, the economy, educational thought, and the fabric of society. Lawrence Stone has gone back to the early sixteenth century to find such preconditions of revolution as the crown's failure to establish a standing army and a paid local bureaucracy, Puritan criticism in the state church, the growing wealth and power of the gentry and the decline of many of the greater nobility, and a crisis of confidence in high government officials. Against this background, he argues, the crown precipitated a revolution by encouraging Laud's campaign against the Puritans, curtailing the political role of the gentry, restricting upward social mobility, and enforcing tighter economic controls. The outbreak of civil war was then triggered by military defeat at the hands of the Scots and financial bankruptcy.

Analysts who hold to the more limited notion of a civil war place the origins much later, either in 1637 and 1638,

when the Scots rebelled against the English liturgy, or even in early 1642, when the king and Parliament failed to agree on control of the militia. According to this interpretation, the civil war was largely an accident that neither side intended. Marxist historians concentrate on economic factors as the primary cause of the revolution, observing that Parliament drew most of its support from the economically advanced south and east of England, while the king's strength was greatest in the more backward regions of the west and north. Marxists have also tried to demonstrate that most of the aristocracy supported the king, whereas the "middling sort" of tradesmen, merchants, and yeoman farmers allied with Parliament. On any interpretation, however, it is clear that the revolutionary period was the gravest and most sustained political and military crisis in English history.

The "Short Parliament" that met briefly in the spring of 1640 was dismissed when it refused the king's demands for money. After the Scots invaded England, Charles had to call another Parliament in the autumn, the so-called Long Parliament. In a series of striking constitutional measures, Parliament abolished courts such as the Star Chamber and the High Commission, whose authority derived directly from the king; outlawed ship money and other questionable forms of revenue that lacked parliamentary sanction; and provided that no more than three years could elapse between Parliaments. By circumscribing royal authority, this legislation prevented the establishment of absolute government. Parliament also imprisoned and tried the king's principal advisers, the earl of Strafford and Archbishop Laud; both were eventually executed for high treason. Although Charles had little choice but to agree to the constitutional reforms and even to the death of his friend Strafford, he refused to surrender control of the militia, his only real military force. Troops had to be raised to suppress a Catholic rebellion that had erupted in Ireland in 1641, but neither side trusted the other with command. This distrust finally persuaded both sides to take up arms, and the civil war began in August 1642.

The Cavaliers supported Charles, while the Roundheads (so called for their short hairstyles) fought for Parliament. Religion was more important than social and economic considerations in persuading people to support one side or the other; Catholics, Arminians, and conservative conformists backed Charles, while Puritans and sectarians such as the Baptists opposed him. Much of Parliament's support came from the middle social orders, but many other segments of society remained neutral. The fighting divided many families. The two sides were roughly equal in strength, but the Roundheads established military supremacy through an alliance with the Scots, more effective military organization, and greater wealth, owing to the support of London and the commercial southeast. Most members of Parliament were required to resign their commissions, promotion was based on merit rather than birth, and strict discipline was imposed. The Cavaliers were badly defeated at the battle of Naseby in 1645, and a year later Charles surrendered. The price of the Scottish alliance was a promise to make the Church of England Presbyterian, but this was unacceptable to the army, which favored religious toleration for Protestants. The army was also impatient over negotiations with the king. In 1648 civil war broke out again, this time with the Scots on Charles' side. Under the leadership of Oliver Cromwell (1599–1658), the parliamentarian army crushed its enemies. After the victorious army purged Parliament of moderates, the remnant—derisively called the Rump Parliament by its critics—appointed a special tribunal to try the king on charges of treason. Found guilty, he was beheaded in London on January 30, 1649. This act, which shocked all Europe, was, said Cromwell, a "cruel necessity."

The Rump proceeded to make England a republic—the Commonwealth—but refused to provide for new elections. In practice it allowed a good deal of religious toleration, particularly for radical Protestants such as the Congregationalists, Baptists, and Quakers. The Quakers were particularly controversial because they not only rejected the traditional ministry and sacraments but also allowed women to preach. The Rump used the army to crush the rebellion in Ireland and then to suppress the Scots when they rallied on behalf of Charles I's son, hoping to impose a Presbyterian state church on England. The Rump also dispatched the navy to fight an inconclusive trade war against Europe's other major republic, the Dutch Netherlands, in 1652. When Cromwell's patience with the Rump finally ran out in 1653, he forcibly dismissed it.

Although handpicked by army officers with the advice of Congregational churches, a new Parliament—nicknamed Barebones after a quaintly named member, Praisegod Barebone—proved ineffective. In 1654 army officers drew up a constitution called the Instrument of Government that made Cromwell Lord Protector. Cromwell, however, fared no better with his Parliaments than the early Stuart kings had. Dissension raged over the structure of the government, the question of religious toleration, the enormous cost of maintaining a standing army, and the appointment of major generals to maintain order throughout the country. A war with Spain brought England both Dunkirk and Jamaica but simultaneously made Cromwell's financial position desperate despite increased taxation. With the political and economic crisis unresolved at his death in 1658, his son Richard, the new Lord Protector, proved unable to govern. By 1660 the propertied classes, fed up with military rule, were prepared to accept the return of monarchy in order to achieve stability and security. Although a good deal of antimonarchical sentiment and popular support for the republic continued, most of the country was relieved when Charles II returned from exile in May 1660.

Although the monarchy was restored, its position was seriously altered. Absolutism such as existed in France had been rendered impossible. The despotic royal courts of the Star Chamber and the High Commission did not return, and the principle of parliamentary approval for taxes was firmly established. Religious toleration ended in the early 1660s, but the dissenters were now strong enough to survive the sporadic persecution that ensued. The Jews, who had been welcomed to England in the 1650s in the expectation that their return signaled the coming of a millennial age, were not expelled. Moreover, the shakeup in the universities left proponents of the new science firmly established and set the stage for the foundation of the Royal Society in 1660. New directions in political thought had also been initiated by the work of the Levellers, who advocated a moderate form of democracy; by Thomas Hobbes, who developed a theory of secular absolutism; and by Gerrard Winstanley (1609–c. 1676), who advocated a commonwealth based on the abolition of property. Most important, the revolution established the principle in England that there must be a government of laws, not of men.

## A WOMAN IN THE ENGLISH REVOLUTION: MARGARET FELL

The collapse of censorship, of the authority of bishops, and ultimately of the monarchy in revolutionary England enabled women who belonged to such Protestant sects as the Congregationalists, Baptists, and Quakers to

## ⊗ Who Should Vote? The Putney Debates ⊗

*During the English revolution the radicals differed sharply among them-
selves on numerous political and religious issues, one of the most crucial
being the extent of the parliamentary franchise. During a debate in the
army council at Putney in the autumn of 1648, the crucial issue was
whether the right to vote should be limited to male property owners.*

**Henry Ireton:** It is not fit that . . . the persons who shall make the law in the kingdom . . . have not a permanent fixed interest in the kingdom. . . .

**John Wildman:** Our case is to be considered thus, that we have been under slavery. . . . Our very laws were made by our conquerors. . . . We are now engaged for our freedom; that's the end of Parliaments. . . . Every person in England has as clear a right to elect his representative as the greatest person in England. I conceive that's the undeniable maxim of government: that all government is in the free consent of the people. . . .

**Ireton:** If a foreigner comes within this kingdom . . . that man may very well be content to submit himself to the law of the land: that is, the law that is made by those people that have a property, a fixed property, in the land. . . . A man ought to be subject to a law [to which he] did not give his consent, but with this reservation, that if this man do think himself dissatisfied to be subject to this law he may go into another kingdom. And so the same reason does extend . . . to that man that has no permanent interest in the kingdom. . . .

**Edward Sexby:** We have engaged in this kingdom and ventured our lives, and it was all for this: to recover our birthrights and privileges. . . . We have had little propriety in the kingdom as to our estates, yet we have had a birthright. But it seems now [that] except a man have a fixed estate in this kingdom, he has no right in this kingdom.

*Source:* After C. H. Firth, ed., *The Clarke Papers*, vol. 1 (London: Camden Society, 1891), pp. 317–323.

---

preach and publish their views in a manner hitherto impossible. Of these groups, however, only the Quakers, with their rejection of a professional ministry and the sacraments, were relatively comfortable with active female participation in ministerial activities. Quaker women crisscrossed England carrying their message of the Inner Light, and the more daring extended their work as far afield as Ireland, Portugal, Malta, the West Indies, and the American colonies, including Massachusetts, which expelled or hanged them. Two Quaker women even went to Adrianople in a futile attempt to convert the Turkish sultan.

The most influential Quaker woman, as well as one of the key figures in the Society of Friends, as the Quakers called themselves, was Margaret Fell (1614–1702), daughter of a Lancashire gentleman. Although she and her first husband, the attorney Thomas Fell, were Congregationalists, the Quaker founder George Fox (1624–1691) persuaded her to adopt his views in 1652, after which she held Quaker meetings in her home. The mother of eight children, she was at first unable to become a traveling minister, but she provided the Friends with an even more important contribution by her extensive correspondence with Quakers of both sexes who sought her advice on religious questions. Enormously influential in shaping the Quaker movement and its ideals, she frequently argued the Friends' case in assertive letters to non-Quaker clergymen and judges.

Fell's wide-ranging activities included the authorship of numerous pamphlets, several of which were translated into Dutch, Hebrew, and Latin. She pleaded with Oliver Cromwell and King Charles II for religious toleration, petitioned the Rump Parliament with 7,000 other women for an end to mandatory tithing, and tirelessly worked for the release of imprisoned Quakers. She was jailed several times, once for four years, because of her religious beliefs. Among her special concerns was the conversion of the Jews to Christianity, a cause for which she wrote five pamphlets, including *A Call unto the Seed of Israel*. Her best-known work, *Women's Speaking Jus-*

CRISIS AND CULTURE, 1598–1670

| Wars and rebellions | Writers | Artists and musicians |
| --- | --- | --- |
| End of the Anglo-Spanish War (1604) | Cervantes (1547–1616) | Caravaggio (1573–1610) |
| Russia's "Time of Troubles" (1598–1613) | Shakespeare (1564–1616) | El Greco (c. 1541–1614) |
| Portuguese revolt (1640) | Lope de Vega (1562–1635) | Rubens (1577–1640) |
| Catalan rebellion (1640–1652) | Grotius (1583–1645) | Monteverdi (1567–1643) |
| English civil wars (1642–1648) | Descartes (1596–1650) | |
| Revolts in Sicily and Naples (1647) | Pascal (1623–1662) | Velázquez (1599–1660) |
| Dutch crisis (1648–1650) | | |
| Cossack revolt in Poland (1648–1654) | Molière (1622–1673) | Rembrandt (1606–1669) |
| First Dutch War (1652–1654) | Milton (1608–1674) | Schütz (1585–1672) |
| Second Dutch War (1665–1667) | Spinoza (1632–1677) | |
| Cossack revolt in Russia (1667–1670) | Hobbes (1588–1679) | Bernini (1598–1680) |

*tified*, which argued for the right of women to preach and prophesy, helped lay the foundation for the establishment of Quaker women's meetings.

Soon after her husband died in 1658, Fell began traveling throughout England on behalf of the Society. In 1669 she married George Fox, partly to end unfounded rumors of an illicit relationship between them but also to symbolize the union of male and female Quakers. Until her death in 1702 she remained active in the Society's work, particularly its women's meetings. The example that she and other sectarian women set made it difficult to force them back into their traditional places in the home, the shop, and the field. Nevertheless, after 1660, with the revolutionary crisis in England essentially concluded, only the Quakers allowed women to preach. In the 1680s and 1690s a flurry of protofeminist works appeared in England by writers such as Mary Astell, but so successful was the restoration of traditional male authority in the 1660s that the new writers were content to plead only for their spiritual equality with men. Viewed in this context, the work and careers of Margaret Fell and her colleagues were an extraordinary product of the midcentury crisis.

# Central and Eastern Europe

Although the institutions of the Holy Roman Empire survived the Thirty Years' War and the Peace of Westphalia, the more powerful German princes subsequently went their own way, leaving the emperors to govern the small German states and their own patrimony in Austria, Bohemia, and Hungary. Increasingly, they concentrated on ruling through ancestral institutions, especially the Austrian Chancellery—where Habsburg policy was formulated—rather than imperial institutions. The result was the gradual establishment of a Danubian state governed from Vienna and mostly Catholic in religion. Because the emperors shared power with the landed aristocracy,

the peasant rebellions of the 1640s and 1650s were doomed, and the empire avoided a serious crisis.

Much of the unrest in central and eastern Europe was sparked by the gradual enserfment of the peasants in the sixteenth and seventeenth centuries. The process of enserfing, carried out by the landed aristocracy with the acquiescence of the monarchs, was intended both to increase agricultural production, particularly for the market in western Europe resulting from the increase in population, and to end the mobility of peasants by binding them to the land. Whereas peasants in western Europe might suffer from heavy debts and eviction from their lands, their counterparts in eastern Europe not only lost their freedom of movement but were also saddled with increasingly heavy burdens, including personal labor on landlords' estates and financial exactions that covered virtually every aspect of their lives. Widespread misery engendered social upheaval.

# Social Unrest in Poland

In common with most of the major states in western Europe, Poland and Russia experienced crises in the mid-1600s. In the case of Poland, the centralization of royal authority was not a factor, for the country was thoroughly fragmented. Real power lay in the hands of the nobles, who secured the principle of elective monarchy in 1572. Their assembly, the Sejm, met at least every two years to determine policy. Poland was also religiously split between Catholics, Greek Orthodox, Jews, and adherents of the Uniate church, who recognized the pope but worshiped according to Greek rites. Under Sigismund III (1587–1632), known as the King of the Jesuits, Catholics tried to destroy Polish Protestantism, causing a civil war in which the Orthodox Cossacks allied with the Protestants. The Jews were cruelly victimized by the wave of religious persecution, with as many as 100,000 murdered in the pogroms, or organized massacres, of the decade 1648–1658.

The Cossacks, free herdsmen and peasants, were the

major cause of unrest in both Poland and Russia. In 1648 one of the great Cossack leaders, Bogdan Khmelnitsky, ignited a major revolt against the Polish government, partly in defense of the Orthodox faith and partly because of economic grievances. In 1654 Khmelnitsky and his supporters in the Ukraine offered their allegiance to the Russian tsar and were incorporated into the Russian state. Refusing to accept the loss of the Ukraine, Poland went to war twice until peace was finally achieved in 1667 by partitioning the Ukraine between Russia and Poland.

## Russia: Centralization and Turmoil

The roots of Russia's troubles in the seventeenth century stemmed primarily from the imposition of serfdom and the centralizing work of Ivan IV, "the Terrible" (1533–1584). When Ivan assumed control of Russia in 1547 at the age of 16, he was crowned "Caesar (*tsar*) of all the Russias." He ruled by divine right in a land dominated by an Orthodox faith that stressed the subservience of the church to the state. At first he governed well, consulting with the great nobles, or boyars, formulating a new law code, instituting direct trade with western Europe, and convening Russia's first consultative assembly, the *zemski sobor*. In the late 1550s, however, he became increasingly paranoid and vindictive. Setting aside a portion of Russia exclusively for himself—the *oprichnina*, or "separate realm"—he used the *oprichnina's* black-garbed military force of 6,000 to brutalize his opponents. Boyars who resisted him were summarily imprisoned and executed, and their estates were confiscated. Ivan tortured priests, slaughtered his enemies while they worshiped, and in a rage killed one of his own sons. Towns were burned, and large numbers of people were forcibly resettled on the frontiers. Following his death in 1584, he was succeeded by his weak son, Fedor I, who died in 1598 without an heir. Russia was plunged into a period of turmoil known as the Time of Troubles. While the boyars struggled to regain their power, peasants rioted, and both the Poles and the Swedes intervened militarily.

Dismayed at the civil war and foreign intervention, the *zemski sobor* resolved the feuding over the crown by awarding it in 1613 to Ivan's grandnephew, 17-year-old Mikhail Romanov. The new dynasty would rule Russia

## ◎ Ivan the Terrible ◎

*One of the earliest descriptions of the court of Tsar Ivan IV, "the Terrible," underscores the extent to which he ruled by inculcating respect and fear in his subjects.*

This emperor uses great familiarity, as well unto all his nobles and subjects, as also unto strangers who serve him either in his wars or in occupations: for his pleasure is that they shall dine oftentimes in the year in his presence, and besides that he is oftentimes abroad, either at one church or another, and walking with his noble men abroad. And by this means he is not only beloved of his nobles and commons, but also had in great dread and fear through all his dominions, so that I think no prince in Christendom is more feared by his own [people] than he is, nor yet better beloved. For if he bids any of his dukes go, they will run; if he gives any evil or angry word to any of them, the party will not come into his majesty's presence again for a long time if he be not sent for, but will fain . . . to be very sick, and will let the hair of his head grow very long, without either cutting or shaving, which is an evident token that he is in the emperor's displeasure: for when they be in their prosperity, they account it a shame to wear long hair, in consideration whereof they used to have their heads shaven. . . .

　　He delights not greatly in hawking, hunting, or any other pastime, nor in hearing instruments or music, but sets . . . his whole delight upon two things: first, to serve God, as undoubtedly he is very devout in his religion, and the second, how to subdue and conquer his enemies.

*Source:* R. Hakluyt, ed., *The Principal Navigations, Voyages, Traffiques and Discoveries of the English Nation,* vol. 2 (Glasgow: MacLehose & Sons, 1903), pp. 438–439.

**Tsar Ivan the Terrible of Russia, as depicted in a contemporary portrait. The period between his reign and that of Mikhail I was an age of turmoil known as the Time of Troubles. [National Museum, Copenhagen]**

until its overthrow in the 1917 revolution. Rather than risk their estates in more civil war, the boyars cooperated with the first Romanovs, enabling them to finish the work of bureaucratic centralization. In return the tsars allowed the boyars to complete the process of enserfing the peasants. Together they placed the overwhelming burden of taxation on the peasants, whose rate was 100 times greater in 1640 than it had been a century earlier.

In a period when peasant disorders were endemic, the greatest peasant uprising in seventeenth-century Europe erupted in 1667. Incited by the Cossack Stenka Razin, runaway serfs and Cossacks proclaimed a message of freedom, equality, and land for all. Stenka led his undisciplined followers up the Volga River, inciting peasant uprisings and replacing local governments with Cossack rule. His ships attacked Muslim villages on the Caspian Sea and even defeated a Persian fleet. The tsar's army finally crushed his forces in 1670, a year before Stenka was captured and beheaded. The resulting repression that ended the last of the midcentury crises entailed the death of as many as 100,000 peasants.

## Old World Rivalries in a Global Setting

The political struggles that enveloped Europe in the century from 1560 to 1660 had profound consequences for the entire world. By 1660 the two countries that had dominated European expansion in the preceding two centuries—Portugal and Spain—had largely been supplanted by the Dutch, the English, and the French. Spain retained control of most of South and Central America, and Brazil remained in Portuguese hands. North America, however, increasingly became the province of the northwestern European powers who would eventually extend their sway over much of the globe.

## The Dutch and English in Asia

The union of Portugal and Spain in 1580 did not materially strengthen what was now their joint effort in the East, but it did highlight the enmity and rivalry between them as Catholic powers and the rising Protestant states of the Netherlands and England. All of the Iberian positions overseas became attractive targets, and Portuguese profits were newly tempting. The Dutch were the first to pick up this challenge effectively in Asia. At this period the Netherlands was a more important center of trade and shipping than England, and Dutch ships had the upper hand in the English Channel. There were more of them, backed by merchant capital earned in trade, and in the course of the sixteenth century they became larger and more powerful, as well as more maneuverable than the Portuguese caravels. Dutch seamen had traveled east on Portuguese ships and learned what they needed to know about sailing to Asia. By the late

1500s their ships began to outnumber those of the Portuguese in Asia, defeating them repeatedly and surpassing them as carriers. Unlike the Portuguese, they concerned themselves only with trade, avoiding any missionary effort or religious conflict, and were generally welcomed as efficient agents to replace the hated Portuguese.

Rival Dutch companies were amalgamated into the Dutch East India Company in 1602, which in the following decades built a highly profitable commercial empire centered on Java, controlling the trade of Southeast Asia far more effectively than the Portuguese had done. Much of this was the work of their able governor-general, Jan Pieterszoon Coen, appointed in 1618, who fixed the naval and administrative capital of the Dutch East Indies at Batavia (now Djakarta), with other bases at strategic points throughout Indonesia and Ceylon, which expelled the Portuguese in 1658. English competitors, excluded from this new empire, increasingly centered their attention on India, while the Dutch successfully competed with them for a share in the trade of mainland Southeast Asia and, more important, at Canton, Formosa, and Nagasaki. Coen and his successors recognized that the long-established trade of Asia would remain in able Asian and Arab hands. They also saw that greater profits could be won by taking whatever part in it they could win, especially in the carrying trade, than by hauling Asian goods to the far smaller European market. The Dutch spice monopoly, however, remained important. Meanwhile, the English East India Company had also been founded, its charter signed by Queen Elizabeth I in December 1600. England was still primarily a country of farmers, unlike the commercially advanced Low Countries, and the scale of its overseas effort was for some time small. The Dutch had little trouble repelling English efforts to break the monopoly of the Asian trade, but the English hung on as minor players at Canton, in some of the mainland Southeast Asian ports, and in India after Dutch attention had shifted to the more profitable East Indies.

The English first concentrated on Surat, where they were obliged to compete with a host of local, Arab, and rival European traders but where much of Indian trade westward was based. The Dutch were not prominent there, and the Mughal governor permitted the English to rent a warehouse. Their ships, though few, were now far more able and maneuverable than those of the Portuguese, and in successive naval battles off Surat in 1612 and 1615 they defeated Portuguese fleets decisively. In 1616 King James I sent Sir Thomas Roe as an ambassador to the Mughal court. Influenced in large part by recent English naval success against both Portuguese and pirates, the emperor, Jahangir, granted the English rights of residence at Surat and limited trade privileges. Roe, however, recognized that the trade goods at Surat were assembled there from all over India, mainly by lo-

cal merchant networks, and that the most desirable of all, fine cotton cloth of the highest quality and much in demand in Europe, came from Bengal, where the Portuguese and some Dutch traders still had a strong position.

> The number of Portuguese residing there is a good argument for us to seek it; it is a sign that there is good doing. An abbey was ever a token of a rich soil, and stores of crows of plenty of carrion. . . . We must fire them out and maintain our trade at the pike's end.[7]

Thus was foreshadowed the English drive to establish a position in eastern India, the founding of Madras in 1639, and the subsequent rise of English power in Bengal.

## Colonial Conflict in the Americas

The Spanish annexation of Portugal in 1580, which was so important for Asia, had less impact on the Americas, where the Portuguese held only Brazil. Because Portuguese settlers, mostly from the islands of the eastern Atlantic, went to Brazil in growing numbers in the seventeenth century, the colonists were strong enough to repulse Dutch and French attempts to establish permanent footholds. Although the Dutch renounced their Brazilian claims in 1661, the French continued their efforts into the eighteenth century, without success. In the meantime, the Dutch began colonizing Guiana, to the north of Brazil, in the 1610s. The Dutch West Indies Company, founded in 1621, subsequently supplied the settlers with slaves for their sugar plantations. The demand for sugar was also a major factor in the colonial efforts of the English and the French in Guiana, the only area in South America where these countries established settlements.

A much stronger challenge to Spanish domination was mounted in the West Indies, strategically important as bases for fleets sailing to and from Mexico and Central America and valuable as well for the raising of tobacco and sugar. The islands attracted so many privateers and smugglers in the late sixteenth century that the Spaniards were forced to build heavy fortifications and organize their shipping in convoys. Beginning with the voyages of John Hawkins in the 1560s, the English intruded themselves into the West Indies trade, though non-Hispanic colonies were not established there until the 1620s. By midcentury the English, Dutch, and French all had colonies in the West Indies, and England added to its holdings when a fleet dispatched by Oliver Cromwell seized Jamaica in 1655. The development of sugar plantations in the mid-1600s meant a growing demand for African slaves, who soon outnumbered Europeans in these "sugar islands."

Apart from Mexico and Florida, where St. Augustine was founded in 1565 to check French incursion, the Spaniards were unable to settle North America. Against a background of deteriorating relations with Spain in the early 1580s, Elizabeth I issued a charter to Sir Walter Raleigh authorizing him to found a North American colony, but his settlement at Roanoke Island lasted only a year. War with Spain prevented further attempts, and not until 1607 did the English establish a permanent colony at Jamestown in Virginia, soon to become famous for its tobacco. Puritan dissatisfaction with the Church of England provided crucial motivation for the founding of colonies at Plymouth (1620) and Massachusetts Bay (1629) in New England, whereas the settlement of Maryland in 1634 was largely made by Catholics. By 1670 English colonies stretched from Maine to South Carolina, the development of which angered Spaniards in Florida.

England's main competitors in North America—the Dutch and the French—could not keep pace. Rebuffed by the Spanish in Florida, the French concentrated their efforts in the north, establishing settlements at Port Royal, Acadia, in 1605, and at Quebec three years later. When France and England went to war in 1627, reverberations were felt in the colonies as Scots from Nova Scotia captured Port Royal and English ships forced Quebec to surrender. Once peace was restored at home, however, both settlements were returned to France in 1632. The decisive struggle for the domination of North America, still more than a century in the future, would not be resolved until 1763.

In the short term the English faced a graver threat from the Dutch, who established New Amsterdam at the mouth of the Hudson River in 1624 and subsequently ended Sweden's bid for a colonial stake on the Delaware River in 1655. Fortunately for the English, however, the Dutch were preoccupied with their Asian trade as well as their African colony on the Cape of Good Hope. The growing commercial and colonial rivalry between the Dutch and the English, which now extended from Asia to the Americas, culminated in a series of three wars, the first of which was instigated by the Rump Parliament in 1652. The Second Dutch War (1665–1667) brought New Jersey and New Amsterdam—henceforth known as New York—to the English and permanently removed the Dutch from North America as a colonial power, though Dutch settlers remained in New York and thousands more made homes in Pennsylvania later in the century. Thereafter, the contest for North America was among the English, the French, and the Spanish, who were exploring northward from Mexico into California. The next three centuries were to demonstrate repeatedly that the struggles for power in Europe could no longer be fought without major ramifications for the rest of the world.

ꗞ   ꗞ   ꗞ

*The century that began in 1560 witnessed the failure of Spanish and Austrian attempts to impose hegemony, the former on western and the latter on central Europe. The frequent wars of the period, normally funded by deficit financing and the imposition of onerous taxes on the peasantry, were a major cause of domestic instability. By the mid-1600s every major state in Europe except the Dutch Netherlands underwent a severe crisis: the vicious destruction of the Thirty Years' War in Germany, the Catalan and Portuguese revolts against the government in Madrid, the Fronde in France, the English revolution, and the Cossack uprisings in Poland and Russia. Although the specific conditions differed in each country, certain common themes stand out: reaction against centralized government, the financial burden of war, and, in most areas, religious conflict. Order was restored when monarchs and nobles discovered a common self-interest, though this realization did not lead to political uniformity. Poland retained its feudal monarchy, England brought its sovereign under the rule of law, and France and Russia, their nobles pacified, were governed by absolute monarchs. Of the major European states, only the Dutch Netherlands was a republic, though even there the House of Orange remained very influential. In the end, except for Poland, the costly quest for centralization was successful. With order restored, Europe in the late seventeenth century was threatened by new visions of hegemony, this time in France, but at the same time European expansion around the world offered dramatic new opportunities for commercial and industrial development.*

# Notes

1. J. H. Elliott, *Imperial Spain, 1469–1716* (New York: New American Library, 1966), p. 250.
2. G. Parker, *Philip II* (London: Hutchinson, 1978), p. 193.
3. D. Howarth, *The Voyage of the Armada: The Spanish Story* (New York: Penguin Books, 1982), p. 23.
4. T. K. Rabb, *The Struggle for Stability in Early Modern Europe* (New York: Oxford University Press, 1975), p. 120.
5. Elliott, *Imperial Spain*, pp. 322–323.
6. R. Zaller, *The Parliament of 1621: A Study in Constitutional Conflict* (Berkeley: University of California Press, 1971), p. 178.
7. J. N. Das Gupta, *India in the Seventeenth Century* (Calcutta: University of Calcutta Press, 1916), p. 212.

# Suggestions for Further Reading

Ashton, R. *The English Civil War: Conservatism and Revolution, 1603–1649.* London: Weidenfeld & Nicolson, 1978.

Aylmer, G. E. *Rebellion or Revolution? England, 1640–1660.* New York: Oxford University Press, 1986.

Beik, W. *Absolutism and Society in Seventeenth-Century France: State Power and Provincial Aristocracy in Languedoc.* Cambridge: Cambridge University Press, 1985.

Bergin, J. *Cardinal Richelieu: Power and the Pursuit of Wealth.* New Haven, Conn.: Yale University Press, 1985.

Braudel, F. *The Mediterranean and the Mediterranean World in the Age of Philip II*, trans. S. Reynolds. 2 vols. New York: Harper & Row, 1972–1973.

Buisseret, D. *Henry IV.* London: Allen & Unwin, 1984.

De Vries, J. *European Urbanization, 1500–1800.* Cambridge, Mass.: Harvard University Press, 1984.

Diefendorf, B. *Beneath the Cross: Catholics and Huguenots in Sixteenth-Century Paris.* New York: Oxford University Press, 1991.

Dunn, R. S. *The Age of Religious Wars, 1559–1715*, 2nd ed. New York: Norton, 1979.

Elliott, J. H. *The Revolt of the Catalans: A Study in the Decline of Spain, 1598–1640.* Cambridge: Cambridge University Press, 1963.

———. *Richelieu and Olivares.* Cambridge: Cambridge University Press, 1984.

Elton, G. R. *The Parliament of England, 1559–1581.* Cambridge: Cambridge University Press, 1986.

Fennell, J. L. I. *Ivan the Great of Moscow.* New York: St. Martin's Press, 1961.

Hill, C. *The World Turned Upside Down: Radical Ideas During the English Revolution.* New York: Viking, 1972.

Hirst, D. *Authority and Conflict: England, 1603–1658.* Cambridge, Mass.: Harvard University Press, 1986.

Kamen, H. *Golden Age Spain.* New York: Humanities Press, 1988.

MacCaffrey, W. T. *Queen Elizabeth and the Making of Policy, 1572–1588.* Princeton, N.J.: Princeton University Press, 1981.

———. *The Shaping of the Elizabethan Regime.* Princeton, N.J.: Princeton University Press, 1968.

Maltby, W. S. *Alba.* Berkeley: University of California Press, 1983.

Mattingly, G. *The Armada.* Boston: Houghton Mifflin, 1959.

Parker, G. *Europe in Crisis, 1598–1648.* Brighton: Harvester Press, 1980.

———. *Philip II.* London: Hutchinson, 1978.

———. *The Thirty Years' War.* London: Methuen, 1985.

Pennington, D. H. *Seventeenth-Century Europe*, 2nd ed. London: Longman, 1989.

Rabb, T. K. *The Struggle for Stability in Early Modern Europe.* New York: Oxford University Press, 1975.

Rodriguez-Salgado, M. *The Changing Face of Empire: Charles V, Philip II, and Habsburg Authority, 1551–1559.* Cambridge: Cambridge University Press, 1988.

Rowen, H. H. *John de Witt: Statesman of the "True Freedom."* Cambridge: Cambridge University Press, 1986.

Russell, C. *The Causes of the English Civil War.* New York: Oxford University Press, 1990.

Schama, S. *The Embarrassment of Riches: An Interpretation of Dutch Culture in the Golden Age.* Berkeley: University of California Press, 1988.

Smith, H. L. *Reason's Disciples: Seventeenth-Century English Feminists.* Champaign: University of Illinois Press, 1982.

Stone, L. *The Causes of the English Revolution, 1529–1642.* London: Routledge & Kegan Paul, 1972.

Stradling, R. A. *Europe and the Decline of Spain: A Study of the Spanish System, 1580–1720.* London: Allen & Unwin, 1981.

———. *Philip IV and the Government of Spain, 1621–1665.* Cambridge: Cambridge University Press, 1988.

Tapié, V. L. *France in the Age of Louis XIII and Richelieu*, trans. D. M. Lockie. New York: Praeger, 1975.

Tracy, J. D. *Holland Under Habsburg Rule, 1506–1566.* Berkeley: University of California Press, 1990.

Wilson, C. *The Transformation of Europe, 1558–1648.* Berkeley: University of California Press, 1976.

Zagorin, P. *The Court and the Country: The Beginning of the English Revolution.* New York: Atheneum, 1970.

———. *Rebels and Rulers, 1500–1660.* 2 vols. Cambridge: Cambridge University Press, 1982.

# Islamic Empires in the Early Modern World

The sixteenth century witnessed extraordinary events in the Middle East and Asia. Under Suleiman the Magnificent (1520–1566), the Ottoman armies made dramatic advances in Syria and North Africa despite their failure to capture Vienna and strike into the heartland of Europe. Under Suleiman, Ottoman imperial power was rivaled only by the Chinese, and despite the Ottomans' later decline, especially in the eighteenth and nineteenth centuries, they remained a force to be reckoned with into the early twentieth century.

Meanwhile, in India the oppressive rule of the Delhi sultanate gave way early in the sixteenth century to a new Islamic dynasty of conquest, the Mughals, who ruled northern India as well as Afghanistan and parts of southern India from 1526 to 1707. At the height of their power, the Mughals restored and added to India's imperial tradition, brought about a notable flowering of cul-

**The coronation of Sultan Selim I, "the Grim." This is a detail from a sixteenth-century manuscript illustration. [Giraudon/Art Resource]**

ture, and reestablished a large measure of political unity. The sixteenth century also saw the restoration of imperial grandeur in Iran under the Safavids, particularly Shah Abbas the Great (1587–1629), who freed western and northern Iran from Ottoman control. As in western Europe, the late sixteenth and early seventeenth centuries were a time of cultural brilliance in the Middle East, India, and Iran.

## The Ottoman Empire

While the Delhi sultans were at the peak of their power in India, a new dynasty of sultans, the Ottomans, was established among another group of Turks who had moved westward into Asia Minor. For nearly three centuries the Ottomans expanded their conquests, until in 1683 they ranged from Hungary to the Persian Gulf and from the Crimea to North Africa and the coasts of Arabia. The followers of the dynasty's founder, Osman (1299–1326), were mostly ghazis, Islamic warriors who saw their sacred duty in extending the faith by attacking unbelievers. Motivated by religion and a thirst for booty, disciplined by a ghazi code of honor, and aided by the weakness of their enemies, the Ottomans were successful out of all proportion to their relatively small numbers. Their success was also aided by their tolerance of other faiths after their first conquests and by the disgust of many Byzantine subjects with the corrupt and oppressive imperial government (see Chapter 8).

From their newly conquered base in western Asia Minor, the Ottomans began in the 1300s by extending their sway over other Turkish states and Byzantine territories in the rest of Asia Minor and adjoining areas. A request for their help by one of the feuding political factions in Constantinople gave them an opportunity to establish a bridgehead on the European side of the Dardanelles, from which they later refused to retreat. Taking advantage of political chaos in the Balkans as well as their own military superiority, the Ottomans defeated the Serbs, Bulgars, and Macedonians in the late 1300s, opening up the Balkans to Turkish immigrants. Europeans were now sufficiently alarmed to send a crusading army. The Ottoman leader Bayezid I, "the Thunderbolt," who had allegedly threatened to feed his horse at the altar of St. Peter's Basilica in Rome, took only three hours to defeat the Europeans at Nicopolis in 1396. As Bayezid prepared to attack the Byzantine capital at Constantinople, the Ottomans themselves became the victims of a new Turco-Mongol invasion led by Tamerlane, who defeated them near Ankara in 1402.

After Tamerlane withdrew and order was restored, the Ottomans renewed their conquests, defeating the Greeks and finally taking Constantinople in 1453. Under Mehmet II, "the Conqueror" (1451–1481), the city, renamed Istanbul, was rebuilt and repopulated with new immigrants, including Jews and Christians as well as Muslims.

## ❦
## MEHMET THE CONQUEROR

Mehmet hoped to make his new capital the center of a world empire far greater than that to which Alexander the Great and Julius Caesar had aspired. In this imperial state Mehmet ruled supreme. He made war—the vehicle to expand his empire—the dominant preoccupation of Ottoman society.

Because of his imperialistic ambitions and his autocratic rule, Mehmet's life was increasingly endangered by foreign agents as well as domestic zealots. The Vene-

Mehmet II, who conquered Constantinople and renamed it Istanbul, as painted by a contemporary artist. [Topkapi Palace Museum, Istanbul]

tian republic organized at least a dozen attempts to assassinate him, but Mehmet's espionage network successfully protected him. Despite the threats to his life, he frequently rode through Istanbul accompanied by only two guards or walked the streets in the company of his slaves. But the strain eventually took its toll, turning the once affable sultan into a suspicious, reclusive despot, afraid even to eat with his viziers for fear of being poisoned. Stories of his cruelty abound. When the Italian Renaissance painter Gentile Bellini showed Mehmet his painting of the beheading of John the Baptist, Mehmet criticized Bellini for making John's neck extend too far and proved his point by having a slave beheaded in Bellini's presence. A serious offender against Mehmet's laws might have a long, sharp pole driven up his rectum with a mallet; if that failed to kill him, the pole, with the victim on it, was erected. Between his military campaigns and his domestic persecution, Mehmet may have been responsible for nearly 30,000 deaths a year during his reign.

Despite the harsher aspects of his rule, Mehmet was tolerant when it came to matters of religion. Perhaps this was due in part to the fact that his mother, who was of Greek, Slavic, or Italian ancestry, had been raised a Christian. Mehmet himself made some effort to comprehend Christian teachings, at least as a means of understanding the faith of a substantial number of his subjects. His own preference was the Shi'ite version of Islam, but as the ruler of a largely Sunni state, he publicly embraced Sunni tenets. Mehmet treated the Jews well; his Jewish physician, Maestro Jacopo, was also a trusted financial adviser.

The Sufis' religious fraternities, or dervishes, did not fare as well. As mystical religious ascetics roughly akin to Christian monks or friars, they were popular with the masses because of their pastoral concerns, their poverty and charitable work, their mystical rites, and in some cases their cult of saints. Because their popularity made Mehmet suspicious, however, he curtailed their activity and occasionally even exiled their leaders, whom he denounced as insane, and confiscated their property.

Mehmet's personality combined intellectual curiosity with superstition and cold calculation. Given his vast imperial ambition—the state he ruled was roughly equivalent to the Byzantine Empire at its height—it was only natural that he should be interested in the study of geography, history, and military strategy. As he grew older, he increasingly enjoyed the company of poets and scholars. Yet he was also keenly superstitious and hired Persian astrologers to prepare horoscopes for him, sometimes even using their predictions as the basis for military decisions. To an artist such as Bellini, who painted his portrait (which the sultan commissioned in defiance of Islamic law), Mehmet attributed virtually supernatural power. Reinforcing the coldness of Mehmet's personality was the constant threat of assassination as

well as his refusal to become involved in long-term relationships with women. Sexually, he enjoyed the company of women and boys, but domestic intimacy he deliberately shunned. Although his modern biographer calls Mehmet's personality "demonic," today many Turks regard the Conqueror as the greatest of the sultans and a holy man who can still intercede with Allah on their behalf.

## Selim the Grim, Suleiman the Magnificent, and Ottoman Expansion

In the decades after the fall of Constantinople the Ottoman armies completed the conquest of Greece and the Balkans. They also established a foothold in the Crimea by supplanting colonies founded by the Genoese so that by the late 1400s the Black Sea was virtually a Turkish lake. In the following century two of the greatest sultans, Selim I, "the Grim" (1512–1520), and Suleiman I, "the Magnificent" (1520–1566), made major new advances. Selim first had to turn his attention eastward, where the expansionist Shi'ite regime in Safavid Iran threatened the Ottomans and offended their Sunni orthodoxy. After pushing back the Safavids, Selim overran Syria, Palestine, and Egypt. These conquests forced the sultan to assume responsibility for protecting the Islamic holy places in Mecca and Medina, now threatened by the advance of the Portuguese into the Red Sea and the Indian Ocean in their quest for bases along the route to India.

Suleiman continued his predecessor's expansionistic program. In a series of brilliant campaigns he captured the island citadel of Rhodes; Belgrade on the Danube, gateway to central Europe; and much of Hungary. He besieged Vienna, but his forces lacked both the supplies and the resolve to take the city, and he was forced to retreat in 1529. Elsewhere his armies were victorious in North Africa as far west as Algeria, and in the Middle East, where they captured Baghdad. In the course of these campaigns Suleiman became an ally of France against the Habsburgs. As a consequence France gained special trade privileges in the Ottoman Empire, and later it acted as protector of Catholic subjects in the empire and of the Christian holy places in Palestine.

Ottoman expansion continued for another century, though at a much slower pace because of domestic conflict, a stronger European maritime presence in the Mediterranean, bitter rivalry with Iran, and a succession of ineffectual sultans. After the Ottomans conquered Cyprus in 1570, the Holy League, comprised of Spain, Venice, and the papacy, successfully challenged and defeated the Ottoman fleet in 1571 at Lepanto, off western Greece. The last major Ottoman conquest in the west was the island of Crete in 1669. A second assault on

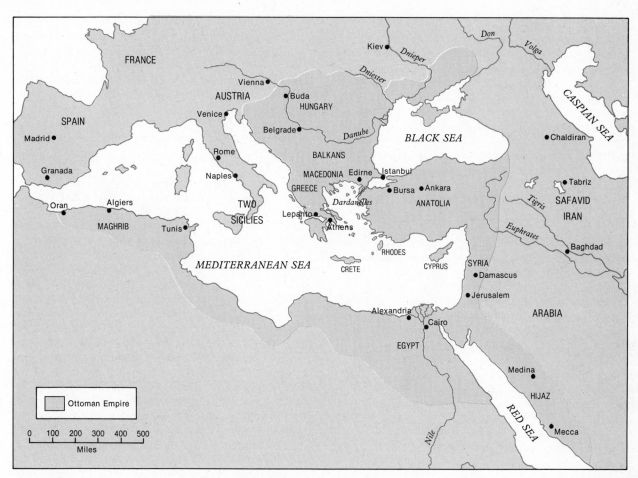

***20.1*** *The Empire of Suleiman I*

## Ottoman Society

Vienna failed in 1683 (see Chapter 23), effectively marking the end of Ottoman expansion. From this point on, the Ottomans, now on the defensive and surpassed by European scientific and technological advances, repeatedly lost territory. The remains of their empire finally crumbled after their defeat in World War I.

## Ottoman Society

The sultans who presided over the empire had supreme authority in matters civil, military, and religious, subject only to divine law. Interpretation of that law was therefore critical, and for this the sultans turned to the grand mufti of Istanbul, a legal expert who interpreted sacred law and issued legal opinions on the secular decrees of the sultans, with the consensus of other religious leaders. Like their counterparts in Europe and Asia, the sultans ruled with the aid of an advisory council, called the divan, which met regularly to handle petitions and to supervise the affairs of state. Beginning in the late 1400s,

the sultans rarely met with the divan, though they sometimes listened to its proceedings behind a grille in the wall of the council chamber. Presiding over the sessions was the grand vizier, the highest-ranking official in the government after the sultan.

Below the divan a highly centralized and immense bureaucracy administered the affairs of state. Because the sultans had huge harems, the problem of succession was potentially explosive, as in Mughal India and Iran. Mehmet II solved the problem by creating the "law of fratricide," which necessitated that each new sultan execute all but one of his brothers and half brothers; one was usually left alive in case a sultan died without a surviving heir. Perhaps no sultan was more thorough in his adherence to this practice than Selim the Grim, who killed his brothers, nephews, and sons, with the exception of his designated heir, Suleiman. Beginning in the mid-1600s, the Ottomans ended the practice of fratricide in preference for selecting the sultan's eldest son as heir. Other sons were made prisoners in palace chambers called the "cage" and kept politically powerless.

A major responsibility of the sultan was to dispense justice, symbolized by a high "tower of justice" in the imperial palace from which the sultan could theoretically see officials acting unjustly and punish them accordingly. In the divan the grand vizier dispensed justice in the sultan's name. Because the empire was ruled chiefly according to Islamic sacred law, even the sultan's decrees had to be rendered in its spirit, and the judicial system in practice involved a close intermingling of legal and religious principles. The two chief justices, second in legal significance only to the grand mufti of Istanbul, were the leaders of the ulema, a body of learned men that included judges, teachers, prayer leaders known as imams, and muftis, who specialized in interpreting the law for judges and public officials. Although the grand mufti was originally not part of the judiciary in order to ensure his objectivity, in time he came to dominate it, even to the point of naming the chief justice.

These officials were drawn from the sultan's ruling class, and most belonged to an elite group known as the "true Ottomans." This group consisted solely of Muslims who served the state and "knew the Ottoman way"; that is, they were Turkish and conformed to Ottoman customs. Membership in the ruling class was not denied by reason of birth; regardless of origin, one could become an Ottoman by acquiring the stipulated qualifications. In an empire that included a wide variety of races and cultures, this was important in attracting support and conveying a sense of shared power.

Beneath the ruling class were the *reaya*, or "subjects"—peasants, townspeople, and nomads, both Muslim and non-Muslim. They were legally distinct from the ruling class. Because sons of that class generally inherited their father's social status, they perpetuated the oligarchy, provided that they acquired the necessary education to serve the state, although recruits from below could be promoted on merit.

The vast numbers of subject communities enveloped by Ottoman expansion were essentially allowed to govern themselves and to retain their institutions as long as they paid their taxes and provided the sultan with military and administrative personnel. The Ottomans even permitted their subjects to retain their traditional religious loyalties. Non-Muslims, including Jews and Greek Orthodox Christians, were organized into communities known as *millets*, which served as the main agencies for tax collection, education, and civil matters such as marriage and inheritance. To encourage the conversion of non-Muslims to Islam, the Ottomans imposed a special tax on all "infidels." Muslim men were permitted to marry non-Muslim women, who did not have to convert, but the children of such unions had to be raised as Muslims. In general the Ottomans proved more tolerant than Christian monarchs in Europe, who subjected heretics and Jews to forcible conversion and sometimes expelled and even executed them.

A characteristic feature of Ottoman society was the institution of slavery. Slavery, as the Ottomans practiced it, was substantially different from the brutal servitude Europeans imposed on blacks in the New World. It was less menial and offered greater opportunities. As elsewhere in the Middle East and parts of Asia, slaves were employed primarily as personal and household attendants or were given assignments in the military and bureaucracy. Some eventually established themselves as judges, philosophers, and poets. A sixteenth-century sultan typically had between 20,000 and 25,000 civil servants and troops in his household, all nominally slaves; the grand vizier had 1,700 in 1561. Slavery was not necessarily considered demeaning in all its circumstances, for some sultans were sons of slaves in their fathers' harems, and sometimes even the grand vizier was a slave.

Because Islamic law did not permit the enslavement of Muslims, slaves necessarily consisted of prisoners of war, people the Ottomans purchased in North Africa and Spain, and young males from Christian families within the empire who were recruited in a periodic levy. This levy, known as the *devshirme*, was imposed by the sultan's personal authority as a special tax, usually on one household in 40 in order to distribute the burden as equitably as possible. The youths selected had to be unmarried and typically between the ages of 8 and 18; orphans and only sons were exempt. Some parents offered bribes to keep their sons out of the levy; some young men resorted to similar means to get in. Once in Istanbul, the youths were forcibly converted to Islam and circumcised; the most promising were then designated to receive special education so that they might assume appointment to a high government office. Many acquired membership in the janissaries, the most elite unit of the Ottoman army; members became especially proficient in the use of firearms, and originally they were not permitted to marry.

Ottoman society, like nearly all societies of the time, was largely geared to benefit the males. Muslim custom permitted polygamy, and women usually wore veils. In sharp contrast with the Byzantine Empire and the western European states, women were excluded as rulers. Wives of the sultans were instead confined to harems, which were organized hierarchically like the rest of society. Presided over by the sultan's mother, who was assisted by mothers of the sultan's children and royal favorites, harems were guarded by eunuchs, men castrated as boys so as to assure no risk of their plotting to put their sons in power and to prevent them from engaging in sexual misconduct with harem members. From the 1500s onward, virtually all eunuchs in the empire were African blacks.

From their position in the harem, powerful women were sometimes able to dominate the government, particularly in the "sultanate of the women" in the mid-

## ◙ *Devshirme:* Turks Drafting Christians ◙

*Europeans were intrigued and horrified by the Turkish practice known as the* devshirme, *by which Christian boys were drafted into slavery by the state. In 1585 a Venetian ambassador described it in these words.*

There are two types of Turks. One is composed of people native-born of Turkish parents, while the other is made up of renegades who are sons of Christians. The latter group were taken by force in the raids . . . on Christian lands, or else harshly levied in their villages from the sultan's non-Muslim subjects and taxpayers. They are taken while still boys, and either persuaded or forced to be circumcised and made Muslims. It is the custom . . . to send men throughout the country every fourth or fifth year to levy one-tenth of the boys, just as if they were so many sheep, and after they have made Turks of these boys they train each one according to his abilities. . . .

Not only is the Turkish army made up of these renegades, but at one time they used to win all the chief positions in the government . . . and the highest commands in the armed forces, because ancient custom forbids that the sons of Turks should hold these jobs. But the present Grand Signor ignores this custom and chooses whatever men he wants. . . .

After they have been taken away as young boys the renegades are sent to different places to be trained according to the jobs they will be given. The handsomest, most wide-awake ones are placed in the seraglio [palace] of the Grand Signor, or in one of two oth-ers . . . and there they are all prepared . . . to rise to the highest government offices. . . .

The other boys . . . [are] in a kind of seminary for the janissary corps. . . . They make them drudge day and night, and they give them no beds to sleep on and very little food. When these boys begin to shave they make them janissaries.

*Source:* J. C. Davis, ed. and trans., *Pursuit of Power: Venetian Ambassadors' Reports on Spain, Turkey, and France in the Age of Philip II, 1560–1600* (New York: Harper Torchbooks, 1970), pp. 135–136.

1600s. One of the most influential of these women was Turhan, mother of Mehmet IV (1648–1687), who seized power by having the boy's grandmother murdered. Be-yond the upper reaches of the imperial harem, however, women were excluded from places of power and even from many of the Islamic religious ceremonies.

Despite their general exclusion from political power, Muslim women in the Ottoman world enjoyed a variety of rights, including the ability to hold and control prop-erty without interference from fathers, husbands, or male relatives. This right extended even to property that was part of their dowry, a right not accorded to French women as late as the nineteenth century. Legally Otto-man women could execute wills, defend their rights in court, and testify, although a man's testimony was con-sidered twice as valid. No Muslim woman could be forced to marry, although various pressures could be applied to attain the family's end. Although divorce was rare among Muslims, a woman who received one was entitled to retain her property. Thus, although Ottoman women shared the generally low status of women else-where, they did possess some basic economic rights and at least a degree of social choice.

## ❦
# ISTANBUL: "THIS PLACE THAT IS LIKE PARADISE"

Before the Muslim conquest in 1453, the population of Constantinople had declined to some 40,000 inhabitants, and it fell to 10,000 immediately thereafter, but within 25 years it had rebounded to nearly 100,000, including its suburbs. By 1600 Istanbul, as the Turks called it, was larger than any city in Europe, with a population of at least 700,000. The initial impetus for the city's growth came from its conqueror, Mehmet II, who was deter-mined to make his new capital the greatest in the world. To increase the population, he offered to return the prop-erty of refugees and to give them freedom to work and worship if they came back, which a great many did.

Mehmet also ordered nearby provincial governors to send 4,000 families to Istanbul (although this goal was never fully achieved), and he attracted merchants and artisans from such conquered cities as Corinth and Ar-gos in Greece and towns in the Crimea. Because of their wealth and trading skills, Jews were also encouraged to emigrate to Istanbul. By 1478 they were the third largest group in the capital, comprising some 10 percent of the population, behind Muslims (58 percent) and Greek Christians (23 percent). To help feed the burgeoning population, Mehmet settled 30,000 captive Balkan peasants, whom he virtually enslaved, in villages near the capital.

Because much of the city had been ruined during the siege, the Ottomans initiated a massive building program that included two palaces and a grand mosque. Around the latter there developed a hospital, an almshouse, and a major center of higher education that provided instruction in theology, law, medicine, and the sciences. The famous Christian church, Hagia Sophia, was transformed into a mosque, minarets were gradually added, the Byzantine mosaics were plastered with a gray limewash, and verses from the Koran were substituted as decorations. The grandest of the new mosques was constructed in the early 1550s at the behest of Suleiman, who employed the leading Ottoman architect, Sinan, de-

signer of more than 300 buildings. When his masterpiece was finished, Sinan reportedly told Suleiman: "I have built for thee, O emperor, a mosque which will remain on the face of the earth till the day of judgment."[1] In addition to such grandiose structures, the Ottomans commissioned many public works, including new roads, bridges, and aqueducts.

The commercial heart of Istanbul was the grand bazaar or *bedestan*, built at Mehmet's command. Consisting of a monumental building with stone domes and iron doors—a secure depository for valuable goods, jewelry, and money—the bazaar was surrounded by groups of shops lining the roads that branched out into the city. Each group of shops housed merchants or artisans who specialized in a particular kind of goods. Mehmet's complex, including the 118 shops in the bedestan and the 984 surrounding it, is today known as Istanbul's covered market.

Crucial to the reconstruction of the capital were the *imarets*, each of which was typically an endowed complex consisting of a mosque, an institution of higher

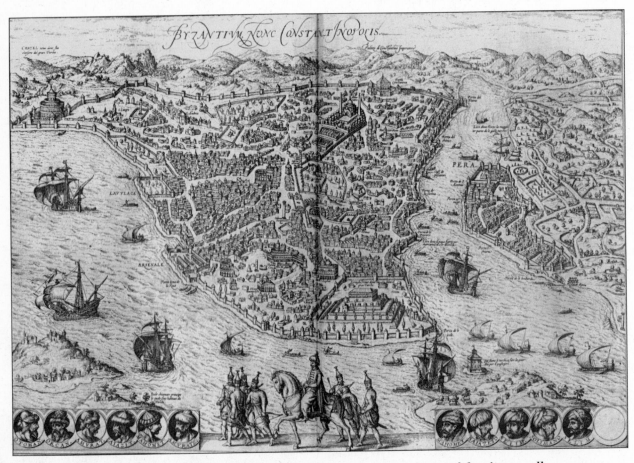

**A view of Istanbul in the sixteenth century. Note the natural defenses of the city as well as the wall at the top of the painting. [British Library]**

learning or *medrese*, a hospital, travelers' lodgings, and appropriate roads and bridges. In 1459 Mehmet required the most prominent citizens to establish imarets in Istanbul, and in time these complexes became the centers of new quarters or suburbs. Istanbul, in fact, grew so rapidly that in the seventeenth century the sultans tried to restrict its expansion and generally succeeded in slowing the rate of growth. By comparison, the English monarchs Elizabeth I and James I were less successful in their efforts to halt the growth of London. A truly cosmopolitan city unlike anything in Europe, some 40 percent of Istanbul's population in the seventeenth century was non-Muslim.

## Urban Life

Though Istanbul was unmistakably the preeminent jewel in the Ottoman crown, a host of other cities contributed to the richness, productivity, and cultural heritage of the empire. Among them by the late 1600s were some of the great cities of antiquity: Alexandria and Baghdad, Athens and Jerusalem. Others, such as Sarajevo and Tatar-Pazarjik in the Balkans, developed from imarets founded in the fourteenth and fifteenth centuries by frontier lords. The largest Ottoman city and commercial center in the Balkans was Edirne (now in European Turkey), which was strategically located on the major overland trade routes between Istanbul and Hungary, Bosnia, and Greece. Its counterpart in Anatolia—Bursa, center of a thriving silk industry—sat astride the overland routes from Europe and western Asia Minor to the Middle East, Iran, and India.

The heart of every major Ottoman city was a great mosque and a bedestan, around which trade centers developed. The endowment of imarets played a key role in the growth of such cities as Edirne and Bursa, underscoring the importance of substantive charitable giving in the expansion of Ottoman urban life and commerce.

Although the people were officially divided into two groups, Muslim and non-Muslim, in practice socioeconomic divisions had little to do with religion. Merchants and artisans in the towns had the same rights, though in theory non-Muslims were required to dress distinctively and were not allowed to ride horses or own slaves. In fact, however, such restrictions were ineffective. Each religious group—Muslim, Jewish, and Christian—was housed in its own quarter, as were the gypsies. Each quarter was typically organized around a religious center or a bedestan and was a community in its own right, its members linked most often by distinctive religious or economic ties. Normally the religious leader of each quarter—imam, rabbi, or priest—was responsible for contacts with the imperial government and would, for example, make the sultan's decrees known to the people. Each quarter had to provide for its own night watchmen, lamplighters, street cleaners, and volunteer firefighters.

Although the Ottoman city was at root a collection of distinctive communities, there were municipal officials who coordinated common services, such as street paving and repair, water supply, building regulations, and refuse disposal. These officials were not, however, representatives of a formal municipal organization, as in modern America, but agents of the imperial government.

## Economy and Culture

Economic life in Ottoman cities was organized around the guilds, whose members comprised a substantial part of the population. Like their medieval European counterparts, the Ottoman guilds regulated their activities, including standards, prices, and competition, and cared for the welfare of their members. They also engaged in a wide variety of social activities ranging from processions and festivals to the provision of relief to the needy. Some guilds were restricted to adherents of a particular religious group, while others embraced Muslims, Jews, and Christians. As in Europe, masters trained apprentices, who in time became journeymen and ultimately masters, so long as their number did not become excessive. Some guilds hired women, principally to wind silk and spin cotton. Other guilds, such as that of the weavers in Bursa, relied heavily on slave labor, promising freedom to slaves who wove a stipulated quantity of cloth. As in Renaissance Florence, these guilds also hired free labor.

The range of guilds was extensive, embracing the usual skilled artisans as well as fishermen, minters, scribes, and religious men. There were even guilds in Istanbul that provided snow, ice, and water from the mountains or made sherbet in such exotic flavors as rhubarb, rose, and lotus. All guilds were subject to strict regulations and substantial taxes.

Merchants in the Ottoman cities generally fell into two groups: those who dealt with local products and belonged to guilds akin to those of the artisans and those engaged in caravan and overseas trade, who were essentially free to pursue their businesses as they wished. Some merchants organized partnerships or corporations, sometimes cornering the market in various commodities and driving up the prices to make substantial profits. Guild members were understandably hostile to such merchants, particularly since profit margins in the guilds normally did not exceed 15 percent. Moreover, the great merchants paid relatively little in taxes, though they used their wealth to benefit their communities in other ways. Some procured raw material for workers and exported their finished products, while others endowed charitable institutions.

## ◉ Jewish Life in the Ottoman Empire ◉

*On his tour of the Ottoman Empire in the sixteenth century, Nicolas De Nicolay, chamberlain and geographer to the king of France, described the Jews in this manner.*

The number of Jews dwelling throughout all the cities of Turkey and Greece, and principally at Constantinople, is so great, that it is a thing marvelous and incredible. For the number of those who trade and traffic in merchandise, likewise who loan money at usury, doth there multiply so from day to day, that the great haunt and bringing of merchandise which arrives there from all parts as well by sea as by land, is such, that . . . they have in their hands the most and greatest traffic of merchandise and ready money that is in all [the] Levant. And likewise their shops and warehouses, the best furnished of all rich sorts of merchandise which are in Constantinople are those of the Jews. Likewise they have among them workmen of all arts and handicrafts most excellent, and especially of the Maranes [Moriscos] of late banished and driven out of Spain and Portugal, who to the great detriment and damage of Christianity, have taught the Turks divers inventions, crafts, and engines of war, as to make artillery, harquebusses [handguns], gunpowder, shot, and other munitions. They have also there set up printing, not before seen in those countries, by the which in fair characters they put in light divers books in divers languages, as Greek, Latin, Italian, Spanish, and the Hebrew tongue, being to them natural, but are not permitted to print the Turkish or Arabic tongue. They . . . speak and understand all other sorts of languages used in [the] Levant, which serves them greatly for the communication and traffic which they have with other strange nations, to whom oftentimes they serve for Dragomans, or interpreters. . . . The Jews which dwell in Constantinople, Adrianople, . . . and other places of the dominion of the great Turk, are all apparelled with long garments, like unto the Greeks and other nations of [the] Levant, but for their mark and token to be known from others, they wear a yellow Tulbant [a turban].

*Source:* N. De Nicolay, *The Navigations into Turkie,* trans. T. Washington (London, 1585), fols. 130v–131v (edited to conform to modern usage).

---

Although charging interest under Islamic law was illegal, merchants of all religious persuasions found ways to provide loans. Among the borrowers were government officials who used the loans to procure higher offices and then rewarded the lenders with such benefits as monopolies or tax farms (the right of private parties to collect taxes for the government). Certain merchants received contracts to establish factories for the production of large amounts of armaments or woolens for the military, thereby depriving the smaller guild shops of business and increasing the friction between merchants and artisans.

The wealthier Ottoman merchants engaged in extensive international trade, particularly from the key centers of Istanbul, Bursa, Edirne, Cairo, and Salonika. Muslim merchants even had their own trading companies in the important cities of northern Italy. The textile merchants of Edirne exported their products as far afield as Florence, Paris, and London and in turn imported European cloth. Cotton from Anatolia, Egypt, Yemen, and India was sold throughout Europe, while the merchants of Bursa exported silk, timber, hides, and ironware to the East. Spices, jewelry, perfume, costly textiles, and dyes were the major commodities in overseas trade. Through the key North African cities of Cairo and Alexandria came ivory, gold, and slaves; Istanbul alone had some 2,000 slave merchants. One of the oddities of the empire was that foreign traders paid fewer taxes than their Ottoman counterparts and thus after the eighteenth century came to dominate international commerce.

Feeding the imperial population, especially the residents of the capital, was a major task. By the mid-seventeenth century Istanbul alone required 250 tons of wheat each day and 2,000 shiploads of food each year. Much of the food, of course, was produced within the empire: wheat from Egypt, Thrace, and especially the Dobrudja region west of the Black Sea; livestock, fish, cereals, and honey from the area north of that sea; wine from the Aegean region; rice, spices, and sugar from Egypt; and cereals from Macedonia and Thessaly. So crucial was the need to find adequate food for the population and sufficient raw materials for the artisans that the imperial government imposed numerous controls. It fixed the price of the food at the point of production, licensed the middlemen who bought it, and supervised its distribution. Smuggling and profiteering were strictly prohibited, and violaters faced the loss of their ships and goods.

Until the end of the sixteenth century the food problem was aggravated by labor shortages in rural areas. The government responded to this by curtailing the mobility of peasants and by offering tax incentives and the right to sell surplus crops on the open market to farmers who brought unused lands under cultivation. Substantial population growth in the sixteenth century finally resolved the labor shortage.

During the golden age of Ottoman culture, which followed the conquest of Constantinople, most leading writers and thinkers belonged to the ulema, although most of the prominent figures in science and medicine were Jews. Ottoman culture was rich and varied, reaching a peak of excellence in the poetry composed for wealthy, powerful patrons. The leading Ottoman poets no longer imitated Persian writers but achieved a creativity of their own, even while extensively borrowing Persian and Arabic words.

The "sultan of the poets," as his contemporaries called him, was Muhammad Abd ul-Baki (1526–1600), a former apprentice to a saddlemaker and hawker of poems in the courtyard of a mosque. His major work was a moving elegy on Suleiman's death:

> *Will not the King awake from sleep? The dawn*
> *    of day has broken.*
> *Will not he come forth from his tent bright as*
> *    heaven's display?*
> *Long have our eyes looked down the road, and*
> *    yet no news is come*
> *From yonder land, the threshold of his*
> *    majesty's array.*[2]

Most of Baki's poems urged readers to enjoy the transitory pleasures of life. Almost as revered as Baki, Mehmet ibn Suleiman Fuzuli (1480–1556) explored the unity of creation and mystic love.

> *Let your grace, my only Lord, forever be my*
> *    only guide;*
> *Lead me not by any path that leads not to*
> *    where You abide.*[3]

There was also poetry for the masses, sung, as in medieval France and Germany, by itinerant troubadours; their themes, however, were mystical rather than secular, as in the West. The greatest of the folk poets was the seventeenth-century minstrel Karacaoglan, whose vigorous verse recounted the lives of the ordinary people of Anatolia:

> *The cranes they circle in the air*
> *The dreams I fear I see anew*
> *Brave comrades, this I have to say*
> *She does not love who is not true.*[4]

Novels, plays, and short stories became important literary forms in the Ottoman world only in the nineteenth century as the result of Western influence, but earlier prose authors made worthy contributions in essays, biographies, and learned treatises on history, geography, and religion. Recognizing the value of history to buttress their claims to expand the empire, Mehmet II and his predecessor, Murat II (1421–1451), sponsored the earliest Ottoman historians, including Ahmedi, whose *Epic of the Histories of the House of Osman* is the earliest source for the rise of the Ottomans. While the major historical writers of Suleiman's era were chroniclers, the distinguished court historian Mustafa Naima Efendi (1665–1716) not only recorded facts but analyzed them as well. "Historians," he insisted, "should speak frankly and fairly. . . . They should not exaggerate . . . , and if, to attain their end, they must criticize and censure great men of praiseworthy works, they should never be unjust."[5]

Two generations earlier, Mustafa ibn Abdullah, known as Katip Chelebi (1609–1657), demonstrated equal respect for sources in compiling his *View of the World*, a compendium of geography that drew not only on Muslim works but also on such European authors as the Flemish geographer Gerardus Mercator. Western scholarship, which owed so much to the Muslim world, was now beginning to repay the debt.

In the area of religion, Muslim authors continued to debate the relationship between philosophy (reason) and religion (faith), in particular whether the two fields could be reconciled. During the late fifteenth century the ulema officially decided that reason could be used in the study of medicine and mathematics but not religion. Religious writers concentrated on the mystical notion of the unity of existence, a theme popular with many poets as well.

The medrese associated with the mosque founded by Suleiman was a boon to science because of its emphasis on mathematics and medicine rather than religion. Its influence is apparent in the large number of hospitals subsequently established in the empire. One of the most influential Ottoman physicians, Ahi Ahmed Chelebi (1436–1523), founded hospitals in 40 villages, encouraged these institutions to train doctors, and established the first Ottoman medical school. Religious leaders, however, continued to threaten scientific inquiry, as in 1580, when their pressure prompted the sultan to destroy the astronomical observatory in Istanbul. Tensions between religious values and secular movements in education and society have continued in Islamic areas to the present day.

## The Decay of the Empire

Beginning in the mid-seventeenth century, the rule of the sultans began to weaken. At the same time the janissaries, who could now marry at will, became more devoted to their families and personal fortunes than to the sultan's welfare. Discipline in the janissary corps eroded, demands for higher pay escalated, and there was a growing reluctance to fight extended campaigns in remote lands. Fortunately for the Ottomans, effective government was restored when Turhan appointed the Albanian Muhammad Kuprili as grand vizier in 1656. Determined to end graft and corruption in the empire, he and his successors dominated Ottoman politics for more than half a century.

After 1716, Ottoman officials, stung by the loss of Transylvania and most of Hungary to Habsburg armies (which had been confirmed in the 1699 Treaty of Karlowitz), began trying to reorganize their decaying army along European lines, but the forces of conservatism, led by the janissaries and the ulema, resisted change. The sultans and some factions at court regularly pressed for reform but were resisted by vested interests and conservative groups. The Ottomans were ultimately unable to stave off the European challenge to their empire. The Treaty of Passarowitz (1718), by which the Ottomans ceded much of Serbia to Austria and Dalmatia to Venice, was a foretaste of things to come.

## The Mughals in India

After Tamerlane's bloody invasion of 1398 (see Chapter 11), the Delhi sultanate never regained its earlier control, and the north of India remained fragmented. An Afghan clan, the Lodis, seized power in Delhi in 1451 but could not extend their rule beyond neighboring Punjab. Their continued oppression of the Hindu population, including temple razing, sparked rebellions that could not be put down. These erupted eastward in the central Ganges valley, westward among the Rajputs of Rajasthan (who still defended Hindu India), and finally in Punjab itself.

## Babur and the New Dynasty

A rebel governor in Punjab asked for help from the central Asian leader Babur (1483–1530), known already as "the Tiger" and by this time established also as ruler of most of Afghanistan. Babur claimed descent on his father's side from Tamerlane and on his mother's from Chinghis Khan. Like many other central Asian Turks, he had acquired a great deal of Persian culture and was a gifted poet in Persian. Babur's tough, mounted Turco-Afghan troops defeated the numerically superior Lodi forces and their war elephants at the battle of Panipat in Punjab, some 70 miles northwest of Delhi, in 1526. The next year Babur routed the Rajput army, which tried to eject him, and in 1529 crushed the Delhi sultanate's last effort to regain power. Babur was master of the north and proclaimed the Mughal dynasty (the name is derived, via Persian, from *Mongol*), which was to restore imperial grandeur in northern India for nearly two centuries.

The greatness of the Mughal period rested on a fortunate combination of able, imaginative rulers, especially the emperor Akbar (1542–1605), and the new infusion of Persian culture into North India. Under Akbar and his immediate successors, Persian, the official language of court, government, and law, merged with the earlier language of the Delhi-Agra area to form modern Hindi, now the largest single language of India, and Urdu, its close equivalent, now the official language of Pakistan. Persian artistic and literary forms blended with earlier traditions in the north and enriched all of Indian culture. The Mughals reestablished firm central control in the north. Within their empire, agriculture and commerce flourished again. Steady revenues and an efficient imperial administration enabled the Mughals to build a network of roads that linked the empire. This was no small task, given India's previous disunity and regional separatism, as well as its size.

The total population in the empire was probably over 100 million, on a par with China's and almost certainly larger than Europe's. To symbolize their power and wealth, the Mughal emperors built magnificent new capitals at both Delhi and Agra. Only 100 miles apart, the cities served alternately as the seat of government. This area, between the Jumna and Ganges rivers, had long been the key to Hindustan, the Ganges valley, and routes southward (see Chapter 11). Successive Delhis had risen and fallen on the same strategic site, controlling, with Agra as its satellite, the heart of repeated imperial efforts. Both cities were built, like sentinels, on the west bank of the Jumna, which flows into the Ganges below Agra after running parallel to it, like a defensive moat, from well north of Delhi.

Each city was dominated by a great walled fort containing the palace and audience halls. Inside and outside the walls the Mughals also constructed great mosques, gardens, tombs (such as the Taj Mahal at Agra), and other monumental buildings in the Persian style, which they developed further and made distinctively Indian. Literature, music, and the graphic arts flourished under

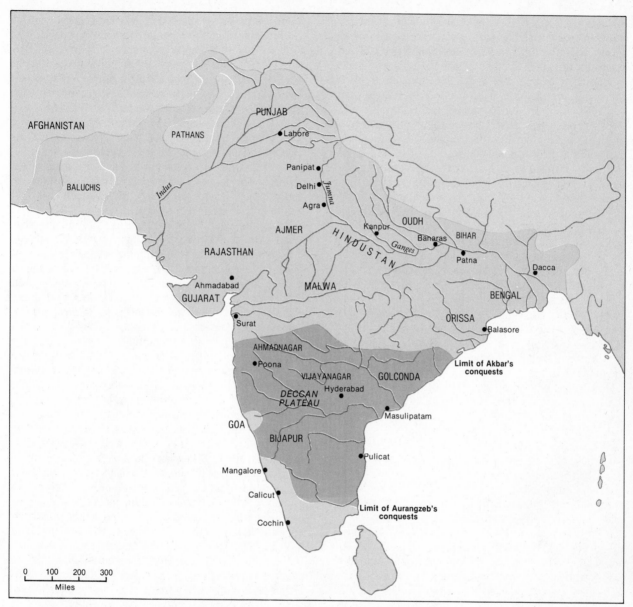

*20.2 India at the Height of Mughal Power*

imperial patronage at both capitals. Strong imperial rule was often oppressive, but it helped ensure an unprecedented period of unity and prosperity that most Indians shared. Hindus too could feel pride in the new imperial grandeur, for they were given an important role in it.

# Akbar and His Achievement

Akbar's success in building a truly Indian empire rather than just another alien conquest was the chief foundation of Mughal greatness, but he had first to establish

his rule. Babur died prematurely in 1530, after offering his life to God in exchange for that of his son Humayun, who was deathly ill. But Humayun (1508–1556) was a weakling who was finally driven out of India in 1540 by one of Babur's Afghan generals and forced to take refuge in Iran. A year after he returned in 1555 at the head of a Persian army to reclaim his father's conquests, he fell on the stone steps of his private astronomical observatory and library, light-headed from opium, and died, leaving the throne to his 13-year-old son Akbar, who had been born in exile in 1542.

Immediately challenged upon his accession in 1556,

Akbar's army defeated yet another Hindu effort to drive out the invaders at Panipat. In 1562, at the age of 20, Akbar assumed full charge of the empire from his advisers. In the same year he married a Rajput princess, beginning what was to be a lifelong campaign to blend the many strands of India's ancient cultural, regional, and religious heritage. Akbar was determined to build both an empire and a new culture that was as nearly as he could make it truly Indian, uniting its various elements under firm Mughal control.

He saw himself as an Indian ruler, not a foreign despot, and understood from the beginning that his own success and that of the dynasty depended on commanding the support and participation of all Indians. But he could be ruthless too if his power was challenged. When the chief Rajput faction resisted his diplomacy, he sacked the Rajput capital in 1568 and massacred the surviving defenders. By 1570 all but a small remnant of the Rajputs had sworn allegiance to him; in return, he made a Rajput, whose military skills he knew well, one of his chief generals, and other Rajputs thereafter also played a strong role in the imperial army. This political wisdom solved what would have otherwise been his major military problem. Rajputs became his comrades rather than his implacable enemies. To mark his policy of religious toleration further, for the four wives allowed to rulers by the Koran, he chose two Hindus (including his Rajput bride), one Christian, and one Muslim, thus symbolically embracing India's religious variety.

With his new Rajput allies, Akbar invaded wealthy Gujarat, capturing Surat, the chief seaport of the west coast, in 1573. Three years later he completed the conquest of Bengal in the east and by 1581 had added most of Afghanistan to his empire. For many years his armies raided south into the northern Deccan but were never able to win permanent control, a goal that also eluded his successors. But northern India and Afghanistan under Akbar and his successors remained until the end of the seventeenth century one of history's greatest empires in size, wealth, and splendor. It was divided into 15 provinces, each under a governor but with a separate set of officials responsible for revenue collection. Provinces were subdivided into districts, where representatives of the governor kept order and dispensed justice. Revenue demands were smaller than under the Delhi sultans, and the large number of Hindus employed in the revenue service, as well as at its head, helped keep taxes from becoming exploitive or unfair. Hindu law was applied in disputes between Hindus. Revenue collectors were ordered to remit taxes in districts that had had a poor harvest.

One reform that endeared Akbar to his subjects was his abolition of two hated taxes: on Hindu pilgrims traveling to sacred sites and on all Hindus as infidels (the *jizya*, or poll tax), both of which had been collected by Muslim rulers for centuries. He abolished the practice of enslaving war prisoners and their families and forbade forcible conversion to Islam, long a bitter issue. Hindus were welcomed at court, and their advice was regularly sought. Akbar patronized Persian and Urdu art and literature, but he also appointed a court poet for Hindi and encouraged Hindu literature and art more generally. Most of the greatest court painters were Hindus, producing beautiful portraits, miniatures, and naturalistic bird, animal, and flower paintings. Orthodox Muslims challenged this defiance of the Islamic ban on the depiction of human or animal forms, but Akbar replied that he could not believe God, "the giver of life," would disapprove of the beauty he had made, which was portrayed in true art.

Like the other Mughal emperors after him, Akbar loved gardens, with which nearly all Mughal buildings, including palaces, forts, and tombs, were surrounded in magnificent blendings of green lawns, gaily colored beds of flowers with flowering trees for shade, and an ingenious use of water in fountains, pools, and fluted channels. These devices enhanced the atmosphere of coolness, restfulness, and greenness, creating an effect that was especially striking in the hot, dry surroundings of the plains of North India. Akbar took a personal interest in the planning and care of the imperial gardens. He is often shown by court painters supervising the planting of flower beds and tending his roses.

Akbar was widely curious and loved to discuss philosophy and religion with all comers, Portuguese Jesuits as well as Hindu Brahmins. He had the Christian Gospels translated into Persian and attended mass. But as he came to reject the dogma of Islam as the only true religion, he could not accept the exclusive truth of any one faith, except a universal faith in an all-powerful creator. In later life he increasingly became a Sufi, or Islamic mystic, blending ideas from many religions and symbolizing his mission to merge the best of all the Indian traditions with those the Mughals brought into India. He was a deeply religious person, but his departures from orthodox Islam shocked many Muslim leaders and provoked a revolt against him in 1581. He suppressed it by force and then in deference to Hindu values forbade the slaughter of cattle and became a vegetarian, even giving up hunting, of which he had been very fond. Akbar founded a new faith that he hoped could unite his varied subjects in the common love of God, without need for a sectarian priesthood, but it did not survive him. If he had been followed by rulers like him, his dream of a united India free of strife might have moved closer to realization.

Much has been written about the fascinating Akbar. He was a contemporary of Elizabeth I of England, Henry IV of France, Shah Abbas of Iran, and the Ming Emperor Wan-li. Europeans who had met them all agreed that as both a human being and a ruler, he towered over his contemporaries. He had great strength of intelligence, character, and will, but he also had the good sense to realize that compromise and cooperation work better than force. He was full of energy and imagination but highly sensitive and often prey to melancholy and fits of depression. He seems to have suffered from epilepsy as well, like Julius Caesar and Napoleon. Astonishingly, he also appears to have been illiterate. As a child he preferred hunting and other sports to lessons, but he had a phenomenal memory, like many unlettered people, and was a great listener. From adolescence he appointed courtiers to read to him several hours a day; he had over 24,000 manuscripts in his library, and the learned men who debated with him often found him better "read" than themselves. He had a broadly inquiring mind, but a complicated one; the Jesuits at his court, who came to know him well, could never fully understand it or predict what he might say or do. He kept his dignity with all but had the knack of making the humblest petitioner feel at ease, and he charmed everyone who met him, high and low.

He was remarkably versatile, not only in his interests but in his skills as well. He was an accomplished polo player, metalworker, draftsman (many of his beautiful drawings have survived), and musician. He even invented a lighted polo ball so that the game could be played at night and a gun with a new mechanism that could fire multiple rounds. But his main preoccupation shifted to religion, especially after he had completed his major conquests, and he spent many nights alone in prayer and meditation. In 1575 he built a hall of worship, to which he invited the widest range of philosophers and theologians for periodic discussions, first from Islamic schools of thought and then from all the religions he could gather, including individual holy men, ascetics and mystics, Hindu sadhus and Muslim Sufis, Jesuit priests and Iranian fire worshipers. In time, these "seminars on religion" were held regularly every Thursday evening, while Akbar continued his own private devotions at sunrise, noon, sunset, and midnight. It was typical of him

## ◉ The Court of Akbar ◉

*One of the many accounts of Akbar and the India of his time is that of the Jesuit Antonio Monserrate, who visited the court from 1580 to 1583. Here are some excerpts from the* Commentary on His Journey to the Court of Akbar.

This prince is of a stature and type of countenance well fitted to his royal dignity, so that one could easily recognize even at first glance that he is the king. . . . His forehead is broad and open, his eyes so bright and flashing that they seem like a sea shimmering in the sunlight. . . . He creates an opportunity almost every day for any of the common people or of the nobles to see him and converse with him. It is remarkable how great an effect this courtesy and affability has in attaching to him the minds of his subjects. . . . He has an acute insight, and shows much wise foresight both in avoiding dangers and in seizing favorable opportunities for carrying out his designs. . . . Unlike the palaces built by other Indian kings, his are lofty [and] their total circuit is so large that it easily embraces four great royal dwellings. . . . Not a little is added to the beauty of the palaces by charming pigeon cotes. . . . The pigeons are cared for by eunuchs and servant maids. Their evolutions are controlled at will, when they are flying, by means of certain signals, just as those of a well trained soldiery. . . . It will seem little short of miraculous when I affirm that when sent out they dance, turn somersaults all together in the air, fly in orderly rhythm, and return to their starting point, all at the sound of a whistle. [Akbar's] empire is wonderfully rich and fertile both for cultivation and pasture, and has a great trade both in exports and imports. . . . Indian towns appear very pleasant from afar; they are adorned with many towers and high buildings in a very beautiful manner. But when one enters them, one finds that the narrowness, aimless crookedness, and ill planning of the streets deprive these cities of all beauty. . . . The common people live in lowly huts and tiny cottages, and hence if a traveller has seen one of these cities, he has seen them all.

*Source:* D. Lach, *Asia on the Eve of Europe's Expansion* (Englewood Cliffs, N.J.: Prentice Hall, 1965), pp. 63–69 passim.

**Akbar's planned capital at Fatehpur Sikri, near Agra. Shown here is part of the women's quarters, open to the view and the breezes, from which the women could overlook the courtyard in the left foreground, marked off as a giant pachisi (Parcheesi) board. The game was played with live pieces—court ladies and members of the harem—whose moves were directed by court or royal players throwing dice. [Rhoads Murphey]**

that although he hoped earnestly that the new mystic religion he founded in 1581 to unite all people would attract a mass following, he never tried to force it on anyone.

Akbar was too intellectually alive and too religiously devout to lapse into the life of extravagant luxury that surrounded him at court, but he was no purist or prude. He enjoyed food and wine, the sherbet brought to him daily by runners from the snowy Himalayas, the dancing girls, the music and plays, and the flourishing literature and art that he so generously patronized. He was, in other words, a truly regal monarch, but a most unusual one in the range of his vision and understanding. It was too much to ask for a succession of others like him, but India was not again to be served by a ruler of his quality until the first prime minister of its modern independence, Jawaharlal Nehru (prime minister, 1947–1964.)

Akbar was still without an heir after six years of marriage. He sought help from a Sufi saint who lived at a place called Sikri, 20 miles west of Agra. A year later his first son was born, and in gratitude Akbar built of red sandstone a magnificent new capital, which he called Fatehpur Sikri, next to the saint's humble cottage. Here he had fresh scope to blend Indian, Persian, Islamic, and Mughal themes in architecture, drawing also on traditional Hindu architecture in the south. But the water supply in this arid region proved inadequate, and Fatehpur Sikri had to be abandoned after only 15 years. The deserted stone city still stands much as Akbar left it, a monument to his vision that still can move visitors.

The last four years of Akbar's life were clouded by the rebellion of his eldest son, whose birth had been such a joyous occasion. The Mughals were never able to work out the problem of succession. From this time on, each emperor was plotted against in his old age by his many sons, who also tore the empire apart by their fighting until the most ruthless had disposed of his rivals. It was a pattern inherited from the Mughals' central Asian origins, and it blighted their otherwise great achievements while also draining the country's resources. In 1605 Akbar reasserted his authority, only to die of poison administered by his rebellious son, who took the throne that year under the name Jahangir ("world-seizer").

## Jahangir and Shah Jahan

Jahangir's Persian wife, Nur Jahan, a power in her own right, further entrenched Persian culture at the court and throughout North India. The administrative system inherited from Akbar continued to run smoothly, and revenues flowed in to pay for the brilliance of the court. Jahangir and Nur Jahan preferred Agra to Delhi and adorned it further with new palaces, gardens, and tombs. Court life took on a more luxurious splendor; Jahangir was no mystic like his father. He and his courtiers delighted in silks and perfumes, jewel-decked costumes, wine, song, and the pleasures of the harem. State processions featured troupes of dancing girls and elephants covered with silk and jewels, and monthlong festivities were held to celebrate the marriages of Jahangir's many sons.

The painting of this era became more naturalistic, and the orthodox Islamic prohibition against representing human or animal forms gave way to older Indian traditions, even including nearly nude figures and embracing couples in classic Rajput and earlier Hindu styles, as well as portraits of the emperor, often in his beloved gardens. For all their use of Persian language, culture, and art forms, the Mughals had become Indian rulers and were increasingly seen as such by most Indians. They were following a traditional maharaja lifestyle, and their pretensions to divine authority were familiar to their subjects; like luxurious living, these were expected of royalty.

A resurgent Iran under Shah Abbas began to challenge the Mughal Empire in the west and conquered most of Afghanistan, but Jahangir was too busy with his gardens, wine, and harems to lead his army over the mountains. He had given his son Shah Jahan command of the army, but Shah Jahan refused to leave the capital because he was plotting to seize the throne, having previously poisoned his elder brother. He knew that his real enemy was Nur Jahan, who had manipulated Jahangir, appointed her own father and brother to the highest offices, and even hoped to occupy the throne herself. Jahangir, entranced by her beauty and wit, had named her Nur Jahan, meaning "light of the world," but she became empress in all but name soon after he married her. She arranged the marriage of her brother's daughter, Mumtaz Mahal, to Shah Jahan as an extension of the power of her clan.

But Shah Jahan openly rebelled in 1623, and when Jahangir died late in 1627, he put to death all of his clos-

## ◉ Festivals in Mughal India ◉

*Jahangir's* Memoirs *include these descriptions of New Year and birthday festivals.*

The feast of the New Year was held near Agra, and at the time of transit of the sun I seated myself on the throne with glory and gladness. The nobles and courtiers all came forward with their congratulations. . . . I determined that this time I would enter Agra [to visit his father Akbar's tomb] and after that would go on foot on this pilgrimage to the shrine, in the same way that my father, on account of my birth, had gone from Agra to Ajmir [Fatehpur]. . . . At an auspicious hour, I returned to Agra, and scattering with two hands 5,000 rupees in small coins along the way, I entered the august place which was inside the fort. . . . On the ninth of the month the feast for my solar weighing, which is the commencement of the 38th year of my age, took place. According to custom, they got ready the weighing apparatus and the scales. At the moment appointed blessings were invoked and I sat in the scales. The first time I was weighed against gold, and then against several metals, perfumes, and essences, up to twelve weighings. Twice a year I weigh myself against gold and silver and other metals, and against all sorts of silks and cloths and various grains, etc., once at the beginning of the solar year and once at that of the lunar. The weight of the money of the two weighings I hand over to the different treasuries for faqirs [holy men] and those in want.

*Source:* J. N. Das Gupta, *India in the Seventeenth Century* (Calcutta: University of Calcutta Press, 1916), pp. 104–105.

est relatives and pensioned off Nur Jahan. He declared himself "emperor of the world," which is the meaning of his regnal name, with three weeks of extravagant coronation ceremonies. He ruled for three decades. His was the most lavish of all the Mughal reigns, especially visible in the royal passion for monumental architecture inlaid with precious stones. Court life under Shah Jahan was sumptuous, in the pattern set by his father, but he was even more attached to his harem, where 5,000 concubines awaited his pleasure. Nevertheless, he was genuinely devoted to his wife, Mumtaz Mahal, who bore him 14 children. When she died in childbirth in 1631 at the age of 39, he was desolate. "Empire has no sweetness, life has no relish for me now," he said when told of her death.

To honor her memory, he built what may be the most famous structure in the world, the Taj Mahal at Agra, which took 20,000 workmen more than 20 years to complete. Designed by two Persian architects, it beautifully blends Iranian and Indian styles and Indian craftsmanship. The emphasis on water and gardens was characteristically Mughal, whereas the use of Rajput canopies around the base of the dome was traditionally Indian. Before the Taj Mahal was finished, Shah Jahan had begun a new capital city at Delhi, site of so many capitals before, modeled on Akbar's Red Fort at Agra and built of the same red sandstone, with similarly massive walls and battlements but on an even larger scale. Inside were beautiful gardens, palaces, audience halls, harems, barracks, stables, and storehouses, and outside he built India's largest mosque, the Jama Masjid. Both still stand, little altered, and still dominate Delhi, the Mughal name of which was Shah Jahanabad ("Shah Jahan's city").

Monumental building and the opulent court were not Shah Jahan's only extravagances. He ordered campaigns to reclaim Afghanistan and to restore Mughal rule in central Asia. Both failed but exhausted the treasury. From his Red Fort palace, on his Peacock Throne, encrusted with the largest jewels ever found, the emperor doubled Akbar's revenue demands, and the empire groaned. Meanwhile, his many sons were already conspiring against one another, impatient to succeed the ailing ruler. His favorite son, Dara, a philosopher and mystic like his great-grandfather Akbar, might have made a fine ruler, but a younger son, Aurangzeb, was insatiably ambitious.

From 1657 open warfare prevailed among rival brothers. Aurangzeb imprisoned his father, Shah Jahan, in the dungeon of Agra's Red Fort while he completed his gruesome work and then sent the old emperor the head of his favorite son, Dara. The aged Shah Jahan could just see through the barred window of his cell a glimpse of his beloved Taj Mahal. Hearing that this gave the elderly man a little comfort, Aurangzeb is said to have had his father's eyes put out.

## The Reign of Aurangzeb: Repression and Revolt

The cold-blooded Aurangzeb ascended the throne in 1658. By poison, intrigue, or assassination he had eliminated a dozen of his own brothers and half brothers, plus uncounted others. He gave as the reason for this slaughter his own devotion to orthodox Islam against the laxer or more tolerant views of his many rivals. But Aurangzeb was also a brilliant and single-minded ruler and admin-

No photograph can do full justice to the Taj Mahal, whose great bulk seems to float weightlessly above the pool that holds its reflection. Mughal cupolas and domes are matched by minarets, the four slender towers on each side in the Islamic tradition, while the central archway beneath the dome is reminiscent of the Persian (Iranian) models on which the archway was based. Inscriptions from the Koran and beautiful inlaid floral patterns cover much of the outer and inner walls. The entire structure is of glistening white marble. [Rhoads Murphey]

istrator and a cunning statesman. Sunni Muslims revered him as much as Hindus hated him. He is said to have had no friends, only servile admirers and bitter enemies.

Civil war on top of Shah Jahan's extravagances had emptied the treasury, but Aurangzeb increased his revenue demands and at the same time extended his own puritanical tastes to the running of court and empire. He stopped all court luxuries, especially the wine, song, and dance forbidden by the Koran, and ended all monumental construction. He also appointed censors of public morals to enforce rigid Islamic law, ordered everyone to pray at the orthodox Islamic intervals every day, tried to abolish gambling and drinking, and began a lifelong campaign to demolish all surviving Hindu monuments and temples. Unfortunately, he largely succeeded in the north, and the only surviving samples of pre-Mughal architecture are in the south, where Aurangzeb never prevailed. Hindus were forbidden to carry arms, forced conversion was resumed for many, and Hindu festivals and public expression were outlawed. Aurangzeb knew the Koran by heart and copied it out twice in his own hand. But his piety and his zealous praying, which mark him as an Islamic zealot, sparked a keen sense of religious intolerance. To increase the revenue needed to maintain his army and to pay for new conquests in the name of Allah, he reimposed the hated *jizya* on Hindus, laid a new tax on Hindu pilgrims, and doubled the taxes on Hindu merchants. When crowds gathered outside the Red Fort in Delhi to protest, he ordered the imperial elephants to crush them to death.

The widespread revolts that arose within a few years merely increased Aurangzeb's pressure for more revenue to put them down. For many years he did so successfully, thanks to his superior generalship and to the fear-induced loyalty of most of his court and army. When revolt failed or the risks of defying Aurangzeb or his tax collectors seemed too great, growing numbers of peasants abandoned their homes and fields and became bandits or joined dissident groups or armies elsewhere, including explicitly Hindu forces such as the Sikhs of Punjab (particularly brutalized by Aurangzeb), the formerly loyal Rajputs, and the Marathas.

Relentless in suppressing rebellion, Aurangzeb was also determined to extend his empire into the south. The last half of his wearily long reign was consumed in bloody but ultimately unsuccessful campaigns into the Deccan, while at the same time his forces tried to stem the rising tide of Sikh, Rajput, Afghan, Bengali, and Maratha revolt. His brief conquests in the south, won at terrible cost in treasure and lives, quickly evaporated. From their mountain fortresses in the northwestern Deccan, the Hindu Marathas became increasingly powerful and took the field to harry Mughal forces retreating from the south near the end of Aurangzeb's reign. His campaigns exhausted the country and left it split among contending powers, who shared an implacable hatred of Mughal rule but were divided by their own differences and rivalries.

# Sects and Rebels: Rajputs, Sikhs, and Marathas

Three groups stood out against Aurangzeb's intolerance and military conquests and as his most effective opponents: the Rajputs, the Sikhs, and the Marathas. Unfortunately for them, they never made a common cause, as they also failed to do later against the British.

Aurangzeb broke the alliance that Akbar had prudently made with the Rajputs and eliminated their role in the Mughal army. Throughout most of his reign they were in revolt, maintaining their reputation as courageous fighters, and were never effectively suppressed. The proximity of their base and its fortresses in Rajasthan to the center of Mughal power in the Delhi-Agra region made them highly vulnerable, and they suffered repeated "annihilation" campaigns, but Rajput resistance survived in the margins of Rajasthan. Each campaign against the Rajputs bred new bitterness and new determination to fight. Aurangzeb's religious zeal and conquering ambition called forth resistance in the name of India and of Hinduism against a Mughal order now seen afresh as alien and hateful. It was a sad sequel to Akbar's vision of a multiracial, multicultural, and multireligious India. The Rajputs throughout their history had been quick to spring proudly to the defense of Hindu India, and now they took the field again, convinced of the rightness of their cause.

The Sikhs of Punjab emerged as a religious group with its own separate identity as an outgrowth of the bhakti movement late in the fifteenth century (see Chapter 11). As elsewhere in India where bhakti ideals spread, a series of nonsectarian saint-reformers preached a puritanical form of life and freedom from priestly domination, discarding the more dogmatic and hierarchical aspects of Hinduism, such as caste, but retaining its devotion to nonviolence. The founder of Sikhism, Guru Nanak (1469–1538), tried at first to work out a compromise between Hinduism and Islam and then to purify Hinduism. He preached the bhakti message of a universal God and his love, to whom everyone has access without the need for priests or rituals. Perhaps his best-known saying is "Man will be saved by his works alone; God will not ask a man his tribe or sect, but what he has done. There is no Hindu and no Muslim. All are children of God."[6] Nanak's rejection of priests as essential intermediaries was akin to the view of his European contemporary Martin Luther, although Nanak was not a formal theologian and, unlike Luther, stressed good works rather than faith.

His disciple and successor, Guru Angad (active 1530–

1552), began the compilation of the Sikh holy book, the Granth Sahib, recording all he had learned from Guru Nanak and adding devotional reflections. Successive Sikh gurus continued their opposition to caste and to all forms of discrimination and met with Akbar, who listened to them with interest and granted them a site for their chief temple in Amritsar, near Lahore. The origins of Sikhism were thus wholly peaceful, but in the sixteenth century some Sikhs were drawn into support for one of Jahangir's rebellious sons, hoping that he would be more tolerant of non-Muslims. When the rebellion failed and Jahangir had the Sikh leader executed in 1606, the Sikhs began to develop a defensive military mentality, to maintain their own identity and their territorial base in Punjab.

By 1650 the Sikhs' numbers had greatly increased, and they began to see themselves as a separate state. Sikh gurus urged their followers to eat meat, in distinction from high-caste Hindus but also to give them strength. Martial skills, bravery, and physical strength began to be cultivated as Sikh hallmarks. Shah Jahan left them largely alone, preoccupied as he was with his ambitious building projects and with the luxurious pleasures of his harem and court. But when the Sikhs supported his favored son Dara's bid for the throne, they became Aurangzeb's enemies. His persecutions of them and his efforts to eliminate them as both a power and a community predictably strengthened their commitment and led to their further militarization. Aurangzeb cruelly tortured to death the ninth Sikh guru, Teg Bahadur, in 1675 when he refused to embrace Islam and ignored the guru's warning against the still tiny but foreboding European threat to India. Teg Bahadur's son and successor, Guru Govind Singh (1675–1708), first organized the Sikhs into a real political power and a great military fraternity. He urged them all to adopt the surname Singh ("lion") as he had done, to swear never to cut their hair (which came to be worn knotted up in a turban) or their beards, and to avoid tobacco and alcohol. The practices of purdah (the veiling and seclusion of women) and *sati* (the burning of widows) were rejected. Sikh women were freer and were seen more nearly as coequals than in most other Indian societies. Govind Singh's four sons were captured by Aurangzeb and tortured to death or executed, steadfastly refusing to convert to Islam.

When Govind Singh himself died in 1708, the line of ten guru leaders ended, and the Sikhs were thereafter ruled by political rather than religious leaders. Many Punjabis and others from neighboring areas had adopted Sikhism, and many more now joined its numbers. A former Rajput, Banda Bairagi, ravaged the Mughal forces as leader of the Sikhs until he was betrayed, captured, and executed in 1716. Nadir Shah's invasion from Iran in 1739 finally eliminated the remnants of Mughal power and gave the Sikhs a new opportunity to extend their domination of Punjab. During the remainder of the eighteenth century the Sikh kingdom became still stronger and stood finally as the last major obstacle to British rule, overcome only in 1849 after two campaigns against it.

The Marathas were probably the most formidable and effective enemies of the Mughals, and for some two centuries they played a major role in India. For a time it seemed as if they would become the dominant power in the subcontinent and would found a new Indian empire. Their home base was well protected by a mountain range behind Bombay, the Western Ghats; by the hilly Deccan Plateau east of the Ghats; and by the central Indian mountain ranges of the Vindhyas and their spurs to the north and east, which were ideally suited to guerrilla warfare. The Marathas gloried in their hardiness, which they attributed to the relative barrenness of their mountain-girt homeland, rather like the Scots or the Gurkhas of Nepal, and like them had a proud military tradition.

The greatest Maratha leader was Shivaji (1627–1680), who rose to prominence as Hindus were beginning to take up arms against Aurangzeb. Shivaji was brought up as a zealous Hindu but combined Hinduism with his martial background and his determination to free India from the Mughals. From the beginning of Aurangzeb's reign, Shivaji and his commando cavalry raided Mughal territory. The Mughal general sent against him captured Poona, the Maratha capital, in 1663, but was surprised there by Shivaji in a daring night attack and routed. A few months later in 1664 Shivaji attacked and looted Surat, then the richest port in India, and carried off immense booty. A second major Mughal campaign against him ended in negotiations after some of Shivaji's feuding adversaries deserted to the Mughal cause. Shivaji visited Agra, expecting to be offered a high post, but when he complained that Aurangzeb's offer was not good enough, he was imprisoned. He smuggled himself out, concealed in a basket, and rebuilt his forces and resources for what he now saw as an inevitable conflict.

When Aurangzeb ordered all Hindu temples and schools demolished and all Hindu public teaching and practice suppressed, Shivaji renewed his raids in 1670 and over the next ten years more than doubled the territory under his control, rivaling the Mughal territory itself as a state to be reckoned with. This achievement inspired the Marathas with renewed pride, and Shivaji remains their greatest hero. Unlike his successors, he was not only a brilliant military strategist and tactician but also an effective organizer and political administrator. He ruled with a council of ministers, made Marathi and Sanskrit the court languages, and banned the use of Urdu and Persian. For nearly 20 years he defied a series of Mughal armies, a considerable accomplishment in itself. Aurangzeb called him "the mountain rat." "My armies have been employed against him for nineteen years," he said, "and nevertheless his state has always been increasing."

But Shivaji did not live to see the death of Aurangzeb and the collapse of Mughal power, and the son who succeeded him neglected the army and the state and spent his time enjoying the luxuries of court life. He was defeated and captured by the Mughals, who executed him and many other Maratha chiefs in 1689. Shivaji's grandson, the next Maratha ruler, defected to the Mughals and was made one of their high officials, but other Marathas renewed the struggle. A younger descendant of Shivaji reorganized the army and resumed his grandfather's devastating raids. In 1699, after his own generals had failed to put them down, Aurangzeb himself marched against the Marathas, but without success. By 1702 the Mughals were on the defensive, and the Marathas were now led by Tara Bai, the remarkable wife of the ruler, who had died in 1700, although she ruled in name through her son, Shivaji III. She rode a horse with fearless skill and led Maratha cavalry charges in battle.

After Aurangzeb's death, however, and the collapse of his crusade, the Marathas were torn by internal civil war, a continuation of the feuding that was also part of their tradition. Successive leaders after 1712 resumed campaigns to the north, south, and east, extending their territory close to Delhi, conquering most of the peninsular south, and raiding even into Bengal.

The Maratha Confederacy, as it was called, had become by far the greatest power in India, but it lacked the firm hand and the administrative skills of Shivaji and was troubled by chronic factionalism. The Maratha army was used as much to raid and plunder as to fight major engagements, and raids or conquests were seldom followed up by responsible government of the areas acquired. In 1761 the army marched north to meet an Afghan invasion on the historic field of Panipat, northwest of Delhi, and was totally defeated. The short-lived Maratha "empire" was dissolved, and its power was never recovered. The real beneficiaries were the English, since the Marathas had been the only major defenders of India against foreign invaders and the only group with the potential to reunite the country. Internal feuding among themselves, lack of commitment to responsible administration, and the exhausting strain of chronic fighting against the Mughals left them unequal to that enormous task. India itself was exhausted by unending warfare, and the Mughals, Marathas, Sikhs, and Rajputs merely bloodied and drained each other and the country as a whole rather than taking any united stand.

## The Mughals and India

By the beginning of the eighteenth century the order and prosperity that had flourished under Akbar and his immediate successors had been fatally weakened. Akbar's carefully designed revenue system, managed by Hindus, had been eroded by the excessive granting of tax-collecting rights for large areas, known as *jagirs*, to people whom the throne wanted or needed to pay off. Especially under Aurangzeb, Mughal attention was concentrated on military conquest, which meant mounting demands for revenue but also decreasing attention to normal administration or its supervision. Hindu revenue officials were eliminated; holders of jagirs (*jagirdars*) became more and more independent and more and more rapacious in extracting everything they could from an oppressed peasantry and merchant class, retaining for themselves any balance beyond the official government tax rates. The same was true for the group known as the *zamindars*, who were also granted tax-collection rights for smaller local areas and used them to enrich themselves, often acquiring the ownership of land from peasants who were unable to pay the tax. This was a disastrous formula for the well-being of most of the agricultural sector, the predominant basis of the economy and the major tax base. The Mughals had built an imperial road system, but it was used mainly for the movement of troops and supplies. Even so, it was not well maintained and became impassable in many sections, especially during the torrential rains of the annual monsoon.

In general, Mughal economic policy concentrated heavily on obtaining revenue and far too little on maintaining or enhancing the system's ability to generate production. In contrast to China, the state did almost nothing to increase irrigation, so badly needed in most of India, or to promote other agricultural improvements. Neglect of agriculture meant neglect of most of the country and its people.

Even before Aurangzeb, what was left over after paying the staggering costs of military campaigns was used primarily for gorgeous display at the capital and the court and for monumental building. The Mughals were at war on a major scale for much more than half of the years from Babur's victory at Panipat in 1526 to Aurangzeb's death in 1707, and fighting continued into the 1750s. Even a prosperous and well-run system would have been fatally weakened by such an outpouring of treasure to no constructive result and by devastation of the countryside on such a scale over two centuries.

Administration as well was increasingly neglected. Court life at Delhi and Agra was sumptuous and brilliant. Officials knew that their money and property would revert to the emperor when they died, and consequently they spent it freely in lavish consumption, with stables full of Arabian horses and harems filled with dancing girls. Massive entertainments and banquets occupied much of their time, complete with music, dance, and poetry readings. Courtiers and the upper classes dressed in magnificent silk outfits, or fine Kashmir wool in the brief northern winter, while the peasants wore coarse sackcloth woven from jute or locally made cottons, if they could afford them. Indian cotton cloth won extensive markets in the rest of Asia and much of Africa as well as in Europe; weavers benefited, but the state's tax collectors benefited still more.

For all the brilliant splendor of court life, however, science and technology were largely neglected after Akbar. What learning there was centered on the Koran and on the cultivation of the arts. There were no changes or improvements in the arts of production, and by the seventeenth century India had fallen behind Europe in science and technology and probably in the productivity of both its agriculture and manufacturing, while at the same time bleeding the economy by virtually continuous warfare. While Shah Jahan was building the Taj Mahal,

at staggering expense, India suffered probably the worst famine in its history, from 1630 to 1632, and another nearly as bad took place in 1702 and 1703 in which over 2 million people died while Aurangzeb was campaigning in the Deccan with a huge army and supply corps.

Aurangzeb had personally moved south in 1683, and for the rest of his life he was primarily concerned with conducting military campaigns from a new capital he established in the Deccan. Annual losses were estimated at 100,000 men and over 300,000 transport animals, mainly requisitioned from the peasantry. Continued Maratha raids and fierce southern resistance sapped his forces. After 1705 he seems to have spent most of his time reading and copying the Koran, preparing himself for death. Until then, he had refused to recognize the

---

# ◉ A Westerner Visits Delhi ◉

*François Bernier, a French traveler in India from 1656 to 1668, included the following description of Delhi in his* Travels in the Mogul Empire.

It is about forty years ago that Shah Jahan, father of the present Great Mogul Aurangzeb, conceived the design of immortalizing his name by the erection of a city near the site of the ancient Delhi. . . . Owing to their being so near at hand, the ruins of old Delhi served to build the new city. Delhi is situated on the Jumna and built on one bank only in such a manner that it terminates in this place very much in the form of a crescent, having but one bridge of boats to cross to the country. Excepting the side where it is defended by the river, the city is encompassed by walls of brick. . . . The suburbs are interspersed with extensive gardens and open spaces. . . . The citadel [Shah Jahan's Red Fort] is defended by a deep ditch faced with hewn stone, filled with water and stocked with fish. . . . Adjoining the ditch is a large garden, filled at all times with flowers and green shrubs, which contrasted with the stupendous red walls produce a beautiful effect. Next to the garden is the great royal square, faced on one side by the gates of the fortress, and on the opposite side of which terminate the two most considerable streets of the city. The tents of such Rajahs as are in the king's pay, and whose weekly turn it is to mount guard, are pitched in this square. . . . In this place also, at break of day, they exercise the royal horses, which are kept in a spacious stable not far distant. . . . Here too is held a bazaar or market for an endless variety of things, which, like the Pont-neuf at Paris, is the rendezvous for all sorts of mountebanks [swindlers] and jugglers. Hither likewise the astrologers resort. These wise doctors remain seated in the sun, on a dusty piece of carpet, handling some old mathematical instruments and having open before them a large book. In this way they attract the attention of the passers-by and impose upon the people, by whom they are considered as so many infallible oracles. . . . Silly women, wrapping themselves in a white cloth from head to foot, flock to the astrologers, whisper to them all the transactions of their lives, and disclose every secret. . . . The rich merchants have their dwellings elsewhere, to which they retire after the hours of business.

*Source:* F. Bernier, *Travels in the Mogul Empire*, trans. A. Constable (London: Constable & Co., 1891), pp. 241–245 passim.

EARLY MODERN ISLAMIC EMPIRES

| The Ottomans | Mughal India | Safavid Iran |
| --- | --- | --- |
| Osman (1299–1326) | | |
| Mehmet II (1451–1481) | | |
| Fall of Constantinople (1453) | Babur (1483–1530) | Safavid dynasty founded (1501) |
| Selim the Grim (1512–1520) | | |
| Suleiman the Magnificent (1520–1566) | Akbar (1542–1605) | Tahmasp I (1524–1576) |
| Siege of Vienna (1529) | | |
| Battle of Lepanto (1571) | | |
| | Jahangir (1605–1627) | Shah Abbas (1587–1629) |
| | Shah Jahan (1627–1658) | |
| Siege of Vienna (1683) | Aurangzeb (1658–1707) | |
| | | End of Safavid rule (1736) |

destructiveness of his policies. At least one anonymous letter reached him after he had restored the poll tax on Hindus, which read in part:

> **Your subjects are trampled underfoot; every province of your empire is impoverished; depopulation spreads and problems accumulate. . . . If your majesty places any faith in those books called divine, you will be instructed there that God is the God of all mankind, not the God of Muslims alone.**[7]

In 1705 he confessed to his son: "I came alone and I go as a stranger. I do not know who I am, or what I have been doing. I have sinned terribly and I do not know what punishment awaits me."[8] The Mughals had come full circle from the inspiring vision of Akbar to the nightmare of Aurangzeb.

The effective power of the Mughals ended with Aurangzeb's death in 1707. India slowly dissolved into civil war, banditry, intergroup rivalry, and mounting chaos, a context in which the English traders, present on the fringes for well over a century, began their own path to ultimate power.

Aurangzeb, whose reign had spanned nearly 50 years, was a contemporary of the Manchu emperor K'ang Hsi in China (Chapter 29) and of Louis XIV of France, the Glorious Revolution in England, Frederick I of Prussia, and Peter the Great of Russia. During these years Europe began its modern development of strong centralized states, continued its commercial and colonial expansion overseas, and rode a wave of unprecedented economic growth, which was reflected in the beginnings of major population increases. Manchu China in Aurangzeb's time also experienced a period of prosperity and vigorous economic growth, with major increases in trade and at least a doubling of agricultural output and population. The modern agricultural revolution was beginning at the same time in Europe, and the foundations were being laid for the later Industrial Revolution. European science and technology leapt ahead of the rest of the world with pioneering discoveries of scientists such as Isaac Newton and Robert Boyle. In these years Europe developed a lead that was to widen greatly in subsequent centuries.

If Akbar's open-minded curiosity and zeal for learning and experimentation had prevailed into Aurangzeb's time, India might have taken part in or at least benefited from these important advances. The early European visitors to India had, like Marco Polo, been drawn to and impressed by its wealth and sophistication. In Akbar's time there seems little question that India was not only richer than Europe but at least on a par with it and with China technologically, economically, and politically. Jahangir and Shah Jahan, however, were preoccupied with the pleasures of the court, monumental building, and intrigue. Aurangzeb was a single-minded zealot who cared nothing for the material welfare of his people and bled the empire to finance his wars. Instead of scholars, as at Akbar's court, Aurangzeb surrounded himself with sycophants, servile yes-men who dared not disagree or suggest alternatives and who flattered the emperor into thinking that he and his empire led the world. He did not deign to correspond with other monarchs, as Akbar had done, or to take an interest in anything but his endless military campaigns, undertaken in the name of Islam, to impose his tyrannical rule over all of India, a goal he never achieved. By the time of his death, India was economically and politically a shambles, and technological development was nonexistent. This was to prove a fatal combination of weaknesses, resulting in a situation of virtual anarchy. The now far more effective and technologically advanced Europeans were able to establish footholds from which their power in India could grow.

# The Safavids in Iran

By about the year A.D. 1000 the Abbasid caliphate began to break up into separate and rival states. At the eastern end of their former domains, a group of central Asian

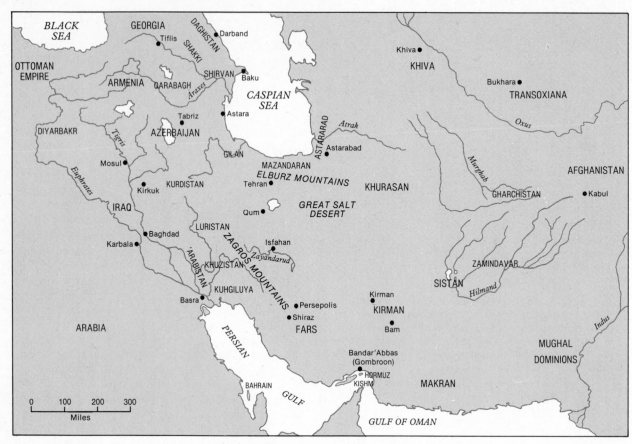

**20.3** *Iran Under the Safavids*

Turks, the Seljuks, took over Iran, accepted Islam, and even captured Baghdad in 1065. The Seljuk rulers of Iran embraced and furthered Persian culture, as did their separate Turkish successors, but all this was swept away by the Mongol onslaught, which also destroyed virtually every city in central Asia in the mid-thirteenth century. A hundred years later, Tamerlane laid waste most of the same area. Through all these catastrophes, Persia's culture and sense of identity survived, much as in China under Mongol rule. Finally, out of the chaos left in the wake of Tamerlane, a new group rose to control Iran and to preside over a new and vigorous period of growth and cultural revival—the Safavids (1501–1736), who claimed descent from a Sufi saint but were in fact founded by yet another central Asian Turkish tribe.

The first Safavid ruler, Ismail, assumed the ancient title of Shah of Iran and briefly incorporated parts of what is now Iraq and southern Russia into his empire. The Safavids were Shi'ite (Shia) Muslims; they forcibly converted the previously Sunni Iranians and came into chronic conflict with the orthodox Sunni Ottomans and with the Mughals in India and Afghanistan.

Shah Ismail's son, Tahmasp I, reigned for 52 years (1524–1576); defended the plateau of Iran, protected by its mountain borders, against continued Ottoman attacks; and presided over a great flowering of Iranian art, especially in miniature painting. In the familiar central Asian pattern, he was poisoned by his overeager son, who also killed off all his other relatives and rivals, only to die himself a year later, in 1577. After a period of civil war, there emerged the most outstanding of the Safavids, Shah Abbas the Great (1587–1629), who was to restore much of Iran's ancient glory. Its art, literature, and philosophy had long played the leading role in the Middle East, as China's had done in East Asia. Shah Abbas had the strength and vision needed to reunite the country and then to ensure economic prosperity and cultural vigor. He was an efficient administrator and a patron of the arts who made Persian culture once more a model for surrounding peoples. The beautiful capital he built at Isfahan in southwestern Iran remains perhaps the finest example of the medieval Persian style. In a series of campaigns between 1595 and 1612 he drove the Ottomans and their allies out of the parts of western and northern Iran they had occupied during earlier periods of disorder and kept them out for the rest of his reign.

Shah Abbas rebuilt much of the imperial structure

Part of the royal mosque at Isfahan, the capital of Safavid Iran. In Iran a great archway is intended to dominate most monumental buildings, as here. [Marburg/Art Resource]

originally laid down by Cyrus and Darius in the sixth century B.C., including the famous network of roads and bridges that crisscrossed the plateau, penetrated its mountain borders, and connected its cities with ports on the Persian Gulf and the Caspian Sea. Agriculture, trade, and cities grew rapidly under the new conditions. In 1617 Shah Abbas began commercial relations with the newly formed English East India Company and with its help in 1622 drove the Portuguese from the port of Hormuz on the gulf. Silks, ceramics, tapestries, carpets, and other exports from Iran could now be sent directly to England and Europe by sea, avoiding the overland route through hostile Ottoman territory and the tolls exacted along it.

Iran under Abbas became the cultural center of the Islamic world. Persian architecture, painting, literature, and the minor arts flourished and exercised a strong influence on Mughal India and on the Ottoman Empire. Rulers in both countries wrote poetry in the Persian style, had their portraits and court scenes painted in the Persian mode, and built palaces, domes, fountains, pools, gardens, and mosques on Persian models. Much of the credit for Iran's revival must go to Shah Abbas. Persian culture was renowned long before his time, but he inherited a weak, poor, war-torn country and gave it new strength, prosperity, and pride.

---

*By the late seventeenth century the Safavids, Mughals, and Ottomans were experiencing serious problems. The Safavid dynasty would collapse in 1736, yet despite Iran's weakened condition, the Ottomans were unable to subjugate their neighbor. In India the last Mughal emperor was not removed by the British until 1858, but for its final 150 years the dynasty increasingly ruled in name only over a progressively shrinking part of northern India. After the death of Emperor Akbar in 1605, successive rulers were more self-indulgent and more concerned with luxury and power than with responsible administration. With the reign of Aurangzeb, Islamic orthodoxy was reasserted, and the empire's wealth was squandered in bloody but fruitless campaigns to control the south and to subdue the rebellious Rajputs, Sikhs, and Marathas. At Aurangzeb's death India was exhausted, impoverished, and torn by civil war. So weak did India become that in 1739 an Iranian army not only defeated the Mughal emperor but also stole the Peacock Throne (later captured by the Ottomans and taken to Istanbul). Thus the simultaneous flowering of western and south-central Asia in the sixteenth century had turned to decline, and in India's case genuine disaster, by the eighteenth.*

*The French traveler François Bernier, who visited India in Aurangzeb's time, reported in his* Travels *that the emperor, after belatedly realizing the potential strength of the Europeans, complained to him that his tutor had told him, "The whole of Feringustan [Europe] was no more than some inconsiderable island, that its kings resembled petty rajahs, and that the potentates of Hindustan eclipsed the glory of all other kings."[9] Bernier's contemporary, the Italian traveler in India, Niccolò Manucci, recorded his impression that Indians believed Europeans "have no polite manners, that they are ignorant, wanting in ordered life, and very dirty."[10] Crude and dirty or not, the Europeans were fast becoming the most effective groups in India, given the ruin of the Mughals and the disorganization of the Marathas and other possible Indian orders. The way was open for the rise of a British-dominated India.*

# Notes

1. B. Lewis, *Istanbul and the Civilization of the Ottoman Empire* (Norman: University of Oklahoma Press, 1963), p. 110.
2. N. Itzkowitz, *Ottoman Empire and Islamic Tradition* (New York: Knopf, 1972), p. 36.
3. N. Menemencioglu, ed., *The Penguin Book of Turkish Verse* (New York: Penguin Books, 1978), p. 80.
4. Ibid., p. 150.
5. S. Shaw, *History of the Ottoman Empire and Modern Turkey*, Vol. 1: *Empire of the Gazis: The Rise and Decline of the Ottoman Empire, 1280–1808* (Cambridge: Cambridge University Press, 1976), p. 289.
6. D. P. Singhal, *A History of the Indian People* (London: Methuen, 1983), p. 206.
7. J. Sarkar, *History of Aurangzeb*, vol. 3 (Bombay: Orient Longman, 1972), p. 34.
8. W. Hansen, *The Peacock Throne* (New York: Holt, Rinehart and Winston, 1972), p. 485.
9. R. Murphey, *The Outsiders: The Western Experience in India and China* (Ann Arbor: University of Michigan Press, 1977), p. 54.
10. Ibid.

# Suggestions for Further Reading

## The Ottomans

Babinger, F. *Mehmed the Conqueror and His Time*, trans. R. Manheim. Princeton, N.J.: Princeton University Press, 1978.

Cook, M. A., ed. *A History of the Ottoman Empire to 1730.* Cambridge: Cambridge University Press, 1976.

Frazee, C. A. *Catholics and Sultans: The Church and the Ottoman Empire, 1453–1923.* London: Oxford University Press, 1983.

Inalcik, H. *The Ottoman Empire: The Classical Age, 1300–1600.* London: Weidenfeld & Nicolson, 1973.

Islamoglu-Inan, H., ed. *The Ottoman Empire and the World Economy.* Cambridge: Cambridge University Press, 1987.

Itzkowitz, N. *Ottoman Empire and Islamic Tradition.* New York: Knopf, 1972.

Lewis, B. *Istanbul and the Civilization of the Ottoman Empire.* Norman: University of Oklahoma Press, 1963.

———. *The Muslim Discovery of Europe.* New York: Norton, 1982.

Lewis, R. *Everyday Life in Ottoman Turkey.* London: Batsford, 1971.

Shaw, S. *History of the Ottoman Empire and Modern Turkey*, Vol. 1: *Empire of the Gazis: The Rise and Decline of the Ottoman Empire, 1280–1808.* Cambridge: Cambridge University Press, 1976.

Vyronis, S., Jr. *The Decline of Medieval Hellenism in Asia Minor and the Process of Islamization from the Eleventh Through the Fifteenth Century.* Berkeley: University of California Press, 1986.

Waddy, C. *Women in Muslim History.* London: Longman, 1980.

## Mughal India

Blake, S. P. *Shajahanabad: The Sovereign City in Mughal India.* Cambridge: Cambridge University Press, 1991.

Edwards, S., and Garrett, H. L. *Mughal Rule in India.* Delhi: Chand, 1962.

Gascoigne, B. *The Great Moghuls.* New York: Harper & Row, 1971.

Habib, I. *The Agrarian System of Mughal India, 1556–1707.* New York: Asia Publishing House, 1963.

———, et al. *The Cambridge Economic History of India*, Vol. 1: *1200–1750.* Cambridge: Cambridge University Press, 1982.

Majumdar, R. C., ed. *An Advanced History of India.* Delhi: Macmillan, 1973.

Prawdin, M. *Builders of the Mughal Empire.* London: Allen & Unwin, 1963.

Sarkar, J. *Shivaji.* Calcutta: Sarkar & Sons, 1952.

———. *A Short History of Aurangzeb.* Calcutta: Sarkar & Sons, 1962.

Shelat, J. M. *Akbar.* Bombay: Bharatiya Bidya Bhavan, 1964.

Singhal, D. P. *A History of the Indian People.* London: Methuen, 1983.

Srivasta, A. L. *The Mughal Empire.* Agra: Agarwala, 1966.

Subrahmanyam, S. *The Political Economy of Commerce: Southern India, 1500–1650.* Cambridge: Cambridge University Press, 1990.

Wolpert, S. *A New History of India.* New York: Oxford University Press, 1989.

## Safavid Iran

*Cambridge History of Iran.* Cambridge: Cambridge University Press, 1983.

Morgan, D. *Medieval Persia, 1040–1797.* New York: Longman, 1988.

Savory, R. M. *Iran Under the Safavids.* Cambridge: Cambridge University Press, 1980.

# Imperial Revival
# in China

With the expulsion of the Mongols in the mid-fourteenth century, the Chinese imperial tradition was reasserted by the founding of the Ming dynasty in 1368. Pride in regained power and wealth led to the building of magnificent new capitals, first at Nanking (Nanjing) and then at Peking (Beijing), as well as to the resumption of the tributary system whereby lesser Asian states sent regular missions to China, acknowledging its superiority and prostrating themselves before the Son of Heaven. Ming armies reconquered the empire of the T'ang and the Sung, and early in the dynasty a series of seven naval expeditions toured Southeast Asia, India, the Persian Gulf, and as far as the east coast of Africa, acquiring new tributaries, trading in Chinese products, and bringing back curiosities from afar.

The growing commercialization of the economy,

**Magnificent paintings of nature continued under the Ming dynasty in the now long established Chinese tradition. This lovely spray of white magnolia is part of a larger painting by the master Wen Cheng-ming (1470–1559). [Metropolitan Museum of Art, bequest of John M. Crawford, Jr.]**

aided from the sixteenth century by imports of silver from the Spanish New World, stimulated urban growth and a rich merchant culture. Literature, philosophy, and the arts flourished, and popular culture also expanded into vernacular writing, opera, plays, and woodblock printing. For at least its first two centuries Ming administration was effective and the country was prosperous. But the dynasty became increasingly conservative and traditional. It was plagued by court intrigues, and a series of weak emperors sapped its vigor. Popular unrest mounted as government became less and less able to provide an equitable order or to move with the times. Rebels took Peking and then were replaced by a new set of alien conquerors, the Manchus from Manchuria, who inaugurated the Ch'ing dynasty in 1644. Manchu rule nevertheless rested consciously and purposefully on the Ming heritage, and most of the trends that began under the Ming continued with little break once order was restored.

## The Ming Dynasty

By the early 1300s Mongol control of China was weakening under the ineffective successors of Kubilai Khan. Chronic feuding within the imperial clan and pressures from rival clans enfeebled Mongol power, and by 1330 civil war had erupted. Beginning in 1333 successive drought-induced famines racked northern China, worsened by unchecked flooding in the Yellow River where the dikes had been neglected. Most Chinese interpreted these natural disasters as portents of divine displeasure and the loss of the Mandate of Heaven by the Yuan dynasty, a response typical of the declining years of all previous dynasties but further fed in this case by bitter Chinese hatred of the alien Mongols and their oppressive rule.

Banditry and rebellion spread rapidly in nearly every province, and rebel leaders vied for Heaven's Mandate in efforts to eliminate their rivals. Many rebel groups were aided by or belonged to secret societies. The most important of these was the White Lotus, a Buddhist sect originating in the Southern Sung period that consistently opposed the ruling dynasty and hence had to remain secret, with its own private rituals. The White Lotus persisted underground or in association with banditry and rebellion until the twentieth century. Another Buddhist secret society, the Red Turbans, so called from their headdress and similarly with origins in the Sung, rose in revolt and played a major role in the lower Yellow River plain while the White Lotus was active in the Yangtze valley. These and other rebel secret societies recruited supporters from among poor peasants and also drew on anti-Mongol sentiments.

| MING CHINA | |
|---|---|
| 1368 | Founding of Ming dynasty |
| 1368–1398 | Hung-wu |
| 1405–1433 | Cheng Ho's expeditions |
| 1472–1529 | Wang Yang-ming, philosopher |
| 1573–1582 | Reforms of Chang Chü-cheng |
| 1644 | Founding of Manchu dynasty |
| 1683 | Fall of Taiwan |

One of the rebel leaders, Chu Yüan-chang (Zhu Yuanzhang, 1328–1398), rose to a commanding position in the 1350s and went on to found a new dynasty. His forces swept the Yangtze valley by the end of the decade, set up a government at Nanking in 1356, and in 1368 captured Peking, proclaiming the Ming ("brilliant") dynasty, which was to last until 1644. The Ming achievement in rebuilding the empire and restoring Chinese pride ushered in a period of unprecedented economic and cultural growth that went far beyond where the Sung had left off. The population probably rose by at least 50 percent by the end of the Ming dynasty, stimulated by major improvements in agricultural technology promoted by the state. The entire economy commercialized rapidly, accompanied by a rise in the number and size of cities and perhaps a doubling of total trade.

### 🪷
### HUNG-WU: THE REBEL EMPEROR

Chu Yüan-chang, the victorious rebel leader who became the first Ming emperor, took the name Hung-wu ("great military power"), by which he is mainly known. Life had been hard for him up to that point. Like Liu Pang, the founder of the Han dynasty, he had been born a peasant. Orphaned early, he entered a Buddhist monastery, where he became literate, and at age 25 joined a rebel band, where his native ability soon brought him to the top. As emperor his strong personality and high intelligence made a deep and lasting impression on the first two centuries of the Ming, whose foundations he largely built. He was an indefatigable worker, concerned with all the details of administering his new empire, but he had few close associates or friends and pursued an austere lifestyle that reflected his difficult and impoverished youth. Having risen to power over rebel rivals, he became paranoid about supposed plots against him and was given to violent rages of temper during which he often ordered harsh punishments for suspected disloyalty or trivial offenses. Irritated by continued Japanese piracy along the China coast, he also wrote to the Ashi-

**Emperor Hung-wu (1328–1398), also known more formally as T'ai-tsu ("Great Progenitor"), in a caricature by an unknown fifteenth-century artist, one of a series of caricatures of notable emperors. Hung-wu's rather piglike face, commented on by many of his contemporaries, bore the traces of smallpox, which had nearly killed him as a younger man. The caricature conveys Hung-wu's forceful personality. [Collection of the National Palace Museum, Taipei, Taiwan, Republic of China]**

kaga shogun (see Chapter 12): "You stupid eastern barbarians! Living so far across the sea . . . you are haughty and disloyal; you permit your subjects to do evil." The Japanese replied simply: "Heaven and earth are vast. They are not monopolized by one ruler."[1] Hung-wu's re-

action, perhaps fortunately, is not recorded. In his last will, he wrote of himself: "For 31 years I have labored to discharge Heaven's will, tormented by worries and fears, without relaxing for a day."[2] One wonders if he felt that winning the Dragon Throne had really been worth the effort!

Hung-wu increasingly concentrated power in his own hands and in 1380 abolished the Imperial Secretariat, which had been the main central administrative body under past dynasties, after suppressing a plot for which he blamed his chief minister. The emperor's role thus became even more autocratic, although Hung-wu necessarily continued to use what were called the Grand Secretaries to assist with the immense paperwork of the bureaucracy, which included memorials (petitions and recommendations to the throne), imperial edicts in reply, reports of various kinds, and tax records.

This group was later more regularly established as the Grand Secretariat, a kind of cabinet, but in Hung-wu's time he supervised everything and made or approved all decisions. He was concerned about the power of eunuchs, remembering the trouble they had often caused in earlier dynasties, and erected a tablet in the palace that read, "Eunuchs must have nothing to do with administration."[3] He greatly reduced their numbers, forbade them to handle documents, insisted that they remain illiterate, and got rid of those who so forgot their place as to offer comments on government matters. Some eunuchs were considered necessary as guards and attendants for the imperial harem, which the emperor was thought to need so as to ensure male heirs. In time eunuch power was to grow again, until in the later Ming period they became once more a scourge of good government.

One policy of Hung-wu's that shocked the Confucians was his resumption of the Mongol practice of having officials publicly beaten when they had displeased him. Confucian doctrine held that corporal punishment was only for the ignorant masses; the "superior man" was to be exempt, because with him one could reason and could expect him to mend his ways if necessary by following the virtuous example of those above him. Hung-wu was a tough ruler and demanded complete submission despite his praise for the Confucian classics. But as a peasant by birth, he never lost his envy and distrust of intellectuals. He also reorganized the army around a new system of elite guard units stationed at strategic points throughout the empire and along the frontiers. While some of his policies seemed extreme to many and his personality forbidding or fearsome, Hung-wu was a strong emperor whose work provided the Ming with a momentum of imperial power and effectiveness that lasted far beyond his time. His concentration of power in the emperor's hands worked well when the emperor was as able and dedicated as he was. When weaker and less conscientious men occupied the throne, the empire was in trouble, as was to happen disastrously in the last decades of Ming rule.

When Hung-wu died in 1398, the provinces within the Great Wall were secure and Chinese power was again dominant in eastern Sinkiang, Inner Mongolia, and southern Manchuria. Vietnam, Tibet, Korea, and Japan accepted tributary status. Hung-wu built a splendid new capital at Nanking with a city wall 60 feet high and 20 miles around. It was the longest city wall in the world, although like most Chinese city walls, it was intended more for symbolic affirmation of imperial power than for defense. Indeed, the Chinese word for *city* also means "wall," to distinguish it from a mere town. Peking was passed over as a capital because of its association with the Mongols and its location on the northern fringe of the country, far from major trade routes and agricultural centers. The Yangtze valley had long been the economic heart of the empire, and it made sense to put the capital there.

The second Ming emperor, Yung-lo (Yongluo, 1403–1424), was also an able and conscientious administrator. Continued prosperity and the new southern orientation of the Ming stimulated the further expansion of trade. Commerce and city life grew rapidly. Ports on the southeast coast acquired new importance as links with the colonies of overseas Chinese in Java, the Philippines, Vietnam, and elsewhere in Southeast Asia.

## Tributaries and Expeditions

To mark the resurgence of empire after the brief Mongol eclipse, the traditional tributary system was enlarged and made more formal. This helped keep peace along the extensive borders as well as assert Chinese overlordship. In theory, Chinese political and cultural superiority was a magnet for all lesser peoples or states. They would willingly acknowledge its greatness and, "yearning for civilization," as the official Chinese phrase went, would model themselves on it. In practice, there was just enough truth in this to warrant saying it. Although, of course, the tributary states had their own pride and culture, they freely recognized that Chinese civilization had a great deal to offer them. Near neighbors such as Korea or Vietnam, and later Burma, Laos, Tibet, and Mongolia, had reason, moreover, to fear Ming military power and hence to accept tributary status. Recognizing China's supremacy cost them little; as long as they did not try to challenge it, they were left to manage their own affairs.

The ritual obeisance to the Chinese emperor required of ambassadors was probably not seen as humiliating, as it might be by a modern diplomat, but in keeping with the way in which they had to deal with their own monarchs at home. Tributary states sent regular missions every few years to the imperial capital, where their representatives knelt before the Son of Heaven in a series of prescribed prostrations known as the *k'e t'ou* (later Westernized as *kowtow*, literally "bang head," placing the head to the floor as a token of respect). They presented a long list of "gifts" and in return were given "presents," often greater in value and number. The missions were in part a polite cloak for trade, combining mutual benefit with diplomacy and the prestige of association with the Celestial Empire. It also fed the Chinese opinion of themselves as the only imperium, the only true civilization, the center of the world, compared with which all other people were barbarians.

At its height, first under the Ming and later in the early Ch'ing period, the tributary system involved over 40 states, including Korea, Vietnam, Tibet, Japan, Java, the Philippines, Burma, Siam, Ceylon, Malacca, and many central Asian kingdoms. The renewed Chinese interest in the wider world was a feature of the first few decades of the Ming, although the tributary system continued into the nineteenth century. The last half or more of Ming rule was, in contrast, a period of retrenchment, preoccupation with the defense of the land frontiers, and cultural conservatism. Such a shift fits the pattern of the dynastic cycle discussed in Chapter 12. All dynasties tended to be open-minded, cosmopolitan, and expansionist in their first century, complacent in their second, and overwhelmed by problems in their third and last, when the effectiveness and vigor of the imperial government deteriorated, corruption mounted, and rebellion spread. The Ming Chinese were no exception to this pattern, and the memory of the Mongol conquest tended in any case to make them antiforeign, conservative in their determination to reaffirm the great tradition of the Chinese past, and inward-centered. All this was understandable and probably benefited the country, at least in the short run, as much as or more than foreign adventuring. China was a huge and productive world in itself. Until late in the 1500s things continued to go well, and general prosperity kept most people content.

Japanese and Korean pirate raids at places all along the coast did worry the Ming, and not only because of what the pirates stole or destroyed. The raids demonstrated that the Chinese government could not keep order locally or defend its people. The raids were regarded as equivalent to rebellion, and the government also knew that a good many renegade Chinese were involved, masquerading as Koreans or Japanese. After much pressure from Peking, the Ashikaga shogunate in Japan, now formally a Ming tributary, suppressed some of the Japanese pirate activity and sent some captured pirates to Peking for execution. A Ming document addressed to the Ashikaga in 1436 acknowledged this and went on to say, in the customary language of the tributary system:

> Since our empire owns the world, there is no country on this or other sides of the seas which does not submit to us. The sage emperors who followed one another had the same regard and uniform benevolence for all countries far and near. You, Japan, are our eastern frontier, and for generations you have performed tributary duties. The longer the time, the more respectful you have become.[4]

## From Southeast Asia to Africa

What distinguished the early Ming period was the outreach of imperial pride, manifested especially in remarkable maritime expeditions. The eunuch admiral Cheng Ho (Zhenghe) mounted seven naval expeditions of Chinese fleets between 1405 and 1433, with up to 60 vessels. They toured much of Southeast Asia, the east and west coasts of India (including Calicut, where 90 years later Vasco da Gama was to make his Asian landfall), Ceylon, the Persian Gulf and the Straits of Hormuz, Aden, Jidda (from which seven Chinese went to Mecca), and East Africa. They may have gone as far as the Cape of Good Hope or even around it. They brought back giraffes, zebras, and ostriches to amaze the court, and tributary agreements with gifts from a host of new states. When the king of Ceylon was considered not deferential enough, he was arrested and taken back to Nanking, and Yung-lo appointed a new king in his place. Tributary missions came several times from the Persian Gulf, East Africa, India, and Southeast Asia.

Cheng Ho's many-decked ships carried up to 500 troops but also cargoes of export goods, mainly silks and porcelains, and brought back foreign luxuries such as spices and tropical woods. The economic motive for these huge ventures may have been important, and many of the ships had large private cabins for merchants. But the chief aim was probably political, to show the flag and command respect for the empire, as well as to enroll still more states as tributaries.

Some of the ships were larger than any previously built in the world, 400 feet long and of 500 tons' burden, with four decks. Despite their size, they were reported to be faster sailers than the Portuguese caravels or Spanish galleons of two centuries later, especially with a favorable wind, and they were designed in accordance with the monsoonal wind patterns of Asia and the Indian Ocean. Properly timed voyages could count on going with the wind for about half the year almost anywhere

---

### ◉ A Ming Naval Expedition ◉

*Here is part of a text engraved on a stone tablet in 1432, commemorating the expeditions of Cheng Ho.*

The Imperial Ming dynasty in unifying seas and continents . . . even goes beyond the Han and the T'ang. The countries beyond the horizon and from the ends of the earth have all become subjects. . . . Thus the barbarians from beyond the seas . . . have come to audience bearing precious objects. . . . The emperor has ordered us, Cheng Ho . . . to make manifest the transforming power of the Imperial virtue and to treat distant people with kindness. . . . We have seven times received the commission of ambassadors [and have visited] altogether more than thirty countries large and small. We have traversed immense water spaces and have beheld huge waves like mountains rising sky-high, and we have set eyes on barbarian regions far away hidden in a blue transparency of light vapors, while our sails loftily unfurled like clouds day and night continued their course, traversing those savage waves as if we were treading a public thoroughfare. . . . We have received the high favor of a gracious commission of our Sacred Lord, to carry to the distant barbarians the benefits of his auspicious example. . . . Therefore we have recorded the years and months of the voyages. [Here follows a detailed record of places visited and things done on each of the seven voyages.] We have anchored in this port awaiting a north wind to take the sea . . . and have thus recorded an inscription in stone . . . erected by the principal envoys, the Grand Eunuchs Cheng Ho and Wang Ching-hung, and the assistant envoys.

*Source:* J. J. L. Duyvendak, "The True Dates of the Chinese Maritime Expeditions in the Early Fifteenth Century," *T'oung Pao* 24 (1938): 349–355.

in that vast region and then returning with the opposite monsoon in the other half of the year.

## The Expeditions in Retrospect

Cheng Ho's ships, like those of the Sung, were built with double hulls and up to a dozen separate watertight compartments. Despite their far-flung voyages and their many encounters with storms and unknown coasts, few were lost. The crews were provided with detailed sailing directions, at least for the waters near home, and compasses. Their exploits of seamanship and exploration were unprecedented in the world. The grand scale and imperial pretension of the expeditions, as well, perhaps, as their commercial ambition, expressed imperial pride and vigor. However, they contributed little to the economy except temporary employment for shipbuilders and crew and luxuries for consumption, and made no lasting impression on the Chinese except to confirm their sense of superiority as the only civilized empire in the world.

The expeditions were also very expensive. They were stopped after 1433, perhaps mainly for that reason, although abuses and corruption in procuring shipbuilding materials and in contracts with shipyards also attracted official criticism. The emperor may have felt that he had made his imperial point, and it is unlikely that trade profits covered the costs. Another factor was the decision to move the capital to Peking in 1421, better to command the chronically troubled northern frontier against the attempted revival of Mongol power and to assert the tradition of a northern capital. The monumental building of Peking also competed for shrinking sources of timber and labor, as well as for treasury allocations.

But the abandonment of the maritime expeditions, like the move to Peking, was a symptom of the Ming's growing interest in consolidation. There were understandable fears of a Mongol resurgence and deep concern as well about the central Asian conquests of the Turkish leader Tamerlane, who was apparently planning to invade China. Tamerlane's death had ended that threat, but the Mongols were still active. Yung-lo personally led five expeditions into the steppe to combat the Mongol revival and remained preoccupied with the northern defenses for the remainder of his reign. In fact, Mongol tribes were to harass the border areas and raid across the frontier until the mid-seventeenth century. The Ming also promoted the spread of Lamaistic Buddhism to the Mongols in an effort to pacify them, a strategy that seems in the end to have been more effective than military confrontation.

The cost of the anti-Mongol campaigns on top of the building of Peking was a strain, and the extravagant oceanic adventures were a logical area for retrenchment. These excursions had also become politically controversial. Cheng Ho's voyages had been supported by his fellow eunuchs at court and strongly opposed by the Confucian scholar-officials; their antagonism was in fact so great that they tried to suppress any mention of the naval expeditions in the official imperial record.

China's relations by sea had always been given a far lower priority than the empire's land frontiers, and this ancient pattern was now reasserted. The Ming expeditions did not, to the Chinese mind, discover anything worth making greater efforts to exploit, and conquest was never part of the plan. Nonetheless, the scale of Cheng Ho's voyages remains impressive. While the Portuguese were just beginning to feel their way cautiously along the West African coast in sight of land, Chinese fleets of far larger ships dominated the Indian Ocean and the western Pacific and traded in most of their ports. They did not try to cross the Pacific or continue westward to Europe, which they were clearly capable of doing, only because to their knowledge there was nothing in either direction to make such a voyage worthwhile.

If they had reached Europe, they probably would have been no more impressed by it than by what they saw in Southeast Asia, India, the Persian Gulf, or Africa, nor any more than they were to be a century later by the early European arrivals in China. Fifteenth-century North America would have seemed to them too primitive even to mention. Like earlier Chinese innovations in science and technology, these maritime achievements were not followed up. The conquest of the seas, global expansion, and a sea-based commercial revolution were left to the poorer and less complacent Europeans, who from both their own and the Chinese point of view had more to gain thereby. The chief early goal of the European expansion overseas was in fact China, whose riches and sophistication had attracted Europe's mind and ambitions since Marco Polo—indeed, perhaps since the first Roman imports of Chinese silk, that symbol of luxury and wealth.

## Prosperity and Conservatism

Meanwhile, the Ming turned inward from their new capital at Peking, rebuilding the Great Wall and its watchtowers in the form it still has today and promoting the development of their own home base. Such domestic concerns had always been the center of Chinese attention. Since Shang times they had called their country the Middle Kingdom, meaning not only that it was the center of the world but also that it combined the advantages of a golden mean, avoiding the extremes of desert, jungle, mountains, or cold around its borders.

In whatever direction one went from China, the physical and cultural environment deteriorated. The Chinese attributed the lack of civilization they noted in all "barbarians" to their far less favorable geographic environment as well as to their distance from the only center of enlightenment. China was indeed the most productive area of comparable size anywhere in the world, especially its great river valleys and floodplains. The empire was bigger than all of Europe in size, held more people, and supported a far greater volume of trade. The Chinese saw their interests best served by embellishing their home base rather than pursuing less rewarding foreign contacts. Domestic and interprovincial trade, between provinces the size of many European states, was far greater than foreign trade and served the world's largest market. Revenues now went increasingly to support domestic projects and to glorify the empire's rulers.

Thus conservatism was growing even before the end of the Ming's first century. Partly this reflected a determination to reestablish the traditional Chinese way in all things after the Mongol humiliation, but it also stemmed from enhanced prosperity. With everything going so well, there was less incentive to seek change or to be innovative, at least in terms of official policy.

The emperors who followed Yung-lo were less able or imaginative and tended to leave policy and administration to the intrinsically conservative Confucian bureaucracy, once again entrenched in power. The imperial censors were revived to keep officials honest and responsible and to keep the capital informed of actual or potential problems. On the whole, this tried-and-true system worked well for another century. In time it became increasingly rigid and less able to respond to change or the need for change, but until the last decades of the Ming, as with other dynasties, it was an impressive form of government that kept order and ensured justice to an admirable degree.

Nor did official conservatism and Confucian-based anticommercialism impede the basic changes at work in the economy. As in every Chinese dynasty, agriculture was regarded as the main source of wealth and worthy of official promotion. Under Hung-wu there was a major effort to rebuild agriculture in the extensive areas devastated by the Mongols and the rebellions against them. Many thousands of reservoirs and canals were constructed or repaired, and depopulated areas were resettled by mass transfers of people. Thousands of acres of farmland were reclaimed. The government undertook new projects to extend irrigation, pave roads, stock public granaries, and construct flood prevention works. Rice yields rose with the use of more productive and earlier-ripening varieties introduced from Southeast Asia and actively promoted by the state. New irrigation and better manuring, plus new land brought under cultivation to feed the growing population, produced a major rise in total output and a marked improvement in average material well-being.

In the sixteenth century new crops, especially maize, peanuts, and sweet and white potatoes, reached China from Spanish America via the Philippines. This increased output still further since the new plants did not replace rice or wheat but grew in hilly or sandy areas little cultivated before.

The Ming government and most of its Confucian magistrates executed duties conscientiously during this period. The tax system was reformed to make it less burdensome for peasants, although the bulk of imperial revenue came from taxes on land and grain in addition to customs duties and the official monopoly taxes on salt and tea. Regular labor service was also required of all districts and households for public works, including the building and maintaining of irrigation and flood prevention systems and the imperial road network. The roughly 2,000 local magistrates, forbidden to serve in their native provinces lest they show favoritism, were necessarily but effectively assisted by a large staff and also by local gentry. The latter were often the major factors in keeping order and ensuring that official policy and projects were carried out. Imperial censors traveling on circuit from the capital watched for irregularities and reported directly to the emperor. A new and comprehensive code of administrative and criminal law was published in 1397.

Food crops were still considered of prime importance, but the state encouraged a boom in commercial crops, such as mulberry (for silkworms) and cotton. Silk was produced in the densely populated Yangtze delta area, where its dependence on intensive hand labor could rest on the family, especially women and older children. The populous Canton (Kwangzhou) area and that of the Red Basin of Szechuan (Sichuan) were other important silk-making regions. All three were close to major urban markets and to navigable waterways to distribute their output throughout the empire at low cost.

Under the Ming, however, for the first time, cotton became the predominant fabric of daily clothing for most people. Cheaper and more durable than silk, it displaced coarser and more laboriously made hemp and linen. Silk remained a luxury item for the wealthy, but cotton became a far larger crop. It was grown and woven in the lower Yangtze, northeastern China, and central China, significantly adding to the income of farmers and providing new employment for weavers and merchants.

## Commerce and Culture

For all the ambitious revival of the imperial bureaucracy, it remained a thin and superficial layer at the top. There were only about 2,000 officials outside the capital, far too few to touch most aspects of daily life in a vast country with a population now well over 100 million. Commerce was officially disparaged, but the most significant

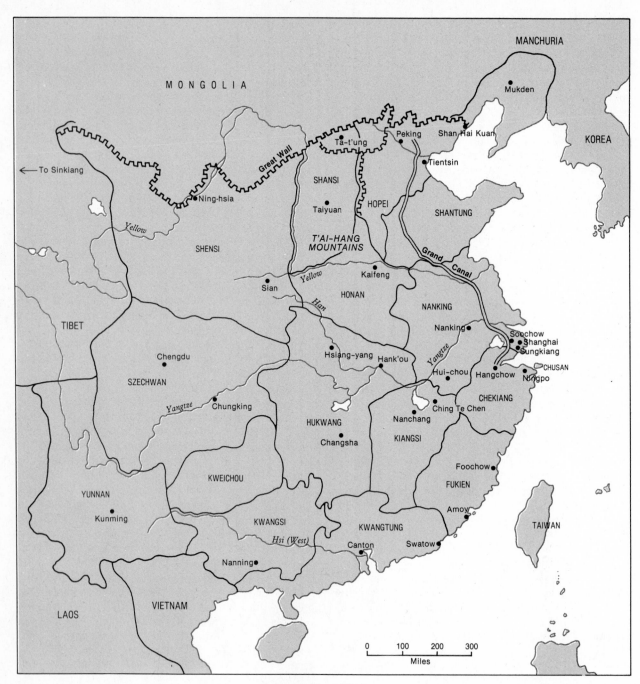

*21.1 Ming China*

changes taking place in Ming China were in the expanding commercialization of the economy. Cheng Ho's expeditions were past, but trade with most of the places he had visited continued to increase, especially with eastern Southeast Asia. Although the largest trade was domestic, new supplies of silver and silver coins came into China to pay for the exports of silk, tea, porcelain, lacquer ware, and other goods and heightened the pace of commercialization and monetarization. More and more production was undertaken for sale, in agriculture and in manufacturing. Most of it was consumed in the rapidly growing cities, but some found its way to Korea, Japan, Java, the Philippines, and farther abroad.

Some of the silver flowing back came from Japan, but

more and more of it came from the Spanish base founded at Manila by the end of the sixteenth century, where it was brought from the mines of Peru and Mexico. Spanish-minted silver dollars began to circulate widely in the China market. By about 1450, silver coins, bars, and smaller ingots had driven paper money out; it was abandoned as people came to prefer increasingly plentiful silver over a paper currency that could not be exchanged for metal. Taxes were commuted from a share of the grain harvest and periods of labor on public works projects to silver. A sweeping reform in the sixteenth and early seventeenth centuries attempted, with considerable success, to simplify the tax system. The reform, known as the "single lash of the whip," lumped what had previously been a great variety of exactions into a few categories and collected them at fixed dates in silver, a major step toward a modern revenue system. At least for a time, this greatly reduced the confusion, corruption, and evasion that had bedeviled the former system, and it also increased the government's net income.

Merchant guilds acquired new though unofficial power in many Chinese cities, especially along the lower Yangtze and the southeast coast, the country's most urbanized and commercialized areas. Guilds controlled much nonagricultural production, marketing, and long-distance trade, informally and often through family or hometown networks, but very effectively. Merchants were still considered parasitic rather than productive. They were formally subject to officials and periodically to special government exactions. However, they were able to secure protection, access to favors, and other informal means of assistance, usually through a member of an extended family who had acquired gentry or official status. Indeed, such contacts were the only secure basis for commercial success in this bureaucratic society. Despite the Confucian disdain for their activity, at least on the surface, many merchants grew rich in this expanding economy. Some were able to buy gentry rank, although they were almost never permitted to hold office. Their money enabled them to live in the style if not with the prestige of the scholar-gentry, as literate connoisseurs of sophisticated art and literature in their great town houses.

After 1520 or so, capital investment increasingly moved away from the ownership and rental of land into commercial enterprises: trade and handicrafts. Prices for land continued to fall, and coastal piracy did not apparently discourage the increase of maritime trade as charges rose to cover those risks, although the biggest growth was in domestic commerce. In agriculture too, commercial or industrial crops such as cotton, indigo (for dyeing fabrics), and vegetable oil for illumination became more important. Handicraft production of tools, furniture, paper, porcelain, and art objects for wider sale became common, distributing finished products to a regional or even national market. Some shops employed several hundred workers—another step toward industrialization.

A major cluster of porcelain workshops that sprang up at Ching Te Chen in the central Yangtze valley made magnificent pieces not only for the imperial household and the court but also for the general domestic market and for export. Iron and steel were made in many places, especially in southern Hopei, in quasi-factories. Large cotton mills producing cloth in major urban centers in the lower Yangtze valley and the highly commercialized delta area sold their output nationwide. There were 50,000 workers in 30 papermaking factories in Kiangsi province alone at the end of the sixteenth century. Skilled workers were in great demand and were recruited over a very wide area. Silk, porcelain, and tea especially, among other products, were exported in growing volume and with great profit. Chinese silk sold in Japan, for example, at five or six times its price in the domestic market, and it continued to be sold in the West at even higher prices.

As would happen two centuries later in Europe, growing commercialization, a widening market, and rising demand for goods provided incentives for improving and speeding up production and the development of new technology to turn out more goods. In the last century of the Ming dynasty a number of technical handbooks were published that show impressive progress in production technology. Some of the new techniques are reminiscent of ones that appeared in eighteenth-century Europe, where the increase in trade and demand helped lead to technological innovation, rising output, and the beginnings of the Industrial Revolution. In Ming China, such innovations included mechanical looms with three or four shuttle winders for producing larger amounts of silk or cotton cloth in less time and without increasing labor requirements. New techniques emerged for the printing of woodblocks in three, four, and five colors to feed the booming market for books and prints. Movable type improved. An alloy of copper and lead made the type sharper and more durable so that it could be used for larger print runs and could be reused many more times. New procedures were worked out even for the manufacture of specially refined grades of sugar, to suit the tastes and the pocketbooks of the greatly increased numbers of the wealthy.

Suspension bridges to carry the booming trade over rivers, making use of iron chains, had been developed by T'ang times. Such bridges became widespread under the Ming dynasty and greatly impressed the early European observers, although they were not successfully copied in Europe until the eighteenth century. The use of a mast and sail on wheelbarrows, important carriers of trade and raw materials on a local scale, especially on the North China plain with its wide expanses of level and treeless areas and its strong winds, also attracted Euro-

# ◉ A Western View of China ◉

*Here is an excerpt from the journal of Matteo Ricci, who observed Ming China from 1583 until his death in 1610.*

The Chinese are a most industrious people, and most of the mechanical arts flourish among them. They have all sorts of raw material and they are endowed by nature with a talent for trading, both of which are potent factors in bringing about a high development of the mechanical arts. . . . Their skill in the manufacture of fireworks is really extraordinary, and there is scarcely anything which they cannot cleverly imitate with them. They are especially adept in reproducing battles and in making rotary spheres of fire, fiery trees, fruit, and the like, and they seem to have no regard for expense where fireworks are concerned. When I was in Nanking I witnessed a display for the celebration of the first month of the year, which is their great festival, and on this occasion I calculated that they consumed enough powder to carry on a sizeable war for a number of years. . . . Their method of making printed books is quite ingenious. The text is written in ink, with a brush made of very fine hair, on a sheet of paper which is inverted and pasted on a wooden tablet. When the paper is thoroughly dry, its surface is scraped off until nothing but a fine tissue bearing the characters remains on the wooden tablet. Then with a steel graver the workman cuts away the surface following the outlines of the characters until these alone stand out in low relief. From such a block a skilled printer can make copies with incredible speed, turning out as many as fifteen hundred copies in a single day. . . . The simplicity of Chinese printing is what accounts for the exceedingly large number of books in circulation here and the ridiculously low prices at which they are sold. Such facts as these would scarcely be believed by anyone who has not witnessed them.

*Source:* M. Ricci, *China in the Sixteenth Century: The Journals of Matthew Ricci, 1583–1610,* trans. L. J. Gallagher (New York: Random House, 1953), pp. 18–21.

pean attention and was soon copied by the Dutch, although the wheelbarrow itself had been invented in Han China, and sails added soon thereafter. A huge network of rivers and canals linked most places from the Yangtze valley south by cheap water transport. In agriculture, new machines were developed under the Ming for cultivating the soil, for irrigation, and even for mechanical sowing, planting, and harvesting. Crops imported from the New World continued to add to total agricultural output. After Hung-wu and Yung-lo, Ming population figures are increasingly unreliable—another symptom of the decline in governmental efficiency—but total population probably increased to something like 130 million by the end of the dynasty.

To serve the needs of an increasingly commercialized economy, guilds of moneychangers and bankers became more important, and some of them developed a national network, with representatives in most major cities and at the capital. Techniques for transferring money through the equivalent of letters of credit, referred to as "flying money," had been used in the Sung dynasty but were refined and greatly expanded in the second half of the Ming period, as were other aspects of banking and the financing of trade. These developments too suggest comparison with what was happening in Europe along similar lines. The Marxist historians of China in the 1970s identified these trends in the Ming era as "early sprouts of capitalism," a description that seems quite reasonable despite the official downgrading of trade and merchants and the state regulation of commerce. Many of the richest merchants in fact grew wealthy through managing what were officially state enterprises or monopolies: supplies for the army, the shipment of rice to feed the capital, and the trade in salt.

## Patronage and Literature

Wealthy merchants patronized literature and the arts, decorated their houses lavishly with art objects, and supported an elegant urban culture. Vernacular literature, too, which had had its major beginnings under the Sung, took on new dimensions and variety, appealing now to a growing mass of urban readers. Ming painting was in

In this beautiful work by the mid-Ming artist
Lu Chi, painted around 1500, autumn mists
veil the rising full moon but do not obscure
the white tree peonies or the nearer two of
the four wild geese by the edge of the stream.
Birds and flowers, especially tree peonies
(native to China), were favorite subjects for
Ming painters. Like so many others, this
painting is deeply restful and at the same
time decorative. The detailed plumage of the
geese is balanced by the simple and
naturalistic single brush strokes of the tall
grasses, as much a trademark of the Chinese
as their renderings of bamboo. [Collection of
the National Palace Museum, Taipei, Taiwan,
Republic of China]

and flowers. Ceramics reached a new level of perfection,
and beautiful pieces were part of every rich merchant
household. This was the period of the famous Ming blue-
and-white porcelain, samples and copies of which were
prominent among Chinese exports to the West.

Yung-lo commissioned an immense encyclopedia of
all knowledge, on which 3,000 scholars worked for five
years. It was followed later in the fifteenth century by a
great medical encyclopedia and others devoted to geography, botany, ethics, and art. The medical volumes,
completed in 1578, listed over 10,000 drugs and prescriptions, most of them unknown in the West, and recorded
the use of inoculation to prevent smallpox, far in advance
of this discovery in eighteenth-century Europe. A handbook of industrial technology printed in 1637, just before
the dynasty collapsed, described methods and tools or
machines in the production of rice, salt, porcelain, metals, coal, weaving, paper, weapons, and many other fruits
of Chinese industry and ingenuity.

In the popular realm, the theater flourished, but the
major advance of Ming literature was in long novels and
other stories of adventure and romance. They still make
excellent reading and give a vivid picture of the life of
the times. Perhaps the best known now is titled *Water
Margins* (translated by Pearl Buck as *All Men Are Brothers*), which tells the story of an outlaw band and its efforts to correct wrongs done by unjust officials. Bandits
of the Robin Hood variety had the same romantic appeal

A sample of the famous Ming blue-and-white
porcelain. [University Museum, Philadelphia]

general less imaginative or innovative than that of the
Sung and tended to rework older themes and styles, but
the later Ming produced its own great painters, especially gifted in their exquisite representations of birds

in China as in the West, and their life as "men of the greenwood" (a phrase identical to that used in medieval England), meaning, of course, the forest, where they had their protected bases, was idealized. Several centuries later, Mao Tse-tung (Mao Zedong), the revolutionary Communist leader, said that *Water Margins* (the title came from the marshes that surrounded the outlaws' base) was his favorite book, probably because it glorified men attempting to defy and replace the existing government. Another still widely read Ming novel, *The Golden Lotus*, is an often pornographic satire about the amorous adventures of a druggist with servants, neighbors, and other men's wives that seems as fresh as today's bestsellers.

Most of the characters in *The Golden Lotus* are members of the leisure class, servants, or concubines in a wealthy household. The novel is generally interpreted as a critical portrayal of decadence, but since the characters are mainly well educated, including the concubines, it includes scenes in which they recite or improvise classical-style poems or songs. Here is one of them:

> *It is evening.*
> *The storm has passed over the southern hall,*
> *Red petals are floating on the surface of the*
>     *pool.*
> *Slowly the gentle thunder rolls away.*
> *The rain is over and the clouds disperse;*
> *The fragrance of waterlilies comes to us over*
>     *the distance.*
> *The new moon is a crescent*
> *Fresh from the perfumed bath, decked for the*
>     *evening;*
> *Over the darkening courtyard it wanes*
> *Yet will not go to rest.*
> *In the shade of the willow the young cicada*
>     *bursts into song,*
> *Fireflies hover over the ancestral halls.*
> *Listen. Whence comes this song of Ling?*
> *The painted boat is late returning,*
> *The jade chords sink lower and lower;*
> *The gentlefolk are silent:*
> *A vision of delight!*
> *Let us rise and take each other by the hand*
> *And dress our hair.*
> *The moon lights up the silken curtains,*
> *But there are no sleepers there.*
> *The mandarin duck tumbles the lotus leaves*
> *On the gently rippling water*
> *Sprinkling them with drops like pearls.*
> *They give out fragrance,*
> *And a perfumed breeze moves softly over the*
>     *flower beds*
> *Beside the summer-house.*
> *How can our spirits fail to be refreshed?*
> *Why crave for the islands of the blest, the home*
>     *of fairies?*
> *Yet when the west wind blows again, Autumn*
>     *will come with it.*[5]

The bandit tales collected in *Water Margins* include a well-known story called "The Birthday Gift Convoy," part of which reads as follows:

**The road had narrowed to mountain paths, but Yang Chih kept the carriers with their pole loads moving. It was almost noon and the sun [was] directly overhead. The men broke out with "Such hot weather! That deadly sun really kills!" but Yang Chih bore down on them shouting, "Hurry along! We have to cross that ridge. Time to worry about the weather later!"**

**On attaining the top of the ridge, the men flung down their poles, loads and all, and stretched themselves at full length under the pine trees. Yang Chih tried to beat them into resuming the march, saying, "This very spot is the haunt of bandits, where even in the best of times robberies are committed in full daylight." Suddenly he dropped his cane, grasped his sword, and dashed into the woods, where he saw seven men with seven wheelbarrows. They said they were date sellers on their way to the capital, resting in the woods in the heat of the day. Soon another man appeared, with two buckets of wine hanging from his shoulder pole, who also sat down to rest in the shade. The carriers of the birthday gift convoy begged to be allowed to buy some wine, but Yang Chih adamantly refused, saying the wine might be drugged. Hearing the commotion, the date sellers came out of the woods, and, after some dickering, persuaded the wine seller to let them have one of his buckets, which they drank from with coconut shell ladles they had in their packs. Yang Chih watched all this and observed that even after some time the date sellers did not seem to be much affected by the wine. Realizing that he still had to get his convoy a long way that day and calculating that a little wine might help get his men back on their feet, he grudgingly permitted them to buy some, and even took a little himself. Within minutes, the date merchants, who had been watching these proceedings, pointed their fingers at the entire party and chanted in chorus, "Sink, sink, sink into heavy slumber!" Instantly the carriers and their guards wobbled at the knees and sank to the ground. The seven strange travelers now brought their wheelbarrows out of the woods, emptied out all the dates, transferred the eleven precious loads of gold, silver, and jewels to the seven wheelbarrows, and were soon out of sight.**

**Yang Chih groaned with rage and bitterness, but his body seemed paralyzed and he could not struggle to his feet. Who were the seven men? Why, they were all famous bandits. How was the wine drugged? Why, by one of the date merchants when he playfully tried to steal another ladleful from the second bucket and in the process added the drug. It was all a carefully worked-out plan to convince Yang Chih and his men, by the date sellers' drinking the first bucket, that the wine was pure. Yang Chih's downfall was like the proverb: Though you be as circumspect as the devil himself, you may unwittingly swallow your own bathwater. Yang Chih tore up his orders. "How can I go back to face my patron? I have no home to return to, no state to serve. Where can I go?" What eventually happened to Yang Chih you will find out in our next chapter.[6]**

## ◉ Folk Wisdom: Maxims from the Chinese ◉

- A wise man adapts himself to circumstances, as water shapes itself to the vessel that contains it.
- Misfortunes issue out where diseases enter in—at the mouth.
- The error of one moment becomes the sorrow of a whole life.
- The gem cannot be polished without friction, nor man perfected without trials.
- A wise man forgets old grudges.
- A mouse can drink no more than its fill from a river. [Enough is as good as a feast.]
- Who swallows quick can chew little. [Applied to learning.]
- What cannot be told had better not be done.
- The torment of envy is like a grain of sand in the eye.
- Dig a well before you are thirsty.
- Better be a dog in peace than a man in anarchy.
- To win a cat and lose a cow—the consequences of litigation.
- Forbearance is a domestic jewel.
- Kindness is more binding than a loan.
- Those who cannot sometimes be unheeding or deaf are not fit to rule.
- Parents' affection is best shown by teaching their children industry and self-denial.
- A truly great man never puts away the simplicity of a child.
- To obtain one leads to wishing for two—enough is always something more than a man possesses.
- If the upper beam be crooked, the lower will be awry. [The example of superiors.]
- One lash to a good horse, one word to a wise man.
- The man who combats himself will be happier than he who contends with others.
- Let every man sweep the snow from before his own door, and not busy himself about the frost on his neighbor's tiles.
- A man need only correct himself with the same rigor that he reprehends in others; and excuse others with the same indulgence he shows to himself.

*Source:* J. R. Davis, ed., *The Chinese*, vol. 2 (London: Charles Knight, 1845), pp. 235–240.

The West as a whole has still not acknowledged that the novel, in much the same form as we know it today, originated in Asia, as did detective stories. But a few westerners were less parochial in their awareness and their tastes. Here is a conversation between the famous German writer Johann Wolfgang von Goethe (1749–1832) and a friend in 1827:

> **"During the days when I did not see you," he said, "I have read a great deal, in particular a Chinese novel with which I am still occupied."**
>
> **"A Chinese novel," I said, "that must be rather curious."**
>
> **"Not as curious as one might be tempted to think," replied Goethe. "These people think and feel much as we do, and one soon realizes that one is like them."**
>
> **"But," said I, "perhaps this Chinese novel is a rather exceptional one?"**
>
> **"Not at all," said Goethe, "the Chinese have thousands of the kind, and they even had a certain number of them**

**already when our forebears were still living in the woods."[7]**

## Popular Culture

By the sixteenth century there was a large and growing number of people who were literate or semiliterate but were not members of any elite or of the official Confucian-style gentry. The latter probably never exceeded 2 percent of the population. These nonelite literates and semiliterates lived in the vast Chinese world that was little touched by the imperial system and its canons, most of them outside the big cities and the circles of the rich merchant elites. Popular literature, stories, novels, and plays produced by and for them probably exceeded in volume and circulation the output in the orthodox classical mode, extensive and varied as that was. Much of it was also read, in private, by the elite, who would hide any "undignified" book under the pillow if someone entered the room. For us today, too, most of it is more fun than the restrained, polished, or formal material that the scholarly gentry were supposed to read and write.

In addition were the number of puppet shows, shadow plays, mystery and detective stories (four or five centuries before they appeared in the West), operas, ballads, the oral tradition of itinerant storytellers, and a wealth of inexpensive woodblock prints, many of them dealing with aspects of daily life, others with mythology or folk religion. Opera, which combined drama, music, dance forms, singing, and gorgeous costumes, could appeal also to illiterates, probably still the large majority (although Ming China may have been the most literate society of its time), as could storytellers, balladeers, and plays. Itinerant groups performed in all these media everywhere, even in small towns. Storytellers would be accompanied by musicians or provide their own music and would end each recital at a moment of suspense: "Come back next time if you want to hear the next episode" or "Pay now if you want to know how it all came out!"

Over 300 different local or regional genres of opera have been identified, intended mainly for nonelite audiences. Many operas, plays, and stories centered on the adventures of heroes and villains of the rich Chinese past, not always historically accurate but always entertaining, and appealing to the deep interest of the Chinese in their own history. Most of the common people learned their history from opera, theater, and storytellers, and they learned a great deal of it. The connection with folk religion was close, including folk versions of Buddhism and Taoism as well as local animist cults and deities, and many of the operas, plays, and stories focused on it.

Operas were commonly performed at festivals celebrating a local god or as part of temple rituals, and many of them, as well as shadow plays, had an explicitly religious or ritual content, like the medieval miracle plays of Europe. Still others satirized daily life: henpecked husbands, jilted or faithless lovers, grasping merchants, corrupt officials, overprotective or authoritarian parents, tyrannical landlords, and so on, set in villages or towns rather than in the more sophisticated and urbane world of the cities.

These operas and plays formed in effect a countertradition to the elite culture. They expressed strong sympathy for the powerless, the oppressed, and the underdogs, especially women, who were often major figures. The works express contempt for wealth without compassion, for power without responsibility, and for all forms of hypocrisy, opportunism, and moral compromise. In this extensive genre, individuals are valued and respected for their achievements and their moral virtue regardless of their social position, in contrast to the hierarchical ordering of individuals that Confucian doctrine supported. This rich and varied literature has a universal flavor and many parallels in the popular culture of most other societies around the world, past and present. But it also reveals the basic good sense, humor, and appealing human qualities of the common people of Ming China.

# Elite Culture and Traditionalism

In monumental architecture the Ming created new glories in their capitals at Nanking and Peking and in temples in every city and many towns, a further indication of prosperity. But in general, particularly after their first century, the Ming looked to the past for guidance. This accounted for their interest in encyclopedias, which collected the wisdom and experience of previous generations as guardians of tradition.

Most Ming scholars and philosophers were traditionalists, mistrusting speculation or innovation. There were exceptions, of course, but orthodoxy tended to dominate thought, reinforced by the system of imperial examinations. As one Ming writer put it: "Since the time of Chu Hsi [the Sung Confucianist] the truth has been made clear. No more writing is needed. We have only to practice."[8] There were nevertheless some important developments in philosophy, especially in the thought of Wang Yang-ming (1472–1529), a scholar-official who went beyond the Neo-Confucianism of Chu Hsi in urging both a meditative and intuitive self-cultivation, much influenced by Buddhism, and an activist moral role in society. Wang's most famous aphorism stresses the organic connection between knowledge and behavior: "Knowledge is the beginning of conduct; conduct is the completion of knowledge"—a maxim still admired by Confucianists in China, Korea, and Japan.

Before Wang's time, Hung-wu had issued six brief imperial edicts that were posted in all villages and towns in 1397, a year before his death. They ordered people to be filial, to respect their elders and ancestors, to teach their children to do the same, and peacefully to pursue their livelihoods. Local gentry, not in office but functioning as local elites and keepers of order and morality, helped make sure that these prescriptions were carried out. The orthodox Confucian denigration of trade and merchants and their subordination to officialdom helped strengthen official disinterest in commerce. Foreign trade was left largely in private hands or was managed by powerful eunuchs at court, which further devalued it in Confucian eyes.

Grain had to be hauled north from the Yangtze valley to feed the swarm of officials, garrison troops, and commoners as well as the elite of Peking. Japanese piracy prompted Yung-lo to restore the Grand Canal, which had silted up and fallen into disrepair, and to abandon the coastal sea route after 1415. The cost was high, but the canal helped generate further increases in interregional trade and in the production of crafted articles and other consumer goods to supply an enlarged market. It also stimulated the growth of cities along its route. Soochow (Suzhou), in the Yangtze delta just west of Shanghai and until the nineteenth century the major city and port of that area after Nanking, became a national financial and commercial center; it was noted for its fine silk goods, which were distributed to the wealthy all over China, especially in fashionable Peking. Cotton cloth, lacquer, magnificent porcelain pieces, iron cooking pots from Canton, and numerous other goods were carried, mainly by water routes, to an increasingly national market. Hankou (now part of the city of Wuhan) on the central Yangtze grew as a major junction of rivers and a national distribution center as well as a major market in itself. Private Chinese merchants went to Southeast Asia in great numbers and managed an increasing overseas trade from bases on the southeast China coast such as Canton, Amoy, Swatow, and Foochow (Fuzhou) despite official discouragement. Tientsin (Tianjin), the port of Peking, grew also as the chief port for trade with Korea. Other booming cities included Chengdu, the capital of the agriculturally rich province of Szechuan with its many rivers, and Changsha, the capital of Hunan on the Hsiang (Xiang) River, a tributary of the Yangtze, which flowed through the productive lowlands of central China known as "China's rice bowl."

Increasingly conservative official attitudes were reflected in the Ming reform of the imperial examination system. In 1487 a set form was established for the writing of examination papers in eight categories using no more than 700 characters altogether, following a prescribed style of polished commentary on the Confucian and Neo-Confucian classics. This was the notorious "eight-legged essay," which in all likelihood intentionally inhibited individual thought or innovation and encouraged a traditionalist orthodoxy.

Government schools at the county and prefectural levels and private academies and tutors for the sons of the wealthy (daughters were given no formal education) passed on the distilled wisdom of the ages to youngsters fortunate enough to attend and shaped their instruction to prepare them to conform to what the examinations now required. Candidates had to pass preliminary examinations at the county level. Success there enabled them to compete at the prefectural city, where they could obtain the lowest principal degree. That constituted admission to the gentry class with, among other things, exemption from labor service and from corporal punishment. The second level of examinations was held in each provincial capital; it lasted several days, during which each candidate was walled into a tiny cell and provided with food and water. Only about one in every 100 passed, earning a higher degree and the right to compete in the final examination offered every three years

at the imperial capital. Success there was rewarded with the highest degree and an interview with the emperor himself, who could appoint those of his choosing to official posts. The lowest degree could be purchased, especially as the dynasty declined and needed money, but such buyers—merchants or landlords—did not serve as officials. The sale of these degrees (akin to the sale of titles in early Stuart England) served to some extent as a concession to wealthy families that might otherwise become restive.

The basic Confucian message of responsibility and human-heartedness continued to be stressed, with its conviction that human nature is fundamentally good and can be molded by education and by the virtuous example of superiors. The ultimate deterioration and collapse of the Ming, and in 1911 of the entire imperial system, should not obscure its positive aspects, especially during its many centuries of relative vigor. Even up to the last years of the Ming, the growing corruption and ineffectiveness of the court were not much reflected in the continued operation of the system elsewhere in the country, which rested far more on the basic Chinese social fabric of family, gentry, and Confucian principles than on the management or intervention of the few imperial officials. The lives and values of most people had their own momentum. Local freedom and good order had relatively little to do with imperial politics at most times and much to do with the traditional Chinese system of a self-regulating society based on respect for tradition and hierarchy.

Local gentry directed and raised money for public works, especially irrigation, roads, canals, bridges, and ferries. Often they organized and funded schools and academies, orphanages, care for the elderly, and relief measures in hard times or after floods. Many of them compiled the local histories or gazeteers that are still a mine of information about local conditions, events, and notable people. This was all done as a manifestation of Confucian morality, without pay or official appointment. When all went well, perhaps half or more of the time during the 2,000 years of dynastic rule, the local gentry thus served as a major supplement to government and an important cement for society.

---

❧

## IMPERIAL PEKING: AXIS OF THE MING WORLD

When Yung-lo decided to move the capital back to the north, Peking was the obvious choice, primarily for its nearness to the most threatened frontiers. It is only about 40 miles from the mountains that surround and protect the city on the west, north, and northeast. The Great Wall runs through them, crossing a narrow lowland strip of coastal plain east of the city that leads to Manchuria and is called Shan Hai Kuan ("mountain sea gate"). Passes to the northwest lead directly into Mongolia. Both areas had been identified by now as the chief trouble spots along the frontier, and it was mainly to guard against them that the Great Wall was rebuilt at tremendous cost.

The Hsiung-nu menace that had plagued the Han had been replaced by that of the Mongols farther east and by early signs of what was to become the next alien conquering group, the Manchus of Manchuria. The gradual eastward progression of China's capital from Chou, Ch'in, Han, and T'ang Ch'ang An (Sian) to Loyang, the Sung move to Kaifeng and Hangchow, and now the Ming choice of Peking reflected these military challenges. The growth of the south, the drought and agricultural deterioration of the northwest, and the provision of canals to bring food from the surplus areas of the Yangtze valley to feed successive northern capitals were also factors in determining where the imperial capital would be located.

The new Peking was designed to make a statement of imperial power and majesty. The older center of the city today is largely a Ming creation, replacing what had been left of the Mongol capital but on a much larger scale. The main outer city walls were 40 feet high and nearly 15 miles around, forming a rectangle pierced by nine gates with watchtowers and outer gates to deter attackers, check permit papers, and awe all who entered. Inside was the Imperial City, within its own walls, 5 miles in circumference. These enclosed in turn the red inner walls of the Forbidden City, which contained the palace and was surrounded by a moat 2 miles around.

Successive courtyards inside the Forbidden City, dominated by throne halls for different purposes, were set on terraces of white marble with gleaming gold-tiled roofs. These led along a north-south axis to the palace. Outside the Forbidden City (so called because it was closed to all except people with official business), a similar succession of elegant stone-paved courtyards, terraces, and audience halls led to the main gates. The outermost walls enclosed gardens, artificial lakes, and even an artificial hill.

The orientation of the city as a whole, based on astronomical principles, followed a north-south axis, thus aligning the court with the order of the universe. The overall plan and its every detail were designed to awe and impress all who approached or entered its series of walls and courtyards. It still has that effect, and partly for that reason, it has been restored by the People's Republic as the centerpiece of the modern capital. The Ming design was accepted and embellished by their successors, the Ch'ing (Qing). That part of Peking remains one of the best-preserved and most impressive planned capitals anywhere. Its splendid courtyards, the gracefulness and yet strength of architectural and roof lines in all of its buildings, and the lavish use of colored porcelain tiles make it aesthetically as well as symbolically overwhelming.

A less planned city grew up outside the walls, where most of the common people lived, and it soon housed most of Peking's residents. The total population, inside and outside the walls, was probably a little over a million under both the Ming and the Ch'ing, fed in part with rice brought from the Yangtze valley by the Grand Canal. Some space was left clear immediately around the outer

The Imperial Palace inside its own wall, looking south across the courtyards of the Forbidden City. The planned rectangular layout of imperial Peking is evident. [Paolo Koch/Photo Researchers]

**Throne room in the Imperial Palace, Peking. Each building in the Forbidden City is fronted by sweeping marble stairs, and courtyards are linked by ornate marble bridges. The buildings are elaborately decorated inside but elegantly simple in their external lines.** [Marc F. Bernheim/Woodfin Camp]

walls for better defense, and there were large military barracks. A maze of streets, alleys, and small courtyards covered most of the area outside the walls, including the small walled compounds with their tiny gardens and living space for extended families. Some of these too can still be seen.

The majestic Imperial City and Forbidden City were formally ordered on a grand scale, in sharp contrast to the unplanned alleys and irregular streets of the city around them. But above all Peking was—and remains—an imperial statement in wood, stone, brick, and tile that dominated the entire urban area physically as well as symbolically.

## Complacency and Decline

Peking was built in the days of Ming power and pride, but as the decades went by, complacency set in, and a number of growing problems were dealt with inadequately or left unattended. Japanese and Korean pirate attacks on the coast proved impossible to control, and the government's feeble response was to order the re-

moval of all settlements 30 miles inland and officially to forbid maritime trade, although the ban was widely ignored. Guns had been in use for centuries, but China had begun to fall behind advances in Western gunnery. Late in the fifteenth century, when a touring censor asked for a demonstration of a garrison's long-neglected cannon, the commander said, "What, fire those things? Why, they might kill somebody!"[9] This may be an exaggerated example, and during most of the dynasty the Ming armies were reasonably effective in keeping the long peace at home and on the frontiers. Yet the failure to control raids by tributary states clearly presaged the decline of the dynasty.

## Strangers at the Gates

China had now to deal with Western visitors as well. The Portuguese reached the South China coast by 1514, but their aggressive behavior led to their expulsion from Canton in 1522, where their envoy died in prison. To the Chinese, they were just another lot of unruly pirates, like the Dutch who followed them later, and their numbers and ships were small enough to be brushed off. The Chinese also found the westerners offensively hairy, misshapen, and very smelly, and although a few military commanders noted that their guns were superior to China's, no one in the government took them very seriously.

The westerners had different ideas. The Jesuits had their eye on China as an immense potential harvest of souls and sent a series of missions there beginning with Matteo Ricci in 1582 (see Chapter 18). He and his successors, notably Adam Schall von Bell and Ferdinand Verbiest, were learned men with a good working knowledge of the rapidly developing science and technology of post-Renaissance Europe. Complacency and pride kept the Chinese from learning what would have been most useful from the Jesuits: new European advances in mathematics, geography (despite the great voyages of the fifteenth century, the Chinese picture of the world was still woefully inaccurate and incomplete), mechanics, metallurgy, anatomy, surveying, techniques and instruments for precise measuring and weighing, and gunnery.

The court was instead fascinated by the clocks and clockwork gadgets or toys that the Jesuits brought and used to ingratiate themselves, while their most useful knowledge was passed over. Von Bell, a trained astronomer and mathematician, was able to decipher and explain the use of some remarkable astronomical instruments built under the Yuan dynasty in Peking; by the late Ming period, the Chinese had lost the secret. Their own astronomers had noticed that their calculations no longer accurately predicted the movements of the heavenly bodies, but instead of questioning their assumptions and methods, they concluded that "the heavens

---

## ◉ Social Customs in Ming China ◉

*Matteo Ricci described a variety of social customs, as in these excerpts.*

When relatives or friends pay a visit, the host is expected to return the visit, and a definite and detailed ceremony accompanies their visiting. The one who is calling presents a little folder in which his name is written and which may contain a few words of address, depending on the rank of the visitor or the host. These folders or booklets consist of about a dozen pages of white paper, with a two inch strip of red paper down the middle of the cover. . . . One must have at least twenty different kinds on hand for different functions, marked with appropriate titles. . . . Men of high station in life are never seen walking in the streets. They are carried about enclosed in sedan chairs and cannot be seen by passers-by, unless they leave the front curtain open. . . . Carriages and wagons are prohibited by law. . . . The whole country is divided up by rivers and canals. People here travel more by boat than we in the West, and their boats are more ornate and more commodious than ours. . . . Sometimes they give sumptuous dinners aboard their yachts and make a pleasure cruise of it on the lake or along the river. . . . Because of their ignorance of the size of the earth and the exaggerated opinion they have of themselves, the Chinese are of the opinion that only China among the nations is deserving of admiration. They look on all other people not only as barbarous but as unreasoning animals.

*Source:* M. Ricci, *China in the Sixteenth Century: The Journals of Matthew Ricci, 1583–1610,* trans. L. J. Gallagher (New York: Random House, 1953), pp. 61, 81, 167.

---

were out of order." All these were symptoms of an increasing tendency to ignore new ideas or troublesome problems or to gloss them over with confident-sounding pronouncements.

## Politics and Corruption

At the capital, decline in administrative effectiveness was clear by the end of the sixteenth century. The court was filled with intriguing factions, including the eunuchs. This was to become a curse of the imperial system. Because they had no heirs, eunuchs were often trusted, given the care of imperial sons, and granted ready access to the emperor and to powerful wives and concubines. The eunuchs also commanded the palace guard and often won high military posts as commanders or served as imperial inspectors in the provinces. They controlled the workshops that made luxury products for the court and supervised the tribute sent by the provinces and foreign countries. Eunuchs were also often appointed to head official missions abroad.

All this gave the eunuchs certain opportunities for graft, which they used to enrich themselves. Eunuchs gained control of the fearsome secret police and used its power to blackmail and corrupt. This was a burden on the treasury as funds were siphoned off from normal revenues. Another serious drain was the huge allowances paid to the numerous relatives of the imperial family and the nobility, altogether many thousands of people and their dependents. By the late sixteenth century these allowances alone consumed over half of the revenues of two provinces, which provides some measure of their gargantuan scope.

Other heavy expenses, including the cost of the expedition to Korea to repulse the invasion of the Japanese warlord Hideyoshi, drained financial resources still further. Subsidies to Mongol and other central Asian princes to keep them quiet and to deter them from new uprisings or raids on Chinese territory added to the financial strain. The already high taxes were raised still more, inciting both urban and rural revolt. The tax burden fell disproportionately on the poor since many families with money and connections had managed to get their names off the tax registers. Peasants also had to perform heavy labor service, including the rebuilding of the Grand Canal and the Great Wall. Many became so desperate that they melted away into the countryside or the towns or became bandits.

Strong rulers, like Hung-wu, could control the eunuchs, but under weaker rulers the eunuchs often assumed real power, which they usually did not use responsibly. Hung-wu had warned his ministers: "Anyone using eunuchs as his eyes and ears will be blind and deaf."[10] After Yung-lo came a succession of undistinguished emperors, most of whom kept to the pleasures of their palaces and left the running of the empire to the eunuchs and the bureaucrats, a disastrous pattern in a system where authority and responsibility had been so heavily centralized in the person of the emperor.

Banditry and piracy proliferated, a response largely to growing poverty but also to the still growing trade, especially with Japan. The Japanese often alternated as traders and as pirates, like their approximate contemporaries Francis Drake and John Hawkins in Elizabethan England. When the Chinese government in 1530 canceled permission for the official Japanese trading missions to Ningpo (Ningbo) on the coast south of Shanghai, piracy and smuggling multiplied. Pirates and smugglers had their major base for the central coast in the Chusan Islands off the mouth of the Yangtze River, conveniently near Ningbo, then the dominant maritime trade center for populous and highly commercialized central China. Other pirate and smuggling bases were scattered along the much indented coast of the south, shifting from one to another as government pressures or other circumstances required.

From the Yangtze southward, the coast was almost impossible to patrol adequately, and it had a long history of piracy. Mountains come down to the sea in most of this area, which meant that there were limited opportunities for agriculture or trade on land but ample forest cover for concealment and timber for ships. Like the shores of much of the Mediterranean, the Dalmatian coast of the Adriatic, or the Caribbean, the southern Chinese coast combined motives and bases for piracy with tempting opportunity: a golden stream of seaborne trade passing just offshore. In fact, piracy along this coast was not finally put down until after 1950, and smuggling continues still.

As an early-twentieth-century report by the Chinese Maritime Customs Office put it, speaking of the south coast, "Piracy and smuggling are in the blood of the people." When hard pressed by the authorities, pirates and smugglers from Amoy or Swatow southward could cross the border into nearby Vietnam, where they could find sanctuaries, supplies, and Vietnamese colleagues. Hainan Island off the coast opposite the border was long notorious as a pirate and smuggling base for desperadoes from both countries, and even modern China has had trouble preventing large-scale smuggling there. The people of the South China coast were the country's principal seafarers in any case, and many earned their living as fishermen and traders. The fleets of Cheng Ho were built in those harbors, using local timber, and their sailors were recruited from this region. As the power of the central government weakened under the later Ming dynasty and as poverty worsened after the fifteenth century, piracy and smuggling once again grew out of control. By the late Ming period, most of the pirates were not Japanese or Korean but Chinese.

A briefly successful effort at reform was led by Chang Chü-cheng (Zhang Juzheng), who became Grand Secretary from 1573 to 1582. Emperor Wan-li had ascended the throne as a boy in 1572 and was guided for some time by Chang, who as a distinguished Confucian scholar stressed the need for economy, justice, and responsibility. Chang tried to increase the now shrinking imperial revenue by once more reforming the tax system to restore exempted lands and families that had slipped off the rolls after the earlier tax reform. He also tried to limit the special privileges and extravagant expenses of the court and the imperial family and to rebuild the authority of the censors to check abuses. But after Chang's death in 1582, Wan-li abandoned all pretense at responsibility and indulged in more extravagance and pleasures, leaving the court eunuchs to run the empire. He avoided even seeing his own ministers for many years and refused to make appointments, conduct business, or respond to abuses.

Unfortunately, he lived and reigned until 1620, and the 15-year-old who succeeded him on the throne was mentally deficient and spent most of his time tinkering with carpentry in the palace. He gave control of the government to an old friend of his childhood nurse, a eunuch named Wei who had been a butler to his mother. Wei then almost certainly poisoned the emperor, although this was never proved; by then people were reluctant to challenge him. Wei put together a small eunuch army to control the palace and set up a spy network all over the empire. By unscrupulous plotting and force he eliminated all his official enemies—most of the Confucianists at court—filled their places with his opportunist supporters, and extorted new taxes to pay for his luxurious lifestyle. There ensued a general persecution of intellectuals, who were branded as "conspirators," and many hundreds were executed. Most of the academies were closed, half the government offices were left vacant, and petitions went unanswered. A group of Confucian scholars calling themselves the Tung Lin (Donglin, from the name of a famous academy) attempted a moral crusade against these evils. Wei responded with terror tactics after the Tung Lin leader accused him of murders, of having forced abortion on the empress, and 24 other "high crimes." In the end Wei won out, and most of the Tung Lin scholars were disgraced, jailed, or beaten to death before he himself was assassinated in 1627.

It was late for reform, and the eunuch stranglehold on the palace was now too strong to break. Eunuch power at court undercut and then virtually eliminated the power and even the role of the imperial censors. Many censors were killed when they dared to speak up. Palace eunuchs went on making most policy, or not making it, after Wei's death. By the 1630s most of the country had lost confidence in the imperial order. The state treasury, drained especially by extravagances at court,

# ◉ An Earthquake at Peking, 1626 ◉

*The Chinese interpreted earthquakes and other natural disasters as symbols of Heaven's displeasure. When they coincided with popular discontent and dynastic decline, they were seen as warnings. Here is a description of an earthquake in 1626 at Peking, in the last corrupt years of the Ming. The partisans referred to were palace eunuchs.*

Just when the . . . partisans were secretly plotting in the palace, there was a sudden earthquake. A roof ornament over the place where they were sitting fell without any apparent reason and two eunuchs were crushed to death. In a moment there was a sound like thunder rising from the northwest. It shook heaven and earth, and black clouds flowed over confusedly. People's dwellings were destroyed to such an extent that for several miles nothing remained. Great stones hurtled down from the sky like rain. Men and women died by the tens of thousands [a phrase that in Chinese means "a great many"]. Donkeys, horses, chickens, and dogs all had broken or cracked limbs. People with smashed skulls or broken noses were strewn about—the streets were full of them. Gunpowder that had been stored in the Imperial Arsenal exploded. This alarmed elephants, and the elephants ran about wildly, trampling to death an incalculable number of people. The court astrologer reported his interpretation of these events as follows: "In the earth there is tumultuous noise. This is an evil omen of calamity in the world. When noise gushes forth from within the earth, the city must be destroyed. . . . The reason why the earth growls is that throughout the empire troops arise to attack one another, and that palace women and eunuchs have brought about great disorder."

*Source:* C. O. Hucker in D. Lach, *Asia on the Eve of Europe's Expansion* (Englewood Cliffs, N.J.: Prentice Hall, 1965), p. 133.

never fully recovered. The results for the efficient operation of all state systems were disastrous.

Inflation aggravated the problem. Officials and local magistrates had to cope with a much larger population, increasingly troubled by discontent, banditry, and even rebellion. Their salaries were increased and special allowances given to discourage them from diverting official funds or taking bribes, but none of this made up for the far heavier work demands, which necessitated their hiring larger and larger staffs to assist them. These aides, though essential, were not official employees, and their wages were not provided by the state, leaving mag-

Street people of the Ming: beggars and hawkers, painted by Chou Ch'en (active c. 1500–1535). [Cleveland Museum of Art, John L. Severance Fund]

istrates and other officials to meet the costs out of their own inadequate salaries and allowances. The inevitable result was increased corruption and bribery, since the greatest of all traditional Confucian virtues was responsibility for one's own family. More and more, the rest of the Confucian morality disappeared as individuals and families strove simply to survive.

The Ming army did not distinguish itself in Korea. It drove the Japanese back but then was ambushed near Seoul, the Korean capital, and the rest of the campaign was largely a stalemate until Hideyoshi providentially died and his army promptly returned to Japan. A few years later, Matteo Ricci found the Ming army unimpressive: "All those under arms lead a despicable life, for they have not embraced this profession out of love of their country or love of honor but as men in the service of a provider of employment."[11] Many Chinese were now saying, "Good iron is not used for nails or good men for soldiers."

Much of the Ming army by this time was composed of ex-prisoners, drifters, former bandits, and idlers. Its size had doubled since the beginning of the dynasty, but its effectiveness had diminished sharply. Military contracts had become an open and expanding field for graft and corruption, and the quality of equipment and other supplies had deteriorated, as had military morale and leadership. One of the reasons for the failure to drive the Japanese out of Korea was what had become the inferiority of most Chinese weapons, including swords, spears, and guns. The Japanese had quickly noted and copied the Portuguese improvements in cannonry, and the development of an early version of the rifle, the harquebus, a cumbersome muzzle-loading weapon that was, however, devastating in close combat.

At the capital under the dissolute Emperor Wan-li, and progressively elsewhere in the empire, effectiveness and morale likewise declined. Despite Chang Chücheng's reforms, corruption had again removed much land and other wealth from the tax rolls, and the new taxes imposed by the eunuch Wei and his successors, together with a growing population, created widespread economic hardship and a rapid growth of tenancy, lawlessness, and regional famine. Banditry, local revolts, and secret societies, always a barometer of impending collapse, multiplied. There was open talk that the Ming had forfeited the Mandate of Heaven.

The incompetent government now faced two major revolts. A famine in Shensi (Shaanxi) in the northwest in 1628 led to arbitrary government economies instead of the needed relief. A postal clerk named Li Tzu-ch'eng (Li Zicheng) was laid off and joined his uncle, a bandit in the nearby mountains. Li and his forces raided widely among three or four adjoining provinces, attracted more followers, set up a government, distributed food to famine victims, appointed officials, and proclaimed a new dynasty. Early in 1644 he advanced on Peking, meeting only weak resistance. Hearing the news that the city had fallen, the last Ming emperor hanged himself in the palace garden, after failing to kill his oldest daughter with a sword.

A rival rebel leader named Chang (Zhang) had meanwhile been raiding and plundering much of northern China. In 1644 he invaded Szechuan, set up a government, and moved to claim the throne. His power plays and his terror tactics, however, lost him the support of the gentry, and without them his cause was lost. Neither Li nor Chang was fated to create a new dynasty; it came instead, as in Mongol times, from the steppe beyond the Great Wall.

# The Manchu Conquest

A non-Chinese steppe people, the Manchus, descendants of the Jurchen, had risen to power in Manchuria despite Ming efforts to keep them divided. A strong leader, Nurhachi (1559–1626), united several previously separate tribes and founded a Chinese-style state, taking the title of emperor and promoting the adoption of the Confucian system and its philosophy. His capital was established at Mukden (now called Shenyang) in southern Manchuria, where his two sons, also capable leaders, succeeded him and continued the Sinification of the Manchu state and culture.

By 1644 the Manchus were for all practical purposes politically and culturally indistinguishable from the Chinese, except for their spoken language. Their administration and army included large numbers of Chinese, who saw them as a coming power. The Manchus made vassals of the Mongols of Inner Mongolia and the Koreans after expeditions had conquered both. They were consciously building their power to take over China, and in 1644 they had their opportunity.

A Ming general invited the Manchu armies waiting on the border at Shan Hai Kuan to help him defeat Li Tzu-ch'eng, who with his army now occupied Peking. The Manchus did so and remained to found a new dynasty, rewarding a number of Chinese collaborators with grants of land. Some of these collaborators later rebelled but were suppressed in heavy fighting. Finally, in 1683 the new dynasty conquered the offshore island of Taiwan, which had clung to the defeated Ming cause, a situation with parallels in the twentieth century. It thus took nearly 40 years before the Manchu conquest was complete. Unlike the Mongols, however, the Manchus ushered in a long period of domestic peace and unprecedented prosperity.

The Manchus called their new dynasty Ch'ing (Qing), a title adopted by Nurhachi's son and continued by his grandson, K'ang Hsi (Kangxi, 1661–1722). *Ch'ing* means "pure," and the name was intended to add legitimacy to an alien rule. But the Manchus had learned their Chinese lessons well. They honored and continued the best of the imperial tradition and could plausibly represent themselves as liberators restoring China's glorious past. While this made them, like the Ming, conservative stewards rather than innovators and in time helped harden them against change, they too presided over a brilliant period in Chinese history for their first two centuries. Ch'ing was the China most westerners first knew well. Although already in its declining years in the nineteenth century, westerners still found it impressive, built as it was on the long foundation of imperial greatness that had preceded it.

*The Ming dynasty ended in ineptness and disgrace, but the positive aspects of its achievements were valued and preserved by its successors. Having begun with great vigor and success, the Ming went on to administer effectively for two centuries or more a new wave of prosperity, cultural growth, commercial and urban development, and the further refinement of taste. Popular culture, aided by cheap printing, enjoyed a notable boom, and in the larger cities rich merchants patronized and participated in elite culture. Although the dramatic maritime expeditions of Cheng Ho were abandoned, private Chinese trade multiplied with Southeast Asia, and domestic commerce thrived. Agriculture was made more productive, in part under state direction, and the population increased substantially. Ming Peking still stands as a monument to the dynasty's wealth and power. But the highly centralized system of government begun under Hung-wu helped sap administrative effectiveness under later and weaker emperors as power came increasingly into the hands of court eunuchs, with disastrous results. In the end the Ming dynasty was easy prey for the far better organized Manchus, who had learned the Confucian lessons that the Ming had forgotten.*

## Notes

1. J. K. Fairbank, E. O. Reischauer, and A. Craig, *East Asia: Tradition and Transformation* (Boston: Houghton Mifflin, 1989), p. 197.
2. Ibid., p. 182.
3. Ibid.
4. W. Bingham, H. Conroy, and F. Ikle, *A History of Asia*, vol. 1 (Boston: Allyn & Bacon, 1964), p. 459.
5. After W. McNaughton, *Chinese Literature: An Anthology* (Tokyo: Tuttle, 1959), pp. 697–698.
6. After H. C. Chang, *Chinese Literature* (Edinburgh: Edinburgh University Press, 1973), pp. 166–177.
7. J. W. von Goethe, *Conversations with Eckermann*, in J. Gernet, *A History of Chinese Civilization*, trans. J. R. Foster (Cambridge: Cambridge University Press, 1985), p. xxvii.
8. C. O. Hucker, *China's Imperial Past* (Stanford, Calif.: Stanford University Press, 1975), p. 373.
9. C. O. Hucker, *China to 1850* (Stanford, Calif.: Stanford University Press, 1980), p. 139.
10. Fairbank et al., p. 182.
11. J. Gernet, *History of Chinese Civilization*, p. 431.

## Suggestions for Further Reading

Berliner, N. *Chinese Folk Art*. Boston: Little, Brown, 1986.

Chang, S. H. *History and Legend: Ideas and Images in the Ming Historical Novels*. Ann Arbor: University of Michigan Press, 1990.

De Bary, W. T., et al. *Self and Society in Ming Thought*. New York: Columbia University Press, 1970.

Duyvendak, J. J. L. *China's Discovery of Africa*. London: Probsthain, 1949.

Eberhard, W. *Moral and Social Values of the Chinese*. Taipei: Chengwen Publishing Co., 1971.

Fairbank, J. K. *The Chinese World Order: Traditional China's Foreign Relations*. Cambridge: Harvard University Press, 1968.

Farmer, E. L. *Early Ming Government: The Evolution of Dual Capitals*. Cambridge, Mass.: Harvard University Press, 1976.

Gernet, J. *A History of Chinese Civilization*, trans. J. R. Foster. Cambridge: Cambridge University Press, 1985.

Hayden, G. *Crime and Punishment in Medieval Chinese Drama*. Cambridge, Mass.: Harvard University Press, 1978.

Huang, R. *Taxation and Government Finance in Sixteenth Century Ming China*. Cambridge, Mass.: Harvard University Press, 1974.

Hucker, C. O., ed. *Chinese Government in Ming Times*. New York: Columbia University Press, 1969.

Idema, W. L. *Chinese Vernacular Fiction*. Leiden: Brill, 1974.

Johnson, A., Nathan, A., and Rawski, E., eds. *Popular Culture in Late Imperial China*. Berkeley: University of California Press, 1985.

Lach, D. F. *China in the Eyes of Europe: The Sixteenth Century*. Chicago: University of Chicago Press, 1968.

Levenson, J. R. *European Expansion and the Counterexample of Asia, 1300–1600*. Englewood Cliffs, N.J.: Prentice Hall, 1967.

Loewe, M. *The Pride That Was China*. New York: St. Martin's Press, 1990.

Mote, F. W., and Twitchett, D., eds. *The Cambridge History of China*, Vol. 7: *The Ming*. Cambridge: Cambridge University Press, 1987.

Parsons, J. B. *The Peasant Rebellions of the Late Ming Dynasty*. Tucson: University of Arizona Press, 1970.

Rawski, E. S. *Agricultural Change and the Peasant Economy of South China*. Cambridge, Mass.: Harvard University Press, 1974.

Ricci, M. *China in the Sixteenth Century: The Journals of Matthew Ricci, 1583–1610*, trans. L. J. Gallagher. New York: Random House, 1953.

So, K. W. *Japanese Piracy in Ming China During the Sixteenth Century*. East Lansing: Michigan State University Press, 1975.

Struve, L. *The Southern Ming*. New Haven, Conn.: Yale University Press, 1984.

Van Gulik, R. *The Chinese Bell Murders*. Chicago: University of Chicago Press, 1984.

# The Societies of the Early Modern World

The richness and variety of the world's societies is abundantly revealed in the period of transition between the medieval and modern worlds that extends from approximately 1400 to 1800. Throughout the Western world in particular, social structures, behavioral patterns, and value systems underwent important changes that helped determine the character of today's societies. The institution of the family also altered, again mostly in the West, whereas in Asia the traditional family remained the bulwark of social hierarchy and stability. The age of women's rights lay in the future, but throughout the world women made significant contributions to their societies, sometimes by exercising political power at the highest levels of government. Women ruled, or were powers behind the throne, in societies as different as western Europe, Africa, and the Ottoman Empire.

**The dress and many of the pursuits of the aristocracy—such as hunting, lawn bowling, and formal afternoon promenades—set them apart from the other social classes. This is a detail from *Le Rendez-vous pour Marly* by Moreau le Jeune. [The Metropolitan Museum of Art, Harris Bisbane Dick Fund, 1933]**

The early modern period saw dramatic educational expansion in the West and a printing revolution in both the West and Asia. For the most part, neither Africa nor the Ottoman Empire effectively shared in these developments. Although patterns of trade became worldwide in the early modern period, most people lived at or near the subsistence level. To alleviate misery, Asians looked primarily to the family; Europeans, to religious, civic, and charitable institutions. In many respects, however, people responded to their social needs in similar ways, as reflected, for example, in the resort of the desperate in virtually all societies to banditry. This was particularly so in areas where governmental power was weak and resentment of urban wealth was strong. Beyond the threads of common human experience, however, differing value systems, rooted in religion and tradition, shaped early modern societies into distinct entities.

# Social Hierarchies

Traditional Asian civilizations were hierarchically based, marked not only by the uniquely Indian institution of caste but also by the status groupings associated with kinship, feudal-style relations, occupation, age, gender, and levels of literacy and learning. In general, apart from caste, the importance of the social hierarchy and the emphasis on achieving status through learning remains a distinctive aspect of Indian, Chinese, Korean, and Japanese civilizations to the present day. Perhaps more than any other characteristic, this emphasis on seeking status and advancement through education distinguishes them from most societies elsewhere. For many Asians, an individual's place in the hierarchy is still the most important single determinant of how to behave, and the proper observance of hierarchical rules remains the most basic means of preserving social and political harmony.

Southeast Asia has always been fundamentally different from China, Korea, India, and Japan, partly because of the influences of Buddhism and Islam, both of which stress equality, and partly because of the indigenous nature of Southeast Asian culture. Kingship and the hierarchies related to it, however, were common in Southeast Asia too.

## Caste and the Social Order in India

In contrast to the merit system of China and its variants in Vietnam, Korea, and Japan, caste was decreed by birth in India. Caste is a sociocultural practice with some religious concepts woven into it. Since it is also practiced by South Asian Muslims, Christians, and Buddhists (in Sri Lanka), it is clearly separable from Hinduism as a nonreligious system evolved later as a means of ordering an otherwise disordered society. The lack of a strong central state was accompanied by chronic disruption. Caste provided a system of social organization, a mutual-benefit society, a trade guild, and a sense of group identity. Ritual pollution and purity became the essence of caste, but its operative units were and are "subcastes," or *jatis*, commonly linked to occupation: potters, weavers, farmers, and so on. Each *jati* was and is endogamous (that is, it restricts marriage to fellow *jati* members), and members are forbidden to eat with or accept food or water from members of other *jatis*. One cannot change one's caste any more than one can change the place where one was born, although caste distinctions seem not to have been observed rigidly until relatively late in Indian history, well after the time of Harsha (seventh century A.D.). However, it has always been possible to escape from caste through religious devotion, again underlining the nonreligious nature of the caste system. The ascetic sadhu, or holy man, was beyond caste and honored by all, regardless of his earthly origins. Such mystics were, and like priests remain, far more numerous in India than elsewhere. South Asians have known for many centuries which *jati* they were born into, but this is not really part of their religion, any more than ancestry, social class, or occupation is for Christians in the West.

Caste has remained a highly flexible system. Although individuals are born into a given *jati*, by sustained group effort the members of a *jati* can raise its status, often by adopting religious, dietary, and other practices of higher-status groups. This process is called "Sanskritization," from the use of Sanskrit rituals associated with the Brahmins. In addition, the power of group action can be a potent weapon, especially in politics. This is particularly characteristic of Asian societies, where the individual is important primarily as a member of a group, be it family, clan, caste, guild, or regional or linguistic division.

Caste also served the need for some form of hierarchical order in a region of complex divisions. As new religions, cultures, and languages came into India, no single one emerged as permanently dominant. In this bewildering context caste provided a sense of group identity, a means of support and defense, and a cultural vehicle as well, since each caste was necessarily local and shared a common language. Occupational associations for most subcastes meant that they also functioned as the equivalent of guilds and mutual-help societies, serving to arbitrate disputes. Caste was less a matter of religious than of social ordering, and the hierarchy it entailed was perhaps less important than the day-to-day support it gave and the social mobility it made possible for group members.

# ◉ Aristocratic Behavior in Japan ◉

*The importance of hierarchical order in Japan is revealed in this 1615 decree of a shogun regulating the behavior of the feudal lords, or dai-myo, and their retainers, the* samurai. *Note the obligation to be aristo-crats rather than mere soldiers.*

Literature, arms, archery, and horsemanship are to be the favorite pursuits. Literature first, and arms next to it, was the rule of the ancients. They must both be cultivated concur-rently. . . . Drinking parties and gambling amusements must be kept within due bounds. . . . Offenders against the law are not to be harbored in the feudal domains. Law is the very foundation of ceremonial decorum and of social order. To infringe the law in the name of reason is as bad as to outrage reason in the name of the law. . . .

The distinction between lord and vassal, between superior and inferior, must be clearly marked by apparel. Vassals may not . . . wear silk stuffs. . . . Miscellaneous persons are not at their own pleasure to ride in palanquins. . . . Lately even sub-vassals and henchmen of no rank have taken to so riding. This is a flagrant impertinence. . . . The *samurai* through-out the provinces are to practice frugality. Those who are rich like to make a display, while those who are poor are ashamed of not being on a par with others. There is no in-fluence so pernicious as this, and it must be kept strictly in check. . . .

*Source:* D. Lach, *Asia on the Eve of Europe's Expansion* (Englewood Cliffs, N.J.: Prentice Hall, 1965), pp. 157–160 passim.

## Social Hierarchy in East Asia

Despite the uniqueness of caste, Indian society con-formed in other respects to the dominant Asian social model, of which China is the principal example. Under the empire in China, which lasted from the third century B.C. to 1911, power, responsibility, and status formed a pyramidal structure, with the emperor at the top as a truly absolute monarch. Below him were appointed of-ficials in a series of grades: councillors, provincial gov-ernors, and generals, down to the district magistrates in some 2,000 counties, all of whom were selected from the ranks of the scholar-gentry who had passed the third level of the imperial examinations.

But this was not merely a political pyramid, and it did not act alone. The emperor and his officials had as their highest duty the setting of a good example, of "virtuous conduct." They were seen, and saw themselves, as fath-ers to the people, since the family was the basis of social order in all of Asia to an even greater extent than in most other societies. In theory, if the emperor and his officials behaved properly and responsibly, others in the social hierarchy would do so as well. In practice, social order—in Chinese parlance, the "Great Harmony"—was pre-served primarily by the family system; this operated in much the same way in the rest of Asia. Younger people deferred to their elders, wives to husbands, and social "inferiors" to "superiors." This was the Confucian for-mula for human happiness and social harmony, but it was accepted in Hindu and Muslim India, too, as well as in Korea and Japan as Confucianism spread.

## Social Hierarchy in Europe

Europeans likewise attached a great deal of significance to a hierarchical society, which they believed was or-dained by both divine and natural law. Civic and reli-gious leaders alike insisted that the duty of each person was to accept his or her place in the social order, an ideal intended to promote social stability and domestic tran-quillity. The hierarchical societies of early modern Eu-rope were not, however, structured according to a class system in which groups were defined by similar levels of income and lifestyles, as in the modern West. In the early modern period the common basis of aristocratic power—landed wealth and the control of labor—was modified by the source of one's wealth, the antiquity of one's title, and the number of armed and paid retainers at one's disposal. A noble, though possibly not as rich as an urban businessman, outranked the latter in pres-tige—so much so that business families often tried to marry their daughters to landed aristocrats as a means of enhancing their social status.

The European system was divided, though less formally than in Asia, into *estates,* or social groups defined by degrees of fixed status, that is, by the dignity and respect with which each group was regarded by society in general. The aristocratic estate was generally expected to possess significant wealth in order to fulfill its social function as leader, exemplar, local ruler, maintainer of order, and reliever of the poor. Whereas in Asia many of these functions resided primarily with the family, in Europe—and among the Aztecs in Mexico—they were largely the province of the aristocracy. It was the duty of the lower orders, both religious and political, to accept the rule of the upper, though in reality there was often resentment and occasionally rebellion. Good behavior demanded deference to superiors, courtesy to equals, and kindness to inferiors. More was expected of, but also tolerated from, the higher orders, where gentility was supposed to entail a combination of birth, breeding, and virtue.

There are some parallels between social hierarchy in the East and the West, including the importance attached to the idea that status entailed responsibility. Europeans too used the analogy of paternal authority to justify monarchical power, especially in the 1600s, but never to the same degree as in Asia, where the family exercised a greater role in the maintenance of social order. In the West the function of the extended family in this regard declined in the early modern period as the emphasis gradually shifted to the nuclear family on the one hand and the state on the other. With the general exception of the Dutch, both Europeans and Asians tried to reinforce the social hierarchy by reserving distinctive styles of dress for the upper orders.

In Europe social distinctions were also reflected in numerous other ways, such as the number of a noble's retainers or clients or the number of coaches in his procession. Even funerals were distinctive pageants designed to reflect the social status of the deceased and their families.

The privileged life of the European aristocracy is reflected in Peter Paul Rubens' portrait of Marchesa Brigida Spinola Doria (1606) clad in a sumptuous gown. [National Gallery of Art, Washington, Samuel H. Kress Collection]

## The European Aristocracy

Prior to the mid-sixteenth century, the aristocracy generally improved its social position and became more involved in public affairs at the local or state level. Most nobility strove to acquire more land, usually by strategic marriages, or greater status, normally by obtaining more elevated titles of nobility. To meet the demand for status, titles such as duke, marquis, and viscount were created, and new chivalric orders, including the Knights of the Garter in England and the Order of the Golden Fleece in Burgundy, were founded. New nobles were usually recruited from the landed gentry (the lesser aristocracy) rather than the bourgeoisie (the upper merchant and professional class), especially in France and England. On the Continent an administrative aristocracy devel-

oped in the early modern period. In France and Milan, for example, officials acquired aristocratic privileges and became known as the nobility of the robe, after their gown of office.

Conditions among the gentry varied widely. Whereas the more successful among them could be as wealthy and powerful as some nobles, others, especially on the Continent, sometimes turned to banditry to improve their sagging fortunes. A notorious gang of English robbers followed the lead of two lesser aristocrats, Sir William Bussy and Sir John de Colseby, while in France similar groups tried unsuccessfully in 1560 to end the political dominance of the Guise family, the head of which, the duke of Guise, was the king's chief adviser. Disaffected knights often supported reform movements, including Lutheranism in Germany and Calvinism in France, hoping to better their position.

Beginning in the mid-sixteenth century, the aristocracy entered a period of difficulty. Incomes from landed estates did not keep pace with excessive expenditures on elaborate dress, rich food, fine jewelry, lavish hospitality, and luxurious buildings. Some governments, especially in France and Spain, pressed the nobility for cash to repay war debts. Raising funds by selling land only reduced the income from rents. Nor did rents keep pace with the rising cost of living due to inflation, especially since many rents were fixed by custom, and in some areas tenants held long-term leases. The position of the aristocracy was further undermined by the growing reliance of governments on talent rather than rank, though no Western country came close to establishing a meritocracy such as existed in China.

The prestige of the older aristocracy was harmed when sovereigns in France, Spain, and England sold titles to raise funds and accommodate the demand for status among newly wealthy elites. The upper aristocracy normally suffered more from these problems than the lower; in England much of the gentry improved their position in this period through careful land management, advantageous marriages, and the purchase of lands from the monasteries dissolved during the Reformation.

## Urban Society

The social eminence of urban merchants, or patricians, stemmed from their involvement with long-distance trade, their ownership of city property, and their control of town government. Patricians intermarried to preserve the exclusiveness of their privileges, though some married off their daughters to aristocrats merely to acquire the unique prestige that went with ownership of the land. Townsfolk treated the patricians as a noble class, particularly in republican Venice, where the absence of a monarch or a landed aristocracy elevated their status. In the Netherlands and the German states too the wealthy patricians were virtually a noble class, though their supremacy was disputed by the landed nobility. In Russia the growth of an autonomous bourgeoisie was delayed by the feudal structure of that society.

In contrast to the patricians, the guildsmen continued, as in the medieval era, to concern themselves primarily with local production and services. In most towns they had considerably less influence than the patricians but were better off than the artisans and unskilled workers, who were poorly organized and had little voice in town government. Only by joining with the guildsmen could the artisans and laborers bring about change. Another urban group, the lawyers, found their services in increased demand as commerce expanded, land transactions became more complex, and landowners sought ways to evade the fiscal payments that were still part of feudal land tenure. Together these middling and upper urban groups began insisting on a greater share of political power in early modern Europe, particularly in France and England, where their demands contributed to the outbreak of civil war in both countries in the 1640s.

## Marriage and the Family

Throughout the early modern world, the family was the basic unit of social organization. The western European aristocracy began to distinguish itself in this period by moving away from the extended family, which remained common in Asia and Africa, toward the conjugal or nuclear family, which was probably already the norm among the lower social orders in Europe. Although family structures varied substantially between Muslims and some Africans and Amerindians, with their polygamous marriages, and Asia and Europe, where monogamy prevailed, all societies valued children for a variety of reasons, including, among the lower orders especially, their function as laborers and eventually as providers for elderly parents. Protestant Europe, by establishing the principle of divorce as we now understand it, planted the seeds for the eventual weakening of the family as the fundamental social unit.

## The Family in Asia

The Asian family was a hierarchical structure in which group welfare took precedence over individual preferences. The father was like a little emperor, with absolute power but also with absolute responsibility. Filial obedience was the cardinal Asian virtue; loyalty and obligation to parents and elders was rigid and inflexible, but it produced a tight-knit unit. In family relations age was the major determinant. Three generations commonly lived under one roof, and the grandfather was thus the dominant figure, although his place might be taken after his death by his widow. Younger sons were subject to their older brothers, wives and sisters to their husbands and brothers, and all to the eldest male. Individual initiative other than by the patriarch was not tolerated; the welfare of the family as he interpreted it came first, and all decisions were accordingly made by the elder members.

A new Asian bride was the servant of the husband's family and was often victimized by a tyrannical mother-in-law. More so than in the West, Asian girls could be married against their wishes and had little or no right of refusal—except suicide. An entire genre of Asian stories was devoted to this theme. In a typical story, an unwilling bride is carried in an enclosed cart or sedan chair to her new husband's family; when the curtains are opened, she is found to have killed herself. Marriage was seen as a business arrangement between families, not as an individual choice or a love match. In later centuries the custom of foot-binding spread through the Chinese population, inflicting dreadful pain on growing girls and emphasizing their role as erotic playthings while reducing them to a hobble that effectively kept them at home. About the same period, the practice of purdah, the veiling and sequestering of women, spread with the Muslim conquerors even through Hindu northern India.

Few Asians questioned the family hierarchy. The family operated as a collective entity; each member was both socially and legally responsible for the behavior of all other members. Collective responsibility, family pride, and the shame of family disgrace are still credited for the relatively low rate of crime in much of Asia. Government from higher levels was far less necessary. Asian societies have been called self-regulating, and to a very large extent that is true. The price of this has been the sacrifice of individual initiative, independence, and self-fulfillment so prized by the modern West and now increasingly attractive in many parts of modern Asia.

Individuals moved through life only as members of families, as did members of larger groups such as castes, clans, or guilds. Yet there was a surprising amount of vertical mobility in Chinese society. Judging from the numerous biographies of successful examination candidates, as many as a third of the gentry group in each generation represented new blood. In Asian countries families and sometimes villages, clans, or guilds squeezed their resources to support promising boys through the lengthy education needed for entry to the scholarly ranks, in effect as their representative and as one who could bring prestige and profit.

The larger society offered few support mechanisms. Without a family or descendants to care for them, the sick, the poor, and the elderly could not survive. In the Hindu and Buddhist countries minimal shelter and food were available to all at temples, as they still are, but in all of Asia the production of offspring, especially sons, was the overriding goal for simple self-preservation. People who did well in life were bound to help not only siblings but also uncles, aunts, cousins, and their families.

The bonds of obligation and collective responsibility reached throughout the extended family, which in Asia included all paternal and maternal relatives, or at least those with whom a given nuclear family was in touch. Each Asian society had a complex variety of name designations for each of these graded kin relationships; one did not refer merely to "brother," "sister," "uncle," "aunt," or "grandmother" but to elder or younger brother, first, second, or third paternal aunt, maternal

grandfather, and so on. This extended network of relationships put a heavy burden on individuals but also provided mutual support.

## The Family in Europe

Extended family linkages were important in Europe as well at the level of the aristocracy, where patterns of ownership, inheritance, and status were complex. Below this level the conjugal or nuclear family was a more or less self-contained unit. Except in eastern Europe, most couples married late, in their mid-twenties, by which time they were usually in a position to establish their own households. A widowed parent might subsequently take up residence with a married child, in contrast with the Asian practice of newlyweds moving in with the bridegroom's parents. The prevalence of the nuclear family pattern at the lower social levels was disadvantageous in the sense that mistreated spouses received less kin support, and smaller family units were more vulnerable to economic hardship if a spouse became unemployed.

The large family network common in Asia provided an important support system that commoners in the West often lacked. Conversely, however, the smaller family units in the West presumably made it easier for many couples to make the personal adjustments necessary for a successful marriage without the intervention of relatives and in-laws.

The nature of the Western family underwent a significant change in the sixteenth and seventeenth centuries, particularly among the aristocracy. The late medieval aristocratic family, in return for loyalty and personal attendance by its retainers and servants, provided patronage and hospitality. The aristocratic household was large because it included not only family members and relatives but also a collection of servants and retainers that might number in the hundreds. The importance of preserving the family's status and property led to the practice of the arranged marriage. Often a young person had no choice in the determination of a partner, for matrimony was a collective decision of the family and kin in which the key issues were property and power. Protestant reformers generally favored the arranged marriage as a means to discourage young people from selecting spouses on the basis of sexual attraction. Some parents allowed their children a veto over the proposed spouse, and occasionally headstrong young people defied the system by eloping, but only at the risk of losing their inheritance. Young men's acceptance of the arranged marriage was aided by the knowledge that once an heir was born, mistresses could be enjoyed. There was a double standard, however, for wives were denied such freedom and were expected to remain sexually loyal to their husbands.

An arranged marriage, in this instance between the son of a financially strapped nobleman and the daughter of a wealthy merchant hungry for social prestige, is the subject of one of the scenes from William Hogarth's series of six paintings titled *Marriage à la Mode* (1744–1745). [National Gallery, London]

Daughters were often an economic liability among the propertied classes since a dowry had to be provided for marriage; in turn, the groom's father guaranteed the bride an annuity if her husband died before she did. As heirs and potential fathers of future heirs, firstborn sons usually married earlier than other young men. In sixteenth-century England men normally wed at about age 28, but aristocratic heirs typically married at 22 in order to facilitate property settlements and enhance the prospects of providing a male heir in the next generation. Because a younger son had considerably less property and wealth than his elder brother, who benefited in England and parts of western Europe from the practice of primogeniture (bequeathing a landed estate to the eldest son), he faced a decline in social position unless he could find a wealthy bride.

About the middle of the sixteenth century the nature of the family began to change among the upper social orders. On the one hand, more significance was attached to the nuclear core (parents and children), and on the other, affection between spouses apparently became more important as a determinant of family relationships. The decline of kinship dominance was manifested in both decreasing hospitality and the diminishing sense of kin responsibility for individual acts. As states such as France, Spain, and England expanded their control of justice, protection, and the preservation of property, the responsibility for social control shifted from kin to state. Simultaneously, Protestantism increased the significance of the nuclear family by stressing marital affection and by treating the family as a miniature parish, with distinct religious responsibilities in instruction and worship. These changes brought about a greater and greater divergence from the Asian model and its associated lack of state control.

In contrast to the modern nuclear family, patriarchal authority was reinforced. The Renaissance state supported the domination of the husband-father on the grounds that his authority was analogous to that of a sovereign over his subjects. The decline of kinship could increase the wife's subordination to her husband by leaving her more exposed to exploitation in the nuclear family. Capitalizing on this, the state relied on husbands to keep their wives law-abiding. Yet the development of the nuclear family could also facilitate better relations between spouses by providing them with more time to be alone, away from the prying eyes of relatives, retainers, and servants.

## Marriage in Asia

In the societies of early modern Asia marital patterns were similar in many ways to those in Europe, particularly with respect to the arranged marriage, the premium placed on sons, and the use of dowries, although considerably less so in areas such as divorce and remarriage. In Asia, however, the average age at marriage was lower than in the West—approximately 21 for males and 17 for females in China; 16 and 14, respectively, in India; and 20 and 16 in Japan and Southeast Asia.

Except for parts of Southeast Asia and a small region of South India, marriage was and remains patrilocal; that is, the bride, who was almost invariably recruited from

## ⊚ "Surplus" Daughters ⊚

*In the eyes of both Asians and Europeans, daughters were much less de-*
*sirable than sons. To avoid the expense of providing dowries, Catholic*
*parents sometimes sought to dispose of "surplus" daughters by coercing*
*them into becoming nuns. Some clergymen strongly protested this*
*practice.*

You have no right to dispose of your children by forcing a vocation on them. . . . It would
cost money to establish this daughter: reason enough to consecrate her as a nun. . . . But
she has no trace of religious calling: the present state of your finances is calling enough for
her. . . . And so the victim is led to the temple, hands and feet tied: by which I mean
against her will, dumb with fear and awe of a father whom she has always honored. Such
murderous fathers are far from imitating Abraham . . . who was ready to sacrifice his son
to God: instead they sacrifice their children to their own estate and to their own cupidity.

*Source:* L. Bourdaloue, *Œuvres complètes*, in *Collection intégrale et universelle des orateurs sacrés*, vol. 15
(Paris, 1845), cols. 374 ff.; English translation in *Not in God's Image*, ed. J. O'Faolain and L. Martines (New
York: Harper Torchbooks, 1973), p. 270.

another village to avoid inbreeding, left her family and
became a member of her husband's family, where she
was the lowest-status member until she had borne a son.
She might visit her parents occasionally, but she was lost
to them as a family member and cost them heavily in
dowry. Girls were often loved as much as boys, but on
practical grounds they were of far less value, although
they were desirable domestic helpers to their mothers.
Sons were essential for family continuity and security.
Since life was an uncertain business and death rates
were high, especially in the early years of life, most families tried to produce more than one son. Girls might be
sold in hard times as servants or concubines in rich
households.

The childless family was truly bankrupt and might
even pay relatively large sums to acquire a son by adoption. A wife who failed to produce a son after a reasonable amount of time was commonly returned to her parents as useless, for the primary purpose of marriage was
perpetuation of the male line. It was not understood until
quite recently that the sex of a child is determined by
the father or that childlessness may result as often from
male as from female sterility. In time, however, most
women became willing and even enthusiastic members
of their husbands' families, passing on these attitudes to
their children. Eventually they might become household
heads and oldest survivors, thereby sometimes achieving considerable power.

All members of the society regarded marriage as a
contract between families for the furthering of their interests. Virtually all marriages were arranged by the

families, usually through a go-between. Bride and groom
had usually not met before their wedding. Sometimes
they might be allowed to express preferences, although
these might be overruled in the family interest. Compatibility was rarely considered, and love marriages
were extremely rare, although affection might grow in
time.

There was a similar willingness to suppress individual
wishes among the Inca of South America, where state
officials chose mates for young people slow to act on
their own. At times the Inca arranged mass marriages.
The rulers themselves could marry only their sisters,
making the royal family a product of considerable
inbreeding.

## Divorce in Asia and Europe

Divorce was rare in Asia, difficult but not impossible.
Unlike the West, remarriage was even more difficult,
and that knowledge probably helped people try harder
to make their marriages work. It doubtless helped too
that romantic expectations were not as high as in the
modern West. People were trained to put individual
wants second to family interest. Biographies, memoirs,
popular literature, and legal records bear out that most
marriages were successful on these terms and that husbands and wives valued and even loved each other and
worked together in the family unit to reproduce the dominant social pattern. Divorce was relatively rare in the
Islamic world as well.

There was no divorce in the modern sense in the medieval West since the canon law of the Catholic church deemed marriage an unbreakable sacrament. If the existence of an impediment or bar to a marriage could be demonstrated, the marriage could be annulled, but any children resulting from the union were thereby made illegitimate. Annulments were granted in such cases as marriage to relatives or in-laws, impotence, or forced marriage. The only other alternative, separation, did not bastardize the children, but neither did it leave the spouses free to remarry. In cases of wife beating, church and state courts in Spain and France permitted legal separation.

The Reformation reduced the grounds for annulment but established divorce in the modern sense in some areas, including the Lutheran states, Zurich, and Geneva. Catholic states retained the medieval canon law, with its absolute prohibition of divorce, until modern times, apart from a brief period during the age of the French Revolution and Napoleon. Among Europe's poor, some unhappy spouses ran away; others committed bigamy. From the medieval period into the nineteenth century a dissatisfied husband in England occasionally put a halter around his wife's neck, took her to the local cattle market, and sold her. The practice underscored the notion that a wife was the property of her husband, although common law never recognized this. In rural Greece well into the twentieth century, a bride might simply be returned to her family if she was discovered or believed to have lost her virginity before marriage.

## Marriage and the Family in Africa

Like the Muslims, Aztecs, and Inca, many African tribes practiced polygamy. A man demonstrated his wealth by having several wives, although in reality women, who typically worked beside men, produced so much by their labor that they virtually supported themselves. The perception of wealth was derived from the fact that a man had to pay "bridewealth"—usually livestock—to a woman's father in order to marry her. As in western Europe, men married relatively late, usually about the age of 30, though brides were typically in their late teens. A new wife would be added at fairly regular intervals of a year or two, and because of the importance attached to fertility, the result was normally a large family.

The high birthrate helped offset the large number of deaths of infants and children and also ensured support for parents in their old age, an ideal no less valued in Asia. Like the early Hebrews, many Africans accepted the practice of leviratic marriage, by which the brother of a deceased man married the widow. In the African family no function was more important for the wife than bearing children, but beyond that she exercised a critical role in providing the food supply and in some instances even conducting local and regional trade.

## The Status of Women

Although many women might have had powers within the family, their role in general was subordinate. There is no question that theirs was a male-dominated world and that their chief claim to status was as breeders of sons. They were less valued from birth virtually everywhere. Females were subject first to their fathers and brothers, then to their husbands and their husbands' male relatives. A new bride was under the authority most directly of her mother-in-law, who was sometimes tyrannical. A wife's status in her husband's family rose only when she produced a son. In time she became a mother-in-law herself, often the role of true power in the family.

## Women in Asia

Much is revealed about the status of women in Asian countries by examining the fate of widows. Unlike their counterparts in the West, Asian widows were not supposed to remarry or even to have male friends. Given the high death rate and the unpredictable fortunes of life, many women—often no more than girls—were thus condemned to celibacy, loneliness, and poverty for most of their lives. "Chaste widows" were praised, and though some managed a little life of their own, most conformed to the expected model and suffered. Some widows committed suicide in China and in the Islamic world; this was carried to its extreme in India, where it often came to be expected among the higher castes. Hindu funeral practice includes the burning of the corpse; a surviving widow was supposed to throw herself on her husband's funeral pyre, a ritual known as *sati* (suttee). Perhaps as many as one-fifth of all childless Indian upper-caste widows actually sacrificed themselves in this way.

As in the West, in hard times female infants might be killed soon after birth so that the rest of the family might survive; Asian female babies could also be sold as servants or potential concubines. The selling of children seems especially heartless, but such a girl might have a better life as a slave-servant or concubine in a wealthy household than starving to death with her own family. Women were rarely given any formal education, and although some acquired it, they were primarily instructed by their mothers and mothers-in-law in how to be good, subservient wives, mothers, and daughters-in-law.

Power within the family brought women rewards that were especially important in this family-centered society. Their key role in ensuring family continuity brought much satisfaction. In most families women, as the chief raisers of children, shaped the future. More directly, they managed most families' finances, as they still do in Asia. Some women achieved public prominence as writers, reigning empresses, and powers behind the throne as imperial consorts or concubines. In India, China, and Southeast Asia, as in England and Scotland, a few women became rulers in their own right, such as the T'ang empress Wu. But only in India could one find women who were brilliant generals and cavalry fighters, such as the Rani of Jhansi. Admittedly, these were a tiny handful within Asia and Europe as a whole. In East and West alike, the crucial role of women in what mattered most—the family, its well-being, and its perpetuation—was, within clear status limits, recognized. Among the peasantry, the overwhelming mass of the population, women played a crucial role in helping with the agricultural labor and were usually the major workers in cottage industries, producing handicraft goods for sale or barter. Upper-class women lived a generally idle life and commonly turned their children over to nurses or tutors.

It remained for the twentieth century, spurred by Western influence, to discourage the traditional subjugation of women in Asia and begin the movement toward equality, or at least more equitable treatment. Southeast Asia has traditionally been freer of sex discrimination than India, China, Korea, or Japan, and most of its regional cultures included some matrilocal marriage, female control and inheritance of property, and female dominance within the family. In the rest of Asia the traditional patterns were formed 4,000 years ago and persisted largely unchanged until this century. (See Chapters 39 and 40.)

## Women in the Middle East and Africa

In the Islamic societies of the Middle East and North Africa, women were discouraged from participating in activities outside the home by the conviction that females should be secluded as well as veiled. The latter practice was obviously a practical way of enforcing anonymity on them when they did appear in public. Women who engaged in trade or educational pursuits were rare exceptions. As in Asian cultures, the woman's primary task was to marry and raise children, especially boys.

Religion was used, as in the West, to legitimate the subordination of women. This point was succinctly stated by a seventeenth-century Iranian theologian, who asserted that a wife's principal spiritual duty was subservience to her husband: "A wife must obey her husband, never disobey his commands, never leave the house without his permission." As early as the 1200s Islamic society was characterized by a separate social

life for men and women, though a small number of women were sometimes able to exert political power in both Ottoman Turkey and Safavid Iran.

In sub-Saharan Africa some tribal societies accorded prominent roles to women. In contrast to the Western world, West African tribes such as the Igbo and the Yoruba in Nigeria were organized on a "dual sex" system in which each sex governed its own affairs at all levels of society. One group of Igbo was ruled by dual monarchs, one female and the other male, each with its own advisory group. The female monarch, or *omu* (literally "mother"), was different from a queen in the Western sense, for she was neither the king's wife nor the reigning daughter of a deceased king who had no male heir. The *omu* represented all women and had special responsibility for the marketplace. Igbo women also had their own organizations at the village level, which functioned as political pressure groups.

Although most African societies were dominated by men, there were important exceptions. Women, for instance, could be chiefs among some of the tribes of West Africa. A number of other West African tribes followed the custom of female descent, by which the throne descended not to the king's son but to the son of his sister. In precolonial African societies, which had no permanent political structure, important matters were routinely decided by a meeting of the heads of households, but because women rarely exercised this responsibility, they were not prominent in making community decisions.

The subordinate role of most African women was underscored by the predominance of patrilineal and patrilocal customs, which traced lineage through the male line and required brides to live in the villages of their husbands. There were exceptions, such as the Senufo of West Africa, whose wives could remain in their native villages and whose divorced women retained custody of the children because the latter belonged to the maternal kin. Generally, however, the traditional African societies treated women as the economic and social dependents of males, as elsewhere.

## Women in Europe

In late medieval Europe aristocratic women were regarded largely as bearers of children, sexual companions, and comrades in social functions. Few administered family estates or raised their own children, a task left to nurses and tutors. Nurturing an infant was turned over to a wet nurse, typically a peasant woman hired for the occasion and often blamed for subsequent medical or psychological problems. Wet nursing freed the mother from the inconvenience of nighttime feeding, it did not interrupt her social engagements, and it permitted her to serve the father's sexual appetites, as nursing mothers tended to shun intercourse for fear that breast feeding would starve an embryo. However, wet-nursing declined sharply in the 1700s.

Aristocratic women had relatively little to occupy their time apart from such leisurely pursuits as reading, social visits, cardplaying, and theatergoing, especially since many had stewards to run their households as well as nurses and tutors to care for their children. However, women of the landed gentry often played a major role in the household economy and managed the family estates when their husbands were away. Because of her social status, a gentlewoman or a merchant's wife had little choice of occupation, for manual labor was incompatible with her position, and the professions were closed to women. Some became ladies-in-waiting to aristocratic women, some governesses of children, and a few, such as the English dramatists Aphra Behn and Susan Centilivre, authors. Two aristocratic English women—Margaret Cavendish, duchess of Newcastle, and Anne, Viscountess Conway—wrote about the new science, and Katherine Boyle, sister of the chemist Robert Boyle, took an active part in it. Some women, such as Judith Leycester (1609–1660) of the Netherlands and Artemisia Gentileschi (1593–c. 1652) of Italy, were accomplished painters. Catholics, of course, had the option of joining a convent or a teaching order.

Near the lower levels of society, the wives of craftsmen and peasants had to labor with their husbands to survive, for most Europeans lived at or near subsistence. As in Asia, Africa, and the Americas, peasant women engaged in virtually every aspect of farming from plowing and spreading manure to reaping and threshing and also handled the household chores and cared for any poultry or dairy animals. In both urban and rural areas many wives supplemented the family income by weaving or other side employments, occasionally even prostitution.

Late medieval craft guilds allowed masters' wives to share in their work, and they often carried on the business when the men died. Although women had been admitted to the guilds, the new forms of business organization were almost exclusively male, and there was mounting hostility to women in the trades because they worked for lower pay. Apart from the cloth industry, women were being pushed out of many trades, such as brewing, at one time largely a female preserve. In England men even moved into the occupation of midwife. Women could practice folk medicine and compete with barber-surgeons, but they were generally excluded from the professions of physician, attorney, and minister. Although women found it increasingly difficult to compete for jobs in most trades, they found employment in the cottage industry concerned with cloth manufacturing, but the pay was poor and the hours long. Life was also difficult for single women. Some worked in the coal and iron mines, where they typically received lower

A self-portrait of the Dutch artist Judith Leycester, one of the most prominent women painters of the seventeenth century. [National Gallery of Art, Washington, gift of Mr. and Mrs. Robert Woods Bliss]

wages than their male peers. Most single women earned their living by spinning yarn, a practice that gave rise to the term *spinster* for an unmarried woman.

In certain respects the legal position of European women declined in the late medieval period. French women could no longer participate in public affairs, testify before various courts, or even act in place of an absentee or insane husband. The laws of Saxony and England prohibited women from undertaking legal actions; an English wife had to be represented by her husband, while a Hamburg statute of 1603 stipulated that "women can neither bring a matter up before the court nor transfer or hand over property without a guardian." Bavarian law prohibited a woman from selling anything without her husband's consent, though beginning in 1616 an exception was made for goods specified for her personal use. In England a husband enjoyed absolute control over his wife's personal property and could profit by leasing her real estate to others.

In the seventeenth century, however, marriage contracts guaranteed the wife "pin money" for her personal expenses, and the courts increasingly recognized the existence of her "separate estate," a handy device if her husband was sued for bankruptcy. French courts similarly began to demonstrate greater concern for a wife's rights, including control over her dowry. A French wife whose husband mismanaged her property could win a legal separation, the most she could expect in a society without divorce. By the eighteenth century Russian noblewomen and the wives of artisans and merchants became the heads of their households when their husbands died, although only in urban areas. Legally, then, the decline in women's rights bottomed out in Europe in the 1500s and improved slowly in the seventeenth and eighteenth centuries.

## Sexual Customs

Sexual customs give us insight into cultural values and provide a benchmark for tracking changes in those values up to modern times. For example, Asian women have always been expected to be modest and chaste. They seldom appeared in public, and any open display of affection with their spouses was taboo. At the same time, the elite Asian cultures, unlike those in the West, are famous for their erotic literature and art and for the development of a courtesan (prostitute) tradition older than any other living civilization. The geisha tradition of Japan and its original, the "singsong" or "flower boat" women of China, are well known, as is the cult of ritual sex among Indian temple priestesses and the orgies of Tantric Buddhism. Explicit portrayals of sex appear in Indian art, and the classic Indian sex manual, the *Kamasutra*, is world famous. But this behavior was reserved for the privileged few.

In contrast to the Judeo-Christian West, India, Tibet, and parts of Southeast Asia had a religious tradition in which sex was used as ritual, in some ways rather like the ancient cult of Dionysus in classical Greece. Representations of sex in Indian sculpture and painting use gods and goddesses as subjects, not ordinary mortals, and celebrate the divine life force, creation. Tantric Buddhist and some Hindu temple sex rites had the same purpose. Western art, beginning in the Renaissance, was less explicit than Indian art but depicted sensuous nudes in the guise of classical deities. All of this—the pleasures of the elite dallying with their concubines, singsong girls, erotic pictures, and the joys of Islamic rulers in their harems—was beyond the experience of the lower social orders, although at least in the West they might find an outlet for their sexual desires in traditional festivals, such as May Day or, in Asia, other celebrations, when promiscuous behavior was reportedly common.

A relationship between sex and religious ritual existed in some African societies, especially in connection with puberty rites. The Kikuyu, who lived in the region of Mount Kenya, not only circumcised boys as part of

such rites but also removed the clitoris from girls. This practice is still widespread in eastern Africa today. In both cases the act of cutting symbolized the rite of passage into adulthood. In the case of the Masai, however, puberty initiation for girls involved elongating the labia by massage and teaching the girls movements to enhance their sexual performance.

Figure of a dancing woman, in painted pottery, from a T'ang dynasty tomb. The elaborate dress and hairstyle and the long floppy sleeves suggest that the figure represented a courtesan-dancer. It was from T'ang China that the Japanese imported much of their culture, and here is, in effect, the origin of the Japanese geisha. [The Nelson-Atkins Museum of Art, Kansas City, Missouri (Nelson Fund)]

European attitudes toward sex were generally determined by the teachings of the church, although these were often merely a veneer imposed on centuries of folk custom and were frequently ignored. For the masses of East and West, sex appears to have been largely oriented toward procreation and usually confined officially to marriage or engagement, although Japanese, Southeast Asian, and Polynesian young people of both sexes were encouraged to experiment with sex before marriage. In the eyes of the medieval Christian church, sexual relations were acceptable only within marriage and were intended primarily for procreation. Little attention was attached to love in a sexual context, and lust was condemned.

During the Reformation, Protestants began to treat love and procreation as related and to regard sexual pleasure in marriage as a legitimate expression of the conjugal relationship. Among the propertied orders, sexual relations before marriage were regarded with disapproval, largely because of the importance of bearing a legitimate heir. Because a woman was regarded as the sexual property of a man, her value diminished if she had been "used" by another male. Despite the church's official disapproval, males of the propertied elite frequently engaged in premarital sex, normally with women from professional or merchant backgrounds whose families had fallen on hard times. The same freedom did not extend to women of their rank. A woman's honor was based on her reputation for chastity, a man's on his word. A wife who committed adultery insulted not only her husband's virility but also his ability to govern her, which resulted in dishonor. In this respect the elites of East and West shared the acceptance of a double standard that enhanced male dominance.

Among the lower orders in Europe, pressure for premarital sex was created by the late ages at which people wed—typically in their upper twenties. Late marriage helped hold down population growth, but figures for illegitimacy indicate relatively little sexual activity apart from engaged and married couples, probably due to religious and socioeconomic pressures. Infanticide may also have contributed to low bastardy levels. The bastardy rate was 3 percent in rural England in the 1590s and 2 percent at Frankfurt in the early 1700s, despite considerable sexual activity by engaged couples. Approximately 21 percent of English brides were pregnant at their weddings in the late sixteenth century.

Because the Catholic church considered the sexual act primarily procreative, it regarded most attempts at contraception as mortal sin. By the sixteenth century, however, many Catholics accepted coitus reservatus—withdrawal before ejaculation—as a permissible technique for the economically destitute, and people did use a variety of physical contraceptives. The church condemned coitus interruptus—ejaculation outside the vagina—as unnatural on biblical grounds, although it became increasingly widespread in the 1700s.

In Protestant lands, religious leaders discouraged birth control methods, believing they were contrary to the biblical command to be fruitful and multiply. Instead, they argued, children should be accepted as blessings from God, means to maintain the commonwealth and the church, and opportunities for women to recover the honor lost to their sex when Eve disobeyed God.

For women with unwanted pregnancies, medical manuals provided information on how to induce abortion, typically through the ingestion of vegetal or mineral poisons, all of which were dangerous to the mother. Interest in the use of birth control methods was undoubtedly strong among women who wanted relief from the repeated cycle of pregnancies that often brought death. In the sixteenth and seventeenth centuries, perhaps one out of every ten pregnancies ended in the mother's death, and 30 to 50 percent of all children died before the age of 5. In France as many as 30 percent were dead before their first birthday.

Because abortion could be as dangerous to the mother as to the fetus, infanticide was a common alternative, particularly since it could be disguised as accidental "overlaying," or accidental suffocation. The problem was so prevalent that in 1784 Austria made it illegal for parents to take children under 5 into bed with them. The punishment for infanticide was often harsh: in the German town of Bamberg a convicted person was drowned or buried alive and then speared. Infanticide figures for Renaissance Florence indicate that more girls than boys died, presumably reflecting the greater value placed on males, though in eighteenth-century Paris there was no significant discrepancy among victims.

Many poverty-stricken parents simply opted to abandon their children in the streets. More foundling hospitals were built to deal with the problem. Milan and Venice had established theirs in the medieval period, and new ones were built in Florence (1445), Paris (1670), London (1739), and St. Petersburg, where two former palaces of the nobility were used to house the children. The availability of the houses seems to have encouraged more parents to abandon their infants. In the 1770s and 1780s the number of children abandoned in Paris reached 4,500 per year, more than double the number at the beginning of the century. By the 1770s more than one out of every five children baptized in Paris had been abandoned. Conditions were so bad in these homes that at times no more than 5 percent of the infants admitted in Paris survived to adulthood.

Catholic and Protestant leaders alike denounced homosexuality. In England the Tudor Parliaments of the sixteenth century made it a capital offense, though the statutes seem not to have been enforced. Magistrates there were more concerned with heterosexual intercourse outside marriage because it could lead to illegitimate children and thus place a financial burden on the community. Homosexuals were found in the court of Elizabeth I and even more extensively in that of her successor, James I, himself bisexual. Homosexuality appears to have been common in secondary schools, where boys often shared beds, and in universities. It was probably also common among servants and in tiny rural communities where access to persons of the opposite sex was severely restricted. In London there were homosexual prostitutes as well as "molly houses" where homosexuals gathered for entertainment. Although Islamic religious writings typically disapproved of homosexuality, the practice itself was generally treated with indifference. In Asia homosexuality was generally considered shameful, and people who were caught at it were condemned or punished, in part because it was held to be unnatural and could not produce offspring, the prime goal of marriage and of society. To Confucius, having no descendants was the ultimate disloyalty to one's parents. Homosexuality was, however, more common and tolerated among the samurai of Japan, many of whom remained unmarried.

By the 1600s organized prostitution was common in European cities such as Paris, Berlin, and Toledo, often with the tacit acceptance of authorities. In Seville brothel keepers and prostitutes were licensed by the city, which even leased houses for this purpose. Church officials tried to close down the brothels, but the city fathers would do no more than require the prostitutes to attend church on Sundays and holy days. In 1676 Cambridge had 13 brothels catering largely to the university community. Many women drawn into a life of prostitution were economically destitute, including unwed mothers and cast-off mistresses, while others opted for it in preference to a 14- to 16-hour day as a seamstress. Some domestics as well were forced out of service and into prostitution when their employers got them pregnant. Other prostitutes were wives whose families were economically destitute or young girls introduced to this life by their mothers, themselves often former prostitutes. Prostitution was typically treated as a criminal offense for which women were pilloried, flogged, imprisoned, and sometimes expelled from a city, though usually to little effect. Nor were punitive measures effective against operators of houses of prostitution.

The late ages at marriage as well as the proximity of family members in small houses tempted some Europeans to commit incest. Apprenticing male children and placing girls in other homes as servants were safety valves, but incest was still sufficiently common to trouble church authorities. Perpetrators caught in the act were usually punished by shaming (public penance), as in the case of other sexual offenses. Usually confined to the lower orders, shaming typically required the offender to appear in church clad only in a white sheet or to ride through town in a cart with a sign proclaiming the offense.

Parents of bastards were treated more harshly because their misdeed was a potential drain on the community's funds; such persons were regularly stripped to

Brothels such as this one, which catered to the aristocracy, became commonplace in early modern Europe. Note that the nobleman is casually giving alms to a beggar. This drawing by Thomas Rowlandson is titled *Charity Covereth a Multitude of Sins.* [Trustees of the British Museum]

the waist, whipped, and placed in the stocks. In keeping with the double standard of the age, mothers but not fathers of bastards were often subjected to punishment, although there were growing efforts to hold fathers fiscally responsible for their illegitimate children. Whether suffering from the double standard or undergoing frequent pregnancies, sexual experience for the early modern woman was fraught with hazard and anxiety and was potentially life-threatening as well.

The dangers sexual intercourse posed to a woman were real whether she lived in Europe, Asia, Africa, or the Americas. Nevertheless, sex was widely valued as the means for procreation. The way in which sex was viewed varied considerably, depending especially on religious traditions. Whereas Roman Catholicism, for instance, exalted the celibate life, sexual elements were incorporated into religious ritual in parts of Africa, India, Tibet, and Southeast Asia, while Hindu elites kept concubines and their Muslim counterparts had harems. Although all societies embraced sex as a life force, for procreative purposes, there was considerable disagreement as to whether it should properly serve as a vehicle for pleasure or for religious expression.

## Education, Literacy, and the Printed Word

Attitudes toward education and learning varied sharply among early modern societies. Until the arrival of Europeans, schools were nonexistent in the Americas and sub-Saharan Africa, while in the Islamic world education was narrowly confined and provided to the few by schools linked to the royal palace or the mosques. The advent of the printing press and the Protestant and Catholic Reformations in Europe spurred the founding of schools, the growth of literacy, and a growing appreciation of learning that has generally continued in the West to the present. Yet nowhere in the early modern world was respect for learning greater than in Asia, both as a means to preserve its philosophical and religious traditions and as a path to achieve worldly success.

## Learning in Asia

Respect for learning was universal in Asia. Written texts in particular or even scraps of paper with writing on them were to be treated reverently and preserved. This was partly due to the importance of the philosophical, moral, and religious texts that played so great a part in each Asian cultural tradition but partly also because literacy and learning were the surest and most prestigious paths to worldly success. In the cultures where religion was more centrally important than in China, especially in India and Buddhist Southeast Asia, literacy and learning also led to an honored status as priest or monk; such persons were second only to the ruler in the status hierarchy. The Indian Brahmin combined the role of scholar and priest, while in Buddhist countries the monkhood has remained the most honorable calling of all. Scholars, priests, and monks were exempt from manual labor, whereas in Europe many clergymen farmed to make ends meet, and monastic labor was often a deliberate part of the ascetic regime. In East and West alike, lip service was paid to the worth and importance of peasant labor and agriculture, but the rewards and status went to people who had risen above the necessity of physical work. In Asia even kings and emperors deferred to the learned holy man or the upright scholar.

Freedom from manual labor for the educated was marked by dress, lifestyle, and the deference of others. In Europe and Asia alike, it was the duty of the rest of society to support monks and priests by regular donations and alms and to finance their temples and rituals. Their activities were connected with ordinary life, including weddings, namings of children, funerals, and religious festivals. Officials, drawn from the ranks of the learned, also wore distinctive clothing and enjoyed special privileges, including exemption from corporal punishment. Especially in China, the masses treated them with respect in deference to their awesome authority as the direct representatives of the emperor. The Chinese gentry, from among whom officials were selected, wore the long blue scholar's gown, hem touching the ground and loose floppy sleeves hanging from the arms. Since no physical exertion could be performed in such a garment, it was in effect a badge of their freedom from manual labor. The scholar-gentry also frequently let their fingernails grow to extreme length, sometimes protecting them with special covers, to make that same point. Throughout Asia and Europe, sumptuary laws prohibited the wearing of upper-class clothing or the use of carriages by the lower orders, the great bulk of the population.

There were three grades of gentry in China, reflecting the three levels of the examination system. Only members who had passed the third level could be selected as officials, but those in the two lower grades were also recognized as educated men and adopted gentry lifestyles and dress. Many of them served as teachers of the next generation of candidates, running both private and government-financed schools where Chinese boys learned their characters and worked their way through the Confucian classics under stern discipline. Most gentry did not become officials but formed an unofficial local elite, serving as teachers, arbiters of disputes, and managers of local enterprises, deferred to by all below them.

Merchants too needed at least some literacy in all Asian cultures, especially since in most of them merchants also had to deal with the state and the official bureaucracy. In any case, they had to keep records and accounts and communicate over long distances. Some of them also acquired a good deal of classical education, and certainly they read poetry and fiction, both classical and popular, as did the scholars. We have no accurate means of measuring literacy in traditional Asian societies. It may have been as high as a quarter of the population, at least in terms of the most basic ability to read and write. Literacy was much higher in Japan after about 1600, and by 1800 it probably reached 50 percent for males. But even a literacy rate of 25 percent would be remarkable, considering the difficulty of learning Chinese characters, which were also the basis of the Japanese, Korean, and Vietnamese written languages.

The gentry group in China, and comparable elites in other Asian societies, probably never constituted more than about 2 percent of the population. To these must be added merchants and petty traders (who often had at least some degree of literacy), clerks and scribes, and some village elders. Despite the fact that they did not attend the regular schools, women sometimes acquired literacy from their brothers or fathers or occasionally on their own. The best evidence is probably the respectable number of female Asian authors, including the famous Lady Murasaki, Japanese author of the world's earliest psychological novel, *The Tale of Genji.* Court ladies such as Lady Murasaki had the leisure to learn to read and write. Literacy was expected of them, as were accomplishments in music, painting, and dance. In the Buddhist countries of Southeast Asia the monkhood claimed virtually all young men for at least two years and at any one time may have included, with older monks, 10 or 15 percent of the population, all of whom were literate. In India the Brahmins, as the sole performers of ritual and the keepers of the Great Tradition, had to be literate.

Paper and printing were both invented in China, the former by the first century A.D. under the Han, the latter by T'ang times. Movable type appeared in the Sung dynasty by about A.D. 1100 and shortly thereafter in Korea. These inventions spread rapidly to Japan, more slowly to India, Southeast Asia, the Islamic areas, and the West. The importance of sacred texts and commentaries for Hinduism, Buddhism, and Islam meant that even before printing, large numbers of copies were made by scribes. As in the West, the spread of printing greatly increased the reading public. The most important result was the increased circulation of literature, first in China, then progressively in other parts of Asia. This included copies of the classics; philosophical and religious texts; epic tales, such as the Indian *Mahabharata* and the *Ramayana*; and similar epics and accounts of heroic deeds from the classical traditions of China, Japan, and Korea.

Literature for a mass audience was being printed by T'ang times in China (A.D. 600–900) and soon thereafter in the rest of Asia, including plays, short stories, poetry, and the first novels. Well before the T'ang period in China, in the splendor of Guptan India (A.D. 300–500), the court poet and playwright Kalidasa had created a brilliant series of dramas. With the spread of printing, his plays and poems were made available to a mass audience. Throughout Asia printing also meant that what had long been present as an oral tradition of storytelling and drama took on new life. Much of it has been lost or is available only in much later printed versions, but from T'ang times on there was a vigorous popular literature in the vernacular, less lofty and more down-to-earth than the classics. Stories and plays about universal human foibles—akin to Chaucer's *Canterbury Tales* in the West—were read avidly by a growing number of people, including scholars to whom such works were supposedly prohibited and who hid them under their pillows. In China there were even detective stories. India produced similar tales, and some of the works of Kalidasa are in this genre. Accounts of adventure and intrigue flourished throughout Asia.

## Learning in the West

Respect for learning in the West was not as pronounced as in the East, though in the early modern period there was a notable increase in literacy, in the number of schools, and in the continued development of the universities. In keeping with their broad range of intellectual and cultural interests, Renaissance humanists not only founded new schools but also reformed the traditional curriculum by challenging its heavy reliance on Aristotle. The success of Protestant reformers ultimately rested on the ability to educate younger generations in their religious principles, and in turn the Catholics relied heavily on education to thwart Protestant expansion and to provide the foundation for their missionary work.

Both religious groups looked to the universities to provide intellectual leadership. The Protestant stress on Bible reading, especially with the availability of new vernacular translations in the sixteenth century, was a powerful incentive to education. The scientific revolution, with its rapid communication of ideas, was also highly dependent on learning, and the rapid growth of state bureaucracies increased the demand for skilled officials, particularly those with some legal training. In England the early modern period was the golden age of the Inns of Court, where aspiring young men studied the common law.

As in the East, many Western educational developments were closely linked to religion. Catholic orders such as the Jesuits and the Ursulines are famous for their educational work, but other groups were active too. The Oratory of Jesus, a society of priests, established colleges and seminaries throughout France, mostly for children of the French nobility, which rejected physical punishment as an educational tool. So did reforming Catholic Jansenists, whose "little schools" normally had no more than 25 boys in classes of six or less. Several Catholic organizations were established in France in the late 1600s to teach the children of the poor. Although Protestants had no teaching orders, they too actively founded schools, including "charity schools" for children of the poor; their curricula concentrated on reading, writing, and religion. One of the greatest Protestant successes was the founding of the University of Halle in eastern Germany in 1694 by Pietists, whose evangelical, devotional faith troubled orthodox Lutherans. By its emphasis on independent thinking, the faculty at Halle helped pioneer the development of modern academic freedom.

The Jewish communities of eastern Europe and Spain were keenly interested in education. At the elementary level, education was mandatory for all boys, and some girls were taught to read, especially after the appearance of printed vernacular literature. Gifted male students were directed into the fields of medicine and religion, the latter being a specialty of rabbinical academies. Because of the importance of rabbinical law in the ghettos, legal studies as well as religion were an important part of the curriculum. Nonreligious subjects often had to be learned from private tutors.

Progress in the founding of schools and the increase of literacy was pronounced in early modern Europe. Between 1580 and 1650 more than 800 schools were en-

Note the use of corporal punishment as a learning device in this 1592 woodcut of a German classroom. [Bettmann Archive]

dowed in England and Wales. By the late seventeenth century the number of parishes with schools was near 90 percent in the diocese of Paris and the lowland counties of Scotland, though the figure was only 42 percent in the diocese of Verdun and even less in some areas. French literacy rates were perhaps 20 percent overall in the seventeenth century, but a third of the population was literate by 1789. The reformer John Knox proposed a program of universal education in the 1560s, but the Scottish Parliament refused to fund it. Nevertheless, a century later Scotland had an impressive system of parish schools where even the poor were welcome.

Universal education effectively began when Prussia made attendance at elementary school mandatory in 1717. The founding of new schools was accompanied by substantial increases in literacy. By 1800 the literacy rate for males approached 90 percent in Scotland and 67 percent in France, whereas in 1600 only one in six Frenchmen had been able to read. Among women, whose educational opportunities were more restricted, literacy rates generally rose more slowly. Only 5 percent of the women in the English counties of East Anglia were literate, compared to 35 percent of the men in the period from 1580 to 1640. In Amsterdam, where literacy greatly enhanced employment opportunities, the rates were 57 percent for men and 32 percent for women in 1630. Because the Swedes required literacy for confirmation and marriage, by the 1690s at least one Swedish diocese had achieved a rate approaching 100 percent, though for many this may have represented little more than the abil-

ity to sign one's name. As in the East, the growth of literacy helped spur the printing industry, which published inexpensive books, ballads, and newspapers, these last appearing for the first time in the seventeenth century. The dramatic increase in Western literacy was not matched in Asia; in Japan, which had the best record, 45 percent of the men and only 15 percent of the women were literate as late as the mid-nineteenth century.

# Education in the Ottoman Empire

Unlike eastern Asia or the West, the Turks, who opposed the publication of Islamic religious literature, did not allow printed books until 1728 or 1729, with the exception of a small number of presses in the non-Muslim communities. The first Turkish newspaper did not appear until 1861. Religious influence dominated the Turkish educational system; most schools were attached to mosques, and the ulema typically supplied the teachers. The Jewish and Christian communities had some schools, but generally the Ottomans discouraged education for their subject peoples. Even among the Muslims, education was essentially the preserve of the well-to-do or the politically important, since the Turks were convinced that too much learning threatened Islam.

Beyond the elementary schools, the more capable Muslim students could pursue the study of Islamic theology, law, and some humanities and science in theological schools known as *medreses.* Here the curriculum lasted as long as 12 years. The sultan also maintained five preparatory and four vocational schools where a full course of study could be as long as 15 years. These palace schools had some Christian teachers, though most of the faculty belonged to the ulema. The curriculum included the study of Turkish, Persian, and Arabic as well as the liberal arts, physical education, calligraphy, and vocational training in such areas as architecture, shipbuilding, and military affairs. There was instruction too in Islam and Turkish etiquette. But the *medreses* and the palace schools were only for the few. The expansion of Islam into North Africa and the Sudan meant that there too education was not encouraged for the masses.

# Poverty, Crime, and Social Control

It is impossible to measure levels of well-being for most periods in the past. We can calculate living standards only roughly, using such evidence as travelers' accounts, estimates of population and production, trade figures, stories reflecting lifestyles, famine records, and remedial measures. Before the modern period these records are fullest for China, where we have a wealth of official and local documents and an extensive literature. Generally, most Chinese seem to have been materially better off in diet, housing, and clothing than most people elsewhere in the world until perhaps as late as the mid-nineteenth century. But the only real defense against absolute poverty was the family system in Asia, which provided its own mutual-assistance network.

Authorities in France and England in the late 1600s probably exaggerated in estimating that over half of their people lived at or below the subsistence level, but the number was high. In the late 1400s more than two-thirds of the taxpayers in Basel and Augsburg were too poor to survive serious economic adversity. The large number of poor seriously strained the ability of religious and civic authorities to provide assistance. In the plague year of 1580, more than half the population of Genoa was on poor relief. In the last decades of the sixteenth century some 20 percent of the inhabitants of Lyons, France's second largest city, needed assistance.

For the poor the greatest problem was often the uncertainty of the food supply, which was frequently threatened by inflationary pressures as well as natural disasters. Malnutrition and disease were the principal reasons for a life expectancy in Europe of only 25 years as late as 1700. Most of the world's population still lived in rural areas in the early modern period, often in mud huts with thatched roofs. Living quarters were severely cramped;

an entire family often lived in a single room. In towns the poor were victims of polluted water and filthy living conditions.

The diet of the poor was simple and, even in Europe, usually devoid of meat. The more fortunate peasants might occasionally have a little mutton or pork, but the poor usually had to survive on a diet of dark bread, peas, beans, and soup. Each day a typical adult peasant ate 2 to 3 pounds of bread made from wheat, rye, barley, or oats; wheat was the most expensive grain. Bread was a valuable source of carbohydrates, vitamins, proteins, and minerals. Many European peasants kept stock simmering in a pot, adding to it whatever foods were available each day. Sometimes cheese, butter, or curds were consumed, but milk was shunned because it was thought to be unhealthy. In general, the lot of the rural poor was marginally better than that of their urban counterparts, since many of the former were able to raise some of their own food. This was not usually true of landless day laborers, who amounted to as much as half the population of some districts in Spain and Switzerland. As the general population increased, it was imperative to find means to relieve the destitute.

## Causes of European Poverty

Various factors contributed to the severity of poverty in early modern Europe. As the population grew, landlords improved the efficiency of their farms to provide additional food, but industry did not expand rapidly enough to absorb the surplus labor displaced as landowners switched from raising crops to grazing sheep. Inflation itself took a heavy toll as rents and prices rose faster than wages, leaving urban workers particularly vulnerable. Short-term increases in poverty were caused by extreme fluctuations in the cloth industry, which was adversely affected by such things as plague, war, and bad harvests. Whereas rural textile workers might weather a slump by finding temporary farm work, urban laborers were typically reduced to poor relief or begging. When harvests failed, the plight of the poor often became desperate. In England from the late fifteenth to the early seventeenth century, harvests failed on an average of every four years. When the harvests were bad several years in a row, the problem was more acute, and food riots were common. Finally, as the size of European armies expanded in the early modern period, the number of demobilized and often unemployable soldiers increased, adding burdens to relief rolls.

## Poor Relief in Europe

There were various attempts to deal with the poor in this period. In the late 1400s local authorities ordered beg-

## ◉ Peasant Poverty: France, 1696 ◉

*The famous French military engineer Sébastien Le Prestre, marquis de Vauban, wrote a moving description of the poor peasants in France in 1696.*

All the so-called *bas peuple* [mean people] live on nothing but bread of mixed barley and oats, from which they do not even remove the bran, which means that bread can sometimes be lifted by the straw sticking out of it. They also eat poor fruits, mainly wild, and a few vegetables from their gardens. . . .

The general run of people seldom drink [wine], eat meat not three times a year, and use little salt. . . . So it is no cause for surprise if people who are so ill-nourished have so little energy. Add to this what they suffer from exposure: winter and summer, three-fourths of them are dressed in nothing but half-rotting tattered linen, and are shod throughout the year with *sabots* [wooden shoes], and no other covering for the foot. . . .

The poor people are ground down in another manner by the loans of grain and money they take from the wealthy in emergencies, by means of which a high rate of usury is enforced, under the guise of presents which must be made after the debts fall due, so as to avoid imprisonment. After the term has been extended by only three or four months, either another present must be produced when the time is up, or they face the *sergent* [debtors' bailiff] who is sure to strip the house bare.

*Source:* Vauban, "Description géographique de l'élection de Vézelay," in P. Goubert, *The Ancien Régime: French Society, 1600–1750,* trans. S. Cox (London: Weidenfeld & Nicolson, 1973), pp. 118–119.

gars to leave their districts, although exceptions were sometimes made for local beggars who were handicapped, ill, or elderly. In Brabant, France, and Venice, vagabonds provided oarpower for the galleys, while in England a 1495 law ordered that the idle be whipped, placed in the stocks for three days, and then returned to their parishes of origin. Intended to keep the destitute from flooding into the towns, virtually all early measures to deal with the poor relied on some form of coercion but failed to provide organized means to relieve the needy.

The widespread social unrest sparked throughout Europe by the harvest failures of the 1520s brought major changes in social policy. Between 1531 and 1541 some 60 cities reformed their welfare policies, and the state imposed reforms in the Netherlands, England, France, Scotland, and Spain. The governments of the first three states prohibited begging and insisted that the able-bodied poor work. Funds for those unable to work were raised through taxes or donations, but there was a clear shift in emphasis from private charity to public welfare. The English Poor Law of 1601, for example, prohibited begging, required the able-bodied poor to work on local projects, centralized poor relief, and provided for the education of paupers' children. Where there was industry to employ the able-bodied at low wages, as in Flanders, France, and England, the new

system achieved some success. In Scotland and Spain, however, there was little need for the labor of unskilled paupers, and licensed begging was used in an attempt to keep them under control. But since licenses could easily be forged, this system was ineffective.

Because employment could not always be found for the able-bodied poor, many European cities established workhouses to discipline the poor as well as to provide job training and moral instruction. Although these institutions could not accommodate all the able-bodied poor, officials hoped to coerce the remainder into finding employment. Some workhouses, such as Bridewell in London and those founded by the papacy in Rome, became little more than places of punishment, while others, such as those in the Netherlands, Scandinavia, and Germany, were sources of cheap labor for private employers. French workhouses at first were used to benefit private business, but after 1640 they were employed primarily to control rebellious peasants and workers. The inmates of these institutions rarely benefited from their enforced stays.

## Poor Relief Outside Europe

The towns of coastal West Africa similarly developed a system of poor relief in the late sixteenth and seven-

In early modern Europe, many indigent persons took to the highways in search of employment, but in so doing they risked severe punishment as vagabonds. This 1520 engraving is by Lucas van Leyden. [Staatliche Museen Preussischer Kulturbesitz, Berlin, Kupferstichkabinett/Jörg P. Anders]

teenth centuries. As the rural poor fled to the towns in search of better opportunities, the number of the indigent was often as high as 40 percent, and in the port of Shama on the Gold Coast it reached 70 or 80 percent.

There were, however, no professional beggars because of a rather extensive system of poor relief. The wealthy took some of the poor into their personal service, while others received assistance from special funds raised by taxes or court fines. Some of the offerings given to priests made their way to the poor as well. Local authorities were required to provide gainful employment for young men, the physically handicapped, and the elderly, usually in the crafts, food processing, and market vending. Because the rural poor who faced severe economic hardship sometimes opted for banditry rather than migration to the towns, in the early 1600s brigandage reached near-epidemic levels in parts of West Africa. By striking at the trading caravans transporting rural produce to the towns, the brigands effectively symbolized the resentment of peasants at their growing subservience to urban merchants, a development that was also common in much of Europe and Asia.

In South America the Inca addressed the problem by systematic regimentation and care of the needy. The state itself owned the land and apportioned it to families based on their size, with a substantial portion of the crops going to storehouses to supply the nobility, the military, state workers, and priests. The government also took much of what the artisans produced. Although the masses were thus deprived of both freedom and initiative, in times of famine or natural disaster the state provided them with food from the public warehouses.

The larger Asian society had pitifully inadequate means beyond the family level to intervene on behalf of the poor. In China the imperial bureaucracy did what its limited local powers allowed, including the remission of taxes, the control of floods, the keeping of order, and the storing of grain for distribution in lean years at uninflated prices, a policy called the "ever-normal granary system." Such efforts flagged or failed when the dynasty was weak or collapsed—perhaps a third of the time— and even in strong periods the state could not cope with a major catastrophe. In India and Southeast Asia, and to a lesser degree in the Buddhist areas of Korea and Japan, temples provided some refuge for the destitute, but this too was inadequate. In general, the family system of mutual support could keep most people from total destitution most of the time, but no means were adequate to deal with the recurrent large-scale disasters to which all premodern societies were subject, such as drought-induced famine, major flooding, or long periods of civil disorder. In the Islamic world, the poor could look to social-service institutions funded primarily by charitable legacies and the obligatory tax, or *zakat*, which was one of the principal duties of a Muslim.

## Crime and Poverty

One of the most striking differences between East and West was in the treatment of crime. In general terms, Asian thought made no place for the Judeo-Christian concept of sin. Correction and, if possible, reform through reeducation or renewed piety were stressed more than repayment or punishment, although these were certainly used and frequently harsh. The incidence of crime or social deviance was almost certainly less in Asia than in other areas, thanks to the self-regulating mechanism of the family and the deterrent power of the shame that individual misbehavior might bring on the group. It is sometimes said that whereas Western societies emphasized individual sin and guilt, the East stressed the unacceptability of antisocial behavior and used shame to enforce moral codes. In addition to the social stigma of misbehavior, public shaming was commonly used as an official punishment both in Asia and in Europe. Both Asian and European criminals were publicly exhibited, often paraded through the streets carrying placards indicating their offenses, and sometimes executed.

As the living standards of European workers and peasants deteriorated, criminal activity increased, especially from the mid-1500s on. In rural areas there was a clear connection between crime and destitution. Records for the Spanish province of Toledo show that nearly all defendants in larceny cases came from the lower ranks of society. Theft was often the most common crime; in the English county of Sussex in the early 1600s stealing accounted for nearly two-thirds of all indictments. Theft was a capital offense, though the death penalty was rarely applied. Most rural felons were common laborers who did not repeat their criminal activity after their initial arrest.

The type of larceny changed somewhat in the early modern period. In medieval times thieves stole mostly subsistence items—food, clothing, and tools—but later they began to prefer luxury goods, increasingly available in the expanding towns. Whereas the poor had hitherto stolen mostly from other poor people, they now increasingly robbed the rich. A major exception to this pattern of crime occurred during the unsettled times of fourteenth- and fifteenth-century Europe when bands of lawless nobles and gentry engaged in robbery and extortion. Victims who refused to pay often had their crops destroyed and their homes burned. Not even the wealthy were immune, for they provided tempting targets for kidnapping and extortion. Known as "fur-collar criminals" because of their noble garb, the culprits thrived until governments were strong enough to stamp most of them out in the 1500s.

Banditry did not cease with the decline of fur-collar crime, but henceforth nearly all bandits were from the lower social orders and included many men unable to find employment. In Granada some of the bandit groups were led by women. As major roads were more effectively patrolled by the seventeenth century, most of these bandits were forced into remote areas. Russia, however, experienced considerable turmoil throughout the 1600s because of large roving bands. Russian bandits were commonly viewed as heroes and defenders of the common people, particularly since most victims were bureaucrats, tax collectors, and wealthy merchants.

In Asia, too, banditry was a common response by people reduced to absolute poverty. It was especially frequent in periods of political disorder and hence virtually endemic in parts of India, while its incidence rose and fell in China with the changing effectiveness of the imperial government and the levels of peasant distress. Bandits operated most successfully on the fringes of state-controlled areas or in frontier zones between provincial jurisdictions, areas that were often mountainous or forested. Bandits exacerbated the poverty of their prey. Although their prime targets were the rich and the

trade routes, these were often better protected than the common people and their villages. Some bandit groups turned into rebels, who built on the support of the disaffected majority to overthrow the government and found a new order that could better serve mass welfare. Much popular fiction dealt with the adventures of bandit groups, often depicted as Robin Hood–type figures but in any case regarded as heroes rather than criminals.

In the West a new literary form, the picaresque novel—celebrating the adventures of an urban rogue, or *picaro*—developed in connection with a trend toward more sophisticated urban crimes. In addition to the usual larceny, physical assault, homicide, and arson, early modern towns were increasingly troubled by business fraud and swindlers. By the mid-1600s novels about these rogues were popular in Spain, from whence they spread to Germany and England.

Another facet of urban crime in the larger European cities was the growth of neighborhoods where a genuine underworld existed. In Paris the criminal sector near the Porte St.-Denis was so extensive that officials dared not enter it until it was subdued by an army detachment in 1667. Curtailing crime in the cities was nearly impossible because the poor were packed into grossly overcrowded slums where shanties filled even the narrow alleys and where criminals could easily hide.

## Controlling Crime

European states responded to the rise in crime by reorganizing the personnel and procedure necessary to control it. In the medieval period criminal control was based on the existence of small populations in compact, mostly isolated areas. As the population expanded and interregional contacts increased, it became imperative to develop more effective government controls beyond the local level. The French met this need by expanding the powers of the royal *procureur*, who handled the prosecution in criminal proceedings. In England the Tudors, who had no police force, enlarged the role of the justices of the peace, who, as unpaid agents of the crown, had the authority to arrest, indict, and grant bail. They also enforced labor codes and social laws that governed such things as alehouses and unlawful games. By the late sixteenth century justices of the peace were responsible for enforcement of the poor law.

Throughout Europe revised criminal procedures had the effect of depersonalizing the judicial process and treating criminal activity as an offense against society rather than the individual. Punishment became more severe. In contrast to the medieval system, where justice was intended to settle disputes between persons, the new criminal proceedings punished the guilty but ignored compensation for the victim. Unlike medieval justice, corporal punishment became more widespread,

## ◉ Capital Punishment and Cruelty ◉

*European justice entailed not only the use of torture to extract confessions but also the application of capital punishment for various crimes against property as well as human life. Here is the account of a French observer sensitive to the cruel suffering inflicted on criminals in eighteenth-century Paris: note his opposition to capital punishment as contrary to natural law.*

I went home by way of rue Saint-Antoine and the Place de Grève. Three murderers had been broken on the wheel there, the day before. . . . As I crossed the square I caught sight of a poor wretch, pale, half dead, wracked by the pains of the interrogation inflicted on him twenty hours earlier; he was stumbling down from the Hôtel de Ville supported by the executioner and the confessor. These two men, so completely different, inspired an inexpressible emotion in me! I watched the latter embrace a miserable man consumed by fever, filthy as the dungeons he came from, swarming with vermin! And I said to myself, "O Religion, here is your greatest glory! . . ." I saw the other as the wrathful arm of the law. . . . But I wondered: "Have men the right to impose death . . . even on the murderer who has himself treacherously taken life?" I seemed to hear Nature reply with a woeful no! . . . "But robbery?" "No, no!" cried Nature. "The savage rich have never felt they devised enough harsh safeguards; instead of being friends and brothers, as their religion commands, they prefer the gallows. . . ." This was what Nature said to me. . . .

*Source:* Nicolas-Edmé, Restif de la Bretonne, *Les Nuits de Paris, or The Nocturnal Spectator,* trans. L. Asher and E. Fertig (New York: Random House, 1964), pp. 7–8.

though a status distinction was generally made in meting out justice; the rich were often fined, the poor imprisoned, flogged, or mutilated. The increased severity of punishments was intended to discipline the lower orders and curb the increase in crimes by the poor against the rich. Public punishment thus had a twofold purpose: to deter crime and to demonstrate the authority of the state to regulate the behavior of its citizens and command their obedience.

In both Asia and Europe criminals were tried and laws and punishments enforced by civil courts run by the state and presided over by magistrates, rulers or their representatives, community elders, or learned men. In Asia and sometimes in Europe there was no prior assumption of guilt or innocence; judgment was made and sentences arrived at on the basis of evidence, including the testimony of witnesses. Asians had no lawyers standing between people and the law; plaintiffs and defendants spoke for themselves. In China and most of the rest of Asia, people charged with criminal behavior could be found guilty and punished only if they confessed their guilt. If they refused to do so despite the weight of evidence against them, they were often tortured to extract a confession. Torture was also used in early modern Europe, though confession was not essential for a conviction. Asian law and the system of official justice, like its European counterpart, was designed to awe all who appeared before its majesty. Plaintiffs, defendants, and witnesses knelt before the magistrate or judge and could be whipped if they were not suitably reverential—another expression of a strongly hierarchical, authoritarian society.

In both Asia and Europe punishment for major crimes of violence was almost invariably death, commonly by beheading or strangulation. Death could also be imposed for many minor crimes. For especially dreadful crimes, such as parricide, treason, rebellion, or, in Asia, other forms of filial and political disloyalty, more gruesome punishments were used: dismemberment, the pulling apart of limbs by horses, the Chinese "death of a thousand cuts," or in India impalement or trampling by elephants. In Europe dismemberment by "drawing and quartering" (sundering limbs from the body) was imposed for treason.

Punishments were seen as deterrents to would-be criminals; the heads of the executed were exhibited on poles until they rotted. For lesser offenses Asian criminals were displayed in painfully small cages or mutilated, practices also used in Europe, or forced to wear a heavy wooden collar that prevented them from feeding them-

Chinese punishment for minor offenses. The heavy wooden collar, the *cangue*, was a burden to support and also prevented the criminal from reaching his mouth with his hands, which meant that he would starve if not fed by others. This man's crime is recorded on the inscription, but all that can be read here are the official title and seal of the imperial magistrate at Shanghai in 1872. [John Thomson/Harvard-Yenching Library, Harvard University]

selves. In East and West alike prisons were often dreadful places where inmates might starve if they were not fed by relatives. For what we might call misdemeanors, Asian sentences tended to stress reeducation and reform. Criminality, or at least misbehavior, was seen as potentially correctible, especially with family help.

People naturally worried about falling into the machinery of the law and the courts, especially in criminal cases. Two important points need to be made. In Asia probably considerably fewer than 10 percent of disputes and minor crimes—perhaps most crimes of all sorts—ever reached the courts since they were settled through family, village, gentry, or other local networks. Second,

modern Western scholars conclude that justice was done by that system, perhaps more consistently than in the West. Most magistrates were judicious, diligent with evidence, and concerned to see justice done, not only to avoid the censure that could ruin their careers but also because of the sense of responsibility they bore. But there was, particularly in the West, a double standard of justice, which was much harder on the poor, whose crimes generally stemmed from poverty, than on their social betters. Laws were made and administered by elite groups, whose interests in the preservation of their privileged status and property were at least as great as their devotion to justice.

*Surveying the societies of the early modern world, perhaps most striking is the contrast between the relative stability of Asian society and the volatility of Europe. As Europeans made crucial economic, political, and educational advances in the early modern period, Western society altered substantially, beginning in western Europe and spreading to the Americas through colonization. Nevertheless, the strikingly numerous social parallels between the different parts of the world in this period underscore the common-ality of much historical development and human experience. Societies were structured hierarchically and embraced the principle that social status entailed special responsibility. In Asia and Europe alike, arranged marriages were common, and precedence was accorded to sons. Capital punishment was commonly imposed for major crimes, and some of the poor in all societies periodically resorted to banditry. Moreover, in their treatment of women, most Asian and Western societies were alike in not granting even a modicum of social equality to women until the twentieth century.*

*Conflicting religious tenets were responsible for some of the most basic social differences in the early modern world. Religious considerations explain at least in part why Aztecs, Inca, Muslims, and some Africans practiced polygamy, whereas non-Muslim Asians and Europeans were primarily monogamous. Religion was also a key factor in views on sex. Many East Asians and Africans, unlike Chris-*

*tians, for instance, linked sex and religious ritual. Religious changes were responsible for altering the way some westerners viewed marriage: divorce (other than through annulment) was not possible in Europe until the Protestant Reformation in the sixteenth century; in Asia, divorce did occur, though rarely. The relative importance attached to education, particularly in Asia, stemmed partly from the desire to preserve its religious and philosophical traditions. The same can be said of Judaism and later of Christianity.*

## Suggestions for Further Reading

Buxbaum, D., ed. *Chinese Family Law and Social Change*. Seattle: University of Washington Press, 1978.

Cahn, S. *Industry of Devotion: The Transformation of Women's Work in England, 1500–1660*. New York: Columbia University Press, 1987.

Ch'u, T. *Law and Society in Traditional China*. Paris: Mouton, 1961.

Cohn, B. S. *India: The Social Anthropology of a Civilization*. Englewood Cliffs, N.J.: Prentice Hall, 1971.

Davidson, B. *The African Genius: An Introduction to Social and Cultural History*. Boston: Little, Brown, 1969.

Dumont, L. *Homo Hierarchicus: An Essay on the Caste System*, trans. M. Sainsbury. Chicago: University of Chicago Press, 1970.

Fildes, V. *Wet Nursing: A History from Antiquity to the Present*. Oxford: Blackwell, 1988.

Foucault, M. *The History of Sexuality*, trans. R. Hurley. New York: Pantheon, 1977.

Fraser, A. *The Weaker Vessel: Woman's Lot in Seventeenth-Century England*. London: Weidenfeld & Nicolson, 1984.

Freedman, M., ed. *Family and Kinship in Chinese Society*. Stanford, Calif.: Stanford University Press, 1970.

Goody, J. *The Oriental, the Ancient and the Primitive: Marriage and the Family in the Preindustrial Societies of Eurasia*. Cambridge: Cambridge University Press, 1990.

Goubert, P. *The French Peasantry in the Seventeenth Century*, trans. I. Patterson. Cambridge: Cambridge University Press, 1986.

Greaves, R. L. *Society and Religion in Elizabethan England*. Minneapolis: University of Minnesota Press, 1981.

Hanawalt, B. A., ed. *Women and Work in Preindustrial Europe*. Bloomington: Indiana University Press, 1986.

Hinsch, B. *Passions of the Cut Sleeve: The Male Homosexual Tradition in China*. Berkeley: University of California Press, 1990.

Houston, R. A. *Literacy in Early Modern Europe: Culture and Education, 1500–1800*. New York: Longman, 1988.

Hunt, D. *Parents and Children in History: The Psychology of Family Life in Early Modern France*. New York: Basic Books, 1970.

Kamen, H. *European Society, 1500–1700*. London: Hutchinson, 1984.

Kea, R. A. *Settlements, Trade, and Politics in the Seventeenth-Century Gold Coast*. Baltimore: Johns Hopkins University Press, 1982.

Ladurie, E. L. *The French Peasantry, 1450–1660*. Berkeley: University of California Press, 1986.

Lannoy, R. *The Speaking Tree: Indian Culture and Society*. New York: Oxford University Press, 1971.

Laslett, P. *The World We Have Lost Further Explored*, 3rd ed. London: Methuen, 1983.

Le May, R. S. *The Culture of Southeast Asia*. London: Allen & Unwin, 1954.

Lewis, R. *Everyday Life in Ottoman Turkey*. New York: Putnam, 1971.

Macfarlane, A. *Marriage and Love in England: Modes of Reproduction, 1300–1840*. New York: Blackwell, 1986.

Mandelbaum, D. G. *Society in India: Continuity and Change*. 2 vols. Berkeley: University of California Press, 1970.

Maynes, M. J. *Schooling in Western Europe: A Social History*. New York: State University of New York Press, 1985.

McKnight, B. *The Quality of Mercy: Amnesties and Traditional Chinese Justice*. Honolulu: University Press of Hawaii, 1981.

Naquin, S., and Rawski, E. S. *Chinese Society in the Eighteenth Century*. New Haven, Conn.: Yale University Press, 1988.

Norberg, K. *Rich and Poor in Grenoble, 1600–1814*. Berkeley: University of California Press, 1985.

Ozment, S. *When Fathers Ruled: Family Life in Reformation Europe*. Cambridge, Mass.: Harvard University Press, 1983.

Pollock, L. A. *Forgotten Children: Parent-Child Relations from 1500 to 1900*. Cambridge: Cambridge University Press, 1984.

Rawksi, E. S. *Education and Popular Literacy in Ch'ing China*. Ann Arbor: University of Michigan Press, 1979.

Rose, M. B., ed. *Women in the Middle Ages and the Renaissance: Literary and Historical Perspectives*. Syracuse, N.Y.: Syracuse University Press, 1986.

Schalk, E. *From Valor to Pedigree: Ideas of Nobility in France in the Sixteenth and Seventeenth Centuries*. Princeton, N.J.: Princeton University Press, 1986.

Shorter, E. *The Making of the Modern Family*. New York: Basic Books, 1977.

Slack, P. *Poverty and Policy in Tudor and Stuart England*. New York: Longman, 1988.

Stone, L. *The Family, Sex, and Marriage in England, 1500–1800*. New York: Harper & Row, 1977.

———. *Road to Divorce: England, 1530–1987*. New York: Oxford University Press, 1991.

———, and Stone, J. C. F. *An Open Elite? England, 1540–1880*. New York: Oxford University Press, 1984.

Traer, J. F. *Marriage and the Family in Eighteenth-Century France*. Ithaca, N.Y.: Cornell University Press, 1980.

Wakeman, F., ed. *Conflict and Control in Late Imperial China*. Berkeley: University of California Press, 1975.

Wiesner, M. E. *Working Women in Renaissance Germany*. New Brunswick, N.J.: Rutgers University Press, 1986.

Woodbridge, L. *Women and the English Renaissance: Literature and the Nature of Womankind, 1540–1620*. Champaign: University of Illinois Press, 1984.